I0005921

A Compendium of Ecclesiastical History, Volume 2

CLARK'S

FOREIGN

THEOLOGICAL LIBRARY.

1st series

VOLUME IX.

Gieseler's Compendium of Ecclesiastical History.

VOL. II.

EDINBURGH:

T. & T. CLARK, 38 GEORGE STREET;

LONDON : SEELEY & CO. ; WARD & CO. ; JACKSON & WALFORD; J. GLADDING.

DUBLIN : JOHN ROBERTSON.—NEW YORK : WILEY & PUTNAM.

BOSTON : CROCKER & BREWSTER.—PHILADELPHIA : J. W. MOORE.

MDCCCXLVIII.

A COMPENDIUM

OF

ECCLESIASTICAL HISTORY.

BY

DR JOHN C. L. GIESELER,

CONSISTORIAL COUNSELLOR AND ORDINARY PROFESSOR OF THEOLOGY
IN GÖTTINGEN.

FOURTH EDITION REVISED AND AMENDED.

TRANSLATED FROM THE GERMAN

BY

SAMUEL DAVIDSON, LL.D.,

PROFESSOR OF BIBLICAL LITERATURE AND ECCLESIASTICAL HISTORY IN THE
LANCASHIRE INDEPENDENT COLLEGE.

VOL. II.

EDINBURGH:

T. & T. CLARK, 38 GEORGE STREET.

LONDON : HAMILTON, ADAMS, AND CO. ; SIMPKIN, MARSHALL, AND CO. ;
DUBLIN : JOHN ROBERTSON.

MDCCCXLVIII.

.

PRINTED BY
M'COSH, PARK, AND DEWARS,
DUNDEE.

CONTENTS.

FOURTH CHAPTER.

HISTORY OF MONACHISM.

FIFTH CHAPTER.

HISTORY OF PUBLIC WORSHIP.

SIXTH CHAPTER.

HISTORY OF MORALS.

SEVENTH CHAPTER.

ATTEMPTS AT REFORMATION.

EIGHTH CHAPTER.

SPREAD OF CHRISTIANITY.

SECOND DIVISION.

FROM THE COUNCIL OF CHALCEDON TO THE BEGINNING OF
THE MONOTHELITIC CONTROVERSIES, AND THE TIME OF MU-
HAMMED, A. D. 451—622.

FIRST CHAPTER.

ENTIRE SUPPRESSION OF PAGANISM IN THE ROMAN EMPIRE.

SECOND CHAPTER.

HISTORY OF THEOLOGY.

THIRD CHAPTER.

HISTORY OF THE HIERARCHY.

FOURTH CHAPTER.

HISTORY OF MONACHISM.

FIFTH CHAPTER.

HISTORY OF PUBLIC WORSHIP.

SIXTH CHAPTER.

SPREAD OF CHRISTIANITY, AND ITS CONDITION WITHOUT THE ROMAN EMPIRE.

THIRD DIVISION.

FROM THE BEGINNING OF THE MONOTHELITIC CONTROVERSY,
AND FROM THE TIME OF MUHAMMED TO THE BEGINNING OF
THE CONTROVERSY CONCERNING THE WORSHIP OF IMAGES
FROM 622—726.

FIRST CHAPTER.

RESTRAINING OF THE CHURCH IN THE EAST.

SECOND CHAPTER.

HISTORY OF THE GREEK CHURCH.

THIRD CHAPTER.

HISTORY OF THE WESTERN CHURCH.

THIRD PERIOD.

FROM THE BEGINNING OF THE CONTROVERSY CONCERNING THE
WORSHIP OF IMAGES TO THE REFORMATION, A. D. 726—1517.

FIRST DIVISION.

TO THE TIME OF NICOLAUS I., OR TO THE APPEARANCE OF THE
PSEUDO-ISIDORIAN DECRETALS.   FROM A. D. 726—858.

FIRST PART.

HISTORY OF THE GREEK CHURCH.

SECOND PART.

HISTORY OF THE WESTERN CHURCH.

FIRST CHAPTER.

CONVERSION OF THE GERMANS BY BONIFACE.

SECOND CHAPTER.

HISTORY OF THE PAPACY.

THIRD CHAPTER.

HISTORY OF THE FRANK EMPIRE.

FOURTH CHAPTER.

SPANISH CHURCH.

FIFTH CHAPTER.

HISTORY OF PUBLIC WORSHIP.

SIXTH CHAPTER.

HISTORY OF CHURCH DISCIPLINE.

SECOND DIVISION.

FROM NICOLAUS I. TO GREGORY VII., A.D. 858—1073.

FIRST PART.

HISTORY OF THE WESTERN CHURCH.

FIRST CHAPTER.

HISTORY OF THE PAPACY.

SECOND CHAPTER.

HISTORY OF THE EPISCOPAL HIERARCHY.

THIRD CHAPTER.

HISTORY OF THEOLOGICAL AND RELIGIO-MORAL CULTURE.

FOURTH CHAPTER.

HISTORY OF MONACHISM.

FIFTH CHAPTER.

HISTORY OF PUBLIC WORSHIP.

SIXTH CHAPTER.

HISTORY OF ECCLESIASTICAL DISCIPLINE.

SEVENTH CHAPTER.

SPREAD OF CHRISTIANITY.

SECOND PART.

HISTORY OF THE GREEK CHURCH.

FIRST CHAPTER.

RELATION OF THE GREEK CHURCH TO THE LATIN.

SECOND CHAPTER.

INTERNAL CONDITION OF THE GREEK CHURCH.

THIRD CHAPTER.

SPREAD OF CHRISTIANITY.

THIRD PART.

HISTORY OF HERETICAL PARTIES,

SECOND PERIOD.

(CONTINUED.)

FOURTH CHAPTER.

Rud. Hospiniani de Monachis h. e. de origine et progressu monachatus libb·
VI. Tiguri 1588. ed II. auct. 1609. Genev. 1669. fol.—Ant. Dadini Alteserrae Asceticâr s. origg. rei monasticae libb. X. Paris. 1674. 4. rec. ac praef.
notasque adjecit Chr. F. Glück. Halae 1782. 8.—Edm. Martene de antiquis monachorum ritibus. Lugd. 1690. 4.—J. Binghami origg. lib. VII.
(vol. iii. p. 1 ss.)—Hippol. Helyot histoire des ordres monastiques, etc.
Paris 1714. 19. t. VIII. 4. translated into German under the title : Aus-
führl. Gesch. aller geistl. u. weltl. Kloster u. Ritterorden Leipzig 1753.
56. 8 Bde. 4.—(Musson) Pragm. Geschichte d. vornehmsten Mönchsorden
aus ihren eigenen Geschichtschreibern (Paris 1751 ss.) i. e. deutschen
Ausz. (v. L. G. Crome) m. e. Vorrede v. Ch. W. Fr. Walch. Leipzig
1774–84. 10 Bde. 8. J. H. Möhler's Gesch. d. Mönchthums in d. Zeit s.
Entstehung u. ersten Ausbildung, in his Schriften u. Aufsätzen herausgeg. von Döllinger II., 165. Neander's Kirchengesch. II, 2, 486 ss.

§ 95.

ORIGIN AND HISTORY OF MONACHISM IN THE EAST.

Solitude and asceticism were universally looked upon in this
age as means of approximation to the Deity. The New Platonists recommended them.[1] The Jewish Essenes and Thera-

---

[1] After Plato's example in the Phædo and Theætetus. Plotinus recommends the μόνον εἶναι, μόνον πρὸς μόνον (θεὸν) γενέσθαι. See Creuzer
ad Plotini opp. ed. Oxon. iii., 140. 276. 412. A. Jahnii Basilius magnus plotinizans. Bernae 1838. 4, p. 19.

A

peutæ lived in this manner.[2] Thus *Anthony* (Div. I. § 73), appeared to have set forth the ideal of *a Christian* wise man : he soon found many imitators, and other hermits fixed themselves in his neighbourhood. Many more were concealed in inaccessible places, of whom one, *Paul of Thebes* († 340), who had lived in the desert ever since the Decian persecution, is said to have become known to Anthony shortly before his death.[3] After a number of hermits had been brought into a kind of connection with one another by Anthony, *Pachomius* founded a place of habitation where they might dwell together (κοινόβιον, μάνδρα, claustrum.—Κοινοβίτης, Συνοδίτης), on the island *Tabenna* in the Nile (about 340), with a system of rules for the government of its inmates, by which strict obedience to the president (Ἀββᾶς, Ἡγούμενος, Ἀρχιμανδρίτης) was particularly enforced. At the same time *Amun* founded a society of monks on *the Nitrian mountain* (τὸ τῆς Νιτρίας ὄρος) ; and *Macarius* the elder[4] in the neighbouring wilderness of *Sketis*.[5] Both were soon peopled by the monks, and became the most celebrated resorts. *Hilarion* assembled in the desert near Gaza, a company of monks, and from thence the system spread through Palestine and Syria.[6] The *Eusebian Eustathius*, afterwards bishop of Sebaste, introduced it into Armenia and Asia Minor.[7] The peculiarities of the monkish life of this period consisted in solitariness, manual labour, spiritual exercises,[8] restraint of the bodily appetites, for the pur-

[2] Still in the time of Nilus, who lived as monk on Sinai A. D. 430. See Nili tract. ad Magnum c. 39. (Nili tractatus ed. J. M. Suaresius, Romae 1673. fol. p. 279), and de monast. exercis. c. 3. (l. c. p. 2.), where they are called Ἰεσσαῖοι.

[3] Vita Antonii by Athanasius, see Div. 1. §. 73. not. 22. Vita Pauli by Jerome.

[4] Probably from him we have the homiliae spirituales 50 ed. J. G. Pritius. Lips. 1698 u. 1714. 8. Comp. Paniel's Gesch. der christl. Beredsamkeit i. 396.

[5] Coptic Schiêt, Greek Σκῆτης, Σκῆτις, ap. Ptolemy Σκίαθις, Latin Scetis, Scithis, Scytiaca, Scythium, means chiefly *the hill* on which Macarius settled, then *the surrounding desert*. Et Quatremère mémoires géograph. et hist. sur l'Egypte. (Paris. T. 2. 1811. 8.) i. 451.

[6] Vita Hilarionis by Jerome.—Λαύραι in Palestine.

[7] On the first monks generally see Socrates iv. 23. 24. Sozomenus i. 12–15. iii. 14. vi. 28 – 34. Palladii (bishop of Helenopolis, afterwards of Aspona, † about 420.) historia Lausiaca in Jo. Meursii opp. vol. viii. (Florent. 1746. fol.) p. 329. Theodoreti φιλόθεος ἱστορια.

Even Tertullian (de orat. c. 25. et adv. Psychicos c. 10.) and Cy-

pose of mortifying the sensual nature, and allowing the spirit with less disturbance to be absorbed in the contemplation of divine things.[9] The rules of the monasteries made, indeed, more moderate demands on the abstinence of the inmates;[10] but the majority of the monks did more than was required, of their own free choice, and many even withdrew from the cells of the convents into the desert (Ἀναχωρηταί), that they might suppress sensual desires by the most ingenious self tortures, and attain the highest degree of holiness. In many cases these measures had only the contrary effect, and temptations increased;[11] many

prian (de orat. domin. p. 154.) recommended the hora tertia, sexta, and nona, as times of prayer, whilst every day, morning and evening, church service was performed. (Const. apost. ii. 59.) Among the monks different usages arose at first. The Egyptians had, on every day of the week, only two meetings for prayer (Cassianus de instit. Coenob. iii. 2. vespertinas ac nocturnas congregationes), and in their cells carried on manual labour, and prayed almost incessantly; those of the East came together for the purpose of singing psalms, hora tertia, sexta, et nona (l. c. c. 3.), the matutina hora was first introduced at a later period into the monastery at Bethlehem (l. c. c. 4.). Athanasius de virginitate (opp. i. 1051 ss.) marks out for the nuns six seasons of prayer, viz., the third, sixth, ninth, twelfth hours (a more solemn assembly in the church at the last hour), μεσονύκτιον and πρὸς ὄρθρον. So also Jerome epituph. Paulae epist. 27. 10. epist 7. ad Laetam; according to Chrysostum. in 1 Tim. hom. xiv. the monks had the same hours. Basil also, de instit. monach. sermo, prescribes these six, but that there may be seven agreeably to Psalm cxviii. 164, the prayer of noon is directed to be divided into that before and that after eating. When six public hours for prayer are prescribed to the churches in the apostolic constitutions, viii. 34. the writer follows the view which arose in the fourth century, viz., that in the apostolic churches for which he pretends to write, a monastic institute prevailed. Even in his day there were daily but two religious services as at an early period (ἐν ἑσπέρᾳ καὶ ἐν πρωΐᾳ, Chrysost. in 1 Tim. hom. vi.)

[9] Respecting the Egyptian monasteries comp. Hieronymi ep. 18. (al. 22.) ad Eustochium (ed. Martian T. iv. P. ii. p. 45.) Jo. Cassiani collationes Patrum, et de institutis coenobiorum. On the labours cf. de inst. coen. x. 23.: Haec est apud Aegyptum ab antiquis patribus sancita sententia: operantem monachum daemone uno pulsari, otiosum vero innumeris spiritibus devastari. cf. Alteserra l. c. lib. v. cap. 7 et 8. Neander's Chrysostomus B. 1. S. 80 ff.

[10] Comp. Pachomius' rule (ap. Pallad. hist. Laus. c. 38.): Συγχωρήσεις ἑκάστῳ κατὰ τὴν δύναμιν φαγεῖν καὶ πιεῖν, καὶ πρὸς τὰς δυνάμεις τῶν ἐσθιόντων ἀνάλογα καὶ τὰ ἔργα αὐτῶν ἐγχείρησον, καὶ μήτε νηστεῦσαι κωλύσῃς μήτε φαγεῖν.

[11] See the confessions of Jerome ep. 18. ad Eustochium: Ille igitur

A 2

monks were driven to despair by a sense of the hopelessness of
their efforts ;[12] in the case of others, complete madness was su-

ego, qui ob gehennae metum tali me carcere ipse damnaveram, scor-
pionum tantum socius et ferarum, saepe choris intereram puellarum.
Pallebant ora jejuniis, et mens desideriis aestuabat in frigido corpore,
et ante hominem suum jam in carne praemortua, sola libidinum incendia bulliebant. Itaque omni auxilio destitutus, ad Jesu jacebam pedes,
rigabam lachrymis, crine tergebam, et repugnantem carnem hebdoma-
darum inedia subjugabam.—Memini me clamantem, diem crebro junx-
isse cum nocte, nec prius a pectoris cessasse verberibus, quam rediret
Domino increpante tranquillitas. Ep. 95. ad Rusticum: Dum essem
juvenis, et solitudinis me deserta vallarent : incentiva vitiorum ardo-
remque naturae ferre non poteram : quem cum crebris jejuniis fran-
gerem, mens tamen cogitationibus aestuabat. Ad quam edomandam
cuidam fratri, qui ex Hebraeis crediderat, me in disciplinam dedi, ut—
alphabetum discerem, et stridentia anhelantiaque verba meditarer. In
like manner Basil admits to his friend Gregory ep. 2. : κατελιπον μὲν τὰς
ἐν ἄστει διατριβὰς ὡς μυρίων κακῶν ἀφορμὰς, ἐμαυτὸν δὲ οὔπω ἀπολιπεῖν ἠδυν-
ήθην.—ὥστε οὐδὲν μέγα τῆς ἐρημίας ἀπωνάμεθα ταύτης. On the temptations
to lust see Nilus lib. ii. ep. 140. (Nili epistolarum libb. iv. Romae
1668. p. 179.) In the quaestt. and responsiones ad orthodoxos among
Justin's works, written after 400, it is asked, qu. 21. whether sensual
dreams exclude from supper : ἐπειδὴ πολλή ἐστι περὶ τούτου καὶ παρ αὐτῶν
(τῶν μοναχῶν) ἡ ζήτησις. Comp. Nilus περὶ διαφόρων πονηρῶν λογισμῶν (tractatus ed. Suaresii p. 512.). Basilii regulae breviores, interrog. 22. Comp.
the experience of Philo, Legis allegor. lib. iii. (properly lib. ii.) p. 1102:
ἐγὼ πολλάκις καταλιπὼν μὲν ἀνθρώπους, συγγενεῖς, καὶ φίλους, καὶ πατρίδα, καὶ
εἰς ἐρημίαν ἐλθων, ἵνα τι τῶν θέας ἀξίων κατανοήσω, οὐδὲν ὤνησα· ἀλλὰ σκορ-
πισθεὶς ὁ νοῦς, ἢ πάθει δηχθεὶς, ἀνεχώρησεν εἰς τἀναντία. Ἔστι δ'ὅτε καὶ ἐν
πλήθει μυριάνδρῳ ἔρημῶ τὴν διάνοιαν, τὸν ψυχικὸν ὄχλον σκεδάσαντος θεοῦ, καὶ
διδάξαντός με, ὅτι οὐ τόπων διαφοραὶ τό τε εὖ καὶ χεῖρον ἐργάζονται, ἀλλ' ὁ
κινῶν θεὸς καὶ ἄγων, ᾗ ἂν προαιρῆται, τὸ τῆς ψυχῆς ὄχημα. Zimmerman on
Solitude, part 2. chapters 6. and 7.

[12] So that some, like the circumcelliones (see §. 86. not. 9.), put an
end to their life, see Nilus lib. ii. ep. 140 : τινὲς μὲν αὐτῶν ξενισθέντες, καὶ
θορυβηθέντες τὸν νοῦν ἐξ ἀπροσεξίας καὶ ἀδιακρισίας, ἑαυτοὺς ἔσφαξαν μαχαίρᾳ,
τινὲς δὲ κατεκρήμνησαν ἑαυτοὺς ἀφορήτῳ λύπῃ καὶ ἀπογνώσει συσχεθέντες, ἕτεροι
δὲ τὰ γεννητικα μόρια κόψαντες, καὶ αὐτοφονευταὶ ἑαυτῶν τῇ προαιρέσει γεγονότες
οἱ τάλανες, ὑπέπεσαν τῇ ἀποστολικῇ ἀρᾷ,—ἄλλοι δὲ καὶ γυναῖκας ἔλαβον συναρ-
πασθέντες ὑπὸ τοῦ Σατανᾶ. Gregor. Naz. carm. xlvii. v. 100 ss. (opp.
T. ii. 107.) :

Θνήσκουσιν πολλοῖς προφρονέως θανάτοις,
Αὐτοὶ ὑπὸ σφετέρης παλάμης, καὶ γαστρὸς ἀνάγκῃ,
Οἱ δὲ κατὰ σκοπέλων βένθεσί τ' ἠὲ βρόχοις,
Μάρτυρες ἀτρεκίης· πολέμου δ'ἀπο καὶ στονόεντος
Χαίρουσιν βιότου τοῦδ' ἀπανιστάμενοι.
Ἵλαθι Χριστὲ ἄναξ πισταῖς φρεσὶν ἀφραδέουσιν !

Pachomius says, Vita Pachomii §.61. (Acta SS. Maji iii. 320. the Greek

perinduced by that excessive asceticism, and by the pride associated with it, under the influence of a burning climate.[13] From that diseased excitement of the imagination, and that spiritual pride, arose also those strange miraculous occurrences which befel the monks only in solitude. The lesser marvellous things which they wrought in the circles of enthusiastic admirers must be explained by the impression they made on the feelings of reverence entertained towards the persons of the monks, and by the magnifying nature of tradition.[14]

Very soon in the East monachism was received with enthusiastic admiration, and the number of monks swelled to an enormous extent.[15] As there were no more persecutions, and no more

original is given in the app. p. 41.) : Ἡ δὲ τῆς βλασφημίας ὑποβολὴ τῶν ἐχθρῶν ἐὰν εὔρῃ τινὰ μὴ νηφάλαιον, κἂν ᾖ ἀγαπῶν θεὸν,—τοῦτον ἀπολέσει. Καὶ πολλοὶ ἐθανάτωσαν ἑαυτοὺς, ὁ μὲν ἐπάνωθεν πέτρας ἑαυτὸν ῥίψας ὡς ἐκστατικὸς, καὶ ἄλλος μαχαίρᾳ ἀπέπτυξεν τὴν κοιλίαν αὐτοῦ καὶ ἀπέθανεν, καὶ ἄλλοι ἄλλως. cf. Chrysostomi ad Stagirium libb. iii. (opp. i. 163.) to a monk who believed that he had been tempted by Satan to commit suicide. Others sought assistance in their struggle against desire in immoderate sleep. Nili lib. iii. ep. 224.

[1] Hieronymi ep. 95. (al. 4.) ad Rusticum : Sunt, qui humore cellarum, immoderatisque jejuniis, taedio solitudinis ac nimia lectione, dum diebus ac noctibus auribus suis personant, vertuntur in melancholiam, et Hippocratis magis fomentis quam nostris monitis indigent. Ejusd. ep. 97. (al. 8.) ad Demetriadem : Novi ego in utroque sexu per nimiam abstinentiam cerebri sanitatem quibusdam fuisse vexatam : praecipueque in his, qui in humectis et frigidis habitaverunt cellulis, ita ut nescirent quid agerent, quove se verterent: quid loqui, quid tacere deberent. Hence his disapprobation of extreme fasting in ep. 57. (al. 7.) ad Laetam and Jo. Cassian. instit. v. 9.

[14] Several hints on this subject may be found in the following passages: Hieron. ep. 59. ad Rusticum : quosdam ineptos homines daemonum pugnantium contra se portenta confingere, ut apud imperitos et vulgi homines miraculum sui faciant, et exinde lucra sectentur. Sozomenus i. 14. : πολλὰ δὲ καὶ θεσπέσια ἐπ᾽ αὐτῷ (Ἀμοῦν) συμβέβηκεν, ἃ μάλιστα τοῖς κατ᾽ Αἴγυπτον μοναχοῖς ἠκρίβωται, περὶ πολλοῦ ποιουμένοις, διαδοχῇ παραδόσεως ἀγράφου ἐπιμελῶς ἀπομνημονεύειν τὰς τῶν παλαιοτέρων ἀσκητῶν ἀρετάς. Sulpicius Severus dial. ii. 4. relates that St Martin often told him, nequaquam sibi in episcopatu eam virtutum gratiam suppetisse, quam prius se habuisse meminisset. Quod si verum est, immo quia verum est, conjicere possumus, quanta fuerunt illa, quae monachus operatus est, et quae teste nullo solus exercuit, cum tanta illum in episcopatu signa fecisse, sub oculis omnium viderimus. For the physiological explanation of the frequent visions seen by these anchorites comp. D. Joh. Müller über die phantastischen Gesichtserscheinungen, Coblenz 1826. 8.

[15] Pachomius had in his convent 1300 monks, and in all upwards of

opportunities of martyrdom; as Christianity had even acquired external dominion; the erroneous notion was spread abroad that there was no longer an opportunity in the world for the full exercise of Christian virtue.[16] The general corruption[17] or consciousness of individual guilt caused many to seek solitude. Many sought escape from the oppressive circumstances of life.[18] Others wished to make a figure and obtain an influence. Others were attracted by sloth;[19] and lastly, others were drawn away by mere

---

7000 under his superintendence (Sozom. iii. 14.). In a monastery at Thebais were 5000 monks (Cass. de instit. iv. l.), in Nitria were 50 convents (Sozom. vi. 31.) &c.

[16] A kindred notion may be found in Origen, see Div. i. §. 70. not. 19.

[17] Chrysostomus adv. oppugnatores vitae monast. i. 7. : Ἐβουλόμην καὶ αὐτὸς—τῶν μοναστηρίων ἀναιρεθῆναι τὴν χρείαν, καὶ τοσαύτην ἐν ταῖς πόλεσι γενέσθαι τὴν εὐνομίαν, ὡς μηδένα δεηθῆναί ποτε τῆς εἰς τὴν ἔρημον καταφυγῆς· ἐπειδὴ δὲ τὰ ἄνω κάτω γέγονε, καὶ αἱ μὲν πόλεις—πολλῆς γέμουσι παρανομίας καὶ ἀδικίας, ἡ δὲ ἐρημία πολλῷ βρύει τῷ τῆς φιλοσοφίας καρπῷ οὐχ οἱ τῆς ζάλης ταύτης καὶ τῆς ταραχῆς τοὺς σωθῆναι βουλομένους ἐξάγοντες, καὶ πρὸς τὸν τῆς ἡσυχίας ὁδηγοῦντας λιμένα, δικαίως ἂν ἐγκαλοῖντο παρ' ὑμῶν.

[18] Isidorus Pelus. (see §. 88. not. 25.) lib. i. ep. 262. Εὐσέβιος (a bishop) καὶ τοῦτο τῇ παροικίᾳ Πηλουσίου παρέχετο, βουνόμοις τισὶ, καὶ αἰπόλοις, καὶ δραπέταις οἰκέταις ἐπιτρέπων μοναχικὰ συμπήγνυσθαι παλαιστήρια, οὐδενὶ μαθητευθεῖσι τὴν μοναχικὴν, ἢ μετελθόντων, ἢ ὅλως ἀγαπώντων, οὐδὲ ὅλως τῆς φιλοσοφίας ταύτης ἢ ἀκηκοόσιν, ἢ μέχρι σχήματος διδαχθεῖσι.

[19] Respecting the reputation which the monks possessed, compare what Chrysostom says to the heathen father of a monk, adv. oppugnatores vitae monast. ii. 4. : Σὺ μὲν οὖν τῶν σαυτοῦ κύριος εἶ μόνον, ἐκεῖνος (ὁ υἱός σου) δὲ τῶν κατὰ τὴν οἰκουμένην ἅπασαν. εἰ δὲ ἀπιστεῖς,—πείσωμεν αὐτὸν κατελθόντα ἀπὸ τοῦ ὄρους—σημᾶναί τινι τῶν σφόδρα πλουτούντων καὶ εὐλαβῶν, πέμψαι χρυσοῦ σταθμὸν, ὅσον ἐθέλεις,—καὶ προθυμότερον ὄψει τὸν πλουτοῦντα ὑπακούοντα καὶ ἐκκομίζοντα, ἢ τῶν οἰκονόμων τινὰ τῶν σῶν. c. 6. : εὑρήσομεν αὐτὸν (τὸν υἱόν σου) οὐ μόνον λαμπρότερον ὄντα νῦν, ἀλλὰ καὶ δι' ἐκεῖνα τιμώτερον, δι' ἅπερ ἄτιμον εἶναι φῇς καὶ εὐτελῆ. εἰ γὰρ βούλει, πείσαντες αὐτὸν ἀπὸ τοῦ ὄρους κατελθεῖν, πείσωμεν καὶ εἰς ἀγορὰν ἐμβαλεῖν, καὶ ὄψει πᾶσαν ἐπιστρεφομένην τὴν πόλιν, καὶ ὑποδεικνύντας αὐτὸν ἅπαντας, καὶ θαυμάζοντας, καὶ ἐκπληττομένους, ὡς ἀγγέλου τινὸς ἐξ οὐρανοῦ παραγενομένου νῦν. c. 7. : τίς μετὰ πλείονος ἐξουσίας διαλέξεται βασιλεῖ, καὶ ἐπιτιμήσει; ὁ τοσαῦτα σὺ κεκτημένος, καὶ ὑπεύθυνος ὢν διὰ ταῦτα καὶ τοῖς ἐκείνου δούλοις,—ἢ οὗτος ὁ τῶν ἐκείνου χειρῶν ἀνώτερος ὤν; βασιλεῦσι μὲν γὰρ οὗτοι μάλιστα διελέχθησαν μετ' ἐξουσίας πολλῆς, ὅσοι πάντων ἐγένοντο τῶν βιωτικῶν ἐκτός. c. 8. : εἰ ταπεινοὶ, καὶ ἐκ ταπεινῶν ὄντες τινὲς ἀγροίκων υἱοὶ καὶ χειροτεχνῶν, ἐπὶ τὴν φιλοσοφίαν ταύτην ἐλθόντες, οὕτως ἐγένοντο τίμιοι πᾶσιν, ὡς μηδένα τῶν ἐν τοῖς μεγάλοις ὄντων ἀξιώμασιν αἰσχυνθῆναι πρὸς τὸ καταγώγιον τούτων ἐλθεῖν, καὶ λόγων μετασχεῖν καὶ τραπέζης·—πολλῷ μᾶλλον, ὅταν ἀπὸ λαμπροῦ μὲν ὁρμώμενον γένους— πρὸς ἐκείνην ἴδωσιν ἐλθόντα τὴν ἀρετὴν, τοῦτο ἐργάσονται. Nilus λόγος ἀσκητικός c. 7. (opusc. ed. Suaresii p. 8.): The striving of many monks

imitation.[20] The measures taken by the emperor Valens[21] against the excessive tendency to this state of things were attended with no lasting consequences, since the following emperors rather showed respect for monachism. The most distinguished teachers of the church, *Athanasius, Ambrose, Basil the great, Gregory of Nazianzum, Chrysostom, Jerome, and Augustine,* were the most zealous panegyrists of the new mode of life (φιλοσοφία, αγγελικὴ διαγωγή.)[22] Examples in favour of it were soon disco-

[20] was even at that time so much directed towards the attainment of possession, ὥστε λοιπὸν τοὺς πολλοὺς πορισμὸν ἡγεῖσθαι τὴν εὐσέβειαν, καὶ δι᾽ οὐδὲν ἕτερον ἐπιτηδεύεσθαι τὸν πάλαι ἀπράγμονα καὶ μακάριον βίον, ἢ ὅπως διὰ τῆς ἐπιπλάστου θεοσεβείας τὰς μὲν ἐπιπόνους λειτουργείας φύγωμεν, ἄδειαν δὲ ἀπολαύσεως πορισάμενοι, ἀκωλύτως ἐπὶ τὰ δοκοῦντα τὰς ὁρμὰς ἐκτείνωμεν, μετὰ πολλῆς ἀναισχυντίας καταλαζονευόμενοι τῶν ὑποδεεστέρων, ἔστι δὲ ὅτε καὶ τῶν ὑπερεχόντων, ὥσπερ ὑπόθεσιν τυραννίδος, ἀλλ᾽ οὐχὶ ταπεινώσεως καὶ ἐπιεικείας τὸν ἐνάρετον βίον εἶναι νομίσαντες. Διὰ τοῦτο καὶ παρὰ τῶν σέβεσθαι ἡμᾶς ὀφειλόντων ὡς εἰκαῖος ὄχλος ὁρώμεθα, καὶ - γελώμεθα,—οὐκ ἐκ πολιτείας, ἀλλ᾽ ἐκ σχήματος γνωρίζεσθαι βουλόμενοι.

[20] Comp. the judgment of Synesius, at that time still a heathen, afterwards bishop of Ptolemais, in his Dion : οἱ δὲ πλείους οὐδ᾽ οἴκοθεν ἐκινήθησαν,—ὥσπερ δὲ ἄλλο τι τῶν εὐδοκιμούντων, τὴν γενναίαν αἵρεσιν ἐζηλώκασι, παντοδαποί τε ὄντες τὰ γένη, καὶ κατὰ χρείαν ἕκαστοι συνιστάμενοι.

[21] Cod. Theodos. xii. 1. 63. (A. D. 365) : Quidam ignaviae sectatores desertis civitatum muneribus captant solitudines ac secreta, et specie religionis cum coetibus monazonton congregantur. Hos igitur atque hujusmodi, intra Aegyptum deprehensos, per comitem Orientis erui et latebris consulta praeceptione mandavimus, atque ad munia patriarum subeunda revocari, aut pro tenore nostrae sanctionis familiarium rerum carere illecebris, quas per eos censuimus vindicandas, qui publicarum essent subituri munera functionum. After the death of his milder brother (Orosii hist. vii. 33 : illico post fratris obitum), Valens became more violent against the monks, see Hieron. chron. ann. 375 : multi monachorum Nitriae per tribunos et milites caesi. Valens enim lege data, ut monachi militarent, nolentes fustibus interfici jussit. This raised the courage of the numerous opponents of monachism, and therefore Chrysostom wrote at that time πρὸς τοὺς πολεμοῦντας τοῖς ἐπὶ τὸ μονάζειν ἐνάγουσιν libb. iii. (ed. Moutf. T. i.)

[22] ὁ τῶν ἀγγέλων βίος, τὰ οὐράνια πολιτεύματα, ἀποστολικὸς βίος (Epiph. haer. lxi. 4.), ἡ ὑψηλὴ φιλοσοφία, ἔργῳ μᾶλλον ἢ λόγῳ κατορθουμένη (Gregor. Nyss. orat. catech. c. 18.), ἡ κατὰ θεὸν φιλοσοφία (Nilus de monast. exercitatione c. 8.). Serapion, bishop of Thmuis, about 350, writes in the epist. ad monachos (spicilegium Romanum iv. p. liv.) to them : ἰσάγγελοι ἐστὲ τῇ πολιτείᾳ· ὥσπερ γὰρ ἐν τῇ ἀναστάσει τῶν νεκρῶν οὔτε γαμοῦσιν οὔτε γαμίσκονται, ἀλλ᾽ ὡς ἄγγελοι εἰσὶν ἐν οὐρανῷ οἱ δίκαιοι, τὸν αὐτὸν τρόπον καὶ ὑμεῖς οὕτω συμβιστεύοντες, προελάβετε τῷ πόθῳ τὸ ἐσόμενον. Entering on the life of a monk is called by Jerome ep. 22. (al. 25.) ad Paulam : secundo quodammodo propositi se baptismo lavare. Subse-

vered even in the Old Testament ;[23] and by new explanations of detached passages and the help of supplementing legends, the original condition of the early Christians was shown to be a completely monastic state.[24]

quently Dionys. Areop. de eccles. hierarch. c. 6. reckons the vow of monks (μυστήριον μοναχικῆς τελειώσεως) among the sacraments.

[23] Hieronymus in vita S. Pauli (about 365) : Inter multos saepe dubitatum est, a quo potissimum Monachorum eremus habitari coepta sit. Quidam enim altius repetentes, a b. Elia et Johanne sumsere principium. Quorum et Elias plus nobis videtur fuisse, quam Monachus : et Johannes ante prophetare coepisse, quam natus sit. Alii autem, in quam opinionem vulgus omne consensit, asserunt Antonium hujus propositi caput, quod ex parte verum est. Non enim tam ipse ante omnes fuit, quam ab eo omnium incitata sunt studia. Amathas vero et Macarius, discipuli Antonii, e quibus superior magistri corpus sepelivit, etiam nunc affirmant, Paulum quemdam Thebaeum principem istius rei fuisse, non nominis; quam opinionem nos quoque probamus. On the contrary, the same Jerome observed about 395. ep. 49. (al. 13.) ad Paulinum : Nos autem habeamus propositi nostri principes Paulos et Antonios, Julianos, Hilarionem, Macarios. Et ut ad scripturarum auctoritatem redeam : noster princeps Helias, noster Helisaeus, nostri duces filii prophetarum, qui habitabant in agris et solitudinibus, et faciebant sibi tabernacula prope fluenta Jordanis. De his sunt et illi filii Rechab (Jerem 35.), qui vinum et siceram non bibebant, qui morabantur in tentoriis etc. Sozomenus i. 12. ταύτης δὲ τῆς ἀρίστης φιλοσοφίας ἤρξατο, ὥς τινες λέγουσιν, Ἡλίας ὁ προφήτης, καὶ Ἰωάννης ὁ βαπτιστής.

[24] The Therapeutae were regarded as Christians (Div. i. §. 17. not. 11.) and for this purpose such passages as Act. ii. 44., iv. 32 ss. were appealed to. Hieron. Catal. c. 11 : Philo—librum de prima Marci Evangelistae apud Alexandriam scribens ecclesia, in nostrorum laude versatus est (he means Philo περὶ βίου θεωρητικοῦ) ; non solum eos ibi, sed in multis quoque provinciis esse commemorans, et habitacula eorum dicens monasteria. Ex quo apparet, talem primam Christo credentium fuisse ecclesiam, quales nunc monachi esse nituntur et cupiunt, ut nihil cujuspiam proprium sit, nullus inter eos dives, nullus pauper : patrimonia egentibus dividuntur, orationi vacatur et psalmis, doctrinae quoque et continentiae : quales et Lucas refert primum Hierosolymae fuisse credentes. Jo. Cassian. collat. 18. c. 5 : Itaque Coenobitarum disciplina a tempore praedicationis apostolicae sumsit exordium. Nam talis extitit in Hierosolymis omnis illa credentium multitudo, quae in Actibus Apostolorum ita describitur (seqq. loci Act. iv. 32. 34. 35.)—Sed cum post Apostolorum excessum tepescere coepisset credentium multitudo, ea vel maxime, quae ad fidem Christi de alienigenis ac diversis gentibus confluebat,—non solum hi qui ad fidem Christi confluxerant, verum etiam illi, qui erant ecclesiae principes, ab illa districtione laxati sunt.—Hi autem, quibus adhuc apostolicus inerat fervor, memores illius pristinae perfectionis, discedentes a civitatibus suis—et ea, quae ab Apostolis per universum corpus ecclesiae generaliter meminerant instituta, privatim ac peculiariter exercere coeperunt etc. Idem de

For a long time the monks appeared to have been able to dwell only in deserts. Individuals, indeed, sometimes shewed themselves in cities to oppose heathens and heretics, but they always withdrew again very soon into their solitude.[25] *Basil the great* was the first who established a company of monks in the vicinity of Caesarea in Cappadocia, in order to suppress Arianism, by their influence with the people.[26] From this time monasteries became more frequent in the neighbourhood of cities; but since there were as yet no strict rules, wandering companies of monks were also found. Thus their influence in Church and State became stronger, but, at the same time, more dangerous.

institut. Coenob. ii. 5 : Cum in primordiis fidei pauci quidem, sed probatissimi, monachorum nomine censerentur, qui sicut a beatae memoriae evangelista Marco, qui primus Alexandrinae urbi Pontifex praefuit, normam suscepere vivendi, non solum illa magnifica retinebant, quae primitus ecclesiam vel credentium turbas in Actibus Apostolorum legimus celebrasse,—verum etiam his multo sublimiora cumulaverant. cf. Sozomenus i. 12. Hence the monks mere said ἀποστολικὸν βίον βιοῦν Epiphan. haer. 61. §. 4.—Legends of the monkish chastity of the saints. Of Mary especially, Protevangelium Jacobi c. 7 ss. From a misunderstanding of Exodus xiii. 1. (2 Macc. iii. 19 ?) it was thought that there were in the temple virgins consecrated to God, among whom Mary had grown up (Epiphan. Ancorat. no. 60. Gregor. Nyss. orat. de sancta Christi nativitate) with the vow of perpetual virginity (Augustinus de virginitate c. 4.) Her marriage with Joseph was only apparent, he being 80 years old (Epiph. haer. 51. c. 10.), and according to Epiph. l. c. a widower, but according to Jerome adv. Helvid. c. 9. a perpetual ascetic. cf. J. A. Schmidii prolusiones Marianae x. Helmst. 1733. 4. p. 21 ss.—1 Cor. ix. 5. was referred to female friends of the apostles (Div. i. §. 27. note 3.)

[25] Antony said : τοὺς μὲν ἰχθύας τὴν ὑγρὰν οὐσίαν τρέφειν· μοναχοῖς δὲ κόσμον φέρειν τὴν ἔρημον· ἐπίσης τὲ τοὺς μὲν ξηρᾶς ἀπτομένους τὸ ζῆν ἀπολιμπάνειν, τοὺς δὲ τὴν μοναστικὴν σεμνότητα ἀπολλύειν τοῖς ἄστεσι προσιόντας. Sozom. i. 13.

[26] Socrates iv. 21. Gregor. Nazianz. orat. xx. in laudem Basilii p. 358 : τοῦ τοίνυν ἐρημικοῦ βίου καὶ τοῦ μιγάδος μαχομένων πρὸς ἀλλήλους ὡς τὰ πολλὰ, καὶ δϋσταμένων, καὶ οὐδετέρου πάντως ἢ τὸ καλὸν, ἢ τὸ φαῦλον ἀνεπίμικτον ἔχοντος· ἀλλὰ τοῦ μὲν ἡσυχίου μὲν ὄντος μᾶλλον, καὶ καθεστηκότος, καὶ θεῷ συνάγοντος, οὐκ ἀτύφου δὲ διὰ τὸ τῆς ἀρετῆς ἀβασάνιστον καὶ ἀσύγκριτον· τοῦ δὲ πρακτικωτέρου μὲν μᾶλλον καὶ χρησιμωτέρου, τὸ δὲ θορυβῶδες οὐ φεύγοντος· καὶ τούτους ἄριστα κατήλλαξεν ἀλλήλοις καὶ συνεκέρασεν· ἀσκητήρια καὶ μοναστήρια δειμάμενος μὲν, οὐ πόρρω δὲ τῶν κοινωνικῶν καὶ μιγάδων, οὐδὲ ὥσπερ τειχίῳ τινὶ μέσῳ ταῦτα διαλαβὼν, καὶ ἀπ' ἀλλήλων χωρίσας, ἀλλὰ πλησίον συνάψας καὶ διαζεύξας· ἵνα μήτε τὸ φιλόσοφον ἀκοινώνητον ᾖ, μήτε τὸ πρακτικὸν ἀφιλόσοφον. On the Ascetica of Basil, the chief parts of which are ὅροι κατὰ πλάτος and ὅροι κατ' ἐπιτομήν (monks' rules) see Garnier in praef. ad Basil. opp. T. ii. p. xxxiv. ss.

It is true that the monks made a strong moral impression by
their strict life dedicated to God in solitude. Even heathens
frequently repaired to them in numbers, for the sake of receiving
their blessing, and were converted by them.[27] But the honour
and power they possessed not unfrequently caused the passions
within them, which were suppressed in regard to their sensual
manifestations, to break forth still more strongly in the form of
spiritual pride,[28] and wild fanaticism, against those who thought
differently from themselves. From the time of Theodosius I., they
opposed heathenism with fury and barbarousness;[29] and they
also mingled in ecclesiastical controversies in a manner no less
violent. Since they despised all learning, and founded their
judgment of orthodoxy merely on an obscure feeling of what looked
like piety, and what did not,[30] it was seldom difficult for a superior
head to excite their fanaticism in favour of a certain view. Thus
the ambitious bishops of Alexandria, *Theophilus*, *Cyril*, and
Dioscurus, knew well how to make use of them, partly to work
upon the people, partly to overpower their opponents by acts of

[27] See Möhler's Schriften u. Aufsätze ii. 219.
[28] Hieronym. ep. 15, (al. 77.) ad Marcum : Pudet dicere, de caver-
nis cellularum damnamus orbem, in sacco et cinere volutati de Episcopis sententiam ferimus. Quid facit sub tunica poenitentis regius animus? Catenae, sordes et comae, non sunt diadematis signa, sed fletus.
Idem ep. 95. (al. 4.) ad Rusticum : In solitudine cito subrepit superbia :
et si parumper jejunaverit, hominemque non viderit, putat se alicujus
esse momenti. Oblitusque sui, unde, et quo venerit, intus corde, lingua foris vagatur. Judicat contra Apostoli voluntatem alienos servos :
quo gula voluerit porrigit manum : dormit quantum voluerit : nullum
veretur : facit quod voluerit : omnes inferiores se putat : crebriusque in
urbibus, quam in cellula est : et inter fratres simulat verecundiam, qui
platearum turbis colliditur. Comp. Nilus above not. 19.
[29] Comp. Libanius above § 78. not. 9. Zosimus v. 23. Eunapius
in vita Aedesii : Μοναχοὺς, ἀνθρώπους μὲν κατὰ τὸ εἶδος, ὁ δὲ βίος αὐτοῖς
συώδης, καὶ εἰς τὸ ἐμφανὲς ἔπασχόν τε καὶ ἐποίουν μυρία κακὰ καὶ ἄφραστα.
Ἀλλ' ὅμως τοῦτο μὲν εὐσεβὲς ἐδόκει τὸ καταφρονεῖν τοῦ θείου· τυραννικὴν γὰρ
εἶχεν ἐξουσίαν τότε πᾶς ἄνθρωπος, μέλαιναν φορῶν ἐσθῆτα, καὶ δημοσίᾳ βουλό-
μενος ἀσχημονεῖν.
[3] Sozomenus i. 12 : ἡ τοιαύτη φιλοσοφία μαθημάτων μὲν πολλῶν καὶ δια-
λεκτικῆς τεχνολογίας ἀμελεῖ, ὡς περιέργου, καὶ τὴν ἐν τοῖς ἀμείνοσι σχολὴν
ἀφαιρουμένης, καὶ πρὸς τὸ βιοῦν ὀρθῶς οὐδὲν συλλαμβανομένης· μόνη δὲ φυσικῇ
καὶ ἀπεριέργῳ φρονήσει παιδεύει τὰ παντελῶς κακίαν ἀναιροῦντα, ἢ μείονα ἐργα-
ζόμενα. Synesius in his Dion designates them by the names of τῶν
ἀμούσων, τῶν μισολόγων, τῶν βαρβάρων, τῶν ἀστεμφῶν καὶ ὑπερόπτων ῥητορι-
κῆς καὶ ποιήσεως, see Clausen de Synesio p. 48.

violence.[31]   The rude mass were as easily excited, in a fanatical manner, against a Chrysostom, at the point of death,[32] as against idolaters and Arians.   The limits of civil law, and the dignity of magistrates, appear to have been disregarded by them.[33]   In them religious fanaticism was united with a cynical indifference to propriety or duty ; and too often indolence and vice also were concealed under this mask of piety.[34]

Contemplation, which was regarded as the most important duty of the monk, as though it led him to an internal union with God, was usually, in the absence of mental cultivation, either a suffering resignation to feeling, without a distinct consciousness of it,[35] or a play of anthropomorphic images of the fancy.   Hence anthropomorphism was very common among them.[36]   But incessant

[31] Witness the insurrection of the Anthropomorphists against Theophilus, Socrates vi. 7, of the Nitrian monks against Orestes in favour of Cyril vii. 13.   Destruction of a Valentinian temple, Ambrosius epist. 40. (al. 29.) ad Theodosium.

[32] In Caesarea, comp. Neander's Chrysost. Bd. 2. S. 238.

[33] They frequently interfered violently in behalf of criminals, ex. gr. for disturbers of the public peace in Antioch, Chrysost. orat. 17, et 18, ad popul. Antioch. Theodoreti h. e. v. 19.   Law of Arcadius, A.D. 398. (Cod. Theod. ix. xl. 16.), see above, § 91, not. 10.

[34] Comp. Neander's Chrysostomus, Bd. 2, S. 108 ff.

[35] Yet Anthony said (Cassiani collat. ix. 31.) : Non est perfecta oratio, in qua se Monachus, vel hoc ipsum quod orat, intelligit.

[36] Theophilus, bishop of Alexandria, rejected the anthropomorphism of the monks, in his Easter letter 399.   Cassiani coll. x. 2 : Quod tanta est amaritudine ab universo propemodum genere Monachorum, qui per totam provinciam Aegypti morabantur, pro simplicitatis errore susceptum, ut e contrario memoratum pontificem, velut haeresi gravissima depravatum, pars maxima Seniorum ab universo fraternitatis corpore decerneret detestandum, quod silicet impugnare Scripturae sanctae sententiam videretur, negans omnipotentem Deum humanae figurae compositione formatum, cum ad ejus imaginem creatum Adam Scriptura manifestissime testaretur.   When Seraphin, an old monk highly esteemed, was convinced of his error, he was so smitten with remorse (cap. 3.) eo quod illam Anthropomorphitarum imaginem Deitatis, quam proponere sibi in oratione consueverat, aboleri de suo corde sentiret, ut in amarissimos fletus crebrosque singultus repente prorumpens, in terramque prostratus, cum ejulatu validissimo proclamaret: heu me miserum, tulerunt a me Deum meum, et quem nunc teneam non habeo, vel quem adorem aut interpellem jam nescio.   So the Anthropomorphites generally (cap. 5.) nihil se retinere vel habere credentes, si propositam non habuerint imaginem quandam, quam in supplicatione positi jugiter interpellent, eamque circumferant mente, ac prae oculis teneant semper

occupation with religious subjects, overstrained views, and self-conceit, joined with the want of culture, occasionally led them to other aberrations also from the doctrine of the Church.[37] *Audius* in Mesopotamia was still worthy of respect, who separated from the Church on account of its corruption, and founded a sect of monks *(Audiani)* about A. D. 340.[38] But the *Messalians* (מְצַלְיָן) or *Εὐχίται*,[39] who also arose in Mesopotamia (about 360), were mere fanatics, wandering hordes of beggars, who supposed that incessant prayer could blot out all sin ; while they undervalued public worship, and were led into the most absurd notions by their coarse imagination. Even *Eustathius*, the founder of monachism in Armenia, came to reject marriage absolutely, and was, on this account, condemned with his followers by the *Synod of Gangra* (between 362 and 370).[40]

In the mean time monachism was developed in forms the most various. Many monks *(Rhemoboth* or *Sarabaitae)*,[41] still continued to live in society[42] like the old ascetics, but were less highly esteemed. Others wandered about in companies *(Βοσκόι)*[43] in

affixam.   On the Anthropomorphism of Abraames see Theodoreti hist. rel. c. 3.

[37] Thus some were led to entertain contempt for public worship and the sacraments, as Valens and Heron (Palladii hist. Lausiaca c. 31, et 32), and the Messalians. One Ptolemy went even so far with his hatching and dreaming over divine things, as to arrive at last at Atheism (Palladius l. c. c. 33.)

[38] Epiphan. haer. 70. cf. Ancoratus c. 14.   Theodoret. h. e. iv. 9. haer. fab. comp. iv. 10.   Walch's Kezerhist. iii. 300.   Neander ii. iii. 1464.   They were Anthropomorphists and Quartodecimani.

[39] Epiphan. haer. 80. Theodoret. h. e. iv. 10. haer. fab. iv. 11.   Extracts in Photius cod. 52.   Walch iii. 481.   Neander ii. ii. 514.

[40] The acts of this synod (ap. Mansi ii. 1095), are the chief source for the knowledge of his doctrines. Socrat. ii. 43. Sozom iv. 24. Walch iii. 536.   In the synodical decree it is also reckoned among their errors in doctrine : πρεσβυτέρων γεγαμηκότων ὑπερφρονοῦντες, καὶ τῶν λειτουργιῶν τῶν ὑπ᾽ αὐτῶν γινομένων μὴ ἁπτόμενοι.   On the contrary, can. 4 : Εἴ τις διακρίνοιτο παρὰ πρεσβυτέρου γεγαμηκότος, ὡς μὴ χρῆναι λειτουργήσαντος αὐτοῦ προσφορᾶς μεταλαμβάνειν, ἀνάθεμα ἔστω.   On the time of the synod of Gangra see Ballerini de ant. collect. canonum P. 1. cap. 4. § 1.

[41] Concerning the former, Hieron. ep. 18. (al. 22.) ad Eustochium, concerding the latter, Cassian. collat. xviii. c. 4 and 7.   Walch de Sarabaitis (novi commentarii Soc. Getting. T. V. Comm. hist. p. 1 ss.)

[42] Also with the συνεισακτα in Ambros. sermo. 65. Gregorii Naz. carm. in several passages. See Walch, l. c. p. 23 s. Moreover, there were still ascetics who abstained from certain meats, but not from mar-

Mesopotamia. Those who lived together in convents were called *coenobites*, each convent having its peculiar constitution, among whom the most distinguished since the fifth century were the ἀκοίμητοι, *watchers*, for whom *Studius*, in 460, founded one of the most celebrated convents in Constantinople (*Studitae*).[44] But amongst the people, the *anchorites* were reckoned the most holy, for they carried their artificial self-tortures the farthest, and vied with each other in inventing new modes of cruelty against their own persons.[45] The highest point in this art was reached by *Simeon*, who, from the year 420, dwelt on a pillar in the neighbourhood of Antioch.[46] In this he was imitated by others, and although at first the example was found by individuals to be hazardous,[47] yet it was wondered at by the mass. Even so late as the twelfth century, similar pillar-saints (στυλίτης or στηλίτης), appeared in the east.

The female sex could not imitate the men in all these kinds of

riage (*abstinentes* apud Tertullian, see div. 1. § 53. not. 31); these also were now occasionally styled monks, Athanasii epist. ad Dracontium: πολλοὶ τῶν ἐπισκόπων οὐδὲ γεγαμήκασι, μοναχοὶ δὲ πατέρες τέκνων γεγόνασιν. Augustin. de haeres. c. 40; utentes conjugibus, et res proprias possidentes—habet catholica Ecclesia et Monachos et Clericos plurimos.

[43] Sozom. vi. 33. Evagr. i. 21.

[44] Nicephori hist. eccl. xv. 23. J. J. Müller Studium coenob. Constantinopol. ex monum. Byzantinis illustratum, diss. Lips. 1721. 4.

[45] An example in Sozom. vi. 28–34.

[46] In like manner in heathen Syria the Φαλλοβατεῖς in the temple at Hierapolis (Lucianus de Dea Syria c. 28. 29.) Respecting Simeon see Theodoreti hist. relig. c. 26, and his biographies by his scholar *Antonius* (in act. SS. ad d. 5. Jan.) and his contemporary Cosmas (in Assemani act. SS. Mart. Occid. et Orient. P. ii. p. 268.) cf. Stylitica; Simeonis Stylitæ senioris biographiam graecam (a later one derived from that of Antonius), junioris orationem graecam prim. ed. et illustr. H. N. Clausen (in the miscellanea Hafniensia ed. F. Münter. Tom. ii. Fasc. 2. Hafn. 1824. 8. p. 227 ss.)

[47] Nili lib. ii. epist. 114. to the Stylite Nicander: ὁ ὑψῶν ἑαυτὸν ταπεινωθήσεται. Σὺ δὲ μηδὲν κατορθώσας ἐπαινούμενον πρᾶγμα, καὶ ὑψώσας σεαυτὸν ἐφ' ὑψηλοῦ τοῦ στύλου, καὶ βούλει μεγίστων τυγχάνειν εὐφημιῶν· ἀλλὰ πρόσεχε σαυτῷ, μήποτε ἐνταῦθα παρὰ ἀνθρώπων φθαρτῶν ἀκρατῶς ἐπαινεθεὶς, ἀρτίως τὸ τηνικαῦτα παρὰ τοῦ ἀφθάρτου θεοῦ ταλανισθῆς ἀθλίως παρ' ἐλπίδας, διότι ὑπὲρ τὴν ἀξίαν ἐνταῦθα ἐνεφορήθης τῶν ἀνθρωπίνων κρότων. Ep. 115. to the same: Ἄτοπον ἂν εἴη ἐφ' ὑψηλοῦ μὲν τοῦ κίονος ἵστασθαι τῷ σώματι τοῖς πᾶσι φαινόμενον ἔνδοξον, κάτω δὲ τοῖς λογισμοῖς σύρεσθαι, μηδὲν ἄξιον τῶν οὐρανίων πραγμάτων διανοεῖσθαι βουλόμενον, μόνον δὲ ταῖς γυναιξὶν ἡδέως προσλαλοῦντα ἐν ταῖς ἡμέραις ταύταις. Πρώην μὲν γὰρ τοῖς ἀνδράσιν ἐκ προθυμίας ἐφθέγγου, νῦν δὲ ὡς ἐπὶ τὸ πλεῖστον τὰ γύναια προσδέχῃ.

asceticism, though there were convents for them as early as for
the male sex (Ascetriæ, Monastriæ, Castimoniales, Sanctimoniales, Nonnæ).[48]

It is true that the resolution of devoting themselves to a monastic life had been now publicly declared, and penance imposed
on those who drew back; but yet the teachers of the Church
looked upon this retractation not merely as possible, without
farther permission, but even advisable under certain circumstances.[49]

---

[48] Pachomius in like manner founded the first.   Pallad. hist. Laus. c.
34. et 38.—Nonna (Hieron. ep. 18. ad Eustoch.) νονίς (Pallad. l. c. c.
(46. were names of honour, as among the monks Nonnus, according to
Arnobius jun. in Psalm. cv. and cxl. the Egyptian for sanctus, castus, or
according to Benedicti regula c. 63. paterna reverentia: according to
Jablonski opusc. ed. te Water T. i. p. 176. properly Ennueneh or
Nueneh, i. e. quae non est hujus saeculi, quae saeculo renunciavit.—
The lady president was called mother, Ἀμμᾶς (Pallad. l. c. c. 42.)

[49] Epiphan. haer. 61. §. 7 : Κρεῖττον τοίνυν ἔχειν ἁμαρτίαν μίαν, καὶ μὴ
περισσοτέρας. κρεῖττον πεσόντα ἀπὸ δρόμου φανερῶς ἑαυτῷ λαβεῖν γυναῖκα κατὰ
νόμον, καὶ ἀπὸ παρθενίας πολλῷ χρόνῳ μετανοήσαντα εἰσαχθῆναι πάλιν εἰς τὴν
ἐκκλησίαν, ὡς κακῶς ἐργασάμενον, ὡς παραπεσόντα, καὶ κλασθέντα, καὶ χρείαν
ἔχοντα ἐπιδέματος, καὶ μὴ καθ' ἑκάστην ἡμέραν βέλεσι κρυφίοις κατασιτρώσ-
κεσθια. Hieronym. ep. 97. (al. 8.) ad Demetriadem : Sanctum virginum
propositum et coelestis angelorumque familiae gloriam quarundam non
bene se agentium nomen infamat.   Quibus aperte dicendum est, ut aut
nubant, si se non possunt continere, aut contineant, si nolunt nubere.
(see above §. 73. not. 6.) Angustinus de bono viduit. c. 10 : Qui dicunt
talium nuptias non esse nuptias, sed potius adulteria, non mihi videntur
satis acute ac diligenter considerare quid dicant.—Fit autem per hanc
minus consideratam opinionem, qua putant lapsarum a sancto proposito
feminarum, si nupserint, non esse conjugia, non parvum malum, ut a
maritis separentur uxores, quasi adulterae sint, non uxores : et cum volunt eas separatas reddere continentiae, faciunt maritos earum adulteros
veros, cum suis vxoribus vivis alteras duxerint. Concil. Chalced. can. 16.
Παρθέναν ἑαυτὴν ἀναθεῖσαν τῷ δεσπότῃ θεῷ, ὡσαύτως δὲ καὶ μονάζοντα, μὴ
ἐξεῖναι γάμῳ προσομιλεῖν· εἰ δέ γε εὑρεθεῖεν τοῦτο ποιοῦντες, ἔστωσαν ἀκοινώνητοι·
ὡρίσαμεν δὲ ἔχειν τὴν αὐθεντίαν τῆς ἐπ' αὐτοῖς φιλανθρωπίας τὸν κατὰ τόπον
ἐπίσκοπον.

§ 96.

MONACHISM IN THE WEST.

Jo. Mabillon observ. de monachis in Occidente ante Benedictum.   (Acta SS. Ord. Bened. Saec. I. Praef. p. 7.)

Monachism was first acknowledged in the West by *Athanasius*, although it was generally looked upon as an excrescence of oriental fanaticism, with a surprise which not unfrequently amounted to contempt and hatred.   Yet it also found numerous warm friends, many of whom went as far as Egypt and Palestine, for the purpose of being initiated into the new mode of life.[1]   *Ambrose* and *Jerome* were the influential promoters of it in Italy. The former established a monastery at *Milan*.[2]   At the same time convents for both sexes were founded in *Rome*,[3] notwith-

---

[1] On this account Jerome translated the rule of Pachomius into Latin, as he says in the preface (Luc. Holstenii codex regularum i. 59.), propterea quod plurimi Latinorum habitant in Thebaidis coenobiis et in monasterio Metanoeae, qui ignorant aegyptiacum graecumque sermonem.

[2] Augustini confess. viii. 6 : Erat monasterium Mediolani plenum bonis fratribus extra urbis moenia sub Ambrosio nutritore.   Id. de moribus eccles. cath. i. 33 : vidi ego diversorium sanctorum Mediolani non paucorum hominum, quibus unus Presbyter praeerat, vir optimus et doctissimus.

[3] Hieron. ep. 96. ad Principiam de laudibus Marcellae A. D. 412: Nulla eo tempore nobilium feminarum voverat Romae propositum Monachorum, nec audebat propter rei novitatem ignominiosum, ut tunc putabatur, et vile in populis nomen assumere.   Haec (Marcella) ab Alexandrinis sacerdotibus, Papaque Athanasio et postea Petro, qui persecutionem Arianae haereseos declinantes, quasi ad tutissimum communionis suae portum Romam confugerant, vitam beati Antonii adhuc tunc viventis, monasteriorumque in Thebaide Pachumii et virginum ac viduarum didicit disciplinam.—Hanc multos post annos imitata est Sophronia, et aliae.—Hujus amicitiis fruita est Paula venerabilis.   In hujus cubiculo nutrita Eustochium, virginitatis decus, ut facilis aestimatio sit, qualis magistra, ubi tales discipulae.—Audivimus te illius adhaesisse consortio, et nunquam ab illa—recessisse.—Suburbanus ager vobis pro Monasterio fuit, et rus electum pro solitudine.   Multoque ita vixistis tempore, ut, ex imitatione vestri, conversatione multarum gauderemus Romam factam Jerosolymam.   Crebra virginum monasteria, Monachorum innumerabilis multitudo, ut pro frequentia servientium Deo, quod prius ignominiae fuerat, esset postea gloriae.   Epist. 54. ad

standing the unfavourable opinion of the people ; and the small
islands near the coast, *Gallinaria* (Galinara), Gorgon (Gorgona),
Capraria (Capraia), *Palmaria* (Palmarola), on the west coast of
Italy,[4] and the islands on the *Dalmatian* coast,[5] became impor-

Pammachium A. D. 398 : Pammachius meus—ἀρχιστρατηγὸς Monachorum. Augustin. de moribus eccl. cath. (388 written in Rome) i. 33 :
Romae plura (diversoria sanctorum) cognovi, in quibus singuli gravitate atque prudentia et divina scientia praepollentes caeteris secum
habitantibus praesunt, christiana caritate, sanctitate et libertate viventi-
bus.   Ne ipsi quidem cuiquam onerosi sunt, sed Orientis more et
Apostoli Pauli auctoritate, manibus suis se transigunt. Jejunia etiam
prorsus incredibilia multos exercere didici, non quotidie semel sub
noctem reficiendo corpus, quod est usquequaque usitatissimum, sed
continuum triduum vel amplius saepissime sine cibo et potu ducere :
neque hoc in viris tantum, sed etiam in foeminis, quibus item, multis
viduis et virginibus simul habitantibus, et lana ac tela victum quaeritan-
tibus, praesunt singulae gravissimae probatissimaeque, non tantum in
instituendis componendisque moribus, sed etiam instituendis mentibus
peritae atque paratae.   These fasts, which were manifestly prejudicial
to the health, stirred up the people.   At the burying of Blaesilla, a
daughter of Paula, a young nun, supposed to have been killed by fasting, A. D. 384, the people cried out (Hieronymi ep. 22. al. 25. ad Paulam) : Quousque genus detestabile monachorum non urbe pellitur ? non
lapidibus obruitur ? non praecipitatur in fluctus ?
  [4] Ambrosii hexaëmeron iii. c. 5 : Quid enumerem insulas, quas velut
monilia plerumque praetexit, id quibus ii, qui se abdicant intempe-
rantiae saecularis illecebris, fido continentiae proposito, eligunt mundum
latere, et vitae hujus declinare dubios anfractus ? Hieronymus ep. 84.
(al. 30.) de morte Fabiolae about 400 : Angusta misericordiae ejus
Roma fuit. Peragrabat ergo insulas et totum Etruscum mare, Vol-
scorumque provinciam et reconditos curvorum littorum sinus, in quibus
monachorum consistunt chori, vel proprio corpore, vel transmissa per
viros sanctos ac fideles munificentia circumibat. Comp. the itinerarium
of the heathen Rutilii Numatiani (A. D. 417) i. 439 ss.

    Processu pelagi jam se Capraria tollit,
    Squallet lucifugis insula plena viris.
    Ipsi se monachos Grajo cognomine dicunt etc.

and respecting Gorgon ibid. v. 517 ss.

    Aversor scopulos, damni monumenta recentis :
    Perditus hic vivo funere civis erat.
    Noster enim nuper, juvenis majoribus amplis,
    Nec censu inferior, conjugiove minor.
    Impulsus furiis, homines divosque reliquit,
    Et turpem latebram credulus exsul amat.
    Infelix putat illuvie coelestia pasci ;
    Seque premit laesis saevior ipse Deis.
    Num, rogo, deterior Circaeis secta venenis ?
    Tunc mutabantur corpora, nunc animi.

  [5] Hieron. ep. 92. ad Julianum : Exstruis monasteria, et multus a te
er insulas Dalmatiae Sanctorum numerus sustentatur.

tant seats of monastic establishments. *Martin's* first established in *Gaul* a monastery at *Poictou*;[7] and afterwards, when he became bishop of *Turonum*, (375–400) another in that city.[8] About 400, *Honoratus* founded the celebrated monastery on the island *Lerina* (now St Honorat).[9] Others rose on the island *Lero*[10] (St Marguerite), and the *Stoechades*[11] on the south coast of Gaul. *John Cassian*,[12] who was educated among the Egyptian monks, founded two cloisters in Massilia (after 410). He died after 432. In *Africa*, notwithstanding *Augustine's* most zealous encomiums on monachism, it found acceptance almost entirely with the lower classes alone;[13] and the hatred of it was kept up there longer than in any other place.[14]

[6] Severi Sulpicii b. Martini vita. Epistolae iii. de Martino Dialogi. iii. de virtutibus monach. orientalium et b. Martini.

[7] The monasterium Locociagense, Gregor. Turon. de miraculis s. Martini iv. 30.

[8] Majus monasterium (Marmoutier).

[9] A. F. Silfverberg hist. monasterii Lerinensis usque ad ann. 731 enarrata. Havn. 1834. 8. The life of Honoratus, who became bishop of Arles in 426, by his disciple and successor Hilary, may be seen in acta SS. ad d. 16. Jan.

[10] Plinius nat. hist. iii. 5. calls the two islands Lerina and Lero, Strabo iv. 1. 10. ἡ Πλανασία καὶ Λήρων. In later authors (Sidonii carm. xvi. 104. Ennodius in vita Epiphanii) they are called Lerinus and Lerus.

[11] To the founders of Monachism on these islands, viz., Jovinianus, Minervius, Leontius, and Theodoretus, Cassian dedicated his last seven collations, as he had done the preceding seven to Honoratus and Eucherius. cf. Praefatt. ad coll. xi. et xiii.

[12] Respecting him see §. 87. not. 48.

[13] Augustin. de opere Monach. c. 22: Nunc autem veniunt ple·rumque ad hanc professionem servitutis Dei et ex conditione servili, vel etiam liberti, vel propter hoc a dominis liberati sive liberandi, et ex vita rusticana, et ex opificum exercitatione et plebejo labore.—Neque enim apparet, utrum ex proposito servitutis Dei venerint, an vitam inopem et laboriosam fugientes vacui pasci atque vestiri voluerint, et insuper honorari ab eis, a quibus contemni conterique consueverant.

[14] Salvianus Massiliensis (about 450) de gubernat. Dei viii. 4: Ita igitur et in monachis.—Afrorum probatur odium, quia inridebant scilicet, quia maledicebant, quia insectabantur, quia detestabantur, quia omnia in illos paene fecerunt, quae in salvatorem nostrum Judaeorum impietas. Intra Africae civitates, et maxime intra Carthaginis muros, palliatum et pallidum et recisis comarum fluentium jubis usque ad cutem tousum videre tam infelix ille populus quam infidelis sine convitio atque execratione vix poterat. Et si quando aliquis Dei servus, aut de Aegyptiorum coenobiis, aut de sacris Hierusalem locis, aut de sanctis eremi venerandisque secretis ad urbem illam officio divini operis accessit,

B

The mode of life of the Western monks was far less strict than that of the Eastern ; partly in consequence of the climate and partly out of regard to the general feeling of the people.[15] Another important point of difference was that the monks in the West soon abandoned mechanical labour.[16] Here also there was not uniformity among them.[17] Besides the monks and nuns who lived in convents, some wandered about,[18] others led an ascetic life, occasionally at considerable expense in the cities,[19] others

simul ut populo apparuit, contumelias, sacrilegia et maledictiones excepit.   Nec solum hoc, sed improbissimis flagitiosorum hominum cachinnis et detestantibus ridentium sibilis quasi taureis caedebatur.

[15] Sever. Sulp. dial. i. 8.   Edacitas in Graecis gula est, in Gallis natura. Cassian de institut. coenob. i. 11 : Nam neque caligis nos, neque colobiis, seu una tunica esse contentos hiemis permittit asperitas : et parvissimi cuculli velamen, vel melotes gestatio derisum potius, quam aedificationem ullam videntibus comparabit.

[16] Sev. Sulp. vita Mart. c. 10. of the monastery at Turonum : Ars ibi exceptis scriptoribus nulla habebatur : cui tamen operi minor aetas deputabatur : majores orationi vacabant.   Yet Augustine de opere monachorum (cf. retractt. ii. c. 21.) and Cassian de instit. coenob. lib. x. recommended the monks to resume manual labour.

[17] As in the east, so there were also in the west, tot propemodum typi ac regulae, quot cellae ac monasteria (Cassian. institt. ii. c. 2.) After Rufinus had translated the rules of St Basil into Latin, they were observed in many monasteries.

[18] Cassianus de institutione Coenobiorum x. 23 : in his regionibus nulla videmus monasteria tanta fratrum celebritate fundata (as in Egypt), quia nec operum suorum facultatibus fulciuntur, ut possint in eis jugiter perdurare : et si eis suppeditari quoquomodo valeat sufficientia victus alterius largitate, voluptas tamen otii et pervagatio cordis diutius eos in loco perseverare non patitur. Augustin. de opere monach. c. 28 : Callidissimus hostis tam multos hypocritas sub habitu monachorum usquequaque disparsit, circumeuntes provincias, nusquam missos, nusquam fixos, nusquam stantes, nusquam sedentes.   Alii membra martyrum, si tamen martyrum, venditant, alii fimbrias et phylacteria sua magnificant : et omnes petunt, omnes exigunt aut sumtus lucrosae egestatis, aut simulatae pretium sanctitatis.   c. 31 : Illi venalem circumferentes hypocrisim, timent ne vilior habeatur tonsa sanctitas quam comata, ut videlicet qui eos videt, antiquos illos quos legimus cogitet, Samuelem et caeteros qui non tondebantur.

[19] Hieron. ep. 95. (al. 4.) ad Rusticum : Vidi ego quosdam, qui postquam renunciavere saeculo vestimentis duntaxat et vocis professione, non rebus, nihil de pristina conversatione mutarunt.   Res familiaris magis aucta quam imminuta.   Eadem ministeria servulorum, idem apparatus convivii.   In vitro et patella fictili aurum comeditur, et inter turbas et examina ministrorum nomen sibi vindicant solitarii.

imitated the most striking asceticism of the orientals, frequently indeed only in appearance.[20]

§ 97.

RELATION OF THE MONKS TO THE CLERGY.

The monks as such belonged to the laity, the convents forming separate churches whose presbyters were usually abbots[1] standing in the same dependent relation to bishops as did the other churches with their people. As monachism was considered the perfection of Christianity, it was natural to choose clergymen from the monks. At first the stricter monks were much dissatisfied with this arrangement;[2] but the aversion to it soon ceased, and even at the end of the fourth century, monastic life was considered to be the usual preparation, and monachism the nursery for the clergy, especially for bishops.[3]

The idea of transferring monachism, as much as possible, entirely to the clergy, was natural in these circumstances; and it was especially adopted in the *West*. The venerable *Paphnutius* had prevented the celibacy of the clergy from being enacted as

[20] Hier. ep. 18. (al. 22.) ad Eustochium : Viros quoque fuge, quos videris catenatos, quibus foeminei contra Apostolum crines, hircorum barba, nigrum pallium, et nudi patientia frigoris pedes. Haec omnia argumenta sunt diaboli. Talem olim Antonium, talem nuper Sophronium Roma congemuit. Qui postquam nobilium introierunt domos, et deceperunt mulierculas oneratas peccatis, semper discentes, et nunquam ad scientiam veritatis pervenientes, tristitiam simulant, et quasi longa jejunia furtivis noctium cibis protrahunt.

[1] Alteserra ascetic. ii. 2. iii. 8. vii. 2.

[2] Cassian. de instit. coenob. xi. 17 : Quapropter haec est antiquitus patrum permanens nunc usque sententia, quam proferre sine mea confusione non potero, qui nec germanam vitare potui, nec episcopi evadere manus, omnimodo monachum fugere debere mulieres et episcopos. Neuter enim sinit eum, quem semel suae familiaritati devinxerit, vel quieti cellulae ulterius operam dare, vel divinae theoriae per sanctarum rerum intuitum purissimis oculis inhaerere. Hence monks were not seldom ordained against their will. Epiphan. ep. ad Joh. Hierosol. Theodoret. hist. relig. c. 13. cf. Bingham lib. iv. c. 7. (vol. ii. p. 189 ss.)

[3] Hieron. ep. 95. ad Rusticum : Ita age et vive in monasterio, ut clericus esse merearis. A law of Arcadius A.D. 398. (Cod. Theod. xvi.

an ecclesiastical law, in Nicœa;[4] but now this regulation took place in the West, first by the influence of *Siricius*, bishop of Rome (385),[5] whom several councils soon followed. *Eusebius*,

ii. 32.) : Si quos forte Episcopi deesse sibi Clericos arbitrantur, ex Monachorum numero rectius ordinabunt. Against the excess of this principle see Augustini ep. 60 : Ordini clericorum fit indignissima injuria, si desertores monasteriorum ad militiam clericatus eligantur:— nisi forte—vulgares de nobis jocabuntur dicentes : malus monachus bonus clericus est. Nimis dolendum, si ad tam ruinosam superbiam monachos surrigamus, et tam gravi contumelia clericos dignos putemus; —cum aliquando etiam bonus monachus vix bonum clericum faciat, si adsit ei sufficiens continentia, et tamen desit instructio necessaria, aut personae regularis integritas.

  [4] Socrates i. 11 : Ἐδόκει τοῖς ἐπισκόποις νόμον νεαρὸν εἰς τὴν ἐκκλησίαν εἰσφέρειν, ὥστε τοὺς ἱερωμένους, λέγω δὲ ἐπισκόπους καὶ πρεσβυτέρους καὶ διακόνους, μὴ συγκαθεύδειν ταῖς γαμεταῖς, ἃς ἔτι λαϊκοὶ ὄντες ἠγάγοντο (just as Can. Illiberit. 33. see Div. 1. §. 73. not. 14. and therefore projected probably by Hosius). Καὶ ἐπεὶ περὶ τούτου βουλεύεσθαι προὔκειτο, διαναστὰς ἐν μέσῳ τοῦ συλλόγου τῶν ἐπισκόπων ὁ Παφνούτιος, ἐβόα μακρὰ, μὴ βαρὺν ζυγὸν ἐπιθεῖναι τοῖς ἱερωμένοις ἀνδράσι, τίμιον εἶναι καὶ τὴν κοίτην καὶ αὐτὸν ἀμίαντον τὸν γάμον (Hebr. xiii. 4.) λέγων, μὴ τῇ ὑπερβολῇ τῆς ἀκριβείας μᾶλλον τὴν ἐκκλησίαν προσβλάψωσιν· οὐ γὰρ πάντας δύνασθαι φέρειν τῆς ἀπαθείας τὴν ἄσκησιν, οὐδὲ ἴσως φυλαχθήσεσθαι τὴν σωφροσύνην τῆς ἑκάστου γαμετῆς (σωφροσύνην δὲ ἐκάλει καὶ τῆς νομίμου γυναικὸς τὴν συνέλευσιν)· ἀρκεῖσθαί τε τὸν φθάσαντα κλήρου τυχεῖν, μηκέτι ἐπὶ γάμον ἔρχεσθαι, κατὰ τὴν τῆς ἐκκλησίας ἀρχαίαν παράδοσιν· μήτε μὴν ἀποζεύγνυσθαι ταύτης, ἣν ἅπαξ ἤδη πρότερον λαϊκὸς ὢν ἠγάγετο. Καὶ ταῦτ' ἔλεγεν ἄπειρος ὢν γάμου, καὶ ἁπλῶς εἰπεῖν γυναικός. Ἐκ παιδὸς γὰρ ἐν ἀσκητηρίῳ ἀνετέθραπτο, καὶ ἐπὶ σωφροσύνῃ, εἰ καὶ τις ἄλλος, περιβόητος ὢν. Πείθεται πᾶς ὁ τῶν ἱερωμένων σύλλογος τοῖς Παφνουτίου λόγοις· διὸ καὶ τὴν περὶ τούτου ζήτησιν ἀπεσίγησαν, τῇ γνώμῃ τῶν βουλομένων ἐπέχεσθαι τῆς ὁμιλίας τῶν γαμετῶν καταλείψαντες. So also Sozom. i. 23. Gelasii hist. Conc. Nic. ii. 32. and historia tripartita ii. 14.—The truth of it is doubted by Baronius, Bellarminus, Jo. Stilting (act. SS. Sept. T. iii. p. 784 ss.). On the other side Natalis Alexander hist. eccl. saec. iv. diss. 19. Calixtus de conj. cler. ed. Henke p. 213 ss.

  [5] Epistola ad Himerium Episc. Tarraconensem c. 7 : Ii vero, qui illiciti privilegii excusatione nituntur, ut sibi asserant veteri hoc lege concessum : noverint se ab omni ecclesiastico honore, quo indigne usi sunt, apostolicae sedis auctoritate dejectos.—Quilibet episcopus presbyter atque diaconus, quod non optamus, deinceps fuerit talis inventus, jam nunc sibi omnem per nos indulgentiae aditum intelligat obseratum : quia ferro necesse est excidantur vulnera, quae fomentorum non senserint medicinam.—c. 9 : Quicumque itaque se ecclesiae vovit obsequiis a sua infantia, ante pubertatis annos baptizari, et lectorum debet ministerio sociari. Qui ab accessu adolescentiae usque ad tricesimum aetatis annum, si probabiliter vixerit, una tantum et ea, quam virginem communi per sacerdotem benedictione perceperit, uxore contentus, acolythus et subdiaconus esse debebit; postque ad diaconii gradum, si se ipse primitus continentia praeeunte dignum probarit, accedat. Unde

bishop of Vercellæ († 371), and *Augustine*, went still farther, and
united with their clergy in adopting a strictly monastic life,[6]

si ultra quinque annos laudabiliter ministrarit, congrue presbyterium
consequatur. Exinde, post decennium, episcopalem cathedram poterit
adipisci, si tamen per haec tempora integritas vitae ac fidei ejus fuerit
approbata.—c. 13 : Monachos quoque, quos tamen morum gravitas et
vitae ac fidei institutio sancta commendat, clericorum officiis aggregari
et optamus et volumus. In the middle ages it was constantly admitted
that this *lex Ecclesiastica* had been unknown to the primitive church. See
Calixtus l. c. p. 3 ss. 304 : Many, however, believed it to be the meaning
of Conc. Nicaeni can. 3. (according to Dionys. exig. translation : Inter-
dixit per omnia magna synodus, non episcopo, non presbytero, non
diacono, nec alicui omnino qui in clero est, licere subintroductam habere
mulierem, nisi forte aut matrem, aut sororem, aut amitam, vel eas tantum
personas, quae suspicionem effugiunt). cf. Aelfrici canones A. D. 970.
(Wilkins. Concil. Magn. Brit. i. p. 250.) c. 5 : At the Nicene synod statuerunt omnes unanimi consensu, quod neque episcopus, neque presbyer,
neque diaconus, nec ullus verus canonicus habeat in domo sua uxorem aliquam, nisi matrem etc. Benedictus viii. in Conc. Ticinensi between 1014
and 1024. (ap. Mansi xix. p. 344.) : Nicaeni patres non solum connubium, sed etiam cum mulieribus habitationem clericis omnibus interdicunt.
So also Alfonsus a Castro († 1550.) tit. Sacerdotium ; Consuetudo,
juxta quam matrimonio alligatus promovebatur ad sacerdotium, invaluit
usque ad tempora Nicaeni concilii, in quo, ut fertur, generali decreto
statutum est, ne aliquis uxorem habens consecretur sacerdos. Quod
statutum cum ab aliquibus minime ut decebat observaretur, Siricius
Papa de hac re illos acerbissime reprehendit. The Jesuits were the
first, in the sixteenth century, who maintained, in opposition to the
Protestants, that the celibacy of the priests originated in apostolic
times. Calixtus l. c. p. 10 ss. 28 ss. J. Gf. Körner vom Cölibat der Geistlichen. Leipzig 1784. 8.   J. A. Theiner u. A. Theiner die Einführung
der erzwungenen Ehelosigkeit b. d. christl. Geistlichen u. ihre Folgen.
Altenburg 1828. 2 Bde. 8.

    [6] Respecting Eusebius see Ambros. ep. 63. ad Vercellenses §. 66 :
Haec enim primus in Occidentis partibus diversa inter se Eusebius
sanctae memoriae conjunxit, ut et in civitate positus instituta Monachorum teneret, et Ecclesiam regeret jejunii sobrietate.   Maximi Ep.
Taurinensis (about 422.) sermo ix. de s. Eusebio, in Muratorii anec-
dotis T. iv. p. 88 : ut universo Clero suo spiritalium institutionum
speculum se coeleste praeberet, omnes illos secum intra unius septum
habitaculi congregavit, ut quorum erat unum atque indivisum in religione propositum, fieret vita victusque communis.   Quatenus in illa
sanctissima societate vivendi invicem sibi essent conversationis suae et
judices et custodes etc. cf. sermo vii. p. 82.—Respecting Augustine
see Augustini vita auct. Possidio c. 5 : Factus ergo presbyter monasterium inter ecclesiam mox instituit, et cum Dei servis vivere coepit
secundum modum et regulam sub sanctis Apostolis constitutam, maxime
ut nemo quidquam proprium in illa societate haberet, sed eis essent

though at first they found no imitators. But we may see how
difficult it was to carry out the law of celibacy, though *Jerome*, *Ambrose*, and *Augustine*, strongly advocated it, from the
frequent repetition of the law, and the mildness with which it
was found necessary to punish transgressors.[7] Still *Leo the Great*
extended the requisition even to the sub-deacons (subdiaconi).[8]

In the East, on the other hand, the Eustathians were opposed
for their very rejection of marriage in the case of priests,[9] and no
law of celibacy was generally adopted. It was the custom, indeed,

omnia communia. After he had become bishop, cap. 11: in monasterio Deo servientes Ecclesiae Hipponensi clerici ordinari coeperunt.
Ac deinde—ex monasterio, quod per illum memorabilem virum et esse
et crescere coeperat, magno desiderio poscere et accipere episcopos et
clericos pax Ecclesiae atque unitas et coepit primo, et postea consecuta
est. Nam ferme decem—sanctos—viros continentes—b. Augustinus
diversis Ecclesiis—rogatus dedit. Similiterque et ipsi ex illorum sanctorum proposito venientes—monasteria instituerunt, et—caeteris Ecclesiis promotos fratres ad suscipiendum sacerdotium praestiterunt.
Comp. August. sermones ii. de moribus Clericorum (at an earlier
period sermo 49 and 50 de diversis, in the Benedictine edition, sermo
355 and 356.) ex. gr. sermo i. c. 1 : nostis omnes,—sic nos vivere in ea
domo, quae dicitur domus episcopii, ut quantum possamus imitemur
eos sanctos, de quibus loquitur liber Actuum Apostolorum : Nemo
dicebat aliquid proprium, sed erant illis omnia communia,—volui habere in ista domo episcopii mecum monasterium clericorum. Ejusd.
epis. 20. 149. 245. cf. Thomassinus P. i. lib. iii. c. 2. and 3. It is a
different thing when other monks, elevated to be bishops, as Martin of
Turonum, had about them establishments of monks, and continued the
monastic life in them.

[7] Siricii ep. ad Episc. Afr. (A. D. 386.) c. 3. Conc. Carthag. (390.)
can. 2. Innocent. I. ep. ad Victricium (404.) cap. 9. Conc. Taurin.
(397.) can. 8. Carthag. v. (398.) can. 3. Toletan. i. (400.) can. 1.
&c. Conc. Turonense i. (461.) can. 2 : Licet a patribus nostris emissa
auctoritate id fuerit constitutum, ut, quicunque sacerdos vel levita
filiorum procreationi operam dare fuisset convictus, a communione
dominica abstineretur : nos tamen huic districtioni moderationem ad-
hibentes, et justam constitutionem mollientes, id decrevimus, ut sacerdos
vel levita conjugali concupiscentiae inhaerens, vel a filiorum procreatione
non desinens ad altiorem gradum non ascendat, neque sacrificium Deo
offerre vel plebi ministrare praesumat.

[8] Leo ep. 14. ad Anastas. episc. Thessalon. (A. D. 446.) c. 4. Still
this was by no means general till the times of Gregory the Great. See
Calixtus l. c. p. 380 ss.

[9] See above §. 93. not. 39. To this refers also Can. Apost. 5 : 'Επίσ-
κοπος, ἢ Πρεσβύτερος, ἢ Διάκονος τὴν ἑαυτοῦ γυναῖκα μὴ ἐκβαλλέτω προφάσει
εὐλαβείας· ἐὰν δὲ ἐκβάλλῃ, ἀφοριζέσθω· ἐπιμένων δὲ καθαιρείσθω. Comp.
Drey über die Constitut. und Canones der Apostel S. 339.

towards the end of the fourth century, in several provinces, to select the unmarried for bishops ; and in some of these this was extended even to the clergy in general,[10] but in most parts, all clergymen had the liberty of living in wedlock.[11]

[10] In the chief countries of Monachism. Hieronum. adv. Vigilantium : Quid facient Orientis ecclesiae ? quid Aegypti et sedis Apostolicae ? quae aut virgines clericos accipiunt, aut continentes, aut si uxores habuerint, mariti esse desistunt. Epiphan. haer. 59. § 4. Expos. fidei cath. §. 21. Synesius, when about to be bishop of Ptolemais, wrote, among other things, even to his brother Euoptius (ep. 105) : ἐμοὶ ὅ τε θεὸς, ὅ τε νόμος, ἥ τε ἱερὰ Θεοφίλου χεὶρ γυναῖκα ἐπιδέδωκε· προαγορεύω τοίνυν ἅπασι καὶ μαρτύρομαι, ὡς ἐγὼ ταύτης οὔτε ἀλλοτριώσομαι καθάπαξ, οὔτε ὡς μοιχὸς αὐτῇ λάθρα συνέσομαι· τὸ μὲν γὰρ ἥκιστα εὐσεβὲς, τὸ δὲ ἥκιστα νόμμον· ἀλλὰ βουλήσομαί τε καὶ εὔξομαι, συχνά μοι πάνυ καὶ χρηστὰ γενέσθαι παιδία. Comp. above §. 84. not. 33. Clausen de Synesio p. 119.

[11] Examples of married bishops in the fourth century. Calixtus p. 253 ss. Theiner I. S. 263 ss. Gregory of Nazianzum was born when his father was a priest, for he makes him say, carmen de vita sua v. 512 :

Οὔπω τοσοῦτον ἐκμεμέτρηκας βίον,
Ὅσος διῆλθε θυσιῶν ἐμοὶ χρόνος.

(Evasions of Papebrochius, Act. SS. Maji T. ii. p. 370, against Tillemont, who explained honestly the Jesuit Mémoires de Trevoux 1707 Avril p. 711. cf. Calixtus l. c. p. 261 ss. Ullmann's Gregor v. Naz. S. 551 ss.) Whether Gregory of Nyssa was married is matter of dispute. Rupp (Gregor's v. Nyssa Leben u. Meinungen S. 24), with Clemencet and others denies it. Nicephorus Callistus first mentions this marriage, Tillemont also recognises it. St. P. Heyns disp. de Gregorio Nysseno. Lugd. Bat. 1835. 4. p. 6., defends it at length, and has even found a son called Basil. Socrates, v. 22 : Ἔγνων δὲ ἐγὼ καὶ ἕτερον ἔθος ἐν Θεσσαλίᾳ. Γενόμενος κληρικὸς ἐκεῖ, ἣν νόμῳ γαμήσας πρὶν κληρικὸς γένηται, μετὰ τὸ κληρικὸς γενέσθαι συγκαθευδήσας αὐτῇ, ἀποκήρυκτος γίνεται· τῶν ἐν ἀνατολῇ πάντων γνώμῃ ἀπεχομένων, καὶ τῶν ἐπισκόπων, εἰ καὶ βούλοιντο, οὐ μὴν ἀνάγκῃ νόμου τοῦτο ποιούντων. Πολλοὶ γὰρ αὐτῶν ἐν τῷ καιρῷ τῆς ἐπισκοπῆς καὶ παῖδας ἐκ τῆς νομίμης γαμετῆς πεποιήκασιν.

FIFTH CHAPTER.

HISTORY OF PUBLIC WORSHIP.

§ 98.

The church had triumphed over heathenism.   It had acquired
riches, external influence, and power.   The effect of this was seen
in the increasing splendour of its ceremonial.   At the same time,
a great number of those who now pressed into the church brought
with them that purely external tendency peculiar to heathen religions, which turned on the sensuous forms of worship, partly
with an interest defectively aesthetic, and partly with a superstitious veneration.   Even those who were capable of higher views
yielded to this propensity, either that the Pagans might be the more
readily won over to Christianity, or from a desire to show honour to
a supposed pious intention.[1] But in proportion as the internal life
evaporated from the Church, and its external reputation increased,
the more usual did it become to impress the character of a law externally binding on ecclesiastical usages which had been gradually developed.   Thus the entire ecclesiastical life was overbur-

---

[1] This irruption of heathen usages into the church is acknowledged
as early as Baptista Mantuanus in Fastis mense Febr. et Novembre,
Beatus Rhenanus ad Tertull. contra Marc. lib. v. and de corona militis,
Polydorus Vergilius de rerum inventoribus lib. v. c. 1. Baronius ann.
58. § 76. ann. 200. §. 5.   It has been shown more at length by (Mus-
sard) les conformitez des ceremonies modernes avec les anciennes.
(Londres) 1667. 8. (new edition, Amsterd. 1744); Conyers Middleton
a letter from Rome, showing an exact conformity between Popery and
Paganism (London 1755. 8.); Jo. Marangonius delle cose gentilesche
e profane transportate ad uso e ad ornamento delle chiese. Rom. 1744.
4. (comp. the continuation of the same, 1752. S. 511 ss.); Ge. Christ.
Hamberger enarratio rituum, quos Romana ecclesia a majoribus suis
gentilibus in sua sacra transtulit. Gotting. 1751. (reprinted in J. P.
Berg museum Duisburgense T. I. P. II. p. 363 ss.)   John James
Blunt vestiges of ancient manners and customs, discoverable in modern
Italy and Sicily.   London 1823.

dened with forms which were merely tolerated at first, but finally converted into laws.[2]

§ 99.

NEW OBJECTS OF WORSHIP.

Jo. Dallaeus adversus Latinorum de cultus religiosi objecto traditionem. Genevae 1664. 4.

Martyrdom,[1] which presented so strong a contrast to the lukewarmness of the present time, was the more highly venerated in proportion to its remoteness.[2] The heathen converts naturally enough transferred to the martyrs the honours they had been accustomed to pay their heroes.[3] This took place the more readily as the scrupulous aversion to excessive veneration of the creature died away in the church after the victory over heathenism; and

[2] Leo M. sermo 77. de jejun. Pentecost. 2. Dubitandum non est, quicquid ab Ecclesia in consuetudinem devotionis est receptum, de traditione apostolica, et de Sancti Spiritus prodire doctrina.

[1] On the increased veneration paid to martyrs comp. Sagittarius de natalitiis martyrum cap. 5. § 19 ss. Bossuet's Gesch. v. Welt u. v. Religion, fortgesetzt von J. A. Cramer. Erste Fortf. S. 493 ss. Dritte Fortf. S. 285 ss. 329 ss.

[2] To which even the apologists of the day contributed. Eusebius praep. evang. xiii. c. 11. cites a passage of Plato concerning the worship of demons, and then continues : Καὶ ταῦτα δὲ ἁρμόζει ἐπὶ τῇ τῶν θεοφιλῶν τελευτῇ, οὓς στρατιώτας τῆς ἀληθοῦς εὐσεβείας οὐκ ἂν ἁμάρτοις εἰπὼν, παραλαμβάνεσθαι. Ὅθεν καὶ ἐπὶ τὰς θήκας αὐτῶν ἔθος ἡμῖν παριέναι, καὶ τὰς εὐχὰς παρὰ ταύταις ποιεῖσθαι, τιμᾷν τε τὰς μακαρίας αὐτῶν ψυχὰς, ὡς εὐλόγως καὶ τούτων ὑφ' ἡμῶν γιγνομένων. Comp. below not. 33.

[3] Respecting the pagan belief that the reliques of distinguished men afforded protection to cities and countries, see Lobeck Aglaophamus T. I. p. 280 s. Thus Ælius Aristides (a rhetorician who lived about 170 A.D.) orat. ii. ad Platonem, ed. Dindorf vol. ii. p. 230, calls the Greeks who had fallen in battle against the Persians, ὑποχθονίους τινὰς φύλακας καὶ σωτῆρας τῶν Ἑλλήνων, ἀλεξικάκους καὶ πάντα ἀγαθοὺς, καὶ ῥύεσθαί γε τὴν χώραν οὐ χεῖρον ἢ τὸν ἐν Κωλωνῷ κείμενον Οἰδίπουν, ἢ εἴ τις ἄλλοθί που τῆς χώρας ἐν καιρῷ τοῖς ζῶσι κεῖσθαι πεπίστευται. Respecting Œdipus Valerius Maximus V. 3, externa 3 : Oedipodis ossa—inter ipsum Areopagum—et—Minervae arcem honore arae decorata, quasi sacrosancta, colis. In Greece worship was paid especially to the founders of cities, which were built for the most part over their graves. Thus Autolycus was worshipped in Sinope, Tenes in Tenedos, Æneas by the Æneates (Liv. xl. 4). See others noticed in Voss de idolol. i. 13, comp. Thucydides v. 11, concerning Brasidas : οἱ Ἀμφιπολῖται, περιέρξαντες αὐτοῦ τὸ μνημεῖον, ὡς ἥρωΐ τε ἐντέμνουσι καὶ τιμὰς δεδώκασιν ἀγῶνας καὶ ἐτησίους θυσίας, καὶ τὴν ἀποικίαν ὡς οἰκιστῇ προσέθεσαν.

the despotic form of government became accustomed to a slavish respect for the powerful.[4]   Thus the old custom of holding meetings for public worship at the graves of the martyrs now gave occasion to the erection of altars and churches (Μαρτύριον, Memoria)[5] over them.   In Egypt, the Christians following an old popular custom, began to preserve the corpses of men reputed to be saints, in their houses;[6] and while the idea of communion with the·mar-

[4] Compare the honours paid to the emperors: their edicts were termed divina, sacra coelestia: their statutes were honoured by adoration and frankincense (Zorn in miscell. Groning. vol. i. p. 186 ss). Consultationum Zachaei Christ. et Apollonii Philos. (after 408) lib. i. c. 28 (in d'Archery spicileg. i. p. 12): Apollonius: cur imagines hominum vel ceris pictas, vel metallis defictas sub Regum reverentia etiam publica adoratione veneramini, et, ut ipsi praedicatis, Deo tantum honorem debitum etiam hominibus datis?   Zacheus: Istud quidem nec debeo probare nec possum, quia evidentibus Dei dictis non Angelos, nec quoslibet coeli ac terrae vel aëris principatus adorare permittimur.   Divini enim speciale hoc nomen officii est, et altior omni terrena veneratione reverentia: sed sicut in hujusmodi malum primum adulatio homines impulit, sic nunc ab errore consuetudo vix revocat; in quo tamen incautum obsequium, non aliquem divinum deprehenditis cultum.   Sed propter similitudinem amabilium vultuum gaudia intenta plus faciunt, quam hi forte exigant, quibus defertur, aut perfungi oporteat deferentes; et licet hanc incautioris obsequii consuetudinem districtiores horreant Christiani, nec prohibere desinant sacerdotes, non tamen Deus dicitur cujus effigies salutatur, nec adolentur thure imagines, aut colendae aris superstant, sed memoria pro meritis exponuntur, ut exemplum factorum probabilium posteris praestent, aut praesentes pro abusione castigent. A law of Theodosius II. A.D. 425.   (Cod. Theod. XV. IV. 1.): Si quando nostrae statuae vel imagines eriguntur,—adsit judex sine adorationis ambitioso fastigio.—excedens cultura hominum dignitatem superno numini reservetur.   cf. de Rhoer dissertt. de effectu relig. christ. in jurisprud. Rom. p. 41 ss.

[5] So called at first by Eusebius de vita Const. III. 48. So also Constantine, on no higher authority, indeed, than the liber pontificalis, vita 34. Sylvestri, written about the year 870, is said to have built the basilics in Rome over the graves of the apostles Peter and Paul. Comp. Jerome, below, not. 8. Afterwards they were called, too, 'Αποστολεῖον, Προφητεῖον.

[6] A practice strongly disapproved by St Anthony.   Comp. Athanasius in vita Antonii (opp. T. II. p. 502): τῶν δὲ ἀδελφῶν βιαζομένων μεῖναι αὐτὸν παρ' αὐτοῖς, κἀκεά τελειωθῆναι, οὐκ ἠνέχετο,— διὰ τοῦτο δὲ μάλιστα· οἱ Αἰγύπτιοι τὰ τῶν τελευτώντων σπουδαίων σώματα, καὶ μάλιστα τῶν ἁγίων μαρτύρων φιλοῦσι μὲν θάπτειν καὶ περιελίσσειν ὀθονίοις, μὴ κρύπτειν δὲ ὑπὸ γῆν, ἀλλ' ἐπὶ σκιμποδίων τιθέναι, καὶ φυλάττειν ἔνδον παρ' ἑαυτοῖς, νομίζοντες ἐν τούτῳ τιμᾶν τοὺς ἀπελθόντας.   Ὁ δὲ 'Αντώνιος πολλάκις περὶ τούτου καὶ ἐπισκόπους ἠξίου παραγγέλλειν τοῖς λαοῖς· ὁμοίως δὲ καὶ λαϊκοὺς ἐνέτρεπεν,

tyrs was always increasingly associated with the vicinity of their mortal remains, the latter were drawn forth from their graves and placed in the churches,[7] especially under the altars.[8] Thus respect for the martyrs received a sensuous object to centre itself on, and became in consequence more extravagant and superstitious. To the old idea of the efficacy of the martyrs' intercession,[9] was now added the belief, that it was possible to communicate the desires to them directly ; an opinion partly founded on the popular notion that departed souls still hovered about the bodies they had once inhabited ;[10] partly on the high views en-

καὶ γυναιξὶν ἐπέπληττεν, λέγων, μήτε νόμιμον, μήτε ὕλως ὅσιον εἶναι τοῦτο. Καὶ γὰρ τὰ τῶν Πατριαρχῶν καὶ τῶν Προφητῶν σώματα μέχρι νῦν σώζεται εἰς μνήματα, καὶ αὐτὸ δὲ τὸ τοῦ κυρίου σῶμα εἰς μνημεῖον ἐτέθη—. Καὶ ταῦτα λέγων ἐδείκνυε, παρανομεῖν τὸν μετὰ θάνατον μὴ κρύπτοντα τὰ σώματα τῶν τελευτώντων, ἐὰν ἅγια τυγχάνῃ· τί γὰρ μεῖζον ἢ ἁγιώτεραν τοῦ κυριακοῦ σώματος ;—Αὐτὸς δὲ τοῦτο γινώσκων, καὶ φοβούμενος, μὴ καὶ τὸ αὐτοῦ ποιήσωσιν οὕτως σῶμα, ἤπειξεν ἑαυτὸν, συνταξάμενος τοῖς ἐν τῷ ἔξω ὄρει μοναχοῖς. In like manner Marcian, Theodoreti hist. relig. c. 3. (ed. Schulz. T. iii. p. 1147 s.), and Akepsimas ibid. c. 15. p. 1221.

[7] Translations of the bodies of the saints into churches. The first instances were those of St Andrew, Luke, and Timothy (359), at the command of Constantine. Hieron. contra Vigilant. (Comp. the discovering and transferring of the bones of Theseus, by Cimon, Plutarch in Thes. ad fin.)

[8] Ambrosii ep. 22. (al. 85. al. 54.) ad Marcellinam sororem § 13 : Succedant victimae triumphales in locum, ubi Christi hostia est. Sed ille super altare, qui pro omnibus passus est: isti sub altari, qui illius redemti sunt passione. Hunc ego locum praedestinaveram mihi : dignum est enim ut ibi requiescat sacerdos, ubi offerre consuevit : sed cedo sacris victimis dexteram portionem, locus iste martyribus debebatur. Hieronymus adv. Vigilant. Male facit ergo Romanus Episcopus, qui super mortuorum hominum Petri et Pauli, secundum nos ossa veneranda, secundum te vilem pulvisculum, offert Domino sacrificia, et tumulos eorum Christi arbitratur altaria ? Sozomenus V. 9. u. 19. cf. Goth. Voigti thysiasteriologia s. de altaribus vett. Christt. Hamb. 1709. 8. p. 260 ss. The passage Apoc. 6. 9. was not yet used, however, in justification of this practice. See Dallaeus adv. Latinorum de cultus relig. objecto traditionem lib. iv. c. 9.

[9] See Div. 1. § 70. not. 13-21.

[10] This was the opinion of the heathen. cf. Platonis Phaedon. Tibullus i. 6, 15. Macrobius de somn. Scip. i. 9. u. 13. Porphyrius de abstin. ii. 47. Lactantius ii. 2 : vulgus existimat, mortuorum animas circa tumulos et corporum suorum reliquias oberrare. cf. Wetstenii Nov. Test. i. p. 364. Hence Conc. Illiberitanum. c. 34. Cereos per diem placuit in coemeterio non incendi : inquietandi enim spiritus Sanctorum non sunt. Among the spiritual Origenists this idea did not na-

tertained of the glorified state of the martyrs[11] who abide only
with the Lord.   As Origen first laid the foundation of this new

turally meet with acceptance.   cf. Macarii Politici (about 370) sermo
de excessu justorum et peccatorum in Cave hist. liter. vol. i. p. 259,
and in J. Tollii insignia itineris Italici (Traj. ad. Rhen. 1696. 4.) p.
196.   But comp. Ambrosii de viduis c. 9 : martyres obsecrandi, quorum
videmur nobis quodam corporis pignore patrocinium vindicare.—isti
enim sunt Dei martyres, nostri praesules, speculatores vitae, actuumque
nostrorum. — Pseudo-Ambrosii (perhaps Maximi Taurinensis about
430) sermo vi. de Sanctis : Cuncti martyres devotissime percolendi
sunt, sed specialiter ii venerandi sunt a nobis, quorum reliquias posside-
mus.   Illi enim nos orationibus adjuvant, isti etiam adjuvant passione :
cum his autem nobis familiaritas est.   Semper enim nobiscum sunt,
nobiscum morantur, hoc est, et in corpore nos viventes custodiunt, et de
corpore recedentes excipiunt : hic ne peccatorum labes absumat, ibi ne
inferni horror invadat.

[11] So that people attributed to them a kind of omnipresence, as the
heathen did to the demons (Hesiodi opera et dies v. 121 ss.), cf. Hieronymus adv. Vigilantium : Tu Deo leges pones ?   Tu Apostolis vin-
cula injicies, ut usque ad diem judicii teneantur custodia, nec sint cum
Domino suo, de quibus scriptum est : Sequuntur agnum, quocunque
vadit (Apoc. 14, 4.) ?   Si agnus ubique, ergo, et hi, qui cum agno sunt,
ubique esse credendi sunt.   Gregorii Naz. orat. xviii. in laudem Cypriani p. 286 : σὺ δὲ ἡμᾶς ἐποπτεύοις ἄνωθεν ἵλεως, καὶ τὸν ἡμέτερον διεξάγοις
λόγον καὶ βίον, καὶ τὸ ἱερὸν τοῦτο ποίμνιον ποιμαίνοις, ἢ συμποιμαίνοις κ.
τ. λ.   Prudentius peristephanon hymn. i. v. 16 ss. ix. v. 97 and often.
Sulpicius Severus ep. ii. de obitu b. Martini (ed Lips. 1709. p. 371) :
non deerit nobis ille, mihi crede, non deerit : intererit de se sermocin-
antibus, adstabit orantibus : quodque jam hodie praestare dignatus est,
videndum se in gloria sua saepe praebebit, et adsidua, sicut ante paullu-
lum fecit, benedictione nos proteget.   Ep. iii. p. 381 : Martinus hic
pauper et modicus coelum dives ingreditur : illinc nos, ut spero, custo-
diens, me haec scribentem respicit, te legentem.   At first Vigilantius
(404) resisted this opinion (see below § 106, note 6) and Jerome defended it against him (see above).   On this Augustine also combated it,
while he endeavoured at the same time to defend independently of it,
the practice of praying to the martyrs which had been already established.   cf. Augustinus de cura gerenda pro mortuis (A. D. 421) c. 13 :
Si rebus viventium interessent animae mortuorum, et ipsae nos quando
eas videmus alloquerentur in somnis ; ut de aliis taceam, me ipsum pia
mater nulla nocte desereret, quae terra marique secuta est, ut mecum
viveret.— Isaias propheta dicit (63, 16) : Tu es enim pater noster : quia
Abraham nescivit nos, et Israel non cognovit nos.   Si tanti Patriarchae
quid erga populum ex his procreatum ageretur ignoraverunt, quomodo
mortui vivorum rebus atque actibus cognoscendis adjuvandisque mis-
centur ?   With regard to the martyrs, he is not indisposed indeed to
allow a miraculous exception (cap. 16), but proceeds : Quamquam ista
quaestio vires intelligentiae meae vincit, quemadmodum opitulentur
Martyres iis, quos per eos certum est adjuvari ; utrum ipsi per se ipsos

kind of respect for martyrs, so the Origenists were the first who addressed them in their sermons as if they were present and besought their intercession.[12] But though the orators were somewhat extravagant in this respect, the poets, who soon after seized upon the same theme, found no colours too strong to describe the power and glory of the martyrs.[13] Even relics soon began to

adsint uno tempore tam diversis locis,—sive ubi sunt eorum Memoriae, sive praetur suas Memorias ubicumque adesse sentiuntur: an ipsis in loco suis meritis congruo ab omni mortalium conversatione remotis, et tamen generaliter orantibus pro indigentiis supplicantium,—Deus—exaudiens Martyrum preces, per angelica ministeria usquequaque diffusa praebeat hominibus ista solatia, quibus in hujus vitae miseria judicat esse praebenda: et suorum merita Martyrum, ubi vult, quando vult, quomodo vult, maximeque per eorum Memorias, quoniam hoc novit expedire nobis ad aedificandum fidem Christi—mirabili atque ineffabilli potestate ac bonitate commendet. Res haec altior est, quam ut a me possit attingi, et abstrusior, quam ut a me valeat perscrutari: et ideo quid horum duorum sit, an vero fortassis utrumque sit, ut aliquando fiant per ipsam praesentiam Martyrum, aliquando per Angelos suscipientes personam Martyrum, definire non audeo; mallem a scientibus ista perquirere. cf. de civit. Dei xxii., c. 9. In his sermons he does not attack the usual opinion, ex. gr. sermo de diversis 316. (al. 94.): Ambo (Paulus et Stephanus) modo sermonem nostrum auditis: ambo pro nobis orate.

[12] Basilii M. hom. 19, in xl. Martyres §. 8: οὗτοί εἰσιν οἱ τὴν καθ' ἡμᾶς χώραν διαλαβόντες, οἱονεὶ πύργοι τινὲς συνεχεῖς, ἀσφάλειαν ἐκ τῆς τῶν ἐναντίων καταδρομῆς παρεχόμενοι· οὐχ ἑνὶ τόπῳ ἑαυτοὺς κατακλείσαντες, ἀλλὰ πολλοῖς ἤδη ἐπιξενωφέντες χωρίοις, καὶ πολλὰς πατρίδας κατακοσμήσαντες. Καὶ τὸ παράδοξον, οὐ καθ' ἕνα διαμερισθέντες τοῖς δεχομένοις ἐπιφοιτῶσιν, ἀλλ' ἀναμιχθέντες ἀλλήλοις, ἡνωμένως χορεύουσιν· ὢ τοῦ θαύματος!—οὔτε ἐλλείπουσι τῷ ἀριθμῷ, οὔτε πλεονασμὸν ἐπιδέχονται· ἐὰν εἰς ἑκατὸν αὐτοὺς διέλῃς, τὸν οἰκεῖον ἀριθμὸν οὐκ ἐκβαίνουσιν· ἐὰν εἰς ἓν συναγάγῃς, τεσσαράκοντα καὶ οὕτω μένουσι, κατὰ τὴν τοῦ πυρὸς φύσιν· καὶ γὰρ ἐκεῖνο καὶ πρὸς τὸν ἐξάπτοντα μεταβαίνει, καὶ ὅλον ἐστὶ παρὰ τῷ ἔχοντι· καὶ οἱ τεσσαράκοντα, καὶ πάντες εἰσὶν ὁμοῦ, καὶ πάντες εἰσὶ παρ' ἑκάστῳ·—ὁ θλιβόμενος ἐπὶ τοὺς τεσσαράκοντα καταφεύγει, ὁ εὐφραινόμενος ἐπ' αὐτοὺς ἀποτρέχει. ὁ μὲν, ἵνα λύσιν εὕρῃ τῶν δυσχερῶν· ὁ δὲ, ἵνα φυλαχθῇ αὐτῷ τὰ χρηστότερα. ἐνταῦθα γυνὴ εὐσεβὴς ὑπὲρ τέκνων εὐχομένη καταλαμβάνεται, ἀποδημοῦντι ἀνδρὶ τὴν ἐπάνοδον αἰτουμένη, ἀῤῥωστοῦντι τὴν σωτηρίαν· μετὰ μαρτύρων γενέσθω τὰ αἰτήματα ὑμῶν—Ὦ χορὸς ἅγιος! ὢ σύνταγμα ἱερόν! ὢ συνασπισμὸς! ὢ κοινοὶ φύλακες τοῦ γένους τῶν ἀνθρώπων! ἀγαθοὶ κοινωνοὶ φροντίδος, δεήσεως συνεωργοί, πρεσβευταὶ δυνατώτατοι, ἀστέρες τῆς οἰκουμένης, ἄνθη τῶν ἐκκλησιῶν! ὑμᾶς οὐχ ἡ γῆ κατέκρυψεν, ἀλλ' οὐρανὸς ὑπεδέξατο κ. τ. λ. cf. Hom. xxiii. in Mamantem Martyrem. Gregorii Naz. orat. xviii. in laudem Cypriani. Gregorii Nysseni orat. in Theodorum Mart. Daniel's Gesch. v. christl. Beredsamkeit i. 281. In the west Ambrose goes farther in extolling the martyrs, Daniel i. 658.

[13] So especially the Spanish writer Aurelins Prudentius Clemens

work miracles, and to become valuable articles of commerce on this account, like the old heathen instruments of magic.[14]

In proportion as men felt the need of such heavenly intercessors, they sought to increase their number. Not only those persons who were inscribed in the Diptycha* for services done to the church, but also the pious of the Old Testament, and particularly distinguished monks,[15] were taken into the catalogue; and thus a still more comprehensive *saint-worship* arose out of the veneration paid to martyrs.[16] Martyrs before unknown announced themselves also in visions; others revealed the places where their bodies were buried. Till the fifth century, prayers had been offered even for the dead saints;[17] but at that time the practice

(about 405. Poemata ed. Nic. Heinsius. Amst. 1667. 12. Chr. Cellarius. Halae 1703. 8.) in his lib. περὶ στεφανῶν, containing 14 hymns to the martyrs, comp. H. Middeldorpf comm. de Prudentio et Theologia Prudentiana in Illgen's Zeitschr. f. hist. Theol. ii., ii., 187; and Pontius Paulinus, bishop of Nola, († 431. Letters and poems ed. J. B. le Brun. Paris, 1685. Tomi ii. 4. in bibl. max. PP. T. vi. p. 163 ss.) especially in the 10 natales S. Felicis.

[14] See Augustine, above § 96, note 18. The Law of Theodosius I. A. D. 386, (Cod. Theod. ix., xvii. 7.): Humatum corpus nemo ad alterum locum transferat: nemo martyrem distrahat, nemo mercetur, Habeant vero in potestate, si quolibet in loco sanctorum est aliquis conditus pro ejus veneratione, quod martyrium vocandum sit, addant quod voluerint fabricarum.

[15] Joannes Cassianus collat. vi. c. 1: In Palaestinæ partibus juxta Tecuae vicum—solitudo vastissima est usque ad Arabiam ac mare mortuum.—In hac summae vitae ac sanctitatis monachi diutissimie commorantes, repente sunt a discurrentibus Saracenorum latrunculis interempti. Quorum corpora—tam a Pontificibus regionis illius quam ab universa plebe Arabum tanta veneratione praerepta, et inter reliquias martyrum condita, ut innumeri populi e duobus oppidis concurrentis gravissimum sibi certamen indixerint, et usque ad gladiorum conflictum, pro sancta rapina sit eorum progressa contentio, dum pia inter se devotione decertant, quinam justius eorum sepulturam ac reliquias possiderent, aliis scilicet de vicinia commorationis ipsorum, aliis de originis propinquitate gloriantibus. Comp. the dispute about the body of James, Theodoreti hist. relig, c. 21. (ed. Schulz. 3 p. 1239.)

[16] Thus Ambrose discovered the bodies of *Protasius* and *Gervasius*. Ambrose, epist. 22, ad sororem August. de civ. Dei. xxii. 8. The populace were inclined to regard every ancient unknown grave as the grave of a martyr, *Sulpicius Severus* de vita Martini, c. 11.

[17] Epiphan. haer. 75. §. 7: καὶ γὰρ δικαίων ποιούμεθα τὴν μνήμην, καὶ

* *Diptycha.* In Rees's Cyclopædia, Diptycha are explained to be " a double catalogue, in one whereof were written the names of the living, and in the other those of the dead, which were to be rehearsed during the office."

was discontinued as unsuitable.[18]   It is true that the more enlightened fathers of the Church insisted on a practical imitation
of the saints in regard to morality as the most important thing
in the new saint-worship,[19] nor were exhortations to address

ὑπὲρ ἁμαρτωλῶν—ὑπὲρ δὲ δικαίων, καὶ πατέρων, καὶ Πατριαρχῶν, Προφητῶν
καὶ Ἀποστόλων, καὶ Εὐαγγελιστῶν, καὶ Μαρτύρων, καὶ Ὁμολογητῶν, Ἐπισκόπων τε καὶ Ἀναχωρητῶν, καὶ παντὸς τοῦ τάγματος, ἵνα τὸν κύριον Ἰησοῦν Χριστὸν ἀφορίσωμεν ἀπὸ τῆς τῶν ἀνθρώπων τάξεως,—ἐν ἐννοίᾳ ὄντες, ὅτι οὐκ ἔστιν
ἐξισούμενος ὁ κύριος τινὶ τῶν ἀνθρώπων, κἂν τε μυρία καὶ ἐπέκεινα ἐν δικαιο-
σύνῃ ἕκαστος ἀνθρώπων.   Cf. Constitt. Apostol. viii. c. 12.   Cyrill. Hieros. catech. Mystag. v. §. 8.   Such intercessions, in their more ancient
form, are preserved in the liturgies of the Nestorians, ex. gr. liturgia
Theodori Interpretis (in Renaudotii liturgiarum orientalium collectio.
Tom. ii. p. 620.): Domine et Deus noster, suscipe a nobis per gratiam
tuam sacrificium hoc gratiarum actionis, fructus scilicet rationabiles la-
biorum nostrorum, ut sit coram te memoria bona justorum antiquorum,
Prophetarum sanctorum, Apostolorum beatorum, Martyrum et Confessorum, Episcoporum, Doctorum, Sacerdotum, Diaconorum, et omnium
filiorum Ecclesiae sanctae catholicae, eorum qui in fide vera transierunt
ex hoc mundo, ut per gratiam tuam, Domine, veniam, illis concedas
omnium peccatorum et delictorum, quae in hoc mundo, in corpore
mortali, et anima mutationi obnoxia peccaverunt aut offenderunt coram te, quia nemo est qui non peccet.   So too liturgia Nestorii ap.
Renaudot. l. c. p. 633.   cf. Bingham lib. xv. c. 3. §. 16, 17 (vol. vi. p.
330 ss.)
    [18] Augustin. serm. 17 : Injuria est enim pro martyre orare, cujus nos
debemus orationibus commendari (quoted by Innocent III., as sacrae
scripturae auctoritas to justify ; decretal. Gregorii lib. iii. tit. 41. c. 6,
the change of the old formula, annue nobis, Domine, ut animae famuli,
tui Leonis haec prosit oblatio, into the modern ; annue, nobis, quaesumus, Domine, ut intercessione b. Leonis haec nobis prosit oblatio.)
    [19] Augustin. de vera religione c. 55 : Non sit nobis religio cultus ho-
minum mortuorum : quia, si pie vixerunt, non sic habentur, ut tales
quaerant honores ; sed illum a nobis coli volunt, quo illuminante laetantur, meriti sui nos esse consortes.   Honorandi sunt ergo propter imitationem, non adorandi propter religionem. contra Faustum xx. 21 : Populus christianus Memorias Martyrum religiosa solemnitate concelebrat,
et ad excitandam imitationem, et ut meritis eorum consocietur, atque
orationibus adjuvetur : ita tamen, ut nulli Martyrum, sed ipsi Deo
Martyrum, quamvis in Memoriis Martyrum, constituamus altaria.
Quis enim antistitum in locis sanctorum corporum adsistens altari, aliquando dixit ; offerimus tibi, Petre, aut Paule, aut Cypriane ? sed quod
offertur, offertur Deo, qui Martyres coronavit, ut ex ipsorum locorum
admonitione major adfectus exsurgat ad acuendam caritatem, et in illos,
quos imitari possumus, et in illum, quo adjuvante possumus. Colimus
ergo Martyres eo cultu dilectionis et societatis, quo in hac vita coluntur
sancti homines Dei, quorum cor ad talem pro evangelica veritate passionem paratum esse sentimus.   At vero illo cultu, qui graece latria di-

prayer directly to God also wanting ;[20] but yet the people attributed the highest value to the intercession of the saints whose efficacy was so much prized.[21] Many heathen customs were incorporated with this saint-worship. Churches, under whose altars their bodies rested, were dedicated to their worship.[22] As gods

citur, latine uno verbo dici non potest, cum sit quaedam proprie divinitati debita servitus, nec colimus, nec colendum docemus, nisi unum Deum.

[20] Ambrosiaster ad Rom. 1, 22. against those who adored the elements, the stars, &c. Solent tamen pudorem passi, neglecti Dei misera uti excusatione, dicentes per istos posse iri ad Deum, sicut per comites pervenitur ad regem. Age, numquid tam demens est aliquis, aut salutis suae immemor, ut honorificentiam regis vindicet comiti, cum de hac re si qui etiam tractare fuerint inventi, jure ut rei damnentur majestatis ? Et isti se non putant reos, qui honorem nominis Dei deferunt creaturae, et relicto Domino conservos adorant ; quasi sit aliquid plus, quod reservetur Deo. Nam et ideo ad regem per tribunos aut comites itur, quia homo utique est rex, et nescit quibus debeat republicam credere. Ad Deum autem, quem utique nihil latet (omnium enim merita novit), promerendum suffragatore non opus est, sed mente devota. Ubicumque enim talis loquutus fuerit ei, respondebit illi. So Chrysostomus in Matth. hom. 52. (al. 53.) §. 3. annexes to the history of the woman of Canaan (Matth. 15, 21.) the admonition : σὺ δέ μοι σκόπει, πῶς τῶν αποστόλων ἡττηθέντων καὶ οὐκ ἀνυσάντων, αὕτη ἤνυσε· τοσοῦτον ἐστι προσεδρεία εὐχῆς· καὶ γὰρ ὑπὲρ τῶν ἡμετέρων παρ᾽ ἡμῶν βούλεται μᾶλλον τῶν ὑπευθύνων ἀξιοῦσθαι ἢ παρ᾽ ἑτέρων ὑπὲρ ἡμῶν. cf. de poenitentia orat. iv. 4 : (ὁ θεὸς) χωρὶς μεσίτου παρακαλεῖται. Comp. Cramer's dritte Forts. ιι. Bossuet. S. 350 ss.

[21] Ambrosius de viduis c. 9 : Aegri, nisi ad eos aliorum precibus medicus fuerit invitatus, pro se rogare non possunt. Infirma est caro, mens aegra est et peccatorum vinculis impedita, ad medici illius sedem debile non potest explicare vestigium. Obsecrandi sunt Angeli pro nobis, qui nobis ad praesidium dati sunt, martyres obsecrandi, quorum videmur nobis quoddam corporis pignore patrocinium vindicare. Possunt pro peccatis rogare nostris, qui proprio sanguine etiam si qua habuerunt peccata laverunt. Isti enim sunt Dei martyres, nostri praesules speculatores vitae actuumque nostrorum. Non erubescamus eos intercessores nostrae infirmitatis adhibere etc. Even Chrysostom recommends (de sanctis martyr. serm. 68. opp. v. 872.) the worship of martyrs and their relics as a means of procuring the forgiveness of sins, and virtues.

[22] The churches were still named in different ways, many after their founders (so in Carthage the basilicae Fausti, Florentii, Leontii, in Alexandria the eccl. Arcadii (the old Serapeum) in Rome the basilicae Constantini and Justiniani), others from other circumstances, thus in Carthage basilica restituta, in Alexandria the Caesareum, in Rome the eccl. triumphalis (the old Church of Peter), eccl. Laterana (because on the site of the palace of Lateranus, a contemporary of Nero) see Bingham vol. iii. p. 329. Thus although originally the calling of churches after mar-

and heroes were formerly chosen for patrons, so patron saints were now selected.[23]   And since the heathen had been so bitterly accused at an earlier period by the Christians of worshipping dead men,[24] they could not now be blamed in thei rturn for ridiculing the new saint-worship.[25]

tyrs did not denote that they were dedicated to them, yet the meaning attached to the names came gradually to be so understood, and even the distinctions made by Augustine admit of this acceptation, comp. de civitate Dei xxii. 10 : An dicent, etiam se habere deos ex hominibus mortuis, sicut Herculem, sicut Romulum, sicut alios multos, quos in deorum numerum receptos opinantur ?   Sed nobis Martyres, non sunt dii. — Nos Martyribus nostris non templa sicut diis, sed memorias sicut hominibus mortuis, quorum apud Deum vivunt spiritus, fabricamus : neque ibi erigimus altaria, in quibus sacrificemus Martyribus, sed uni Deo et Martyrum et nostro sacrificia immolamus : ad quod sacrificium, sicut homines Dei, qui mundum in ejus confessione vicerunt, suo loco et ordine nominantur, non tamen a sacerdote qui sacrificat invocantur.   Deo quippe, non ipsis, sacrificat, quamvis in memoria sacrificet eorum. cf. viii. 27.

[23] Theodoreti graec. affect. curat. disp. 8. (ed Schultze. T. iv. p. 902.) αἱ μὲν γενναῖαι τῶν νικηφόρων ψυχαὶ περιπολοῦσι τὸν οὐρανὸν,—τὰ δὲ σώματα, οὐχ εἰς ἑνὸς κατακρύπτει τάφος ἑκάστου· ἀλλὰ πόλεις καὶ κῶμαι ταῦτα διανειμάμεναι, σωτῆρας καὶ ψυχῶν καὶ σωμάτων, καὶ ἰατροὺς ὀνομάζουσι, καὶ ὡς πολιούχους τιμῶσι καὶ φύλακας· καὶ χρώμενοι πρεσβευταῖς πρὸς τὸν τῶν ὅλων δεσπότην, διὰ τούτων τὰς θείας κομίζονται δωρεάς.   pag. 921 : οἱ δέ γε τῶν καλλινίκων μαρτύρων σηκοὶ, λαμπροὶ καὶ περίβλεπτοι, καὶ μεγέθει διαπρεπεῖς, καὶ παντοδαπῶς πεποικιλμένοι, καὶ κάλλους ἀφιέντες μαρμαρυγάς· εἰς δὲ τούτους οὐχ ἅπαξ ἢ δίς γε τοῦ ἔτους ἢ πεντάκις φοιτῶμεν· ἀλλὰ πολλάκις μὲν πανηγύρεις ἐπιτελοῦμεν, πολλάκις δὲ καὶ ἡμέρας ἑκάστης τῷ τούτων Δεσπότῃ τοὺς ὕμνους προσφέρομεν· καὶ οἱ μὲν ὑγιαίνοντες αἰτοῦσι τῆς ὑγείας τὴν φυλακήν· οἱ δέ τινι νόσῳ παλαίοντες, τὴν τῶν παθημάτων ἀπαλλαγήν· αἰτοῦσι δὲ καὶ ἄγονοι παῖδας, καὶ στέριφαι παρακαλοῦσι γενέσθαι μητέρες.—καὶ οἱ μὲν εἴς τινα ἀποδημίαν στελλόμενοι, λιπαροῦσι τούτους ξυνοδοιπόρους γενέσθαι, καὶ τῆς ὁδοῦ ἡγεμόνας· οἱ δὲ τῆς ἐπανόδου τετυχηκοτες, τὴν τῆς χάριτος ὁμολογίαν προσφέρουσαν· οὐχ ὡς θεοῖς αὐτοῖς προσιόντες, ἀλλ᾽ ὡς θείους ἀνθρώπους ἀντιβολοῦντες, καὶ γενέσθαι πρεσβευτὰς ὑπὲρ σφῶν παρακαλοῦντες.   ὅτι δὲ τυγχάνουσιν ὧνπερ αἰτοῦσιν οἱ πιστῶς ἐπαγγέλλοντες, ἀναφανδὸν μαρτυρεῖ τὰ τούτων ἀναθήματα, τὴν ἰατρείαν δηλοῦντα· οἱ μὲν γὰρ ὀφθαλμῶν, οἱ δὲ ποδῶν, ἄλλοι δὲ χειρῶν προσφέρουσιν ἐκτυπώματα· καὶ οἱ μὲν ἐκ χρυσοῦ, οἱ δὲ ἐξ ὕλης ἀργύρου πεποιημένα. pag. 923 : τοὺς γὰρ οἰκείους νεκροὺς ὁ Δεσπότης ἀντεισῆξε τοῖς ὑμετέροις θεοῖς· καὶ τοὺς μὲν φρούδους ἀπέφηνε, τούτοις δὲ τὰ ἐκείνων ἀπένειμε γέρα· ἀντὶ γὰρ δὴ τῶν Πανδίων, καὶ Διασίων, καὶ Διονυσίων, καὶ τῶν ἄλλων ὑμῶν ἑορτῶν, Πέτρου καὶ Παύλου καὶ Θωμᾶ καὶ Σεργίου—καὶ τῶν ἄλλων μαρτύρων, ἐπιτελοῦνται δημοθοινίαι κ. τ. λ. Comp. Neander's Chrysostomus Bd. 2. S. 128 f.

[24] Arnobius adv. gentiles vi. 6.—multa ex his templa—comprobatur, contegere cineres atque ossa, et functorum esse corporum sepulturas, etc.

[25] Julianus ap. Cyrill. adv. Jul. x. p. 335 : ὅσα δὲ ὑμεῖς ἑξῆς προσευρή-

In the fourth century no peculiar reverence above other saints was as yet shown to *the Virgin Mary*. In consequence of monastic ideas (see § 95, note 23), the Christians merely attributed a high value to her perpetual virginity; and for this reason began to declare the opinion that she had afterwards borne children to Joseph[26] to be heretical; as, for instance, Epiphanius (haer. 78) against the Ἀντιδικομαριανῖται, in Arabia (367); Jerome against *Helvidius*, in Rome (383);[27] and the Macedonian bishops against *Bonosus*, bishop of Sardica (392)[28]; while it was also shown in what way she did not cease to be a virgin, notwithstanding the birth of Christ.[29] Besides, the teachers of the

κατε, πολλοὺς ἐπεισάγοντες τῷ πάλαι νεκρῷ τοὺς προσφάτους νεκρούς, τίς ἂν πρὸς ἀξίαν βδελύξηται; Πάντα ἐπληρώσατε τάφων καὶ μνημάτων.—Εἰ ἀκαθαρσίας Ἰησοῦς ἔφη εἶναι πλήρεις τοὺς τάφους (Matth. xxiii. 27.), πῶς ὑμεῖς ἐπ᾽ αὐτῶν ἐπικαλεῖσθε τὸν θεόν; cf. vi. p. 201. Misopogon p. 344. Eunapius in vita Aedesii ed. Genev. 1616. p. 65. Ammian. Marcell. xii. 11. Comp. Maximus §. 79. not. 1.

[26] Basilius M. hom. in sanctam Christi generationem c. 5. (opp. T. ii. p. 598), remarks, however, on Matth. i. 25: οὐκ ἐγίνωσκε αὐτὴν, ἕως οὗ ἔτεκε τὸν υἱὸν αὐτῆς τὸν πρωτότοκον the following: τοῦτο δὲ ἤδη ὑπόνοιαν παρέχει, ὅτι μετὰ τὸ καθαρῶς ὑπηρετήσασθαι τῇ γεννήσει τοῦ κυρίου τῇ ἐπιτελεσθείσῃ διὰ τοῦ πνεύματος τοῦ ἁγίου, τὰ νενομισμένα τοῦ γάμου ἔργα μὴ ἀπαρνησαμένης τῆς Μαρίας· ἡμεῖς δὲ, εἰ καὶ μηδὲν τῷ τῆς εὐσεβείας παραλυμαίνεται λόγῳ, (μέχρι γὰρ τῆς κατὰ τὴν οἰκονομίαν ὑπηρεσίας ἀναγκαία ἡ παρθενία, τὸ δ᾽ ἐφεξῆς ἀπολυπραγμόνητον τῷ λόγῳ τοῦ μυστηρίου,) ὅμως διὰ τὸ μὴ καταδέχεσθαι τῶν φιλοχρίστων τὴν ἀκοὴν, ὅτι ποτὲ ἐπαύσατο εἶναι παρθένος ἡ θεοτόκος, ἐκείνας ἡγούμεθα τὰς μαρτυρίας αὐτάρκεις.

[27] Hieron. adv. Helvidium lib. in opp. ed. Martinay T. iv. P. ii. p. 129, ed. Vallarsi T. ii. Concerning the Antidicomarianites and Helvidius see Walch's Kekerhist. iii. 577.

[28] Siricii ep. 9 (comp. above, § 94. not. 14.) Walch iii. 598.

[29] Tertullianus de carne Christi c. 23: Agnoscimus ergo signum contradicibile (according to Luc. ii. 34.) conceptum et partum virginis Mariae: de quo Academici isti: peperit, et non peperit; virgo, et non virgo.— Peperit enim, quae ex sua carne: et non peperit, quae non ex virili semine. Et virgo, quantum a viro; non virgo, quantum a partu. Clemens Alex. strom. vii. p. 889: τοῖς πολλοῖς καὶ μέχρι νῦν δοκεῖ ἡ Μαριὰμ λεχὼ εἶναι διὰ τὴν τοῦ παιδίου γένησιν, οὐκ οὖσα λεχώ· καὶ γὰρ μετὰ τὸ τεκεῖν αὐτὴν μαιωθεῖσαν φασί τινες παρθένον εὑρεθῆναι. Epiphanius haer lxxviii. §. 19. does not hesitate to say, in reference to Luke ii. 23, Exod. xiii. 2: οὗτός ἐστιν ἀληθῶς ἀνοίγων μήτραν μητρός. On the contrary, Ambrosius ep. 42. (al. 81. al. 7.) ad Siricium P.: Haec est virgo, quae in utero concepit: virgo, quae peperit filium. Sic enim scriptum est: Ecce virgo in utero accipiet, et pariet filium (Es. 7, 14.), non enim concepturam tantummodo virginem, sed et parituram virginem dixit. Quae autem est illa porta sanctuarii, porta illa exterior ad Orientem, quae

Church in the fourth century did not refrain from speaking of the faults of Mary;[30] and Epiphanius includes certain enthusiastic women in his catalogue of heretics for their extravagant adoration of the Virgin (Κολλυριδιανοί.)[31] The Nestorian controversy first led men to set her at the top of the host of saints, as the mother of God, θεοτόκος.

Though it was the general belief that *angels* guarded men, and presented their prayers to God, it was still thought unallowable to address them, because of the passages, *Coloss.* ii. 18, *Revelation of John* xix. 10 ; xxii. 8, 9.[32] *Ambrose* is the first who

manet clausa; et nemo, inquit, pertransibit per eam, nisi solus Deus Israel (Ezech. xliv. 2.) ? Nonne haec porta Maria est, per quam in hunc mundum redemtor intravit ?...de qua scriptum est, quia Dominus pertransibit per eam, et erit clausa post partum ; quia virgo concepit et genuit. Hieronymus adv. Pelagianos lib. ii. (Opp. ed. Martian. T. iv. P. ii. p. 512.) : Solus enim Christus clausas portas vulvae virginalis aperuit quae tamen clausae jugiter permanserunt. Haec est porta orientalis clausa, per quam solus Pontifex ingreditur et egreditur, et nihilominus semper clausa est.

[30] After the example of Irenaeus iii. 18. Tertull. de carne Christi 7. Origenes in Luc. hom. 17 :—Basilius ep. 260. (al. 317.) ad Optimum. Chrysostomus Hom. 45. in Matth. et Hom. 21. in Joh. On the other hand Augustin. de nat, et grat. c. 36 : Excepta sancta virgine Maria, de qua propter honorem Domini nullam prorsus, cum de peccatis agitur, haberi volo quaestionem,—si omnes illos sanctos—congregare possemus, et interrogare, utrum essent sine peccato, quid fuisse responsuros putamus ?

[31] Concerning them Epiphan. haer. 78. §. 23. Haer. 79. Anacephal. c. 79. Comp. Walch's Ketzerhistorie iii. 625. F. Münter de Collyridianis in the miscellanea Hafniensia t. i. Fasc. 2. Hafn. 1818. p. 153 ss. Their heresy was : ἀντὶ θεοῦ ταύτην παρεισάγειν σπουδάζοντες,—ὡς εἰς ὄνομα τῆς δειπαρθένου κολλυρίδα τινὰ ἐπιτελεῖν, καὶ συνάγεσθαι ἐπὶ τὸ αὐτὸ,—καὶ εἰς ὄνομα αὐτῆς ἱερουργεῖν διὰ γυναικῶν. This usage is perhaps explained by Jerem. xliv. 19. where the women offer cakes to the Queen of heaven ; perhaps by Conc. Quinisexti can. 79 : "The birth of the Virgin was ἀλόχευτος : hence no cake (σεμίδαλις) shall be presented after the birthday of Christ προφάσει τιμῆς λοχειῶν τῆς ἀχράντου παρθενομήτορος."

[32] Concil. Laodic. can. 35 : ὅτι οὐ δεῖ Χριστιανοὺς ἐγκαταλείπειν τὴν ἐκκλησίαν τοῦ θεοῦ καὶ ἀπιέναι καὶ ἀγγέλους ὀνομάζειν κ. τ. λ. Dionys. exig. translates :—atque angelos (var. lect. angulos) nominare. cf. Theodoret. ad Coloss. ii. 18 : Οἱ τῷ νόμῳ συνηγοροῦντες, καὶ τοὺς ἀγγέλους σέβειν αὐτοῖς εἰσηγοῦντο, διὰ τούτων λέγοντες δεδόσθαι τὸν νόμον. ἔμεινε δὲ ταῦτο τὸ πάθος ἐν τῇ Φρυγίᾳ καὶ Πισιδίᾳ μέχρι πολλοῦ· οὗ δὴ χάριν καὶ συνελθοῦσα σύνοδος ἐν Λαοδικείᾳ τῆς Φρυγίας νόμῳ κεκώλυκε τὸ τοῖς ἀγγέλοις προσεύχεσθαι· καὶ μέχρι δὲ τοῦ νῦν εὐκτήρια τοῦ ἁγίου Μιχαὴλ παρ᾽ ἐκείνοις καὶ τοῖς ὁμόροις ἐκείνων ἐστὶν ἰδεῖν. τοῦτο τοίνυν συνεβούλευον ἐκεῖνοι γίνεσθαι, ταπεινοφροσύνῃ δῆθεν κεχρημένοι, καὶ λέγοντες, ὡς ἀόρατος ὁ τῶν ὅλων θεὸς ἀνέφικτός τε καὶ ἀκατά-

C 2

recommends the intercession of the *guardian* angel ;[33] but as yet the Christians had not adopted a more general worship of angels.[34]

The cross, always a highly honoured symbol among Christians,[35] had been more superstitiously venerated ever since the time when Constantine believed that he owed to it his victory over Maxentius.[36] But after the tradition had spread, from the end of the fourth century, that Helena (326) had discovered the true cross of Christ,[37] relics and even pictures of it

λῃστος, καὶ προσήκει διὰ τῶν ἀγγελων τὴν θείαν εὐμένειαν πραγματεύεσθαι. Augustini confess. x. 42 : Quem invenirem, qui me reconciliaret tibi? Abeundum mihi fuit ad angelos? Multi conantes ad te redire, neque per se ipsos valentes, sicut audio, tentaverunt haec, et inciderunt in desiderium curiosarum visionum, et digni habiti sunt illusionibus. cf. Keilii opusc. acad. T. ii. p. 548 ss.

[33] Ambros. de viduis c. 9: Obsecrandi sunt angeli, qui nobis ad praesidium dati sunt. See not. 21.

[34] Augustini collatio cum Maximino c. 14. (Opp. viii 467.) : Nonne si templum alicui sancto Angelo excellentissimo de lignis et lapidibus faceremus, anathematizaremur a veritate Christi et ab Ecclesia Dei, quoniam creaturae exhiberemus eam servitutem, quae uni tantum debetur Deo? In the time of Sozomen there was, it is true, a church in Constantinople named Μιχαήλιον, but solely for this reason (Sozom. ii. 3.) : καθότι πεπίστευται ἐνθάδε ἐπιφαίνεσθαι Μιχαὴλ τὸν θεῖον Ἀρχάγγελον.

[35] But Minucius Felix c. 29: cruces nec colimus, nec optamus.

[36] Euseb. de vit. Const i. 40. ii. 6-9. 16. iv. 21. Sozom. i. 8. in fine.

[37] This story is false. Eusebius de vita Const. iii. 25. relates at great length how the holy sepulchre was cleared out at the command of Constantine, not of Helena, and the church of the resurrection built over it, but says nothing of the discovery of the cross. Then not till c. 41 ss. does he speak of the journey of Helena to Palestine, and how she built churches at the spot where Christ was born in Bethlehem, and on the locality of the ascension on the Mount of Olives. The Gaul also, who was in Jerusalem A.D. 333, and mentions all the holy objects in the city in his itinerarium (vetera Rom. itineraria ed. P. Wesseling p. 593.), knew nothing of the holy cross and its finding. The oldest testimony alleged for it, but which notwithstanding does not speak of Helena, is in Cyrilli Hieros. epist. ad Constantium, professedly written about A. D. 351, is a later interpolation. It cannot have been known before the fifth century, for Jerome in catal. s. v. Cyrillus does not mention it, and Ambrose orat. de obitu Theodosii, Jo. Chrysostomus hom. 85. (al. 84.), Paulinus Nolanus epist. 31. (al. 11.), Rufinus hist. eccl. x. 7. 8. Socrates i. 17. Sulpic. Sever. hist. sacr. ii. 34. are ignorant of it, since otherwise they would not have related the circumstances of the finding, and especially the recognition of the true cross so differently. The credulous Sozomen (ii. 1.) first speaks of this letter of Cyril. The conclusion of it, in which the Emperor is designated as δοξάζων τὴν

began to work miracles,[38] became objects of the highest adoration, and were finally put on altars.[39]

Helena set the first example of a pilgrimage to Palestine, which was soon extensively imitated.[40] By this means ideas of *the holiness of that country* had increased so much, even to the grossest superstition,[41] that many teachers of the Church openly discouraged these pilgrimages.[42]

ὁμοούσον τριάδα, is decidedly adverse to its authenticity. For Cyril, in the time of Constantius, was not an adherent of the Nicene faith, and that this Emperor was not so might have been unknown a considerable time after, in different places. Comp. Dallaeus adv. Latinorum de cultus religiosi objecto traditionem, Genevae 1664. 4. p. 704. Witsii miscellan. sacra ii. 364.

[38] Paulinus Nolanus ep. 31. (al. 11.): The bishop of Jerusalem alone could bestow splinters of the cross, ad magnam fidei et benedictionis gratiam. Quae quidem crux in materia insensata vim vivam tenens, ita ex illo tempore innumeris paene quotidie hominum votis lignum suum commodat, ut detrimenta non sentiat, et quasi intacta permaneat.

[39] First mentioned by Sozomen ii. 3. and Nilus. See not. 48. cf. Bingham vol. iii. p. 236.

[40] Partly in order to be baptised in Jordan (Euseb. de locis Ebr. s. v. Βηθαβαρά), which was also the purpose of Constantine (Euseb. de vit. Const. iv. 62.); but also attracted by the marvellous, and the love of relics. Paulinus Nol. ep. 11: the holy cross was shown only at Easter, nisi interdum religiosissimi postulent, qui hac tantum causa illo peregrinati advenerint, ut sibi ejus revelatio quasi in pretium longinquae peregrinationis deferatur. Epist. 36: religiosa cupiditas est loca videre, in quibus Christus ingressus et passus est, et resurrexit, et unde conscendit: et aut de ipsis locis exiguum pulverem, aut de ipso Crucis ligno aliquid saltem festucae simile sumere et habere, benedictio est. As the wood of the cross suffered no diminution (note 38.), so also the footsteps of the Lord at his ascension were not worn away. Sulpic. Sever. hist. sacr. ii. 33: cum quotidie confluentium fides certatim Domino calcata diripiat, damnum tamen arena non sentit: et eadem adhuc sui speciem, velut impressis signata vestigiis terra custodit.

[41] Ex. gr. Augustin. de civ. Dei xxii. 8. Respecting the wonderful power of the terra sancta de Hierosolymis allata.

[42] Hieron. ep. 13. ad Paulinum: Non Hierosolymis fuisse, sed Hierosolymis bene vixisse laudandum est.—Et de Hierosolymis et de Britannia aequaliter patet aula coelestis.—Beatus Hilarion cum Palaestinus esset et in Palaestina viveret: uno tantum die vidit Hierosolymam, ut nec contemnere loca sancta propter viciniam, nec rursus, dominum loco claudere videretur. (On the other hand epist. 47. ad Desiderium: adorasse, ubi steterunt pedes domini, pars fidei est, et quasi recentia nativitatis et crucis ac passionis vidisse vestigia.) Especially zealous is Gregorii Nyseuni epist. περὶ τῶν ἀπιόντων εἰς Ἱεροσόλυμα against these pilgrimages (reprinted also as an appendix to J. H.

Aversion to pictures ceased among Christians in the fourth century. They allowed not merely likenesses of emperors,[43] but also of other distinguished men.[44] On the other hand, it was still reckoned a heathen practice to represent objects of worship by *images*.[45] At first, allegorical representations of sacred doctrines, and historical pictures taken from the Scriptures or from the his-

Heidegger dé peregrinationibus religionis. Turici 1670. 8.) We see from his letters that even then, Jerusalem was remarkable for corruption of morals, as places of pilgrimage usually are: εἰ ἦν πλέον ἡ χάρις ἐν τοῖς κατὰ Ἱεροσόλυμα τόποις, οὐκ ἂν ἐπεχωρίαζε τοῖς ἐκεῖ ζῶσιν ἡ ἁμαρτία. Νῦν μέντοι οὐκ ἔστιν ἀκαθαρσίας εἶδος, ὃ μὴ τολμᾶται παρ᾽ αὐτοῖς, καὶ πονηρίαι, καὶ μοιχεῖαι, καὶ κλοπαί, καὶ εἰδωλολατρεῖαι, καὶ φαρμακεῖαι, καὶ φθόνοι, καὶ φόνοι.

[43] Likenesses of Constantine and his children were brought into the Labarum, Euseb. de vita Const. i. 31, iv. 69, comp. above, not. 4.

[44] Thus the Christians of Antioch had likenesses of their bishop Meletius († 381) even during his lifetime, on the seals, rings, vessels, and walls. See Chrysostomi orat. encomiastica in s. Meletium, opp. ii. 519.

[45] See Div. 1. §. 70. not. 5. Euseb. Caesariensis ep. ad. Constantiam. (Conc. Nicaeni ii. actio 6. Published more complete by J. Boivin in the notes to Nicephori Gregorae Byzant. histor. ed Bonn. T. ii. p. 1301): Ἐπεὶ δὲ καὶ περί τινος εἰκόνος ὡς δὴ τοῦ Χριστοῦ γέγραφας, εἰκόνα βουλομένη σοι ταύτην ὑφ᾽ ἡμῶν πεμφθῆναι· τίνα λέγεις καὶ ποίαν ταύτην, ἣν φῂς τοῦ Χριστοῦ εἰκόνα ;—πότερον τὴν ἀληθῆ καὶ ἀμετάλλακτον, καὶ φύσει τοὺς αὐτοῦ χαρακτῆρας φέρουσαν ἢ ταύτην ἣν δι᾽ ἡμᾶς ἀνείληφε, τῆς τοῦ δούλου μορφῆς περιθέμενος τὸ σχῆμα ;—ἀλλὰ τοῦ πρὸ τῆς μεταβολῆς σαρκίον αὐτοῦ δὴ τοῦ θνητοῦ τὴν εἰκόνα φῂς παρ᾽ ἡμῶν αἰτεῖν· ἆρα γὰρ τοῦτό σε μόνον διέλαθεν τὸ ἀνάγνωσμα, ἐν ᾧ ὁ θεὸς νομοθετεῖ μὴ ποιεῖν ὁμοίωμα μήτε τῶν, ὅσα ἐν τῷ οὐρανῷ, μήτε τῶν, ὅσα ἐν τῇ γῇ κάτω ; ἢ ἔστιν ὅτε ἐν ἐκκλησίᾳ τὸ τοιοῦτον ἢ αὐτὴ, ἢ καὶ παρ᾽ ἄλλου τοῦτο ἤκουσας ; οὐχὶ δὲ καθ᾽ ὅλης τῆς οἰκουμένης ἐξώρισται καὶ πόρρω τῶν ἐκκλησιῶν πεφυγάδευται τὰ τοιαῦτα, μόνοις τε ἡμῖν μὴ ἐξεῖναι τὸ τοιοῦτον ποιεῖν παρὰ πᾶσι βεβόηται ;—οὐκ οἶδα γὰρ, ὅπως γύναιόν τι μετὰ χεῖράς ποτε δύο τινὰς φέρουσα καταγεγραμμένους, ὡς ἂν φιλοσόφους, ἀπέρριψε λόγον, ὡς ἂν εἶεν Παύλου καὶ τοῦ Σωτῆρος· οὐκ ἔχω λέγειν, οὔτε ὁπόθεν λαβοῦσα, οὔτε ὅθεν τοῦτο μαθοῦσα· ἵνα μηδὲ αὐτὴ, μηδὲ ἕτεροι σκανδαλίζοιντο, ἀφελόμενος ταύτην παρ᾽ ἐμαυτὸν κατεῖχον, οὐχ ἡγούμενος καλῶς ἔχειν εἰς ἑτέρους ὅλως ἐκφέρειν ταῦτα, ἵνα μὴ δοκῶμεν δίκην εἰδωλολατρούντων τὸν θεὸν ἡμῶν ἐν εἰκόνι περιφέρειν. Epiphanius ep. ad Johannem Hierosol. ex vers. Hieronymi (Epiph. opp. ii. 317) relates, that when he had come into the church in Anablatha, a village of Palestine, inveni ibi velum pendens in foribus ejusdem Ecclesiae tinctum atque depictum, et habens imaginem, quasi Christi, vel sancti cujusdam. Non enim satis memini, cujus imago fuerit. Cum ergo hoc vidissem, in Ecclesia Christi contra auctoritatem Scripturarum hominis pendere imaginem, scidi illud, et magis dedi consilium custodibus ejusdem loci, ut pauperem mortuum eo obvolverent et efferrent. He promises them a new velum which he herewith sends and asks John deinceps praecipere, in Ecclesia Christi ejus-

tory of martyrs, were allowed in the churches. Of these the earliest instances in the East are mentioned by *Gregory* of Nyssa;[46] in the West, by *Paulinus*, bishop of Nola (409–431, A.D.)[47] Such pictures were not intended to be worshipped, but were merely for instruction and exhortation.[48] The likenesses of individuals only were capable of leading the minds of the illiterate astray, so as to worship them. The first pictures of this kind which we find in a Gallic Church at the end of the fifth century do not, it is

modi vela, quae contra religionem nostram veniunt, non appendi. Asterius, bishop of Amasea (about 400. See Homilies in the auctarium PP. ed. Combefisii) hom. in divitem et Lazarum : Μὴ γράφε τὸν Χριστόν. ἀρκεῖ γὰρ αὐτῷ ἡ μία τῆς ἐνσωματώσεως ταπεινοφροσύνη, ἣν αὐθαιρέτως δι' ἡμᾶς κατεδέξατο· ἐπὶ δὲ τῆς ψυχῆς σου βαστάζων νοητῶς τὸν ἀσώματον λόγον περίφερε. cf. Suiceri thes. eccl. i. 1014. Jo. Dallaei de imaginibus libb. iv. Lugd. Bat. 1642. 8. p. 163 ss. Frid. Spanhemii hist. imaginum. Lugd. Bat. 1686. 8. (Opp. iii. 707). Neander's Chrysostomus ii. 143.

[46] Greg. Nyss. orat. de laudibus Theodori Mart. c. 2. (Opp. ii. 1011.) in describing the church built in honour of Theodore : Ἐπέχρωσε δὲ καὶ ζωγράφος τὰ ἄνθη τῆς τέχνης ἐν εἰκόνι διαγραψάμενος, τὰς ἀριστείας τοῦ μάρτυρος, τὰς ἐνστάσεις, τὰς ἀλγηδόνας, τὰς θηριώδεις τῶν τυράννων μορφὰς, τὰς ἐπηρείας, τὴν φλογοτρόφον ἐκείνην κάμινον, τὴν μακαριωτάτην τελείωσιν τοῦ ἀθλητοῦ, τοῦ ἀγωνοθέτου Χριστοῦ τῆς ἀνθρωπίνης μορφῆς τὸ ἐκτύπωμα· πάντα ἡμῖν, ὡς ἐν βιβλίῳ τινὶ γλωττοφόρῳ, διὰ χρωμάτων τεχνουργησάμενος σαφῶς διηγόρευσε τοὺς ἀγῶνας τοῦ μάρτυρος. In the orat. de deitate Filii et Spir. s. (l. c. p. 908), he describes a picture of the sacrifice of Isaac. (Augustin. contra Faustum xxii. 73 : factum ita nobile,—ut tot linguis cantatum, tot locis pictum, et aures et oculos dissimulantis feriret.) Comp. Cramer's Forts. v. Bossuet's Weltgesch. Th. 4, S. 442 ss. Münter's Sinnbilder u. Kunstvorstellungen der alten Christen. Heft 1. S. 9 ss.

[47] Paulin. natal. ix. Felicis :

> Propterea visum nobis opus utile, totis
> Felicibus domibus pictura illudere sancta :
> Si forte attonitas haec per spectacula mentes
> Agrestum caperet fucata coloribus umbra etc.

cf. natalis vii. et x. epistl. 30. (al. 12.) Prudentius περὶ στεφανῶν hymn. ix. v. 10, hymn. xi. v. 127. Münter i. 18.

[48] Nilus (see § 85. not. 1.) advised the Eparch Olympiodorus who intended to build a Martyrion and to adorn it with a number of pictures lib. iv. cp. 61.), ἐν τῷ ἱερατείῳ μὲν κατὰ ἀνατολὰς τοῦ θειοτάτου τεμένους ἕνα καὶ μόνον τυπῶσαι σταυρόν· δι' ἑνὸς γὰρ σωτηριώδους σταυροῦ τὸ τῶν ἀνθρώπων διασώζεται γένος, καὶ τοῖς ἀπηλπισμένοις ἐλπὶς πανταχοῦ κηρύσσεται· ἱστοριῶν δὲ παλαιᾶς καὶ νέας διαθήκης πληρῶσαι ἔνθεν καὶ ἔνθεν χειρὶ καλλίστου ζωγράφου τὸν ναὸν τὸν ἅγιον, ὅπως ἂν οἱ μὴ εἰδότες γράμματα, μηδὲ δυνάμενοι τὰς θείας ἀναγινώσκειν γραφὰς τῇ θεωρίᾳ τῆς ζωγραφίας μνήμην τε λαμβάνωσιν τῆς τῶν γνησίως τῷ ἀληθινῷ θεῷ δεδουλευκότων ἀνδραγαθίας, καὶ πρὸς ἅμιλλαν διεγείρωνται τῶν εὐκλεῶν καὶ ἀοιδίμων ἀριστευμάτων, δι' ὧν τῆς γῆς τὸν οὐρανὸν ἀπηλλάξαντο.

true, imply that they were worshipped;[49] but soon after, superstition connected itself with the likenesses of miracle-working
persons, which were placed in houses.[50]   Under Leo the Great,
we find the first image of Christ in a Romish Church.[51]

[49] Severus caused pictures of Martin of Tours and Paulinus of Nola
to be brought into the baptistery of the church in Bourges, while the
former was probably alive, the latter, certainly so.   Pauli Nol. ep. 32.
cf. Bingham vol. iii. p. 305.
[50] Thus Augustine mentions pictures of Peter and Paul, (de consensu
evangel. i. 10.) but says of them : Sic omnino errare meruerunt, qui
Christum et Apostolos ejus non in sanctis codicibus, sod in pictis parietibus quaesierunt. Comp. de moribus eccl. cath. i. 34 : Novi, multos
esse sepulchrorum et picturarum adoratores.   Nunc vos illud admoneo,
ut aliquando Ecclesiae catholicae maledicere desinatis, vituperando
mores hominum, quos et ipsa condemnat, et quos quotidie tanquam
malos filios corrigere studet.   According to Theodoreti hist. relig. c. 26.
(ed. Schultze iii. 1272.)   Simeon Stylita was held in such honour at
Rome even during his lifetime, ὡς ἐν ἅπασι τοῖς τῶν ἐργαστηρίων προπυ-
λαίοις εἰκόνας αὐτῷ βραχείας ἀναστῆσαι, φυλακήν τινα σφίσιν αὐτοῖς καὶ ἀσφάλειαν ἐντεῦθεν πορίζοντας.
[51] According to Severianus (about 400) an opponent of Chrysostom,
subsequently bishop of Gabala (tract. in s. crucem in s. Jo. Chrysost, de
educandis liberis lib. etc. ed Franc. Combefis. Paris 1656. 8. p. 129),
the cross is ἡ τοῦ ἀθανάτου βασιλέως εἰκών.   In the churches of Paulinus of
Nola, Christ appears only in the symbolic form of the lamb at the foot
of the cross.   In the picture belonging to the S. Maria Maggiore, the
oldest extant, which was made under Sixtus III., 432-440, a throne
with a book roll, and behind it a cross, forms the central point.   In the
back ground, Christ appears only as a child, in historical representations
from the accounts of his childhood.   In the Basilica of St Paul, which
was built under Leo I., in the picture of the triumphal arch he is first
made to occupy the exact centre as a Saviour (see die bild). Darstellungen
im Sanctuarium d. christl. Kirchen vom 5ten bis zum 14ten Jahrh von J.
G. Müller, Trier 1835. 8, S. 42 ss.)   These Salvator pictures continue
for a long time the only ones.   Pictures of the crucified, the Eccehomo,
the dead Christ in the bosom of the mother, belong to the middle ages.
The caput radiatum or the Nimbus was taken from heathen and transferred
to Christian art.   See Schoepflini-comment. hist. et crit. p. 69. Münter's
Sinnbilder ii. 28.—The Thomas-Christians in India suppose that Cyril
introduced the, to them hateful, pictures.   See La Croze hist. du Christianisme des Indes, a la Haye 1724. 4. p. 243.   Assemanus bibl. orient.
iii. ii. 401. endeavours indeed to prove that this tradition cannot be very
old ; but it is a remarkable fact that it is also related by the Copt *Elmacin* (about 1250) on whose authority it is repeated by Makriz (about
1400.)   See Renaudot hist. Patr. Alex. p. 114, Makrizii hist. coptorum
ed Wetzer. Solisb. 1828. 8. p. 53.)   On any supposition, it is historically established that pictures were introduced into churches in the time
of Cyril.

§ 100.

PLACES AND TIMES OF PUBLIC WORSHIP.

Since *basilicae*[1] had frequently been converted into churches after the time of Constantine, and churches had been built in the form of *basilicae*,[2] the name *basilica* was also the more readily transferred to the churches themselves,[3] because it was susceptible in this instance of a signification so appropriate. The churches, now large and splendid, were divided into three parts : the *νάρθηξ* (*πρόναος*, ferula) *porch*, from which the *beautiful gates*, *πύλαι ὡραῖαι*, (according to Acts iii. 2-10) led into the *body of the church*, *ναός*, navis (where was the *ἄμβων*, pulpitum), which again was divided from the *βῆμα,* sacrarium, *sacristy*, by cancelli, *κιγκλίδες*, a lattice-work. There were usually other buildings attached to the churches, and especially a baptistery, *βαπτιστήριον*, with the font, piscina, fons, *κολυμβήθρα*. All the buildings were situated in an inclosed court (*αἴθριον*, *αὐλή*, atrium), in which was also a *reservoir* or large vessel of water (*κρήνη*, cantharus) for washing the hands before entering the church, after the ancient Jewish fashion.

Fasts, hitherto voluntary, were now prescribed by the Church.[4] *Festival days* were more equally distributed, and, at the same

[1] The Roman basilica, an imitation of the *στοὰ βασιλική* in Athens, consisted partly of an oblong four cornered space, which served principally for a place of merchandize, and partly of a second space situated over against the entrance which formed a semicircle, and in which a court was held, the so called *tribunal*. See Vitruv. v. i. Hirt's Baukunst iii. 180. Dr F. Kugler's Handbuch der Kunstgeschichte. Stuttgart 1842.

[2] On the form of the churches, see the description of the city of Rome by Platner, Bunsen, Gerhard, and Röstell i. 419. Die Basiliken des christl. Roms. Kupfertafeln u. Erklärung (von Bunsen). München 1843. Fol.

[3] Hieronymus ep. 35. epitaph. Nepotiani: basilicas ecclesiae.

[4] The older and more liberal view (see Div. i. § 73. not. 1.) is still maintained by Victor Antiochenus (about 400), comm. in. ev. Marci c. 2. (bibl. PP. max. T. iv.): Enimvero inter eos, qui in Moysis, et eos rursum, qui in gratiae lege jejuniis dant operam, hoc praeter caetera interest, quod illi quidem jejunia a Deo praefinita habebant, quae proinde modis omnibus explere obligabantur, etiamsi alias noluissent ; hi vero virtutis amore, liberaque voluntatis electione jejunant verius, quam ulla legis coactione. Quodsi vero quadragesimale vel aliud quodcunque je-

time, multiplied.   In the East, *the Epiphany* was celebrated
as the festival[5] both of the birth and baptism of our Lord ;
in the West, the 25th December had been adopted as the
birth-day ever since the middle of the fourth century ;[6] the
custom proceeding from Rome and spreading into the differ-

junium definitum habemus, propter ignavos et negligentes, quo nimirum quoque ii officium faciant, praefinitum habemus.   Chrysostomus
hom. lii. in eos qui primo Pascha jejunant.   Cassianus collat. xxi. c. 30 :
Sciendum sane hanc observantiam quadragesimae, quamdiu ecclesiae
illius primitivae perfectio inviolata permansit, penitus non fuisse.   Non
enim praecepti hujus necessitate nec quasi legali sanctione constricti,
arctissimis jejuniorum terminis claudebantur, qui totum anni spatium
aequali jejunio concludebant.   Socrates v. 22.   On the contrary Epiphanius haer. lxxv. 6.   Expos. fidei c. 22, derives the Wednesday's and
Friday's fasts from an apostolic arrangement.   Hieronymus ep. 27. (al.
54.) ad Marcellam : Nos unam quadragesimam secundum traditionem
Apostolorum, toto nobis orbe congruo, jejunamus.   Leo P. serm. 43, de
Quadrages. 6 : Apostolica institutio xl. dierum jejunio impleatur.
While in the Oriental church all fasting was prohibited on the Saturday,
the custom of fasting on this day arose in the West, especially in Rome,
perhaps even in the third century (Neander i. 1, 510 : Tertullian de jejun. c. 14, does not, however, prove this.   See my remarks in the Theol.
Stud. and Kritik. 1833, iv. 1149.)   In the fourth century, Saturday as a
fast day entirely took the place of Wednesday at Rome (Innocent i. ep.
25, ad Decentium. c. 4.   Augustini ep. 36. ad Casulanum). cf. Quesnel.
diss. de jejunio Sabbati in Eccl. Rom. observato in his edition of the opp.
Leonis ii. 544.

[5] Cassian. collat. x. c. 2.   Intra Aegypti regionem mos iste antiqua
traditione servatur, ut peracto Epiphaniorum die, quem provinciae illius
sacerdotes vel dominici baptismi, vel secundum carnem nativitatis esse
definiunt, et idcirco utriusque sacramenti solemnitatem non bifarie, ut
in occiduis provinciis, sed sub una diei hujus festivitate concelebrant,
epistolae pontificis Alexandrini per universas dirigantur Aegypti ecclesias, quibus et initium quadragesimae et dies paschae non solum per civitates omnes, sed etiam per universa monasteria designentur.

[6] According to epist. Johannis episc. Nicaeni in the auctar. bibl. Patr.
ed Combessius t. ii. p. 297, and an Anonymus ap. Cotelerius ad Constitt.
Apost. v. 13, which, however, are too modern to be regarded as proper
witnesses, although they certainly come near the truth, this day was
established by Julius, bishop of Rome (337-352.)   An expression of
his successors, Liberius (352-366) in Salvatoris natali is adduced by
Ambrosius de virginibus iii. c. 1.   Even an ancient Syrian in Assemani
bibl. orient. ii. 164, states that the natalis solis invicti falling on this
day (Winter-solstice, according to the erroneous reckoning of the Julian
calendar on the 25th December, see Ideler's Chronologie ii. 24), was
the reason why the natalis Christi was assigned to the same day.   So
also Jo. Harduin (Acta SS. Junii iv. 702. D.) and especially Jablonski
de origine festi nativit. Christi diss. ii. §. 2. (Opusc. ed. te Water iii.

ent parts of the empire. This festival began now to obtain
in the East;[7] and at last, also (shortly before 431) in Egypt.[8]
The Epiphany was observed in addition as the day of baptism,
and came to be kept as such even in the West.[9] The celebration of the passover, as customary in Asia Minor, had been rejected at the council of Nice;[10] and since that time, those who
still retained it were regarded as heretics, Τεσσαρεσκαιδεκα-
τῖται, Quartodecimani.[11] With respect to the appointment of
the Easter festival, they followed for the most part the patriarch
of Alexandria;[12] yet not always, especially in the West; and

348.) Even so late as the times of Leo the Great, there were many in
Rome quibus haec die solemnitatis nostrae non tam de nativitate Christi,
quam de novi, ut dicunt, solis ortu honorabilis videatur (Leonis M. sermo xxi. c. 6.) According to Credner de natalitiorum Christi et rituum
in hoc festo celebrande solemnium origine, in Illgen's Zeitschr. f. d. hist.
Theol. iii. ii. 228, this festival began in Egypt in the fourth century.

[7] For example, in Antioch about 380. Chrysost. hom. 31. de natali
Christi (ed. Montfauc. ii. 355.): οὕπω δέκατόν ἐστιν ἔτος, ἐξ οὗ δῆλη καὶ
γνώριμος ἡμῖν αὕτη ἡ ἡμέρα γεγένηται. What follows furnishes a remarkable illustration of the ease with which customs of a recent date could assume the character of apostolic institutions: παρὰ μὲν τοῖς τὴν ἑσπέραν
αἰκοῦσιν ἄνωθεν γνωριζομένη—παλαιὰ καὶ ἀρχαία ἐστι, καὶ ἄνωθεν τοῖς ἀπὸ
Θράκης μέχρι Γαδείρων οἰκοῦσι κατάδηλος καὶ ἐπίσημος γέγονε.

[8] Comp. Cassian collat. x. 2. above note 5. On the other hand, in
the Acts of the Ephesian council (ap. Mansi iv. 293.) Pauli Episc. Emi-
seni homilia λεχθεῖσα κθ Χοιὰκ (25. Dec.) ἐν τῇν μεγάλη ἐκκλησίᾳ Ἀλεξανδρείας—εἰς τὴν γέννησιν τοῦ Κυρίου κ. τ. λ. About the same time under
bishop Juvenalis the festival was also adopted in Jerusalem, which was
united with Alexandria against Antioch. See Basilides Seleuc. de s. Stephano, in S. Joannis Chrysostomi de educandis liberis lib. ejusdem tractatus alii quinque etc. ed. Franc. Combefis. Paris 1656. 8. p. 302.

[9] The first trace of it is in 360, when Julian, according to Ammian.
Marcell. xxi. c. 2. celebrated the Epiphany in the church at Vienne. In the
West, the commemoration of the arrival of the Magi (i. e., three kings,
according to Psalm lxxii. 10), and the first miracle in Cana were united
with this feast. Bingham vol. ix. p. 80. Neander ii. 2, 657 ss.

[10] Comp. Div. 1. §. 60. not. 15. Constantini epist. ad ecclesias
de decretis syn. Nic. (ap. Eusebius de vita Const. iii. 18.) et epist. Syn.
Nic. ad eccl. Alexandr. ap. Socrates i. 9. ὡς πάντας τοὺς ἐν τῇ ἑῴᾳ ἀδελφοὺς
τοὺς μετὰ τῶν Ἰουδαίων τὸ πρότερον ποιοῦντας, συμφώνως Ῥωμαίοις καὶ ἡμῖν—
τὸ πάσχα ἐκ τοῦ δεῦρο ἄγειν. There is nothing more precise on the subject.
This Nicene decree was confirmed by the Conc. Antioch. ann. 341.
can. 1.

[11] The name first occurs in Conc. Laodic. (about 364) can. 7. Conc.
Constant. oec. ii. ann. 381, c. 2. Epiphan. haer. 50. On the other
hand Philastrius haer. 87. knows nothing of it.

[12] Leonis ep. 121. (ed Quesn. 94.): Paschale festum—quamvis in

thus Easter was sometimes observed on different Sundays in different provinces.[13]   The Paschal festival, which was announced
at the Epiphany, was preceded by the Quadragesima (τεσσαρα-
κοστή)[14] and divided into the πάσχα σταυρώσιμον, hebdomas magna, *the great week*, in which the feria quinta, (ἡ ἁγία πέμπτη), the
παρασκευή, and the Sabbatum magnum were distinguished from
one another ; and into the πόσχα ἀναστάσιμον, *the week of the
resurrection*, which ended with the Dominica in albis (καινὴ
κυριακή).   This festival was followed by the Quinquagesima (πεντηκοστή), which included the ascension (ἀνάληψις), and ended
with pentecost (πεντηκοστή.)

The nightly service (vigiliæ, παννυχίδες) which preceded the

primo semper menso celebrandum sit, ita tamen est lunaris cursus conditione mutabile, ut plerumque sacratissimae diei ambigua occurrat electio, et ex hoc fiat plerumque quod non licet, ut non simul omnis Ecclesia
quod nonnisi unum esse oportet observet.   Studuerunt itaque sancti
Patres occasionem hujus erroris auferre, omnem hanc curam Alexan-
drino Episcopo delegantes (quoniam apud Aegyptios hujus supputationis antiquitus tradita esse videbatur peritia), per quem quotannis dies
praedictae solemnitatis Sedi apostolicae indicaretur, cujus scriptis ad
longinquiores Ecclesias iudicium generale percurreret.

[13]   Ambrosii ep. 23. (al. 83.)   On the different paschal cycles see
Bingham vol. ix. p. 99.   Ideler's Chronologie Bd. 2. S. 200 ss.   In
Alexandria a cycle of nineteen years invented by Anatolius was used (ἐννεα-
καιδεκαετηρίς.)   In Rome, to the time of Leo the Great, and in the
West, the cycle of 84 years.   With the Alexandrians, Easter festival
must fall between 22d March and 25th April ; with the Latins, between
the 18th March and the 21st April.   Hence there was a difference in
the keeping of Easter, and hence arose the discussions respecting it.
Ideler ii. 254 ff.   For this reason, Leo M. ep. 121. (see note 12) applied to the emperor Marcian : obsecro clementiam vestram, ut studium
vestrum praestare dignemini, quatenus Aegyptii, vel si qui sunt alii, qui
certam hujus supputationis videntur habere notitiam, scrupulum hujus
solicitudinis absolvant, ut in eum diem generalis observantia dirigatur,
qui nec paternarum constitutionum normam relinquat, nec ultra prae-
fixos terminos evagetur.   Quicquid autem pietas vestra de hac consultatione cognoverit, ad meam jubeat mox notitiam pervenire, ut in divinis
mysteriis nulla dissonantiae culpa nascatur.

[14]   Among the Orientals seven weeks, among the Westerns who fast-
ed also on the Sabbath (see above, note 6) six ; in both cases, therefore,
thirty-six days.   Cassiani collat. xxi. 24. 25. (qui substantiarum nostrarum omniumque fructuum decimas offerre praecipimur, multo magis
necesse est, ut ipsius quoque conversationis nostrae, et humani usus,
operumque nostrorum decimas offeramus, quae profecto in supputatione
quadragesimae implentur,) 27. 28.   Comp. Socrates v. 22.

Easter festival, was observed with great splendour;[15] but now similar vigils were also annexed to other festivals, especially to those in honour of martyrs.

§. 101.

RITES AND CEREMONIES OF WORSHIP.

Christian worship was now invested with a splendour hitherto unknown. The clergy began to wear a peculiar costume while engaged in holy things.[1] In some of the services lights were also used in the day time ;[2] and in the fifth century frankincense began to be employed.[3] More attention was paid to the music. The custom of singing in responses, first introduced into the Church at Antioch,[4] soon spread in the East, and was transferred

[15] Euseb. de vit. Const. iv. 22.   Gregor. Nyss. orat. 5. de Paschate Gregor. Naz. orat. 19 et 42.

[1] All the clergy wore the στιχάριον (vestis alba tunica) ; bishops, presbyters, and deacons wore over that the ὠράριον, (according to Jo. Morinus de sacris Ecclesiae ordinationibus p. 174. ὠράριον, according to Suicer thes. eccl. ii. 498. ὀράριον lat. orarium, afterwards Stola), bishops and presbyters over that the φελόνης or φαιλόνης (planeta, casula. comp. Morinus p. 176. Suicer ii. 1422). The ὠμοφόριον (pallium) distinguished the bishops in the East; in the West it was not yet in use (cf. Pertsch de origine, usu et auctoritate pallii archiepiscopalis. Helmst. 1754. 4. p. 91 ss.) That no tonsure was ever practised either by monks or clergymen may be inferred from Hieronymus ad Ezech. 44, 20 : Quod sequitur ; caput suum non radent neque comam nutrient, sed tondentes attondebunt capita sua, perspicue demonstratur, nec rasis capitibus, sicut sacerdotes cultoresque Isidis ac Serapis nos esse debere, nec rursum comam demittere, quod proprie luxuriosorum est, barbarorumque et militantium, sed ut honestus habitus sacerdotum facie demonstretur etc.   Comp. Bingham vol. ii. p. 413. iii. 50.

[2] Before the relics of martyrs, and in the East also during the reading of the Gospel. See Hieronymus adv. Vigilantium.   Lactantius (institutt. vi. 2) still mocks the heathens on account of it.

[3] The first certain trace of it is found in Pseudodionys. Areop. de eccl. hier. c. 3.   It had been used before as a mark of honour to the emperors. See §. 99, note 4.

[4] According to Theodoretus h. e. ii. 19.   Flavianus and Diodorus, two monks in Antioch, in the time of Constantine, were its originators : οὗτοι πρῶτοι, διχῇ διελόντες τοὺς τῶν ψαλλόντων χορούς, ἐκ διαδοχῆς ᾄδειν τὴν Δαυιτικὴν ἐδίδαξαν μελῳδίαν· καὶ τοῦτο ἐν Ἀντιοχείᾳ πρῶτον ἀρξάμενον πάντοσε διέδραμε, καὶ κατέλαβε τῆς οἰκουμένης τὰ τέρματα.   According to Theodore of Mopsvestia in Nicetae Acomin, thesaurus orthodoxiae v. 30. they

to the Western Church by Ambrose.[5]   The *disciplina arcani*
(distinction between the initiated and uninitiated) reached its
highest development in the fourth century,[6] but afterwards gradually disappeared as heathenism ceased.   Public worship (λει-
τουργία,[7] missa)[8] was divided on account of it into several parts

first only translated Antiphonies from the Syriac into Greek : and Socrates vi. 8. attributes the first introduction of this kind of music to Ignatius
(Augusti diss. de hymnis Syrorum. Vratisl. 1814. 8. Hahn über den Ge-
sang in der syrischen Kirche, in the Kirchenhist. Archive für 1823. iii.
52.) The custom of singing in responses was especially diffused by
the monks, (τὸ ἀντίφωνον, ἀντίφωνοι ὕμνοι.) Comp. generally M. Ger-
bertus de cantu et musica sacra (tomi ii. typis San-Blasianis 1774. 4.)
i. 40.   Schöne's Geschichtsforschungen über die kirchl. Gebräuche
ii. 191.
   [5] Augustini confess. ix. 6, 7.   Paulinus in vita Ambros. p. iv.   On
the musical character of the Ambrosian singing see Kiesewetter's Gesch.
d. europäisch-abendländischen Musik. Leipzig 1834, 4. S. 3.
   [6] Comp. Div. 1. §. 67, not. 3. Basilius de Spir. sancto c. 27.
Comp. especially Cyrilli Hieros. catecheses. Hence the formula so
frequent among the orators, ἴσασιν οἱ μεμυημένοι or οἱ συμμύσται in opposition to the ἀμύητοι : in Augustine, norunt fideles : Frommann de disciplina arcani p. 43.
   [7] Comp. Suiceri thes. eccl. ii. 220.   Bingham v. 16, particularly the
solemnity of the Lord's Supper, but in other respects every religious
service too.
   [8] Missa i. e. missio : as remissa, offensa, for remissio, offensio.   Avitus (archbishop of Vienne about 490) in epist. i. : in Ecclesiis, Pala-
tiisque, sive Praetoriis missa fieri pronunciatur, cum populus ab observatione dimittitur.   In the first part of the service, which consisted of
psalms, readings, and sermon, even the unbelieving portion of the people
were permitted to join. After their retiring, the proper missa catechumenorum followed, which was a series of prayers, whereby the catechu-
mens, penitents, and possessed, were dismissed in classes (by the call
οἱ ἀκοινώνητοι μεριπατήσατε. μή τις τῶν κατηχουμένων,) &c. (cf. Conc. Carthag. iv. ann. 398. can. 84 : Ut Episcopus nullum prohibeat ingredi
Ecclesiam, et audire verbum Dei, sive gentilem, sive haereticum, sive
Judaeum, usque ad missam catechumenorum. Augustini sermo 49.
§. 8 : Ecce post sermonem fit missa catechumenis : manebunt fideles,
venietur ad locum orationis.)   According to this analogy, the last part
of public worship was called missæ fidelium, *i.e.*, the service with which
the fideles were dismissed, and which ended with the call ἀπολύεσθε, ite,
missa est (this dismissal was among the Greeks ἡ ἀπόλυσις τῆς ἐκκλησίας.)   Since the last part was the most important, it was also called
in particular missa (cf. Ambrosii ep. 20. al. 14. ad Marcellinam sororem : post lectiones atque tractatum dimissis catechumenis—missam
facere coepi). Finally, the name was transferred to every public service.   Thus it is applied to the meetings of the monks for prayer, Cassian. institt. ii. c. 13, missa nocturna, iii. c. 5, missa canonica.

(missa catechumenorum, and missa fidelium),[9] and received more definite formularies.[10]

Baptism, now preceded by unction, was frequently delayed as long as possible.[11] Against this abuse several teachers of the Church zealously remonstrated.[12] The baptism of infants did not

[9] See not. 8. The Greeks distinguished the parts of public worship in a different manner. See Conc. Laodic. can. 19: περὶ τοῦ δεῖν ἰδίᾳ πρῶτον μετὰ τὰς ὁμιλίας τῶν Ἐπισκόπων, καὶ τῶν κατηχουμένων εὐχὴν ἐπιτελεῖσθαι, καὶ μετὰ τὸ ἐξελθεῖν τοὺς κατηχουμένους τῶν ἐν μετανοίᾳ τὴν εὐχὴν γίνεσθαι, καὶ τούτων προσελθόντων ὑπὸ χεῖρα καὶ ὑποχωρησάντων οὕτως τῶν πιστῶν τὰς εὐχὰς γίνεσθαι τρεῖς,—καὶ μετὰ τὸ Πρεσβυτέρους δοῦναι τῷ Ἐπισκόπῳ τὴν εἰρήνην, τότε τοὺς Λαϊκοὺς τὴν εἰρήνην διδόναι, καὶ οὕτω τὴν ἁγίαν προσφορὰν ἐπιτελεῖσθαι.

[10] The arrangement of public worship and single formularies had been already established for a long time; but now there were added to them formularies of prayer too; complete liturgies were made, and those of the apostolic churches were soon derived from their founders. Proclus Episc. Constantinop. (about 440) de traditione divinae Missae (in Gallandii bibl. PP. ix. 680): Πολλοὶ μὲν τινὲς καὶ ἄλλοι τῶν τοὺς ἱεροὺς Ἀποστόλους διαδεξαμένων θεῖοι ποιμένες καὶ διδάσκαλοι τῆς Ἐκκλησίας τὴν τῆς μυστικῆς λειτουργίας ἔκθεσιν ἐγγράφως καταλιπόντες, τῇ Ἐκκλησίᾳ παραδεδώκασιν. ἐξ ὧν δὲ πρῶτοι οὗτοι καὶ διακρύσιοι τυγχάνουσιν ὅ,τε μακάριος Κλήμης, ὁ τοῦ κορυφαίου τῶν Ἀποστόλων μαθητὴς καὶ διάδοχος, αὐτῷ τῶν ἱερῶν Ἀποστόλων ὑπαγορευσάντων. (This is the liturgy found in the Constitut. apost. viii. 16, the oldest extant.) καὶ ὁ θεῖος Ἰάκωβος, ὁ τῆς Ἱεροσολυμιτῶν Ἐκκλησίας τὸν κλῆρον λαχών.—Ὁ δὲ μέγας Βασίλειος μετὰ ταῦτα τὸ ῥάθυμον καὶ κατωφερὲς τῶν ἀνθρώπων θεωρῶν, καὶ διὰ τοῦτο τὸ τῆς λειτουργίας μῆκος ὀκνούντων,—ἐπιτομώτερον παρέδωκε λέγεσθαι.—Μετ' οὐ πολὺ δὲ πάλιν ὁ ἡμέτερος πατὴρ ὁ τὴν γλῶτταν χρυσοῦς Ἰωάννης—εἰς τὴν τῆς ἀνθρωπίνης φύσεως ῥᾳθυμίαν ἐφορῶν—τὰ πολλὰ ἐπέτεμε, καὶ συντομώτερον τελεῖσθαι διετάξατο. In the fifth century the liturgy of Basil had been spread almost over all the East. But in addition to it, that of Chrysostom also, proceeding from Constantinople, gradually obtained acceptance. The Alexandrians derived their liturgy from Mark, the Romans from Peter, the Milanites from Barnabas and Ambrose. No liturgy of this period, with the exception of that in the Constitutt. apost., has been preserved free from alteration. Comp. Leonis Alatii de libris ecclesiasticis Graecorum diss. ii. Paris 1645. 4. (with Fabricius' remarks in the old edition of his biblioth. graeca appended to vol. v.) Jac. Goar εὐχολόγιον s. rituale Graecorum. Paris 1647. and Venet. 1730. fol. Eus. Renaudotii liturgiarum orientalium collectio. T. ii. Paris 1716. 4. J. A. Assemani codex liturgicus Eccl. universae. P. vi. Romae 1749 ss. 4.

[11] Constitt. apostoll. vii. c. 41. Cyrill. Hieros. catech. myst. ii. c. 3. n. 4. This unction was with ἐλαίῳ ἁγίῳ; the unction after baptism, which had been practised before (see Div. 1. §. 53, not. 25), with μύρῳ or χρίσματι, see Suicer thes. eccl. i. 1077, u. ii. 1534. Bingham vol. iv. p. 303.

[12] Gregor. Nazianz. orat. 40. Comp. Ullmann's Gregor v. Naz. 8.

become universal till after the time of Augustine. The baptism
of heretics was still, in the fourth century, rejected for the most
part in the East; and afterwards the baptism of single parties
only was excepted.[13] On the contrary, Augustine established
the milder practice of the west on firm principles.[14]

As to *the Lord's Supper*, the Christians of that period recognised in it the flesh and blood of Christ, and even spoke of a
transformation; but only in a figurative sense.[15] As this rite

466 ss. (On the baptism of children : δίδωμι γνώμην, τὴν τριετίαν ἀνα-
μείναντας – ἡνίκα καὶ ἀκοῦσαί τι μυστικὸν, καὶ ἀποκρίνεσθαι δυνατὸν,—οὕτως
ἁγιάζειν.) Basilii M. orat. 13 (Walli hist. bapt. infant. i. 136. 181.)
Gregorii Nyss. orat. in eos qui differunt baptismum. Chrysostom
(Neander's Chrys. i. 74.)
[13] Comp. Div. 1. §. 72. not. 22. Athanasius, Cyril of Jerusalem,
and Basil rejected it. Münscher's Dogmengesch. iv. 368. The Synod
of Laodicea can. 7. and the second oecumenical Synod of Constantinople, can. 7. made exceptions. whose consistency is not obvious. Comp.
Drey über apost. Constit. S. 260. Gass in Illgen's Zeitschr. f. hist.
Theol. 1842, iv. 120.
[14] Augustinus de baptismo contra Donatistas vi. 47 : dicimus, baptismum Christi, i. e. verbis evangelicis consecratum, ubique eundem esse,
nec hominum quorumlibet et qualibet perversitate violari. c. 61 : Manifestum est, iniquos, quamdiu iniqui sunt, baptismum quidem posse
habere; sed salutem, cujus sacramentum baptisma est, habere non
posse. c. 78 : Dicimus, accipientibus non prodesse (baptismum), cum
in haeresi accipiunt consentientes haereticis : et ideo veniunt ad catholicam pacem atque unitatem, non ut baptismum accipiant, sed ut eis prodesse incipiat quod acceperant.
[15] We find the expressions : μεταβολή, μεταβάλλεσθαι, μεταμορφοῦσθαι,
μεταστοιχειοῦσθαι (similar expressions with regard to the consecrated oil,
Münscher iv. 387, and the baptismal water, same author, p. 352.
Wundemann ii. 417), and again, τύπος, ἀντίτυπον, figura, signum. Hence
all churches appeal to the fathers in their favour Comp. especially the
dispute between A. Arnauld, P. Nicole (chief work la perpétuité de
la foi de l'église catholique touchant l'eucharistie, 3. T. 1669-1672. T.
4 et 5. par Eus. Renaudot, 1711-1713 4). and J. Claude (réponse aux
deux traités intitulés : la perpétuité etc. Charent. 1666. Réponse au
livre de M. Arnauld intitulé : la perpétuité etc. Charent, 1671 2 voll.
8). Clear passages on this subject are : Augustinus epist. 98. (al. 23.)
ad Bonifacium §. 9 : Nempe saepe ita loquimur, ut Pascha propinquante
dicamus crastinam vel perendinam Domini passionem, cum ille ante tam
multos annos passus sit, nec omnino nisi semel illa passio facta sit.—
Nonne semel immolatus est Christus in se ipso, et tamen in sacramento
non solum per omnes Paschae solemnitates, sed omni die populis im-
molatur, nec utique mentitur, qui interrogatus eum responderit immolari ? Si enim sacramenta quandam similitudinem earum rerum, quarum sacramenta sunt, non haberent, omnino sacramenta non essent. Ex

hac autem similitudine plerumque etiam ipsarum rerum nomina accipiunt. Sicut ergo secundum quendam modum sacramentum corporis Christi corpus Christi est, sacramentum sanguinis Christi sanguis Christi est, ita sacramentum fidei fides est. Contra Adimantum Manich. c. 12 : Non enim Dominus dubitavit dicere hoc est corpus meum, cum signum daret corporis sui. Ad Ps. iii : figuram corporis et sanguinis sui. in Joan. tract. xxvi. 18 : Qui non manet in Christo, et in quo non manet Christus, procul dubio nec manducat carnem ejus, nec bibit ejus sanguinem, etiamsi tantae rei sacramentum ad judicium sibi manducet et bibat (so all MSS. The editions have interpolations). cf. contra Faustum xx. c. 18. and 21. De doctrina christiana iii. 16. A fragment in Fulgentius in bibl. max. PP. T. ix. p. 177 s. While the Catholic theologians endeavour to explain away these passages by a forced interpretation P. de Marca in his traité du sacrament de l'Eucharistie (published after his death by his relative, the abbot Paul Faget, Paris 1668, and though suppressed soon, reprinted in the Netherlands), candidly acknowledged that the fathers to Chrysostom, and particularly Augustine, did not teach the doctrine of transubstantiation. Very clear passages on this subject are furnished by the polemical demonstrations against Eutyches and the Monophysites, so far as they had been always accustomed to compare the union of the earthly with the heavenly in the Supper, with the incarnation of Christ, and now borrowed a proof from the rite in favour of the fact, that the human nature in Christ did not cease to exist after the union. So Theodoreti Eranistes dial. ii. (ed. Schulze t. iv. p. 126) : οὐδὲ μετὰ τὸν ἁγιασμὸν τὰ μυστικὰ σύμβολα τῆς οἰκείας ἐξίσταται φύσεως· μένει γὰρ ἐπὶ τῆς προτέρας οὐσίας καὶ τοῦ σχήματος, καὶ τοῦ εἴδους·— νοεῖται δὲ ἅπερ ἐγένετο, καὶ πιστεύεται καὶ προσκυνεῖται, ὡς ἐκεῖνα ὄντα ἅπερ πιστεύεται. To these polemics belongs also first of all Chrysostom's epist. ad Caesarium, although even Leontius Hierosolym. (or Byzantium, about 600) in Maji scriptt. vett. coll. vii. i. 130, 135. Joannes Damasc. and others cite this letter as belonging to Chrysostom. The same is preserved in Latin in a codex Florentinus, and was first discovered and employed by Peter Martyr. The first edition by Bigot (appended to Palladii vita Chrystom, see above, § 85, not. 6.) was torn out of the copies by royal command (see Chaufepié and Bayle in their dictionnaires art. Bigot). The second edition appeared, according to a copy of Scipio Maffei, with Greek fragments, in Canisii lectt. ant. ed. Basnage i. 235. Comp. especially Salig de Eutychianismo ante Eutychen p. 367. In this letter it is said : antequam sanctificetur panis, panem nominamus, divina autem illum sanctificante gratia, mediante sacerdote, liberatus est quidem appellatione panis, dignus autem habitus est dominici corporis appellatione, etiamsi natura panis in ipso permansit. Comp. R. Hospiniani historia sacramentaria. (T. ii. Tiguri 1602. Genev. 1681. fol.) J. A. Ernesti Antimuratorius 1755. (Opusc. theol. p. 1.) Münscher iv. 377. Wundemann ii. 419. How value was still attributed to the fact, that the laity also received the cup, may be seen from Leo I. sermo iv. de Quadrages. (§ 86, not. 6.) Chrysostom. in epist. ii. ad Cor. hom. 18 : ἔστι δὲ ὅπου οὐδὲ διέστηκεν ὁ ἱερεὺς τοῦ ἀρχομένου, οἷον ὅταν ἀπολαύειν δέῃ τῶν φρικτῶν μυστηρίων· ὁμοίως γὰρ πάντες ἀξιούμεθα τῶν αὐτῶν· οὐ καθάπερ ἐπὶ τῆς παλαιᾶς τὰ μὲν ὁ ἱερεὺς ἤσθιε, τὰ δὲ

D

was looked upon in the light of a sacrifice,[16] the idea was naturally suggested, that God could be propitiated by it, and in this
way it was even already abused, and that frequently, by superstition.[17] The Agapæ had been, for a considerable time past, in
most countries separated from the Supper,[18] and converted into
entertainments which families prepared on the death of relatives,
churches on the anniversaries of martyrs, and at which clergy and
poor were regular guests.[19] But because the heathen notions of

ὁ ἀρχόμενος, καὶ θέμις οὐκ ἦν τῷ λαῷ μετέχειν, ὧν μετεῖχεν ὁ ἱερεύς· ἀλλ' οὐ
νῦν· ἀλλὰ πᾶσιν ἐν σῶμα πρόκειται, καὶ ποτήριον ἕν.

[16] How far see Münscher iv. 400. Wundemann ii. 441. Neander's KG. ii. 2. 707.

[17] Especially as the bread was often taken home (in Egypt universally, see Basilii ep; 93, ad Caesarium). Thus Satyrus, brother of Ambrose, during a shipwreck, took the holy bread, ligari fecit in orario, et
orarium involvit collo, utque ita se dejecit in mare :—his se tectum atque
munitum satis credens, alia auxilia non desideravit (Ambrosius de obitu
fratris sui Satyri c. 13) : A certain Acatius (August. opus imp. contra
Julian. iii. c. 162), related to Augustine that he had been born blind,
and a surgeon was about to perform an operation for him, neque hoc
permisisse religiosam matrem suam, sed id effecisse impositio ex Eucharistia cataplasmate. Comp. Gregor. Naz. orat. xi. in laudem Gorgo-
niae, p. 186, s. epist. 240. Comp. Münscher iv. 403. Wundemann
ii. 446. Neander ii. 2, 705. In like manner the heathen, cf. Etym.
Magn. : Ὑγίειαν καλοῦσιν Ἀττικοὶ τὰ πεφυραμένα οἴνῳ καὶ ἐλαίῳ ἄλφιτα καὶ πᾶν
ὅ, τι ἐξ ἱεροῦ φέρεται, οἷον θαλλόν τινα ἢ ἄλειμα. Simplicius (about 530.)
comm. ad Epictet. c. 38. ed. Schweigh. p. 351 : τὰ προσαγόμενα καὶ ἀνα-
τιθέμενα—μεταλαμβάνει καὶ αὐτὰ τῆς θείας ἀγαθότητος, ὡς καὶ θείας ἐνεργείας
ἐπιδείκνυσθαι. καὶ γὰρ ἐπιληψίας τις ὡμολόγησεν ἀπηλλάχθαι δαὶ τῆς τῶν
τοιούτων μεταλήψεως, καὶ χαλάζας καὶ θαλάσσης ἐλύθωνας ἔπαυσε. cf. Lobeck
Aglaophamus i. p. 766 ss.

[18] As it was now an ecclesiastical law that the Lord's Supper should
be taken fasting, so it was also believed that even in the time of the
Apostles the agapae were observed after the Supper. Chrysost. hom.
xxvii. in 1. Cor. (on xi. 27.) Pelagius in 1. Cor. xi. 20. Theodoret. in
1. Cor. xi. 16.—Remains of the old custom were still found in several
parts of Egypt, in which the Lord's Supper was observed on the Sabbath after the evening meal, Socrates v. 22. Sozom. vii. 19. and in the
African mode to celebrate the Supper after the evening meal on the
Thursday before Easter. Conc. Carthag. iii. ann. 397. c. 29 : Ut
sacramenta altaris nonnisi a jejunis hominibus celebrentur, excepto uno
die anniversario, quo coena domini celebratur. cf. Augustin. ep. 54.
ad Januarium c. 9.

[19] Comment. in Job (among the works of Origen, belonging to the
fourth century) lib. iii. p. 437 : Celebramus (diem mortis) religiosos cum
sacerdotibus convocantes, fideles una cum clero, invitantes adhuc egenos
et pauperes, pupillos et viduas saturantes, ut fiat festivitas nostra in

the people saw in them the reappearance of their Parentalia and sacrificial festivals, drunkenness soon pervaded them.[20] Hence they

memoriam requiei defunctis animabus, quarum memoriam celebramus, nobis autem efficiatur in odorem suavitatis in conspectu aeterni Dei. Augustini ep. xxii. ad Aurelium c. 6 : istae in coemeteriis ebrietates et luxuriosa convivia non solum honores martyrum a carnali et imperita plebe credi solent, sed etiam solatia mortuorum.   Id. contra Faustum xx. 20 : Agapes nostrae pauperes pascunt sive frugibus, sive carnibus. —plerumque in agapibus etiam carnes pauperibus erogantur.   Theodoret. graec. affect. curat. disp. viii. (ed. Schulze iv. 923.): Ἀντὶ τῶν Πανδίων καὶ Διασίων καὶ Διονυσίων καὶ τῶν ἄλλων ὑμῶν ἑορτῶν, Πέτρου καὶ Παύλου—καὶ Ἀντωνίνου καὶ Μαυρικίου καὶ τῶν ἄλλων μαρτύρων ἐπιτελοῦνται δημοθοινίαι· καὶ ἀντὶ τῆς πάλαι πομπείας καὶ αἰσχρουργίας—σώφρονες ἑορτάζονται πανηγύρεις, οὐ μέθην ἔχουσαι, καὶ κῶμον, καὶ γέλωτα, ἀλλ᾽ ὕμνους θείους, καὶ ἱερῶν λογίων ἀκρόασιν, καὶ προσευχὴν ἀξιεπαίνοις κοσμουμένην δακρύοις. Juliani Imp. fragm. (ed. Spanhem. p. 305.): ὥσπερ οἱ τὰ παιδία διὰ τοῦ πλακοῦντος ἐξαπατῶντες—πείθουσιν ἀκολουθεῖν ἑαυτοῖς·—τὸν αὐτὸν καὶ αὐτοὶ τρόπον ἀρξάμενοι (οἱ δυσσεβεῖς Γαλιλαῖοι) διὰ τῆς λεγομένης παρ᾽ αὐτοῖς ἀγάπης καὶ ὑποδοχῆς καὶ διακονίας τραπεζῶν—πιστοὺς ἐπήγαγον εἰς τὴν ἀθεότητα.   The use of these Agapae was defended by the council of Gangra against the darker asceticism of the Eustathians. can. 11 : Εἴ τις καταφρονοίη τῶν ἐκ πίστεως ἀγάπας ποιούντων καὶ διὰ τιμὴν τοῦ κυρίου συγκαλούντων τοὺς ἀδελφοὺς, καὶ μὴ ἐθέλοι κοινωνεῖν ταῖς κλήσεσι, διὰ τὸ ἐξευτελίζειν τὸ γινόμενον, ἀνάθεμα ἔστω.

[20] Even teachers of the church compared them with those heathen festivities.   See Theodoret note 19.   Chrysostom (hom. xlvii. in s. Julianum) advises his hearers to partake of the meal to be appointed in honour of the martyr beside his church (τοῦ μαρτυρίου πλησίον ὑπο συκὴν ἢ ἄμπελον) instead of joining in the heathen feasts in Daphne, a suburb of Antioch.   Hence some even supposed that they had been appointed by their ancestors as a substitute for those heathen banquets.   See Gregorius Nyss. in vita Gregor. thaumat. Div. i. §. 70. not. 9.   So also Augustine explains the origin of them to his church (ep. xxix. ad Alypium, c. 9.) : post persecutiones—cum facta pace turbae gentilium in christianum nomen venire cupientes hoc impedirentur, quod dies festos cum idolis suis solerent in abundantia epularum et ebrietate consumere, nec facile ab his—voluptatibus se possent abstinere, visum fuisse majoribus nostris, ut huic infirmitatis parti interim parceretur, diesque festi post eos quos relinquebant alii in honorem ss. Martyrum vel non simili sacrilegio, quamvis simili luxu celebrarentur.   On the drunkenness at these meals, Ambrosius de Elia et jejunio c. 17 : calices ad sepulcra Martyrum deferunt, atque illic ad vesperam bibunt, et aliter se exaudiri posse non credunt.   Augustin ep. 22. ad Aurelium c. 3 : Comessationes et ebrietates ita concessae et licita putantur, ut in honorem etiam beatissimorum Martyrum non solum per dies solemnes, sed etiam quotidie celebrentur.   Gregorius Naz. carm. ccxvii. thus addresses those who took part in such feasts :

Νῦν δὲ τί τάρβος ἔχει με, ἀκούσατε ὦ φιλόκωμοι, Πρὸς τοὺς δαιμονικοὺς αἰτομολεῖτε τύπους.
D 2

began to be discountenanced and opposed, and even banished from
the Church where it could be done without offence, while the
clergy were forbidden to take part in them.[21] Thus these festivals

On the festivals of the martyrs, sellers in the sanctuary regarded as venal
that which was necessary for the feasts, Basilii M. regula major, qu.
xl : 'Αλλ' οὐδὲ τὰς ἐν τοῖς μαρτυρίοις γινομένας ἀγορασίας οἰκείας ἡμῖν ὁ λόγος
δείκνυσιν (he then mentions how Christ drove the sellers out of the temple.)
Paulinus Nol. nat. s. Felicis ix.: Divendant vina tabernis.   Sancta precum domus est Ecclesia.   Thus the Manichaean Faustus, not without
reason, reproached the Catholics (Augustin. contra Faust. xx. 4.) : sacrificia eorum (gentilium) vertistis in agapas, idola in Martyres, quos
votis similibus colitis: defunctorum umbras vino placatis et dapibus.
    [21] In the East, the Laodicean council enacted (probably 363) can. 28. :
ὅτι οὐ δεῖ ἐν τοῖς κυριακοῖς ἢ ἐν ταῖς ἐκκλησίας τὰς λεγομένας ἀγάπας ποιεῖν, καὶ
ἐν τῷ οἴκῳ τοῦ θεοῦ ἐσθίειν καὶ ἀκούβιτα στρωννύειν.   Accordingly they were,
even in Antioch, celebrated beside the places dedicated to the martyrs.
See Chrysostom note 20.   About 392 they were no longer observed in
the greatest part of the West out of Africa.   See Augustini ep. xxii. ad
Aurelium. c. 4.: per Italiae maximam partem, et in aliis omnibus aut
prope omnibus transmarinis Ecclesiis partim nunquam facta sunt, partim vel orta vel inveterata—Episcoporum diligentia et animadversione
exstincta atque deleta sunt.   In Milan, Ambrose had forbidden them
(Augustin. confess. vi. 2., ne ulla occasio se ingurgitandi daretur ebrio-
sis, et quia illa quasi parentalia superstitioni gentilium essent simillima.)
In Rome, Alethius, at the funeral of his wife, entertained all the poor in
the basilica s. Petri (Paulinus Nol. ep. 33.); Pammachius on the contrary gave rich alms on a similar occasion (Hieron. ep. 26. ad Pammach.
c. 2.)   In Nola they kept vigils on the festival of the birth of St Felix,
while all the night through they ate and drank in the church of the
saint.   Paulinus, since he could not abrogate this practice, endeavoured
by means of pictures which he brought into the church to give a more
serious direction to the joy (Paulini nat. Felicis ix.   Compare above §.
99. not. 47.)   In Africa, where those festivals were universal (August. de
moribus eccl. cath. i. 34) : Novi—multos esse qui luxuriosissime super
mortuos bibant, et epulas cadaveribus exhibentes, super sepultos se
ipsos sepeliant, et voracitates ebrietatesque suas deputent religioni.
Augustine used his influence against them.   He first of all motioned
for their abolition from Aurelius, bishop of Carthage, in the epist. xxii.
ad Aurelium cf. c. 6.: mihi videtur facilius illic dissuaderi posse istam
foeditatem,—si—oblationis pro spiritibus dormientium, quas vere aliquid adjuvare credendum est, super ipsas memorias non sint sumtuosae,
atque omnibus petentibus sine typhő et cum alacritate praebeantur :
neque vendantur (that is, when that which was intended to serve as oblations is not offered for sale there), sed si quis pro religioni aliquid pecuniae offerre voluerit, in praesenti pauperibus eroget.   Afterwards he
effected their abrogation in Hippo ; in what way is related by him ep.
xxix. ad Alypium in the year 395.   Finally it was enacted by the Conc.
Carthag. iii. ann. 397. c. 30: Ut nulli Episcopi vel Clerici in Ecclesia

ceased in most countries, though in some they still continued beyond the present period.[22]

SIXTH CHAPTER.

HISTORY OF MORALS.

§ 102.

HISTORY OF CHRISTIAN ETHICS.[1]

Stäudlin's Gesch. d. Sittenlehre Jesu Bd. 3.—de Wette Gesch. d. christl. Sittenlehre.   Erste Hälfte S. 334 ss.

THE disposition already manifested in the preceding period to
lay too much stress on certain forms of external discipline, had
now been much increased by the influence of monachism.   Fasting and almsgiving,[2] as well as prayer, were regarded as expia-

conviventur, nisi forte transeuntes hospitiorium necessitate illic refician-
tur : populi etiam ab hujusmodi conviviis quantum fieri potest prohibe-
antur.

[22] In Syria they are mentioned at a time so late as that of Theodoret,
without blame, see note 19, and Theodoret's hist. eccles. iii., 11, where
he relates how the martyrs Juventinus and Maximinus in Antioch were
honoured : μέχρι δέ τήμερον έτησίᾳ δημοθοινίᾳ γεραίρονται.—The council
Quinisextum, A. D. 692, repeats can. 74 of the can. Laodic. 28 (see note
21.)—L. A. Muratori de agapis sublatis, in his anecdota graeca. Patav.
1709. 4. p. 241.   Bingham vol. vi. p. 516. ix. 147. x. 69.   Drescher
de agapis comm. Giessae 1824. p. 39.

[1] There was an ancient controversy concerning the morals of the
fathers occasioned by the unfavourable view taken of them by J. Barbeyrac in the preface to the translation of Puffendorf: le droit de la nature et des gens. Amst. 1712. 4.   On the other side, Remig. Ceiller apo-
logie de la morale des pères de l'église contre J. Barb. Paris 1718. 4. J.
F. Buddeus isag. ad univers. theolog. p. 620.   Replied to by Barbeyrac traitè de la morale des pères de l'èglise. Amst. 1728. 4.

[2] Münscher's Dogmengesch. iv. 314. de Wette i. 354.   Ambrosius
de Elia et jejunio c. 20 : Pecuniam habes, redime peccatum tuum.
Non venalis est Dominus, sed tu ipse venalis es : redime te operibus
tuis, redime te pecunia tua.   Vilis pecunia, sed pretiosa est misericordia
(according to Dan 4. 24 : peccata tua eleemosynis redime et iniquitates
tuas misericordiis pauperum.) Salvianus (about 450) adv. avaritiam libb.

tery of sins.   The theatre, dancing, and other amusements,[3] were
branded as absolutely sinful ; oaths,[4] the taking of interest for
money lent,[5] every kind of self-defence,[6] capital punishments,[7]
and second marriages,[8] were rejected.   In the fourth century, indeed, those who had been legally divorced were still universally
allowed to marry again,[9] though this was discouraged as well as
second marriages generally ; but in the fifth century, the Latin
church began to forbid the divorced person to marry as long as
the other party lived.[10]   So prevalent was now the spirit of mona-

iv. expressly makes generosity to churches and convents the surest redemtio peccatorum.

[3] De Wette i. 349.   Stäudlin's Gesch. d. Vorstellungen v. d. Sitt-
lichkeit des Schauspiels.   Gött. 1823.

[4] Jerome, Basil, especially Chrysostom.   See Stäudlin's Gesch. d.
Sittenlehre Jesu iii. 111. 220. 244., same author's Gesch. der Vorstellungen und Lehren vom Eide.   Gott. 1824.   Hence the Lex Marciani
A. D. 456 (Cod. Justin. i. 3, 25) : ecclesiasticis regulis, et canone a bea-
tissimis Episcopis antiquitus instituto, clerici jurare prohibentur.

[5] Basilius M. in Ps. 14. et contra foeneratores.   Gregor. Nyss. ep.
can. ad Letojum can. 6.   Ambrosius de Tobia, c. 2. ss.

[6] Ambrosius, Augustinus, Basilius, see Stäudlin's Gesch. der Sittenlehre Jesu iii. 65. 149, 219.

[7] Ambrosius ep. 25 and 26. (al. 51 and 52.)   Augustin. ep. 153. ad
Macedonium.

[8] Forbidden by Ambrose and Jerome, disadvised by Chrysostom,
a state of widowhood preferred by Augustine, cf. Cotelerius ad Hermae
Pastor. lib. ii. Mand. 4. c. 4. and in Constit. apost. iii. 2.   Stäudlin
iii. 60. 92. 141. 146.   Hence penances were imposed on those who married twice.   Conc. Neocaesar. can. 1. 3.   Laodic. can. 1.   Basilii epist.
188. (ep. can. 1.) can. 4.   Comp. ep. can. ii. c. 50. respecting those
who married three times, and ep. can. iii. c. 80. respecting those who
married more than three times.

[9] Ambrosiaster in 1. Cor. 7. 15.: Si infidelis discesserit, liberum ha-
bebit arbitrium, si voluerit, nubere legis suae viro, Contumelia enim
creatoris solvit jus matrimonii circa eum, qui relinquitur etc.   Epiphan.
haer. 59. §. 4.: ὁ δὲ μὴ δυνηθεὶς τῇ μιᾷ ἀρκεσθῆναι τελευτησάσῃ, [ἢ] ἕνεκέν
τινος προφάσεως, πορνείας ἢ μοιχείας, ἢ κακῆς αἰτίας χωρισμοῦ γενομένου,
συναφθέντα δευτέρᾳ γυναικὶ ἢ γυνὴ δευτέρῳ ἀνδρὶ, οὐκ αἰτιᾶται ὁ θεῖος λόγος,
οὐδὲ ἀπὸ τῆς ἐκκλησίας καὶ τῆς ζωῆς ἀποκηρύττει, ἀλλὰ διαβαστάζει διὰ τὸ
ἀσθενὲς, οὐχ ἵνα δύο γυναῖκας ἐπὶ τὸ αὐτὸ σχῇ ἔτι περιούσης τῆς μιᾶς, ἀλλ' ἀπὸ
μιᾶς ἀποσχεθεὶς, δευτέρᾳ, εἰ τύχοιεν, νόμῳ συναφθῆναι.   cf. Asterius below
§. 105. not. 18.   Bingham vol. ix. p. 301 ss. 349 ss.

[10] The transition to this view may be traced in Augustinus de fide
et opere c. 19 :   In ipsis divinis sententiis ita obscurum est, utrum et
iste, cui quidem sine dubio adulteram licet dimittere, adulter tamen habeatur, si alteram duxerit, ut, quantum existimo, venialiter ipi quisque
fallatur.   Still the Conc. Milevitanum ii. ann. 416, at which also Augus-

chism, that the married state began to be considered as something impure,[11] and only a tolerated evil.[12]   Even certain kinds of food were forbidden.[13]

By means of such excrescences, whose foundations could not be shown in the moral consciousness of mankind, Christian morals now assumed the aspect of a series of arbitrary, divine, despotic, commands.[14]   And since those rigorous principles were not at all observed by most people, they promoted the spirit of indifference towards the Divine precepts generally, and prepared the way for the unfortunate distinction between a higher virtue, which was solely for the monks, and a lower, which was sufficient for common Christians.[15]

It seems at first sight contradictory to this external strictness,

tine was present resolved, quite unanimously, can. 17 : Placuit, ut secundum evangelicam et apostolicam disciplinam, neque dimissus ab uxore neque dimissa a marito, alteri conjugantur : sed ita maneant, aut sibimet reconcilientur.   Quod si contempserint, ad poenitentiam redigantur. In qua causa legem imperialem petendam promulgari.   Such too was the opinion of Innocentius I. epist. 6. ad Exsuperium c. 6 : De his etiam requisivit dilectio tua, qui interveniente repudio alii se matrimonio copularunt.   Quos in utraque parte adulteros esse manifestum est etc.

[11] As Origen.   See Div. 1. §. 73. not. 12.   Hence Conc. Carthag. iv. c. 13. enacts that the newly-married pair, cum benedictionem acce· perint, eadem nocte pro reverentia ipsius benedictionis in virginitate permaneant.

[12] Hieronymus adv. Jovinian. i. 4. with reference to 1. Cor. 7, 1 : Si bonum est mulierem non tangere, malum est ergo tangere : nihil enim bono contrarium est nisi malum.   Si autem malum est, et ignoscitur; ideo conceditur, ne malo quid deterius fiat.—Oro te, quale illud bonum est, quod orare prohibet ? quod corpus Christi accipi non permittit ? Quandiu impleo mariti officium, non impleo Christiani.   Yet he was obliged in the epist. 30. (al. 50.) ad Pammachium, pro libris adv. Jovinianum apologia to make some concession.   Among other things he writes : Cum toties et tam crebro lectorem admonuerim,—me ita recipere nuptias, continentes viduas virginesque praeferrem : debuerat prudens et benignus lector etiam, ea, quae videntur dura, aestimare de caeteris etc.   Augustine is more moderate in the work called forth by this very controversy between Jovinian and Jerome, de bono conjugali.   Among other things, he writes c. 8 : duo bona sunt connubium et continentia, quorum alterum est melius. cap. 10 : Certe dubitare fas non est, nuptias non esse peccatum.   Non itaque nuptias secundum veniam concedit Apostolus (1. Cor. 7, 6.)

[13] Against the use of flesh and wine Hieronymus adv. Jovinian. lib. ii.

[14] Comp. de Wette i. 340.

[15] Münscher's Dogmengesch. iv. 311. de Wette i. 346.

yet it is in fact intimately connected with it, that most of the
church fathers of this period maintained, in addition to that apparent moral severity,[16] lax principles concerning veracity which
threatened the very foundations of genuine virtue.[17]

§ 103.

MORALS OF THE CLERGY.

As ecclesiastical offices were no longer attended with dangers
and persecutions, but with honour and power, there was a general pressing towards them :[1] all the arts of unworthy flattery and

[16] See Div. 1. §. 63. not. 7.
[17] Ex. gr. Hieronymus epist. 30. (al. 50.) ad Pammachium : Aliud
esse γυμναστικῶς scribere, aliud δογματικῶς. In priori vagam esse disputationem, et adversario respondentem nunc haec nunc illa proponere, argu-
mentari ut libet, aliud loqui, aliud agere, panem, ut dicitur, ostendere,
lapidem tenere. In sequenti autem aperta frons, et, ut ita dicam, in-
genuitas necessaria est etc. In particular they stretched the limits of
allowed accommodation quite too far (οἰκονομία), and believed that they
could attribute it in the same extent even to Jesus and the apostles.
Comp. Suicer s.'v. συγκατάβασις. ii. 1067. Münscher's Dogmengesch. iv.
154 s. Jahn's Nachträge zu s. theolog. Werken. Tübingen 1821. S. 15
ss. 28 ss. In this way Jerome comm. ad Gal. ii. 11 ss. thought that he
could explain the transaction between Peter and Paul by a mere accommodation, but was opposed by Augustine who held stricter principles.
(Comp. his writings de mendacio and contra mendacium.) Comp. the
correspondence between them on this subject in epistt. Hieron. ep. 65.
67—73. 76. see Jahn l. c. P. 31 ff.—Even Chrysostom lays down very
questionable principles respecting the allowableness of deception and
lying, in certain cases. In this he is followed by his disciple John Cassian coll. xvii. 8. ss. ex. gr. cap. 17 : Itaque taliter de mendacio sentiendum, atque ita eo utendum est, quasi natura ei insit hellebori. Quodsi
imminente exitiali morbo sumtum fuerit, fit salubre : caeterum absque
summi discriminis necessitate perceptum praesentis exitii est.—Non
enim Deus verborum tantum actuumque nostrorum discussor et judex,
sed etiam propositi ac destinationis inspector est. Qui si aliquid causa
salutis aeternae ac divinae contemplationis intuitu ab unoquoque vel factum viderit vel promissum, tametsi hominibus durum atque iniquum
esse videatur ; ille tamen intimam cordis inspiciens pietatem, non verborum sonum, sed votum dijudicat voluntatis, quia finis operis et affectus considerandus est perpetrantis : quo potuerunt quidam, ut supra dictum est, etiam per mendacium justificari (for example Rahab Jos. 2), et
alii per veritatis assertionem peccatum perpetuae mortis incurrere (De-
lilah Jud. 16.)
[1] Comp. above, § 91, not. 15. cf. Gregorius Naz. below, not. 4.

low intrigue were put in requisition to obtain them, and to rise
from a lower to a higher station.[2] In this way not merely the
unprepared but even many absolutely immoral pushed themselves
into the clerical office ;[3] an objectionable, worldly spirit pervaded
the whole order, which frequently perverted what was holy to its
own purposes ;[4] and since that monkish morality required of the

[2] Gregor. Naz. orat. xliii. (al. xx.) in laudem Basilii c. 26. (ed. Colon. p. 335) : νῦν δὲ κινδυνεύει τὸ πάντων ἁγιώτατον τάγμα τῶν παρ ἡμῖν παν-
των εἶναι καταγελαστότατον· οὐ γὰρ ἐξ ἀρετῆς μᾶλλον, ἢ κακουργίας ἡ προεδρία·
οὐδὲ τῶν ἀξιωτέρων, ἀλλὰ τῶν δυνατωτέρων οἱ θρόνοι. Ullmann's Gregor v.
Naz. S. 511 ss. Conc. Sardic. c. 1. and 2. against the striving of the
bishops for better and richer bishoprics. Basilius ep. 76. ad Eipscopos
suos against simony in the choice of bishops. Can. Chalced. 2. and Can.
Apost. 30. against simony generally.
[3] Hieron. in ep. ad Titum i. 8. (opp. iv. p. 417) : vere nunc est cer-
nere—in plerisque urbibus, Episcopos, sive Presbyteros, si laïcos viderint hospitales, amatores bonorum, invidere, fremere, excommunicare,
de Ecclesia expellere, quasi non liceat facere quod Episcopus non faciat ; et tales esse laïcos damnatio Sacerdotum sit. The Can. apost.
26, 64, 71, are directed against roughnesses and common offences in the
clergy, which, however, must have taken place at this time. See Drey,
apost. Constitut. S. 339, 344.
[4] Comp. Hieronymus ep. 34. (al. 2.) ad Nepotianum concerning
the law of Valentinian against underhand dealing with inheritances,
given above, § 91. not. 14. He then continues : Ignominia omnium
Sacerdotum est, propriis studere divitiis. Natus in paupere domo, et
in tugurio rusticano, qui vix milio et cibario pane rugientem saturare
ventrem poteram, nunc similam et mella fastidio. Novi et genera et
nomina piscium, in quo littore concha lecta sit calleo : saporibus avium
discerno provincias ; et ciborum preciosorum me raritas, ac novissime
damna ipsa delectant. Audio praeterea in senes et anus absque liberis
quorumdam turpe servitium. Ipsi apponunt matulam, obsident lectum,
purulentiam stomachi et phlegmata pulmonis manu propria suscipiunt.
Pavent ad introitum medici, trementibusque labiis, an commodius habeant, sciscitantur : et si paululum senex vegetior fuerit, periclitantur :
simulataque laetitia, mens intrinsecus avara torquetur. He describes
the life of rich widows ep. 18. (al. 22.) ad Eustochium : Plena adulato-
ribus domus, plena conviviis. Clerici ipsi, quos in magisterio esse opor-
tuerat doctrinae pariter et timoris, osculantur capita matronarum, et ex-
tenta manu, ut benedicere eos putes velle, si nescias, pretia accipiunt
salutandi. In an oration of that time which is found among the sermons of Ambrose (sermo in dominicam xxii. post Pentecosten, and of
Augustine (tom. v. app. sermo 82.) it is said on Luc iii. 14 : Si (clericus) non contentus stipendiis fuerit, quae de altario, Domino jubente,
consequitur ; sed exercet mercimonia, intercessiones vendit, viduarum
munera libenter amplectitur : hic negotiator magis potest videri, quam
clericus. Gregorii Naz. carmen de se ipso et adv. Episcopos v. 331

clergy many external things to keep up the appearance of spi-
ss. (in J. Tollii insignia itineris Italici, Traj. ad Rhen. 1696. 4. p.
34 ss.) :

331. Ἄγνοια γὰρ κακὸν μὲν, ἀλλ' ἧσσον κακόν.
     Τί δ' ἂν τις εἴποι καὶ κακῶν μεμνημένος ;
     Εἰσὶν γὰρ, εἰσὶν ἀθλιώτεροί τινες,
     Δύστην', ἀπευκτὰ τοῦ βίου κυβεύματα,
     Τὴν πίστιν ἀμφιδέξιοι, καιρῶν νόμους,
     Οὐ τοὺς θεοῦ σέβοντες, εὕρισοι λόγων
     Παλιῤῥοοῦντες, ἢ κλάδων μετακλίσεις,
     Θῶπες γυναικῶν, τερπνὰ δηλητήρια,
     Μικροῖς λέοντες, τοῖς κρατοῦσι δ' αὖ κύνες,
     Πάσης τραπέζης εὐφυεῖς ἰχνεύμονες,
341. Θύρας κρατούντων ἐκτρίβοντες, οὐ σοφῶν.—
361. Αἰσχρὸν μὲν εἰπεῖν, ὡς ἔχει, φράσω δ' ὅμως.
     Ταχθέντες εἶναι τοῦ καλοῦ διδάσκαλοι,
     Κακῶν ἁπάντων ἐσμὲν ἐργαστήριον·
     Σιγῇ βοῶντες, κἂν δοκῶμεν μὴ λέγειν·
     Πρόεδρος ἡ κακία, ποινείτω μηδὲ εἷς·
     Κακὸν γίνεσθαι, τοῦτο συντομώτατον,
367. Καὶ λῷον.— — — — —
375. Ἡμεῖς δὲ πάντας ῥᾳδίως καθίζομεν,
     Ἐὰν μόνον θέλωσι, λαοῦ προστάτας,
     Οὐδὲν σκοποῦντες τῶν νέων, ἢ τῶν πάλαι,
378. Οὐ πρᾶξιν, οὐ λόγον τιν', οὐ συνουσίαν.—
382. Εἰ γὰρ τόδ' ἴσμεν, ὡς τὸν ἐξειλεγμένον
     Χείρω τίθησιν ὡς τὰ πολλ' ἐξουσία.
384. Τίς ἂν προβάλοιτ' εὖ φρονῶν, ὃν ἀγνοεῖ ;—
393. Ὁ δὲ πρόεδρος ῥᾳδίως εὑρίσκεται,
     Μηδὲν πονηθεὶς, πρόσφατος τὴν ἀξίαν.
395. Ὦ τῆς ταχείας τῶν τρόπων μεταστροφῆς !—
402. Χθὲς ἦσθα μίμων καὶ θεάτρων ἐν μέσῳ,
     (Τὰ δ' ἐκ θεάτρων ἄλλος ἐξεταζέτω)
     Νῦν αὐτὸς ἡμῖν εἶ ξένη θεωρία.
     Πρώην Φίλιππος, καὶ θεῷ πέμπων κόνιν,
406. Ὡς ἄλλος εὐχὰς, ἢ νοήματ' εὐσεβῆ.—
411. Νῦν εὐσταλής τις, καὶ βλέπων αἰδὼ μόνην,
412. Πλὴν εἰ λαθών που πρὸς ἀρχαῖον δράμοις.—
415. Χθὲς ῥητορεύων τὰς δίκας ἀπημπόλεις,
416. Στρέφων ἄνω τε καὶ κάτω τὰ τῶν νόμων.—
419. Νῦν μοι δικαστὴς, καὶ Δανιήλ τις ἀθρόως.
     Χθές μοι δικάζων σὺν ξίφει γυμνουμένῳ
     Τὸ βῆμ' ἐποίεις ἔννομον λῃστήριον,
     Κλέπτων, τυραννῶν, καὶ πρὸ πάντων τοὺς νόμους.
     Ὡς ἡμερός μοι σήμερον ! οὐδ' ἐσθῆτά τις
     Οὕτως ἀμείβει ῥᾳδίως, ὡς σὺ τρόπον
     Χθὲς ἐν χορευταῖς ἐστρέφου θηλυδρίαις,
     Γάμων δὲ κήρυξ ἦσθα Λυδαῖς ἐν μέσαις,
     Ὠιδὰς λυγίζων, καὶ ποτοῖς γαυρούμενος.

rituality, low hypocrisy pervaded the clerical order.[5]   This corruption of the clergy was not a little increased by the interference of the emperors with ecclesiastical disputes.   While on the one

> Νῦν σωφρονιστὴς παρθένων καὶ συζύγων.
> Ὡς σου τὸ καλὸν ὑπόπτον ἐκ τοῦ πρὶν τρόπου !
> Σίμων μάγος χθές, σήμερον Πέτρος Σίμων !
> 431.   Φεῦ τοῦ τάχους ! φεῦ, ἀπ' ἀλώπεκος λέων !

The remark is worthy of attention v. 382 s. comp. v. 634 ss.

> Οὖτοι μὲν οὖτως· καὶ τάχ' ἂν καὶ βελτίους
> Αὐτῶν γενόμενοι κωλύονται τοῖς θρόνοις.
> Τὸ γὰρ κρατεῖν τὸν ἄφρονα ποιεῖ χείρονα.

Gregorii Naz. orat. ii. (al. 1.) Apologeticus de fuga sua (ed. Col. p. 4 s.) : ὅσοι μηδὲν τῶν πολλῶν ὄντες βελτίονς, μέγα μὲν οὖν εἰ καὶ μὴ πολλῷ χείρους, ἀνίπτοις χερσὶν, ὃ δὴ λέγεται, καὶ ἀμυήτοις ψυχαῖς, τοῖς ἁγιωτάτοις ἑαυτοὺς ἐπεισάγουσι, καὶ πρὶν ἄξιοι γενέσθαι προσιέναι τοῖς ἱεροῖς, μεταποιοῦνται τοῦ βήματος, θλίβονταί τε καὶ ὠθοῦνται περὶ τὴν ἁγίαν τράπεζαν, ὥσπερ οὐκ ἀρετῆς τύπον, ἀλλ' ἀφορμὴν βίου τὴν τάξιν ταύτην εἶναι νομίζοντες, οὐδὲ λειτουργίαν ὑπεύθυνον, ἀλλ' ἀρχὴν ἀνεξέταστον. Isidor. Pelus. lib. v. ep. 21 : Μεταπεπτωκέναι λοιπὸν τὸ ἀξίωμα ἔδοξεν ἀπὸ ἱερωσύνης εἰς τυραννίδα, ἀπὸ ταπεινοφροσύνης εἰς ὑπερηφανίαν, ἀπὸ νηστείας εἰς τρυφὴν, ἀπὸ οἰκονομίας εἰς δεσποτείαν· οὐ γὰρ ὡς οἰκονόμοι ἀξιοῦσι διοικεῖν, ἀλλ' ὡς δεσπόται σφετερίζεσθαι.

[5] Especially as monachism led them to place so great value en external forms.   Gregor. Naz. carmen de seipso et adv. Episc. v. 647 ss. thus describes the spiritual hypocrite :—

> 647.   Ἔπειτα χαλκὸς χρυσὸν ἠμφιεσμένος,
> Ἢ καὶ χαμαιλέοντος ἄστασις χρόας,
> Πώγων, κατηφὲς ἦθος, αὐχένος κλάσις,
> Φωνὴ βραχεῖα, πιστὸς ἐσκευασμένος,
> 651.   Νωθρὸν βάδισμα, πάντα, πλὴν φρενὸς, σοφάς.
> 696.   Αἰσχρῶν μὲν οὖν αἴσχιστον ἡ τρόπου πλάσις.

Thus it became the custom, especially in consequence of the example of the monks (see Bingham vol. ii. p. 189 ss.), seemingly to decline r eceiving ecclesiastical honours when presented. cf. lex Leonis A.D. 469 (Cod. Justin. i. 3, 31.) : Nemo gradum sacerdotii pretii venalitate mer. cetur :—Cesset altaribus imminere profanus ardor avaritiae, et a sacris adytis repellatur piaculare flagitium.—Nec pretio, sed precibus ordinetur antistes. Tantum ab ambitu debet esse sepositus, ut quaeratur cogendus, rogatus recedat, invitatus effugiat : sola illi suffragetur necessitas excusandi. Profecto enim indignus est sacerdotio, nisi fuerit ordinatus invitus. This priestly decorum led of course, very frequently, merely to a mock reluctance and hesitation. cf. Gregorius Naz. orat. xvii. de se ipso p. 466 : οὐ γὰρ ἵνα ζητηθῶμεν ἀποκρυπτόμεθα· οὐδ' ἵνα πλείονος ἄξιοι δόξωμεν τιμῆς.

-side, the clergy were always carrying their spiritual pride higher ;[6] on the other, they frequently changed their opinions at the beck of the court. Synods were the theatre on which this new pharisaism of Christian spirituality, added to a rough passionateness, was chiefly exhibited.[7]

In the meantime, however, zeal for morality among the clergy was not rare. This zeal for morality fearlessly found fault with sin where it existed, opposed with spirit tyrannical barbarity,[8] took under its powerful protection all that needed help,[9] and left behind even permanent monuments of benevolence and concern for the public good.[10]

[6] See above, § 91. not. 24.

[7] Comp. the ironical discourse of Gregory of Nazianzum at the second oecumenical council (carmen de vita sua, opp. ii. 27):

> — — — ὃς θέλει δεῦρ' εἰσίτω,
> Κἂν δίστροφός τις ἢ πολύστροφος τύχῃ·
> Πανήγυρις ἕστηκεν, ἀπίτω μηδεὶς
> Ἀπραγμάτευτος. ἂν μεταστραφῇ κύβος
> (Καιροῦ γὰρ οὐδέν ἐστιν εὐστροφώτερον),
> Ἔχεις τὸ τεχνύδριον, ἔκδραμε πάλιν·
> Οὐκ εὐμαθὲς πίστει τὸ προσκεῖσθαι μιᾷ,
> Βίων δὲ πολλὰς εἰδέναι διεξόδους.

Comp. carmen de se ipso et adv. Episc. v. 152. (ap. Tollius p. 18.) on the same council :

> — — — καὶ γὰρ ἦν αἶσχος μέγα,
> Τούτων τιν' εἶναι τῶν καπήλων πίστεως.

In like manner he calls forth the bishops (carmen de vita sua p. 28) Χριστέμποροι. When he was invited to the synod at Constantinople, A.D. 382, he replied, epist. 55. ad Procopium : Ἔχω μὲν οὕτως, εἰ δεῖ τἀληθὲς γράφειν, ὥστε πάντα σύλλογον φεύγειν ἐπισκόπων, ὅτι μηδεμιᾶς συνόδου τέλος εἶδον χρηστὸν, μηδὲ λύσιν κακῶν μᾶλλον ἐσχηκυίας, ἢ προσθήκην. Αἱ γὰρ φιλονεικίαι καὶ φιλαρχίαι (ἀλλ' ὅπως μήτε φορτικὸν ὑπολάβῃς οὕτω γράφοντα) καὶ λόγου κρείττονες· καὶ θᾶττον ἂν τις ἐγκληθείη κακίαν ἑτέραν δικάζων, ἢ τῶν ἐκείνων λύσειε. Διὰ τοῦτο εἰς ἐμαυτὸν συνεστάλην κ. τ. λ.—Carmen x. v. 92 ss. (opp. ii. 81):

> Οὐδέ τί που συνόδοισι ὁμόθρονος ἔσσομ' ἔγωγε
> Χηνῶν ἢ γεράνων ἄκριτα μαρναμένων·
> Ἔνθ' ἔρις, ἔνθα μόθος τε, καὶ αἴσχεα κρυπτὰ πάροιθεν
> Εἰς ἕνα δυσμενέων χῶρον ἀγειρόμενα.

Comp. Ullmann's Gregor v. Naz. S. 269 s.

[8] See § 91, not. 8.

[9] See § 91, not. 9.

[10] ξενῶνες or ξενοδοχεῖα, πτωχοτροφεῖα, γηροκομεῖα, νοσοκομεῖα, ὀρφανοτροφεῖα. The institution which Basil founded in Caesarea for strangers

§. 104.

MORAL INFLUENCE OF THE CHURCH ON THE PEOPLE.

The clergy thus sinking into degeneracy were now called to solve the most difficult problem that could ever, perhaps, be presented to an order of Christian teachers. A highly cultivated people, but one sunk in unbelief and superstition of every kind, now crowded into the church,[1] impelled, for the most part, by interested motives ; a people either for the most part fully devoted to paganism in their heart[2] or apprehending Christianity from a heathen point of view,[3] and transferring into it even heathen customs or Jewish practices.[4] In addition to this, the new con-

---

and the sick was very large. After him it was called Βασιλειάς (Basil. ep. 94. Gregor. Naz. orat. 30 u. 27). Basil also caused to be established, smaller ones of the same kind in the country (Basil. ep. 142, 143). Theodoret got colonnades and bridges built, and a canal made. (Theod. ep. 81.) See Neander ii. i. 292.

[1] See above, § 75, not. 7 and 35.

[2] Chrysost. in ep. ad Ephes. c. 3. hom. vii. (opp. xi. 44) : οἱ μὲν γὰρ ὀρθῶς βιοῦντες—τὰς κορυφὰς τῶν ὁρίων κατειλήφασι, καὶ ἐκ μέσου γεγόνασιν (the monks).—φθόροι δὲ καὶ μυρίων γέμοντες κακῶν εἰσεπήδησαν εἰς τὰς ἐκκλησίας.—Εἴ τις κατὰ τὴν ἡμέραν τοῦ Πάσχα πάντας τοὺς προσιόντας—ἐξήτασε σὺν ἀκριβείᾳ,—πολλὰ ἂν εὑρέθη βαρύτερα τῶν Ἰουδαϊκῶν κακῶν. καὶ γὰρ οἰωνιζομένους, καὶ φαρμακείαις καὶ κληδονισμοῖς καὶ ἐπῳδαῖς κεχρημένους, καὶ πεπορνευκότας, καὶ μοιχεύσαντας, καὶ μεθύσους, καὶ λοιδόρους εὕρεν ἄν.

[3] P. E. Müller comm. hist. de genio, moribus et luxu aevi Theodosiani (P. ii. Lips. 1797. 98. 8.) P. i. p. 33 ss. Neander's Chrisostomus Bd. 1. S. 236 ss. Abuse of holy things as charms. cf. Hieronymus in Matth. c. 23 (ed. Martian. iv. p. 109 : Haec in corde portanda sunt, non in corpore. Hoc apud nos superstitiosae mulierculae in parvulis Evangeliis et in crucis ligno et istiusmodi rebus usque hodie factitant. Chrysostom. ad. pop. Antioch. hom. xix. (T. ii. p. 197) : αἱ γυναῖκες καὶ τὰ μικρὰ παιδία ἀντὶ φυλακῆς μεγάλης εὐαγγέλια ἐξαρτῶσι τοῦ τραχήλου, καὶ πανταχοῦ περιφέρουσιν, ὅπου περ ἂν ἀπίωσιν. See above § 99. not. 38. 41. 50. § 101. not. 17. Many of the clergy made use of and fostered this superstition. cf. Conc. Laodic. c. 36 : ὅτι οὐ δεῖ ἱερατικοὺς, ἢ κληρικοὺς, μάγους ἢ ἐπαοιδοὺς εἶναι, ἢ μαθηματικοὺς, ἢ ἀστρολόγους, ἢ ποιεῖν τὰ λεγόμενα φυλακτήρια. Heineccius Abbildung der alten u neuen griech. Kirche. Leipzig 1711. 5. Th. 3. S. 461. Du Resnel treatise on the pagan sortes Homericae, sortes Virgilianae etc. and the Christian sortes Sanctorum in the Mémoires de l'Acad. des Inscriptions t. xix. p. 287 ss.

[4] See especially Chrysostomi adv. Judaeos oratt. viii. Bingham vol. vii. p. 274 ss. Neander's Chrysostomus Bd. 1. S. 256 ss.

verts were demoralized by all the vices which follow in the train of over-refinement, and confirmed in them by the example of the court which had been growing more corrupt ever since its removal to the East, and by the example of the nobility.[5]   Christian knowledge and Christian faith, in place of unbelief and superstition, and piety for vice, had to be infused into this spiritually dead mass.   To be successful, the gospel needed to be proclaimed in its spiritual aspect with apostolic zeal ; but the greater portion of the clergy depended for the most part on external means ; and thereby gave Christianity the character of a compulsory institute, promoting the superstitious and external view of it.

The Christians soon forgot the principles of religious endurance which they had so prominently exhibited and insisted on in their former persecutions ;[6] and fanatical voices were raised among them calling for a violent suppression of paganism.[7]   It was not

[5] Comp. the description of the court at Julian's accession.   Ammian. Marcell. xxii. 4 : Namque fatendum est pleraeque eorum (Palatinorum) partem vitiorum omnium seminarium effusius aluisse, ita ut rempublicam inficerent cupiditatibus pravis, plusque exemplis quam peccandi licentia laederent multos.   Pasti enim ex his quidam templorum spoliis, et lucra ex omni odorantes occasione, ab egestate infima ad saltum sublati divitiarum ingentium, nec largiendi, nec rapiendi, nec absumendi tenuere aliquem modum, aliena invadere semper adsuefacti. Unde fluxioris vitae initia pullularunt, et perjuria, et nullus existimationis respectus, demensque superbia fidem suam probrosis quaestibus polluebat.   Inter quae ingluvies et gurgites crevere praerupti conviviorum etc.   An orator of the day (Augustini tom. v. app. sermo 82, also in Ambrosii opp. as sermo in dom. xxii. post Pentecosten) complains : Usque adeo autem hoc inolevit malum, ut jam quasi ex consuetudine vendantur leges, corrumpantur jura, sententia ipsa venalis sit, et nulla jam causa possit esse sine causa.   Salvianus de gubern. Dei is particularly full of complaints of the corruption of his time, ex. gr. iv. 5, 7 ; vi. 11 ; vii. 12, 15.

[6] For example, Justin. apol. i. 2, 4, 12.   So still under Constantine, Luctantius institutt. v. 19 : religio cogi non potest : verbis potius quam verberibus res agenda est, ut sit voluntas.—Nihil est tam voluntarium, quam religio.   c. 20: nos non expetimus, ut Deum nostrum, qui est omnium, velint, nolint, colat aliquis invitus: nec, si non coluerit, irascimur.   Epitome c. 54 : Religio sola est, in qua libertas domicilium collocavit.   Res est enim praeter caeteras voluntaria, nec imponi cuiquam necessitas potest, ut colat quod non vult.   Potest aliquis forsitan simulare, non potest velle.

[7] So even Julius Firmicus Maternus under Constantine.   See § 75, not. 21.   Hilarii Pictav. contra Auxentium Mediol. liber init.   Ac primum misereri licet nostrae aetatis laborem et praesentium temporum

without the co-operation of the Christian clergy that the prohibitions of *heathenism* were always assuming a stricter tone, and that the laws against *Judaism* were more and more circumscribing.[8] The treatment of heretics, too, became more severe.[9] At first, the Catholic Christians were contented to render them innocuous by interdicting their meetings or by banishment.[10] The execution of Priscillian (§. 86) was still universally regarded with abhorrence.[11]

congemiscere: quibus patrocinari Deo humana creduntur, et ad tuendam Christi Ecclesiam ambitione saeculari laboratur.   Oro vos, Episcopi, qui hoc vos esse creditis, quibusnam suffragiis ad praedicandum Evangelium Apostoli usi sunt ?   Quibus adjuti potestatibus Christum praedicaverunt, gentesque fere omnes ex idolis ad Deum transtulerunt ? Anne aliquam sibi assumebant e palatio dignitatem, hymnum Deo in carcere, inter catenas, et post flagella cantantes ?   Edictisque Regis Paulus cum in theatro-spectaculum ipse esset, Christo ecclesiam congregabat ?—Aut non manifesta se tum *Dei* virtus contra odia humana porrexit : cum tanto magis Christus praedicaretur, quanto magis praedicari inhiberetur ?   At nunc, proh dolor ! divinam fidem suffragia terrena commendant : inopsque virtutis suae Christus, dum ambitio nomini suo conciliatur, arguitur.   Terret exiliis et carceribus Ecclesia, credique sibi cogit, quae exiliis et carceribus est credita : pendet a dignatione communicantium, quae persequentium est consecrata terrore : fugat sacerdotes, quae fugatis est sacerdotibus propagata : diligi sese gloriatur a mundo, quae Christi esse non potuit, nisi eam mundus odisset.   Haec de comparatione traditae nobis olim Ecclesiae, nunc quam deperditae, res ipsa, quae in oculis omnium est atque ore, clamavit.

[8] C. W. de Rhoer dissert. de effectu relig. christianae in jurisprudentiam Romanam p. 157 ss.   Meysenbug de christ. relig. vi et effectu in jus civile. (Gottingae 1828. 4.) p. 42.

[9] Bingham vol. vii. p. 285 ss. de Rhoer p. 170 ss.   Meysenbug p. 38.   Riffel geschichtl. Darstellung des Verhaltnisses zwischen Kirche und Staat i. 669.

[10] It is true that Julianus (ap. Cyrill. c. Jul. lib. vi. ed. Spanh. p. 206) accuses the Christians, even in his time : ἀπεσφάξατε οὐχ ἡμῶν μόνον τοὺς τοῖς πατρῴοις ἐμμένοντας, ἀλλὰ καὶ τῶν ἐξίσης ὑμῖν πεπλανημένων αἱρετικῶν τοὺς μὴ τὸν αὐτὸν τρόπον ὑμῖν τὸν νεκρὸν θρηνοῦντας. Epist. 52. that under Constantius τοὺς πολλοὺς αὐτῶν καὶ φυγαδευθῆναι, καὶ διωχθῆναι, καὶ δεσμευθῆναι· πολλὰ δὲ ἤδη καὶ σφαγῆναι πλήθη τῶν λεγομένων αἱρετικῶν ὡς ἐν Σαμοσάτοις, καὶ Κυζίκῳ, καὶ Παφλαγονίᾳ, καὶ Βιθυνίᾳ, καὶ Γαλατίᾳ, καὶ πολλοῖς ἄλλοις ἔθνεσιν ἄρδην ἀνατραπῆναι πορθηθείσας κώμας. Perhaps, however, this should be understood of extra-judicial murders.

[11] Not only by Latinus Pacatus, in his Panegyricus Theodosio dictus c. 29, but also by bishops : Sulpic. Severus hist. sacr. ii. 50 : Namque tum Martinus (bishop of Turonum) apud Treveros constitutus, non desinebat increpare Ithacium, ut ab accusatione desisteret : Maximum orare, ut sanguine infelicium abstineret : satis superque sufficere, ut Episcopali sententia haeretici judicati Ecclesiis pellerentur : novum

In the meantime, however, Augustine allowed himself to be persuaded that corporal punishments against heretics were allowable and fit;[12] and Leo the Great went so far as to approve the

esse et inauditum nefas, ut causam Ecclesiae judex saeculi judicaret.
How he behaved when he came again to Treves, after the murder of
Priscillian, may be seen in Sulpic. Sever. dial. iii. c. 11-13.   Maximus
wished that the persecution of the Priscillianists should be continued in
Spain; but pia erat solicitudo Martino, ut non solum Christianos, qui
sub illa erant occasione vexandi, sed ipsos etiam haereticos liberaret.
Besides cavit cum illa Ithacianae partis communione misceri.   Ambrose, too, who was with Maximus as ambassador from Valentinian II.,
A. D. 387, endeavoured there (Ambros. ep. 24. ad Valentin.) abstinere
ab episcopis,—qui aliquos devios licet a fide ad necem petebant.   cf.
ep. 26.   Indeed, at that time every kind of capital punishment was
pretty generally regarded as forbidden.
    [12] Augustini ep. 93. ad Vincentium § 17: mea primitus sententia
non erat, nisi neminem ad unitatem Christi esse cogendum, verbo esse
agendum, disputatione pugnandum, ratione vincendum, ne fictos catholicos haberemus, quos apertos haereticos noveramus.   Sed haec opinio
mea non contradicentium verbis, sed demonstrantium superabatur exemplis.   Nam primo mihi opponebatur civitas mea, quae cum tota esset
in parte Donati, ad unitatem catholicam timore legum imperialium con-
versa est, quam nunc videmus ita hujus animositatis perniciem detes-
tari, ut in ea nunquam fuisse credatur etc.   cf. retractt. ii. 5.   How the
Donatists attack these new principles, and how Augustine defends them,
may be seen in ejusd. contra litt. Petiliani lib. ii.   Contra Gaudentium
lib. i.   Epist. 185. ad Bonifacium, among other things, § 21, it is written: Melius est quidem—ad Deum colendum doctrina homines duci,
quam poenae timore vel dolore compelli.   Sed non quia isti meliores
sunt, ideo illi qui tales non sunt, negligendi sunt.   Multis enim profuit
(quod experimentis probavimus et probamus) prius timore vel dolore
cogi, ut postea possent doceri.   Then he refers § 24 the cogite intrare
(Luc. xiv. 23.) to this point: ipse Dominus ad magnam coenam suam
prius adduci jubet convivas, postea cogi.—In illis ergo, qui leniter primo adducti sunt, completa est prior obedientia, in istis autem, qui co-
guntur, inobedientia coërcetur.   Still epist. 100. ad Donatum, Procons.
Africae: unum solum est, quod in tua justitia, pertimescimus, ne forte
—pro immanitate facinorum, ac non potius pro lenitatis christianae consideratione censeas coërcendum, quod te per Jesum Christum ne facias
obsecramus.—Ex occasione terribilium judicum ac legum ne in aeterni
judicii poenas incidant, corrigi eos cupimus, non necari; nec disciplinam
circa eos negligi volumus, nec suppliciis, quibus digni sunt, exerceri.
So, too, epist. 139, ad Marcellinum: Poena sane illorum, quamvis de
tantis sceleribus confessorum, rogo te, ut praeter supplicium mortis sit,
et propter conscientiam nostram, et propter catholicam mansuetudinem
commendandam.   cf. Ph. a Limborch historia inquisitionis.   (Amst.
1692. fol.) lib. i. c. 6.   J. Barbeyrac traité de la morale des pères c. 16,
§ 19.   Jerome, however, says, epist. 37. (al. 53.) ad Riparium adv.

putting of them to death.[13] Besides, the bishops endeavoured, by means of ecclesiastical laws, not only to prevent all contact of the faithful with the opponents of the church,[14] but ventured even to absolve individuals from the obligation of duties which they manifestly owed to heretics.[15]

At the same time, the church did not the less continue to deviate from the right path, in her regulations which were instituted for the purpose of gaining over the masses of external professors which had been obtained by external measures, to the side of Christianity internally. She endeavoured to give her *service* the external attractions of the heathen worship, and thus only strengthened the tendency to externalities ; while she even invited men to substitute for a genuine interest in religion and the service of God, a feeling quite foreign to piety. On the one hand, many were confirmed in the heathenish, superstitions

Vigilantium: Non est crudelitas pro Deo pietas. Unde et in lege dicit: si frater tuus et amicus et uxor, quae est in sinu tuo, depravare te voluerit a veritate, sit manus tua super eos, et effunde sanguinem eorum, et auferes malum de medio Israel (Deut. xiii. 6 ss.) Chrysostom, indeed, recommends Christian love towards heretics and heathens (hom. 29. in Matth.), but would yet have them restrained, and their assemblies forbidden, and declares himself only against putting them to death (hom. 46. in Matth.) Thus, also, he caused their churches to be taken from the Novatians, Quartodecimani, and other heretics in Asia, and many considered his misfortunes a righteous retribution for this. Socrates vi. 19.—Stäudlin's Gesch. d. Sittenlehre Jesu iii. 238. de Wette Gesch. d. christl. Sittenlehre i. 344.

[13] The first law of a Christian emperor, authorising capital punishment against certain heretics, is that of Theodosius I. A. D. 382, against the Manichaeans. Sozomen, however, vii. 12, says of all the laws of this emperor against heretics : χαλεπὰς τοῖς νόμοις ἐπέγραφε τιμωρίας, ἀλλ' οὐκ ἐπεξῄει· οὐ γὰρ τιμωρεῖσθαι, ἀλλ' εἰς δέος καθιστᾶν τοὺς ὑπηκόους ἐσπούδαζεν. (cf. Socrates v. 20.) : and Socrates vii. 8, still maintains : οὐκ εἰωθὸς διώκειν τῇ ὀρθοδόξῳ ἐκκλησίᾳ. On the other hand, Leo M. epist. 15. ad Turribium :—etiam mundi principes ita hanc sacrilegam amentiam (Priscillianistarum) detestati sunt, ut auctorem ejus cum plerisque discipulis legum publicarum ense prosternerent.—Profuit diu ista districtio ecclesiasticae lenitati, quae etsi sacerdotali contenta judicio, cruentas refugit ultiones, severis tamen christianorum principum constitutionibus adjuvatur, dum ad spiritale nonnumquam recurrunt remedium, qui timent corporale supplicium.

[14] Bingham, vol. vii. p. 276 ss. 294 ss.

[15] For example, Concil. Carthag. iii. ann. 397. can. 13 : Ut Episcopi vel clerici, in eos qui catholici Christiani non sunt, etiamsi consanguinei fuerint, nec per donationes, nec per testamentum rerum suarum aliquid conferant.

E

notion of looking for works acceptable to God in the external rites of his worship ; on the other hand, there were not a few, especially in the cities, who went to the churches as if to the theatre, with a mere aesthetic interest ; and followed the spiritual orators as they would rhetoricians ;[16] while, on the contrary, they did not remain to be present at the Lord's supper,[17] a circumstance which necessarily led to a prohibition of their partaking of it.[18] Meetings for public worship began to be even abused, as occasions for sensual excesses.[19] Finally, *the theological disputes* of this period were also an important obstacle in preventing Christianity from exercising its full power on the men of the age. While they were contending about definitions, as if the essence of Christianity consisted in them ; the interest of the understanding being in a one-

[16] Gregor. Naz. orat. 42. (ed. Colon. or. 22, p. 596) : οὐ γὰρ ζητοῦσιν ἱερεῖς, ἀλλὰ ῥήτορας. How the clergy themselves promoted this direction may be seen in orat. 36. (ed. Col. or. 27. p. 465) : ὁρῶ πολλοὺς τῶν νῦν ἱερατεύειν ὑπισχνουμένων, οἱ τὴν ἁπλῆν καὶ ἄτεχνον ἡμῶν εὐσέβειαν ἔντεχνον πεποιήκασι, καὶ πολιτικῆς τι καινὸν εἶδος ἀπὸ τῆς ἀγορᾶς εἰς τὰ ἅγια μετενηνεγμένης, καὶ ἀπὸ τῶν θεάτρων ἐπὶ τὴν τοῖς πολλοῖς ἀθέατον μυσταγωγίαν, ὡς εἶναι δύο σκηνὰς, εἰ δεῖ τολμήσαντα τοῦτο εἰπεῖν, τοσοῦτον ἀλλήλων διαφερούσας, ὅσον τὴν μὲν πᾶσιν ἀνεῖσθαι, τὴν δὲ τισί· καὶ τὴν μὲν γελᾶσθαι, τὴν δὲ τιμᾶσθαι· καὶ τὴν μὲν θεατρικὴν, τὴν δὲ πνευματικὴν ὀνομάζεσθαι. Chrysostom. de sacerdot. v. 1. of the hearers of sermons : οὐ πρὸς ὠφέλειαν, ἀλλὰ πρὸς τέρψιν ἀκούειν εἰθίσθησαν οἱ πολλοί, καθάπερ τραγῳδῶν ἢ κιθαρῳδῶν καθήμενοι δικασταί. Id. hom. 30. in Act. Apost. Hieronym. adv. Luciferianos (opp. iv. 296.) : Ex litteratis quicunque hodie ordinantur, id habent curae, non quomodo Scripturarum medullas ebibant : sed quomodo aures populi declamatorum flosculis mulceant. Id. praef. in lib. iii. comm. in epist. ad Ephes. Comp. Neander's Chrysostomus i. 118. 320 ss. 327. Ullmann's Gregor v. Naz. S. 155 ss. Daniel's Gesch. d. christl. Beredtsamkeit i. 331. Concerning the applause by clapping of hands during the sermon see B. Ferrarii de ritu sacrarum eccl. vet. concionum. (Mediolani 1621. c. praef. J. G. Graevii. Ultraj. 1692. 8.) lib. ii. c. 24. Bingham vol. vi. p. 187 ss. Daniel i. 334. 605. 677.

[17] Chrysostom. hom. iii. in epist. ad Ephes. (opp. xi. 23) : εἰκῆ θυσία καθημερινὴ, εἰκῆ παρεστήκαμεν τῷ θυσιαστηρίῳ, οὐδεὶς ὁ μετέχων. Id. de incomprehensibili hom. iii. 6. (opp. i. 462.)

[18] Conc. Antioch. (341) can. 2. Can. apost. 8 and 9. See Drey über die apost. Constitutionen S. 255.

[19] Hieronymus adv. Vigilantium (ed. Martian. T. iv. P. ii. p. 285), says de vigiliis et pernoctationibus in basilicis Martyrum celebrandis in defence of them : Error autem et culpa juvenum vilissimarumque mulierum, qui per noctem saepe deprehenditur, non est religiosis hominibus imputandus : quia et in vigiliis Paschae tale quid fieri plerumque convincitur, et tamen paucorum culpa non praejudicat religioni, etc.

sided way excited in favour of it ;[20] it was no wonder that among
many Greeks the interest in favour of Christianity was of the
same nature with an interest in sophistical problems ;[21] the
holiest relations being torn asunder at the same time by hatred
and discord.[22]   And then, again, as the prevailing systems changed, sometimes one and sometimes another being enforced by
worldly power, it was almost an unavoidable consequence that the
people should either be made suspicious of Christianity and indifferent to it, or else tempted to employ falsehood and hypocrisy
in the most sacred things.[23]

It is true that *monachism* appeared likely to subordinate
everything to a striving after the highest, by means of its example in giving a wholesome stimulus to the enervated race ;[24] but it
was itself too impure in most of its manifestations to be able to
give pure impressions, while it brought confusion into moral ideas
by its arbitrary mode of worship.   In former times, this external strictness of morals had found a corresponding internal basis
in the spirits of men ; but now it was to be made prominent
among a people devoid of faith in a degree much increased by
monachism.   Of course the people endeavoured to make the im-

[20] Hilarius ad Constantium ii. 5: Dum in verbis pugna est, dum de
novitatibus quaestio est, —dum de studiis certamen est, dum in consensu
difficultas est, dum alter alteri anathema esse coepit ; prope jam nemo
Christi est.
[21] Gregor. Naz. orat. xxxiii. p. 530: ὡς ἕν τι τῶν ἄλκων καὶ τοῦτο
φλυαρεῖται ἡδέως, μετὰ τοὺς ἱππικούς, καὶ τὰ θέατρα, καὶ τὰ ᾄσματα, καὶ τὴν
γαστέρα, καὶ τὰ ὑπὸ γαστέρα, οἷς καὶ τοῦτο μέρος τρυφῆς, ἡ περὶ ταῦτα ἐρεσ-
χελία καὶ κομψεία τῶν ἀντιθέσεων. cf. orat. xxi. p. 376. or. xxvi. Gregor.
Nyss. orat. de deitate Fil. et Spir. sancti, opp. iii. 466.   The law of
Theodosius A. D. 388. (Cod. Theod. xvi. iv. 2.) : Nulli egresso ad publicum vel disceptandi de religione, vel tractandi, vel consilii aliquid de-
ferendi patescat occasio (cf. Gothofred. ad h. l.), of Marcian A. D. 452.
(in Actis Conc. Chalced. ap. Mansi vii. 476. and Cod. Justin. i. 1. 4.)
Neander's Chrysost. ii. 118.   Ullmann's Gregor. v. Naz. S. 158 ss.
[22] Gregor. Naz. orat. xxxii. 4. says of the theological controversies :
καὶ τοῦτό ἐστιν, ὡς ἐπὶ τὸ πλεῖστον, ὃ διέσπασε μέλη, διέστησεν ἀδελφούς,
πόλεις ἐτάραξε, δήμους ἐξέμηνεν, ὥπλισεν ἔθνη [ἐπὶ] βασιλεῖς, ἐπανέστησεν
ἱερκεῖς λαῷ καὶ ἀλλήλοις, λαὸν ἑαυτῷ καὶ ἱερεῦσι, γονεῖς τέκνοις, τέκνα γονεῦσιν,
ἄνδρας γυναιξὶ, γυναῖκας ἀνδράσι.
[23] Gregorii Naz. carmen de se ipso et adv. Episc. v. 333 ss. above,
§ 103, not. 4.
[24] Neander's Chrysost. Bd. 1. S. 78, 90.

E 2

press of the new law as light as possible,[25] to which monachism
itself contributed most readily by making a distinction between
a higher and lower virtue.[26]   To introduce a christian morality into the life of society, the church began to extend its penance to smaller offences likewise,[27] and at the numerous councils
an extensive code of laws was formed, which fixed certain ecclesiastical punishments for different ecclesiastical and moral trans-
gressions, according to their external form.   In the Eastern
church, this penance was left to the free-will of the transgressors, in the case of private offences ; particularly after *Nec-
tarius*, bishop of Constantinople, had abolished (about 391)

---

[25] Chrysostom. orat. de baptismo Christi (opp. ii. 366), complains
that many went to the churches : οὐ καθ' ἑκάστην σύναξιν, ἀλλ' ἐν ἑορτῇ
μόνον ἅπαξ ἢ δεύτερον μόλις τοῦ παντὸς ἐνιαυτοῦ.   Id. hom. in princip. Act.
1. (opp. iii. 50.) Salvianus de gubern.   Dei lib. vi. p. 113 : Nos Ecclesiis Dei ludicra anteponimus, nos altaria spernimus et theatra honora-
mus.—Omni enim feralium ludierorum die si quaelibet Ecclesiae festa
fuerint, non solum ad Ecclesiam non veniunt qui Christianos se esse
dicunt ; sed si qui inscii forte venerint, dum in ipsa Ecclesia sunt, si
ludos agi audiunt, Ecclesias derelinquunt.

[26] Comp. an unknown preacher of the day, (Augustini tom. v. app.
sermo 82, also in Ambrosii opp. as sermo in dom. xxii. post Pentecost.)
on Luc. 3, 12 ss.   Nonnulli fratres, qui aut militiae cingulo detinentur,
aut in actu sunt publico constituti, cum peccant graviter, hac solent a
peccatis suis prima se voce excusare, quod militant.—Illud autem quale
est, quod cum ob errorem aliquem a senioribus arguuntur, et imputatur,
alicui de illis, cur ebrius fuerit, cur res alienas pervaserit, caedem cur
turbulenter admiserit ; statim respondeat : Quid habebam facere, homo
saecularis et miles ?   Numquid monachum sum professus aut clericum ?
Quasi omnis, qui clericus non est aut monachus, possit ei licere, quod
non licet.   Chrysostom frequently inveighs against the abuses of this
distinction, for example. de Lazaro orat. iii. (op. i. 737) in ep. ad Hebr.
hom. vii. c. 4. (opp. xii. 79.)   Neander's Chrysost. i. 95.   Augustin.
in Psalm. 48. sermo ii. §. 4. : Cum coeperit Deo quisque vivere, mundum contemnere, injurias suas nolle ulcisci, nolle hic divitias, non hic
quaerere felicitatem terrenam, contemnere omnia, Dominum solum cogitare, viam Christi non deserere ; non solum a paganis dicitur insanit,
sed quod magis dolendum est, quia et intus multi dormiunt, et evigilare
nolunt, a suis, a Christianis audiunt *quid pateris?* in Psalm. 90. sermo.
i. §. 4. : Quomodo inter Paganos qui fuerit Christianus, a Paganis audit
verba aspera,—sic inter Christianos qui voluerint esse diligentiores et
meliores, ab ipsis Christianis audituri sunt insultationes,—dicunt : magnus tu justus, tu es Elias, tu es Petrus, de caelo venisti.   Insultant ;
quocumque se verterit, audit hinc atque inde verbum asperum.

[27] Cramer's Fort. v. Bossuet's Weltgesch. Th. 5. Bd. 1. S. 379 ss.

the πρεσβύτερος ἐπὶ τῆς μετανοίας (see Div. i. §. 71. note 1].)[28]
But in the Western church, they began to consider it a necessary
condition of forgiveness for all gross sins,[29] and in order to set

[28] Socrates v. 19. Sozomenus vii. 16. According to Socrates the
decree was : περιελεῖν μὲν τὸν ἐπὶ τῆς μετανοίας πρεσβύτερον· συγχωρῆσαι
δὲ, ἕκαστον τῷ ἰδίῳ συνειδότι τῶν μυστηρίων μετέχειν. So Chrysost. in ep.
ad Hebr. hom. 31. c. 3. (opp. xii. 289) : μὴ ἁμαρτωλοὺς καλῶμεν ἑαυτοὺς
μόνον, ἀλλὰ καὶ τὰ ἁμαρτήματα ἀναλογιζώμεθα, κατ᾽ εἶδος ἕκαστον ἀναλέγοντες.
οὐ λέγω σοι "ἐκπόμπευσον σαυτόν," οὐδὲ παρὰ τοῖς ἄλλοις κατηγόρησον, ἀλλὰ
πείθεσθαι συμβουλεύω τῷ προφήτῃ λέγοντι "ἀποκάλυψον πρὸς κύριον τὴν ὁδόν
σου (Ps. xxxvi. 5.)." ἐπὶ τοῦ θεοῦ ταῦτα ὁμολόγησον, ἐπὶ τοῦ δικαστοῦ ὁμο-
λόγει τὰ ἁμαρτήματα, εὐχόμενος, εἰ καὶ μὴ τῇ γλώττῃ, ἀλλὰ τῇ μνήμῃ. In like
manner ad illuminandos catech. ii. c. 4. (opp. ii. 240.), de poenitentia
hom. vi. c. 5. (ibid. p. 326.), non esse ad gratiam concionandum c. 3.
(ibid. p. 663.), in ep. i. ad Corinth. hom. 28. c. 1. ad 1. Cor. xi. 28.
(opp. x. 250.) et passim.

[29] Augustinus serm. 351. (de poenitentia 1.) § 2 ss. distinguishes tres
actiones poenitentiae. Una est, quae novum hominem parturit, donec
per baptismum salutare omnium praeteritorum fiat ablutio peccatorum.
—Altera,—cujus actio per totam istam vitam, qua in carne mortali degi-
mus, perpetua supplicationis humilitate subeunda est.—Tertia, quae pro
illis peccatis subeunda est, quae legis decalogus continent. Respecting
the latter : § 9 : Implicatus igitur tam mortiferorum vinculis peccatorum detrectat, aut differt, aut dubitat confugere ad ipsas claves Ecclesiae, quibus solvatur in terra, ut sit solutus in caelo; et audet sibi post
hanc vitam, quia tantum Christianus dicitur, salutem aliquam polliceri ?
—Judicet ergo se ipsum homo—et mores convertat in melius.—Et cum
ipse in se protulerit severissimae medicinae, sed tamen medicinae sententiam, veniat ad antistites, per quos illi in Ecclesia claves ministran-
tur : et tamquam bonus jam incipiens esse filius, maternorum membrorum ordine custodito, a praepositis sacramentorum accipiat satisfactionis
suae modum.—Ut si peccatum ejus non solum in gravi ejus malo, sed
etiam in tanto scandalo aliorum est, atque hoc expedire utilitati Ecclesiae videtur antistiti, in notitia multorum, vel etiam totius plebis agere
poenitentiam non recuset, non resistat, non letali et mortiferae plagae per
pudorem addat tumorem. However, de Symbolo ad Catechumenos c.
7 : Illi, quos videtis agere poenitentiam, scelera commiserunt, aut adulteria, aut aliqua facta immania : inde agunt poenitentiam. Nam si levia
peccata (above : venialia, sine quibus vita ista non est, and : levia, sine
quibus esse non possumus) ipsorum essent, ad haec quotidiana oratio
delenda sufficeret. Leo M. epist. 108. ed Ball. (83. ed. Quesn.) ad
Theodorum c. 2 : Multiplex misericordia Dei ita lapsibus subvenit hu·
manis, ut non solum per baptismi gratiam, sed etiam per poenitentiae
medicinam spes vitae, reparetur aeternae, ut qui regenerationis dona
violassent, proprio se judicio condemnantes, ad remissionem criminum
pervenirent : sic divinae bonitatis praesidiis ordinatis, ut indulgentia
Dei nisi supplicationibus Sacerdotum nequeat obtineri. Mediator enim
Dei et hominum homo Christus Jesus hanc praepositas Ecclesiae tradi-

aside all difficulties, to change public confession into a private
one in the case of private sins.[30]

It cannot be denied, that this system of penance promoted a
certain external propriety of conduct ; and as little can it be dis-
allowed that the church awakened and animated a sympathy,
which had almost entirely disappeared from Paganism, by its care
for the oppressed and suffering part of humanity, for the poor, the
captives, the sick, widows and orphans.[31] But yet by this new system of legislation, Christian freedom, and genuine morality which
has its root in it, were robbed of their true life. A comparison
of the present with earlier times in this particular, would yield
none but melancholy results.[32]

dit potestatem, ut et confitentibus actionem poenitentiae darent; et eosdem salubri satisfactione purgatos ad communionem sacramentorum
per januam reconciliationis admitterent. Cui utique operi incessabili-
ter ipse Salvator intervenit, nec umquam ab his abest, quae ministris
suis exequenda commisit, dicens : Ecce ego vobiscum sum etc. (Matth.
xxviii. 20.), ut si quid per servitutem nostram bono ordine et gratulando impletur effectu, non ambigamus per Spiritum sanctum fuisse donatum. cf. Hieronymus comm. in Matth. xvi. 19 : Istum locum : Et dabo tibi claves regni caelorum, Episcopi et Presbyteri non intelligentes,
aliquid sibi de Pharisaeorum assumunt supercilio, ut vel damnent innocentes, vel solvere se noxios arbitrentur, cum apud Deum non sententia
sacerdotum, sed eorum vita quaeratur.

[30] Leo M. epist. 168. ed. Ball. (ed. Quesn. 136.) c. 2 : Illam etiam
contra apostolicam regulam praesumtionem, quam nuper agnovi, a quibusdam illicita usurpatione committi, modis omnibus constituo submo-
veri. De poenitentia scilicet, quae a fidelibus postulatur, ne de singulorum peccatorum genere libello scripta professio publice recitetur : cum
reatus conscientiarum sufficiat solis sacerdotibus indicari confessione
secreta.—Quia non omnium hujusmodi sunt peccata, ut ea, qui poenitentiam poscunt, non timeant publicare ; removeatur tam improbabilis
consuetudo : ne multi a poenitentiae remediis arceantur, dum aut eru-
bescunt, aut metuunt inimicis suis sua facta reserari, quibus possint legum constitutione percelli. Sufficit enim illa confessio, quae primum
Deo offertur, tum etiam, Sacerdoti, qui pro delictis poenitentium preca-
tor accedit. Tunc enim demum plures ad poenitentiam poterunt provocari, si populi auribus non publicetur conscientia confitentis.

[31] Comp. §. 91. not. 9. §. 103. not. 10. Thomassinus p. ii. lib. 3. c.
87. and c. 95 s. Stäudlin's Gesch. d. Sittenlehre Jesu iii. 404.

[32] E. g. Chrysostomus hom. 26. in epist. ii. ad Corinth. (opp. x. 623.)
ἂν τὰ ἡμέτερά τις ἐξετάσῃ τὰ νῦν, ὄψεται ἡλίκον τῆς θλίψεως τὸ κέρδος. νῦν
μὲν γὰρ εἰρήνης ἀπολαύοντες ἀναπεπτώκαμεν, καὶ διερρύημεν, καὶ μυρίων τὴν
ἐκκλησίαν ἐνεπλήσαμεν κακῶν· ὅτε δὲ ἠλαυνόμεθα, καὶ σωφρονέστεροι, καὶ
ἐπιεικέστεροι, καὶ σπουδαιότεροι· καὶ περὶ τοὺς συλλόγους τούτους ἦμεν προ-
θυμότεροι, καὶ περὶ τὴν ἀκρόασιν· ὅπερ γὰρ τῷ χρυσίῳ τὸ πῦρ, τοῦτο ἡ θλίψις

§ 105.

INFLUENCE OF THE CHURCH ON LEGISLATION.

C. W. de Rhoer dissertt. de effectu religionis christianae in jurisprudentiam Romanam. Fasc. I. Groningae 1776. 8. H. O. Aem. de Meysenbug de christianae religionis vi et effectu in jus civile, speciatim in ea, quae Institutiones in primo libro tractant. Gotting. 1828. 4. De l'influence du Christianisme sur le droit civil. des Romains par M. Troplong. Paris 1843. 8.

Though the great changes which had taken place in Roman legislation since Constantine had not been effected by Christianity alone,[1] yet Christian principles and Christian customs, even respect to the Mosaic law,[2] had an important influence on it; while several laws were directly owing to representations made by the bishops.[3] A stop was put to sensual excesses,[4] rape was punished with death,[5] immoral *plays* were abolished or checked.[6]

ταῖς ψυχαῖς κ. τ. λ. Hieronymus in vita Malchi init. Scribere disposui, —ab adventu Salvatoris usque ad nostram aetatem,—quomodo et per quos Christi Ecclesia nata sit, et adulta, persecutionibus creverit, et martyriis coronata sit : et postquam ad christianos principes venerit, potentia quidem et divitiis major, sed virtutibus minor facta sit. Verum haec alias. Salvianus de avaritia i. 1. cf. Rittershusius sacr. lectt. vi. c. 17. Venema hist. eccl. t. iv. p. 260 ss.

[1] de Rhoer p. 39 ss.
[2] de Rhoer p. 65. 77 s.
[3] de Rhoer p. 89 s.—On the influence of Christianity on Constantine's laws (νόμους ἐκ παλαιῶν ἐπὶ τὸ ὁσιώτερον μεταβάλλων ἀνενεοῦτο) cf. Euseb. de vita Const. iv. 26.
[4] Cod. Theodos. lib. xv. tit. 8 de lenonibus. Riffel's Gesch. Darstellunge des Verhältnisses zwischen Kirche und Staat i. 108. Laws for lessening concubinage. Meysenbug p. 51.
[5] Cod. Theod. lib. ix. tit. 24. de raptu virginum vel viduarum. Riffel i. 110.
[6] Comp. the laws Cod. Theodos. lib. xv. tit. 5. de spectaculis ; tit. 6. de Majuma ; tit. 7. de scenicis. Stäudlin's Gesch. d. Sittenlehre Jesu. Bd. 3. S. 388. Yet it is evident from the law, Cod. Justin. iii. 12, 11. A. D. 469, that at that time, in addition to the scena theatralis and the circense theatrum, the ferarum lacrymosa spectacula also still continued : probably only in the West, for in the East, they appear to have ceased even before Theodosius I. See Müller comm. de. genio, moribus et luxu aevi Theodosiani. Havn. 1797. P. ii. p. 87.

Contests of gladiators, which had been already prohibited by Constantine, still continued, it is true, at Rome;[7] but they were entirely abolished by Honorius.   Classes of society which had been heretofore almost unrecognised by the laws, were now embraced within their operation.   The condition of *slaves*[8] and of *prisoners*[9] was improved ; the unlimited *power of fathers over their children* abridged ;[10] *women*, who had been kept till now in a very inferior position, were invested with greater rights ;[11] and the *widow* and *orphan* protected.[12]   On the other hand, legislation did not comply every where or in every respect with the peculiar requirements of the Christian morals of this age.   The laws became *more bloody* and strict than before.[13]   *Swearing* assumed Christian forms, but was more frequently practised.[14]   And though *restrictions to certain marriages* were established, agreeably to Christian principles,[15] the laws against *celibacy* abolished,[16] and *second marriages* rendered difficult,[17] yet the old *liberty of divorce* was but partially limited ; and from fear of still greater crimes, the emperors were obliged to admit many causes of valid separation, besides unfaithfulness to the marriage contract.[18]

[7] Cod. Theod. lib. xv. tit. 12. de gladiatoribus.   The self-sacrifice of Telemachus, Theodoret, hist. eccl. v. 26.   Comp. Neander's Chrysost. i. 383.

[8] de Rhoer p. 117 ss.   Meysenbug p. 34.

[9] Cod. Theod. lib. ix. tit. 3. de custodia reorum. de Rhoer p. 72.

[10] de Rhoer p. 137 s. Meysenbug p. 45.

[11] de Rhoer p. 124.

[12] de Rhoer, p. 111.

[13] de Rhoer p. 59 ss.

[14] J. F. Malblanc doctrina de jurejurando e genuinis fontibus illustrata.   Norimberg. 1781. ed. 2. Tübing. 1820. 8. p. 342. C. F. Stäudlin's Gesch. der Lehren vom Eide. Göttingen 1824. 8. S. 81.

[15] Cod. Theod. lib. iii. tit. 12, de incestis nuptiis, on forbidden degrees of affinity.   de Rhoer p. 248.   Besides, marriage between Christians and Jews was forbidden (l. c. iii. 7. 2.)   A proposal of marriage made to a nun was punished with death (ix. 25, 2.)

[16] Cod. Theod. viii. 16, 1. s. Div. 1. §. 56. not. 35.

[17] On the poenas secundarum nuptiarum see de Rhoer p. 240.   Meysenbug p. 61.   v. Löhr in the Archive f. d. civilistische Praxis Bd. 16. (1833) S. 32.

[18] Cod. Theodos. lib. iii. tit. 16. de repudiis.   Theodosii ii. Novell. tit. 12.   Bingham vol. ix. p. 356 ss. de Rhoer p. 287 ss.   Asterii Amaseni (about 400) homil. v. (in Combefisii auct. nov. i. 82) : ἀκούσατε δὲ νῦν οἱ τούτων κάπηλοι, καὶ τὰς γυναῖκας ὡς ἱμάτια εὐκόλως μετενδυόμενοι· οἱ

SEVENTH CHAPTER.

ATTEMPTS AT REFORMATION.

§ 106.

The new tendencies of Christian life could not be unperceived, especially as it is certain that the Catholic church was frequently reproached with them by the older Christian parties.[1] Nor were the morally dangerous aspects of these tendencies entirely over-looked by the more acute ; though they were too often excul-pated on the ground of pious intentions.[2]   The men who looked

τὰς παστάδας πολλάκις καὶ ῥᾳδίως πηγνύντες, ὡς πανηγύρεως ἐργαστήρια.—Οἱ μικρὸν παροξυνόμενοι καὶ εὐθὺς τὸ βιβλίον τῆς διαιρέσεως γράφοντες. οἱ πολλὰς χήρας ἐν τῷ ζῆν ἔτι καταλιμπάνοντες· πείσθητε, ὅτι γάμος θανάτῳ μόνῳ καὶ μοι-χείᾳ διακόπτεται.   Hieronymi epist. 84. (al. 30.) ad Oceanum de morte Fabiolae, c. 1 : Aliae sunt leges Caesarum, aliae Christi : aliud Papini-anus, aliud Paulus noster praecipit etc.

[1] Faustus (ap. Augustin. contra Faust. xx. 4.) : Vos, qui desciscentes a gentibus monarchiae opinionem primo vobiscum divulsistis, id est, ut omnia credatis ex Deo ; sacrificia vero eorum vertistis in agapas, idola in Martyres, quos votis similibus colitis ; defunctorum umbras vino placatis et dapibus ; solemnes gentium dies cum ipsis celebratis, ut ca-lendas, et solstitia ; de vita certe mutastis nihil : estis sane schisma, a matrice sua diversum nihil habens nisi conventum.   The Novatians also rejected the worship of martyrs and relics.   See Eulogius Patr. Alex. (about 580) contra Novatianos lib. Vto. (ap. Photius cod. 280. cf. cod. 182) : perhaps also Eustathius (Conc. Gangr. c. 20, comp. however Dallaeus adv. Latinorum de cultus religiosi objecto tradit. p. 151.) Eunomius was an opponent of martyr-worship (auctor hujus haereseos. Hieron. adv. Vigilant.) and of monachism (Gregor. Nyssen. contra Eunom. lib. ii.)

[2] As Hieronym. adv. Vigilant. (opp. iv. ii. p. 284) : Cereos autem non clara luce accendimus, sicut frustra calumniaris, sed ut noctis tene-bras hoc solatio temperemus.—Quod si aliqui per imperitiam et sim-plicitatem saecularium hominum, vel certe religiosarum feminarum, de quibus vere possumus dicere : confiteor, zelum Dei habent, sed non se-cundum scientiam (Rom. x. 1.) hoc pro honore Martyrum faciunt, quid inde perdis ? Causabantur quondam et Apostoli, quod periret unguen-tum ; sed Domini voce correpti sunt (Matth. xxvi. 8 ss.)   Neque enim Christus indigebat unguento, nec Martyres lumine cereorum : et tamen illa mulier in honore Christi hoc fecit, devotioque mentis ejus recipitur ; et quicumque accedunt cereos, secundum fidem suam habent mercedem, dicente Apostolo : unusquisque in suo sensu abundet (Rom. xiv. 5.)

into the ecclesiastical and religious errors of the time more pro-
foundly, and attacked them publicly, were declared heretics by
the offended hierarchy ; and their voice soon died away without
being able to give another direction to the incipient development of ecclesiastical life. To these latter belonged *Aërius*, presbyter in Sebaste, and friend of bishop Eustathius (about 360) ;[2]
Jovinian, monk at Rome, (about 388) first condemned there by

Augustin. ad Januarium lib. ii. (epist. 55.) § 35 : Quod autem institui-
tur praeter consuetudinem, ut quasi observatio sacramenti sit, approbare
non possum, etiamsi multa hujusmodi propter nonnullarum vel sanctarum vel turbulentarum personarum scandala devitanda, liberius impro-
bare non audeo. Sed hoc nimis doleo, quod multa, quae in divinis
libris saluberrime praecepta sunt, minus curantur ; et tam multis praesumtionibus sic plena sunt omnia, ut gravius corripiatur, qui per octavas
suas terram nudo pede tetigerit (namely neophytus. cf. Tert. de cor. mil.
c. 3. See Div. 1. § 53. not. 25), quam qui mentem vinolentia sepeli-
erit. Omnia itaque talia, quae neque sanctarum scripturarum auctoritatibus continentur, nec in conciliis episcoporum statuta inveniuntur,
nec consuetudine universae ecclesiae roborata sunt, sed pro diversorum
locorum diversis moribus innumerabiliter variantur, ita ut vix aut omnino
nunquam inveniri possint causae, quas in eis instituendis homines secuti sunt, ubi facultas tribuitur, sine ulla dubitatione resecanda existimo.
Quamvis enim neque hoc inveniri possit, quomodo contra fidem sint :
ipsam tamen religionem, quam paucissimis et manifestissimis celebrati-
onum sacramentis misericordia Dei esse liberam voluit, servilibus oneri-
bus premunt, ut tolerabilior sit conditio Judaeorum, qui, etiamsi tempus
libertatis non agnoverunt, legalibus tamen sarcinis, non humanis praesumtionibus subjiciuntur. Sed ecclesia Dei inter multam paleam mul-
taque zizania constituta, multa tolerat, et tamen quae sunt contra fidem
vel bonam vitam non approbat, nec tacet nec facit. Id. contra Faustum
xx. 21 : Aliud est quod docemus, aliud quod sustinemus, aliud quod
praecipere jubemur, aliud quod emendare praecipimur, et donec emen-
demus, tolerare compellimur. Alia est disciplina Christianorum, alia
luxuria vinolentorum, vel error infirmorum.

[3] Only authority Epiphan. haer. 75. His doctrines *ib.* §. 3 : I. τί
ἐστιν ἐπίσκοπος πρὸς πρεσβύτερον ; οὐδὲν διαλλάττει·οὗτος τούτου· μία γάρ ἐστι
τάξις, καὶ μία τιμὴ καὶ ἓν ἀξίωμα (proofs from New Testament passages,
§ 5.) II. τί ἐστι τὸ πάσχα, ὅπερ παρ᾽ ὑμῖν ἐπιτελεῖται ;—οὐ χρὴ τὸ πάσχα
ἐπιτελεῖν· τὸ γὰρ πάσχα ὑμῶν ἐτύθη Χριστός (1 Cor. v. 7.)—III. τίνι τῷ
λόγῳ μετὰ θάνατον ὀνομάζετε ὀνόματα τεθνεώτων ;—εἰ δὲ ὅλως εὐχὴ τῶν ἐνταῦθα τοὺς ἐκεῖσε ὤνησεν, ἄρα γοῦν μηδεὶς εὐσεβείτω, μηδὲ ἀγαθοποιείτω, ἀλλὰ
κτησάσθω φίλους τινὰς,—καὶ εὐχέσθωσαν περὶ αὐτοῦ, ἵνα μή τι ἐκεῖ πάθῃ.—
IV. οὔτε νηστεία ἔσται τεταγμένη· ταῦτα γὰρ Ἰουδαϊκά ἐστι, καὶ ὑπὸ ζυγὸν
δουλείας.— εἰ γὰρ ὅλως βούλομαι νηστεύειν, οἵαν δ᾽ ἂν αἱρήσομαι ἡμέραν ἀπ᾽
ἐμαυτοῦ νηστεύω διὰ τὴν ἐλευθερίαν. The Protestants were frequently accused of the heresy of Aërius. Walch's Ketzerhist. iii. 321.

Siricius, afterwards by Ambrose at Milan ;[4] some of whose opinions were soon after adopted by two monks of Milan, *Sarmatio* and *Barbatianus* (about 396) ;[5] but especially *Vigilantius* (shortly before 404) of Calagurris in Gaul (now Caseres in the district Commenges in Gascogne), presbyter in Barcelona.[6]

[4] Siricii epist. ad diversos episcopos adv. Jovinianum (about 389) ap. Constant. epist. 7. Ambrosii rescriptum ad Siricium (epist. 42. ap. Constant. ep. Siric. 8.)   Hieronymi libb. ii. adv. Jovinianum A. D. 392. Augustinus de haeres. c. 82. and in other writings. Doubtless Jovinian was greatly strengthened by the prevailing voice against monachism which was at Rome, and by the death of Blaesilla (384). See §. 96. note 3. He was thus excited to reflection, and was brought to deny the advantages which the monastic state claimed in its favour. Hence also he met with so much acceptance in Rome. See his doctrines in Jerome i. 2 : Dicit, virgines, viduas et maritatas, quae semel in Christo lotae sunt, si non discrepent caeteris operibus, ejusdem esse meriti (August. l. c. virginitatem etiam sanctimonialium, et continentiam sexus virilis in sanctis eligentibus caelibem vitam conjugiorum castorum atque fidelium meritis adaequabat : ita ut quaedam virgines sacrae provectae jam aetatis in urbe Roma, ubi haec docebat, eo audito nupsisse dicantur). Nititur approbare, eos, qui plena fide in baptismate renati sunt, a diabolo non posse subverti (farther below:—non posse tentari : quicunque autem tentati fuerint, ostendi, eos aqua tantum et non spiritu baptizatos, quod in Simone mago legimus : more accurately Jerome adv. Pelag. ii. posse hominem baptizatum, si voluerit, nequaquam ultra peccare : *i. e.* divine grace is communicated fully to man in baptism, and is not increased by the monastic state). Tertium proponit, inter abstinentiam ciborum et cum gratiarum actione perceptionem eorum nullam esse distantiam. Quartum, quod et extremum, esse omnium, qui suum baptisma servaverint, unam in regno caelorum remunerationem. Augustine adds l. c. : Omnia peccata, sicut stoici philosophi, paria esse dicecat. (Jovinian said : Hieron. adv. Jov. ii. 20 : Qui fratri dixerit fatue et raca, reus erit Geennae : et qui homicida fuerit et adulter, mittetur similiter in Geennam), and virginitatem Mariae destruebat, dicens eam pariendo fuisse corruptam.—Comp. Augustin. retract. ii. 22 : Remanserant autem istae disputationes ejus (Joviniani) in quorundam sermunculis ac susurris, quas palam suadere nullus audebat :—jactabatur, Joviniano responderi non potuisse cum laude, sed cum vituperatione nuptiarum (cf. §. 102. not. 12). Propter hoc librum edidi, cujus inscriptio est de bono conjugali. Walch iii. 655. Neander's KG. ii. ii. 574. Gu. B. Lindner de Joviniano et Vigilantio diss. Lips. 1839. 8. p. 10.

[5] Ambrosii epist. 63. (al. 82. al. 25.) ad Vercellensem ecclesiam : Audio venisse ad vos Sarmationem et Barbatianum, vaniloquos homines, qui dicunt nullum esse abstinentiae meritum, nullum frugalitatis, nullam virginitatis gratiam, pari omnes aestimari pretio, delirare eos, qui jejuniis castigent carnem suam, et menti subditam faciant etc.

[6] Concerning his earlier abode in Palestine (396), and his disputes

with Jerome, whom he considered to be a follower of Origen, Hieron.
ep. ad Vigilantium (ap. Martian. ep. 36. ap. Vallarsi ep. 61.)—Against
the later assertions of Vigilantius Hieron. ep. ad Riparium a. d. 404.
(ap. Martian. ep. 37. ap. Vallarsi ep. 109.) adv. Vigilantium lib. a. d.
406.—In the latter it is said : Martyrum negat sepulchra veneranda
(in ep. ad Riparium : Ais, Vigilantium, qui κατ' ἀντίφρασιν hoc vocatur
nomine, nam Dormitantius rectius diceretur, os foetidum rursus aperire,
et putorem spurcissimum contra sanctorum martyrum proferre reliquias:
et nos, qui eas suspicimus, appellare cinerarios et idololatras, qui mortuorum hominum ossa veneremur), damnandas dicit esse vigilias nunquam nisi in pascha alleluja cantandum (cf. Bingham vol. vi. p. 41 ss.),
continentiam haeresin, pudicitiam libidinis seminarium.—Proh nefas,
episcopos sui sceleris dicitur habere consortes, si tamen episcopi nomi-
nandi sunt, qui non ordinant diaconos, nisi prius uxores duxerint, nulli
caelibi credentes pudicitiam. Extracts from the writings of Vigilantius :
Quid necesse est, te tanto honore non solum honorare, sed etiam adorare
illud nescio quid, quod in modico vasculo transferendo colis ?—Quid
pulverem linteamine circumdatum adorando oscularis ?—Prope ritum
gentilium videmus sub praetextu religionis introductum in ecclesiis, sole
adhuc fulgente moles cereorum accendi, et ubicunque pulvisculum
nescio quod in modico vasculo pretioso linteamine circumdatum oscu-
lantes adorant. Magnum honorem praebent hujusmodi homines bea-
tissimis martyribus, quos putant de vilissimis cereolis illustrandos, quos
agnus, qui est in medio throni cum omni fulgore majestatis suae illustrat,—Vel in sinu Abrahae, vel in loco refrigerii, vel subter aram Dei
animae Apostolorum et Martyrum consederunt, nec possunt suis tumulis,
et ubi voluerint, adesse praesentes.—Dum vivimus, mutuo pro nobis
orare possumus : postquam autem mortui fuerimus, nullius est pro alio
exaudienda oratio. Jerome adds still farther : Praeterea iisdem ad me
relatum est epistolis, quod contra auctoritatem Pauli—tu prohibeas,
Hierosolymam in usus sanctorum aliqua sumtuum solatia dirigi;—hoc
unumquemque posse in patria sua facere ; nec pauperes defuturos, qui
ecclesiae opibus sustentandi sint.—Asseris, eos melius facere, qui utuntur
rebus suis, et paulatim fructus possessionum suarum pauperibus di-
vidunt, quam illos, qui possessionibus venumdatis—semel omnia largi-
untur.—Dicis : si omnes se clauserint et fuerint in solitudine : quis
celebrabit ecclesias ? quis saeculares homines lucrifaciet ? quis peccantes ad virtutes poterit cohortari ? Comp. the writings quoted in
§. 102. note 1. Barbeyrac pref. p. 48. Ceillier p. 339 ss. Barbeyrac
traité p. 251 ss.—Bayle diction. s. v. Vigilantius. Walch de Vigilantio
haeretico orthodoxo. Goett. 1756. (in Pottii syll. comm. theol. vii. 326.)
Walch iii. 673. Lindner de Joviniano et Vigilantio p. 40.

EIGHTH CHAPTER.

SPREAD OF CHRISTIANITY.

§. 107.

IN THE EAST.

In *Persia*, where there were numerous churches under the metropolitan bishop of *Seleucia* and *Ctesiphon*, Christianity had become an object of suspicion ever since it had prevailed in the Roman empire. The recommendation of Constantine therefore, in favour of the Persian Christians, had no permanent or good influence with the king (*Schabur* ii. 309–381.)[1] When a war broke out soon after between the Romans and Persians, Schabur began a tedious and horrible persecution of the Christians with the execution of *Simon bishop of Seleucia* and *Ctesiphon* (343), under the pretence of his being a spy of the Romans.[2] After *Schabur's* death, indeed, this persecution ceased, *Jezdcdscherd* i. (400–421) being at first even a friend to the Christians; but the fanatic *Abdas, bishop of Susa,* by the destruction of a *Pyreion* (404) brought on another persecution as severe, which was finally extinguished by Theodosius II. making war on the Persians (422.)[3] The Persian church was always in close connection with the Syrian, and exhibited the same theological tendency. When, therefore, Nestorianism in its native land was forced to give way to violence, it found a secure asylum among Persian Christians; from which time the Persian church separated itself from that of the Roman empire.[4]

[1] Constantini epist. ad regem Persarum ap. Euseb. de vit. Const. iv. 9-13. et ap. Theodoret. i. 24.
[2] Sozomen. ii. 9-14. Steph. Evod. Assemani acta sanctorum Martyrum orientalium et occidentalium. Romae 1784. fol. Neander's KG. ii. i. 222.
[3] Theodoretus v. 38. Socrates vii. 18-21. Neander S. 235 ss.
[4] §. 88. at the end.

Christianity had also been introduced into *Armenia* as early
as the second century.[5]   In the time of Diocletian, it was spread
universally by *Gregory the illuminator*,[6] who gained over king
Tiridates himself to its side, and was consecrated first metropolitan of Armenia in 302 by Leontius, bishop of Caesarea.[7]   The
long contests that followed, with the adherents of the old religion,
had an important political character, so far as the one party was
supported by the Persian, the other by the Roman emperors.[8]
But when, after the greatest part of Armenia had come under the
Persian dominion (428), the Persian kings wished to procure by
violence a victory for the Zend-doctrine over Christianity, they
found such determined opposition, that they were at last obliged
to allow the Christians the free exercise of their religion, after a
lengthened war (442–485.)[9] In the fifth century, *Mesrop* gave the
Armenians their alphabet and a version of the Bible.[10]—Christianity was carried into *Iberia* under Constantine the Great.[11]
   At the same time it was introduced into *Ethiopia* by *Frumen-*

[5] Dionysius Corinthius according to Eusebius vi. 46. wrote τοῖς κατὰ
'Αρμενίαν περὶ μετανοίας, ὃν ἐπεσκόπευε Μερουζάνης.
[6] Armenian Lusaworitsch, illuminator.   Respecting him see C. F.
Neumann's Gesch. der armen. Literatur, Leipzig 1836. S. 13.
[7] Sozomenus ii. 8.   Mosis Chorenensis (about 440) historiae Armeniacae libb. iii. ed. Guilelmus et Georgius Guil Whistoni filii.
Londini 1736. 4. p. 256 ss.   Bekehrung Armeniens durch d. heil.
Gregor Illuminator, nach national histor. Quellen bearbeitet von P.
Mal. Samueljan. Wien 1844. 8.
[8] Mémoires historiques et géographiques sur l'Armenie par M. J.
Saint-Martin. (T. ii. Paris 1818. 19. 8.) T. i. p. 306 ss.
[9] A history of these persecutions, from 439-451, and of the general
of the Armenians, Wartan, written by a contemporay, Elisä, bishop of
the Amadunians, is: The history of Vartan, by Elisaeus, bishop of
the Amadunians, translated from the Armenian by C. F. Neumann.
Lond. 1830. 4.   Comp. St Martin i. 321.   The proclamation in com-
mendation of the Zend-religion, issued before the beginning of the persecution by the Persian general Mihr-Nerseh, is especially deserving of
notice, ap. Saint-Martin ii. 472. more correctly in the history of Vartan p. 11.
[10] Goriun's (a disciple of Mesrop) Lebensbeschr. des. heil. Mesrop,
aus d. Arm. übersetst u. erläutert von Dr B. Welte (Programm.)
Tübingen 1841. 4.   Neumann's Gesch. d. arm. Literatur S. 30.   Concerning the many Armenian versions of Greek writers in the succeeding
period see Saint-Martin i. 7.   Neumann S. 71.
[11] Rufini hist. eccl. x. 10.   Socrates i. 20.   Sozomenus ii. 7.   Theodoretus i. 23.   Moses Chorenensis ii. c. 83.

tius ; first at court, and, very soon after, throughout the country.[12] In *southern Arabia* under the *Hamdschars,* Constantine endea voured to establish Christianity by means of *Theophilus* (about 350.)[13] He seems, however, not to have produced any considerable effect.

§ 108.

IN THE WEST.

In the preceding period Christianity had been known among the *Goths* (Div. i. § 57), and there was even a Gothic bishop at the council of Nice.[1] After Arianism had been fathered upon them by their ecclesiastial connection with Constantinople,[2] *Ulfila,* who was consecrated bishop in 348 at Constantinople, became their apostle.[3] When the Christian Goths were oppressed by a persecution, he led a great multitude of them into the habitation about Nicopolis in Moesia, which Constantius had assigned them (355), where, after inventing the Gothic alphabet, he translated the Bible into Gothic.[4] Afterwards, Fridigern broke off from Atha-

[12] Rufinus x. 9. Socrates i. 19. Sozomenus ii. 24. Theodoretus i. 22. Hiobi Ludolfi historiae Aethiopicae libb. iv. Francof. 1681. fol. lib. iii. c. 2. Ejusdem commentarius ad hist. Aethiopicam. ibid. 1691. fol. p. 283 ss.

[13] Philostorgius ii. 6. iii. 4. Since it was an Arian Christianity, orthodox historians are silent on the subject.

[1] Among the signatures preserved in Latin : Theophilus Gothorum Metropolis (sc. Episc.) Socrates also mentions the signature of Θεόφιλος τῶν Γότθων ἐπίσκοπος.

[2] According to Theodoret h. e. iv. 33. Ulfila led away the Goths to Arianism, while he told them ἐκ φιλοτιμίας γεγενῆσθαι τὴν ἔριν, δογμάτων δὲ μηδεμίαν εἶναι διαφοράν. It is true, indeed, that the Goths had such a view of the controversy.

[3] Respecting him Socrates iv. 33. Sozomenus vi. 37. Theodoretus iv. 33. Philostorgius ii. 5. Jordanis (about 550 in the Eastern Roman Empire, incorrectly called Jornandes, and reckoned a bishop of Ravenna) de rebus Geticis (in Muratorii rerum Italicarum scriptores i. p. 187.) c. 25. More exact information respecting him was first furnished by the letter of Auxentius, bishop of Dorostorus, his disciple, which, transferred to a work of the Arian bishop Maximin, has been again found along with it in a cod. Paris, and printed and explained in : G. Waitz über das Leben u. die Lehre des Ulfila. Hannover, 1840. 4.

[4] The most complete edition : Ulfilas. Veteris et Novi Test. versionis gothicae fragmenta quae supersunt, edd. H. C. de Gabelentz et Dr J. Loebe. Altenburgi et Lips. vol. i. and vol. ii. P. i. 1836. 1843. 4. Comp. Hug's Einleit. in d. N. T. i. 492.

narich, the leader of the Visigoths, who persecuted the Christians, with a part of the people, was supported by Valens, and
spread Christianity among his subjects. And when the Huns
pressed upon the Goths, this portion of the Visigoths received a
place of residence from Valens, in Thrace, on condition of their
becoming Christians (375); and Ulfila was especially active in
their conversion. Soon after, Arianism was overthrown by Theodosius. Ulfila died in Constantinople (388), where he endeavoured in vain to revive it. Efforts were now made at Constantinople to procure acceptance for the Nicene confession among
the Goths, but without much success.

Arian Christianity was diffused by the *Visigoths* with surprising rapidity among the other wandering German tribes, while
it was suppressed in the Roman empire.[5] The fact of the Arian
doctrine being more easily apprehended, and hatred to the Romans, procured the confidence of the Germans in Arianism ; and
it soon obtained the reputation of being as generally the Christianity of the Germans as Homousianism was of the Romans.

The *Ostrogoths* and *Vandals* first received Arian Christianity
from their countrymen.[6] *The Burgundians* had passed indeed
into the Catholic Church after their wandering into Gaul (413);
but they afterwards (about 450) adopted Arianism, along with
their kings belonging to the Visigothic race. In like manner,
Catholic Christianity had been at first received by the *Suevi* in
Spain ; but Arianism was subsequently disseminated among them
by the Visigoths. The older Catholic inhabitants of the countries
in which these German tribes had settled, suffered oppression
only from the *Visigoths* and *Vandals*.[7] They were especially

----

[5] Walch's Ketzerhistorie Th. 2. S. 553 ss. cf. Prosper in Chron.
Imperiali ad ann. 404. (Chronica medii aevi ed. Roesler. Tübing.
1798, 8. T. i. p. 199): Radagaius Rex Gothorum Italiae limitem
vastaturus transgreditur. Ex quo Ariani, qui Romano procul fuerant
orbe fugati, barbararum nationum, ad quas se contulere, praesidio erigi
coepere.
[6] Jordanis c. 25: Sic quoque Vesegothae a Valente Imp. Ariani
potius quam Christiani effecti. De caetero tam Ostrogothis quam
Gepidis parentibus suis per affectionis gratiam evangelizantes hujus
perfidiae culturam edocentes, omnem ubique linguae hujus nationem ad
culturam hujus sectae invitavere.
[7] Sidonius Apollinaris (Episc. Arvernorum 472.) lib. vii. ep. 6.

persecuted by the latter in a most horrible manner after Africa (431–439) had been conquered by them under their first two kings *Geiserich* († 477) and *Hunerich* († 484.)[8] The Christianity of the Germans was still mixed, to a considerable degree, with heathenism; what rude notions they entertained of the former may be seen in the practice of buying off crimes with money, which they soon transferred to Christian repentance.[9]

Christianity in Britain (Div. i. § 57) was in the meantime very much retarded by the Anglo-Saxons, who had established themselves there from A. D. 449. The Britons still held out in *Wales*, in the mountains of *Northumberland* and *Cornwall*, where alone Christianity was preserved. Shortly before this Christianity had been established in Ireland by *Patricius*[10] (about 430) and spread with rapidity over the island.[11] The seat of the bishop soon arose at *Armagh*.

[8] Victor Episc. Vitensis wrote 487 hist. persecutionis Africanae sub Genserico et Hunnerico Vandalorum regibus reprinted in Th. Ruinarti historia persecutionis Vandalicae. Paris. 1694. 8. (Venet. 1732. 4.) Neander's Denkwürdigkeiten iii. 1. S. 3 ff. F. Papencordt's Gesch. d. vandal. Herrschaft in Afrika. Berlin 1837. S. 66. 113. 269.

[9] cf. Homilia de haereticis peccata vendentibus in Mabillon museum Italicum T. i. P. ii. p. 27. (according to Mabillon's conjecture, p. 6. belonging to Maximus Taurinensis about 440): Nec mirari debemus, quod hujusmodi haeretici in nostra aberrare coeperint regione.—Nam ut eorum interim blasphemias seponamus, retexamus, quae sint ipsorum praecepta vivendi. Praepositi eorum, quos Presbyteros vocant, dicuntur tale habere mandatum, ut si quis laicorum fassus fuerit crimen admissum, non dicat illi: age poenitentiam, deplora facta tua, defle peccata; sed dicat: pro hoc crimine da tantum mihi, et indulgetur tibi.—Suscipit ergo dona Presbyter, et pactione quadam indulgentiam de salvatore promittit. Insipiens placitum, in quo dicitur, minus deliquisse Domino, qui plus contulerit Sacerdoti. Apud hujusmodi praeceptores semper divites innocentes, semper pauperes criminosi.

[10] According to Ussher, belonging to Kilpatrick in Dumbarton in Scotland; according to John Lanigan ecclesiastical history of Ireland (2 ed. Dublin 1829. 4 voll.) i. 93. belonging to Bonavem Taverniae i. e. Boulogne in Picardy.

[11] Respecting him see particularly his Confessio (in Patricii opusculis ed. Jac. Waraeus. Lond. 1658. 8. and Acta SS. Mart. ii. 517. after an older text in Betham P. ii. App. p. xlix.) In this work nothing is found about his journey to Rome, nor of a papal authorization of a mission to Ireland, of which we find a relation first of all in Hericus vita S. Germani i. 12. (Act. SS. Jul. vii.) about 860. Jocelin, in the 12th century, has introduced still more fables in his vita Patricii (Acta SS. Mart. ii. 540.) Jac. Usserii britani carum ecclesiarum antiquitates.

F

SECOND DIVISION.

FROM THE COUNCIL OF CHALCEDON TO THE BEGINNING OF THE
MONOTHELITIC CONTROVERSIES, AND THE TIME OF MUHAMMED.
A. D. 451—622.

SOURCES.

I. *Ecclesiastical historians:* The works of the two Monophysites
are lost, viz., the presbyter John Ægeates, hist. eccles. lib. x.
of which the first five books comprised the period between
428 and 479 (see Photius cod. 41. cf. 55) ; ·and of Zacharias
Rhetor, bishop of Meletina in lesser Armenia, an excerpt
from Socrates and Theodoret, and a continuation to 547
(Greek fragments in Evagrius : 19 Syrian fragments, of
which Assemanus bibl. orient. ii. 53, gave an account, communicated in A. Maji scriptt. vett. nova coll. x. 361) ; as
also of the Nestorian Basil of Cilicia (presbyter in Antioch,
Photius cod. 107.) eccles. hist. libb. iii. from 450 to 518
(Photius cod. 42.)

Still extant are : Theodorus lector in fragments, Evagrius
Scholasticus, Nicephorus Callistus (comp. the preface of
section 1.)

Gennadius, presbyter in Marseilles, † after 495, and Isidore,
bishop of Hispalis, † 636, de scriptoribus ecclesiasticis, both
in Fabrici bibliotheca eccles. Hamb. 1718. fol.

II. Profane historians : Procopius Caesariensis († after 522.
de bello Persico libb. ii., de bello Vandalico libb. ii., de bello
Gothico libb. iv., historia arcana Justiniani, de aedificiis
Justiniani Imp. libb. vi. Opp. ex rec. Gu. Dindorfii voll. iii.
Bonnae 1833—38. 8.)—Agathias Myrinaeus (historiarum
libb. v., written about 580. ed. B. G. Niebuhr. Bonnae 1828. 8.)

Chronicon paschale (comp. the preface of section 1.)

Theophanes Confessor († 817, chronographia from 285 to 813
ex rec. Jo. Classeni, voll. ii. Bonnae 1839. 41. 8.

Dublin. 1639. 4. auctius Lond. 1687.   fol.   Neander's Denkwürdigkeiten iii. ii. 19.   Irish antiquarian researches by Sir Will. Betham.
P. ii. Dublin 1826 and 27. 8.

III. Latin Chroniclers (comp. preface to section 1): Marcellinus Comes till 534, continued by another till 566 (in Sirmondi opp. ii. Bibl. PP. Lugd. ix. 517.) Victor, bishop of Tunnuna, from 444 till 566 (ap. Canisius-Basnage i. 321, best printed in Henr. Florez Espanna Sagrada vi. 382.) Isidore, bishop of Hispalis, from the creation of the world till 614 (in Esp. Sagr. vi. 445.)

IV. Imperial decrees : Codex Justinianeus, see preface to section 1.—Novellae (νεαραὶ διατάξεις μετὰ τὸν κώδικα.)

FIRST CHAPTER.

ENTIRE SUPPRESSION OF PAGANISM IN THE ROMAN EMPIRE.

§ 109.

In *the East*, the remains of paganism disappeared under Justinian I. (527–565), who abolished the new Platonic school at Athens (529),[1] and compelled the heathens to submit to baptism.[2] Only the free Maenotts in Peloponnesus clung obstinately to it.[3] Even in *the West* it was not yet completely extirpated. Theodorich was obliged to prohibit sacrifices to the gods on pain of

[1] Joh. Malala (about 600) historia chronica (libb. xviii. from the creation of the world to the death of Justinian I.) ex rec. Lud. Dindorfii, Bonnae 1831. 8. p. 451. Exile of the philosophers Damascius, Isidorus, Simplicius, Eulamius, Hermias, Diogenes, and Priscian, into Persia, Agathias ii. 30. cf. Wesselingii observationum variarum (Traj. ad Rhen. 1740. 8.) lib. i. c. 28.

[2] Cod. Justin. lib. i. tit. xi. (de paganis et sacrificiis et templis) l. 10. Theophanes i. 276. activity of Johannes Episc. Asiae (probably a missionary bishop for the conversion of the heathen in Asia Minor) see Assemani bibl. orient. ii. 85. As late as the year 561 heathens were discovered in Constantinople (Jo. Malala p. 491.)

[3] Till the ninth century.   See Div. 1. § 44.—According to J. Ph. Fallmerayer Gesch. d. Halbinsel Morea während des Mittelalters (2 Th. Stuttg. u. Tübingen 1830. 36.) i. 169, 189. heathen Slavonians had seized upon, from 578 till 589, the interior of Macedonia, Thessaly, Hellas, and the Peloponnesus; but this first happened about 746, though single Slavonian colonies in those parts may have been older.   See J. W. Zinkeisen's Gesch. Griechenlands v. Anfange geschichtl. Kunde bis auf unsere Tage. Th. 1. (Leipzig 1832.) S. 689. 741.

F 2

death ;[4] and at the end of the fifth century many heathen practices were still continued at Rome, and could not be abolished
without resistance.[5] Still longer did various superstitions adhere
to those heathen temples which were not destroyed.[6] In many
distant places paganism was mantained for a long time undis-
turbed. Sacrifices were offered in a temple of Apollo on mount
Cassinum, until Benedict (529) transformed it into a chapel of
St Martin.[7] In Sicily,[8] but especially in Sardinia[9] and Corsica,[10]
there were still many heathens about A. D. 600. Even Gregory
the Great did not hesitate now to advise violent measures, with
the view of effecting their conversion.[11]

[4] See Lindenbrogii cod. legum antt. p. 255.
[5] cf. Salvianus Massil. above § 79. not. 23. Gelasius P. (492-496)
adv. Andromachum Senatorem caeterosque Romanos, qui Lupercalia
secundum morem pristinum colenda constituebant (ap. Mansii viii.
p. 95 ss.). He shows of what a sacrilege he is guilty, qui cum se
Christianum videri velit, et profiteatur, et dicat, palam tamen publiceque
praedicare non horreat, non refugiat, non pavescat, ideo morbos gigni,
quia daemonia non colantur, et deo Februario non litetur.—Quando
Anthemius Imperator Romam venit (about 470), Lupercalia utique
gerebantur.—dum haec mala hodieque perdurant, ideo haec ipsa im-
peria defecerunt, ideo etiam nomen Romanorum, non remotis etiam
Lupercalibus, usque ad extrema quaeque pervenit. Et ideo nunc ea
removenda suadeo.—Postremo si de meorum persona praescribendum
aestimas praedecessorum : unusquisque nostrorum administrationis suae
redditurus est rationem.—Ego negligentiam accusare non audeo praedecessorum, cum magis credam fortasse tentasse eos, ut haec pravitas
tolleretur, et quasdam extitisse causas et contrarias voluntates, quae
eorum intentionibus praepedirent : sicut ne nunc quidem vos istos
absistere insanis conatibus velle perpenditis. Beugnot hist. de la dés-
truction du Paganisme en Occident ii. 273.
[6] Palladium in the temple of Fortune, Procop. de bello goth. i. 15.
The temple of Janus i. 25. The Pantheon continued till 610 with its
idololatriae sordibus, Paulus Diac. hist. Longob. iv. 37. Beugnot
ii. 288.
[7] Gregorii M. dialog. lib. ii. Beugnot ii. 285. At a still later period
heathen rites of worship in holy groves were practised in the diocese of
Terracina. Gregorii M. viii. ep. 18. ad Agnellum Episc. Terracin.
[8] Gregor. M. lib. iii. epist. 62.
[9] Gregor. M. lib. iv. epist. 26. and lib. ix. epist. 65. ad Januar. Episc.
Caralitanum lib. v. epist. 41. ad Constantinam Augustam.
[10] Gregor. M. lib. viii. epist. 1.
[11] He prescribes lib. iv. ep. 26. in case a peasant should obstinately
persist in heathenism: tanto pensionis onere gravandus est, ut ipsa
exactionis suae poena compellatur ad rectitudinem festinare. And lib.
ix. epist. 65: Contra idolorum quoque cultores vel aruspices atque

SECOND CHAPTER.

HISTORY OF THEOLOGY.

§ 110.

MONOPHYSITE CONTROVERSIES.

Sources: Fragments of Acts of Councils collected by Mansi vii. 481.—ix. 700. Liberati breviarium (see preface to §. 88.)—Breviculus hist. Eutych. (see preface to §. 89.)—Leontii Byzantini (about 600?) de sectis liber, in x. actiones distributus (prim. ed. Jo. Leunclavius in legat. Manuelis Comneni ad Armenos. Basil. 1578. 8. in Gallandii bibl. PP. T. xii. p. 621 ss.), actio v.—x. Ejusdem contra Eutychianos et Nestorianos libb. iii. (lat. ex. Fr. Turriani versione ap. Canisius-Basnage, i. 535. ap. Gallandius xii. 658. in Greek Ang. Maji spicileg. roman, x. ii. 1). Zachariae rhet. et Theodori lect. hist. eccl. fragmenta.—Evagrius ii. 5 ss. Theophanes ed. Paris. p. 92 ss.

Works: Walch's Ketzerhistorie vi. 461. vii. and viii. Baur's Lehre v. d. Dreieingkeit und Menschwerdung Gottes ii. 37.

The decisions of the council of Chalcedon were regarded by the Egyptian party as completely Nestorian.[1] There was therefore an insurrection of monks in *Palestine,* led on by one of their number, Theodosius, against Juvenal, bishop of Jerusalem, and favoured by the widowed empress Eudoxia, which was finally

sortilegos Fraternitatem vestram vehementius pastorali hortamur invigilare custodia, atque publice in populo contra hujus rei viros sermonem facere, eosque a tanti labe sacrilegii et divini intentatione judicii, et praesentis vitae periculo, adhortatione suasoria revocare. Quos tamen si emendare se a talibus atque corrigere nolle repereris, ferventi comprehendere zelo te volumus: et siquidem servi sunt, verberibus cruciatibusque quibus ad emendationem pervenire valeant, castigare. Si vero sunt liberi, inclusione digna districtaque sunt in poenitentiam dirigendi; ut qui salubria et a mortis periculo revocantia audire verba contemnunt, cruciatus saltem eos corporis ad desideratam mentis valeat reducere sanitatem.

[1] So also the Monophysites related that Leo the Great and Theodoret had been completely reconciled to Nestorius; that the latter had been invited to the Synod of Chalcedon by the Emperor Marcian, but had

quashed after much bloodshed (451–3.)[2]   But in *Alexandria*, a considerable party, headed by the presbyter *Timothy* ὁ αἴλου-ρος, and the deacon *Peter* ὁ μογγός, (*i. e.* blaesus Liberat. c. 16) separated from the newly-appointed bishop Proterius.   The greatest part of this faction continued to maintain the doctrine of one nature, rejected the council of Chalcedon, and considered Dioscurus as unjustly deposed;[3] while, on the contrary, they ap-

---

died on the way. See Zachariae hist. eccl. in Maji scriptt. vett. nova coll. x. 361. and Xenayas, bishop of Mabug, about 500, in Assemani bibl. or. ii. 40.   On the other hand, it is remarked by Evagrius ii. 2. that Nestorius had died previously.

[2] Zachariae fragm. ap. Majus x. 363.   Vita S. Euthymii Abbatis († 472) by Cyril of Scythopolis (about 555), in an enlarged form by Simeon Metaphrastes in Cotelerii monum. Eccles. graec. ii. 200. in a shorter, perhaps a genuine form, in the analectis graecis (ed. Benedictini mon. Jac. Lopinus, B. Montfaucon, Ant. Pugetus. Paris. 1688. 4.) p. 1 ss. Juvenal had before sided with the Egyptians, and was also at first at Chalcedon on the side of Dioscurus: but (Zacharias l. c.) accepta demum ab Imperatore promissione de subjiciendis tribus Palaestinae sedibus honori cathedrae hierosolymitanae, mentis oculos sibi obstruxit, solum destituit in certamine Dioscorum, et adversariorum in partes transiit.

[3] The most important representative of this tendency which we have is Severus monophysite patriarch of Antioch, from A. D. 513. (See below note 19.) Comp. my comm. qua Monophysitarum veterum variae de Christi persona opiniones inprimis ex ipsorum effatis recens. editis illustrantur (Partic. ii. Gotting. 1835. 38. 4.) i. 9 ss. Severi locus (prim. ed. Mansi vii. 831. Gallandius xii. 733. is, according to Maji scriptt. vett. nova coll. vii. i. 136. from Severi lib. contra Grammaticum, Joannem Ep. Caesareae) : Δύο τὰς φύσεις ἐν τῷ Χριστῷ νοοῦμεν, τὴν μὲν κτιστήν, τὴν δὲ ἄκτιστον· ἀλλ᾽ οὐδεὶς ἐγράψατο τὴν ἐν Χαλκηδόνι σύνοδον τὴν ἄλογον ταύτην γραφήν, τί δήποτε δύο φύσεις ὠνόμασαν περὶ τῆς τοῦ Ἐμμανουὴλ ἑνώσεως διαλαμβάνοντες. οὐδεὶς ταύτην ἔστησε τὴν κατηγορίαν, ἀλλ᾽ ἐκείνην μάλα δικαίως, τί δήποτε μὴ ἀκολουθήσαντες τῷ ἁγίῳ Κυρίλλῳ ἐκ δύο φύσεων ἔφασαν εἶναι τὸν Χριστόν. Οὐ παυσόμεθα λέγοντες, ὡς δειξάτω τις τὴν ἐν Χαλκηδόνι σύνοδον ἢ τὸν τόμον Λέοντος τὴν καθ᾽ ὑπόστασιν ἕνωσιν ὁμολογήσαντας, ἢ σύνοδον φυσικήν, ἢ ἐξ ἀμφοῖν ἕνα Χριστὸν, ἢ μίαν φύσιν τοῦ θεοῦ λόγου σεσαρκωμένην· καὶ τότε γνωσόμεθα, ὡς κατὰ τὸν σοφώτατον Κύριλλον θεωρίᾳ μόνῃ ἀνακρίνοντες τὴν οὐσιώδη διαφορὰν τῶν συνενεχθέντων ἀπορρήτως εἰς ἓν ἴσασι· καὶ ὡς ἑτέρα ἡ τοῦ λόγου φύσις, καὶ ἑτέρα ἡ τῆς σαρκὸς, καὶ ὡς δύο τὰ ἀλλήλοις συνενηνεγμένα καθορῶσι τῷ νῷ, διϊστῶσι δὲ οὐδαμῶς.   Ex ejusd. ad Jo. Grammat. lib. ii. c. 1. ap. Majum l. c. p. 138 : καὶ τῶν, ἐξ ὧν ἡ ἕνωσις, μενόντων ἀμειώτων καὶ ἀναλλοιώτων, ἐν συνθέσει δὲ ὑφεστώτων καὶ οὐκ ἐν μονάσιν ἰδιοσυστάτοις.   Ex ejusd. epist. iii. ad Joannem ducem ap. Majum l. c. p. 71 : Ἕως ἂν οὖν εἷς ἐστιν ὁ Χριστὸς, μίαν ὡς ἑνὸς αὐτοῦ τήν τε φύσιν καὶ τὴν ὑπόστασιν καὶ τὴν ἐνέργειαν σύνθετον ἐπ᾽ ὄρους ὑψηλοῦ, τὸ δὴ λεγόμενον, ἀναβάντες κηρύττομεν, ἀναθεματίζοντες καὶ πάντας τοὺς ἐπ᾽ αὐτοῦ

proved of the condemnation of Eutyches, for his supposed doce-
tism.[4]   But as the doctrine of one nature had before led in some
cases to the idea of considering the body of Jesus as something

μετὰ τὴν ἕνωσιν δυάδα φύσεων καὶ ἐνεργειῶν δογματίζοντας.—Collatio Catholicorum cum Severianis habita Constantinop. anno 531 ap. Mansi viii.
822: Quod ex duabus quidem naturis dicere unam significat Dei verbi
naturam incarnatam, secundum b. Cyrillum et ss. patres: in duabus
autem naturis duas personas et duas subsistentias significat. At the
same time they allowed that Christ is κατὰ σάρκα ὁμοούσιος ἡμῖν (Leontius
de sectis act. 5. Evagrius iii. 5.)—Severus ap. Anastasius Sinaita
(about 560) in the Ὁδηγὸς adv. Acephalos (prim. ed. J. Gretser. Ingolst.
1606. 4.) c. 18: ὥσπερ ἐπὶ τῆς μιᾶς τοῦ ἀνθρώπου φύσεως μέρος μὲν ταύτης
ἐστὶν ἡ ψυχή, μέρος δὲ τὸ σῶμα, οὕτω καὶ ἐπὶ τοῦ Χριστοῦ, καὶ τῆς μιᾶς αὐτοῦ
φύσεως, μέρους τάξιν ἐπέχει ἡ θεότης, καὶ μέρους τὸ σῶμα. This comparison
was frequently used by the Monophysites generally after Cyril's example
(see ep. ad Succensum above § 88. note 21.), and in like manner by
Philoxenus or Xenayas, bishop of Mabug (488-518) in Assemani bibl.
orient. ii. 25. Gelasius I. (bishop of Rome 492-496) de duabus naturis
in Christo adv. Eutychen et Nestorium (in bibl. PP. and in Jo. Heroldi
haereseologia. Basil. 1556. p. 686.): Adhuc autem etiam illud adjiciunt, ut sicut ex duabus rebus constat homo, id est ex anima et corpore, quamvis utriusque rei sit diversa natura, sicut dubium non habetur,
plerumque tamen usus loquendi singulariter pronunciet, simul utrumque
complectens, ut humanam dicat naturam, non humanas naturas: sic
potentiam in Christi mysterio, et unitionem divinitatis atque humanitatis unam dici vel debere vel posse naturam: non considerantes, quia
cum una natura dicatur humana, quae tamen ex duabus constet, id est
ex anima et corpore principaliter, illa causa est, quia nec initialiter
anima alibi possit existere, quam in corpore, nec corpus valeat constare
sine anima: et merito, quae alterutro sibi sit causa existendi, pariter
unam abusive dici posse naturam, quae sibi invicem causam praebeat, ut
ex alterutro natura subsistat humana, salva proprietate duntaxat duarum.
According to the decrees of the synod at Chalcedon φύσις and οὐσία are
synonymous, while τὸ ἄτομον and ἡ ὑπόστασις are different from them.
But the monophysites took φύσις, ὑπόστασις and ἄτομον synonymously,
and separated ἡ οὐσία from them. See Muji scriptt. vett. nova coll.
vii. 1. 11 ss. my Comm. i. 11. That this was also the phraseology employed by Cyril is acknowledged by Eubulus, bishop of Lystra, ap.
Majus l. c. p. 31. who endeavours to exculpate him on that account.
And that this controversy was more about correctness of expression
than of idea, even the monk Eustathius, with all his bitterness against
Severus, is obliged to allow. See Majus l. c. p. 291. and my Comm.
i. 23.
  [4] Collatio Cathol. cum Severianis ap. Mansi t. viii. p. 818: qualem
opinionem de Eutyche habetis? Orientales dixerunt: Tanquam haereticus, magis autem princeps haeresis. Zacharias (ap. Evagrium
iii. 5.): οἱ τὴν Εὐτυχοῦς φαντασίαν νοσοῦντες ἀνὰ τὴν βασιλεύουσαν, καὶ τὸν
μονήρη διώκοντες βίον, ὥσπερ ἑρμαίῳ τινὶ περιτυχεῖν οἰηθέντες Τιμοθέῳ (Aeluro),

superhuman,[5] so also now, many attributed peculiar excellencies to it.[6]   To the most influential advocates of the doctrine of one nature, Athanasius and Cyril, was now added *Pseudo-Dionysius the Areopagite*, whose writings were doubtless composed in Egypt towards the end of the fifth century,[7] and therefore coin-

—δρομαῖοι παρ αὐτὸν ἀφικνοῦνται, καὶ ὡς διελεγχθέντες πρὸς Τιμοθέου, ὁμοού-σιον ἡμῖν εἶναι κατὰ σάρκα τὸν τοῦ θεοῦ λόγον, καὶ τῷ πατρὶ ὁμοούσιον κατὰ τὴν θεότητα, ἐς τοὐπίσω ἀνεχώρουν.   Prevailing notion respecting the doctrine of Eutyches: Hormisdae P. epist. 30. ad Caesarium: Eutyches carnis negans veritatem,—ut Manichaeam phantasiam ec-clesiis Christi—insereret etc.   Justinianus in Codice i. i. 5: (anathe-matizamus) et Eutychetem mente captum, *phantasiam inducentem.* Vigilius Tapsensis (about 484) adv. Eutychen libb. v. (opp. ed. P. F. Chiffletius. Divione 1664. 4.) in the beginning of lib. iii.: Euty-chiana haeresis in id impietatis prolapsa est errore, ut non solum verbi et carnis unam credat esse naturam, verum etiam hanc eandem carnem non de sacro Mariae virginis corpore adsumtam, sed de coelo dicat, juxta infandum Valentini et Marcionis errorem, fuisse deductam.   Ita pertinaciter verbum carnem adserens factum, ut per virginem, ac si aqua per fistulam, transisse videatur, non tamen ut de virgine aliquid, quod nostri sit generis, adsumsisse credatur.   Liberatus c. 11. Samuel pres-byter in Edessa went so far as to attempt to prove to the Eutychians veram humani generis carnem a Deo assumtam, et non de coelo exhi-bitam, nec crassi aëris substantiam in carne incessisse formatam (Gen-nadius de vir. illustr. c. 82.)

[5] See Theodoreti eranistes et Isidor. Pelus. § 89. not. 2.

[6] So said Dioscurus (in Maji nova coll. vii. i. 289.): Ἰ. Χρ. γενόμενος ἄνθρωπος—τοῖς ἀνθρωπίνοις κεκοινώνηκε πάθεσιν οὐ κατὰ φύσιν, ἀλλὰ κατὰ χάριν.   And μὴ γένοιτο ἑνὸς τῶν κατὰ φύσιν λέγειν ἡμᾶς ὁμοούσιον τὸ αἷμα Χριστοῦ.   Timotheus Aelurus (l. c. p. 277.): Φύσις δὲ Χριστοῦ μία μόνη θεότης (consequently not as according to Severus: φύσις σύνθετος), and: εἰ γὰρ ἦν ἄνθρωπος κατὰ φύσιν καὶ νόμον ὁ μέλλων ἀποτελεῖσθαι ἄνθρωπος ἐν μήτρᾳ τῆς παρθένου, οὐκ ἂν ἐτέχθη ἐξ αὐτῆς εἰ μὴ πρῶτον τῆς παρθενίας διαλυ-θείσης.

[7] De hierarchia coelesti, de hierarchia ecclesiastica, de nominibus divinis, de theologia mystica, epistolae (ed. Paris. 1644. 2 voll. fol.) falsely ascribed to the Dionysius mentioned in Acts xvii. 34, who, accord-ing to Dionys. Corinth. ap. Euseb. iii. 4. iv. 23. was the first bishop of Athens.   The first trace of these writings which has been preserved to us belongs to the beginning of the 6th century, when Joannes Scytho-politanus wrote scholia on them (Le Quien disert. Damasc. prefixed to his edition of Joannes Damasc. i. fol. xxxviii. verso).   The Monophy-site patriarch of Antioch, Severus, cites them (see note 8.), and the no less respectable orthodox writer Ephraemius, who, from 526, was patri-arch of Antioch, refers to them (ap. Photius cod. 229. ed. Hoeschel. p. 420.)   When, however, in the collatio Catholicorum cum Severianis in the year 531, the Monophysites appealed to them (Mansi viii. 817.), Hypatius, archbishop of Ephesus, judged ostendi non posse, ista vera

cided with the mode of expounding the doctrine of Christ's person adopted by Cyril.[8] Among the many heretical names which the party received from its opponents,[9] the appellation Μονοφυσῖται was the most common. On the other hand they called the opposite party Δυοφυσῖται, or Διφυσῖται.[10]

The death of Marcian inspired († 457) the Monophysites with new hopes. At *Alexandria*, Proterius was killed in an insurrec-

esse, quae nullus antiquus memoraverit. Subsequently many were found in the Greek Church who always asserted the spuriousness of these writings (Maximi prol. in schol. Dionys. p. 45, Photius cod. 1.). In the Latin Church, in which they had been widely diffused from the 9th century, Laurentius Valla († 1457) was the first that detected the imposition. He was followed in his opinion by the ablest scholars of the day; and Jo. Dallaeus de scriptis, quae sub Dionysii Areop. et Ignatii Ant. nominibus circumferuntur. Genevae 1666. 4. finally exhibited in a copious form the evidence of their spuriousness. cf. le Quien l. c. Salig de Eutychianismo ante Eutychen. Wolfenbuttelae 1723. 4. p. 159 ss. J. G. V. Engelhardt diss. de Dionysio Plotinizante. Erlang. 1820. 8. Id. de origine scriptorum Areopagiticorum. Erl. 1823. 8. The same writer's Die angebl. Schriften des Areopagiten Dionysius, überf. u. m. Abhandlungen begleitet. Sulzbach 1823. 2 Theile. 8. Baumgarten-Crusius de Dionysio Areop. comm. 1823 (opusc. theol. p. 261.) departing from the opinions of others, attributes these writings to the third century, and thinks they were written with the object of transferring the Greek mysteries to Christianity. See against this hypothesis Ritter Gesch. d. christl. Philos. ii. 519.

[8] He combats the excrescences of it, the doctrines of a confusion and transmutation de eccles. hierarchia c. 3. (opp. i. 297. 299), de divinis nominibus c. 2. (l. c. p. 501). The principal passage is in epist. iv. ad Cajum (opp. ii. 75) : οὐδὲ ἄνθρωπος ἦν, οὐχ ὡς μὴ ἄνθρωπος, ἀλλ' ὡς ἐξ ἀνθρώπων, ἀνθρώπων ἐπέκεινα, καὶ ὑπὲρ ἄνθρωπον ἀληθῶς ἄνθρωπος γεγονώς. Καὶ τὸ λοιπὸν, οὐ κατὰ Θεὸν τὰ θεῖα δράσας, οὐ τὰ ἀνθρώπεια κατὰ ἄνθρωπον, ἀλλ' ἀνδρωθέντος Θεοῦ, καινήν τινα τὴν θεανδρικὴν ἐνέργειαν ἡμῖν πεπολιτευμένος. The last words of this passage are addressed by Severus epist. ad Joannem ducem in Maji collect. vii. 1, 71, as a φωνὴν τοῦ πανσόφου Διονυσίου τοῦ Ἀρεοπαγητικοῦ, and enlarged by the addition of τὸν ἀνδρωθέντα Θεὸν, τὴν ταύτην (ἐνέργειαν) καινοπρεπῶς πεπολιτευμένον, μίαν ὁμολογοῦμεν φύσιν τε καὶ ὑπόστασιν θεανδρικὴν, ὥσπερ καὶ τὴν μίαν φύσιν τοῦ θεοῦ λόγου σεσαρκωμένην. The Monophysites obtained from Dionysius a new formula in addition to the old Athanasian one.

[9] At different times and places, for example, Acephali Severiani, Aegyptii, Jacobitae, Timotheani, etc.—Facundus Episc. Hermianensis (about 540) pro defensione iii. capitulorum (libb. v. prim. ed. Jac. Sirmond. Paris. 1629. 8. ap. Gallandius T. xi. p. 665) libb. i. c. 5. et iv. c. 3: Acephali vocantur a Graecis, quos significantius nos Semieutychianos possumus appellare. This name, however, never became usual.

[10] So Timotheus Aelurus in Maji coll. vii. 1, 277.

tion; and *Timotheus Ælurus*, chosen bishop. The emperor, *Leo I.* (457–474) actually requested a new decision of the bishops respecting adherence to the decrees of the council of Chalcedon. But as the majority declared themselves in favour of the synod,[11] Timotheus Ælurus was banished, and *Timotheus σαλοφακίαλος* nominated in his place (460), who succeeded in maintaining the tranquillity of Alexandria by his prudent, conciliating conduct towards the opposite party. It is true, that new commotions

---

[11] The letters are collected in the codex encyclius. Mansi T. vii. p. 777 ss. gives their form, and the writings themselves also in the same volume, p. 521 ss. Most remarkable is the epist. Episcoporum Pamphyliae. Ibid. p. 573 ss. :—doctrina—quae a S. Nicaeno concilio gratia spiritali prolata est—omnia complet et omnibus valde sufficit—Nos et Nicaenum synodum debito honore veneramur, et Chalcedonensem quoque suscipimus, veluti scutum eam contra haereticos opponentes, et non anathema (leg. mathema, μάθημα) fidei existentem. Non enim ad populum a papa Leone et a S. Chalcedonensi concilio scripta est, ut ex hoc debeant scandalum sustinere, sed tantummodo sacerdotibus, ut habeant quo possint repugnare contrariis. Duarum namque naturarum sive substantiarum unitatem in uno Christo declaratam invenimus a pluribus apud nos consistentibus sanctis et religiosissimis patribus, et nequaquam veluti mathema aut symbolum his qui baptizantur hoc tradimus, sed ad bella hostium reservamus. Si vero propter medelam eorum, qui per simplicitatem scandalizati noscuntur, placuerit vestrae potentiae, Christo amabilis imperator, S. Leoni Rom. civ. episcopo, nec non aliorum pariter sanctitati, propter istorum (sicut dixi) condescensionem et satisfactionem, quatenus idem sanctissimus vir literis suis declaret, quia non est symbolum neque mathema epistola, quae tunc ab eo ad sanctae memoriae nostrum archiepiscopum Flavianum directa est, et quod a sancto concilio dictum est, sed haereticae pravitatis potius increpatio: simul et illud, quod ab eis est dictum, "in duabus naturis," quod forte eis dubium esse dignoscitur, dum a patre prolatum sit propter eos, qui veram Dei verbi incarnationem negant, his sermonibus apertius indicatum, ita tamen, ut in nullo sanctae synodo fiat injuria. Nihil enim differt, sive duarum naturarum unitas inconfusa dicatur, sive ex duabus eodem modo referatur. Sed neque si una dicatur verbi natura, inferatur autem incarnata, aliud quid significat, sed idem honestiori sermone declarat. Nam et invenimus saepius hoc dixisse ss. patres. Apud vestrae pietatis imperium, quod significat vestra potentia decenter ago, quia ipsa synodus permanebit, sicut ecclesiae membra discerpta copulabuntur hoc sermone curata, et ea, quae contra sacerdotes nefanda committuntur, cessabunt, et ora haereticorum contra nos aperta damnabuntur, et omnia reducentur ad pacem, et fiet, sicut scriptum est, unus grex et unus pastor. Quoniam et dominus Christus multa condescensione circa nos usus, et humanum salvavit genus: et quia cum dives esset, utique divinitate, pauper factus est pro nobis, secundum quod homo fieri voluit, ut nos illa paupertate ditaremur, sicut b. Paulus edicit etc.

arose soon after even in Antioch. *Peter* the Fuller (ὁ γναφεύς), a monk of Constantinople, and an enemy of the council of Chalcedon, endeavoured to carry through here, the favourite formula of the Monophysites θεὸς ἐσταυρώθη, and even to introduce it into the *Trishagion;*[12] succeeded in gaining over the monks to his party ; and put himself in the place of the deposed patriarch ; but not long after he was banished by an imperial decree (about 470), and there was hope of seeing the schism gradually disappear and be every where forgotten.   But it proved incurable when *Basiliscus,* having driven the Emperor Zeno Isauricus from the throne (476. 477), declared in favour of the Monophysites, reinstated Timotheus Ælurus and Peter the Fuller in their dignities, and by the *Encyclion,* required all bishops (476) to condemn the synod of Chalcedon.[13]

It was not long, indeed, before the persevering *Acacius,* patriarch of Constantinople, succeeded in exciting a popular tumult,

---

[12] The elder τρισάγιον consisted of the words Jes. 6, 3.   cf. Constitt. apost. viii. 12.   Miraculous origin of the later one under Theodosius II.   (Felicis Papae ep. ad Petrum Full. ap Mansi vii. 1041.   Acacii ep. ad. eund. ibid. p. 1121) : Ἅγιος ὁ θεὸς, ἅγιος ἰσχυρὸς, ἅγιος ἀθάνατος (ὁ σταυρωθεὶς δι' ἡμᾶς), ἐλέησον ἡμᾶς.   cf. Suiceri thes. ii. 1310.   Bingham vi. p. 37 ss.   Walch's Ketzerhistorie vii. 239.

[13] In the 'Εγκύκλιον (ap. Evagrius iii. 4), it is said : θεσπίζομεν τὴν κρηπίδα καὶ βεβαίωσιν τῆς ἀνθρωπίνης εὐζωΐας, τουτέστι τὸ σύμβολον τῶν τιή ἁγίων πατέρων τῶν ἐν Νικαίᾳ πάλαι μετὰ τοῦ ἁγίου πνεύματος ἐκκλησιασθέντων— μόνον πολιτεύεσθαι καὶ κρατεῖν ἐν πάσαις ταῖς ἁγιωτάταις τοῦ θεοῦ ἐκκλησίαις τὸν ὀρθόδοξον λαὸν, ὡς μόνον τῆς ἀπλανοῦς πίστεως ὅρον, καὶ ἀρκοῦν εἰς ἀναίρεσιν μὲν καθόλου πάσης αἱρέσεως, ἕνωσιν δὲ ἄκραν τῶν ἁγίων τοῦ θεοῦ ἐκκλησιῶν· ἐχόντων δηλαδὴ τὴν οἰκείαν ἰσχὺν, καὶ τῶν εἰς βεβαίωσιν αὐτοῦ τοῦ θείου συμβόλου πεπραγμένων ἔν τε τῇ βασιλευούσῃ πόλει ταύτῃ—παρὰ τῶν ρν' ἁγίων πατέρων, ἔτι δὲ καὶ πάντων τῶν πεπραγμένων ἐν τῇ 'Εφεσίων μητροπόλει κατὰ τοῦ δυσσεβοῦς Νεστορίου, καὶ τῶν μετὰ ταῦτα τὰ ἐκείνου φροηησάντων·   τὰ δὲ διελόντα τὴν ἕνωσιν καὶ εὐταξίαν τῶν ἁγίων τοῦ θεοῦ ἐκκλησιῶν καὶ εἰρήνην τοῦ κόσμου παντός, δηλαδὴ τὸν λεγόμενον τόμον Λέοντος, καὶ πάντα τὰ ἐν Χαλκηδόνι ἐν ὅρῳ πίστεως ἢ ἐκθέσει συμβόλων—εἰρημένα καὶ πεπραγμένα εἰς καινοτομίαν κατὰ τοῦ μνημονευθέντος ἁγίου συμβόλου τῶν τιή ἁγίων πατέρων, θεσπίζομεν ἐνταῦθά τε καὶ πανταχοῦ καθ' ἑκάστην ἐκκλησίαν παρὰ τῶν ἁπανταχοῦ ἁγιωτάτων ἐπισκόπων ἀναθεματίζεσθαι, καὶ πυρὶ παραδίδοσθαι παρ' οἷς ἂν εὑρίσκηται.— θεσπίζομεν τοὺς πανταχοῦ ἁγιωτάτους ἐπισκόπους ἐμφανιζομένῳ τῷ θείῳ τούτῳ ἡμῶν ἐγκυκλίῳ γράμματι καθυπογράφειν σαφῶς καταμηνύοντας, ὅτι δὴ μόνῳ τῷ θείῳ στοιχοῦσι συμβόλῳ τῶν τιή ἁγίων πατέρων, ὅπερ ἐπεσφράγισαν οἱ ρν' πατέρες ἅγιοι, ὡς ἔδοξεν ὁριστικῶς καὶ τοῖς μετὰ ταῦτα συνελθοῦσι κατὰ τὴν 'Εφεσίων μητρόπολιν ὀρθοδόξοις καὶ ὁσίοις πατράσιν.   cf. J. Gu. Berger henotica Orientis.   Vitemb. 1723. 4. p. 1 ss.

which was the means of restoring *Zeno Isauricus* to the throne (477–491); but in the meantime, the principles of the Monophysites had been so firmly established in Egypt by those occurrences, that Zeno, by the advice of Acacius, issued the *Henoticon*[14] (482), in which both parties were to be brought into a state of peace and union by reducing the points at issue to more general principles. *Peter Mongus* was patriarch of Alexandria, and subscribed the Henoticon. Many Monophysites, however, displeased at this, separated from him, and were called 'Ακέφαλοι, without a head.[15] *Peter the Fuller* was once more appointed patriarch of Antioch (485); though many Syrian bishops were deposed because they would not subscribe the Henoticon. The most decided opposition to church fellowship with the Mo-

---

[14] Ap. Evagrius iii. 14 : Αὐτοκράτωρ Καῖσαρ Ζήνων—τοῖς κατὰ ᾿Αλεξάνδρειαν καὶ Αἴγυπτον, καὶ Λιβύην καὶ Πεντάπολιν κ. τ. λ.—γινώσκειν ὑμᾶς ἐσπουδάσαμεν, ὅτι καὶ ἡμεῖς καὶ αἱ πανταχοῦ ἐκκλησίαι ἕτερον σύμβολον, ἢ μάθημα, ἢ ὅρον πίστεως, ἢ πίστιν πλὴν τοῦ εἰρημένου ἁγίου συμβόλου τῶν τιή ἁγίων πατέρων, ὅπερ ἐβεβαίωσαν οἱ μνημονευθέντες ρν´ ἅγιοι πατέρες, οὔτε ἐσχήκαμεν, οὔτε ἔχομεν, οὔτε ἕξομεν.—ᾧ καὶ ἐξηκολούθησαν οἱ ἅγιοι πατέρες οἱ ἐν τῇ ᾿Εφεσίων συνελθόντες, οἱ καὶ καθελόντες τὸν ἀσεβῆ Νεστόριον, καὶ τοὺς τὰ ἐκείνου μετὰ ταῦτα φρονοῦντας· ὅντινα καὶ ἡμεῖς Νεστόριον ἅμα καὶ Εὐτυχῆ, τἀναντία τοῖς εἰρημένοις φρονοῦντας, ἀναθεματίζομεν, δεχόμενοι καὶ τὰ ιβ´ κεφάλαια τὰ εἰρημένα παρὰ τοῦ τῆς ὁσίας μνήμης γενομένου Κυρίλλου ἀρχιεπισκόπου τῆς ᾿Αλεξανδρέων ἁγίας καθολικῆς ἐκκλησίας. ῾Ομολογοῦμεν δὲ τὸν μονογενῆ τοῦ θεοῦ υἱὸν καὶ θεὸν τὸν κατὰ ἀλήθειαν ἐνανθρωπήσαντα, τὸν κύριον ἡμῶν ᾿Ιησοῦν Χριστὸν, τὸν ὁμοούσιον τῷ πατρὶ κατὰ τὴν θεότητα καὶ ὁμοούσιον ἡμῖν τὸν αὐτὸν κατὰ τὴν ἀνθρωπότητα, κατελθόντα καὶ σαρκωθέντα ἐκ πνεύματος ἁγίου καὶ Μαρίας τῆς παρθένου καὶ θεοτόκου, ἕνα τυγχάνειν καὶ οὐ δύο· ἑνὸς γὰρ εἶναι φαμὲν τά τε θαύματα καὶ τὰ πάθη, ἅπερ ἑκουσίως ὑπέμεινε σαρκί. τοὺς γὰρ διαιροῦντας, ἢ συγχέοντας, ἢ φαντασίαν εἰσάγοντας οὐδὲ ὅλως δεχόμεθα· ἐπείπερ ἡ ἀναμάρτητος κατὰ ἀλήθειαν σάρκωσις ἐκ τῆς θεοτόκου προσθήκην υἱοῦ οὐ πεποίηκε.—πάντα δὲ τὸν ἕτερόν τι φρονήσαντα, ἢ φρονοῦντα, ἢ νῦν ἢ πώποτε, ἢ ἐν Χαλκηδόνι, ἢ οἵᾳ δήποτε συνόδῳ, ἀναθεματίζομεν. Berger henotica Orientis p. 42 ss.

[15] These considered Timothy Ælurus as the last legitimate patriarch. See Eustathii mon. epist. ad Timoth. Scholasticum, in Maji coll. vii. 1, 277 : Τούτῳ (Τιμοθέῳ Αἰλούρῳ) καὶ τοῖς ἀπ᾿ αὐτοῦ μέχρι τῆς σήμερον οὐ κοινωνοῦσιν οἱ Σευήρου, ἀκεφάλους αὐτοὺς προσαγορεύοντες. However, Timotheus himself seems to have died before the division, since Severus esteems him highly. See his words l. c. Διοσκόρου δὲ καὶ Τιμοθέου, τῶν τῆς ἀληθείας ἀγωνιστῶν—τοὺς ἀγῶνας τιμῶ καὶ ἀσπάζομαι. It might be expected that the strictest Monophysites should have belonged to the Acephali, who considered even the body of Jesus as something higher, and these found passages in Timotheus Ælurus, which agreed with them (see note 6), though he had maintained that the body of Christ is of like essence with our own.

nophysites was presented by the Roman patriarchs, who had become entirely independent of the emperor since the downfall of the Western empire (476). All remonstrance proving vain, *Felix II.* issued an anathema (484)[16] against Acacius, and communion between the Eastern and Western churches was entirely broken off.

But even in the East, the Henoticon proved but a weak bond of union, since the questions left indeterminate in it, were continually employing the minds of men. At Constantinople, the council of Chalcedon stood high in estimation; and *the Acoemetae* even continued in communion with the Church of Rome. In Alexandria, the decrees of this council were rejected. In the East, opinions on the subject were divided. Among all these churches. it is true, external fellowship was for the most part maintained by the Henoticon; but it could not be otherwise than that there should be coldness between the parties, which often led to open quarrels. Such was the situation of affairs at the accession of the emperor *Anastasius* (491–518). He adopted the principle of avoiding all interference in religious matters, except to protect the peace of the citizens against fanaticism.[17] But he could

[16] Felicis epist. ad Acacium ap. Mansi vii. p. 1053. The conclusion: Habe ergo cum his, quos libenter amplecteris, portionem ex sententia praesenti, quam per tuae tibi direximus ecclesiae defensorem, sacerdotali honore, et communione catholica, nec non etiam a fidelium numero segregatus; sublatum tibi nomen et munus ministerii sacerdotalis agnosce, S. Spiritus judicio et apostolica auctoritate damnatus, numquamque anathematis vinculis exuendus.—Theophanes p. 114: Ἀκάκιος δέ ἀναισθήτως ἔσχε περὶ τὴν καθαίρεσιν, καὶ τὸ ὄνομα αὐτοῦ (τοῦ Φιλικος) ἐξῆρε τῶν διπτύχων.

[17] Evagrius iii. 30: Οὗτος ὁ Ἀναστάσιος εἰρηναῖός τις ὤν, οὐδὲν καινουργεῖσθαι παντελῶς ἠβούλετο, διαφερόντως περὶ τὴν ἐκκλησιαστικὴν κατάστασιν.— Ἡ μὲν οὖν ἐν Χαλκηδόνι σύνοδος ἀνὰ τούτους τοὺς χρόνους οὔτε ἀναφανδὸν ἐν ταῖς ἁγιωτάταις ἐκκλησίαις ἐκηρύττετο, οὔτε μὴν ἐκ πάντων ἀπεκηρύττετο. ἕκαστοι δὲ τῶν προεδρευόντων, ὡς εἶχον νομίσεως, διεπράττοντο. Κἂν ἔνιοι μὲν τῶν ἐκτεθειμένων αὐτῇ μάλα γεννικῶς ἀντείχοντο, καὶ πρὸς οὐδεμίαν ἐνεδίδοσαν συλλαβὴν τῶν ὁρισθέντων παρ᾽ αὐτῆς, οὐ μὴν γράμματος ἀλλαγὴν παρεδέχοντο, ἀλλὰ καὶ μετὰ πολλῆς ἀπεπήδων τῆς παρρησίας, καὶ κοινωνεῖν παντελῶς οὐκ ἠνείχοντο τοῖς μὴ δεχομένοις παρ᾽ αὐτῆς τὰ ἐκτιθέμενα. Ἕτεροι δὲ οὐ μόνον οὐκ ἐδέχοντο τὴν ἐν Χαλκηδόνι σύνοδον καὶ τὰ παρ᾽ αὐτῆς ὁρισθέντα, ἀλλὰ καὶ ἀναθέματι περιέβαλον αὐτήν τε καὶ τὸν Λέοντος τόμον. Ἄλλοι τοῖς ἑνωτικοῖς Ζήνωνος ἐνισχυρίζοντο καὶ ταῦτα πρὸς ἀλλήλους διερρωγότες τῇ τε μιᾷ καὶ ταῖς δύο φύσεσιν, οἱ μὲν τῇ συνθήκῃ τῶν γραμμάτων ἐλαπένντες, οἱ δὲ καὶ πρὸς τὸ εἰρηνικωτέρων μᾶλλον ἀποκλίναντες· ὡς πάσας τὰς ἐκκλησίας εἰς ἰδίας ἀποκριθῆναι μοίρας,

not prevent all outbreaks of the latter.   In Constantinople itself,
he was threatened by the seditious *Vitalianus*, who put himself
forth as a defender of the Chalcedonian synod (514), and was
obliged to promise to him that he would effect a restoration of
communion with Rome.   But all negotiations to bring this about
were frustrated by the extravagant demands of the Roman see;
and Anastasius carried with him to the grave the hatred of all
the friends of the council of Chalcedon, as may be seen by many
narratives written after his death.[18]

Under *Justin I.* (518–527), a popular tumult finally compelled
the general and solemn adoption of the Chalcedonian council at
Constantinople, and the renewal of Church-communion with Rome
(519).   The same measures were soon after taken in the East;
the Monophysite bishops were deposed, particularly *Severus*, patriarch of Antioch,[19] *Xenayas* or *Philoxenus*, bishop of Mabug,

καὶ μηδὲ κοινωνεῖν ἀλλήλοις τοὺς προεδρεύοντας.—Ἅπερ ὁ βασιλεὺς Ἀναστάσιος
θεώμενος τοὺς νεωτερίζοντας τῶν ἐπισκόπων ἐξωθεῖτο, εἴ που κατειλήφει ἢ παρὰ
τὸ εἰωθὸς τοῖς τόποις τινὰ τὴν ἐν Χαλκηδόνι σύνοδον κηρύττοντα, ἢ ταύτην ἀναθέματι περιτιθέντα.

[18] Evagrius iii. 32: ὁ Ἀναστάσιος δόξαν μανιχαϊκῆς (νομίσεως) παρὰ τοῖς
πολλοῖς εἶχεν.   Theodor. lect. ii. 6: Μανιχαῖοι καὶ Ἀρειανοὶ ἔχαιρον Ἀνα-
στασίῳ.   Μανιχαῖοι μὲν, ὡς τῆς μητρὸς αὐτοῦ ζηλούσης αὐτοὺς (Symmachi
P. ep. ad Orientales ap. Mansi viii. p. 220: Declinemus sacrilegum
Eutychetis errorem cum Manichaea malitia congruentem), Ἀρειανοὶ δὲ
ὡς Κλέαρχον τὸν θεῖον πρὸς μητρὸς Ἀναστασίου ὁμόδοξον ἔχοντες.   Victor
Episc. Tununensis (about 555) in his Chronicon (in Canisii lectt. ant.
ed. Basnage, vol. i. p. 326): Messala V. C. Cos. Constantinopoli, jubente Anastasio Imperatore, sancta Evangelia, tamquam ab idiotis Evan-
gelistis composita, reprehenduntur et emendantur.   (P. Wesselingii
diss. de Evangeliis jussu Imp. Anast. non emendatis append. to his diatribe de Judaeorum Archontibus. Traj. ad Rh. 1738.)   On the contrary,
Liberati breviarium c. 19: Hoc tempore Macedonius Constantinopolitanus episcopus ab imperatore Anastasio dicitur expulsus, tamquam
evangelia falsasset, et maxime illud Apostoli dictum: qui apparuit in
carne, justificatus est in spiritu (1 Tim. iii. 16.)   Hunc enim immutasse,
ubi habet ΟΣ id est Qui, monosyllabum graecum, littera mutata Ο in Θ,
vertisse et fecisse ΘΣ, id est Deus, ut esset: Deus apparuit per carnem.
Tamquam Nestorianus ergo culpatus expellitur per Severum monachum.
—P. E. Jablonski exercit. de morte tragica Anastasii Dicori, Francof.
ad Viadr. 1744.   (Opusc. ed. te Water. T. iv. p. 353.)   Among the
Monophysites Zeno and Anastasius were reckoned orthodox.   See
Zachariae hist. ecci. in Maji coll. x. i. 366.

[19] To the fragments of his works which were known before (a list is
given in Cave i. 500), many new ones have been added, which are scattered through A. Maji scriptt. vett. nova coll. vii. i.   Fragments of his

Julian, bishop of Halicarnassus ; and the greater number of them fled to Alexandria ; for in Egypt, Monophysitism was so generally prevalent, that Justin durst not undertake any thing against it there.

This very congregating of so many bishops in Alexandria now led to internal divisions among the Monophysites themselves.[20] From the controversy between Severus and Julian respecting the question whether the body of Christ was subject to that corruption, $τ\tilde{η}\ φθορ\tilde{α}$, and was therefore $φθαρτόν\ τι$, or not,[21] which has come upon human bodies by the fall, arose the first and most obstinate dispute, that of the *Severians* (Theodosiani,[22] $Φθαρτολάτραι$) and the *Julianists*[23] (Gajanitae, $'Αφθαρτοδοκῆται$, Phantasiastae). Soon after there sprang from the former the $'Αγνοηταί$, or Themistiani.[24] On the other hand, the Julianists were divided into the $'Ακτιστηταί$ and $Κτιστολάτραι$. About 530, the celebrated *John Philoponus*[25] promulgated his errors respecting the Tri-

comm. in Lucam and in Acta Apost. are given in Maji classicorum auctorum x. 408. Fragments and a Confession of Faith, addressed to the Emperor Anastasius, out of the Arabic in the Spicilegium romanum T. iii. (Romae 1840. 8.) p. 722. Liber ad Julian. Episc. Halicarn. out of the Syriac in the Spicileg. rom. x. 169.

[20] Concerning them as a peculiar source : Timotheus presb. de variis haereticis ac diversis eorum in Ecclesiam recipiendi formulis, in Cotelerii monum. Eccles. gr. iii. 377. Comp. Walch's Ketzerhist viii. 520. Baur's Dreieinigkeit ii. 73.

[21] Comp. my comm. qua Monophysitarum variae de Christi persona opiniones illustrantur. Partic. ii. Gotting. 1835. 38. 4.

[22] A fragment of Theodosius, patriarch of Alexandria, which extends over this disputed question, is given out of the Arabic in the Spicileg. rom. iii. 711. Among other things it is written, Nisi Christus—in sua carne eas qualitates habuisset, quae sine peccato consistere possunt, scil. nisi ejus caro par nostrae esset, tum quod ad essentiam attinet, tum etiam quod ad patiendum ;—nunquam stimulus mortis destructus fuisset i. e. peccatum. Comp. especially Severi liber ad Julianum, quo demonstrat, quid sacri libri doctoresque Ecclesiae docuerint circa incorruptibilitatem corporis J. Chr. out of the Syriac in the Spicileg. rom. x. 169.

[23] Juliani anathematismi x. in Syriac in J. S. Assemani biblioth. Vatic. codd. mss. catal. P. I. T. iii. (Romae 1759. fol.) p. 223. in Lat. in my Comm. ii. 5.

[24] Fragments of Themistius in Maji coll. vii. 1, 73. In order to perceive his view, the following sentences are of importance : Μία τοῦ Λόγου θεανδρικὴ ἐνέργειά τε καὶ γνῶσις. But τὰ μὲν θεῖκῶς, τὰ δὲ ἀνθρωπίνως ὁ αὐτὸς ἐνήργησεν (consequently also ἐγίνωσκεν.)

[25] That a great part of his life does not belong to the seventh cen-

nity[26] and the resurrection,[27] drawn from the Aristotelian philosophy, among the Monophysites (Philoponiaci, Tritheitae; on the other side, Condobauditae and Cononitae) in opposition to whom *Damian*, patriarch of Alexandria, appeared to fall into the Sabellian error (Damianitae). At the same time, the doctrine of *Stephanus Niobes*, who removed all distinction of natures in Christ after their union, was condemned by the other Monophysites (Niobitae).[28]

§ 111.

CONTROVERSIES UNDER JUSTINIAN I.

Justinian I. (527–565) a zealous adherent of the council of Chalcedon[1] endeavoured to restore unity and order both in state

tury, as has been usually assumed, is shown by Ritter Gesch. d. christl. Philos. ii. 501, and confirmed by a letter which he wrote, when an old man, to the Emperor Justinian. Seè Spicileg. rom. iii. 739.—His writings were: In Hexaëmeron, disp. de Paschate (ed. B. Corderius. Vienn. 1630. 4. more correctly printed in Gallandius xii. 471), de aeternitate mundi contra Proclum lib. (Venet. 1535), Commentaries on Aristotle.— Among other lost books was one adv. Synod. Chalcedonensem (Photius cod. 55.) Fabricii bibl. gr. vol. ix. p. 359 ss. (ed. Harles vol. x. p. 639 ss.

[26] Leontius de sectis act. v. § 6, makes Philoponus say to the church : εἰ δύο λέγετε φύσεις ἐν τῷ Χριστῷ, ἀνάγκη ὑμᾶς καὶ δύο ὑποστάσεις εἰπεῖν.— ναὶ ταὐτό ἐστι φύσις καὶ ὑπόστασις. Εἶτα πάλιν ἡ ἐκκλησία· εἰ ταὐτό ἐστι φύσις καὶ ὑπόστασις, οὐκοῦν λέγομεν καὶ τῆς ἁγίας τριάδος τρεῖς φύσεις, ἐπειδὴ ὁμολογουμένως τρεῖς ὑποστάσεις ἔχει.—Ἀπεκρίνατο ὁ Φιλόπονος· ὅτι καὶ ἔστω τρεῖς φύσεις λέγειν ἡμᾶς ἐπὶ τῆς ἁγίας τριάδος. Ἔλεγε δὲ ταῦτα λαβὼν τὴν ἀφορμὴν ἀπὸ τῶν Ἀριστοτελικῶν ὁ γὰρ Ἀριστοτέλης φησὶν, ὅτι εἰσὶ τῶν ἀτόμων καὶ μερικαὶ οὐσίαι, καὶ μία κοινή· οὕτως οὖν καὶ ὁ Φιλόπονος ἔλεγεν, ὅτι εἰσὶ τρεῖς μερικαὶ οὐσίαι ἐπὶ τῆς ἁγίας τριάδος, καὶ ἔστι μία κοινή. Comp. the important fragments out of Philoponi dial. Διαιτητὴς ap. Joh. Damascenus de haeresibus c. 83.—His book on the Trinity against John, patriarch of Constantinople (Photius cod. 75.) is lost. J. G. Scharfenberg de Joh. Philop. Tritheismi defensore diss. Lips. 1768. 4. Joh. Philoponus, eine dogmenhist. Erörterung von F. Trechsel in the theol. Studien u. Kritiken 1835. i. 95. Baur's Dreieigkeit ii. 13. Ritter ii. 512.

[27] Timotheus in Cotelerii monum. Eccl. gr. iii. 413. Philoponus's book περὶ ἀναστάσεως (Photius cod. 21.) is lost. Ritter ii. 511.

[28] Dionysius Patr. Antioch. in Assemani bibl. orient. ii. 72. Timotheus l. c. p. 397. 407 ss. 417 ss. Baur ii. 92.

[1] A new memorial of it is his λόγος δογματικὸς πρὸς τοὺς ἐν τῷ ἐνάτῳ τῆς Ἀλεξανδρέων μοναχούς, which Majus Scriptt. vett. nova coll. vii. i. 292, has published.

and church by means of laws ; for which purpose he tried to bring
back the Monophysites in particular, into the church. These
endeavours were turned to advantage by a secret Monophysite
court party, at whose head stood his spouse, *Theodora*,[2] who exercised great influence over him, and who, in the hope of bringing
the Catholic Church, step by step, to Monophysitism, persuaded
the emperor that the Monophysites took offence simply at points
in the Catholic Church, which could be removed without a violation of orthodoxy. But since the dominant church had also its
representatives at court, the emperor was led sometimes by the
one party, sometimes by the other, to enact regulations, whose
natural consequence was to increase rather than remove the causes
of dispute.

The conferences between Catholic and Monophysite bishops,
which Justinian[3] caused to be held, were, on the whole, fruitless.
The original Monophysite formula—"God was crucified"—which
had been approved of by many, even among the Catholics in the
East ($\theta\epsilon o\pi a\sigma\chi\hat{\iota}\tau a\iota$),[4] but which some Scythian monks under Justin I. had in vain attempted to introduce both at Rome and Con-
stantinople (519–521),[5] was declared orthodox by Justinian (533),

---

[2] Respecting her see Procopii hist. arcana c. 9.
[3] The protocol of the one A. D. 531 : collatio Catholicorum cum Severianis ap. Mansi viii. 817.—Johannes Episc. Asiae speaks of several
in Assemani bibl. orient. ii. 89.
[4] See Walch's Ketzerhist. vii. 261. 311 ff.
[5] Walch vii. 262. Under Anastasius the addition in the Trishagion
(see § 110, not. 12) was also introduced at Constantinople, (see Zachariae hist. eccl. ap. Assemani bibl. or. ii. 59, and in Maji nova coll. x.
375, comp. Dioscuri Diac. ep. ad Hormisdam ap. Mansi viii. 480.) Its
abrogation during the reaction under Justin doubtless occasioned the
monks to defend the formula. Hormisdae Ep. Rom. ep. ad Possessorem Episc. Afric. Constantinopoli exulantem (ap. Mansi viii. 498) :
Ubi non variae tentationis aculei ? Quales per hunc fere jugem annum
quorundam Scytharum, qui monachos prae se ferebant specie non veritate, professione non opere, subtili tectas calliditate versutias, et sub
religionis obtentu famulantia odiis suis venena pertulimus.—Nunquam
apud eos caritas novo commendata praecepto, nunquam pax dominico
relicta discessu : una pertinacis cura propositi, rationi velle imperare,
non credere : contemtores auctoritatum veterum, novarum cupidi qua-
estionum ; solam putantes scientiae rectam viam, qualibet concepta
facilitate sententiam : eousque tumoris elati, ut [ad] arbitrium suum
utriusque orbis putent inclinandum esse judicium etc. The answer of
one of the Scythian monks to this, Joh. Maxentii ad epist. Hormisdae

with the evident purpose of conciliating the Monophysites.[6] This
step, however, was without success. In Egypt the Monophysites

responsio (Bibl. PP. Lugdun. T. ix. p. 539 ss.):—Non est facile credendum, hanc esse epistolam cujus fertur nomine titulata, praesertim
cum in ea nihil, ut diximus, rationis aut consequentiae reperiatur, sed
tota criminationibus obtrectationibusque vanis—videatur referta.—Quod
monachis responsum quaerentibus Romanus Episcopus dare omnino
distulerit, eosdemque post multa maris pericula, longique itineris vexationem, nec non etiam afflictionem prolixi temporis, quo eos apud se
detinuit, vacuos et sine ullo effectu ad has partes venire compulerit,
quod omnibus paene catholicis notum est, nec ipsi queunt haeretici de-
negare.—Nam et ipsi haeretici ad hoc ubique hanc ipsam, cui respon-
dimus, epistolam proferunt, quatenus et saepedictis monachis invidiam
concitent, et omnes quasi ex auctoritate ejusdem Romani Episcopi pro-
hibeantur Christum filium Dei unum confiteri ex trinitate. Sed quis
hanc sententiam catholicam non esse ausus est profiteri, quam universa
veneratur et amplectitur Dei ecclesia? Confidenter etenim dicere audeo,
non quod, si per epistolam, seu quod, si viva voce hic in praesenti positus idem Romanus prohiberet Episcopus Christum filium Dei unum
confiteri ex sancta et individua trinitate, nunquam eidem Dei ecclesia
acquiesceret, nunquam ut Episcopum catholicum veneraretur, sed omnino ut haereticum penitus execraretur. Quia quisquis hoc non confitetur non est dubium, quod Nestorianae perfidiae tenebris excaecatus,
quartum et extraneum a sancta et ineffabili Trinitate eum, qui pro nobis
crucem sustinuit, praedicare contendat.—An forte illos rationi credere,
non imperare judicat, qui Christum unam personam quidem ex Trinitate, non autem unum ex Trinitate esse fatentur? Sed hi qui hoc
dicunt, potius rationi velle imperare, non credere, penitus convincuntur,
etc. The Episcopi Africani in Sardinia exules also sided with the
Scythian monks: comp. their book composed by Fulgentius Ruspensis
lib. de incarnatione et gratia Dom. nostri J. C. ad Mon. Scyth. (Fulgentii opera ed. Paris. 1684. 4. p. 277 ss.) Fulgentius Ferrandus Diac.
Carthag. ad Anatolium Diac. Rom. Dionysius exiguus praef. ad versi-
onem epistolae Procli Archiep. Const. ad Armenos (ap. Mansi v. 419.)
    [6] The Monophysites accused the orthodox, before the emperor, of not
acknowledging dominum passum carne, nec unum eum esse de sancta
Trinitate, nec ejusdem esse personae tam miracula quam passiones (cf.
collatio Cathol. cum Sever. ap. Mansi viii. 832.) The Acoemetae did
really deny esse confitendum, b. Mariam vere et proprie Dei genetri-
cem; et unum de Trinitate incarnatum et carne passum (Liberatas c.
20.) evidently misled by their adherence to Rome (Sam. Basnage annal.
politico-eccles. iii. 701.) Justiniani lex A. D. 533. (Cod. i. i. 6.)—Unius
ac ejusdem passiones et miracula, quae sponte pertulit in carne, agnoscentes. Non enim alium Deum Verbum, et alium Christum novimus,
sed unum et eundem.—Mânsit enim Trinitas et post incarnatum unum
ex Trinitate Dei verbum: neque enim quartae personae adjectionem
admittit sancta Trinitas.—Anathematizamus—Nestorium anthropola-
tram, et qui eadem cum ipso sentiunt—qui negant nec confitentur Dominum nostrum J. C. filium Dei et Deum nostrum incarnatum et homi-

continued to be the prevailing party, though Justinian (536) again appointed a Catholic patriarch of Alexandria, *Paul*. But on the other hand, the secret endeavours of Theodora to spread Monophysitism in Rome and Constantinople were equally fruitless. *Anthimus*, who had been promoted to the see of Constantinople by her (535), was soon after (536) deposed for being a Monophysite.[7] *Vigilius*, elevated to the see of Rome, with the secret understanding that he was to declare in favour of Monophysite doctrines (538),[8] soon found it expedient to break through his agreement.

nem factum et crucifixum unum esse ex sancta et consubstantiali Trinitate.—Epist. Joannis Ep. Romae ad Justin. (ibid. L. 8. et. ap. Mansi viii. 797): comperimus, quod fidelibus populis proposuistis Edictum amore fidei pro submovenda haereticorum intentione, secundum apostolicam doctrinam, fratrum et Coëpiscoporum nostrorum interveniente consensu. Quod, quia apostolicae doctrinae convenit, nostra auctoritate confirmamus. The formula, however, was still suspected in the West of being Monophysite, and Bishop Cyprian of Toulon (about 550) was obliged to defend himself against Bishop Maximus of Geneva, quod beatitudo Vestra imperitiam nostram judicat esse culpandam, eo quod Deum hominem passum dixerim (the document is communicated by Schmidt in Vater's kirchenhist. Archive für 1826. S. 307.) The addition to the Trishagion (§ 110, not. 12) continued to be used by the Catholics in Syria (see Ephraem. Patr. Antioch. about 530 apud Photius cod. 228. Assemani bibl. orient. i. 518), till it was rejected by the Conc. Quinisextum can. 81. After that time it was retained only by the Monophysites and Monothelites (Walch's Ketzerhist. ix. 480.) Among the Catholics the idea arose that a quaternity, instead of a Trinity, was introduced by it. See Jo. Damasc. de fide orthod. iii. 10. See Royaards in the Nederlandsch Archief voor kerkel. Geschiedenis ii. 263. (1842.)

[7] Acta Syn. Constantinop. ann. 536 ap. Mansi viii. 873 ss.

[8] Liberatus c. 22. In him and in Victoris Tunun. Chronic. (ap. Canisius-Basnage i. 330) is found the epist. Vigilii to the Monophysite bishops, Theodosius, Anthimus, and Severus, where we read among other things: me eam fidem, quam tenetis, Deo adjuvante et tenuisse et tenere significo.—Oportet ergo, ut haec, quae vobis scribo, nullus agnoscat, sed magis tanquam suspectum me sapientia vestra ante alios existimet habere, ut facilius possim haec, quae coepi, operari et perficere. In the Confession of Faith appended to it in Liberatus: Non duas Christum confitemur naturas, sed ex duabus naturis compositum unum filium, unum Christum, unum Dominum. Qui dicit in Christo duas formas, unaquaque agente cum alterius communione, et non confitetur unam personam, unam essentiam, anathema. Qui dicit: quia hoc quidem miracula faciebat, hoc vero passionibus succumbebat (Leo § 89. not: 7): et non confitetur miracula et passiones unius ejusdemque, quas

G 2

In the meantime these theological proceedings were increased by the revival of *the Origenist controversy.* Origen had, by degrees, obtained many devoted admirers among the monks in Palestine. One of them, *Theodorus Ascidas,* bishop of Caesarea in Cappadocia, who had come to court, and gained the confidence of the emperor, protected the Origenists in propagating their doctrines in Palestine, sometimes by violent means.[9] But at last the opposite party prevailed, by the aid of *Mennas,* patriarch of Constantinople, and obtained from Justinian a condemnation of the Origenist errors (about 544).[10] It was more with the design of diverting attention from Origenism than of being revenged on his orthodox opponents, that Theodorus now persuaded the emperor[11] that the reconciliation of the Monophysites with the or-

sponte sua sustinuit, carne nobis consubstantiali, anathema sit. Qui dicit, quod Christus velut homo misericordia dignatus est, et non dicit ipsum Deum Verbum et crucifixum esse, ut misereatur nobis, anathema sit. Anathematizamus ergo Paulum Samosatenum, Dioscorum (leg. Diodorum), Theodorum, Theodoritum et omnes, qui eorum statuta coluerint, vel colunt. Soon after this, however, he proved his orthodoxy to the Emperor and the Patriarch of Constantinople. Epist. ad Justinian. ap. Mansi ix. 35, ad Mennam ibid. p. 38.

[9] Chief authority, vita s. Sabae by Cyrillus Scythopolitanus (in Coterlerii monum. Eccles. graec. T. iii.) from cap. 36 . cf. Walch de Sabaitis (novi comm. Soc. Gotting. vii. 1.)

[10] In the epist. ad Mennam Archiepisc Const. adv. impium Origenem ap. Mansi ix. 487. Here, p. 524, Mennas is ordered, συναγαγεῖν ἅπαντας τοὺς ἐνδημοῦντας κατὰ ταύτην τὴν βασιλίδα πόλιν ὁσιωτάτους ἐπισκόπους, καὶ τοὺς—μοναστηρίων ἡγουμένους, καὶ παρασκευάσαι πάντας—τὸν—'Ωριγένην—ἀναθεματίσαι, and from this σύνοδος ἐνδημοῦσα proceeded, without doubt, the 15 canons against Origen (prim. ed. Petr. Lambecius in comment. bibl. August. Vindob. viii. 435, ap. Mansi ix. 395), though their title favours the fifth oecumenical council. See M. Lequien Oriens christianus iii. 210. Walch's Ketzerhist. vii. 660.

[11] The Origenist Domitian, bishop of Ancyra, himself admitted in libello ad Vigilium (in Facundi Episc. Hermianensis pro defens. trium capitul. lib. iv. c. 4): prosiluerunt ad anathematizandos sanctissimos et gloriosissimos doctores sub occasione eorum, quae de praeexistentia et restitutione mota sunt, dogmatum, sub specie quidem Origenis, omnes autem, qui ante eum et post eum fuerunt, sanctos anathematizantes. Hi vero, qui proposuerant hujusmodi dogma defendere, id implere nullo modo voluerunt: sed talem relinquentes conflictum, conversi sunt, ut moverent adversus Theodorum, qui fuit Mopsvestenus episcopus, et moliri coeperunt, quatenus anathematizaretur et ille, ad abolitionem, ut putabant, eorum, quae contra Origenem mota constiterant. Liberatus c. 24 : Theodorus Caesareae Cappadociae episcopus, dilectus et famili-

thodox would be much facilitated by a public condemnation not only of *Theodore of Mopsuestia*,[12] who had been long in somewhat evil repute among the orthodox, but also of *Theodoret's* writings against Cyril and the letter of *Ibas* to Maris, though the two latter had been expressly pronounced orthodox by the council of Chalcedon.[13] Justinian accordingly condemned, in an edict (544), the three chapters (τρία κεθάλαια, tria capitula).[14] In the East they very easily coincided with this measure; but in the West it was so much the more obstinately resisted.[15] On this account Justinian summoned *Vigilius*, bishop of Rome, to Constantinople (546), and prevailed on him there to condemn, in like manner, the three chapters (518)[16] in a document called

aris principum,—cognoscens Origenem fuisse damnatum, dolore damnationis ejus, ad ecclesia conturbationem, damnationem molitus est in Theodorum Mopsvestenum, eo quod Theodorus multa opuscula edidisset contra Origenem, exosusque et accusabilis haberetur ab Origenistis.

[12] The enmity of the abbot Sabba to him Vita Sabae (see note 9), c. 72, 74.—A Synod convened for the purpose at Mopsuestia by the imperial command (550), came to the conclusion, Theodorum veterem, qui per istam civitatem fuit episcopus, in antiquis temporibus extra praedicationem divini mysterii fuisse, et sacris diptychis ejectum esse: et—in illius vocabulum, inscriptum esse Cyrillum sanctae memoriae (see Mansi ix. 286.) The testimonies of the ancients against Theodorus, collected in the collatio v. of the fifth oecumenical council, must be very cautiously received; for instance, Theodore's name, in the two laws of Theodosius II. against Nestorius (p. 249 ss.) is a later addition.

[13] Theodoret in the actio viii. (ap. Mansi vii. 189.) Ibas after a long investigation, act. ix. and x. after which the Roman ambassadors expressly declare: ἀναγνωσθείσης τῆς ἐπιστολῆς αὐτοῦ (that very epist. ad Marin.) ἐπέγνωμεν αὐτὸν ὑπάρχειν ὀρθόδοξον.

[14] *i. e.* three points, articles: not as J. H. Mücke de tribus capitulis concilii Chalced. Lips. 1766. 4. p. 6. thinks, the three decrees of the council of Chalcedon, for there was no such decree respecting Theodore. The first edict of Justinian is lost, except fragments in Facundus ii. 3, iv. 4. See Norisii diss. de synodo quinta c. 3. Walch's Ketzerhist. viii. 150.

[15] Their leading reasons are given by Fulgentius Ferrandus epist. vi. ad Pelagium et Anatolium at the conclusion of the following sentences: Ut concilii Chalcedonensis, vel similium nulla retractatio placeat, sed quae semel statuta sunt, intemerata serventur. Ut pro mortuis fratribus nulla generentur inter vivos scandala. Ut nullus libro suo per subscriptiones plurimorum dare velit auctoritatem, quam solis canonicis libris ecclesia catholica detulit.

[16] The particulars are related by Facundus lib. contra Mocianum scholast.—The Judicatum is no longer extant, except in a fragment in

judicatum. But Vigilius was soon induced to hesitate, by the decided opposition of the greater number of the Western bishops;[17] and he refused to adopt the emperor's second edict against the three chapters (551).[18]

Justinian now convened *the fifth oecumenical council at Constantinople* (553),[19] at which Vigilius not only refused to attend, but even defended the three chapters in the so-called *Constitutum*.[20] The Synod, therefore, broke off all Church communion with him,[21] and approved without qualification all the decrees of the emperor hitherto made respecting religion.[22] No farther

the Latin translation of the epist. Justin. ad Concilium oecum. v. (ap. Mansi ix. 181.)

[17] Victor Tunnun. in Chron. (l. c. p. 332): Post Consulatum Basilii V. C. anno ix. (549). Illyriciana Synodus in defensione iii. capitum Justiniano Aug. scribit, et Benenatum, primae Justinianae Civitatis episcopum, obtrectatorem eorundem iii. capitum condemnat.—Post Cons. Bas. V. C. anno x. (550) Africani Antistites Vigilium Romanum Episcopum, damnatorem iii. Capitulorum synodaliter a catholica communione, reservato ei poenitentiae loco, recludunt, et pro defensione memoratorum iii. Capitulorum literas satis idoneas Justiniano Principi per Olympium Magistrianum mittunt. Also defences of the three chapters by Facundus and Rusticus.

[18] Or the ὁμολογία πίστεως Ἰουστ. Αὐτοκράτορος, preserved in the Chronic. Alexandr. ed. du Fresne p. 344 ss. ap. Mansi ix. 537.—Concerning the conduct of Vigilius see especially epistola legatis Francorum, qui Constantinopolim proficiscebantur, ab Italiae clericis directa A. D. 551. ap Mansi xi. 151.

[19] Acta in Mansi ix. 157 ss. Natalis Alexander hist. eccl. saec. vi. T. v. p. 502 ss. J. Basnage histoire de l'église liv. x. c. 6. Norisii diss. de synodo v. (Patav. 1673. opp. ed. Ballerini, Veron. 1729. T. i. p. 437.) Against him Garnerii diss. de syn. v. (first appended to his Liberatus. Paris. 1675. improved in the auctar. opp. Theodoreti p. 493. also in Theodoret. ed. Schultze v. 512.) On the other side the Ballerini: defensio diss. Noris. adv. Garn. (in Noris. opp. iv. 985.)

[20] Ap. Mansi ix. 61-106.

[21] Justinian declared, with reference to Vigilius, to the synod in a rescript (in the Acta of the Synod collatio vii. ap. Mansi ix. 367.): ipse semetipsum alienum catholicae ecclesiae fecit, defendens praedictorum capitulorum impietatem, separans autem semetipsum a vestra communione. His igitur ab eo factis, alienum Christianis judicavimus nomen ipsius sacris diptychis recitari [leg. resecari], ne eo modo inveniamur Nestorii et Theodori impietati communicantes.—Unitatem vero ad apostolicam sedem et nos servamus, et certum est quod et vos custodietis. Without sufficient reason the Ballerini, in their defensio (Norisii opp. iv. 1035.) declare this writing to be spurious.

[22] The 13 anathemas appended to Justinian's ὁμολογία (ap. Mansi

notice was taken of the Origenists,[23] a circumstance which we shall not be far from the truth in attributing to the artful management of Theodorus Ascidas, who was the leading person at the council. Vigilius at length (554) assented to the decisions of the council,[24] to which step he was doubtless influenced chiefly by the success of the imperial arms in Italy under Narses. Immediately after he set out on his return to Rome, but died by the way in Syracuse (555). His successor, *Pelagius* I., acknowledged at once the authority of the fifth Synod,[25] which led to a tedious schism between several Western Churches and Rome. Among the writers who, during this controversy, opposed the condemnation of the three chapters, the most distinguished are *Fulgentius Ferrandus*, deacon in Carthage, († before 551);[26]

ix. 557.) are for the most part verbally repeated in the 14 anathemas of the Synod (l. c. p. 376 ss.) So also the 6th imperial anathema in the 10th of the council: Εἴ τις οὐχ ὁμολογεῖ τὸν ἐσταυρωμένον σαρκὶ κύριον ἡμῶν Ἰησοῦν Χριστὸν εἶναι θεὸν ἀληθινὸν καὶ κύριον τῆς δόξης, καὶ ἕνα τῆς ἁγίας τριάδος, ὁ τοιοῦτος ἀνάθεμα ἔστω.

[23] Though as early as Cyrillus Scythopolit. in vita Sabae c. 90. and Evagrius iv. 37. the formal condemnation of Origen is attributed to the 5th council by confounding it with the synod under Mennas (see note 10.), as was afterwards generally believed. See on the other side Walch's Ketzerh. viii. 280.

[24] Vigilii epist. ad Eutychium Archiepisc. Constant. prim. ed. P. de Marca in diss. de decreto Papae Vigilii pro confirmatione v. Syn. (in ejusd. dissert. iii. a Baluzio editis. l'aris. 1669. 8. and appended to Boehmer's edition of the concord. Sac. et Imp. p. 227.) ap. Mansi ix. 413 ss. The remarkable commencement: Τά σκάνδαλα, ἅπερ ὁ τοῦ ἀνθρωπίνου γένους ἐχθρὸς τῷ σύμπαντι κόσμῳ διήγειρεν, οὐδεὶς ἀγνοεῖ, οὕτως ὡς τὸ οἰκεῖον βούλημα πρὸς τὸ ἀνατρέψαι τὴν τοῦ θεοῦ ἐκκλησίαν—πληρῶσαι οἵῳ δήποτε τρόπῳ σπουδάζοντα, οὐ μόνον ἐξ ὀνόματος ἰδίου, ἀλλὰ καὶ ἐξ ἡμετέρου καὶ ἐξ ἄλλων, διὰ τοῦ λέγειν ἢ τοῦ γράφειν, διάφορα πλάσασθαι πεποίηκεν· εἰς τοσοῦτον, ὅτι ἡμᾶς μετὰ τῶν ἀδελφῶν καὶ συνεπισκόπων ἡμῶν – ἐν τῇ τῶν τεσσάρων συνόδων μιᾷ καὶ τῇ αὐτῇ πίστει ἀμώμως διατελοῦντας, τοῖς σοφίσμασι τῆς οὕτω πονηρᾶς πανουργίας, αὐτῶν ἐπεχείρισε διελεῖν.—'Αλλ' ἐπειδὴ Χριστὸς ὁ θεὸς ἡμῶν—πάσης συγχύσεως τῆς ἡμῶν διανοίας ἀποκινηθείσης, πρὸς εἰρήνην τὴν οἰκουμένην ἀνεκαλέσατο κ. τ. λ.

[25] Victor Tunnun. in Chron. Post consulatum Basilii V. C. anno xviii. Pelagius Romanus archidiaconus, trium praefatorum defensor Capitulorum, Justiniaui principis persuasione de exsilio redit: et condemnans ea, quae dudum constantissime defendebat Romanae Ecclesiae Episcopus a praevaricatoribus ordinatur.

[26] Opp. ed. Fr. Chiffletius. Divione 1649. Bibl. PP. Lugd. T. ix. Bibl. PP. Gallandii xi. 329. Among his letters the most remarkable are those in answer to questions addressed to him from Rome · ad Ana-

Facundus, bishop of Hermiane († about 570) ;[27] *Rusticus*, deacon in Rome ;[28] *Liberatus*, deacon in Carthage (about 553) ;[29] *Victor*, bishop of Tunnuna († after 565).[30]

Shortly before his death (564), Justinian was misled by his excessive desire to bring back the Monophysites to the Church, so as to elevate to the rank of orthodoxy the doctrine of the *Apthartodocetae*. *Eutychius*, patriarch of Constantinople, was deposed for his opposition to this measure ; and the like fate awaited *Anastasius Sinaita*, patriarch of Antioch ; when the death of the emperor (565) became the death likewise of the new doctrine.[31]

§ 112.

DEVELOPMENT OF MONOPHYSITE CHURCHISM.

The efforts of Justinian to reunite the Monophysites with the Catholic Church were so far from successful, that the sect was always becoming more distinct under his reign, and internally established. The later dominion of the Arabians, by which the Monophysites were especially favoured, rendered the breach incurable.

Only a small part of the Egyptians followed the Catholic patriarch of Alexandria, who had been appointed by Justinian. The

tolium, quod unus de Trinitate passus dici possit, et ad Pelagium et Anatolium [546] pro tribus capitulis.

[27] By whom is the chief work in favour of the three chapters pro defensione iii. Capitulorum libb. xii. (about 548), and contra Mocianum scholasticum (opp. prim. ed. Jac. Sirmond. Paris. 1629. 8. emendatius in bibl. PP. Gallandii xi. 665.)

[28] Lib. adv. Acephalos ad Sebastianum (in bibl. PP. ap. Gallandius xii. 37.)

[29] Breviarium causae Nestorianorum et Eutychianorum (ed. Jo. Garnerius. Paris. 1675. 8. Ap. Mansi ix. 659. and ap. Gallandius xii. 119.)

[30] Chronicon ab orbe condito, only the second part is extant from 444 to 565 (ap. Canisius-Basnage i. 321. plur. in locis restitut. ap. Gallandius xii. 221.)

[31] Evagrius iv. 38-40. Eutychii vita, composed by one of his adherents Eustathius or Eustratius (in the Greek original Acta SS. April. Tom. i. append. p. 59.), has been dressed out with praises even to the miraculous. Walch's Ketzerhist. viii. 578. According to Eustathius, Justinian was misled by Origenists.

more numerous Monophysites chose another patriarch; and thus they continued till the present day under the name of *Copts*.[1] The *Æthiopian Church* was always in connexion with them.[2]

The Christians in *Armenia*[3] also attached themselves ecclesiastically in the fifth century to the Greek emperors, by whose aid they held out against the Persians, and accordingly agreed to the Henoticon of Zeno.[4] After Monophysitism had obtained acceptance among them, in consequence of these proceedings, they remained all the more faithful to it from the time of Justin I., since the Persians favoured all parties separated from the Greek Church. In vain did Kyrion, patriarch of Georgia, endeavour to procure an approval of the council of Chalcedon in Armenia also;[5] a Synod at *Twin* (595)[6] declared itself decidedly in favour of

[1] Taki-eddini Makrizii (a lawyer in Cairo † 1441) hist. Coptorum Christianorum in Aegypto, arab. et lat. ed. H. J. Wetzer. Solisbaci 1828. 8. (A complete and more accurate edition, with a translation, may be shortly expected from Prof. Wüstenfeld.) Eusebii Renaudot historia patriarcharum Alexandrinorum Jacobitarum. Paris. 1713. 4. Michael Le Quien Oriens christianus in iv. patriarchatus digestus, quo exhibentur ecclesiae patriarchae caeterique praesules totius Orientis. (Paris. 1740. 3. T. fol.) T. ii. p. 357.

[2] Jobi Ludolf historia Aethiopica. Francof. ad M. 1681. Commentarius ad hist. Aeth. 1691. and appendix ad hist. Aeth. 1693. All in fol.— Maturin Veyssier la Croze histoire du christianisme d'Ethiopie et d'Arménie. à la Haye 1739. 8.

[3] The older literature respecting Armenian church history in Clem. Galani hist. Armena eccl. et polit. Colon. 1686. Francof. et Lips. 1701. 8. (a reprint of vol. i. of the Conciliatio eccl. Armenae cum Romana, Romae 1651. 3 voll. fol.), la Croze, le Quien l. c. is almost useless, since the Mechitarists, united Armenian monks, have begun to publish on the island of S. Lazzaro at Venice, the numerous Armenian historians, and to prepare an Armenian history. Their principal work is the history of Armenia by P. Michael Tschamtschean († 1823) in the Armenian language, 3 volumes 4to. 1784. With it are connected the works of Saint-Martin and C. F. Neumann. Comp. Mémoires sur l'Arménie par J. Saint-Martin. Tomes ii. Paris 1828. 29. Histoire d'Arménie par le patriarche Jean VI., dit Jean Catholicos († 925) trad. de l'arménien en français par J. Saint-Martin. Paris 1841. 8. C. F. Neumann's Gesch. d. armen. Literatur. Leipzig 1836. 8.

[4] In the year 491, at a synod at Edschmiadsin, the Heneticon was adopted, and the decress of the council of Chalcedon rejected, Tschamtschean ii. 225. Mémoires sur l'Arménie par J. Saint-Martin i. 329.

[5] See respecting him Neumann's Gesch. d. arm. Lit. S. 94.

[6] Twin (also written Thevin or Thovin), in the provine of Ararat, at that time the residence of the Armenian kings and patriarchs. Galanus

Monophysitism; and thus the *Armenian Church* still continues, to the present day, as a sect separated from the other Monophysite Churches,[7] merely by peculiar customs.

In *Syria* and *Mesopotamia* the Monophysites had nearly become extinct by persecution and want of a clergy, when *Jacob Baradai*, or Zanzalus, by unwearied diligence (from 541 to 578), set in order their churches, and supplied them with pastors. From him the Syrian Monophysites received the name *Jacobites*.[8]

§ 113.

CONTROVERSY BETWEEN AUGUSTINISM AND SEMIPELAGIANISM.

G. F. Wiggers pragm. Darstellung des Augustinismus und Pelagianismus. Th. 2. (Hamburg 1833.) S. 224.

The Western Churches were but little disturbed by the Monophysite controversy. On the contrary, the struggle between Augustinism and Semipelagianism continued especially in Gaul (comp. § 87, note 47, and following) though without leading to actual schisms in the Church. At first the Semipelagians had so much the advantage that their most distinguished defender *Faustus*, formerly abbot of the monastery at Lerins, afterwards *bishop of Reji (Reiz)* († after 490), compelled a certain presbyter, *Lucidus*, to retract the Augustinian doctrines,[1] and his Semipelagian creed was generally approved at the councils of *Arelate* and *Lyons* (475).[2] Hence *Arnobius* the younger,[3] author of the

hist. arm. c. 10. Le Quien i. 1360. and other older writers, place this synod earlier. Comp. however, Aug. Majus in the spicilegium Rom. x. ii. 450. annotation 3.

[7] Comp. Eccl. Armeniacae canones selecti in Ang. Maji vett. scriptt. nova coll. x. ii. 269. One of the most remarkable of these customs is that the Armenians use unmixed wine at the Lord's Supper, p. 303, and keep the day of Epiphany as the festival of the birth and baptism of Jesus, p. 307.

[8] Assemani bibl. orient. T. ii.—Le Quien. l. c. T. ii.

[1] Fausti Rejensis epist. ad Lucidum, and Lucidi errorem emendantis libellus ad Episcopos ap. Mansi vii. 1008. Comp. Walch's Ketzerhist. v. 90.

[2] His chief work de gratia Dei et hummanae mentis libero arbitrio libb. 2. (Bibl. Patr. Lugd. viii. 525.) was subscribed there. His creed is given by Wiggers ii. 235.

[3] See his comm. in Psalmos (bibl. PP. Lugd. viii. 238.) Wiggers ii. 348.

Praedestinatus[4] (both about 460), and *Gennadius*, presbyter at Massilia († after 495),[5] express these sentiments without disguise. They had even penetrated to Upper Italy ; and *Magnus Felix Ennodius*, bishop of Ticinum, from 511–521, professed them.[6]

Augustinism was hated in Gaul, especially on account of the doctrine of an unconditional decree of God, which, in the form it had there assumed, distorted by the consequences drawn from it by its obstinate defenders on the one hand, and still more by its too eager opponents on the other,[7] was completely and necessarily fatal to all morality.[8] Some, indeed, did not hesitate to attribute

[4] Prim. ed. J. Sirmond. Paris. 1643. 8. (recus. in bibl. PP. Lugd. xxvii. 543. Bibl. PP. Gallandii x. 357.) The first book contains a short sketch of 90 heresies (the 90th that of the Praedestinatorum), the second a liber sub nomine Augustini confictus, in which the Augustinian doctrine was presented with great exaggeration (as it had been previously in the capitulis calumniantium, which Prosper refuted, see § 87. note 52. Wiggers ii. 184.), the third a refutation of this book. Walch v. 227. Wiggers ii. 329. Perhaps Arnobius was the author, as Sirmond and the Benedictines histoire littéraire de la France ii. 349. suppose. Comp. however Wiggers ii. 349.
[5] De scriptoribus ecclesiasticis, continuation of Jerome (in biblioth. eccl. J. A. Fabricii. Hamb. 1718) : de fide s. de dogmatibus ecclesiasticis liber ad Gelasium Papam (ed. Ehmenhorst. Hamburg. 1614. 4.) Wiggers ii. 351.
[6] cf. lib. ii. epist. 19. (see opera best in Sirmondi opp. T. i.) Wiggers ii. 356.
[7] Lucidus was forced to condemn the following propositions : quod praescientia Dei hominem violenter compellat ad mortem, vel quod cum Dei pereant voluntate, qui pereunt,—alios deputatos ad mortem, alios ad vitam praedestinatos. The Pseudo-Augustinus Praedestinatus lib. ii. says : Quem voluerit Deus sanctum esse, sanctus est, aliud non erit : quem praescierit esse iniquum, iniquus erit, aliud non erit. Praedestinatio enim Dei jam et numerum justorum, et numerum constituit peccatorum, et necesse erit constitutum terminum praeteriri non posse.— De Deo Apostolus dicit : Quos vocavit, hos praedestinavit (Rom. viii. 30.) Si praescientem et praedestinantem et vocantem in Apostolo legitis ; nobis ut quid impingitis crimen ob hoc, quod dicimus, praedestinasse Deum homines sive ad justitiam sive ad peccatum ?—Invictus enim in sua voluntate permanet Deus, cum homo adsidue superetur. Si ergo invictum confitemini Deum, confitemini et hoc, quia quod eos voluit ille, qui condidit, aliud esse non possunt. Unde colligimus apud animum, quia quos Deus semel praedestinavit ad vitam, etiamsi negligant, etiamsi peccent, etiamsi nolint, ad vitam perducentur inviti : quos autem praedestinavit ad mortem, etiamsi currant, etiamsi festinent, sine causa laborant. cf. § 87. note 31.
[8] Praefatio Praedestinati :—Quis hanc fidem habens sacerdotum

these errors directly to Augustine ;[9] but for the most part it was usual, in order not to tread too closely on the honoured man, to distinguish between himself and his adherents at that time,[10] that these last could be the more safely condemned as heretics under the name of *Predestinarians.*[11]

In Rome and Africa, on the other hand, the doctrines of Augustine were strictly followed.[12] Thus Gallic Semipelagianism was threatened with extinction from this quarter, and that the more readily, inasmuch as even in Gaul were many adherents of

benedictionibus caput inclinare desideret, et eorum sibi precibus et sacrificiis credat posse succurri? Si enim haec nec prodesse volentibus, nec obesse nolentibus incipiant credi, cessabunt omnia Dei sacerdotum studia, et universa monitorum adminicula vana videbuntur esse figmenta: atque ita unusquisque suis erit vitiis occupatus, ut criminum suorum delectationem Dei praedestinationem existimet, et ad bonum a malo transitum, nec per sacerdotum Dei (studia?), nec per conversionem suam, nec per legem dominicam se posse invenire confidat.

[9] Faustus only alludes to him (if Lucidus be not meant, as Wiggers ij. 232. assumes) de grat. Dei et hum. ment. lib. arb. i. 4 : si ergo unus ad vitam, alter ad perditionem, ut asserunt, deputatus est, sicut quidam Sanctorum dixit, non judicandi nascimur, sed judicati. Ibid. c. 11 : igitur dum liberi interemtor arbitrii in alterutram partem omnia ex praedestinatione statuta et definita esse pronunciat etc.—Gennadius de script. eccl. c. 38. speaking of Augustine : Quis tanto studio legat, quanto ille scripsit ? Unde et multa loquenti accidit, quod dixit per Salomonem Spir. S.: In multiloquio non effugies peccatum (Prov. x. 19.)—Error tamen illius sermone multo, ut dixi, contractus, lucta hostium exaggeratus, necdum haeresis quaestionem dedit.—Ennodius lib. ii. ep. 19. contradicts the doctrine that man has freedom only to do evil, and adds : Video, quo se toxica libycae pestis extendant: arenosus coluber non haec sola habet perniciosa, quae referat.

[10] So particularly Praedestinatus.   In the praef.: Silerem—si non etiam audacter sub Augustini nomine libros ederent.—Quis enim nesciat, Augustinum orthodoxum semper fuisse doctorem, et tam scribendo quam disputando omnibus haereticis obviasse ?

[11] Violent controversy in the 17th century on the question whether there ever was a particular sect of the Predestinarians, as the Jesuits (particularly J. Sirmond historia Praedestinatiana. Paris. 1648. in ej. opp. t. iv. and in Gallandii bibl. PP. x. 401.) and the older Lutherans asserted, while the Jansenists (especially G. Mauguin accurata historiae Praedestinatianae J. Sirmondi confutatio, in his vindiciis praedestinationis et gratiae p. 443 ss.), Dominicans, and Reformed, denied it. Modern impartial historians agree with the latter (comp. Semler in the historical introduction prefixed to Baumgarten's Polemik iii. 312.)—Comp. Sagitarii introd. in hist. eccl. i. 1148. Walch's Ketzerhist. v. 218.

[12] Wiggers ii. 365.

Augustine, and among them two distinguished bishops, *Avitus*, archbishop of Vienne (490–523), and *Caesarius*, bishop of Arles (502–542).[13] Those same Scythian monks who had raised so much disturbance by their efforts to introduce the formula, " one of the Trinity was crucified " (§ 111. note 5.), also renewed the struggle against Pelagianism, which seemed to them to be closely connected with Nestorianism, and against Semipelagianism.[14] After they had been banished from Rome, because Hormisdas had pronounced judgment too indefinitely on Faustus, they brought the question of the latter's orthodoxy before the African bishops living in Sardinia (523); in whose name *Fulgentius*, bishop of Ruspe († 533), now defended Augustine against the writings of Faustus.[15] In consequence of this, Semipelagianism was rejected in Gaul also, under the leadership of *Caesarius* at the synod of *Arausio* (Oranges, 529), and the Augustinian system adopted, though in a form essentially modified.[16] Thus also no teacher of Semipelagianism was condemned by name ;[17] and

[13] Alcimi Ecdicii Aviti opera (poems, letters, homilies) ed. J. Sirmond. Paris. 1643. (Bibl. PP. Lugd. ix. 560.) Caesarii opp. (especially homilies, many incorrectly attributed to him) in the bibl. PP. Lugd. viii. 819. 860. xxvii. 324. Wiggers ii. 368.

[14] Walch v. 117. Wiggers ii. 394.

[15] Epistola synodica Episc. Afric. in Sardinia exulum ad Jo. Maxentium etc. ap. Mansi viii. 591.—Fulgentii Ruspensis libb. iii. de veritate praedestinationis et gratia dei (his libb. vii. adv. Faustum are lost) together with his other works (libb. iii. ad Monimum—several writings against the Arians, and other doctrinal treatises) published. Paris 1684. 4. in bibl. PP. Lugd. ix. 16.

[16] The 25 capitula of the Synod, to which a sketch of the doctrine of grace, in the form of a Confession of Faith, is annexed, ap. Mansi viii. 711. Here the Augustinian doctrines of original sin, and of grace, as the only source of all that is good, are introduced ; afterwards it is said in the Confession of Faith : Quam gratiam—omnibus, qui baptizari desiderant, non in libero arbitrio haberi, sed Christi novimus simul et credimus largitate conferri.—Hoc etiam secundum fidem catholicam credimus, quod accepta per baptismum gratia omnes baptizati, Christe auxiliante et cooperante, quae ad salutem animae pertinent possint et debeant, si fideliter laborare voluerint, adimplere. If sufficient grace be granted to all in baptism, it depends on man to embrace or to resist it, and there is no gratia irresistibilis and no decretum absolutum. These latter, therefore, do not result, as Wiggers ii. 441, supposes, as necessary consequences from the positions of the Synod. The Synod does not teach them, because it does not recognise them.

[17] Hence Faustus is still honoured in Provence as a saint, which is

not long after the principles were again taught without giving offence,[18] although even rigid Augustinism continued to have its adherents.[19]

§. 114.

HISTORY OF THE THEOLOGICAL SCIENCES.

After the Roman Empire had been annoyed and overrun by barbarians, the necessity of struggling against paganism no longer calling forth spiritual activity, and the study of the so-called heathen sciences having become increasingly suspicious, especially in the eyes of the monks, scientific cultivation was deteriorated more and more, inasmuch as the free movement of the spirit was hindered by the narrowing restraints of orthodoxy, and attention exclusively directed to single barren speculations, by the disputes carried on with so much zeal.[1] How narrowly they began in the West to judge of the writings of the older fathers, according to the standard of the new orthodoxy, is proved by the so called Decretum Gelasii de libris recipiendis et non recipiendis.[2]

indeed censured by some (for example, Baronius ad ann. 490, § 42), but defended by others. Comp. J. Stilting de S. Fausto comm. hist. in Actis SS. Sept. vii. 651.

[18] So by the African bishop Junilius (about 550), de partibus divinae legis (bibl. PP. Lugd. x.) ii. 12, 15, by Gregory, archbishop of Tours († 595) Miraculorum (bibl. PP. xi.) ii. 1, vii. 1, 2, 9, 11, 13, by Gregory the Great, bishop of Rome († 604). Comp. G. F. Wiggers de Gregorio M. ejusque placitis anthropologicis comm. ii. Rostochii 1838–40. 4.

[19] To these belong Fulgentius Ferrandus—see § 111, note 26. Comp. his Paraeneticus ad Reginum comitem; Facundus, bishop of Hermiane —see § 111, note 27, contra Mocianum ap. Gallandius xi. 811; Isidore, archbishop of Seville († 636) Sententt. ii. 6.

. [1] Bossuet's Weltgesch. continued by J. A. Cramer v. ii. 52. L. Wachler's Handbuch der Geschichte der Literatur. (Zweite Umarbeit. Frankf. a. M. 1823) ii. 5. Münscher's Dogmengesch. iii. 44.

[2] In some MSS. it is attributed to Damasus (366–384), in the Spanish MSS. to Hormisdas (514–523), but commonly to a Roman Synod under Gelasius (496). On the contrary, it is wanting in the Dionysian collection of decrees (525), and in the Spanish (about 600) is placed entirely at the end, behind the decrees of Gregory the Great, which points to a later addition. It is afterwards first mentioned, but without

The writers who were engaged in the various controversies have been already named. In the Western Church, *Faustus Rejensis* (§ 113. note 1. 2.), *Fulgentius Ruspensis* (§ 113. note 15.), *Fulgentius Ferrandus, Facundus Hermianensis, Liberatus* (§ 111. note 26 ff.) ; among the Orientals, *Leontius Byzantinus* (preface to § 110), and *Johannes Philoponus* (§ 110. note 25.)

There was now less and less of independent investigation ; and instead of it men were content with compilations from the highly esteemed older fathers.[3] By way of exegesis began the series of the so-called catenae ;[4] in the East with *Procopius of Gaza* (about 520),[5] in the West with *Primasius*, bishop of Adrumetum

the name of an author, by the English bishop Adhelmus (about 680) de virginitate c. 11, first attributed to Gelasius by Hincmar, archbishop of Rheims (about 860) opusc. L. capitulorum c. 24. That it was gradually enlarged is shown by the different existing texts (three in Mansi viii. 153). In like manner, the difference of authors may be inferred from the fact that the opera Cypriani are placed both among the libris recipiendis and the non-recipiendis. At the time of Hormisdas the basis of this list was already in existence (Horm. ep. ad Possessorem ap. Mansi viii. 499: Non improvide veneranda patrum sapientia fideli potestati quae essent catholica dogmata definiit, certa librorum etiam veterum in auctoritatem recipienda, sancto Spiritu instruente, praefigens), but not in the form of a decree, since, in the latter case, Dionysius would have adopted it. At the time of Hormisdas the opera Fausti were also not yet in it, since Hormisdas hesitates to condemn Faustus. The decree, however, must have received its present form substantially in the first half of the sixth century, because in it no writings and heretics of this century whatever are mentioned, and only the first four general councils. Single interpolations were freely made afterwards. Thus, in Hincmar's time the canones Apostolorum were not yet adduced among the Apocryphis. cf. Mansi viii. 145, 151. Regenbrecht de canonibus Apostolorum et codice Eccl. hispanae diss. Vratisl. 1828. 8. p. 52.—In this decree are mentioned, among other things, the historia Eusebii Pamph. the opuscula Tertulliani, Lactantii, Clementis Alex., Arnobii reckoned among the libris apocryphis, qui non recipiuntur.

[3] Cassiodorus institt. div. praef. Quapropter tractatores vobis doctissimos indicasse sufficiat, quando ad tales remisisse competens plenitudo probatur esse doctrinae. Nam et vobis quoque erat praestantius praesumpta novitate non imbui, sed priscorum fonte satiari.

[4] J. F. S. Augustin de catenis PP. graec. in N. T. observationes. Halae 1762. (in J. A. Noesselti iii. commentatt. ad hist. eccl. pertinent. Halae 1817. 8. p. 321 ss.)

[5] Comm. in Octateuchum, in Esaiam, Proverbia, in xii. Proph. minores etc. cf. Fabricii bibl. gr. vol. vi. p. 259, (ed. Harles vol. vii. p. 563.) Augustin l. c. p. 385. In Ang. Maji classicorum auctorum e

(about 550).[6] Most of the works, too, of *Magnus Aurelius Cassiodorus Senator* († after 562),[7] and of *Isidore, bishop of Hispalis* († 636),[8] are written in the compilation method. The χριστιανικὴ τοπογραφία of the Nestorian *Cosmas Indicopleustes* (about 535), in its remarkable theologico-geographical part, is only a compilation, chiefly from the works of Diodorus of Tarsus and Theodorus of Mopsuestia.[9]

Distinguished as an independent thinker in this age of imitation and authorities was the Aristotelian philosopher *Anicius Manlius Torquatus Severinus Boethius* († 525), who, however, in his philosophical writings,[10] refers so little to Christianity, that one is led to doubt not only of the authenticity of the theological

Vaticanis codd. editorum T. vi. (Romae 1834. 8.)' are published besides comm. in Genesin usque ad cap. xviii. and fragm. in cant. Salomonis ; T. ix. (1837) comm. in Salom. Proverbia, catena in cant. cant.

[6] Comm. in epistolas Pauli.

[7] Thus his comment. in Psalmos is drawn from Augustine; his historia eccl. tripartita in 12 books (see preface to § 1.)—De institutione divinarum literarum libb. ii. (a more correct title is : Institutiones quemadmodum divinae et humanae debeant intelligi lectiones libb. ii. See Credner's Einl. in d. R. T. i. i. 15.) Historically important are his variae epistolae libb. xii. Of his de rebus gestis Gothorum libb. xii. there remains only the extract by Jordanis (see § 108, note 3.) His book de vii. disciplinis was much used in the middle ages. Opp. ed. J. Garetius. Rothomagi 1679. (Venet. 1729) 2 vol. fol. La vie de Cassiodore par F. D. de Ste Marthe. Paris 1694. 12. Cassiodorus by Ständlin, in the Kirchenhist. Archive for 1825, p. 259 ff. and 381 ff. Ritter's Gesch. d. christl. Philos. ii. 598. Bähr's christl. römische Theologie, S. 418.

[8] Comm. in libros hist. Vet. Test.—De ecclesiasticis officiis libb. ii.—Sententiarum s. de summo bono libb. iii. (important for the middle ages. Sententiarii.)—Regula Monachorum.—De scriptoribus eccles.—and many others. See the chief work Originum s. Etymologiarum libb. xx. —Hist. Gothorum, Vandalorum et Suevorum in Hispania.—Opp. ed. J. Grial. Madr. 1599. (Paris. 1601. Colon. 1617) fol. Faust. Arevalo. Romae 1797. vii. voll. 4. Bähr. S. 455.

[9] Prim. ed. B. de Montfaucon in collect. nov. PP. Graec. T. ii. (Paris. 1706) : recus. in Gallandii bibl. PP. T. xi. p. 401 ss. The Nestorianism of Cosmas was first pointed out by La Croze hist. du Christianisme des Indes T. i. p. 40 ss. cf. Semler hist. eccl. selecta capita i. p. 421 ss.

[10] His principal work : de consolatione philosophiae libb. v. Besides this, translations from the writings of Porphyry and Aristotle, and commentaries on the same. He laid the foundation of the predilection for the Aristotelian philosophy in the West, as John Philoponus did at the same time in the East (§ 110. note 25.)

works[11] ascribed to him, but even whether he could have been a Christian.[12]

The prevailing dialectic development of Christian doctrine must have been as unsatisfactory as it was injurious to deeper religious spirits, and therefore mysticism, in opposition to it, obtained a fuller and better developed form in the works of *Pseudodionysius Areopagita*,[13] which appeared towards the end of the fifth century. These writings, tracing up the divine essence, in the manner of the new Platonists, above all existence and perception, and representing all things to proceed in regular gradation out of it as their essence, proposed to teach how man, rightly apprehending his own position in the chain of being, might elevate himself through the next higher order to communion with still higher orders, and finally with God himself. At present they spread but gradually in the oriental church, till they penetrated in the middle ages into the west also, and so became the basis of all the later Christian mysticism.

There were now but few institutions for the advancement of theological learning any where; in the West none whatever.[14]

[11] Adv. Eutychen et Nestor. de duabus naturis et una persona Christi. —Quod Trinitas sit unus Deus et non tres dii ad Symmachum.—Utrum Pater, Filius et Sp. S. de divinitate substantialiter praedicentur. Comp. Hand in the Encyclopädie of Ersch and Gruber xi. 283. Bähr's christl. römische Theologie S. 423. On the other hand, Gust. Baur de A. M. S. Boëthio christianae doctrinae assertore, Darmst. 1841. 8. is in favour of the authenticity.

[12] Much used in the schools of the middle ages. In the eighth century he was even enrolled among the saints, and in addition to two other Severini, worshipped on the 23d October. That he was a Christian is denied by Gottf. Arnold, (Kirchen u. Ketzerhist. Th. i. B. 6. cap. 3. § 7.) and Hand l. c. On the contrary, G. Baur asserts that he was at least outwardly a Christian. Comp. Ritter's Gesch. d. christl. Philos. ii. 580.

[13] Comp. § 110, not. 7, and Engelhardt's works there quoted. Ritter's Gesch. d. christl. Philosophie ii. 515. Die christl. Mystik in ihrer Entwickelung u. in ihren Denkmalen von A. Helfferich (2 Th. Gotha 1842) i. 129, ii. 1.

[14] Cassiodor. de inst. div. lit. praef. : Cum studia saecularium literarum magno desiderio fervere cognoscerem (comp. Sartorius Versuch über die Regierung der Ostgothen während ihrer Herrschaft in Italien. Hamburg 1811. S. 152 ss. Manso Gesch. des ostgoth. Reichs in Italien. Breslau 1824. S. 132), ita ut multa pars hominum per ipsa se mundi prudentiam crederet adipisci; gravissimo sum (fateor) dolore permotus, quod scripturis divinis magistri publici deessent, cum mun-

H

The monkish contempt displayed by *Gregory the Great*, bishop of Rome (from 590–604),[15] for the liberal sciences,[16] contributed much to the daily increasing neglect of them; but the later

dani auctores celeberrima procul dubio traditione pollerent. Nisus sum ergo cum b. Agapito Papa urbis Romae, ut sicut apud Alexandriam multo tempore fuisse traditur institutum, nunc etiam in Nisibi civitate Syrorum ab Hebraeis sedulo fertur exponi (see below § 122, not. 5), collatis expensis in urbe Romana professos doctores scholae potius acciperent christianae, undo et anima susciperet aeternam salutem, et casto atque purissimo eloquio fidelium lingua comeretur. Sed cum per bella ferventia et turbulenta nimis in Italico regno certamina desiderium meum nullatenus valuisset impleri: quoniam non habet locum res pacis temporibus inquietis; ad hoc divina caritate probor esse compulsus, ut ad vicem magistri introductorios vobis libros istos, Domino praestante, conficerem etc. What substitute was adopted may be seen from Conc. Vasense iii. ann. 529 can. 1: Hoc enim placuit, ut omnes presbyteri, qui sunt in parochiis constituti, secundum consuetudinem, quam per totam Italiam satis salubriter teneri cognovimus, juniores lectores—secum in domo—recipiant: et eos—psalmos parare, divinis lectionibus insistere, et in lege domini erudire contendant: ut sibi dignos successores provideant. In Spain we find the first trace of a kind of episcopal seminaries, Conc. Tolet. ii. ann. 531 can. 1: De his, quos voluntas parentum a primis infantiae annis clericatus officio manciparit, hoc statuimus observandum, ut mox detonsi vel ministerio lectorum cum traditi fuerint, in domo Ecclesiae sub episcopali praesentia a praeposito sibi debeant erudiri.

[15] Pauli Warnefridi (about 775) de vita S. Gregor. Papae libb. iv. (prim. ed. Jo. Mabillon in the annales Ord. S. Bened. saec. i. p. 385) and Johannis Eccl. Rom. Diaconi (about 875) de vita S. Greg. libb. iv. both in the iv. tome of the Benedictine edition of Gregory's works. Comp. the life composed by the Benedictines, and given in that volume. G. F. Wiggers de Gregorio M. ejusque placitis anthropologicis comm. ii. Rostoch. 1838. 4. p. 11.—Gregory's most important works (see Bähr's christl. röm. Theologie. S. 442. Wiggers p. 35): Expositionis in Job. s. moralium libb. xxxv.—Liber pastoralis curae ad Job. Ravennac Episc. (by Anastasius Sinaita, patriarch of Antioch, immediately translated into Greek.)—Dialogorum de vita et miraculis Patrum Ital. et de aeternitate animarum libb. iv. (translated into Greek by Pope Zacharias about 744).—Epistolarum libb. xiv. (according to the older arrangement libb. xii.)—Liber Sacramentorum de circulo anni s. Sacramentarium.—Antiphonarius s. gradualis liber.—Opp. ed. Petr. Gussanvillaeus. voll. iii. Paris 1675. fol. studio et labore Monachorum Ord. S. Bened. e Congr. S. Mauri voll. iv. Paris 1705. fol. locupletata a J. B. Galliccioli. Venet. 1768 ss. voll. xvii. 4. Concerning the modern abbreviators of Gregory see Oudinus de scriptt. eccl. ant.i. 1544.

[16] For example, in the epistola ad Leandrum prefixed to his exposit. libri Jobi: Non barbarismi confusionem devito, situs motusque praepositionum casusque servare contemno, quia indignum vehementer existimo, ut verba caelestis oraculi restringam sub regulis Donati.—Lib. xi.

traditions of his hostility to all literature, are not to be fully believed.[17]

New fields were now opened to ecclesiastical writers in collecting and arranging *the saints' traditions*, in which *Gregory, archbishop of Tours* (573–595),[18] and *Gregory the Great*,[19] led the way ; and in the preparation of *ecclesiastical law*.[20] In the Greek Church,[21] soon after the council of Chalcedon, appeared the

epist. 54. ad Desiderium, Episc. Viennensem : pervenit ad nos, quod sine verecundia memorare non possumus, Fraternitatem tuam grammaticam quibusdam exponere. Quam rem ita moleste suscepimus, ac sumus vehementius aspernati, ut ea, quae prius dicta fuerant, in gemitus et tristitiam verteremus : quia in uno se ore cum Jovis laudibus Christi laudes non capiunt etc.

[17] Joannes Sarisburiensis (about 1172) in his Policraticus lib. ii. c. 26 : Doctor sanctus ille Gregorius—non modo Mathesin jussit ab aula, sed, ut traditur a majoribus, incendio dedit probatae lectionis scripta Palatinus quaecumque recepit Apollo. Lib. viii. c. 19. fertur b. Gregorius bibliothecam combussisse gentilem, quo divinae paginae gratior esset locus, et major auctoritas, et diligentia studiosior. Barthol. Platina (about 1480) de vitis Pontificum, in vita Gregorii : Neque est cur patiamur, Gregorium hac in re a quibusdam—carpi, quod suo mandato veterum aedificia sint dirupta, ne peregrini et advenae—posthabitis locis sacris, arcus triumphales et monumenta veterum cum admiratione inspicerent. Platina tries to defend him from the charge. Id. in vita Sabiniani : Paululum etiam abfuit, quin libri ejus (Gregorii) comburerentur, adeo in Gregorium ira et invidia exarserat homo malevolus. Sunt qui scribant, Sabinianum instigantibus quibusdam Romanis hoc in Gregorium molitum esse, quod veterum statuas tota urbe, dum viveret, et obtruncaverit et disjecerit, quod quidem ita vero dissonum est, ut illud, quod de abolendis aedificiis majorum in vita ejus diximus. Against the credibility of these stories see P. Bayle dictionnaire hist. et crit. Art. Gregoire not. H. and M. Jo. Barbeyrac de la morale des Pères c. 17, § 16. What Brucker hist. phil. iii. 560, says in their defence is of no importance.

[18] De gloria Martyrum libb. ii. de gloria Confessorum lib. i. de virtutibus et miraculis s. Martini libb. iv. de vitis Patrum lib. i. in his opp. ed. Theod. Ruinart, Paris 1699. fol. (comp. Div. 1, § 53, not. 46.) Dr C. G. Kries de Greg. Tur. Episc. vita et scriptis, Vratisl. 1839. 8.

[19] Dialogorum libb. iv. see above, not. 15.

[20] A. Gallandii de vetustis canonum collectionibus dissertationum sylloge (Dissertations of Coustant, de Marca, the Ballerini, Berard, Quesnell, etc.) Venetiis 1778. fol. recus. Moguntiaci 1790. T. ii. 4. (L. T. Spittler's) Geschichte des kanonischen Rechts bis auf die Zeiten des falschen Isidorus. Halle 1778. 8.

[21] Jos. Sim. Assemani bibliotheca juris orientalis, civilis et canonici. Romae 1762—66. T. v. 4. (incomplete, contains merely the Codex canonum eccl. Graecae and the Codex juris civilis eccl. Graecae.) F. A. Biener de collectionibus canonum Eccl. Graecae schediasma litterarium. Berol. 1827. 8.

so-called *apostolic canons*,[22] claiming to form the unalterable
basis of all ecclesiastical arrangements. About the same time
the Christians began to put together the decrees of councils in
the order of the subjects, instead of in the old chronological way.
The oldest collection of this kind now extant is that of *Johannes
Scholasticus* of Antioch (afterwards patriarch of Constantinople
† 578),[23] which was in great repute for several centuries. Justinian's code was also so rich a source for ecclesiastical matters,
that particular collections of church laws were made soon after
his time, out of his institutes.[24] Those of John Scholasticus were
at a later period adapted to Justinian's by a new collection of
canons,[25] and thus arose the first *Nomocanon*.[26]

In the Latin Church there was not even a tolerably complete
chronological collection of the canons till that made after the
council of Chalcedon, since known as the *prisca translatio*.[27] A
still fuller collection was afterwards made by *Dionysius Exiguus*
(about 500)[28] in a better translation, to which was added, in a
second part, a collection of the papal decretals. In *Spain* there
had been a collection of canons, between 633 and 636, on the
model of that by Dionysius (the Greek ones in a particular version), and of papal decretals for the use of the Spanish Church,[29]

[22] See Div. 1, § 67, not. 5.
[23] Published in Guil. Voëlli et H. Justelli bibliotheca juris canonici
veteris (T. ii. Paris 1661. fol.) ii. 449.
[24] The collectio lxxxvii. capitulorum, collected by Johannes Scholasticus from the novellae; the coll. xxv. capitt. from the codex and
novellae (published in G. E. Heimbach anecdota. T. ii. Lips. 1840. 4.);
and that erroneously published under the name of Theod. Balsamon in
Voëlli et Justelli bibl. juris ii. 1223 collectio constitt. ecclesiasticarum,
which was compiled at the time of Heraclius, perhaps also of Justin II.
from the pandects, codex and novellae. Comp. F. A. Biener's Gesch.
d. Novellen Justinians, Berlin 1824. 8. S. 166.
[25] In this form it is found in Voëlli et Justelli bibl. ii. 603.
[26] Though this name is much more modern. See Biener's Gesch. d.
Novellen S. 194. Heimbach anecd. T. ii. Prolegom. p. lv.
[27] Best edition that of the Ballerini opp. Leonis iii. 473, from which
Mansi vi. 1105. Concerning it comp. Ballerini de ant. collectionibus
canonum (before T. iii. opp. Leonis and in Gallandii sylloge), P. ii.
cap. 2, § 3. Spittler S. 129.
[28] Published in Voëlli et Justelli biblioth. i. 101. Ballerini l. c. P.
iii. cap. 1—3. Spittler S. 134. According to Drey, über die Constit. u. Kanones d. Apostel p. 203, even before the end of the fifth
century.
[29] Published by Ant. Gonzalez in 2 Div. Collectio canonum Eccl.

which was afterwards called the collection of *Isidore*,[30] because it was erroneously ascribed to the most celebrated man of that time, Isidore, archbishop of Hispalis († 636). The laws respecting penance had gradually become so numerous as to require a separate work. *Johannes jejunator* (ὁ νηστευτής), patriarch of Constantinople (from 585–593), wrote the ἀκολουθία καὶ τάξις ἐπὶ ἐξομολογουμένων,[31] the first libellus poenitentialis (rules of penance).

THIRD CHAPTER.

HISTORY OF THE HIERARCHY.

§ 115.

PRIVILEGES OF THE CLERGY.

The clergy, and particularly the bishops, received new privileges from *Justinian*. He entrusted the latter with civil jurisdiction over the monks and nuns, as well as over the clergy.[1]

hispanae, Matriti 1808, and epistolae decrotales ac rescripta Rom. Pontiff. Matriti 1821. fol. comp. Ballerini l. c. P. ii. cap. ii. § 2. P. iii. c. 4. M. E. Regenbrecht de cann. Apostolorum et codice Eccl. hispanae diss. Vratisl. 1828. 8. Eichhorn on the Spanish collection of the sources of ecclesiastical jurisprudence, in the Transactions of the Royal Academy of Sciences at Berlin for the year 1834. (Berlin 1836. 4to.) historical and philosophical class, p. 89.

[30] According to Eichhorn, p. 113, since Pseudoisidore.

[31] Afterwards variously interpolated; published in J. Morini comm. hist. de disciplina in administratione Sacramenti Poenitentiae. Paris 1651, fol. in append.

[1] Novellae Justin. 79 et 83 (both A. D. 539.) More particular notices are given in Nov. 123, cap. 21 : Si quis autem litigantium intra x. dies contradicat iis, quae judicata sunt, tunc locorum judex causam examinet.—Si judicis sententia contraria fuerit iis, quae a Deo amabili Episcopo judicata sunt: tunc locum habere appellationem contra sententiam judicis.—Si vero crimen fuerit, quod adversus quamlibet memoratarum reverendissimarum personarum inferatur,—judex ultionem ei inferat legibus congruentem. Further, in a criminal accusation : Si Episcopus distulerit judicare, licentiam habeat actor civilem judicem adire. cf. B. Schilling de origine jurisdictionis eccles. in causis civilibus. Lips. 1825. 4. p. 41 ss.

Episcopal *oversight of morals*, and particularly *the duty of pro-viding for all the unfortunate* (§ 91, notes 8–10), had been esta-blished till the present time only on the foundation of ecclesiasti-cal laws ; but Justinian now gave them a more general basis, by founding them on the civil law also.[2] He made it the duty of the bishops, and gave them the necessary civil qualifications, to un-dertake the care of *prisoners, minors, insane persons, found-lings, stolen children,* and *oppressed women* ;[3] and invested them with the power of upholding good morals[4] and impartial administration of justice. It is true, that he established a mutual inspection of the bishops and of the civil magistrates ; but he gave in this respect to the latter considerably smaller privileges than to the former.[5] For example, he gave the bishops a legal influence over the choice of magistrates,[6] and security against general oppression on their part ;[7] allowed them to interfere in case of refusal of justice ;[8] and, in special instances, even consti-tuted them judges of those official personages.[9] In like manner,

[2] C. W. de Rhoer de effectu relig. christ. in jurisprudentiam rom. fasc. 1.   Groningae 1776. 8. p. 94.   C. Riffel's geschichtl. Darstellung des Verhältnisses zwischen Kirche und Staat.   (Mainz 1836) i. 622.

[3] Cod. Justin. lib. i. tit. iv. de episcopali audientia (*i. e.* judicio.) l. 22.—l. 30.—l. 27. l. 28.—l. 24.—l. 33.

[4] In addition to their former powers against pimps (Cod. Th. xv. viii. 2) and sorcerers (Cod. Th. ix. xvi. 12) Justinian gave them also the privilege of interfering against gaming (Cod. Just. i. iv. 25.)

[5] The Praesides provinciarum were obliged to see to it that bishops observed ecclesiastical laws relating to ecclesiastical things (Cod. Just. i. iii. 44, § 3. Nov. cxxxvii. c. 6), particularly those relating to the un-alienableness of Church possessions (Nov. vii. in epil.) and the regular holding of synods (Nov. cxxxvii. c. 6.)   They could only, however, put the bishops in mind of their duty, and then notify the emperor.

[6] Nov. cxlix. c. 1.

[7] Cod. Just. i. iv. 26, Nov. cxxxiv. c. 3.

[8] Nov. lxxxvi. c. 1.

[9] Nov. lxxxvi. c. 4. (A. D. 539) : Quodsi contingat aliquem ex sub-ditis nostris ab ipso clarissimo provinciae praeside injuria affici, jubemus eum sanctissimum illius urbis Episcopum adire, ut ille inter cl. praesi-dem, eumve, qui se ab eo injuria affectum putat, judicet.   If the presi-dent (of a province) were condemned, and gave no satisfaction, the mat-ter was referred to the emperor, and in case he found the episcopal sentence just, the president was condemned to death.   According to Nov. viii. c. 9. cxxviii. c. 23, every magistrate, after laying down his office, was obliged to remain fifty days in the province to satisfy any claims that might be made against him.   If he removed sooner, every one injured might complain to the bishop.

he conveyed to them the right of concurrence in the choice of city officials,[10] and a joint oversight of the administration of city funds, and the maintenance of public establishments.[11] Thus the bishops became important personages even in civil life ; and were farther honoured by Justinian, in freedom from parental violence,[12] from the necessity of appearing as witnesses, and from taking oaths.[13]

Finally, *Heraclius* committed to them jurisdiction over the clergy in criminal cases also (628).[14]

§ 116.

DEPENDENCE OF THE HIERARCHY ON THE STATE.

Notwithstanding these great privileges, the hierarchy became still more dependent on the State. As the emperors sent their civil laws to be promulgated by the Praetorian prefects, so, in like manner, ecclesiastical laws went forth from them to the patriarchs,[1] and the magistrates were directed to watch the observance of them by the bishops.[2] None doubted the emperor's

[10] Cod. Just. i. iv. 17, Nov. cxxviii. 16.

[11] Cod. Just. i. iv. 26.

[12] Novell. lxxxi.

[13] Novell. cxxiii. c. 7.

[14] The law issued to the patriarch of Constantinople, Sergius, of which merely the contents are given in the Constitutt. Imper. appended to the Codex Justin. is found complete iu Jo. Leunclavii juris Graeco Romani (tomi ii. Francof. 1596. fol.) i. 73, and in Voëlli et Justelli biblioth. juris can. ii. 1361 : The offences (ἐγκλήματα) of clergymen are to be judged by the bishop κατὰ τοὺς θείους κανόνας. εἰ δέ γε νομίσοι σφοδροτέρας ἐπεξελεύσεως ἄξιον καθιστάναι τὸν κρινόμενον, τηνικαῦτα τὸν τοιοῦτον—τοῦ περικειμένου κελεύομεν γυμνοῦσθαι σχήματος, καὶ τοῖς πολιτικοῖς ἄρχουσι παραδιδόσθαι, τὰς τοῖς ἡμετέροις διωρισμένας νόμοις τιμωρίας ὑποσχησόμενον.

[1] For example, Nov. 6, epilogus : Sanctissimi igitur Patriarchae cujusque dioecesis haec in sanctissimis Ecclesiis sub se constitutis. proponant, et Dei amantissimis Metropolitanis quae a nobis sancita sunt nota faciant. Hi vero ipsi in sanctissima Ecclesia metropolitana haec rursus proponant, et Episcopis, qui sub ipsis sunt, manifesta faciant. Quilibet vero illorum in Ecclesia sua haec proponat, ut nemo in nostra sit republica, qui ea—ignoret. F. A. Biener's Gesch. der Novellen Justinian's. Berlin 1824. S. 31 f. comp. S. 25 ss.

[2] See § 115, not. 5.

right to enact laws touching the external relations of the Church,
and even subjects connected with its internal constitution ;[3] but
it was more suspicious when the emperors began now to decide
questions of faith by edicts, and when Synods were assembled
almost entirely for the purpose of adopting imperial articles of
faith.   The Greek bishops became more and more accustomed to
sacrifice their conviction to circumstances ;[4] but the bishops of
Italy, favoured by the political condition of their country, were
able for the most part to assert a firmer position.

§ 117.

HISTORY OF THE PATRIARCHS.

Ever since the beginning of the Monophysite controversy in
the East, the sees of Alexandria and Antioch had become so

[3] Biener l. c. S. 157 ss. 161 ss. Thus Justinian, Nov. 123, c. 3,
where he fixes the amount to be given by the bishops pro inthronisticis,
uses the expression : Κελεύομεν τοίνυν τοὺς μὲν μακαριωτάτους ἀρχιεπισκό-
πους καὶ πατριάρχας, τουτέστι τῆς πρεσβυτέρας Ῥώμης, καὶ Κωνσταντινουπόλεως, καὶ Ἀλεξανδρείας, καὶ Θεουπόλεως, καὶ Ἱεροσολύμων. When the Emperor Maurice had made a law, ut quisquis publicis administrationibus
fuerit implicatus, ei neque ad ecclesiasticum officium venire, neque in
monasterium converti liceat : Gregory the Great, lib. iii. ep. 65, ad
Mauricium Aug. remonstrated against the second part of the prohibition. Ex. gr. Ego vero haec Dominis meis loquens, quid sum nisi pulvis
et vermis ?   Sed tamen quia contra auctorem omnium Deum hanc in-
tendere constitutionem sentio, Dominis tacere non possum.—Ad haec
ecce per me servum ultimum suum et vestrum respondebit Christus
dicens : Ego te de notario comitem excubitorum, de comite excubitorum, Caesarem, de Caesare Imperatorem, nec solum hoc, sed etiam
patrem Imperatorum feci. Sacerdotes meos tuae manui commisi, et tu
a meo servitio milites tuos subtrahis ? Responde, rogo, piissime Domine, servo tuo, quid venienti et haec dicenti responsurus es in judicio
Domino tuo ?—Ego quidem jussioni subjectus eandem legem per diversas terrarum partes transmitti feci : et quia lex ipsa omnipotenti Deo
minime concordat, ecce per suggestionis paginam serenissimis
Dominis nuntiavi. Utrobique ergo quae debui exsolvi, qui et Imperatori obedientiam praebui, et pro Deo quod sensi minime tacui.

[4] Epistola Legatis Francorum, qui Constantinopolim proficiscebantur,
ab Italiae clericis directa A. D. 551 ap. Mansi ix. p. 153 : Sunt graeci
Episcopi habentes divites et opulentas ecclesias, et non patiuntur duos
menses a rerum ecclesiasticarum dominatione suspendi : pro qua re
secundum tempus, et secundum voluntatem principum, quidquid ab eis
quaesitum fuerit, sine altercatione consentiunt. Comp. § 92, not. 1 and 2.

weak that the patriarchs of Constantinople only, upheld by the privileges granted them at the council of Chalcedon,[1] were able to vie with the Roman patriarchs.[2]   But while the former were dependent on imperial caprice, and constantly harassed by the Greek spirit of controversy, the latter enjoyed the most perfect freedom in ecclesiastical things, and the advantage of standing at the head of the West, which was less inclined to controversies about faith, and therefore more united.[3]   After the extinction of the West Roman empire (476), by which, however, they had been never molested, but often furthered,[4] the Roman bishops became subject to German princes, who left them at perfect liberty to manage all affairs within the Church according to their pleasure.   This was particularly the case with *Theoderich*, king of the Arian Ostrogoths (493–526),[5] to whom the schism between Rome and Constantinople gave sufficient security from all dangerous combinations of the Catholic hierarchy.   And when, on the death of Bishop Anastasius, there was a contested election

[1] The Monophysite party which predominated under Basiliscus suspended these privileges in part, Evagrius iii. 6: (Timotheus Aelurus) ἀποδίδωσι τῇ Ἐφεσίων καὶ τὸ πατριαρχικὸν δίκαιον, ὅπερ αὐτὴν ἀφεῖλεν ἡ ἐν Χαλκηδόνι σύνοδος : but by the law Cod. Justin. i. ii. 16, (by Zeno, not, as the title has it, by Leo) the decrees of Chalcedon were revived, to be in force ever after.

[2] Order of the Roman bishops: Leo I. the Great † 461, Hilary † 468, Simplicius † 483, Felix II. † 492, Gelasius I. † 496, Anastasius II. † 498, Symmachus † 514, Hormisdas † 523, John I. † 526, Felix III. † 530, Boniface II. † 532, John II. † 535, Agapetus I. † 536, Silverius banished by Belisarius 537, Vigilius † 555, Pelagius I. † 560, John III. † 573, Benedict I. † 578. Pelagius II. † 590, Gregory I. the Great † 604, Sabinianus † 606, Boniface III. † 607, Boniface IV. † 615, Deusdedit † 618, Boniface V. † 625.

[3] See above, p. 205.

[4] See above, § 94, not. 12, and 66.

[5] On the course pursued by the Ostrogoth kings towards the Church, see G. Sartorius Versuch über die Regierung der Ostgothen während ihrer Herrschaft in Italien.   Hamburg 1811. S. 124 ss. 306 ss.   J. C. F. Manso Gesch. des ostgoth. Reichs in Italien.   Breslau 1824. S. 141 ss.   Theoderich says (Cassiodori variarum lib. ii. ep. 27): Religionem imperare non possumus : quia nemo cogitur, ut credat invitus.   King Theodahat to the emperor Justinian (Ibid. x. ep. 26): Cum divinitas diversas patiatur religiones esse, nos unam non audemus imponere. Retinemus enim legisse nos, voluntarie sacrificandum esse Domino, non cujusquam cogentis imperio.   Quod qui aliter facere tentaverit, evidenter caelestibus jussionibus obviavit.

between Symmachus and Laurentius (498),[6] he waited till required by both parties to decide,[7] and then quietly allowed a Roman synod under Symmachus to declare all interference of the laity in the affairs of the Roman Church entirely inadmissible.[8]

[6] According to Theodorus lector lib. ii. (ed. Vales. Amstelod. p. 560) Laurentius was chosen by an imperial party on condition of subscribing the Henoticon.   cf. Anastasii lib. pontificalis c. 52, in vita Symmachi.

[7] Anastasii lib. pontificalis c. 52, in vita Symmachi : Et facta contentione hoc constituerunt partes, ut ambo ad Ravennam pergerent ad judicium Regis Theodorici.   Qui dum ambo introissent in Ravennam, hoc judicium aequitatis invenerunt, ut qui primo ordinatus fuisset, vel ubi pars maxima cognosceretur, ipse sederet in sede apostolica.   Quod tandem aequitas in Symmacho invenit.

[8] Synodus Romana iii. sub Symmacho (in the collections cited erroneously as the Syn. Rom. iv. s. palmaris, see Pagi ad ann. 502 num. 3 ss.) ap. Mansi viii. 266 ss. The protocol of a synod held after the death of Pope Simplicius was here read, and the decrees passed at it declared nugatory as proceeding from a layman. This protocol is given in the Acta of the synod referred to, and runs thus : Cum in unum apud b. Petrum Apostolum resedissent, sublimis et eminentissimus vir, praefectus praetorio atque patricius, agens etiam vices pracellentissimi regis Odoacris, Basilius dixit : Quamquam studii nostri et religionis intersit, ut in episcopatus electione concordia principaliter servetur ecclesiae, ne per occasionem seditionis status civitatis vocetur in dubium : tamen admonitione beatissimi Papae nostri Simplicii, quam ante oculos semper habere debemus, hoc nobis meminstis sub obtestatione fuisse mandatum, ut propter illum strepitum, et venerabilis ecclesiae detrimentum, si eum de hac luce transire contigerit, non sine nostra consultatione cujuslibet celebretur electio.   Nam et cum quid confusionis atque dispendii venerabilis ecclesia sustineret, miramur praetermissis nobis quidquam fuisse tentatum, cum etiam sacerdote nostro superstite nihil sine nobis debuisset assumi.   Quare si amplitudini vestrae vel sanctitati placet, incolumia omnia, quae ad futuri antistitis electionem respiciunt, religiosa honoratione servemus, hanc legem specialiter praeferentes, quam nobis haeredibusque nostris christianae mentis devotione sancimus : Ne unquam praedium, seu rusticum seu urbanum, vel ornamenta aut ministeria ecclesiarum—ab eo qui nunc antistes sub electione communi fuerit ordinandus, et illis qui futuris saeculis sequentur, quocumque titulo atque commento alienentur.   Si quis vero aliquid eorum alienare voluerit, inefficax atque irritum judicetur ; sitque facienti vel consentienti, accipientique anathema etc.   At this enactment the following voices were now raised at the synod under Symmachus : Perpendat s. Synodus, uti praetermissis personis religiosis, quibus maxime cura est de tanto pontifice, electionem laici in suam redegerint potestatem, quod contra canones esse manifestum est.—Scriptura evidentissimis documentis constat invalida.   Primum quod contra patrum regulas a laicis, quamvis religiosis, quibus nulla de ecclesiasticis facultatibus aliquid disponendi legitur unquam attributa facultas, facta videtur.   Deinde quod nullius

Thus the Roman bishops were so far from being hindered by any superior power, that it proved an advantageous circumstance to them in the eyes of their new masters, that they steadfastly resisted innovations of faith made in Constantinople, till they gained a new victory over the changeable Greeks under the emperor Justin. The natural consequence of this was, that while the patriarchs of Constantinople were constantly sinking in ecclesiastical esteem on account of their vacillation in these controversies, the bishops of Rome still maintained their ancient reputation of being the defenders of oppressed orthodoxy.[9]

Under these favourable circumstances, *the ecclesiastical* pretensions of the Roman bishops, who now formed the only centre of Catholic Christendom in the West, in opposition to the Arian conquerors, rose high without hindrance. They asserted that not only did the highest ecclesiastical authority in the West belong to them, but also superintendence of orthodoxy and maintenance of ecclesiastical laws throughout the whole Church. These claims they sometimes founded on imperial edicts[10] and decrees of synods;[11] but for the most part on the peculiar rights

praesulis apostolicae sedis subscriptione firmata docetur. The arrangement was declared null, and, on the contrary, another of similar import was passed to secure ecclesiastical property from the synod.

[9] Cod. Just. i., i. 7, below not. 23.

[10] Hilarii P. epist. xi. (Mansi vii. 939): Fratri enim nostro Leontio nihil constituti a sauctae memoriae decessore meo juris potuit abrogari: —quia Christianorum quoque principum lege decretum est, ut quidquid ecclesiis earumque rectoribus—·apostolicae sedis antistes suo pronunciasset examine, venerantur accipi tenaciterque servari, cum suis plebibus caritas vestra cognosceret: nec unquam possent convelli, quae et sacerdotali ecclesiastica praeceptione fulcirentur et regia.

[11] Epist. synod. Rom. ad Clericos et Monachos Orient. A. D. 485 (Mansi vii. 1140): Quotiens intra Italiam propter ecclesiasticas causas, praecipue fidei, colliguntur domini sacerdotes, consuetudo retinetur, ut successor praesulum sedis apostolicae ex persona cunctorum totius Italiae sacerdotum juxta solicitudinem sibi ecclesiarum omnium competentem cuncta constituat, qui caput est omnium; Domino ad b. Petrum dicente: Tu es Petrus etc. Quam vocem sequentes cccxviii. sancti patres apud Nicaeam congregati confirmationem rerum atque auctoritatem sanctae Romanae ecclesiae detulerunt (comp. above, § 94, not. 28, 35, 60): quam utramque usque ad aetatem nostram successiones omnes, Christi gratia praestante, custodiunt. Gelasii ep. iv. ad Faustum (Mansi viii. 19): Quantum ad religionem pertinet, nonnisi apostolicae sedi juxta canones debetur summa judicii totius. Ejusd. ep. xiii. ad Episc. Dardaniae (Mansi viii. 54): Non reticemus autem, quod cuncta

conferred on Peter by the Lord.[12] After the *synodus palmaris*,
called by Theoderich to examine the charges newly raised by the
Laurentian party against Symmachus (503), had acquitted him
without examination, in consequence of the circumstances;[13] the

[12] per mundum novit ecclesia, quoniam quorumlibet sententiis ligata pontificum, sedes b. Petri Apostoli jus habeat resolvendi, utpote quod de
omni ecclesia fas habeat judicandi, neque cuiquam de ejus liceat judicare judicio, siquidem ad illam de qualibet mundi parte canones appellari voluerint, ab illa autem nemo sit appellare permissus.

[12] Gelasii decretum de libris recipiendis et non recipiendis (Mansi
viii. 157, comp. on it § 114, not. 2): quamvis universae per orbem
catholicae diffusae ecclesiae unus thalamus Christi sit, sancta tamen
Romana ecclesia nullis synodicis constitutis caeteris ecclesiis praelata
est, sed evangelica voce Domini et Salvatoris nostri primatum obtinuit :
Tu es Petrus etc. Cui data est etiam societas b. Pauli Apostoli,—qui
non diverso, sicut haeretici garriunt, sed uno tempore, uno eodemque
die gloriosa morte cum Petro in urbe Roma sub Caesare Nerone ago-
nizans, coronatus est. Et pariter supradictam s. Romanam ecclesiam
Christo domino consecrarunt, aliisque omnibus in universo mundo sua
praesentia atque venerando triumpho praetulerunt. (Gregorii M. lib.
iv. in 1 Reg. 5, ed. Bened. iii. ii. 250 : Saulus ad Christum conversus
caput effectus est nationum, quia obtinuit totius ecclesiae principatum.
Comp. above § 94, not. 37.)

[13] Syn. Rom. iv. sub Symmacho s. palmaris, in the collections falsely
cited as Syn. iii. See Pagi ad ann. 503, num. 2 ss. C. L. Nitzschii
disp. de Synodo palmari. Viteberg. 1775 (reprinted in Pottii sylloge
commentt. theoll. iv. 67.)—The Acts ap. Mansi viii. 247. After Symmachus had been in danger of his life at the synod from his enemies,
he declared (relatio Episcopp. ad Regem p. 256): Primum ad conventum vestrum—sine aliqua dubitatione properavi, et privilegia mea voluntati regiae submisi, et auctoritatem synodi dedi : sicut habet ecclesiastica disciplina, restaurationem ecclesiarum regulariter poposci : sed
nullus mihi a vobis effectus est. Deinde cum venirem cum clero meo,
crudeliter mactatus sum. Ulterius me vestro examini non committo :
in potestate Dei est, et domini regis, quid de me deliberet ordinare.
(Compare above, § 92, not. 15.) The synod having reported this to the
king, he answered (l. c. p. 257): miramur denuo fuisse consultum :
cum si nos de praesenti ante voluissemus judicare negotio, habito cum
proceribus nostris de inquirenda veritate tractatu, Deo auspice, potuisse-
mus invenire justitiam, quae nec praesenti saeculo, nec futurae forsitan
displicere potuisset aetati.—Nunc vero eadem, quae dudum, praesentibus intimamus oraculis.—Sive discussa, sive indiscussa causa, proferte
sententiam, de qua estis rationem divino judicio reddituri : dummodo,
sicuti saepe diximus, haec deliberatio vestra provideat, ut pax Senatui
populoque Romano, submota omni confusione, reddatur. For the further proceedings of the synod see their protocol, p. 250: Dei mandata
complentes Italiae suum dedimus rectorem, agnoscentes nullum nobis
laborem alium remansisse, nisi ut dissidentes cum humilitate propositi

apologist of this synod, *Ennodius*, bishop of Ticinum (511), first gave utterance to the assertion, that the bishop of Rome is subject to no earthly judge.[14]   Not long after an attempt was made to give a historical basis to this principle by supposititious *Gesta* (acts) of former popes ;[15] and other falsifications of older docu-

nostri ad concordiam hortaremur.   They proceed to consider quanta inconvenienter et praejudicialiter in hujus negotii principio contigissent :— maxime cum illa quae praemisimus inter alia de anctoritate sedis obstarent : quia quod possessor ejus quondam b. Petrus meruit, in nobilitatem possessionis accessit :—maxime cum omnem paene plebem cernamus ejus communioni indissociabiliter adhaesisse : and therefore concluded : ut Symmachus Papa sedis apostolicae praesul, ab hujusmodi propositionibus impetitus, quantum ad homines respicit (quia totum causis obsistentibus superius designatis constat arbitrio divino fuisse dimissum), sit immunis et liber.—Unde secundum principalia praecepta, quae nostrae hoc tribuunt potestati, ei, quidquid ecclesiastici intra sacram urbem Romam vel foris juris est, reformamus totamque causam Dei judicio reservantes etc.   Just as before also the Conc. Cirtense A. D. 305 (see Augustin. contra Cresonium iii. 27) put down the accusation against several bishops of their being Traditores, with the asseveration : habent Deum, cui reddant rationem.

[14] Magni Felicis Ennodii (opp. ed. J. Sirmond. Paris 1611, recusa in Gallandii bibl. PP. xi. 47) libellus apologeticus pro Synodo iv. Romana (Mansi viii. 274) : Non nos b. Petrum, sicut dicitis, a Domino cum sedis privilegiis, vel successores ejus, peccandi judicamus licentiam suscepisse.   Ille perennem meritorum dotem cum haereditate innocentiae misit ad posteros : quod illi concessum est pro actuum luce, ad illos pertinet, quos par conversationis splendor illuminat.   Quis enim sanctum esse dubitet, quem apex tantae dignitatis attollit ? in quo si desint bona acquisita per meritum, sufficiunt quae a loci decessore praestantur : aut enim claros ad haec fastigia erigit, aut qui eriguntur illustrat. Praenoscit enim, quid Ecclesiarum fundamento sit habile, super quem ipsa moles innititur. p. 284 : Aliorum forte hominum causas Deus voluerit per homines terminare : sedis istius presulem suo, sine quaestione, reservavit arbitrio, in direct contradiction to the epist. Rom. Conc. A. D. 378, above § 92, not 15.

[15] Namely Conc. Sinuessanum de Marcellini P. condemnatione (quod thurificasset) pretended to be held A. D. 303. (Mansi i. 1249 ss. The bishops say to him : Tu eris judex : ex te enim damnaberis, et ex te justificaberis, tamen in nostra praesentia.—Prima sedes non judicabitur a quoquam) : Constitutio Silvestri Episc. urbis Romae et Domini Constantini Aug. in Concil. Rom. pretended to be in 324 (Mansi ii. 615 ss. Cap. 20 : Nemo enim judicabit primam sedem, quoniam omnes sedes a prima sede justitiam desiderant temperari. Neque ab Augusto, neque ab omni clero, neque a regibus, neque a populo judex judicabitur) : Synodi Rom. (alleged to be held A. D. 433) acta de causa Sixti iii. stupro accusati, et de Polychronii Hierosolym. accusatione (Mansi v. 1161.) Comp. P. Constant diss. de antiquis canonum collectionibus

ments in favour of the Roman see now appeared in like manner.[16]
Still the Roman bishops (or as they were already called in Italy,
by way of distinction, *papa*)[17] did not yet demand any other
kind of honour than was paid to the other apostolic sees,[18] ac-

§ 97–99, (in Gallandii de vetustis canonum collectionibus dissertationum sylloge i. 93.)

[16] Thus the passage in Cyprian's lib. de unit. eccl. (see Div. i. § 68,
not. 10) appears already corrupted in Pelagii ii. ep. vi. ad Episc. Istriae
(Mansi ix. 898.)

[17] Thus, for instance, as early as in the councils held under Symmachus (see above notes 8 and 13) and in Ennodius (see note 14. Sirmond ad Ennod. lib. iv. ep 1): In the other regions of the West, however, the title Papa continued for a long time to be a name of honour
applied to every bishop (Walafrid Strabo about 840 de rebus eccl. c. 7,
in Hittorp's collection, p. 395: Pabst a Papa, quod cujusdam paternitatis nomen est, et Clericorum congruit dignitati) till Gregory VII.
forbade it, A. D. 1075.   Comp. Jo. Diecmann de vocis Papae aetatibus
diss. ii. Viteberg. 1671. 4.   In the East Πάπας was especially the title
of the patriarchs of Rome and Alexandria.—Just so in Italy the see of
Rome was especially Sedes apostolica ; in other countries of the West
every episcopal see was so styled, cf. Gregorii Tur. hist. Franc. iv. 26:
Presbyter—Regis praesentiam adiit et haec effatus est: Salve, Rex gloriose, Sedes enim apostolica eminentiae tuae salutem mittit uberrimam.
Cui ille, numquid, ait, Romanam adisti urbem, ut Papae illius nobis
salutem deferas ? Pater, inquit Presbyter, tuus Leontius (Ep. Burde-
galensis) cum provincialibus suis salutem tibi mittit.

[18] Pelagius i. ad Valerianum (Mansi ix. 732): quotiens aliqua de
universali synodo aliquibus dubitatio nascitur, ad recipiendam de eo
quod non intelligunt rationem,—ad apostolicas sedes pro recipienda
ratione conveniant.—Quisquis ergo ab apostolicis divisus est sedibus, in
schismate eum esse non dubium est.   Comp. above § 94, not. 5.   Gregorii M. lib. vii. ep. 40. ad Eulogium Episc. Alexandr.   Suavissima
mihi Sanctitas vestra multa in epistolis suis de s. Petri Apostolorum
principis cathedra locuta est, dicens, quod ipse in ea nunc usque in suis
successoribus sedeat.—Cuncta quae dicta sunt in eo libenter accepi,
quod ille mihi de Petri cathedra locutus est, qui Petri cathedram tenet.
Et cum me specialis honor nullo modo delectet, valde tamen laetatus
sum, quia vos, sanctissimi, quod mihi impendistis, vobismetipsis dedis-
tis.—Cum multi sint Apostoli, pro ipso tamen principatu solo Apostolorum principis sedes in auctoritate convaluit, quae in tribus locis unius
est.   Ipse enim sublimavit sedem, in qua etiam quiescere, et presen-
tem vitam finire dignatus est (Rome) ; ipse decoravit sedem, in qua
Evangelistam discipulum misit (Alexandria) ; ipse firmavit sedem, in
qua septem annis, quamvis discessurus, sedit (Antioch.)   Cum ergo
unius atque una sit sedes, cui ex auctoritate divina tres nunc Episcopi
praesident, quidquid ego de vobis boni audio, hoc mihi imputo.   Si
quid de me boni creditis, hoc vestris meritis imputate, quia in illo unum
sumus, qui ait: ut omnes unum sint etc.   (Jo. 17, 21.)   cf. Wiggers

knowledging that they were subject to general councils,[19] and
that the bishops were bound by duty to hear them only in case
of delinquency. In other respects, they admitted that these
bishops were equal to them in dignity.[20]

de Gregorio M. ejusque placitis anthropologicis comm. ii. Rostoch.
1838. 4. p. 29. The flattery of Eulogius may be explained by his
straitened condition, which Gregory relieved even by presents (cf. lib.
vi. ep. 60, vii. 40, viii. 29.) Isidorus Hisp. etymol. vii. 12 (in Gratiani
decreto dist. xxi. c. 1): Ordo Episcoporum quadripartitus est, id est in
Patriarchis, Archiepiscopis, Metropolitanis atque Episcopis. Patriarcha graeca lingua summus patrum interpretatur, quia primum *i. e.*
apostolicum retinet locum: et ideo quia summo honore fungitur, tali
nomine censetur, sicut Romanus, Antiochenus et Alexandrinus. Here,
therefore, the pope still stands in the same rank completely with the
other patriarchs.
 [19] Gelasius ep. xiii. (Mansi viii. 51): confidimus, quod nullus jam
veraciter Christianus ignoret, uniuscujusque synodi constitutum, quod
universalis ecclesiae probavit assensus, non aliquam magis exsequi sedem prae caeteris oportere, quam primam, quae et unamquamque synodum sua auctoritate confirmat, et continuata moderatione custodit, pro
suo scilicet principatu, quem b. Petrus apostolus domini voce perceptum, ecclesia nihilominus subsequente, et tenuit semper et retinet.
 [20] Gregorii M. lib. ix. epist. 59, ad Joh. Episc. Syracus. Si qua culpa
in Episcopis invenitur, nescio quis ei (Sedi apostolicae) subjectus non
sit: cum vero culpa non exigit, omnes secundum rationem humilitatis
aequales sunt. Lib. xi. ep. 37. ad Romanum defensorem: Pervenit ad
nos, quod si quis contra clericos quoslibet causam habeat, despectis
eorum Episcopis, eosdem clericos in tuo facias judicio exhiberi. Quod
si ita est, quia valde constat esse incongruum, hac tibi auctoritate praecipimus, ut hoc denuo facere non praesumus.—Nam si sua unicuique
Episcopo jurisdictio non servatur, quid aliud agitur, nisi ut per nos, per
quos ecclesiasticus custodiri debuit ordo, confundatur? (Lib. ii. ep. 52:
mihi injuriam facio, si fratrum meorum jura perturbo.)—Lib. viii. ep.
30, ad Eulogium Episc. Alexandr. Indicare quoque vestram Beatitudo
studuit, jam se quibusdam (the patriarch of Constantinople) non scribere superba vocabula, quae ex vanitatis radice prodierunt, et mihi
loquitur, dicens: sicut jussistis. Quod verbum jussionis peto a meo
auditu removere, quia scio, qui sum, qui estis. Loco enim mihi fratres
estis, moribus patres. Non ergo jussi, sed quae utilia visa sunt, indicare
curavi. Non tamen invenio vestram Beatitudinem hoc ipsum, quod
memoriae vestrae intuli, perfecte retinere voluisse. Nam dixi, nec mihi
vos, nec cuiquam alteri tale aliquid scribere debere: et ecce in praefatione epistolae, quam ad me ipsum qui prohibui direxistis, superbae
appellationis verbum, universalem me Papam dicentes, imprimere cu-
rastis. Quod peto dulcissima mihi Sanctitas vestra ultra non faciat,
quia vobis subtrahitur, quod alteri plus quam ratio exigit praebetur.—
Nec honorem esse deputo, in quo fratres meos honorem suum perdere
cognosco.—Si enim universalem me Papam vestra Sanctitas dicit, negat

After ecclesiastical peace had been restored between Rome and
Constantinople, the kings of the Ostrogoths became suspicious of
their Catholic subjects generally, and, in particular, of the Romish
bishops, because the latter had broken off communion with Constantinople. *John I.*, indeed, in his capacity of regal ambassador, procured the restoration of their Churches to the Arians in
the Greek Church; yet he was obliged to end his life in prison.[21]
The kings maintained a strict oversight of the choice of the
Catholic bishops, reserving to themselves the confirmation, or
absolute nomination of them.[22]   Yet even now the Gothic rule
was not so dangerous to the papacy as the Byzantine, which
latter began after the conquest of Italy (553–554).   It is true
that Justinian honoured the Roman see,[23] but he distinguished
the Constantinopolitan with no less favour;[24] and endeavoured in

se hoc esse, quod me fatetur universum.   Sed absit hoc.   Recedant
verba, quae vanitatem inflant et caritatem vulnerant.
   [21] Anastasii lib. pontific. c. 54, in vita Joannis.   Historia miscella lib.
15, (in Muratori scriptt. Ital. i. 103.)   Manso Gesch. d. ostgoth.
Reiches in Italien S. 163 ss.
   [22] Thus Theoderich appointed the Romish bishop, Felix III.   Cassiodori variarum lib. viii. ep. 15.   Comp. Sartorius Vers. über die Regierung der Ostgothen in Italien S. 138 ss. 308 s.—Athalarich's edict
addressed to John II. against bribery at the election of popes and
bishops A. D. 533.   Cassiod. variar. ix. ep. 15, with a commentary ap.
Manso l. c. P. 416 ff.
   [23] Justinian, A. D. 533, to the patriarch of Constantinople.   Cod.
Justin. i. i. 7 : οὔτε γὰρ ἀνεχόμεθά τι τῶν εἰς ἐκκλησιαστικὴν ὁρώντων κατάστασιν, μὴ καὶ τῇ αὐτοῦ (τοῦ πάπα τῆς πρεσβυτέρας Ῥώμης καὶ πατριάρχου)
ἀναφέρεσθαι μακαριότητι, ὡς κεφαλῇ οὔσῃ πάντων τῶν ὁσιωτάτων τοῦ θεοῦ
ἱερέων, καὶ ἐπειδὴ, ὁσάκις ἐν τούτοις τοῖς μέρεσιν αἱρετικοὶ ἀνεφύησαν, τῇ γνώμῃ
καὶ ὀρθῇ κρίσει τοῦ ἐκείνου σεβασμίου θρόνου κατηργήθησαν.   Ibid. l. 8. Justinianus ad Joannem ii. P.   Nec enim patimur quicquam, quod ad
Ecclesiarum statum pertinet, quamvis manifestum et indubitatum sit,
quod movetur, ut non etiam vestrae innotescat sanctitati, quae caput
est omnium sanctarum Ecclesiarum.   Per omnia enim (ut dictum est)
properamus, honorem et auctoritatem crescere vestrae sedis.
   [24] Cod. Justin. i. ii. 25 : Ἡ ἐν Κωνσταντινουπόλει ἐκκλησία πασῶν τῶν
ἄλλων ἐστὶ κεφαλή.   On the other hand, the right of the highest ecclesiastical court, which was conveyed to the patriarch of Constantinople at
Chalcedon (comp. above § 93, not. 15), if indeed it ever extended beyond the dioceses of Pontus, Asia, and Thrace, appears to have fallen
into oblivion.   The right of appeal is thus fixed by Justinian Cod. i.
iv. 29 : Bishop—Metropolitan and his Provincial synod—Patriarch.
From the decision of the last, as from that of the Praetorian prefect,
there could be no appeal (Cod. Just. vii. lxii. 19.)   No complaint is to

the end to convert both merely into instruments to enable him to rule both in church and state. Two of his creatures, *Vigilius* and *Pelagius I.*, successively filled the Roman see; and in the controversy concerning the three chapters it soon became apparent how hazardous to Rome this dependence on Byzantium was. For a long time in the Western Church the rejection of the three chapters was considered a violation of orthodoxy; and on this account the bishops of the diocese of Italy broke off communion with Rome. The bishops of *Milan* and *Ravenna* were indeed reconciled; when, oppressed by the Arian Lombards, they were compelled to set greater value on communion with the Catholic Church (570–580); but the archbishop of *Aquileia* (who, since the incursions of the Lombards into Italy (568), resided on the island Grado) and the Istrian bishops were more obstinate, and did not renew their fellowship with Rome till the year 698.[25]

But even this dangerous period of dependence on Byzantium ceased for Rome, after the incursion of the Lombards into Italy

be brought before the patriarch first, πλὴν εἰ μὴ τὴν αἰτίασίν τις ἐπὶ τούτῳ θείη, ἐφ᾽ ᾧτε παραπεμφθῆναι τὴν ὑπόθεσιν τῷ τῆς χώρας θεοφιλεστάτῳ ἐπισκόπῳ· τηνικαῦτα γὰρ ἄδεια μὲν ἔσται τὴν αἰτίασιν ἀποτίθεσθαι καὶ παρὰ τοῖς θεοφιλεστάτοις πατριάρχαις, *i.e.*, unless accompanied with the petition that the matter shall be delegated to the bishop of the province. For in that case it shall be allowed to bring the complaint before the patriarch. Then § 2 : Εἰ μέντοι παραπεμφθείσης τῆς ὑποθέσεως παρὰ τοῦ θεοφιλεστάτου πατριάρχου ἤ τινι τῶν θεοφιλεστάτων μητροπολιτῶν, ἢ ἄλλῳ τῶν θεοφιλεστάτων ἐπισκόπων, ἐνεχθείη ψῆφος, καὶ μὴ στερχθείη παρὰ θατέρου μέρους, ἐκκλητός τε γένηται· τηνικαῦτα ἐπὶ τὸν ἀρχιερατικὸν θρόνον (*Vers. lat.* ad Archiepiscopalem *hanc* sedem) φέρεσθαι τὴν ἔφεσιν, κἀκεῖσε κατὰ τὸ μέχρι νῦν κρατοῦν ἐξετάζεσθαι, *i.e.*, if the complaint is delegated by the patriarch to a metropolitan or another bishop, and a sentence passed which the one party is dissatisfied with, and an appeal is made; then the appeal shall be to the archbishop (consequently with the omission of some intermediate courts, according to the rule Cod. Just. vii., lxii., 32, § 3 : eorum sententiis appellatione suspensis, qui ex delegatione cognoscunt, necesse est eos aestimare—qui causas delegaverint judicandas). ὁ ἀρχιερατικὸς θρόνος, is every delegating patriarch, not exclusively, (as has been assumed after the Latin translation of Anton. Augustinus, which in this law is entirely false,) the patriarch of Constantinople. Even Ziegler Geschich. der Virchl. kerfassungsformen S. 232 ss. has entirely misunderstood this law.

[25] J. F. B. M. de Rubeis de schismate eccl. Aquilejensis diss. hist. Venet. 1732. 8. Republished in an enlarged form in ejusd. monimenta eccl. Aquilejensis. 1740. fol. Walch's Ketzerhist. viii. 331. N. C. Kist de Kerk en het Patriarchaat van Aquileja in de Archief voor kerkelijke Geschiedenis, i. 118.

I

(568). From that time the Greek dominions in this country
were confined to *the exarchate of Ravenna, the Duchy of Rome
and Naples, the cities on the coast of Liguria, and the extreme
provinces of Lower Italy*. Continually threatened by the Lombards, and often forsaken by the Greek emperors, these districts
were frequently obliged to protect themselves. At the head of
all measures for defence appeared the popes as the richest possessors,[26] whose own interest it was to avert the rule of those
Arian barbarians. Thus they not only gained great political
influence in Grecian Italy,[27] but also obtained a more indepen-

[26] As the emperors called their fortunes patrimonium (namely patrimonium privatum s. dominicum their private property, and patrim. sacratum s. divinae domus, their domains. See Gutherius de offic. dom. Aug.
lib. iii. c. 25. Pancirolius ad notit. dignitatum Imp. orient. c. 87) ; so
the churches called their possessions patrimonia of their saints. That
of the Roman church was therefore patrimonium s. Petri: at the same
time also the single estates which were managed by defensoribus or rectoribus were called patrimonia. cf. Zaccaria diss. de patrimoniis s. Rom.
Eccl. in his commentationes de rebus ad hist. atque antiquitt. Ecclesiae pertinentibus dissert. latinae (Fulginiae. Tomi. ii. 1781. 4.) ii. 68.
Planck's Gesch. d. christl. kirchl. Gesellschaftsverf. i. 629. C. H.
Sack de patrimoniis Eccl. Rom. circa finem saeculi vi. in his commentationes, quae ad theol. hist. pertinent, tres. Bonnae 1821. 8. p.
25. ss. For an account of the activity of the Popes in protecting
Italy comp. Gregorii M. lib. v. ep. 21. ad Constantinam Aug.:
Viginti autem jam et septem annos ducimus, quod in hac urbe inter
Langobardorum gladios vivimus. Quibus quam multa hac ab Ecclesia quotidianis diebus erogantur, ut inter eos vivere possimus, suggerenda non sunt. Sed breviter indico, quia sicut in Ravennae partibus
Dominorum Pietas apud primum exercitum Italiae saccellarium habet,
qui causis supervenientibus quotidianas expensas faciat, ita et in hac
urbe in causis talibus eorum saccellarius ego sum. Et tamen haec Ecclesia, quae uno eodemque tempore Clericis, monasteriis, pauperibus,
populo, atque insuper Langobardis tam multa indesinenter expendit,
ecce adhuc ex omnium Ecclesiarum premitur afflictione, quae de hac
unius hominis (Johannis Jejunat.) superbia multum gemunt, etsi nihil
dicere praesumunt.
[27] Gregorii M. lib. ii. ep. 31. ad cunctos milites Neapolitanos: Summa
militiae laus inter alia bona merita haec est, obedientiam sanctae Reipublicae utilitatibus exhibere, quodque sibi utiliter imperatum fuerit,
obtemperare: sicut et nunc devotionem vestram fecisse didicimus, quae
epistolis nostris, quibus magnificum virum Constantium Tribunum custodiae civitatis deputavimus praeesse, paruit, et congruam militaris
devotionis obedientiam demonstravit. Unde scriptis vos praesentibus
curavimus admonendos, uti praedicto viro magnifico Tribuno, sicut et
fecistis, omnem debeatis pro serenissimorum Dominorum utilitate, vel conservanda civitate obedientiam exhibere etc. Comp. the excerpt from the

dent position in ecclesiastical matters in relation to the Greek emperors. As citizens, they remained subject to the Greek emperors, and their representatives, the exarchs of Ravenna.[28]

Towards the end of this period the flame of controversy was again kindled between the two first patriarchs of Christendom, when *John Jejunator* began to assume the title of a Patriarcha universalis, οἰκουμενικός (587).[29] Even *Pelagius II.* grew very warm respecting it,[30] and still more *Gregory the Great.* These popes rejected that appellation altogether, as antichristian and devilish; without, however, making the desired impression on the Emperor Maurice and the court patriarch.[31] So much the

acts of Honorius i.(625, 638), by Muratori, antiquitt. Ital. v. 834 from Cehcii Camerarii lib. de censibus, and published more fully by Zaccaria l. c. p. 131. from the collect. Cann. of Cardinal Deusdedit. Idem in eodem (*i. e.,* Honorius in suo Registro) Gaudisso Notario et Anatolio Magistro militum Neapolitanam civitatem regendam committit, et qualiter debeat regi, scriptis informat. It does not follow from these passages, as Dionysius de Ste Marthe in vita Gregorii lib. iii. c. 9. no. 6. (Gregg. opp. iv. 271.) and Zaccaria l. c. p. 112. 131. conclude from them that the city of Naples belonged to the patrimonium s. Petri; but that the popes who had important possessions there (a patrimonium Neapolitanum and Campanum, Zaccaria p. 111.) when the city was hard pressed (cf. Gregor. M. lib. ii. ep. 46. ad Johannem Episc. Ravennae: De Neapolitana vero urbe, excellentissimo Exarcho instanter imminente, vobis indicamus, quia Arigis—valde insidiatur eidem civitati, in quam si celeriter dux non mittatur, omnino jam inter perditas habetur) and required speedy aid, took the necessary measures instead of the exarch. cf. Sack l. c. p. 52.

[28] Cf. Gregorii M. lib. iii. ep. 65. above § 116. not. 3. For the official authorities concerning the relations of the ecclesiastical to the civil power, especially concerning the right of the exarchs to confirm the choice of a pope, see the liber diurnus Romanorum Pontiff. See on this subject on the following period.

[29] At first applied by flatterers to all patriarchs. See § 93. not. 20. § 94. not. 72. Ziegler Gesch. der kirchl. Verfassungformen, S. 259. Justinian gives the patriarch of Constantinople the title, τῷ ἁγιωτάτῳ καὶ μακαριωτάτῳ ἀρχιεπισκόπῳ τῆς βασιλίδος ταύτης πόλεως καὶ οἰκουμενικῷ πατριάρχῃ. Cod. i. 1. 7. Novell. iii. v. vi. vii. xvi. xlii.

[30] Gregorii M. lib. v. ep. 18. 43. ix. 68. The letter viii. Pelagii ad universos Episcc. (Mansi. ix. 900.) relative to this point is pseudo-isidorian. See Blondelli Pseudoisidorus p. 636 ss.

[31] Gregorii M. lib. v. ep. 18. ad Johann.—Si ergo ille (Paulus) membra dominici corporis certis extra Christum quasi capitibus, et ipsis quidem Apostolis subjici partialiter evitavit (1 Cor. i. 12. ss.): tu quid Christo, universalis scilicet Ecclesiae capiti, in extremi judicii es dicturus examine, qui cuncta ejus membra tibimet conaris universalis appellatione supponere? Quis, rogo, in hoc tam perverso vocabulo, nisi ille

I 2

more, therefore, did Gregory thank Providence when *Maurice's* murderer *Phocas* (602) ascended the throne;[32] and Phocas repaid the pope's favour by taking his part against the patriarch,[33]   .

ad imitandum proponitur, qui despectis Angelorum legionibus secum socialiter constitutis, ad culmen conatus est singularitatis erumpere, ut et nulli subesse et solus omnibus praeesse videretur? Certe Petrus Apostolorum primus, membrum sanctae et universalis Ecclesiae, Paulus, Andreas, Johannes, quid aliud quam singularium sunt plebium capita? et tamen sub uno capite omnes membra—Numquid non—per venerandum Chalcedonense Concilium hujus apostolicae sedis Antistites, cui Deo disponente deservio, universales oblato honore vocati sunt? (Comp. § 94. not. 72.)   Sed tamen nullus umquam tali vocabulo appellari voluit, nullus sibi hoc temerarium nomen arripuit: ne si sibi in Pontificatus gradu gloriam singularitatis arriperet, hanc omnibus fratribus denegasse videretur. Ep. 19. ad Sabinianum Diac. (Apocrisiarium.) Ep. 20. ad Mauricium Aug. ep. 21. ad Constantinam Aug. ep. 43. ad Eulogium Ep. Alexandr. et Anastasium Antiochenum. Lib. vii. ep. 4. 5. and 31. ad Cyriacum Ep. Constant. ep. 27. ad Anastas. Antioch. ep. 33. ad Mauricium Aug.: De qua re mihi in suis jussionibus Dominorum Pietas praecipit, dicens, ut per appellationem frivoli nominis inter nos scandalum generari non debeat.   Sed rogo, ut Imperialis Pietas penset, quia alia sunt frivola valde innoxia, atque alia valde nociva.   Numquidnam cum se Antichristus veniens Deum dixerit, frivolum valde erit, sed tamen nimis perniciosum?   Si quantitatem sermonis attendimus, duae sunt syllabae; si vero pondus iniquitatis, universa pernicies.   Ego autem fidenter dico, quia quisquis se universalem Sacerdotem vocat, vel vocari desiderat, in elatione sua Antichristum praecurrit, quia superbiendo se caeteris praeponit.   Nec dispari superbia ad errorem ducitur, quia sicut perversus ille Deus videri vult super omnes homines: ita quisquis iste est, qui solus Sacerdos appellari appetit, super reliquos Sacerdotes se extollit.   Ep. 34. ad Eulogium Alex. et Anastas. Ant.   How earnestly Gregory rejected for himself this title, may be seen in lib. viii. ep. 30. ad Eulogium Ep. Alex. above not. 18.   According to Joannes Diac. (about 825) in vita Greg. M. ii. 1. Gregory may have assumed the title servus servorum Dei, to put to shame the patriarch of Constantinople. Even Augustine called himself ep. 130 and 217. servus servorum Christi, Fulgentius ep. 4. servorum Christi famulus.   Among Gregory the Great's etters, there are now only three before which he so styles himself.   But even so late as the eleventh century other bishops too, as well as kings and emperors, employed this title.   See du Fresne glossar. ad scriptt. med. et. inf. lat. s. v. servus.

[32] Comp. the congratulatory letter of Gregory lib. xiii. ep. 31. ad Phocam Imp. ep. 38. ad Leontiam Aug.

[33] The patriarch Cyriacus was an adherent of Maurice (Theophanes i. 446. 453.)   Anastasius de vitis Pontific. c. 67. Bonifacius iii.: Hic obtinuit apud Phocam Principem, ut Sedes apostolica B. Petri Apostoli caput esset omnium ecclesiarum, *i. e.*, Ecclesia Romana, quia Ecclesia Constantinopolitana primam se omnium Ecclesiarum scribebat.   With

though after him that disputed title was constantly assumed by the see of Constantinople.[34]

At this time the popes also began to bestow the pallium (which all bishops in the East received at their consecration)[35] on the most distinguished bishops of the West, for the purpose of symbolising and strengthening their connection with the Church of Rome.[36]

the same words Paulus Warnefridi de gestis Longob. iv. 37. Doubted by J. M. Lorenz examen decreti Phocae de primatu Rom. Pont. Argent. 1790. Schröckh xvii. 72. Remarkable is the view of the subject taken by the Ghibelline Gotfridus Viterbiensis (about 1186) in his Pantheon p. xvi. (Pistorii rer. Germ. scriptt. ed. Struve ii. 289).

> Tertius est Papa Bonifacius ille benignus,
> Qui petit a Phoca munus per secula dignum,
> Ut sedes Petri prima sit; ille dedit.
> Prima prius fuerat Constantinopolitana;
> Est modo Romana, meliori dogmate clara.

[34] Even Heraclius, successor of Phocas, in his laws gives again this title to the patriarch of Constantinople. See Leunclavii jus Graeco-Romanum. T. i. p. 73 ss.

[35] See above § 101. not. 1. Against the opinion almost universally adopted from Petrus de Marca de conc. Sac. et Imp. lib. vi. c. 6. that the old pallium, a splendid mantle, was a part of the imperial dress, and therefore bestowed only by the emperors, or with their permission by the patriarchs, see J. G. Pertsch de origine, usu, et auctoritate, pallii archiepiscopalis. Helmst. 1754. 4. p. 56 ss.

[36] The oldest document on the subject is Symmachi P. ep. ad Theodorum Laureacensem (Mansi viii. p. 228) about 501: Diebus vitae tuae palli usum, quem ad sacerdotalis officii decorem et ad ostendendam unauimitatem, quam cum b. Petro Apostolo universum gregem dominicarum ovium, quae ei commissae sunt, habere dubiuni non est, ab apostolica sede, sicut decuit, poposcisti, quod utpote ab eisdem Apostolis fundatae ecclesiae majorum more libenter indulsimus ad ostendendum te magistrum et archiepiscopum, tuamque sanctam Laureacensem ecclesiam provinciae Pannoniorum sedem fore metropolitanam. Idcirco pallio, quod ex apostolica caritate tibi destinamus, quo uti debeas secundum morem ecclesiae tuae, solerter admonemus pariterque volumus, ut intelligas, quia ipse vestitus, quo ad missarum solemnia ornaris, signum praetendit crucis, per quod scito te cum fratribus debere compati ac mundialibus illecebris in affectu crucifigi etc. (The formula in the liber diurnus cap. iv. tit. 3. is abbreviated from this epistle.) According to Vigilii P. ep. vii. ad Auxanium Arelatensem (Mansi ix. p. 42.) Symmachus also invested Caesarius, bishop of Arles, with the pallium. These investitures became more frequent under Gregory the Great, not only of metropolitans, as John of Corinth, Leo of Prima Justinianea, Vigilius of Arles, Augustine of Canterbury, but also simple bishops, as of Donus of Messina, John of Syracuse, John of Palermo, &c. See Pertsch l. c. p. 134 ss. Though

FOURTH CHAPTER.

HISTORY OF MONACHISM.

§. 118.

THE LITERATURE MAY BE SEEN IN THE PREFACE TO § 95.

In the East, monachism continued in its manifold forms.[1] Justinian favoured it by his laws,[2] though he endeavoured to re-

Vigilius P. ep. vi. ad Auxanium Arelatensem (Mansi ix. p. 40.) writes : De his vero, quae Caritas vestra tam de usu pallii, quam de aliis sibi a nobis petiit debere concedi, libenti hoc animo etiam in praesenti facere sine dilatione potuimus, nisi cum christianissimi Domini filii nostri imperatoris hoc, sicut ratio postulat, voluissemus perficere notitia ; and Gregorius i. lib. ix. ep. 11. ad Brunichildem Reginam, while he mentions to Synagrius, bishop of Autun, gifted with the pallium, the necessity of the imperial approbation ; yet it was probably sought for only when hostile relations existed with the kingdom to which the pallium was sent. See Pertsch l. c. p. 196 ss. That a tax was early connected with this investiture, see Gregorii i. lib. v. ep. 57. ad Johannem Ep. Corinth. (also ap. Gratianus dist. C. c. 3.) : Novit autem Fraternitas vestra, quia prius pallium nisi dato commodo non dabatur. Quod quoniam incongruum erat, facto Concilio tam de hoc quam de ordinationibus aliquid accipere sub districta interdictione vetuimus. The decree referred to is in Mansi ix. p. 1227.

[1] Comp. the description, Evagrius i. 21. The spirit of the oriental monks of this period may be gathered from Johannis Moschi (about 630) λειμών, pratum spirituale (in Latin in Herib. Rosweydi vitae patrum. Antverp. 1615. fol. p. 855 ss. The Greek original, though defective, is found in Frontonis Ducaei auctarium bibl. PP. ii. 1057. The chasms are supplied in Cotelerii monum. Eccl. Gr. ii. 341). Even here complaints of the decay of monachism appear ex. gr. c. 130: οἱ πατέρες ἡμῶν τὴν ἐγκράτειαν καὶ τὴν ἀκτημοσύνην μέχρι θανάτου ἐτήρησαν, ἡμεῖς δὲ ἐπλατύναμεν τὰς κοιλίας ἡμῶν καὶ βαλάντια κ. τ. λ. cf. cap. 52 and 168.

[2] Cod. Justin. i. 3. 53. (A. D. 532) forbids, μηδένα παντελῶς, μήτε βουλευτὴν μήτε ταξεώτην ἐπίσκοπον ἢ πρεσβύτερον τοῦ λοιποῦ γίνεσθαι, but adds : πλὴν εἰ μὴ ἐκ νηπίας ἡλικίας, καὶ οὔπω τὴν ἔφηβον ἐκβάσης, ἔτυχε τοῖς εὐλαβεστάτοις μοναχοῖς ἐγκαταλελεγμένος, καὶ διαμείνας ἐπὶ τούτου τοῦ σχήματος· τηνικαῦτα γὰρ ἐφίεμεν αὐτῷ καὶ πρεσβυτέρῳ γενέσθαι, καὶ εἰς ἐπισκοπὴν ἐλθεῖν,—τὴν τετάρτην μέντοι μοῖραν τῆς αὐτοῦ περιουσίας ἁπάσης παρέχων τοῖς

strain the irregular wanderings of the Coenobites.[3]   While the
Stylites in the East still attracted the highest wonder, especially
one *Daniel*,[4] in the neighbourhood of Constantinople, under the
Emperors Basiliscus and Zeno, an attempt in the neighbourhood
of Treves to imitate them was interdicted by the bishops of the
place.[5]   On the other hand, the κατειργμένοι of the East, especi-.
ally in Gaul, found many admirers (Reclausi, Recluses).[6]

§ 119.

BENEDICTINES.

Jo. Mabillonii annales ordinis S. Benedicti, vi. tomi (the 6th edited by Edm.
Martene reaches to the year 1157.) Paris. 1703—1739. auct. Luccae
1739—1745. fol.—Lucae Dacherii et Jo. Mabillonii acta Sanctorum Ord.
S. Benedicti (six centuries to 1100.) ix. voll. 1668—1701: fol.

In the West, *Benedict,* a native of Nursia in Umbria,[1] gave a

βουλευταῖς, καὶ τῷ δημοσίῳ. § 3 ; Ἔτι θεσπίζομεν, εἴτε ἀνὴρ ἐπὶ μονήρη βίον
ἐλθεῖν βουληθείη, εἴτε γυνὴ τὸν ἄνδρα καταλιποῦσα πρὸς ἄσκησιν ἔλθοι, μὴ τοῦτο
αὐτὸ ζημίας παρέχειν πρόφασιν, ἀλλὰ τὰ μὲν οἰκεῖα πάντως λαμβάνειν. cf.
Novell. cxxiii. c. 40 : Εἰ δὲ συνεστῶτος ἔτι τοῦ γάμου ὁ ἀνὴρ μόνος ἢ ἡ γυνὴ
μόνη εἰσέλθῃ εἰς μοναστήριον, διαλυέσθω ὁ γάμος, καὶ δίχα ῥεπουδίου. (On the
other hand Gregorius M. lib. xi. ep. 45: Si enim dicunt, religionis
causa conjugia debere dissolvi, sciendum est, quia etsi hoc lex humana
concessit, divina lex tamen prohibuit. cf. Bingham vol. iii. p. 45).
Cod. Just. i. 3. 55: Ut non liceat parentibus impedire, quominus liberi
eorum volentes monachi aut clerici fiant, aut eam ob solam causam ex-
heredare (cf. Nov. cxxiii. c. 41). Nov. v. c. 2. allows slaves to go into
convents contrary to the will of their masters.

3 Novella v. de Monachis (A. D. 535) cap. 4 : Εἰ δέ τις ἅπαξ ἑαυτὸν
καθιερώσας τῷ μοναστηρίῳ, καὶ τοῦ σχήματος τυχὼν, εἶτα ἀναχωρῆσαι τοῦ μοναστηρίου βουληθείη, καὶ ἰδιώτην τυχὸν ἐλέσθαι βίον· αὐτὸς μὲν ἴστω, ποίαν ὑπὲρ
τούτου δώσει τῷ θεῷ τὴν ἀπολογίαν, τὰ πράγματα μέντοι ὁπόσα ἂν ἔχοι ἡνίκα εἰς
τὸ μοναστήριον εἰσῄει, ταῦτα τῆς δεσποτείας ἔσται τοῦ μοναστηρίου καὶ οὐδ'
ὁτιοῦν παντελῶς ἐξάξει. cap. 7. : Εἰ δὲ ἀπολιπὼν τὸ μοναστήριον, καθ' ὅπερ
τὴν ἄσκησιν εἶχεν, εἰς ἕτερον μεταβαίνοι μοναστήριον, καὶ οὕτω μὲν ἡ αὐτοῦ
περιουσία μενέτο τε καὶ ἐκδικείσθω ὑπὸ τοῦ προτέρου μοναστηρίου, ἔνθα ἀποταξ-
άμενος τοῦτο κατέλιπε. προσῆκον δέ ἐστι τοὺς εὐλαβεστάτους ἡγουμένους μὴ
εἰσδέχεσθαι τὸν τοῦτο πράττοντα.
4 Acta Danielis ap. Surium ad d. 11 Dec.
5 Gregor. Turon. hist. Franc. viii. 15.
6 Ex. gr., Gregor. Tur. ii. 37. v. 9. 10. vi. 6.
1 His biographer is Gregorius M. in dialogorum lib. secundo.

new form to the monastic life. After he had long lived a hermit's life, he founded a convent on a mountain in Campania, where the old castrum Cassinum was situated (hence called monasterium Cassinense, monte Cassino). Here he introduced a new system of rules (529)[2] which mitigated the extreme rigour of the Eastern monks,[3] prescribed a variety of suitable employments,[4] but was distinguished especially by this, that it exacted

[2] Regula Benedicti in 73 Capp. in Hospinian and many others, best in Luc. Holstenii codex regularum monastic. et canon. (Romae 1661. iii. voll. 4). auctus a Marian. Brockie (August. Vindel. 1759. vi. tomi fol.) i. 3. and thence in Gallandii bibl. PP. xi. 298. Among the numerous commentaries the best are by Edm. Martene. Paris. 1690. 4. and by Augustin Calmet. Paris. 1734. T. 2. 4. General regulations: cap. 64 : In Abbatis ordinatione illa semper consideretur ratio, ut hic constituatur, quem sibi omnis concors congregatio secundum timorem Dei, sive etiam pars, quamvis parva, congregationis, saniori consilio, elegerit. Cap. 65 : Quemcunque elegerit Abbas cum consilio fratrum timentium Deum, ordinet ipse sibi Praepositum. Qui tamen Praepositus illa agat cum reverentia, quae ab Abbate suo ei injuncta fuerint, nihil contra Abbatis voluntatem aut ordinationem faciens. Cap. 21 : Si major fuerit congregatio, eligantur de ipsis fratres boni testimonii et sanctae conversationis, et constituantur Decani, qui solicitudinem gerant super Decanias suas. Cap. 3 : Quoties aliqua praecipua agenda sunt in monasterio, convocet Abbas omnem congregationem, et dicat ipse unde agitur. Et audiens consilium fratrum, tractet apud se, et quod utilius judicaverit faciat. Si qua vero minora agenda sunt in monasterii utilitatibus, seniorum tantum utatur consilio. Cap. 5 : Primus humilitatis gradus est obedentia sine mora. Haec convenit iis, qui nihil sibi Christo carius aliquid existimant: propter servitium sanctum, quod professi sunt, seu propter metum gehennae, vel gloriam vitae aeternae, mox ut aliquid imperatum a majore fuerit, ac si divinitus imperetur, moram pati nesciunt in faciendo.

[3] Cap. 39. Appoints for the daily food cocta duo pulmentaria (ut forte, qui ex uno non poterit edere, ex alio reficiatur). Et si fuerint inde poma aut nascentia leguminum, addatur et tertium. Farther panis libra una and cap. 40. hemina vini. (different opinions concerning the hemina, see in Martene comm. in Reg. S. Bened. p. 539 ss.) On the other hand carnium quadrupedum ab omnibus abstineatur comestio, praeter omnino debiles et aegrotos. Cap. 36 : balneorum usus infirmis, quoties expedit, offeratur. Sanis autem, et maxime juvenibus, tardius concedatur.

[4] Cap. 48 : Otiositas inimica est animae : et ideo certis temporibus occupari debent fratres in labore manuum, certis iterum horis in lectione divina. Between these the horae canonicae, namely the Nocturnae vigiliae, Matutinae, Prima, Tertia, Sexta, Nona, Vespera and Completorium (see respecting them Cap. 8-19.), Cap. 16. justified by Ps. 118. 164. Septies in die laudem dixi tibi, and v. 62. media nocte surgebam ad confitendum tibi. Comp. § 95. not. 8.

a promise from all who entered, never to leave the monastery again, and strictly to observe its rules.[5] This system was soon diffused in Italy, Gaul, and Spain. Instead of the former diversity of monasteries, unity now appeared ; and thus arose the first proper monastic order or association of many monasteries under a peculiar rule. The straitening of vows in this Benedictine rule was followed by the declaration of marriage being invalid in the case of monks ;[6] while the monks and nuns who had left their monasteries began to be violently brought back into them.[7]

[5] Cap. 58: After ordering a probation time of the noviter venientis ad conversionem: si habita secum deliberatione promiserit se omnia custodire et cuncta sibi imperata servare, tunc suscipiatur in congregatione, sciens se jam sub lege regulae constitutum, quod ei ex illa die non liceat egredi de monasterio, nec collum excutere de subjugo regulae, quam sub tam morosa deliberatione licuit aut excusare, aut suscipere. Suscipiendus autem in oratorio coram omnibus promittat de stabilitate sua, et conversione morum suorum, et obedientia coram Deo et sanctis ejus, ut si aliquando aliter fecerit, ab eo se damnandum sciat, quem irridet. De qua promissione sua faciat petitionem ad nomen Sanctorum, quorum reliquiae ibi sunt, et Abbatis praesentis. Quam petitionem manu sua scribat, aut certe, si non scit literas, alter ab eo rogatus scribat, et ille novitius signum faciat, et manu sua eam super altare ponat. Cap. 59 : Si quis forte de nobilibus offert filium suum Deo in monasterio, si ipse puer minori aetate est, parentes ejus faciant petitionem, quam supra diximus. Et cum oblatione ipsam petitionem et manum pueri involvant in palla altaris, et sic eum offerant. Cap. 66 : Monasterium autem, si possit fieri, ita debet construi, ut omnia necessaria, id est aqua, molendinum, hortus, pistrinum, vel artes diversae intra monasterium exerceantur, ut non sit necessitas Monachis vagandi foras, quia omnino non expedit animabus eorum.

[6] The older appointment (see § 95. note 49.), that the breaking of the vow should be punished with church-penance, is still repeated by Leo I. ep. 90. ad Rusticum c. 12. (Propositum monachi—deseri non potest absque peccato. Quod enim vovit Deo, debet et reddere. Unde qui relicta singularitatis professione ad militiam vel ad nuptias devolutus est, publicae poenitentiae satisfactione purgandus est), and Gelasius I. ep. 5. ad Episc. Lucaniae (ap Gratian. Causa xxvii. Qu. 1. c. 14.) Also Conc. Aurelian. i. ann. 511. c. 21. pre-supposes the validity of marriage. (Monachus si in monasterio conversus vel pallium comprobatus fuerit accepisse, et postea uxori fuerit sociatus, tantae praevaricationis reus nunquam ecclesiastici gradus officium sortiatur.)   On the contrary, first, the Conc. Turonicum ii. ann. 567. c. 15: (Monachus) si —uxorem duxerit, excommunicetur, et de uxoris male sociatae consortio etiam judicis auxilio separetur.—Qui infelix monachus,—et illi, qui eum exceperint ad defensandum, ab ecclesia segregentur, donec revertatur ad septa monasterii, et indictam ab Abbate—agat poenitentiam, et post satisfactionem revertatur ad gratiam.

[7] Thus Gregory the Great ordered, with reference to a married nun

Of literary pursuits among the monks we find no trace, either in Benedict's rule, or among the first Benedictines.[8] It was *Cassiodorus* who made the first attempt of this kind in the· convent built by him called *Vivarium* (Coenobium Vivariense. 538) near Squillacci in Bruttia, whither he had withdrawn ;[9] and where, in addition to other useful employments, an endeavour was made to introduce learned occupations also into a monastery.[10]

(ap. Gratian. C. xxvii. Qu. 1. c. 15.), and with reference to another who had merely returned ad saecularem habitum, lib. vii. ep. 9. ad Vitalianum Ep. A. D. 597. (ap. Gratian. l. c. c. 18): Instantiae tuae sit, praedictam mulierem una cum Sergio defensore nostro comprehendere, et statim non solum ad male contemptum habitum sine excusatione aliqua revocare, sed etiam in monasterio, ubi omnino districte valeat custodiri, detrudere.   And lib. i. ep. 40. A. D. 591: Quia aliquos Monachorum usque ad tantum nefas prosiliisse cognovimus, ut uxores publice sortiantur, sub omni vigilantia eos requiras, et inventos digna coërcitione in monasteriis, quorum monachi fuerant, retransmittas.

[8] See Rich. Simon critique de la bibliothéque de Mr. Ell. du Pin. (Paris 1730. 4 Tom. 8.) i. 212.

[9] That he introduced the rules of Benedict into his convent, as the Benedictines (see Garetius in the vita Cass. prefixed to his opp. p. 27.) supposed, has been justly denied by Baronius ad ann. 494.

[10] For this purpose he wrote in particular his works de institutione divinarum litterarum, and de artibus ac disciplinis liberalium litterarum, comp. § 114. note 7.   He exhorts, above all things, to study the Holy Scriptures and the fathers.   But then he adds de instit. div. litt. c. 28: Verumtamen nec illud Patres sanctissimi decreverunt, ut saecularium litterarum studia respuantur : quia exinde non minimum ad sacras scripturas intelligendas sensus noster instruitur.—Frigidus obstiterit circum praecordia sanguis, ut nec humanis nec divinis litteris perfecte possit erudiri : aliqua tamen scientiae mediocritate suffultus, eligat certe quod sequitur :

Rura mihi et rigui placeant in vallibus amnes.

Quia nec ipsum est a Monachis alienum hortos colere, agros exercere, et pomorum foecunditate gratulari.   Cap. 30 : Ego tamen fateor votum meum, quod inter vos quaecumque possunt corporeo labore compleri, Antiquariorum mihi studia (si tamen veraciter scribant) non immerito forsan plus placere ; quod et mentem suam relegendo scripturas divinas salubriter instruant, et Domini praecepta scribendo longe lateque disseminent.   (Comp. the directions for copying and revising manuscripts cap. 15. and the treatise de orthographia.)—Cap. 31 : Sed et vos alloquor fratres egregios, qui humani corporis salutem sedula curiositate tractatis, et confugientibus ad loca sanctorum officia beatae pietatis impenditis.   Et ideo discite quidem naturas herbarum, commixtionesque specierum sollicita mente tractate.   He recommends to them the writings of Dioscorides, Hippocrates, and Galen.   Comp. Stäudlin in the Kirchenhist. Archive für 1825. S. 413 ss.

The Benedictines, already accustomed to a well regulated activity, very soon followed this example; and thus they could now be useful to the West in many ways.

They reclaimed many waste lands, actively advanced the cause of education,[11] handed down to posterity the history of their time in chronicles, and preserved to it by their copyists, for the most part indeed as dead treasures, the writings of antiquity.[12]

§ 120.

RELATION OF THE MONKS TO THE CLERGY.

Though the clergy continued to be very often chosen from among the monks, yet there were in the convents no more ordained monks than were required by the necessities of the monks' congregation; and many convents had no presbyter whatever.[1] The old rule that all convents should be under the inspection of the bishops of the dioceses in which they were situated,[2] was first

[11] The permission to undertake the care of pueros oblatos, given by Benedict in his rule c. 59. (see above note 5.) was soon and often taken advantage of. See Gregory M. dial. ii. cap. 3: Coepere etiam tunc ad eum Romanae urbis nobiles et religiosi concurrere, suosque ei filios omnipotenti Deo nutriendos dare. For these pueri oblati in particular, the monastery schools were erected, of which the first intimation is found in the so-called Regula Magistri c. 50. (ap. Holstenius-Brockie t. i. p. 266) composed about 100 years after Benedict, where it is prescribed in the three hours from the first to the third, infantuli in decada sua in tabulis suis ab uno litterato litteras meditentur.

[12] cf. Mabillon acta SS. Ord. Ben. T. i. Praef. no. 114 et 115.

[1] Presbyters were sent into the convents by the bishops (directi, deputati) ad missas celebrandas. Gregor. M. lib. vi. ep. 46. vii. 43.—Abbots prayed and received permission in monasterio Presbyterum, qui sacra Missarum solemnia celebrare debeat, ordinari. Ibid. vi. 42. ix. 92: or a presbyter was appointed to the convent, quem et in monasterio habitare, et iudo vitae subsidia habere necesse fuit, ibid. iv. 18.—On the other hand Gregory lib. vi. ep. 56. praises a convent of which he had heard, et Presbyteros et Diaconos cunctamque congregationem unanimes vivere ac concordes.

[2] Conc. Chalced. c. 4:—ἔδοξε μηδένα μὲν μηδαμοῦ οἰκοδομεῖν μηδὲ συνιστᾶν μοναστήριον ἢ εὐκτήριον οἶκον παρὰ γνώμην τοῦ τῆς πόλεως Ἐπισκόπου· τοὺς δὲ καθ᾽ ἑκάστην πόλιν καὶ χώραν μονάζοντας ὑποτετάχθαι τῷ Ἐπισκόπῳ. can. 8: Οἱ κληρικοὶ τῶν πτωχείων καὶ μοναστηρίων καὶ μαρτυρίων ὑπὸ τῶν ἐν

departed from in Africa, where many put themselves under the
superintendence of distant bishops, especially the bishop of Carthage, to keep themselves secure against oppression.[3]   In the
remaining part of the West, the duty of the monasteries to be
spiritually subject to the diocesan bishops was still strictly enforced.[4]   On the other hand, synods and popes took them under
their protection in opposition to episcopal oppression, and made
it a fundamental principle that the bishops should not interfere
with their internal administration.[5]   *Gregory the Great*, in particular, was distinguished for his protection of convents.[6]

ἑκάστῃ πόλει Ἐπισκόπων τὴν ἐξουσίαν, κατὰ τὴν τῶν ἁγίων πατέρων παράδοσιν,
διαμενέτωσαν, καὶ μὴ κατανθαδιάζεσθαι ἢ ἀφηνιᾷν τοῦ ἰδίου Ἐπισκόπου.
[3] Conc. Carthag. ann. 525. diès secunda (ap. Mansi viii. 648.)   The
prayer of Abbas Petrus to Bishop Boniface of Carthage, p. 653 :—hu-
miles supplicamus, ut—a jugo nos clericorum, quod neque nobis neque
patribus nostris quisquam superponere aliquando tentavit, eruere dig-
neris.   Nam docemus, monasterium de Praecisu, quod in medio plebium
Leptiminensis ecclesiae ponitur, praetermisso eodem Episcopo vicino,
Vico Ateriensis ecclesiae Episcopi consolationem habere, qui in longinquo positus est. —Nam et de Adrumetino monasterio nullo modo silere
possumus, qui praetermisso ejusdem civitatis Episcopo de transmarinis
partibus sibi semper presbyteros ordinaverunt.—Et cum sibi diversa
monasteria, ut ostenderent libertatem suam, unicuique prout visum est,
a diversis Episcopis consolationem quaesierint : quomodo nobis denegari poterit, qui de hac sede sancta Carthaginensis ecclesiae, quae prima
totius Africanae ecclesiae haberi videtur, auxilium quaesivimus? etc.
cf. Concil. Carthagin. ann. 534. (Mansi viii. 841.)   cf. Thomassinus
P. i. L. iii. c. 31.
[4] Conc. Aurelian. i. (511) can. 19.   Epaonense (517) can. 19.
Arelatense v. (554) can. 7.
[5] So first Concil. Arelatense iii. A. D. 456. (Mansi vii. 907.), which
limited the rights of the bishop of the diocese in the convent of Lerins
as follows, ut clerici, atque altaris ministri a nullo, nisi ab ipso, vel cui
ipse injunxerit, ordinentur; chrisma non nisi ab ipso speretur; neo-
phyti si fuerint, ab eodem confirmentur ; peregrini clerici absque ipsius
praecepto in communionem, vel ad ministerium non admittantur.   Monasterii vero omnis laica multitudo ad curam Abbatis pertineat : neque ex
ea sibi Episcopus quidquam vindicet, aut aliquem ex illa clericum, nisi
abbate petente, praesumat.   Hoc enim et rationis et religionis plenum
est, ut clerici ad ordinationem Episcopi debita subjectione respiciant ;
laica vero omnis monasterii congregatio ad solam ac liberam Abbatis
proprii, quem sibi ipsa elegerit, ordinationem dispositionemque pertineat ; regula, quae a fundatore ipsius monasterii dudum constituta est,
in omnibus custodita.
[6] Comp. especially Greg. M. lib. viii. ep. 15. ad Marinianum Ravennae Episc.: Nullus audeat de reditibus vel chartis monasterii minuere.

FIFTH CHAPTER.

HISTORY OF PUBLIC WORSHIP.

§ 121.

How much the sensuous tendency of public worship,[1] of which we have already spoken, was farther developed in this period, and how many new superstitious notions sprung from it,[2] is best seen in the writings of *Gregory the Great*, a man who, with much real piety, had also very many monkish prejudices and great credulity ; while by his high reputation in the Western Church,

—Defuncto Abbate non extraneus nisi de eadem congregatione, quem sibi propria voluntate congregatio elegerit, ordinetur.—Invito Abbate ad ordinanda alia monasteria aut ad ordines sacros tolli exinde monachi non debent.—Descriptio rerum aut chartarum monasterii ab Ecclesiasticis fieri non debet.—Quia hospitandi occasione monasterium temporibus decessoris vestri nobis fuisse nunciatum est praegravatum: oportet ut hoc Sanctitas vestra decenter debeat temperare.   He orders a bishop to restore what he had taken from a convent xenii quasi specie. lib. viii. ep. 34.   On the other hand he admonishes all bishops to keep a strict watch over the discipline and morals of the convents, lib. vi. ep. 11. viii. ep. 34.—Other privileges which Gregory is alleged to have granted to convents, for instance the celebrated privilegium monasterii S. Medardi in Soissons (see appendix to his letters in the Benedictine edition No. 4.) are spurious.   cf. Launoji opp. iii. ii. 90.   Thomassinus. P. i. lib. iii. c. 30.

[1] For it there is a decree Gregorii M. (Opp. ed. Maur. ii. 1288. Mansi x. 434. also in Gratianus dist. 92. c. 2.) characteristically: In sancta Romana Ecclesia—dudum consuetudo est valde reprehensibilis exorta, ut quidam ad sacri altaris ministerium Cantores eligantur, et in Diaconatus ordine constituti modulationi vocis inserviant, quos ad praedicationis officium eleemosynarumque studium vacare congruebat.   Unde fit plerumque, ut ad sacrum ministerium dum blanda vox quaeritur, quaeri congrua vita negligatur, et cantor minister Deum moribus stimulet, cum populum vocibus delectat.   He therefore arranges that not deacons but sub-deacons and minores ordines should be employed in the singing.

[2] Comp. Neander's Denkwürdigkeiten aus der Gesch. des Christenthums. Bd. 3. Heft 1. (Berlin 1824.) S. 132 ss.

he did much to introduce new forms of worship, and diffuse a multitude of superstitions.

The chief part of the reverence paid to saints came more and more to consist in the superstitious worship of relics,[3] of whose miraculous power the most absurd stories were told. The consequence of this was, that *the moral aspect* of saint-reverence was still farther lost sight of by an age which longed only for the marvellous. As this tendency now began to give rise to impos-

---

[3] Gregor. M. lib. iv. ep. 30. ad Constantinam Aug. : Serenitas vestra—caput S. Pauli Apostoli, aut aliud quid de corpore ipsius, suis ad se jussionibus a me praecepit debere transmitti.—Major me moestitia tenuit, quod ille praecipitis, quae facere nec possum, nec audeo. Nam corpora SS. Petri et Pauli App. tantis in Ecclesiis suis coruscant miraculis atque terroribus, ut neque ad orandum sine magno illuc timore possit accedi.—Examples. Among other things, that in opening the grave of Laurentius monachi et mansionarii, qui corpus ejusdem Martyris viderunt, quod quidem minime tangere praesumserunt, omnes intra X. dies defuncti sunt (Exod. xxxiii. 20.)—Romanis consuetudo non est, quando Sanctorum reliquias dant, ut quidquam tangere praesumant de corpore : sed tantummodo in pyxide *brandeum* mittitur, atque ad sacratissima corpora Sanctorum ponitur. Quod levatum in Ecclesia, quae est dedicanda, debita cum veneratione reconditur : et tantae per hoc ibidem virtutes fiunt, ac si illuc specialiter eorum corpora deferantur (in like manner Gregor. Turon. de gloria Martyr. i. 28.) Unde contigit, ut b. recordationis Leonis P. temporibus, sicut a majoribus traditur, dum quidam Graeci de talibus reliquiis dubitarent, praedictus Pontifex hoc ipsum brandeum allatis forficibus inciderit, et ex ipsa incisione sanguis effluxerit. In Romanis namque vel totius Occidentis partibus omnino intolerabile est atque sacrilegum, si Sanctorum corpora tangere quisquam fortasse voluerit. Quod si praesumserit, certum est, quia haec temeritas impunita nullo modo remanebit.—Sed quia serenissimae Dominae tam religiosum desiderium esse vacuum non debet, de catenis, quas ipse S. Paulus Ap. in collo et in manibus gestavit, ex quibus multa miracula in populo demonstrantur, partem aliquam vobis transmittere festinabo, si tamen hanc tollere limando praevaluero. namely quibusdam petentibus, diu per catenas ipsas ducitur lima, et tamen ut aliquid exinde exeat non obtinetur.—Lib. ix. ep. 122. ad Recharedum Wisigoth. Regem : Clavem vero parvulam a sacratissimo b. Petri Ap. corpore vobis pro ejus benedictione transmisimus, in qua inest ferrum de catenis ejus inclusum ; ut quod collum illius ad martyrium ligaverat, vestrum ab omnibus peccatis solvat. Crucem quoque dedi latori praesentium vobis offerendam, in qua lignum Dominicae crucis inest, et capilli b. Joannis Baptistae. Ex qua semper solatium nostri Salvatoris per intercessionem praecursoris ejus habeatis. cf. lib. iii. ep. 33. A number of similar miraculous stories are found in the works of Gregory of Tours, see note 6.

ture in introducing false relics,[4] it had also the effect of developing, to a much greater extent, the saints' sayings relating to the miraculous. The old martyrs, of whom for the most part the names alone were handed down,[5] were furnished with new descriptions of their lives, while the new saints were dressed out with wonderful narratives; even martyrs, with the histories of martyrs, were entirely fabricated anew.[6]

In the worship of saints, *angels* were now without hesitation made to participate, to whom also churches were dedicated.[7]

Pictures became more common in the churches. In the East authentic likenesses of Christ now appeared in public,[8] and were

[4] Gregor. M. lib. iv. epist. 30. ad Constantinam Aug.: Quidam Monachi Graeci huc ante biennium venientes nocturno silentio juxta ecclesiam S. Pauli corpora mortuorum in campo jacentia effodiebant, atque eorum ossa recondebant, servantes sibi dum recederent. Qui cum tenti, et cur hoc facerent diligenter fuissent discussi, confessi sunt quod illa ossa ad Graeciam essent tanquam Sanctorum reliquias portaturi. Concil. Caesaraugust. ii. (592) can. 2: Statuit S. Synodus ut reliquiae in quibuscunque locis de Ariana haeresi inventae fuerint, prolatae a Sacerdotibus, in quorum ecclesiis reperiuntur, pontificibus praesentatae igne probentur (the old German ordeal.)

[5] Gregor. M. lib. viii. ep. 29. see Div. 1. § 53. not. 46.

[6] The writings of Gregory, archbishop of Tours, afford abundant proofs of all this. See above § 114. not. 18. Among many other things we find also in him for the first time (de gloria mart. i. 95). the legend belonging to the Decian persecution de septem dormientibus apud urbem Ephesum. It had been derived from an old tradition which is even found in Pliny nat. hist. vii. 52. but which being afterwards transferred to Christian martyrs, was differently localized. Thus it appears in the Coran (Surat 18.) to be transplanted into Arabia, subsequently it was carried into Gaul (Pseudo-Gregor. Tur. epist. ad Sulpic. Bituric.), to Germany (Nicephori Call. hist. eccl. v. 17), and also to the north (Paulus Diac. de gestis Longob. i. 4).

[7] Comp. § 99. not. 34. As presents had been made to the deities in heathen Rome, so now they were frequently made to saints and angels. cf. lex Zenonis (Cod. Just. i. ii. 15).: Si quis donaverit aliquam rem— in honorem Martyris, aut Prophetae, aut Angeli, tanquam ipsi postea oratorium aedificaturus, — cogitur opus, quamvis nondum inchoatum fuerit, perficere per se vel per heredes. Justiniani A. D. 530. (l. c. l. 26.): in multis jam testamentis invenimus ejusmodi institutiones, quibus aut ex asse quis scripserat Dominum nostrum Jesum Christum heredem: then the inheritance of the church of the place was to be applied to the benefit of the poor. Si vero quis unius ex Archangelis meminerit, vel venerandorum Martyrum, in that case the nearest church dedicated to him shall be heir.

[8] The picture of Christ by Luke first mentioned by Theodorus lector

the principal means of establishing there the worship of images ;[9] but in the West the latter was still rejected.[10]

Justinian was distinguished for building splendid *churches*.[11]

To the festivals were added the two feasts of Mary, *festum purificationis* (ὑπαπαντή) on the second of February ; and *festum annunciationis* (ἡ τοῦ εὐαγγελισμοῦ ἡμέρα) on the 25th March.[12]

On the three days before the ascension (jejunium rogationum),

about 518, which was soon followed by pictures of other holy persons from the same hand. But after this appeared the εἰκόνες ἀχειροποίητοι, a counterpart of the ἀγάλματα διοπετῆ of heathenism, first noticed in Evagrius iv. 27. See Div. i. § 21. not. 4.

[9] Comp. especially the fragment of Leontii (bishop of Neapolis in Cyprus † about 620) apologia pro Christianis adv. Judaeos in the Acts of the Conc. Nic. ii. ann. 787. Act. 4. (Mansi xiii. 43.) where he defends προσκύνησις before the pictures, mentions even αἱμάτων ῥύσεις ἐξ εἰκόνων and designates the pictures as πρὸς ἀνάμνησιν καὶ τιμὴν καὶ εὐπρέπειαν ἐκκλησιῶν προκείμενα καὶ προσκυνούμενα. Neander's Kirchengesch. ii. 2. 627 ss.

[10] Gregorii Magni lib. ix. ep. 105. ad Serenum Massiliensem Ep.: Praeterea indico dudum ad nos pervenisse, quod Fraternitas vestra, quosdam imaginum adoratores adspiciens, easdem in Ecclesiis imagines confregit atque projecit. Et quidem zelum vos, ne quid manufactum adorari posset, habuisse laudavimus, sed frangere easdem imagines non debuisse indicamus. Idcirco enim pictura in Ecclesiis adhibetur, ut hi, qui litteras nesciunt, saltem in parietibus videndo legant, quae legere in codicibus non valent. (as Paulinus Nilus § 99. not. 47. and 48.) Tua ergo Fraternitas et illas servare, et ab earum adoratu populum prohibere debuit : quatenus et litterarum nescii haberent, unde scientiam historiae colligerent, et populus in picturae adoratione minime peccaret. Lib. xi. ep. 13. ad eundem : quod de scriptis nostris, quae ad te misimus, dubitasti, quam sis incautus apparuit. Amplification of the above. Among other things, frangi ergo non debuit, quod non ad adorandum in ecclesiis, sed ad instruendas solummodo mentes fuit nescientium collocatum. cf. lib. ix. ep. 52. ad Secundinum : Imagines, quas tibi dirigendas per Dulcidum Diaconum rogasti, misimus. Unde valde nobis tua postulatio placuit : quia illum toto corde, tota intentione quaeris, cujus imaginem prae oculis habere desideras, ut te visio corporalis quotidiana reddat exercitatum : ut dum picturam illius vides, ad illum animo inardescas, cujus imaginem videre desideras. Ab re non facimus, si per visibilia invisibilia demonstramus. Scio quidem, quod imaginem Salvatoris nostri non ideo petis, ut quasi Deum colas, sed ob recordationem filii Dei in ejus amore recalescas, cujus te imaginem videre desideras. Et nos quidem non quasi ante divinitatem ante illam prosternimur, sed illum adoramus, quem per imaginem aut natum, aut passum, sed et in throno sedentem recordamur.

[11] Procopius Caesariensis de aedificiis Justiniani libb. vi.

[12] Bingham. vol. ix. p. 170 ss. J. A. Schmidii prolusiones Marianae sex. Helmst. 1733. 4. p. 116 ss. 103 ss.

Mamercus or *Mamertus*, bishop of Vienne (452), had instituted solemn rites of penance and prayer, accompanied by fasting and public worship (litaniae, rogationes), appointed for the three days before the ascension (jejunium rogationum).[13] To this festival *Gregory the Great* added new ceremonies (litania septiformis).[14] He also improved the church-music (cantus Gregorianus).[15]

Justinian first transferred to the spiritual relationship (cognatio spiritualis) between the god-father and the god-child, the civil consequences arising from corporeal affinities.[16]

Gregory the Great, in his *Sacramentarium*, gave that form to the Roman *liturgy relative to the Lord's Supper*, which it has substantially preserved ever since.[17] The earlier notions of this rite, and of its atoning power, became more exaggerated in proportion as the idea became general, which was thrown out by *Augustine* as a conjecture,[18] that men would be subjected to a

[13] Sidonius Apollinaris Ep. Arvernorum (✝ 482) epistolarum lib. vii. ep. 1. lib. v. ep. 14. Gregor. Tur. ii. 34. Bingham. vol. v. p. 21.

[14] Appendix ad Gregorii epistolas no. iii. and sermo tempore mortalitatis (in the older edition, lib. xi. ep. 2.)

[15] Joannes Diac. de vit. Gregorii lib. ii. c. 7. Martin. Gerbert de cantu et musica sacra (Bambergae et Frib. 1774. t. ii. 4), t. i. p. 35 ss. Jos. Antony's archäologisch-liturg. Lehrbuch d. gregorian. Kirchengesanges. Münster 1829. 4.

[16] Ideas of regeneration in baptism, of spiritual generation, of the brotherly relation of Christians, had before led men to compare the relations of the baptiser, of the godfather, and the baptized, with corporeal relationship. cf. Fabii Marii Victorini (about 360) comm. in ep. ad Gal. (in Maji scriptt. vett. nova coll. iii. ii. 37): per baptismum, cum regeneratio fit, ille qui baptizatum perficit, vel perfectum suscipit, pater dicitur. cf. Gothofr. Arnoldi hist. cognationis spiritualis inter Christianos receptae. Goslar. 1730. 8. p. 44 ss. From this now proceeded the decree of Justinian, Cod. lib. v. tit. 4. de nuptiis l. 26 :—Ea persona omnimodo ad nuptias venire prohibenda, quam aliquis—a sacrosancto suscepit baptismate : cum nihil aliud sic inducere potest paternam affectionem et justam nuptiarum prohibitionem, quam hujusmodi nexus, per quem Deo mediante animae eorum copulatae sunt. The relation was considered as a sort of adoption. See du Fresne Glossar. s. v. Adoptio et Filiolatus.

[17] Joannes Diac. de vita Greg. ii. 17. Sed et Gelasianum codicem, de missarum solemniis multa subtrahens, pauca convertens, nonnulla superadjiciens, in unius libelli volumine coarctavit. Jo. Bona rerum liturg. libb. ii. Colon. 1764. 8. and frequently. Best edited in his Opp. omnibus. Antverp. 1723. fol. Th. Christ. Lilienthal de canone Missae Gregoriano. Lugd. Bat. 1740. 8.

[18] Entirely distinct from the purifying fire of the last day, the belief

K

purifying fire immediately after death.[19]   *Gregory the Great* did
much to confirm these notions by descriptions of the tortures of
departed souls, and the mitigation of such tortures by the sacrifice offered in the Supper.[20]   In proportion as the latter assumed

in which has been general since Origen (see Div. i. § 63, not. 12), and
in which even Augustine seems to believe, August. de civ. Dei xx. 25,
apparere in illo judicio quasdam quorundam purgatorias poenas futu-
ras. On the other hand, liber de viii. quaestionibus ad Dulcitium § 13:
Tale aliquid (ignem, tribulationis tentationem) etiam post hanc vitam
fieri incredibile non est, et utrum ita sit, quaeri potest, et aut inveniri
aut latere, nonnullos fideles per ignem quendam purgatorium, quanto
magis minusve bona pereuntia dilexerunt, tanto tardius citiusve salvari. De civ. Dei xxi. 26: Post istius sane corporis mortem, donec
ad illum veniatur, qui post resurrectionem corporum futurus est damnationis et remunerationis ultimus dies, si hoc temporis intervallo spiritus
defunctorum ejusmodi ignem dicuntur perpeti,—non redarguo, quia
forsitan verum est.   Dallaei de poenis et satisfactionibus humanis libb.
vii. Amst. 1649. 4. J. G. Chr. Hoepfner de origine dogmatis de pur-
gatorio. Hal. 1792. 8. Münscher's Dogmengeschichte Th. 4. S. 425.

[19] Caesarius Arelat. hom. viii. on 1 Cor. iii. 11–15, (in Bibl. PP.
Lugd. viii. 826,) has the Augustinian distinction between peccata capitalia and minuta, and teaches that the latter are expiated by an ignis
transitorius or purgatorius; but yet he places the latter in the time of
the final judgment.   Ille ipse purgatorius ignis durior erit, quam quicquid potest poenarum in hoc saeculo aut cogitari, aut videri, aut sentiri.
Et cum de die judicii scriptum sit, quod erit dies unus tanquam mille
anni, et mille anni tanquam dies unus: unde scit unusquisque, utrum
diebus aut mensibus, an forte etiam et annis per illum ignem sit transi-
turus.   Et qui modo unum digitum suum in ignem mittere timet, quare
non timeat, ne necesse sit tunc non parvo tempore cum animo et corpore (consequently after the resurrection) cruciari ?   Et ideo totis viribus unusquisque laboret, ut et capitalia crimina possit evadere, et minuta
peccata ita operibus bonis redimere, ut aut parum ex ipsis, aut nihil
videatur remanere, quod ignis ille possit absumere.—Omnes sancti, qui
Deo fideliter serviunt,—per ignem illum—absque ulla violentia transi-
bunt.   Illi vero, qui, quamvis capitalia crimina non admittant, ad perpetranda minuta peccata sint faciles, ad vitam aeternam—venturi sunt ;
sed prius aut in saeculo per Dei justitiam vel misericordiam amarissimis
tribulationibus excoquendi, aut illi ipsi per multas eleemosynas, et dum
inimicis clementer indulgent, per Dei misericordiam liberandi, aut certe
illo igne, de quo dixit Apostolus, longo tempore cruciandi sunt, ut ad
vitam aeternam sine macula et ruga perveniant. Illi vero, qui aut,
homicidium, aut sacrilegium, aut adulterium, vel reliqua his similia
commiserunt, si eis digna poenitentia non subvenerit, non per purgatorium ignem transire merebuntur ad vitam, sed aeterno incendio prae-
cipitabuntur ad mortem. cf. Oudinus de scriptoribus eccl. i. 1514.

[20] Greg. M. dialog. lib. iv. c. 39: Qualis hinc quisque egreditur, talis
in judicio praesentatur. Sed tamen de quibusdam levibus culpis esse

the form of a *tremendi mysterii*, the seldomer did the people partake of it, so that it was necessary for the Church to enact laws on the subject.[21]   In other respects the ideas of the nature of the elements in the Supper suffered no change (§ 101. note 15.)[22]

ante judicium purgatorius ignis credendus est, pro eo quod veritas dicit, quia si quis in S. Spiritu blasphemiam dixerit, neque in hoc seculo remittetur ei, neque in futuro (Matth. xii. 31.)   In qua sententia datur intelligi, quasdam culpas in hoc seculo, quasdam seculo vero in futuro posse laxari.—Instances of such tormented souls, ibid. ii. 23, iv. 40, especially iv. 55 : Si culpae post mortem insolubiles non sunt, multum solet animas etiam post mortem sacra oblatio hostiae salutaris adjuvare, ita ut hanc nonnumquam ipsae defunctorum animae expetere videantur, with two examples.   Peter listening artlessly asks (iv. 40) : Quid hoc est, quaeso, quod in his extremis temporibus tam multa de animabus clarescunt, quae ante latuerunt : ita ut apertis revelationibus atque ostensionibus venturum saeculum inferre se nobis atque aperire videatur ?   To which Gregory replies (c. 41) : Ita est : nam quantum praesens saeculum propinquat ad finem, tantum futurum saeculum ipsa jam quasi propinquitate tangitur, et signis manifestioribus aperitur.

[21] Conc. Agathense (506) can. 18 : Saeculares, qui natale domini, pascha, et pentecosten non communicaverint, catholici non credantur, nec inter catholicos habeantur.

[22] Gelasius P. de duabus in Christo naturis adv. Eutychen et Nestorium (cited as genuine even by his contemporaries Gennadius de script. c. 94, and Fulgentius Rusp. in epist. xiv. ad Fulgentium Ferrandum cap. 19, in Gallandii bibl. T. xi. p. 334, and therefore doubted without reason by Baronius, Bellarminus, and others.   It is found in the bibl. PP., in Heroldi haereseologia.   Basil. 1556. fol. p. 683 etc.) : Certe sacramenta, quae sumimus, corporis et sanguinis Christi, divina res est, propter quod et per eadem divinae efficimur consortes naturae, et tamen esse non desinit substantia vel natura panis et vini.   Et certo imago et similitudo corporis et sanguinis Christi in actione mysteriorum celebrantur.   Satis ergo nobis evidenter ostenditur, hoc nobis in ipso Christo Domino sentiendum, quod in ejus imagine profitemur, celebramus et sumimus, ut sicut in hanc, scilicet in divinam transeant Spiritu S. perficiente substantiam permanente tamen in sua proprietate natura, sic illud ipsum mysterium principale, cujus nobis efficientiam virtutemque veraciter repraesentant.   Facundus Hermian. pro defens. iii. capitul. ix. 5 : Nam sacramentum adoptionis suscipere dignatus est Christus, et quando circumcisus est, et quando baptizatus est : et potest sacramentum adoptionis adoptio nuncupari, sicut sacramentum corporis et sanguinis ejus, quod est in pane et poculo consecrato, corpus ejus et sanguinem dicimus : non quod proprie corpus ejus sit panis, et poculum sanguis : sed quod in se mysterium corporis ejus et sanguinis contineant. Hinc et ipse Dominus benedictum panem et calicem, quem discipulis tradidit, corpus et sanguinem suum vocavit. Cramer's Forts. v. Bossuet Th. 5. Bd. 1. S. 200 ff.

SIXTH CHAPTER.

SPREAD OF CHRISTIANITY, AND ITS CONDITION WITHOUT THE
ROMAN EMPIRE.

I. IN ASIA AND AFRICA.

§ 122.

During the reign of Justinian I., the people dwelling on the Black Sea, viz., the *Abasgi, Alani, Lazi, Zani,* and *Heruli,* declared themselves in favour of Christianity, and for the Catholic Church. But the *Nestorians* and *Monophysites* made much more important acquisitions to the cause, during this period, in Asia and Africa.

The *Nestorians*[1] not only maintained themselves in *Persia,* where they enjoyed exclusive protection (§ 88. at the end), but also spread themselves on all sides in Asia, particularly into *Arabia*[2] and *India,*[3] and it is said, in the year 636, even as far as *China.*[4] Along with the theological tendencies of the Syrian

---

[1] Concerning them, compare especially Jos. Sim. Assemani diss. de Syris Nestorianis, Part ii. tom. iii. of the biblioth. orientalis.

[2] Assemanus l. c. p. 607 s.

[3] Cosmas Indicopleustes (about 535) christ. topographiae lib. iii. says that there was a Christian Church ἐν τῇ Ταπροβάνῃ νήσῳ ἐν τῇ ἐσωτέρᾳ Ἰνδίᾳ, (namely lib. xi. : ἐκκλησία τῶν ἐπιδημούντων Περσῶν χριστιανῶν with a πρεσβύτερος ἀπὸ Περσίδος χειροτονούμενος) : οὐκ οἶδα δὲ εἰ καὶ περαιτέρω. So too in Male. But ἐν τῇ Καλλιάνᾳ—ἐπίσκοπός ἐστιν ἀπὸ Περσίδος χειροτονούμενος. So also ἐν τῇ νήσῳ τῇ καλουμένῃ Διοσκορίδους.—Ὁμοίως δὲ καὶ ἐπὶ Βάκτροις, καὶ Οὔννοις, καὶ Πέρσαις, καὶ λοιποῖς Ἰνδοῖς, καὶ Περσαρμενίοις, καὶ Μήδοις, καὶ Ἐλαμίταις καὶ πάσῃ τῇ χώρᾳ Περσίδος καὶ ἐκκλησίαι ἄπειροι, καὶ ἐπίσκοποι, καὶ χριστιανοὶ λαοὶ πάμπολλοι κ. τ. λ. Hence the Christiani S. Thomae. cf. Assemanus.l. c. p. 435 ss. again discovered in the sixteenth century by the Portuguese in Malabar (about A. D. 780 all the Persian Christians, among whom were the Indian, declared themselves disciples Thomae Apostoli. See Abulpharagius ap. Assem. l. c. p. 438.)

[4] That is, if the monumentum Syro-Sinicum be genuine, which is said to have been erected A. D. 781, and discovered 1625 in the city

Church, whence they had come forth, they preserved its learning likewise; and were thus the introducers of Greek science into Asia. Their school in *Nisibis* was the only theological institution of Christendom in the sixth century.[5]

The *Monophysites*, on the other hand, spread themselves from Alexandria towards the south. Among the *Hamdschars* or *Homerites* Christianity had been early established (§ 107); though it did not become general till the time of Anastasius.[6] But when Dhu-Nowas, a Jewish king of this people, afterwards persecuted the Christians with violence (522), the Æthiopian king Elesbaan came to their aid (529); in consequence of which the Homerites were subject to Æthiopian rulers for 72 years.[7]

Si-an-fu in the province Schen-si, copies of the inscription on it having been sent to Europe by the Jesuit missionaries. First published in Athanas. Kircheri prodromus Copticus. Rom. 1636. 4. p. 74 and in ejusd. China illustrata. ibid. 1667. fol. p. 43 ss. also in Mosheim hist. Tartarorum eccl. Helmst. 1741. 4. App. p. 4. The genuineness of the monument has always been doubted by many. So in particular by La Croze, against whom Assemanus bibl. orient. iii. ii. 538 defends it. Renaudot anciennes relations des Indes et de la Chine, Paris 1718, p. 228; Mosheim hist. Tart. eccl. p. 9. Deguignes Untersuchung über die in 7ten Jahrh. in Sina sich aufhaltenden Christen. Greifsw. 1769. 4; Abel Remusat nouveaux mélanges. Paris 1829, ii. 189; and Saint Martin on Lebeau hist. du Bas-Empire (new edition, Paris 1824. voll. xi.) vi. 69, hold it to be genuine. On the contrary, Beausobre (hist. de Manichée c. 14), Neumann in the Jahrbüchern f. wissenschaftl. Kritik 1829. S. 592, and Von Bohlen (das alte Indien, Königsberg 1830, Th. 1. S. 383) have once more declared it to be a work of the Jesuits.

[5] It was formed at the end of the fifth century out of the exiled remains of the school of Edessa (comp. § 88 at the end.) Respecting it comp. Assemani bibl. orient. iii. ii. 927 ss. cf. p. 80, and the passage of Cassiodorus given above, § 114, not. 14. The African bishop, Junilius, (about 550), relates in the preface to his work de partibus divinae legis respecting the origin of it, that he had become acquainted with quendam Paulum nomine, Persam genere, qui in Syrorum schola in Nisibi urbe est edoctus, ubi divina lex per magistros publicos, sicut apud nos in mundanis studiis Grammatica et Rhetorica, ordine ac regulariter traditur. He had read, drawn up by him, regulas quasdam, quibus ille discipulorum animos, divinarum scripturarum superficie instructos, priusquam expositionis profunda patefaceret, solebat imbuere, ut ipsarum interim causarum, quae in divina lege versantur, intentionem ordinemque cognoscerent, ne sparsim et turbulente, sed regulariter singula discerent. These regularia instituta he gives here with some alteration of the form.

[6] Theodori Lect. hist. eccl. ii. where they are called Ἰμμιρηνοί.

[7] Comp. the varying accounts of the contemporaries Johannis Episc.

As the Homerite Christians were Monophysites, the Monophysite doctrines were carried to other parts of Arabia.[8] Under Justinian the *Nubians* were also converted to Christianity by the Monophysites of Alexandria.[9]

II. AMONG THE GERMAN NATIONS.

Planck's Gesch. d. christl. kirchl. Gesellschaftsverfassung. B. 2.

§ 123.

‑SPREAD OF CHRISTIANITY AMONG THE GERMAN NATIONS.

The first German people converted to the Christianity of the Catholic Church were the *Franks*, who since 486 had been masters of the greatest part of Gaul. *Chlodowich*, King of the Salian Franks, influenced by his Queen Chrotechildis, and by a vow made at the battle of *Tolbiacum* (Zülpich 496), was bap-

---

Asiae in Assemani bibl. orient. i. 359 ; Simeonis Episc. in Perside epist., preserved in Zachariae hist. eccl. ap. Assemani l. c. p. 364, and in Maji coll. x. i. 376 ; and Procopius de bello Persico i. c. 17 and 20. Martyrium Arethae (Arethas, head of the Christian city Nadschran), hitherto known only in the work of Simeon Metaphr. but recently published in the original in J. Fr. Boissonade anecdota graeca v. 1. (Paris 1833.) Walchii hist. rerum in Homeritide seculo sexto gestarum, in the novis commentariis Soc. Reg. Gottingensis iv. 1. Johannsen historia Jemanae (Bonnae 1828) p. 88 ss. Jost's Gesch. der Israeliten v. 253, 354. Lebeau hist. du Bas-Empire ed. Saint Martin viii. 48. On the chronology, see De Sacy in the Mémoires de l'Acad. des Inscript. L. 531, 545.—Respecting Gregentius, archbishop of Taphara, who was in the highest repute under the Christian viceroy, Abraham, see Gregor. disp. cum Herbano Judaeo ed. Nic. Gulonius. Lutet. 1586. 8. and νόμοι τῶν 'Ομηριτῶν, composed by Gregentius, ap. Boissonade v. 63.

[8] Assemani bibl. orient. iii. ii. 605. The Arab tribes among whom Christianity was propagated, are pointed out in Ed. Pocockii spec. hist. Arabum ed. Jos. White. Oxon. 1806, p. 141.

[9] Abulpharagius in Assem. bibl. orient. T. ii. p. 330. Comp. Letronne nouvel examen de l'inscription grecque du roi nubien Silco, considerée dans ses rapports avec la propagation de la langue grecque et l'introduction du christianisme parmi les peuples de la Nubie et de l'Abyssinie, in the Mémoires de l'institut royal de France, Acad. des inscriptions. T. ix. (1831) p. 128.

tized by Remigius, bishop of Rheims, and his people followed his example.[1] From the Franks Christianity was propagated among the *Allemanni*, who were subject to them.[2]

So far as the inclination of all Romans that had been subjected to the yoke of the Germans leaned immediately to the Franks as Catholic Christians,[3] the latter obtained an important predominance of influence over the other German people. For this reason the others successively came over at this time to the Catholic Church.[4] This took place in regard to the *Burgundians*, under their King Sigmund (517); the *Suevi*, under their Kings Carrarich (550–559) and Theodemir I. (559-569) ;[5] the *Visigoths*, under their King Reccared at the council of Toledo (589).[6] Since the *Vandalic* kingdom in Africa (534), and that of the *Ostro-*

[1] Gregorii Turonensis († 595) historiae Francorum (libb. 10, till the year 591, best edited in Dom Martin Bouquet rerum Gallicarum et Francicarum scriptores. T. ii. Paris 1739, fol.) lib. ii. c. 28-31. F. W. Rettberg's Kirchengesch. Deutschlands Bd. i. (Göttingen 1845. 8.) S. 270. Dr C. G. Kries de Greg. Tur. vita et scriptis. Vratisl. 1839. 8. Gregor v. Tours u. s. Zeit, Von J. W. Löbell. Leipzig 1839. 8.—Tradition of the oil flask brought by a dove found first in Hincmar in vita Remigii cap. 3. The Ampulla itself first came to light at the coronation of Philip II., 1179, and was broken in the year 1794, at Rhül's command. Comp. de Vertot diss. au sujet de la sainte ampulle (Mémoires de l'Acad. des Inscr. T. ii. Mém. p. 669.) C. G. v. Murr über die heil. Ampulle in Rheims. Nürnberg u. Altdorf 1801. 8.

[2] Bishopric of Vindonissa (now Windisch in the canton Aargau) transferred to Constance in the 6th century. Sosimus, the first known bishop of Augsburg, A. D. 582. C. J. Hefele's Gesch. d. Einführung des Christenth. im südwestl. Deutschland. Tübingen 1837. S. 112.

[3] Gregor. Tur. hist. ii. 36 : Multi jam tunc ex Gallis habere Francos dominos summo desiderio cupiebant. Unde factum est, ut Quintianus Rutenorum (Rodez) Episcopus per hoc odium ab urbe depelleretur (by the Visigoths.) Dicebant enim ei : quia desiderium tuum est, ut Francorum dominatio possideat terram hanc. Hence Chlodowich gave his war against the Visigoths the appearance of being undertaken chiefly from religious zeal. He said to his people l. c. c. 37 : Valde moleste fero, quod hi Arriani partem teneant Galliarum. Eamus cum Dei adjutorio, et superatis redigamus terram in ditionem nostram.

[4] A history of Arianism among the German nations in Walch's Ketzerhist. ii. 553.

[5] The history of Carrarich's conversion in Gregor. Turon. de miraculis S. Martini i. c. 11 ; but Theodemir first propagated the catholic faith among the people, and therefore Isidorus Chron. Suevorum even makes him the first catholic king of the Suevi. See Ferrera's span. Geschichte. Bd. 2.

[6] Aschbach's Gesch. d. Westgothen. Frankf. a. M. 1827. S. 220 ff.

goths in Upper Italy (553), had been destroyed, Arianism also lost its dominion in those territories.

On the contrary, it revived under the rule of the *Lombards* in Italy (from 568), and was longest maintained among this people.[7]

In other parts, the amalgamation of the German conquerors with the older inhabitants of their land,[8] and the development of the new European nations, were universally effected by similarity of faith.[9]

At the end of this period began the conversion of the *Anglo-Saxons* in Britain. Augustine, sent thither by Gregory the Great with 40 Benedictines (596), was first received by Ethelbert, King of Kent, through the influence of his Queen Bertha, who was a Frank. From Kent Christianity was gradually diffused in the other Anglo-Saxon kingdoms.[10]

---

[7] Paulus Warnefridi, Diaconus (about 774) : de gestis Longobardorum libb. vi. (best in Muratori scriptor. Italic. Tom. i. Mediol. 1723, fol.)

[8] Formerly marriages between the two parties were universally forbidden by the Church ; but among the Visigoths they were also prohibited by the civil code : See leges Visigothorum (best edition : Fuero juzgo en latin y castellano, por la real Academia española. Madrid 1815. fol.) iii. i. 2. (a law of king Recesvinth from 649–672) : priscae legis remota sententia hac in perpetuum valitura lege sancimus, ut tam Gothus Romanam, quam etiam Gotham Romanus, si conjugem habere voluerit,—facultas eis nubendi subjaceat.

[9] H. I. Royaard's über d. Gründung u. Entwickelung der neueurop. Staaten im Mittelalter, bes. durch d. Christenth. aus d. Archief Deel 2. übersetzt v. G. Kinkel, in Illgen's Zeitchr. f. d. hist. Theol. v. i. 67.

[10] Beda Venerabilis († 735) historia ecclesiastica gentis Anglorum libb. v. ed. Fr. Chiffletius. Paris 1681. 4. Joh. Smith. Cantabrig. 1722. fol. Jos. Stevenson (Bedae opp. hist. T. i.) Lond. 1838. 8. J. A. Giles (Bedae opp. vol. 2 et 3.) Lond. 1843. 8. Das erste Jahrh. d. engl. Kirche, od. Einführung und Befestigung des Christenthums bei den Angelsachen in Britannien, v. D. K. Schrödl. Passau 1840. 8. [Sharon Turner's History of the Anglo-Saxons, 3 vols. 8vo, London 1823, fourth edition. Lingard's History of the Anglo-Saxon Church, second edition, 2 vols. 8vo, 1845. Lond.]

§ 124.

HIERARCHY IN THE GERMAN EMPIRE.

Eugen Montag's Gesch. der deutschen staatsbürgerlichen Freiheit. (Bamb. u. Würzb. 1812. 8.) Bd. 1. Th. 1. S. 205 ff. Th. 2. S. 1 ff. K. F. Eichhorn's deutsche Staats- u. Rechtsgeschichte. (4 Theile. 4te Ausg. Göttingen 1834–36. 8.) i. 217. 478. Gregor v. Tours u. s. Zeit von T. W. Löbell S. 315. 8. Sugenheim's Staatsleben des Klerus im Mittelalter. Bd. 1. Berlin 1839.

Although the ecclesiastical constitution and code which had been formed in the Roman Empire were adopted by the German nations,[1] yet the relations of the hierarchy received a peculiar form. The kings soon saw how much their power could be supported and strengthened by the reputation of the clergy;[2] and they endeavoured therefore to bind more closely to themselves the heads of the clergy, the bishops and abbots. Churches and monasteries received considerable possessions from their hands,[3] while the bishops and abbots, as the temporary possessors, became *the vassals* (ministeriales) of the king,[4] were often employed in affairs of the state, and were thus invested with a very important political influence. The possessions of the Church were

[1] As all conquered nations lived according to their own law (Lex Ripuariorum tit. xxxi. § 3), so the clergy, according to Roman law, Lex Ripuar. tit. lviii. § 1: Legem Romanam, qua Ecclesia vivit. Comp. Eichhorn i. 172, 217.

[2] Chlodovaei praeceptum pro Monasterio Reomaensi, in Bouquet rerum gall. scriptt. iv. 615 : Servos Dei, quorum virtutibus gloriamur et orationibus defensamur, si nobis amicos acquirimus, honoribus sublimamus atque obsequiis veneramur, statum regni nostri perpetuo angere credimus, et saeculi gloriam atque caelestis regni patriam adipisci confidimus. Löbell S. 318.

[3] Gregor. Turon. hist. Franc. vi. 46 : Chilperich, king in Soissons (from 561–584), ajebat plerumque : Ecce pauper remansit fiscus noster, ecce divitiae nostrae ad Ecclesias sunt translatae : nulli penitus nisi soli Episcopi regnant : periit honor noster et translatus est ad Episcopos civitatum. Comp. Hüllmann's Gesch. des Ursprungs der Stände in Deutschland (2te Ausg. Berlin 1830) S. 114 ff.

[4] Fredegarii (about 740) chron. c. 4 : Burgundiae barones, tam Episcopi quam caeteri leudes. c. 76 : Pontifices caeterique leudes. G. I. Th. Lau on the influence which the feudal tenure system has exercised on the clergy and papacy in Illgen's Zeitschr. f. hist. Theol. 1841. ii. 82.

only by degrees freed from all taxes ; but those bestowed out of
the royal exchequer continued to be devoted to military services,[5]
which were in some instances rendered in person.[6]   Besides,
the kings regarded them as feudal tenures (beneficia), and frequently did not scruple to resume them.[7]   It was stipulated by
law, that the choice of a bishop should be confirmed by the
king ;[8] but for the most part, the kings themselves appointed to
vacant sees.[9]   Synods could not assemble without the royal per-

[5] Gregor. Tur. v. 27. Chilpericus rex de pauperibus et junioribus
Ecclesiae vel basilicae bannos jussit exigi, pro eo quod in exercitu non
ambulassent.   Non enim erat consuetudo, ut hi ullam exsolverent publicam functionem. From this it does not follow, as Löbell says (p. 330),
that in general the church was not required by duty to furnish troops
from its property. Rather does the erat shew that it had not been usual
only till the time of Chilperich. Comp. Planck ii. 222. Montag i. i.
314. Eichhorn i. 202, 506, 516. Sugenheim i. 315.
[6] In a battle against the Lombards (572) there were the bishops Sa-
lonius and Sagittarius, qui non cruce caelesti muniti, sed galea aut lorica
saeculari armati, multos manibus propriis, quod pejus est, interfecisse
referuntur. Gregor. Turon. iv. 43. (al. 37.)
[7] Conc. Arvernense (at Clermont) ann. 535. c. 5.   Qui reiculam
ecclesiae petunt a regibus, et horrendae cupiditatis impulsu egentium
substantiam rapiunt; irrita habeantur quae obtinent, et a communione
ecclesiae, cujus facultatem auferre cupiunt, excludantur. Comp. Conc.
Parisiens. (about 557) against those qui facultates ecclesiae, sub specie
largitatis regiae, improba subreptione pervaserint.   Even judicial miracles take place, ex. gr. when Charibert, king of Paris (562-567) wished
to take away a property belonging to the church at Tours. Gregor. Tur.
de miraculis S. Martini i. 29.   Planck ii. 206.   Hüllmann S. 123 ff.
[8] Conc. Aurelian. v. ann. 549. c. 10 : cum voluntate regis, juxta electionem cleri ac plebis—a metropolitano—cum comprovincialibus pontifex consecretur.
[9] Ex. gr. Gregor. Turon. de SS. Patrum vita c. 3. de S. Gallo : Tunc
etiam et Apronculus Treverorum episcopus transiit. Congregatique
clerici civitatis illius ad Theodoricum regem (king of Austrasia 511-534)
S. Gallum petebant episcopum. Quibus ille ait : Abscedite et alium
requirite, Gallum enim diaconum alibi habeo destinatum. Tunc eli-
gentes S. Nicetium episcopum acceperunt. Arverni vero clerici consensu insipientium facto cum multis muneribus ad regem venerunt.
Jam tunc germen illud iniquum coeperat pullulare, ut sacerdotium aut
venderetur a regibus, aut compararetur a clericis. Tunc ii audiunt a
rege, quod S. Gallum habituri essent episcopum.—The Concil. Paris
ann. 615 wished indeed (can. 1) to have the choice by canons restored ;
but king Chlotarius II. modified that decree in his confirmatory edict,
as follows (Mansi x. p. 543) : Episcopo decedente in loco ipsius, qui a
metropolitano ordinari debet cum provincialibus, a clero et populo eligatur ; et si persona condigna fuerit, per ordinationem principis ordi-

mission ; their decrees had to be confirmed by the king, being previously invalid. In the mean time they began to consult about the affairs of the Church even in the meetings of the king's vassals or council (Placitum regis, Synodus regia, Synodale concilium).[10] Synods became more rare, and at length ceased entirely.

This arrangement completed the downfall of the metropolitan system, which had been already weakened in many ways. The king became the only judge of the bishops.[11] But in proportion as *they* rose higher in civil relations, the other clergy sank so much the deeper. No free man was allowed to enter the church without the royal permission.[12] Hence the clergy were chosen for the most part from among the serfs ; and on this very account the bishop acquired an unlimited power over them, which frequently manifested itself in the most tyrannical conduct.[13] The

netur : vel certe si de palatio eligitur, per meritum personae et doctrinae ordinetur. Comp. the formulas in Marculfi (about 660) formularum l. i. c. 5, (in Baluzii Capitularia Regum Franc. T. ii. p. 378) : Praeceptum Regis de Episcopatu c. 6. Indiculus Regis ad Episcopum, ut alium benedicat ; and in the Formulis Lindenbrogii c. 4 : carta de Episcopatu (ibid. p. 509.) Sugenheim i. 86. Löbell S. 335.

[10] Just. F. Runde Abhandlung v. Ursprung der Reichsstandschaft der Bischöfe u. Aebte, Göttingen 1775. 4. (The treatise on the same subject, appended, p. 93, is by Herder, and is also reprinted in his works on philosophy and history. Calsruhe edition. Part 13, p. 219.) Planck ii. 126. Hüllmann S. 186 ff. Montag i. ii. 54.

[11] Gregory Turon. says to king Chilperich : Si quis de nobis, o Rex, justitiae tramitem transcendere voluerit, a te corrigi potest : si vero tu excesseris, quis te corripiet ? Loquimur enim tibi, sed si volueris, audis : si autem nolueris, quis te condemnabit, nisi is qui se pronunciavit esse justitiam ? Gregor. Tur. hist. Franc. v. 19.

[12] See Marculfi formularum lib. i. c. 19. (Baluzii Capitul. ii. p. 386) and Bignon's remarks on it (ibid. p. 901.)

[13] Even before this time, it appears that monks had been punished with blows by their abbots, Cassian. collat. ii. 16. Palladii hist. Lausiaca c. 6, Benedicti regula c. 70. Bishops were now instructed by synods to punish in this manner also the offences of the inferior clergy. See Concil. Agathense ann. 506, can. 41. Epaonense ann. 517, c. 15. The Concil. Matisconense i. ann. 581, c. 8, prescribes the Mosaic number uno minus de quadraginta ictus. How the bishops often treated their clergy may be seen from Concil. Carpentoractense (527) : hujusmodi ad nos querela pervenit, quod ea quae a quibuscunque fidelibus parochiis conferuntur, ita ab aliquibus Episcopis praesumantur, ut aut parum, aut prope nihil ecclesiis, quibus collata fuerant, relinquatur.

administration of justice among the clergy was at first conducted according to Roman principles of legislation, as they were in force before Justinian (§ 91. note 5 ff.),[14] till *the Synod of Paris* (615) gave the clergy the privilege of being brought before a mixed tribunal, in all cases which hitherto belonged to the civil judge alone.[15] A wider influence was given to the bishops by committing to them an oversight of the entire administration of justice,[16] while their spiritual punishments were made more effectual by connecting with excommunication civil disadvantages also.[17] On the other hand, in the application of their discipline they were bound to regard the intercession of the king.[18]

Concil. Toletanum iii. (589) capitul. 20 : cognovimus Episcopos per parochias suas non sacerdotaliter deservire, sed crudeliter desaevire.

[14] Planck ii. 161. Montag i. ii. 106. Schilling de orig. jurisdictionis eccles. in causis civilibus. Lips. 1825. 4. p. 46.

[15] In the Edictum Clotarii ii., confirming this synod, we have : Ut nullus judicum de quolibet ordine clericos de civilibus causis, praeter criminalia negotia, per se distringere aut damnare praesumat, nisi convincitur manifestus, excepto presbytero aut diacono. Qui vero convicti fuerint de crimine capitali, juxta canones distringantur, et cum pontificibus examinentur. Comp. Planck. ii. 165. Rettberg's Kirchengesch. Deutschl. i. 294.

[16] Chlotarii Regis constitutio generalis A. D. 560 (in Baluzii Capitularia Regum Franc. i. 7. Walter corpus juris Germ. ant. ii. 2) : VI. Si judex aliquem contra legem injuste damnaverit, in nostri absentia ab Episcopis castigetur, ut quod perpere judicavit, versatim melius discussione habita emendare procuret. Conc. Toletanum iii. (589) cap. 18 : —judices locorum vel actores fiscalium patrimoniorum ex decreto gloriosissimi domini nostri simul cum sacerdotali concilio autumnali tempore die Kal. Nov. in unum conveniant, ut discant, quam pie et juste cum populis agere debeant, ne in angariis aut in operationibus superfluis sive privatum onerent, sive fiscalem gravent. Sint enim prospectores· episcopi secundum regiam admonitionem, qualiter judices cum populis agant ; ut aut ipsos praemonitos corrigant, aut insolentias eorum auditibus principis innotescant. Quodsi correptos emendare nequiverint, et ab ecclesia et a communione suspendant.

[17] Decretio Childeberti Regis A. D. 595 : II.—Qui vero Episcopum suum noluerit audire, et excommunicatus fuerit, perennem condemnationem apud Deum sustineat, et insuper de palatio nostro sit omnino extraneus, et omnes facultates suas parentibus legitimis amittat, qui noluit sacerdotis sui medicamenta sustinere.

[18] Conc. Parisiense v. (615), can. 3 : Ut si quis clericus—contemto episcopo suo ad principem vel ad potentiores homines—ambularit, vel sibi patronos elegerit, non recipiatur, praeter ut veniam debeat promereri. Chlotar II. repeats in his edict confirming this canon, but adds : Et si pro qualibet causa principem expetierit, et cum ipsius principis

Under these circumstances, the popes could not directly interfere in ecclesiastical matters; and their communication with
the established church of the country depended entirely on the
royal pleasure.[19]

§ 125.

MORAL INFLUENCES OF CHRISTIANITY AMONG THE GERMAN NATIONS.

As is usual among rude people when coming into closer contact with the more enlightened, there proceeded from the Romans,

epistola ad episcopum suum fuerit reversus, excusatus recipiatur. Conc.
Toletan. xii. ann. 681, c. 3 : quos regia potestas aut in gratiam benigni-
tatis receperit, aut participes mensae suae effecerit, hos etiam sacerdotum et populorum conventus suscipere in ecclesiasticam communionem
debebit : ut quod jam principalis pietas habet acceptum, neque a sacerdotibus Dei habeatur extraneum.   Confirmed in Conc. Tolet. xiii. ann.
683, c. 9.   cf. J. G. Reinhard de jure Principum Germaniae circa sacra
ante tempora Reformationis exercito. ʻHalae 1717. 4. p. 359.

[19] Hence Pelagius I. was obliged to use the utmost pains in defending himself to king Childebert against the suspicion of heresy which he
had drawn on himself by condemning the three chapters.   Pelagii i.
ep. 16, ad Childeb. Reg. (Mansi ix. p. 728) : Since one must give no
offence even to the little ones : quanto nobis studio ac labore satagen-
dum est, ut pro auferendo suspicionis scandalo obsequium confessionis
nostrae regibus ministremus; quibus nos etiam subditos esse sanctae
Scripturae praecipiunt ?   Veniens etenim Rufinus vir magnificus, legatus excellentiae vestrae, confidenter a nobis, ut decuit, postulavit, qua-
tenis vobis aut beatae recordationis papae Leonus tomum a nobis per
omnia conservari significare debuissemus, aut propriis verbis nostrae
confessionem fidei destinare.   Et primam quidem petitionis ejus partem,
quia facilior fuit, mox ut dixit, inplevimus.—Ut autem nullius deinceps,
quod absit, suspicionis resideret occasio, etiam illam aliam partem, quam
memoratus vir illustris Rufinus admonuit, facere mutavi, scilicet propriis verbis confessionem fidei, quam tenemus, exponens.   Then follows
a diffused confession of faith, in which, however, he mentions only four
oecumenical synods, not the fifth.   At the same time he writes to Sa-
paudus Episc. Arelat. (Ep. 15, l. c. p. 727) praying, ut, si epistola,
quam—ad—Childebertum regem direximus, in qua de institutis beatissimorum patrum nostrorum fidem catholicam nostro per Dei gratiam
sermone deprompsimus, tam ipsi gloriosissimo regi, quam caritati tuae,
vel aliis fratribus coëpiscopis nostris placuit, rescripto tuae caritatis
celerius agnoscamus. cf. Preuves des libertés de l'église Gallicane c. 3.
Planck ii. 673.

then greatly corrupted, pernicious influences rather than enlightenment to the Germans, which were exhibited among the
latter in the roughest form, less hidden in their case by the external rites prevalent among the Romans.   Christianity, as it
was then proclaimed, a series of dogmas and laws, could not re-
strain this corruption.   While it presented *expiations* for all
offences, in addition to its prohibitions of them, there was opened
up to wild barbarity a way of first enjoying the lust of sin, and
then of procuring exemption from the guilt of it.   There was
little concern for instruction.   The public services of religion
by means of their pomp and the use of a foreign, *i. e.*, the Latin
language, awakened dark feelings rather than right ideas.   As
the grossest notions were entertained of hell, so also were similar
ideas prevalent respecting the power of the church, the influence
of the saints,[1] the merit of ecclesiastical and monkish exercises,
the value of alms to the church and to the poor.[2]   These notions

---

[1] Even under them an aristocracy was formed.   When the Huns
approached Metz (Gregor. Tur. hist. ii. 6.), Saint Stephen implored
in the heavenly regions the Apostles Peter and Paul to protect the
town, and received from them the answer: vade in pace, dilectissime
frater, oratorium tantum tuum carebit incendio.   Pro urbe vero non
obtinebimus, quia dominicae sanctionis super eam sententia jam processit.

[2] cf. vita s. Eligii Episc. Noviomensis libb. iii. written A. D. 672. by
his contemporary Audoënus Archiep. Rotomag. in Luc. d'Achery spicilegium ed. ii. Tom. ii. p. 76 ss.   Eligius, bishop of Noyon, was considered a man of extraordinary sanctity (vitae lib. ii. c. 6. p. 92 : Huic
itaque viro sanctissimo inter caetera virtutum suarum miracula id etiam
a Domino concessum erat, ut sanctorum Martyrum corpora, quae per
tot saecula abdita populis hactenus habebantur, eo investigante ac nimio
ardore fidei indagante patefacta proderentur: siquidem nonnulla vene-
rabantur prius a populo in locis, quibus non erant, et tamen quo in loco
certius humata tegerentur, prorsus ignorabatur.)   The more remarkable,
therefore, is his exhortation, contained in the vitae lib. ii. c. 15, p. 96 ss.
He refers first to the judgment-day, then to the points of faith, then to
the duty of performing opera christiana, and thus continues : Ille itaque
bonus Christianus est, qui nulla phylacteria, vel adinventiones diaboli
credit.—Ille, inquam, bonus Christianus est, qui hospitibus pedes lavat,
et tamquam parentes carissimos diligit ; qui juxta quod habet pauperibus eleemosynam tribuit ; qui ad Ecclesiam frequentius venit, et obla-
tionem quae in altari Deo offeratur exhibet ; qui de fructibus suis non
gustat, nisi prius Deo aliquid offerat ; qui stateras dolosas et mensuras
duplices non habet ; qui pecuniam suam non dedit ad usuram ; qui et
ipse caste vivit, et filios vel vicinos docet, ut caste et cum timore Dei

were strengthened by legends and miracles, which were certainly in part an imposition of the clergy,[3] but were far from exerting any good moral influence on the people.[4] Crimes of

vivant; et quoties sanctae solemnitates adveniunt, ante dies plures castitatem etiam cum propria uxore custodit, ut secura conscientia ad Domini altare accedere possit; qui postremo symbolum vel orationem dominicam memoriter tenet, et filios ac filias eadem docet. Qui talis est, sine dubio verus Christianus est.—Ecce audistis, Fratres, quales sint Christiani boni : ideo quantum potestis cum Dei adjutorio laborate, ut nomen christianum non sit falsum in vobis. Sed ut veri Christiani esse possitis, semper praecepta Christi et cogitate in mente, et implete in operatione. Redimite animas vestras de poena, dum habetis in potestate remedia; eleemosynam juxta vires facite, pacem et charitatem habete, discordes ad concordiam revocate, mendacium fugite, perjurium expavescite, falsum testimonium non dicite, furtum non facite, oblationes et decimas Ecclesiis offerte, luminaria sanctis locis juxta quod habetis exhibete, symbolum et orationem dominicam memoria retinete, et filiis vestris insinuate.—Ad Ecclesiam quoque frequentius convenite, Sanctorum patrocinia humiliter expetite, diem dominicam pro reverentia resurrectionis Christi absque ullo servili opere colite, Sanctorum solemnitates pio affectu celebrate, proximos vestros sicut vos ipsos diligite etc.—Quod si observaveritis, securi in die judicii ante tribunal aeterni judicis venientes dicetis: Da, Domine, quia dedimus; miserere, quia misericordiam fecimus; nos implevimus quod jussisti, tu redde quod promisisti.

[3] The Arians blamed the catholic clergy for this. So Gregorius Turon. de glor. mart. i. 25 : Theodegisilus hujus rex regionis, cum vidisset hoc miraculum, quod in his sacratis Deo fontibus gerebatur, cogitavit intra se dicens, quia ingenium est Romanorum (Romanos enim vocitant homines nostrae religionis) ut ita accidat, et non est Dei virtus. c. 26 : Est enim populus ille haereticus, qui videns haec magnalia non compungitur ad credendum, sed semper callide divinarum praeceptionum sacramenta nequissimis interpretationum garrulationibus non desinit impugnare. On the contrary, the catholics related many impostures of miracles wrought by the Arian priests, Gregor. Tur. hist. ii. 3, de gloria Confess. c. 13. Comp. the miraculous histories in Löbell, p. 274, and the judgment delivered respecting them, p. 292. The reason why cures performed at the graves of saints should be credible it is impossible to perceive. The presents which those gifted with miraculous power had to expect from pious simplicity induced deception even here.

[4] Gregor. de glor. mart. i. 26. While a person was filling his vessel with that wonder-working water from a priest, manum alterius extendit ad balteum, cultrumque furatus est.—How holy rites were made instrumental in crime may be seen from the words of the monster Fredegundis, the spouse of Chilperich, to the assassins she had hired to murder king Sigbert (575. See Gesta Regum Franc. c. 32, in Bouquet rer. Gall. scriptt. T. ii. p. 562) : Si evaseritis vivi, ego mirifice honorabo vos

the grossest kind were common among the clergy,[5] as well as
the kings[6] and the people, without aversion to them being exhibited, while public opinion did not declare against them in a
manner conformable to the spirit of Christianity.[7]   The moral
influence of Christianity on the multitude was confined to the
external influence of church laws and church discipline, so far as
these were respected.   The period of legal discipline, as a preparation for the gospel, was now restored.

Though every thing heathen was strictly forbidden,[8] yet secret

ot sobolem vestram : si autem corrueritis, ego pro vobis eleemosynas
multas per loca Sanctorum distribuam.

[5] Löbell's Gregor v. Tours S. 309.

[6] Assassination was an every-day occurrence, and even the clergy
were employed as instruments : Gregor. Tur. hist. Franc. vii. 20, viii.
29.   Several Frankish kings lived in polygamy ; Chlotar, for instance,
with two sisters, Gregor. Tur. iv. 3.   Dagobert tres habebat ad instar
Salomonis reginas maxime et plurimas concubinas.   Fredegarii Chronicon c. 60.   Löbell S. 21.

[7] Thus Gregory Tur. relates, without disguise, the crimes of Chlodowich, and yet he passes this judgment on him, ii. 40 : Prosternebat enim
quotidie Deus hostes ejus sub manu ipsius, et augebat regnum ejus,
eo quod ambularet recto corde coram eo, et faceret, quae placita erant
in oculis ejus. Löbell's (p. 263) exculpation of this judgment is of no
avail.   It is nothing but moral barbarousness, when Gregory admits
and disaproves the crimes of Chlodowich, and yet designates him as
pious on account of his confession.   Comp. iii. 1 : Velim, si placet,
parumper conferre, quae Christianis beatam confitentibus Trinitatem
prospera successerint, et quae haereticis eandem scindentibus fuerint in
ruinam.—Hanc Chlodovechus Rex confessus, ipsos haereticos adjutorio
ejus oppressit, regnumque suum per totas Gallias dilatavit : Alaricus
hanc denegans, a regno et populo, atque ab ipsa, quod majus est, vita
multatur aeterna.   Moral barbarousness is also shewn in the sentiments
expressed concerning Guntramnus Boso v. 14 : Guntchramnus alias
sane bonus, nam ad perjuria nimium praeparatus erat.   Comp. ix. 10 :
fuit in actu levis, avaritiae inhians, rerum alienarum ultra modum cupi-
dus, omnibus jurans, et nulli promissa adimplens.   In like manner,
concerning king Theudebert, iii. 25 : magnum se atque in omni bonitate
praecipuum reddidit.   Erat enim regnum cum justitia regens, sacerdotes venerans, Ecclesias munerans, pauperes elevans, et multa multis
beneficia pia ac dulcissima accommodans voluntate.   Omne tributum,
quod in fisco suo ab Ecclesiis in Arverno sitis reddebatur, clementer indulsit.   Comp. de vitis Patrum c. 17, §´2 : Nam Theudebertus—(cum)
multa inique exerceret, et ab eodem (Nicetio) plerumque corriperetur,
quod vel ipse perpetraret, vel perpetrantes non argueret etc.

[8] Theodorich's prohibition, see § 109, not. 4.   Childebert's I. law,
de abolendis idololatriae reliquiis A. D. 554, in Baluzii capitul. i. 5.

idolatry[9] and apostacy from Christianity[10] frequently appeared. It was still more common for the new Christians to be unable entirely to lay aside reverence for their old gods, and the power they were supposed to possess.[11]   Thus the remains of old pagan superstition were preserved among the people along with Christianity.[12]   In civil legislation, all traces of heathenism were like-

[9] Even as late as the time of Gregory of Tours, an image of Diana was worshipped at Treves. (Greg. Tur. hist. viii. 15.)   In Herbadilla at Nantes, about the same time, were statues of Jupiter, Mercury, Venus, Diana and Hercules.   (Mabillon Acta SS. Ord. s. Bened. i. 683.)   In like manner there was found in Luxovium, when Columbanus came thither about 590, imaginum lapidearum densitas, quas cultu miserabili rituque profano vetusta paganorum tempora honorabant (Jonas in vita Columbani c. 17. in Mabillon Acta SS. Ord. s. Bened. ii. 13.)   Martinus Ep. Bracarensis (about 570) wrote de origine idolorum (ed. A. Majus, classicorum auctorum iii. 379), pro castigatione rusticorum, qui adhuc pristina paganorum superstitione detenti, cultum venerationis plus daemoniis quam Deo persolvunt.   The Roman names of deities were frequently transferred to Celtic and German deities also; and therefore the peculiar character of this worship cannot always be perceived.   Beugnot hist. de la destruction du Paganisme en Occident. (Paris 1835) ii. 307.
[10] Conc. Aurelian, ii. ann. 533. can. 20.
[11] Thus said the Arian Agilanes, ambassador of the Visigoths, to Gregory of Tours (hist. Franc. v. 43) : sic vulgato sermone dicimus, non esse noxium, si inter gentilium aras et Dei ecclesiam quis transiens utraque veneretur.
[12] Conc. Turon. ii. ann. 567. c. 22. against the heathen mode of celebrating the Calends of January.   Then : Sunt etiam, qui in festivitate cathedrae domni Petri Apostoli cibos mortuis offerunt, et post missas redeuntes ad domos proprias ad gentilium revertuntur errores, et post corpus Domini sacratas daemoni escas accipiunt.   Conc. Autissiodorense ann. 578. c. 1 : Non licet Kalendis Januarii vetula aut cervolo facere, vel strenas diabolicas observare.   c. 4 : Non licet ad sortilegos vel ad auguria respicere, non ad caragios, nec ad sortes, quas sanctorum vocant, vel quas de ligno aut de pane faciunt, adspicere.   Conc. Narbon. ann. 589. c. 14 : against viros ac mulieres divinatores, quos dicunt esse caragios atque sorticularios.   c. 15 : Ad nos pervenit, quosdam de populis catholicae fidei execrabili ritu diem quintam feriam, quae dicitur Jovis, multos excolere, et operationem non facere.   On the celebration of the Kal. Jan. Isidorus Hisp. de eccles. officiis i. 40 : Tunc miseri homines, et quod pejus est etiam fideles, sumentes species monstruosas in ferarum habitu transformantur ; alii foemineo gestu demutati, virilem vultum effoeminant ; nonnulli etiam de fanatica adhuc consuetudine, quibusdam ipso die observationem auguriis profanantur: perstrepunt omnia saltantium pedibus, tripudiantium plausibus, et quod his turpius est nefas, nexis inter se utriusque sexus choris, inops animi, furens vino turma

L

wise rejected,[13] though the most extended freedom of divorce remained,[14] and *the ordeal*[15] still continued.   The attempt of
Gregory the Great to adopt into the services of the church par-

miscetur.   On belief in auspices and sorcery among the Franks, see
Löbell's Gregor v. Tours, S. 271.

[13] On the history of ancient national privileges, the Salic law under
Chlodwig, the Burgundian under King Gundobald, † 516, the Ripua-
rian under King Theoderich 511-534, the Alemannic under Chlotar II.
in 613-628, the Bavarian under Chlotar II. or Dagobert I. 613-638.
See Eichhorn's Deutsche Staats und Rechtsgesch. i. 220.   Editions
of the laws in Baluzii Capitularia Reg. Franc. T. i.   J. P. Canciani
barbarorum leges antiquae.   Venet. 1781-92. 5 Tomi fol.   Walter corp.
juris Germ. ant. T. i.   cf. prologus Leg. Ripuar (in many editions incorrectly printed as prol. Leg. Sal.):   Theodoricus Rex Francorum,
cum esset Cathalaunis, elegit viros sapientes;—ipso autem dictante
jussit conscribere legem Francorum, Alamannorum et Bojoariorum, et
unicuique genti, quae in ejus potestate erat, secundum consuetudinem
suam: addiditque addenda, et improvisa et incomposita resecavit; et
quae erant secundum consuetudinem Paganorum, mutavit secundum
legem Christianorum.   Et quidquid Theodoricus Rex propter vetustis-
simam Paganorum consuetudinem emendare non potuit, posthaec Hil-
debertus rex inchoavit corrigere; sed Chlotharius rex perfecit.   Haec
omnia Dagobertus rex—renovavit, et omnia veterum legum in melius
transtulit; unicuique quoque genti scriptam tradidit.

[14] By the lex Burgund. tit. 34. c. 3. the husband could put away an
adulteram, maleficam, vel sepulcrorum violatricem without ceremony;
if he does so without these reasons, he was obliged to make her indem-
nification (c. 2. 4. and Lex Bajuvar, tit. vii. c. 14).   By agreement of
both parties, however, marriage could be annulled without any difficulty.
See the formulae in the Formulis Andegavensibus (from the sixth century prim. ed. Mabillon analect. iv. 234) c. 56, and Marculfi formularum lib. ii. c. 30.   The libellus repudii adopted by Marculf runs thus:
Certis rebus et probatis causis inter maritum et uxorem repudiandi locus
patet.   Idcirco dum et inter illo et conjuge sua illa non caritas secundum Deum, sed discordia regnat, et ob hoc pariter conversare minime
possunt, placuit utriusque voluntas, ut se a consortio separare deberent.
Quod ita et fecerunt.   Propterea has epistolas inter se uno tenore con-
scriptas fieri et adfirmare decreverunt, ut unusquisque ex ipsa, sive ad
servitium Dei in monasterio, aut ad copulam matrimonii se sociare voluerit, licentiam habeat etc.

[15] Which was used even in questions belonging to Christianity itself.
Comp. Can. Caesaraugust. § 121. not. 4.—Gregor. Tur. de glor. mart.
i. 81: Arianorum presbyter cum diacono nostrae religionis altercationem
habebat.   At ille—adjecit dicens: Quid longis sermocinationum intentionibus fatigamur?   Factis rei veritas adprobetur: succendatur igni
aeneus, et in ferventi aqua annulus cujusdam projiciatur.   Qui vero eum
ex ferventi unda sustulerit, ille justitiam consequi comprobatur: quo
facto pars diversa ad cognitionem hujus justitiae convertatur etc.

ticular heathen rites, at the time of the conversion of the Anglo-Saxons, is quite singular.[16]

III. OLD BRITISH CHURCH.

§ 126.

Since the invasion of the Anglo-Saxons, ecclesiastical as well as social order had been subverted among the Britons, who manfully strove for their freedom.[1] But the Irish Church was still in a very prosperous state. Their convents were distinguished for their discipline and learning,[2] as well as their efforts to diffuse Christianity towards the north. The monk *Columba* in particular (about 565 † 597) converted a great part of the northern *Picts*, became their spiritual leader as abbot of the monastery

---

[16] Gregor. M. lib. xi. Ep. 76. ad Mellitum Abbatem (also in Bedae hist. eccl. Angl. i. 30.) : Cum vos Deus omnipotens ad—Augustinum Episcopum perduxerit, dicite ei, quid diu mecum de causa Anglorum cogitans tractavi, videlicet, quia fana idolorum destrui in eadem gente minime debeant, sed ipsa, quae in eis sunt, idola destruantur.   Aqua benedicta fiat, in eisdem fanis aspergatur, altaria construantur, reliquiae ponantur : quia si fana eadem bene constructa sunt, necesse est ut a cultu daemonum in obsequium veri Dei debeant commutari : ut, dum gens ipsa eadem fana non videt destrui, de corde errorem deponat, et Deum verum cognoscens ac adorans, ad loca, quae consuevit, familiarius concurrat.   Et quia boves solent in sacrificio daemonum multos occidere, debet his etiam hac de re aliqua solemnitas immutari : ut die dedicationis vel natalitiis SS. Martyrum, quorum illic reliquiae ponuntur, tabernacula sibi circa easdem ecclesias, quae ex fanis commutatae sunt, de ramis arborum faciant et religiosis conviviis solemnitatem celebrent. Nec diabolo jam animalia immolent, sed ad laudem Dei in esum suum animalia occidant, et donatori omnium de satietate sua gratias referant : ut, dum eis aliqua exterius gaudia reservantur, ad interiora gaudia consentire facilius valeant.   Nam duris mentibus simul omnia abscidere impossibile esse non dubium est : quia is, qui locum summum adscendere nititur, necesse est ut gradibus vel passibus, non autem saltibus elevetur.

[1] Gildas Badonicus (560-580) de excidio Britanniae liber querulus (in three parts historia ; epistola ; increpatio in clerum), best edited in Thom. Gale historiae Britannicae, Saxon., Anglo-Danicae scriptores xv. Oxon. 1691, thence in Gallandii bibl. PP. xii. 189.

[2] Jo. Ph. Murray de Britannia atque Hibernia saeculis a sexto inde ad decimum litterarum domicilio, in the novis commentariis Soc. Reg. Gotting. T. i. comm. hist. et philol. p. 72 ss.

founded by him on the island *Hy* (*St Iona*), and transmitted
this relation to his successors.[3]

Close as the union was between the British and Irish Churches,
they could yet have little connexion of importance, on account of
their remoteness, with other Churches.   Hence they had retained
many old arrangements, and developed them in a peculiar way,
after such usages had been altered in other countries.[4]   Since the

[3] Beda hist. eccl. iii. 4 : Habere autem solet ipsa insula rectorem
semper Abbatem Presbyterum, cujus juri et omnis provincia, et ipsi
etiam Episcopi, ordine inusitato, debeant, esse subjecti, juxta exemplum primi doctoris illius, qui non Episcopus, sed Presbyter exstitit et
Monachus.

[4] These appear in the following controversy, and relate to (a) the
reckoning of Easter.   The Britons were by no means Quarto-decimani,
though they were often called so from ignorance (ex. gr. Bedae chron.
ad ann. 4591), and appealed too, themselves, to John and the Asiatics
(for example, Colman, Beda, h. e. iii. 25).   Beda hist. eccl. iii. 4 : Paschae diem non semper in luna quartadecima cum Judaeis, ut quidam
rebantur, sed in die quidem dominica, alia tamen quam decebat hebdo-
mada, celebrabant.   Namely, ii. 2 : Paschae diem a decimaquarta usque ad vicesimam lunam observabant.   Quae computatio octoginta quatuor annorum circulo continetur.   The Romans, on the other hand (ii.
19), adstruebant, quia dominicum Paschae diem a quintadecima luna
usque ad vicesimam primam lunam oporteret inquiri.   The difference,
therefore, was, that the Easter festival fell on different Sundays in many
years.   The cause of this was, that owing to the previous confusion on
the subject, and for the purpose of removing it (see above, § 100, not.
13), the Aquitanian Victorius first (457), and afterwards the Roman
abbot, Dionysius Exiguus (525), had made new Easter tables, which,
in succession, were brought into use, first in Italy, and then in the other
Western churches (see Ideler's Chronologie ii. 275).   On the contrary,
the British church had retained the old cycle of 84 years.   The state
of the controversy is more minutely developed by Jac. Usserius britan-
nicarum Ecclesiarum antiquitt.   Dublin, 1639, 4. p. 925.   Humphr.
Prideaux connexion of Scripture history, ii. 273.   Ideler's Chronol. ii.
295. (b.)   The tonsure.   The Roman clergy were in coronam atton-
si ; the British, as also the monks elsewhere, in older times, see Paulini
Nol. ep. vii., had the fore part of the head bald.   The former called
their tonsure tonsuram Petri, and that of the Britons tonsuram Simonis
Magi (Beda h. e. v. 21).   Usserii brit. Eccl. antiqu. p. 921. (c) Lanfrancus ep. ad. Terdelvacum Hibern. regem, written 1074 (in J. Usserii vett. epistolarum hibernicarum syll. Dublin, 1632, 4. p. 72), accuses
them, quod quisque pro arbitrio suo legitime sibi copulatam uxorem,
nulla canonica causa interveniente, relinquit, et aliam quamlibet, seu
sibi vel relictae uxori consanguinitate propinquam, sive quam alius simili
improbitate deseruit, maritali seu fornicaria lege, punienda sibi temeritate conjungit.   Quod Episcopi ab uno Episcopo consecrantur.   Quod

condemnation of the three chapters, a great mistrust of the Romish orthodoxy had arisen here also.[5]

When *Augustine* formed a new Church with Roman arrangements among the Anglo-Saxons, he required the British clergy

infantes baptismo sine chrismate consecrata baptizantur. Quod sacri ordines per pecuniam ab Episcopis dantur. But from these the abuses 1 and 4, which afterwards prevailed, may have sprung. We have also to direct attention to the following peculiarities of the British-Irish church, which are not touched on in the disputes. They had (a) no celibacy of the priests. Patrick himself was sprung from priests, see Patricii confessio : patrem habui Calpurnium Diaconum, filium quondam Potiti Presbyteri. Synodus Patricii about 456, can. 6. (in D. Wilkins concilia Magnae Britanniae et Hiberniae i. 2) : Quicunque clericus ab ostiario usque ad sacerdotem — si non more romano capilli ejus tonsi sint (i. e., cut short generally, the differences of tonsure arose subsequently), et uxor ejus si non velato capite ambulaverit, pariter a laicis contemnantur, et ab Ecclesia separentur. Synodus Hibern. in d'Achery spicilegium i. 493 : Qui ab accessu adolescentiae usque ad trigesimum annum aetatis suae probabiliter vixerit, una tantum uxore virgine sumta contentus, quinque annis Subdiaconus, et quinque annis Diaconus, quadragesimo anno Presbyter, quinquagesimo Episcopus stet. The Irish Clement defended the marriage of a bishop as late as the eighth century. Bonifacii ep. 67. (b) A peculiar liturgy. Usser brit. Eccles. antiqu. p. 916. (c) The monks had a peculiar system of rules. Usser p. 918.—That the British-Irish Church derived its origin from Asia Minor, and had preserved a purer, simpler Christianity, are mere empty conjectures, which have been carried to an extravagant length, especially by Münter in the Theol. Studien u. Krit. 1833, iii. 744. The opinion that the Britains, as Quarto-decimani, had the Asiatic mode of celebrating the passover, an opinion which principally lies at the foundation of that belief, is obviously false.

[5] Comp. § 111. not. 25. § 117. not. 25. § 124. not. 19. Gregorii magni ep. ad Episcopos Hiberniae A. D. 592 (lib. ii. ep. 36) : Reducat caritatem vestram tandem integritas fidei ad matrem, quae vos generavit, Ecclesiam.—Nam in synodo, in qua de tribus capitulis actum est, aperto liquet nihil de fide convulsum esse vel aliquatenus immutatum, sed (sicut scitis) de quibusdam illic solummodo personis est actitatum.—Quod autem scribitis, quia ex illo tempore inter alias provincias maxime flagellatur Italia, non hoc ad ejus debetis intorquere exprobrium, quoniam scriptum est : quem diligit Dominus castigat.—Ut igitur de tribus capitulis animis vestris ablata dubietate possit satisfactio abundanter infundi, librum, quem ex hac re sanctae memoriae decessor meus Pelagius Papa scripserat, vobis utile judicavi transmittere. Quem si deposito voluntariae defensionis studio, puro vigilantique corde saepius volueritis relegere, eum vos per omnia secuturos, et ad unitatem nostram reversuros nihilominus esse confido. However, at a later period, Columbanus defended, with zeal, the three chapters against Boniface IV. See below, note 13.

(Culdees)[6] to adopt the Roman ecclesiastical arrangements, especially with regard to the mode of reckoning Easter ; and to yield
to him, as archbishop of Canterbury, the primacy of all Britain. [7]
But the negotiations at two meetings (603) led to no agreement ;[8] they gave rise rather to bitter hatred between the two
parties.[9]

[6] Keledei, Kyledei, Latinised Colidei, the British appellation for
priests and monks (Kele-De *i. e.* servus Dei, as elsewhere too, for example, in Gregory the Great, the clergy are often called servi Dei).
When the Roman regulations were subsequently adopted generally in
these lands, the name continued to be applied principally to the clergy,
who in their corporations held fast by the old British modes. It was,
however, given also to all priests to the time of the Reformation, by
those who spoke in British. See Hector Boëthius hist. Scotorum lib.
vi. p. 95 : Invaluit id nomen apud vulgus in tantum, ut sacerdotes omnes
ad nostra paene tempora vulgo Culdei, i. e. cultores Dei, sine discrimine vocitarentur. Comp. historical account of the ancient Culdees of
Iona and of their settlements in Scotland, England, and Ireland, by
John Jamieson. Edinburgh, 1811, 4. J. W. J. Braun de Culdeis
comm. Bonnae 1840, 4.
[7] Gregory the Great had conferred this on him (lib. xi. ep. 65. Beda
h. e. i. 29 : Tua vero fraternitas—omnes Britanniae sacerdotes habeat
—subjectos. He derived the right of doing so from this fact, that the
British church, as well as the Anglo-Saxon, was a daughter of the Roman (see note 5).
[8] Respecting them see Beda h. e. ii. 2. The Britons had not only a
different mode of celebrating the Easter festival, sed et alia plurima uni-
tati ecclesiasticae contraria faciebant. Qui cum, longa disputatione habita, neque precibus, neque hortamentis, neque increpationibus Augustini ac sociorum ejus assensum praebere voluissent, sed suas potius traditiones universis, quae per orbem sibi in Christo concordant, ecclesiis
praeferrent, sanctus pater Augustinus—finem fecit. At the second
meeting Augustine said to them : Quia in multis quidem nostrae con-
suetudini, imo universalis Ecclesia, contraria geritis ; et tamen si in tribus his mihi, obtemperare vultis, ut Pascha suo tempore celebretis, ut
ministerium baptizandi—juxta morem sanctae Romanae et apostolicae
Ecclesiae compleatis, ut genti Anglorum una nobiscum verbum Domini
praedicetis ; caetera quae agitis, quamvis moribus nostris contraria, ae-
quanimiter cuncta tolerabimus. At illi nil horum se facturos, neque
illum pro Archiepiscopo habituros esse respondebant. The papal primacy was not at all a subject of dispute. The first rank among the
bishops was conceded to the popes by the Britons, but they believed so
in an erroneous way (see note 5). But the popes themselves did not
yet lay claim to a greater ecclesiastical power than that of other apostolic sees (see § 117, note 18-20) ; and so one appealed against the
Britons not to papal authority but to the statuta canonica quaternae sedis Apostolicae, Romanae videlicet, Hierosolymitanae, Antiochenae,
Alexandrinae, to the old councils, and to the universalis Ecclesiae catho-

At this time the Irish monk *Columbanus* came into the king-dom of Burgundy (about 590), where he acquired great reputa-tion by his strict piety and cultivated mind, and founded several convents, particularly that at *Luxovium* (Luxeuil). Here he not only introduced a peculiar system of monastic rules, but also con-tinued faithful to the peculiarities of his mother Church, and de-fended the Irish mode of celebrating Easter with great zeal.[10] At length he displeased king Theodorich II., on account of his boldness; was banished (about 606); laboured some years in the conversion of the Alemanni at the lake of Constance; then trans-ferred this task to his pupil *Gallus;* founded the convent *Bobium* in a valley in the Appenines in Liguria, where he inspired the same desire for learning for which the monks of his country were

licae unanimem regulam (see Cummiani ep. ad Segienum Huensem Abbatem, in J. Usserii vett. epistt. hibernicarum sylloge p. 27, 28). The Britons did not consider the pope as the sole successor of Peter, but all bishops: Gildas de excidio Britanniae P. iii. cap. 1., describes bad priests as sedem Petri Apostoli inmundis pedibus usurpantes (comp. § 94, note 36). That the Britons acknowledged no ecclesiastical power of the pope over them, is proved by their opposition to the Roman re-gulations, an opposition which continued in Ireland down to the twelfth century. Spelman (Conc. Brit. i. 108) has published for the first time, from a Cottonian MS. in the old British language, the following decla-ration of Dinooth, abbot of the monastery of Bangor, which he is said to have made to Augustine: Notum sit et absque dubitatione vobis, quod nos omnes sumus et quilibet nostrum obedientes et subditi eccle-siae Dei, et Papae Romae, et unicuique vero Christiano et pio, ad aman-dum unumquemque in suo gradu in caritate perfecta, et ad juvandum unumquemque eorum verbo et facto fore filios Dei. Et aliam obedien-tiam, quam istam, non scio debitam ei, quem vos nominatis esse Papam; nec esse patrem patrum vindicari et postulari : et istam obedientiam nos sumus parati dare et solvere ei et cuique Christiano continuo. Prae-terea nos sumus sub gubernatione episcopi Caerlionis super Osca, qui est ad supervidendum sub Deo super nobis, ad faciendum nos servare viam spiritualem. It is however spurious. See Döllinger's Gesch. d. christl. Kirche i. ii. 218. Stevenson on Bedae h. e. ii. 2. p. 102.

⁹ Thus Augustine's successor, Laurentius (Beda ii. 4), complained that the Scottish bishop, Dagamus, ad nos veniens, non solum cibum nobiscum, sed nec in eodem hospitio, quo vescebamur, sumere voluit. Comp. Beda ii. 20 : usque hodie moris est Brittonum, fidem religion-emque Anglorum pro nihilo habere, neque in aliquo eis magis commu-nicare quam paganis.

¹⁰ Columbani epist. i. ad Gregor. Papum (among Gregory's letters, lib. ix. ep. 127), and epist 2. ad Patres Synodi cujusd. Gallicanae.

chiefly distinguished.[11]   He died A. D. 615.[12]   His letter to Gregory the Great on the subject of the celebration of Easter, as well as that to Boniface IV. against the condemnation of the three chapters, still attest the free spirit of the Irish Church.[13]

[11] cf. Antiquissimus quatuor Evangeliorum Codex Sangallensis ed· H. C. M. Rettig. Turici 1836, 4. praef.   Hence the important discoveries of modern times in the Codd. Bobiensibus, at present very much scattered.   See Amad. Peyron de bibliotheca Bobiensi comm. prefixed to his Ciceronis orationem fragmenta inedita. Stuttg. et Tubing. 1824. 4.

[12] His life by his pupil Jonas, abbot of Luxovium, in Mabillon Acta Sanct. Ord. Bened. ii. 3.   Neander's Denkwürdigk. iii. ii. 37 ff.   Gu. Chr. Knottenbelt disp. hist. theol. de Columbano. Lugd. Bat. 1839. 8. —His works (regula coenobialis, sermones xvi., epistolae vi., carmina iv.), ed. Patricius Flemingus.   Lovanii 1667. recensita et aucta in Gallandii bibl. PP. xii. 319.

[13] Ep. ad Gregor. : Forte notam subire timens Hermagoricae novitatis, antecessorum et maxime Papae Leonis auctoritate contentus es. Noli te quaeso in tali quaestione humilitati tantum aut gravitati credere, quae saepe falluntur.   Melior forte est canis vivus in problemate Leone mortuo (Eccl. ix. 4).   Vivus namque sanctus emendare potest, quae ab altero majore emendata non fuerint.—non mihi satisfacit post tantos, quos legi auctores, una istorum sententia Episcoporum dicentium tantum : " Cum Judaeis Pascha facere non debemus."   Dixit hoc olim et Victor Episcopus, sed nemo Orientalium suum recepit commentum. Epist. 5. ad Bonifacium iv. cap. 4 : Vigila itaque quaeso, Papa, vigila, et iterum dico, vigila : quia forte non bene vigilavit Vigilius, quem caput scandali isti clamant, qui vobis culpam injiciunt.   c. 10 : ex eo tempore, quo Deus et Dei filius esse dignatus est, ac in duobus illis ferventissimis Dei Spiritus equis, Petro scilicet et Paulo Apostolis—per mare gentium equitans, turbavit aquas multas, et innumerabilium populorum miîlibus multiplicavit quadrigas; supremus ipse auriga currus illius, qui est Christus,—ad nos usque pervenit.   Ex tunc vos magni estis et clari, et Roma ipsa nobilior et clarior est; et, si dici potest, propter Christi geminos Apostolos—vos prope caelestes estis, et Roma orbis terrarum caput est ecclesiarum, salva loci dominicae resurrectionis singulari praerogativa (comp. Firmilianus Div. 1. § 68, not. 12.   Augustinus § 94. not. 5).   Et ideo sicut magnus honor vester est pro dignitate cathedrae, ita magna cura vobis necessaria est, ut non perdatis vestram dignitatem propter aliquam perversitatem.   Tamdiu enim potestas apud vos erit, quamdiu recta ratio permanserit : ille enim certus regni caelorum clavicularius est, qui dignis per veram scientiam aperit, et indignis claudit.   Alioquin, si contraria fecerit, nec aperire nec claudere poterit.   c. 11 : Cum haec igitur vera sint, et sine ulla contradictione ab omnibus vera sapientibus recepta sint (licet omnibus notum est, et nemo est qui nesciat, qualiter Salvator noster sancto Petro regni caelorum contulit claves, et vos per hoc forte superciliosum nescio quid, prae

THIRD DIVISION.

FROM THE BEGINNING OF THE MONOTHELITIC CONTROVERSY, AND FROM THE TIME OF MUHAMMED TO THE BEGINNING OF THE CONTROVERSY CONCERNING THE WORSHIP OF IMAGES.

FROM 622—726.

FIRST CHAPTER.

RESTRAINING OF THE CHURCH IN THE EAST.

§ 127.

Though the Persians tolerated the Nestorians, they hated the Catholic Christians, as was apparent in the war which *Kesra* (Chosröes) *II. Parviz* carried on against the East Roman empire from A. D. 604, and especially in the taking of Jerusalem (614). On this account the victories of *Heraclius* from 621, ending with the dethronement of Chosröes by his son *Schirujeh* (Siröes) (628) were of importance in relation to the Church. Besides, Heraclius brought back the wood of the true cross which had been carried off ; and instituted a festival in commemoration of it, the σταυρώσιμος ἡμέρα, festum exaltationis (14th of September).[1]

In the meantime, a far more dangerous enemy of the Church had appeared in Arabia. *Muhammed*, in the year 611, began to preach Islamism, at first in private, and then publicly among the Koreish in Mecca. At first, indeed, he was

caeteris vobis majoris auctoritatis, ac in divinis rebus potestatis vindicatis) ; noveritis minorem fore potestatem vestram apud Dominum, si vel cogitatis hoc in cordibus vestris : quia unitas fidei in toto orbe unitatem fecit potestatis et praerogativae ; ita ut libertas veritati ubique ab omnibus detur, et aditus errori ab omnibus similiter abnegetur etc.

[1] Theophanis Chronographia p. 245-273, among other things says, of the conduct of Chosröes in the conquered lands, p. 263. ἠνάγκαζε τοὺς Χριστιανοὺς γενέσθαι εἰς τὴν τοῦ Νεστορίου θρησκείαν πρὸς τὸ πλῆξαι τὸν βασιλέα.

obliged to give way to his enemies (15th July 622 *Hedschra*),[2] but gained over the city *Yatschreb* (Medina al Nabi) in his favour; extended his dominion and his doctrines thence, prince and prophet in one person, till they spread far into Arabia; at length conquered Mecca (630); consecrated the *Caaba* as the chief temple of Islamism; and bequeathed to his successors (*Chalifs*) Arabia, as a country completely subject to their faith and their dominion († 632).[3]

Islamism, whose holy writings are contained in the *Koran*,[4] collected by Abubekr, was a compound of Judaism and Christianity in its essential features.[5] But it made the doctrine of the infinite sublimity of God its basis, in a way so much one-sided as that *an absolute dependence* of man on God resulted from it; and ideas of a likeness and an inward union between man and God, and consequently the fundamental principles of all the higher morality, found no place in the system. By making it a religious duty to wage war on infidels, by its fatalism, and its

---

[2] Ideler's Chronologie Bd. 2. S. 482 ff.

[3] Abulfeda de vita Muhammedis ed. J. Gagnier. Oxon. 1723. fol. La vie de Mohammed par J. Gagnier. Amsterd. 1732. 2 voll. 8. translated into German by Ch. F. R. Vetterlein, Köthen 1802-1804. v. Hammer-Purgstall's Gemäldesaal der Lebensbeschreibungen grosser moslimischer Herrscher. Bd. 1. Mohammed d. Prophet. Leipzig 1837 (Comp. Umbreit in the theol. Studien u. Krit. 1841. i. 212). Gust. Weil's Mohammed d. Prophet, s. Leben u. s. Lehre, aus handschriftl. Quellen u. d. Koran geschöpft. Stuttgart 1843. 8.—On the miracles of Muhammed and his character, see in Tholuck's vermischten Schriften i. 1.

[4] Arab. et lat. ed. Lud. Maraccius, Patav. 1698 fol. French par Savary, Paris 1783. 2 voll. 8. German by F. E. Boysen, Halle 1775. 8. by F. S. G. Wahl, Halle 1828. 8. literally translated with annotations by Dr L. Ullmann. Bielefeld u. Crefeld, 3te Aufl. 1844. 8.—G. Weil's hist. krit. Einleit. in den Koran. Bielefeld 1844. 8. [English by G. Sale.]

[5] Weil's Mohammed see not. 3. Muhammed's Religion nach ihrer innern Entwickelung und ihrem Einflusse auf das Leben der Völker, von I. I. I. Döllinger. Regensburg 1838. 4. Dettinger's Beiträge zu einer Theologie des Korans, in the Tübingen Zeitschr. f. Theol. 1831. iii. 1.—Was hat Mohammed aus dem Judenthume angenommen? von Abr. Geiger, Bonn 1833. 8.—Maier's christl. Bestandtheile des Koran, in the Freiburger Zeitschr. f. Theol. Bd. 2. Heft. 1. S. 34. (1839). C. F. Gerock's Darstellung der Christologie des Koran. Hamburg und Gotha 1839. 8.—On the relation of Islamism to the gospel, in Möhler's Schriften u. Aufsätzen, herausgeg. v. Döllinger i. 348.

sensual promises, it excited among the rude and powerful people of the Arabs so unconquerable a spirit for war, and so wild a desire for conquest,[6] that the two neighbouring kingdoms, the Persian and the Byzantine, could not withstand such resistance amid their internal weaknesses. The provinces of the Byzantine empire, which lay nearest, were the more easily conquered, inasmuch as the greater number of the inhabitants consisted of Monophysites who joyfully met the Arabians as their deliverers. The conquest of *Syria* was begun under the first Chaliph *Abubekr* († 634), and completed under the second, *Omar* (639), under whom the valiant Amru also overcame Egypt (640). Under *Osman* the Persian empire was conquered (651). During the reign of the *Ommiades*, their general *Musa*, brought first the entire northern coast of Africa (707), and then Spain also (711), under the Arabian dominion ; while, on the other side, the Arabians advanced several times as far as Constantinople, and twice besieged the city for a long time (669 till 676, and 717 till 718).

Jews and Christians were tolerated by the Arabs on condition of paying a poll·tax ; and though sometimes severely oppressed, yet they were not compelled to change their religion.[7] Still,

---

[6] Mohamed. See a representation of the influence of his faith on the middle ages by K. E. Oelsner. Frankf. a. M. 1810. 8. Muhammed's religion by Döllinger, see not. 5.

[7] Muhammed was tolerant at first of other religions (cf. Sura ii. et v.) : afterwards, however, he made it the duty of believers, by the 9th and 67 Surats, to carry on religious war, for the purpose of exterminating idolaters and making Jews and Christians tributary (comp. Gerock's Christologie des Koran S. 118). Before this he had granted the Christians of some parts of Arabia, as well as the Jews and Sabaeans, letters of freedom, though doubtless both the Testamentum et pactiones initae inter Mohammedem et christianae fidei cultores (first brought from the East by the capuchin Pacificus Scaliger, and printed at Paris 1630, 4to. and often afterwards), and the Pactum Muhammedis, quod indulsit Monachis montis Sinai et Christianis in universum (in Pococke descr. of the East. Lond. 1743. fol. i. 268. translated into German, 2d edition, Erlangen 1771. 4. i. 393), in which distinguished privileges are secured to all Christians, are spurious. The humiliating terms under which Omar, at the taking of Jerusalem 637, allowed freedom of religion to the Christians there (Le Beau hist. du Bas-Empire xii. 421), express, on the contrary, the spirit with which the subjugated Christians were treated at a later time. cf. Th. Chr. Tychsen comm. qua disquiritur, quatenus Muhammedes aliarum religionum sectatores toleraverit, in the commentationes Soc. Reg. Gotting. xv. 152.

however, the advantages held out to those who adopted Islamism attracted many converts ; and thus Christianity not only lost all political importance in the conquered provinces, but the number of its confessors was always diminishing in proportion to that of the Moslems.   The catholic patriarchates of Antioch, Jerusalem, and Alexandria, remained unoccupied ; for their possessors, living in the Greek empire, were merely titulars.

SECOND CHAPTER.

HISTORY OF THE GREEK CHURCH.

§ 128.

MONOTHELITIC CONTROVERSY.

Original Documents in the Acts of the first Lateran Synod, A. D. 649 (ap. Mansi x. 863,) and the sixth General Council, A. D. 680 (ap. Mansi xi. 190.) Anastasii bibliothecarii (about 870) collectanea de iis quae spectant ad histor. Monothelit. (prim. ed. J. Sirmond. Paris 1620. 8. in Sirm. opp. T. iii. in bibl. PP. Lugdun. xii. 833. ap. Gallandius T. xiii. and scattered in Mansi T. x. and xi.)

Historical authorities : Theophanes (comp. the preface to section 2.)

Works : F. Combefisii hist. haeresis Monothelitarum ac vindiciae actorum sextae synodi in his nov. auctarium Patrum. ii. 3.   (Paris 1648.)   Walch's Ketzerhist. ix. 3.   Neander's KG. iii. 353.

A fresh attempt to bring the Monophysites back to the Catholic Church was followed by no other consequence than that of introducing into the latter a new element of controversy.

When the emperor *Heraclius* (A. D. 611–641) during his Persian campaign abode in Armenia and Syria (from 622), he thought he perceived that the Monophysites were particularly stumbled at the consequence arising from the catholic doctrine, viz., *two manifestations of will* (ἐνέργειαι) in the person of Christ. *Sergius*, patriarch of Constantinople, having been applied to on the point, declared that the adoption of an *active will*, and a *manifestation of will*, was not inconsistent with the received creed of the Church ; and therefore the emperor, as well as several bishops, decided in favour of this opinion.[1] But when one of these bishops, *Cyrus*, whom the emperor had appointed patriarch of Alexandria, reunited (633)[2] the Severians of that place with the Catholic Church by articles of agreement, in which the Monophysite doctrine of one volition was expressed ; *Sophronius*, a Palestinian monk, who happened to be there at the time, raised the first opposition to this doctrine, which he afterwards continued with zeal after he became patriarch of Jerusalem (634).[3] Sergius now advised that nothing should be said on the disputed point.[4] Pope Honorius agreed with him, not only in this advice, but in the doctrinal view of the matter.[5] Sophronius was quieted by

[1] Cyri Episc. Phasidis epist. ad Sergium (ap. Mansi xi. 561.) mentions κέλευσις of Heraclius to Arcadius, archb. of Cyprus, δύο ἐνεργείας ἐπὶ τοῦ δεσπότου ἡμῶν Ἰ. Χ. μετὰ τὴν ἕνωσιν λέγεσθαι κωλύουσα. Sergius ad Cyprum (ibid. p. 525.) rests on the authority Cyril of Alexandria, who speaks of μίαν ζωοποιὸν ἐνέργειαν, and on Mennas' letter to Virgilius, which says, ἓν τὸ τοῦ Χριστοῦ θέλημα καὶ μίαν ζωοποιὸν ἐνέργειαν, though he is willing to be instructed by stronger reasons in favour of the contrary opinion. More decidedly Theodorus episc. Pharan. (Fragments ibid. p. 567 ss.) εἶναι μίαν ἐνέργειαν· ταύτης δὲ τεχνίτην καὶ δημιουργὸν τὸν θεόν, ὄργανον δὲ τὴν ἀνθρωπότητα.

[2] Cyri epist. altera ad Sergium (ap. Mansi xi. 561.) with the nine articles of agreement appended, p. 563. In the seventh we read : τὸν αὐτὸν ἕνα Χριστὸν καὶ υἱὸν ἐνεργοῦντα τὰ θεοπρεπῆ καὶ ἀνθρώπινα μιᾷ θεανδρικῇ ἐνεργείᾳ, κατὰ τὸν ἐν ἁγίοις Διονύσιον (Dionys. Areopag. epist. iv. ad Cajum. Comp. § 110. not. 8. The orthodox read καινῇ θεανδρικῇ ἐνεργείᾳ).

[3] Sophronii Synodica ap. Mansi xi. 461.—His other extant writings (saints' lives, discourses, &c.), to which many have been added in the Spicilegium Romanum T. iii. and iv. (1840) do not refer to Monothelitism.

[4] Sergii ep. ad Honorium (ap. Mansi xi. 529), contains the most credible account of the beginning of the controversy. He assures Cyrus that his advice was, μηκέτι τοῦ λοιποῦ τινι συγχωρεῖν, μίαν ἢ δύο προφέρειν ἐνεργείας ἐπὶ Χριστοῦ τοῦ θεοῦ ἡμῶν· ἀλλὰ μᾶλλον, καθάπερ αἱ ἅγιαι καὶ οἰκουμενικαὶ παραδεδώκασι σύνοδοι, ἕνα καὶ τὸν αὐτὸν υἱὸν μονογενῆ τὸν κύριον ἡμῶν Ἰ. Χ. τὸν ἀληθινὸν θεὸν ἐνεργεῖν ὁμολογεῖν τά τε θεῖα καὶ ἀνθρώπινα, καὶ πᾶσαν θεοπρεπῆ καὶ ἀνθρωποπρεπῆ ἐνέργειαν ἐξ ἑνὸς καὶ τοῦ αὐτοῦ σεσαρκωμένου θεοῦ λόγου ἀδιαιρέτως προϊέναι, καὶ εἰς ἕνα καὶ τὸν αὐτὸν ἀναφέρεσθαι· διά τὸ τὴν μὲν μιᾶς ἐνεργείας φωνὴν—θορυβεῖν τὰς τινων ἀκοὰς, ὑπολαμβανόντων, ἐπ᾽ ἀναιρέσει ταύτην προφέρεσθαι τῶν ἐν Χριστῷ—ἡνωμένων δύο φύσεων.—ὡσαύτως δὲ καὶ τὴν τῶν δύο ἐνεργειῶν ῥῆσιν πολλοὺς σκανδαλίζειν.—ἕπεσθαι ταύτῃ τὸ καὶ δύο πρεσβεύειν θελήματα ἐναντίως πρὸς ἄλληλα ἔχοντα,—δύο τοὺς τἀναντία θέλοντας εἰσάγεσθαι, ὅπερ δυσσεβές.

Honorii epist. i. ad Sergium (ap. Mansi xi. 537). Extracts from the epist. ii. ad eundem, ibid. p. 579.

the incursions of the Arabs; but the spark which had fallen on spirits so susceptible of dogmatic speculation could not be extinguished. In vain did the emperor now issue the Ἔκθεσις (638),[6] composed by Sergius for the purpose of putting down the controversy. The West, too, now rose up against the new doctrine. The monk *Maximus*,[7] a former companion of Sophronius, roused up Africa against it; Pope *John IV.* refused to adopt the *Ecthesis*;[8] and Pope *Theodore* excommunicated *Paul*, patriarch of Constantinople (646). Equally unsuccessful was the attempt of *Constans II.* (A. D. 642–668) to restore internal tranquillity by means of the edict called Τύπος (648),[9] which merely

[6] Ap. Mansi x. 992.—ὅθεν ἕνα ἴσμεν υἱὸν τὸν κύριον ἡμῶν Ἰ. Χ.—καὶ ἑνὸς καὶ τοῦ αὐτοῦ τάτε θαύματα καὶ τὰ πάθη κηρύττομεν, καὶ πᾶσαν θείαν καὶ ἀνθρωπίνην ἐνέργειαν ἑνὶ καὶ τῷ αὐτῷ σεσαρκωμένῳ τῷ λόγῳ προσνέμομεν,— οὐδαμῶς συγχωροῦντες τινὶ τῶν πάντων μίαν ἢ δύο λέγειν ἢ διδάσκειν ἐνεργείας ἐπὶ τῆς θείας τοῦ κυρίου ἐνανθρωπήσεως, ἀλλὰ μᾶλλον, καθάπερ αἱ ἅγιαι καὶ οἰκουμενικαὶ παραδεδώκασι σύνοδοι. What follows is word for word the same as the passage from Sergii ep. ad Honor., given in note 4. But he continues, εἰ γὰρ ὁ μιαρὸς Νεστόριος καίπερ διαιρῶν τὴν θείαν τοῦ κυρίου ἐνανθρώπησιν, καὶ δύο εἰσάγων υἱοὺς, δύο θελήματα τούτων εἰπεῖν οὐκ ἐτόλμησε, τοὐναντίον δέ ταυτοβουλίαν τῶν ἐπ᾽ αὐτοῦ ἀναπλαττομένων δύο προσώπων ἐδόξασε, πῶς δυνατὸν, τοὺς τὴν ὀρθὴν ὁμολογοῦντας πίστιν, καὶ ἕνα υἱὸν τὸν κύριον ἡμῶν Ἰ. Χ. τὸν ἀληθινὸν θεὸν δοξάζοντας δύο καὶ ταῦτα ἐναντία θελήματα ἐπ᾽ αὐτοῦ παραδέχεσθαι; ὅθεν τοῖς ἁγίοις πατράσιν ἐν ἅπασι καὶ ἐν τούτῳ κατακολουθοῦντες, ἓν θελῆμα τοῦ κυρίου ἡμῶν Ἰ. Χ.—ὁμολογοῦμεν, ὡς ἐν μηδενὶ καιρῷ τῆς νοερῶς ἐψυχωμένης αὐτοῦ σαρκὸς κεχωρισμένως καὶ ἐξ οἰκείας ὁρμῆς, ἐναντίως τῷ νεύματι τοῦ ἡνωμένου αὐτῇ καθ᾽ ὑπόστασιν θεοῦ λόγου, τὴν φυσικὴν αὐτῆς ποιήσασθαι κίνησιν, ἀλλ᾽ ὁπότε καὶ οἵαν καὶ ὅσην αὐτὸς ὁ θεὸς λόγος ἠβούλετο.

[7] Who is also worthy of notice as a commentator on Pseudo-Dionysius the Areopagite. See Neander's KG. iii. 344. Ritter's Gesch. d. christl. Phil. ii. 535. His works, for the most part, against the Monothelites were edited by Franc. Combefisius. Paris. 1675. 2 voll. fol. Prefixed to the first volume is the Greek life of Maximus, important in the history of the Monothelites. The doctrines of the Duothelites and Monothelites are most clearly represented in contrast in Maximi disp. cum Pyrrho, opp. ii. 159.

[8] Johannis ep. ad Constantinum Imp. in Anastasii collectan. ap. Mansi x. 682.

[9] Ap. Mansi x. 1029.—ἔγνωμεν ἐν πολλῷ καθεστάναι σάλῳ τὸν ἡμέτερον ὀρθόδοξον λαόν, ὡς τινῶν μὲν ἓν θέλημα ἐπὶ τῆς οἰκονομίας τοῦ μεγάλου θεοῦ καὶ σωτῆρος ἡμῶν Ἰησοῦ δοξαζόντων, καὶ τὸν αὐτὸν ἐνεργεῖν τάτε θεῖα καὶ τὰ ἀνθρώπινα· ἄλλων δὲ δογματιζόντων δύο θελήματα καὶ ἐνεργείας δύο ἐπὶ τῆς αὐτῆς ἐνσάρκου τοῦ λόγου οἰκονομίας· καὶ τῶν μὲν ἐν ἀπολογίᾳ προτιθεμένων διὰ τὸ ἐν πρόσωπον ὑπάρχειν τὸν κύριον ἡμῶν Ἰ. Χ. ἐν δύο ταῖς φύσεσιν ἀσυγχύτως καὶ ἀδιαιρέτως θέλοντα καὶ ἐνεργοῦντα τάτε θεῖα καὶ τὰ ἀνθρώπινα· τῶν δέ διὰ τὰς

recommended silence on the point, without giving a preference to either view; although that tranquillity was most desirable in the kingdom so severely oppressed from without.[10] Pope *Martin I.* at *the first Lateran synod* (649),[11] even ventured to anathematise the doctrine of one will, and the two imperial decrees relating to it. *Martin I.* indeed was now deposed, and, together with Maximus, brought to Constantinople (653), where both were condemned to end their life in exile after much severe treatment.[12] This had the effect of restoring communion between Rome and Constantinople, at least for a time,[13] though it was broken off again under *Constantine Pogonatus* (668–685). To remove this, the emperor summoned *the sixth general council* (680), where pope *Agatho* triumphed in procuring a confirmation by the synod of the doctrine of two wills,[14] as copiously unfolded by him in an

ἀδιαιρέτως ἐν τῷ αὐτῷ καὶ ἑνὶ προσώπῳ συνελθούσας φύσεις, καὶ τοῦ τὴν αὐτῶν σώζεσθαι καὶ μένειν διαφορὰν, καταλλήλως καὶ προσφυῶς ταῖς φύσεσι τὸν αὐτὸν καὶ ἕνα Χριστὸν ἐνεργεῖν τάτε θεῖα καὶ τὰ ἀνθρώπινα.—θεσπίζομεν, τοὺς ἡμετέρους ὑπηκόους—μὴ ἄδειαν ἔχειν πρὸς ἀλλήλους ἀπὸ τοῦ παρόντος περὶ ἑνὸς θελήματος ἢ μιᾶς ἐνεργείας, ἢ δύο ἐνεργειῶν καὶ δύο θελημάτων, οἰανδήποτε προφέρειν ἀμφισβήτησιν, ἔριν τε, καὶ φιλονεικίαν. There is said to be τὸ πρὸ τῆς ἀνωτέρω τῶν εἰρημένων ζητήσεως προελθούσης φιλονεικίας ἁπανταχοῦ φυλαχθῆναι σχῆμα. Sharp threats against those who disobey.

[10] The opponents derided the Typus as: ἀνενέργητον πάντη καὶ ἀνεθέλητον, τουτέστιν ἄνουν, καὶ ἄψυχον, καὶ ἀκίνητον αὐτὸν τὸν τῆς δόξης θεὸν τὸν κύριον ἡμῶν Ἰ. Χ. ἐδογμάτισαν, τοῖς τῶν ἐθνῶν ἀψύχοις παραπλησίως εἰδώλοις (Epistola Abbatum et Monachorum in Synodo Lateranensi ap. Mansi x. 908). So too Martin in his address. Ibid. p. 880.

[11] The Acts in Mansi x. 863. On the bad state of the Latin text see Walch's Ketzerhist. ix. 222. The 20 canons in the fifth Secretarius, can. x. ss. are directed against the Monothelites. Can. xiv. runs thus: Si quis secundum scelerosos haereticos cum una voluntate et una operatione, quae ab haereticis impie confitetur, et duas voluntates pariterque et operationes, hoc est, divinam et humanum, quae in ipso Christo Deo in unitate salvantur, et a sanctis patribus orthodoxe in ipso praedicantur, denegat et respuit, condemnatus sit.

[12] See Martini epist. xv. et xvi. and the commemoratio eorum, quae saeviter acta sunt in Martinum, given together from Anastasii collectan., in Mansi x. 851. Neander iii. 375. For an account of the sufferings of Maximus see acts and letters ap. Mansi xi. 3. Anastasii Presb. epist. ad Theodosium in opp. Maximi i. 67. Neander iii. 386.

[13] Namely, between the patriarch Peter and pope Vitalianus. cf. Acta Synodi oecum. vi. Actio xiii. ap. Mansi xi. 572: Ἔτι ἀνεγνώσθη—ἐπιστολὴ Πετρου—πρὸς Βιταλιανὸν—ἧς ἡ ἀρχὴ πνευματικῆς εὐφροσύνης πρόξενον ἡμῖν τὸ γράμμα τῆς ὑμετέρας ὁμοψύχου καὶ ἁγίας ἀδελφότητος γέγονεν.

[14] Agathonis epistola ad Imperatores ap. Mansi xi. 233-286.—p.

epistle, after an examination which terminated in peace and order.[15] An anathema was pronounced on all *Monothelites*,[16] and

239 : Cum duas naturas, duasque naturales voluntates, et duas naturales operationes confitemur in uno domino nostro J. Ch., non contrarias eas, nec adversas ad alterutrum dicimus (sicut a via veritatis errantes apostolicam traditionem accusant, absit haec impietas a fidelium cordibus), nec tanquam separatas in duabus personis, vel subsistentiis, sed duas dicimus unum eundemque dominum nostrum J. Ch., sicut naturas, ita et naturales in se voluntates et operationes habere, divinam scilicet et humanam etc.—p. 243 : Apostolica ecclesia—unum dominum nostrum J. Ch. confitetur ex duabus et in duabus existentem naturis—et ex proprietatibus naturalibus unamquamque harum Christi naturarum perfectam esse cognoscit, et quidquid ad proprietates naturarum pertinet, duplicia omnia confitetur.—Consequenter itaque—duas etiam naturales voluntates in eo, et duas naturales operationes esse confitetur et praedicat. Nam si personalem quisquam intelligat voluntatem, dum tres personae in s. Trinitate dicuntur, necesse est, ut et tres voluntates personales, et tres personales operationes (quod absurdum est et nimis profanum) dicerentur.—Ipse dominus noster J. Ch.—in sacris suis evangeliis protestatur in aliquibus humana, in aliquibus divina, et simul utraque in aliis de se patefaciens.—orat quidem ad Patrem ut homo, ut calicem passionis transageret, quia in eo nostrae humanitatis natura absque solo peccato perfecta est, Pater, inquiens, si possibile est etc. (Matth. xxvi. 39).   Et in alio loco Non mea voluntas, sed tua fiat (Luc. xxii. 42).   Farther, the passages Phil. ii. 8. obediens usque ad mortem, Luc. ii. 51. obediens parentibus, Jo. vi. 38. descendi de coelo, ut non faciam voluntatem meam, sed voluntatem ejus qui misit me, cf. Jo. v. 30. also from the Old Testament, Ps. xl. 9, Ut faciam voluntatem tuam, Deus meus, volui. Ps. liv. 8. voluntario sacrificabo tibi. Then follow testimonies from the fathers.   On the mode in which the two wills co-operate Agatho says nothing.

[16] The definitio (ὅρος) of the sixth council in the actio xviii. ap Mansi xi. 631 ss.—p. 637 : ἕνα καὶ τὸν αὐτὸν Χριστὸν, υἱὸν κύριον μονογενῆ, ἐν δύο φύσεσιν ἀσυγχύτως, ἀτρέπτως, ἀχωρίστως, ἀδιαιρέτως γνωριζόμενον, οὐδαμοῦ τῆς τῶν φύσεων διαφορᾶς ἀνῃρημένης διὰ τὴν ἕνωσιν, σωζομένης δὲ μᾶλλον τῆς ἰδιότητος ἑκατέρας φύσεως, καὶ εἰς ἓν πρόσωπον καὶ μίαν ὑπόστασιν συντρεχούσης.—Καὶ δύο φυσικὰς θελήσεις ἤτοι θελήματα ἐν αὐτῷ, καὶ δύο φυσικὰς ἐνεργείας ἀδιαιρέτως, ἀτρέπτως, ἀμερίστως, ἀσυγχύτως κατὰ τὴν τῶν ἁγίων πατέρων διδασκαλίαν ὡσαύτως κηρύττομεν καὶ δύο μὲν φυσικὰ θελήματα οὐχ ὑπεναντία, μὴ γένοιτο, καθὼς οἱ ἀσεβεῖς ἔφησαν αἱρετικοὶ ἀλλ' ἑπόμενον τὸ ἀνθρώπινον αὐτοῦ θέλημα, καὶ μὴ ἀντιπίπτον, ἢ ἀντιπαλαῖον [ἀντίπαλον], μᾶλλον μὲν οὖν καὶ ὑποτασσόμενον τῷ θείῳ αὐτοῦ καὶ πανσθενεῖ θελήματι.—ὥσπερ γὰρ ἡ αὐτοῦ σὰρξ, σὰρξ τοῦ θεοῦ λόγου λέγεται καὶ ἔστιν, οὕτω καὶ τὸ φυσικὸν τῆς σαρκὸς αὐτοῦ θέλημα ἴδιον τοῦ θεοῦ λόγου λέγεται καὶ ἔστι, καθά φησιν αὐτός· " ὅτι καταβέβηκα ἐκ τοῦ οὐρανοῦ, οὐχ ἵνα ποιῶ τὸ θέλημα τὸ ἐμὸν, ἀλλὰ τὸ θέλημα τοῦ πέμψαντός με πατρός" (Jo. vi. 38.), ἴδιον λέγων θέλημα αὐτοῦ τὸ τῆς σαρκὸς, ἐπεὶ καὶ ἡ σὰρξ ἰδία αὐτοῦ γέγονεν· ὃν γὰρ τρόπον ἡ παναγία καὶ ἄμωμος ἐψυχωμένη αὐτοῦ σὰρξ θεωθεῖσα (deificata) οὐκ ἀνῃρέθη, ἀλλ' ἐν τῷ ἰδίῳ αὐτῆς ὅρῳ τε καὶ λόγῳ διέμεινεν, οὕτω καὶ τὸ ἀνθρώπινον αὐτοῦ θέλημα θεωθὲν οὐκ

also on Honorius ;[17] and thus Church unity was restored in the Roman empire.

ἀνῃρέθη, σέσωσται δὲ μᾶλλον κατὰ τὸν θεολόγον Γρηγόριον λέγοντα· " τὸ γὰρ ἐκείνου θέλειν τὸ κατὰ τὸν σωτῆρα νοούμενον οὐδὲ ὑπεναντίον σεῷ θεωθὲν, ὅλον." δύο δὲ φυσικὰς ἐνεργείας ἀδιαιρέτως, ἀτρέπτως, ἀμερίστως, ἀσυγχύτως ἐν αὐτῷ τῷ κυρίῳ ἡμῶν Ἰ. Χ. τῷ ἀληθινῷ θεῷ ἡμῶν δοξάζομεν, τουτέστι θείαν ἐνέργειαν καὶ ἀνθρωπίνην ἐνέργειαν κατὰ τὸν θεηγόρον Λέοντα τρανέστατα φάσκοντα· " ἐνεργεῖ γὰρ ἑκατέρα μορφὴ μετὰ τῆς θατέρου κοινωνίας ὅπερ ἴδιον ἔσχηκε, τοῦ μὲν λόγου κατεργαζομένου τοῦτο, ὅπερ ἐστὶ τοῦ λόγου, τοῦ δὲ σώματος ἐκτελοῦντος ἅπερ ἐστὶ τοῦ σώματος" (comp. § 89. not. 7).
[16] The name Μονοθελῆται first in Johannes Damasc.
[17] John IV., in the epist. ad Constantin. (note 8), had endeavoured to exculpate Honorius on the ground that he merely asserted quia in salvatore nostro duae voluntates contrariae, id est, in membris ipsius (cf. Rom. vii. 23.) penitus non consistant, quoniam nihil vitii traxit ex praevaricatione primi hominis. So too Maximus in epist. ad Marinum ap. Mansi x. 687. and in the disputatio cum Pyrrho ibid. p. 739. In all the measures afterwards taken in Rome against the Monothelites, no mention was made of Honorius. On the other hand, Synodus oecum. vi. actio xiii. (ap. Mansi xi. 556.), pronounces an anathema on Sergius, Cyrus, Pyrrhus, Petrus, Paulus, Theodorus, bishop of Pharan, καὶ Ὀνώριον τὸν γενόμενον πάπαν τῆς πρεσβυτέρας Ῥώμης διὰ τὸ εὑρηκέναι ἡμᾶς διὰ τῶν γενομένων παρ' αὐτοῦ γραμμάτων πρὸς Σέργιον κατὰ πάντα τῇ ἐκείνου γνώμῃ ἐξακολουθήσαντα καὶ τὰ αὐτοῦ ἀσεβῆ κυρώσαντα δόγματα. This anathema was repeated act. xvi. p. 622. act. xviii. p. 655, &c. Leo II., in his epist. ad Constant. Imp., in which he confirms the council (ap. Mansi xi. 731): Anathematizamus—nec non et Honorium, qui hanc apostolicam ecclesiam non apostolicae doctrina lustravit, sed profana proditione immaculatam subvertere conatus est. cf. ejusd. epist. ad Episc. Hispaniae ap. Mansi xi. 1052, and ad Ervigium Regem Hispaniae ibid. p. 1057. Also in the confession of faith subscribed by the following popes at their accession (liber diurnus cap. ii. tit. 9. professio 2,), the anathema was pronounced against auctores novi haeretici dogmatis, Sergium etc.—una cum Honorio, qui pravis eorum assertionibus fomentum impendit.—Anastasius biblioth. ep. ad Joannem Diaconum (collectanea ed. Sirmond. p. 3.), is the first that endeavours again, after the example of John IV., whose letter he reproduced, to excuse Honorius, licet huic sexta sancta Synodus quasi haeretico anathema dixerit. But later Catholic historians deny even this fact. Platina in vita Honorii I. : Ferunt Heraclium—Pyrhi—et Cyri fraudibus deceptum in haeresim Monothelitarum incidisse.—Hos tamen postea tanti erroris auctores, hortante Honorio et veram ante oculos literis et nunciis ponente, relegavit Heraclius. According to Baronius, the acts of the sixth council have been corrupted, and instead of Honorius we should read Theodorus. Bellarmine maintains that the letters of Honorius are either spurious or interpolated. According to Pagi, Garnier, the Ballerini, and others, Honorius was not condemned for heresy, but for negligence ; and according to Combefisius and others, even with the consent of Pope Agatho. Against all these evasions see Richer historia

M

§ 129.

CONCILIUM QUINISEXTUM.

At the last two general councils, no attention had been paid to the laws affecting the constitution of the Church. To supply this defect, and to receive a complete synodical code, the emperor *Justinian II.* (reigned from 685–695, and from 705–711,) called a new oecumenical council in the Trullus at Constantinople (692),[1] at which 102 canons were passed, for the most part giving legal expression merely to older Church usages, and repeating older canons. It appears that the Greek bishops had expressly entertained the design, both here and at Chalcedon, of reminding the Roman patriarchs, again exalted by their new victory, of the limits of their power. Particularly unacceptable to the Romans were the six canons *concerning the Church laws to be esteemed valid,*[2] *the marriage of priests,*[3] *the rank of the*

concil. general. i. 296.   Du Pin de antiqua eccl. discipl. p. 349.   Bossuet defensio declar. Cleri Gallic. ii. 128.

[1] Names : Concilium Trullanum, Σύνοδος πενθέκτη, Conc. quinisextum. The Greeks consider it merely as a continuation of the sixth council, and call its decisions κανόνες τῆς ἔκτης συνόδου. The Acts are given in Mansi xi. 921.

[2] Can. ii. confirms 85 canones Apost., while the Roman church, after Dionysius, adopted only the first 50. This council also sanctioned, as church laws, the canons of the councils of Nice, Ancyra, Neocaesarea, Gangra, Antioch, Laodicea, Constantinople in A. D. 381, Ephesus, Chalcedon, Sardica, Carthage and Constantinople, A. D. 394.   Also the canons of Dionysius Alexandrinus, Petrus Alex., Gregory Thaumaturgus, Athanasius, Basil the Great, Gregory Nyssene, Gregory of Nazianzum, Amphilochius of Iconium, Timotheus Alex., Cyril Alex., and Gennadius patriarch of Constantinople. Lastly, also of Cyprian and his synod. All other canons are prohibited as not genuine. (μηδενὶ ἐξεῖναι—ἑτέρους παρὰ τοὺς προκειμένους παραδέχεσθαι κανόνας ψευδεπιγράφως ὑπό τινων συντεθέντας τῶν τὴν ἀλήθειαν καπηλεύειν ἐπιχειρησάντων.) : In that list, however, many western synods, and all decretals of Romish bishops, are passed over.

[3] Can. xiii. : Ἐπειδὴ ἐν τῇ Ῥωμαίων ἐκκλησίᾳ ἐν τάξει κανόνος παραδεδόσθαι διέγνωμεν, τοὺς μέλλοντας διακόνου ἢ πρεσβυτέρου ἀξιοῦσθαι χειροτονίας καθομολογεῖν, ὡς οὐκέτι ταῖς αὐτῶν συνάπτονται γαμεταῖς· ἡμεῖς τῷ ἀρχαίῳ ἐξακολουθοῦντες κανόνι τῆς ἀποστολικῆς ἀκριβείας καὶ τάξεως, τὰ τῶν ἱερῶν ἀνδρῶν κατὰ νόμους συνοικέσια καὶ ἀπὸ τοῦ νῦν ἐρρῶσθαι. βουλόμεθα· μηδαμῶς αὐτῶν τὴν πρὸς γαμετὰς συνάφειαν διαλύοντες, ἢ ἀποστεροῦντες αὐτοὺς τῆς πρὸς ἀλλήλους κατὰ καιρὸν τὸν προσήκοντα ὁμιλίας. Ὥστε εἴ τις ἄξιος εὑρεθείη πρὸς

patriarch of Constantinople,[4] *against fasting on Saturday,*[5] *against the eating of blood and things strangled,*[6] *and against pictures of the Lamb.*[7] Though the papal legates had subscribed

χειροτονίαν ὑποδιακόνου ἢ διακόνου ἢ πρεσβυτέρου, οὗτος μηδαμῶς κωλυέσθω ἐπὶ τοιοῦτον βαθμὸν ἐκβιβάζεσθαι γαμετῇ συνοικῶν νομίμῳ, μήτε μὴν ἐν τῷ τῆς χειροτονίας καιρῷ ἀπαιτείσθω ὁμολογεῖν, ὡς ἀποστήσεται τῆς νομίμου πρὸς τὴν οἰκείαν γαμετὴν ὁμιλίας. ἵνα μὴ ἐντεῦθεν τὸν ἐκ θεοῦ νομοθετηθέντα καὶ εὐλο-γηθέντα τῇ αὐτοῦ παρουσίᾳ γάμον καθυβρίζειν ἐκβιασθῶμεν, τῆς τοῦ εὐαγγελίου φωνῆς βοώσης· ἃ ὁ θεὸς ἔζευξεν, ἄνθρωπος μὴ χωριζέτω (Matth. xix. 6.) καὶ τοῦ ἀποστόλου διδάσκοντος τίμιον τὸν γάμον καὶ τὴν κοίτην ἀμίαντον (Heb. xiii. 4.) καὶ δέδεσαι γυναικί, μὴ ζήτει λύσιν (1 Cor. vii. 27.)—χρὴ τοὺς τῷ θυσιαστηρίῳ προσεδρεύοντας ἐν τῷ καιρῷ τῆς τῶν ἁγίων μεταχειρήσεως ἐγκρα-τεῖς εἶναι ἐν πᾶσιν.—Εἴ τις οὖν τολμήσαι, παρὰ τοὺς ἀποστολικοὺς κανόνας κι-νούμενος, τινὰ τῶν ἱερωμένων, πρεσβυτέρων φαμὲν ἢ διακόνων ἢ ὑποδιακόνων, ἀποστερεῖν τῆς πρὸς νόμιμον γυναῖκα συναφείας τε καὶ κοινωνίας, καθαιρείσθω. Ὡσαύτως καὶ εἴ τις πρεσβύτερος ἢ διάκονος τὴν ἑαυτοῦ γυναῖκα προφάσει εὐλα-βείας ἐκβάλλει, ἀφοριζέσθω, ἐπιμένων δὲ καθαιρείσθω (cf. Can. Apostol. v. § 97. not. 9.) Bellarmin. de. cler. i. 10. supposes, respecting this sub-ject : Tempore hujus synodi (Trullanae) coepit mos Graecorum, qui nunc est.—Besides, can. iii. forbids the clergy marrying a second time, and marriage with a widow.   Can. vi. forbids marriage after ordination. Can. xii. forbids bishops to remain in the married state : εἰς γνῶσιν ἡμε-τέραν ἦλθεν, ὡς ἔν τε Ἀφρικῇ καὶ Λιβύῃ καὶ ἑτέροις τόποις οἱ τῶν ἐκεῖσε θεοφι-λέστατοι πρόεδροι συνοικεῖν ταῖς ἰδίαις γαμεταῖς, καὶ μετὰ τὴν ἐπ᾽ αὐτοῖς προελ-θοῦσαν χειροτονίαν, οὐ παραιτοῦνται.—ἔδοξεν ὥστε μηδαμῶς τὸ τοιοῦτον ἀπὸ τοῦ νῦν γίνεσθαι· τοῦτο δέ φαμεν, οὐκ ἐπ᾽ ἀθετήσει ἢ ἀνατροπῇ τῶν ἀποστολικῶς προνενομοθετημένων, ἀλλὰ τῆς σωτηρίας καὶ προκοπῆς τῆς ἐπὶ τὸ κρεῖττον τῶν λαῶν προμηθούμενοι κ. τ. λ.   cf. Can. lxviii.   According to Zonaras and Theod. Balsamo ad Can. Apost. v. these were the first ecclesiastical prohibitions against the marriage of bishops, though Justinian had for-bidden them by a civil law (Cou. i. iii. 48). cf. Calixtus de conjugio Clericorum ed. Henke p. 389 ss.

[4] Can. xxxvi., referring to Can. Constant. iii. (§ 93. not. 9.) and Can. Chalced. xxviii. (ibid. not. 14.), and in the same words as the lat-ter.   So, too, in Can. xxxviii. the 17th canon of Chalced. (ibid. note 3.) is repeated word for word.

[5] Can. lv. : Ἐπειδὴ μεμαθήκαμεν, ἐν τῇ Ῥωμαίων πόλει ἐν ταῖς ἁγίαις τῆς τεσσαρακοστῆς νηστείαις τοῖς ταύτης σάββασι νηστεύειν παρὰ τὴν παραδοθεῖσαν ἐκκλησιαστικὴν ἀκολουθίαν (comp. § 100. not. 14.)   ἔδοξε τῇ ἁγίᾳ συνόδῳ, ὥστε κρατεῖν καὶ ἐπὶ τῇ Ῥωμαίων ἐκκλησίᾳ ἀπαρασαλεύτως τὸν κανόνα τὸν λέ-γοντα· " εἴ τις κληρικὸς εὑρεθείη τῇ ἁγίᾳ κυριακῇ νηστεύων ἢ τὸ σάββατον πλὴν τοῦ ἑνὸς καὶ μόνου, καθαιρείσθω· εἰ δὲ λαϊκός, ἀφοριζέσθω." (Can. Apostol. lxvii.)

[6] Can. lxvii.

[7] Can. lxxxii. : Ἔν τισι τῶν σεπτῶν εἰκόνων γραφαῖς ἀμνὸς δακτύλῳ τοῦ προδρόμου δεικνύμενος ἐγχαράττεται (according to Joh. i. 29.)—τὸν τοῦ αἴ-ροντος τὴν ἁμαρτίαν τοῦ κόσμου ἀμνοῦ Χριστοῦ τοῦ θεοῦ ἡμῶν κατὰ τὸν ἀνθρώ-πινον χαρακτῆρα καὶ ἐν ταῖς εἰκόσιν ἀπὸ τοῦ νῦν ἀντὶ τοῦ παλαιοῦ ἀμνοῦ ἀνασ-τηλοῦσθαι ὁρίζομεν.   See § 99. not. 51.

M 2

them, yet Pope *Sergius I.* refused to accept them. Justinian meant to have him brought to Constantinople, but was prevented by the rebellion of the garrison of Ravenna, and soon after by his deposition.[8] Thus this council was acknowledged only in the East, but not in the West;[9] and was the first public step which led to the separation of the two Churches.

§ 130.

FORTUNES OF MONOTHELITISM.

The emperor *Philippicus Bardanes* (711–713) revived once more the Monothelitic doctrine, and made it the prevailing faith, though merely for a short time.[1] Only Rome withstood him.[2] But the Greek bishops were as ready to subscribe a Monothelitic confession of faith as they were to return to orthodoxy at the command of the next emperor, *Anastasius II.*[3]

[8] cf. Anastas. biblioth. in vita Sergii.
[9] Ap. Beda de sex aetatibus and Paulus Diac. hist. Longob vi. 11. it is called Synodus erratica. By degrees, however, several of the less offensive canons began to be cited, as Canones Syn. vi., those who did so being misled by the example of the Greeks (see note 1). Gratian (Decret. P. I. dist. xvi. c. 6.) translates a Greek account of this Synod, and then naïvely adds : Ex his ergo colligitur, quod sexta synodus bis congregata est : primo sub Constantino Imp., et nullos canones constituit, secundo sub Justiniano filio ejus, et præfatos canones promulgavit. Thus, then, he also adopts several of the canons. It was not till after the Reformation that the conciliabulum pseudosextum was again discovered. cf. Calixtus p. 401 ss.
[1] The chief authority on this subject is the epilogus ad Acta Syn. vi. of the contemporary Agathon, deacon and librarian of the church at Constantinople (prim. ed. F. Combefisius in the nov. auctar. PP. ii. 199. ap. Mansi xii. 189.) Farther, Theophanes p. 319 ss. Walch's Ketzerhist. ix. 449.
[2] Anastasii bibl. vita Constantini. Paulus Diac. hist. Longob. vi. 33.
[3] The miserable spirit of the Greek bishops is particularly expressed in the exculpatory letter which John, who had been elevated to the see of Constantinople by Philippicus, addressed to pope Constantine, after the state of things had been entirely changed (appended to Agathon's Epilogus ap. Combefis. p. 211 ss. Mansi p. 195 ss.) Among other things he says : οἴδατε γὰρ καὶ ὑμεῖς,—ὡς οὐ λίαν ἀντιτύπως καὶ σκληρῶς ἔχειν πρὸς τὴν τῆς ἐξουσίας ἀνάγκην ἐν τοῖς τοιούτοις, ἄνευ τινὸς τέχνης καὶ περινοίας καθέστηκεν εὐμαρές· ἐπεὶ καὶ Νάθαν ὁ προφήτης οὐκ ἀπερικάλυπτον τὸν ἔλεγχον τὸν περὶ τῆς μοιχείας τε καὶ τοῦ φόνου προσήγαγε τῷ Δαβὶδ, καίτοι καὶ αὐτοῦ τοῦ Δαβὶδ προφητικῷ τετιμημένου χαρίσματι. Κατὰ τοῦτο καὶ ἡμεῖς, ὅπερ φησὶν ὁ μέγας Βασίλειος, ἐνδιδόναι μικρὸν τῷ ἤθει τοῦ ἀνδρὸς κατεδεξάμεθα,

In Syria, however, a small party of Monothelites remained for a long time. Here all Christian parties had a political importance. The *Jacobites* were favourable to the Arabians ; the *Catholics* to the Greek emperors, hence called *Melchites* (from מֶלֶךְ). On the other hand, an independent party had collected in mount Libanus, about the monastery of St *Maro*, who adopted the Monothelitic doctrines, chose for themselves a patriarch of Antioch (the first was *John Maro* † 701), and under the name of *Maronites*[4] continued to hold the doctrine of one will in Christ till the time of the Crusades.[5]

ὥστε τὴν ἐν τοῖς καιρίοις τῆς πίστεως ὁμολογίαν, εἰ καὶ μὴ λέξεσιν, ἀλλάγε ταῖς ἐννοίαις φυλάττεσθαι ἀπαράβατον. Οὐ γὰρ ἐν λέξεσιν ἡμῖν, ἀλλ᾽ ἐν πράγμασιν ἡ ἀλήθεια, ὁ θεῖος Γρηγόριος βοᾷ· καὶ πάλιν ἱκανῶς ἄτοπον καὶ λίαν αἰσχρὸν διορίζεται, τὸ περὶ τὸν ἦχον σμικρολογεῖσθαι.—Κατὰ τοῦτον δὴ τὸν τῆς οἰκονομικῆς καὶ κατὰ περίστασιν συμβάσεως τρόπον καὶ τὰ λοιπὰ τῶν γεγενημένων προελθεῖν πειθόμενοι, ἁγιώτατοι, μὴ ἀσύγγνωστον ἡμῖν τὸ ἐπὶ τούτοις ἔγκλημα προσαγαγεῖν καταδέξησθε· ἀλλὰ κἄν τι τῆς ἀκριβείας ἡμῖν ἡμαρτῆσθαι ὑπονοῆται, τῇ παραθέσει τῶν ἐκ τῶν ἁγίων πατέρων ἡμῶν οἰκονομικῶς προελθόντων ἀπολύεσθω ἀνεύθυνον καὶ πάσης ἐλεύθερον κατακρίσεως. He then appeals to the bishops of the Robber Synod at Ephesus, who had condemned Flavian unjustly, καὶ ὅμως ἐν τῇ κατὰ Χαλκηδόνα ἁγίᾳ συνόδῳ ἤρκεσε τούτοις πρὸς τελείαν ἀποτροπὴν τοῦ ἐγκλήματος ἡ τῆς ὑγιοῦς ὁμολογίας σύνθεσις, &c., and concludes that he has offered an ἀπολογίαν ἰσχυράν τε καὶ ἔννομον.

[4] Johann. Damasc. lib. de vera sententia c. 8. Epist. de hymno trishagio c. 5. Eutychii annal. Alex. T. ii. p. 192.

[5] The modern Maronite writers, namely, Abraham Echellensis in several works, Faustus Nayron diss. de origine et religione Maronitarum. Rom. 1679. 8. Ejusd. enoplia fidei catholicae. Ibid. 1694. 8. Assemani bibl. orient. i. 496, have introduced confusion into the history of their sect, 1. By asserting that the Maronites were never Monothelites, but were always orthodox (in addition to the opposite reasons given by Renaudot histor. patr. Alexandr. p. 149 ss. is the testimony of Germanus, patriarch of Constantinople, about 725, de haeresibus et synodis, in the spicilegium Romanum vii. 65. that the Maronites rejected the sixth synod. The grounds given by both parties may be found in M. Le Quien oriens christ. iii. 1. Walch's Ketzerhist. ix. 474.) ; 2. By identifying the Mardaites (whose name is erroneously derived from מֶרֶד) with the Maronites. On the contrary, Anquetil Duperron recherches sur les migrations des Mardes, ancien peuple de Perse in the Mémoires de l'Acad. des Inscript. Tome 50. p. 1., has shown that the Mardaites, or Mards, a warlike people in Armenia, were placed as a garrison on Mount Libanus by Constantine Pogonatus A. D. 676. (Theophanes p. 295), but withdrawn as early as 685 by Justinian ii. (Theoph. p. 302 s.)

THIRD CHAPTER.

§ 131.

ECCLESIASTICAL STATE OF ITALY.

Important for the history of this and the following period is Anastasii bibliothecarii (about 870) liber pontificalis s. vitae Rom. Pontif.[1]) ed. C. Annib.
Fabrotus in the corp. hist. Byz. T. xix. Paris 1649. fol., Fr. Blanchini. Rom.
1718—35. iv. T. fol. Jo. Vignolius. Romae 1724. 4. with the biographies
of the later popes in L. A. Muratorii rerum Ital. scriptor. T. iii. p. i.—Liber

---

[1] The liber pontificalis has arisen from former catalogis Pontificum
which we know only in part. The first known catalogus, which was
composed under Liberius, 354, and contains few other notices besides
those relating to chronology, furnished ground for subsequently attributing to Damasus the first collection of the vitae Pontificum. The
second known catalogus under Felix iv. (526-530) has taken the former
into itself only in part, but enlarged it by other accounts. From these
catalogis arose, at the end of the seventh century, the first edition of the
liber pontificalis, which concludes with Conon († 687) and is still extant
in a Veronese and a Neapolitan MS. (see Pertz in the Archiv. d. Gesellschaft für ältere deutsche Geschichtskunde V. 68). The second
edition of it in the Cod. Vatican 5269, concludes with Constantine
(† 714). The lives that follow were appended successively by contemporaries, and Anastasius can only have composed the last till Nicolaus I. († 868), and have published the book anew in this form. The
lives of Hadrian II. and Stephen VI. († 891), subsequently added, are
attributed to one Gulielmus Bibliothecarius. From what has been said,
it may be seen how even Beda, Rabanus Maurus, Walafrid Strabo, could
cite the liber pontificalis ; and how Pseudoisidorus could use it. Just as
the older shorter lives, which merely furnish notices of time, and short accounts of ordinations, church buildings, regulations and arrangements of
popes, and respecting martyrdoms and heresies, have become uncertain by
the mixing up of doubtful traditions with true accounts ; so, on the other
hand, the more copious lives, from the end of the seventh century and
onward, have great historical value, as they were written by contemporaries. cf. Emm. a Schelstrate de antiquis Rom. pont. catalogis, ex
quibus lib. pontificalis concinnatus fuit, et de lib. pont. auctore ac prae-
stantia. Jo. Ciampini examen lib. pontif. Fr. Blanchini praef. in lib.
pont., all together prefixed to Muratori's edition. See a description of
the city of Rome by Platner, Bunsen, Gerhard, and Röstell i. 207.

diurnus Roman. Pontificum, collected about 715, prim. ed. Luc. Holstenius. Rom. 1658. 8.²) J. Garnerius. Paris 1680. 4. (Supplementum in J. Mabillon museum Italicum, i. i. 32. Paris 1687. 4.) reprinted in Chr. G. Hoffmanni nova scriptorum ac monumentorum collect. T. ii. Lips. 1733. 4.

The political consequence of the *popes*³ in Italy increased, in proportion as the Greek emperors, now pressed by the Saracens too, were forced to leave to them chiefly the defence of their Italian possessions against the Lombards.⁴ Still they continued subjects of the emperors, had to be confirmed by them in office,⁵ and

³ This edition, better than that of Garnier, was immediately suppressed by the Romish censors. Its history (see especially Baluzii. not. ad de Marca de concord Sac. et Imp. lib. i. c. ix. § 8.), and an account of its variations may be seen in Schoepflini commentt. hist. crit. Basil. 1741. 4. p. 499 ss. In addition to the two codd. used by Holsten and Garnier, a third is noticed by Launojus diss. de Lazari et Magdal. in provinciam adpulsu cap. 10. obs. 10.

³ Honorius I. from 625-638, Severinus † 640, John IV. † 642, Theodore † 649, Martin I. banished 654, † 655, but even in 654 Eugenius I. was again chosen, † 657, Vitalianus † 672, Adeodatus † 676, Domnus I. † 678, Agatho † 682, Leo II. † 683, Benedict. II. † 685, John V. † 686, Conon † 687, Sergius I. † 701, John VI. † 705, John VII. † 707, Sisinnius † 708, Constantine † 714, Gregory II. † 731.

⁴ Comp. above, § 117. not. 26. cf. liber diurnus cap. ii. tit. iv. Account of the Romans de electione Pontificis ad Exarchum:—Et ideo supplicantes quaesumus, ut inspirante Deo celsae ejus dominationi, nos famulos voti compotes celeriter fieri praecipiat: praesertim cum plura sint capitula, et alia ex aliis quotidie procreentur, quae curae solicitudinem et pontificalis favoris expectant remedium.—Propinquantium quoque inimicorum ferocitas, quam nisi sola Dei virtus atque Apostolorum Principis per suum Vicarium, hoc est Romanum Pontificem, ut omnibus notum est, aliquando monitis comprimit. aliquando vero flectit ac modigerat hortatu, singulari interventu indiget, cum hnjus solius pontificalibus monitis, ob reverentiam Apostolorum Principis, parentiam offerant voluntariam: et quos non virtus armorum humiliat, pontificalis increpatio cum obsecratione inclinat. The popes possessed already some small forts; probably erected, in the first place, for protection of their patrimony. Thus Anastasius in vita xc. Gregorii II., relates, that the Lombards had taken from him the Cumanum castrum, and that the pope having in vain required them to surrender it, John, Dux Neapolitanus, retook it from them, and gave it back to the former possessor. Pro cujus redemptione lxx. auri libras ipse Sanctissimus Papa, sicut promiserat antea, dedit.

⁵ As had become customary under the Ostrogoth kings. Agatho, however, received from Constantine Pogonatus divalem jussionem, per quam relevata est quantitas, quae solita erat dari pro ordinatione Pontificis facienda: sic tamen, ut si contigerit post ejus transitum electionem

paid them taxes.⁶ While the Monothelitic troubles gave the
popes an opportunity of even appointing a vicar in Palestine now
overrun by the Saracens,⁷ *Martin I.* was still made to feel bitterly the emperor's power ; and *Vitalianus* was compelled to
bow to Monothelitism supported by imperial patronage. But
by their triumph at the sixth synod the popes strengthened anew
their ancient calling as defenders of the true faith ;⁸ and began at
this time to attribute to themselves the title *Episcopus Universalis*, which Gregory the Great had declared to be antichristian.⁹
The *Quinisextum* could ·no longer humble them in the West.
When Justinian II. attempted to bring Pope Sergius I. to Con-

fieri, non debeat ordinari qui electus fuerit, nisi prius decretum generale
introducatur in regiam urbem secundum antiquam consuetudinem, et
cum eorum conscientia et jussione debeat ordinatio provenire (Anastasius in vita lxxx. Agathonis).   Benedict II. received from the same
emperor the privilege ut persona, qui electus fuerii ad Sedem Apost. e.
vestigio absque tarditate Pontifex ordinetur (Anastasius in vita lxxxii.
Bened.).   Still, however, this did not obviate the necessity of confirmation.   See the forms in liber diurnus, cap. ii. de ordinatione Summi
Pontificis.   Namely, tit. 1. Nuntius ad Exarchum de transitu Pontificis.   Tit. 2. Decretum de electione Pontificis.   (Subscribed by totus
Clerus, Optimates, et Milites seu Cives).   Tit. 3. Relatio de electione
Pontificis ad Principem.   Tit. 4. De electione Pontificis ad Exarchum.
On the same subject, tit. 5. ad Archiepisc. Ravennae, tit. 6. ad Judices
Ravennae, tit. 7. ad Apocrisiarium Ravennae, to effect the speedy con-
firmation.   Tit. 8. Ritus ordinandi Pontificis, and tit. 9. Professio pon-
tificia.

⁶ Ex. gr. Anastas. in vita lxxxiv. Cononis : Hujus temporibus pietas
Imperialis relevavit per sacram jussionem suam ducenta annonae capita
(i. e. capitationem), quae patrimonii custodes Brutiae et Lucaniae annue
persolvebant.

⁷ This was done by the popes Theodore and Martin I. during a va-
cancy in the see of Jerusalem, though the patriarchs of Antioch and
Jerusalem protested against it.   See lib. Stephani Episc. Dorensis ad
Synod. Rom. (Mansi T. X. p. 899), and Martini P. epist. ad Johannem
Episc. Philadelphiae (ibid. p. 805 ss.), comp. Walch's Ketzerhistorie
Th. 9. S. 280. comp. S. 214 and 240.

⁸ Comp. Agathonis P. ep ad Imperatores (see above, § 128. not. 14) ap.
Mansi xi. p. 239: Petrus spirituales oves ecclesiae ab ipso redemptore
omnium terna commendatione pascendas suscepit : cujus annitente praesidio haec apostolica ejus ecclesia nunquam a via veritatis in qualibet
erroris parte deflexa est, cujus auctoritatem, utpote Apostolorum omnium
principis, semper omnis catholica Christi ecclesia, et universales synodi
fideliter amplectentes, in cunctis secutae sunt etc.

⁹ So first in the liber diurnus cap. iii. Tit. 6. ap. Hoffmann ii. 95. in
the promissio fidei Episcopi, which falls between 682 and 685.

stantinople to compel him to subscribe the decrees of the Quinisextum, the garrison of Ravenna rose in rebellion,[10] and soon
after (701) the mere suspicion of such an intention caused a new
uproar against the exarch.[11]   Hence, in order to confirm his own
authority in Italy, Justinian II. invited Pope *Constantine* to visit
him, and overloaded him with exceedingly high marks of honour
(710).[12]   The loose connexion between Rome and the empire was
soon after shown in the refusal of the former to obey the heretic
Philippicus Bardanes (711–713).[13]

   The oppressed Church of Africa now yielded to the claims of
Rome without resistance.[14]   On the other hand they still met
with much opposition in Italy.   *The bishops of Ravenna* ventured to build higher claims on the fact that their city was the
seat of the exarch, in accordance with Grecian principles, and
even maintained for some time the independent management of
the Church of the exarchate, when Rome would not accommodate
herself to the imperial Monothelitism.[15]   Among the *Lombards*

   [10] Anastasius vit. lxxxv. Sergii says : Sed misericordia Dei praeve-
niente, beatoque Petro Apostolo et Apostolorum Principe suffragante,
suamque ecclesiam immutilatam servante, excitatum est cor Ravennatis
militiae etc.
   [11] Anastas vit. lxxxvi. Joannis VI.
   [12] Anastas. vit. lxxxix. Constant.: In die autem, qua se vicissim viderunt, Augustus Christianissimus cum regno in capite se prostravit,
pedes osculans Pontificis.
   [13] Anastasii vit. lxxxix. Constant.—Pauli Diac. hist. Longobard. vi.
34.
   [14] Comp. the letter of the African bishops to Pope Theodore in the
Acts of the Conc. Lateran. ann. 649. Secretarius ii. (Mansi x. 919.) :
Magnum et indeficientem omnibus Christianis fluenta redundantem,
apud apostolicam sedem consistere fontem nullus ambigere possit, de
quo rivuli prodeunt affluenter, universum largissime irrigantes orbem
Christianorum, cui etiam in honorem beatissimi Petri patrum decreta
peculiarem omnem decrevere reverentiam in requirendis Dei rebus.—
Antiquis enim regulis sancitum est, ut quidquid, quamvis in remotis vel
in longinquo positis ageretur provinciis, non prius tractandum vel acci-
piendum sit, nisi ad notitiam almae sedis vestrae fuisset deductum, ut
hujus auctoritate, juxta quae fuisset pronunciato, firmaretur, indeque
sumerent caeterae ecclesiae velut de natali suo fonte praedicationis exordium, et per diversas totius mundi regiones puritatis incorruptae maneant fidei sacramenta salutis.   Taken almost word for word from the
letters of Innocent I. and Zosimus to the African bishops.   Comp. the
passages § 94. not. 20. 35.
   [15] Anastas. vit. lxxix. Domini I. (676-678) : Hujus temporibus Ec-

catholicism found many adherents since the time of Queen Theo-
delinda and her son King *Adelwald* (616–620) ; and from the
time of King *Grimoald* († 671) became the prevailing system
among them.[16]   Still, however, they remained at variance with
the popes ;[17] and Upper Italy asserted its ecclesiastical independence.[18] Theological learning continued to be in a low state in
Italy.[19]

§ 132.

ECCLESIASTICAL STATE OF FRANCE AND SPAIN.

The superior dignity of the Romish Church was the more
readily admitted in the West on account of its being the only
apostolic Church in that region, as well as the only medium of

clesia Ravennatum, quae se ab Ecclesia Romana segregaverat causa autocephaliae, denuo se pristinae Sedi Apostolicae subjugavit. Vit. lxxxi.
Leonis II. (683-684) : Hujus temporibus percurrente divali jussione
clementissimi Principis restituta est Ecclesia Ravennatis sub ordinatione Sedis Apostolicae.—typum autocephaliae, quem sibi elicuerant, ad
amputanda scandala Sedis Apostolicae restituerunt.

[16] Though always mixed with idolatry still. See vita s. Barbati
(bishop of Benevent † 682) in the Actis Sanct. Febr. iii. 139 : His diebus quamvis sacri baptismatis unda Longobardi abluerentur, tamen
priscum gentilitatis ritum tenentes, sive bestiali mente degebant, bestiae
simulacro, quae vulgo Vipera nominatur, flectebant colla, quae debite
suo debebant flectere creatori.   Quin etiam non longe a Beneventi mo-
enibus devotissime sacrilegam colebant arborem, in qua suspenso corio,
cuncti qui aderant terga vertentes arbori, celerius equitabant, calcaribus
cruentantes equos, ut unus alterum posset.praeire, atque in eodem cursu
retroversis manibus in corium jaculabantur, sicque particulam modicam
ex eo comedendam superstitiose accipiebant.   Et quia stulta illic persolvebant vota, ab actione nomen loco illi, sicut hactenus dicitur, Votum
imposuerunt.

[17] Planck's Gesch. d. kirchl. Gesellschaftsverf. ii. 669 ff.

[18] It is true that there is also found an indiculum (sacramenti) Episcopi de Longobardia in the liber diurnus cap. iii. Tit. 8, but such an
oath was taken only by the bishops of the Roman patriarchal territory
(the middle and south of Italy), who were now under the Lombard dominion.

[19] This is clear, particularly from Agathonis ep. ad Impp. in the Actis
Syn. Constantinop. ann. 680. Act. iv. (ap. Mansi xi. 235.), where he
repeatedly says of the legates whom he sends to the council : non nobis
eorum scientia confidentiam dedit, with the general remark : nam apud
homines in medio gentium positos et de labore corporis quotidianum
victum cum summa haesitatione conquirentes, quomodo ad plenum poterit inveniri scripturarum scientia ?

ecclesiastical connexion with the East. But the greatest impression was made by the halo of holiness which surrounded that city in the eyes of the Westerns; so that everything proceeding from it was regarded as sacred.[1]

The connexion of the *French Church* with Rome was slight since the time of Gregory the Great. The chief authority lay continuously in the hand of the king; and thus all traces of metropolitan government had disappeared. Among the political disturbances of the French empire in the 7th century, the Church also fell into great disorder; the bishops took part in the feuds of the nobles; clergy and monasteries became ungovernable; and the better few, who wished to call attention to morality and discipline, were persecuted.[2] The robbing of Churches was not uncommon; and *Charles Martell* (major-domus from 717–741) even distributed ecclesiastical revenues and offices in usufruct to valiant soldiers (as beneficium, precarium.)[3]

[1] For example, Anastas. vit. xc. Gregor. ii., after the account of the great victory gained by Duke Eudo of Aquitania over the Saracens at Toulouse (721): Eudo announced it to the pope, adjiciens, quod anno praemisso in benedictionem a praedicto viro eis directis tribus spongiis, quibus ad usum mensae (perhaps the altar?) Pontificis apponuntur, in hora, qua bellum committebatur, idem Eudo Aquitaniae princeps populo suo per modicas partes tribuens ad sumendum eis, nec unus vulneratus est, nec mortuus ex his, qui participati sunt.

[2] So Leodegar, bishop of Autün, who was put to death by the major-domus Ebrün 678. Aigulf, abbot of a monastery at Lerins, wished merely to keep order among his monks, but was therefore abused, banished, and, in 675, murdered. See the lives of both in Mabillon Act. SS. Ord. Benedicti, saec. ii. p. 679 ss. 656 ss.

[3] Comp. above, § 124. not. 7. Bonifacius ep. 132 (ed Würdtwein ep. 51.) ad Zacharjam about 742: Franci enim, ut seniores dicunt, plus quam per tempus lxxx. annorum Synodum non fecerunt, nec Archiepiscopum habuerunt, nec Ecclesiae canonica jura alicui fundabant vel renovabant. Modo autem maxima ex parte per civitates Episcopales sedes traditae sunt Laicis cupidis ad possidendum, vel adulteratis Clericis, scortatoribus, et publicanis saeculariter ad perfruendum. De Majoribus domus regiae libellus vetusti scriptoris in, du Chesne hist. Francorum scriptt. T. ii. p. 2: Carolus—res Ecclesiarum propter assiduitatem bellorum laicis tradidit. Hadriani P. I. ep. ad Tilpinum Archiep. Rhem. in Flodoardi hist. eccl. Rhem. lib. II. c. 17, and ap. Mansi xii. p. 844. Hincmar epist. vi. ad Episc. diocesis Remensis c. 19: Tempore Caroli Principis,—in Germanicis et Belgicis ac Gallicanis provinciis omnis religio Christianitatis paene fuit abolita, ita ut, Episcopis in paucis locis residuis, Episcopia Laicis donata et rebus di-

The *Spanish Church* appears to have gradually relaxed in
humble subjection to the Roman see since catholicism had prevailed among the Goths likewise; although that subordination
had been shewn as long as the Church stood under the pressure
of Arianism.[4]   Here also the king, as feudal lord of the bishops,

visa fuerint; adeo ut Milo quidam tonsura Clericus, moribus, habitu et
actu irreligiosus laicus Episcopia, Rhemorum ac Trevirorum usurpans
simul per multos annos pessumdederit, et multi jam in orientalibus regionibus (East Franks) idola adorarent et sine baptismo manerent.   cf.
Chronicon Virdunense (written about 1115) in Bouquet rer. Gall. et
Franc. script. T. iii. p. 364.   But for this even the clergy abused him
after his death.   Boniface wrote to Athelbald, king of Mercia, to deter
him from a similar course (Baronius ann. 745 no. 11.): Carolus quoque
Princeps Francorum, multorum monasteriorum eversor, et ecclesiasticarum pecuniarum in usus proprios commutator, longa torsione et ve-
renda morte consumtus est.   (This passage, however, is wanting in the
editions of Boniface's letters, ap. Serarius ep. 19).   A hundred years
later, on the contrary, Hincmar, archbishop of Rheims, in the prologus
in vitam b. Remigii (written about 854), and still more fully in his
epist. Synodi Carisiacensis ad Ludov. Germ. Regem. A. D. 858 (Capitularia Caroli Calvi tit. xxvii. c. 7. ap. Baluzius ii. p. 108.   Bouquet l.
c. p. 659): Carolus Princeps, Pipini Regis pater, qui primus inter omnes Francorum Reges ac Principes res Ecclesiarum ab eis separavit atque divisit, pro hoc solo maxime est aeternaliter perditus.   Nam S.
Eucherius Aurelianensium Episc.—in oratione positus ad alterum est
saeculum raptus, et inter caetera, quae Domino sibi ostendente con-
spexit, vidit illum in inferno inferiori torqueri.   Cui interroganti ab
Angelo ejus ductore responsum est, quia Sanctorum judicatione, qui in
futuro judicio cum Domino judicabunt, quorumque res abstulit et divisit, ante illud judicium anima et corpore sempiternis poenis est deputatus, et recipit simul cum suis peccatis poenas propter peccata omnium,
qui res suas et facultates in honore et amore Domini ad Sanctorum loca
in luminaribus divini cultus, et alimoniis servorum Christi ac pauperum
pro animarum suarum redemtione tradiderant.   Qui in se reversus s.
Bonifacium et Fulradum, Abbatem monasterii s. Dionysii, et summum
Capellanum Regis Pipini ad se vocavit, eisque talia dicens in signum
dedit, ut ad sepulchrum illius irent, et si corpus ejus ibidem non repe-
rissent, ea quae dicebat, vera esse concrederent.   Ipsi autem—sepulchrum illius aperientes, visus est subito exisse draco, et totum illud sepulchrum interius inventum est denigratum, ac si fuisset exustum.   Nos
autem illos vidimus, qui usque ad nostram aetatem duraverunt, qui huic
rei interfuerunt, et nobis viva voce veraciter sunt testati quae audierunt
atque viderunt.   cf. Acta SS. Februarii t. iii. p. 211 ss.
 [4] Planck's Gesch. d. christl. kirchl. Gesellschaftsverfassung Bd. ii.
692 ff.   On the Romish vicars in Spain who appeared during the Arian
period, see P. de Marca de concordia Sac. et Imp. lib. v. c. 42.   Caj.
Cenni de antiquitate Eccl. Hispanae (2 Tomi. Romae 1741. 4.) i. 200.

was the head of the Church ;[5] but at the same time the bishops
attained to a peculiarly great importance, both by their weighty
voice in the election of the king, and by the necessity of sup-
porting a tottering throne by means of spiritual authority.[6] Thus
the connexion with Rome ceased.[7] The bishop of the royal metropolis, Toledo, was primate of the Spanish Church,[8] and raised
himself to a self-importance, which exhibited itself very decidedly
even in opposition to the Roman see.[9] King *Witiza* (701–710)

[5] The king called councils, Cenni ii. 89, and was supreme judge,
even of bishops, ii. 153.

[6] Planck ii. 235. 246. Gregor. Tur. hist. Franc. iii. c. 30: Sump-
serant enim Gothi hanc detestabilem consuetudinem, ut si quis eis de
regibus non placuisset, gladio eum adpeterent: et qui libuisset animo,
hunc sibi statuerent regem. Comp., in particular, Concil. Tolet. iv.
(633) cap. 75. (ap. Mansi x. p. 637 ss.): Post instituta quaedam ecclesiastici ordinis—postrema nobis cunctis sacerdotibus sententia est, pro
robore nostrorum regum et stabilitate gentis Gothorum pontificale, ultimum sub Deo judice ferre decretum. A long admonition to maintain
fidelity to the kings. Then: Nullus apud nos praesumtione regnum
arripiat, nullus excitet mutuas seditiones civium, nemo meditetur interi-
tus regum: sed et defuncto in pace principe, primates totius gentis cum
sacerdotibus successorem regni concilio communi constituant. Then
follows the solemn condemnation of every one who should resist: Anathema sit in conspectu Dei Patris et angelorum, atque ab ecclesia catholica, quam profanaverit perjurio, efficiatur extraneus, et ab omni coetu
Christianorum alienus cum omnibus impietatis suae sociis etc. Finally:
Anathema sit in conspectu Christi et apostolorum ejus, atque ab ecclesia
cath. etc. as above. Finally, Anathema sit in conspectu Spiritus sancti,
et martyrum Christi etc.—But further on also: Te quoque praesentem
regem, futurosque sequentium aetatum principes humilitate qua debemus deposcimus, ut moderati et mites erga subjectos existentes cum
justitia et pietate populos a Deo vobis creditos regatis.—Ne quisquam
vestrum solus in causis capitum aut rerum sententiam ferat, sed consensu publico, cum rectoribus, ex judicio manifesto delinquentium culpa
patescat.—Sane de futuris regibus hanc sententiam promulgamus, ut si
quis ex eis contra reverentiam legum, superba dominatione et fastu regio, in flagitiis et facinore, sive cupiditate crudelissimam potestatem in
populis exercuerit, anathematis sententia a Christo domino condemnetur, et habeat a Deo separationem atque judicium etc.

[7] Cenni. ii. 46. 62. 154.

[8] Cenni ii. 197.

[9] From Gregorii M. lib. vii. ep. 125. 126. it is plain that the same
sent the pallium to Archbishop Leander of Hispalis. It may be that
the latter was already dead († 599) when it came to him, so that for
this reason no trace is found of his assuming it, as Cenni ii. 225, supposes. That little value generally was attributed to the Roman pallium, is proved by the fact, that the succeeding archbishops did not seek

at length broke off all connection with it ;.[10] but this step was

for it, and that, before the invasion of the Saracens, no other Roman
pallium came to Spain, Cenni ii. 252.—That self-consciousness and independence are expressed particularly in the explanations of Archbishop
Julian of Toledo, respecting the remarks made by Benedict II. against
his confession of faith, in Conc. Toletan xv. (688) ap. Mansi xii. 9.
They conclude with the words p. 17 : Jam vero si post haec et ab ipsis
dogmatibus patrum, quibus haec prolata sunt, in quocumque [Romani]
dissentiant, non jam cum illis est amplius contendendum, sed, majorum
directo calle inhaerentes vestigiis, erit per divinum judicium amatoribus
veritatis responsio nostra sublimis, etiamsi ab ignorantibus aemulis censeatur indocilis.

[10] Witiza is a remarkable example of the manner in which the clergy,
treating of the historical persons of the middle ages, handled those who
displeased them. The oldest writer of his history Isidorus Pacensis
(about 754. Chronicon in España Sagrada por Henrique Florez T. viii.
p. 282 ss.), speaks in highly commendatory terms of his reign. He
notices the ecclesiastical regulations made under his sanction in two
places ; first at the Aera 736 (698 p. C.), when Witiza reigned along
with his father Egica, p. 296: Per idem tempus Felix, urbis Regiae
Toletanae Sedis Episcopus, gravitatis et prudentia excellentia nimia
pollet, et Concilia satis praeclara etiam adhuc cum ambobus Principibus
agit. (To these councils also belongs Conc. Toletan. xviii. (701) at which,
perhaps, the decrees above alluded to were enacted. cf. Roderici Ximenii
hist. Hispan. iii. c. 15: Hic [Witiza] in ecclesia S. Petri, quae est extra Toletum, cum episcopis et magnatibus super ordinatione regni concilium celebravit, quod tamen in corpore canonum non habetur.) The
second passage of Isidorus p. 298: Per idem tempus (towards the end
of Witiza's reign) divinae memoriae Sinderedus urbis Regiae Metropolitanus Episcopus sanctimoniae studio claret : atque longaevos et merito
honorabiles viros, quos in suprafata sibi commissa Ecclesia repetit, non
secundum scientiam zelo sanctitatis stimulat (probably he was zealous
against unchastity) atque instinctu jam dicti Witizae Principis eos sub
ejus tempore convexare non cessat. The first aspersions of Witiza appear in the Frankish Chron. Moissiacense (about 818) ad ann. 715, in
Pertz monumenta Germaniae hist. i. 290 : His temporibus in Spania
super Gothos regnabat Witicha.—Iste deditus in feminis, exemplo suo
sacerdotes ac populum luxuriose vivere docuit, irritans furorem Domini.
Sarraceni tunc in Spania ingrediuntur.   In Spain these aspersions first
appear in the Chron. Sebastiani Episc. Salmanticensis seu Alphonsi iii.
Regis (about 866 in España Sagrada T. xiii.) They have been extended and exaggerated by Rodericus Ximenius, archbishop of Toledo,
in the historia Hispaniae (A. D. 1243) lib. iii. c. 15–17, and Lucas,
Episc. Tudensi, in the continuation of Isidore's Chronicon (A. D. 1236).
After relating many infamous deeds of Witiza, it is stated by Rodericus
l. c. c. 16. in Andr. Schotti Hispania illustrata (Francof. 1603. 4 Tomi.
fol.) ii. 62 : Verum quia ista sibi in facie resistebant, [clerici] propter
vexationem pontificis [Episc. Toletani] ad Romanum pontificem appel-
labant. Vitiza facinorosus timens, ne suis criminibus obviarent, et po-

attended with no important consequence, inasmuch as an incursion of the Saracens took place soon after.

§ 133.

ECCLESIASTICAL CONDITION OF THE BRITISH ISLANDS.

Among the Anglo-Saxons, Christianity had at first to struggle against heathenism with various fortune, but was afterwards diffused by degrees in all the Anglo-Saxon states. Those who preached it were for the most part Roman missionaries; *Northumberland* alone being converted by the Scottish clergy, who introduced here the regulations of the ancient British Church. Old controversies between them and the Roman-English clergy were soon renewed; however, after a conference between both parties at the synod of *Streaneshalh* (now Whitby, not far from York, Synodus Pharensis 664), the king of Northumberland, *Oswiu*, decided in favour of the Roman ordinances.[1] And since

pulum ab ejus obedientia revocarent, dedit licentiam, immo praeceptum, omnibus clericis, ut uxores et concubinas unam et plures haberent juxta libitum voluptatis, et ne Romanis constitutionibus, quae talia prohibent, in aliquo obedirent, et sic per eos populus retineretur. Lucas Tudensis (ibid. iv. 69.): Et ne adversus eum insurgeret s. ecclesia, episcopis, presbyteris, diaconibus et caeteris ecclesiae Christi ministris carnales uxores lascivus Rex habere praecepit, et ne obedirent Romano Pontifici sub mortis interminatione prohibuit. The state of the matter appears to have been this. Witiza, in conjunction with Sinderedus, archbishop of Toledo, opposed licentiousnes in priests, and perceived that it could be eradicated only by allowing them to marry. The latter had been general among the Arians, and abolished when they joined the Catholic Church (cf. Conc. Tolet. iii. ann. 589 c. 5): Compertum est a sancto Concilio, Episcopos, Presbyteros et Diaconos venientes ex haerese carnali adhuc desiderio uxoribus copulari : ne ergo de cetero fiat etc. Thus the prejudicial alteration which had taken place for 100 years, by the prohibition of the council, could be clearly noticed. Hence Witiza allowed priests to marry, and declared the Roman decretals, forbidding it, to be of no binding force. Comp. a defence of King Witiza by Don Gregorio Mayans y Siscar, translated into German, from the Spanish, in Büsching's Magazin für die neue Historie und Geographie i. 379 ff. Aschbach's Gesch. der Westgothen S. 303 ff.

[1] Bedae hist. eccl. gentis Anglorum iii. 25. The remarkable conclusion of the dispute between the Scotch bishop, Colman, and the English presbyter, Wilfrid. The former appealed to Anatolius and Columba, the latter to Peter, and closed with the passage, Matth. xvi. 18: tu es Pe-

the well-ordered schools of the Irish monasteries always attracted
many young Anglo-Saxons to Ireland,[2] and by this means might
become dangerous to the Roman regulations, Rome sent forth
into England, for the purpose of giving a check to this influence,
the learned *Theodore*, born at Tarsus, as archbishop of Canterbury (668–690), and the abbot *Hadrian*, who everywhere
strengthened the Roman ordinances, and, by the erection of
schools, rendered those journies to Ireland superfluous.[3]   No less

trus etc.   King Oswiu then said: Verene, Colmane, haec illi Petro dicta sunt a Domino ?   Qui ait: vere, Rex.   At ille: habetis, inquit, vos
proferre aliquid tantae potestatis vestro Columbae datum ?   At ille ait:
nihil.   Rursum autem Rex: si utrique vestrum, inquit, in hoc sine ulla
controversia consentiunt, quod haec principaliter Petro dicta, et ei claves
regni caelorum sunt datae a Domino ?   Responderunt: etiam utique.
At ille ita conclusit: et ego vobis dico, quia hic est ostiarius ille, cui ego
contradicere nolo, sed in quantum novi vel valeo, hujus cupio in omnibus obedire statutis, ne forte me adveniente ad fores regni caelorum, non
sit qui reseret, averso illo qui claves tenere probatur.   Haec dicente
Rege faverunt assidentes quique sive adstantes, majores una cum mediocribus, et abdicata minus perfecta institutione, ad ea quae meliora
cognoverant, sese transferre festinabant.
   [2] Beda iii. 27: multi nobilium simul et mediocrium de gente Anglorum.—relicta insula patria, vel divinae lectionis vel continentioris vitae
gratia illo secesserant.   Et quidam quidem mox se monasticae conver-
sationi fideliter mancipaverunt, alii magis circumeundo per cellas magis-
trorum lectioni operam dare gaudebant: quos omnes Scoti libentissime
suscipientes, victum eis quotidianum sine pretio, libros quoque ad legendum et magisterium gratuitum praebere curabant.   cf. Murray in nov.
comm. Soc. Gott. (see above, § 126. not. 3) T. I. p. 109.
   [3] Beda iv. 2.   (Theodorus) peragrata insula tota, quaquaversum Anglorum gentes morabantur,—rectum vivendi ordinem, ritum celebrandi
pascha canonicum, per omnia comitante et cooperante Adriano dissemi-
nabat.   Isque primus erat archiepiscopus, cui omnis Anglorum ecclesia
manus dare consentiret.   Et quia literis sacris simul et saecularibus, ut
diximus, abundanter ambo erant instructi, congregata discipulorum ca-
terva, scientiae salutaris quotidie flumina irrigandis eorum cordibus
emanabant: ita ut etiam metricae artis, astronomicae et arithmeticae
ecclesiasticae disciplinam inter sacrorum apicum volumina suis auditoribus contraderent.   Indicio est, quod usque hodie supersunt de eorum
discipulis, qui latinam graecamque linguam aeque ut propriam, in qua
nati sunt, norunt.   Neque unquam prorsus ex quo Britanniam petierunt
Angli, feliciora fuere tempora, dum et fortissimos christianosque habentes reges cunctis barbaris nationibus essent terrori, et omnium vota ad
nuper audita caelestis regni gaudia penderent: et quicunque lectionibus
sacris cuperent erudiri, haberent in promtu magistros qui docerent: et
sonos cantandi in ecclesia—ab hoc tempore per omnes Anglorum ecclesias discere coeperunt etc.

active in favour of the Roman Church was also *Wilfrid*, a noble Anglo-Saxon,[4] who even, when a young priest, had turned the scale at the synod of Streaneshalh, had been afterwards for a time bishop of York; and, driven thence, had preached, not without fruit, to the Frieslanders; and, lastly, had converted *Sussex* (about 680 † 709) where heathenism remained longest among the Anglo-Saxons.

It is true that the original missionary-dependence of the Anglo-Saxon Church on Rome gradually ceased; here also the kings put themselves in possession of the same ecclesiastical privileges, which kings asserted in the other German kingdoms;[5] the Latin language connecting with Rome was obliged to suffer along with itself, even in the Liturgy, the Anglo-Saxon tongue;[6] but notwithstanding such considerations, Rome continued to maintain an authority in the Anglo-Saxon Church which it did not now exercise in any other German Church.[7]

Emulation with the Irish institutions for educational purposes also introduced into the Anglo-Saxon schools a very great activity. Not only did they distinguish themselves by the study of the Greek language, which Theodore had established in the whole of the West, but its revival unquestionably contributed to the development of the Anglo-Saxon dialect, even as the language of writing.[8] At the end of this period, England possessed the most

[4] Vita s. Wilfridi by the contemporary Eddius (Æddi), cognomento Stephanus (cantandi magister in Northumbrorum Ecclesiis, invitatus de Cantia a reverendissimo viro Wilfrido, Beda hist. eccl. iv. 2.), in Th. Gale historiae britannicae, saxonicae, anglodanicae scriptores xv. Oxon. 1691. fol. p. 40. Lappenberg's Geschichte von England. Bd. 1. (Hamburg 1834) S. 167.

[5] Theodore was still in Rome when nominated archbishop of Canterbury, after Wighard, who had been sent thither to be ordained, had died (Beda iii. 29. iv. 1). But the decision of Rome in favour of Wilfrid, who had been expelled from the see of York (Eddius in vita Wilfridi ap. Gale i. 67), was not regarded; Wilfrid, on the contrary, was put in captivity (l. c. p. 69). The bishops were for the most part appointed by the kings (Lappenberg's Gesch. v. England i. 183), who had also the power of confirming the decrees of synods, and the highest judicial power over the clergy (Lappenberg i. 194).

[6] Lappenberg i. 196.

[7] Planck's christ. kirchl. Gesellchaftsverf. ii. 704 ff.

[8] Caedmon, a monk in the monastery of Streaneshalh † 680 (Beda iv. 24. non ab hominibus,—sed divinitus adjutus gratis canendi donum

N

learned man of the West, *the venerable Bede,* a monk in the
monastery of *Peter and Paul* at Yarrow († 735).[9] The new
branch of ecclesiastical literature founded by John the Fas-
ter, in his penitential law-book, had been first adopted by the

accepit), author of poetical paraphrases of biblical books, especially of
Genesis. See Caedmon's metrical paraphrase of parts of the Holy
Scriptures, in Anglo-Saxon, by Benj. Thorpe. London, 1832. 8.—Aldhelm, abbot of Malmesbury, afterwards bishop of Sherborne † 709,
translated the Psalms (King Alfred said of him, according to Wilhelm.
Malmesb. ap. Gale i. 339 : nulla unquam aetate par ei fuit quisquam
poësin anglicam posse facere, tantum componere, eadem apposite vel
canere vel dicere). As early as the year 680, there existed a version of
the four gospels by Aldred. (Selden praef. ad scriptt. hist. angl. ed.
Twysden p. 25) : also Ekbert, bishop of Lindisfarne, translated the
gospels; Bede, the gospel of John.—Beowulf, a heroic poem, received
its present form at this time from the hands of Christians (ed. G. F.
Thorkelin, Kopenh. 1817. 4. translated into German by L. Ettmüller,
Zurich 1840. 8.) In like manner, about the year 700, there existed a
poem (by Aldhelm ?) descriptive of the conversion of the Myrmidoni-
ans by the apostle Andrew, and another on the finding of the cross by
the empress Helena, composed by one Cynewulf. See Andrew and
Elene, published by J. Grimm. Cassel 1840. 8vo.

[9] As a proof of his wide-spread fame is adduced Sergii P. I. ep. ad Ceol-
fridum (abbot of the cloister there), A. D. 700, quoted in Guilelmi Malms-
buriensis († 1143) de reb. gestis Regum Angl. i. 3. :—hortamur Deo
dilectam bonitatis tuae religiositatem, ut, quia exortis quibusdam ecclesiasticarum causarum capitulis (without doubt the cloister in question),
non sine examinatione longius innotescendis, opus nobis sunt ad con-
ferendum artis literatura imbuti,—absque aliqûa immoratione religiosum
famulum Dei (Bedam) venerabilis monasterii tui ad veneranda limina
Apostolorum principum dominorum meorum Petri et Pauli, amatorum
tuorum ac protectorum, ad nostrae mediocritatis conspectum non mo-
reris dirigere. Stevenson, however, in his Introduction prefixed to
Bedae opp. hist. Tom. 1. p. x., shews that the word Bedam is wanting
in an old MS. of this epistle, and was inserted by William of Malmesbury, but that Bede could not have been called at that time.—Bede's
writings embrace Natural Philosophy, Chronology, Philosophy, Grammar, Astronomy, Arithmetic, &c., and give a view of all the learning of
the time. In particular, Historia ecclesiast. gentis Anglorum libb. v.,
from Julius Cæsar till 731. (ed. Fr. Chiffletius. Paris, 1681. 4. Joh.
Smith. Cantabrig. 1722. fol.) De sex aetatibus mundi liber. Lives of
English monks. (Opera historica ad fidem Codd. MSS. rec. Jos. Stevenson, T. ii. Lond. 1838. 41. 8). Numerous commentaries on the
Holy Scriptures, homilies, letters, &c. Opp. ed. Basil. 1563. T. viii.
fol. Colon. 1688. T. iv. fol. ed. J. A. Giles, 5 voll. Lond. 1843.
8. H. Gehle disp. de Bedae ven. vita et scriptis. Lugd. Bat.
1838. 8.

British Church in the West,[10] and, after its example, was also used among the Anglo-Saxons by *Theodore, Bede,* and *Egbert* of York († 767).[11] On the other hand, these *libelli pœnitentiales* do not seem to have as yet obtained currency any where out of England.

Endeavours were always proceeding from the Anglo-Saxon states to reconcile the Britons and Irish with the Roman Church as the common mother-church,[12] and to unite them with the Church of the Anglo-Saxons. But although the abbot *Adamnan,* at the beginning of the eighth century, had laboured to effect this object, not without success, among the Britons and in the south of Ireland,[13]

[10] These libelli poenitentiales were constantly altered, that they might continue useful in practice: on the other hand, the earlier were transferred more or less verbally into the later. Hence hardly any one has come down to us entirely free from alterations; and in many cases it is difficult to decide to what author an extant poenitentiale is to be attributed. Among the Irish the oldest known was that of Columbanus, a part of which was published in Columb. opp. ed. Patric. Fleming. Lovan. 1667. (See F. F. Mone's Quellen u. Forschungen zur Gesch. d. teutschen Literatur u. Sprache. Bd. 1. Aachen u. Leipzig 1830. S. 494), another by Cumin († 661), an extract from which was published by Fleming l. c. and Bibl. PP. Lugd. xii. 42. (see Mone, S. 490), and which is the same work as the so-called Canones poenitentiales Hieronymi (opp. ed. Martianay v. 5.) (Mone S. 497.)

[11] Theodori liber poenitentialis printed in its oldest existing form in the ancient laws and institutes of England. London 1840. fol. and taken from this in Dr F. Kunstmann's latein. Pönitentialbücher der Angelsachsen. Mainz 1844. S. 43. Theodori capitula de redemptione peccatorum (ap. Kunstmann P. 106.) give the oldest instructions how to purchase penitential seasons by singing, prayer, and by money.— Beda de remediis peccatorum (ap. Kunstmann S. 142), elaborated, perhaps, by Egbert; and therefore Bede's canons are also occasionally attributed to the latter, and the Ballerini de ant. collectionibus canonum p. iv. c. 6, have assigned the whole to him. Egbert's Poenitential Latin and Anglo-Saxon is given in Wilkin's Conc. M. Brit. i. A fourth book was published by Mone l. c. i. 501. Comp. Ballerini l. c. Wasserschleben's Beiträge zur Gesch. u. Kenntnissz der Beichtbücher in dess. Beitr. zur Gesch. d. vorgratianischen Kirchenrechtsquellen. Leipzig 1839. S. 78.

[12] Hence the fable which first appears in Beda i. 4., that the British king, Lucius, in the second century, applied to Pope Eleutherus, obsecrans, ut per ejus mandatum Christianus efficeretur, and that the British church was thus founded. cf. D. Thiele de Ecclesiae britann, primordiis partt. 2. (Halae 1839. 8.) i. 10. ii. 14.

[13] Beda v. 16.

and the monk *Ekbert* had gained over the northern Picts to
the side ˙of Rome,[14] yet the breach was not removed by this
means.[15] It was not till the decline of the Irish Church amid
the continued civil wars,[16] that, towards the end of the eleventh
century, Dublin first came to attach itself to the archbishop of Canterbury;[17] afterwards the archbishop of Armagh, *Malachy* (†1148),
was active in favour of Rome ;[18] till at last Ireland and Wales

[14] Beda v. 23.

[15] Beda v. 24. says, when he speaks of the condition of his times
(735): Brittones maxima ex parte domestico sibi odio gentem Anglorum et totius catholicae Ecclesiae statum pascha minus recto moribus-
que improbis impugnant. About the same time Gregory III. (731-
741.) warns the German bishops of the British errors. See an epistle
among those of Boniface ep. 129 : Gentilitatis ritum et doctrinam, vel
venientium Britonum abjiciatis.

[16] Bernardus Claraevall. de vita s. Malachiae c. 10. (opp. ed. Montfaucon i. 673): Mos pessimus inoleverat quorundum diabolica ambitione procerum, sedem sanctam (Armachanam) obtentum iri haereditaria
successione. Nec enim patiebantur episcopari, nisi qui essent de tribu
et familia sua.— Et eousque firmaverat sibi jus pravum—generatio mala,
—ut etsi interdum defecissent clerici de sanguine illo, sed Episcopi
nunquam. Denique jam octo exstiterant ante Celsum viri uxorati, et
absque Ordinibus, literati tamen. Inde tota illa per universam Hiberniam—dissolutio ecclesiastieae disciplinae, censurae enervatio, religionis
evacuatio.—Nam—sine ordine, sine ratione mutabantur et multiplica-
bantur Episcopi pro libitu Metropolitani, ita ut unus Episcopatus uno
non esset contentus, sed singulae paene Ecclesiae singulos haberent
Episcopos. Hence also, perhaps, may be explained the statement of
Ekkehardus († 1070, a monk in St Gallen, to which place many Irish
came at that time) in his liber benedictionum : In Hibernia Episcopi et
Presbyteri unum sunt (ex MS. in Arx Gesch. v. St Gallen i. 267).

[17] Lanfranc, A. D. 1074, consecrated Patricius, who was chosen bishop
of Dublin, and obtained from him the promise of canonical obedience.
All subsequent bishops of Dublin were consecrated by the Archbishop
of Canterbury. See J. Usserii veterum epistolarum hibernicarum sylloge, Dublinii 1632. 4. p. 68. 118. 136, but for this very reason hated
by the other Irish bishops. After this, Gillebertus Ep. Lunicensis (of
Limerick) endeavoured, as well as Anselm, Archbishop of Canterbury,
to induce the other Irish also to come to the same conclusion, l. c. p.
77 ss. The church of Waterford also attached itself to England 1096,
p. 92.

[18] He stood in close connection with St Bernard, and died in a journey to Rome in Clairvaux. Bernard wrote on this lib. de vita et rebus
gestis s. Malachiae (Opp. ed. Montf. i. 663.) Malachy was legatus
sedis Apost. per totam Hiberniam, but did not desire the pallium. In
Clairvaux he educated young Irishmen, and then founded, by their in-
strumentality, Cistercian monasteries in Ireland (vita Mal. c. 16. Us-

were conquered by Henry II.,[19] and thus the complete association of the British and Irish Church with Rome was effected.

§ 134.

SPREAD OF CHRISTIANITY IN GERMANY.

Schmidt's Kirchengesh. iv. 10. Neander's Kirchengesch. iii. 72. Rettberg's Gesch. d. Kirche Deutschlands. Bd. i. Göttingen 1845.

The attempts to convert the Germans, whether made by Franks, or by Irish and Anglo-Saxons, were as yet but partially successful.

The Irish *Kilian*[1] lost his life in the cause at Würzburg (689) ; as also *Emmeram*[2] at Ratisbon (654). In Bavaria, however, better success attended *Rupert*,[3] bishop of Worms, who baptized Duke

serii vett. epist. hibern. p. 102). Immediately after him came the first pallia to Ireland. See Chronica de Mailros (ed. Edinburgi 1835. 4.) p. 74: Anno MCLI Papa Eugenius quatuor pallia per legatum suum Johannem Papirum transmisit in Hiberniam, quo nunquam antea pallium delatum fuerat.

[19] Pope Hadrian IV. made a gift of Ireland, A. D. 1155, to the king. See the Bull in Usserii vett. epist. hib. p. 109. comp. Johannis Sarisburiensis (who, as royal ambassador, had prevailed on the pope to do so) Metalogicus lib. iv. in fine. Giraldi Cambrensis (about 1190) expugnatio Hiberniae (in the Historicis Angl. Normannicis. Francof. 1602. fol.) M. Chr. Sprengel's Gesch. v. Grossbritanniën. Th. 1. (a continuation of the Universal History of the world, part 47) S. 433.—Wales was conquered since 1157. See Giraldi Cambr. descriptio Cambriae (in the above quoted collection). Sprengel l. c. P. 378.

[1] Acta SS. ad d. 8. Jul. C. F. Hefele's Gesch. d. Einführung des Christenth. im südwestl. Deutschland. Tübingen 1837. S. 372.

[2] See life of Aribo, fourth bishop of Freisingen († 753). See Acta SS. ad d. 22. Sept. B. A. Winter's Vorarbeiten zur Beleuchtung d. baier. u. österr. Kirchengesch. (2 Bde. München 1805. 1810), ii. 153. According to Winter ii. 169, he was not a native of Pictavium, in West Franconia, as has been usually assumed, but of Petavio, now Petau, in Pannonia.

[3] Act. SS. ad d. 27. Mart. Rupert came to Bavaria at the time of a Frankish King Childebert. According to the Salzburg tradition, the king was Childebert II., at the end of the sixth century ; but, according to Valesius, Mabillon, Pagi, and especially Hansiz (Germania sacra ii. 51.) Childebert III. a hundred years later. On the contrary, M. Filz, a Benedictine, and Prof. in Salzburg, has reasserted, conformably

Theodore II. (†696), and founded the Church of Salzburg (†718);
as also *Corbinian*,[4] who gathered a church in Freisingen (†730).

On the other hand, Anglo-Saxon monks endeavoured to spread
Christianity among the kindred north-German races. *Wilfrid*
was the first who preached among the Frieslanders (†677).[5]
Afterwards *Willebrord*, first bishop of Wiltaburg (Utrecht) from
696–739 laboured, along with his associates,[6] with much success,
under the protection of the Franks, among the West Frieslanders
and the surrounding territories; but the East Frieslanders remained steadfast to paganism. The Saxons even murdered the
two *Ewalds* who visited them;[7] and *Suidbert*,[8] who had at first
been received among the Boructiarii, was afterwards obliged to
retreat, when they were subdued by the Saxons; and obtained
from Pipin an island in the Rhine to establish a convent on it
(Kaiserswerth) †713.

to the ancient tradition, that Rupert came to Bavaria A. D. 580, and died
in 623. See his treatise on the true period of the apostol. Wirksamkeit
d. heil. Rupert in Baiern. Salzburg 1831. 8. The same writer in the
Anzeigelblätt. d. Wiener Jahrb. d. Literatur, Bd. 64. (1833) S. 23. Bd.
80. (1837.) S. 1. In the meantime, however, the younger age of Rupert is maintained by Blnmberger, Benedictine in Göttweih, in the
Vienna Jahr. Bd. 73. S. 242, u. Bd. 74. S. 147, and by Rudhart in the
Munich gel. Anzeigen. Bd. 5. 1837. S. 587.

[4] See life of Aribo, Bishop of Freisingen. See Acta SS. ad d. 8
Sept.

[5] See § 133. not. 4. Beda hist. eccl. v. 19. Eddius ap. Gale p. 64.
H. J. Royaards Geschiedenis der invoering en vestiging van het Christendom in Nederland 3te Uitg. Utrecht 1844. p. 127.

[6] Beda hist. eccl. v. c. 10 ss. Villebrord's life by Alcuin in Mabillonii Act. SS. Ord. Bened. Saec. iii. P. i. p. 601. Royaards p. 159. ·

[7] Beda v. c. 11. Acta SS. ad. 3 Oct. L. v. Ledebur das Land u.
Volk der Bructerer. Berlin 1827. S. 277. Royaards p. 201.

[8] Beda v. c. 12. Acta SS. ad d. 1 Mart. Ledebur S. 280. Royaards p. 197.

THIRD PERIOD.

FROM THE BEGINNING OF THE CONTROVERSY CONCERNING THE
WORSHIP OF IMAGES TO THE REFORMATION.

FROM A.D. 726—1517.

FOR THE GENERAL LITERATURE OF THE MIDDLE AGES, SEE THE LITERATURE
PREFIXED TO THE SECOND PERIOD.

FIRST DIVISION.

TO THE TIME OF NICOLAUS I. OR TO THE APPEARANCE OF THE
PSEUDO-ISIDORIAN DECRETALS.

FROM 726—858.

FIRST PART.

HISTORY OF THE GREEK CHURCH.

Sources are, the Byzantines : Nicephorus (patriarch of Constantinople, † 828)
till 769, Theophanes († 817) till 813, and his continuator, Constantinus
Porphyrogenneta († 959), Josephus Genesius about 940 (A.D. 813-867),
Georgius Monachus (till 959), Simeon Logotheta (till 967), Leo Gramma-
ticus (till 1013). From these Georgius Cedrenus (1057), Joh. Zonaras
(1118), and Michael Glykas (1450 ?) have drawn their histories.

§ 1.

CONTROVERSY CONCERNING IMAGE-WORSHIP.

Imperialia decreta de cultu imaginum in utroque imperio promulgata, col-
lecta et illustrata a Melch. Haiminsfeldio Goldasto, Francof. 1608. 8.
Jo. Dallaeus de imaginibus, Lugd. Bat. 1642. 8. Lud. Maimbourg. hist.
de l'heresie des iconoclastes, Paris 1679. u. 83. 2 voll. 12. Frid. Spanhemii historia imaginum restituta, Lugd. Bat. 1686. 8. (recus. in ejusd.

opp. T. ii., p. 707). Walch's Ketzerhistorie, Th. 10, u, 11. Neander's KG.
iii. 398. Gfrörer's KG. iii. 1. 97. F. Ch. Schlosser's Geschichte der bilder-
stürmenden Kaiser des ostromischen Reichs, Francf. a. M. 1812. 8. The
Roman Catholic point of view is maintained by J. Marr, der Bilderstreit
der Byzant. Kaiser. Trier 1839. 8.

The worship of images had long assumed a very unchristian
form,[1] when *Leo III. Isauricus* (716–741), an intelligent and
powerful prince, became opposed to it,[2] but in what way is uncertain.[3] At first he was satisfied with a simple prohibition (726),
but afterwards he commanded the pictures themselves to be taken
away (730).[4] The measure was enforced by the removal of *Germanus*,[5] patriarch of Constantinople, who opposed him, in whose

[1] Comp. p. 1. Div. 2. Even the author of the oratio adv. Constantinum Cabalinum, a fanatical image worshipper of the 8th century,
knew of no other reply, c. 13. to the objection of opponents: ἡ γενεὰ
αὕτη ἐθεοποίησεν τὰς εἰκόνας than ὀφείλεις διδάξαι τὸν ἀγράμματον λαόν. cf.
Joannis Damasc. opp. ed. Le Quien ii. 621 and 622.

[2] Attempts at explanation may be found in Walch x. 202. Schlosser
S. 161. Deserving of attention is Theophanes ad. ann. vi. Leonis p.
336.: Τούτῳ τῷ ἔτει ἠνάγκαζεν ὁ βασιλεὺς τοὺς Ἑβραίους καὶ τοὺς Μοντα-
νοὺς βαπτίζεσθαι,.and then ad. ann. vii. follow the first declarations against
images in which the renegade Beser, and Constantine, bishop of Nakolia,
were principal assistants of the emperor. In the Synodicon vet. c. 138.
(in Fabricii bibl. graec. xi. 248) Leo is said: τῇ πλάνῃ Κωνσταντίνου
ἐπισκόπου Νακωλείας, καὶ Βίσηρ Πατρικίου σαρακηνόφρονος τῶν αἱρεσιαρχῶν
χραινόμενος. It is worthy of remark that Leo considered the ravages of
a volcano that arose in the Cretan sea as a punishment for the worship
of images. Nicephori breviar. p. 37: ὡς ἐκ τῶν εἰκονισμάτων ἱδρύσεώς τε
καὶ προσκυνήσεως γεγονέναι οἰόμενος τὸ τεράστιον, cf. Theophanes p. 339.

[3] The emperor's own explanations in a letter to Gregory II., bishop
of Rome, cf. Gregorii epist. i. ad. Leonem. ap. Mansi xii. 959: αἱ εἰκόνες εἰδώλων τόπον ἀναπληροῦσι·— οἱ προσκυνοῦντες αὐτὰς εἰδωλολάτραι·—οὐ
δεῖ προσκυνεῖν χειροποίητα, καὶ πᾶν εἶδος καθ᾿ ὁμοίωμα, καθὼς εἶπεν ὁ θεός,
μήτε ἐν οὐρανῷ, μήτε ἐπὶ τῆς γῆς (Exod. xx. 4.)—πληροφόρησόν με τίς ἡμῖν
παρέδωκε σέβεσθαι καὶ προσκυνεῖν χειροποίητα· κἀγὼ ὁμολογῶ, ὅτι θεοῦ νομο-
θεσία ἐστί.

[4] Comp. especially Theophanes p. 336, 343. Nicephorus p. 37, 38.

[5] Subservient as he had shown himself under Philippicus in acknowledging the Monotheletic doctrines, and afterwards renouncing them
(Theophanes p. 320. Nicephorus p. 31. Walch's Ketzergesch. ix.
466), he was now immovable in favour of images. Three letters of his
are in the Actis Council. Nicaeni ii. Actio iv. ap. Mansi xiii. 99. The
third ad. Thomam Episc. Clandeopoleos is a long defence in favour of
the use of pictures. In p. 125 he dwells particularly on the miracles
wrought by them, among which the greatest in his view was ἡ ἐν Σωζο-

place was put the pliant *Anastasius* ; and by the vigorous suppression of some tumultuous movements.[6] He was obliged to allow his measures to be blamed with impunity only in Rome, which refused obedience to him,[7] and in the East, which was now subject to the Saracens ;[8] but in his own empire, *the friends of images* (εἰκονολάτραι, ξυλολάτραι, εἰδωλολάτραι) were soon compelled to conceal themselves, and the fanatics who resisted the imperial power had to repent bitterly of their opposition. Another superstition also was threatened by means of the enlightenment party, *the opponents of images*, (εἰκονομάχοι, εἰκονοκλάσται, εἰκονοκαύσται, χριστιανοκατήγοροι) ;[9] but since it was not created by a religious feeling, but merely by the emperor's will, this party

πόλει τῆς Πισιδίας τὸ πρὶν ὑπάρχουσα εἰκὼν τῆς παναχράντου θεοτόκου, ἐκ τῆς γεγραμμένης παλάμης αὐτῆς τὴν τοῦ μύρου βλύσιν προχέουσα. Also in his lib. de synodis et haeresibus he speaks in brief terms respecting the image controversy in the Spicilegium Romanum T. vii. (Romae 1842. 8.) i. 59. Here the only thing he maintains against the opponents of images is: εἰ, ὡς φατὲ ὑμεῖς, εἰδώλων δίκην τὰ σεπτὰ τῶν ἁγίων ἀπείργετε εἰκονίσματα, μικροῦ καὶ αὐτὰ τὰ καίρια τῆς πίστεως ἀνατρέπετε·—οὐδὲν ἀπὸ τοῦ νῦν βέβαιόν τι ἡ τῆς ἐκκλησίας ἡμῶν παράδοσις ἕξειν δυνήσεται, τὰ πρὶν ἀθετήσασα.

[6] Namely, the revolt in Greece and the Cyclades (Theophanes p. 339. Nicephorus p. 37), and the rebellion in Constantinople at the taking down of the crucifix (called ὁ Ἀντιφωνητής) ἐν τοῖς Χαλκοπρατείοις Gregor. ii. ep. i. ad. Leonem ap. Mansi xii. 969. Theophanes 339 (who calls it τὴν τοῦ Κυρίου εἰκόνα τὴν ἐπὶ τῆς χαλκῆς πύλης), comp. Walch x. 178. Schlosser S. 177.

[7] Gregorii. epistolae 2 ad Leonem Imp. (not. 726, but written after 730. Walch x. 173) iu the Actis Concil. Nicaeni ii. ap. Mansi xii. 959. On the ignorance and indecency in them see Bower's lives of the popes iv. 365. Walch xi. 271. ex. gr. p. 966 : καὶ τὰ μικρὰ παιδία καταπαίζουσί σου· γύρωσον εἰς τὰς διατριβὰς τῶν στοιχείων, καὶ εἰπέ· ὅτι ἐγώ εἰμι ὁ καταλύτης καὶ διώκτης τῶν εἰκόνων· καὶ εὐθὺς τὰς πινακίδας αὐτῶν εἰς τὴν κεφαλήν σου ῥίψουσι, καὶ ὅπερ οὐκ ἐπαιδεύθης ὑπὸ τῶν φρονίμων, παιδευθήσῃ ὑπὸ τῶν ἀφρόνων. Ἔγραψας, ὅτι Ὀζίας ὁ βασιλεὺς τῶν Ἰουδαίων (Rather Hezekiah 2 Kings 18, 4.) μετὰ ὀκτακοσίους ἐνιαυτοὺς ἐξήγαγε τὸν χαλκοῦν ὄφιν ἐκ τοῦ ναοῦ, κἀγὼ μετὰ ὀκτακοσίους ἐνιαυτοὺς ἐξήγαγον τὰ εἴδωλα ἐκ τῶν ἐκκλησιῶν. Ἀληθῶς καὶ Ὀζίας ἀδελφός σου ἦν, καὶ τὸ σὸν πεῖσμα εἶχε, καὶ τοὺς τότε ἱερεῖς ἐτυράννησεν ὥσπερ σύ (Uzziah 2 Chron. 26, 16-18.)· ἐκεῖνον γὰρ τὸν ὄφιν ὁ ἡγιασμένος Δαβὶδ εἰσήγαγεν εἰς τὸν ναὸν μετὰ τῆς ἁγίας κιβωτοῦ.—p. 967: συνέφερέ σοι, βασιλεῦ, τῶν δύο προκειμένων, αἱρετικόν σε ὀνομάζεσθαι, ἢ διώκτην καὶ καταλυτὴν τῶν ἱστοριῶν καὶ ζωγραφιῶν τῶν εἰκόνων καὶ παθημάτων τοῦ κυρίου.

[8] Johannis Damasceni λόγοι γ' ἀπολογητικοὶ πρὸς τοὺς διαβάλλοντας τὰς ἁγίας εἰκόνας in opp. ed. Le Quien. T. i. p. 305 ss.

[9] Germanus lib. de synodis et haeres. im Spicil. Rom. vii. i. 61 :

fostered a superficial free-thinking, rather than a beneficial refor-
matory tendency.   The measures taken against images were also
honestly prosecuted by *Constantius Copronymus* (741–775),
equally honoured by his subjects as a prince, and beloved by his

'Απ' αὐτῆς τῆς βασιλείας, καὶ πάντων τῶν ἐν ὑπεροχῇ κρατούντων τὰ πραγ-
ματα, ἐκμανὴς ἀγανάκτησις τοῖς εὐλαβῶς διάγειν προαιρουμένοις ἐπινενόηται.
Τοῦ γε χάριν καὶ κίνδυνος οὐχ ὁ τυχὼν ἀλλὰ καὶ λίαν ὀλέθριος, πᾶσαν σχεδὸν
τὴν οἰκουμένην ἐμπεριείληχε, πλείστων ἱερέων τε καὶ λαϊκῶν, περισσοτέρως δὲ
τῶν τῷ μοναχικῷ ἀσκουμένων τάγματι θεοσεβεστάτων ἀνδρων, μεταναστῶν τῶν
οἰκείων γεγενημένων, καὶ ἐν ἐξορίᾳ καὶ γυμνητεύσει, μετὰ καὶ τῶν τοῦ σώματος μελῶν ἀφαιρέσεως, εἰς διασποραν καὶ ἐρήμωσιν παραπεμφθέντων.   Οὐ γὰρ
ἠρκέσθησαν οἱ τὰ νῦν τοῦ κηρύγματος τὸν λόγον ἐπιδεικτικῶς ὑποφαίνοντες τῇ
τῶν σανίδων μόνον ἐκποιήσει τὰ τῶν ἁγίων περιαίρεθαι εἰκονίσματα, ἀλλὰ καὶ
τὴν ἐν γραφίδι ἐφάμιλλον τούτοις κόσμησιν τῶν σεπτοτάτων νεῶν ὁλικῶς ἐξο-
ρύττέσθαι· καὶ ἔμπαλιν τοῖς θείοις θυσιαστηρίοις τὰ τῶν σεβασμίων καὶ ἱερῶν
τραπεζώσεων συμβολικὰ ἐπενδύματα, ἐν χρυσῷ καὶ πορφύρᾳ συμποικιλθέντα,
χύδην ἀπομορξάμενοι, ἐν τοῖς ἑαυτῶν οἴκοις ἀνέθεσαν, ὅτι καὶ χαρακτῆρες ἁγίων
εὕρηνται ἱστορούμενοι.   Πρὸς δὲ τούτοις καὶ τὸ πάσης ἀνοσιουργίας ἀνάμεστον
δρᾶν οὐκ ἐνάρκησαν· τὰ γὰρ τῶν μακαρίων καὶ ἀοιδίμων Μαρτύρων λείψανα,
ὑπὸ τῶν τῆς Ἐκκλησίας διδασκάλων συγκομισθέντα, καὶ ἐν τιμίοις κιβωρίοις
σωρηδὸν ἐντεθέντα ἀπογυμνώσαντες, πυρὶ κατανάλωσαν, τὸ ὅσον ἐπ' αὐτοῖς
τοὺς διὰ πίστιν ἠθληκότας καταπατῆσαι καὶ ἀτιμάσαι σπουδάσαντες.   Holy
vessels furnished with images and clothes cannot have been taken away
in consequence of general measures, but only occasionally by zealous
enemies to images; for the Conc. Constant. of 754 forbids such things,
καθὼς τοιαῦτα ὑπό τινων ἀτάκτως φερομένων προγέγονεν (Mansi xiii. 332.)
How far the fanaticism of individual foes to pictures had proceeded may
be seen from the fact, that at this synod, even a bishop was accused (vita
Stephani jun. in Analecta Graeca ed. Mon. Bened. Congr. S. Mauri.
Paris 1688, 4. i. 480), ὡς ὅτι ἅγιον δίσκον τῶν ἀχράντων τοῦ θεοῦ μυστηρίων κατεπάτησεν, διότιπερ ἐκτετύπωτο εἰκόνας σεπτὰς τοῦ τε Χριστοῦ καὶ τῆς
αὐτοῦ μητρὸς καὶ τοῦ προδρόμου.   So also relics may have been attacked
by individuals, but certainly very rarely, because traces of it must have
been found in the polemics of the period.   The tendency, it is true, of
the enemies of images must have turned itself also in consistent development against relic and saint worship, and several may have even proceeded so far as to reject and renounce it.   But the party, on the whole,
dependent on the imperial will, did not go so far, without doubt even
with regard to the general, popular disposition.   It even expressly
warded off from itself the suspicion of wishing to attack the worship of
saints, Conc. Const. ann. 754 Anath. ix. and xi., see not. 11 at the end.
It is therefore a very exaggerated statement, when Theophanes p. 340.
says of Leo: οὐ μόνον γὰρ περὶ τὴν σχετικὴν τῶν σεπτῶν εἰκόνων ὁ δυσσεβὴς
ἐσφάλλετο προσκύνησιν, ἀλλὰ καὶ περὶ τῶν πρεσβειῶν τῆς παναγίου θεοτόκου,
καὶ πάντων τῶν ἁγίων καὶ τὰ λείψανα αὐτῶν ὁ παμμίαρος, ὡς οἱ διδάσκαλοι
αὐτοῦ Ἄραβες, ἐβδελύττετο.   The persecutions also of the opponents of
images have been greatly exaggerated by later historians, see Walch x.
286.

soldiers as a general. After *Artabasdus*, who had endeavoured to procure more adherents to his cause by favouring image-worship, had been conquered (741–743),[10] and while this practice was constantly assuming a more fanatical character, especially among the monks, the emperor procured its solemn rejection, by calling a general council at *Constantinople* (754),[11] though the decrees of this council were not admitted in the East,[12] and at Rome.[13] And because the monasteries were the places of resort to which

[10] Theophanes p. 347 ss.

[11] The ὅρος of this council in the Acta Concilii Nic. ii. ap. Mansi xiii. 205 ss. cf. p. 216 : Ἀπέστησεν ἡμᾶς (ʼΙ. Χ.) ἐκ τῆς φθοροποιοῦ τῶν δαιμόνων διδασκαλίας ἤτοι τῆς τῶν εἰδώλων πλάνης τε καὶ λατρείας καὶ τὴν ἐν πνεύματι καὶ ἀληθείᾳ προσκύνησιν παραδέδωκεν. p. 221: Πάλιν δὲ—ὁ τῆς κακίας δημιουργὸς οὐκ ἠπόρησε κατὰ διαφόρους καιρούς τε καὶ τρόπους πονηρᾶς ἐπινοίας, ὥστε ὑπὸ χεῖρα δι᾽ ἀπάτης ἑαυτῷ ποιῆσαι τὸ ἀνθρώπινον· ἀλλ᾽ ἐν προσχήματι Χριστιανισμοῦ τὴν εἰδωλολατρείαν κατὰ τὸ λεληθὸς ἐπανήγαγε, πείσας τοῖς ἰδίοις σοφίσμασι τοὺς πρὸς αὐτὸν ὁρῶντας μὴ ἀποστῆναι τῆς κτίσεως, ἀλλὰ ταύτην προσκυνεῖν καὶ ταύτην σέβεσθαι, καὶ θεὸν τὸ ποίημα οἴεσθαι τῇ τοῦ Χριστοῦ κλήσει ἐπονομαζόμενον. p. 225 : Διὸ δὴ καθὼς πάλαι ὁ τῆς σωτηρίας ἡμῶν ἀρχηγὸς καὶ τελειωτὴς Ἰησοῦς τοὺς ἑαυτοῦ πανσόφους μαθητάς καὶ ἀποστόλους τῇ τοῦ παναγεστάτου πνεύματος δυνάμει ἐπὶ ἐκμειώσει τῶν τοιούτων κατὰ παντὸς ἐξαπέστειλεν, οὕτως καὶ νῦν τοὺς αὐτοῦ θεράποντας, καὶ τῶν ἀποστόλων ἐφαμίλλους, πιστοὺς ἡμῶν βασιλεῖς ἐξανέστησε, τῇ τοῦ αὐτοῦ πνεύματος σοφισθέντας δυνάμει, πρὸς καταρτισμὸν μὲν ἡμῶν καὶ διδασκαλίαν, καθαίρεσιν δὲ δαιμονικῶν ὀχυρωμάτων ἐπαιρομένων κατὰ τῆς γνώσεως τοῦ θεοῦ, καὶ ἔλεγξιν διαβολικῆς μεθοδείας καὶ πλάνης. p. 251 : that they who painted pictures of Christ fell either into the Eutychian, or p. 255 : into the Nestorian heresy, p. 324 : ὁμοφώνως ὁρίζομεν, ἀπόβλητον εἶναι καὶ ἀλλοτρίαν καὶ ἐβδελυγμένην ἐκ τῆς τῶν Χριστιανῶν ἐκκλησιας πᾶσαν εἰκόνα ἐκ παντοίας ὕλης καὶ χρωματουργικῆς τῶν ζωγράφων κακοτεχνίας πεποιημένην· (p. 328) : μηκέτι τολμᾶν ἄνθρωπον τὸν οἱονδήποτε ἐπιτηδεύειν τὸ τοιοῦτον ἀσεβὲς καὶ ἀνόσιον ἐπιτήδευμα. ὁ δὲ τολμῶν ἀπὸ τοῦ παρόντος κατασκευάσαι εἰκόνα, ἢ προσκυνῆσαι, ἢ στῆσαι ἐν ἐκκλησίᾳ ἢ ἐν ἰδιωτικῷ οἴκῳ, ἢ κρύψαι, εἰ μὲν ἐπίσκοπος ἢ πρεσβύτερος ἢ διάκονος εἶεν, καθαιρείσθω· εἰ δὲ μονάζων ἢ λαϊκὸς ἀναθεματιζέσθω, καὶ τοῖς βασιλικοῖς νόμοις ὑπεύθυνος ἔστω ὡς ἐναντίος τῶν τοῦ θεοῦ προσταγμάτων, καὶ ἐχθρὸς τῶν πατρικῶν δογμάτων. Among the thirteen anathemas affixed are to be remarked ix. (p. 345) : Εἴ τις οὐχ ὁμολογεῖ τὴν ἀειπάρθενον Μαρίαν κυρίως καὶ ἀληθῶς θεοτόκον, ὑπερτέραν τε εἶναι πάσης ὁρατῆς καὶ ἀοράτου κτίσεως, καὶ μετὰ εἰλικρινοῦς πίστεως τὰς αὐτῆς οὐκ ἐξαιτεῖται πρεσβείας ὡς παρρησίαν ἐχούσης πρὸς τὸν ἐξ αὐτῆς τεχθέντα θεὸν ἡμῶν, ἀνάθεμα. xi. (p. 348) : Εἴ τις οὐχ ὁμολογεῖ ἅπαντας τοὺς ἀπ᾽ αἰῶνος καὶ μέχρι τοῦ νῦν ἁγίους, πρὸ νόμου, καὶ ἐν νόμῳ, καὶ ἐν χάριτι τῷ θεῷ, εὐαρεστήσαντας, τιμίους εἶναι ἐνώπιον αὐτοῦ ψυχῇ τε καὶ σώματι, καὶ τὰς τούτων οὐκ ἐξαιτεῖται προσευχὰς ὡς παρρησίαν ἐχόντων ὑπὲρ τοῦ κόσμου πρεσβεύειν, κατὰ τὴν ἐκκλησιαστικὴν παράδοσιν, ἀνάθεμα.

[12] Συνοδικὸν of Theodore, patriarch of Jerusalem, about 766, in Actis Conc. Nic. ii. ap. Mansi xii. 1135. comp. Walch x. 376.

[13] Cf. Concilium Lateranense A.D. 769 ap. Mansi xii. 713 ss.

the picture-worshippers now fled, and which nourished their fanaticism that frequently broke forth into tumultuous resistance,
severer measures against the monks followed, amounting in some
provinces to absolute persecution.[14] By this means, Constantine
has become the object of monkish abhorrence; and they have
revenged themselves richly on him by historical misrepresenta-
tions.[15]

Under *Leo IV. Chazarus* (775–780), the laws against image-
worship were still rigidly enforced. *Irene*, on the contrary, was
friendly to it (780–802). At first, indeed, she was compelled to
be cautious, by the voice of the capital and the soldiery; but
afterwards, in conjunction with the new patriarch *Tarasius*,[16] she
called a synod, which was broken up by an insurrection at Constantinople,[17] but met again at *Nice* (Conc. œcumenic vii., 787),
and restored image-worship.[18] The decrees of this synod remained

[14] Constantine (762) first put Andrew to death, ἐλέγχοντα αὐτοῦ τὴν
ἀσέβειαν, καὶ Οὐάλεντα νέον καὶ Ἰουλιανὸν ἀποκαλοῦντα αὐτόν. Theophanes
p. 363. Continued obstinacy called forth a series of cruelties from 766
to 775. Theophan. p. 367 ss. Nicephorus p. 45 ss. Acta S. Stephani
in the Analectis graecis ed. Monach. Benedict. Paris. 1688. 4. p. 396
ss. Comp. Walch x. 403. Schlosser S. 228 ff.
[15] Comp. Walch x. 413. On the surnames Copronymos (see the
account of Theoph. p. 334) and Caballinus see Walch x. 356.—Against
Theophanes, p. 370 : πανταχοῦ μὲν τάς πρεσβείας τῆς παρθένου καὶ θεοτόκου
καὶ πάντων τῶν ἁγίων ἐγγράφως, ὡς ἀνωφελεῖς, καὶ ἀγράφως ἀποκηρύττων, δἰ ὧν
ἡμῖν πηγάζει πᾶσα βοήθεια· καὶ τὰ ἅγια λείψανα αὐτῶν κατορύττων, καὶ ἀφανῆ
ποιῶν κ. τ. λ. (cf. not. 9) see Walch x. 401. But much superstition
connected with the relics certainly disappeared. Concil. Nic. ii. can. 7.
ap. Mansi xiii. 427 : τῇ οὖν ἀσεβεῖ αἱρέσει τῶν Χριστιανοκατηγόρων καί ἄλλα
ἀσεβήματα συνηκολούθησαν·—ἕτερά τινα ἔθη παραλελύκασιν, ἃ χρὴ ἀνανεωθῆναι·
—ὅσοι οὖν σεπτοὶ ναοὶ καθιερώθησαν ἐκτὸς ἁγίων λειψάνων μαρτύρων, ὁρίζομεν
ἐν αὐτοῖς κατάθεσιν γενέσθαι λειψάνων μετὰ καὶ τῆς συνήθους εὐχῆς.
[16] S. Tarasii vita by his pupil Ignatius Acta SS. Febr. iii. 576.
[17] See in particular the συγγραφὴ σύντομος δηλωτικὴ τῶν πραχθέντων πρὸ
τῆς συνόδου ap. Mansi xii. 990 ss. Theophanes p. 389.
[18] Its acts in Mansi xii. 951—xiii. 820. In the ὅρος Actio vii. ap.
Mansi xiii. 377 it is said : ὁρίζομεν σὺν ἀκριβείᾳ πάσῃ καὶ ἐμμελείᾳ παραπλησίως τῷ τύπῳ τοῦ τιμίου καὶ ζωοποιοῦ σταυροῦ ἀνατίθεσθαι τὰς σεπτὰς καὶ ἁγίας
εἰκόνας—ἐν ταῖς ἁγίαις τοῦ θεοῦ ἐκκλησίαις, ἐν ἱεροῖς σκεύεσι καὶ ἐσθῆσι, τοί-
χοις τε καὶ σανίσιν, οἴκοις τε καὶ ὁδοῖς,—(ὅσῳ γὰρ συνεχῶς δἰ εἰκονικῆς ἀνατυ-
πώσεως ὁρῶνται, τοσοῦτον καὶ οἱ ταύτας θεώμενοι διανίστανται πρὸς τὴν τῶν
πρωτοτύπων μνήμην τε καὶ ἐπιπόθησιν) καὶ ταύταις ἀσπασμὸν καὶ τιμητικὴν προσκύνησιν ἀπονέμειν, (οὐ μὴν τὴν κατὰ πίστιν ἡμῶν ἀληθινὴν λατρείαν, ἣ πρέπει μόνῃ
τῇ θείᾳ φύσει, ἀλλ᾽ ὃν τρόπον τῷ τύπῳ τοῦ τιμίου καὶ ζωοποιοῦ σταυροῦ καὶ τοῖς
ἁγίοις εὐαγγελίοις καὶ τοῖς λοιποῖς ἱεροῖς ἀναθήμασι) καὶ θυμιαμάτων καὶ φώτων

also in force under *Nicephorus* (802–811) and *Michael Rhangabe* (811–813), though there were always many opposed to such worship, especially among the troops.[19]

Leo V. Armenus (813–820), one of the best princes,[20] appeared against image-worship,[21] which had been carried by the heat of controversy to the greatest absurdities,[22] caused it to be prohibited

προσαγωγὴν πρὸς τὴν τούτων τιμὴν ποιεῖσθαι, καθὼς καὶ τοῖς ἀρχαίοις εὐσεβῶς εἴθισται· ἡ γὰρ τῆς εἰκόνος τιμὴ ἐπὶ τὸ πρωτότυπον διαβαίνει, καὶ ὁ προσκυνῶν τὴν εἰκόνα προσκυνεῖ ἐν αὐτῇ τοῦ ἐγγραφομένου τὴν ὑπόστασιν. In the confession of faith of the synod, ib. p. 132, it is said : τὰς ἁγίας καὶ σεπτὰς εἰκόνας ἀποδεχόμεθα καὶ ἀσπαζόμεθα, καὶ περιπτυσσόμεθα,—τιμῶμεν καὶ ἀσπα-ζόμεθα, καὶ τιμητικῶς προσκυνοῦμεν·—Exclamations of the synod : Νέου Κωνσταντίνου καὶ νέας Ἑλένης αἰωνία ἡ μνήμη, and τῷ μὴ ἀσπαζομένῳ τὰς ἁγίας εἰκόνας ἀνάθεμα.

[19] Comp. the relation of Theophanes p. 425 : some (τινὲς τῶν δυσσεβῶν τῆς μιαρᾶς αἱρέσεως τοῦ θεοστυγοῦς Κωνσταντίνου) broke into the imperial tomb, προσέπιπτον τῷ τοῦ πλάνου μνήματι τοῦτον ἐπικαλούμενοι, καὶ οὐ θεόν· ἀνάστηθι, λέγοντες, καὶ βοήθησον τῇ πολιτείᾳ ἀπολλυμένῃ.

[20] Particular sources : The chronographica narratio eorum quae tempore Leonis contigerunt annexed to Theophanes ; S. Nicephori Patr. vita by Ignatius in the Actis SS. Mart. ii. 296, Greek in the Append. p. 704 ; S. Nicetae vita by Theosterictus Acta SS. April. i. 261, Greek in the Append. p. xxii. ; S. Theophanis vita prefixed to his chronography and Act. SS. Mart. ii. 218 ; S. Theodori Studitae vita by Michael Monachus in Sirmondii opp. v. i. S. Nicolai Studitae vita in Act. SS. Febr. i. 538.

[21] Chronograph. narratio p. 435 : λέγων πρός τινας ὁμόφρονας αὐτοῦ, ὅτι τίνος ἕνεκέν, φησι, ταῦτά πως ἔχουσιν οἱ Χριστιανοὶ κατακυριευόμενοι ὑπὸ τῶν ἐθνῶν ; ἐμοὶ δοκεῖ διὰ τὸ προσκυνεῖσθαι τὰς εἰκόνας, καὶ ἄλλο οὐδέν· καὶ βούλομαι αὐτὰς καταστρέψαι· βλέπετε γάρ, φησιν, ὅσοι βασιλεῖς ἐδέξαντο καὶ προσεκύνησαν αὐτὰς, ἀπέθανον, οἱ μὲν ἐκδιωχθέντες, οἱ δὲ ἐν πολέμῳ πεσόντες· μόνοι δὲ οἱ μὴ προσκυνήσαντες αὐτὰς ἰδίῳ θανάτῳ ἕκαστος εἰς τὴν βασιλείαν αὐτοῦ ἐτελεύτησε, καὶ μετὰ δόξης προκομισθεὶς εἰς τὰ τῶν βασιλέων κοιμητήρια ἐτάφη ἐν τοῖς Ἀποστόλοις. λοιπὸν ἐκείνους κἀγὼ βούλομαι μιμήσασθαι, καὶ καταστρέψαι τὰς εἰκόνας κ. τ. λ. Still more remarkable are the words of the emperor to the patriarch Nicephorus ib. p. 437 : ὁ λαὸς σκανδαλίζεται διὰ τὰς εἰκόνας, λέγοντες, ὅτι κακῶς αὐτὰς προσκυνοῦμεν, καὶ ὅτι διὰ τοῦτο τὰ ἔθνη κυριεύουσιν ἡμῶν· συγκατάβα τι μικρὸν, καὶ ποίησον οἰκονομίαν εἰς τὸν λαὸν, καὶ τὰ χαμηλὰ περιέλωμεν· εἰ δὲ μὴ βούλει, πεῖσον ἡμᾶς δι' οὗ ἕνεκεν [leg. ἐκεῖνα] προσκυνεῖτε, τῆς γραφῆς μὴ ἐχούσης ῥητῶς πώποτε. The patriarch had no other answer than : ἡμεῖς αὐτὰ, καλῶς ἐξ ἀρχῆς καὶ ἄνωθεν ὁρισθέντα ὑπό τε τῶν Ἀποστόλων καὶ τῶν πατέρων, οὔτε παρασαλεύομεν, οὔτε περισσότερόν τι ἐν αὐτοῖς οἰκονομοῦμεν.

[22] Cf. Michaelis Balbi et Theophili Impp. epist. ad Ludov. Pium A. D. 824 (preserved in Latin in the Acts of the Paris Synod, A. D. 825) ap. Goldast. l. c. p. 610 ss. Mansi xiv. 417 : There we read : multi de ecclesiasticis seu et laicis viris alieni de apostolicis traditionibus facti,

by a synod at Constantinople (815),[23] and punished the disobedient, for the most part, monks, under the leadership of the fanatical *Theodore Studita. Michael II. Balbus* (820–829), tolerated
the practice in private,[24] without, however, satisfying the friends
of images by that concession.   But since such toleration led to
increasing encroachments, *Theophilus* (829–842) renewed vigorous measures against images, and their zealous defenders, the
monks.[25]   Soon after his death, *Theodora* once more allowed the
worship of images to be ecclesiastically adopted (842),[26] and
caused the memory of this triumph to be perpetuated by a yearly

et neque paternos terminos custodientes, facti sunt inventores malarum
rerum.   Primum quidem honorificas et vivificas cruces de sacris templis
expellebant, et in eadem loca imagines statuebant ponebantque lucernas coram eis, simul et incensum adolebant, atque eas in tali honore
habebant, sicut honorificum et vivificum lignum, in quo Christus verus
Deus noster crucifigi dignatus est propter nostram salutem.   Psallebant
et adorabant, atque ab eisdem imaginibus auxilium petebant.   Plerique
autem linteaminibus easdem imagines circumdabant, et filiorum suorum
de baptismatis fontibus susceptrices faciebant.   (One Spatharius, who
had done this, is almost elevated to the rank of a saint by Theodorus
Stud. lib. i. epist. 17).   Alii vero religiosum habitum monasticum
sumere volentes, religiosiores personas postponebant, qui prius comam
capitis eorum suscipere solebant, adhibitis imaginibus quasi in sinum
earum decidere capillos eorum sinebant.   Quidam vero sacerdotum et
clericorum colores de imaginibus radentes, immiscuerunt oblationibus
et vino, et ex hac oblatione post missarum celebrationem dabant communicare volentibus.   Alii autem corpus Domini in manus imaginum
ponebant, unde communicare volentes accipere fecerunt.   Nonnulli
vero spreta ecclesia, in communibus domibus tabulis imaginum pro
altariis utebantur, et super eas sacrum ministerium celebrabant, et alia
multa his similia illicita, et nostrae religioni contraria in ecclesiis fiebant,
quae a doctioribus et sapientioribus viris satis indigna esse videbantur.
A counterpart of fanaticism in the Iconoclasts may be seen in vita
Stephani jun. above not. 9.
   [23] Cf. Mansi xiv. 235 ss.   Walch x. 687.   Especially Michaelis ep.
ad Lud. P. (l. c.) : Propterea statuerunt orthodoxi Imperatores et doctissimi Sacerdotes, locale adunare concilium.—Talia ubique communi
consilio fieri prohibuerunt, et imagines de humilioribus locis efferri
fecerunt, et eas, quae in sublimioribus locis positae erant, ut ipsa pictura pro scriptura haberetur, in suis locis consistere permiserunt, ne ab
indoctioribus et infirmioribus adorarentur, sed neque eis lucernas accen-
derent, neque incensum adolerent, prohibuerunt.
   [24] Theodori Studitae vita c. 102—122 et Nicolai Stud. vita.
   [25] Still there are no instances of capital punishments, Walch x. 715.
   [26] Walch x. 764 u. S. 784 ff.   Schlosser S. 544 ss.

festival (ἡ κυριακὴ τῆς ὀρθοδοξίας).[27] Still opponents of images appear afterwards in the Greek Church ;[28] but as the opposition to them did not arise from a true development of the popular mind, but solely from the emperor's will, it left no traces of a deep awakening in the direction of reform.

§ 2.

CONDITION OF THE GREEK CHURCH.

In this period of controversy about images, when orthodoxy was so frequently changed according to court-caprice, the Greek clergy, yielding to the fear of man and immoderate ambition, sank to an abandoned condition;[1] while, on the other hand, the compulsion exercised towards the monks, called forth the most fearful fanaticism.   Hence every thing bowed before such fanaticism at the times in which the monks' cause was triumphant. As the Church had lost her free characteristic nature, so also had the theological sciences.   The only person worthy of distinction is *Johannes Damascenus (Chrysorrhoas, Mansur)* from the year

[27] Leo Allatius de dominicis et hebdomadibus Graecorum appended to his work de eccl. occid. atque orient. perpetua consensione, Colon. Agripp. 1648. 4. p. 1432.   Walch x. 799.

[28] According to Nicolai Papae i. epist. ad universos Catholicos (ap. Mansi xv. 161) he had been assured by the Byzantine ambassadors who invited him to the synod of Constantinople A. D. 861. maxime eandem ecclesiam (Constantinopolitanam) ab Iconomachis redivivam contentionem excitantibus vexari, Christumque per singula conventicula blasphemari.   Hence the decrees in favour of images at the synod of Constantinople A. D. 869. can. iii. and vii. ap. Mansi xvi. 400 and 401, and at that of A. D. 879, ap. Mansi xvii. 494.   Comp. Walch x. 808.

[1] For example, the patriarch Anastasius, at first a tool of Leo Isaurus, but afterwards changed under the pretender Artabasdus (Theophanes p. 348 : κρατήσας τὰ τίμια καὶ ζωοποιὰ ξύλα ὤμοσε τῷ λαῷ· ὅτι μὰ τὸν προσηλωθέντα ἐν αὐτοῖς, οὕτως μοι εἶπε Κωνσταντῖνος ὁ βασιλεὺς, ὅτι μὴ λογίσῃ υἱὸν θεοῦ εἶναι, ὃν ἔτεκεν ἡ Μαρία, τὸν λεγόμενον Χριστὸν, εἰ μὴ ψιλὸν ἄνθρωπον· ἡ γὰρ Μαρία αὐτὴν ἔτεκεν, ὡς ἔτεκεν ἐμὲ ἡ μήτηρ μου ἡ Μαρία).   Constantine punished him in the severest manner, Theoph. p. 353 : πάλιν δὲ ὡς ὁμόφρονα αὐτοῦ ἐκφοβήσας καὶ δουλώσας ἐν τῷ θρόνῳ τῆς ἱερωσύνης ἐκάθισε.—Comp. the mode in which the bishops, who, just before the synod of Nice, had been violently opposed to the worship of pictures (Theoph. p. 389. and the συγγραφὴ σύντομος ap. Mansi xii. 990), retracted their sentiments at it, Act. 1. ap. Mansi xii. 1015 ss.

730, a monk in the Laura of St Sabas, † about 760.[2]   On the other hand, the works of the fanatical *Theodore*, abbot of the monastery Studium from 798, † 826,[3] are only of historical importance.

§ 3.

PAULICIANS.

Petri Siculi (about 870) historia Manichæorum (gr. et lat. ed. Matth. Rade-rus, Ingolst. 1604. 4.   J. C. L. Gieseler.   Gotting. 1846. 4.)   Photius adv. recentiores Manichaeos libb. iv. (in J. Christ. Wolfiianeodotis gr. T. i. et ii. Hamb. 1722. 23. 8. and in Gallandii bibl. pp. xiii. 603.)   Armenian accounts respecting the Paulicians,[1] in the Tübingen Quartalschrift. 1835. S. 54.   F. Schmidii hist. Paulicianorum orientalium diss.   Hafniae. 1826. 8. Die Paulicianer, a treatise in Winer's u. Engelhardt's neuem krit. Journ. d. theol. Literat.   Bd. 7. St. 1. u. St. 2.   Gieseler's Untersuchungen über die Geschichte der Paulicianer, in the theol. Studien u. Kritiken.   Jahrg. 1829. Heft. 1. S. 79 ss.   Neander's KG. iii. 492.   Gfrörer's KG. iii. i. 196.

In Armenia, the struggle of Christianity with Parsism[2] had also favoured the blending together of both religions, and thus the dualist-christian parties called *children of the sun*, *i.e.*, *sun-worshippers* by the other Armenian Christians, had maintained

---

[2] His principal work Πηγὴ γνώσεως in three parts, 1) τὰ φιλοσοφικά, 2) περὶ αἱρέσεων, 3) ἔκδοσις ἀκριβὴς τῆς ὀρθοδόξου πίστεως. (cf. C. J. Lénström de expositione fidei orthodoxae auct. Jo. Damasceno. Upsal. 1839.   Ritter's Gesch. d. christl. Philos. ii. 553.)—Besides ἱερὰ παράλληλα.   Controversial writings against heretics, discourses, letters, ed. Michael le Quien, Paris. 1712.   2 voll. fol.

[3] His numerous writings, discourses, and letters, against the Iconoclasts are for the greater part collected in Jac. Sirmondii opp. T. v. Besides these the κατηχήσεις (lat. ed. J. Livinejus, Antverp. 1602. 8. cf. J. J. Müller Studium coenob. Constant. illustratum diss. philol. hist. Lips. 1721. p. 32 ss.) and much beside in part unprinted, cf. Fabricii bibl. gr. T. ix. p. 234.

[1] The oldest in the treatise of Johannes v. Ozun (patriarch of Armenia from 718-729) against the Paulicians, in Domini Johannis Philos. Ozniensis, Armenorum Catholici, opera, ed. J. N. Aucher. Venet. 1834. 8.   Comp. Neumann's Gesch. der armen. Literatur S. 107.   In this work, however, there is less a representation of the peculiarities of the Paulicians than reports of scandalous actions which were every where circulated respecting the Dualists.

[2] Comp. above Div. 2. § 107.

their existence longest in this country.[3] About 660, one *Constantine* appeared as a reformer, proceeding from a dualistic, probably a Marcionite Church, in Mananalis in Samosata. This man had been moved by reading the New Testament writings, especially those of Paul; and made his public appearance in the like-minded church at *Kibossa*, situated in the province of Colonia in *Armenia prima*. His design was, without renouncing his dualistic fundamental principle, to restore, as a genuine disciple of Paul (Sylvanus), a genuine Pauline Church (Macedonia), († about 684). He found successors like himself (*Symeon*, Titus † about 690. *Paulus* † about 715. *Gegnäsius*, Timotheus † about 745. *Josephus*, Epaphroditus † about 775. *Baanes* till 801), under whom the *Paulicians* (Παυλικιανοί)[4] continued to spread themselves farther into Asia Minor, and had *Phanaröa* in Helenopontus as their chief settlement. In addition to the peculiar dualistic doctrines, their characteristic marks were the affixing of a high value to the universal use of the Holy Scriptures,[5] and a rejection of all externalities in religion.[6] Their abhorrence of

[3] Tschamtschean's (respecting him see Div. 2. § 112, not. 3.) Gesch. Armenieus i. 765. Neander iv. 451.

[4] Ap. Germanus de haeresibus et synodis in the Spicil. Rom. vii. i. 70 (comp. § 1, not. 5) Παυλιανίται. The affirmation, that they received these names from two Manicheans, Paul and John, sons of Callinice, who are said, at an earlier but uncertain period, to have spread Manicheism from Samosata to Phanaröa, is nothing but a later Catholic fiction. Doubtless, the name was originally given by them by the Catholic Church on account of the high value they attached to Paul. See Theol. Studien u. Krit. 1829. S. 82 ff. They did not so style themselves, Photius i. c. 6: τοὺς μὲν ἀληθῶς ὄντας Χριστιανοὺς Ῥωμαίους οἱ τρισαλιτήριοι ὀνομάζουσιν, ἑαυτοῖς δὲ τὴν κλῆσιν—τῶν Χριστιανῶν περιάπτουσιν. c. 9: καθολικὴν δὲ ἐκκλησίαν τὰ ἑαυτῶν καλοῦσι συνέδρια.

[5] To Sergius, the Paulician female, who converted him, said (Petrus Sic. p. 56): ἴνατι τὰ θεῖα οὐκ ἀναγινώσκεις Εὐαγγέλια; to which he replied: οὐκ ἔξεστιν ἡμῖν κοσμικοῖς οὖσιν ταῦτα ἀναγινώσκειν, εἰ μὴ τοῖς ἱερεῦσι μόνοις. (It was not an ecclesiastical regulation, but a popular delusion, like that refuted by Chrysostomus de Lazaro orat. iii. Opp. iii. 56, that the reading of the bible is only for monks.) On which she said: οὐκ ἔστιν οὕτως ὡς σὺ ὑπολαμβάνεις· οὐ γάρ ἐστι προσωποληψία παρὰ τῶ θεῷ· πάντας γὰρ θέλει σωθῆναι ὁ Κύριος, καὶ εἰς ἐπίγνωσιν ἀληθείας ἐλθεῖν.

[6] Their errors were according to Petrus Sic. p. 16 ss.: Πρῶτον μὲν γάρ ἐστι τὸ κατ' αὐτοὺς γνώρισμα τὸ δύο ἀρχὰς ὁμολογεῖν, πονηρὸν θεὸν καὶ ἀγαθόν· καὶ ἄλλον εἶναι τοῦδε τοῦ κόσμου ποιητὴν καὶ ἐξουσιαστήν, ἕτερον δὲ τοῦ μέλλοντος (namely τὸν πατέρα ἐπουράνιον). To the Catholics they

o

images might have brought many a vigorous opponent of image-worship nearer to them ;[7] but under the image-assailing emperors they could the less reckon on their being spared, because the enemies of images had to avoid the danger of being classed with them.[8] At first, gross immorality of various kinds was also charged against the Paulicians, into which, bye-paths from their system may have certainly led them ;[9] but afterwards, when

said : ὑμεῖς πιστεύετε εἰς τὸν κοσμοποιητήν· ἡμεῖς δὲ εἰς ἐκεῖνον περὶ οὗ ἐν Εὐαγγελίοις ὁ Κύριος λέγει, ὅτι οὔτε φωνὴν αὐτοῦ ἀκηκόατε οὔτε εἶδος αὐτοῦ ἑωράκατε.—Δεύτερον τὸ τὴν πανύμνητον καὶ ἀειπάρθενον θεοτόκον μηδὲ κἂν ἐν ψιλῇ τῶν ἀγαθῶν ἀνθρώπων τάττειν ἀπεχθῶς ἀπαριθμήσει, μηδὲ ἐξ αὐτῆς γεννηθῆναι τὸν Κύριον, ἀλλ' οὐρανόθεν τὸ σῶμα κατενεγκεῖν (Photius i. c. 7 : δι' αὐτῆς δὲ, ὡς διὰ σωλῆνος, διεληλυθέναι.) Καὶ ὅτι μετὰ τὸν τοῦ Κυρίου τόκον καὶ ἄλλους, φασὶν, υἱοὺς ἐγέννησεν ἐκ τοῦ Ἰωσήφ. (According to Photius they were fond of expressing themselves thus : πιστεύομεν εἰς τὴν παναγίαν θεοτόκον, ἐν ᾗ εἰσῆλθεν καὶ ἐξῆλθεν ὁ κύριος, and understood this with reference to Gal. iv. 26, τὴν ἄνω Ἱερουσαλήμ, and said, ἐν αὐτῇ πρόδρομον ὑπὲρ ἡμῶν εἰσελθεῖν τὸν Χμιστόν.)—Τρίτον τὸ τὴν θείαν καὶ φρικτὴν τῶν ἁγίων μυστηρίων τοῦ σώματος καὶ αἵματος τοῦ Κυρίου καὶ θεοῦ ἡμῶν μετάληψιν ἀποτρέψαι· οὐ μόνον δὲ, ἀλλὰ καὶ ἄλλους περὶ τοῦτο πείθειν οἴεσθαι· λέγοντες, ὅτι οὐκ ἦν ἄρτος καὶ οἶνος, ὃν ὁ Κύριος ἐδίδου τοῖς μαθηταῖς αὐτοῦ ἐπὶ τοῦ δείπνου, ἀλλὰ συμβολικῶς τὰ ῥήματα αὐτοῦ αὐτοῖς ἐδίδου, ὡς ἄρτον καὶ οἶνον. (Phot. i. 9 : τὸ σωτήριον διαπτύοντες βάπτισμα, ὑποπλάττονται παραδέχεσθαι αὐτὸ, τὰ τοῦ Εὐαγγελίου ῥήματα τῇ τοῦ βαπτίσματος φωνῇ ὑποβάλλοντες· καὶ γάρ φασιν, ὁ Κύριος ἔφη· ἐγώ εἰμι τὸ ὕδωρ τὸ ζῶν.)—Τέταρτον τὸ τὸν τύπον καὶ τὴν ἐνέργειαν καὶ δύναμιν τοῦ τιμίου καὶ ζωοποιοῦ σταυροῦ μὴ ἀποδέχεσθαι, ἀλλὰ μυρίαις ὕβρεσι περιβάλλειν. (Phot. i. 7 : τὸν σταυρὸν, ἅτε δὴ ξύλον φασὶ, καὶ κακούργων ὄργανον, καὶ ὑπὸ ἀρὰν κείμενον, οὐ δεῖ προσκυνεῖν καὶ ἀσπάζεσθαι.)—Πέμπτον τὸ μὴ ἀποδέχεσθαι αὐτοὺς τὴν οἱανοῦν βίβλον παλαιὰν, πλάνους καὶ λῃστὰς τοὺς προφήτας ἀποκαλοῦντες. Of the New Testament they adopted four gospels, fourteen epistles of Paul, the epistles of James, John, and Jude, and the Acts of the Apostles, with unaltered text : τὰς δύο καθολικὰς τοῦ μεγάλου—Πέτρου τοῦ πρωταποστόλου οὐ δέχονται, ἀπεχθῶς πρὸς αὐτὸν διακείμενοι, καὶ ὕβρεσι καὶ ὀνειδισμοῖς μυρίοις περιβάλλοντες. (Phot. i. 8 : ὅτι γέγονεν ἐξαρνός, φασι, τῆς εἰς τὸν διδάσκαλον καὶ Χριστὸν πίστεως, perhaps with reference to Gal. ii. 11 ff. See Theol. Studien und Krit. 1829. S. 109.)—Ἕκτον τὸ τοὺς πρεσβυτέρους τῆς ἐκκλησίας ἀποτρέπεσθαι· φασὶ δὲ, ὅτι τηνικαῦτα οἱ πρεσβύτεροι κατὰ τοῦ Κυρίου συνήχθησαν, καὶ διὰ τοῦτο οὐ χρὴ αὐτοὺς ὀνομάζεσθαι, ψιλῷ τῷ ὀνόματι καὶ μόνῳ ἀπεχθανόμενοι. According to Photius i. 9, they called their houses of meeting προσευχάς.

[7] John of Ozun (see note 1) says, that the Paulicians begin their attempts at conversion with attacking image-worship (p. 79), and that many Iconoclasts, driven out from the Catholic Church, had gone over to them (p. 89).

[8] Theol Stud. u. Krit. 1829. S. 89.

[9] Theol. Stud. u. Krit. 1829. S. 120 ff.

Sergius, as **Tychicus**, set himself in antagonism to Baanes surnamed ὁ ῥυπαρός on account of his immorality (801), a beneficial reform was effected in the greater part of the sect who sided with him,[10] and he procured for himself the reputation of a second founder, not only by this antagonism, but by the unwearied and successful efforts he put forth for the extension of the sect.[11] But this very enlargement gave rise to new persecutions, which were so violent, under Leo the Armenian, that many Paulicians, and with them Sergius too, fled from lesser Armenia to the territories of the Saracens. The Emir in Melitene assigned to them, as a place of residence, the little town of *Argaum*; from which place, notwithstanding the dissuasions of Sergius,[12] they began unceasing predatory marches into the Byzantine territory. After Sergius's death († 835), they resolved to entrust the spiritual oversight of the Church to all the συνεκδήμοις of it, instead of to one person.[13] But after a political character also had now been

[10] Petrus Sic. p. 58 ss.: οἱ γὰρ πρὸ αὐτοῦ (Σεργίου) ἀναφανέντες, εἰ καὶ διὰ τὸν δυσώδη βόρβορον τῆς ἀκολασίας καὶ τὴν αἰσχρουργίαν τῶν μιασμάτων καὶ τὰς εἰς θεὸν βλασφημίας ἐξαίρετοι τῇ κακίᾳ ὑπῆρχον, ἀλλ' ὅμως φευκταῖοι τοῖς ἀνθρώποις καὶ βδελυκτοὶ πᾶσιν ἐφαίνοντο· ὅθεν καὶ ὀλίγοι οἱ ἐξ αὐτῶν ἀπατώμενοι· οὗτος δὲ τοὺς μὲν μιασμοὺς καὶ τὰς πολλὰς ἀκολασίας αὐτῶν ἀποβαλόμενος, τὰς δυσφημίας δὲ πάσας ὡς σωτήρια περιπτυξάμενος δόγματα, ἀρετάς τινας δολίως ὑπεκρίνετο, καὶ εὐσεβείας μόρφωσιν περικαλύψας τὸν λύκον ὡς ἐν κωδίῳ προβάτου,—ἐδόκει τοῖς ἀγνοοῦσιν ἄριστος ὁδηγὸς σωτηρίας καταφαίνεσθαι.—Ἐν τοιαύταις τοίνυν ταῖς μεθοδείαις μέχρι τῆς δεῦρο τοὺς ἀστηρίκτους ἐξαπατῶσιν.
[11] He himself said on this point in one of his letters (Petrus Sic. p. 60. Phot. i. c. 21): ἀπὸ ἀνατολῶν καὶ μέχρι δυσμῶν, καὶ βορρᾶ καῖ νότου ἔδραμον κηρύσσων τὸ Εὐαγγέλιον τοῦ Χριστοῦ, τοῖς ἐμοῖς γόνασι βαρήσας. In another letter he says, respecting the establishment of the different churches (Petrus Sic. p. 66): τὴν ἐν Κορίνθῳ (probably Episparis in Phanaröa. See Phot. i. 18) ἐκκλησίαν ᾠκοδόμησε Παῦλος, τὴν δὲ Μακεδονίαν (Kibossa) Σιλουανὸς (Constantinus) καὶ Τίτος (Symeon)· καὶ Ἀχαΐαν (Mananalis) ἀνιστόρισε Τιμόθεος (Gegnasius). Τὴν τῶν Φιλιππησίων ἐκκλησίαν ἐλειτούργησεν Ἐπαφρόδιτος (Josephus)· τὴν Λαοδικέων καὶ Ἐφεσίων ἐκκλησίαν, ἔτι δὲ καὶ τὴν τῶν Κολασσέων ἐμαθήτευσε Τυχικός (Sergius). Petrus adds: Κολασσαεῖς μὲν λέγει τοὺς Ἀργαούτας, Ἐφεσίους δὲ τοὺς ἐν Μοψουεστίᾳ, Λαοδικεῖς δὲ τοὺς κατοικοῦντας κύνας τὴν τοῦ κυνὸς χώραν (i. e., τοὺς Κυνοχωρίτας).
[12] He said (Petrus Sic. p. 62): ἐγὼ τῶν κακῶν τούτων ἀναίτιός εἰμι· πολλὰ γὰρ παρήγγελλον αὐτοῖς ἐκ τοῦ αἰχμαλωτίζειν τοὺς Ῥωμαίους ἀποστῆναι, καὶ οὐχ ὑπήκουσάν μοι.
[13] Petrus Sic. p. 70 s: Μαθηταὶ δὲ τούτου (Σεργίου) ὑπῆρχον μυστικώτεροι Μιχαὴλ κ. τ. λ. οὗτοι τοίνυν οἱ μαθηταὶ αὐτοῦ, οἱ καὶ συνέκδημοι (cf. Act.

o 2

forcibly impressed on it, it soon after received a temporal head. When the bigoted empress Theodora caused persecution to be renewed against them, fresh crowds of them fled to Argaum, under the leadership of *Karbeas* (about 844), who soon stepped forth at the head of the whole sect. Their power increased, partly by the union of the Baanites and Sergiots,[14] hitherto divided, and partly by the founding of new settlements, among which *Tephrica* soon became a border establishment very dangerous to the Byzantine territory.[15] Thus Karbeas, at the head of armies, could now give regular battle to the Byzantine generals, allied as he was with the Saracens.[16] During this time, there proceeded from the Paulicians an impulse towards a reform of the old dualistic parties in Armenia; and the sect of the *Thontrakians*, in the province of Ararat, was formed by one *Sembat*, between 833 and 854.[17]

.xix. 29, 2 Cor. viii. 19, in the same way as Marcion addressed his adherents, συνταλαίπωροι καὶ συμμισούμενοι. Tertull. adv. Marc. iv. 9 and 36) παρ᾽ αὐτοῖς λεγόμενοι, ὡς μιερεῖς (i. e., μιαροὶ ἱερεῖς) τινες, τὸν ἅπαντα λαὸν τὸν συναθροισθέντα ἐν τῷ ᾿Αργαοῦ, μετὰ τὸν τοῦ διδασκάλου αὐτῶν Σεργίου θάνατον, ταῖς διδασκαλίαις αὐτοῦ τε καὶ τῶν προηγησαμένων λυμαινόμενοι, ἰσότιμοι πάντες ὑπῆρχον, μηκέτι ἕνα διδάσκαλον ἀνακηρύξαντες, καθάπερ οἱ πρώην, ἀλλὰ πάντες ἴσοι ὄντες. ῎Εχουσι δὲ καὶ ὑποβεβηκότας μιερεῖς, νοταρίους παρ᾽ αὐτοῖς ὀνομαζομένους. Photius i. c. 9 : Τοὺς παρ᾽ αὐτοῖς ἱερέων τάξιν ἐπέχοντας οὐχ ἱερεῖς, ἀλλὰ συνεκδήμους καὶ νοταρίους ἐπονομάζουσιν. Οὗτοι δὲ οὔτε σχήματι, οὔτε διαίτῃ, οὔτε τινὶ ἄλλῳ τρόπῳ βίον σεμνότερον ἐπιτελοῦντι τὸ διάφορον αὐτῶν πρὸς τὸ πλῆθος ἐπιδείκνυνται.

[14] Petrus Sic. p. 70 : Μετὰ τὸν θάνατον Σεργίου, μὴ φέροντες οἱ αὐτοῦ μαθηταὶ ἑαυτῶν τὴν αἰσχύνην καὶ τὸν ὀνειδισμόν, ὃν παρὰ πάντων ὠνειδίζοντο, ἤρξαντο ἀποκτείνειν τοὺς Βανιώτας, ὅπως ἐξαλείψωσιν ἐξ ἑαυτῶν τὸν ὀνειδισμὸν αὐτῶν. Εἷς δέ τις, Θεόδοτος ὀνόματι, ὁ συνέκδημος Σεργίου, λέγει· " μηδὲν ὑμῖν καὶ τοῖς ἀνθρώποις τούτοις· πάντες γὰρ μέχρις ἀναδείξεως τοῦ διδασκάλου ἡμῶν μίαν πίστιν εἴχομεν." καὶ οὕτως τοῦ φονεύειν ἀπαύσαντο. Cf. Photius i. c. 23.

[15] Constantini Porphyrog. Continuator iv. c. 16.   Cedrenus p. 541.
[16] Constantini Porph. Cont. iv. c. 16. 23—25.
[17] Tschamtschean's Gesch. v. Armenien ii. 884.   Neander iv. 451. Neumann's Gesch. d. armen.   Liter. S. 127.

SECOND PART.

HISTORY OF THE WESTERN CHURCH.

Anastasii bibliothecarii (about 870) liber pontificalis (see Vol. i. Div. ii. preface, § 131). The Frank historians, especially Annales Laurissenses (usually called plebeji or Loiseliani) from 741—829 (the second part from 788 composed by Einhard): and Annales Einhardi from 741—829, a corrected version of the Laurissenses :—Annales Fuldenses from 680—901, the original reaches to 830, and continued in successive portions till 838, 863, 882, 887, and 901, by contemporaries.— Annales Bertiniani from 741—882, the original likewise to 830, from 835—861 composed by Prudentius, bishop of Troyes, and from 861—882 by Hincmar, archbishop of Rheims. All these works are best edited in the Monumenta Germaniae historica ed. G. H. Pertz. Scriptorum Tom. i. Hanover, 1826. fol.

Einhardi († 844) vita Caroli M. (Einhardi omnia quae exstant opera ed. A. Teulet. Tomi ii. Paris 1840. 43. 8. Life and conduct of Charlemagne described by Einhard. Introduction, original, explanation, collection of original documents, by J. C. Ideler. 2 Bde. Hamburg u. Gotha 1839. 8.) Monachi Sangallensis de gestis Caroli M. libb. ii. (884—887 probably not written by Notkerus balbulus, see Pertz Monum. Germ. ii. p. 729.) Thegani vita Ludovici Pii (written 835, with additions to 838). (Astronomii) Vita Imp. Lud. P. (Pertz ii. p. 604). Nithardi historiarum libb. iv. (written 841—843). All in the Monumenta Germaniae T. ii.

On the entire sources see J. Chr. F. Bähr's Gesch. d. röm. Literatur im karoling. Zeitalter (Carlsruhe 1840. 8.) S. 143 ss.

FIRST CHAPTER.

CONVERSION OF THE GERMANS BY BONIFACE.

Sources: Bonifacii epistt. ed. Nic. Serarius, Mogunt. 1605. recus. 1629. 4. Steph. Würdtwein, ibid. 1789. fol. (comp. Allgem, Lit.-Zeit. Octob. 1790. S. 49 ff.) Bonifacii vita by Willibald (about 760) in Monumenta Germaniae hist. ii. 331. by Othlonus (about 1050) ap. Canisius-Basnage iii. 337. cf. Acta SS. Junii i. 452. Mabillon Act. SS. Ord. Bened. saec. iii. ii. 1.

Works: Nic Serarii Moguntiacarum rerum [libri V. Mog. 1604. 4. denuo ed. G. Chr. Johannes, Francof. 1722. fol.] lib. tertius. Casp. Sagittarii antiquitates gentilismi et christianismi Thuringici, Jenae 1685. 4. H. Ph Gudenii diss. de. Bonif. Germanorum Apost. and ejusd. observatt. miscell. ex historia Bonifacii selectae. both Helmst. 1720. 4. J. S. Semler diss. de propagata per Bonifacium inter Germanos relig. chr. Hal. 1765.

J. F. Chr. Loffler's Bonifacius,Gotha 1812. 8. Bonifacius, d. Apostel. d.
Deutschen, v. J. Ch. A. Seiters. Mainz 1845. 8. H. J. Royaards Geschiedenis der Invoering en vestiging van het Christendom in Nederland. 3te
Uitg. Utrecht 1844 p. 219. F. W. Rettberg's Kirchengesch. Deutschlands. Bd. 1. (Göttingen 1846) S. 330.

§ 4.

In proportion as the influence of the Franks on the different German tribes was greater or less, Christianity met with
greater or less acceptance among them, not so much by general
organised plans, as by the voluntary activity of individuals.
Hence ecclesiastical discipline was still entirely unknown, and
heathenism was not unfrequently mixed with Christianity.[1]   At
this time *Winfried* (Boniface), an English monk, full of the piety
of an age which consisted in mingling together an attachment to
external forms, and, in the English Church in particular, subjection to the Roman See, resolved to be apostle of Germany. After
an unsuccessful attempt in Friesland (715), he went to Rome
(718), to procure there full powers for the conversion of the Germans.[2] The first successful fruit of his labours he met with
among the *Hessians* about *Amoeneburg* (722).   Highly pleased
with this, Pope Gregory II. consecrated him bishop (723), and
thus bound him and his active ministry still more closely to the
Roman See.[3] Recommended by the pope to Charles Martell,

[1] Comp. Gregorii Papae II. capitulare datum Martiniano Episcopo
caet. in Bavariam ablegatis A. D. 716, ap. Mansi xii. p. 257. Sterzinger v. d. Zustande der baier. Kirche unter Theodo II. in the Abhandl.
d. churf. baier. Academie Bd. 10. [München 1776] S. 137 ff.
[2] The document giving him full power (Othlon. lib. i. c. 12, Bonif.
ep. ed. Serarii 118, ed. Würdtw. 2) closes thus : Disciplinam denique
sacramenti, quam ad initiandos Deo praevie credituros tenere studeas,
ex formula officiorum sanctae nostrae sedis apostolicae, instructionis tuae
gratia praelibata, volumus ut 'intendas. Quod vero actioni susceptae
tibi deesse perspexeris, nobis, ut valueris, intimare curabis.
[3] Boniface's oath, Othlon. i. 14, in Bonif. epist. l. c.   In nomine
Domini Dei et Salvatoris nostri Jesu Christi. Imperante domno Leone
a Deo coronato magno imperatore anno septimo post consulatum ejus.
Sed et Constantini magni imperatoris ejus filii anno iy. indictione vi.
Promitto ego Bonifacius, Dei gratia episcopus, tibi beato Petro Apostolorum principi, vicarioque tuo beato Gregorio Papae et successoribus
ejus, per Patrem, et Filium, et Spiritum Sanctum, Trinitatem insepara-

and provided by the latter with a letter of safety, he first completed the conversion of the Hessians, and then went into *Thuringia.* Gregory III. appointed him archbishop and apostolic vicar (732),[4] and in this capacity Boniface began, after a third journey to Rome (738), to arrange the ecclesiastical relations of Germany. He first divided *Bavaria* into four dioceses (*Salzburg, Freisingen, Regensburg, Passau,* 739);[5] then he established (741) for East Franconia, Hesse, and Thuringia, the bishoprics of *Würzburg, Eichstädt, Buraburg* (at Fritzlar, 787 united with Mainz), and *Erfurt;*[6] and at *the first German coun-*

bilem, et hoc sacratissimum corpus tuum, me omnem fidem et puritatem sanctae fidei catholicae exhibere, et in unitate ejusdem fidei Deo operante persistere, in qua omnis Christianorum salus sine dubio esse comprobatur *:* nullo modo me contra unitatem communis et universalis ecclesiae suadente quopiam consentire : sed, ut dixi, fidem et puritatem meam atque concursum tibi, et utilitatibus ecclesiae tuae, cui a Domino Deo potestas ligandi solvendique data est, et praedicto vicario tuo, atque successoribus ejus per omnia exhibere. Sed et si cognovero, antistites contra instituta antiqua sanctorum patrum conversari, cum eis nullam habere communionem aut conjunctionem, sed magis, si valuero prohibere, prohibeam : sin minus, fideliter statim Domno meo Apostolico renuntiabo. Quod si, quod absit, contra hujus promissionis meae seriem aliquid facere quolibet modo, seu ingenio vel occasione tentavero, reus inveniar in aeterno judicio, ultionem Ananiae et Sapphirae incurram, qui vobis etiam de rebus propriis fraudem facere vel fulsum dicere praesumserunt. Hunc autem indiculum sacramenti ego Bonifacius exiguus episcopus manu propria scripsi, atque ponens supra sacratissimum corpus beati Petri, ita ut praescriptum est, Deo teste et judice, praestiti sacramentum, quod et servare promitto. This oath is, with a few alterations, entirely like the Indiculus Episcopi which the pope exacted from the bishops belonging to his patriarchal diocese, of which two formulas have been preserved in the lib. diurnus cap. iii. tit. 8 and 9. Similar oaths it was usual to take in Spain, even at an earlier period, the bishops to the metropolitan and the inferior clergy to the bishop. Conc. Tolet. iv. ann. 633, can. 17. Conc. Tolet. xi. ann. 675, can. 10. cf. Zaccaria diss. de jurejurando, quo Archiepiscopi pallio donati, et Episcopi in sacra ipsorum ordinatione obedientiam Romano Pontifici pollicentur cap. 1–3 (in ejusd. de rebus ad. hist. atque antiquitt. ecclesiae pertinentibus dissertt. latinae Fulginiae 1781. 4. Tom. ii. p. 264 ss.)

4 Bonif. epist. 122, ed. Serar. 25 Würdtw.

5 Sterzinger's Entwurf v. d. Zustande der baier. Kirche v. 717. b. 800. in d. Neuen hist. Abhandl. d. churf. baier. Academie. Bd. 2. S. 315.

6 Boniface consecrated no bishop for Erfurt, but probably reserved

cil (742), subordinated the new church, so far as the ecclesiastical government of the Frankish rulers allowed, to the pope.[7] As seminaries and resting points of Christianity, he founded monasteries : *Ohrdruf* for Thuringia (724) ; *Fritzlar* and *Amöneburg* for Hesse (732). The most celebrated was *Fulda* (744.) In the meantime Boniface had entered into an association with the new Frankish rulers, Karlmann and Pipin, which proved of no small importance in the course of the great ecclesiastical developments of this century. He made *Mainz* (745) his archiepiscopal seat, but resigned it (753) to his pupil Lullus, for the sake of preach-

this diocese for himself, since otherwise he would have been without a diocese till 745, till he united it after his elevation to the see of Mainz with this archbishopric. Thus all difficulties are most readily solved. Comp. Seiters p. 306 ff.

[7] The seven resolutions of this synod were announced by Karlmann as capitularies (Mansi xii. 365. Pertz Monum. Germ. iii. 16) : Ego Carlmannus, dux et princeps Francorum—cum consilio servorum Dei et optimatum meorum Episcopos, qui in regno meo sunt, cum Presbyteris—congregavi,—ut mihi consilium dedissent, quomodo lex Dei et ecclesiastica religio recuperetur, quae in diebus praeteritorum principum dissipata corruit ; et per consilium sacerdotum et optimatum meorum ordinavimus per civitates Episcopos, et constituimus super eos Archiepiscopum Bonifacium, qui est Missus s. Petri. Statuimus per annos singulos synodum congregare, ut nobis praesentibus canonum decreta et Ecclesiae jura restaurentur, et religio chrisiana emendetur etc. The additional measures taken by Boniface are related by him in his epist. ed. Serar. 105. ed. Würdtw. 73. ad Cudberthum : Decrevimus autem in nostro synodali conventu et confessi sumus fidem catholicam et unitatem, et subjectionem Romanae Ecclesiae, fine tenus vitae nostrae, velle servare : sancto Petro et Vicario ejus velle subjici : synodum per omnes annos congregare : Metropolitanos pallia ab illa sede quaerere : et per omnia, praecepta Petri canonice sequi desiderare, ut inter oves sibi commendatas numeremur. Et isti confessioni universi consensimus et subscripsimus, et ad corpus sancti Petri principis Apostolorum direximus, quod gratulando Clerus et Pontifex Romanus suscepit. —Et unusquisque Episcopus, si quid in sua dioecesi corrigere vel emendare nequiverit, itidem in synodo coram Archiepiscopo et palam omnibus ad corrigendum insinuet, eodem modo, quo Romana Ecclesia nos ordinatos cum sacramento constrinxit, ut si-Sacerdotes vel plebes a lege Dei deviasse viderim, et corrigere non potuerim, fideliter semper sedi apostolicae et Vicario S. Petri ad emendandum indicaverim. Sic enim, ni fallor, omnes Episcopi debent Metropolitano, et ipse Romano Pontifici, si quid de corrigendis populis apud eos impossibile est, notum facere : et sic alieni fient a sanguine animarum perditarum.

ing among the Frieslanders.[8]   He died the death of a martyr at
Dockum (5th June, 755).

The chief traits in Boniface's character are, an exaggerated
notion of the external unity of the church, and obedience to its
statutes, as well as a deep reverence for the Roman See, without
which he undertook nothing.   As he himself sought for ecclesiastical laws, even with regard to the most indifferent actions of
daily life,[9] so was he severe and persecuting against all who departed from Roman-ecclesiastical regulations,[10] as in the instance
of the two clergymen, *Adelbert* and *Clement*.[11]   Thus he bound

[8] Till the death of the Friesian king Radbod (719), Utrecht still belonged to Friesland ; Wiltaburg, which lay opposite to it, to Franconia.
(vita Bonifacii auct. Wilibaldo § 13. Pertz ii. p. 839. Gesta abb.
Fontanell. c. 3. l. c. p. 277.)   From this time Frankish rule spread
more and more towards the east, especially after Charles Martel's victory, 734 (Fredeger c. 109).   Thus, therefore, a much better prospect
of success presented itself here since the first missionary labours of Boniface.

[9] Which had been abundantly furnished to him by Rome, because
such fetters of the conscience bound at the same time to the Roman
See.   For example, Gregorii iii. epist. ad Bonif. [ed. Serar. 122.
Würdtw. 25, ap. Mansi xii. 277] : agrestem caballum aliquantos adjunx-
isti comedere, plerosque et domesticum.   Hoc nequaquam fieri deinceps, sanctissime frater, sinas, sed quibus potueris modis Christo juvante
per omnia compesce, et dignam eis indicito poenitentiam. Immundum
enim est et execrabile. Zachariae epist. ad Bon. [ed. Serar. 142.
Würdtw. 87, ap. Mansi xii. 345] : ·flagitasti a nobis, quae recipienda,
quae respuenda sint. Imprimis de volatilibus, *i. e.*, graculis et corni-
culis atque ciconiis, quae omnino cavendae sunt ab esu Christianorum.
Etiam et fibri et lepores et equi salvatici multo amplius vitandi. Attamen, sanctissime frater, de omnibus e Scripturis sacris bene compertus
es.—Et hoc inquisisti, post quantum temporis debet lardum comedi.
Nobis a Patribus institutum pro hoc non est.   Tibi autem petenti consilium praebemus, quod non oporteat illud mandi, priusquam super fu-
mo siccetur aut igne coquatur.   Si vero libet, ut incoctum manducetur,
post Paschalem festivitatem erit manducandum.—Seiters, p. 226, 451,
would consider these regulations as directed merely against impedi-
ments to civilization. In this way, certainly, the use of raw flesh generally, not of single beasts, might be accounted for, but not the entire use
of certain beasts. Besides, Zacharias expressly refers to holy Scripture
and the fathers. It is obvious that he makes his Italian usages, respecting meats, Christian laws relative to food.

[10] Particularly also against married priests, who are designated as
fornicatores. Rettberg i. 323.

[11] Bonif. ep. ad Zachariam P. [ed Serar. ep. 135. Würdtw. 67] :

the new German Church to Rome still more firmly than the En-

Maximus tamen mihi labor fuit contra duos haereticos pessimos et
publicos et blasphemos contra Deum et contra catholicam fidem. Unus
qui dicitur Adelbert natione generis Gallus est; alter qui dicitur Clemens genere Scotus est: specie erroris diversi, sed pondere peccatorum pares. Contra istos obsecro apostolicam auctoritatem vestram,
quod meam mediocritatem defendere et adjuvare, et per scripta vestra
populum Francorum et Gallorum corrigere studeatis,—ut per verbum
vestrum isti duo haeretici mittantur in carcerem,—et nemo cum eis loquatur vel communionem habeat.—Propter istos enim persecutiones et
inimicitias et maledictiones multorum populorum patior.—Dicunt enim
de Adelberto, quod eis sanctissimum Apostolum abstulerim, patronum
et oratorem, et virtutum factorem, et signorum ostensorem abstraxerim.
Sed pietas vestra audiens vitam ejus judicet. In primaeva enim aetate
hypocrita fuit, dicens quod sibi angelus Domini in specie hominis de
extremis finibus mundi mirae et tamen incertae sanctitatis reliquias at-
tulerit, et exinde posset omnia quaecunque a Deo posceret impetrare :
et tunc demum—domos multorum penetravit et captivas post se mulierculas duxit oneratas peccatis,—et multitudinem rusticorum seduxit,
dicentium quod ipse esset vir apostolicae sanctitatis, et signa atque prodigia faceret.   Deinde conduxit Episcopos indoctos qui se contra praecepta canonum absolute ordinaverunt.   Tum demum in tantam superbiam elatus est, ut se aequipararet Apostolis Christi.   Et dedignabatur
in alicujus honore Apostolorum vel Martyrum ecclesiam consecrare,
improperans hominibus etiam, cur tantopere studerent sanctorum Apostolorum limina visitare.   Postea, quod absurdum est in proprii nominis
honore dedicavit oratoria, vel, ut verius dicam, sordidavit. Fecit quoque
cruciculas et oratoriola in campis, et ad fontes, vel ubicumque sibi
visum fuit : et jussit ibi publicas orationes celebrari, donec multitudines
populorum, spretis caeteris Episcopis, et dimissis antiquis ecclesiis, in
talibus locis conventus celebrarent, dicentes : Merita sancti Adelberti
adjuvabunt nos.   Ungulas quoque et capillos suos dedit ad honorifi-
candum et portandum cum reliquiis S. Petri principis Apostolorum.
Tum demum, quod maximum scelus, et blasphemia contra Deum esse
videbatur, fecit.   Venienti enim populo et prostrato ante pedes ejus, et
cupienti confiteri peccata sua dixit : Scio omnia peccata vestra, qui mihi
cognita sunt omnia occulta. Non est opus confiteri, sed dimissa sunt
peccata vestra praeterita: securi et absoluti redite ad domos vestras
cum pace.   Alter autem haereticus, qui dicitur Clemens, contra catholicam contendit ecclesiam, et canones ecclesiarum Christi abnegat et re-
futat : tractatus et sermones SS. Patrum, Hieronymi, Augustini, Gregorii recusat.   Synodalia jura spernens, proprio sensu affirmat, se post
duos filios, in adulterio natos sub nomine Episcopi esse posse christianae legis Episcopum.   Judaismum inducens judicat justum esse
Christiano, ut, si voluerit, viduam fratris defuncti accipiat uxorem. Contra fidem quoque SS. Patrum contendit, dicens, quod Christus filius
Dei descendens ad inferos omnes, quos inferni carcer detinuit, inde
liberavit, credulos et incredulos, laudatores Dei simul et cultores idolorum : et multa alia horribilia de praedestinatione Dei contraria fidei

glish was.[12]   On the other hand, his true Christian piety, which
shone forth under all external forms, and his strict morality,
which exceeded even his reverence for Rome, are worthy of all
respect.[13]

catholicae affirmat.   This led to the assembling of a synod at Rome,
whose acts are in Mansi. xii. 373.   Zachariae P. epist. iii. ad Bonif.
[ed. Serar. ep. 144, 139, 138, b. Mansi xii. 321, 334, 336.] Walch's
Ketzerhist. x. 1. Neander's KG. iii. iii. Rettberg i. 314, 324.

[12] Neander's Denkwürdigkeiten iii. ii. 76.

[13] Bonifacii ep. ad Zachariam [ed. Serar. ep. 132. ed. Würdtw. 51] :
After complaining that a layman in Rome wished to obtain a dispensa-
tion, ut in matrimonium acciperet viduam avunculi sui, quae et ipsa fuit
uxor consobrini sui, et ipsa illo vivente discessit ab eo, he continues :
carnales homines, idiotae Alemanni vel Bajoarii vel Franci, si juxta
Romanam urbem aliquid facere viderint ex his peccatis, quae nos pro-
hibemus, licitum et concessum a sacerdotibus esse putant, et nobis improperium deputant, sibi scandalum vitae accipiunt.   Sicut affirmant,
se vidisse annis singulis in Romana urbe, et juxta ecclesiam in die vel
nocte quando, Kalendae Januarii intrant, paganorum consuetudine choros ducere per plateas, et acclamationes ritu Gentilium, et cantationes
sacrilegas celebrare : et mensas illa die vel nocte dapibus onerare : et
nullum de domo sua vel ignem vel ferramentum vel aliquid commodi
vicino suo praestare velle.   Dicunt quoque, se vidisse ibi mulieres
pagano ritu phylacteria et ligaturas, et in brachiis et cruribus ligatas,
habere, et publice ad vendendum venales ad comparandum aliis offerre.
Quae omnia eo, quod ibi, a carnalibus et insipientibus videntur, nobis
hic et improperium et impedimentum praedicationis et doctrinae perfi-
ciunt.—Si istas paganias ibi paternitas vestra in Romana urbe prohi-
buerit, et sibi mercedem et nobis maximum profectum in doctrina
ecclesiastica acquiret.   Other traits of liberal thinking against Rome
may be seen in Rettberg i. 413.

SECOND CHAPTER.

HISTORY OF THE PAPACY.

§ 5.

EXTENSION OF THE PAPAL POWER IN THE WEST, TO THE TIME OF CHARLEMAGNE.

Sources : Codex Carolinus in Muratorii script. rerum Ital. T. iii. P. 2. p. 73 ss., best besides other original documents in : Cajet. Cenni monumenta dominationis pontificiae, (Romae 1760. 61. Tomi ii. 4. Comp. Ritter's review in Ernesti's theol. Bibl. vi. 524. 911.) T. i.

François Sabbathier essai historique-critique sur l'origine de la puissance temporelle des Papes, a la Haye 1765. 8. J. R. Becker, über den Zeitpunct der Veränderung in der Oberherrschaft über die Stadt Rom, Lübeck 1769. 8. Die Karolinger u. die Hierarchie ihrer Zeit, v. J. Ellendorf. 2 Bde. Essen 1838. 8. Planck's Gesch. d. christl. kirchl. Gesellschaftsverf. Bd. 2. S. 714 ff.

The prohibition of image-worship by the emperor *Leo the Isaurian* (see § 1.) was the cause of Rome, under the guidance of the popes,[1] being in a state of rebellion against the emperors,

---

[1] Gregory II. from 715-731, Gregory III. † 741, Zachary † 752, Stephanus II. † 757, Paul I. † 767, Constantine II. † 768, Stephanus III. † 772, Hadrian I. † 795, Leo III. † 816, Stephanus IV. † 817, Paschalis I. † 824, Eugenius II. † 827, Valentinus † 827, Gregory IV. † 844, Sergius II. † 847, Leo IV. † 855, Benedict III. † 858. The female pope, Johanna (Johannes Anglicus or Johann VIII.), who is said to have sat in the chair between Leo IV. and Benedict III., is a later fable. It is disputed when this story first appeared. In some MSS. of the liber pontificalis, it has been interpolated from Martinus Polonus. Kist (Nederlandsch Archief voor kerkelijke Geschienis III. 27) has drawn attention to the circumstance that, in two Milan Codd. of it, the texts of the vitae of Leo IV., Benedict III., and Nicolaus I., differ very much from the printed texts, and that the design of preventing the possibility of making a female pope appears to have had an influence in part on the printed texts of these lives. But when, p. 39, he wishes to find in a remark of Muratori's, the text of these MSS. relating to the female pope, he ventures to bring the words of Muratori

to allude to the point without sufficient authority. In the older editions of the Chronicles of Marianus Scotus († 1086) and of Sigebertus Gemblacensis († 1113) is found a short passage respecting the female pope, but in the MSS. it is wanting, and was probably inserted at first by the original editors (Monum. Germ. hist. ed. Pertz, Scriptorum v. 551, vi. 340, 470). Thus there appears to remain, as the first voucher for the fact, a person who has been for the most part overlooked, viz., Stephanus de Borbone lib. de vii. donis Spir. S. (written about 1225, in Lyons) in J. Quetifii et A. J. Echardi scriptores Ord. Praedicat. i. 367: Accidit autem, mirabilis audacia, imo insana, circa ann. Dom, MC. [CM ?] ut dicitur in chronicis. Quaedam mulier literata, et in arte nõndi (notandi ?) edocta, adsumto virili habitu, et virum se fingens, venit Romam, et tam industria, quam literatura accepta, facta est notarius curiae, post diabolo procurante cardinalis, postea Papa. Haec impraegnata cum ascenderet peperit. Quod cum novisset Romana justitia, ligatis pedibus ejus ad pedes equi distracta est extra urbem, et ad dimidiam leucam a populo lapidata, et ubi fuit mortua, ibi fuit sepulta, et super lapidem super ea positum scriptus est versiculus: "Parce pater patrum papissae edere partum." The same story appears in an enlarged form in Martini Poloni († 1278) chron., and here the passage is perhaps genuine, although it is also wanting in several MSS. (Murator. ad Anastas. p. 247. cf. Ptolemaeus Lucensis about 1312) hist. eccl. xvi. 8. (in Muratori scriptt. rer. Ital. xi. 1013): Omnes, quos legi, praeter Martinum, tradunt, post Leonem IV. fuisse Benedictum III. Martinus autem Polonus ponit Johannem Anglicum VIII. Even John XX. († 1227) called himself John XXI. See G. G. Leibnitii flores sparsi in tumulum Papissae (in the Biblioth. hist. Goetting. first part 1758 p. 297 ss.) p. 330. From this time forward, the story was generally believed (comp. the list of writers who repeat it down to the Reformation in Sagitarii introd. i. 679) (see Leibnitius l. c. p. 303-309), the sella stercoraria belonging to her was pointed to (Platina de vitis Pont. no. 106. Leibnit. l. c. p. 335), and statues of her were shown (Mabillon iter Italicum p. 157. Leibnit. p. 333): till in the fifteenth century some (Aeneas Sylvius in ep. 130. Platina l. c.) doubted, and Jo. Aventinus († 1534) in the Annal. Bojorum lib. iv. first rejected it. From this time, being denied by the Catholics, it was adopted and defended by self-entangling Protestant polemics till Dav. Blondel (Question si une femme a été assise en siège papal de Rome entre Léon IV. et Bénoit III. Amsterd. 1649, 8. Joanna Papissa s. famosae quaestionis, an foemina ulla inter Leonem IV. et Bened. III. RR. PP. media sederit ἀνάκρισις. Amstelod. 1657. 8.), whom Ph. Labbeus (cenotaphium Jo. Papissae in diss. de scriptoribus eccl. Paris, 1660. i. 385. ap. Mansi xv. 38) transcribed, settled the matter, though the female pope was still defended by F. Spanheim (diss. de Joh. Pap. in Opp. ii. 577 ss., in French, histoire de la Papesse Jeanne, by J. Lenfant 1694., second edition by A. des Vignoles, à la Haye 1720. 2 T. in 12.) The copious literature of this topic may be seen in Sagittarii introd. i. 676. ii. 626. Fabricii bibl. gr. vol. x. p. 935. At the head of the numerous grounds that lie against the existence of a female pope stand those from which it is inferred that Benedict III. immediately succeeded Leo IV. 1. Prudentius, bishop of Troyes († 861), author of the part of the

Anales Bertiniani that relates to this topic, **says ad ann. 855** (Monum. German. hist. ed. Pertz. i. 449): **Mense Augusto Leo, apostolicae sedis antistes, defunctus est, eique Benedictus** successit: and ad ann. 858 (p. 452): **Benedictus Romanus** pontifex moritur: Nicolaus—substitutur. By **these testimonies** from a contemporary are also obviated the general **doubts** raised by Kist (Nederlandsch Archief iii. 53) **against the received** chronology of these popes. 2. Hincmari epist. xxvi. ad. Nicolaum i. A.D. 867. (ed. Sirmond. ii. 298): Missos meos cum literis Romam direxi. Quibus.in via nuntius venit de obitu P. Leonis. Pervenientes autem Romam cum praefatis literis, et intervenientibus praedictis Episcopis, Domnus nomine et gratia Benedictus mihi, quod nostis, privilegium inde direxit. 3. Diploma Bened. in confirmationem privilegiorum Corbejae (ap. Mansi xv. 113, but it was given even by Mabillon de re diplom. p. 436., much more minutely, from the original) at the conclusion: Scriptum—in mense Octobri indictione quarta. Bene valete. Datum Nonas Octobrias—Imp. Dn.—Aug. Hlothario—anno tricesimo nono, et P. C. (post Consulatum) ejustanno xxxix., sed et Hludovico novo Imp. ejus filio anno vii., Ind. quarta. sign. Benedicti Pape (consequently, the 7th Oct. 855. Leo IV. † 17th July 855. Lotharius † 28th Sept. 855. in Prüm). 4. A Roman denarius, on one side of which is: Hlotharius Imp., on the other, the inscription round it S. Petrus, and in the middle B. N. E. P. A. (Benedictus Papa). See J. Garampi de nummo argent. Bened. III. P. M. Rom. 1749. 4. Köhler's Münzbelustig. Bd. xx. S. 305. That the people in Rome knew nothing of the female pope, in the middle of the eleventh century follows. 5. From an epist. Leonis P. IX. ad. Michaelem Constantinop. Patriarch. opist. A.D. 1054 c. 23 (ap. Mansi xix. 649): Absit autem, ut velimus credere, quod publica fama non dubitat asserere, Constantinopolitanae ecclesiae contigisse, ut ennuchos contra primum Nicaeni concilii capitulum passim promovendo, foeminam in sede Pontificum suorum sublimasset aliquando. Hoc tam abominabile scelus, detestabileque facinus etsi enormitas ipsius vel horror fraternaque benevolentia non permittit nos credere etc. Origin of the fable: according to Baronius ann. 869, no. 5. a satire on John VIII. ob nimiam ejus animi facilitatem et mollitudinem ; according to others, on the dissolute popes John X. (so Aventinus l. c.), or John XI. or XII. (Onuphrius Panvinius in notis ad Platinam); according to Bellarminus de Rom. Pont. iii. 24, transferred from the see of Constantinople to the Roman (cf. Leon. ix. epist.); according to Leibnitz (l. c. p. 367), true of some one Pontifex (bishop) Joannes Anglicus ; according to C. Blascus de collect. can. Isidor. Merc. cap. xvi. § 2 and Henke (KG. ii. 23), a satirical representation of the origin of the Pseudo-Isidorian decretals; according to Gfrörer KG. iii. ii. 978, it also referred, in a reproving spirit, to a connection which Leo IV. wished to conclude with the Byzantines. According to Schmidt (KG. iv. 379), it arose from a misrepresentation of the sella stercoraria (respecting it see Mabillon comm. in ordinem Rom. in the Museum Ital. T. II. p. cxxi). Recently the Genevan, Galiffe Pictet, has declared the female pope to be the honourable widow of Leo IV. (Nederlandsch Archief iii. 78. 87). But the Romish Jesuit, Secchi, has declared it to be an invention of the schismatic Greeks, particularly of Gregory As-

without, however, entirely separating itself from the empire.[2]
For they feared the dominion of the Lombards ; who, under *Luit-prand* (712–744), were only waiting for a favourable opportunity
of forthwith extending their sway over Rome and the Exarchate
of Ravenna; while the popes had been endeavouring to prevent
them by every means in their power.

It is true that the Greek emperors avenged themselves for
this rebellion on the popes, by separating from the latter the
provinces of the Greek empire which had been hitherto subject
to Rome's ecclesiastical oversight, and stretched out their arm so
far as to confiscate the Roman patrimonies ;[3] but the popes

besta, and Photius ! When Prof. Kist, in his treatises on the female
pope (Nederl. Archief voor kerk. Geschiedenis iii. 1. v. 461), endeavours to show that the inquiry on this subject cannot yet be considered
as finished ; he is only correct so far, as the occasion and origin of the
fable are not yet explained. It is probable that it will never be possible
to arrive at certainty respecting them.

[2] Anastasius in vit. xc. Gregorii ii.: Cognita vero Imperatoris nequitia, omnis Italia consilium iniit, ut sibi eligerent Imperatorem, et
Constantinopolim ducerent. Sed compescuit tale consilium Pontifex,
sperans conversionem Principis.—blando omnes sermone, ut bonis in
Deum proficerent actibus et in fide persisterent, rogabat. Sed ne de-
sisterent ab amore vel fide Romani Imperii, admonebat. Theophanes
p. 338 : Γρηγόριος ὁ Πάπας ʿΡώμης τοὺς φόρους ʾΙταλίας καὶ ʿΡώμης ἐκώλυσε,
et p. 342 : ἀπέστησε ʿΡώμην τε καὶ ʾΙταλίαν καὶ πάντα τὰ ἐσπέρια τῆς πολιτικῆς καὶ ἐκκλησιαστικῆς ὑπακοῆς Λέοντος καὶ τῆς ὑπ᾽ αὐτὸν βασιλείας. The
last passage, which is repeated by all the Byzantine writers, must be
corrected and explained by that from Anastasius. Still Baronius ad ann.
730. § 5. follows the Greek writers with the application : Sic dignum
posteris idem Gregorius reliquit exemplum, ne in ecclesia Christi reg-
nare sinerentur haeretici principes, si saepe moniti in errore persistere
obstinato animo invenirentur. So too Bellarminus de Rom. Pont. v. 8 :
Gregorius Leoni Imp. iconomacho a se excommunicato prohibuit vecti-
galia solvi ab Italis, et proinde mulctavit eum parte imperii. This
Ultramontane view, defended even so late as the 18th century by A.
Sandini, J. S. Assemani, and others, is controverted, particularly by the
Gallican Natalis Alexander, L. E. du Pin, J. B. Bossuet, etc. Comp.
Walch's Ketzerhist. x. 263.

[3] Theophanes, p. 343. merely mentions the confiscation of the Roman
patrimonies in Sicily and Calabria. On the contrary, Hadrianus P. i.
ep. ad Carol R. de imaginibus in fine (Mansi xiii. 808), says that he
has reminded the Greek emperors de dioecesi tam Archiepiscoporum
quam et Episcoporum sanctae catholicae et apostolicae Romanae Ecclesiae, and prayed for their restitution, quae tunc cum patrimoniis
nostris abstulerunt, quando sacras imagines deposuerunt. That the

gained proportionably in the new western kingdoms. At the commencement of this period England was the only one of the countries in the West which was closely united with the popes; and the numerous pilgrimages of the English to Rome caused (A. D. 794) *Offa*, king of Mercia, to erect an English establishment in that city.[4] But the notions entertained of Peter, heaven's porter, who considered what was done to his successors as done to himself, made a deep impression even out of England, and were therefore unceasingly insisted on by the popes.[5] *Boniface*, having been invited (743) by *Carlmann* and *Pipin* to assist in restoring order to the Frankish Church, which had got into wild confusion under *Charles Martell*, appeared in this new task also as the papal legate,[6] and thus brought the Frank rulers, as well as the newly-ordered Frankish Church, into closer connection with Rome.[7] Afterwards, as archbishop of Mainz, and most dis-

vicariat-relation of the bishop of Thessalonica, in particular, was abolish-ed at that time, may be fairly concluded from Nicolai i. epist. ad Michael. Imp. (ap. Mansi xv. 167.)

[4] That it was not Ina, King of Wessex, 726, but Offa, King of Mercia, who introduced Peter's pence, may be seen from Sprengel, in the allg. Weltgesch. Th. 47. S. 123.

[5] Comp. Div. 2. § 133. note 1. Gregorii ii. epist. i. ad Leonem Imp. (ap. Mansi xii. 971): τὸν ἅγιον Πέτρον αἱ πᾶσαι βασιλεῖαι τῆς δύσεως Θεὸν ἐπίγειον ἔχουσι. Comp. the addresses of the popes to the Frankish kings, in which they constantly refer to beatum Petrum clavigerum regni caelorum, or janitorem r. c.; and, in particular, Claudi locum, below § 11. note 11.

[6] Bonifac. epist. ad Zachariam P. ed. Serar. 132: Notum similiter sit paternitati vestrae, quod Carolomannus, Dux Francorum, me accersitum ad se rogavit, ut in parte regni Francorum, quae in sua est potestate, synodum facerem congregari: et promisit, se de ecclesiastica religione, quae jam longo tempore i. e. non minus quam per lx. vel lxx. annos calcata et dissipata fuit, aliquid corrigere et emendare velle. Quapropter si hoc, Deo insipirante, veraciter implere voluerit, consilium et praeceptum vestrae auctoritatis i. e. apostolicae habere et sapere debeo.

[7] At first not without doubts and scruples on the part of many Frankish bishops. Thus Boniface wished even to send pallia to the new metropolitans of Rheims, Rouen, and Sens (743). Zacharias was ready at once (op. ad Bonif. in Bonif. epp. 144. Mansi xii. 321): Qualiter mos pallii sit, vel quomodo fidem suam exponere debeant hi, qui pallio uti conceduntur, eis direximus. But soon after two drew back, and Zacharias asks Boniface with surprise about the original cause (Bonif. epp. 143. Mansi xii. 324), quod antea nobis una cum memoratis prin-

tinguished bishop of the kingdom, his efforts were constantly directed to the establishment of the papal authority in this country also. When therefore Pipin wished for *the title* as well as *the power* of king, and needed a priestly declaration that this transference of loyalty was consonant with the divine laws, partly in order to obviate the conscientious scruples of the Franks,[8] and partly not to render insecure all succeeding oaths of allegiance by one act of perjury; he could only seek for this sanction from the pope, as the acknowledged high priest; and Zacharias, by his ready consent (752),[9] laid the new kings under an obligation to render still more important services to Rome.

cipibus Galliarum pro tribus palliis suggessisti, et postea pro solo Grimone (Archbp. of Rouen). In the mean time, 748, Zachariae ep. ad diversos Episc. Galliae et Germaniae, particularly to the bishops of Rouen, Beauvais, Noyon, Tongern, Speyer, Terouanne, Cambray, Würzburg, Laon, Meaux, Cöln, and Strassburg (Mansi xii. 344): Gaudeo in vobis, charissimi, quoniam fides vestra, et unitas erga nos pretiosa est et manifesta,—dum ad fautorem et magistrum vestrum a Deo constitutum beatum Apostolorum principem Petrum benignissima voluntate conversi estis.—Et nunc Deo cooperante est aggregata Sanctitas vestra nostrae societati in uno pastorali ovili etc.

[8] How firmly and truly the Franks adhered to the Merovingian kingly race may be seen from Löbell's Gregorius von Tours, S. 220. It was natural for Pipin to wish that this loyalty should be transferred to his family.

[9] Respecting this are the accounts of contemporaries: the author of the Appendix to Fredegarii chron. concludes with this occurrence, and probably wrote immediately after (Bouquet ii. 460): Quo tempore una cum consilio et consensu omnium Francorum, missa relatione a sede apostolica auctoritate percepta, praecelsus Pippinus electione totius Franciae in sedem regni cum consecratione Episcoporum et subjectione Principum una cum Regina Bertradane, ut antiquitus ordo deposcit, sublimatur in regno. The conclusion which a copyist has attributed to him from a Codex of Gregor. Turin. de gloria confessorum in the year 767, transcribed by the former (Bouquet v. 9): Pippinus, Rex pius, per auctoritatem et imperium sanctae recordationis domni Zachariae Papae, et unctionem sancti chrismatis per manus beatorum sacerdotum Galliarum, et electionem omnium Francorum,—in regni solio sublimatus est. Postea (754 in St Denys) per manus ejusdem Stephani pontificis —in Regem et Patricium, una cum praedictis filiis Carolo et Carlomanno in nomine sanctae Trinitatis unctus et benedictus est.—Pontifex—Francorum principes benedictione et Spiritus sancti gratia confirmavit, et tali omnes interdictu et excommunicationis lege constrinxit, ut numquam de alterius lumbis Regem in aevo praesumant eligere sed ex ipsorum, quos et divina pietas exaltare dignata est, et sanctorum Apos-

P

When the Lombard king, *Aistulph* (752) had already overrun the Exarchate, and threatened Rome, *Stephen II.* flew to Pipin for aid.[10] This was readily granted, and in two campaigns (754

tolorum intercessionibus per manus vicarii ipsorum beatissimi Pontificis confirmare et consecrare disposuit. The Annales Laurissenses, written in the first years of Charlemagne, ad ann. 749 [751] (Pertzii monum. Germaniae hist. i. 136): Burghardus Wirzeburgensis Episcopus et Folradus Capellanus missi fuerunt ad Zachariam Papam, interrogando de Regibus in Francia, qui illis temporibus non habentes regalem potestatem, si bene fuisset, an non. Et Zacharias Papa mandavit Pippino, ut melius esset illum Regem vocari, qui potestatem haberet, quam illum, qui sine regali potestate manebat; ut non conturbaretur ordo, per auctoritatem apostolicam jussit Pippinum Regem fieri. Ad ann. 750 [752]: Pippinus secundum morem Francorum electus est ad Regem, et unctus per manum sanctae memoriae Bonifacii Archiepiscopi (denied by Le Cointe, Eckhart, and Rettberg K. G. Deutschl. i. 380), et elevatus a Francis in regno in Suessionis civitate. Hildericus vero, qui false Rex vocabatur, tonsoratus est et in monasterium missus. A later ultramontane view, Gregorii VII. (in Gratiani decret. P. ii. Causa xv. qu. vi. c. 3): Alius etiam Romanus Pontifex, Zacharias scilicet, Regem Francorum, non tam pro suis iniquitatibus, quam pro eo, quod tantae potestati erat inutilis, a regno deposuit; et Pipinum, Caroli magni Imp. patrem, in ejus locum substituit, omnesque Francigenas a juramento fidelitatis, quod illi fecerant, absolvit. Cf. J. Gu. Loebell disp. de causis regni Francorum a Merovingis ad Carolingos translati. Bonnae 1844. 4.

[10] Anastasius in vit. xciv. Stephani ii.: cernens ab imperiali potentia nullum esse subveniendi auxilium, tunc quemadmodum praedecessores ejus, beatae memoriae domnus Gregorius, et Gregorius alius, et domnus Zacharias, beatissimi Pontifices, Carolo, excellentissimae memoriae, Regi Francorum, direxerunt, petentes sibi subveniri propter oppressiones ac invasiones, quas et ipsi in hac Romanorum provincia a nefanda Longobardorum gente perpessi sunt: ita modo et ipse—clam per quendam peregrinum suas misit literas Pipino etc. Comp. the pope's address between the first and second campaigns. Cod. Carol. no. iii. iv. vi. vii. especially no. iii. : Ego Petrus Apostolus—qui vos adoptivos habeo filios, ad defendendum de manibus adversariorum hanc Romanam civitatem et populum mihi a Deo commissum, sed et domum, ubi secundum carnem requiesco, de contaminatione gentium eruendam, vestram omnium dilectionem provocans adhortor, et ad liberandam Ecclesiam Dei mihi a divina potentia commendatam omnino protestans admoneo.—Sed et domina nostra, Dei genitrix semper virgo Maria, nobiscum vos magnis obligationibus adjurans protestatur, atque admonet et jubet, sicut simul etiam throni atque dominationes, et cunctus caelestis militiae exercitus, nec non et martyres atque confessores Christi et omnes omnino Deo placentes, et hi nobiscum adhortantes et conjurantes protestantur etc.— Praestate ergo populo meo Romano, mihi a Deo commisso,—praesidia totis vestris viribus, ut ego Petrus vocatus Dei Apostolus, in hac vita, et in die futuri examinis vobis alterna impendens patrocinia, in regno Dei

and 755) the Lombards were compelled to give up all they had taken. Pipin himself assumed the Patriciate of Rome,[11] and made the Pope *Patricius* of the Exarchate,[11] both, however, tacitly acknowledging the supremacy of the Greek empire. It now became a part of the papal policy to prevent all friendly connection between the Lombards, whom they still feared, and the Franks;[13] in which design they succeeded so well, that when new

lucidissima ac praeclara vobis praeparem tabernacula, atque praemia aeternae retributionis, et infinita paradisi gaudia vobis polliceus adinvicem tribuam.—Non separemini a populo meo Romano : sic non sitis alieni aut separati a regno Dei, et vita aeterna. Quidquid enim poscetis a me, subveniam vobis videlicet, et patrocinium impendam.—Si autem, quod non credimus, et aliquum posueritis moram ;—sciatis vos ex auctoritate sanctae et unicae Trinitatis per gratiam apostolatus, quae data est mihi a Christo Domino, vos alienari pro transgressione nostrae adhortationis a regno Dei et vita aeterna.

[11] The patriciate was a dignity established by Constantine the Great, the highest after the imperial, which was bestowed for life, and was capable of being united with different offices. Patricius Romae was properly governor of Rome, who at the same time possessed the authority of a Patricius. Before this time German kings had received the title of a consul or Patricius from emperors (Eichhorn's deutsche Rechtsgesch. i. 170.) Pipin received it from Stephen as representative of the Roman people. See the appendix to Gregor. Tur. not. 9.

[12] Anastasius in vit. Stephani ii. Comp. Savigny's Gesch. des röm. Rechts im Mittelalter Bd. i. (2te Ausg. Heidelberg 1834) S. 357. Pertz in the Monum. iv. ii. 7. Gfrörer's K. G. iii. ii. 571. Hence Hadrianus ad Carol. M. (Cod. Car. no. 85. ed. Cenni p. 521) A. D. 790, contrasts the Patriciatus b. Petri with the Patriciatus Caroli.

[13] Comp. Stephani iii. ep. ad Carolum et Carolomannum respecting a marriage projected between the two royal families A. D. 770, in the Cod. Carol. no. 45 : Quod certe si ita est, haec propria diabolica est immissio, et non tam matrimonii conjunctio, sed consortium nequissimae adinventionis esse videtur.—Quae est enim, praecellentissimi filii, magni Reges, talis desipientia, ut penitus vel dici liceat, quod vestra praeclara Francorum gens, quae super omnes gentes enitet, et tam splendiflua ac nobilissima regalis vestrae potentiae proles, perfida, quod absit, ac foetentissima Langobardorum gente polluatur, quae in numero gentium nequaquam computatur, de cujus natione et leprosorum genus oriri certum est ?—Quapropter et b. Petrus, princeps Apostolorum, cui regni caelorum claves a Domino Deo traditae sunt, et caelo ac terra ligandi solvendique concessa est potestas, firmiter Excellentiam vestram per nostram infelicitatem obtestatur, —ut nullo modo quisquam de vestra fraternitate praesumat filiam jam dicti Desiderii, Langobardorum Regis, in conjugium accipere, nec iterum vestra nobilissima germana, Deo amabilis Gisila, tribuatur filio saepe fati Desiderii.—Praesentem itaque

P 2

inroads were made by the Lombards under *Desiderius*, *Charlemagne* having been summoned to his assistance by *Hadrian I.*, appeared immediately in order to destroy the kingdom of the Lombards (774). After Charles had confirmed and enlarged the grants made by Pipin,[14] he exercised in Italy all imperial rights,[15] even in ecclesiastical matters,[16] till at length the very

nostram exhortationem atque adjurationem in confessione b. Petri ponentes, et sacrificium super eam atque hostias Deo nostro offerentes, vobis cum lacrymis ex eadem sacra confessione direximus. Et si quis, quod non optamus, contra hujusmodi nostrae adjurationis atque exhortationis seriem agere praesumserit, sciat, se auctoritate Domini mei b. Petri, Apostolorum principis, anathematis vinculo esse innodatum et a regno Dei alienum, atque cum diabolo et ejus atrocissimis pompis, et ceteris impiis, aeternis incendiis concremandum deputatum. At vero qui observator et custos istius nostrae exhortationis exstiterit, caelestibus benedictionibus a Domino Deo nostro illustratus, aeternis praemiorum gaudiis, cum omnibus Sanctis et electis Dei particeps effici mereatur. Still Charlemagne married Desideria, though he put her away a year after.

[14] Anastasius in vita Hadriani i. Pertz in the Monum. iv. ii. 8.

[15] Gfrörer's K. G. iii. ii. 581.

[16] In the disputes about investiture, it was asserted by the imperial party that these ecclesiastical rights had been formally bestowed on King Charles by the Pope and a Roman synod. They referred to Leonis p. viii. privilegium, given in 963 to the emperor Otto (in Pertz monum. vi. ii. 166) : B. Hadrianus—domno Carolo, victoriosissimo Regi Francorum ac Longobardorum, ac Patricio Romanorum, ac ordinationem apostolicae sedis .et episcopatum concessit. This document, however, is probably spurious. See Pertz l. c. Dönniges Jahrbücher des deutschen Reiches unter Otto i. (Berlin 1839) S. 102. More copious accounts are found in several works belonging to the end of the eleventh and beginning of the twelfth century. So in the Collectio cann. tripartita, written in the time of Urban II., and in Ivo's decree (in Pertz monum. iv. ii. 160 note) : after Desiderius was taken captive, Carolus Romam reversus, constituit ibi synodum cum Adriano Papa.—Adrianus autem Papa cum universa synodo tradiderunt Carolo jus et potestatem eligendi Pontificem et ordinandi apostolicam sedem, dignitatem quoque Patriciatus ei concesserunt. Insuper Archiepiscopos, Episcopos per singulas provincias ab eo investituram accipere diffiniverunt, et ut, nisi a Rege laudetur et investiatur Episcopus, a nemine consecretur. Et quicunque contra hoc decretum esset, anathematis eum vinculo innodaverunt, et nisi resipisceret, bona ejus publicari praeceperunt. This account was also inserted in the Chronicle of Siegbert of Gemblours in the monastery of Anchin at Douay 1113, (Pertz monum. scriptt. vi. 393. Hence poor Siegbert was accused by Baronius ann. 774 no. 10 of a deceitful fabrication. Pagi, however, critt. iii. 343, perceived that this passage was interpolated by others). The same account

appearance of the supremacy of the Greek emperor vanished,[17] so that Charles (novus Constantinus)[18] received the West Roman imperial crown from the hands of Leo III. (25th Dec. 800.)[19] The Pope, assuming all the rights of the former Exarch, began to

also appears in somewhat different words in a treatise composed A. D. 1109 at Naumburg by the bishop Waltram, or the abbott Conrad (Tüb. theol. Quartalschr. 1838 S. 348) de investitura Episcoporum (in Schardii syntagma tractatuum de imperiali jurisdictione p. 72, and in the Tübingen theol. Quartalschr. 1837 S. 187). The truth of the case is, that Charles now began to exercise in Italy also in the capacity of governor-general of the country, the same rights which he had always exercised in the empire of the Franks. It was not till a later time that the opinion was entertained that these rights must have been established by papal concessions; though Charles had not to receive privileges from the pope, but the pope from him.

[17] That they were still acknowledged as late as 785 is proved by Hadriani P. ep. ad Constantinum et Irenen (in Actis Conc. Nic. ii. Actio iii. ap. Mansi xii. 1056).

[18] Hadriani p. i. ep. ad Carolum A. D. 777 (Cod. Carol. no. 49): Et sicut temporibus b. Sylvestri Rom. Pont. a sanctae recordationis piisimo Constantino M. Imperatore per ejus largitatem sancta Dei catholica et apostolica Romana ecclesia elevata atque exaltata est, et potestatem in his Hesperiae partibus largiri dignatus est: ita et in his vestris felicissimis temporibus atque nostris S. Dei Ecclesia, i. e., b. Petri Apostoli, germinet atque exsultet:—quia ecce novus christianissimus Dei Constantinus Imperator his temporibus surrexit, per quem omnia Deus sanctae suae Ecclesiae bb. Apostolorum principis Petri largiri dignatus est. Sed et cuncta alia, quae per diversos Imperatores Patricios etiam et alios Deum timentes, pro eorum animae mercede et venia delictorum—b. Petro Apostolo—concessa sunt, et per nefandam gentem Langobardorum per annorum spatia, abstracta atque ablata sunt, vestris temporibus restituantur. Unde et plures donationes in sacro nostro scrinio Lateranensi reconditas habemus etc. Many find here a reference to the Donatio Constantini M., namely, de Marca de conc. Sac. de et Imp. lib. iii. c. 12 (according to whom it was forged, A. D. 767, jussu Romanorum Pontiff. pia quadam industria.) On the contrary, it is shown by Cenni monum. domin. Pontiff. i. 304, that Hadrian had here before his eyes only the Acta Sylvestri, to which he also refers in the ep. ad. Constantinum et Irenen (in the Actis Conc. Nic. ii. Act ii., ap. Mansi xiii. 529), and which first served for the basis of the later Donatio Constantini. Probably, too, the expression in the prominent treatise, viz. potestatem in his Hesperiae partibus largiri dignatus est had also an influence on the later forgery.

[19] Annales Laurissenses ad ann. 801: Ipsa die sacratissima natalis Domini cum Rex ad Missam ante confessionem b. Petri Apostoli ab oratione surgeret, Leo P. coronam capiti ejus imposuit, et a cuncto Romanorum populo acclamatum est: Karolo Augusto a Deo coronato, magno et pacifico Imperatori Romanorum, vita et victoria! Et post

exerciso the patriciate of Rome also.   Rome itself continued an
imperial city,[20] the popes were obliged to swear fidelity to the
emperor, acknowledging him as their lord and judge ;[21] though
the papal dignity was held to be superior to all ecclesiastical
courts,[22] and the first in the world.[23]

Laudes ab Apostolico more antiquorum principum adoratus est, atque
ablato Patricii nomine, Imperator et Augustus est appellatus.   Alcuins
Leben von D. F. Lorenzt.   Halle 1829.   S. 218 ff.
    [20] In Charlemagne's will (vita Car. M. per Einhardum c. 33) stand
the nomina metropolium civitatum : Roma, Ravenna, Mediolanum etc.
    [21] Comp. Caroli M. ep. ad Leonem iii. P. (Alcuini epist. 84.   Mansi
xiii. 980) referring to his entering on the episcopal see, A. D. 795 :
Perlectis Excellentiae vestrae litteris, et audita decretali chartula, valde,
ut fateor, gavisi sumus, seu in electionis unanimitate, sue in humilitatis
vestrae obidientia, et in promissionis ad nos fidelitate.—Sicut enim cum
beatissimo praedecessore vestrae sanctae paternitatis pactum inii, sic
cum beatitudine vestra ejusdem fidei et caritatis inviolabile foedus sta-
tuere desidero.—Nostrum est, secundum auxilium divinae pietatis,
sanctam ubique Christi Ecclesiam ab incursu paganorum, et ab infidelium devastatione armis defendere foris et intus catholicae fidei agni-
tione munire.   Vestrum est, sanctissime pater, elevatis ad Deum cum
Moyse manibus, nostram adjuvare militiam, quatenus vobis interceden-
tibus, Deo ductore et datore, populus christianus super inimicos sui
sancti nominis ubique semper habeat victoriam, et nomen Domini nostri Jesu Christi toto clarificetur in orbe.   Vestrae vero auctoritatis prudentia canones ubique sequatur ; quatenus totius sanctitatis exempla
omnibus evidenter in vestra fulgeant conversatione, et sanctae admonitionis exhortatio audiatur ab ore ; quatenus sic luceat lux vestra coram
hominibus, ut videant opera vestra bona, et glorificent Patrem vestrum
qui in caelis est (Matth. v. 16).   The abbot Angilbert, who had to con-
vey this letter to the pope, he at the same time charges (Caroli. ep. ad
Angilb. ap. Mansi xiii. 981): Domnum apostolicum Papam nostrum
admoneas diligenter de omni honestate vitae suae, et praecipue de sanctorum observatione canonum, de pia sanctae Dei Ecclesiae gubernatione.
—Ingerasque ei saepius, quam paucorum honor ille, quem praesentialiter habet, annorum, quam multorum est perpetualiter merces, quae-
datur bene laboranti in eo.   Et de simoniaca subvertendo haeresi diligentissime suadeas illi, quae sanctum ecclesiae corpus multis male ma-
culat in locis.   Et quidquid mente tenes saepius querelis agitasse inter
nos.   On the oath to be taken by the popes to the emperor, see below
§. 6, not. 4 and 5.   Baluzius in notis ad Agobardum. ii. 122. ejusd.
praef. in Capitularia §. 21 ss.   On the Missi dominici in Rome, see
Muratorii antiqu. Ital. medii aevi diss. ix. Tom. i. p. 455 ss. Ch. G. F.
Walchii diss. hist. de missis dominicis Pontificis Romani judicibus.
Jenae 1749. 4.
    [22] When A.D. 800, Leo III. had been maltreated and fled to Charle-
magne, and when many accusations were brought against him, the em-

§ 6.

PROGRESS OF THE PAPAL POWER AFTER CHARLEMAGNE.

The immediate successors, too, of Charlemagne maintained their civil lordly rights over Rome[1] and the Pope.[2] But the

peror assembled a synod in St Peter's Church to examine the case. This synod, however, declared: Nos sedem apostolicam, quae est caput omnium Dei Ecclesiarum, judicare non audemus. Nam ab ipsa nos omnes, et Vicario suo judicamur, ipsa autem a nemine judicatur, quemadmodum et antiquitus mos fuit. And Leo spontaneously cleared himself by an oath, Anastasius in vita Leonis III. On the origin of that view, see vol. i. Div. 2, § 117, not. 14, 15.

²⁵ The relations of that time are plainly described by Alcuinus epist. 80. [ed. Froben.] ad Carolum R. A. D. 799: Tres Personae in mundo altissimae hucusque fuerunt : apostolica sublimitas, que b. Petri principis Apostolorum sedem vicario munere regere solet.—Alia est imperialis dignitas, et secundae Romae secularis potentia.—Tertia est regalis dignitas, in qua vos Domini nostri J. C. dispensatio rectorem populi christiani disposuit, caeteris praefatis dignitatibus potentia excellentiorem, sapientia clariorem, regni dignitate sublimiorem. Ecce in te solo tota salus Ecclesiarum Christi inclinata recumbit. Tu vindex scelerum, tu rector errantium, tu consolator moerentium, tu exaltatio bonorum, etc.

¹ The Act of Lewis the Debonaire (in Pertz monum iv. ii. 6), in which he, among other things, makes a present of the civitatem Romanam cum ducatu suo et surburbanis, etc., also to the pope was interpolated in the eleventh century, cf. Ch. G. F. Walch censura diplomatis, quod Ludov. P. Paschali i. concessisse fertur. Lips. 1749. also in Pottii sylloge comm. theoll. vi. 278, and Pertz. l. c.

² Examples: An inquiry instituted against Leo III., who had executed some Romans. See vita Ludov. Pii per Astronomum c. 25 ap. Pertz. ii. 619.—Stephanus iv. statim postquam pontificatum suscepit, jussit omnem populum Romanum fidelitatem cum juramento promittere Hludowico (Theganus de gestis Ludov. P. c. 16, ib. p. 594), and when he travelled to the emperor, praemisit legationem, quae super ordinatione ejus Imperatori satisfaceret. (Astonomus c. 26).—When Lothar was crowned in Rome (823) the abbot of the monastery Farfa complained to him, suum monasterium ablata pristina libertate sub tributo ac pensione a Romanis Pontificibus constrictum, multasque possessiones eidem monasterio violenter ablatas. The result of the inquiry was, quod praedictum monasterium nullatenus sub jure et dominatione praefatae Romanae Ecclesiae, vel sub tributo et pensione esse

natural effect of their situation was to inspire the popes with the desire of bringing their power into some proportion with the honour assigned them ; the aversion of the Romans to the rule of the barbarous Franks aided them in this ; and it needed only weak and disunited princes to insure success to their efforts. Traces of such an endeavour were exhibited even under the government of Lewis the Debonaire.[3]   Though *Eugenius II.*, in addition to the Romans, had been expressly reminded by the Emperor Lothar (824) of his allegiance,[4] yet *Gregory IV.*, at

deberet, and Paschalis I. was obliged to restore omnes res, quas ex eodem monasterio potestas antecessorum ejusdem injuste abstulerat. See the diplomata Lotharii in the Chronicon Farfense in Muratorii scriptt. rer. Ital. ii. ii. 386.

[3] Astronomus c. 37 : Sub hoc tempore [ann. 823] perlatum est Imperatori, Theodorum Primicerium S. Ecclesiae Romanae et Leonem Nomenclatorem luminibus privatos, ac deinde decollatos in domo episcopali Lateranensi.   Invidia porro interfectoribus inurebatur, eo quod diceretur, ob fidelitatem Lotharii eos, qui interfecti sunt, talia fuisse perpessos.   In qua re fama quoque Pontificis laedebatur, dum ejus consensui totum adscriberetur.   Missi were sent to Rome and Paschalis P. ab interfectorum nece se cum plurimis Episcoporum sacramento purgavit.

[4] Astronomus c. 38 : Immediately after Eugenius II. ascended the episcopal throne (824), Lotharius comes to Rome, cumque de his, quae accesserant, quereretur, quare scilicet hi, qui Imperatori sibique et Francis fideles fuerant, iniqua nece peremti fuerint, et qui superviverent ludibrio reliquis haberentur : quare etiam tantae querelae adversus Romanorum Pontifices judicesque sonarent ; repertum est, quod quorundam Pontificum vel ignorantia vel desidia, sed et judicum caeca et inexplebili cupiditate, multorum praedia injuste fuerint confiscata.   Ideoque reddendo quae injuste sublata erant, Lotharius magnam populo Romano creavit laetitiam.   Statutum etiam juxta antiquum morem, ut ex latere Imperatoris mitterentur, qui judiciariam exercentes potestatem, justitiam omni populo, tempore quo visum foret Imperatori, aequa lance penderent.   The Constitutio Romana, by which Lotharius at that time restored order in Rome, may be seen in Pertz monum. iii. 239.   At that time clergy and people were obliged even swear anew, Continuator supplementi Longobardicorum Pauli Diac. ap. Bouquet vi. 173 : Et hoc est juramentum, quod Romano clero et populo ipse. (Lotharius) et Eugenius P. facere imperavit : Promitto ego ille per Deum omnipotentem et per ista sacra iv. Evangelia, et per hanc crucem D. N. J. C. et per corpus beatissimi Petri principis Apostolorum, quod ab hac die in futurum fidelis ero dominis nostris Imperatoribus Hludowico et Hlothario diebus vitae meae, juxta vires et intellectum meum, sine fraude atque malo ingenio, salva fide, quam repromisi domino Apostolico : et quod

the rebellion of the sons of Lewis (833), appeared willing to interfere as a superior mediator in their favour.[5] But he was withstood in the attempt.   By the treaty of *Verdun* (843) the popes received in the Emperor *Lothar* a less powerful master, who besides was frequently employed out of Italy, while Rome was often threatened by the invasions of the Saracens now commencing.

non consentiam, ut aliter in hac sede Romana fiat electio Pontificis nisi canonice et juste, secundum vires et intellectum meum : et ille qui electus fuerit, me consentiente, consecratus Pontifex non fiat, priusquam tale sacramentum faciat in praesentia Missi domini Imperatoris et populi, cum juramento, quale dominus Eugenius Papa sponte pro conservatione omnium factum habet per 'scriptum.

[5] Astronomus c. 48. . When it was reported of Gregory, who was in the camp of the sons, quod ideo adesset, ut tam Imperatorem quam Episcopos excommunicationis irretire vellet vinculis, si qui inobedientes essent suae filiorumque Imperatoris voluntati : parum quid subripuit Episcopis Imperatoris praesumtionis audaciae, asscrentibus nullo modo se velle ejus auctoritati succumbere : sed si excommunicans adveniret, excommunicatus abiret : cum aliter se habeat antiquorum auctoritas Canonum.   Paschasius Radbertus in vita Walae Abb. lib. ii. (in Pertz monum. ii. 562) says of the bishops on Lewis's side : insuper consiliabantur firmantes, proh dolor, quod eundem Apostolicum, quia non vocatus venerat, deponere deberent.—Quibus auditis Pontifex plurimum mirabatur ac verebatur.   Unde et ei dedimus (the bishops and monks of Lothar's party) nonnulla SS. Patrum auctoritate firmata, praedecessorumque suorum conscripta, quibus nullus contradicere possit, quod ejus esset potestas, immo Dei et b. Petri Apostoli, suaque auctoritas, ire, mittere ad omnes gentes pro fide Christi et pace Ecclesiarum, pro praedicatione Evangelii et adsertione veritatis, et in eo esset omnis auctoritas b. Petri excellens, et potestas viva ; a qua oporteret universos judicari, ita ut ipse a nemine judicandus esset (comp. § 5. not. 22). Quibus profecto gratanter acceptis valde confortatus est.   Agobard, though on the pope's side, yet writes to Lewis, de comparatione utriusque regiminis c. 4 : Certe, clementissime domine, si nunc Gregorius Papa inrationabiliter et ad pugnandum venit, merito et pugnatus et repulsus recedet.   Si autem pro quiete et pace populi et vestra laborare nititur, bene et rationabiliter obtemperandum est illi, non repugnandum. —Gregorii ep. ad Episcop. regni Francorum (ap. Mansi xiv. 521, a reply to a writing of Lewis's bishops, which is now lost) : Bene autem subjungitis, memorem me esse debere jurisjurandi causa fidei facti Imperatori.   Quod si feci, in hoc volo vitare perjurium, si annuntiavere ei omnia, quae contra unitatem et pacem Ecclesiae et regni committit : quod si non fecero, perjurus ero, sicut et vos, si tamen juravi.   Hincmar epist. 41. ad Hadrianum II.: Et quomodo Gregorius subreptus cum Lothario patri suo repugnante in Franciam venit, et pax postea in Francia ut antea non fuit, et ipse Papa cum tali honore, sicut decuerat, et sui antecessores fecerunt, Romam non rediit.

Thus attempts could now be made to avoid the legal sanction of
the emperor at the election of popes.[6]   At the choosing of
Sergius II. (844) this neglect of the imperial authority was indeed blamed,[7] but yet it was repeated at that of *Leo IV.* (847).[8]
This pope even manifested an ambitious design, by means of new
forms which he had · inserted in the writing addressed to the
princes,[9] though he still saw himself under the necessity of giving
valid assurances of his allegiance,[10] perhaps in consequence of the
examination of a conspiracy which was alleged to have been projected at Rome.[11]   Hence, at the election of *Benedict III.* (855)

[6] See above, note 4.   So still in Gregory IV. Einhardi annales ann.
827 : Gregorius—electus, sed non prius ordinatus est, quam legatus
Imperatoris Romam venit, et electionem populi, qualis esset. examin-
avit.

[7] Prudentii Trecensis ann. (or ann. Bertiniani) ann. 844 : Quo (Sergio) in sede apostolica ordinato, Lotharius filium suum Hludovicum
Romam cum Drogone, Mediomatricorum Episcopo, dirigit, acturos,
ne deinceps decedente Apostolico quisquam illic praeter sui jussionem
missorumque suorum praesentiam ordinetur antistes.   Qui Romam venientes, honorifice suscepti sunt etc.   Anastasius bibl. in vita Sergii :
Tunc demum in eadem Ecclesia (s. Petri) sedentes pariter tam beatissi-
mus Pontifex, quam magnus Rex, et omnes Archiepiscopi atque Episcopi—fidelitatem Lothario magno Imperatori semper Augusto promi-
serunt.

[8] When Rome was just threatened by the Saracens (Anastasius in vita
cv. Leonis IV.) : Romani—novi electione Pontificis congaudentes, coeperunt iterum non mediocriter contristari, eo quod sine imperiali non
audebant auctoritate futurum consecrare Pontificem, periculumque Romanae urbis maxime metuebant, ne iterum, ut olim, aliis ab hostibus
fuisset obsessa.   Hoc timore et futuro casu perterriti, eum sine permissu
Principis Praesulem consecraverunt, fidem quoque illius, sive honorem
post Deum per omnia et in omnibus conservantes.

[9] He first put his name before the names of the princes, and avoided
the appellation Dominus, hitherto used towards them.   cf. Garnerius ad
libr. diurnum Pontiff. Rom. p. 151.

[10] Anastasius in vita Leonis IV. in fine : A Roman leader, Daniel,
complained of another, Gratian, before the Emperor Lewis, that he had
said privately to him : Franci nihil nobis boni faciunt, neque adjutorium
praebent, sed magis quae nostra sunt violenter tollunt.   Quare non advo-
camus Graecos, et cum eis foedus pacis componentes Francorum Regem
et gentem de nostro regno et dominatione expellimus ?   The emperor
immenso furore accensus hastened to Rome, instituted an enquiry, but
found the accusation groundless.   It had been, however, calculated from
probability, and may lead us to infer what was the general voice in Rome.

[11] Leo IV. ad. Ludov. Imp. (so according to Pius II. in d'Archery
spicileg. iii. 811) in Gratiani decreto P. ii. C. 2 Qu. 7 c. 41 : Nos si in-

they did not venture to proceed again without the emperor's sanction.[12] But inasmuch as the Carlovingian princes generally, with the full consciousness of mastery over their clergy, allowed themselves to be misled into the practice of yielding up to them even rights superior to their own, with the view of employing them as an instrument so much the more powerful in their hands; inasmuch as they allowed themselves by turns to be deposed by their bishops,[13] thinking that they could again make their

competenter aliquid egimus, et in subditis justae legis tramitem non conservavimus, vestro ac Missorum vestrorum cuncta volumus emendare judicio. Leo IV. Lothario Augusto (ap. Gratianus P. i. dist. x. c. 9.): De capitulis vel praeceptis imperialibus vestris, vestrorumque (pontificum) praedecessorum irrefragabiliter custodiendis et conservandis, quantum valuimus et valemus Christo propitio, et nunc, et in aeternum nos conservaturos modis omnibus profitemur. Et si fortasse quilibet aliter vobis dixerit vel dicturus fuerit, sciatis eum pro certo mendacem. On this document see Baluzzii praef. ad T. I. Capitularium § 21 ss. On the interpolation pontificum see Antonii Augustini de emendatione Gratiani lib. i. dial. 19.

[12] Anastas. in vita Benedictii III.: Clerus et cuncti proceres decretum (electionis) componentes propriis manibus roboraverunt, et, consuetudo prisca ut poscit, invictissimis Lothario ac Ludovico destinaverunt Augustis. Imperial Missi appeared, and were introduced with solemnity, and in their presence finally Benedict was consecrated.

[13] The Concil. Paris. ann. 829, in an epistle to the emperors Lewis and Lothar, lib. iii. c. 8 (Mansi xiv. 597), first asserts that bishops are the judges of kings: Petimus humiliter vestram Excellentiam, ut per vos filii et proceres vestri nomen, potestatem, vigorem et dignitatem sacerdotalem cognoscant.—Illud etiam ad exemplum eis reducendum est, quod in ecclesiastica historia (Rufini x. 2) Constantinus Imp. Episcopis ait Deus, inquit, constituit vos sacerdotes, et potestatem vobis dedit de nobis quoque judicandi: et ideo nos a vobis recte judicamur; vos autem non potestis ab hominibus judicari caet. This doctrine was first brought into life by the Synod of Compiegne (833), by which the sons of Lewis caused their father to be condemned to do public penance (Conventus Compendiensis ap. Mansi xiv. 647. Pertz iii. 365), for the purpose of making him unfit to reign (Capitull. lib. vi. c. 338: Quod ad militiam saecularem post poenitentiam redire nemo debeat). Afterwards a council at Aix-la-Chapelle 842 deposed the emperor (Nithard histor. iv. 1 bei Pertz ii. 668). When Lewis the German 858 had invaded the kingdom of Charles the Bold, he procured a decree approving of his conquest, from a council at Attigny, under Archbishop Wenilo of Sens. When afterwards he was overpowered by Charles, the latter caused him to be brought to penitence by his bishops; but he would not declare his sentiments till he had asked his bishops, quia, Deo gratias, nihil sine illorum consilio feci (legatio Episcoporum ap. Baronius

authority inviolable, by episcopal unction ;[14] so also the emperors believed that they could place themselves in a secure position if they derived a peculiar divine right in their favour from papal unction, and by this means established the dangerous opinion that the imperial dignity was communicated by the pope.[15]

ann. 859. no. 6. Pertz iii. 458). All these episcopal decisions, how-ever, were only valid so far as the princes who had procured their en-actments were able or willing to maintain them with uprightness.

[14] Caroli Calvi libellus proclamationis adv. Wenilonem Archiepisc. Senonum. A. D. 859. c. 3. (ap. Baronius ann. 859 no. 25. Pertz. iii. 462): A qua consecratione vel regni sublimitate supplantari vel projici a nullo debueram, saltem sine audientia et judicio Episcoporum, quo-rum ministerio in Regem sum consecratus, et qui throni Dei sunt dicti, in quibus Deus sedet, et per quos sua decernit judicia ; quorum pater-nis correptionibus et castigatoriis judiciis me subdere fui paratus, et in praesenti sum subditus.

[15] Charlemagne himself crowned his son Lewis the Debonaire as emperor (Annales Einhardi ad ann. 813) : evocatum ad se apud Aquas-grani filium suum Hludovicum Aquitaniae Regem. coronam illi impos-suit et imperialis nominis sibi consortem fecit. When Stephen IV. visited the emperor, 816, he bestowed on him spiritual consecration (Astronomus c. 26). In the same manner Lewis appointed his son Lo-tharius emperor, who was crowned by Pope Paschalis at his visit to Rome (Annalis Einhardi ad ann. 823) : Lotharius again caused his son, Lewis II., to be crowned in Rome by Leo IV. (Prudentii Trec. ann. ad ann. 850). But this Lewis II. himself writes as early as the year 871 to the Greek emperor Basil (Muratorii scriptt. Ital. ii. ii. 243) : unctione et sacratione per summi Pontificis manus impositionem divinitus sumus ad hoc culmen provecti.—Carolus M. abavus noster unctione hujusmodi per sumum Pontificem delibutus primus ex gente et genealogia nostra—et Imperator dictus et christus Domini factus est —Si calumniaris Rom. Pontificem, quod gesserit : calumniari poteris et Samuel, quod spreto Saule, quem ipse unxerat, David in Regem un-gere non renuerit.

THIRD CHAPTER.

HISTORY OF THE FRANK EMPIRE.

Capitularia regum Francorum,[1] preserved partly in the original, partly in the Capitularium libb. vii., of which the first four books were collected by Abbot Ansegisus 827, and the last three books[2] by Benedictus Levita about 845, ed. Steph. Balusius. Paris. 1677. ed. nova cura Petri de Chiniac. Paris. 1780. ii. voll. fol. The Capitularia enlarged and improved in Pertz monum. iii., the Capitularium libri by Ansegisus, ibid. iii. 256. those by Benedictus Levita ibid. iv. ii. 39.

§ 7.

CHURCH GOVERNMENT.

Since the Frank Church had been raised from its decayed condition by Carlmann and Pipin, it began to develop its resources with freshness and power under the management of the Carlovingians, and to exercise a most important influence among the churches of the West.

The general belief was, that there must be a return to the old laws of the church, in order that men might have a secure guide in this renovation. But many decisions of that ancient church could not be brought into harmony with the fundamental principles of civil and feudal law, by which the relations of churches and clergy had been principally established, and which it was thought impossible to abandon without endangering the state. Hence arose an antagonism between the rights of the church resuscitated, and the prevailing rights of the state—an antago-

---

[1] On the capitularia generally, see Eichhorn's deutsche Rechtsgeschichte. i. 626.

[2] Benedictus Levita drew not merely from the capitularies but also from other secular and ecclesiastical laws, and has adopted in particular many Pseudo-isidoriana likewise. See the accurate specification of his services by Knust in Pertz monum. iv. ii. 19.

nism which could only be prevented from breaking forth by powerful rulers, but which, under weak princes, threatened to produce a dangerous contest between church and state.

Carlmann and Pipin immediately reinstated metropolitans in their ancient rights,[3] and endeavoured, if possible, to diminish the evil of commendator-bishops and abbots;[4] but the feudal relations of churches and monasteries remained unaltered.[5] Charlemagne, it is true, wished to restore the ancient mode of choosing bishops;[6] the laws issued on that point were not, however, universally carried out; for no choice could be made without the king's special permission,[7] and most of the bishops continued to be appointed by the kings.[8] In the opinion, indeed,

---

[3] Capit. ann. 742. c. 1. ann. 755. c. 2.

[4] Carlomanni capitulare Liftinense ann. 743. c. 2 : Statuimus quoque cum consilio servorum Dei et populi christiani, propter imminentia bella et persecutiones caeterarum gentium quae in circuitu nostro sunt, ut sub precario et censu aliquam partem ecclesialis pecuniae (goods, possessions) in adjutorium exercitus nostri cum indulgentia Dei aliquanto tempore retineamus, ea conditione, ut annis singulis de unaquaque casata (farmhouse) solidus, i. e., xii. denarii, ad Ecclesiam vel ad Monasterium reddatur; eo modo, ut si moriatur ille cui pecunia commodata fuit, Ecclesia cum propria pecunia revestita sit. Et iterum, si necessitas cogat, ut princeps jubeat, precarium renovetur, et rescribatur novum. Et omnino observetur, ut Ecclesiae vel Monasteria penuriam et paupertatem non patiantur, quorum pecunia in precario praestita sit : sed si paupertas cogat, Ecclesiae et domui Dei reddatur integra possessio. Eugen Montag's Gesch. d. deutschen staatsbürgerl. Freiheit (2 Bde. Bamb. u. Würzb. 1812) i. i. 333.

[5] The fealty-duties were so severe in many monasteries that Lewis the Debonaire, 817, lightened them, and established three classes, monasteria, quae dona et militiam facere debent,—quae tantum dona dare debent sine militia,—quae nec dona nec militiam dare debent, sed solas orationes pro salute Imperatoris vel filiorum ejus et stabilitate imperii, see the list in Baluz. capit. i. 589, and the commentary annexed, ii. 1092

[6] Capit. Aquisgranense A. D. 803 c. 2. (Baluz. cap. i. 379), repeated word for word capit. Aquisgr. A. D. 817 c. 2. (Baluz. i. 564. Pertz. monum iii. 206). Comp. Formulae diversae in Episcoporum promotionibus usurpatae post restitutam electionum libertatem ap. Baluz. ii. 591. Especially on the management of the choice by royal missi : Adlocutio Missorum Imp. Ludov. P. ad clerum et plebem electionis causa congregatum, ib. p. 601.

[7] Conc. Valentinum ann. 855 c. 7. (Mansi xv. 7.)

[8] Baluzius ad Concilia Galliae Narbonensis (Paris. 1668. 8.) p. 34. Ejusd. not. ad capitul. ii. 1141. Comp. Thegani vita Ludovici Imp. c.

of ecclesiastics, this was regarded as an abuse; but that bishops should be confirmed and invested by kings was universally held to be necessary.[9] The Carlovingians allowed the possessions of the church to be continually set apart to foreign purposes. Bishoprics, indeed, were no longer bestowed in usufruct, but single estates and abbeys were conferred in this way on valiant soldiers (Abbacomites).[10] The feudal system was also introduced

20: Consiliariis suis magis credidit quam opus esset; quod ei fecit occupatio psalmodiae et lectionum assiduitas, et aliud quod ille non incipiebat. Quia jam dudum illa pessima consuetudo erat, ut ex vilissimis servis fiebant summi pontifices: hoc non prohibuit. Leo IV. epist. ad Lothar. et Ludov. Aug. about 853 (in Gratiani decret. P. I. dist. 63. c. 16.):—Vestram mansuetudinem deprecamur, quatenus Colono humili diacono eandem Ecclesiam [Reatinam] ad regendum concedere dignemini; ut vestra licentia accepta, ibidem eum Deo adjuvante consecrare valeamus Episcopum. Sin autem in praedicta Ecclesia nolueritis ut praeficiatur Episcopus, Tusculanam Ecclesiam, quae viduata existit, illi vestra Serenitas dignetur concedere; ut consecratus a nostro praesulatu, Deo omnipotenti vestroque imperio grates peragere valeat. So, too, John VIII. petitions King Carlmann, 879, to bestow the bishopric of Vercelli on one Conspertus (ap. Mansi xvii. 125), and afterwards announces the appointment to the inhabitants of Vercelli (l. c. p. 166), with the remark, quoniam—Carolomanus—ipsum Vercellensem episcopatum more praecessorum suorum regum et imperatorum concessit huic Consperto, etc.

[9] Hincmar epist. 12. ad Ludov. iii. Franc. Regem: Episcopi talem eligant, qui et s. Ecclesiae utilis, et regno proficuus et vobis fidelis ac devotus cooperator existat; et consentientibus clero et plebe eum vobis adducant, ut secundum ministerium vestrum res et facultates Ecclesiae, quas ad defendendum et tuendum vobis Dominus commendavit, suae dispositioni committatis, et cum consensu ac litteris vestris eum ad metropolitanum Episcopum ac coëpiscopos ipsius dioeceseos, qui eum ordinare debent, transmittatis.

[10] For this Lewis the Debonaire was very much blamed as early as 828, at Worms, by Wala, abbot of Corvey (Paschasius Radbertus in vita Walae ii. 3. in Pertz monum. ii. 549): Ecce Rex noster, ut saepe ostensum est, de facultatibus Ecclesiarum multa in suis suorumque praesumit usibus.—Si respublica sine suffragio rerum Ecclesiarum subsistere non valet; quaerendus est modus et ordo cum summa reverentia et religione Christianitatis, si quid vos vestrique ab Ecclesiis ob defensionem magis quam ad rapinam accipere debeatis. The Concil. Paris. ann. 829. lib. iii. c. 15. (Mansi xiv. 600) requests the emperor, ut—quasdam sedes episcopales, quae rebus propriis viduatae, immo annullatae esse videntur, dum tempus habetis, et opportunitas se praebuerit, de earum sublevatione et consolatione cogitetis. That they were not deficient also in lay abbots may be seen from capitul. ann. 825. c. 10. (ap. Pertz

into the lower situations of the church. Not only were candidates for ordination obliged to take a sort of oath of fealty to the bishop,[11] but even civil rulers considered the churches founded by them as loans, which they had at their disposal, and thus *the right of patronage*[12] was developed.

iii. 294. according to Baluz. i. 635. ann. 823. c. 8) : Abbatibus quoque et laicis specialiter jubemus, ut in monasteriis, quae ex nostra largitate habent, Episcoporum consilio et documento ea quae ad religionem canonicorum, monachorum, sanctimonialium pertinent, peragant. Agobardus de dispensatione ecclesiasticarum rerum c. 4. exculpates Lewis the Debonaire on this account : quoniam de sacris rebus in laicales usos illicite translatis dicimus, non fecit iste dominus Imperator, sed praecessores ejus, et propterea isti impossibile est omnia emendare, quae antecedentes male usurpata dimiserunt. Frequently, perhaps, did powerful laymen themselves take possession of church property, Conc. Aquisgran. ann. 836 ad Pippinum Regem Aquitaniae lib. i. c. 3 : Sunt etiam quidam —sibi in Deo oblatis sacratisque rebus auferendis impunitatem inaniter promittentes, qui—solent dicere : Quid mali, quidve discriminis est, si rebus ecclesiasticis in nostris pro libitu nostro utimur necessitatibus ? Quid curae est inde Deo sanctisque ejus, ob quorum amorem Deo dicantur oblatae, cum utique in eorundem sanctorum usus nihil ex his cedat ? · Et ubi Deus haec, quae Ecclesiarum rectores opponunt, jussit sibi offerri, praesertim cum omnia quae in terris sunt sua sint, et ille ea ad usus hominum creaverit ? Under Lewis's sons the case was still worse. See the complaints of the bishops A.D. 844 in the Conventus ad Theodonis villam c. 4. and the Concilio in Verno palatio c. 12. (Baluzii capit. ii. 10. 18. Pertz monum. iii. 382. 385.) Conc. Valentinum ann. 855. c. 8. Planck ii. 542. Montag's Gesch. d. deutschen staatsbürgerlichen Freiheit i. i. 337. Möhler's Schriften i. 322.

[11] See an example of such an oath in the Deutschen Abschwörungs-Glaubens-Beich-tund Betformeln vom 8ten bis 12ten Jahrh., herausgeg. von. H. F. Massmann, Quedlinb. u. Leipzig 1839. S. 182.

[12] To the builder of a church remained by law the possession of it (Conc. Francof. ann. 794. c, 54. in Baluz. capit. i. 270. Pertz monum. iii. 75), and the privilege of appointing to it a suitable presbyter, who, however, was obliged to obtain the bishop's approval, and to continue subject to his superintendence like other clergymen (Conc. Rom. ann. 826 and 853 c: 21. ap. Mansi xiv. 1006). However, so early as between the years 649 and 664 the Conc. Cabilon. c. 14. complains, quod oratoria per villas potentum jam longo constructa tempore et facultates ibidem collatas ipsi, quorum villae sunt, Episcopis contradicant, et jam nec ipsos clericos, qui ad ipsa oratoria deserviunt, ab Archidiacono coërceri permittant. Agobardus de privilegio et jure sacerdotii c. 11 (Opp. i. 134) : increbuit consuetudo impia, ut paene nullus inveniatur anhelans et quantulumcunque proficiens ad honores et gloriam temporalem, qui non domesticum habeat sacerdotem, non cui obediat, sed a quo incessanter exigat licitam simul atque inlicitam obedientiam, non solum

Ecclesiastical legislation,[13] the highest judicial power in church affairs,[14] the management and confirmation of ecclesiastical decrees,[15] remained with the king, who summoned the spiritual as

in divinis officiis, verum etiam in humanis; ita ut plerique inveniantur, qui aut ad mensas ministrent, aut saccata vina misceant, aut canes ducant, aut caballos, quibus feminae sedent, regant, aut agellos provideant. Et quia tales, de quibus haec dicimus, bonos sacerdotes in domibus suis habere non possunt,—non curant omnino quales clerici illi sint, quanta ignorantia coeci, quantis criminibus involuti ; tantum ut habeant presbyteros proprios, quorum occasione deserant Ecclesias, seniores et officia publica. Quod autem non habeant eos propter religionis honorem, apparet ex hoc, quod non habent eos in honore. Unde et contumeliose eos nominantes, quando volunt illos ordinari Presbyteros, rogant nos aut jubent, dicentes : habeo unum clericionem, quem mihi nutrivi de servis meis propriis, aut beneficialibus, sive pagensibus, aut obtinui ab illo vel illo homine, sive de illo vel illo pago : volo, ut ordines eum mihi Presbyterum. Comp. Isidor Kaim's Kirchenpatronatrecht nach seiner Entstehung, Entwickelung und heutigen Stellung im Staate. Th. i. die Rechtsgeschichte. Leipzig 1845.

[13] The numerous ecclesiastical regulations in the Capitularies afford proof of this. When Charlemagne, A.D. 802, caused a general revision of legislation to be undertaken (Eichhorn's deutsche Rechtsgesch i. 613), several capitularies respecting ecclesiastical things proceeded from it also.

[14] Capitulare Francofordiense A.D. 794 c. 4 : Statutum est a domino Rege et s. Synodo, ut Episcopi justitias faciant in suas parochias. Si non obedierit aliqua persona Episcopo suo de Abbatibus, Presbyteris, Diaconibus etc., veniant ad Metropolitanum suum, et ille dijudicet causam cum suffraganeis suis. Comites quoque nostri veniant ad judicium Episcoporum. Et si aliquid est, quod Episcopus metropolitanus non possit corrigere vel pacificare, tunc tandem veniant accusatores cum accusato cum litteris Metropolitani, ut sciamus veritatem rei. Capitulare tertium ann. 812 c. 1 : Ut Episcopi, Abbates, Comites, et potentiores quique si causam inter se habuerint ac se pacificare noluerint ad nostram jubeantur venire praesentiam.

[15] De Marca lib. vi. c. 24-28. Comp. the acts of the councils called together by Charlemagne, at Arles, Rheims, Tours, Chalons, and Mainz, (ap. Mansi xiv. 55 ss.) in the introductory and concluding addresses. Ex. gr. praef. ad Conc. Mogunt. ann. 813 (p. 64) : Gloriosissimo Imp. Carolo Aug. verae religionis rectori ac defensori s. Ecclesiae.—venimus secundum jussionem vestram in civitatem Moguntinam : gratias agimus Deo, quia s. Ecclesiae suae tam pium ac devotum in servitio Dei concessit habere rectorem, qui suis temporibus sacrae sapientiae fontem aperiens, oves Christi indesinenter sanctis reficit alimentis, ac divinis instruit disciplinis etc.—After enumerating their employments : De his tamen omnibus valde indigemus vestro adjutorio atque sana doctrina, quae et nos jugiter admoneat, atque clementer erudiat, quatenus ea quae paucis subter perstrinximus capitulis, a vestra auctoritate firmentur si

well as the civil feudatories to diets,[16] conducted spiritual causes
by the *Apocrisiarius* (or *Archicapellanus*, afterwards *Archi-
cancellarius*),[17] as he did civil causes by the *Comes Palatii* ; and
sent round into every province two extraordinary judges (*missi*),
a bishop and a count,[18] to exercise in common the highest over-

tamen vestra pietas ita dignum esse judicaverit : et quidquid in eis emendatione dignum reperitur, vestra—imperialis dignitas jubeat emendare.
Concluding words of the Conc. Arelat. (p. 62) : Haec igitur sub brevi-
tate, quae emendatione digna perspeximus, quam brevissime annotavi-
mus, et domino Imperatori praesentanda decrevimus, poscentes ejus
clementiam, ut si quid hic minus est, ejus prudentia suppleatur : si quid
secut quam se ratio habet, ejus judicio emendetur : si quid rationabiliter
taxatum est, ejus adjutorio divina opitulante clementia perficiatur.   Accordingly Charlemagne says, in the libr. Carolinis praef. ad lib. i. : Ecclesiae in sinu regni gubernacula suscepimus:—nobis (Ecclesia) ad regendum commissa est ; and Lewis the Debonaire declares, in the prologus ad
capit. Aquisgr. ann. 816 (Baluz. i. 562), it to be his duty, ut quicquid
sive in ecclesiasticis negotiis, sive in statu republicae, emendatione dignum prospexissemus, quantum Dominus posse dabat, nostro studio
emendaretur.

[16] For which, since 811, the clergy begin to form a proper curia (hall)
for deliberation on ecclesiastical matters, Planck ii. 139.

[17] Walafrid. Strabo de rebus eccles. c. 31. : Quemadmodum sunt in
palatiis praeceptores vel comites palatii, qui saecularium causas ven-
tilant, ita sunt et illi quos summos Capellanos Franci appellant, Clericorum causis praelati. Hincmar de ordine palatii § 13. calls the spiritual
minister Apocrisiarium i. e. responsalem negotiorum ecclesiasticorum.
See Eichhorn's deutsche Rechtsgesch. i. 194.

[18] Comp. Eichhorn's deutsche Rechtsgesch, i. 681.   Cf. capitulare
iii. ann. 789. c. 11. (Baluz. capitul. i 244), capitula data Missis dominicis belonging to the year 802 (p. 375), capitulare Noviomagense belonging to the year 806 cap. 4. (p. 453), capitulare anni 828 (p. 657) :
Haec sunt capitula, quae volumus ut diligenter (Missi) inquirant.
Primo de Episcopis quomodo ministerium expleant, et qualis sit illorum
conversatio vel quomodo Ecclesias et clerum sibi commissum ordinatum
habeant atque dispositum, vel quibus rebus maxime studeant, in spiritualibus videlicet aut in saecularibus negotiis.   Deinde quales sint adjutores ministerii eorum, i. e. Chorepiscopi, Archipresbyteri, Archidiaconi et Vicedomini, et Presbyteri per parochias eorum, quale scilicet
studium habeant in doctrina, vel qualem famam habeant secundum
veritatem in populo.   Similiter de omnibus monasteriis inquirant juxta
uniuscujusque qualitatem et professionem.   Similiter et de caeteris
Ecclesiis nostra auctoritate in beneficio datis.   Utrum Episcopi in circumeundo parochias suas caeteras minores Ecclesias gravent, aut populo
oneri sint, et si ab ipsis aut a ministris eorum indebita exenia a Presbyteris exigantur.—Quae personae vel de quibus causis culpabiles ad
praesentiam nostram venire debeant, discernendum est.   Exceptis Epis-

sight and power in things ecclesiastical as well as civil. Bishops and counts were every where instructed to work in common, and mutually to support one another;[19] while ecclesiastical usurpations were not endured.[20] The pope's supremacy was acknowledged. The kings inquired of him in matters of ecclesiastical legislation,[21] and consulted him in difficult questions;[22] but till

copis, Abbatibus, Comitibus, qui ad placita nostra semper venire debent isti venient, si in talibus culpis et criminibus deprehensi fuerint quales inferius adnotatae sunt. Capitula Misso cuidam data A.D. 803. c. 5. (Baluz. i. 402. Pertz monum. iii. 122): referebatur de Episcopis, Abbatibus, vel caetris nostris hominibus, qui ad placitum vestrum venire contempserint. Illos vero per bannum nostrum ad placitum vestrum bannire faciatis. Et qui tunc venire contempserint, eorum nomina annotata ad placitum nostrum generale nobis repraesentes. Cf. Franc. de Roye de Missis dominicis, eorum officio et potestate. Andegavi 1672. 4. iter. ed. J. W. Neuhaus. Lips. 1744. 8.

[19] Capitulare Bajoaricum ann. 803 c. 4. (Baluz. i. 450. Pertz monum. iii. 127): Ut Episcopi cum comitibus stent, et Comites cum Episcopis, ut uterque pleniter suum ministerium peragere possint. Comp. Ludovici Germ. Regis conventus Mogunt. ann. 851. I. De concordia Episcoporum Comitumque fidelium (Pertz, monum. iii. 411).

[20] Thus preventions of the administration of justice by the privilege of Asylum. Capitulare ann. 779. c. 8. (Baluz. i. 197. Pertz iii. 36), capitula, quae in lege Salica mittenda sunt, ann. 803. (Baluz. i. 387. Pertz iii. 113) c. 2: Si homo furtum fecerit, aut homicidium vel quodlibet crimen foras committens infra immunitatem fugerit, mandet Comes vel Episcopo, vel Abbati, vel Vicedomino,—ut reddat ei reum.—Si—eum reddere noluerit, in prima contradictione solidis xv. culpabilis judicetur.—Si nec ad tertiam inquisitionem consentire voluerit, quicquid reus damnum fecerit, totum ille, qui eum infra immunitatem retinet,—solvere cogatur. Et ipse Comes veniens licentiam habeat ipsum hominem infra immunitatem quaerendi, ubicunque eum invenire potuerit.

[21] So Pipin in Zacharias, about 747. See Zachar. epist. ad Bonifacium (in epist. Bonif. ed. Serarii epist. 139. ed. Würdtwein ep. 74. ap. Mansi xii. 334): Agnoscas, charissme, flagitasse a nobis Pippinum, excellentissimum majorem domus gentis Francorum, per suum hominem, nomine Ardobanium, religiosum Presbyterum, aliquanta capitula de sacerdotali ordine, et quae ad salutem animae pertinent: simul etiam et pro illicita copula qualiter sese debeant custodire juxta ritum Christianae religionis, et sacrorum canonum instituta.—Illius vocibus aurem accommodantes, in brevi eloquio conscripta apostolica documenta direximus etc. These capitula Zachariae P. ad Pippinum missa, besides an epistle to the same, are given in Serarius, Mansi, and Würdtwein ll. cc. —A more copious Codex canonum, namely, an enlarged Dionysian collection, was received from Charlemagne, 774, by Hadrian I. An epitome of the first part, or the synodical decrees, may be seen in Canisii lectt. ant. ed. Basnage ii. 266. Mansi xii. 859 ss. The first part is

the time of Lewis the Debonaire they allowed him no other influence over the Frank church, than that of advice, admonition,
and remonstrance.[23] Under that weak prince, however, the Frank
bishops felt that they were partly threatened, by the continued
civil disturbances,[24] and partly instigated, to enlarge the power
of the church. Hence they began to assert the church's supremacy,[25] and to adduce the Roman see as the natural point of its

printed complete in J. Hartzheim Concilia Germaniae i. 131 ss. A
description of the entire Codex see in Ballerini de antt. Canonum collect.
P. iii. c. 2.   J. C. Rudolph nova comm. de cod. cann. quem Hadr. I.
Carolo M. dono dedit. Erlangg. 1777. 8.   Spittler's Gesch. d. canon.
Rechts S. 168 ss.

[23] Comp. epist. Caroli. M. ad Episc. A.D. 799 (in Baluzii capit. i.
327): Et hoc vobiscum magno studio pertractandum est, quid de illis
Presbyteris, unde approbatio non · est et semper negant, faciendum sit.
Nam hoc saepissime a nobis et progenitoribus atque antecessoribus nostris ventilatum est, sed non ad liquidum hactenus definitum.   Unde ad
consulendum Patrem nostrum Leonem Papam sacerdotes nostros mittimus. Et quicquid ab eo vel a suis perceperimus, vobis una cum illis
quos mittimus, renuntiare non retardabimus.   Vos interdum vicissim
tractate adtentius, quid ex his vobiscum constituamus una cum praedicti
s. Patris institutionibus etc.   So respecting the ordinations performed
by the country bishops, capit. Aquisgr. A.D. 803. l. c. p. 380): quod
jurgium cum enucleatius discutere voluissemus, placuit nobis ex hoc
apostolicam sedem consulere, jubente canonica auctoritate atque dicente:
Si majores causae in medio fuerint devolutae, ad sedem apostolicam, ut
a. Synodus statuit, et beata consuetudo exigit, incunctanter referatur.
Comp. vol. i. § 94. note 20.

[23] Therefore, many capitularia were issued, apostolicae sedis hortatu,
monente Pontifice, ex praecepto Pontificis.   At the Synod of Frankfurt, 794, two papal legates were present, Theophylactus ac Stephanus
Episcopi, vicem tenentes ejus, a quo missi sunt, Hadriani Papae (Ann.
Einhardi ap. Pertz. i. 181): but yet Charlemagne had the presidency.
See Synodica Concilii ad Episc. Galliae et Germaniae ap. Mansi xiii.
884: congregatis nobis,—praecipiente piissimo et gloriosissimo domino
nostro Carolo rege.

[24] During the reign of Lewis the Debonaire, bishops were frequently
deposed for taking part in insurrections, ex. gr. in 818 the bishops of
Milan, Cremona, and Orleans, as being concerned in Bernhard's conspiracy, 835; Ebbo, archbishop of Rheims, &c. The sentences, it is true,
proceeded from synods; but these were called by the emperor, and
composed of the political opponents of the accused.

[25] Thus the Concil Paris. ann. 829 lib. i. c, 3. (Mansi xiv. 537) again
brings forward the passage ep. Gelasi. P. ad Anastasium Imp. ann. 494
(Mansi viii. 31.): Duo sunt,—quibus principaliter mundus hic regitur,
auctoritas sacrata Pontificum et regalis potestas.   In quibus tanto gravius est pondus sacerdotum, quanto etiam pro ipsis regibus Domino in

support.[26] And since the bishops certainly needed protection against worldly tyranny, the right of appeal in particular, which had been transferred to the pope at Sardica, was recalled,[27] but soon enlarged, so that every bishop might choose the pope to be his judge instead of his own provincial synod.[28] Civil govern-

divino reddituri sunt examine rationem; and the passage from Fulgentius de veritate praedestinationis et gratiae (lib. ii.): Quantum pertinet ad hujus temporis vitam in Ecclesia nemo Pontifice potior, et in saeculo Christiano Imperatore nemo celsior invenitur. Accordingly, the council demands, for the future, that suitable respect should be paid to the bishops. Moreover, the original cause of the perplexities are given with perfect justice and truth (Mansi xiv. 603): Specialiter unum obstaculum ex multo tempore jam inolevisse cognovimus: id est, quia et principalis potestas diversis occasionibus intervenientibus, secus quam auctoritas divina se habeat, in causas ecclesiasticas prosilierit, et sacerdotes partim negligentia, partim ignorantia, partim cupiditate in saecularibus negotiis et sollicitudinibus mundi, ultra quam debuerant, se occupaverint. Et hac occasione aliter quam divina auctoritas doceat in utraque parte actum extitisse dubium non est.

[26] Conc. Parisiensis ann. 849. Synodica ad Nomenojum Ducem (ap. Mansi xiv. 923): omnem laesisti Christianitatem, dum vicarium b. Petri apostolicum, cui dedit Deus primatum in omni orbe terrarum sprevisti.

[27] In the codex presented by Hadrian to Charlemagne were found certainly (see Hartzheim Concil. Germ. i. 190) the Canones Sardicenses (see vol. i. § 94, note 7); but there was also the African prohibition of appeal, ad transmarina (Hartzheim i. 228), and the epist. Conc. Afric. ad Coelestin. (Hartzheim i. 233), see vol. i. § 94, note 61. Out of this codex Charlemagne inserted the most important conoues in the Capitulare Aquisgram. s. primum ann. 789; but here we do not find those Sardican canons that establish the right of appeal to Rome, but rather the Nicene and Antiochian canons, which attribute the highest authority to the provincial synod. Accordingly, even all complaints against bishops were decided by synods, Thomassina vetus et nova Ecclesiae disciplina de beneficiis P. ii. lib. 3. c. 109. Benedictus Levita is the first who has in his collection of capitularies the Sardican decrees. Cap. lib. vi. c. 64: Et judicato in aliqua causa Episcopo liceat iterare judicium, et, si necesse fuerit, libere Episcopum adire Romanum. Cf. lib. vii. c. 103, c. 412.

[28] The theory which Benedictus Levita has adopted in addition to the Sardican regulation, was developed, lib. vii. c. 315: Placuit, ut, si Episcopus accusatus appellaverit Romanum Pontificem, id statuendum, quod ipse censuerit (a manifest falsification of the expression of the Epitome Codicis ab Hadriano Carolo M. donati ap. Mansi xii. 872: Si Episcopus damnatus appellaverit Rom. Pont., id observandum, quod ipse censuerit.) Cf. lib. vii. c. 173. Addit. iv. c. 27. Accordingly, Gregory IV., as early as the year 835, raised his claims, while he asserted, in reference to the accused Aldricus, bishop of Mans (epist. ad universos Episcc. ap. Mansi xiv. p. 513): Liceat illi post auditionem

ments themselves, by calling in the papal authority to their aid,
when they felt their weakness on the occasion of unusual ecclesiastical matters, furnished ground for the opinion that such authority could not be dispensed with in important ecclesiastical regulations.[29] Thus papal influence over the Frank church increased
very perceptibly,[30] and new ideas of church polity arose, to which
Pseudoisidore, in his decretals, tried to give a historic basis.

Primatum dioeceseos, si necesse fuerit, nos appellare :—nullusque illum
ante haec judicet aut judicare praesumat. And Leo IV. (epist. ad.
Episcc. Britanniae ap. Mansi xiv. p. 882) : Nullam damnationem Episcoporum esse unquam censemus, nisi aut ante legitimum numerum
Episcoporum, qui fit per xii. Episcopos, aut certe probata sententia per
lxxii. idoneos testes.—Et si inter eos, quos damnandos esse dixerunt
homines, fuerit Episcopus, qui suam causam in praesentia Romanae sedis Episcopi petierit audiri, nullus super illum finitivam praesumat dare
sententiam : sed omnino eum audiri decernimus.

[29] When, for example, Ebbo, who had been deposed from the archbishopric of Rheims, on account of a rebellion, 835, was appointed, after
844, bishop of Hildesheim by Lewis the German, (Conc. Tricassini
ann. 867, ep. ad Nicolaum P. ap. Mansi xv. 794) auctoritate cujusdam
privilegii—a b. Gregorio Papa sibi collati, connivente supra—sua restitutione, ministerium pontificale fine tenus exercuit. In this privilege
was contained in transmigratione alterius parochiae ut episcopali et
praedicationis licenter fungeretur officio. (The doubts which Baluzius
in his Regino p. 599, raises against the genuineness of this privilegium
are unsatisfactory ; even Rhabanus, Ebbo's metropolitan, in ep. ad Heribaldum c. 34, ibid. p. 518, attests, eum ab apostolica sede in locum
suum restitutum esse). Thus, now, in an unusual case, a pope had
both restored a deposed bishop to his office, and sanctioned his removal.
By this means, the rule that had been hitherto observed was broken
through (capitul. vi. ann. 806, c. 10, ap. Baluz. i. 456) : ne de uno loco
ad alium transeat Episcopus sine decreto Episcoporum : we find it afterwards even in Hincmar, the opponent of the Pseudoisidorian principles, de translationibus Episcoporum c. 7. (written 872) Opp. ii. 744.
Episcopus de civitate, in qua ordinatus est, transferatur ad aliam civitatem synodali dispositione, vel apostolicae sedis consensione. Comp.
Thomassinus P. ii. lib. 2, c. 63.

[30] Respecting the earlier limits of Roman influence, and its gradual
enlargement, see Agobard de dispensatione eccles. rerum c. 20. (Cf.
adv. legem. Gundobadi c. 12) : Verum quia sunt, qui Gallicanos canones aut aliarum regionum putent non recipiendos, eo quod legati Romani seu Imperatoris in eorum constitutione non interfuerint (adv. leg.
Gund. l. c. quod neoterici Romani eos non commendaverint) : restat, ut
etiam SS. Patrum doctrinas et expositiones diversosque tractatus, ut
sunt Cypriani, Athanasii etc., doceant non esse recipiendos : quia cum
haec tractarent,—legati Romani s. Imperatoris non aderant. Melius
mihi sentire videntur, qui secundum Domini dictum, ubi duo vel tres in

§. 8.

RESTORATION OF ECCLESIASTICAL ORDER.

The Carlovingians chiefly sought to reform the state of morals among the laity[1] as well as the clergy,[2] but met with great opposition in consequence of the grossness of the age.[3] For this end

nomini Domini congregatos agnoscunt, Dominum quoque inter eos affuisse non dubitant.—Ubicunque enim catholici Ecclesiarum rectores pro Ecclesiarum utilitatibus cum Dei timore in ejus nomine et honore conveniunt, quicquid consonanter s. scripturis statuunt, nulli proculdubio spernenda, immo veneranda omnibus esse debent.

[1] Prohibitions of heathenism capit. Liftinense ann. 743, c. 4, Pertz iii 18, comp. the Indiculus superstitionum et paganiarum ibid. p. 19, and in the capitularies very often.—Statuta Salisburgensia ann. 799: Ut omnis populis honorifice cum omnibus supplicationibus devotione, humiliter et cum reverentia absque pretiosarum vestium ornatu vel etiam illecebroso cantico et lusu saeculari cum lactaniis procedant, et discant Kyrieeleyson clamare, ut non tam rustice, ut nunc usque, sed melius discant.

[2] So Carlomanni capit. i. ann. 742, c. 2 (ap. Baluz. i. 146): Servis Dei per omnia omnibus armaturam portare vel pugnare, aut in exercitum et in hostem pergere omino prohibuimus.—Nec non et illas venationes et sylvaticas vagationes cum canibus omnibus servis Dei interdiximus. Similiter ut accipitres et falcones non habeant. c. 6. Punishments for lewdness in the clergy, Pipini capit. ann. 744, c. 8 (ibid. p. 158): Similiter diximus, ut neque clericus mulierem habeat in domo sua, quae cum illo habitet, nisi matrem, aut sororem, vel neptem suam. All these laws were frequently repeated.

[3] Respecting Gewillieb, archbishop of Mainz, see Othlonus in vita Bonif. i. c. 44. Comp. especially capitulare viii. ann. 803, ap. Baluz. i. 405 ss. Petitio populi ad Imperatorem: Flexis omnes precamur poplitibus majestatem vestram, ut Episcopi deinceps, sicut hactenus, non vexentur hostibus, sed quando vos nosque in hostem pergimus, ipsi propriis resideant in parochiis, Deoque fideliter famulari studeant etc. —Quosdam enim ex eis in hostibus et praeliis vulneratos vidimus, et quosdam perisse cognovimus.—Illud tamen vobis et omnibus scire cupimus, quod non propterea haec petimus, ut eorum res aut aliquid ex eorum pecuniis, nisi ipsis aliquid sponte nobis dare placuerit, aut eorum Ecclesias viduari cupiamus.—Scimus enim res Ecclesiae Deo esse sacratas etc. In consequence of this petition, it was resolved at a synodalis conventus (p. 409), ut nullus sacerdos in hostem pergat, nisi duo vel tres tantum Episcopi—propter benedictionem et praedicationem populique reconciliationem, et cum illis electi sacerdotes, qui bene sciant populis poenitentias dare, Missas celebrare, de infirmis curam habere, sacratique olei cum sacris precibus unctionem impendere, et hoc maxime

they found a weighty support in the *vita canonica*[4] first introduced by *Chrodegang* (bishop of Metz from 742–766) among his clergy. This system of rules having been confirmed by Charlemagne,[5] and with some additions by Lewis the Debonaire at Aix-la-chapelle, 816,[6] was soon adopted in almost all the cities of the Frank empire (Canonici[7] cathedrales and collegiati,

praevidere, ne sine viatico quis de saeculo recedat. Hi vero nec arma ferant, nec ad pugnam pergant,—sed tantum sanctorum pignora et sacra ministeria ferant et orationibus pro viribus insistant, ut populis qui pugnare debet, auxiliante Domino victor existat.——Reliqui vero, qui ad Ecclesias suas remanent, suos homines bene armatos nobiscum, aut cum quibus jusserimus, dirigant; et ipsi pro nobis et cuncto exercitu nostro Missas, letanias, oblationes, eleemosynas faciant, orantes Deum caeli, ut proficiamus in itinere quo pergimus, victoresque Deo adminiculante existamus.   Gentes enim et Reges earum, quae sacerdotes secum pugnare permiserunt, neque praevalebant in bello, nec victores extiterunt, quia non erat differentia inter laicos et sacerdotes, quibus pugnare non est licitum.   Haec vero Galliarum, Hispaniarum, Langobardorum, nonnullasque alias gentes et Reges earum fecisse cognovimus, quae propter praedictum nefandissimum scelus nec victores extiterunt, nec patrias retinuerunt.   To this is attached the following regulation : Quia instante antiquo hoste audivimus, quosdam nos suspectos habere propterea quod concessimus—sacerdotibus—, ut in hostes—non irent,— nec arma ferrent,—quod honores sacerdotum et res Ecclesiarum auferre vel minuere eis voluissemus, quod nullatenus facere velle vel facere volentibus consentire omnes scire cupimus.——Et ut haec certius credantur et per futura tempora conserventur, praecipimus, ut nullus res Ecclesiae nisi precario possideat etc.——Novimus multa regna et Reges eorum propterea cecidisse, quia Ecclesias spoliaverunt, resque earum vastaverunt, abstulerunt—et pugnantibus dederunt etc.   We see here how the prejudices of a people, accustomed to war and feudal duties, were overpowered by religious prejudices.   The petitio in question had been, doubtless, brought about artfully.

[4] Chrodogangi regula sincera ap. Mansi xiv. 313.   Cf. Thomassini vet. et nov. Eccl. discipl. P. i. lib. iii. c. 9.   Rettberg's Kirchengesch. Deutschlands i. 495.

[5] Capit. Aquisgr. ann. 789. c. 71. (ap. Baluz. i. 238): Qui ad clericatum accedunt, quod nos nominamus canonicam vitam, volumus, ut illi canonice secundum suam regulam omnimodis vivant, et Episcopus eorum regat vitam, sicut Abba Monachorum.   Capit. i. ann. 802. c. 22. (ibid. p. 369.)

[6] The regula Aquisgranensis in Hartzhemii Conc. Germ. i. 430.

[7] The title Canonicus was indeed already in use, but in the sense of canoni s. matriculae Ecclesiae adscriptus, or canonem frumentarium percipiens (see Muratori diss. de Canonicis in the antiquitt. Itall. medii aevi v. 183): and was now first used in the signification of a clerici regulariter i. e. canonice viventis.

Monasteria canonicorum). In like manner the maintenance of order among the country clergy was secured by the division of dioceses into *Archidiaconatus*,[8] which began to be made about the same time as the preceding regulation, and of these again into *Archipresbyteratus* or *Decanias*.[9] On the other hand, the *Chorepiscopi*, who were often used as helps instead of the bishops, were, for the most part, removed;[10] and finally it was

[8] Heddo first divided his bishopric of Strassburg into seven arch-deaconries, and received for this, 774, the approval of Hadrian I. Grandidier hist. de l'église de Strasbourg, vol. i. p. 176. 291. vol. ii. original document no. 66. Planck ii. 584.

[9] Thomassinus P. i. l. ii. c. 5. The clergy of every deanery came together on the calends of every month, chiefly for spiritual exercises and deliberations (Hincmari capitula anno xii. Episcopatus superaddita c. 1. opp. ed. Sirmond. i. 731: Et semper de Kalendis in Kalendis mensium, quando Presbyteri de Decaniis simul conveniunt, collationem de poenitentibus suis habeant, qualiter uuusquisque suam poenitentiam faciat): but to these were soon joined luxurious banquets. See Hincmari capitula Presbyteris data ann. 852. c. 15. (opp. i. 714).: Ut, quando Presbyteri per Kalendas simul convenerint, post peractum divinum mysterium et necessariam collationem non quasi ad prandium ibi ad tabulam resideant, et per tales inconvenientes pastellos (meal-times) se invicem gravent, quia inhonestum est et onerosum. Saepe enim tarde ad Ecclesias suas redeuntes majus damnum de reprehensione conquirunt, et de gravedine mutua contrahunt, quam lucrum ibi faciant.—Et ideo peractis omnibus, qui voluerint, panem cum caritate et gratiarum actione in domo confratris sui simul cum fratribus suis frangant, et singulos biberes (drunk) accipiant, maxime autem ultra tertiam vicem poculum ibi non contingant, et ad Ecclesias suas redeant.—In Germany the archdeaconship coincided with the province, the deanship with the aut (centen. orig.)

[10] Hence Hincmar, archbishop of Rheims, had complained of this in a letter to Pope Leo IV. (see Flodoardi, canon in Rheims, † 966, hist. Eccl. Remensis lib. iii. c. 10), quod terrena potestas hac materia saepe offenderet, ut videlicet Episcopo quolibet defuncto per Chorepiscopum solis Pontificibus debitum ministerium perageretur, et res ac facultates Ecclesiae saecularium usibus expenderentur, sicut et in nostra Ecclesia jam secundo actum fuisset. Besides, many bishops of this kind also consecrated themselves at their convenience. See Benedictus Levita in capitularium lib. vi. c. 121: Placuit ne Chorepiscopi a quibusquam deinceps fiant, quoniam hactenus a nescientibus sanctorum patrum et maxime Apostolicorum decreta, suisque quietibus ac delectationibus inhaerentibus facti sunt. Thus, then, the decisions of ancient councils were renewed for the purpose of checking the country bishops (see vol. i. § 91. not. 19.) See capit. ecclesiast. ann. 789. c. 9. Cap. Francof. ann. 794. c. 20. (ap. Pertz c. 22.)

established that those still existing should not have episcopal
dignity and privileges, but only sacerdotal authority.[11] For the
amelioration of the monastic institutions, *Benedict*, abbot of Ani-
ane († 821),[12] was very active in his endeavours, who accordingly
reformed several monasteries, and at whose instance the *capitulare Aquisgranense de vita et conversatione monachorum*[13]
was issued by Lewis the Debonaire A. D. 817.

In general, Charlemagne chose the Church of Rome as the
most ancient church of the West for his model in the ecclesiastical enactments he made. As he had received from *Adrian I.*
a *codex canonum*,[14] so he afterwards sent to the same person
for the *Sacramentarium Gregorii M.*[15] and two singers, that he
might introduce the Roman church-music into his empire.[16]

---

[11] In the controversy whether the spiritual rights of bishops belonged
to the country bishops, Hincmar declared his opinion against the latter
(Flodoardus l. c.), so also Pseudoisidorus, from whom Benedictus Levita
capitul. lib. vi. c. 369, compiled a decision to this effect. On the other
hand, those rights were defended by Rabanus Maurus lib. de Chorepis-
copis et dignitate atque officio eorum (appended to de Marca de concordia sacerd. et Imp., ed Böhmer p. 1261.) However Albericus mon.
Triumfontium (about 1240) in chron. ad ann. 849, Audradus Chore-
piscopus Senonensis—Parisius ad concilium evocatus est, et non solum
ipse, sed etiam omnes alii Chorepiscopi, qui erant in Francia, in eodem
concilio depositi sunt.

[12] From him proceeded Codex regularum ed. Luc. Holstenius, Romae
1661. recus. Paris. 1664. 4. Concordia regularum ed. Hugo Menardus.
Paris. 1638. Bähr's Gesch. d. röm. Liter. im karolingischen Zeitalter,
S. 366.

[13] Baluz. cap. i. 579.

[14] See above § 7. not. 21.

[15] Hadriani epist. ad Car. in Cod. Carol. no. 82. ap. Mansi xii. 798.
Landulphus Senior (about 1070) hist. Mediolan. lib. ii. c. 10. (Muratorii scriptt. rer. Ital. iv. 73) first speaks of a Roman council under
Hadrian, which had rejected the Ambrosian ritual, on which Charlemagne, at the destruction of the Lombard empire, omnes libros Ambro-
siano titulo sigillatos—alios comburens, alios trans montes secum detulit. This narrative is given in excerpt by Gulielm. Durandus (1286)
rationale divin. offic. lib. v. c. 2. See Carolus M. below not. 16.

[16] Monachus Sangallensis de gestis Car. M. lib. i. c. 11. Ann. Laurissenses ad ann. 787. (Pertz. i. 170.) Vita Adriani in Mabillonii
museum Ital. i. ii. 41. (cf. capit. eccles. ann. 789. c. 79. Capit. in
Theodonis villa promulgatum ann. 805. c. 2.) Carolus M. contra
Synodum Graeciae pro adorandis imaginibus gestam lib. i. c. 6: Nostrae
partis ecclesia dum a primis fidei temporibus cum ea [Eccl. Romana]
perstaret in sacrae religionis unione,—venerandae memoriae genitoris

The laws concerning marriage were also conformed to the principles of the Roman church,[17] the benediction of a priest was made necessary to its legality,[18] and points about marriage, as matters referring to the making of wills, were referred to the bishops.[19] The old freedom of divorce[20] was restricted by laws.[21] Until the time of Charlemagne the party not accused of crime was permitted to marry again;[22] but afterwards the Roman notion began to prevail more and more, viz., that divorced persons could not marry

nostri—Pipini regis cura et industria, sive adventu in Gallias—Stephani Romanae urbis antistitis, est etiam ei in psallendi ordine copulata, ut non esset dispar ordo psallendi, quibus erat compar ardor credendi.—Quod quidem et nos, conlato nobis a Deo Italiae regno, fecimus, S. Romanae Ecclesiae fastigium sublimare cupientes, et reverendissimi Papae Adriani salutaribus exhortationibus parere nitentes : scil, ut plures illius partis Ecclesiae, quae quondam apostolicae sedis traditionem in psallendo suscipere recusabunt, nunc eam omni diligentia amplectantur :—quod non solum omnium Galliarum provinciae, et Germania, sive Italia, sed etiam Saxones et quaedam Aquilonaris plagae gentes, per nos Deo annuente ad verae fidei rudimenta conversae, facere noscuntur.—Singing schools in Metz and Soissons. Mon. Sang. : ut nunc usque—ecclesiastica cantilena dicatur Metensis, apud nos vero qui Teutonica s. Teutisca lingua loquimur, aut vernacule Met aut Mette, vel secundum Graecam derivationem usitato vocabulo Metisca nominetur. Cf. Thomassinus P. i. l. ii. c. 80.

[17] G. W. Böhmer über die Ehegesetze im Zeitalter Karls d. G. und seiner nächsten Regierungsnachfolger. Göttingen 1826. 8.

[18] Capitt. lib. vi. c. 130. 327. 408. lib. vii. c. 179.

[19] Planck ii. 275 ff. Böhmer S. 126 ff.

[20] See vol. i. § 125. not. 14.

[21] The lawful causes of divorce see in Böhmer S. 89 ff.

[22] Thus Pipin allowed the husband who had put away his wife for adultery capit. ann. 757. c. 8 : si vult, potestatem habet accipere aliam. Capit. ann. 752, c. 5 : Si qua mulier mortem viri sui cum aliis hominibus consiliavit,—ille vir potest ipsam uxorem dimittere, et, si voluerit, aliam accipiat. The same thing is even allowed the husband, cap. 9, si quis necessitate inevitabili cogente in alium ducatum s. provinciam fugerit,—et uxor ejus—eum sequi noluerit. At that time, however, they were less strict even in Rome, cf. Gregorii ii. ep. ad Bonifacium A. D. 726. c. 2. ap. Mansi xii. 245. (also in Gratianus caus. xxxii. qu. 7. c. 18) : si mulier infirmitate correpta non voluerit debitum viro reddere, —ille, qui se non poterit continere, nubat magis. Zacharias P. about 744 (ap. Gratian. l. c. c. 23. and in Lombardi sent. lib. iv. dist. 34) : Concubuisti cum sorore uxoris tuae ? Si fecisti, neutram habeas : et si illa, quae uxor tua fuerit, conscia sceleris non fuit, si se continere non vult, nubat in Domino, cui velit. Still Pope Leo VII. († 939) writes in epist. ad Eberhardum ducem Bojariae (in Aventini annal. Bajorum lib

again so long as the other party was alive.[23]   The discipline of the church was enforced not only by spiritual terrors,[24] but also by secular punishments.[25]   In particular, *the yearly visitations* made by the clergy to inspect the churches (*Synodi*)[26] served to preserve a certain outward decency.

iv. c. 23. ed. Gundling. p. 461) : Si quispiam uxori adulterae repudium remiserit, nec hi conjuges in gratiam redigi conniverint, nulla lex, nulla religio vetat illum novas facere nuptias.   Satius enim est casto connubio frui, quam multarum amore deperire aut scortari. This epist. ad Eberh., which Aventinus gives in excerpt, is still extant (ap. Mansi xviii. 379) ; but this passage, and another which Aventinus had, is wanting in it ; a circumstance that must make one very suspicious about the integrity of the printed papal letter.

[23] So first Conc. Paris. ann. 829. lib. iii. c. 2.   (Mansi xiv. 596) : quod nisi causa fornicationis, ut Dominus ait, non sit uxor dimittenda, sed potius sustinenda.   Et quod hi, qui causa fornicationis dimissis uxoribus suis alias ducunt, Domini sententia adulteri esse notentur. This regulation is adopted by Benedictus Levita in his collection of Capitularies (Capitt. lib. vi. c. 235) but he perverts the sense of the first sentence by leaving out nisi, so as to make it have the opposite sense.   Benedict has preserved several capitula of older synods against the remarrying of divorced persons (lib. vi. c. 63. c. 87. vii. c. 73. c. 381), though he does not omit to give also the opposite regulations of Frank kings (Ex. gr. lib. v. c. 21. from capit. ann. 757. c. 8. see above not. 22.)   But the civil law did not yet go as far as the ecclesiastical view.   See Lotharii i. legg. Langobard. c. 92. (in Walter corp. juris germ. T. iii. p. 656) : Nulli liceat excepta causa fornicationis adhibitam sibi uxorem relinquere, et deinde aliam copulare.   S. Böhmer S. 108 ff.

[24] Comp. the epistola Jesu Christi (in Baluzii capitul. ii. 1396) fabricated in Charlemagne's time, with horrible threats against those who did not keep Sunday holy, who observed heathen usages, &c.

[25] Childebert's decretio A. D. 595. c. 2. (see vol. 1. Div. 2. § 124. note 17.) against those excommunicated for incest, who continued obstinate.   More general Pipini capit. vern. ann. 755. c. 9 : Si aliquis ista omnia contemserit, et Episcopus emendare minime potuerit, Regis judicio exilio condemnetur.   Cf. capitt. lib. vii. c. 215.—Synodus Regiaticinia [Pavia] A. D. 850. c. 12. (ap. Mansi xiv. 934) : Hoc autem omnibus Christianis intimandum est, quia hi, qui sacri altaris communione privati, et pro suis sceleribus reverendis adytis exclusi publicae poenitentiae subjugati sunt, nullo militiae secularis uti concilio, nullamque reipublicae debent administrare dignitatem etc.

[26] An improvement of the old church visitation (cf. Conc. Taracon. ann. 516 c. 8 : ut antiquae consuetudinis ordo servetur, et [Ecclesiae] annuis vicibus ab Episcopo dioceses visitentur).   Carol. M. capit. ann. 769 c. 7 : Statuimus, ut singulis annis unusquisque Episcopus parochiam suam solicite circumeat, et populum confirmare et plebes docere, et investigare et prohibere paganas observationes, divinosque vel sortilegos, aut auguria, phylacteria, incantationes, vel omnes spurcitias gentilium

§ 9.

PRIVILEGES OF THE CLERGY.

To the Carlovingians the clergy were indebted for new possessions and privileges. *The tithes* granted to the Church by Charlemagne, 779, were at first, indeed, reluctantly and irregularly paid,
but yet they were carried out into execution.[1] Parishes received

studeat. Capit. ii. ann. 813 c. 1 : Ut Episcopi circumeant parochias
sibi commissas, et ibi inquirendi studium habeant de incestu, de parrici-
diis, fratricidiis, adulteriis, cenodoxiis et aliis malis, quae contraria sunt
Deo, quae in sacris Scripturis leguntur quae Christiani devitare debent.
Capitt. lib. vii. c. 148, 465. Conc. Arelatense ann. 813 c. 17. (Mansi
xiv. 61) : Ut unusquisque Episcopus semel in anno circumeat parochiam suam. Noverint sibi curam populorum et pauperum in protegendis
ac defendendis'impositam. Ideoque dum conspiciunt, judices ac potentes
pauperum oppressores existere, prius eos sacerdotali admonitione redar-
guant; et si contempserint emendari, eorum insolentia Regis auribus in-
timetur, ut quos sacerdotalis admonitio non flectit ad justitiam, regalis
potestas ab improbitate coërceat. A description of the synods in Regino de disciplina eccl. lib. ii. c. 1. ss. Hartzhemii Conc. Germ. ii.
511. Jo. Morini comm. hist. de disciplina in administratione sacramenti poenitentiae lib. vii. c. 3. F. A. Biener's Beitr. zu d. Gesch. d.
Inquisitionsprocesses. Leipz. 1827. S. 28 ss. Eichhorn's Kirchenrecht
ii. 73.

[1] People had very early begun to consider ecclesiastical oblations as
a continuation of the Old Testament first fruits and tithes (vol. i. § 53,
note 16), and to assert that the laity should proportion the greatness of
their oblations to that standard. For a long time this was only enforced
as a moral duty, but subsequently it was demanded on pain of ecclesiastical punishment (Conc. Matisconense ann. 585, c. 5) : let the disobedient person a membris Ecclesiae omni tempore separetur. . A letter
of Pipin's to Lullus, archbishop of Mainz, A. D. 764, ap. Baluz. i. 185,
desires that the bishops should institute a thanksgiving feast, on account
of a rich harvest, et faciat unusquisque homo sua eleemosyna, et pauperes pascat. Et sic praevidere faciatis et ordinare de verbo nostro, ut
unusquisque homo, aut vellet, aut nollet, suam decimam donet, viz., to the
poor. Charlemagne made the church law, which required a tenth, the
law of the state also, capit. ann. 779, c. 7 : De decimis, ut unusquisque
suam decimam donet, atque per jussionem Pontificiis dispensetur. Capitulatio de partibus Saxoniae (Pertz iii. 49) c. 16 : Et hoc Christo propitio placuit, ut undecunque census aliquid ad fiscum pervenerit, sive
in frido, sive in qualicunque banno, et in omni redibutione [*i.e.*, reditu]
ad Regem pertinente, decima pars Ecclesiis et Sacerdotibus reddatur, c.
17 : Similiter secundum Dei mandatum praecipimus, ut omnes decimam
partem substantiae et laboris sui Ecclesiis et Sacerdotibus donent, tam

a secure endowment, to which, in particular, a certain extent of
land (mansus ecclesiasticus) free of all rent and taxes also belonged.[2] To this were added, not only many donations,[3] but, as the

nobiles quam ingenui, similiter et liti, juxta quod Deus unicuiqui dederit Christiano, partem Deo reddant ; subsequently also often repeated.
According to a capit. anni inc. in Martene et Durand coll. ampl. vii.
10, the disobedient shall first be excommunicated, and if then they will
not submit, they shall be compelled by civil punishments, succeeding
one another by gradation. This ecclesiastical tithe must be' distinguished from that tenth which, at the time of the Romans, colonists had
to pay from the ager publicus to the state as rent, and which subsequently had come with the possession of that ager into many other
hands, and had also in a great measure fallen into the hands of the church
(Birnbaum die rechtl. Natur der Zehnten. Bonn 1831. 8). Such
colonists had now to pay a double tithe decimam et nonam ; hence capit. Francof. ann. 794, c. 23 : Ut decimas et nonas sive census omnes
generaliter donent, qui debitores sunt ex beneficiis et rebus Ecclesiarum.—Et omnis homo ex sua proprietate legitimam decimam ad Ecclesiam conferat. Experimento enim didicimus, in anno, quo illa valida
fames irrepsit, ebullire vacuas annonas a daemonibus devoratas, et voces
exprobrationis auditas. Planck ii. 397. Gfrörer iii. ii. 609. Kühlen-
thal's Gesch. des deutschen Zehntens. Heilbronn 1837. 8.
    [2] Ludov. P. capit. ann. 816, c. 10 : Statutum est, ut unicuique Ec-
clesiae unus mansus integer absque ullo servitio adtribuatur, et Presbyteri in eis constituti non de decimis, neque de oblationibus fidelium, non
de domibus, neque de atriis vel hortis juxta Ecclesiam positis, neque de
praescripto manso aliquod servitium faciant praeter ecclesiasticum. Et
si aliquid amplius habuerint, inde Senioribus suis debitum servitium
impendant. On Mansus see Eugen Montag's Gesch d. deutschen
staatsbürgerl. Freiheit, i. 1. 273 u. 325. The Conc. Rom. ann. 826, c.
16 (repeated ann. 853, ap. Mansi xiv. 1005) forbids the bishop res im-
mobiles de subjectis plebibus seu aliis piis locis in proprio usu habere.
    [3] Also by contractus precarios, Planck ii. 390. Montag i. i. 278.
Kunstmann's Rabanus Maurus S. 20.—What means were employed in
part to obtain these donations may be seen from Caroli M. capitulare
ii. ann. 811, c. 5 : Inquirendum etiam, si ille saeculum dimissum habeat, qui quotidie possessiones suas augere quolibet modo et qualibet
arte non cessat, suadendo de caelestis regn ibeatitudine, comminando de
aeterno supplicio inferni, et sub nomine Dei aut cujuslibet sancti tam
divitem quam pauperem, qui simplicioris naturae sunt, et minus docti
atque cauti inveniuntur, si rebus suis exspoliant, et legitimos heredes
eorum exheredant, ac per hoc plerosque ad flagitia et scelera propter inopiam, ad quam per hoc fuerint devoluti, perpetranda compellunt, ut
quasi necessario furta et latrocinia exerceant, cui paternarum [rerum]
hereditas, ne ad eum perveniret, ab alio praerepta est. Cap. 6 : Iterum
inquirendum, quomodo seculum reliquisset, qui cupiditate ductus propter adipiscendas res, quas alium videt possidentem, homines ad perjuria
et falsa testimonia pretio conducit ; et Advocatum sive Praepositum non

feudal system prevailed, many private estates were converted into ecclesiastical fiefs.[4] Many churches received judicial power over their colonists,[5] perhaps also over the free men that dwelt among them ; many also received other *Regalia*[6] (rights belonging to royalty). From *Charlemagne's* time all prelates were obliged to keep *advocates* (Advocati Ecclesiae)[7] for transacting the secular affairs incompatible with their spiritual calling.

justum ac Deum timentem, sed crudelem ac cupidum, ac perjuria parvipendentem inquirit etc.

[4] Capit. iii. ann. 811, c. 3 : Dicunt etiam, quod quicunque proprium suum Episcopo, Abbati, vel Comiti aut Judici vel Centenario dare noluerit, occasiones quaerunt super illum pauperem, quomodo eum condemnare possint, et illum semper in hostem faciant ire, usque dum pauper factus volens nolens suum-proprium tradat aut vendat, alii vero, qui traditum habent, absque ullius inquietudine domi resideant. Charles the Bald desired, on the contrary, that every one should come under the feudal obligations, conventus apud Marsnam ann. 847 (Baluz. ii. 44. Pertz iii. 395) : Volumus etiam, ut unusquisque liber homo in nostro regno seniorem qualem voluerit, in nobis et in nostris fidelibus accipiat. Eichhorn's deutsche Rechtsgesch. i. 724.

[5] Such cases had already happened singly among the Merovingians, but now they were more frequent. Thus Treves received the privilege of immunity from the jurisdiction of counts, for church possessions from Pipin 761 (Hontheim hist. dipl. i. 120, confirmed by Charlemagne 773, p. 132, and Lewis the Debonaire, 816, p. 167). Osnabruck received from Charlemagne, 804, immunity from all judicial courts, even from that of Missi (Möser's osnabrück. Gesch. 3te Aufl. Berlin 1819, i. 405). Montag i. i. 220. Eichhorn i. 735.

[6] Comp. Montag i. 285. Thus Lewis the Debonaire in particular bestowed on many monasteries and churches, the right of tolls, markets, and coinage (Walch diss. de pietate Lud. P. 1748, in Pottii syll. comm. theol. iv. 280). Therefore Heimoldus in chronic. Slav. lib. i. c. 4, § 2, says that Lewis was so indulgent to the clergy, ut Episcopos, qui propter animarum regimen principes sunt caeli, ipse eosdem nihilominus principes efficeret regni.

[7] Caroli capit. ii. ann. 813 c. 14 : Ut Episcopi et Abbates Advocatos habeant. Et ipsi habeant in illo comitatu propriam hereditatem. Et ut ipsi recti et boni sint, et habeant voluntatem recte et juste causas perficere. Cf. Lotharii capit. tit. iii. c. 7. c. 9. c. 18. Pippini Ital. Reges. leges Langobard. c. 7. These Advocati had to appear in courts on behalf of the church they represented, to attend to the administration of justice in them (Montag i. i. 232 ss. 244 ss.) Many churches had for protection also Defensores Ecclesiae (Montag. S. 250): Both offices, however, were soon united (Montag. S. 254 ff.), and the expressions, Advocati, Defensores, Vicedomini, became synonymous. The appointment of such officers originated in the older, particularly African, synodical decrees, though the new Advocati were quite differ-

Charlemagne *exempted* the clergy more than ever from the jurisdiction of the civil courts; but the king continued to be supreme judge of all clergymen, even of bishops.[8] And since a more accurate distinction of the peculiar limits belonging to the rights of the clergy did not take place as Charles had intended,[9] spiritual aspirings after greater freedom and power were certainly the more encouraged by this means under the feeble government of his successors. The bishops strove to obtain the pope for their spiritual judge ;[10] and, on the other hand, to raise

ent from the earlier subordinate Defensores. Cf. Thomassinus P. i. lib. ii. cap. 97 ss. Planck ii. 452. Eichhorn's deutiche Rechtsgesch. i. 787. Kaim's Kirchenpatronatrecht i. 70.

[8] Comp. vol. i. Div. ii. § 124, note 15. Caroli M. alia capitula add. ad leg. Longob. ann. 801. c. 1 : Volumus primo, ut neque Abbates, neque Presbyteri, neque Diaconi, neque Subdiaconi, neque quislibet de clero, de personis suis ad‘ publica vel ad secularia judicia trahantur vel distringantur, sed a suis Episcopis judicati justitiam faciant. (Cf. capit. Aquisgran. ann. 789 c. 37 : Ut Clerici ecclesiastici ordinis, si culpam incurrerint, apud ecclesiasticos judicentur, non apud seculares). Si autem de possessionibus, sive ecclesiasticis, sive suis propriis, super eos clamor ad judicem venerit, mittat judex clamantem cum Misso suo ad Episcopum, ut faciat ei per advocatum justitiam percipere. Si vero talis aliqua inter eas exorta fuerit intentio, quam per se pacificare non velint aut non possint, tunc per advocatum Episcopi, qualem lex jusserit, causa ipsa ante Comitem vel judicem veniat, et ibi secundum legem finiatur, anteposito quod dictum est de persona clericorum. (Cf. capit. Francof. ann. 794 c. 28. Et si forte inter clericum et laicum fuerit orta altercatio, Episcopus et Comes simul conveniant, et unanimiter inter eos causam definiant secundum rectitudinem). Still the final decision belonged to the king and his ministers. Lothar. imp. in lege Longobard. lib ii. tit. 45. c. 2. (Baluz. ii. 337) : Ut omnes Episcopi, Abbates et Comites, excepta infirmitate vel nostra jussione, nullam habeant excusationem, quin ad placita Missorum nostrorum veniant, aut talem vicarium mittant, qui in omnibus causis pro illis rationem reddere possit. Caroli Calvi capit. tit. 40 ann. 859 c. 7. (ibid. p. 211) : Ut si Episcopi suis laicis injuste fecerint, et ipsi laici se ad nos inde reclamaverint, nostrae regiae potestati secundum nostrum et suum ministerium ipsi Archiepiscopi et Episcopi obedient,—sicut temporibus avi et patris nostri juxta et rationabilis consuetudo fuit. Eichhorn i. 177.

[9] Capitulare interrogationis de iis, quae C. M. pro communi omnium utilitate interroganda constituit [ann. 811] c. 4 :—discutiendum est atque inveniendum, in quantum se Episcopus aut Abbas rebus secularibus debeat inserere, vel in quantum Comes vel alter laicus in ecclesiastica negotia. Hic interrogandum est acutissime, quid sit quod Apostolus ait : " Nemo militans Deo implicat se negotiis secularibus. (2 Tim. ii. 4), vel ad quos sermo iste pertineat.

[10] See above § 7. not. 27 ff.

themselves to be judges of kings;[11] an attempt was also made
to change the previously existing right of arbitration possessed
by the bishops (vol. i. § 91, note 4) into a compulsory judicial
power over the laity, in certain cases.[12] The royal authority,
however, over spiritual fief holders was still too firmly established

[11] See above § 6. not. 13.
[12] Capitt. lib. vi. c. 366: Volumus atque praecipimus, ut omnes
ditioni nostrae Deo auxiliante subjecti, tam Romani, quam Franci, Ala-
manni, Bajuvarii, Saxones, Thuringii, Fresones, Galli, Burgundiones,
Britones, Langobardi, Wascones, Benventani, Gothi, et Hispani—hanc
sententiam, quam ex 16mo Theodosii Imp. libro—sumsimus, et inter
nostra capitula—posuimus, legem cunctis perpetuo tenendam; id est:
Quicunque litem habens, sive possessor sive petitor fuerit, vel in initio
litis, vel decursis temporum curriculis, sive cum negotium peroratur,
sive cum jam coeperit promi sententia, si judicium elegerit sacrosanctae
legis Antistitis, illico sine aliqua dubitatione, etiamsi alia pars refragatur,
ad Episcoporum judicium cum sermone litigantium dirigatur.—Omnes
itaque causae, quae vel praetorio jure vel civili tractantur, Episcoporum
sententiis terminatae, perpetuo stabilitatis jure firmentur; nec liceat ulterius retractari judicium, quod Episcoporum sententia deciderit. That
this law which also belongs to the 18 extravagancies of the Cod.
Theod. published in Jac. Sirmondi appendix Codicis Theodosiani,
Paris 1631. 8. (see novellae constitutiones Impp. Theodosii ii. etc.
xviii. constitutiones quas J. Sirmondus divulgavit ed. G. Haenel. Bonnae 1844. 4. p. 445), is not at all a lex Constantini, which it pretends
to be, may be seen from Gothofred. in Cod. Theod. ed Ritteri vi. 339.
Savigny Gesch. d. röm. Rechts im Mittelalter ii. 281, 296. Eichhorn's
Kirchenrecht ii. 131. (although it has been recently pronounced genuine by Jungk diss. de originibus et progressu episcopalis judicii in causis
civilibus laicorum, Berol. 1832. 8. and by G. Haenel l. c. p. 429).
But even the capitulary form which is only met with in Benedict's collection proceeds neither from Charlemagne (to whom it has often been
referred) nor from any other Frank king. C. S. Berardus (Gratiani
canones genuini ab apocryphis discreti. Taurini 1752. T. iv. 4.) i.
444, and Jodocus le Plat diss. de spuriis in Gratiano canonibus P. iii.
c. 14. (in Gallandii sylloge ed. Mogont. ii. 843 not. 8.) declare it to be
a fabrication of Benedict; Schmidt Kirchengesch. v. 161 and Eichhorn
deutsche Rechtsgesch. i. 776, which says the same thing, declare it to be a
Pseudoisidorianum. Since that lex Const. is also found in Codd. of brevi-
arii Alaricii, since moreover Benedict used for his collection of capitularies
the documents collected by Archbishop Riculf (see preface), and since
such records were brought from Spain by Riculf (see Hincmar. Laud.
c. 24); this law may have arisen among the Visigoths, with whom the
bishop's power was very considerable (see vol. i. Div. 2. §. 132, note 6.)
Thus even the subsequent royal renewing and confirmation of it may
have been originally a Visigothic deed, so that Benedict only added the
names of several states, to make it a Frank regulation.

R

for them to succeed in obtaining anything in opposition to the will of the king.

§ 10.

EFFORTS OF THE CARLOVINGIANS TO PROMOTE THEOLOGICAL CULTURE.

Jo. Launoji de scholis eelebrioribus s. a Carolo Magno s. post eundem Car. per Occidentem instauratis liber, Paris. 1672. 8. (in addition to Jo. Mabillonii iter German. republished by J. A. Fabricius, Hamb. 1717. 8). L. Thomassini vet. et nov. Eccl. discipl. P. ii. lib. i. c. 96-100. Histoire literaire de la France par des religieux Benedictins de la Congrég. de S. Maur, (Paris 1733 ss. 20 Tomes 4. is continued). T. iv. et v. Bossuet's Weltgeschichte, continued by J. A. Cramer, v. ii. 118-180. C. H. van Herwerden comm. de iis, quae a Carolo M. tum ad propagandam religionem christ. tum ad emendandam ejusdem docendi rationem acta sunt. Lugd. Bat. 1825. 4. Dr J. Chr. F. Bähr's Gesch. d. röm. Literatur im karoling Zeitalter, Carlsruhe 1840. 8.

As soon as Charlemagne had become acquainted with the liberal sciences in Italy, he became anxious to introduce them immediately into his own kingdom, and in particular among the clergy. Accordingly he invited to his court learned foreigners,[1] for instance *Petrus Pisanus, Paulus Warnefridi,* († 799)[2] *Paulinus,* patriarch of Aquileia († 804),[3] and in 782, the most distinguished of all, *Flaccus Alcuinus* or *Albinus* († 804).[4] By precept and example, he excited a zeal for those studies, and

---

[1] Annales Laurissenses ad ann. 787 (ap. Pertz. i. 171): Et domnus Rex Carolus a Roma artis gramaticae et computatoriae magistros secum adduxit in Franciam, et ubique studium literarum expandere jussit. Ante ipsum enim domnum Regem Carolum in Gallia nullum studium fuerat liberalium artium.

[2] From him we have de historia Longobardorum libb. vi. et historiae miscellae lib. xvi., afterwards enlarged by the addition of 8 books (both best edited in Muratorii rer. Ital. scriptor. T. I.) Vitae Gregorii M., Benedicti, etc. Excerpta de primis Metensium Episcopis (in Pertz. monum. Germ. hist. ii. 260). Homiliarium.

[3] Bähr S. 356.

[4] Controversial writings against Adoptians. Biblical commentaries. Doctrinal writings, especially de fide S. Trinitatis libb. iii. ad. Car. M. De Virtutibus et vitiis l. Vitae S. Willebrordi, Martini, etc. Homiliae. De vii. artibus. Carmina. Espec. epistolae 232. Opp. ed Frobenius. Ratisbon, 1777. Tomi ii. fol. Alcuin's life by Dr F. Lorenz. Halle 1829. 8. Bähr S. 302. 78. 192.

erected schools attached to cathedrals and monasteries,[5] in which the *trivium* and *quadrivium*[6] were taught. Monastic schools were divided from A. D. 817 into external and internal.[7] Though

[5] Car. M. epist. ad Baugulfum Abb. Fuldensem, or rather a circular letter to all bishops and abbots A. D. 787 (Baluz. i. 201. Pertz. iii. 52): Notum sit—devotioni vestrae, quia nos una cum fidelibus nostris consideravimus utile esse, ut episcopia et monasteria—etiam in literarum meditationibus, eis qui, donante Domino, discere possunt, secundum uniuscujusque capacitatem, docendi studium debeant impendere : qualiter sicut regularis norma honestatem morum, ita quoque docendi et discendi instantia ordinet et ornet seriem verborum, ut qui Deo placere appetunt recte vivendo, ei etiam placere non negligant recte loquendo. Quamvis enim melius sit bene facere quam nosse, prius tamen est nosse quam facere. Nam cum nobis in his annis a nonnullis monasteriis saepius scripta, dirigerentur, cognovimus in plerisque—eorumdem et sensus rectos et sermones incultos. Unde factum est, ut timere inciperemus, ne forte, sicut, minor erat in scribendo prudentia, ita quoque et multo minor esset, quam recte esse debuisset, in eis ss. Scripturarum ad intelligendum sapientia. Quamobrem hortamur vos literarum studia non solum non negligere, verum etiam humillima et Deo placita intentione ad hoc certatim discere, ut facilius et rectius divinarum Scripturarum mysteria valeatis penetrare. Tales vero ad hoc opus viri eligantur, qui et voluntatem et possibilitatem discendi et desiderium habeant alios instruendi, etc. Capitul. Aquisgr. ann. 789. c. 70. (Baluz. i. 237) :—non solum servilis conditionis infantes sede etiam ingenuorum filios (Canonici et Monachi) adgregent sibique socient. Et ut scholae legentium puerorum fiant. Psalmos, notas, cantus, computum, grammaticam per singula monasteria vel episcopia discant.—Mentioned repeatedly by Concil. Cabilonense [A. D. 813] can. 3. T. König's geschichtl. Nachrichten über das Gymnas. zu Münster in Westphalen seit Stiftung dess. durch. Karl d. G. bis auf die Jesuiten. Münster 1821. 8. Respecting Charlemagne's literary occupations see Alcuin's life by Lorenz. pp. 20, 164; on his alleged Academy ibid. p. 169.

[6] The notion of seven artes liberales, though previously indicated, proceeds from Augustine de ordine lib. ii. Encyclopaedie of Martianus Capella (about 460) containing the seven liberal sciences, Satyricon libb. ix. ; Boëthius († 524) de arithmetica libb. iii. (where i. 1. the name and establishment of the Quadrivium are first met with); Cassiodorus († after 562) de vii. disciplinis ; the first manuals and those much used in the middle ages proceeded from him. See Jac. Thomasius in the Observationibus select. Halens. T. ii. p. 40 ss. F. Cramer's Gesch. d. Erziehung und des Unterrichts in d. Niederlanden während des Mittelalters, Stralsund 1843. 8. 5. The division into the trivium and quadrivium is given in the memorial lines :—

> Gram. loquitur, Dia. verba docet, Rhe verba colorat;
> Mus canit, Ar numerat, Geo. ponderat, As. collt astra.

[7] Scholae exteriores or canonicae, and interiores, in consequence of

Lewis the Debonaire,[8] *Lotharius*, and *Charles the Bald*,[9] were friends and patrons of the sciences no less than their great ancestor, yet in their times those institutions suffered from internal disturbances,[10] and fell into still greater disorder in the suc-

---

the regulation in the capitulare of the year 817. § 45, (Pertz. iii. 202), ut schola in monasterio non habeatur, nisi eorum, qui oblati sunt. Comp. Kunstmann's Rabanus Maurus S. 54. R. v. Raumer's Einwirkung des Christenth, aus die althochdeutsche Sprache. Stuttgart 1845. S. 199.

  [8] Capit. Altiniacense ann. 822 c. 3. (ap. Pertz. iii. 231). Capit. Aquisgr. ann. 825. c. 6. (ap. Pertz. iii. 243). Conc. Paris. vi. ann. 829 lib. i. c. 30. (ap. Mansi xiv. 558). The passage of the epist. of this council ad Ludov. Imp. [lib. iii. c. 12] : Similiter obnixe ac suppliciter vestrae celsitudini suggerimus, ut morem paternum sequentes saltem, in tribus congruentissimis imperii vestri locis scholae publicae ex vestra auctoritate fiant : ut labor patris vestri et vester per incuriam, quod absit, labefactando non pareat, must be understood of the higher places of education. C. E. Bulaei hist. Acad. Paris i. 159.

  [9] Herici Mon. ad Car. Calvum, about A. D. 876 (Dedication prefixed to his lib. vi. carminum de vita S. Germani, see Bouquet vii. 562): Illud vel maxime vobis aeternam parat memoriam, quod famatissimi avi vestri Caroli studium erga immortales disciplinas non modo ex aequo repraesentatis, verum etiam incomparabili fervore transcenditis : dum quod ille sopitis eduxit cineribus, vos fomento multiplici tum beneficiorum, tum auctoritatis usquequaque provehitis, immo, ut sublimibus, sublimia conferam, ad sidera perurgetis. Ita vestra tempestate ingenia hominum duplici nituntur adminiculo, dum ad sapientiae abdita persequenda omnes quidem exemplo allicitis, quosdam vero praemiis invitatis. Id vobis singulare studium effecistis, ut sicubi terrarum magistri florerent artium,—hos ad publicam eruditionem undecunque vestra celsitudo conduceret, comitas attraheret, dapsilitas provocaret. Dum te tuosque ornamentis sapientiae illustrare contendis, cunctarum fere gentium scholas et studia sustulisti. Spretis ceteris in eam mundi partem, quam vestra potestas complectitur, universa optimarum artium studia confluxerunt.

  [10] Conc. Valentinum iii. [ann. 855] c. 18. (ap. Mansi xv. 11.): Ut de scholis tam divinae quam humanae literaturae, necnon et ecclesiasticae cantilenae, juxta exemplum praedecessorum nostrorum, aliquid inter nos tractetur, et si potest fieri, statuatur atque ordinetur : quia ex hujus studii longa intermissione, pleraque Ecclesiarum Dei loca et ignorantia fidei et totius scientiae inopia invasit. Conc. Lingonense ann. 859, c. 10. (Mansi xv. 539): Ut scholae ss. Scripturarum, et humanae quoque literaturae, unde annis praecedentibus per religiosorum Imperatorum studium magna illuminatio, Ecclesiae et eruditionis utilitas processit, deprecandi sunt pii principes nostri, et omnes fratres et coëpiscopi nostri instantissime commonendi, ut—constituantur undique scholae publicae, scilicet ut utriusque eruditionis, et divinae scilicet et humanae,

ceeding stormy reigns. Among the schools which flourished from the time of Charlemagne, besides the *Schola Palatina*,[11] those of *Tours, Lyons, Orleans, Rheims, Fulda, old and new Corbey, Hirschau, Reichenau,* and *St Gallen*,[12] are especially deserving of notice. Among the learned men, by the number and importance of whom the Frank empire was distinguished in the ninth century above all the West, the most worthy of mention are, *Agobard*, archbishop of Lyons († 841)[13] *Rabanus Maurus*, 822, abbot in Fulda, 847, archbishop of Mainz, († 856),[14] *Haimo*, bishop of Halberstadt, († 853),[15] *Walafrid Strabo*, a scholastic in Fulda, 842 abbot in Reichenau, († 849),[16] *Servatus Lupus*, abbot at Ferrierers, († 862),[17] *Ratramnus*, monk in Corbie, (†

in Ecclesiae Dei fructus *t*aleat accrescere : quia, quod nimis dolendum est et perniciosum maxime, divinae Scripturae verax et fidelis intelligentia jam ita delabitur, ut vix ejus extrema vestigia reperiantur.

[11] Bähr S. 19. 31. 42.

[12] Hüllmann's Städtewesen des Mittelalters. iv. 307. Bähr S. 21. 43.

[13] Among his writings are four against the Jews, several against the superstitions of the time (adv. legem Gundobadi, et impia certamina, quae per eam geruntur. Liber contra judicium Dei. De grandine et tonitruis. Epist. ad Barthol. Episc. Narbon. de quorundam illusione signorum. De picturis et imaginibus) and on the contemporary political events (de divisione imperii Francorum inter filios Lud. Imp. flebilis epistola. Liber apologeticus pro filiis Lud. P. Chartula porrecta Lotharia Aug. in Syn. Compendiensi). Opp. prim. ed. Papir. Masson, Paris. 1605. 8. castigatius St. Baluzius, Paris. 1666. 2 voll. 8. and by this ap. Gallandius xiii. 405. C. B. Hundeshagen de Agobardi vita et scriptis. P. i. vita. Giessae 1831. 8. Bähr S. 383. Gfrörer iii. ii. 747.

[14] Writings: Commentaries on almost all the biblical books. Homilies. Moral writings. On the customs of the church (De clericorum institutione et ceremoniis eccl. libb. iii. De sacris ordinibus, sacramentis divinis, et vestimentis sacerdot. De disciplina eccl. libb. iii.) Opp. ed. G. Colvenerius. Colon. 1627. vi. T. fol. Hrabanus Magnentius Maurus, v. D. F. Kunstmann, Mainz 1841. 8. Hrab. Maurus, der Schöpfer des deutschen Schulwesens, Programm von R. Bach. Fulda 1835. 4. Bähr S. 415. 105.

[15] Biblical Commentaries.—Historiae eccl. breviarium libb. x. (ed. Jo. Maderus, Helmst. 1671.) Bähr S. 408.

[16] De exordiis et incrementis rerum ecclesiasticarum (in scriptt. de div. offic. ed. Melch. Hittorp, Colon. 1568.) Glossa ordinaria in Biblia (ed. Antverp. 1634. 6 voll. fol.) Vitae S Galli, Othmari et al. Bähr S. 100. 217. 398.

[17] A work on predestination. Epistolae 132. Opp. ed. St. Baluz., Paris. 1664. emend. Antverp. 1710. 8. Bähr S, 456.

after 868),[18] *Claudius*, bishop of Turin, († 839),[19] and *Christianus Druthmar*, monk in Corbie, († abont 840),[20] are distinguished as grammatical scholars ; as a philosopher, *John Scotus orErigena*, at the court of Charles the Bald († after 877).[21]

[18] Called Bertramus merely by a continued error of the copyists. He was not abbot at Orbais, nor should be confounded with Ratramnus, abbot of Neuvillers in Elsace. Hist. lit. de la France v. 333. De partu virginis. De praedestinatione libb. ii. Contra Graecorum errores libb. iv. De corpore et sanguine Domini. Bähr S. 471.

[19] The following works of his have been published : Praefatio in libros informationum literae et spiritus super Leviticum, ad Theodemirum Abb. and the conclusion of this work (in Mabillonii vett. analecta ed. ii. p. 90); comm. in libros Regum ad Theodemirum Abb. (in Bedae et Claudii Taur. aliorumque opuscula a Canonicis regul. s. Salvatoris edita. Bononiae 1755. fol. p. 4. From this commentary nothing more than the introductions to separate books had been published before in F. A. Zachariae biblioth. Pistoriensis, Aug. Taurin. 1752. fol. p. 60. the complete edition has remained quite unnoticed in Germany) ; praef. in catenam ad Matthaeum, ad Justum Abb. (in the spicilegium Romanum T. iv. Romae 1840. 8. p. 301) ; praef. in commentarios ad epistt. Pauli ad Theodemirum Abb. (in Maji scriptt. vett. nova collectio vii. i. 274) ; praef. in epist. ad Rom. (in Fabricii bibl. mediae et infimae Latin. i. 1087); comm. in epist. ad Galatas (Paris. 1542. 8. Bibl. Patrum, Lugd. xiv. p. 134) ; praefatio exposit. in epist. ad Ephesios ad Ludov. Pium (ap. Mabillon. l. c. p. 91) ; expositio epist. ad Philemonem (in the spicileg. Rcm.-ix. i. 109); dicta in lectionem s. Evangelii sec. Matthaeum viii. 1-13 ; xi. 25-29 ; xx. 1-16; and in ep. ad Rom. viii. 1-27 (in Claudii Taur. Ep. ineditorum operum specimina, praemissa de ejus doctrina scriptisque diss., exhibuit A. Rudelbach, Havn. 1824. 8.) Many are still lying in the libraries. Cf. Rich. Simon. hist. cri. des principaux commentateurs du N. T. p. 353. The same author's critique de la bibliothèque de Mr. du Pin. i. 284. Oudinus de scriptt. eccl. ii. 26. Claudius of Turin by Dr T. Schmidt in Illgen's Zeitschr. f. d. hist. Theol. 1843. ii. 39.

[20] Comm. in evang. Matthaei, ed. Argentorati 1514. op. Jo. Secerii, Hagenoae 1530. Bibl. PP. Lugd. xv. 86. cf. Rich. Simon hist. des princip. comm. du. N. T. p. 370. The same author's critique de la bibl. de Mr. du Pin. i. 299. That Druthmar does not belong to the 11th century, as after Fabricius bibl. med. et inf. Latin. i. 374. is assumed even by Wachler Gesch. d. Literatur, Th. 2. (2te Umarbeit. S. 59) may be seen in histoire lit. de la France, v. 85. Bähr S. 401.

[21] The contemporaries Hincmar and Anastasius (ep. ad Carolum in Usherii vett. epist. Hibern. sylloge. Dublin. 1632. p. 40 ss.) call him Scottigena, Trithemius for the first time Erigena. The story of his return to England and violent death has been often derived from the act of confounding him with one Johannes presbyter et monachus ex Ealdsaxonum genere (Asserii hist. Alfredi regis) s. Mabillon ann. Benedict.

For the instruction of the people little could be done, since the requirements demanded of the pastors[22] must still have been very low were it for.no other reason than the want of books.[23]

lib. xxxv. § 39. lib. xxxviii. § 72. Hist. lit. de la France, v. 418. Hjort S. 44. See on the opposite side Staudenmaier S. 115. Works: De divisione naturae libb. v. (ed. Th. Gale, Oxon. 1681. fol.) De praedestinatione Dei.—Opera S. Dionysii latine versa. Joh: Scotus Erig., od. v. d. Ursprung einer christlichen Philosophie u. ihrem heill. Beruf, v. D. Peder Hjort, Kopenh. 1823. 8. H. Schmid der Mysticismus des Mittelalters in seiner Entstehungsperiode, Jena 1824. 8. S. 114 ff. Joh. Scot. Erig. u. die Wissenschaft seiner Zeit v. Dr F. A. Staudenmaier Th. 1. Frkf. a. M. 1834. Dr Nic. Möller, Joh. Scot. Erig. Mainz 1844. Philosophia Erigenae ex ipsius principiis delineata ab A. Torstrick. P. i. Gotting. 1844. 8. Helfferich die christl. Mystik. Gotha 1842. 2 Th. Baur's Lehre von der Dreieinigkeit ii. 274. Ritter's Gesch. der christl. Philos. iii. 206. Die Lehre des Joh. Scotus Erigena vom Wesen des Bösen von M. Fronmüller, in Steudel's Tübinger Zeitschrift s. Theol. 1830. i. 49. iii. 74.

[22] Freculph, bishop of Lisieux, writes to Rabanus (Rab. opp. ii. 4): nulla nobis librorum copia suppeditat,—dum in episcopio nostrae parvitati commisso nec ipsos novi veterisque testamenti reperi libros, multo minus horum expositiones.

[23] Capit. Aquisgran. ann. 789. cap. 68. especially capitula de doctrina clericorum in the capitulare Aquense ann. 802. (Pertz iii. 107): Haec sunt, quae jussa sunt discere omnes ecclesiasticos: 1. fidem catholicam s. Athanasii et caetera quaecunque de fide; 2. symbolum etiam apostolicum; 3. orationem dominicam ad intelligendum pleniter cum expositione sua; 4. librum sacramentorum pleniter tam canonem missasque speciales ad commutandum pleniter; 5. exorcismum super catechumenum sive super daemoniacos; 6. commendationem animae; 7. poenitentialem; 8. computum; 9. cantum Romanorum in nocte; 10. et ad missa similiter; 11. Evangelium intelligere, seu lectiones libri comitis; 12. homilias dominicis diebus et solemnitatibus dierum ad praedicandum canonem; monachi regulam similiter et canonem firmiter; 13. librum pastoralem canonici atque librum officiorum; 14. epistolam Gelasii pastoralem; 15. scribere chartas et epistolas. Hincmar's (archbp. of Rheims) capitula Presbyteris data ann. 852. may be considered a commentary on these (ap. Mansi xv. 475) c. 1: Ut unusquisque Presbyterorum expositionem symboli, atque orationis dominicae juxta traditionem orthodoxorum patrum plenius discat, exinde praedicando populum sibi commissum sedulo instruat. Praefationem quoque canonis et eundem canonem intelligat, et memoriter ac distincte proferre valeat, et orationes missarum, Apostolum quoque et Evangelium bene legere possit; psalmorum etiam verba et distinctiones regulariter, et ex corde cum canticis consuetudinariis pronuntiare sciat. Nec non et sermonem Athanasii de fide, cujus initium est: "Quicunque vult salvus esse," memoriae quisque commendet et sensum illius intelligat, et verbis communibus enuntiare queat. Farther, he must know by

Charles particularly recommended frequent preaching,[24] and to
this end caused a *homilarium* to be compiled;[25] which plan of
popular instruction was followed under his successors.[26] *Theo-*

heart c. 2. ordinem baptizandi, c. 3. exorcismos et orationes ad catechumenos faciendum, ad fontes quoque consecrandum, et caeteras preces
super masculos et feminas, pluraliter atque singulariter, c. 4. ordinem
reconciliandi atque unguendi infirmos, orationes quoque eidem necessitati competentes, similiter ordinem et preces in exequiis atque agendis
defunctorum, nec minus exorcismos et benedictiones aquae et salis.
c. 8. homilias xl. Gregorii quisque Presbyter studiose legat et intelligat :
et ut cognoscat, se ad formam lxxii. discipulorum in ministerio ecclesiastico esse promotum, sermonem praedicti doctoris de lxxii. discipulis
a Domino ad praedicandum missis plenissime discat ac memoriae tradat.
Computo etiam necessario et cantu per anni circulum plenissime in-
struatur.   Similar are the capitula Walterii Episc. Aurelianensis (Mansi
xv. 503).
   [24] Capit. i. ann. 813. c. 14. and the synods held in the same year.
Arelatens. c. 10. Mogunt. c. 25. Rhemens. c. 14. 15. Turon. c. 4.
c. 17: quilibet Episcopus habeat homilias continentes necessarias ad-
monitiones, quibus subjecti erudiantur.—Et ut easdem homilias quisque
aperte transferre studeat in rusticam Romanam linguam, aut Theotiscam,
quo facilius cuncti possint intelligere quae dicuntur.   Cabilonense c. 2.
Theodulphi capit. ad parochiae suae sacerdotes c. 28. (ap Mansi xiii.
28) : Hortamur vos paratos esse ad docendas plebes.   Qui Scripturas
scit, praedicet Scripturas : qui vero nescit, saltem hoc, quod notissimum
est, plebibus dicat, ut declinent a malo et faciant bonum, inquirant
pacem et sequantur eam etc. Neander's K. G. iii. 246. iv. 219. Schmidt
in the theol. Stud. u. Krit. 1846. ii. 250. K. v. Raumer's Einwirkung
des Christenth. auf die althochdeutsche Sprache. Stuttgart 1845. S. 250.
   [25] Carol. M. in homiliarium Pauli Diac. about 788. (ap. Baluz. i.
203. Bouquet v. 622) : quia curae nobis est, ut Ecclesiarum nostrarum
ad meliora semper proficiat status, obliteratam paene majorum nostrorum desidia reparare vigilanti studio literarum satagimus officinam, et
ad pernoscenda sacrorum librorum studia nostro etiam quos possumus
invitamus exemplo.—quia ad nocturnale officium compilatas quorundam
casso labore, licet recto intuitu, minus tamen idonee reperimus lectiones ;
earundem lectionum in melius reformare tramitem, mentem intendimus,
idque opus Paulo Diacono familiari nostro elimandum injunximus.—
Qui nostrae celsitudini devote parere desiderans, tractatus atque sermones et homilias diversorum catholicorum Patrum perlegens, et optima
quaeque decerpens in duobus voluminibus per totius anni circulum congruentes cuique festivitati distincte et absque vitiis nobis obtulit lectiones.   Quarum omnium textum nostra sagacitate perpendentes, nostra
etiam auctoritate eadem volumina constabilimus, vestraeque religioni in
Christi Ecclesiis tradimus ad legendum.   The homiliarium was printed,
Spirae 1482. Basil. 1493 fol. and in the 16th century frequently.
   [26] Ludov. P. capit. Aquisgr. ann. 816. c. 28. Syn. Mogunt. ann.
847. c. 2. repeats the can. 17. Conc. Turon. ann. 813. [see note 24].

dulph, bishop of Orleans († 821), one of the trustiest assistants of Charlemagne, also established schools for the common people in his diocese.[27] His example was followed by some, but probably not many.[28] It was generally believed, that the people were sufficiently furnished with knowledge if they knew the *pater noster* and the creed;[29] and even this small requirement was enforced by punitive laws.[30] Spiritual compositions which

How low the state of preaching had fallen about this time in Italy may be seen from the rescriptum consultationis Epp. ad domn. Ludovic. ii. Imp. [about 855] c. 3. ap. Baluz. ii. 352.

[27] On Theodulph see hist. lit. de la France iv. 459. Bähr S. 359. See capitulare ad parochiae suae sacerdotes (ap. Mansi xiii. 993 ss.) c. 20: Presbyteri per villas et vicos scholas habeant, et si quilibet fidelium suos parvulos ad discendas literas eis commendare vult, eos suscipere et docere non renuant, sed cum summa caritate eos doceant.—Cum ergo eos docent, nihil ab eis pretii pro hac re exigant, nec aliquid ab eis accipiant, excepto quod eis parentes caritatis studio sua voluntate obtulerint.

[28] Herardi Archiep. Turonensis capitula A. D. 858. c. 17. (Baluz. i. 1286): Ut scholas Presbyteri pro posse habeant et libros emendatos. Walterii Episc. Aurelian. cap. c. 6. (Mansi xv. 506): Ut unusquisque Presbyter suum habeat clericum, quem religiose educare procuret: et si possibilitas illi est, scholam in Ecclesia sua habere non negligat.

[29] The precept to learn both was often repeated, Ex. gr. Conc. Mogunt. 813. c. 45. (Mansi xiv. 74): Symbolum, quod est signaculum fidei, et orationem dominicam discere semper admoneant sacerdotes populum christianum. Volumusque, ut disciplinam condignam habeant, qui haec discere negligunt, sive in jejunio, sive in alia castigatione emendentur. Propterea dignum est, ut filios suos donent ad scholam, sive ad monasteria, sive foras Presbyteris, ut fidem catholicam recte discant, et orationem dominicam, ut domi alios edocere valeant. Et qui aliter non potuerit, vel in sua lingua hoc discat. Properly it should have been also learned in Latin, and hence arose the popular belief combated by Charlemagne in the capitul. Francof. ann. 794. c. 50: Ut nullus credat, quod nonnisi in tribus linguis Deus orandus sit: quia in omni lingua Deus adoratur, et homo exauditur, si justa petierit. In particular, every one was to teach his godsons, Raumer's Einwirkung des Christenthums auf die ahdeutsche Sprache S. 266. A written exhortation to learn both, and to teach their godchildren, belonging to this period, in German and Latin, is published in Massmann's deutschen Abschwörungs-, Glaubens-, Beicht und Betformeln vom 8ten bis zum 12ten Jahrh. Quedlinb. u. Leipz. 1839. S. 150.

[30] Cap. Aquens. ann. 802, c. 15 (Pertz iii. 106): Ut nullus infantem vel alium ex paganis de fonte sacro suscipiat, antequam symbolum et orationem dominicam Presbytero suo reddat. Capit. ann. 804, c. 2 (Pertz iii. 130): Et si quis ea nunc non teneat, aut vapulet, aut jejunet de omni potu excepta aqua, usque dum haec pleniter valeat. Et

now began to appear in the native language,[31] *i.e.*, in the German, could only influence the multitude, in the first instance, through the priests.[32]   Spiritual poems were especially adapted to bring Christian ideas into the living consciousness of the people.[33] Among these, two poetical *Harmonies of the gospels* must be noticed, the one in the old Saxon language, and in the alliteration form (about 830), which in a true poetic spirit attaches itself to the popular poesy;[34] the other, by the Weissenburg monk *Otfried* (868) in the Frankish dialect and in rhyme, which

qui ista consentire noluerit, ad nostram praesentiam dirigatur. Feminae vero aut flagellis aut jejuniis constringantur.   Quod Missi nostri cum Episcopis praevideant ut ita perficiatur : et Comites similiter adjuvant Episcopis, si gratiam nostram velint habere, ad hoc constringere populum, ut ista discant. Cf. Conc. Mogunt. not. 28.

[31] On the fragments of an old (?) German Matthew see Räumer's Einwirk. d. Christenth. auf die ahdeutsche Sprache S. 35, the Gospel Harmony of Tatian (ed. J. A. Schmeller, Viennae 1841. 4), Raumer S. 36, catechetical memorials (published in Massmann's deutschen Abschwörungs-, Glaubens-, Beicht-und Betformeln), Raumer S. 47, fragments of sermons, Raumer S. 66.   An interlinear version of the Benedictine rule by Kero, and a translation of Isidorus de nativitate Domini, Raumer S. 42.

[32] The German glosses on Biblical and ecclesiastical writers were intended for the clergy in particular. See Raumer S. 81, 218.

[33] Hymnorum veteris Ecclesiae xxvi. interpretatio theotisca. ed. Jac. Grimm. Gottingae 1830. 4. Spiritual songs belonging to the 9th century, in Hoffmann's Fundgruben f. Gesch. deutscher Sprache u. Literatur. Th. 1. (Breslau 1830) S. 1 ff. A translation of the Psalms in the low German dialect, published by F. H. v. d. Hagen. Breslau 1816, 4. Dr K. G. P. Mackernagel's deutsches Kirchenlied. Stuttgart 1841 gr. 8. S. 38.

[34] Heliand, or the old Saxon Gospel Harmony, published by J. A. Schmeller, two parts, München 1830 and 39, 4to. Without doubt what the praef. in librum ant. lingua Saxonica conscriptum in Flacii catalog. testium veritatis no. 101, p. 126, relates of Lewis the Debonaire, refers to it : Praecepit cuidam viro de gente Saxonum, qui apud suos non ignobilis vates habebatur, ut vetus ac novum Testamentum in germanicam linguam poëtice transferre studeret, quatenus non solum literatis, verum etiam illiteratis sacra divinorum praeceptorum lectio panderetur. Qui jussis imperialibus libenter obtemperans—ad tam difficile tamque arduum se statim contulit opus.—Igitur a mundi creatione initium capiens, juxta historiae veritatem quaeque excellentiora summatim decerpens, et interdum quaedam ubi commodum duxit mystico sensu depingens, ad finem totius Veteris ac Novi Testamenti interpretando more poëtico satis faceta eloquentia perduxit etc. Cf. Walch de pietate Ludov. P. diss. § 20, in Pottii syll. comm. theol. iv. 309.   Dr

maintains a spiritual didactic tone.[35]   The Latin Church music
was studied by the clergy alone ;[36] while the people sang simply
Kyrieeleison.[37]

§ 11.

POSITION OF THE FRANK CHURCH IN THE CONTROVERSY CON-
CERNING IMAGE-WORSHIP.

See the literature before § 1. especially Walch's Ketzer hist. xi. 1.

In the controversy concerning images, the Frank Church gave
evident proof, not only of its independence of the Romish see, but
of its higher theological culture.   Of the transactions, indeed, of
the synod at *Gentiliacum* (767),[1] connected with a Greek embassy,
we know nothing further ; but Charlemagne caused a refutation
of the decrees of the second Nicene council (libri Carolini),[2] to be

A. F. C. Vilmar's deutsche Alterthümer im Heliand als Einkleidung
der evangel. Geschichte.   Marburg 1845. 4.

[35] Krist, das älteste von Otfried im 9ten Jahrh. verfasste hochdeutsche
Gedicht, kritisch herausgeg. von C. G. Graff.   Königsberg 1831. 4.
On both Gospel Harmonies see Gervinus Gesch. d. poet. National-Li-
teratur der Deutschen Th. i. (3te Ausg. Leipz. 1846) S. 81.   Vilmar's
Vorlesungen über die Gesch. d. deutschen National-Literatur.   Mar-
burg u. Leipzig 1845. S. 33.

[36] Of whom many were exclusively occupied with this department.
See Agobardus de correctione antiphonarii c. 18, (ed. Baluz. ii. 99) :
quamplurimi ab ineunte pueritia usque ad senectutis canitiem omnes
dies vitae suae in parando et confirmando cantu expendunt, et totum
tempus utilium et spiritalium studiorum, legendi videlicet et divina eloquia perscrutandi, in istiusmodi occupatione consumunt ; quodque animabus eorum proculdubio valde est noxium, ignari fidei suae, inscii
Scripturarum sanctarum, et divinae intelligentiae inanes ac vacui, hoc
solum sibi sufficere putant ; et ob hoc etiam ventosi et inflati incedunt,
si sonum et vocem decantationis utcunque addiscant, et in numero can-
torum deputari videantur.

[37] Stat. Salisb. ann. 799, f. § 8, not. 1.   Dr H. Hoffmann's Gesch.
d. deutschen Kirchenliedes bis auf Luthers Zeit.   Breslau 1832, S. 3.

[1] Annales Lauriss. ad ann. 767 : Tunc habuit domnus Pippinus Rex
in supradicta villa [Gentiliaco] Synodum magnam inter Romanos et
Graecos de s. Trinitate et de Sanctorum imaginibus.

[2] Prim. ed. Eli. Phili. (Elias Philyra, *i. e.*, Jean du Tillet, afterwards
bishop of Brieux, then of Meaux.   See du Chesne scriptt. Franc. ii. p.
352) 1549.   Reprinted in Goldasti imperial. decret. de cultu imaginum

drawn up (790),[3] and, without being satisfied with Pope Hadrian's reply,[4] the worship of pictures was rejected at *the Synod of Frank-*

p. 67 ss., and in his collectio constitutionum imperialium i. 23 ss. Last: Augusta Conc. Nic. ii. censura h. e. Caroli M. de impio imaginum cultu libb. iv. ed. Ch. A. Heumann. Hanover, 1731. 8. Mentioned by the Syn. Paris (see below, note 8), and Hincmar opusc. adv. Hincmar. Laudunensem c. 20.—Sixti Senensis praef. in biblioth. sanctam (Venet. 1566) p. 3, advances the singular opinion, in which, however, others have followed him, that Andr. of Carlstadt was the author. On the other hand, Baronius ad ann. 794, § 30. Bellarmine and many others say, that they were the work of a heretic, and sent to Rome by Charlemagne for condemnation. Correct is the opinion of Sirmond Concil. Gall. ii. 19. Natalis Alex. diss. de imaginibus in his hist. eccl. v. 782. Hist. lit. de la France iv. 410, &c. Comp. chiefly Walch's Ketzerhist. xi. 49. that these books were written in 790 follows from the praef. ad. libr. i., according to which the Nicene synod was held ferme ante triennium. Charlemagne alone appears as the speaker, for example, lib. i. c. 6 : Venerandae memoriae genitoris nostri—Pipini regis cura etc. Certainly he got assistance, according to the usual assumption, from Alcuin, which has been recently defended against Frobenius's doubts, expressed in his edition of opp. Alcuini ii. 459, by Lorenz in Alciun's Leben (life) p. 132. Neander K. G. iii. 475. Gfrörer K.G. iii. ii. 624.

[3] Fundamental principles of these books : lib. ii. c. 21 : Solus igitur Deus colendus, solus adorandus, solus glorificandus est, de quo per Prophetam dicitur : " Exaltatum est nomen ejus solius " (Ps. cxlviii. 13): cujus etiam Sanctis, qui triumphato diabolo cum eo regnant, sive quia viriliter certaverunt, ut ad nos incolumis status Ecclesiae perveniret, sive quia eandem Ecclesiam assiduis suffragiis et intercessionibus adjuvare noscuntur, veneratio exhibenda est : imagines vero, omni sui cultura et adoratione seclusa, utrum in basilicis propter memoriam rerum gestarum et ornamentum sint, an etiam non sint, nullum fidei catholicae adferre poterunt praejudicium : quippe cum ad peragenda nostrae salutis mysteria nullum penitus officium habere noscantur. Lib. iii. c. 16 : Nam dum nos nihil in imaginibus spernamus praeter adorationem, quippe qui in basilicis Sanctorum imagines non ad adorandum, sed ad memoriam rerum gestarum et venustatem parietum habere permittimus : illi vero paene omnem suae credulitatis spem in imaginibus collocent ; restat, ut nos Sanctos in eorum corporibus vel potius reliquiis corporum, seu etiam vestimentis veneremur, juxta antiquorum Patrum traditionem : illi vero parietes et tabulas adorantes in eo se arbitrentur magnum fidei habere emolumentum, eo quod operibus sint subjecti pictorum. Nam etsi a doctis quibusque vitari possit hoc, quod illi in adorandis imaginibus exercent, qui videlicet non quid sint, sed quid innuant venerantur, indoctis tamen quibusque scandalum generant, qui nihil aliud in his praeter id quod vident venerantur et adorant.

[4] Epist. Hadriani P. ad Carol. R. de imaginibus, qua confutantur illi, qui Synodum Nicaenam ii. oppugnarunt, ap. Mansi xiii. 759. (p.

furt (794),[5] according to later accounts, with the approbation of the English Church.[6] An embassy which King Michael *Balbus* sent to Lewis the Debonaire, and to Rome,[7] led to another declaration of *the Synod of Paris* (825) against image-worship, at this

795: praedecessores nostri saepius dicti sanctissimi pontifices in sacris conciliis talem dedere sententiam : si quis sanctas imagines Domini nostri J. Chr. et ejus genitricis, atque omnium Sanctorem secundum ss. Patrum doctrinam venerari noluerit, anathema sit. Cf. Conc. Lateran. ann. 769.   Act. iv. ap. Mansi xii. 720).

[5] Conc. Francofordiensis can. ii. prim. ed. du Tillet in praef. ad libr. Carol. (from an old Cod. Ecclesiae Remensis, see Baluz. ad capitt. ii. 753) ap. Mansi xiii. 909 : Allata est in medium quaestio de nova Graecorum synodo, quam de adorandis imaginibus Constantinopoli fecerunt, in qua scriptum habebatur, ut qui imaginibus Sanctorum, ita ut deificae Trinitati, servitium aut adorationem non impenderent, anathema judicarentur.   Qui supra, sanctissimi Patres nostri, omnimodis et adorationem et servitutem eis renuentes contemserunt atque consentientes condemnaverunt.   Comp. Annales Laurissenses ad ann. 794 of the Frankfurt Synod : Pseudosynodus Graecorum, quam falso septimam vocabant, et pro adorandis imaginibus fecerunt, rejecta est a Pontificibus.   Einhard. de. gest. Car. M. ad ann. 794.   Synodus etiam, quae ante paucos annos in Constantinopoli sub Irene et Constantino filio ejus congregata, et ab ipsis non solum septima, verum etiam universalis erat appellata, ut nec septima nec universalis haberetur diceretur, quasi supervacua in totum omnibus abdicata est (the Nicene synod was closed at Constantinople).   Basquez, Suarez, Surius, Vinius, and others, pretend that the decrees of the Nicene synod were confirmed at Frankfurt, and, on the contrary, the Pseudoseptima, A. D. 754, rejected.   Baronius, Bellarmine, Natalis Alex., and others, think that the Nicene decrees were misunderstood and rejected in a false sense.   Barruel du Pape et de ses droits religieux, Paris 1803, ii. 402, declares the Frankfurt Acts supposititious.   Correct is the opinion of Sirmond ad Conc. Francof. Petav. dogmat. theol. lib. xv. c. 11.   J. Mabillon de cultu sacrarum imaginum, prefixed to his Act. SS. Ord. S. Bened. saec. iv. vol. i.

[6] So first Simeon Dunelmensis (about 1100) hist. de gestis regum Anglorum (in Twysden hist. Angl. scriptores decem i. 111), from whom first Rogerus de Hoveden (about 1198) in his annal. Anglican. ad. ann. 792, drew. comp. Wilkins Conc. magn. Britann. i. 73.   Dallaeus de imag. lib. iii. c. 2, p. 380.   Gfrörer K. G. iii. ii. 621.

[7] Its object see in Michaelis Balbi ep. ad Ludov. P. A. D. 824 (cf. § 1. not. 22) : Propterea quidam illorum, qui noluerunt suscipere Concilia localia et a veritate redargui, fugerunt hinc et venerunt ad antiquam Romam,—injuriam et calumnias Ecclesiae inferentes et verae religioni detrahentes.—Unde honorem Ecclesiae Christi quaerentes fecimus literas ad s. Papam antiquae Romae, et eas missimus per praedictos Missos nostros ad eum.—De caetero ordinet vestra spiritalis Dilectio, ut cum omni honore et illaesione ad eum veniant, auxilium eis

time accompanied with an express rebuke of the pope.[8] The
Franks, indeed, were not successful in reconciling the pope and

ferentes in his, quae Deo placeant,—jubentes ei, ut si amodo manifesti
fuerint quidam seductores pseudo-christiani, Ecclesiae calumniatores,
illuc eos expellere etc.

[8] Acta Synod. Paris. prim. ed. (Jac Bongars) Francof. 1596. 12.
Also in Goldasti imp. decret. p. 623. First included in the collections
of Councils, by Mansi xiv. 415. Comp. Walch xi. 96. Synod. Paris.
ad. Ludov. et Lotharium Imp. (ap. Goldast. p. 626 ss.) :—primum
epistolam domini Hadriani Papae, quam pridem pro imaginibus erigen-
dis Constantino Imp. et Herenae matri ejus ad eorum precationem in
transmarinis partibus direxit, coram nobis legi fecimus, et quantum
nostrae parvitati res patuit, sicut juste reprehendit illos, qui imagines
Sanctorum temerario ausu in illis partibus confringere et penitus abo-
lere praesumserunt, sic indiscrete noscitur fecisse in eo, quod superstitiose eas adorare jussit. Inseruit etiam in eadem epistola quaedam
testimonia ss. Patrum, quantum nobis datur intelligi, valde absona, et
ad rem, de qua agebatur, minime pertinentia. Eandem porro Synodum
[Nicaenam] cum s. memoriae genitor vester coram se suisque perlegi
fecisset, et multis in locis, ut dignum erat, reprehendisset, et quaedam
capitula, quae reprehensione patebant, praenotasset, eaque per Angil-
bertum Abbatem eidem Hadriano Papae direxisset, ut illius judicio et
auctoritate corrigerentur; ipse rursus favendo illis, qui ejus instinctu
tam superstitiosa quamque incongrua testimonia memorato operi inse-
ruerant, per singula capitula in illorum excusationem respondere quae
voluit, non tamen quae decuit, conatus est. Talia quippe quaedam sunt,
quae in illorum objectionem opposuit, quae remota pontificali auctoritate, et veritati auctoritate refragantur. Sed licet in ipsis objectioni-
bus aliquando absona, aliquando inconvenientia, aliquando etiam reprehensione digna testimonia defensionis gratia proferre nisus sit; in fine
tamen ejusdem apologiae sic sentire et tenere et praedicare ac praecipere
de his quae agebantur professus est, sicut a b. Papa Gregorio institutum
esse constabat (see vol. i. Div. 2, § 121, not. 10). Quibus verbis liquido
colligitur, quod non tantum scienter, quantum ignoranter in eodem facto
a recto tramite deviaverit. Venerabilis namque Freculfus Episc. subtiliter prudenterque, qualiter ipse et Adegarius socius illius (the two Frank
ambassadors, who had accompanied the Greek ambassadors to Rome),
egissent, viva voce parvitati nostrae innotuit. Sed cum prudenti relatu
illius cuncta cognovissemus, qualiter partim veritatis ignorantia, partim
pessimae consuetudinis usu hujus superstitionis pestis illis in partibus
(Rome and Italy) inolevisset, et priora et posteriora studiosissime consi-
derassemus, intelleximus, quantum nobis res patuit, quo zelo ad haec
consideranda vestra s. Devotio excitata fuerit. Non enim ignoramus
animum vestrum magno taedio posse affici, cum illos a recto tramite
quoquo modo conspicitis deviare, qui, summa auctoritate praediti, devi-
antes quosque debuerant corripere (the Pope). Sed quoniam maximum
vobis in eo obstaculum erat, eo quod pars illa, quae debebat errata corrigere, suaque auctoritate hujusce superstitionis errori obniti, ipsa prorsus

the Greeks by means of their views ;[9] but, on the other hand, neither did the popes venture to treat the Franks, as their predecessors treated the Greeks. Throughout the ninth century, the worship of images continued to be rejected in the empire of the Franks,[10] without Rome excommunicating any one on that account.

eidem superstitioni non solum resistere, verum etiam incauta defensione contra auctoritatem divinam et ss. Patrum dicta nitebatur suffragari, aperuit vobis Dominus ostium juxta optatum vobis desiderium, ut licentiae vobis ab eadem tribueretur auctoritate tantae rei cum vestris quaerendi familiariter veritatem—quatenus sancto vestro desiderio ac vigilanti studio veritas patefacta, dum se in medium ostenderet, etiam ipsa auctoritas volens nolensque veritati cederet atque succumberet.

[9] This was the object, the Parisian fathers advising for this end the following l. c. p. 631: Credimus itaque, quod illos reprehendendo, illisque compatiendo, istos vero demulcendo, laudando et praeferendo, eorumque auctoritatem magnis laudum praeconiis efferendo, et s. Romanae Ecclesiae condignam laudem deferendo, veritatem tamen ex testimoniis ss. Scripturarum et sententiis ss. Patrum in medium proferendo, et veraciter sobrieque exponendo, poterit vestra sanctissima Devotio, sicut optat, utrisque consulere. Sic quippe refragator vinculis veritatis modo blandiendo, modo honorando, modo secundum rationem veritatem demonstrando subtiliter adstrictus, non audebit aliter docere, quam quod veritas habet etc. In the same spirit also Lewis issued his letter to Eugenius II. and the commonitorium [instruction] to the ambassadors sent to Rome, Jeremy, archbishop of Sens and Jonas, bp. of Orleans (ap. Goldast. p. 747. Baluzii capitull. I. 643, and thence, in Mansi in the app. ad T. xv. 435.) In these instructions we read among other things : Sed et vos ipsi tam patienter ac modeste cum eo de hac causa disputationem habeatis, ut summopere caveatis, ne nimis ei resistendo eum in aliquam inrevocabilem pertinaciam incidere compellatis, sed paulatim verbis ejus quasi obsequendo magis quam aperte resistendo ad mensuram, quae in habendis imaginibus tenenda est, eum deducere valeatis. Postquam vero hanc rationem de earundem imaginum causa consummaveritis, si tamen hoc ad nihilum Romana pertinacia permiserit,—eum interrogetis, si ei placeat, ut nostri Legati pariter cum suis in Graeciam pergant etc.

[10] Anastasius in his praef. in septimam Synodum ad Joann. viii. Papam about 880 (ap. Mansi xii. 983) : Quae enim super venerabilium imaginum adoratione praesens Synodus docet, haec et apostolica sedes vestra—antiquitus tenuit, et universalis Ecclesia semper venerata est et hactenus veneratur: quibusdam dumtaxat Gallorum exceptis, quibus utique nondum est harum utilitas revelata. Ajunt namque, quod non sit quodlibet opus manuum hominum adorandum etc. The annales Mettenses (towards the end of the 10th century) write ad ann. 794, still without ever stumbling at them, after the old annalists, Pseudosynodus

This is the more remarkable, inasmuch as the Frank Churches, in some cases, went still farther than the Greeks themselves, in the ninth century, in opposing this practice. *Claudius*, as bishop of Turin (from 820-839) opposed the reigning prejudices with such freedom as soon to provoke the opposition,[11] (before 424) of

Graecorum pro adorandis imaginibus habita, et falso septima vocata, ab Episcopis damnatur (ap. Pertz. I. 335).

[11] Comp. above, § 10, not. 19. The root of his doctrines was Augustinism, comp. his praef. in comm. ad epistt. Pauli (in Maji scriptt. vett. nova coll. vii. i. 275): De admonitione fratrum et exhortatione, unde rogasti quod scriberem, ut votum quod voverunt Domino reddant, —nullam admonitionem meliorem potui invenire, quam epistolae primae Pauli Apostoli, quam misi, quia tota inde agitur, ut merita hominum tollat, unde maxime nunc monachi gloriantur, et gratiam Dei commendat, per quam omnis qui vovit, quod vovit, Domino reddat. Expositio epist. ad Philem. (Spicileg. Rom. ix. i. 110): Gratia est, quia nullo merito, nec opere salvamur. To this also his opponents point, Jonas de cultu imag. lib. 1. (Bibl. PP. Lugd. xiv. 169): Patet, te dicta b. Augustini,—de cujus dictis nihil te latere jactitabas, penitus ignorasse. Dungali liber respons. (l. c. p. 204): Augustinum adsumit, a cujus subtilitate ingenii christianique sensus rectitudine longissime distat. Alios quidem praeter eum solum paene omnes abjicit. On his peculiar doctrines see Claudii libri informationum literae et spiritus super Leviticum ad Theodemirum Abbatem A. D. 823, at the conclusion (in Mabillonii vett. annal. p. 91): Et quia ita est, non jubemur ad creaturam tendere, ut efficiamur beati, sed ad ipsum Creatorem: de quo si aliud quam oportet ac sese res habet nobis persuadetur, perniciosissimo errore decipimur.—Beatitudine autem alterius hominis non fit alter beatus.—Neque prudentia cujusdam fit prudens alius, aut fortis fortitudine, aut temperans temperantia, aut justus justitia hominis alterius quisquam efficitur : sed coaptando animum illis incommutabilibus regulis luminibusque virtutum, quae incorruptibiliter vivunt in ipsa veritate sapientiaque communi, quibus et ille coaptavit et fixit animum, quem istis virtutibus praeditum sibi ad imitandum proposuit. Voluntas ergo adhaerens communi atque incommutabili bono impetrat prima et magna hominis bona, cum ipsa sit medium quoddam bonum. Et ideo non sit nobis religio cultus hominum mortuorum, quia si pie vixerunt non sic habentur, ut tales quaerant honores, sed illum a nobis coli volunt, quo illuminati laetantur, meriti sui nos esse consortes etc. (from Augustin. de vera relig. c. 55). Hanc adstruendo et defendendo veritatem, opprobrium factus sum vicinis meis, et timor notis meis : in tantum, ut qui videbant nos, non solum deridebant, sed etiam digito unus alteri ostendebant. Sed consolatus est nos Pater misericordiarum et Deus totius consolationis in omni tribulatione nostra etc. Claudii comm. in Gal. 6. 5. (Bibl. PP. Lugd. xiv. 164): Obscure licet docemur per hanc sententiolam novum dogma, quod latitat: dum in praesenti saeculo sumus, sive orationibus, sive consiliis invicem posse nos adjuvari ; cum autem

ante tribunal Christi venerimus, nec Job, nec Daniel, nec Noe rogare posse pro quoquam, sed unumquemque portare onus suum.—Claudii apologeticum atque rescriptum adv. Theodemirum Abb. was, in 1461, still in the monastery of Bobbio (see Tull. Ciceronis oratt. fragm. inedita ed. Am. Peyron. Stuttg. 1824. 4. p. 13): The codex is now in the Ambrosiana, but the Apologeticum is wanting in it (ibid. p. 167). Even Papirius Masson employed a complete codex, for he says, after the extracts which he gives before his edition of Dungal, Paris 1608: liber, de quo ista excerpisimus, tantae magnitudinis est, quantum liber Psalmorum et L. Psalmi plus. These extracts only were known before Dungal, and scattered in the answer of Jonas, also in Goldasti imper. decr. p. 764:—postquam coactus suscepi sarcinam pastoralis officii, missus a pio Principe—Ludovico, veni in Italiam, civitatem Taurini, inveni omnes basilicas, contra ordinem veritatis, sordibus anathematum et imaginibus plenas. Et quia, quod homines colebant, ego destruere solus coepi, idcirco aperuerunt omnes ora sua ad blasphemandum me, et nisi adjuvisset me Dominus, vivum deglutissent me.—Dicunt isti, contra quos Dei Ecclesiam defendendam suscepimus, " non putamus imagini, quam adoramus, aliquid inesse divinum. Sed tantummodo pro honore ejus, cujus effigies est, tali eam veneratione adoramus." Cui respondeo, quia, si Sanctorum imagines hi qui daemonum cultum reliquerunt, venerantur, non idola reliquerunt, sed nomina mutaverunt. —Si omne lignum schemate crucis factum volunt adorare, pro eo quod Christus in cruce pependit ;—adorentur ergo puellae virgines, quia virgo peperit Christum, adorentur et praesepia, quia mox natus in praesepio est reclinatus, adorentur et veteres panni, quia continuo cum natus est pannis veteribus est involutus etc.—Redite praevaricatores ad cor, qui recessistis a veritate et diligitis vanitatem, et estis vani facti, qui rursum crucifigitis Filium Dei, et ostentui habetis, et per hoc catervatim animas miserorum socias factas daemonum habetis ; alienando eas per nefanda sacrilegia simulacrorum a creatore suo, habetis eas dejectas et projectas in damnationem perpetuam.

Quod vero ais, quod ego prohibeam, homines poenitentiae causa pergere Romam, falsum tu loqueris. Ego enim iter illud nec adprobo nec improbo, quia scio, quod nec omnibus obest, nec omnibus prodest. Scimus enim, quod non intellecta evangelica verba Domini Salvatoris, ubi ait b. Apostolo Petro : " Tu es Petrus et super hanc petram aedificabo Ecclesiam meam, et tibi dabo claves regni caelorum," propter ista jam dicta Domini verba imperitum hominum genus pro adquirenda vita aeterna, postposita omni spiritali intelligentia, volunt pergere Romam. Si proprietatem verborum Domini subtiliter consideramus, non est ei dictum : " Quodcunque solveris in caelo, erit solutum et in terra, et quodcunque ligaveris in caelo, erit ligatum super terram." Ac per hoc sciendum est, quod tam diu antistitibus Ecclesiae istud ministerium concessum est, usque dum ipsi peregrinantur in hoc mortali corpore: cum vero debitum mortis reddiderint, alii succedunt loco ipsorum, qui eandem obtinent judiciariam potestatem. Audite et hoc insipientes in populo, et stulti aliquando sapite, qui intercessionem Apostoli Romam pergendo quaeritis, quid contra vos dicat idem saepe dictus b. Augustinus, etc. Promittente Deo debet fidelis quisque credere quanto magis

S

the abbot *Theodemir*,[12] and (827) of one *Dungal*.[13]   Still, he was

jurante quidem dicere : " Si fuerint in medio ejus Noe, Daniel et Job,"
i. e., si tantae sanctitatis, tantae justitiae, tantique meriti sint, quanti illi
fuerunt, " non liberabunt filium neque filiam" (Ezech. xiv. 20). Haec
idcirco dicit, ut nemo de merito vel intercessione Sanctorum confidat,
quia nisi eandem fidem, justitiam, veritatemque teneat, quam illi tenu-
erunt, per quam illi placuerunt Deo, salvus esse non poterit. Quinta
tua in me objectio est, et displicere tibi dicis, eo quod Domnus Apostolicus indignatus sit mihi.   Hoc dixisti de Paschali Ecclesiae Romanae
Episcopo, qui praesente jam corruit vita.   Apostolicus autem dicitur,
quasi Apostoli custos.   Certe non ille dicendus est Apostolicus, qui in
cathedra sedet Apostoli, sed qui apostolicum implet officium.   De illis
enim, qui eum locum tenent, et non implent officium, Dominus dixit :
" Super cathedram Moysi sederunt Scribae et Pharisaei, etc." (Matth.
xxiii. 1. 2.) Comp. Rudelbach's and Schmidt's treatises cited above §.
10. note 19.   Walch's Ketzerhist. xi. 140.   Neander's KG. iv. 225.

[12] Abbot of psalmody in the diocese of Nismes.   To him Claudius
dedicated many of his commentaries, and Theodemir had mentioned to
him what approbation they met with from the Frank bishops.   (See
epist. prefixed to Claudii comm. in libros Regum, in Bedae et Claudii
Taur. opuscula, Bononiae 1755 fol. p. 7).   But subsequently he took
offence at the commentary on the epistles to the Corinthians, Claudii
epist. ad Theutmirum (l. c. p. 164) : pervenit ad manus meas epistola ex
Aquis, regio directa palatio, qualiter tu librum tractatus mei, quem tibi
ante biennium praestiti, in epistolas ad Corinthios, Episcoporum judicio atque Optimatum damnandum ad eundem jam dictum palatium
praesentari feceris.   Quem tractatum ibidem non damnandum, sed scri-
bendum amici mei non solum humiliter, sed etiam amabiliter susceperunt.   Ignoscat tibi Dominus, testis vitae meae, et largitor operis mei,
qui non timuisti sermonibus detrahere veritatis, et sedens adversum
me loqueris mendacium, etc.   On this followed an epistle of Theodemir
in which he designates several opinions of Claudius as errors : and
against him Claudius set forth his apologeticum.

[13] Dungali liber responsionum adv. Claudii Taur. Ep. sententias ed.
Pauperius Masson. Paris. 1608, in Bibl. PP. Lugdun, xiv. 197. (comp.
Bähr S. 372).   In the prologue an account of the differences of opinion
caused by Claudius, de sancta pictura, de cruce : Pari ratione de memoriis Sanctorum causa orationis adeundis, et reliquiis eorum venerandis
obnituntur : aliis adfirmantibus, bonam et religiosam esse consuetudinem, basilicas Martyrum frequentare, ubi eorum sacri cineres et sancta
corpora—cum honore eorum meritis congruo condita habentur, ubique
ipsis intervenientibus corporales ac spiritales quotidie languores, divina
operante manu et gloria coruscante, copiosissime et praesentissime sanantur : alii vero resistunt, dicentes, Sanctos post obitum nullum adjuvare, nullique posse intercedendo succurrere, nihil eorum duntaxat
scientes, quae in terris geruntur, illorumque reliquias nullum alicujus
reverentiae gratiam comitari, sicut nec ossa villissima quorumlibet, animalium reliquamve terram communem.

not molested, though, perhaps, even in France, many believed
that he went too far, and though, after his death, even there
Jonas, bishop of Orleans, (840) wrote against him.[14] *Agobard*,
archbishop of Lyons (from 816-840), the liberal opponent of all
superstition, was little behind Claudius in his views of image and

[14] Jonae de cultu imaginum libb.' iii. in bibl. PP. Lugdun. xiv. 167.
(Comp. Bähr S. 394). In the praefatio : Deo dilectissimus Princeps
[Ludovicus] inter caetera bonitatis suae studia erga divinum cultum
amplificandum multiplici modo ferventia, quendam Presbyterum, natione Hispanum, nomine Claudium, qui aliquid temporis in Palatio suo
in Presbyteratus militaverat honore, cui in explanandis ss. Evangeliorum
lectionibus quantulacunque notitia inesse videbatur, ut Italicae plebis
(quae magna ex parte a ss. Evangelistarum sensibus procul aberat) sacrae doctrinae consultum ferret, Taurinensi praesulem subrogari fecit
Ecclesiae. Lib. i. above : Qui dum super gregem sibi creditum pro
viribus superintenderet,—vidit eum inter caetera, quae emendatione
digna gerebat, superstitiosae, imo perniciosae imaginum adorationi, qua
plurimum nonnulli illarum partium laborant, ex inolita consuetudine
deditum esse. Unde immoderato et indiscreto zelo succensus non solum
picturas sanctarum rerum gestarum, quae non ad adorandum sed solummodo (teste b. Gregorio) ad instruendas nescientium mentes, in Ecclesiis suis antiquitus fieri permissae, verum etiam cruces materiales, quibus ob honorem et recordationem redemptionis suae sancta consuevit uti
Ecclesia, a cunctis Parochiae suae basilicis dicitur delevisse, evertisse et
penitus abdicasse. Sed quia errorem gregis sui ratione corrigere ne-
glexit, et eorum animis scandalum generavit, et in sui detestationem
eos quodammodo prorumpere coëgit.—Dicitur etiam, Claudium eundem
adversus reliquias Sanctorum—eorumque sepulcra—quaedam nefanda
dogmatizasse, et usque nunc dogmatizare. Quae licet series literarum
suarum manifeste non indicit, ex his tamen, quae innuit, et ex veridica
quorundam fidelium relatione, ita se rem habere liquido claret. Theo-
demirus—eidem Claudio, ut ab his se—compesceret, literis caritate re-
fertis mandari curavit. Ille e contra fraternae admonitionis impatiens,
turbidaque indignatione permotus, non solum in illum juste se redargu-
entem, verum etiam in omnes s. catholicae et apostolicae Ecclesiae sin-
cerissimos cultores Galliam Germaniamque incolentes,—et ab imaginum superstitiosa adoratione immunes, diversarum reprehensionum ac
vituperationum jacula intorsit, eosque et idololatriae abominatione, et
falsae religionis superstitione et innumeris aliis sceleribus irretitos, sicut
textus suarum literarum demonstrat, appellare non erubuit. Praefatio :
The book of Claudius against Theodemir had been brought to the emperor Lewis, qui ab eo suique palati prudentissimis viris examinatus
justo judicio est repudiatus. On this Jonas received extracts from it
from the emperor for the purpose of refuting them, but at the news of
Claudius's death abandoned the task. Sed quia, ut relatione veridica didici, non modo error, de quo agitur, in discipulorum suorum mentibus reviviscit, quin, potius haeresis Ariana pullulare deprehenditur, de
qua fertur, quaedam monumenta librorum congessisse, et—in armario

s 2

saint worship, without giving much offence in his circle.[15] Even
in Rome itself, this tendency appears to have found adherents.[16]

episcopii sui clandestina calliditate reliquisse; non sum ausus, quiu—
opus, quod praetermiseram, enucleatim discutiendum repeterem, etc.

   [15] Agobardi lib. contra eorum superstitionem, qui picturis et imaginibus SS. adorationis obsequium deferendum putant (Comp. § 10.
not. 13.) It is said c. 17: Non solum vero divinum deferre honorem,
quibus non licet, sed et ambitiose honorare Sanctorum memorias ob
captandam gloriam popularem, reprehensibile est.   Arguit super his
Dominus Pharisaeos in Evangelio, teste b. Hieronymo, his verbis:
"Vae vobis, Scribae et Pharisaei hypocritae, qui aedificatis sepulcra
Prophetarum," etc. (Matth. xxiii. 29. 30.) c. 23: Si serpentem aeneum
quem Deus fieri praecepit, quoniam errans populus tamquam idolum
colere coepit, Ezechias religiosius rex cum magna pietatis laude contrivit; multo religiosius Sanctorum imagines (ipsis quoque Sanctis
faventibus, qui ob sui honorem cum divinae religionis contemtu eas
adorari more idolorum indignantissime ferunt) omni genere cou-
terendae, et usque ad pulverem sunt eradendae: praesertim cum non
illas fieri Deus jusserit, sed humanus sensus excogitaverit.   c. 30: Adoretur, colatur, veneretur a fidelibus Deus; illi soli sacrificetur, vel mysterio corporis et sanguinis quo sumus redemti, vel in sacrificio cordis
contriti et humiliati.   Angeli vel homines sancti amentur, honorentur
caritate, non servitute.   Non eis corpus Christi offeratur, cum sint hoc
et ipsi.   Non ponamus spem nostram in homine sed in Deo, ne forte
redundet in nos illud propheticum: "Maledictus homo qui confidit in
homine," etc. (Jer. xvii. 5.) c. 31: Agit hoc nimirum versutus et calli-
dus humani generis inimicus, ut sub praetextu honoris Sanctorum rursus
idola introducat, rursus per diversas effigies adoretur; ut avertat nos ab
spiritalibus, ad carnalia vero demergat; ac per omnia simus digni ab
Apostolo audire: "O insensati, quis vos fascinavit?" etc.   c. 35: flec-
tamus genu in nomine solius Jesu, quod est super omne nomen; ne si
alteri hunc honorem tribuimus, alieni judicemur a Deo, et dimittamur
secundum desideria cordis nostri ire in adinventionibus nostris.   The
verbal agreement of Claudius and Agobard in several sentences deserves
particular attention.   Claudius has, for example: Certe si adorandi
fuissent, vivi potius quam mortui adorandi esse debuerunt, i. e. ubi
similitudinem Dei habent, non ubi pecorum vel, quod verius est, lapidum
seu lignorum, vita, sensu et ratione carentium.   Agobard c. 28. exactly
the same, only he says: vivi magis quam picti.—Controversy concerning the sanctity of St Agobard Act. SS. Junii ii. 748.   Hist. lit. de la
France iv. 571.

   [16] A Roman cardinal priest, Anastasius, was deposed under Leo IV.
(Anastasius vita Leonis), because he had left his parish and remained
five years abroad, and did not appear though he had been cited even by
two councils.   After the death of this pope, he entered Rome with the
imperial messengers who had been sent to the new election, destroyed
the images in Peter's church (imagines confregit, ignique concremavit,
—Dominique Jesu Christi, ejusque semper virginis genitricis iconam
bipenni, quod non debuerat, ad ima dejecit), met with adherents, and by
the aid of the legates had almost become pope (l. c. vita Benedicti iii.)

§ 12.

ON THE ADDITION FILIOQUE IN THE CREED.

G. J. Vossii de tribus Symbolis (ed. ii. Amstel. 1662. 4.) diss. iii. § 15 ss. Mich. L. Quien diss. de processione Sp. S. is the first of his dissertatt Damascen. prefixed to the opp. Joh. Damasc. i. 1. J. G. Walchii hist. controversiae Graecorum Latinorumque de processione Spir. S. Jenae 1751. 8. W. C. L. Ziegler's Geschichtsentwickelung des Dogma vom h. Geiste, in his theologischen Abhandl. i. 204.

An older doctrine, peculiar to the Latin fathers, viz., that the Holy Spirit proceeds from the Father and *the Son*,[1] had been inserted before this time in the Nicene-Constantinopolitan creed, in Spain ;[2] but now, for the first time, it excited the attention of the Greeks.[3] What was decided respecting it, at the Synod of *Gentilly*,[4] is not known. As to the insertion in the symbolum which had by degrees obtained in the Frank Church, opinions were [5]

[1] Supported especially by the example of Augustine (de Trinit. iv. 20 : Nec possumus dicere, quod Sp. S. et a Filio non procedat, neque enim frustra idem Spiritus et Patris et Filii Spiritus dicitur. v. 14. xv. 26 : De utroque procedere sic docetur etc.) and Leo the great. (epist. xv. ad Turibium c. 1.—tamquam—nec alius sit, qui genuit, alius, qui genitus est, alius, qui de utroque processit.) Comp. Wundemann's Gesch. der Glaubenslehren, i. 383. Münscher's Dogmengesch. iii. 500.

[2] First appeared at the Concil. Tolet. iii. ann. 589 (ap. Mansi ix. 981):—Credimus et in Spiritum S. dominum et vivificatorem ex Patre et Filio procedentem etc. In like manner the Conc. Tolet. viii. ann. 653, Bracar. iii. 675, Tolet. xii. 681, xiii. 683, xv. 688, xvii. 694. The Conc. Tolet. iii. c. 2. had also decreed ut per omnes Ecclesias Hispaniae—secundum formam orientalium Ecclesiarum, Concilii Constantinopolitani—symbolum fidei recitetur, ut priusquam dominica dicatur oratio voce clara a populo decantetur etc.

[3] It had been so at an earlier period (about 650) Maximi epist. ad Marinum. See Ziegler S. 208.

[4] Comp. § 11. not. 1. More plainly Ado in chron. ad ann. 767 : quaestio ventilata est inter Graecos et Romanos de Trinitate, et utrum Spir. S. sicut procedit a Patre ita procedat a Filio.

[5] Walafrid Strabo de rebus eccles. c. 22 : apud Gallos et Germanos post dejectionem Felicis haeretici sub gloriosissimo Carolo Francorum Rectore damnati, idem Symbolum latius et crebrius in Missarum coepit officiis iterari. Paulinus Patr. Aquilejensis in Concil. Forojuliensi ann. 791 (ap. Mansi xiii. 829) expresses himself violently indeed against additions to the creed, but what he thereby understands see in p. 836 :

divided.   The doctrine, however, was generally defended, for instance, by *Alcuin* and *Theodulph*.⁶ It had strong support, in
particular, in the so-called *Athanasian creed*, which had also been
probably brought from Spain into France.⁷ When Charlemagne,

addere vel minuere est subdole contra sacrosanctum eorum sensum,
aliter quam illi, callida tergiversatione diversa sentire. Explanatory
additions therefore he does not include. Si recenseatur Nicaeni symboli series veneranda, nihil aliud de Spiritu S. in ea nisi hoc modo
reperiri poterit promulgatum: et in Sanctum, inquiunt, Spiritum.—
Suppleverunt tamen [cl. Patres] quasi exponendo eorum sensum, et in
Spiritum S. confitentur se credere, Dominum et vivificatorem, ex Patre
procedentem.—Sed et postmodum propter eos videlicet haereticos, qui
susurrant Spiritum S. solius esse Patris et a solo procedere Patre, ad-
ditum est : Qui ex Patre Filioque procedit. Et tamen non sunt hi ss.
Patres culpandi, quasi addidissent aliquid vel minuissent de fide cccxviii.
Patrum, quia non contra eorum sensum diversa senserunt, sed immacu-
latum eorum intellectum sanis moribus supplere studuerunt etc. Ziegler
p. 211. is wrong in supposing that here there is any rejection of the
addition ; the reading in the symbol inserted among the Synodical Acts
p. 842 : qui ex Patre Filioque procedit, is not interpolated. On the
other hand Alcuinus epist. 75. (ed. Froben.) ad fratres Lugdun. : His-
panici erroris sectas tota vobis cavete intentione.—Et Symbolo catholicae fidei nova nolite inserere, et in ecclesiasticis officiis inauditas priscis
temporibus traditiones nolite diligere.
    ⁶ Alcuini lib. de processione Spir. S. ad Car. M. first printed in opp.
Alcuin. ed. Froben i. 743.   Theodulphi de Spir. S. liber (in Theodulphi opp. ed. J. Sirmond.   Par. 1646. 8. and in Sirmondii opp. ii. 695).
Cf. libr. Carolin. lib. iii. c. 3 : ex Patre et Filio—omnis universaliter
confitetur et credit Ecclesia eum procedere.
    ⁷ G. J. Vossius de tribus symbolis. Amstelod. 1662. 4. diss. ii. Guil.
E. Tentzelii judicia eruditorum de symb. Athanas. Gothae 1687. 12.
Dan. Waterland critical history of the Athanasian creed. Cambridge 1724.
ed. 2. 1728. 8.   Quesnelli diss. de variis fidei libellis in antiquo Rom. Ecclesia Codice contentis (diss. xiv. in Leon. M. and in Gallandii de vetustt.
canonum collectionibus dissertatt. syll. ed. Mogunt. i. 829) and Balleri-
norum obss. ad. Quesnelli diss. (ib. p. 842).   D. M. Speroni de symb.
vulgo s. Athanasii dicto diss. ii. Patav. 1750. 51.   D. E. Köllner's Sym-
bolik d. luth. Kirche S. 53.   All the testimonies respecting the existence
of this creed before the end of the 8th century are insecure.   A sermo
which has fallen among the Augustinian (opp. v. ap. Sermo 244), refers
to it ; but that it belongs to Caesarius Arelat, about 520, is a mere
conjecture.   The expositio fidei catholicae Fortunati, published by
Muratori anecdota ii. 212, cannot be from Venantius Fortunatus about
560, since it presupposes the Symb. Quicunque as a confession of faith
already adopted in general, and endeavours to justify polemically Filioque.   Probably Fortunati expositio symb. apostol. was the reason why
this expositio was also erroneously attributed to him.   Respecting a
Canon Augustodunensis, which mentions the fides s. Athanasii, it is un-

at a synod in Aix-la-Chapelle (809), brought forward the matter, Pope *Leo III.* decided in favour of the doctrine, but against its insertion in the symbol.[8]

§ 13.

ADOPTIAN CONTROVERSY.

Chr. G. F. Walchii hist. Adoptianorum. Gotting. 1755. 8. Frobenii diss. hist. de haeresi Elipandi et Felicis in his. opp. Alcuini i. ii. 923. Walch's Ketzerhist. ix. 667. Neander iii. 314.

Since Christ could only be the adopted Son of God according to the Arian creed, the Catholic Church had often asserted pole-

certain to what time it belongs; many even regard it as spurious. The first certain witnesses are Theodulphus de Spir. S., a contemporary anonymous author, whom Sirmond cites in the notes to Theodulf and Agobardus adv. Felicem. c. 3. Probably, too, so early as the Conc. Francof. ann. 794, c. 31 (Baluzii capit. i. p. 268 : ut fides catholica sanctae Trinitatis et oratio dominica atque Symbolum fide omnibus praedicetur et tradatur) the fides cath. s. Trin. is this symbol, which characterises itself at the beginning and end as fides catholica. It is most likely that we should seek for the origin of it in Spain. The councils of Toledo all begin with a confession of faith, several with the unaltered Nicene creed ; others enlarge it, especially in the articles respecting the Trinity and incarnation of Christ, first in the dialectic manner of the Symb. Quicunque, and coincide in single sentences with it, without, however, being dependent on it. So Conc. Tolet. iv. ann. 633, c. 1., vi. ann. 638, c. 1., xi. ann. 675, praef. (a similar dialectic development respecting the incarnation is in the Conc. Tolet. xiv. ann. 684, c. 8). Hence that symbol appears to have been formed after these patterns, in the 7th and 8th centuries, in Spain, and from thence to have been transferred to France towards the end of the 8th. Even the old appellation, fides Athanasii, which was afterwards misunderstood, as if Athanasius were the author, points to Spain. For the catholic faith could only at first have been designated by the Arians as fides Athanasii, in opposition to fides Arii, as their creed was named by opponents ; and in Spain, the party of Arius continued the longest opposed to that of Athanasius.

[8] On the disputes of the monks at Jerusalem Baluzii miscellan. vii. 14. Collatio cum Papa Romae a legatis habita et epist. Caroli Imp. ad Leonem P. iii. utraque a Smaragdo Abb. edita (ap. Mansi xiv. 17 ss). Anastasii vita xcviii. Leonis iii. (ap. Muratori p. 208) : Hic vero pro amore et cantela orthodoxae fidei fecit in basilica s. Petri scuta argentea duo, scripta utraque Symbolo, unum quidem literis Graecis, et aliud Latinis etc. The same is also related by Photius epist. ad Patriarcham Aquilej. in Combefisii auctario noviss. i. 529, and Petrus Lomb. sen-

mically against the Arians in Spain his natural sonship.[1] To this *Elipand*, archbishop of Toledo, and *Felix*, bishop of Urgel, appealing to older authorities,[2] now attached the assertion, that Christ, as God, was the natural, and, as man, the adopted, son of God.[3]

tent. lib. i. diss. xi. (in quo quidem symbolo in processione Spiritus solus commemoratur Pater his verbis : et in Spir. S. dominum et vivificatorem ex Patre procedentem).

[1] Conc. Tolet. ann. 675, in the confessio fidei, which is found in the preface : Hic etiam Filius Dei natura est Filius, non adoptione.

[2] Comp. especially Walchii hist. Adopt. cap. 1.   Fabius Marius Victorinus [about 360] adv. Arium. lib. i. : non sic Filius, quemadmodum nos.   Nos enim adoptione filii, ille natura.   Etiam quadam adoptione filius et Christus, sed secundum carnem.   Isidorus Hispalensis originn. s. etymologg. lib. vii. c. 2 : Unigenitus autem vocatur secundum Divinitatis excellentiam, quia sine fratribus : Primogenitus secundum susceptionem hominis, in qua per adoptionem gratiae fratres habere dignatus est, de quibus esset primogenitus.   Authorities of the Adoptians enumerated in the epist. Episcoporum Hispan. ad Episc. Galliae, and in the epist. Elipandi ad Alcuinum (see note 3 and 11), Ambrose, Hilary, Jerome, Augustine, Isidore of Spain, mostly inapplicable.   At the close : Item praedecessores nostri Eugenius, Ildephonsus, Julianus, Toletenae antistites, in suis dogmatibus ita dixerunt in Missa de Coena Domini : " Qui per adoptivi hominis passionem, dum suo non indulsit corpori, nostro demum—pepercit."—Item in Missa de Ascensione Domini : " Hodie Salvator noster post adoptionem carnis sedem repetit Deitatis."   Item in Missa defunctorum : " Quos fecisti adoptionis participes, jubeas hereditatis tuae esse consortes."   These passages are actually found in the liturgia Mozarabica ed. Alex. Lesle. Romae 1755. 4.—The passage of Hilarius de Trinit. ii. c. 29, has become critically remarkable : Parit virgo : partus a Deo est.   Infans vagit : laudantes angeli audiuntur.   Panni sordent : deus adoratur.   Ita potestatis dignitas non amittitur, dum carnis humilitas adoptatur.   Alcuinus c. Felicem lib. vi. c. 6, complains of corruption, and would read adoratur Agobardus adv. Felic. c. 40, explains it correctly by adsumitur (juxta hunc modum et caeteros doctores dixisse et sensisse, ubicumque nomen et verbum adoptionis in fidei dogmatibus inseruerunt, credimus).   On the controversy between P. Coustant, who, in his edition of Hilary, defended adoptatur and the Jesuit Barth. Germonius, who with great vehemence would have adoratur, see Walch hist. Adopt. p. 26 ss. (Germonius went so far as to accomplish the falsification of the oldest MS. of Hilary in the Vatican in favour of his reading, by means of the royal confessor, which was discovered immediately after, and judicially authenticated.   See Le Bret's pragmatische Gesch. d. Bulle in Coena Domini Bd. 1. 2te Aufl. 1772. S. 52.

[3] Epist. Episc. Hisp. ad Episc. Galliae etc. c. 2 (in Alcuini opp. ed. Froben. ii. 568) : Nos—confitemur et credimus, Deum Dei filium ante omnia tempora sine initio ex Patre genitum—non adoptione sed genere, neque gratia sed natura :—pro salute vero humani generis, in fine tem-

Having been long contested in Spain,[4] Adoptianism, by penetrating into France, caused Charlemagne to interfere in the matter.

poris ex illa intima et ineffabili Patris substantia egrediens, et a Patre non recedens, hujus mundi infima petens, ad publicum humani generis apparens, invisibilis visibile corpus adsumens de virgine, ineffabiliter per integra virginalia Matris enixus: secundum traditionem Patrum confitemur et credimus, eum factum ex muliere, factum sub lege, non genere esse filium Dei sed adoptione; neque natura sed gratia, idipsum eodem Domino attestante, qui ait: Pater major me est (Jo. xiv. 28, farther, Luc. i. 80, Jo. i. 14).—cap. 9. Credimus igitur et confitemur Deum Dei Filium, lumen de lumine, Deum verum ex Deo vero, ex Patre Unigenitum sine adoptione; Primogenitum vero in fine temporis, verum hominem assumendo de Virgine in carnis adoptione: Unigenitum in natura: Primogenitum in adoptione et gratia. Proofs from Rom. viii. 29 (primogenitus in multis fratribus). Ps. xxii. 23. Unde fratres, nisi de sola carnis adoptione, per quod fratres habere dignatus est? Then especially 1 Joh. iii. 2 (similes ei erimus): Similes atique in carnis adoptione, non similes ei in Divinitate. For the Filius unigenitus were quoted Ps. cx. 4 (Ex utero ante Luciferum genui te), xliv. 2, Jes. xlv. 23, Prov. viii. 25; for the Filius primogenitus et adoptivus Deut. xviii. 15 (Prophetam suscitabit Dominus Deus de fratribus vestris). Matth. xvii. 5; Ps. lxxxix. 27 ss.; Ps. ii. 8; Jes. xlv. 2, 3; Mich. vi. 7, &c. Cap. 10: (credimus) in uno eodemque Dei et hominis Filio in una persona; duabus quoque naturis plenis atque perfectis, Dei et hominis, domini et servi, visibilis atque invisibilis, tribus quoque substantiis, verbi scilicet, animae et carnis.—Felix (ap. Alcuin. contra Felicem lib. iv. c. 2): Secundo autem modo nuncupative Deus dicitur, sicut superius dictum est de sanctis praedicatoribus, de quibus Salvator Judaeis ait: Si enim illos dixit deos, ad quos Dei sermo factus (Jo. x. 35): qui tamen non natura ut Deus, sed per Dei gratiam ab eo, qui verus est Deus, deificati dii sunt sub illo vocati: in hoc quippe ordine Dei Filius dominus et redemtor noster juxta humanitatem, sicut in natura ita et in nomine, quamvis excellentius cunctis electus, verissime tamen cum illis communicat, sicut et in caeteris omnibus i. e., in praedestinatione, in electione, in gratia, in susceptione, in adsumtione nominis servi atque applicatione, seu caetera, his similia, ut idem qui essentialiter cum Patre et Spiritu Sancto in unitate Deitatis verus est Deus, ipse in forma humanitatis cum electis suis per adoptionis gratiam deificatus fieret, et nuncupative Deus.

[4] First contradicted by Beatus and Eutherius. Elipandi ep. ad Fidelem Abbatem, A.D. 785 (preserved in the following answer, best edited in Alcuini opp. ed. Froben. ii. 587). On the other side, Beati et Etherii adv. Elipandum libb. ii. (in Canisii lect. antt. ed. Basnage ii. i. 269. and ap. Gallandius xiii. 290, but might still be corrected from Codd. Toletanis, cf. Gregor. Majans in Alcuini opp. ed. Froben. ii. 592 ss.)—Hadriani P. i. epist. ad Episcopos per universam Spaniam commorantes in the Cod. Carol. no. 97. ap. Mansi xii. 814. Doubts of the genuineness Walch's Ketzerhist. Bd. ix. 747.

Felix was obliged to recant at *Ratisbon* (792), and then at Rome.[5] Elipand having complained to Charles of this treatment,[6] the latter called *the Synod of Frankfurt* (794), at which Adoptianism was rejected anew.[7] After many fruitless attempts of various writers, of whom *Alcuin* was the most important,[8] to con-

---

[5] In the Acts of the Synod of Narbonne A.D. 788 (ed. Baluz. ad de Marca concord. Sac. et Imp. lib. vi. c. 25. ap. Mansi xiii. 821.) the introduction and the signatures, which have reference to this subject, are perhaps spurious. Walch ix. 687. 749. Concerning the transactions at the Synod of Ratisbon and in Rome see the accounts: Alcuinus adv. Elipandum lib. c. 16. Acta Conc. Rom. ann. 799 (ap. Mansi xiii. 1031) and all the Frank annals.

[6] Epist. Episcop. Hispaniae ad Carol. M. (prim. ed. H. Florez in Espanna sagrada v. 558. Walch hist. Adopt. p. 154. With emendations in opp. Alcuini ed. Froben. ii. 567). Epist. Episcop. Hispaniae ad Episc. Galliae, Aquitan. et Austriae (l. c. p. 568 ss).

[7] Acta Conc. Francofordensis (ap. Mansi xiii. 863). To this belong Epist. Hadriani P. i. ad Episc. Hispaniae (p. 865), libellus Episcoposum Italiae contra Elipandum or Paullini Aquilej. libellus sacrosyllabus (p. 873. and in the works of Paullinus), Synodica Concilii ab Episc. Galliae et Germaniae ad Praesules Hispaniae missa (p. 883), then Can. Francof. i. (p. 909), and lastly Caroli M. epist. ad Elipandum et caeteros Episc. Hispaniae (p. 899).

[8] First, Alcuini libellus adv. haeresin Felicis ad Abbates et Monachos Gothiae missus (prim. ed. Froben. in opp. Alcuini i. ii. 759 ss.) and epist. ad. Felicem (l. c. p. 783 ss).—Against the latter, Felicis libellus contra Alcuinum, of which remain only fragments in the works written against it. Of this work Alcuini epist. 68. ad domnum Regem: Hujus vero libri, vel magis erroris responsio multa diligentia et pluribus adjutoribus est consideranda. Ego solus non sufficio ad responsionem. Praevideat vero tua sancta Pietas huic operi tam arduo et necessario adjutores idoneos etc. Ejusd. epist. 69. ad eund. : De libello vero Infelicis, non magistri sed subversoris, placet mihi valde, quod vestra sanctissima Voluntas et Devotio habet curam respondendi ad defensionem fidei catholicae. Sed obsecro, si vestrae placeat Pietati, ut exemplarium illius libelli domno dirigatur Apostolico, aliud quoque Paullino Patriarchae, similiter Richbono, et Teudulfo Episcopis, doctoribus et magistris, ut singuli pro se respondeant. Flaccus vero tuus tecum laborat in reddenda ratione catholicae fidei. Tantum detur ei spatium, ut quiete et diligenter liceat illi cum pueris suis considerare Patrum senus ; quid unusquisque diceret de sententiis, quas posuit praefatus subversor in suo libello. Et tempore praefinito a vobis ferantur vestrae auctoritati singulorum responsa. This was followed by the Conc. Roman ann. 799., at which Leo III. pronounces an anathema against Felix, ap. Mansi xiii. 1029. Works written against it by Paullinus Aquilej. libb. iii. adv. Felicem Orgelitanum (best in Paulini opp. ed. J. F. Madrissi, Venet. 1737,

vince the Adoptians of their error,[9] Felix was at last persuaded by Alcuin to yield, at a synod at *Aix-la-Chapelle* (799) ;[10] while Elipand violently resisted all the exhortations of Alcuin.[11] Felix, indeed, left proofs after his death at Lyons († 818) that he had

p. 95 ss.) and Alcuini libb. vii. adv. Felicem (ed. Froben. i. ii. 783) first appeared after the synod of Aix-la-Chapelle.

[9] The greatest reproach against the Adoptians was constantly that of Nestorianism. For example, Alcuinus contra Felicem lib. i. c. 11 : Sicut Nestoriana impietas in duas Christum dividit personas propter duas naturas :—ita et vestra indocta temeritas in duos eum dividit filios, unum proprium, alterum adoptivum. Si vero Christus est proprius Filius Dei Patris et adoptivus : ergo est alter et alter. Similiter si in divinitate Deus verus est, et in humanitate Deus nuncupativus, alter et alter est, et nullatenus sic sentientes potestis vobis evitare impietatem Nestorianae doctrinae : quia quem ille in duas personas dividit propter duas naturas. hunc vos dividitis in duos filios, et in duos Deos per adoptionis nomen et nuncupationis. Lib. iv. c. 5 : Nam si duas personas in uno Christo propter apertam blasphemiam timeas fateri, tamen omnia, quae duabus personis inesse necesse est, in tua confessione confirmare non metuis. On the other hand, lib. ii. c. 12 : Adsumsit namque sibi Dei Filius carnem ex Virgine, et non amisit proprietatem, quam habuit in Filii nomine : sed quamquam duas habuisset post nativitatem ex Virgine naturas, tamen unam proprietatem in Filii persona firmiter tenuit. Accessit humanitas in unitatem personae Filii Dei, et mansit eadem proprietas in duabus naturis in Filii nomine, quae ante fuit in una substantia. In adsumtione namque carnis a Deo persona perit hominis, non natura. In nobis est persona adoptionis, non in Filio Dei : quia singulariter ille unus homo ex Deo conceptus et in Deum adsumtus habet proprietatem Filius Dei esse, quod omnes Sancti habent per adoptionem gratiae Dei.—Nec in illa adsumtione alius est Deus, alius homo, vel alius Filius Dei, et alius Filius Virginis : sed idem est Filius Dei, qui et Filius Virginis ;—ut sit unus Filius etiam proprius et perfectus in duabus naturis Dei et hominis.

[10] See on this, confessio fidei Felicis, Orgelitanae sedis Episcopi, quam ipse post spretum errorem suum in conspectu Concilii edidit, et eis, qui in ipso errore ei dudum consentientes fuerant, direxit (ap. Mansi xiii. 1035 ss. and in Alcuini opp. ed. Froben. i. ii. 917 ss.) and Alcuinus adv. Elipandum lib. i. c. 16.

[11] First epist. Alcuini ad Elipandum (opp. ed. Froben. i. ii. 863) and epist. Elipandi ad Alcuinum (ib. p. 868), both A.D. 799. The latter begins : Reverendissimo fratri Albino Diacono, non Christi ministro, sed Antiphrasii Beati foetidissimi discipulo, tempore gloriosi Principis in finibus Austriae exorto, novo Arrio, sanctorum venerabilium Patrum Ambrosii, Augustini, Isidori, Hieronymi doctrinis contrario, si se converterit ab errore viae suae, a Domino aeternam salutem : et si noluerit, aeternam damnationem. After this Alcuini adv. Elipandum libb. iv. (ib. p. 876 ss.)

not entirely given up his opinions ;[12] but with the death of its leaders, Adoptianism sank into oblivion.[13]

§ 14.

CONTROVERSIES OF PASCHASUS RADBERT.

The ecclesiastical mode of speaking, that bread and wine in the Lord's Supper became by consecration the body and blood of Christ, may have been frequently understood of a transformation of substance by the uneducated ; but among the theologians of the West, this misconception could not so readily find acceptance,[1] in consequence of the clear explanations given by the celebrated Augustine.[2]   When, therefore, *Paschasius Radbert*, a monk and abbot of Corbey, from 844-851 († 865),[3] expressly. taught such a transformation,[4] he met with considerable opposi-

---

[12] A posthumous work of his given in extracts, and refuted in Agobardi liber adv. dogma Felicis Episc. Urgellensis ad Ludovicum Pium Imp.

[13] In the middle ages, Folmar was accused of Adoptian or Nestorian opinions (about 1160) (Walch hist. Adopt. p. 247.   Comp. Cramer's Forts. v. Bossuet's Weltgesch. vii. 43).   Duns Scotus (1300) and Durandus a S. Porciano (1320) allow the expression Filius adoptivus in a certain sense to Christ (Walch l. c. p. 253).—In modern times, the Adoptians have been defended among the Catholics, particularly by the Jesuit Gabr. Vasquez commentar. in Thomam (Ingolst. 1606. fol.) in P. iii. diss. 89. c. 7. ; among the Protestants, by G. Calixtus (a Helmstadt programme of 1643, reprinted in his de persona Christi dissertationum fasciculus ed. F. U. Calixtus. Helmst. 1663. p. 96.) and others (Walch l. c, p. 256 ss).

[1] The views of the time immediately preceding Radbert (Bede, Alcuin, Charlemagne) see in Cramer's continuation of Bossuet v. i. 222. Münscher's Lehrb. d. Dogmengesch. von v. Cölln ii. i. 223.

[2] See vol. i. div. 2. § 101. note 15.

[3] Concerning him see hist. lit. de la France v. 287.   Bähr's Gesch. d. röm. lit. im karoling. Zeitalter S. 462.—Opera (among which the commentar. in Evang. Matthaei lib. xii. is still worthy of notice) ed. J. Sirmond. Paris. 1618. fol. and afterwards in bibl. PP. Lugd. xiv. 352 ss.

[4] Pasch. Radb. lib. de corpore et sanguine Domini, 831, dedicated to Marinus, abbot of New Corvey : in a second edition, 844, presented to Charles the Bald.   The earliest printed editions (prim. ed. Hiob. Gastius Hagenoae 1528. 4.) are mutilated.   The first genuine edition ed. Nicol. Mameranus. Colon. 1550. 8.   Afterwards many editions; the

tion. *Rabanus Maurus* rejected the new doctrine as erroneous.[5] *Ratramnus*, in the opinion for which he was asked by the

best in Edm. Martene et Ursini Durand veterum script. et monument.
amplissima collectio ix. 367. Cf. hist. lit. de la Fr. v. 294.—Cap. 1:
Patet igitur quod nihil extra vel contra Dei velle potest, sed cedunt illi
omnia omnino. Et ideo nullus moveatur de hoc corpore Christi et sanguine, quod in mysterio vera sit caro et verus sit sanguis, dum sic voluit
ille qui creavit. Omnia enim quaecunque voluit fecit in caelo et in terra (Ps. cxxxv. 6.): et quia voluit, licet in figura panis et vini maneat,
haec sic esse omnino, nihilque aliud quam caro Christi et sanguis post
consecrationem credenda sunt: unde ipsa Veritas ad discipulos:
"Haec, inquit caro mea est pro mundi vita:" et ut mirabilius loquar,
non alia plane, quam quae nata est de Maria, et passa in cruce et resurrexit de sepulcro. Ca.p 4.: sed quia Christum vorari fas dentibus non
est, voluit in mysterio hunc panem et vinum vere carnem suam et sanguinem consecratione Spiritus Sancti potentialiter creari, creando vero
quotidie pro mundi vita mystice immolari, ut sicut de Virgine per Spiritum vera caro sine coitu creatur, ita per eundem ex substantia panis ac
vini mystice idem Christi corpus et sanguis consecretur: de qua videlicet carne et sanguine: "Amen, amen," inquit, "dico vobis, nisi manducaveritis carnem filii hominis etc. (Jo. vi. 53)."—Si carnem illam vere
credis de Maria virgine in utero sine semine potestate Sp. S. creatam,
ut Verbum caro fieret; vere crede, et hoc, quod conficitur in verbo
Christi per Sp. S., corpus ipsius esse ex Virgine.—potentia divinitatis
contra naturam ultra nostrae rationis capacitatem efficaciter operatur.
Cap. 8.: Substantia panis et vini in Christi carnem et sauguinem efficaciter interius commutatur. Cap. 14.: Examples, quod haec mystica
corporis et sanguinis sacramenta—visibili specie in agni formam aut in
carnis et sanguinis colorem monstrata sint, or tamquam puerulus jacens
super altare etc. Cap. 20.:—non modo caro aut sanguis Christi in nostram convertuntur carnem aut sanguinem, verum nos a carnalibus elevant
et spirituales efficiunt. Hoc sane nutriunt in nobis, quod ex Deo natum
est, et non quod ex carne et sanguine.—Frivolum est ergo—in hoc mysterio cogitare de stercore, ne commisceatur in digestione alterius cibi.
Denique ubi spiritalis esca et potus sumitur, et Spiritus S. per eum in
homine operatur, ut si quid in nobis carnale adhuc est, transferatur in
spiritum, et fiat homo spiritualis, quid commixtionis habere poterit? Sirmond confesses at least in his vita Paschacii: genuinum Ecclesiae catholicae sensum ita primus explicuit, ut viam caeteris aperuerit, qui de
eodem argumento multa postea scripserunt. Cf. histoire de l'eucharistie
par Matth. Larroque. Amst. 1669. 4. p. 357. H. Reuter de erroribus,
qui aetate media doctrinam Christ. de s. Eucharistia turpaverunt. Berol.
1840. 8. p. 26. It is surprising that Dr A. Ebrard (das Dogma vom
heil Abendmal u. s. Geschichte, Bd. 1. Frankf. a. M. 1845. S. 406)
finds in Paschasius not a substantial transformation, but only the doctrine that bread and wine became the body and blood of Christ, according to potentia (potentially).

[5] Rab. M. epist. ad Heribaldum Antissidorensem Episc. (written

emperor,[6] and which has subsequently been often attributed er-

853) cap. 33. (Reginonis Abb. libb. ii. de ecclesiast. disciplinis ed.
Baluzius p. 516. the passage corrected by MSS. in Mabillonii iter Germ.
in his vett. analectis ed. ii. p. 17): " Quod autem interrogasti, utrum
Eucharistia, postquam consumitur, et in secessum emittitur more aliorum
ciborum, iterum redeat in naturam pristinam, quam habuerat, antequam
in altari consecraretur : superflua est hujusmodi quaestio, cum ipse Salvator dixerit in Evangelio : " Omne quod intrat in os, in ventrem vadit,
et in secessum emittitur," (Matth. xv. 17.)   Sacramentum ergo corporis et sanguinis Domini ex rebus visibilibus et corporalibus conficitur,
sed invisibilem tam corporis quam animae efficit sanctificationem et
salutem.   Quae est enim ratio, ut hoc, quod stomacho digeritur, et in
secessum emittitur, iterum in statum pristinum redeat, cum nullus hoc
unquam fieri asseruerit.   Nam quidam nuper de ipso Sacramento corporis et sanguinis Domini non rite sentientes dixerunt, hoc ipsum esse
corpus et sanguinem Domini, quod de Maria Virgine natum est, et in
quo ipse Dominus passus est in cruce, et resurrexit de sepulcro.   Cui
errori quantum potuimus, ad Eigilum Abbatem scribentes, de corpore
ipso quid vere credendum sit aperuimus. This epistle to Eigilus, abbot
of Prüm, is lost.   Mabillon supposes it to be the dicta cujusdam sapi-
entis de corpore et sanguine Domini adv. Radbertum, edited by him
from a Cod. Gemblac. (Act. SS. Ord. Bened. saec. iv. ii. 591.)   Comp.
the praef. ad h. tom. no. 57-60. See on the other hand v. Cölln on
Münscher's Lehrbuch d. Dogmengesch. ii. i. 229.—Cf. Rab. Maur. de
institutione clericorum lib. i. c. 31. (ap. Hittorp p. 324) : Maluit enim
Dominus corporis et sanguinis sui sacramenta fidelium ore percipi, et
in pastum eorum redigi, ut per visibile opus invisibilis ostenderetur
effectus. Sicut enim cibus materialis forinsecus nutrit corpus et vegetat,
ita etiam verbum Dei intus animam nutrit et roborat.—aliud est sacramentum, aliud virtus sacramenti.   Sacramentum enim ore percipitur,
virtute sacramenti interior homo satiatur : sacramentum in alimentum
corporis redigitur, virtute autem sacramenti aeterna vita adipiscitur.
Quia panis corpus confirmat, ideo ille corpus Christi congruenter nuncupatur, vinum autem, quia sanguinem operatur in carne, ideo ad sanguinem Christi refertur : haec autem dum sunt visibilia, sanctificata tamen
per Spiritum S., in sacramentum divini corporis transeunt. Lib. iii.
c. 13. Among the examples of oratio figurata : " Nisi manducaveritis,"
inquit, " carnem filii hominis," etc. (Jo. vi. 53.) Facinus vel flagitium
videtur jubere. Figurata ergo est, praecipiens passioni Domini esse
communicandum : et suaviter atque utiliter recolendum in memoria,
quod pro nobis caro ejus crucifixa et vulnerata sit (taken word for word
from Augustin. de doctr. christ. iii. c. 16.)

    [6] Ratr. de corpore et sang. Domini liber ad Carol. R. (prim. ed. cum
praef. Leonis Judae. Colon. 1532. 8. frequently published in the original and in translations, especially by the Reformed ; best by Jac.
Boileau. Paris 1712. in 12.) Quod in Ecclesia ore fidelium sumitur
corpus et sanguis Christi, quaerit vestrae Magnitudinis Excellentia, in
mysterio fiat an in veritate ? i. e. utrum aliquid secreti contineat, quod
oculis fidei solummodo pateat,—et utrum ipsum corpus sit, quod de

Maria natum est et passum. According to these two questions the
book is divided into two parts. On the first :—ille panis, qui per sacerdotis ministerium Christi corpus efficitur, aliud exterius humanis sensibus ostendit, et aliud interius fidelium mentibus clamat. Exterius
quidem panis, quod ante fuerat, forma praetenditur, color ostenditur,
sapor accipitur : ast interius longe aliud, multoque pretiosius multoque
excellentius intimatur, quia caeleste, quia divinum, i. e. corpus Christi
ostenditur, quod non sensibus carnis, sed animi fidelis contuitu vel ad-
spicitur vel accipitur, vel comeditur. § 2 :—Haec ita esse dum nemo
potest abnegare, claret, quia panis ille vinumque figurate Christi corpus
et sanguis exsistit.—Nam si secundum quosdam figurate nihil hic acci-
piatur, sed totum in veritate conspiciatur ; nihil hic fides operatur, quoniam nihil spirituale geratur : sed quicquid illud est, totum secundum
corpus accipitur.—At quia confitentur et corpus et sanguinem Christi
esse, nec hoc esse potuisse, nisi facta in melius commutatione ; neque
ista commutatio corporaliter, sed spiritualiter facta sit : necesse est, ut
jam figurate facta esse dicatur, quoniam sub velamento corporei panis
corporeique vini spirituale corpus Christi spiritualisque sanguis exsistit.
Non quod duarum sint exsistentiae rerum inter se diversarum, corporis
videlicet et spiritus : verum una eademque res secundum aliud species
panis et vini consistit, secundum aliud autem corpus et sanguis Christi.
Secundum namque, quod utrumque corporaliter contingitur, species
sunt creaturae corporea, secundum potentiam vero, quod spiritualiter
factae sunt, mysteria sunt corporis et sanguinis Christi. Consideremus
fontem sacri baptismatis, qui fons vitae non immerito nuncupatur.—si
consideretur solummodo, quod corporeus aspicit sensus, elementum
fluidum conspicitur.—Sed accessit S. Spiritus per sacerdotis consecrationem virtus.—Igitur in proprietate humor corruptibilis, in mysterio
vero virtus sanabilis. Sic itaque Christi corpus et sanguis superficie
tenus considerata creatura est mutabilitati corruptelaeque subjecta, si
mysterii vero perpendis virtutem, vita est, participantibus se tribuens
immortalitatem. Non ergo sunt idem, quod cernuntur, et quod creduntur. Secundum enim quod cernuntur, corpus pascunt corruptibile,
ipsa corruptibilia : secundum vero quod creduntur, animas pascunt in
aeternam victuras, ipsa immortalia. To the second question :—Ait enim
(Ambrosius) : "in illo sacramento Christus est;" non enim ait : "ille
panis et illud vinum Christus est."—Est quidem corpus Christi, sed
non corporale sed spirituale ; est sanguis Christi, sed non corporalis sed spiritualis.—Corpus Christi, quod mortuum est et resurrexit et immortale factum, jam non moritur,—aeternum est nec jam
passibile. Hoc autem, quod in Ecclesia celebratur, temporale est, non
aeternum, corruptibile est non incorruptum.—quodsi non sunt idem,
quomodo verum corpus Christi dicitur et verus sanguis ?—De vero corpore Christi dicitur, quod sit verus Deus et verus homo, qui in fine
saeculi ex Maria virgine genitus. Haec autem dum de corpore Christi,
quod in Ecclesia per mysterium geritur, dici non possunt, secundum
quendam modum corpus Christi esse cognoscitur. Et modus iste in
figura est et imagine, ut veritas res ipsa sentiatur. In orationibus, quae
post mysterium sanguinis corporisque Christi dicuntur, et a populo respondetur amen, sic sacerdotis voce dicitur : " Pignus aeternae vitae

roniously to *John Scotus*,[7] declared against it; and the most

capientes humiliter imploramus, ut quod imagine contingimus, sacramenti manifesta participatione sumamus." Et pignus nempe et imago alterius rei sunt, i. e. non ad se, sed ad aliud adspiciunt. Pignus nempe illius rei est, pro qua donatur, imago illius, cujus similitudinem ostendit. Significant nempe ista rem, cujus sunt, non manifeste ostendunt. Quod cum ita est, apparet, quod hoc corpus et sanguis pignus et imago rei sunt futurae, ut quod nunc per similitudinem ostenditur, in futuro per manifestationem reveletur.—Item alibi : " Perficiant in nobis, Domine, quaesumus, tua sacramenta, quod continent, ut quae nunc specie gerimus, rerum veritate capiamus." Dicit quod specie gerantur ista, non veritate, i. e. per similitudinem, non per ipsius rei manifestationem. Differunt autem a se species et veritas. Quapropter corpus et sanguis, quod in Ecclesia geritur, differt ab illo corpore et sanguine, quod in Christi corpore per ressurrectionem jam glorificatum cognoscitur. Et hoc corpus pignus est et species, illud vero ipsa veritas.—Videmus itaque multa differentia separari mysterium sanguinis et corporis Christi, quod nunc a fidelibus sumitur in Ecclesia, et illud quod natum est de Maria virgine, quod passum, quod sepultum, quod resurrexit, quod caelos ascendit, quod ad dexteram Patris sedet. Docemur a Salvatore nec non a S. Paulo Apostolo, quod iste panis et iste sanguis, qui super altare ponitur, in figuram sive memoriam dominicae mortis ponatur, ut quod gestum est in praeterito, praesenti revocet memoriae, ut illius passionis memores effecti, per eam efficiamur divini muneris consortes, per quam sumus a morte liberati. Cognoscentes, quod ubi pervenerimus ad visionem Christi, talibus non opus habebimus instrumentis, quibus admoneamur etc.—The older Catholic theologians universally considered this work as heretical, and believed that it had been in part interpolated by Protestants. Hence it stands in the index libr. prohibit. of 1559. De Sainte Boeuve first endeavoured to shew that it was Catholic, in which opinion he was followed particularly by Jo. Mabillon act. SS. Ord. Bened. saec. iv. P. ii. praef. p. 44. and ann. Bened. lib. xxxv. § 40. and J. Boileau in his edition.

[7] All the writers of the next succeeding centuries speak either of a work of Ratramnus, or of John Scotus, on the Lord's Supper; those who mention the one say nothing of the other. All the citations suit the only extant one, which in Codd. is attributed to Ratramnus. Afterwards, indeed, both works were spoken of together as distinct, and that of Scotus declared to be lost. P. de Marca (epist. ad d'Acherium, in the spicileg. iii. 852, ed. 2) of the latter, first asserted correctly, that the alleged two works were only one and the same, but he attributed it to the heterodox Scotus, in order to weaken its importance. But this author has quite another doctrine respecting the Supper de divis naturae ii. 11, v. 38, comp. Ebrard's Dogma vom heil. Abendmal, S. 420. The identity of both writings, and, at the same time, that Ratramnus was the author, is shown by F. W. Laufs uber die fur verloren gehaltene Schrift des Johannes Scotus von der Eucharistie, in the Theol. Studien u. Kritiken. Bd. 1. (1828.) Heft 4. S. 755 ss. Gfrörer's (KG. iii. ii. 921) objections may not be set aside by the consideration, that

distinguished theologians of this period firmly adhered to the Augustinian view,[8] so that Paschasius saw that he was called upon to defend his sentiments, for many reasons.[9] Still the mys-

the work of Ratramnus, as having been directed against his abbot, was doubtless circulated anonymously at first, and that therefore even contemporaries as Hincmar (de praedest. c. 31.) and Adrevaldus (de corpore et sanguine Christi contra ineptias Jo. Scoti ap. d'Achery i. 150. a fragment, but which may have been intended to oppose the eucharistic opinions of the book de divis. naturae) might have erroneously regarded John Scotus as the author, because in such cases he was often interrogated by Charlemagne.

[8] For example Walafrid. Strabo de rebus eccles. c. 16: (Christus) corporis et sanguinis sui sacramenta in panis et vini substantia eisdem discipulis tradidit, et ea in commemorationem sanctissimae suae passionis celebrare perdocuit (c. 17) : illius unitatis perfectae, quam cum capite nostro jam spe, postea re, tenebimus, pignora. Christiani Druthmar expos. in Matth. xxvi. 26 ss. (Bibl. PP. Lugd. xv. 165) : Dedit discipulis sacramentum corporis sui—ut memores illius facti semper hoc in figura facerent, quod pro eis acturus erat, et hujus caritatis non obliviscerentur. " Hoc est corpus meum," i. e. in sacramento (Sixt. Senensis bibl. sanct. lib. vi. p. 158. would read after a Cod. Lugd. hoc est vere in sacramento subsistens).—Vinum et laetificat et sanguinem auget.) Et idcirco non inconvenienter sanguis Christi per hoc figuratur.—Sicut denique si aliquis peregre proficiscens dilectoribus suis quoddam vinculum dilectionis relinquit, eo tenore, ut omni die haec agant, ut illius non obliviscantur : ita Deus praecepit agi a nobis, transferens spiritualiter (Sixt. Sen. l. c. would have the word spiritualiter left out) corpus in panem, vinum in sanguinem, ut per haec duo memoremus, quae fecit pro nobis etc. (That the edition by J. Wimpheling, Strasb. 1514, really exists, and has the common text, see Cave ii. 25. hist. lit. de la Fr. v. 89. J. G. Schelhorn amoenitates hist. eccl. et literariae i. 823). Florus Magister de expositione Missae (for the first time complete in Martene et Durand amplissima collect. T. ix. p. 577 ss.) c. 4 : Hujus sacrificii caro et sanguis ante adventum Christi per victimas similitudine promittebatur, in passione Christi per ipsam veritatem reddebatur, post ascensum Christi per sacramentum memoria celebratur. Idem adv. Amalarium (ibid. p. 641 ss.) c. 9 : prorsus panis ille sacrosanctae oblationis corpus est Christi, non materie vel specie visibili, sed virtute et potentia spirituali.—Simplex e frugibus panis conficitur, simplex e botris vinum liquatur, accedit ad haec offerentis Ecclesiae fides, accedit mysticae precis consecratio, accedit divinae virtutis infusio : sicque miro et ineffabili modo, quod est naturaliter ex germine terreno panis et vinum, efficitur spiritualiter corpus Christi, i. e. vitae et salutis nostrae mysterium, in quo aliud oculis corporis, aliud fidei videmus obtentu [leg. obtuitu], nec id tantum, quod ore percipimus, sed quod mente credimus, libamus.—Mentis ergo est cibus iste, non ventris, non corrumpitur, sed permanet in vitam aeternam.—Corpus igitur Christi —non est in specie visibili, sed in virtute spirituali etc.

[9] Exposit. in Matth. lib. xii. ad Matth. xxvi. 26. (Bibl. PP. Lugd.

T

tical, and apparently pious, doctrine, which was easier of appre-
hension, and seemed to correspond better to the sacred words,
obtained its advocates too ;[10] and it was easy to see, that it only
needed times of darkness, such as soon followed, to become general.

In the same spirit Radbert also taught *a miraculous delivery
of Mary*,[11] but here again he was opposed by Ratramnus.[12]

xiv. 668): Audiant qui volunt extenuare hoc verbum corporis, quod
non sit vera caro Christi, quae nunc in sacramento celebratur in Ecclesia
Christi, neque verus sanguis ejus, nescio quid volentes plaudere aut
fingere, quasi quaedam virtus sit carnis et sanguinis in eo tantummodo
sacramento.—Miror, quid velint nunc quidam dicere, non in re esse
veritatem carnis Christi vel sanguinis : sed in sacramento virtutem
quandam carnis et non carnem, virtutem fore sanguinis et non sanguinem,
figuram et non veritatem, umbram et non corpus.—Haec idcirco pro-
lixius dixerim et expressius, quia audivi quosdam me reprehendere,
quasi ego in eo libro, quem de sacramentis Christi edideram, aliquid his
dictis (namely, Hoc est corpus m. etc.) plus tribuere voluerim aut aliud,
quam ipsa veritas repromittit etc.   Ejusd. epist. de corpore et sanguine
Domini ad Frudegardum (l. c. p. 754): Quaeris de re, ex qua multi
dubitant.   Quam si forte ad plenum intelligunt, utique credere debuerant verba Salvatoris, quia non mentitur verax Deus, cum ait: nisi
manducaveritis carnem filii hominis,—non habebitis vitam.—Cum ait:
hoc est corpus meum vel caro mea, seu hic est sanguis meus, non aliam
puto insinuasse, quam propriam et quae nata est de Maria virgine, et
pependit in cruce, neque sanguinem alium, quam qui profusus est in
cruce, et tunc erat in proprio corpore.—Alias autem qualitercunque intelligitur, si alius esset sanguis, et alia esset caro in hoc mysterio, non
in eo esset remissio peccatorum.   Then he enters particularly on a consideration of several passages in Augustine, which Frudegard had adduced against him.

[10] Especially Haimonis tract. de corp. et sang. Dom. or rather a
fragment of a commentary on the first epistle to the Corinthians (in
d'Achery spicileg. i. 42.) and Hincmari ep. ad Carol. Calv. de cavendis
vitiis et virtutibus exercendis c. 12.

[11] Pasch. Radb. opusc. de partu Virginis addressed to a venerabilis
matrona Christi una cum sacris virginibus Vesonae monastice degentibus
(in d'Achery spicil. i. 44): Dicunt enim (namely his opposers), non
aliter b. virginem Mariam parere potuisse, neque aliter debuisse, quam
communi lege naturae, et sicut mos est omnium feminarum, ut vera
nativitas Christi dici possit.—Non dico, quod dicant, virginitatem
amisisse, quae nesciens virum virgo concepit, virgo peperit et virgo permansit: sed quia idipsum, quod confitentur, negant, dum dicunt, eam
communi lege naturae puerperam filium edidisse.   Quod si ita est, ut
astruunt et affirmant, quod absit, Maria virgo non est, Christus sub male-
dicto natus est, irae filius de carne peccati etc.—Nam et ipsa lex naturae, sub qua nunc mulieres concipiunt et pariunt, ut ita dicam, vere

§ 15.

CONTROVERSY OF GOTTSCHALK.

Jac. Usserii Gotteschalci et praedestinatianae controversiae ab eo motae hist. Dublini 1631. 4. Hanov. 1662. 8. Gilb. Maugnini vett. auctorum, qui saec. ix. de praedestinatione et gratia scripserunt, opera et fragm. Paris. 1650. Tomi ii. 4. (im Tom. ii.: Gotteschalcanae controversiae historica et chronica dissertatio). Lud. Cellotii hist. Gottschalci praedestinatiani. Paris. 1655. fol. Natalis Alex. diss. de causa Gottschalci (in hist. eccl. saec. ix. et x. diss. Vta.) Jo. Jac. Hottingeri diatribe hist. theol. qua praedestinatianam et Godeschalci pseudohaereses commenta esse demonstratur. Tiguri 1710. 4. Ejusd. fata doctrinae de praedestinatione et gratia Dei (Tig. 1727. 4.) p. 397 ss. W. F. Gess Merkwürdigk. aus dem Leben Hinkmars. (Gotting. 1806. 8.) S. 15 ff.

Strict Augustininism had never been generally adopted even

non est lex naturae quodammodo, sed maledictionis et culpae.—Ideo sicut (Christus) clausis visceribus jure creditur conceptus, ita omnino et clauso utero natus.—sicut mirabiliter conceptus ita mirabiliter Deus et homo natus.—Non est credendum, quod ejus (Mariae) puerperium doloribus et gemitibus more feminarum subjacuerit. Christus de Virgine speciali et ineffabili quodam modo procreatus, absque vexatione matris ingressus est mundum—sine dolore et sine gemitu et sine ulla' corruptione carnis. Cf. (Ch. W. F. Walchii) hist. controversiae saec. ix. de partu Virginis (a programm) Goett. 1758. 4.

[12] Ratr. lib. de eo, quod Christus ex Virgine natus est (in d'Achery i. 52.) c. 1: Fama est, et quorundam non contemnenda cognovimus relatione, quod per Germaniae partes serpens antiquus perfidiae novae venena diffundat, et catholicam super nativitate Salvatoris fidem, nescio qua fraudis subtilitate subvertere molitur; dogmatizans Christi infantiam, per virginalis januam vulvae, humanae nativitatis verum non habuisse ortum, sed monstruose de secreto ventris incerto tramite luminis in auras exisse, quod non est nasci, sed erumpi. Jam ergo nec vere natus Christus, nec vere genuit Maria. He concludes, c. 10: Ergo omnifariam adversario devicto, teneamus vera fide, confiteamur ore veridico, Verbum carnem factum, per ministerium vulvae naturaliter natum, et secundum rationis consequentiam, et secundum divinarum testimonia Scripturarum et secundum doctorum non contemnendam auctoritatem. Satis abundeque, ut aestimo, monstratum est, Dominum Salvatorem de Virgine sicut hominem natum, non ut integritatem violaret illa nativitas, quia Maria virgo fuit ante partum, virgo in partu, virgo mansit et post partum ; sed ut qui de virgine corpus assumsit, et intra gremium virginale concrevit, per aulam quoque virgineam naturaliter nasceretur.

T 2

in the West ;[1] and, therefore, *Gottschalk*,[2] a monk of Orbais, a faithful follower of Augustine and Fulgentius, while on a pilgrimage to Rome, by teaching the doctrine of a twofold predestination, excited the attention of *Rabanus Maurus*, who thought he perceived in it a predestination to sin.[3] Gottschalk was therefore condemned by *a synod at Mainz* (848),[4] and delivered

[1] See vol. i. div. i. § 113. not. 16 ff.

[2] Concerning an earlier controversy of Gottschalks, then a monk at Fulda, with his abbot Raban, and respecting the decision of the synod of Mainz, 829, see the extracts of the Centur. Magdeburg. from the epistola Rabani, since lost, and ep. Hattonis ad Otgarium, centur. ix. cap. 9. p. 404, and cap. 10. p. 543 and 546. This was no doubt the occasion of Raban's work contra eos qui repugnant institutis b. P. Benedicti (prim. ed. J. Mabillon in append. annal. Bened. T. ii. no. li.) See Mabillon annal. Bened. lib. xxx. c. 30. Kunstmann's Hrabanus Maurus S. 69.

[3] See Rabani epist. ad Notingum Episc. Veronensem and ad Eberardum comitem A.D. 847, both published first by J. Sirmond: Rabani de praedestinatione Dei contra Gotteschalcum epistolae iii. Paris. 1647. 8, (in Sirm. opp. ii. 1289) ap. Mauguin i. i. 3. Kunstmann S. 119.

[4] Fragments of the writing handed over by Gottschalk, at this synod, to Rabanus, are preserved in Hincmar de praedestin. c. 5 : Ego Gothescalcus credo et confiteor,—quod gemina est praedestinatio, sive electorum ad requiem, sive reproborum ad mortem (word for word from Isidori Hispal. sent. lib. ii. c. 6) : quia sicut Deus incommutabilis ante mundi constitutionem omnes electos suos incommutabiliter per gratuitam gratiam suam praedestinavit ad vitam aeternam, similiter omnino omnes reprobos, qui in die judicii damnabuntur propter ipsorum mala merita, idem ipse incommutabilis Deus per justum judicium suum incommutabiliter praedestinavit ad mortem merito sempiternam.—c. 21 : De quo videlicet libero arbitrio quid Ecclesiae Christi tenendum sit,—cum a caeteris catholicis Patribus evidenter sit Deo gratias disputatum, tum praecipue contra Pelagianos et Caelestianos a b. Augustino plenius et uberius diversis in opusculis, et maxime in Hypomnesticon esse cognoscitur inculcatum. Unde te [Rabane] potius ejusdem catholicissimi doctoris fructuosissimis assertionibus incomparabiliter inde quoque malueram niti, quam erroneis opinionibus Massiliensis, Genadii, qui—praesumpsit—fidei catholicae,—infelicis Cassiani perniciosum nimis dogma sequens, reniti.—c. 27 : Illos omnes impios et peccatores, quos proprio fuso sanguine filius Dei redimere venit, hos omnipotentis Dei bonitas ad vitam praedestinatos irretractibiliter salvari tantummodo velit : et rursum illos omnes impios et peccatores, pro quibus idem filius Dei nec corpus assumsit, nec orationem, ne dico sanguinem fudit neque pro eis ullo modo crucifixus fuit, quippe quos pessimos futuros esse praescivit, quosque justissime in aeterna praecipitandos tormenta praefinivit, ipsos omnino perpetim salvari penitus nolit. Of the synod of Mainz we have only Rabani epist. synodalis ad Hincmarum (in Sirmondi opp. ii. 1293. ap. Mansi xiv. 914.) according to which

over to his metropolitan, *Hincmar*, archbishop of Rheims, for punishment*; by whom, after much ill-treatment, he was sentenced to imprisonment, at *the synod of Chiersy* (849).[5] Gottschalk maintained that he had merely abided by the doctrine of Augustine*;[6] and, indeed, there were not a few who thought that Hincmar had encroached on it. Hence *Prudentius*, bishop of Troyes,[7] *Ratramnus*,[8] and *Servatus Lupus*,[9] came forward in

Gottschalk taught, quod praedestinatio Dei, sicut in bono, sic ita et in malo: et tales sint in hoc mundo quidam, qui propter praedestinationem Dei, quae eos cogat in mortem ire, non possent ab errore et peccato se corrigere; quasi Deus eos fecisset ab initio incorrigibiles, et poenae obnoxios in interitum ire. On the other hand, Hincmar de praedestin. c. 15. concedes: Dicunt [moderni Praedestinatiani]: praedestinavit Deus reprobos ad interitum, non ad peccatum. Cf. Remigius in libro de tribus epistolis not. 13. below.

[5] Conc. apud Carisiacum ap. Mansi xiv. 919. According to Flodoardus (about 940) hist. Ecclesiae Rhemensis lib. iii. c. 28. Hincmar afterwards called on Gottschalk to confess, Deum et bona praescire et mala; sed mala tantum praescire, bona vero et praescire et praedestinare. Unde praescientia esse potest sine praedestinatione: praedestinatio autem esse non potest sine praescientia: et quia bonos praescivit et praedestinavit ad regnum, malos autem praescivit tantum, non praedestinavit, nec ut perirent sua praescientia compulit. Gottschalk refused to subscribe this.

[6] His two confessions written in prison (prim. ed. J. Usserius l. c. in append. p. 211 ss. ap. Mauguin i. i. 7). In the longer one he says of his opponents: Te precor, Domine Deus, gratis Ecclesiam tuam custodias, ne sua diutius eam falsitate pervertant, haereseosque suae pestifera de reliquo pravitate subvertant, licet se suosque secum lugubriter evertant. Ego vero gratis edoctus ab ipsa veritate—hic evidenter expressam de praedestinatione tua fidem catholicam fortiter teneo, veraciter patenterque defendo: et quemcunque contraria dogmatizare cognosco, tamquam pestem fugio, et tamquam haereticum abjicio.—Porro conflictum cujuslibet eorum, si semel his lectis et intellectis cedere noluerit, et instar Pharaonis induratus haeretico videlicet more, tam manifestae veritati acquiescere contemserit, secundum consilium vel potius praeceptum Apostoli, jam mihi vitandum censeo —Attamen propter minus peritos, et ob id ab eis illectos, et nisi corrigantur, perditos, optarem publicum, si tibi Domine placeret, fieri conventum: quatenus adstructa palam veritate, et destructa funditus falsitate, gratias ageremus communiter tibi. Namely, quatuor doliis uno post unum positis atque ferventi sigillatim repletis aqua, oleo, pingui, et pice, et ad ultimum accenso copiosissimo igne, liceret mihi—ad adprobandam hanc fidem meam, immo fidem catholicam, in singula introire, et ita per singula transire etc.

[7] Prudentii Trecassini epistola ad Hincmarum Rhem. et Pardulum Laudunensem (about 849) prim. ed. Lud. Cellot in hist. Gottesch. p. 425 ss. Comp. Raban's judgment thereupon ep. ad. Hincmarum in Sirmondi opp. ii. 1295. Mauguin i. i. 5.

defence of the Augustinian orthodoxy ; Rabanus could no longer
come to the proposed refutation of these writings ;[10] while *John
Scotus*, who attempted to answer them,[11] could only do injury to

[8] Ratramni de praedestinatione libb. ii. (about 850) prim. ed. G.
Mauguin i. i. 27.

[9] Serv. Lupi lib. de tribus quaestionibus (namely de libero arbitrio,
de praedestinatione bonorum et malorum and de sanguinis Christi superflua taxatione), besides a collectaneum de tribus quaest. after 850.
The first faulty edition by Donatus Candidus 1648. 16.　A corrected
text by J. Sirmond. Paris. 1650. 8. (Opp. ii. 1227) and G. Mauguin
i. ii. 9. cf. hist. lit. de la France. v. 262., where Cave's statements are
corrected.

[10] See his two letters to Hincmar, published by Kunstmann, in the
Tübingen theol. Quartalschrist 1836 S. 445., and also appended to his
Rabanus Maurus p. 215.

[11] Jo. Scotus de praedestinatione Dei contra Gotteschalcum (851)
prim. ed. G. Mauguin i. i. 103.　Comp. Fronmüller's above. § 10. note
21. cited treatise : ex. gr. the following assertions cap. 6. § 1 : Firmissime igitur tenendum, nullum peccatum—nullamque ejus poenam aliunde nasci, nisi propria hominis voluntate, libero male utentis arbitrio.
Cap. 7. § 1 : Non ergo liberum arbitrium malum est, cum eo quisque
male utatur, sed est numerandum inter bona, quae homini divina largitate donata sunt : praesertim cum potius ad bene utendum eo datum
sit : in hoc enim maxime arguitur humana voluntas, quod eo dono, quod
ei datum est ad recte utendum, maluit perverse uti.　Cap. 8. § 7 : Si
omne quod movet plus est quam quod movetur, necessario majora a minoribus moveri non sinunt, simili ratione paria non possunt paria mo-
vere.—Restat plane, humanam voluntatem aut a se ipsa moveri, aut ab
ea, quae eam condidit .—§ 9 : Hoc ergo nisi fallor prolixae ratiocinationis ambitu confectum est, causas omnium recte factorum—in libero
humanae voluntatis arbitrio, praeparante ipsum ipsique cooperante
gratuito divinae gratiae multiplicique dono constitutas esse : malefacto-
rum vero—in perverso motu liberi arbitrii suadente diabolo principalem
radicem esse fixam.　Quanta igitur dementia est eorum, qui talium
causas inevitabiles, coactivasque necessitates in praedestinatione divina
falsissime fingunt, impudentissime adstrunt.　Cap. 9. § 5. The expressions praescire and praedestinare cannot be used of God proprie : in eo
enim sicut nulla locorum spatia sunt, ita nulla temporum intervalla.
Cap. 10. § 3 : Omne igitur malum aut peccatum est aut poena peccati :
quae duo si nulla ratio vera sinit Deum praescire, quanto magis
praedestinare quis audeat dicere, nisi e contiario ? (κατ’ ἀντίφρασιν,
namely, according to § 1., in the sense, quod Deus in creatura, quam
ipse condidit, fieri sinit motu proprio liberoque rationalis naturae perverse utentis naturalibus bonis).　Quid enim, numquid possumus recte
sentire de Deo,—eorum quae nec ipse est, nec ab eo sunt, quia nihil
sunt praescientiam seu praedestinationem habere ?　Si enim nihil aliud
est scientia, nisi rerum, quae sunt, intelligentia, qua ratione in his,
quae non sunt scientia vel praescientia dicenda est ? — Deinde si
nihil aliud est malum nisi boni corruptio,—omnis autem corruptio

Hincmar by his own heterodoxy.[12] At length *Remigius*, archbishop of Lyons from 852, appeared in the name of his church,
expressly as defender of the unfortunate Gottschalk.[13] Hincmar

nihil appetit, nisi ut bonum non sit : quis dubitare potest, esse
malum, quod appetit bonum delere ne sit ?—§ 4 : Quis non videat,—
totum quod dicitur peccatum, ejusque consequentias in morte atque
miseria constitutas, non aliud esse, quam integrae vitae beataeque cor-
ruptiones : ita ut singula singulis opponantur, integritati quidem peccatum, vitae mors beatitudini miseria. Illa sunt, ista penitus non sunt.—
§ 5 : Omnino igitur non sunt, ac per hoc nec praesciri, nec praedesti-
nari ab eo, qui summus est, possunt. Cap. 11. and 12. that praescientia
and praedestinatio are one in God, that there is only a praedestinatio
ad vitam, not ad mortem.—Cap. 16. § 1 : In magno aeterni ignis
ardore nihil aliud sit poenalis miseria, quam beatae felicitatis absentia, in qua tamen nullus erit qui non habeat insitam sibi naturaliter
absentis beatitudinis notionem, ejusque desiderium, ut eo maxime tor-
queatur, quo ardenter appetat, quod justum Dei judicium comprehendere non sinat.—Cap. 17. § 8 : Sive itaque ignis ille corporeus (ut
ait Augustinus), sive incorporeus (ut Gregorio placet) ;—idem ignis
bonus profecto, quoniam a bono factus. Non ergo ille ignis est poena,
neque ad eam praeparatus, vel praedestinatus, sed qui fuerat praedestinatus, ut esset in universitate omnium bonorum, sedes factus est impiorum. In quo proculdubio non minus habitabunt beati, quam miseri :
sed sicut una eademque lux sanis oculis convenit, impedit dolentibus
etc. Quid enim bonorum illi non noceret, quando ei auctor omnium
placere non poterat ?—§ 9 : Proinde si nulla beatitudo est, nisi vita
aeterna : vita autem aeterna est veritatis cognitio : nulla igitur beatitudo
est nisi veritatis cognitio. Ita si nulla miseria est, nisi mors aeterna : aeterna autem mors est veritatis ignorantia : nulla igitur miseria est nisi
veritatis ignorantia.—Cap. 18. § 1. Errorem itaque saevissimum eorum,
qui venerabilium Patrum, maximeque s. Augustini sententias confuse,
ac per hoc mortifere ad suum pravissimum sensum redigunt, ex utilium
disciplinarum—ignorantia crediderim sumpsisse primordia insuper etiam
ex Graecarum literarum inscita. In quibus praedestinationis interpretatio nullam ambiguitatis caliginem gignit. for προοράω means both praevidere and praedestinare etc.
   [12] Scotus was answered by (852) Prudentius : tructatus·de praedestinatione contra Jo. Scot. (prim. ed. Mauguin i. 1, 191, afterwards in the
bibl. PP. Lugdun. xv. 467), and Florus Magister : lib. de praedestinatione contra Jo. Scoti erroneas definitiones (also called Ecclesiae Lugd.
lib. etc., because written in the name of it ; best edited ap. Mauguin
i. 1, 575, and in the bibl. PP. Lugd. xv. 611) ; comp. Staudenmaier's
Joh. Scotus Erig. S. 183.
   [13] Hincmar and Pardulus, bishop of Laon, had written on this occasion to Amolo, archbishop of Lyons, two letters (preserved in part in
the following work of Remigius), and accompanied them with Rabani
epist. ad Nottingum (cf. not. 3). On this Remigius, who had already
begun to officiate, wrote in the name of his church : liber de tribus epis-

procured the confirmation of his doctrinal creed at the synod of
Chiersy (853), in presence of the emperor Charles the Bald ;[14] but

tolis (ap. Mauguin i. ii. 61, Bibl. PP. Lugd. xv. 666).   Here it is said
directly, cap. 24 : videtur nobis sine dubio, quod illa, quae [Gottes-
chalcus] de divina praedestinatione dixit, juxta regulam catholicae fidei
vera sint, et a veridicis Patribus manifestissime confirmata, nec ab ullo
penitus nostrum, qui catholicus haberi vult, respuenda sive damnanda.
Et ideo in hac re dolemus non hunc miserabilem, sed ecclesiasticam veritatem esse damnatam.   Rabanus is reproached with the false interpretation he had put on Gottschalk's system (com. not. 4).   Cap. 41:
Tertia epistola—assumit, quantum nobis videtur, non necessarium, nec
ullatenus ad rem, de qua quaeritur, pertinentem disputationem.   Quaeritur namque—non illud, utrum impios Deus et iniquos praedestinave-
rit ad ipsam impietatem et iniquitatem, i. e. ut impii et iniqui essent, et
aliud esse non possent : quod nullus omnino moderno tempore dicere
vel dixisse invenitur, quod est utique immanis et detestabilis blasphemia : sed illud potius quaeritur, utrum eos, quos veraciter omnino praescivit, proprio vitio impios et iniquos futuros, et in suis impietatibus
atque iniquitatibus usque ad mortem perseveraturos, justo judicio prae-
destinaverit aeterno supplicio puniendos.

[14] The capitula iv. Carisiacensia from Hincmar de praedest. c. 2, ap.
Mansi xiv. 920, (by Sirmond. in concill. Gall. T. iii. and the succeeding editors of councils falsely assigned to the Conc. Carisiac. l. 819 ;
comp. on the other side, ann. Bertiniani ad ann. 853, ap. Mansi xiv.
995), cap. i. ; Deus omnipotens hominem sine peccato rectum cum libero arbitrio condidit, et in paradiso posuit, quem iu sanctitate justitiae
permanere voluit.   Homo libero arbitrio male utens peccavit et cecidit,
et factus est massa perditionis totius humani generis.   Deus autem bonus et justus elegit ex eadem massa perditionis, secundum praescientiam suam, quos per gratiam praedestinavit ad vitam, et vitam illis praedestinavit aeternam : caeteros autem, quos justitiae judicio in massa
perditionis reliquit, perituros praescivit, sed non ut perirent praedestinavit : poenam autem illis, quia justus est, praedestinavit aeternam. Ac
per hoc unum Dei praedestinationem tantummodo dicimus, quae aut ad
donum pertinet gratiae, aut ad retributionem justitiae.   Cap. ii. : Libertatem arbitrii in primo homine perdidimus, quam per Christum Dominum nostrum recepimus : et habemus liberum arbitrium ad bonum,
praeventum et adjutum gratia : et habemus liberum arbitrium ad malum, desertum gratia.   Liberum autem habemus arbitrium, quia gratia
liberatum, et gratia de corrupto sanatum.   Cap. iii. : Deus omnipotens
omnes homines sine exceptione vult salvos fieri, licet non omes salven-
tur.   Quod autem quidam salvantur, salvantis est donum : quod autem
quidam pereunt, pereuntium est meritum.   Cap. iv. : Christus Jesus
Dominus noster, sicut nullus homo est, fuit vel erit, cujus natura in illo
assumta non fuerit, ita nullus est, fuit, vel erit homo, pro quo passus
non fuerit ; licet non omnes passionis ejus mysterio redimantur.   Quod
vero omnes passionis ejus mysterio non redimuntur, non respicit ad
magnitudinem et pretii copiositatem, sed ad infidelium, et ad non cre-

Remigius at once protested against it,[15] and the *synod of Valence* (855) sanctioned, in opposition to it, a twofold predestination as an ecclesiastical dogma.[16] But the two archbishops soon after came to an understanding (859)[17] and Gottschalk's situa-

dentium ea fide, quae per dilectionem operatur, respicit partem: quia poculum humanae salutis, quod confectum est infirmitate nostra, et virtute divina, habet quidem in se, ut omnibus prosit: sed si non bibitur, non medetur.

[15] In the libellus de tenenda immobiliter s. Scripturae veritate, et ss. orthodoxorum Patrum auctoritate fideliter sectanda, in which Remigius, in the name of the Church of Lyons, condemns those four chapters (ap. Mauguin i. ii. 178, Bibl. PP. Lugd. xv. 701).

[16] Conc. Valeutinum (ap. Mansi xv. 1 ss.) can. iii.: fidenter fatemur praedestinationem electorum ad vitam, et praedestinationem impiorum ad mortem: in electione tamen salvandorum misericordiam Dei praecedere meritum bonum: in damnatione autem periturorum meritum malum praecedere justum Dei judicium. Praedestinatione autem Deum ea tantum statuisse, quae ipse vel gratuita misericordia, vel justo judicio facturus erat, secundum Scripturam dicentem: "qui fecit quae futura sunt" (Jes. xlv. 11, according to the LXX.): in malis vero (Deum) ipsorum malitiam praescisse, quia ex ipsis est; non praedestinasse, quia ex illo non est. Poenam sane malum meritum eorum sequentem, uti Deum, qui omnia prospicit, praescivisse, et praedestinasse, quia justus est etc. Can. iv.: Item de redemtione sanguinis Christi propter nimium errorem, qui de hac causa exortus est, ita ut quidam, sicut eorum scripta indicant, etiam pro illis impiis, qui a mundi exordio usque ad passionem Domini in sua impietate mortui aeterna damnatione puniti sunt, effusum eum definiant—: illud nobis simpliciter et fideliter tenendum ac docendum placet—, quod pro illis hoc datum pretium teneamus, de quibus ipse Dominus noster dicit: "Sicut Moyses exaltavit serpentem in deserto, ita exaltari oportet filium hominis, ut omnis qui credit in ipso non pereat," etc. (Joh. iii. 14-16) et Apostolus, "Christus," inquit, "semel oblatus est ad multorum exhaurienda peccata" (Hebr. ix. 28). Porro capitula iv. quae a concilio fratrum nostrorum minus prospecte suscepta sunt, propter inutilitatem vel etiam noxietatem et errorem contrarium veritati: sed et alia xix. syllogismis ineptissime conclusa, (namely, the writing of John Scotus), et, licet jactetur, nulla saeculari literatura nitentia, in quibus commentum diaboli potius, quam argumentum aliquod fidei deprehenditur, a pio auditu fidelium penitus explodimus, et ut talia et similia caveantur per omnia auctoritate Spiritus S. interdicimus. Can. v.: Item firmissime tenendum credimus, quod omnis multitudo fidelium ex aqua et Spiritu S. regenerata—et in morte Christi baptizata, in ejus sanguine sit a peccatis suis abluta.—Ex ipsa tamen multitudine fidelium et redemtorum, alios salvari aeterna salute, quia per gratiam Dei in redemtione sua fideliter permanent;—alios, quia noluerunt permanere in salute fidei,—ad plenitudinem salutis et ad perceptionem aeternae beatitudinis nullo modo pervenire.

[17] At the Conc. Tullense apud Saponarias (Mansi xv. 527), at

tion was no better than before, especially as he had provoked
Hincmar anew by blaming him for altering one of the church
hymns.[18] Gottschalk's defenders were silent, after Hincmar had
published several works in justification of his conduct and
creed.[19] An appeal of the unfortunate man to Pope Nicolaus I.
was without success.[20] He at last died during his imprisonment,
and under the ban of the church, A. D. 868.[21]

which, according to the titulis canonum iii., still extant, the subjects dis-
cussed were : de stabili unione principum Caroli et Lotharii atque Caroli Regum, et x. ; de capitulis quibusdam in synodo relectis, de quibus
inter quosdam Episcopos erat controversia.   In the can. Valentinus iv.,
the passage levelled at the capitula Carisiac., had been expressed by
Remigius and his bishops at the Conc. Lingonense held a few days before, and in this form it was presented to Hincmar and his bishops at
Savonnieres. Cf. Mansi xv. 525 and 538.   Hincm. poster. diss. de
praedest. in praefat.

[18] Te, trina Deitas unaque, poscimus, Hincmar wished, as an Arian,
to have altered into Te summa Deitas.   Even Rabanus declared himself in the letters referred to in note 10 against that expression. Gottschalk's little treatise in defence of the expression, is contained in Hincmar's refutation, de una et non trina Deitate about 857 (in Hincm. opp.
ed. Sirmond. i. 413), in which also Ratramnus's defence of the trina
Deitas (since lost) is combated.

[19] Since 856.   First de praedestinatione Dei et libero arbitrio libb.
iii. against Gottschalk and all his defenders, (Flodoard. hist. Eccl. Rhem.
c. 15) is no longer extant.   Then posterior de praedest. Dei et libero
arbitrio diss. contra Gotesc. et caeteros Praedestinatianos (begun 859,
finished before 863), in opp. ed. Sirmond. i. 1.

[20] Comp. Hincmari ep. ad Nicolaum i. A. D. 864, preserved by Flodoard. iii. 12-14 (in ed. Sirm. ii. 244), and Hincm. epist. ad Egilonem
Archiep. Senonsem A. D. 866 (in ed. Sirm. ii. 290, ap. Manguin ii. i.
237).

[21] Obstinacy and vanity, strengthened by external oppression, may
always have produced in Gottschalk such dreams as Hincmar de non
trina Deit. p. 550. describes : Scripsit quoque ad Deum loquens, et dicens ei, quod ipse illi praeceperit, ut pro me non oraret, et quia primum
filius in eum intraverit, postea Pater, deinde Spiritus S., qui in illum intrans ei circa os barbam adussit.—Ante hos annos revelatum sibi quibusdam familiaribus suis scripsit, quod ego statim post tres semisannos
suae revelationis, sicut Antichristus usurpans sibi potestatis potentiam,
mori, et ipse Remorum Episcopus fieri, et post septennium veneno interfici, et sic gloriae martyrum adequari deberet etc.—Gottschalk is defended by the reformed (Usser, Hottinger, &c.), the Jansenists (Corn.
Jansenii Augustinus T. i. lib. 8, c. 23, Mauguin etc.), and also by the
Roman Catholic Morisius, who was inclined to Augustinian sentiments ;
on the other hand, he is most violently opposed as a predestinarian by

The subordinate critical dispute respecting the genuineness of the Hypognosticon lib. vi.,[22] ascribed to Augustine, developed in this controversy, is worthy of notice, so far as it affords a favourable proof of the learned education of the period.

§ 16.

SPREAD OF CHRISTIANITY BY THE CARLOVINGIANS.

Charlemagne endeavoured to spread Christianity in like degree with the extension of his dominions. But by this means he made it an object of suspicion and hatred to the neighbouring free states. Thus his wars against *the Saxons*[1] from 772, had for their object both their subjection and conversion. A peace of eight years' duration ensued, on *Wittekind's* and *Alboin's* baptism (785). From that time, the Frieslanders continued loyal to the Frank sovereignty, and faithful in their adherence to Christianity;[2] but a new rebellion of the Saxons (793) could not be

the Jesuits (Sirmond, Petavius, Cellot, and others). Comp. vol. i. Div. 2, § 113, not. 11.

[22] After Gottschalk had candidly appealed to them against Rabanus (Hincmar de praed. c. 21, see above, not. 4). John Scotus de praedest. c. 14, § 4, adduced passages from them to prove quod Deus neminem praedestinavit ad poenam. On the other hand, it was asserted by Florus de praedest. contra Jo. Scot. c. 18, (ap. Mauguin i. i. 726), and still more with historical and critical reasons by Prudentius de praedest. contra Jo. Scot. c. 14, (ap. Mauguin i. i. 398), that they were not written by Augustine. It is true that Hincmar in ep. ad Amolonem (ap. Remigius de tribus epistt. c. 34) appealed again to these books, and Pardulus ep. ad Amolonem (l. c. cap. 39) went so far as to endeavour to defend their authenticity; but Remegius (de tribus epistt. c. 35, ap. Mauguin i. ii. 124, and lib. de tenenda s. Scripturae veritate c. 9, l. c. p. 204), proved their spuriousness by so decisive arguments, that Hincmar's defence (posterior de praedest. Dei diss. ed. Sirmond. p. 10 ss.) on the other side, remains quite insignificant. Cf. J. W. Feuerlini disqu. hist. crit. de libris hypognosticon, an ab Hincmaro, in Augustana confessione et alibi recte tribuantur divo Augustino, Altorf. 1735. 4.

[1] Nic. Schaten historia Westphaliae, Neuhusii 1690. fol. p. 417 ss. H. A. Meinders tract. de statu relig. et reipubl. sub Car. M. et Lud. P. in veteri Saxonia. Lemgo 1711. 4. Just. Möser's Osnabrück. Geschichte Tb. 1. A. F. H. Schaumann's Gesch. d. niedersächsischen Volks bis 1180. Götting. 1839. S. 338.

[2] St Ludgerus had already preached here, a man descended from a leading Friese family. Now he completed the conversion of the Frieslanders. See vita s. Liudgeri, written by his second successor in the

quieted till 803. The Saxons were invited to embrace Christianity, not in the way of conviction, but of the rudest compulsion ;[3] and it was therefore natural that heathenism found secret adherents among them for a long time. The principal mission-

see of Münster, Altfried († 849), in the Act. SS. ad 26. Mart. and in Pertz-mon. ii. 403.

[3] Cf. capitulatio de partibus Saxoniae ap. Baluz. i. 249. Pertz iii. 48. (according to Baluz ii. 1039. A. D. 788. According to Pertz A. D. 785.) with a commentary ap. Meinders l. c. p. 23 ss. ex. gr. cap. iv.: Si quis sanctum quadragesimale jejunium pro despectu christianitatis contemserit, et carnem comederit, morte moriatur. cap. vii.: Si quis corpus defuncti hominis secundum ritum paganorum flamma consumi fecerit, et ossa ejus ad cinerem redegerit, capite punietur. cap. viii.: Si quis deinceps in gente Saxonum inter eos latens non baptizatus se abscondere voluerit, et ad baptismum venire contemserit, paganusque permanere voluerit, morte moriatur. Then follow laws against heathen images. c. xvi. and xvii. concerning tithes see § 9. note 1. The remarks of Alcuin on this subject in his letters are very appropriate. Ex. gr. epist. xxviii. (ed. Froben.) ad domnum Regem (A. D. 796): Sed nunc praevideat sapientissima et Deo placabilis Devotio vestra pios populo novello praedicatores, moribus honestos, scientia sacrae fidei edoctos et evangelicis praeceptis imbutos: ss. quoque Apostolorum in praedicatione verbi Dei exemplis intentos, qui lac, i. e. suavia praecepta, suis auditoribus in initio fidei ministrare solebant, dicente Apostolo Paulo: " Et ego, fratres, non potui vobis loqui quasi spiritalibus," etc. [1 Cor. iii. 1. 2.] Hoc enim totius mundi praedicator, Christo in se loquente, significavit, ut nova populorum ad fidem conversio mollioribus praeceptis, quasi infantilis aetas lacte, esset nutrienda : ne per austerioa praecepta fragilis mens evomat, quod bibit.—His ita consideratis, vestra sanctissima Pietas sapienti consilio praevideat, si melius sit, rudibus populis in principio fidei jugum imponere decimarum, ut plena fiat per singulas domus exactio illarum : an Apostoli quoque ab ipso Deo Christo edocti et ad praedicandum mundo missi exactiones decimarum exegissent, vel alicubi demandassent dari, considerandum est. Scimus quia decimatio substantiae nostrae valde bona est. Sed melius est illam amittere, quam fidem perdere. Nos vero in fide catholica nati, nutriti et edocti vix consentimus, substantiam nostram pleniter decimare. Quanto magis tenera fides, et infantilis animus, et avara mens illarum largitati non consentit? Roborata vero fide et confirmata consuetudine christianitatis, tunc quasi viris perfectis fortiora danda sunt praecepta, quae solidata mens religione christiana non abhorreat. Illud quoque maxima considerandum est diligentia, ut ordinate fiat praedicationis officium et baptismi sacramentum : ne nihil prosit sacri ablutio baptismi in corpore, si in anima ratione utenti catholicae fidei agnitio non praecesserit in corde. Ipse Dominus in Evangelio discipulis suis praecipiens ait: " Ite, docete omnes gentes, baptizantes eos," etc. (Matth. xxviii. 19. 20.) Hujus vero praecepti ordinem b. Hieronymus in commentario suo—ita exposuit : Primum doceant omnes gentes, deinde

stations which had been established here and there in Saxony, and placed at first under the superintendence of Frank bishops, [4]

doctas intinguant aqua. Non enim potest fieri, ut corpus baptismi capiat sacramentum, nisi ante anima fidei susceperit veritatem. Epist. xxxi. ad Arnonem (bishop of Salzburg, to whom the conversion of the Avari was entrusted): Idcirco misera Saxonum gens toties baptismi perdidit sacramentum, quia nunquam fidei fundamentum habuit in corde. Sed et hoc sciendum est, quod fides, secundum quod s. Augustinus ait, ex voluntate fit, non ex necessitate. Quomodo potest homo cogi, ut credat, quod non credit? Impelli potest homo ad baptismum, sed non ad fidem etc. Epist. xxxvii. ad Megenfridum : Si tanta instantia suave Christi jugum et onus ejus leve durissimo Saxonum populo praedicaretur, quanta decimarum redditio, vel legalis pro parvissimis quibuslibet culpis edicti necessitas exigebatur, forte baptismatis sacramenta non abhorrerent. Sint tandem aliquando doctores fidei apostolicis eruditi, sint praedicatores, non praedatores etc. Epist. lxxii. ad Arnonem : Tu vero—perge in opus Dei,—et esto praedicator pietatis, non decimarum exactor.—Decimae, ut dicitur, Saxonum subverterunt fidem. Quid injungendum est jugum cervicibus idiotarum, quod neque nos, neque fratres nostri sufferre potuerunt ?

[4] Translatio s. Liborii, written about 890, c. 2 (Pertz mon. vi. 160): (Carolus) Ecclesias per omnem regionem illam—sub quanta potuit celeritate construi fecit, atque parochias diligenti ratione suis quasque terminis servandas designans, quia civitates, in quibus more antiquo sedes episcopales constituerentur, illi penitus provinciae deerant, loca tamen ad hoc, quae et naturali quadam excellentia et populi frequentia prae caeteris opportuna videbantur, elegit. Tum vero vix reperiebantur, qui barbarae et semipaganae nationi praesules ordinarentur ; cujus interdum ad perfidiam relabentis cohabitatio nulli clericorum tuta videbantur. Quocirca unamquamque praedictarum pontificalium sedium cum sua dioecesi singulis aliarum regni sui Ecclesiarum praesulibus commendavit, qui et ipsi, quotiens sibi vacaret, ad instruendam confirmandamque in sacra religione plebem eo pergerent, et ex clero suo personas probabiles cujuscunque ordinis, cum diverso rerum ecclesiasticarum apparatu, ibidem, mansuros jugiter destinarent ; et hoc tamdiu, donec annuente Domino salutaris illic fidei doctrina convalesceret, et ita divini usus ministerii proveheretur, ut proprii quoque in singulis parochiis digna et fiducialiter possent manere pontifices. Vita s. Sturmi (written by his pupil Eigil about 800) c. 22. (ap. Pertz. ii. 376) : Congregato grandi exercitu, invocato Christi nomine, (Carolus) Saxoniam profectus est, adsumtis universis sacerdotibus, Abbatibus, Presbyteris et omnibus orthodoxis atque fidei cultoribus, ut gentem, quae ab initio mundi daemonum vinculis fuerat obligata, doctrinis sacris mite et suave Christi jugum credendo subire fecissent. Quo cum rex pervenisset, partim bellis, partim suasionibus, partem etiam muneribus, maxima ex parte gentem illam ad fidem Christi convertit ; et post non longum tempus totam provinciam illam in parochias episcopales divisit, et servis Domini ad docendum et baptizandum potestatem dedit. Tunc

obtained by degrees bishops of their own, whose dioceses, however, were not very securely fixed till after the peace of *Sals* (804). These Saxon bishoprics, the years of whose foundations have been very differently stated, on account of their gradual origination,[5] were, for Westphalia, *Osnabrück* (year of foundation variously marked 783, 788, 793, 803);[6] *Nimigardeford*, afterwards Münster (791, 801),[7] for Hungary (?) *Minden* (stated

pars maxima beato Sturmi populi et terrae illius ad procurandum committitur.—Quo cum multum temporis praedicando et baptizando cum suis Presbyteris peregisset, et per regiones quasque singulas Ecclesias construxisset: then the Saxons rebelled, and Sturm was obliged to flee. After they were vanquished, Ehresburg was assigned to him and his friends as a place of abode by Charlemagne, but there Sturm died as early as 779.

[5] Original documents alleged to have been executed by Charlemagne, 1. A deed of foundation of the Bremen Church, A. D. 788 (in Adami Brem. hist. eccl. I. c. 10. Chronik der freien Hansestadt Bremen von Carsten Miesegaes i. 169. J. M. Lappenberg's hamburgisches Urkundenbuch Bd. 1. (Hamburg 1842, 4.) 8. 4. 2. A similar foundation-deed of the Church of Verden A. D. 786 (first published by J. J. Maderus after his Adamus Brem. 1670, then ex Verdensis Ecclesiae tabulario by N. Schaten hist. Westph. 505. ap. Lappenberg i. 1). 3. Two titles bestowed on the Osnabrück Church A. D. 804 (from the alleged original in Ferd. de Fürstenberg monumenta Paterbornensia ed ii. Amstelod. 1672, 4. p. 325 ss. also in Schaten p. 607 and p. 612, and in Möser's Osnabrück Gesch. Th. 1. Urkunden S. 3 ff.). 4. Praeceptum pro Trutmanno Comite, by which the right of advocacy for all Saxon bishopricks is made over to it A. D. 789 (Baluzii cap. i. 249). When the older Protestants after Gryphiander's (de Weichbildis Saxonicis c. 33.) example even deny that Charlemagne founded the Saxon bishoprics generally; Catholics, on the other hand, such as Fürstenberg, and with especial violence Nic Schaten, undertook to defend the untenable authenticity of those patents. The more impartial of both parties, Papebroch, Car. le Cointe, Mabillon, J. G. Eccard, as also Meinders and Ludewig perceived on the contrary, that they could not be genuine, at least in their present form. See Meinder's tract. de statu religionis et reipubl. sub. Car. M. et Lud. Pio in veteri Saxonia p. 217 ss.

[6] Möser l. c. Th. 1. 275.

[7] In the Southerngau (the present province of Münster) a monk Bernard first preached. After his death Charlemagne sent thither the apostle of the Frieslanders Ludger, about 791, who first became bishop 802. (Even in 801 he is still called Presbyter or Abbas. Niesert's Münsterische Urkundensammlung ii. 1). See vita s. Liudgeri (comp. note 2) ap. Pertz ii. 411. comp. (F. M. v. Raet's) Münsterische Geschichte Th. 1. (Göttingen 1788) S. 127, 142. T. König's geschichtl. Nachrichten uber das Gymnasium zu Münster (Münster 1821) S. 20 ff. H. A. Erhard's Geschichte Münsters. (Münster 1837) S. 28.

to be 780), and *Paderborn* (usually 795);[8] for Eastphalia *Verden* (786),[9] *Bremen* (788),[10] and *Hildesheim* (said to have been established 796 in Elze, and removed under Lewis the Debonaire);[11] for North Thuringia *Halberstadt* (said to have been established at Seligenstadt, 781, and soon after removed).[12]

[8] It was probably this diocese in particular which was assigned to the monastery of Fulda to be converted (see vita Sturmi above note 4): In Paderborn, as early as 777, Charles built a church (ann. Petav. and Sangallenses ap. Pertz i. 16. 63). Subsequently (after Pope Leo III. had been with Charles in Paderborn, consequently about 800) this church was assigned to the superintendence of the bishop of Würzburg, and received, about 810, its first bishop Hathumar. See translatio s. Liborii c. 5: Hic ex praecepto Principis (Caroli) primus est Patherbrunnensis Ecclesiae ordinatus Episcopus. Post cujus ordinationem paucis annis transactis idem gloriosissimus Princeps ab hac luce migravit. Among other things we find G. T. Bessen's Gesch. des Bisthums Paderborn (2 Bde. Paderb. 1820) i. 78.

[9] The first seat of it was Kuhfeld, not far from Salzwedel. See Chronography of the Bishops at Verden. in A. Chr. Wedekind's Noten zu einigen Geschichtschreibern des deutschen Mittelalters Heft. i. (Hamb. 1821) S. 92. On the extent of the bishopric see Asmussen in the Archiv f. Staats- und Kirchengesch. der Herzogthümer Schleswig, Holstein, Lauenburg. Bd. 1. Heft 1. (Kiel 1833) S. 214. P. v. Kobbe's Gesch. und Landesbeschreibung der Herzogthümer Bremen und Verden (Göttingen 1824) Th. 2. S. 260. Pfannkuche ältere Gesch. d. vormal. Bisth. Verden. Verden 1830.

[10] Willehad, an English Benedictine, first preached among the Frieslanders, afterwards, from 780, among the Saxons in the pagus Wigmodia (the present duchy of Bremen). So early as the succeeding year, Christianity had been generally diffused there externally; but at the rebellion of Wittekind, 782, there succeeded an apostacy as general, and the priests who could not flee were murdered. After Wittekind's baptism, Willehad, in 785, was again sent to Wigmodia, restored the churches and Christianity, and was consecrated first bishop of Bremen 788. See vita s. Willehadi, written by his later successor Anschar, best given in Pertz monum. ii. 378. Leben des St. Willehad's u. St. Ansgar's übers. mit Anm. v. Carsten Miesegaes, Bremen 1826. 8. v. Kobbe ii. 58. Delius in Ersch u. Gruber's Encyclop. xii. 436.

[11] J. B. Lauenstein's diplomat. Historie des Bisthums Hildesheim (2 Th. Hildesh. 1740. 4.) Th. 1. S. 199.

[12] Ann. Quedlinburg. ad ann. 781 (Pertz v. 38): Eodem anno Carolus de Roma reversus in Franciam, terram Saxonum inter Episcopos divisit, et terminos Episcopis constituit: et s. Stephano protomartyri in loco, qui dicitur Seliganstedi monasterium construxit, quod postea in locum translatum est, qui dicitur Halverstede, ubi nunc est sedes episcopalis. Idque ad corrigendum et propagandum Catalaunensi Episcopo Hildegrimo, qui frater erat b. Liudgeri confessoris, commendavit. This

Lewis the Debonaire founded the monasteries of *Corbeia nova* (822, a colony from Corbeia vetus)[13] and *Herford*.

Against the *Slavonians* and *Avari* Charles' wars were as unsuccessful as his attempts to effect their conversion.

The appearance of the banished Jütland prince, *Harald Klak*, at Lewis' court, drew the attention of this emperor to the conversion of the north. Harald was baptized in the year 826 at Ingelheim, and then returned to his native country, attended by *Anschar*.[14] This apostle of the north diffused Christianity chiefly in *North Albingia*; in *Jutland* and *Sweden*, which he visited 829 and 855, he laid a foundation which was still insecure. For the management of these new churches, the recently founded archbishoprick of *Hamburg* was bestowed on Anschar 831, which was united with the bishoprick of *Bremen* in 849.[15] Anschar died A. D. 865.

Hildegrin was, up to 782, assistant to his brother Ludgerus, among the Frieslanders (vita Liudgeri i. 18. ap. Pertz ii. 410), consequently he cannot have been at that time bishop of Chalons. The immunities and boundaries of the bishopric of Halberstadt were confirmed in a diploma of 814 (ap. Leukfeld antt. Groning. p. 10). Hildegrin continued bishop of Chalons till his death, 827, and Halberstadt was his benefice in commendam. Hence he is designated by Thietmar iv. 45. (Pertz v. 787) in the account of his death as Cathelaunensis Episcopus sanctaeque Halverstadensis Ecclesiae rector primus.—Seligenstadt is not Osterwyk. See Delius in Ledebur's Archiv. f. d. Geschichtskunde d. preutz. Staats Bd. 9. no. 1 and 5. Niemann's Gesch. Halberstadts Bd. 1. (Halberstadt 1829) S. 19.

[13] See the contemporaries, a monk of Corvey, the author of the hist. translationis s. Viti c. 5 ss. (ap. Pertz ii. 577), and Paschasius Radbert in his vita Adalhardi c. 65 (ap. Pertz ii. 531). Wigand's Gesch. v. Corvey Bd. 1. (Höxter 1819). S. 36 ff.

[14] Vita s. Anskarii by his pupil Rimbertus (Act. ss. Febr. i. 559. ed. Dahlmann in Pertz monumenta Germ. historica ii. 683. translated by Miesegaes. See above note 10). Moeller hist. Cimbriae literaria iii. 8. Langebeck chronol. aevi Anschar. in script. rer. Dan. i. 496. Münter's Kirchengesch. v. Dänem. u. Norweg. i. 266. St Anschar von G. Ch. Kruse. Altona 1823. F. C. Kraft narratio de Ansgario Aquilonarium gentium Apostolo, Hamb. 1840. 4. (also in his Kleinen Schulschriften, neue Folge, Stuttgart 1843. S. 98). Dr. G. H. Klippel's Lebensbeschreibung des. Erzb. Ansgar, Bremen 1845.—It is to be regretted that Anschar's diarium is lost, as also all his letters except one. See Münter's Kirchengesch. i. 319. Kruse S. 227.

[15] L. Giesebrecht's wendische Geschichte v. 780. bis 1182. Bd. 1. (Berlin 1843) S. 161. J. Asmussen über den Umfang der Hamburger

FOURTH CHAPTER.

SPANISH CHURCH.

Eulogii Cordubensis [† 859] opera (Memoriale Sanctorum lib. iii. Apologeti-
cus pro martyribus. Exhortatio ad martyrium. Epistolae) ed. cum
scholiis Ambros. Morales. Compluti 1574. also in the bibl. PP. and in A.
Schotti Hispan. illustr. iv. 217. best in ss. PP. Toletanorum opera (2 Tomi.
Matriti 1782. 85 fol.) ii. 391.—Petri Alvari Cordubensis († 862) opera
(Confessio. Epistolae. Indiculus luminosus. Versus) in the España sagrada
por Henr. Florez (Madrid 1747—1801. 42. T. 4.) xi. 62.   Neander iv. 89.
Gfrörer iii. ii. 810. iii. iii. 1590.

§ 17.

The Spanish Christians (Mozarabes)[1] had enjoyed legal religious freedom under their Saracen rulers,[2] but they had to
suffer in various ways from the fanatical hatred of the Moslem,
which had been excited chiefly by the wars of the free Spaniards.
While many Christians devoted themselves to Arabic literature,
endeavoured to attain prosperity in the service of the sovereigns,
and avoided every thing which was offensive to the Arabians,
though at the same time they were also lukewarm in their Christianity ;[3] others felt, in consequence of the success with which

Diöcese und Archidiöcese, in Michelsen's u. Asmussen's Archiv f. Gesch.
d. Herzogthümer Schleswig, Holstein, Lauenburg. Bd. 1. Heft. 1. (Kiel
1833) S. 109.
   [1] Not, as Rodericus, archbishop of Toledo († 1245) in histor. Hispan. iii. c. 22. supposes, Mixtiarabes, eo quod mixti Arabibus convive-
bant, but Arabi Mustaraba (i. e. Ar. insititii) in opposition to the Arabi
Araba, cf. Ed. Pocockii spec. histor. Arabum, Oxon. 1650. p. 39. Her-
belot s. v. Arab and Mostarab.
   [2] Comp. Ant. Morales de statu christ. relig. etc. in Schotti Hispan.
illustr. iv. 220.
   [3] Alvari Indiculus luminosus (written 854) c. 9. (ap. Florez xi. 232):
Nunc ad teporem nostrorum reflectamus narrationis articulum.   Numquid ipsi nostri, qui palatino officio illorum jussis inserviunt, eorum non
sunt implicati palam erroribus, eorumque inquinati fulgentes se dicunt
esse foetoribus ? cum enim palam coram ethnicis orationem non faciunt,

U

their brethren in the faith fought for the cross and their freedom, that they were called upon to make a decided stand as Christians against their oppressors.[4]   This disposition increased so much under the Ommajad *Abd-er-Rhaman* II. (822–852) that many were filled with a fanatical zeal for the glories of martyrdom (850), in consequence of the execution of a monk.[5]   This conduct again provoked the Saracens to redoubled hatred and new attacks.[6]   In vain did the moderate, and even *a national synod*

signo crucis oscitantes frontem non muniunt, Deum Christum non aperte coram eos, sed fugatis sermonibus proferunt, Verbum Dei et Spiritum, ut illi asserunt (as also the Koran), profitentes, suasque confessiones corde, quasi Deo omnia inspiciente, servantes.   Quid his omnibus nisi varietatem pardi zelo Dei zelantibus, sibi inesse ostendunt, dum non integre, sed medie Christianismum defendunt ?   Cap. 35 : Quis rogo hodie solers in nostris fidelibus laicis invenitur, qui Scripturis sanctis intentus volumina quorumcumque Doctorum latine conscripta respiciat ? —Nonne omnes juvenes Christiani vultu decori, lingua diserti, habitu gestuque conspicui, gentilicia eruditione praeclari, Arabico eloquio sublimati, volumina Chaldaeorum avidissime tractant, intentissime legunt, ardentissime disserunt,—Ecclesiae flumina de paradiso manantia quasi vilissima contemuentes ?   Heu proh dolor linguam suam nesciunt Christiani, et linguam propriam non advertunt Latini, ita ut omni Christi collegio vix inveniatur unus in milleno hominum numero, qui salutatorias fratri possit rationabiliter dirigere literas.   Et reperitur absque numero multiplex turba, quae erudite chaldaicas verborum explicet pompas.

[4] Thus, even about the year 780, one Migetius asserted, quod cibus infidelium polluat mentes fidelium, and was accordingly reproved for it by Elipand, archbishop of Toledo (Elipandi epist. ad. Migetium c. 11. ap. Florez iii. 552).

[5] The first martyr Perfectus (Eulogii memor. ii. c. 1.) was certainly provoked by the Mahometans.   Res vero tanti facinoris in sacerdote commissi multos otio securae professionis per deserta montium et nemora solitudinum in Dei contemplatione fruentes ad sponte et publice detestandum et maledicendum sceleratum vatem (Mohammed) exsilire coëgit : majorisque ardoris fomitem moriendi pro justitia cunctis ministravit.   Ex. gr. (Eulog. epist. ad Wiliesindum c. 11.) : Quidam Presbyterorum, Diaconorum, Monachorum, Virginum et Laicorum repentino zelo divinitatis armati in forum descendentes, hostem fidei repulerunt, detestantes atque maledicentes, nefandum et scelerosum ipsorum vatem Mahomat, et hoc modo contra eum animosum spiritum erigentes, testimonium protulerunt.   " Virum hunc, quem vos summa veneratione excolitis,—magum adulterum et mendacem esse cognovimus ejusque credulos aeternae perditionis laqueis mancipandos confitemur" etc.   It was natural that omnes gladio vindice interemti sunt.

[6] Eulogius memor, Sanctorum lib. i. (written 851) c. 21. complains of diruptiones basilicarum, opprobria sacerdotum, et quod lunariter sol-

assembled at Corduba (852),[7] declare against this longing for martyrdom;[8] the fanaticism which had for its spokesmen *Eulogius* and *Alvarus* still brought many to death.[9]   Under the succeed-

vimus cum gravi moerore tributum.—nemo nostrum (i. e. sacerdotum) inter eos securus ingreditur, nemo quietus permeat, nemo septum eorum nisi dehonestatus pertransit etc.   Adeo ut multi ex eis tactu indumentorum suorum nos indignos dijudicent, propiusque sibimet accedere execrentur.   Alvari indiculus luminosus c. 6. : Quotidie opprobriis et mille contumeliarum fascibus obruti, persecutionem nos dicimus non habere.   Nam, ut alia taceam, certe dum defunctorum corpora a sacerdotibus vident—humo dando portare ; nonne—dicunt : Deus non miserearis illis : et lapidibus sacerdotes Domini impetentes, ignominiosis verbis populum Domini denotantes, spurcitiarum fimo christicolas transeuntes paedore infando adspargunt ?   Sic itidem et cum sacerdotes Dei casu quo quem obviant perviantes, lapides testasque—ante vestigia eorum revolventes, ac improperioso et infami nomine derogantes, vulgari proverbio et cantico inhonesto sugillant, et fidei signum, opprobrio +o elogio decolorant.   Sed cum Basilicae signum, h. e. tinnientis aeris sonitum—audiunt,—Christi Domini gregem non uniformi subsannio, sed milleno contumeliarum infamio maledice impetunt et derident.

    [7] Respecting it see J. S. de Aguirre collect. concill. omn. Hispaniae (T. iv. Rom. 1693 und 1694 fol.) iii. 149.   Ferreras histoire générale d'Espagne ii. 604. Eulogii memoriale SS. ii. c. 14 : Of the Metropolitanorum judicio, qui ob eandem causam tunc. e. diversis provinciis a rege fuerant adunati.   Their determination : inhibitum esse martyrium, nec licere quiquam deinceps ad palaestram professionis discurrere, praemisso pontificali decreto ipsae literae nuntiarunt.

    [8] The views of this synod on the subject are given by its bitterest opponent, Eulogius, memor. lib. i. c. 18 : jubent eos non recipi in catalogo Sanctorum, inusitatum scilicet atque profanum asserentes hujusmodi martyrium.   Quippe quos nulla violentia praesidalis fidem suam negare compulit, nec a cultu sanctae piaeque religionis amovit, sed propria se voluntate discrimini offerentes, ob superbiam suam (ita dicunt), quae initium est omnis peccati, interemti suarum parricidae effecti sunt animarum.   Praeceptis etiam Evangelicis eos arguendos esse credunt (Matth. v. 44, Luc. iii. 14, 1 Pet. ii. 23, 1 Cor. vi. 10), p. 247 : non debere esse martyres, aut haberi, qui non violenter tracti sunt ad martyrium, sed sponte sua venientes his convitium intulerant, qui eos in nullo molestia affecerint.—Id. in apologetico pro martyrib. (c. 3). They said : Isti tirones et nostrorum temporum confessores ab ictu mucronis celeremt antummodo excipientes interitum, nullam furentium acerbitatem perpessi tortorum, non sub diutinum desudarunt stimulum. Praesertim cum ab hominibus Deum colentibus et caelestia jura fatentibus compendiosa morte peremti sint.   Unde sat eis est, si praeteritorum curationem adepti sunt criminum etc.

    [9] Eulogius memor. i. c. 6 : Et licet formidolosis facultas collata sit declinandi rabiem persecutionis, non tamen passim hoc observandum

U 2

ing prince *Mohammed* (852–886), as long as the fanaticism of
the Christians continued,[10] their oppressions also continued ; and

est a perfectis, qui jam praescia Redemtoris potentia denotati et conscripti, quasi ab immensis legionibus ad exercitium proeliorum Dei
electi sunt.—secundum Apostolum dissolvi cupiunt et esse cum Christo,
viam compendii requirentes, qua de corpore mortis hujus eruti propere
ad caelestem patriam pervenirent, et pia violentia regnum Dei arriperent.   Sic quoque armati lorica justitiae in forum prosiliunt, praedi-
cantes Evangelium Dei principibus et nationibus mundi.—ideo perfecto
odio contra adversarios Ecclesiae insurgentes, arguunt impios de falsi-
dica vatis iniqui doctrina, praestigiis, sacrilegiis;—detestantur quoque,
et maledictionibus auctorem tantae perversitatis impugnant, eundemque
coetum talibus inservientem culturis perenni anathemate damnant.   c.
20 : Idcirco huic perdito atque spurcissimo vati resistere, virtus mactae
coronae est : summumque trophaeum tanti derisoris cultum evertere :
adeo ut si illum aetas nostra superstitem haberet, nequaquam ab ejus
esset interitu christicolis resiliendum.—Foretque (ut reor) tunc melius
poenitudinem unius occisi homunculi gerere, quam tot nationum luere
perniciem.—Quoniam quemadmodum sine culpa non est maledicere
justos, pios persequi, adversitatem parare electis : ita magni meriti esse
credo, subvertere impios, Ecclesiae hostibus contraire, bellum parare
incredulis, et framea verbi Dei concidere adversarios fidei etc.—c. 24 :
Et idcirco, ut quidam sapientium meminit, inter primas dignitates regnorum caelestium sunt ponendi, qui ad passionem venerunt non quae-
siti : et excellentis voti est inter tormenta prosilire, ubi non est criminis
latuisse.   Against the milder view of Mohammedanism apolog. pro
mart. c. 12 : Deum ergo et legem isti vanitatis cultores ullo modo habere credendi sunt, qui evangelicae institutionis per totum orbem vitalia
diffusa praecepta non solum non credunt, verum etiam omni zelo perversitatis magnum discrimen ea fatentibus ingerunt, exosum et iniquum
putantes, Christum verum Deum et verum hominem credere ? etc.   Alvari indiculus luminosus c. 2 : Fugiant debiles et infirmi, certent fortes
et animi honestate praecincti.   Et certe non eos veritatem supprimere,
sed tergum persequentibus ob seminarium Evangelii jussit praebere :
fugiant de una civitate in aliam (Matth. x. 23), praedicando quae vera
sunt et honesta, non (quod absit) tegendo quae sancta sunt et modesta.
c. 10 : Nec tantum illa apostolica tempora praedicationi fidei sunt con-
tradenda, imo quousque omnis gens et lingua Christi Evangelio credant,
praedicatio Ecclesiae est per omne saeculum seminanda.   Puto, quod
in hac Ismaelitica gente nullus hactenus extitit praedicator, per quod
debitores fidei tenerentur.—Et evangelizantibus genti justitiam, in qua
nullius praedicatio hactenus praebuit viam, insaniae vociferamus esse
vecordiam, non complementum evangelizantium praescientiam praesa-
gatam !

[10] In the year 864, Samson, presbyter in Corduba, wrote with this
view.   See apologeticus contra Hostegisum Episc. Malacitanum (ap.
Florez iii. 325).

consequently many of the indifferent went over to Islamism.[11] Gradually, however, a calmer state of things returned.[12]

FIFTH CHAPTER.

HISTORY OF PUBLIC WORSHIP.

Particular Sources: 1. Liturgical: Ordo Romanus de divinis officiis per totius anni circulum (belonging to the 8th century). Amalarii Chorepiscopi Metensis de divinis officiis libb. iv. ad Ludov. Imp. (written 819. 2d ed. after 827) and de ordine antiphonarii lib. after 827), comp. Bähr's Gesch. d. röm. Lit. im. karol. Zeitalter S. 381. Rabani Mauri de clericorum institutione et ceremoniis eccl. libb. iii. (written 819) and de sacris ordinibus, sacramentis divinis et vestimentis sacerdotalibus, see above § 10. note 14. Walafridi Strabonis de exordiis et incrementis rerum ecclesiasticarum, see above § 10. note 16. All collected in: De divinis cathol.

[11] Memor. SS. ii. c. 15: Qui [Mahomad] ingenito quodam odio saepius quaestionem adversus fideles proponens, non illo inferior esse meritis apparuit, cujus nomine insignitus ostenditur. Nam ipso die, quo sceptrum regni adeptus est, Christianos abdicari Palatio jussit, dignitate privavit, honore destituit. III. c. 2: Multi autem sua se sponte a Christo divertentes adhaerebant iniquis, sectamque diaboli summo colebant affectu. C. 3: [Mahomad] jubet ecclesias nuper structas dirure, et quicquid novo cultu in antiquis basilicis splendebat, fueratque temporibus Arabum rudi formatione adjectum elidere. Eulogius was put to death in 859. See life by his friend Alvarus in Schotti Hisp. illustr. iv. 223. Patres Tolet. ii. 394.

[12] To Johannes Abb. Gorziensis, who in 959 came to Spain, as legate of the Emperor Otto I., it was said by a bishop of the country (see vita Johannis § 122, in the act. SS. Feb. iii. 713. Pertz monum vi. 372): Resistere potestati verbo prohibemur Apostoli: tantum hoc unum relictum est solatii, quod in tantae calamitatis malo legibus nos propriis uti non prohibent; qui quos diligentes christianitatis viderint observatores, colunt et amplectuntur, simul ipsorum convictu delectantur, cum Judaeos penitus exhorreant. Pro tempore igitur hoc videmur tenere consilii, ut, quia religionis nulla infertur jactura, caetera eis obsequamur, jusssique eorum in quantum fidem non impediunt, obtemperemus. The Christians, in the meantime, must have been very accommodating to the Moslims at that time, if what John reproaches them with be true: ad ritum eorum vos audio circumcisos.

Eccl. officiis varii vetustorum Patrum ac scriptt. libri. editi per Melch. Hittorpium. Colon. 1568. Paris. 1610 fol.

2. Martyrologies: especially the kalendarium Rom. belonging to the 8th century (in Jo. Frontonis epistt. et dissert. eccl. ed. J. A. Fabricius. Hamb. 1720. 8.) The martyrolŏgium Aquilejense (not Romanum, see H. Valesii diss. at the end of his Eusebius), which Ado prefixes to his as of great antiquity, and which is at least as old as the beginning of the 9th century. Wandelberti mon. Prumiensis martyrologium rhythmicum about 850 (erroneously inserted in Bede's works as ephemerides Bedae) best edited in d'Achery spicileg. ii. 39, comp. Bähr S. 114. Adonis Archiep. Vienn. († 875) written about 858 martyrologium (ed. Herib. Rosweydus appended to Baronii martyrol. Rom. Antverp. 1613 fol.) Comp. Bähr S. 501. In part also the later martyrologies of Usuardus (about 876) and Notker (892—895).

§ 18.

Though Charlemagne withstood particular tendencies of ecclesiastical superstition,[1] others had taken too deep root to be perceived by him, especially an exaggerated veneration of saints and their relics.[2] The latter, the legends concerning which became

---

[1] Cap. i. ann. 789, c. 76 : De pseudographiis et dubiis narrationibus. c. 77. De magonibus et nudis cum ferro. Capit. iii. ann. 789, c. 4 : ut nullus in Psalterio vel in Evangelio vel in aliis rebus sortire praesumat, nec divinationes aliquas observare. c. 18: Ut clocas non baptizent, nec chartas per perticas appendant propter grandinem. Capit. Francof, ann. 794, c. 40: ut nulli novi Sancti colantur, aut invocentur, nec memoriae eorum per vias erigantur; sed ii soli in Ecclesia venerandi sunt, qui ex auctoritate passionum aut vitae merito electi sunt. Comp. his principles concerning images of the saints, § 11, not. 3.

[2] Comp. the controversial writings Christ. Nifanii ostensio hist. theol. quod Car. M. in quamplurimis fidei articulis formaliter non fuerit Papista. Francof. 1670. 8. On the other side, Nic. Schaten Carolus M. Rom. Imp. romano-cathol. libb. iv. explicatus et vindicatus. Neuhus. 1674. 4. In reply to this, Nifanii Car. M. confessor veritatis evangel. Francof. 1679. 8. Other works see in Walchii bibl. theol. ii. 369. Karlomanni capit. i. ann. 742, c. 2. The army must be accompanied by priests, qui propter divinum ministerium, Missarum scilicet solemnia adimplenda, et Sanctorum patrocinia portanda, ad hoc electi sunt, i. e. unum vel duos Episcopos cum capellanis Presbyteris Princeps secum habeat etc. In like manner Caroli M. capit. viii. ann. 803 (see above, § 8, not. 3. Capellani a Capa, see Du Fresne glossar, ad scriptt. med. et inf. Latin. s. v.) cf. Monachus Sangall. de gestis C. M. I. c. 4. Even an Alcuin (homil. de natali s. Willibrordi ed. Froben. ii. 195) says : Te continuis, o pater, prosequimur laudibus, tu nobis assiduis auxiliare pre-

more and more marvellous,[3] were brought chiefly from the East[4] and from Rome.[5]   As they worked miracles of all kinds,[6] so were magic powers also ascribed to the mass ;[7] *private masses*[8] began,

cibus.   Credimus te in praesentia Domini Dei tui omnia posse impetrare, quae poscis ; dum tanta potuisti in praesentia nostra per ejus gratiam efficere miracula etc.

[3] Thus Angilbertus Abb. Centulensis, about 801, in a long series of relics of his cloister, speaks (in Mabillon act. SS. ord. s. Bened. saec. iv. i. 114), among other things : De ligno Domini, de veste ejus, de sandaliis ejus, de praesepe ejus, de spongia ejus, de Jordane ubi baptizatus est, de petra ubi sedit, quando quinque millia hominum pavit, de pane unde distribuit discipulis suis, de templo Domini, de candela quae in nativitate ejus accensa est,—de monte Horeb, de lignis trium tabernaculorum.   De lacte s. Mariae, de capillis ejus, de veste ejus, de pallio ejus.   De barba s. Petri, de sandaliis ejus, de casula ejus, et de mensa ejus.   De mensa s. Pauli, de orario ejus, de cippo in quo missus fuit etc.

[4] Ex. gr. annales Laurissenses ad ann. 799 : Monachus quidam de Hierosolymis veniens, benedictionem et reliquias de sepulchro Domini, quas Patriarcha Hierosolymitanus domno Regi miserat, detulit.

[5] Gregor. IV. epist. ad Otgar. (in Mabillonii analectt. vett. ed. ii. p. 570), confesses that in Rome there remained no bodies of the saints unappropriated.

[8] Miraculous relics in the monasteries became often a source of annoyance to serious monks.   When among the Voges the body of a monk who had died there, called Spinulus, attracted, by the miracles it wrought, too many people, in the monast. Medianum (Moyen Moutier), the abbot Hildulf († 707) spoke seriously to the saint on this account (vita Hildulfi in the historia Mediani in monte Vosago monasterii, Argentor. 1724. 4. p. 62) : Si hac populorum confluentia pressi fuerimus, non parum a proposito declinabimus : licet enim Domino cooperante subsidia nostro conferantur loco, tamen animarum timemus pericula.   Unde concurrentium comprime turbas etc.   Tunc ergo videres spiritum carne solutum et vita potitum obedire mortali :—nam signis cessantibus frequentia quoque desivit.   Cf. Mabillon acta SS. ord. Ben saec iii. P. i.   Praef. p. 87 s.   The expression of Autpertus Abbas monast. s. Vincentii ad Vulturnum in Benevento, in the biography of his three predecessors, is also worthy of notice († 778), ap. Mabillon l. c. p. 430 : Et quidem narrantur de eis quaedam digna miraculis, sed nostrum ad hoc tantum fuit studium incitatum, ut quibus modis saeculum ac diabolum vicerint apicibus prosequamur.—Et quia multi videntur miraculorum esse participes, sed nullatenus nomina habent scripta in caelis : nequaquam hoc in tempore virtutes in Ecclesia, sed perfectam vitam requirimus.

[7] Lulli epist. ad Presbyteros in Thuringia (in Bonifacii epist. ed. Serar. ep. 62.   Würdtw. ep. 107) : Admonemus Vos, ut rogetis omnes, —ut in communi misericordiam Domini deprecentur, quatenus ab imminenti pluviarum flagello liberemur, i. e. ut unam hebdomadam absti-

and in consequence of this measure altars were multiplied in the
churches.[9] To the festivals[10] were added that of the *Birth of the*

neant se ab omni carne, et ab omni potu, in quo mel sit : secunda feria,
iv. feria et vi. feria jejunetis usque ad vesperum : et unusquisque servorum Dei et sanctimonialium ·L. psalmos cantet omni die in illa sep-
timana, et illas Missas,'quae pro tempestatibus fieri soleant, celebrare Vos,
Presbyteri, recordamini.; Missimus Vobis nomina domini Romani Episcopi, pro quo unusquisque Vestrum xxx. Missas cantet et illos psalmos,
et jejunium juxta constitutionem nostram.   Similiter pro duobus laicis
nomine Megenfrith et Hraban x. Missas unusquisque Vestrum cantet.
    [8] Walafridus Strabo de reb. eccles. c. 22 : per totam Missam pro eis
quam maxime et quasi nominatim oratur, qui ibi offerunt atque communicant.   Possumus autem et debemus—dicere, caeteros in fide et in
devotione offerentium et communicantium persistentes ejusdem oblationis et communionis dici et esse participes.   Quamvis autem, cum
soli sacerdotes Missas celebrant, intelligi possit, illos ejusdem actionis
esse co-operatores, pro quibus tunc ipsa celebrantur officia, et quorum
personam in quibusdam responsionibus sacerdos exequitur : tamen fatendum est, illam esse legitimam Missam, cui intersunt sacerdos, re-
spondens, offerens atque communicans, sicut ipsa compositio precum
evidenti ratione demonstrat.   Even Pseudoisidore directs (Anacleti P.
epist. i. c. 2, in Gratiani decreto P. iii. dist. ii. c. 10) : Peracta consecratione omnes communicent, qui noluerint ecclesiasticis carere limini-
bus.   Sic enim et Apostoli statuerunt, et s. Romana tenet Ecclesia. Cf.
J. F. Buddeus de origine Missae pontificiae in his miscellaneis sacr. i.
1.   Karl d. G. und seine Bischöfe, die Synode von Mainz i. J. 813 (in
the Tübinger kath. theol. Quartalschrift, 1824, iii. 416).   Some priests
went so far as to begin to read mass without any one being present, but
this was forbidden, Conc. Mogunt. ann. 813, c. 43.   (Mansi xiv. 74.)
Conc. Paris. ann. 829, c. 48 (l. c. p. 567) : Irrepsit in plerisque locis,
partim incuria, partim avaritia, reprehensibilis usus,—eo quod nonulli
Presbyterorum sine ministris Missarum solemnia frequentent.—Unde
—interrogandus nobis videtur hujusmodi corporis et sanguinis Domini
solitarius consecrator, quibus dicit : Dominus vobiscum, et a quo illi
respondetur : Et cum spiritu tuo : vel pro quibus supplicando Domino
inter caetera : Memento, Domine, et omnium circumstantium, cum
nullus circumstet, dicit.
    [9] Capitulare in Theodonis villa ann. 805 promulgatum i. c. 6. (Ba-
luz. i. 422.   Pertz iii. 132) : De altaribus, ut non superflua sint in
Ecclesiis.
    [10] Capitularium lib. i. c. 158 : Hac sunt festivitates in anno, quae
per omnia venerari debeant.   Natalis Domini, s. Stephani, s. Johannis
Evangelistae, Innocentum, Octabas Domini, Epiphania, Octabas Epi-
phaniae, Purificatio s. Mariae, Pascha dies octo, Letania major, Ascen-
sio Domini, Pentecosten, s. Johannis Bapt., s. Petri et Pauli, s. Martini, s. Andreae.   De adsumtione s. Mariae interrogandum relinquimus.
Conc. Mogunt. ann. 813, can. 36 (Mansi xiv. 73) : Festos dies in anno celebrare sancimus.   Hoc est diem dominicum Paschae cum omni

Virgin on the 8th September ;[11] *the Festival of Mary's ascension* on the 15th August ;[12] and the feast of *All Saints* on the

honore et sobrietate venerari, simili modo totam hebdomadem illam observari decrevimus. Diem Ascensionis Domini pleniter celebrare. Item Pentecosten similiter ut in Pascha. In natali App. Petri et Pauli diem unum, nativitatem s. Joannis Baptistae, assumtionem s. Mariae, dedicationem s. Michaelis, natalem s. Remigii, s. Martini s. Andrae. In natali Domini dies quatuor, octavas Domini, epiphaniam Domini, purificationem s. Mariae. Et illas festivitates martyrum vel confessorum observare decrevimus, quorum in unaquaque parochia sancta corpora requiescunt. Similiter etiam dedicationem templi.

[11] Celebrated in the Greek Church as early as the seventh century (see Andreae Cretensis homil. ii. in Gallandii bibl. PP. xiii. 93), at Rome in the eighth century (kalendar. Frontonis ed. Fabric. p. 226), and under Charles the Bald, adopted also in the Gallican Church. See Augusti's Denkwürdigk. iii. 102.

[12] Very early there were conjectures respecting the end of Mary. At first it was supposed from Luke ii. 35, that she suffered martyrdom. In opposition to this Origenes hom. xvii. in Lucam : Nulla docet historia, b. Virginem gladii occisione migrasse : praesertim cum non anima sed corpus ferro soleat interfici. In like manner Ambros. comm. in Luc. 2. Isidorus Hisp. de vita et obitu SS. Bedae comm. in Luc. 2. The fable introduced by Epiphan. haer. lxxviii. § 11 : ζητήσωσι τὰ ἴχνη τῶν γραφῶν, καὶ εὕρωσιν ἂν οὔτε θάνατον Μαρίας, οὔτε εἰ τέθνηκεν, οὔτε εἰ μὴ τέθνηκεν· οὔτε εἰ τέθαπται, οὔτε εἰ μὴ τέθαπται·—ἀλλ' ἁπλῶς ἐσιώπησεν ἡ γραφή, διὰ τὸ ὑπερβάλλον τοῦ θαύματος· ἵνα μὴ εἰς ἔκπληξιν ἀγάγῃ τὴν διάνοιαν τῶν ἀνθρώπων.—τάχα γάρ που καὶ ἴχνη εὕρομεν τῆς ἁγίας ἐκείνης καὶ μακαρίας, ὡς οὔτε εὑρεῖν ἐστι τὸν θάνατον αὐτῆς. πῆ μὲν γὰρ ὁ Συμεὼν φάσκει περὶ αὐτῆς· " καὶ σοῦ αὐτῆς τὴν ψυχὴν διελεύσεται ῥομφαία" (Luc. ii. 35)—πῆ δὲ τῆς Ἀποκαλύψεως Ἰωάννου φασκούσης, ὅτι καὶ ἔσπευδεν ὁ δράκων ἐπὶ τὴν γυναῖκα τὴν γεννήσασαν τὸν ἄῤῥενα, καὶ ἐδόθησαν αὐτῇ πτέρυγες ἀετοῦ, καὶ ἐλήφθη εἰς τὴν ἔρημον, ὅπως ἂν μὴ λάβῃ αὐτὴν ὁ δράκων (Apoc. xii. 13, 14). Τάχα δὲ δύναται ἐπ' αὐτῇ πληροῦσθαι· οὐ πάντως δὲ ὁρίζομαι τοῦτο, καὶ οὐ λέγω, ὅτι ἀθάνατος ἔμεινεν· ἀλλ' οὔτε διαβεβαιοῦμαι εἰ τέθνηκεν. ὑπερέβαλε γὰρ ἡ γραφὴ τὸν νοῦν τὸν ἀνθρώπινον καὶ ἐν μετεώρῳ εἴασε κ. τ. λ. (Similarly Hilarius can. 20, and Ambrosius de Cain et Abel i. c. 2. respecting the death of Moses). The use of ambiguous expressions (ex. gr. Euseb. de vit. Const. iv. c. 64. Βασιλεὺς—πρὸς τὸν αὑτοῦ θεὸν ἀνελαμβάνετο· Gregor. Tur. de gloria confess. c. 99 : anniversarius assumtionis s. Aviti dies) contributed probably to the existence of such a fable. It is first found in apocryphal books, in Joannis Ap. εἰς τὴν κοίμησιν τῆς ὑπεραγίας δεσποίνης (according to Thilo, belonging to the end of the fourth or beginning of the fifth century), Melitonis Ep. Sard. de transitu Virginis Mariae (cf. Thilo acta s. Thomae Apost. Lips. 1823, in the notitia uberior novae Cod. Apocr. editionis p. xvi. ss.) The Roman bishop Gelasius (about 495) declares however in his decretum de libris sacris et apocryphis : librum, qui appellatur transitus s. Mariae, apocryphum, but Gregorius Turon. de glor. Mart. i. c. 4, unhesitatingly adopts the fabulous

tradition: Impleto a b. Mariae, hujus vitae cursu cum jam vocaretur a saeculo, congregati sunt omnes Apostoli de singulis regionibus ad domum ejus. Cumque audissent, quia esset adsumenda de mundo, vigilabant cum ea simul: et ecce Dominus Jesus advenit cum angelis suis, et accipiens animam ejus tradidit Michaeli angelo et recessit. Dilu·culo autem levaverunt Apostoli cum lectulo corpus ejus, posueruntque illud in monumento, et custodiebant ipsum, adventum Domini praestolantes. Et ecce iterum adstitit eis Dominus, susceptumque corpus sanctum in nube deferri jussit in Paradisum: ubi nunc resumta anima cum electis ejus exultans aeternitatis bonis nullo occasuris fine perfruitur. In the Greek Church it is true that even Andreas Cretensis (about 650) hom. in dormitionem Mariae (ap. Galland xiii. 147) hints at the fable; but it is found complete for the first time in Jo. Damasceni λόγοι γ´ εἰς τὴν κοίμησιν τῆς—Θεοτόκου and in Nicephori Callisti hist. eccl. ii. c. 21 ss. et xv. c. 14. According to Niceph. Call. xvii. c. 28. the emperor Maurice commanded the celebration of the κοίμησις τῆς Θεοτόκου on the 15th August. So also in the Kalendar. Rom. of the eighth century, ed Fronto-Fabricius. p. 221: Die xv. mens. Aug. sollemnia de pausatione s. Mariae. The Frank Church, on the other hand, celebrated it on the 18th January (Mabillon liturg. Gallican. p. 118 ss. 211 ss.) In the eighth century they did not go beyond the pausatio or dormitio, Beda de locis sanctis, an extract from the account of the travels of a Frank bishop, Arculf, who had been in Palestine shortly before 700, c. 7: In the valley of Josaphat was a church of Mary, and in it an altar, ad eius dexteram monumentum vacuum, in quo s. Maria aliquamdiu pausasse dicitur, sed a quo vel quando sit ablata, nescitur. Introduction of the festum assumptionis into the Frank Church, see note 10. Anastasius in vita C. Paschalis:—fecit—vestem de chrysoclavo, habentem historiam, qualiter b. Dei Genetrix Maria corpore est assumta. vita cv. Leonis iv.: octavam Assumptionis b. Dei Genetricis diem, quae minime Romae antea colebatur, celebrari praecepit. Hincmari carmen ad b. Virg. Mariam in A. Maji classicorum auctorum v. 455:—

> Quae caro sancta Dei non est corrupta sepulchro,
> Nec tua, qua corpus sumpserat ipse Deus.
> Cum quo stella maris resides in culmine caeli,
> Concelebrata piis laudibus angelicis.

Wandelberti martyrolog. ad. 18. kal. Sept.:—

> Octava et decima mundi lux flosque Maria
> Angelico comitata choro petit aethera Virgo.

Supperstitious writings contributed to recommend the festival. Thus the sermo b. Hieronymi do ipsius Dominae assumtione, which a monk of Corbey affirmed to be spurious, but Hincmar defended (Flodoardi hist. eccl. Remensis lib. iii. c. 5. Mabil. ann. Bened. T. iii. lib. 35, no. 100). There were also a lib. and a sermo. de assumt b. Mariae falsely attributed to Augustine (in the old edition serm. de Sanctis 34 and 35, in the Benedictine edition, T. v. ap. sermo. 208, and T. vi. app. p. 249). However, Hunfried, bishop of Terouanne, A. D. 862, still needed a miracle for introducing this festival into his diocese. See annal. Bertin. ad ann. 862. Notker balbulus in Martyrologio (Canisii lectt. ant ed. Bas-

1st November.[18] The circumstance that the French, after *Dio-*

nage ii. iii. 167) defends the account of Gregor. Tur., but adds : De
quibus quia doctissimi tractatores videntur inter se dissidere, non est
meum in tam brevi opusculo definire : hoc tamen certissime cum universali Ecclesia et credimus et confitemur, quia si reverendissimum illud
corpus, ex quo Deus est incarnatus, adhuc alicubi in terra celatur, revelatio utique ipsius ad destructionem Antichristi reservatur. But still
we find about 1004 Atto Vercellensis in assumptionem b. Mariae (in
A. Maji vett. scriptt. nova collectio vi. ii. 39) : Corporis vero ejus jam
factam resurrectionem affirmare minime audemus, quia nec a ss. Patribus hoc declaratum esse cognoscimus. Denique in valle Josaphat ejus
sepulturae manet locus, ubi tamen ejus non reperitur corpus. Sed qui
de ea ineffabiliter carnem eduxit, ipse quid de ejus sit corpore novit.
Tamen sive in corpore, sive extra corpus, super choros angelorum in
caelis exaltatam confitemur.

[13] In the Greek Church the Sunday after Whitsuntide is called ἡ κυριακὴ τῶν ἁγίων πάντων (Heineccius Abbild. der griech. Kirche iii. 183)
as early as the time of Chrysostom (cf. his ἐγκώμιον εἰς τοὺς ἁγίους
πάντας ed. Montf. ii. 711. Leo Allad. de hebd. et domin. Graec. c. 31.)
In the Latin Church erroneously derived from Boniface IV. cf. Paulus
Diac. hist. Longob. lib. iv. c. 37: (Focas) Papa Bonifacio petente jussit
in veteri fano, quod Pantheon vocabant, ablatis idololatriae sordibus Ecclesiam beatae semper Virginis Mariae et omnium Martyrum fieri, ut
ubi quondam omnium non deorum sed daemonum cultus erat ibi deinceps omnium fieret memoria Sanctorum. In like manner Anastas. vit.
lxviii. Bonif. iv. This church was called s. Mariae ad Martyres (Anastas.
vit. lxxvii. Vitaliani and vit. lxxxii. Benedicti ii.), the festival of its dedication on the 13th May. Comp. the Martyrol. Aquilejense ap. Ado belonging to the beginning of the ninth century : iii.id. Maj. s. Mariae ad Martyres dedicationis dies agitur a Bonifacio Papa statutus. So also the
kalend. Rom. of the eighth century, ed 'Fronto-Fabricius, p. 198. Besides this festival the Martyrol. Aquil. of Ado mentions ad Kal. Nov.
Festivitas Sanctorum, quae celebris et generalis agitur Romae, which is
wanting in Fronto's calendar. (See Frontonis nota in ed Fabric. p. 233).
Consequently, 1. The festival oo. ss. is different from the dedic. Mariae
ad Martt. 2. It was celebrated in Rome as early as the eighth century,
and in addition to the dedic. Mariae ad Martt. Probably the celebration of it is connected with the oratorium in honorem omnium Sanctorum (see Anastasius in vita Greg. iii.) erected by Gregory III. Ado is
the first to confound the two festivals. Adonis martyrol. ad. iii. idus
Maj. : Natalis s. Mariae ad Martyres. Phoca Imperatore b. Bonifacius
Papa in veteri fano quod Pantheon vocabatur,—ecclesiam beatae semper
virginis Mariae et omnium Martyrum dedicavit. Cujus dedicationis
sacratissima dies agitur Romae iii. idus Maji. Id. ad. kal. Nov. Festivitas SS. omnium. Petente namque P. Bonifacio jussit Phocas Imp.
in veteri fano, quod Pantheon vocabatur,—ecclesiam b. semperque virg.
Mariae et omnium Martyrum fieri, ut ubi quondam omnium non Deorum sed daemoniorum cultus agebatur, ibi deinceps omnium fieret me-

nysius the Areopagite had become known to them in the writings
attributed to him,[14] confounded him with their own Dionysius,[15]

moria Sanctorum : quae ab illo tempore kal. Nov. in urbe Roma celebris et generalis agitur.   Sed et in Galliis, monente s. recordationis
Gregorio Pontifici, piissimus Ludovicus Imp. omnibus regni et imperii
sui Episcopis consentientibus, statuit, ut solenniter festivitas oo. SS. in
praedicta die annuatim perpetuo ageretur.   As the dedicatio s. Mar. ad
Martt. was not observed in other countries, Usuardus in martyrol. explained the matter thus : Kal. Novemb. Festivitas b. Dei genetricis et
omnium Martyrum, quam Bonifacius Papa celebrem et generalem instituit agi omnibus annis in urbe Roma.   Sed et Gregorius Pontifex
postmodum decrevit, eandem in honore omnium Sanctorum solemniter
observari ab omni Ecclesia.   Ptolomaeus Luc. hist. eccl. ix. c. 6.
(Murat scriptt. rer. Ital. xi. 921) and Durandus (rationale divin. offic.
lib. vii. c. 34) ; that Boniface had fixed the festum b. Mariae ad Martyres for the iv. [iii.] idus Maji, but that Gregory IV. transferred it to
the Kal. Nov. and converted the festival into a fest. omnium SS.   This
opinion, though frequently repeated, is manifestly erroneous.

[14] As soon as the Franks heard of the writings of Dionysius they
were eager after them, because they immediately called to their thoughts
the patron saint of the country.   Pauli P. ep. ad Pipinum (cod. Car.
no. 65. ap. Mansi xii. 612) in Embolo : Direximus etiam Praecellentiae
vestrae et libros, quantos reperire potuimus, i. e.—Dionysii Ariopagiti
libros etc. (Neander Denkwürdigkeiten iii. ii. 54. even supposes a
trace of the Pseudodionys. in Columbanus.)   Pope Hadrian I. presented these writings to Fulradus, abbot of St Denys (Mabillon ann.
Bened. lib. xxxi. c. 42.)   King Michael sent them, 827, to Lewis the
Debonaire.   See rescriptum Hilduini ad Ludov. [in the Areopagiticis]
§ 4.   Caeterum de notitia librorum ejus, quos patrio sermone conscripsit,—lectio nobis per Dei gratiam et vestram ordinationem, cujus dispensatione interpretatos scrinia nostra petentibus reserant, satisfacit.
Authenticos autem eosdem libros Graeca lingua conscriptos, quando
Oeconomus Ecclesiae Constantinop. et caeteri missi Michaelis, legatione
publica ad vestram gloriam Compendio functi sunt, in ipsa vigilia solen-
nitatis s. Dionysii pro munere magno suscepimus.   Hence Michael did
not send them in a Latin translation, as Mabillon ann. Bened. lib. xxix.
c. 59. and the hist. liter. de la France T. v. p. 425. represent.   John
Scotus translated them anew at the instance of Charles the Bald, about
859 (comp. his two dedications addressed to Charles, and Anastasii bibl.
ep. ad Carol. in Jac. Usserii vett. epistolarum Hibernic. sylloge, Dublini 1632. p. 58. and Nicolai P. i. ep. ad Car. Calv. in Bulaei hist. univ.
Paris. i. 184), and wrote expositions of them (see Ang. Maji classicorum auctorum v. p. xlvi.), comp. Bähr röm. Lit. im karol. Zeitalter
S. 486.

[15] First in the (written under Charlemagne) gestis Dagoberti c. 3.
(ap. Bouquet ii. 580), that Dionysius Episc. Parisiensis temporibus
Domitiani was martyred : and Synod. Paris. A. D. 824 (ap. Mansi xiv.
466), that he a. s. Clemente in Gallias cum duodenario numero primus

praedicator directus et—martyrio coronatus est. Hincmar relates (823) that he had read something of the same kind in the actis s. Sanctini (Hincmari epist. ad Carol. in the Areopagiticis and in Mabillonii vett. analect. ed. ii. p. 212.) The two Dionysii were completely confounded in the Actis Dionysii, which were first printed in the act. SS. mens. Octob. iv. 792, and are older than Hilduin (see act. SS. l. c. p. 790. no. 17 ss. p. 701. no. 23 ss.) The fable indeed was completed and made more general by Hilduin's vita et passio Dionysii etc. This Hilduin was abbot of St Denys, and the work was written by order of Lewis the Debonaire 834. (Areopagitica ed. Matth. Galenus, Colon. 1563. 8. and contained in Surii vitis SS. ad ix. Oct. : Epist. Ludov. P. ad Hilduinum—Rescriptum Hild. ad Lud. Imp.—Ep. Hild. ad cunctos s. cath. matris Ecclesiae filios et fidelos—Passio Dionysii—Revelatio facta s. P. Stephano—Ep. Hincmari Rhem. ad Carol. Imp. de Dion. Ar.—Ep. Anastasii bibl. ad Carol. Imp. contra falsas quorundam opiniones, asserentium b. Dionys. Parisiorum Episc. non esse Areopagitam.) That Hilduin was not a lying impostor originating the fable, as is maintained by J. Launoji judicium de Areopagiticis, Paris. 1641. 8. and is frequently asserted, may be seen from act. SS. mens. Oct. iv. 696. The fable was doubted for a long time on account of Gregor. Tur. hist. Fr. i. 28. (See vol. i. Div. i. § 57. not. 2), and because the martyrologies, as also Usuardus, Ado, Notker (other instances in Launoji discussio responsionis de duobus Dionys. Paris. 1642. 8. cap. 19), distinguished two Dionysii, the Areopagita on the 3d October, and the Parisiensis on the 9th October. John Scotus epist. ad Car. Imp. (see note 14) says : Fertur praefatus Dionysius (Areopagita) fuisse discipulus atque adjutor Pauli Apostoli,—cujus Lucas commemorat in Act. Apost. et Dionysius Corinth. etc. Hunc eundem quoque non praefati viri, sed alii moderni temporis asserunt—temporibus P. Clementis—Romam venisse, et ab eo—in partes Galliarum directum fuisse etc. For the purpose of overthrowing these doubts the Roman abbot Anastasius, about 875, translated a Greek vita Dionysii, in which the same fable appears. Cf. Anastasii ep. ad Carol. Imp. in Areopagiticis : Passionem s. hieromartyris Dionysii quondam Areopagitae—latino eloquio tradidi,—etsi non ex toto verbum e verbo, sensum tamen penitus hauriens. Cesset ergo jam quorundam opinio, perhibentium, non esse Areopagitam Dionysium eum, qui prope Parisium corpore ac virtutibus redolet, cum hoc et Graecorum quoque stylus—testetur et praedicet. Hujus autem textum b. Methodius, qui a sede apostolica Constantinopolin Presbyter missus, ejusdem urbis tenuit pontificium,—edidit, pauca de multis praecedentibus scriptis excerpens. This Methodius (from 842 patriarch of Constantinople) had formerly been deputy of the patriarch Nicephorus in Rome, and was always in close connection with Rome. It is therefore beyond a doubt that he drew the materials for his vita Dionysii from Western sources, perhaps, as Sirmond and Launoi think, from Hilduini Areopagiticis. Since this time the fable obtained general belief, till in the 17th century Sirmond, and especially Launoi, detected the groundlessness of it. See the numerous controversial writings on the subject in Fabricii salutaris lux Evang. p. 386. and Walchii bibl. theolog. iii. 195.

helped to obtain acceptance for the Dionysian mysticism. About the same time the free Spaniards discovered their apostle *James the elder* in the person afterwards called Compostella,[16] and found in him a powerful ally against the Saracens.

SIXTH CHAPTER.

HISTORY OF CHURCH DISCIPLINE.

Particular Sources: Besides the capitularies of the French kings, and the decrees. of synods and individual bishops: Halitgarii ep. Cameracensis († 831) opus de vitiis et virtutibus, remediis peccatorum, et ordine vel judiciis poenitentiae, libb. vi. (in Canisii lectt. ant. ed. Basnage. T. ii. P. ii. p. 87.)

§ 19.

By the laws concerning penance, which had long ago become milder, it was now established, that only *public* sins should be visited with public penance, and that too by bishops in synodi-

[16] Even Isidore Hispal. de ortu ac obitu Patrum c. 71. (opp. ed. Arevalo v. 183.) says, that this apostle preached the gospel to the Spaniards. Respecting the finding of his body the oldest source is the historia Compostellana of Munno, bishop of Montognedo, written in the beginning of the 12th century, published in Florez España sagrada xx. 8. an extract in the act. SS. mens. Jul. vi. 16. The discovery belongs therefore to the time of Adefonsi Casti (Alfonso el Casto v. 791-842) and Charlemagne. It is put sometimes in the year 798, sometimes 808, sometimes 816 (so Baronius ad h. a. no. 48-52), sometimes still later. Ado, however (about 858), has in his martyrolog. ad viii. kal. Aug. merely: Natalis b. Jacobi Zebedaei Apostoli. On the other hand Usuardus (about 876) adds: Hujus b. Apostoli sacratissima ossa ab Hierosolymis ad Hispanias translata, et in ultimis earum finibus condita, celeberrima illarum gentium veneratione excoluntur. The battle of Clavijo said to have been won by his miraculous assistance, 849 [first narrated by Rodericus rer. Hisp. lib. iv. c. 13), is doubted even by Spanish historians. See act. SS. Jul. vi. 37.

cal judicatures ;[1] while *private* offences were confessed to the
priests, who immediately granted absolution under the condition
of a time of penance to be expected afterwards,[2] without, however, holding confession to be an indispensable condition of the
forgiveness of sins.[3]   The substitution of other so-called pene-

---

[1] See above § 8. not. 26.

[2] S. Bonifacii statuta (A. D. 745, first in d'Achery spicil. i. 507, ap.
Mansi xii. 386.) c. 31. and thence extracted in capitularium lib. vi.
c. 206. where the corrupted text must be corrected after that source :
Quia varia necessitate praepedimur, Canonum statuta de reconciliandis
poenitentibus pleniter observare, propterea emnino non dimittatur. Cu-
ret unusquisque Presbyter [an addition in the capit. : jussione Episcopi de
occultis tantum, quia de manifestis Episcopos semper convenit judicare],
statim post acceptam confessionem poenitentium, singulos data oratione
reconciliari.   Capitula Rodulfi Archiep. Bituricensis (in Baluzii miscell. vi. 139.   Mansi xiv. 962) c. 44 : Quorum peccata in publico sunt,
in publico debet esse poenitentia per tempora, quae Episcopi arbitrio
poenitentibus secundum differentiam peccatorum decernuntur. Quorum
autem peccata occulta sunt, et spontanea confessione soli tantummodo
Presbytero ab eis fuerint revelata, horum occulta debet esse poenitentia
secundum Presbyteri judicium, cui confessi sunt, ne infirmi in Ecclesia
scandalizentur videntes eorum poenas, quorum penitus ignorant causas.
The procedure at confession is described by Alcuinus de divinis officiis
(de div. off. libri, ed. M. Hittorp. Colon. 1568. fol. p. 51.) How much
rarer public penance had become is shewn by the decrees of the three
councils A. D. 813, Arelat. c. 26, Rhem. c. 31, Cabillon. c. 25, Jonas
Episc. Aurelian. († 843) de institutione laicorum lib. i. c. 10. (d'Achery
spicileg. i. 258), Rhaban. de instit. cleric. c. 30. cf. J. Morinus de disciplina in administratione sacramenti poenitentiae, Paris. 1651. fol.
R. v. Raumer's Einwirkung des Christenth. auf die althochdeutsche
Sprache, Stuttgart 1845. S. 254.

[3] Theodulfi Episc. Aurelian. capitulare ann. 797 ad parochiae suae
sacerdotes c. 30. (Mansi xiii. p. 1001) : Omni etenim die Deo in oratione nostra, aut semel, aut bis, aut quanto amplius possumus, confiteri
debemus peccata nostra.   Quia confessio, quam sacerdotibus facimus,
hoc nobis adminiculum affert, quia accepto ab eis salutari consilio, salu-
berrimis poenitentiae observationibus, sive mutuis orationibus peccatorum
maculas diluimus.   Confessio vero, quam soli Deo facimus, in hoc
juvat, quia quanto nos memores sumus peccatorum nostrorum, tanto
horum Deus obliviscitur : et e contrario, quanto nos horum obliviscimur,
tanto Dominus reminiscitur.   Conc. Cabilon. ann. 813. can. 33 : Quidam Deo solummodo confiteri debere dicunt peccata, quidam vero sacerdotibus confitenda esse percensent : quod utrumque non sine magno
fructu intra sanctam fit Ecclesiam.   Ita dumtaxat et Deo, qui remissor
est peccatorum, confiteamur peccata nostra, et cum David dicamus :
" Delictum meum cognitum tibi feci," etc. (Ps. xxxii. 5.)   Et secundum institutionem Apostoli confiteamur alterutrum peccata nostra, et

tential works for the penitential time, the conditions for doing
which acts had already found their way into the *libri poenitentiales,*[4] was still considered an abuse.[5]   As excommunication be-

oremus pro invicem, ut salvemur (Jac. v. 16.)   Confessio itaque, quae
Deo fit, purgat peccata : ea vero, quae sacerdoti fit, docet, qualiter ipsa
purgentur peccata.   Deus namque salutis et sanitatis auctor et largitor,
plerumque hanc praebet suae potentiae invisibili administratione, plerumque medicorum operatione.

[4] Particularly in England, first in Theodori Cantuar. lib. poenit. (see
vol. i. div. 2. § 133. not. 11.   Then similar insertions are found in the
lib. poen, Romanus, as well as in the shorter edition, which Halitgar.
Camerac. appended to his books de poenitentia (ap. Canissius-Basnage
ii. ii. 134), as well as in the more copious edition (ibid. p. 122. and
129).

[5] Conc. Cloveshov. ann. 747 (under Cuthbert, the second successor
of Theodore in the see of Canterbury) can. 26. (ap. Mansi xii. 403) :
Postremo igitur (sicuti nova adinventio, juxta placitum scilicet propriae
voluntatis suae, nunc plurimis periculosa consuetudo est) non sit eleemosyna porrecta ad minuendam vel ad mutandam satisfactionem per
jejunium et reliqua expiationis opera, a sacerdote Dei pro suis criminibus jure canonico indictam, sed magis ad augmentandam emendationem
suam, ut eo citius placetur divinae indignationis ira.   Bonum est
omnino psalmodiae insistere, bonum est genua saepius veraci flectere
intentione, bonum est eleemosynas quotidie dare : sed pro his non est
abstinentia remittenda, non est jejunium impositum semel juxta Ecclesiae regulam, sine qua non remittuntur ulla peccata, relaxandum.
Can. 27 : Non eis eo licentius—peccare,—vel jejunium pro peccatis
indictum relaxare, vel eleemosynas minus largire, ullo modo licet, quo
pro ipsis alios psalmos cantare putant, vel jejunare.   Nuper quidam
dives secundum hoc saeculum, petens reconcilationem pro magno quodam facinore suo citius sibi dari, affirmans in suis literis idem nefas
juxta multorum promissa in tantum esse expiatum, ut si deinceps vivere
possit, trecentorum annorum pro eo plene jejunium, satisfactionum
modis per aliorum scilicet psalmodiam, et jejunium, et eleemosynas,
persolutum esset, excepto illius jejunio, et quamvis ipse utcumque vel
parum jejunaret.   Ergo si ita placari per alios potest divina justitia, cur
divites—difficilius voce veritatis regnum intrare caelorum—dicuntur ?
etc. Conc. Cabilonense ann. 813 can. 36. against those, qui ex industria
peccantes propter eleemosynarum largitionem quandam sibi promittunt
impunitatem.   Can. 38 : Modus autem poenitentiae peccata sua confitentibus aut per antiquorum canonum institutionem, aut per s. Scripturarum auctoritatem, aut per ecclesiasticam consuetudinem—imponi debet, repudiatis ac penitus eliminatis libellis quos poenitentiales vocant,
quorum sunt certi errores, incerti auctores.   Qui dum pro peccatis gra-
vibus leves quosdam et inusitatos imponunt poenitentiae modos, con-
suunt pulvillos secundum propheticum sermonem, sub omni cubito
manus, et faciunt cervicalia sub capite universae 'aetatis ad capi-
endas animas, Ezech. 13. 18. (repeated in Conc. Mogunt, ann. 847.

came less frequent, in consequence of this arrangement in the system of penance,[6] it had become more fearful by the civil forfeitures which were connected with it,[7] and by the distinction which began to be made in the ninth century between *excommunication* and *anathema*.[8] Besides, in all mat-

c. 31. and in the Capitulis Rodulfi Archiepisc. Bituricensis c. 33. ap. Mansi xiv. 958; similarly Conc. Paris. ann. 829. lib. i. c. 32). Can. 45 : Nam et a quibusdam, qui Romam Turonumve, et alia quaedam loca sub praetextu orationis inconsulte peragrant, plurimum erratur. Sunt Presbyteri et Diacones et caeteri in clero constituti, qui negligenter viventes, in eo purgari se a peccatis putant, et ministerio suo fungi debere, si praefata loca attingant. Sunt nihilominus laici, qui putant se impune peccare aut peccasse, quia haec loca oraturi frequentant,—non attendentes quod ait b. Hieronymus : Non Hierosolymam vidisse sed Hierosolymis bene vixisse laudandum est. Qui vero peccata sua sacerdotibus, in quorum sunt parochiis, confessi sunt, et ab his agendae poenitentiae consilium acceperunt, si orationibus insistendo, eleemosynas largiendo, vitam emendando, mores componendo, Apostolorum limina, vel quorumlibet Sanctorum invisere desiderant, horum est devotio modis omnibus collaudanda.

6 Caroli M. capit. iii. anni 803, and thence extracted in capitul. lib. i. c. 136. lib. vi. c. 217 : Ut excommunicationes passim (for which capit lib. vi. subito) et sine causa non fiant.

7 Cf. § 8. not. 25.

8 The germs of such a distinction in Augustin. hom. 50. de poenitentia : prohibitio (a communione) mortalis and medicinalis. Syn. Rom. v. sub Symmacho A.D. 504 (Mansi viii. 298) : si vero monachus aut laicus fuerit, communione privetur, et si non emendaverit vitium, anathemate feriatur. Cf. du Pin de ant. eccl. discipl. p. 261 ss. Synodus Regiaticina A.D. 850 can. 12 : Hoc autem omnibus Christianis intimandum est, quia hi, qui sacri altaris communione privati, et pro suis sceleribus reverendis adytis exclusi publicae poenitentiae subjugati sunt, nullo militiae saecularis ut concilio, nullamque reipublicae debent administrare dignitatem. Qui vero administratione Episcopi seu sacerdotum perpetrato palam scelere poenitentiae remedium suscipere noluerint, magis abjiciendi sunt, anathematizandi scilicet, tamquam putrida ac desperata membra ab universalis Ecclesiae corpore dissecandi, cujusmodi jam inter Christianos nulla legum, nulla morum, nulla collegii participatio est, quibus neque in ipso exitu communicatur, et quorum neque post mortem saltem inter defunctos fideles commemoratio fit. Sed si ad hoc irrevocabile judicium obdurati cordus contemtus trahit, non sine magna tamen examinatione veniendum est, et omnia sacerdoti prius experienda, nec absque metropolitani cogitatione, et provincialium Episcoporum communi judicio quemlibet anathematizandum esse permittimus. Comp. Arsenii Episc. (legate of Nicol. I.) ep. gener. ad omnes Episc. (ap. Mansi xv. 326). Planck's Gesch. d. kirchlichen Gesellschaftsverfassung. iii. 507.

X

ters of this kind the highest appeal was to the diocesan bishop.[9]

[9] Ahytonis Episc. Basiliensis capitulare (about 820) c. 18. (Mansi xiv. 396): Nullus ordinatus sive ordinandus migret de sua parochia ad aliam nec ad limina Apostolorum causa orationis, Ecclesiae suae cura derelicta, nec ad palatium causa interpellandi, nec a communione suspensus ab alio communionem recipiendi, sine permissione et praescientia Episcopi sui: quod si fecerit, nihil valet hujusmodi communio, aut ordinatio, aut demigratio. Et hoc omnibus fidelibus denuntiandum, ut qui causa orationis ad limina Apostolorum pergere cupiunt, domi confiteantur peccata sua et sic proficiscantur: quia a proprio Episcopo aut sacerdote ligandi aut exsolvendi sunt, non ab extraneo.

SECOND DIVISION.

FROM NICOLAUS I. TO GREGORY VII.

A.D. 858—1073.

MOST IMPORTANT SOURCES.

1. Byzantines: Georg. Cedrenus and Joh. Zonaras (see preface of Division I.)
2. Latins: Annales Fuldenses and Bertiniani (see pref. to Div. I. Part II.) Regino, abbot of Prüm († 915), Chronicon from the birth of Christ till 907, important from 870, with continuation till 967, best edited in Pertzii monum. i. 537. Flodoardus, canon and keeper of the archives in Rheims, afterwards abbot of a neighbouring monastery († 966), hist. Ecclesiae Remensis libb. iv. till 948 ed. J. Sirmond. Paris 611. 8. G. Colvenerius. Duaci 1617. 8. Bibl. pp. Lugd. xvii. 500. Annales from 919—966. ap. Pertz v. 363. Comp. Bähr's Rom. Liter. in karol. Zeitalter. S. 274. 188.—Luitprandus, bishop of Cremona († 972) wrote the history of his time from 893 to 964 : Antapodosis libb. vi. and de rebus gestis Ottonis M. best ap. Pertz. v. 264. The credibility of this source which is often underestimated by those who follow Muratori, is vindicated by Martini in the Denkschr. d. K. Akad. zu München für 1809 and 10. Hist. Class. S. 3 ff. R. A. Koepke de vita et scriptis Liudprandi. Berol. 1842. 8.—Richerus, monk in the monastery of St. Remigius in Rheims, a friend of Gerbert's wrote about 995 historiarum libb. iv. from 888 till 995, especially important from 969 and onward, ap. Pertz. v. 561. Riches historie de son temps par Guadet T. i. Paris 1845. 8. (Latin and French with introduction and commentary)—Thietmarus, bishop of Merseburg († 1018) chronicon, embracing the period of the Saxon emperors, first ed. complete in Leibnitii scriptt. Brunsvecens, T. i., then 'ed. J. A. Wagner, Norimb. 1807. 4. in German by M. Ursinus, Dresd. 17 0. 8. and J. M. Lappenberg in Pertz monum. v. 723.—Comp. M. Th. Contzen, die Geschichtschreiber d. sächs. Kaiserzeit nach ihrem Leben u. ihren Schriften Regensburgh 1837. 8.—Hermannus Contractus, monk in Reichenau († 1054), chronicon from the birth of Christ till 1054, important for chronology, especially from 1045, an important source of history (ap. Pertz vii. 67), continued by Bertholdus, Hermann's disciple, and likewise monk of Reichenau, till 1080 (ap. Pertz vii. 264) : both abbreviated and continued till 1100 by Bernoldus, Bernaldus, or Bernardus, monk in St Blascia (ap. Pertz. vii. 385). Hermann and his continuator were first edited complete by P. Aem. Ussermann in the monumenta res Alemannicas illustrantia. 2. Tomi. Typis San-Blasianis 1790 and 1792. 4to. Comp. Docen in the Archive. für ältere deutsche Geschichtkunde iii. 1. Stenzel's Gesch. Deutschlands unter den fränkischen Kaisern, ii. 99.—Marianus Scotus, monk, last in Mentz (†1082), chron. from the creation of the world to the year

X 2

1082, continued by Dodechinu till 1200 in Pistorii rerum Germ. scriptor. T. i. (Mar. Scoti lib. iii. from 1.—1082 ed. G. Waitz ap. Pertz vii. 841). —Lambertus, monk in Hersfeld, usually but incorrectly styled Schafna-burgensis, annales, fullest from 1040—1077. ap. Pistorius T. i., then ed. J. C. Krause. Hal. 1797. 8. in German by F. B. Buchholz, Frankf. a. M. 1819. 8. ed. Hesse ap. Pertz vii. 134. Comp. Stenzel ii. 101. Locherer, in the Giessener Jahrbuchern f. Theol. und christliche Philosophie 1834. ii. 3.—Sigebertus, monk in Gemblours († 1113), chronicon, continua-tion of Jerome from 381—1112. ap. Pistorius T. i. ed. L. C. Bethmann ap. Pertz viii. 268. cf. S. Hirsch. comm. de. Sigeb. Gembl. vita et scriptis. Berol. 1841. 8.

FIRST PART.

HISTORY OF THE WESTERN CHURCH.

FIRST CHAPTER.

HISTORY OF THE PAPACY.

§ 20.

PSEUDOISIDORIAN DECRETALS AND CONSTANTINE'S DEEDS OF GIFT.

Dav. Blondelli Pseudo-Isidorus et Turrianus vapulantes. Genev. 1628. 4. C. Blasci comm. de collect. cann. Isid. Merc. in Gallandii sylloge. ed. Ma-gont. ii. 1. (Spittler's) Gesch. des canon. Rechts bis auf die Zeiten des fals-chen Isidorus. Halle 1778. S. 220 ff. (in Spittler's Werken, herausgeg. v. Wächter Bd. i.)   Planck's Gesch. d. christl. kirchl. Gesellschaftsverf. ii. 800 ff.   F. Walter's Lehrbuch des Kirchenrechts, vierte Ausl. (Bonn. 1829). S. 135 ff.   Möhler's Fragmente aus und über Pseudo-Isidor, in his Schriften u. Aufsatzen, herausgegeben v. Döllinger (Regensburg 1839. 2 Bde.) i. 283.   F. H. Knust de fontibus et consilio pseudoisidorianae collectionis. Götting. 1832. 4.

About the middle of the ninth century appeared gradually an Isidorian collection,[1] enlarged with many false decretals,

---

[1] The preface begins : Isidorus Mercator servus Christi lectori conservo suo et parenti in Domino fidei salutem. The Merlin editor omits Merca-

whose object generally tended to counteract the oppression and the disorder of the clergy[2] as well as ecclesiastical irregularities generally, which were the consequences of political divisions and disturbances under the successors of Charlemagne.[3]

tor, some Codd. have, partly as a gloss, Peccator (as, for example, Rabanus calls himself before some of his letters Rabanus peccator. See Kunstmann's Rab. Maurus S. 215, 219). See Ballerini de ant. collection. canonum (prefixed to T. iii. opp. Leonis, and in Gallandii syll.) P. iii. c. 6, no. 18. Blascus l. c. cap. 6, p. 35. The Pseudo-isidorian collection has undergone many additions, omissions, and alterations, and appears therefore perfectly pure in few codices. So also not even in the only complete edition where it is found undivided : J. Merlini tom. prim. iv. concilior. generall. xlvii. conc. provinc. decrett. lxix. Pontificum ab Apostolis usque ad Zachariam I. Isidoro autore, Paris. 1523. fol. (reprinted Colon. 1530. fol. Paris. 1535. 8). Inquiries respecting its original form see in Ballerini l. c. P. iii. c. 5-8. Spittler l. c. S. 221 ff. Comp. the description of five Pseudo-isidorian MSS., especially a Cod. Vatican, written about 868 in France, in the notices et extraits vi. 265. A critical edition, such as Coustant designed in the second part of his epistt. Pontiff., is still wanting. It consisted of three parts : I. 61 epistolae decretales of the popes of the first three centuries, from Clement to Melchiades (two from Clement to James were before forged, but newly interpolated, 59 Pseudoisidoriana). II. Canons of councils, chiefly from the genuine Isidorian collection. III. Epist. decrett. from Sylvester till Gregory the great, of which 35 Pseudoisid., the others mostly from the Isidorian collection. Many regulations were fabricated after the accounts of the liber pontificalis. These, which were intended only to give credibility to the imposture, must therefore be left out of the question in determining the object of the imposture. Blascus l. c. cap. 15. How rich this period generally was in such forgeries may be seen in Spittler l. c. S. 243 and 252.

[2] The contents and sources in general are pointed out ap. Knust p. 22 ; the sources of individual documents are indicated ibid. p. 33.

[3] Comp. § 7, not. 24. Agobardus de privilegio et jure sacerdotii c. 1 : pressurae, odia et despectio Ecclesiarum atque Clericorum nunc infervescere coeperunt saeculis inaudito et inusitato modo. Idem de dispensatione ecclesiasticarum rerum c. 15 : Nunc in quibusdam locis nullus ordo hominum, sive sint liberi, sive servi, de habitatione sua tam infidus est, ut sacerdotes : utpote qui nullo modo securi esse possint, nec scire, quot diebus Ecclesiam vel habitaculum suum eis habere sit licitum. Nunc non solum possessiones ecclesiasticae, sed ipsae etiam Ecclesiae cum possessionibus venundantur. Thus the synod at Thionville 844 complained to the other assembled kings (Pertz iii. 380, Baluz. cap. ii. 7) c. 1 : constat hanc sanctam Ecclesiam,—praedecessorum vestrorum multo labore redintegratam ac adunatam atque gubernatam, vestra discordia esse discissam et perturbatam atque afflictam. c. 2 : monemus ut sedes, quae vestra discordia—sine Episcopis viduatae manent, submota funditus peste simoniacae haereseos —aut Episcopos—a vobis re-

These decretals consisted of admonitions, instructions, and regulations, compiled for the most part from existing ecclesiastical literature. But they are of historical importance, only in consequence of the new principles of ecclesiastical law by which, developing a tendency that had arisen already in the Church amid the weakness and disunion of worldly power (see § 7, note 25 ff.) they were meant to make the Church independent of the state, and to give it a self-dependent centre of protection in the Romish see. Exaltation of the episcopal dignity ;[4] numerous definitions for the purpose of securing the clergy, and in particular, the bishops against attacks ;[5] limitation of the metropolitans,[6] who were

gulariter designatos—accipiant, aut quae suis Episcopis quacunque occasione privatae sunt, canonice eos—recipiant. c. 5: On the restoration of the monasteries bestowed on laymen. In like manner the Concil. in Verno palatio 844. (Pertz iii. 383. Baluz. ii. 13). The Synod of Mainz 847 to Lewis the German (Mansi xiv. 901): Proh dolor, his temporibus nec loca sancta venerantur, neque ministri Dei condigne honorantur : sed versa vice illi, qui honorari debuerunt, flagellantur, spoliantur, atque diversis calumniis franguntur.   Comp. Möhler i. 321.   Such a condition is also presupposed and indicated in the Pseudoisidorianis. See Möhler i. 294.   Ex. gr. Pii i. ep. ii.: Ad sedem apostolicam perlatum est, quod—praedia divinis usibus tradita quidam humanis applicant usibus, et Domino Deo, cui tradita sunt, ea subtrahunt, ut suis usibus inserviant.   Zephyrini ep. ii.: Nuntiatum est sedi apostolicae per apocrisiarios vestros, quosdam fratrum nostrorum Episcoporum videlicet, ab ecclesiis et sedibus propriis pelli, suaque eis auferri supellectilia, et sic nudos et exspoliatos ad judicia vocari.

[4] Ex. gr. Urbani P. (A.D. 222) ep. unic.: Ideo ista praetulimus, carissimi, ut intelligatis potestatem Episcoporum vestrorum, in eisque Dominum veneremini, et eos ut animas vestras diligatis, et quibus illi non communicant, non communicetis, et quos ejecerint non recipiatis. Valde enim timenda est sententia Episcopi, licet injuste liget aliquem, quod tamen summopere providere debet. Pontiani P. (A.D. 230) ep. 1: De illis enim dictum est, " qui vos contristabit, me contristabit, et qui vobis facit injuriam, recipiet id, quod inique gessit;" et alibi : " Qui vos audit, me audit, et qui vos spernit, me spernit. Qui autem me spernit, spernit eum, qui me misit." Hi enim non sunt infestandi, sed honorandi. In eis quoque Dominus honoratur, cujus legatione funguntur. Hi ergo si forte ceciderint, a fidelibus sunt sublevandi et portandi. Accusandi autem non sunt ab infamibus, aut sceleratis, vel inimicis, aut alterius sectae hominibus vel religionis. Si peccaverint, a reliquis arguantur sacerdotibus, sed et a summis pontificibus constringantur, et non a saecularibus aut malae vitae hominibus arguantur vel arceantur.

[5] Here belong the many declamations against robbing clergymen, and the new principles respecting accusations brought against them,

often very much independent of the civil power ; elevation of the

the last derived in part from the Roman law, cf. Blascus cap. 8, p. 54 ss. Walter S. 151 ss. Ex. gr. Pii P. ep. i. [ann. 147] : Oves pastorem suum non reprehendant, plebs vero Episcopum non accuset, nec vulgus eum arguat, quum non est discipulus super magistrum, neque servus supra dominum. Episcopi autem a Deo sunt judicandi, qui eos sibi oculos elegit, nam a subditis aut pravae vitae hominibus non sunt arguendi vel accusandi aut lacerandi, ipso domino exemplum dante' qui per se ipsum, et non per alium vendentes sacerdotes, et ementes ejecit de templo etc. Eleutherii P. ep. De accusationibus Clericorum,—quia omnes eorum accusationes difficile est ad sedem apostolicam deferre, finitiva Episcoporum tantum judicia huc deferantur, ut hujus s. sedis auctoritate finiantur. Nec in eorum Ecclesiis alii aut praeponantur aut ordinentur, antequam hic eorum juste terminentur negotia. Quoniam quamvis liceat apud Provinciales et Metropolitanos atque Primates eorum ventilare accusationes vel criminationes, non tamen licet diffinire secus quam praedictum est. Reliquorum vero Clericorum causas apud Provinciales et Metropolitanos ac Primates et ventilare et juste finire licet. Eusebii P. ep. ii. : In scripturis vestris reperimus, quosdam Episcopos vestris in partibus a propriis ovibus accusatos, aliquos videlicet ex suspicione, et aliquos ex certa ratione : et idcirco quosdam esse rebus suis exspoliatos, quosdam vero a propria sede pulsos. Quos sciatis nec ad synodum—posse vocari, nec in aliquo judicari, antequam cuncta, quae eis sublata sunt, legibus, potestati eorum redintegrentur. Prius ergo oportet omnia illis legibus redintegrari, et ecclesias, quae eis sublatae sunt, cum omni privilegio sibi restitui, et postmodum non sub angusti temporis spatio, sed tantum temporis spatium eis indulgeatur, quantum exspoliati vel expulsi esse videntur, antequam ad synodum convocentur, et ab omnibus quibusque suae provinciae Episcopis audiantur. Nam nec convocari ad causam, nec dijudicari potest exspoliatus vel expulsus, quia non est privilegium, quo exspoliari possit jam nudatus. Zephyrini P. ep. i. (A.D. 208): Patriarchae vero vel Primates accusatum discutientes Episcopum, non ante sententiam proferant finitivam, quam apostolica fulti auctoritate, aut reum seipsum confiteatur, aut per innocentes et regulariter examinatos convincatur testes. Qui minori non sint numero, quam illi discipuli fuerunt, quos Dominus ad adjumentum Apostolorum eligere praecepit, i e. septuaginta duo. (Even earlier it appears that this number of bishops was called to the condemnation of a bishop, either with reference to the 70 disciples, or to the great Jewish Sanhedrim. So Macedonius was deposed by 72 bishops, chron. Pasch. ad ann. 360 ; so Chronopius by 70, cod. Theod. xi. 36, 20, cf. Gothofred. ad h. l. So also the constitutio Sylvestri (cap. iii. ap. Mansi ii. 623), which had been previously inserted, demands : non damnabitur praesul nisi in septuaginta duobus ; but even Alcuinus ep. 92, ad Arnonem A.D. 800, interprets this sentence, non minus LXXII. testibus Pontificem accusandum esse. In like manner, too, Leo IV., about 850, see above, § 7, note 28. Since this regulation was carried out into practice in none of the two forms before Pseudoisidore in the west, we cannot suppose a change of the custom ; but the later acceptation of it

primates to be the first instruments of the popes ;[7] and in particular, an enlargement of the privileges of the Roman see ;[8] these

is merely a consequence of the ambiguity of the expression in the constit. Sylvestri.)   Accusatores autem eorum omni careant suspicione,
quia columnas suas Dominus firmiter stare voluit, non a quibuslibet
agitari.   Duodecim enim judices quilibet Episcopus accusatus, si necesse fuerit, eligat (so the Conc. Carthag. i. A.D. 348, can. 11, determines that a deacon shall be judged by three, a presbyter by six bishops:
si Episcopus, a XII. consacerdotibus audiatur, i. e. a successor of the
apostles by the apostolic number.   Also Leo IV. requires 12 bishops as
judges, or 72 witnesses.   See above, § 7, not. 28), a quibus ejus causa
juste judicetur : nec prius audiatur, aut excommunicetur, vel judicetur,
quam ipsi per se eligantur, et regulariter vocato ad suorum primo conventum Episcoporum, per eos ejus causa juste audiatur et rationabiliter
discernatur.   Finis vero ejus causae ad sedem apostolicam deferatur, ut
ibidem terminetur.   Nec antea finiatur, sicut ab Apostolis vel successoribus eorum olim statutum est, quam ejus auctoritate fulciatur.

    [6] Against these and provincial synods the objection in Sixti ii. ep. ii.
is valid : fratres, quos timore terreno injuste damnastis, scitote a nobis
juste esse restitutos.

    [7] Aniceti P. ep. (in part ap. Gratian. ii. ix. iii. 6): Nulli Archiepis-
copi Primates vocentur, nisi illi, qui primas tenent civitates, quarum
Episcopos, Apostoli et successores Apostolorum regulariter Patriarchas
et Primates esse constituerunt, nisi aliqua gens deinceps ad fidem convertatur, cui necesse sit propter multitudinem eorum Primatem constitui.   Reliqui vero, qui alias metropolitanas sedes adepti sunt, non Primates sed Metropolitani nominentur.   Si autem aliquis Metropolitanorum inflatus fuerit, et sine omnium comprovincialium praesentia vel
consilio Episcoporum, aut eorum aut alias causas, nisi eas tantum, quae
ad propriam suam parochiam pertinent, agere aut eos gravare voluerit :
ab omnibus districte corrigatur, ne talia deinceps praesumere audeat. Si
vero incorrigibilis, eisque inobediens apparuerit, ad hanc apostolicam
sedem, cui omnia Episcoporum judicia terminare praecepta sunt, ejus
contumacia referatur, ut vindicta de eo fiat, et caeteri timorem habeant.
Si autem propter nimiam longinquitatem, aut temporis incommoditatem,
vel itineris asperitatem grave ad hanc sedem ejus causam deferre fuerit,
tunc ad ejus Primatem causa deferatur, et penes ipsum hujus sanctae
sedis auctoritate judicetur.   Comp. Stephani P. ep. ii., where it is added besides: si prohiberi non potuerunt accusationes Episcoporum, ad
memoratos Primates debent ab accusatoribus deferri.   Comp. Blascus
cap. 12, p. 99 ss., and cap. 13, p. 111 ss., the just remark that the object of this provision was to exalt the archbishop of Mainz. In fact a
distinction began to be made already between primates and metropolitans (de Marca de primatu Lugdunensi c. 23 ss. in his dissertatt. appended to de concord. Sac. et Imp. ed. Boehmer p. 23) ; but this did
not prevent the rights taken from the metropolitans eventually falling
into the net of Rome.

    [8] For Sixti i. ep. ii. : Ab hac enim sancta sede a sanctis Apostolis

form the chief ecclesiastical and legal contents of the *Pseudoi-*

tueri, defendi et liberari Episcopi jussi sunt. On the Pseudoisidorian
papal system see Planck ii. 815. Knust p. 30. Designation of the
pope as universalis Ecclesiae Episcopus in Sixti i. ep. ii., Victoris ep. i.,
Stephani ep. ii., Pontiani ep. ii. Vigilii ep. ad Profuturum (where cap.
6 and 7 are pseudoisidorian) c. 7. (partly ap. Grat. ii. ii. vi. 12) :
Nulli vel tenuiter sentienti vel pleniter sapienti dubium est, quod
Ecclesia Romana fundamentum et forma sit Ecclesiarum (τύποι τοῦ
ποιμνίου 1. Petr. 5. 3. Vulg. forma gregis), a qua omnes Ecclesias principium sumsisse nemo recte credentium ignorat, cum licet omnium
Apostolorum par esset electio, beato tamen Petro concessum est, ut caeteris praemineret, unde et Cephas vocatur, quia caput est et primus omnium Apostolorum. Et quod in capite praecessit, in membris sequi
necesse est. Quamobrem s. Romana Ecclesia ejus merito Domini voce
consecrata, et ss. Patrum auctoritate roborata primatum tenet omnium
Ecclesiarum, ad quam tam summa Episcoporum negotia et judicia atque
querelae, quam et majores Ecclesiarum quaestiones, quasi ad caput,
semper referenda sunt. Nam et qui se scit aliis esse praepositum, non
moleste ferat aliquem esse sibi praelatum : ipsa namque Ecclesia, quae
prima est, ita reliquis Ecclesiis vices suas credidit largiendas, ut in partem sint vocatae solicitudinis, non in plenitudinem potestatis (this remarkable expression borrowed from Leonis M. ep. xii. ad Anastas.
Thessal. : Vices enim nostras ita tuae credimus Caritati, ut in partem
sis vocatus solicitudinis, non in plenitudinem potestatis, namely, as papal
vicar in Illyria, cf. de Marca conc. Sac. et Imp. lib. v. c. 26. § 5 ss.
Gibert corp. jur. can. Tom. i. Proleg. p. 261. Sect. 3).—Anacleti i. ep.
iii. : Haec vero apostolica sedes cardo et caput omnium Ecclesiarum a
Domino, et non ab alio est constituta. Et sicut cardine ostium regitur
sic hujus sanctae sedis auctoritate omnes Ecclesiae Domino disponente
reguntur. Besides, the expression borrowed from Cyprian is singularly
remarkable (see vol. i. div. i. § 68. note 10). Anacleti i. ep. ii. (Gratian. i. xxi. 2) : In novo testamento post Christum Dominum a Petro
sacerdotalis coepit ordo : quia ipsi primo pontificatus in Ecclesia Christi
datus est (Matth. xvi. 18). Hic ergo ligandi atque solvendi potestatem
primus accepit a Domino. Caeteri vero Apostoli cum eodem pari consortio honorem et potestatem acceperunt, ipsumque principem eorum
esse voluerunt. New papal rights : 1. regarding the power of making
laws : Damasi ep. v. (Grat. ii. xxv. i. 12.) : Omnia decretalia et cunctorum decessorum nostrorum constituta, quae de ecclesiasticis ordinibus
et canonum promulgata sunt disciplinis ; ita a vobis et ab omnibus
Episcopis ac cunctis generaliter sacerdotibus custodiri debere mandamus,
ut, si quis in illa commiserit, veniam sibi deinceps noverit denegari.
This passage is from Leonis i. ep. iv. c. 5, but is there addressed to the
bishops of the Roman patriarchal jurisdiction, here to the Numidian
bishops, and, accordingly, contains here an obligation devolving on all
bishops, which the forger has made still more remarkable by this circumstance, that he changed Leo's more modest formula, a vestra dilectione, for the other a vobis—sacerdotibus.) 2. Regarding ecclesiastical
judicature : Julii ep. i. (Grat. ii. iii. vi. 9) : Dudum a ss. Apostolis, suc-

sidoriana. They must have been written between 829[9] and 845[10]

cessoribusque eorum in antiquis decretum fuerat statutis, quae hactenus
s. et universalis apostolica tenet Ecclesia, non oportere praeter sententiam Romani Pontificis concilia celebrari, nec Episcopum damnari, quoniam s. Romanam Ecclesiam primatem omnium Ecclesiarum esse
voluerunt, et sicut b. Petrus Ap. primus fuit omnium Apostolorum, ita
et haec Ecclesia suo nomine consecrata (Domino instituente) prima et
caput sit caeterarum, et ad eam, quasi ad matrem atque apicem, omnes
majores Ecclesiae causae et judicia Episcoporum recurrant et juxta ejus
sententiam terminum sumant : nec extra Romanum quicquam ex his
debere decerni Pontificem. Zephyrini ep. 1. (Grat ii. ii. vi. 8.): Ad
Romanam Ecclesiam ab omnibus, maxime tamen ab oppressis, appel-
landum est et concurreudum quasi ad matrem, ut ejus uberibus nutrian-
tur, auctoritate defendantur, et a suis oppressionibus releventur; quia
nec potest nec debet mater oblivisci filium suum. Cf. Damasi ep. iv.:
Discutere namque Episcoporum et summorum ecclesiasticorum negotiorum causas Metropolitanos una cum omnibus suis comprovincialibus,
ita ut nemo ex eis desit et omnes in singulorum concordent negotiis,
licet ; sed definire eorum atque ecclesiasticarum summas querelas causarum, vel damnare Episcopos absque hujus s. sedis auctoritate minime
licet, quam omnes appellare, si necesse fuerit, et ejus fulciri auxilio
oportet. Nam, ut nostis, synodum sine ejus auctoritate fieri, non est
catholicum etc. Julii ep. ii. (Gratian. i. xvii. 2): Nec ullum [conci-
lium] ratum est aut erit unquam quod non fultum fuerit ejus [Romanae
Ecclesiae] auctoritate. How the way had been gradually prepared for
the doctrine : praeter sententiam Rom. Pont. non oportere Episcopum
damnari, since the time of Gregory IV., may be seen above, § 7. not.
28. de Marca lib. vii. c. 21. The position : non oportere praeter sententiam Romani Pontificis concilia celebrari, is borrowed from the historia tripartita, &c. (see vol. i. div. 2. § 94. note 28), there, perhaps,
meant only of general councils, but was also never in force in respect to
provincial and diocesan synods. 3. Relating to the ecclesiastical administration Calixti ep. ii. (Grat. ii. vii. i. 39) : Si utilitatis causa fuerit
mutandus [Episcopus], non per se hoc agat, sed fratribus invitantibus,
et auctoritate hujus sanctae sedis faciat, non ambitus causa, sed utilitatis et necessitatis. However, the Pseudoisidore does not continue here
to observe uniformity of sentiment. See Anteri ep. : Sicut Episcopi
habent potestatem ordinare regulariter Episcopos et reliquos sacerdotes,
sic quoties utilitas aut necessitas coëgerit, supradicto modo et mutare et
inthronizare potestatem habent. Gratian, who adopts this passage
causa vii. qu. i. c. 34, has for the first time appended to it the words :
non tamen sine sacrosanctae Romanae sedis auctoritate et licentia.

[9] For passages of the synod of Paris of 829 are inserted in the letters
of Urban I. and John III. Blascus, however, l. c. p. 39 ss. is of another opinion.

[10] Because in this year Benedictus Lev. began to compile his collection of capitularies (comp. the pref. to § 7), in which Pseudoisidoriana
first appear in great numbers, but without being quoted by name as if
they were taken from capitularies. Comp. Bened. praef. (ap. Baluz. i.

in Eastern France ;[11] and were first published, in a pretended Isidorian collection which Archbishop *Riculf* (786–814) is said to have
brought from Spain, at Mainz, in the time of Archbishop *Autcarius* (826–847.)[12]   They were soon circulated in various collec-

803) : Haec vero capitula, quae in subsequentibus tribus libellis coadu-
nare studuimus, in diversis locis et in diversis schedulis, sicut in diversis
synodis ac placitis generalibus edita erant, sparsim invénimus, et maxime
in s. Magontiacensis metropolis ecclesiae scrinio a Riculfo ejusdem s.
sedis Metropolitano (from 786-814) recondita, et demum ab Autcario secundo ejus successore atque consanguineo inventa reperimus.
    [11] So Blondellus, Ballerini, Spittler, Planck.   On the other hand,
their origin is put in the time of Charlemagne by Natalis Alexander,
Baluzius, Petrus de Marca, Mabillon, and Blascus l. c. cap. 6.—Febro-
nius de statu Eccles. T. i. p. 643. supposes that they were composed in
Rome soon after 744 ; Theiner de Pseudo-Isidoriana canonum collec-
tione diss. Vratislav. 1827. 8. p. 71. 79., that they were written between
774 and 785 in Rome at the instigation of the popes ; Eichhorn Grund-
sätze des Kirchenrechts i. 158, that they appeared in Rome in the 8th
century, and were subsequently foisted into the Isidorian collection, in
the Frank empire.
    [12] Hence Hincmar. adv. Hincm. Laud. c. 24. designates it as liber
collectarum epistolarum ab Isidoro, quem de Hispania allatum Riculfus,
Moguntinus Episcopus,—obtinuit, et istas regiones ex illo repleri fecit.
Hincmar, however, was wrong in this, that Riculf had already circulated
it, for, according to Benedictus Levita (note 10), it was in s. Magontiacensis ecclesiae scrinio a Riculfo recondita, et demum ab Autcario inventa.   Probably Riculf had received the genuine Spanish collection
from Spain ; for it is this which his suffragan bishop Rachio, bishop of
Strasburgh, caused to be copied in the year 787.   This genuine
collection was afterwards transformed into the pseudoisidorian, which
was then put forward, pretending to be the other.   Benedictus
Levita has frequently been looked upon as the forger, who certainly was
the first that made use of the false decretals in his collection of capitularies, and gave them more extended circulation.   But, in any case,
Autcarius must have been privy to it.   It is probable, indeed, that he
was the proper author, and that he employed Benedict solely as an instrument.   As an instrument for the propagation of them, he was the more
useful, the less he suspected the forgery.   Petr. de Marca (de conc.
Sac et Imp. lib. iii. c. 5.) and Blascus (l. c. cap. 6) regard Riculf as the
forger, but incorrectly.
    [13] Rabanus Maurus, however, does not mix any Pseudoisidoriana in
his liber poenitentiarum between 841 and 847.   See Ballerini de ant.
coll. can. P. iv. cap. 8. § 4.   Collections in which they are found are
besides Bened. capitul. libb. iii. the additio quarta capitularium (see
Spittler Gesch. des canon. Rechts S. 247.)   Hadriani P. i. capitula
Angilramno tradita or capitula Angilramni, ap. Mansi xii. 903 ss., supposed to belong to A. D. 785, were first brought to light about 870 by

tions,[13] appealed to without suspicion in public transactions,[14] and used by the popes, from Nicolaus I., immediately after he had

Hincmar of Laon. See Hincm. Rhem. opusc. adv. Hincm. Laud. c. 24. see below note 16. evidently spurious, Ballerini P. iii. cap. vi. § 2. not. 8. Blascus p. 151, but not perhaps by Hincmar of Laon as Spittler Gesch. des canon. Rechts S. 235. 271. assumes.   See Gfrörer iii. ii. 1079.   According to Wasserschleben (Beiträge zur Gesch. d. vorgratian. Kirchenrechtsquellen, Leipz. 1839, S. 14.) they proceeded really from Angilramnus and Hadrian, and the Pseudoisidorian was a later interpretation: on the other hand Rettberg KG. Deutschlands i. 647, holds that the chapters were composed by the author of the false decretals, but earlier than the latter.   Comp. generally Rettberg i. 501 and 646.   Capitula Remedii (in Goldast. scriptt. rer. Alem. ii. ii. 119. Die Kanonensammlung des Remedius v. Chur zuerst vollständig heraus-gegeben u. krit. erläutert v. Dr F. Kunstmann, Tübingen 1836. 8.), alleged to belong to the time of Charlemagne.   On the other side see Ballerini P. iii. c. 4. § 13.   Spittler Gesch. des canon. Rechts S. 236: according to Knust in the Theol. Stud. u. Krit. 1836, i. 161, the series of canons drawn from Pseudoisidore belonged to a Bavarian synod, pro-bably at Ratisbon A. D. 895 ; according to Kunstmann l. c. p. 58. they were composed about 870 in Bretagne, by a clergyman addicted to the metropolitan of Tours.   Capitula Isaaci Ep. Lingonensis (in Baluzii capitul. i. 1233, about the year 859.   See Ballerini P. iv. c. 9. § 8. Spittler S. 281.)   A MS. collection in the royal library at Paris, No. 3859, belonging to the end of the 9th century.   See Dr Aug. Theiner über Ivo's vermeintl. Decret, Mainz 1832, S. 9.   Collectio Auselmo dedicata between 883 and 897 (cf. Coustant diss. de ant. ca-nonum collect. no. 169 s. Ballerini P. iv. c. 10), from which Burchard has borrowed the greatest part of his work, Theiner p. 13.—Subse-quently Regino Prumiensis in his de disciplinis· eccles. libb. ii. (about 906) made indeed little use of the Pseudoisidoriana (Ballerini P. iv. c. 11): but Burcardus Ep. Wormatiensis took so much the more pains to introduce them into the general usage of the church, by his decre-torum volumen (about 1020).

[14] First A. D. 857 in the epistola synodalis (written by Hincmar at the Syn. Carisiaca) sub nomine Caroli R. ad Episc. et Com. Galliae scripta ap. Baluz. ii. 92. Pertz iii. 453. Mansi xv. 127): Audiant rap-tores et praedones rerum ecclesiasticarum, quod s. Anacletus P. ab ipso Petro Apostolo Presbyter ordinatus cum totius mundi sacerdotibus judi-cavit etc.   Item s. Urbanus Papa et martyr etc.   Item s. Lucius Papa etc.   About 860, when Hermann, bishop of Nevers, was to be deposed on account of fatuity, Wenilo, archbishop of Sens, sent by Servatus Lupus to Nicolaus I. to ask (ap. Mansi xv. 397. Serv. Lup. epist. 130. ed. Baluz. p. 194. comp. Baluz's remarks p. 466 ss.): Dici-tur autem Melchiades P. decrevisse, ne quis unquam Pontifex sine con-sensu Papae Romani deponeretur.   Unde supplicamus, ut statuta illius, sicut penes vos habentur, nobis dirigere dignemini etc.   Nicolaus in his reply (ap. Mansi l. c.) praises highly his determination to send to

become acquainted with them (864),[15] without any opposition be-

Rome: antequam ad consulta vestra mentis oculum inclinemus, parumper in laudibus vestris stylum operae pretium duximus immorandum,
and goes on to speak of Hermann's case, but gives not one syllable of
reply to his question. Respecting the proceedings see Blascus l. c.
p. 17.

[15] Leo IV. says, as late as the year 850, in ep. ii. ad Episc. Britann.
c. 6. (ap. Mansi xiv. 884, ap. Gratian. P. i. dist. xx. c. 1) : De libellis
et commentariis aliorum non convenit aliquem judicare, et ss. Conciliorum canones relinquere, vel decretalium regulas, i. e. quae habentur
apud nos simul cum illis in canone, et quibus in omnibus ecclesiasticis
utimur judiciis, i. e. Apostolorum, Nicaenorum etc. : et cum illis regulae
praesulum Romanorum Sylvestri (the constit. Sylv. were forged still
earlier than the Pseudoisidorian, see vol. i. Div. 2. § 117. not. 15.
Blascus l. c. p. 11. 25), Siricii, Innocentii, Zosimi, Caelestini, Leonis,
Gelasii, Hilarii, Symmachi, Simplicii. Isti omnino sunt, per quos
judicant Episcopi, et per quos Episcopi simul et clerici judicantur.
Even Nicolaus I. neither knew of those decretals in 860 (see note 14),
nor does he know in 863, in. ep. v. ad Hincmarum (ap. Mansi xv. 374)
of older constitutiones Rom. sedis Pontiff. than those of Siricius, Innocentii, etc. In like manner he refers in Rothad's case (863) only to the
Sardican canons ; in his sermo made on the day before Christmas, 864.
he first appeals to the Pseudoisidoriana. See below § 21. not. 15. 16.
Hence it is probable, as Gfrörer iii. ii. 1022 assumes, Rothad, who
came to Rome in June 864, had brought thither the false decretals. In
the year 865 Nicolaus demonstrates their validity in the following manner. Ep. ad univ. Episc. Gall. (Mansi xv. 694) : etsi (Rothadus Episc.]
sedem apostolicam nullatenus appellasset, contra tot tamen et tanta vos
decretalia efferri statuta, et Episcopum inconsultis nobis deponere nullo
modo debuistis. Absit enim, ut—decretalia constituta—debito cultu et
cum summa discretione non amplectamur opuscula, quae dumtaxat et
antiquitus s. Romana Ecclesia conservans, nobis quoque custodienda
mandavit, et penes se in suis archivis et vetustis rite monumentis recondita veneratur. Absit ut scripta eorum quoquomodo parvipendenda
dicamus, quorum videmus Deo auctore s. Ecclesiam aut roseo cruore
floridam, aut rorifluis sudoribus et salubribus eloquiis adornatam.—
Quamquam quidam vestrum scripserunt, haud illa decretalia priscorum
pontificum in toto codicis canonum corpore contineri descripta, cum
ipsi, ubi suae intentioni haec suffragari conspiciunt, illis indifferenter
utantur, et solum nunc, ad imminutionem potestatis sedis apostolicae,
et ad suorum augmentum privilegiorum, minus accepta esse perhibeant.
Nam nonnulla eorum scripta penes nos habentur, quae non solum quorumcumque Romanorum Pontificum, verum etiam priorum decreta in
suis causis praeferre noscuntur.—decretales epistolae Rom. Pontificum
sunt recipiendae, etiamsi non sunt canonum codici compaginatae. Hadrianus ii. ep. xxxii. ad Episc. Synodi Duziacensis (ap. Mansi xv. 852)
expressly cites A. D. 871, epistolam Auteri P. etc. In other points not
affecting the papal dignity, the popes did not at once adopt the Pseu-

ing made to their authenticity,[16] and continued in undiminished
doisidorian principles.   Thus not only Nicolaus I., but even Gregory
VII. (epist. lib. vii. ep. 34.), decided that priests convicted of crimes
should be expelled from the clergy, though Pseudo-Callistus ep. 2. had
written : Errant itaque, qui putant, sacerdotes post lapsum, si condignam
egerint poenitentiam, Domino non posse ministrare.   Comp. Blascus
l. c. p. 18 ss.

[16] Even Hincmar did not doubt the authenticity but the validity of
those decretals (cf. Blascus l. c. p. 16) : he appealed to them, 857,
against robbers of churches (note 14), and, 868, against Charles the
Bald, when the latter had summoned the younger Hincmar before a
civil tribunal, and had imposed taxes on his revenues (Hincm. ep. 29.
ad Car. Calv. Opp. ed. Sirmond. ii. 223. cites Lucii ep. and Stephani
ep. ii.) : On this account the objection of Nicolaus I. held good against
him in particular (note 15), that he sometimes made use of those letters,
sometimes disowned them, according as they favoured or not his own
interest.   The authority of these decretals is combated by Hincmar in
regard to the rights of metropolitans, especially in his opusc. adv.
Hincmar. Laudun. A. D. 870.   The Pseudoisidorian positions of the
capitula Angilramni, to which the younger Hincmar had appealed, are
with him c. 10. (Opp. ii. 413) circumposita nobis omnibus Metropolitanis a te muscipula.   Cap. 24. p. 475 : De sententiis vero, quae dicuntur ex Graecis et Latinis canonibus, et synodis Romanis atque decretis praesulum ac ducum Romanorum collectae ab Adriano Papa, et
Engelramno Metensium Episcopo datae, quando pro sui negotii causa
agebatur, ex quibus quaedam tuis commentis interposuisti, quam dis-
sonae inter se habeantur,—et quam diversae a sacris canonibus, et quam
discrepantes in quibusdam ab ecclesiasticis judiciis habeantur,—evi-
dentor manifestatur.   Proofs, that they were even opposed to Hincmar
of Laon.   Si vero ideo talia, quae tibi visa sunt de praefatis sententiis
ac saepe memoratis epistolis, detruncando et praeposterando atque dis-
ordinando, collegisti, quia forte putasti, neminem alium easdem sententias, vel ipsas epistolas praeter te habere, et idcirco talia libere te existi-
masti posse colligere, res mira est, cum de ipsis sententiis plena sit ista
terra, sicut et de libro collectarum epistolarum ab Isidoro, quem de
Hispania allatum Riculfus Moguntinus Episcopus, in hujusmodi sicut
et in capitulis regiis studiosus, obtinuit, et istas regiones ex illo repleri
fecit.   Cap. 25. p. 482 : Animadvertenda est discretio ex verbis b.
Gelasii (in the decretum de libris recipiendis et non recipiendis) inter
synodalia Concilia et apostolicorum virorum epistolas, quas ante Concilia celebrata diversis temporibus pro diversorum Patrum consolatione
dederunt, quasque venerabiliter suscipiendas dicit : si qua sunt antem
Concilia a sanctis Patribus instituta post quatuor Conciliorum auctoritatem, custodienda et observanda decrevit.   Quantum enim distet inter
illa scilicet Concilia—et illas epistolas,—nemo in dogmatibus ecclesiasticis exercitatus ignorat.   Si enim quaedam ex his, quae in quibusdam
illis epistolis continentur, tenere et custodire velle inceperimus, contra
alia plurima illarum epistolarum facere incipiemus.   Et rursus si alia,
contra quae feceramus, tenere et custodire inceperimus,—a Conciliis

reputation[17] till the Reformation led to the detection of the cheat.[18] On these false decretals were founded the pretensions of the popes[19] to universal sway in *the Church ;*[20] while the pretend-

sacris, quae perpetuo nobis recipienda, tenenda, ac custodienda, atque sequenda sunt, deviabimus: sed et a consuetudine, quam catholica Ecclesia habuit, ex quo in sacrum Nicaenum Concilium patres nostri convenerunt,—perniciosissime discedemus, et nihil certi tenentes in⁻ sectam Genethliacianorum i. e. Mathematicorum offendemus, qui diffinierunt omnia in incertum. Nam et b. Gelasius easdem epistolas non solum sacris canonibus in quibusdam adversas, sed etiam sibi ipsis diversas ostendit cum dicit, illas diversis temporibus pro diversorum consolatione datas. Et hinc forte adversum me dices: ergo calumniaris apostolicam sedem in sanctis ejus Pontificibus, eo quod male senserint, et non tenenda decreverint. Unde tibi respondeo, quod de lege non judaice servanda, contradicentibus sibi et dicentibus: lex ergo adversus promissa Dei ? (Gal. iii. 21) respondit Apostolus : Absit : lex quidem sancta, et mandatum sanctum, et justum et bonum (Rom. vii. 12), sed personis et temporibus suis congrua : quae propter transgressiones posita est, donec veniret semen (Gal. iii. 19.) Et illas epistolas sanctorum et apostolicorum virorum, diversis temporibus pro diversorum consolatione—a sede apostolica datas,—venerabiliter suscipiendas dico. Quae suis temporibus congruentes fuerunt, donec per sacra Concilia patres nostri in unum convenientes—suggerente sibimet sancto Spiritu —mansuras usque in finem saeculi leges condiderunt. That Hincmar suspected the spuriousness of these decretals, but said nothing on the subject from motives of prudence, as Gfrörer iii. ii. 1081 assumes, is in my opinion improbable ; for a combating of the authenticity could not be looked on as contempt of the holy see, but probably, if the authenticity were conceded, a denial of their validity might be so regarded.

[17] Concerning those who are supposed to have doubted the authenticity of the forged decretals, in the middle ages, Petrus Comestor [1170], Marsilius Patavinus [1324] (not Wicliffe, he asserted : decretales epistolae sunt apocryphae et seducunt a Christi fide, also apocryphae = erroneae), Gobelinus Persona [1418], Heinr. v. Kalteisen [1432, comp. however Spittler's doubts l. c. p. 259], Nicolaus Cusanus [1448], Erasmus, see Blascus l. c. cap. 5. p. 30 ss.

[18] Calvin institutt. iv. c. 7. § 11. 20. the spuriousness; the Magdeburg centuries (centur. ii. c. 7. and cent. iii. c. 7.) first gave a copious proof of it, which opinion was also adopted about the same time by Anton. Contius and Antonius Augustinus, archbp. of Tarragona (see Blascus l. c. p. 33), while the Jesuit Franc. Turrianus wrote libb. v. adv. Magdeburgenses Centuriatores pro canonibus Apostolorum et epistolis decretalibus Pontificum apostolicorum, Florent. 1572. Colon. 1573. 4. Bellarmine (de Pont. Rom. lib. ii. c. 14.) and Baronius (ad ann. 865. § 8.) abandoned these decretals. The question was decided by Dav. Blondelli Pseudoisidorus et Turrianus vapulantes, Genev. 1628. 4.

[19] The Ultramontanists, though they admit the deception, deny the revolution of ecclesiastical principles caused by it. So Ballerini l. c.

ed *donatio Constantini M.*,[21] a fiction of an earlier time, but soon adopted into them, was the first step from which the papacy endeavoured to elevate itself even above *the state.*

P. iii. c. 6. § 3. and P. Ballerini de potest. eccl. summ. Pontif. et Concill. generall. una cum vindiciis contra J. Febronium. Veron. 1768. Aug. Vindel. 1770 in the vindiciis cap. 5. On the other side see Jo. Gerbasii diss. de causis majoribus. Paris. 1679. 4. Fleury hist. eccl. T. xvi. diss. préliminaire. Justification des discours et de l'hist. ecclés. de M. l'Abbé de Fleury. 1736. P. ii. Tübinger kath.-theol. Quartalschrift, 1823. 2tes Quart. S. 277 ff.

[20] Comp. vol. i. Div. 1. § 56. note 40. Above § 5. note 18. It is found so early as in the collectio cann. Colbertina, which is older than Pseudoisidore (see Coustant diss. de ant. canonum collectionibus no. 103). There are also obvious references to it by Hincmar ep. iii. c. 13 : Constantinus M.—propter amorem et honorem ss. Apostolorum Petri et Pauli—locum et sedem suam, urbem scilicet Romanam, Papae Sylvestro edicto privilegii tradidit, et sedem suam in civitate sua, quae antea Byzantium vocabatur,—aedificavit. Aeneae Paris. liber adv. Graecos (A. D. 868) c. 209. (in d'Achery spicileg. i. 147) : singulare privilegium et mirabile testamentum toto tunc orbe vulgatum apostolicae sedi conscribi jussit,—cujus exemplaribus Ecclesiarum in Gallia consistentium armaria ex integro potiuntur. Blascus cap. 2. p. 13. rightly shows indeed that this act cannot have originated with Pseudoisidore as many suppose, but he erroneously assumes, that because it appears first in Leonis ix. ep. ad Michael. Const. Patriarch. (a. 1054) c. 13 et 14. (ap. Mansi xix. 643.) it was forged long after Pseudoisidore. Worthy of notice is Ottonis iii. diploma ann. 999 (see below § 22. not. 28) : Haec sunt etiam commenta ab illis ipsis inventa, quibus Joannes Diaconus, cognomento digitorum mutius (mozzo, mutilus), praeceptum aureis literis scripsit, sub titulo magni Constantini longa mendacii tempora finxit. This John is discovered (Marqu. Freherus) Constantini donatio integre edita. 1610. 4. in the author of the life of s..Gregorii M. about 875 ; Jo. Morinus hist. de la délivrance de l'égl. chret. par l'Emp. Constantin. Paris 1630. fol. identifies him with Johannes Diaconus about 963. On the other side is de Marca lib. iii. c. 12, according to whom the original document was composed A. D. 767 at the command of Pope Paul I. Against the opinion of Baronius ann. 324. no. 117 ss. that the document was forged by Greeks, see Morinus l. c. Comp. E. Münch über die Schenkung Constantin's, in his vermischte Schriften, Ludwigsburg 1828. ii. 183.) The original document was meant in part to establish an older right than the Donatio of Pipin and Charles, and to favour the efforts of the popes to obtain independence (see § 6); partly also to justify the views of the papal coronation of emperors which then appeared (see § 6. note 15.)

[21] There is one old Latin text of it, but four Greek texts. See F. A. Biener de collectionibus cann. Ecclesiae Graecae. Berol. 1827. 8. p. 72 ss. The first alone is of historical importance, being found in the Pseudoisidorian decretals under the title of edictum domini Constantini

§ 21.

PAPACY UNDER NICOLAUS I. (858–867), HADRIAN II. (TILL 872), AND JOHN VIII. (TILL 882).

Planck's Gesch. der kirchl. Gesellschaftsverf. iii. 1. Neander iv. 112. Gfrörer iii. ii. 983.

The rulers of the divided Frank empire,[1] unable to withstand

Imp., and extracts from it in the decret. Gratiani dist. xcvi. c. 13. Among other things we read : Et sicut nostram terrenam imperialem potentiam, sic ejus (Petri) sacrosanctam Romanam Ecclesiam decrevimus veneranter honorari, et amplius quam nostrum imperium terreunmque thronum, sedem sacratissimam b. Petri gloriose exaltari : tribuentes ei potestatem et gloriae dignitatem, atque vigorem et honorificentiam imperialem. Therefore he gives him palatium Lateranense and all imperial insignia. Unde ut pontificalis apex non vilescat, sed magis quam imperii dignitas, gloria et potentia decoretur, ecce tam palatium nostrum, ut praedictum est, quam Romanam urbem, et omnes Italiae, seu occidentalium regionum provincias, loca et civitates (i. e. the western empire, as it was still limited to some provinces of Italy, in the eighth century, and was transferred to the Franks : the forger knows only of this, and puts it back in the times of Constantine) praefato beatissimo Pontifici nostro Sylvestro, universali Papae, contradimus atque relinquimus : et ab eo et a successoribus ejus per hanc divalem nostram, et pragmaticum constitutum decernimus disponenda, atque juri s. Romanae Ecclesiae concedimus permansura. Unde congruum perspeximus nostrum imperium, et regni potestatem in orientalibus transferri regionibus, et in Byzantinae provinciae optimo loco, nomini nostro civitatem aedificari, et nostrum illic constitui imperium : quoniam ubi principatus sacerdotum, et christianae religionis caput ab Imperatore caelesti constitutum est, justum non est, ut illic Imperator terrenus habeat potestatem. That there never was any such donatio was acknowledged by Otto III. in the year 999 (note 20) and in 1152 by the Romans (see below, Div. 2. § 51. note 18.) In the fifteenth century this was shown to be the case by Nicolaus Cusanus de concordantia catholica (about 1432), and in particular by Laurentius Valla († 1457) de falso credita et ementita Constantini donatione declamatio (in S. Schardii syntagma tractatuum de imperiali jurisdictione. Argentor. 1609. fol. p. 401.) (see Münch verm. hist. Schriften ii. 214.) Since then the document is universally given up as spurious, but the donation itself is still defended by Baronius, and the Jesuits Jac. Gretser, Nic. Schaten, and others, ex. gr. Blanchini ad Anastas. de vitis Pontiff. ii. ii. 295. and Mamachii antiquitt. christ. ii. 232.

[1] After the death of the emperor Lothar I. († 855), his sons received, the emperor Lewis II., Italy († 875), Lothar II., Lorraine († 869),

the attacks of foreign enemies and the encroachments of their
own nobles, were obliged, in consequence, to seek protection from
the Church ; and had been long since induced to invest their
bishops with important rights.[2]   How much the position of the
pope, as the highest bishop, was heightened by this means,
Nicolaus I.[3] was the first fully to perceive.   The success of his
new pretensions and encroachments was made more certain by his
appearing not only as the champion of the oppressed, and thus
securing a powerful ally in public opinion, but in being also assist-
ed by the disunion of the civil princes, who, mutually suspicious
and ambitious, were ready to aid in humbling one another.   The
first opportunity for interference was presented to him by King
Lothar II., who, out of love to his mistress, Waldrade, had long
treated his spouse, Teutberg, most shamefully, till he at length
divorced her at a synod held at Aix-la-Chapelle (862).[4]   Charles
the Bald and his bishops having sided with the persecuted one,[5]
Nicolaus, to whom she had long ago applied for aid,[6] ventured to

and Charles († 863), Provence, which last, however, was divided, after
his death, by the two older brothers.   Lewis the German reigned over
the East Franks († 876), and Charles the Bald over the West Franks
(† 877).

[2] For instance, bishops judges of kings, comp. § 6. note 13. 14.

[3] He was the first pope who, without doubt, allowed himself to be
crowned agreeably to the donatio Constantini (remarkably short is
Anastasius vita cvii. Nicolai i.: coronatur denique), and to whom an
emperor, Lewis II., performed the office of equerry (Anastasius l. c.
frenum Caesar equi Pontificis suis manibus apprehendens pedestri more,
quantum sagittae jactus extenditur, traxit).   A description of Nicolaus
I. ap Regino ad ann. 868: post b. Gregorium usque in praesens nullus
Praesul in Romana urbe pontificali honore sublimatus illi videtur aequi-
parandus: regibus ac tyrannis imperavit, eisque, ac si dominus orbis
terrarum, auctoritate praefuit: Episcopis et Sacerdotibus religiosis ac
mandata Domini observantibus humilis, blandus, pius, mansuetus apparuit; irreligiosis et a recto tramite exorbitantibus terribilis atque auste-
ritate plenus extitit, ut merito credatur alter Helias, Deo suscitante,
nostris in temporibus resurrexisse, etsi non corpore, tamen spiritu et
virtute.

[4] After church penance had been imposed on Teutberg, at a synod
held at Aix-la-Chapelle (Mansi xv. 547), the synod of 862 gave Lothar
permission to marry again (l. c. p. 611).

[5] Hincmar, archbishop, wrote against the proceedings of the conc.
Aqnisgr. A.D. 860 his work de divortio Hlotharii Regis et Teutbergae
Reginae, in opp. ed. Sirmond i. 557.

[6] Nic. epist. ad Carol. Calv. 867 (Mansi xv. 319) : cum nos ex utra-

send legates to Lotharingia to examine the matter anew. But when these legates, having been bribed, confirmed the former decision at the synod of Metz (863),[7] Nicolaus went so far as to declare this synod null; and to depose the heads of the Lorraine clergy, Archbishops Gunthar of Cöln, and Thietgaud of Treves.[8] The danger with which he was threatened from the emperor Lewis for this presumption soon passed;[9] but Lothar submitted through fear of his uncles, who were desirous to seize on his territories.[10] When afterwards he endeavoured to con-

que parte, i. e. tam a Teutberga quam a Lothario fuerimus provocati judices,—ad nullos alios convenit super hoc negotio judices convolare : cum secundum sacros canones a judicibus, quos communis consensus elegerit non liceat provocare.

[7] Ann. Bertiniani (i. e. Hincmari) ad ann. 863.

[8] Concil. Romanum ann. 863 ap. Mansi xv. 649.

[9] Regino ad ann. 865 : Qui tam turpiter dehonestati [the two archbishops] Hludovicum Imp.—adeunt, qui ea tempestate Beneventanis morabatur in partibus, scriptis ac dictis vociferantes, se injuste esse depositos : ipsi Imperatori et omni s. Ecclesiae injuriam esse factam, cum numquam auditum sit, vel uspiam lectum quod ullus Metropolitanus sine conscientia Principis vel praesentia aliorum Metropolitanorum fuerit degradatus. Concerning Lothar's expedition against Rome, see especially annal. Bertin. ad ann. 864, where, too, may be found the protest of the two archbishops laid on Peter's grave, in which they prove the invalidity of their deposal, c. 3. in this manner: sine Synodo et canonico examine, nullo accusante, nullo testificante, nullaque disputationis districtione dirimente, vel auctoritatem probatione convincente, absque nostri oris confessione, absentibus aliis Metropolitanis et dioecesanis Coëpiscopis et confratribus nostris extra omnium omnino consensum, tuo solius arbitrio et tyrannico furore damnare nosmet voluisti. c. 4. : Sed tuam maledictam sententiam—nequaquam recipimus : immo cum omni coetu fraterno—contemnimus atque abjicimus. Te ipsum quoque—in nostram communionem nostrumque consortium recipere nolumus, contenti totius Ecclesiae communione et fraterna societate, quam tu arroganter te superexaltans despicis, teque ab ea elatione tumore indignum faciens sequestras. The conclusion in the annal. Fuld. ad ann. 863 : scies nos non tuos esse, ut te jactas et extollis, Clericos, quos ut fratres et Coëpiscopos recognoscere, si elatio permitteret, debueras. Et haec tibi nostri ordinis non inscii, nimium tua improbitate compulsi respondemus, non quasi ad illitam nobis contumeliam provocati, sed contra tuam iniquitatem ecclesiastico zelo accensi, nec nostrae vilitatis personam attendentes, sed omnem nostri ordiniis universitatem, cui vim inferre conaris, prae oculis habentes.

[10] Capitula quae Hlud. et Car. Reges in Tusiaco villa populo annuntiaverunt xi. kal. Mart. 865. cap. 6. (Baluz. capit. ii. 203). Ann. Bertinn. (Hincmar) ad ann. 865. Nicolaus was the first pope who en-

tinue his illicit intercourse with Waldrade, and at the same time
to conciliate the pope by crouching affectations of humility,[11] the
severity of the latter was the less blamed on account of the king's
cowardly voluptuousness.[12]   At the same time, Nicolaus also

joyed the triumph of protecting a king. Ann. Bert. l. c. Nicolaus P.
Arsenium—cum epistolis ad Hludovicum et Carolum fratres, sed et ad
Episcopos ac Primores regnorum illorum, ea quae Lotharius per fratrem
petierat continentibus (namely, ann. Fuld. : ob pacem et concordiam
inter Hlud. et Car., necnon Hlotharium nepotem eorum, renovandam
atque constituendam), non cum apostolica mansuetudine, et solita hono-
rabilitate, sicut Episcopi Romani Reges consueverant in suis epistolis
honorare, sed cum malitiosa interminatione transmittit. The letters are
not extant, as Pagi ad. ann. 865 no. 8. believes.

[11] Comp. his letter to Nicolaus ap. Baronius ad ann. 866. no. 36.

[12] Nic epist. ad univ. Episcopos A.D. 863 (Mansi xv. 649) begins:
Scelus, quod Lotharius Rex, si tamen rex veraciter dici possit, qui nullo
salubri regimine corporis appetitus refraenavit, sed lubrica enervatione
magis ipsius illicitis motibus cedit, in duabus feminis, Teutberga scilicet
et Waldrada, commisit, omnibus manifestum est. He wrote to Adven-
tius, bishop of Metz, with reference to the synod at that place (Mansi
xv. 373) : Verumtamen videte, utrum reges isti et principes, quibus vos
subjectos esse dictis, veraciter reges et principes sint. Videte, si primum
se bene regunt, deinde subditum populum : nam qui sibi nequam est,
cui alii bonus erit ?   Videte si jure principantur ; alioqui potius tyranni
credendi sunt, quam reges habendi ; quibus magis resistere, et ex ad-
verso ascendere, quam subdi debemus. Alioquin si talibus subditi, et
non praelati fuerimus nos, necesse est eorum vitiis faveamus. Nic. ep.
li. ad Lothar. R. (ap. Mansi xv. 324) : Igitur consilium nostrum accipe,
—praecipue Waldradae pellicis tuae et dudum a te repudiatae communionem declinans. Excommunicata est enim. Quamobrem cavendum
est, ne cum ea pari mucrone percellaris sententiae, ac pro unius mulieris
passione, et brevissimi temporis desiderio, vinctus et obligatus ad sulfu-
reos foetores et ad perenne traharis exitum. Praecave—ne hoc Ecclesiae sanctae dicamus, et, quod non optamus, de caetero fias cunctis sicut
ethnicus et publicanus. Such conduct, however, was entirely consistent
with the prevailing principles, comp. note 2. So also Hincmar de divort.
Hlot. et Tentb., to the question which had been propounded to him :
Dicunt quoque etiam aliqui sapientes quia iste princeps Rex est, et nullorum legibus vel judiciis subjacet, nisi solius Dei, qui eum—Regem
constituit :—et sicut a suis Episcopis, quicquid egerit, non debet excom-
municari, ita ab aliis Episcopis non potest judicari quoniam solius Dei
principatui debet subjici etc. To this he replies: Haec vox non est
catholici Christiani, sed nimium blasphemi, et spiritu diabolico pleni.—
Quod dicitur, " quia Rex nullorum legibus, vel judiciis subjacet, nisi
solius Dei," verum dicitur, si Rex est, sicuti neminatur. Rex enim a
regendo dicitur, et si se ipsum secundum voluntatem Dei regit, et bonos
in viam rectam dirigit, malos autem de via prava ad rectam corrigit,
tunc Rex est, et nullorum legibus vel judiciis nisi solius Dei subjacet—

humbled the proud archbishop of Rheims, *Hincmar*, who had
first suspended from his office, (861) *Rothad*, bishop of Soissons,
perhaps, without sufficient reason ;[13] and afterwards, without regarding his appeal to the pope, had deposed him at a synod held
at Soissons (863).[14] While the pope annulled these decisions and
called Rothad to Rome (864), he appealed at first for his justification in such a course to the canons[15] of Sardica, and afterwards
for the first time to the Pseudoisidorian decretals,[16] and met with
the less enduring opposition in proportion as they appeared to
promote the interests of the suffragan bishops.[17]   The Pseudoi-

"quia lex non est posita justo sed injustis, etc. (1 Tim. i. 9)." Alioquin
adulter, homicida, injustus, raptor, et aliorum vitiorum obnoxius quilibet, vel secrete vel publice, judicabitur a sacerdotibus, qui sunt throni
Dei etc.

[13] See Annal. Bertin. ad ann. 861.   Comp. generally W. F. Gess
Merkwürdigkeiten aus d. Leben u. d. Schriften Hincmar's. Götting.
1806. S. 233.   E. Rossteuscher de Rothado Ep. Suessionensi Part. ii.
Marburgi 1845. 8.

[14] Both sides of this controversy are narrated in Hincmari epist. ad
Nicol. i. A.D. 864 in ejusd. opp. ed. Sirmond ii. 244. and Rothadi libellus
proclamationis in the acts of the Roman synod of 865 (Mansi xv. 681).
—As Hincmar had declared against the Lorrain bishops in the affair of
Lothar, they now took the part of Rothad. Cf. epist. synod. Episcopo-
rum regni Loth. ad Episc. regni Ludovici (Mansi xv. 645).

[15] There was certainly a violation of these, since Hincmar had forthwith consecrated a successor to Rothad, without regarding his appeal.
See Nicolai epist. 28 ad Hincmarum (Mansi xv. 294), and still more
fully in his epist. ad Episcopos Synodi Silvanectensis (Mansi xv. 302),
where the constituta Sardicensis concilii, namely, c. iv. and viii. are expressly given.

[16] Sermo Nic. preached on the day before Christmas, 864 (Mansi xv.
686):—facto concilio generali, quod sine apostolicae sedis praecepto
nulli fas est vocandi vocaverunt hunc [Rothadum] Episcopi etc.—
Quamvis et ipse sedem apostolicam si nullatenus appellasset ; contra
tot tamen et tanta decretalia se efferre statuta, et Episcopum inconsulte
deponere, sicut vos bene nostis, non debuerunt.   Comp. the epist. ad
univ. Episc. Gall, § 20. not. 15. Hincmar's judgment on it in the annal.
Bertin. ad ann. 865 (Pertz monum. i. 468) : Rothadum canonice a
quinque provinciarum Episcopis dejectum, et a Nicolao Papa non regulariter sed potentialiter restitutum etc.

[17] To this Nicholas himself adverts as early as 863 in epist. xxxii. ad
Episc. Synod. Silvanectensis (Mansi xv. 305): privilegia sedis apostolicae tegmina sunt, ut ita dicamus, totius Ecclesiae catholicae ; privilegia, inquam, hujus Ecclesiae munimina sunt circa omnes impetus
pravitatum.   Nam quod Rothado hodie contigit, unde scitis, quod cras
cuilibet non eveniat vestrum ?—Quod si contigerit,—ad cujus, rogo,

sidorian principle, that obedience was due to all the papal decrees as such, must have been particularly advanced by the fact,[18]
that Nicolaus began to have such obedience in the metropolitans
praised at their investiture with the pallium.[19]

But that these new papal pretensions owed much of their success to the peculiar relations of the times, and that they had obtained very little general approbation,] is clear from the fact,
that immediately after Nicolaus's death, his arrangements were
very much endangered,[20] and that his successor, *Hadrian II.*, who

confugietis auxilium?   Hence the Synod of Troyes, 867, wrote on
another occasion ep. conc. Tricassini ad Nic. P. i. (Mansi xv. 795):
exoramus magnificam beatitudinem, ut—more b. praedecessorum vestrorum, quae de statu sacri pontificalis ordinis ab eis statuta—sunt, ut im-
mota de caetero maneant, mucrone apostolico quorumcunque Metropolitanorum temeraria praesumtione suppressa, quin etiam reliquorum
Episcoporum—audaci conniventia penitus summota, privilegia et decreta servari innovata constitutione decernatis : ita ut nec vestris nec
futuris temporibus, praeter consultum Rom. Pontificis de gradu suo
quilibet Episcoporum dejiciatur, sicut eorundem ss. antecessorum mul-
tiplicibus decretis et numerosis privilegiis stabilitum modis mirificis
extat.
    [18] Nicol. I. ep. ad univ. Episc. Gall. A.D. 865 (above § 20. not. 15.):
decretales epistolae Rom. Pontificum sunt recipiendae, etiamsi non sunt
canonum codici compaginatae.
    [19] The first case is that of Anschar.   He had before received the
Pallium as archbishop of Hamburg, 835, from Gregory IV., without
any such condition annexed (St Auschar by Kruse, p. 277); but when
Nicolaus I. confirmed the junction of the two dioceses of Hamburg and
Bremen, and sent a new pallium to Anschar (864), he announced to
him, at the same time, in the deed issued respecting it (Staphorst's
Hamburg. Kirchengesch. i. 41.   Hartzheim Conc. Germ. ii. 172):
Porro te (Anscharium) pallio uti nonnisi more sedis concedimus apostolicae, scil. ut successores tui per semetipsos, vel per legatos spos et
scriptum fidem nobiscum tenere, ac sanctas sex synodos recipere, atque
decreta omnium Romanae sedis Praesulum et epistolas, quae sibi dela-
tae fuerint, venerabiliter observare atque perficere omnibus diebus suis,
scripto se et juramento profiteantur.
    [20] Anastasius, librarian of the Roman Church, writes, in the letter in
which he mentions the death of Nicolaus to Ado, archbishop of Vienne
(Mansi xv. 453): Verum nunc congregatio omnis, quos ille vel pro diverso adulterii genere, vel pro aliis criminibus redarguit, ad hoc exarse-
runt, ut universa ejus opera destruere, et cuncta scripta delere meditari
non metuant.   And in the Embolo: Adjuro autem, ut omnibus Metropolitis Galliarum intimetis, ne, si hic factum fuerit concilium, sic quasi
recuperationem sui status assequantur, ut in derogationem defuncti praesulis prosiliant.

proceeded completely in the same spirit, met with much less success. After the death of Lothar II. (869), *Charles the Bald* having conquered Lorraine and divided it with Lewis of Germany (870), the pope sought to defend the rights of the lawful heir, the emperor Lewis II. with spiritual weapons;[21] but was insultingly repulsed, especially by Hincmar.[22] When afterwards he

[21] Hadr. ep. 19. ad Proceres regni Lotharii (Mansi xv. 838) : Quem ex vobis—apostolicae sedis monitis in contemtum b. Petri Apostoli, caelestis regni clavigeri, spretis, ad aliam se partem conferre cognoverimus, velut infidelem et ecclesiasticae paci ac saluti contrarium, a nostri apostolatus communione non solum alienum habebimus, sed etiam anathematis vinculo jure meritoque alligare omnino curabimus : et nos secundum apostolicae privilegium dignitatis et potestatis ipsum—domnum Hludovicum—regni hujus provinciae—Regem, dominum et Imperatorem, sicuti jam olim a Deo praeordinatum esse constat, et ab antecessoribus nostris Pontificibus statutum multis videtur indiciis habemus et quosque superfuerit ipse eum habere studebimus. Quod sane regnum si tyrannus aliquis contra divinam et apostolicam voluntatem invadere praesumserit,ᶠapostolicae sine mora sustinebit ultionis censuram. So too, the letters to Proceres and ad Episcopos regni Caroli Calvi, ad Hincmarum, ad Car. Calv., ad Ludov. Reg. epist. 20-28. Comp. generally Gess Merkwürdigk. Hincmar's S. 331.

[22] Hincm. ep. ad Hadr., A.D. 870 (opp. ed Sirm. ii. 689 Bouquet vii. 537.) He puts the answers to the assumptions of the pope into the mouth of others : Dicunt saecularem scripturam dicere, quia omne regnum saeculi hujus bellis quaeritur, victoriis propagatur, et non Apostolici vel Episcoporum excommunicationibus obtinetur, et Scripturam divinam proponunt dicere, quia Domini est regnum, per quem Reges regnant, et cui voluerit dat illud. Et cum potestatem a Christo s. Petro primo Apostolorum, et in eo suis successoribus datam, sed et Apostolis, et in eis, Episcopus pontificium ligandi et solvendi collatum illis insinuare volumus, respondent : " Et vos ergo solis orationibus vestris regnum contra Nortmannos et alios impetentes defendite, et nostram defensionem nolite quaerere : et si vultis ad defensionem habere nostrum auxilium, sicut volumus de vestris orationibus habere adjutorium, nolite quaerere nostrum dispendium, et petite domnum Apostolicum, ut, quia Rex et Episcopus simul esse non potest, et sui antecessores ecclesiasticum ordinem, quod suum est, et non rempublicam, quod Regum est, disposuerunt, non praecipiat nobis habere Regem, qui nos in sic longinquis partibus adjuvare non possit contra subitaneos et frequentes paganorum impetus, et nos Francos non jubeat servire, cui nolumus servire : quia istud jugum sui antecessores nostris antecessoribus non imposuerunt, et nos illud portare non possumus, qui scriptum esse in sacris libris audimus, ut pro libertate et hereditate nostra usque ad mortem certare debeamus. Et si aliquis Episcopus aliquem Christianum contra legem excommunicat, sibi potestatem ligandi tollit ; et nulli vitam aeternam potest tollere, si sua peccata illi eam non tollunt. Et non

sought to interfere with the measures of Charles the Bald against his rebellious son Carlmann,[23] his presumptuous letter remained disregarded.   And finally, *Hincmar*, bishop of Laon, having been deposed by the synod of·*Duziacum* (871)[24] for disobedience to his king and to his metropolitan and uncle Hincmar of Rheims,[25]

convenit ulli Episcopo dicere, ut Christianum, qui non est incorrigibilis non propter propria crimina, sed pro terreno regno ulicui tollendo vel acquirendo, nomine Christianitatis debeat privare, et eum cum Diabolo collocare—Propterea si domnus Apostolicus vult pacem quaerere, sic pacem quaerat, ut rixam non moveat: quia non nos concredemus, ut aliter ad regnum Dei pervenire non possimus, si illum, quem ipse commendat, terrenum Regem non habuerimus.''

[23] Respecting the history, see Hincmar in the annal. Bertin. ad ann. 870. 873, and ep. ad Episc. prov. Lugdun. A.D. 871 (opp. ii. 353, complete in de la Lande suppl. concill. ant. Gall. Par. 1660. fol. p. 204).— Hadr. ep. xxix. ad Carol. Calv. A D. 871, (Mansi xv. 850) : Inter caetera excessuum tuorum, quibus aliena usurpando invasisse crederis, illud, quoque nihilominus objicitur, quod etiam bestiarum feritatem excedens, contra propria viscera, *i.e.*, contra Carolomannum genitum tuum saevire minime verearis, etc.   In the same tone, ep. xxx. ad Proceres and ep. xxxi. ad Episc. regni Car.

[24] Comp. annal. Bertin. ad ann. 868 et 869.   The earlier writers concerning this affair, see in Hincmar's opp. ii. 316—352, in particular, Hincm. Rhem. opusculum lv. capitulorum adv. Hincm. Laudun. A. D. 870.   Opp. ii. 377.   Gess Merkwürdigk. S. 271.

[25] Acta conc. Duziacensis prim. ed. Lud. Cellot. Par. 1658. 4. ap. Mansi. xvi. 569 ss.   In the ep. synod. ad Hadr. P. (p. 680), it is said : Et si forte, quod non putamus, visum vobis necessario fuerit, ut secundum Sardicenses canones renovetis judicium, et detis judices, scribendo Episcopis, qui in finitimis et vicinis provinciis sunt, ut et ipsi diligenter omnino requirant, et juxta fidem veritatis definiant : vel, si decreveritis mittere a latere vestro habentes auctoritatem vestram, qui cum Episcopis judicent, eo in gradu adhuc non restituto, sicut sacri Sardicensis canones praecipiunt; non abnuimus.   Verumtamen quanta possumus devotionis humilitate deposcimus, ut etiam in hac causa nobis canonicam definitionem servetis.   Videlicet ut si, quod non credimus, ea quae regulariter definivimus,—vobis praesentialiter non placuerit vestra sententia roborare, non antea communioni sacerdotali, a qua separatus est, restituatur, antequam secundum regulas et leges in provincia, in qua causae gestae et judicatae sunt, requirantur.   Quia usque ad nostra tempora nulla Patrum definitione hoc Ecclesiis Gallicanis et Belgicis est derogatum ; praesertim quia decreta Nicaena, sive inferioris gradus clericos, sive Episcopos ipsos, ut Africanum scribit concilium, suis Metropolitanis aptissime commiserunt. Comparison with the ep. conc. Tric. above not. 17. shows, how circumstances threw the chief influence at councils sometimes into the hands of the metropolitan, sometimes into the hands of the suffragans.

the pope, to whom he had appealed, undertook to interfere in his favour, as Nicolaus I.[26] had done in the case of Rothad; but in this new contest in favour of the Pseudoisidorian principles he was so unexpectedly repulsed,[27] that he found it expedient to make every effort in his power to pacify the enraged king.[28]

[26] Hadr. ep. xxxii. ad Episc. Syn. Duziacensis (Mansi xv. 852) and ep. xxxiii. ad Carol. Calv. (p. 855). In the latter he says: jubemus ipsum Hincm. Laud. Episc., vestra fretum potentia, ad limina ss. Apostolorum, nostramque venire praesentiam. Quo sane veniente, veniat pariter accusator idoneus, qui nulla possit auctoritate legitima respui. Nos in depositione Hincmari, quamdiu vivimus, nullatenus consentiemus, nisi, ad nostram ipso veniente praesentiam, causa ejus depositionis nostro fuerit examine diligenter inquisita atque finita. Quibus nimirum admonitis, aliter in praesenti de praedicto Hincmaro, nisi eum Romam veniendi, vobis mandare distulimus.

[27] Car. c. ep. ad. Hadr. ii., composed by Hincmar (in Hincm. opp. ii. 701 and ap. Bouquet vii. 542): Cogitis nos, indecentibus potestati regiae literis vestris inhonoratum, inconvenientibus episcopali modestiae vestrae mandatus gravatum, contumeliis et opprobriis dehonestatum, aliter quam vellemus mente pacifica vobis rescribere: ut tandem animadvertatis, quamquam perturbationibus humanis obnoxium, in imagine tamen Dei ambulantem esse nos hominem, habere sensum paterna et avita successione Dei gratia, regio nomine ac culmine sublimatum, et quod his majus est, Christianum, Catholicum, fidei orthodoxae cultorem. Valde mirati sumus, ubi hoc dictator epistolae—scriptum invenerit, esse apostolica auctoritate praecipiendum, ut Rex, corrector iniquorum, et districtor reorum, ac secundum leges ecclesiasticas atque mundanas ultor criminum, reum legaliter ac regulariter pro excessibus suis damnatum, sua fretum potentia, Romam dirigat: maxime autem illum, qui et ante depositionem contra custodiam publicam et contra quietem moliri in tribus synodis extitit deprehensus,—et post depositionem suam—a sua pervicacia non quievit. Reges Francorum ex regio genere nati, non Episcoporum vicedomini, sed terrae domini hactenus fuimus computati: et ut Leo ac Romana Synodus scripsit: "Reges et Imperatores, quos terris divina potentia praecepit praeesse, jus distinguendorum negotiorum Episcopis sanctis juxta divalia constituta permiserunt;" non autem Episcoporum villici extiterunt. Et si revolveritis regesta decessorum ac praedecessorum vestrorum, talia mandata, sicut habentur in literis ex nomine vestro nobis directis,—decessores nostros a decessoribus vestris accepisse nullatenus invenietis,—iterato scribimus—deprecantes vos,—ut tales inhonorationis nostrae epistolas, taliaque mandata, sicut hactenus ex nomine vestro suscepimus, nobis et regni nostri Episcopis ac Primoribus de caetero non mandetis, et non compellatis nos mandata et epistolas vestras inhonorandas contemnere, et missos vestros dehonorare, qui vobis in his, quae ad vestrum ministerium pertinent (si tamen ministerium vestrum) cupimus obtemperare.

[28] Hadr. ep. xxxiv. ad Car. C. (Mansi xv. 857):—Et quidem quia

On the other hand, *John VIII.* enjoyed the triumph of having
plainly dared to affirm the pope's right to bestow the imperial
crown, after he had crowned as emperor Charles the Bald, subsequently to the death of Lewis II. († 875), notwithstanding the
opposition of Lewis of Germany.[29] The new emperor, too, proved

quasi tumores et laesiones vestras palpitare sensimus, has oleo consolationis per melos dulcissimae caritatis, et sanctae dilectionis unguentum
fovere, lenire, et ad integritatis sanitatem perducere medicamento, quo
valemus, optamus. Praedicatur enim de te, et longe lateque diffunditur,
quod sis sapiens et Deum timens,—quod sis justus,—quod sis amator,
exaltator et illustrator specialis in orbe terrarum et permaximus Ecclesiarum Dei, etc.—vobis confitemur devovendo, et notescimus affirman-
do, salva fidelitate Imperatoris nostri, quia, si superstes ei fuerit vestra
nobilitas, vita nobis comite, si dederit nobis quislibet multorum modio-
rum auri cumulum, nunquam acquiescemus, exposcemus, aut sponte
suscipiemus alium in regnum et imperium Romanum, nisi te ipsum.
He even yielded the disputed point. Hincmar of Laon, it is true, was
still ordered to come to Rome to see whether he persisted in his inno-
cence : tunc electis judicibus, non tamen eo prius in gradu restituto,
aut ex latere nostro directis legatis, cum auctoritate nostra refricentur
quae gesta sunt, et negotia in qua orta sunt provincia canonice terminentur. Entirely according to the first proposition. But even this did
not take place. Johannes viii. ep. 314. ad Hincm. Rhem. (Mansi
xvii. 226) A.D. 876 confirmed the decision : agnovimus justum fuisse
omnino judicium. Neque enim tantus princeps, nisi veritate fultum
quidquam poterat affirmare. Unde nefas esse duximus ejus relationi
non praebere incunctanter auditum. Hincmar of Laon was kept in prison and even blinded. See reclamatio Hincm. in actis conc. Tricassini,
A. D. 878 (Mansi xvii. 352), and at this council, Pope John VIII.,
merely out of pity for him, permitted ut Hincm. caecus, si vellet, missam
cantaret, et partem de rebus episcopii Laudunensis haberet, see annal.
Bertin. ad ann. 878.

[29] Joh. viii. epist. 315. ad Episcop. regni Ludov., A. D. 876, (Mansi
xvii. 227) : imperium, quod Carolo constat non humano collatum beneficio, licet per nostrae mediocritatis ministerium, sed divino. [Deus] per
apostolicae sedis privilegium, cunctorum favoribus approbatum sceptris
imperialibus sublimavit. Reproaches that they had not prevented Lewis
from invading Charles' realms: ubi est, qaesumus, quod vicem Christi
in Ecclesia fungimur, si pro Christo contra insolentiam principum non
luctamur ; praesertim cum secundum Apostolum non sit nobis colluc-
tatio adversus carnem et sanguinem, sed adversus principes et potestates
(Eph. vi. 12 ! !) Ejusd. epist. 316. ad Comites in regno Ludov. (ib.
p. 230). Synodus apud Ticinum ad Carol. Imp. A. D. 876 (ib. p. 310) :
Jam quia divina pietas vos, bb. Principum Apostolorum Petri et Pauli
interventione, per vicarium ipsorum, domnum videlicet Joannem summum Pontificem et universalem Papam, spiritalemque patrem vestrum
—ad imperiale culmen s. Spiritus judicio provexit: nos unanimiter vos
protectorem, dominum ac defensorem omnium nostrum eligimus.

his gratitude by many regulations in favour of the Roman see and church.[30] He even appointed *Ansegisus*, archbishop of Sens,

[3] At the Conventus Ticinensis in the year 876 (Pertz iii. 530) Charles ordains c. 1 : ut s. Rom. Ecclesia, sicut est caput omnium Ecclesiarum, ita ab omnibus honoretur et veneretur ; neque quisquam contra jus et potestatem ipsius aliquid injuste agere praesumat : sed liceat ei debitum tenere vigorem, et pro universali Ecclesia pastoralem exhibere curam. c. 2 ut honor domno et spiritali patri nostro Johanni, summo Pontifici et universali Papae ab omnibus conservetur ; et quae secundum sacrum ministerium suum auctoritate apostolica decreverit, cum summa veneratione ab omnibus suscipiantur, et debita illi obedientia in omnibus conservetur. Then c. 4 ecclesiasticus honor, et sacerdotalis atque clericalis reverentia, and finally c. 5. imperialis honor are inculcated. At the Conventus Carisiacensis, A. D. 877, (Pertz iii. 541) the emperor took under his protection the honours and rights of the Church of his country. Thus even the pope relying on the emperor, could advance with new ecclesiastical arrangements. He commanded in Synodo Ravenn. ann. 877. c. 1. (Mansi xvii. 337) : QuisquisMetropolitanus intra tres menses consecrationis suae ad fidem suam exponendam palliumque suscipiendum ab apostolica sede—non miscerit, commissa sibi careat dignitate. cap. 4 : Nulli Ducum liceat quemlibet Episcopum in praesentiam Romani praesulis introducere (this might have taken place with reference to the laws of Gratian. See vol. i. Div. 2, § 94, note 12, and Valentinian iii. ibid. note 66), vel census ab eo, sumtus publicos, et dona quaelibet exigere : sed nec coram laicis Episcopum objurgare concedimus. Clericos et sanctimoniales, pupillos et viduas sub tutela Episcoporum esse decernimus, et eos ad saecularia trahi modis omnibus interdicimus. Quemlibet autem Ducum vel alium contra haec agentem excommuuicandum esse decernimus, perseverantem vero anathematis vinculo innodandum. Hence the superabundant praise which the pope in Synodo Romanna ann. 877 (Baluz. capit. ii. 261) pronounces on this emperor : Carolus—Imperator,—tanquam splendidissimum astrum ab arce polorum illuxit, non solum monumenta progenitorum—aequiperavit, verum etiam omne prorsus avitum studium vicit, et universum paternum certamen in causa religionis atque justitiae superavit. Quapropter et nos—non immerito intelleximus, istum esse proculdubio, qui a Deo constitutus esset salvator mundi. Et quia pridem apostolicae memoriae decessori nostro Papae Nicolao idipsum jam inspiratione caelesti, revelatum esse comperimus, eligimus hunc merito et approbavimus una cum annisu et voto omnium fratrum et Coëpiscoporum nostrorum,—amplique Senatus totiusque Romani populi gentisque togatae, et secundum priscam consuetudinem solemniter ad Imperii Romani sceptra proveximus, et augustali nomine decoravimus. That Charles gained over the pope and the Romans by rich presents, see proved in annal. Fuldenses ann. 875 (Pertz i. 389) : omnem Senatum populi Romani pecunia more Jugurthino corrupit sibique sociavit ; ita ut etiam Johannes Papa—eum Imperatorem et Augustum appellare praecepisset. Hincmari annales ad ann. 876 (Pertz i. 498) : b. Petro

Pseudoisidorian primate of the Gallican and German church,[31] against the opposition of his bishops; but was not able to give steadfastness to this new institute, since he died soon after († 877). Still, however, even Charles the Bald did not think of conceding to the pope a Pseudoisidorian subjection of the Frank church.[32]

multa et pretiosa munera offerens in Imperatorem unctus et coronatus est. But yet the appendix to Eutropius, who belongs to the first half of the tenth century, is very exaggerated (see Wilman's Jahrb. d. deutschen Reichs unter Otto iii. S. 235) ap. Pertz v. 722: Qui veniens Romam, renovavit pactum cum Romanis, perdonans illis jura et consuetudines illius. Patrias autem Samniae et Calabriae simul cum omnibus civitatibus Beneventi eis contulit, insuper ad decorem regni totum ducatum Spoletinum cum duabus civitatibus Tusciae,—i.e., Aricium et Clusium, quatenus ut is, qui praeerat regia vice ante, Romanis videretur post esse subjectus. Removit etiam ab eis regias legationes, assiduitatem vel praesentiam apostolicae electionis. Quid plura? cuncta illis contulit, quae voluerunt, quaemadmodum dantur illa, quae nec recte adquiruntur nec possessura sperantur. Ab illo autem die honorificas consuetudines regiae dignitatis nemo Imperatorum, nemo Regum acquisivit. Comp. Gfrörer iii. ii. 1096. In the wild times of the tenth century, the Romans may have reconveyed to Charles the Bald, the rights which they appropriated to themselves.
[31] At the conc. Pontigonense [876] capitul. Caroli Calvi tit. xlviii. c. 7. Hincmari tract. ad Episcopos de jure Metropolitanorum, cum de primatu Ansegisi ageretur (opp. ed. Sirm. ii. 719), especially Hincmari annales (ann. Bertin.) ad ann. 876: The new primate was empowered, ut, quoties utilitas ecclesiastica dictaverit, sive in evocanda synodo, sive in aliis negotiis exercendis per Gallias et per Germanias apostolica vice fruatur, et decreta sedis apostolicae per ipsum Episcopis manifesta efficiantur: et rursus quae gesta fuerint, ejus relatione, si necesse fuerit, apostolicae sedi pandantur, et majora negotia ac difficiliora quaeque suggestione ipsius a sede apostolica disponenda et enucleanda quaerantur (word for word from the epist. Joh. P. ad. Episc. Galliae et Germ. in Sirmondii concil. Gall. iii. 422, ap. Bouquet vii. 459.) The French bishops merely declared, ut servato singulis Metropolitanis jure privilegii secundum sacros canones—domni Joannis Papae apostolici jussionibus obedirent. Et cum Imp. ut legati apostolici satagerent, ut absolute Archiepiscopi responderent, se obedituros de primatu Ansegisi, sicut Apostolicus scripsit, aliud, nisi quod praedictum est, responsum ab eis extorquere non potuerunt. In the seventh session the matter was taken up again; but the bishops declared:—quod veluti sui antecessores illius [Johannis] antecessoribus regulariter obedierunt, ita ejus decretis vellent obedire. Cf. Marca de conc. Sac. et Imp. lib. iv. c. 5, § 5, lib. vi. c. 29, § 5. Ejusd. diss. de Primatibus § 56.
[32] Caroli Calvi de Presbyteris ex criminibus diffamatis ad Joannem P. ann. 876 (Hincmari opp. ii. 768, and in Goldasti collectio constitut.

§. 22.

PAPACY IN THE STORMY TIMES TILL THE SYNOD OF SUTRI, (1046.)

V. E. Löscher's Historie des röm. Hurenregiments, Leipzig 1707. 4. (2d
edition with the title die Historie der mittlern Zeiten als ein Licht aus
der Finsterniss. 1725. 4.) Gfrörer's K.G. iii. iii. 1133. On the chronology
of the popes from 885—972, see R. A. Koepke de vita et scriptis Liudprandi, Berol. 842. 8. p. 155.

From the time that the Italian nobles, whose power gradually

imperialium ii. 34) : cap. 2 : Cum non longe ante hos annos nepos
noster Hludovicus Italiae Imperator instinctu quorundam contra nos se
commovit, missae sunt nobis epistolae, quasi ex apostolicae hujus sedis
auctoritate ac nomine, quas tenoris inconvenientia hanc sanctam et dis-
cretissimam sedem non misisse ostendit. Cap. 3 : Et quoniam pravis
saepius prava quam recta innotesci solent, nacta hinc occasione trans-
alpinarum regionum Presbyteri, a suis Episcopis de certis criminibus
regulariter ab ordine sacerdotali dejecti, et poenitentiae subacti, sine
licentia et conscientia Primatum et Episcoporum suorum huc venire, et
hinc epistolas, quae regulis non conveniunt, referre coeperunt. Quas
non jussione apostolica, sed—quorumque ministrorum quasi pia miseratione factas, et nos, et illius regionis putant Episcopi. Therefore he
wishes to lay before the pope the fundamental principles of the transalpine churches on this point. There are those of the Nicene, Sardican,
and African synods, whose canons are adduced in full. Namely, cap. 7.
Episcopum judicari debere a suis judicibus Episcopis. Then cap. 8.
can. Sardic. 7. respecting the appeal to Rome at that time allowable.
On the other hand, cap. 13. Sacrae leges ac regulae Presbyteros et
caeteros inferioris gradus clericos non alibi, quam ad suos Episcopos
praecipiunt accusari : then according to can. Sardic. 17, the appeal to
finitimos Episcopos is still open to them. Cap. 18. A judicibus autem,
sive quos juxta Africanos canones Primates dederint, sive quos ipsi
vicinos ex consensu delegerint causa finienda, regulariter provocari non
potest. These are the principles of the transalpine church, without
which all discipline would come to nothing. For else (c. 19) faciet
licenter quisque Presbyterorum quodlibet. Unde si fuerit redargutus,
veniat Romam. Cap. 22 : Legimus etiam quamvis rarissime praeceptum a sede apostolica, quosdam de longinquioribus parochiis specialis
dioceseos Romani Pontificis—propter contumaces contentiones aliquos
invitatos fuisse : sed de transalpinis regionibus—tale quid pro Presbyterorum et Diaconorum appellatione a sede apostolica praeceptum fuisse
non legimus etc.

increased under the last Carlovingians after the deposal of Charles
the Stout (887), had become entirely independent, the popes [1]
were also involved in the wild strife of parties which now began
in Italy.[2]   They were obliged, as creatures of the reigning party,
to give their spiritual sanction to its objects, but were by this
means involved in all its fortunes, and were therefore frequently
compelled to end their career by a violent death or in prison.

When the dukes Guido of Spoleto, and Berengarius of Friaul,
strove for the Italian crown, *Stephen V.*[3] favoured the former,
and crowned him emperor (891).   It is true that *Formosus* summoned the German king, Arnulf (894)[4] against Guido's son,
the emperor Lambert : but after Arnulf's departure, Lambert was
again recognised, and Formosus, even in the grave, was blamed

---

[1] Martin II. (properly Marinus) from 882-884, Hadrian III. † 885,
Stephanus V. (VI.) † 891, Formosus † 896, Bonifacius VI. only 15
days, Stephanus VI. (VII.) strangled 897, Romanus only 4 months,
Theodore II. only 20 days, John IX. † 900, Benedict IV. † 903,
Leo V. after one month banished by his successor, Christophorus like-
wise banished after 7 months, Sergius III. from 904-911.

[2] At first there was a struggle between a Frank and a national party,
in which the latter, even at the time of Charles the Stout, endeavoured
to make the choice of a pope independent of the emperors. Thus it
chose, 885, Stephen V.   See annal. Fuldenses ad h. a. (Pertz i. 402) :
Unde Imperator iratus, quod eo inconsulto illum ordinare praesumserunt, misit Liutwartum et quosdam Romanae sedis Episcopos, qui
eum deponerent : quod perficere minime potuerunt. When Martinus
Polonus [1277] ad ann. 884 says of Hadrian III. : Hic constituit ut,
Imperator non intromitteret se de electione, what some later writers
have followed him in (see on the opposite side Muratori annali d'Italia
v. 148), and when Sigonius de regno Ital. lib. v. even ascribes to him
the constitution, ut moriente rege Crasso sine filiis, regnum Italicis
principibus una cum titulo Imperii traderetur ; they rightly designate
the strivings of the national party, which however have hardly found a
formal expression in papal decrees.

[3] In what manner the popes, even at this time, when they were at
Rome the playthings of parties, established their claims externally, is
shown by the regulation Stephani V. ap. Gratian. P. i. dist. xix. c. 4 :
Enimvero, quia in speculum et exemplum s. Romana Ecclesia, cui nos
Christus praeesse voluit, proposita est, ab omnibus quicquid statuit,
quicquid ordinat, perpetuo et irrefragabiliter observandum est.

[4] Oath which the Romans took to Arnulf at the imperial coronation,
in the annal. Bertin. and Fuldens. ad ann. 896 : Juro per haec omnia
Dei mysteria, quod salvo honore et lege mea atque fidelitate domini
Formosi P. fidelis sum et ero omnibus diebus vitae meae Arnolfo Imperatori etc.

by *Stephen VI.*[5] After Lambert's death († 898)[6] Berengar renewed his attempts, and having defeated Lewis, king of Provence whom the Spoletan party had put up against him, and who had even been crowned emperor (901) by *Benedict IV.*, was at length successful in becoming king of Italy, and was crowned emperor by *John X.* (915).

In the meantime, a party led by Adelbert Margrave of Tuscany and by the notorious Theodora with her two daughters, Marozia and Theodora, were endeavouring to obtain dominion over Rome. The decided ascendency of this party began with the elevation of the vile *Sergius III.* to the papal see (904). The succeeding popes were nominated by it.[7] *John X.*, elevated by his relation to Theodora (914)[8] was murdered, when he be-

[5] Concerning the conc. Rom. held against Formosus 897, see especially the contemporaries Auxilius de ordinationibus Formosi P. libb. ii. (in bibl. PP. Lugd. xvii. 1. and ap. J. Morinus de sacris Ecclesiae ordinationibus p. 282) and super causa et negotio Form. P. (in Mabillonii analectis p. 28.) Farther, an unknown individual's Invectiva in Romam pro Formoso Papa (in Anastas. de vitis Rom. Pont. ed. Blanchini iv. lxx.) and Syn. Rom. A. D. 898 (not 904. ap. Mansi xviii. 221), where John IX. cashiered the acts of that Synod.

[6] To this Italian emperor a co-operation in the choice of a pope had been formally conceded by John IX., in order to check the usurpations of the Roman nobles. Syn. Rom. ann. 898. c. 10. (Mansi xviii. 225. Pertz iv. ii. 158) : Quia s. Romana Ecclesia, cui Deo auctore praesidemus, plurimas patitur violentias Pontifice obeunte, quae ob hoc inferuntur, quis absque Imperatoris notitia, et suorum legatorum praesentia Pontificis fit consecratio, nec canonico ritu et consuetudine ab Imperatore directi intersunt nuntii, qui violentiam et scandala in ejus consecratione non permittant fieri : volumus, id ut deinceps abdicetur, et constituendus Pontifex convenientibus Episcopis et universo clero eligatur, expetente senatu et populo, qui ordinandus est, et sic in conspectu omnium celeberrime electus ab omnibus, praesentibus legatis imperialibus, consecretur. Nullusque sine periculo juramentum vel promissiones nova adinventione ab eo audeat extorquere, nisi quae antiqua exigit consuetudo, ne Ecclesia scandalizetur, vel Imperatoris honorificentia minuatur.

[7] Anastasius III. † 913, Landus † 914, John X. murdered in prison 928, Leo VI. † 929, Stephen VII. (VIII.) † 931, John XI. † 936, Leo VII. † 939, Stephen VIII. (IX.) † 942, Martin III. (Marinus II.) † 946, Agapetus II. † 956, John XII. deposed 963.

[8] Luitprandi antapodosis ii. 48 (Pertz v. 297) : Theodora scortum impudens, hujus Alberici, qui nuper hominem exiit, avia (quod dictu etiam foedissimum est), Romanae civitatis non inviriliter monarchiam obtinebat. Quae duas habuit natas, Marotiam atque Theodoram, sibi

trayed symptoms of a disposition to act independently (928).[8]
Soon after, *Marozia's* son, *John XI.*[10] (931), was made pope ; and
her second son, *Alberich*, possessed himself of the chief power
of Rome[11] as patricius and senator (932–954).   The latter's son
Octavianus, not content with succeeding to his father's power,
assumed the papal dignity also as *John XII.* (956) which he dis-
graced by the most shameful excesses.[12]   In an evil hour for him—

non solum coaequales, verum etiam Veneris exercitio promptiores.   Harum Marotia ex Papa Sergio—Joannem, qui post Joannis Ravennatis
obitum Rom. Ecclesiae obtinuit dignitatem, nefario genuit adulterio :
ex Alberico autem Marchione Albericum, qui nostro post tempore ejusdem Romanae urbis principatum sibi usurpavit.   (Petrus Ravennatis
sedis Archiepiscopus) dum subjectionis officio debitae Joannem Papam,
qui suae minister Ecclesiae tunc temporis habebatur, Romam saepius
et iterum domino dirigeret Apostolico : Theodora—meretrix satis impu-
dentissima, Veneris calore succensa, in hujus speciei decorem vehementer exarsit ; secumque hunc scortari non solum voluit, verum etiam atque
etiam post compulit.   Haec dum impudentur aguntur, Bonoviensis
Episcopus moritur, et Joannes iste loco ejus eligitur.   Paulo post ante
hujus diem consecrationis nominatus Ravennas Archipraesul mortem
obiit, locumque ejus Johannes hic, Theodorae instinctu—sibi usurpavit.
Romam quippe adveniens mox Ravennatis Ecclesiae ordinatur Episcopus.   Modica vero temporis intercapedine, Deo vocante, qui eum injuste
ordinaverat Papa defunctus est.   Theodorae autem Glycerii mens per-
versa, ne amasii CC. milliarium interpositione, quibus Ravenna seques-
tratur a Roma, rarissimo concubitu potiretur, Ravennatis hunc sedis
archiepiscopium coëgit deserere, Romanumque (proh nefas !) summum
pontificium usurpare.   On Luitprand's credibility in this passage, see
Martini's (cited before section 2) Abhandl. S. 54 ff.   John's campaign
against the Saracen fort at Fl. Garigliano (916).   Luitpr. ii. 14.   Martini S. 24.   Schlosser's Weltgesch. ii. i. 595.
    [9] Luitpr. iii. 43. (Pertz v. 312).   Martini S. 27.
    [10] According to Luitprand (note 8), son of Pope Sergius and Marozia.
Leo of Ostia (about 1100) according to whom Albericus Rom. Consul.
was the father, cannot disprove this account, since he (as well as Schlosser ii. ii. 201) confounds John xi. with John xii.   See Martini p. 53.
    [11] Luitpr. iii. 44.   Martini S. 27.   Schlosser ii. ii. 164.
    [12] Concerning him, Luitpr. de rebus gestis Ottonis (Pertz v. 340.)
Martini, p. 68, shows that there is no ground for questioning the authenticity of the last chapters of Luitprand, as had been frequently done, after
Baronius ad. ann. 963 no. 2 ss.   His manners, c. 4 : Joannes P. his
omnibus (moribus et legibus) adversatur.   Non clam est populo, quod
fatemur.   Testis est Rainerii, sui ipsius militis, vidua, quam caeco captus igne, multis praefectam urbibus, sacrosanctis b. Petri donavit aureis
crucibus atque calicibus.   Testis est Stephana, ejus amita, quae in effu-
sione, quod ex eo conceperat, recens hominem exivit.   Quod se cuncta
taceant, Lateranense palatium, Sanctorum quondam hospitium, nunc

self, he summoned the German King Otto I. to protect him
against the oppressions of Berengar II., king of Italy, (960) and
crowned him emperor (962) ;[13] for when he acted treacherously
towards him, Otto caused him to be deposed[14] (963), appointing

prostibulum meretricum, non silebit, amitam conjugem, Stephaniae alterius concubinae sororem. Testis omnium gentium, praeter Romanar-
um, absentia mulierum, quae ss. Apostolorum limina orandi gratia
timent visere, cum nonnullas ante dies paucos hunc audierint conjuga-
tas, viduas, virgines vi oppressisse. Testes sunt ss. Apostolorum Ecclesiae, quae non stillatim pluviam, sed totum tectum intrinsecus, supra
ipsa etiam sacrosancta altaria imbrem admittunt.
    [13] Schlosser ii. ii. 202. W. Dönniges Jahrbücher des deutschen
Reichs unter Otto i. Berlin 1839. 8. S. 81. Luitpr. de rebus gest
Ottonis c. 3 : Jusjurandum vero (Otto) ab eodem P. Joanne supra pre-
tiosissimum corpus Petri, atque omnibus civitatis proceribus, se nunquam
Berengario atque Adelberto auxiliaturum, accepit. On the contrary,
Gratian P. i. dist. lxiii. c. 33. has a juramentum Ottonis, before he was
emperor (three texts in Pertz monum iv. 28) : quod si—Romam venero,
s. Rom. Ecclesiam, et te rectorem ipsius exaltabo secundum posse
meum, et numquam vitam, aut membra, et ipsum honorem, quem habes, mea voluntate—aut meo consensu—perdes : et in Romana urbe
nullum placitum, aut ordinationem faciam de omnibus, quae ad te aut
ad Romanos pertinent, sine tuo consilio, et quicquid de terra s. Petri
ad nostram potestatem pervenerit, tibi reddam, etc. Dönniges, p. 203,
believes that this oath, whose tenor is certainly striking, in an oath of allegiance, was forged at the time of the investiture controversy. On the
other hand, Gfrörer iii. iii. 1242 declares it to be authentic. The investiture act of Otto, given by Baronius ad ann. 962, no. 3 professedly
from the original (ap. Pertz iv. ii. 164), has been pronounced spurious,
especially by Goldast, Conring (de Germanorum Imp. Romano 1643.
Opp. i. 76), and Muratori; but defended on the other side by Gretser,
Cenni and Marini (Rom. 1822). Probably the genuine original document
was subsequently falsified, Pertz iv. ii. 159. The expression of the investiture is significant for the relations of this period, ut ea in illius
[Pontifices] ditione ad uttendum et fruendum atque disponendum firmiter valeant obtineri, salva in omnibus potestate nostra, et filii nostri,
posterorumque nostrorum, secundum quod in pacto et constitutione ac
promissionis firmitate Eugenii Pontificis (see above § 6 not, 4), succes-
sorumque illius continetur. The fictitious investiture of Lewis the debonaire (see § 6 note 1), which appears to have been adopted into this
of Otto has certainly flowed first from it. Comp. Le Bret Geschichte
Italien i. 476.
    [14] See the Acts of the conc. Rom. ap. Luitprand de rebus gestis Ot-
tonis c. 10 ss. (Pertz v. 342). Comp. Dönniges, Jahrbucher d. deutschen Reichs unter Otto i. S. 93. The older writers always acknowledged the legitimacy of this council (even as late as Platina in the fifteenth, and Onuphrius Panvinius in the sixteenth century) ; on the con-

as pope[15] Leo VIII., whom he maintained in spite of all the opposition of John XII. and Benedict V.

trary most of the later catholic historians, after Baronius ad ann. 963, declare it to be a Pseudosynodus and Conciliabulum, and Leo VIII., who was there elected, a Pseudo-papa. Comp. particularly Nat. Alex. hist. eccl. ad saec. ix. et x. diss. xvi.

[15] Luitprand. c. 8 : Cives vero sanctum Imperatorem cum suis omnibus in Urbem suscipiunt, fidelitatemque repromittunt: hoc addentes et firmiter jurantes, nunquam se Papam electuros aut ordinaturos praeter consensum atque electionem domni Imperatoris Ottonis. Constitutio Leonis P. (by Theodoricus de Niem about 1400 communicated, with scholia, in the privilegia et jura Imperii circa investituras Episcopatuum et Abbatiarum in S. Schardii syntagma tractatuum de imperiali jurisdictione, p. 249, in extracts, ap. Gratian. P. i. dist. lxiii. c. 23, in an older form after Codd. of the eleventh century ap. Pertz iv. ii. 167) :—Idcirco ad exemplum b. Adriani, sedis apostolicae Episcopi, cujus vitam et actionem satis discretam audivimus, et rationabilem admodum in suis spiritalibus sanctionibus recognovimus : qui ejusmodi s. Synodum constituit, et domno Carolo—Patriciatus dignitatem ac ordinationem apostolicae sedis et Episcopatuum concessit ; nos quoque Leo, servus servorum Dei, Episcopus, simul cum cuncto Clero et universo populo Romano, omnibus ordinibus hujus almae Urbis,—constituimus, confirmamus, corroboramus, et per nostram Apostolicam auctoritatem concedimus atque largimur domno Ottoni Primo, Teutonico Regi, dilectissimo spirituali in Christo Filio nostro, ejusque successoribus hujus regni Italiae in perpetuum, tam sibi facultatem successorem eligendi, quam summae sedis apostolicae Pontificem ordinandi : ac per hoc Archiepiscopos seu Episcopos, ut ipsi tamen ab eo investituram suscipiant, et consecrationem recipiant undecunque pertinuerit, exceptis his, quos Imperator Pontifici et Archiepiscopis concessit. Ita demum asserimus, ut nemo deinceps, cujuscunque gradus vel conditionis, sive aignitatis sive religiositatis, eligendi Regem vel Patricium sive Pontificem summae sedis apostolicae, aut quemcunque Episcopum, vel ordinandi habeat facultatem, sed soli regi Romani Imperii hanc reverentiae tribuimus facultatem, absque omni pecunia haec omnia superius disponenda ; et ut ipse sit Rex, et Patricius. Quodsi a Clero et populo quis eligatur Episcopus, nisi a supradicto Rege laudetur et investiatur, non consecretur. Unde si quis contra hanc apostolicam auctoritatem et traditionem aliquid molitur,—sciat se in iram b. Petri, Apostolorum Principis, et filii nostri domni Ottonis, ejus successorum, et nostram casurum, et sub anathematis vinculo emersurum, ac per hoc excommunicationi universalis Ecclesiae omnisque populi christiani eum subjacere decrevimus. Insuper nisi a malo resipuerit, irrevocabili exilio puniatur, vel ultimis suppliciis feriatur.—Baronius, ad ann. 964 no. 22. and 23, denies the genuineness of this document, though he refers to it again ann. 996, no. 35 and 42. The genuineness is specially defended by Goldast, rationale constitutt. imp. p. 29 ss. Comp. also Chr. W. F. Walchii diss. de Ottone M. p. 46 ss. Le Bret Geschichte von Italien i. 486. The contents of the

As long as Otto I. lived, he preserved tolerable order in Rome ;[16] but immediately after his death (973), the Tuscan party elevated itself anew under *Crescentius* son of *the younger Theodora*.[17] *Otto II.* († 983) maintained in some measure the imperial dignity ; but during the minority of *Otto III.* Crescentius exercised full sway over Rome.[18] The power of the pope seems to have sunk not only in this city but also in other countries ;[19] for at the instance of Hugo Capet a *Synod at Rheims*[20] did not hesitate to depose Archbishop Arnulf of Rheims, and to

document correspond with the relations which were actually established at that time, but the form of it is perhaps spurious. Pertz l. c. Dönniges S. 102. However, Gfrörer, iii. iii. 1254, defends the latter also. Another document, in which Leo is said to have restored to the emperor all former imperial gifts (Pertz iv. ii. 168), is doubtless wholly fictitious.

[16] Popes: Leo VIII. † 965. Contin. Regin. ad ann. 965 : Tunc legati Romanorum—Imperatorem pro instituendo, quem vellet, Romano Pontifice, in Saxoniam adeuntes, honorifice suscipiuntur et remittuntur. Et Otgerus, Spirensis Episc. et Linzo, Cremonensis Episc. cum eisdem Romam ab Imp. diriguntur. Tunc ab omni plebe Romana Joannes, Narniensis Ecclesiae Episc., eligitur. John XIII. † 972. Benedict VI.

[17] Benedict VI., murdered by the Tuscan party 974 ; Boniface VII. expelled by the people, 974 ; Benedict VII. † 983 ; John XIV., chosen by imperial influence. .On the chronology see W. Giesebrecht in den Jahrbüchern des deutschen Reichs unter Otto ii. S. 141.

[18] Immediately after Otto II.'s death, Boniface VII. returned, and John XIV. died in prison, 984, Boniface VII. (cf. Arnulf. Aurel. in the discourse about to be quoted, note 19, below ; horrendum monstrum Bonifacius, cunctos mortales nequitia superans, etiam prioris pontificis sanguine cruentus—fugatus—redit—virum Apostolicum—squalore carceris affectum perimit) † 985. John XV. † 996, Gregory V. owed his election to his relative, Otto III. (See Schlosser ii. ii. 291.) On the chronology see Wilman's Jahrb. des deutschen Reichs unter Otto III. S. 207.

[19] The chief authority for the following is the newly-discovered Richerus iv. 25. ap. Pertz v. 636. Gerbert od. Papst Sylvester II. u. s. Jahrhundert, v. Dr C. F. Hock, Wien 1837. S. 80. Wilman's Jahrb. des deutschen Reichs unter Otto III., Berlin, 1840. S. 51. On Gerbert's letters belonging to this period see Wilman's, p. 167. On Richer see p. 175. Gfrörer iii. iii. 1441.

[20] The acts of this memorable synod have been preserved by Gerbert (Pope Sylvester II). He says in the prologus : Accingar igitur, et summarum quidem genera causarum, in Remensi concilio exposita, breviter attingam, ut et gestorum veritas innotescat, et quae a summis viris retractata sunt agnoscantur.—triplici genere interpretationis utendum

z 2

appoint the celebrated *Gerbert* his successor, in a manner that showed their utter contempt for the papal authority.[21] *John XV.*

fore censeo, scilicet ut quaedam ad verbum ex alia in aliam transferantur linguam : in quibusdam autem sententiarum gravitas et eloquii dignitas dicendi genere conformentur : porro in aliis una dictio occasionem faciat, et abdita investigari, et in lucem ipsos affectus manifeste proferri. It seems, then, from this that Gerbert had before him the protocol composed in the vulgar tongue.   These acts were first published by the Magdeburg Centuriators, Cent. x. cap. 9. p. 457 ss., best with new appendices, ap. Pertz. v. 658.   Baronius declared them to be spurious. Hence they are wanting in the older collections.   Mansi xix. 107. was the first to adopt them and declare : censent vulgo omnes, Gerbertum reipsa et sincere recitasse acta Concilii vere habiti etc.

   [21] Arnulf was accused of having betrayed Rheims, A.D. 989, to Charles, duke of Lorrain, who pretended to the crown.   Hugo Capet at first applied to the pope (letters in the act. Syn. Rhem. cap. 25 and 26) : but having got Arnulf into his power, he summoned that council.   At it an attempt was made by certain monks at first to prove from the Pseudo-isidoriana that Arnulf ought, first of all, to be restored to his bishopric, and that the negotia Episcoporum belonged to the see of Rome (cap. 19-23).   This was specially opposed by Arnulphus Ep. Aurelianensis (qui ordinis custos ac omnium gerendorum interpres declaratus est, eo quod inter omnes Galliarum Episcopos sapientia et eloquentia clarior haberetur. cap. 1).   He said, cap. 28., among other things : Nos—Rom. Ecclesiam—semper honorandam decernimus—salva tamen auctoritate Nicaeni concilii.   Si nova constitutio Rom. Pontificis promulgatis legibus canonum praejudicare potest, quid prosunt leges conditae, cum ad unius arbitrium omnia dirigantur ?   O lugenda Roma, quae nostris majoribus clara patrum lumina protulisti, nostris temporibus monstruosas tenebras futuro saeculo famosas offudisti !   Olim accepimus claros Leones, magnos Gregorios.   Eorum itaque dispositioni, qui vitae merito et scientia cunctos mortales anteirent, recte universalis Ecclesia credita est: quamvis et in hac ipsa felicitate hoc privilegium tibi ab Africanis Episcopis contradictum sit (see vol. i. div. 2. § 94. not. 61.), has credo quas patimur miserias magis, quam typhum dominationis formidantibus. Nam quid sub haec tempora non vidimus ?   Vidimus Johannem cognomento Octavianum, in volutabro libidinum versatum etc. etc.   Num talibus monstris hominum ignominia plenis, scientia divinarum et humanarum rerum vacuis, innumeros sacerdotes Dei per orbem terrarum, scientia et vitae merito conspicuos subjici decretum est ?   Quid hunc, rev. Patres, in sublimi solio residentem, veste purpurea et aurea radiantem, quid hunc, inquam, esse censetis ?   Nimirum si caritate destituitur, solaque scientia inflatur et extollitur, Antichristus est, in templo Dei sedens, et se ostendens tamquam sit Deus.   Si autem nec caritate fundatur, nec scientia erigitur, in templo Dei tamquam statua, tamquam idolum est, a quo responsa petere, marmora consulere est.   Quo ergo consultum ibimus ?   Certe in Belgica et Germania—summos sacerdotes Dei, religione admodum praestantes, inveniri, in hoc sacro conventu

declared indeed the decrees of this synod void ; but, as it seems, without effect.[22] On the other hand, the new king, Robert, found

testes quidam sunt.   Proinde, si regum dissidentium animositas non prohiberet, inde magis Episcoporum judicium petendum fore videretur, quam ab ea urbe, quae nunc emtoribus venalis exposita, ad nummorum quantitatem judicia trutinat.   He then shows, in answer to the epist. Pseudo-Damasi cited by the monks, that, according to Gregory the Great, certainly bishops and metropolitans could be judged by provincial councils.   Further, in opposition to the rule of Pseudo-Damasus, Synodum sine ejus Rom. sedis auctoritate fieri, non est catholicum : among other things : Nicaenus canon bis in anno concilia debere fieri dicit, nihilque inde ad Rom. Episcopi auctoritatem spectare praescribit. But no suspicion that that decree might have been supposititious !   At length, Arnulf of Rheims acknowledged his offence, and voluntarily resigned his place. Comp. Gerbert's Rechtfertigungsschreiben für d. Concil ad Wilderodum Episc. Argentinae ap. Mansi xix. 163.

[22] The French bishops united at the synod of Chela, 992, for this end (Richerius iv. 89. ap. Pertz. v. 651), ut ab ea die idem sentirent, idem vellent, idem cooperarentur, secundum id quod scriptum est : erat eis cor unum et anima una (Act. 4. 32).   Placuit quoque sanciri, si quid a Papa Romano contra Patrum decreta suggereretur, cassum et irritum fieri, juxta quod Apostolus ait : haereticum hominem et ab Ecclesia dissentientem penitus devita (Tit. iii. 10).   Nec minus abdicationem Arnulfi et promotionem Gerberti, prout ab eis ordinatae et peractae essent, perpetuo placuit sanciri, juxta quod in canonibus scriptum habetur : Synodo provinciali statutum a nullo temere labefactandum. Comp. Gerbert's three letters ap. Mansi xix. 173 ss. ad Constantinum Miciacensem Abb. :—Majus est, quod quaeritur, et quod appetitur, quam ego humilis et parvus ; verumque proverbium est : tua res agitur, paries cum proximus ardet.   Hoc enim concesso, dignitas vel potius gravitas confunditur sacerdotalis, status regni periclitatur etc.   Ad Siquinum Archiep. Senon. : Quomodo ergo nostri aemuli dicunt, quod in Arnulfi dejectione Romani Episcopi judicium expectandum fuit ?   Poteruntne docere Romani Episcopi judicium Dei majus esse ?   Constanter dico, quod si ipse Romanus Episcopus in fratrem peccaverit, saepiusque admonitus Ecclesiam non audierit, hic inquam, Rom. Episc. praecepto Dei est habendus sicut ethnicus et publicanus.   Quod si propterea sua communione nos indignos ducit, quia contra Evangelium sentienti nullus nostrum consentit ; non ideo a communione Christi nos separare poterit.   Non est ergo danda occasio nostris aemulis, ut sacerdotium, quod ubique unum est, sicut Ecclesia catholica una est, ita uni subjici videatur, ut et pecunia, gratia, metu vel ignorantia corrupto nemo sacerdos esse possit, nisi quem sibi hae virtutes commendarint.   Sit lex communis Ecclesiae catholicae Evangelium, Apostoli, Prophetae, Canones spiritu Dei constituti, et totius mundi reverentia consecrati, Decreta sedis apostolicae ab his non discordantia.   Ad Adelaidem Imperatricem : neque enim Ecclesiam, quam Episcoporum judicio regendam accepi, sine Episcoporum judicio relinquere volo.

a reconciliation with the pope desirable, amid the hostile designs of the emperor Otto III. against him. *Gregory V.*[23] had the triumph of seeing Arnulf restored to freedom, and Gerbert compelled to yield (997);[24] so that he even met with obedience when he desired to annul Robert's marriage with Bertha, on account of their too near consanguinity.[25]

When Crescentius violated the lauded obedience *Otto III.* put an end to his dominion (998),[26] and elevated after Gregory's death his own teacher Gerbert to the papal see, as *Sylvester II.* ;[27] but at the same time took up his residence in Rome for

[23] Respecting him see die deutschen Päpste v. C. Höfler (2 Th. Regensburg 1839. 8.) i. 94. Martinus Polonus in chron. ad Ottonem III. makes the remark : Licet tres Ottones per successionem generis regnaverunt, post tamen institutum fuit, ut per officiales imperii Imperator eligeretur, qui sunt septem etc. In the work de regimine Principum (attributed to St Thomas) lib. iii. cap. 19. this becomes : Otto imperium tenuit ad tertiam generationem, quorum quilibet vocatus est Otto. Et tunc, ut historici tradunt, per Gregorium V. genere similiter Teutonicum, provisa est electio, ut videlicet per VII. principes Alemanniae fiat etc. This passage has been copied by succeeding writers, even defended by Baronius ad ann. 996 n. 38 ss. and Bellarmine de translat. Rom. imp. lib. iii. but is now universally abandoned, cf. Natalis Alexander hist. eccl. ad saec. ix. et x. diss. xvii.

[24] Richerus in fine ap. Pertz v. 657.

[25] Conc. Rom. ann. 998 can. 1. (Mansi xix. 225) ut rex Robertus consanguineam suam Bertam, quam contra leges in uxorem duxit, derelinquat et VII. annorum poenitentiam agat.—Quod si non fecerit, anathema sit, idemque de eadem Berta fieri praeceptum est. The contemporary Helgaldus Floriacensis Mon. relates in vita Roberti R. c. 17. (ap Bouquet x. 107) merely this : Abbonis Floriacensium Abbatis increpatio tam diu perstitit, donec Rex mitissimus reatum suum agnosceret, et quam male sibi copulaverat mulierem prorsus derelinqueret, et paccati maculam grata Deo satisfactione dilueret. The credulous Petrus Damiani († 1072) first tells us, epist. lib. ii. ep. 15. (ap. Bouquet x. 492) : Robertus—propinquam sibi copulavit uxorem, ex qua suscepit filium, anserinum per omnia collum et caput habentem. Quos etiam, virum scilicet et uxorem, omnes fere Galliarum Episcopi communi simul excommunicavere sententia. Cujus sacerdotalis edicti tantus omnem undique populum terror invasit, ut ab ejus universi societate recederent, nec praeter duos sibi servulos ad necessarii victus obsequium remanerent. Qui tamen et ipsi omnia vasa, in quibus rex edebat vel bibebat, percepto cibo, abominabilia judicantes, pabulum ignibus exhibebant. His tandem Rex coactus angustiis, ad sanum consilium rediens, divortit incestum, iniitque legale connubium.

[26] Thietmari chron. iv. 21. ap. Pertz v. 776. Schlosser ii. ii. 294.

[27] Gregory V. † 999, Sylvester II. † 1003, (Gerbert oder Papst

the purpose of restoring the old Roman dominion in Byzantine forms.[28] Yet much as he purposed to favour *the Romans*, he

Sylvester II. u. s. Jahrhundert. v. Dr. C. F. Hock. Wien 1837. S. 129), John XVII. † 1003, John XVIII. † 1009, Sergius IV. † 1012, Benedict VIII. † 1024, John XIX. † 1033, Benedict IX.

[28] Thietmari chron. iv. 29 : Imperator antiquam Romanorum consuetudinem jam ex parte magna deletam suis cupiens renovare temporibus, multa faciebat, quae diversi diverse sentiebant. Wilmans Jahrb. d. deutschen Reichs unter Otto iii. S. 133. Gfrörer iii. iii. 1510. Remarkable fragments respecting form of government and ceremonials which were introduced into Rome at this time have been discovered by Pertz in the Vatican, and published by Blume in the Rheinisches Museum für Jurisprudenz v. 123. Ottonis iii. diploma A. D. 999 (ap. Baronium ad ann. 1191 no. 57. Pertz iv. ii. 162) : Romam caput mundi profitemur, Rom. Ecclesiam matrem omnium Ecclesiarum esse testamur, sed incuria et inscientia Pontificum longe suae claritatis titulos obfuscasse. Nam non solum quae extra urbem esse videbantur vendiderunt,—sed—si quid in hac nostra urbe regia habuerunt, ut majori licentia evagarentur, omnibus cum vindicante pecunia in commune dederunt, et s. Petrum et s. Paulum, ipsa quoque altaria spoliaverunt, et pro reparatione semper confusionem duxerunt. Confusis vero papaticis legibus, et jam abjecta Ecclesia Rom. in tantum quidam Pontificum irruerunt, ut maximam partem Imperii nostri apostolatui suo conjungerent.—Haec sunt enim commenta ab illis ipsis inventa, quibus Joannes Diaconus, cognomento Digitorum mutius [mozzo, mutilus, perhaps that John Diaconus whom John XII. first employed as a tool, Cont. Regin. ann. 960, and whose right hand he afterwards caused to be cut off, id. ad ann. 964, Luitpr. hist. Ottonis c. 19. ap. Pertz v. 346] praeceptum aureis literis scripsit, sub titulo magni Constantini longa mendacii tempora finxit (see above § 20. note 21.) Haec sunt etiam commenta, quibus dicunt, quendam Carolum s. Petro nostra publica tribuisse (see above § 21. note 30.) Sed ad haec respondemus, ipsum Carolum nihil dare jure potuisse, utpote jam a Carolo meliore fugatum, jam imperio privatum, jam destitutum et annullatum.—Spretis ergo commentitiis praeceptis, et imaginariis scriptis ex nostra liberalitate s. Petro donamus quae nostra sunt : non sibi, quae sua sunt, veluti nostra conferimus. Sicut enim pro amore s. Petri dominum Sylvestrum magistrum nostrum Papam elegimus, et Deo volente ipsum serenissimum ordinavimus et creavimus : ita pro amore ipsius domini Sylvestri Papae, s. Petro de publico nostro dona conferimus—octo comitatus,— Pisaurum, Fanum, Senogalliam, Anconam, Fossabrunum, Callium, Esium et Ausimum. This diploma was copied and authenticated by command of the pope, from the archives at Assisi 1339 (the protocol ap. Baron. l. c.)—is declared spurious by Baronius, Gretser, Pagi, and others, and recently by Wilmans Jahrb. des deutschen Reichs unter Otto iii. S. 233, defended by Muratori in his controversial writings concerning Commachio, by Pertz l. c. and Gfrörer iii. iii. 1570.

only incurred their hatred, with his German associations.[29] After his death (1002), the German dominion was cast off, the Tuscan party were again triumphant, and even from *Benedict VIII.* (1012), the papal dignity was for a long time hereditary in the family of the counts of Tuscany. Henry II.[30] was merely able to exercise imperial rights in Rome temporarily at his coronation (1014).[31] To Benedict succeeded (1024) his brother *John XIX.*

[29] Comp. the Roman fragments belonging to this time in the Rheinischen Museum für Jurisprudenz v. 131 : Postquam peccatis nostris exigentibus Romanorum imperium barbarorum patuit gladiis feriendum, Romanas leges penitus ignorantes illiterati ac barbari judices legis peritos in legem cogentes jurare, judices creavere, quorum judicio lis ventilata terminaretur. Hi accepta abusiva potestate, dum stipendia a republica non accipiunt, avaritiae face succensi jus omne confundunt. Comes enim illiteratus ac barbarus nescit vera a falsis discernere, et ideo fallitur. Alberici chron. ad ann. 1002. (ed. Leibnit. ii. 26.) Otto Imp. degens Romae, dum cum Romanis remissius agit, tractans, qualiter jura Regni et Ecclesiae ad antiquum statum reformaret ; Romani per hoc ad contemptum ejus adducti, subito contra eum conspirant, et aliquot militum ejus peremtis eum in palatio obsident, unde—vix egressus Roma discedit cum Sylvestro (comp. Thietmar iv. 30.)—moritur. Milites transalpini corpus Imperatoris defuncti cum insignibus Imperii ad Galliam [Germaniam] transferentes, crebris Italorum incursibus lacessiti armis sibi viam parant.

[30] Thietmar vii. 1. Glaber Radulphus (monk in Clügny about 1045) historiarum sui temporis lib. i. c. 5 : Anno igitur Dominicae incarnationis MXIV. licet insigne illud imperiale diversis speciebus prius figuratum fuisset, a venerabili tamen P. Benedicto—fieri jussum est admodum intellectuali specie idem insigne. Praecepit fabricari quasi aureum pomum, atque circumdari per quadrum pretiosissimis quibusque gemmis, ac desuper auream crucem inseri. Erat autem instar hujus mundanae molis,—ut dum siquidem illud respiceret Princeps terreni imperii, foret ei documentum, non aliter debere imperare vel militare in mundo, quam ut dignus haberetur vivificae crucis tueri vexillo ; in ipso etiam diversarum gemmarum decoramine videlicet Imperii culmen plurimarum virtutum speciebus exornari oportere. Cumque postmodum praedictus Papa Imperatori videlicet Henrico—obviam—processisset—eique hujusmodi insigne scilicet Imperii—tradisset, etc.

[31] Thietmar lib. vi. in fine :

> Ista dies pulchro signetur clara lapillo,
> Qua Regi nostro se subdit Roma benigno.

Hugo Farfensis Abbas de imminutione rerum monasterii sui (in Mabillonii ann. ord. s. Bened. T. iv. App. p. 701. 704.) related of Henry's verdicts pertaining to the monastery of Farfa.—The act of investiture by Henry II. (ap. Mansi xix. 331. Pertz iv. ii. 173), which agrees with that of Otto I. (see note 13), except some few additions, is declared

though yet a layman,[32] and to him, even as early as 1033, a boy *Benedict IX.* one of the vilest men.[33] Having been expelled (1044) and *Sylvester III.* chosen in his place, he sold his right to the papal dignity to *Gregory VI.*[34] To this confusion the emperor *Henry*

spurious by Conring de Germ. Imp. Rom. c. x. § 15, Muratori annal. d'Italia vi. 46. See F. Hahn deutsche Staats- Reichs- und Kaiserhist. ii. 208, defended on the contrary by Cenni monum. dominationis pontif. ii. 165, Borgia breve istoria del dominio temporale della sede apostolica nelle due Sicilie (Roma 1788. 4) p. 269. According to Pertz it belongs to the year 1020, but is interpolated.

[32] Glaber Radulph. iv. c. 1 : Johannes iste cognomento Romanus, frater illius Benedicti, cui in Episcopatum successerat, largitione pecuniae repente ex laïcali ordine neophytus constitutus est Praesul. Sed insolentia Romanorum adinvenit palliandae subdolositatis ridiculum, scilicet ut, quemcunque pro suo libitu inpraesentiarum ad Pontificatus officium delegerint, mutato nomine quod illi prius fuerat, aliquo magnorum Pontificum nomine illum appellari decernant : re vera quem si non meritum rei, saltem nomen extollat. The first pope who changed his name was John XII.

[33] From this time onward the following works of two decided adherents of Gregory VII. are important for history : lib. ad amicum s. de persecutione Ecclesiae libb. ix. of Bonizo, bishop of Sutri, afterwards of Piacenza († 1089), where from lib. *v.* we meet with a history of the popes from Benedict IX. to Gregory VII. (in Oefelii scriptores rerum Boicarum ii. 794. Comp. Stenzel's Geschichte Deutschlands unter den fränkischen Kaisern ii. 67), and the work of Desiderius, abbot of Cassino, who was afterwards Pope Victor III. († 1086), entitled de miraculis a s. Benedicto aliisque monachis Casinensibus gestis dialogorum lib. iii. init. (Bibl. PP. Lugd. xviii. 853.) Besides annales Romani from 1044 in the spicileg. Rom. T. vi. (Romae 1841), p. 282, ap. Pertz vii. 468. Bonizo lib. v. p. 801. relates : Urbis Romae Capitanei et maxime Tusculani per patriciatus inania nomina Romanam vastabant Ecclesiam, ita ut quodam hereditario jure viderentur sibi possidere pontificatum. Enimvero mortuo Joanne Benedicti Papae fratre, qui uno eodemque die Praefectus fuit et Papa, cum successisset ei Theophylactus, qui Alberici fuit filius, Gregorius frater ejus nomen sibi vendicabat patriciatus. Desiderius l. c.: Dum per aliquot annos nonnulli solo nomine Pontificum cathedram obtinerent ; Benedictus quidam nomine, non tamen opere, cujusdam Alberici Consulis filius, Magi potius Simonis, quam Simonis Petri vestigia sectatus, non parva a patre in populum profligata pecunia, summum sibi sacerdotium vindicavit (and even according to Glaber Radulph. iv. c. 5. when puer ferme decennis or duodecennis) : cujus quidem post adeptum sacerdotium vita quam turpis, quam foeda, quamque execranda extiterit, horresco referre.

[34] Desiderius l. c. Denique cum rapinas, caedes, aliaque nefanda in Romanum populum aliquanta per tempora sine ulla dilatione ageret (Benedictus), congregati in unum populi, quia ejus nequitiam amplius

III. put an end, when he appeared before Rome with an army.
Having called *the Synod of Sutri* (1046) he deposed all the three

ferre nequibant, eum a pontificatus cathedra exturbantes, urbe pellunt,
alterumque in locum ejus, Joannem videlicet Sabinensem Episcopum
(Sylvestrum), non tamen vacua manu, canonica parvipendentes decreta,
substituunt.   Qui tribus, non amplius, mensibus Romanae usus est
cathedrae successione ; Benedicto undique suis cum propinquis infest-
ante urbem, quia ex consulibus terrae ortus erat, et in eis maxima
virtus ; urbe cum dedecore pulsus suum ad Episcopatum reversus est.
Benedictus igitur, quod amiserat, sacerdotium recepit, pristinos tamen
mores minime mutavit.—Cumque se a clero simul et populo propter
nequitias suas contemni respiceret, et fama suorum facinorum omnium
aures impleri cerneret : tandem reperto consilio (quia voluptati deditus,
ut Epicurus magis, quam ut Pontifex vivere volebat) cuidam Joanni
Archipresbytero, qui tunc in urbe religiosior caeteris clericis videbatur,
non parva ab eo accepta pecunia, summum sacerdotium relinquens, tradidit : ipse vero in propriis se castellis recipiens, urbe cessit.   Interea
Joannes, cui Gregorius nomen inditum est, cum II. annis et VIII.
mensibus sacerdotium administrasset, Henricus Rex—Romanam adiit
urbem.   Extracts from the work of this contemporary in Leo Ostiensis
chron. monasterii Casinensis lib. ii. c. 79 (in Muratorii rer. Ital. scriptt.
iv. 395), and Hermannus Contractus ad ann. 1044 agrees with them.
See Muratorii excursus hist. l. c. p. 396.   On the other hand there is
much that is erroneous in Otto Frisingensis vi. c. 32.   Tribus ibi inva-
soribus (Benedicto, Sylvestro et Johanne)—sedem illam simul occu-
pantibus, atque ad majoris miseriae cumulum divisis simul cum reditibus
patriarchiis, uno ad s. Petrum, altero ad s. Mariam majorem, tertio, i. e.
Benedicto, in palatio Lateranensi sedente, flagitiosam et turpem vitam,
ut egomet in Urbe Romanis tradentibus audivi, duxere.   Hunc miser-
rimum statum Ecclesiae religiosus quidam Presbyter Gratianus nomine
videns—praefatos viros adiit, eisque a se de s. Ecclesia cedere pecunia
persuasit, Benedicto reditibus Angliae, quia majoris videbatur auctoritatis esse, relictis.   Ob ea cives praefatum Presbyterum, tanquam
Ecclesiae Dei liberatorem in summum Pontificem elegerunt, eumque
mutato nomine Gregorium VI. vocaverunt.   That Gregory VI. was at
last the only acknowledged pope, and excited the best hopes by his
personal character and acts is proved by Peter Damiani's letter to him
(lib. i. epist. 1. for example reparetur nunc aureum Apostolorum saeculum, et praesidente vestra prudentia, ecclesiastica refloreat disciplina
etc.) and by Glaber Radulphus, who concludes his history with the
words v. c. 5 : Benedictus—ejectus est a sede, et in loco ejus subrogatus
est vir religiosissimus ac sanctitate perspicuus Gregorius,—cujus videlicet bona fama, quicquid prior foedaverat, in melius reformavit.   Stenzel's Gesch. Deutschlands unter den fränkischen Kaisern i. 104. Engelhardt observationes de Syn. Sutriensi, and Erlangen Easter programme
1834.   Th. Mittler de schismate in Eccl. Rom. sub pontificatu Benedicti ix. orto disp. Turici 1835. 8.

popes, and elevated to the Roman see Suidger, bishop of Bamberg, under the name of *Clement II.*[35]

[35] Desiderius l. c. continues : Sed antequam (Henricus) Urbem ingrederetur, plurimorum Episcoporum, necnon Abbatum, Clericorum quoque ac religiosorum Monachorum in Sutrina urbe concilio congregato, Joannem, qui Gregorius dictus est, missis ad eum Episcopis, ut de ecclesiasticis negotiis, maximeque de Romana Ecclesia, quae tres simul tunc Pontifices habere videbatur, ipso praesidente, tractaretur, venire rogavit. Sed haec de industria agebantur : jam enim dudum regio animo insederat, ut tres illos, qui injuste apostolicam sedem invaserant, cum consilio et auctoritate totius Concilii, juste depelleret.—Praedictus itaque Pontifex, exoratus a Rege, caeterisque Pontificibus, Sutrium, ubi Synodus congregata erat, allectus spe, quod aliis duobus depositis, sibi soli pontificatus confirmaretur, gratanter perrexit. Sed postquam eo ventum est, et res agitari ac discuti a Synodo coepta est ; agnoscens, se non posse juste honorem tanti sacerdotii administrare, ex pontificali sella exsiliens ac semetipsum pontificalia indumenta exuens, postulata venia, summi sacerdotii dignitatem deposuit. Post haec Rex, Urbem ingressus, congregato in ecclesia b. Petri Apostoli Romano clero et populo una cum Episcopis, qui in praedictam convenerant Synodum, communi consilio Clementem Bambergensem Episc. elegerunt, quia in Romana Ecclesia non erat tunc talis reperta persona, quae digne posset ad tanti honorem sufficere sacerdotii. This is related more fully by Bonizo l. c. p. 801 s. Hermannus contractus ad ann. 1046 goes so far as to say : Henricus—elegit Pontificem ; Lambertus ad ann. 1047 : tribus depositis—Suitgerum—vicarium Apostolorum constituit ; Arnulfus Mediol. rerum sui temporis iii. 2 : Henricus Papa—abjecto unum ex Teutonibus praesulem illius loco substituit : On the other hand, those Romans who wrote during the disputes about investiture, endeavoured to conceal the fact that popes had been previously appointed by the emperor, Walthramus Numburgensis de investitura Episc. A.D. 1109 (in M. Goldastii apologiae pro Henrico iv. p. 232), Sigebertus Gemblac. and Martinus Polonus ad ann. 1046 add : ab eo rex Henricus in Imperatorem benedicitur, jurantibus Romanis, se sine ejus consensu nunquam Papam electuros. That is to say, according to Benzonis panegyricus in Henricum iii. Imp. lib. vii. c. 2. (in Menckenii script. rer. Germ. i. 1062), it was resolved at a synod in Peter's Church at Rome, ut rex Henricus cum universis in monarchia imperii sibi succedentibus fieret Patricius, sicuti de Carolo (Magno) factum legimus.—Indutus igitur rex viridissima chlamyde, desponsatur patriciali annulo, coronatur ejusdem praelaturae aureo circulo. As Patricius he now elects the pope, and is crowned emperor by him. Even Peter Damiani in his disceptatio synodalis (A. D. 1062 in Petri Dam. opp. ed. Cajetani iii. 23) admits the assertion of the regius advocatus, quod—Henricus Imperator factus est Patricius Romanorum, a quibus accepit in electione super ordinando Pontifice principatum. (in like manner in the lib. gratissimus c. 36.) Bonizo l. c. p. 802, narrates the occurrence thus : postquam imperiali est Rex auctus dignitate, calamitatibus reipublicae compatiens,

§ 23.

PAPACY UNDER HILDEBRAND'S INFLUENCE.

Bonizonis liber ad amicum, in Oefelii scriptt. rer. Boicarum ii. 794. Desiderii Abb. Casinensis de miraculis s. Benedicti dialogi in the bibl. PP. Lugd. xviii. (see § 22. not. 33). Leonis Ostiensis (monk and librarian in Monte Cassino, 1101, cardinal of the Roman Church) chronicon monasterii Casinensis libb. iii. in Muratorii scriptt. rer. Italicarum iv. Free from partiality for Hildebrand are the contemporary annales Romani ap. Pertz vii. 469.

Planck iv. i. 1. J. Voigt's Hildebrand als Papst Gregorius VII. 2te Aufl. Weimar, 1846. S. 5. Schlosser's Weltgesh. ii. ii. 642. Schmidt's Kirchengesch. vi. 1. Neander iv. 150. Stenzel's Gesch. Deutschlands unter d. fränk. Kaisern i. 116. C. Höfler's deutsche Päpste (2te Abth. Regensb. 1839) i. 251. Annales Altahenses, hergestellt von W. Giesebrecht, Berlin, 1841. S. 132.

Despicable as many popes had made themselves during the past period, the papacy itself was not so. These stormy times were rather propitious to it, by cutting off all opportunity of frequent discussion respecting the new principles contained in the Pseudo-isidorian decretals, which every year of undisputed authority naturally contributed to confirm. When the more worthy popes,[1] chosen under imperial influence, now began to oppose the

civitatem a patriciorum liberavit tyrannide, quod valde esset laudabile, nisi subsequens post macularet commissum. Nam rumoribus populi illectus—tyrannidem patriciatus arripuit, quasi aliqua esset in laicali ordine dignitas constituta, quae privilegii possideret plus imperatoria Majestate.—Quid namque est, quod mentem tanti viri ad tantum traxit delictum, nisi quod credidit per patriciatus ordinem se Romanum posse ordinare Pontificem. The patricius was originally deputy of the emperor, even in the choosing of a pope. In stormy times the Roman nobles had made an independent authority out of the patriciate, with the right of appointing the pope. Hence it now appeared advisable to transfer it to the emperor himself, lest it should be again abused by petty tyrants.

[1] Leo Ostiensis in chron. monast. Casin ii. c. 81 : Clemente vero post ix. menses ultra montes defuncto (Clemens ii. † 1047), praefatus Benedictus iterum in pontificatum reversus per viii. circiter menses illum retinuit, donec ab Imperatore transmissus ex Germania Damasus Brexenorum Episcopus illi in papatu successit. Henry asked advice of Wazo, bishop of Lüttich, at this new election. The

two evils of the Church, *simony* and *the immorality of the clergy*,[2] supported as they were by the general feeling of the necessity of reform, they found no difficulty in establishing their entire supremacy over the whole Church, even by new encroachments on the rights of the bishops. These struggles began under *Leo IX.*,[3] and were, from the first, so directed by *Hildebrand*, the soul of this as well as of succeeding papal reigns, as to make the hierarchy independent of civil power.[4] As long as Henry III.

bishop replied (Anselmus Leod. gesta Pontiff. Leod. c. 106 in Jo. Chapeavilli auctt. de gestis Pontiff. Tungrens. i.) : credimus, per ecclesiasticos ministros absque potentia seculari electiones et promotiones Apostolicorum fiere debere. But when his messenger arrived, the new pope had been already nominated. Damasus II. sat 23 days, † 1048. Leo IX. † 1054. Victor II. † 1057. Stephen IX. † 1058. Nicolaus II. † 1061. Alexander II. † 1073.

[2] Desiderii de miraculis s. Bened. dialog. lib. iii. init.: Dum igitur negligentia sacerdotum, maximeque Romanorum Pontificum, Italia a recto religionis tramite paulatim devians labefactaretur, in tantum mala consuetudo adolevit, ut sacrae legis auctoritate posposita, divina humanaque omnia miscerentur: adeo ut populus electionem, et sacerdotes consecrationem donumque Spiritus Sancti, quod gratis accipere et dare divina auctoritate statutum fuerit, data acceptaque per manus pecunia, ducti avaritia venderent, ita ut vix aliquanti invenirentur, qui non hujus simoniacae pestis contagione foedati—existerent. Itaque cum vulgus clericorum per viam effraenatae licentiae, nemine prohibente, graderetur: coeperunt ipsi Presbyteri ac Diacones (qui tradita sibi sacramenta dominica mundo corde castoque corpore tractare debebant) laicorum more uxores ducere, susceptosque filios heredes testamento relinquere: nonnulli etiam Episcoporum, verecundia omni contemta, cum uxoribus domo simul in una habitare: et haec pessima et exsecranda consuetudo intra Urbem maxime pullulabat, unde olim religionis norma ab ipso Apostolo Petro ejusque successoribus ubique diffusa processerat. In Glaber Radulph v. 5, Henry III. reproaches the bishops: Omnes quippe gradus ecclesiastici a maximo Pontifice usque ad ostiarium opprimuntur per suae damnationis pretium, ac juxta vocem dominicam in cunctis grassatur spiritale latrocinium. Glaber adds: non solum in Gallicanis Episcopis haec pessima pullulaverat nequitia, verum etiam multo amplius totam occupaverat Italiam: omnia quippe ministeria ecclesiastica ita eo tempore habebantur venalia, quasi in foro saecularia mercimonia.

[3] Desiderius l. c.: Leo—qui, quaemadmodum scriptum est, coepit invocare nomen Domini; a quo omnia ecclesiastica studia renovata ac restaurata; novaque lux mundo visa est exoriri.—Vita Leonis ix., by his former archdeacon in Toul, in 2 BB. in the act. SS. ad. d. 19, Apr. and in Muratorii rer. Ital. scriptt. iii. i. 278; and by Bruno, bishop of Segni about 1100, ap. Murator. iii. ii. 346.

[4] Wibert. in vit. Leonis ix. lib. ii. c. 2 : Leo IX. was chosen pope

lived, the popes were obliged to content themselves with combating those two evils of the day, with an unwonted earnestness, and
in unusual forms.   *Leo IX.* did so at several synods,[5] where he

at a Diet at Worms (Bruno Tullensis Episcopus, Teutonicus natione, et
stirpe regali progenitus, see Leo Ostiensis ii. 81), and consented at
length to accept the dignity, ea conditione, si audiret, totius cleri ac
Romani populi communem esse sine dubio consensum.   He then travelled back to Toul, and thence to Rome, pedes longinquo itinere nudis
plantis incedit,—adstanti clero et populo Romano imperialem de se electionem—brevi sermunculo promulgat, eorum, voluntatem, qualiscun-
que erga se sit, pandere expostulat.   Dicit electionem cleri et populi
canonicali auctoritate aliorum dispositionem praeire : affirmat se gratanti
animo in patriam rediturum, nisi fiat electio ejus communi omnium
laude.   Bruno in vita Lonis ix. makes him even express that resolution
at the election in Worms, but then he relates in addition the following,
which he himself had heard, as is highly probable, from Hildebrand.
Illis autem diebus erat ibi monachus quidam Romanus, Ildebrandus
nomine, nobilis indolis adolescens, clari, ingenii, sanctaeque religionis.
Iverat autem illuc, tum discendi gratia, tum etiam ut in aliquo religioso
loco sub b. Benedicti regula militaret.   Hunc igitur b. Episcopus vocavit ad se, cujus propositum, voluntatem et religionem mox ut cognovit
rogavit eum, ut simul cum eo Romam rediret.   Cui ille, " non facio,"
inquit.   Respondit Episcopus: " Quare non ?"   At ille : " Quia non
secundum canonicam institutionem, sed per saecularem et regiam potestatem Romanam Ecclesiam arripere vadis."   Ille autem, ut erat natura
simplex atque mitissimus, patienter ei satisfecit, reddita de omnibus,
sicut ille voluerat, ratione.   Et tunc Episcopus Romam veniens praedictum monachum secum adduxit, multum in hoc ipso b. Petro Apostolo serviens, quod illum hominem secum reducebat, cujus consilio et
sapientia Romana Ecclesia aliquando regenda et gubernanda erat.
Otto Frisingensis vi. c. 33, incorrectly makes the monastery of Clügny
the scene of this conversation.   See Mabillon annal. Bened. lib. lviii. no.
113.
    [5] On the first council in Rome 1049, see Wibert. ii. c. 4 : Simonia-
cam haeresim damnavit—et in eodem concilio quosdam deposuit Episcopos, quos praedicta haeresis naevo suae nequitiae maculaverat : and
Petrus Damiani opusc. vi. c. 35. (Opp. ed. C. Cajetani, iii. 68) : Cum
omnes simoniacorum ordinationes synodalis vigoris auctoritate cassasset,
protinus a Romanorum multitudine sacerdotum magnae seditionis tumultus exortus est : ita ut non solum ab ipsis, sed a plerisque diceretur
Episcopis, omnes paene basilicas sacerdotalibus officiis destitutas, et
praecipue missarum solemnia, ad subversionem christianae religionis et
desperationem omnium circumquaque fideHum, funditus omittenda.
Quid plura ?   Post longa sane disceptationum hinc inde volumina tandem suggestum est, reverendae memoriae nuper ejusdem sedis Episcopum decrevisse Clementem : ut quicumque a simoniaco consecratus
esset, in ipso ordinationis suae tempore non ignorans, simoniacum esse
cui se obtulerit promovendum, XL. nunc dierum poenitentiam ageret, et
sic in accepti ordinis officio ministraret.   Quam nimirum sententiam

presided in person; and his successor, *Victor II.*,[6] by legates.[7]

protinus venerabilis Leo ratam percensuit, etc. (That Leo afterwards
wavered between this and reordination required by Humbert, see
Berengarius Turon. de sacra coena ed. Vischer, Berol. 1834, p. 40).
In 1049, he held councils for the same object at Rheims and Mainz,
1050 at Vercelli and Sipontum, 1051 at Rome, 1052 at Mantua.
The most complete account of the Concil. Rhemense is extant
(prim. ed. Baron. in append. tomi xi. ad ann. 1049 ap. Mansi xix.
727): When the pope came to France, some noblemen of the kingdom
and some bishops and abbots applied to the king and, Regi suggerunt,
regni sui decus annihilari, si in eo Romani Pontificis auctoritatem dominari permitteret; vel si eidem, ut decreverat, occurrens praesentiae suae
favorem ad cogendum concilium exhiberet. Addunt etiam, quod nullus
antecessorum ejus id reperiatur aliquando concessisse, ut ob similem
causam in Franciae urbes ingressus pateret alicui Papae. But when the
pope could not be induced to put off the council, the king summoned
his bishops to attend the army to quell certain insurrections, and hence
only 19 bishops presented themselves in Rheims. The object of the
council was to treat (Mansi xix. 737) de multis illicitis, quae contra canonum instituta in Gallicis finibus exercebantur, i. e. de simoniaca
haeresi etc. Post haec ad Episcopos sermone converso commonuit illos
sub anathemate apostolicae auctoritatis, ut si quis eorum ad sacros ordines per simoniacam haeresim pervenisset, vel praemio quemlibet ad
eandem dignitatem promovisset, publica confessione patefaceret. Finally, edictum est sub anathemate auctoritatis apostolicae, ut si quis as-
sidentium quempiam universalis Ecclesiae primatem praeter Romanae
sedis antistitem esse assereret, ibidem publica satisfactione patefaceret.
Cumque ad haec universi reticerent, lectis sententiis super hac re olim
promulgatis ab orthodoxis Patribus, declaratum est, quod solus Romanae
sedis Pontifex universalis Ecclesiae Primas esset et Apostolicus. After
having deposed several of the bishops for simony, habitus est sermo de
Episcopis, qui invitati ad synodum venire noluerant.—poena damnati
sunt excommunicationis, cum omnibus illis, qui ipsius Papae formidan-
tes adventum, hac de re profecti erant in expeditionem Regis. Excommunicatus est etiam s. Jacobi Archiepiscopus Galliciensis, quia contra
fas sibi vindicaret culmen apostolici nominis.

    6 The annales Altahenses (restored by Giesebrecht p. 89), and Lam-
bertus ad ann. 1054 say merely that the emperor appointed him pope.
But Leo Ostiens. in chron. Casinensi ii. c. 89: Defuncto praeterea s.
memoriae P. Leone Hildebrandus, tunc Romanae Ecclesiae Subdiaconus, ad Imperatorem a Romanis transmissus est, ut, quoniam in Romana
Ecclesia persona ad tantum officium idonea reperiri non poterat, de partibus illis, quem ipse, tamen vice cleri populique Romani, in Pontificem
Romanum elegisset, auduceret. Quod cum Imperator assensus fuisset,
et Gebhardum Aistettensem Episcopum—Hildebrandus ex industria et
consilio Romanorum expetivisset, tristis super hoc valde Imperator effectus est: nimis enim illum carum habebat. Et cum eundem sibi
omnimodis necessarium Imperator assereret, et alium atque alium huic

But after Henry III.'s death († 1056) *Nicolaus II.*[8] secured the
election of popes by committing it to *the college of cardinals,*[9]

officio magis idoneum judicaret ; Hildebrando tamen, ut alterum reciperet, persuaderi nullatenus potuit.   Erat enim idem Episcopus, super
id quod prudentia multa callebat, post Imperatorem potentior ac ditior
cunctis in regno.   Hunc ergo Hildebrandus, invito licet Imperatore,
invito etiam eodem ipso Episcopo,—Romam secum adduxit, eique Victoris nomen imponens, Romanum Papam cunctorum assensu constituit ;
cum jam ferme a transitu P. Leonis annus elaberetur.   Qui, quoniam
eidem praedecessori suo, ut supra diximus (cap. 84), impedimento
maximo fuerat (unquestionably the chief ground of Hildebrand's choice)
quotiens a circumpositis molestiam aliquam patiebatur, dicere solitus
erat : " Merito haec patior," etc.

[7] Hildebrand held the synod of Tours 1054 as the legate of Leo IX.
(not as legate of Victor II. 1055, see Berengarius below, § 29, note 9),
then the synod of Lyons 1055, as legate of Victor ; other legates were
those at Licieux 1055, at Toulouse 1056.

[8] Concerning his election Leo Ostiens. in chron. Casin. ii. c. 100 :
Stephen IX. had communicated before his death, ut, si antequam Hildebrandus—ab Imperatrice, ad quam—mittebatur, rediret, se obire contingeret, nullus omnino eligere Papam praesumeret, sed usque ad illius
reditum apostolica sedes intacta vacaret, ejus demum consilio ordinanda
(this account is from Petr. Damiani lib. iii. ep. 4) c. 101 : The opposite
party led by the count of Tusculum, immediately elected Benedict X.
Petrus Damiani—uno cum Cardinalibus coepit obsistere, reclamare ac
anathematizare ; sed omnes hi tandem—per diversa coacti sunt latibula
fugere.   III. c. 13 : Cum—Hildebrandus reversus ab Imperatrice—
invasam a pessimis hominibus Ecclesiam comperisset, Florentiae sub-
stitit, suisque literis super hoc Romanorum meliores conveniens, eorumque ad omnia consensum recipiens, mox annitente Gotfrido Duce,
Girardum Florentinum Episcopum in Romanum Papam elegit, simulque cum ipso et Duce Romam mense jam Januario venit, ubi praefatus
electus a Romano clero et populo apostolica sede inthronizatus et Nicolai nomen indeptus est.   According to Lambert von Aschaffenburg ad
ann. 1059, Nicolaus had been nominated by the empress, and the cun-
ning Hildebrand availed himself of this pretext.   Benedict X. was
obliged to submit at once.   Stenzel's Gesch. Deutschlands unter den
fränk. Kaisern i. 195.   Voigt's Hildebrand S. 39.

[9] Clericus Cardinalis or incardinatus is Clericus primarius certo coe-
tui addictus, Titularis, as opposed to the Commends, vicars and assistant clergy.   The expression, Cardinalis Pontifex, is found to have been
first employed by Pope Gelasius, in the sense of Episcopus ordinarius
(dist. xxiv. c. 3).   Afterwards, frequently in Gregory the Great, Cardinalis episcopus, c. sacerdos, c. presbyter, c. diaconus, also the expression
incardinare aliquem.   A bishop whose church was taken by enemies, and
who is provisionally set over another vacant church as bishop, in illa
Ecclesia incardinatur, and becomes Cardinalis illius Ecclesiae, see liber
diurnus c. iii. Tit. xi.   In like manner, Gregorius M. lib. ii. ep. 37.   In

(1059), contrary to the predominance of civil influence hitherto existing, and gained at once, as vassal and protector of the papal see,[10] *Robert Guiscard*, duke of the Normans, in southern Italy.[11]

an old ritual, ap. Baronius ann. 1057, it is said of the Lateran Church: haec vii. Cardinales Episcopos habebat, qui dicebantur collaterales et hebdomadarii, eo quod singulis hebdomadibus per vices explerent munus Pontificis. In Pope John VIII. is found Cardinis Ecclesiae Romanae Presbyter (ep: 89), Diaconus cardinis Ecclesiae Ravennatensis (ep. 220). The Conc. Meldense ann. 845 c. 45. (Mansi xiv. 831) calls the offices of them tituli cardinales. So in all churches (but remarkable in Leonis ix. ep. i. ad Michael Patr. Const. c. 32. ap. Mansi xix. 653 : Unde clerici summae sedis Cardinales dicuntur : cardini utique illi, quo caetera moventur, vicinius adhaerentes), abolished in Ravenna as late as 1568 by Pius V. Comp. Onuphrius Panvinius de Cardinalium origine in the spicileg. Rom. ix. 469. Thomassini vet. et nov. Ecclesiae discipl. P. i. lib. ii. cap. 113-116. J. F. Buddeus de origine cardinalitiae dignitatis, Jenae, 1693. 12. Muratori antiquitt. Ital. medii aevi v. 156.

[10] Decretum de electione Rom. Pontificis, passed at a Roman synod in April 1059 (Henricus Episc. Spirensis ad Hildebrandum P., Codex Udalrici no. 162. in Eccardi corpus hist. medii aevi ii. 172 : hujus consilii, seu decreti tu ipse auctor, persuasor subscriptorque fuisti), preserved in two different texts. The one in the chronicon Farfense (composed about 1100) in Muratorii rer. Ital. scriptt. ii. ii. 645 ; in Udalrici Babenberg. codex epistolaris (collected 1125) no. 9. in Eccardi corpus historic. medii aevi ii. 21 ; and in the Cod. Vatican. no. 1984, written about 1100, best in Pertz iv. ii. 176 runs thus :—decernimus atque statuimus, ut obeunte hujus Romane universalis Ecclesiae Pontifice, in primis Cardinales diligentissima simul consideratione tractantes, salvo debito honore, et reverentia dilectissimi filii nostri Heinrici, qui in praesentiarum Rex habetur, et futurus Imperator Deo concedente speratur, sicut jam sibi, mediante ejus nuntio Longobardiae Cancellario W. (Wibert who was afterwards rival pope of Clement III., who was present, see Bonizo ap. Oefele ii. 806) concessimus, et successorum illius, qui ab hac apostolica sede personaliter hoc jus impetraverint, ad consensum novae electionis accedant : ut nimirum, ne venalitatis morbus qualibet occassione subrepat, religiosi viri cum reverendissimo filio nostro Rege Heinrico praeduces sint in promovenda Pontificis electione ; reliqui autem sequaces. Eligant autem de ipsius Ecclesiae gremio, si reperitur idoneus ; vel si de ipsa non invenitur, ex alia assumatur. Quod si pravorum atque iniquorum hominum ita perversitas invaluerit, ut pura, sincera, atque gratuita electio fieri in Urbe non possit ; licet tantum pauci sint, jus tamen potestatis obtineant eligere apostolicae sedis Pontificem, ubi cum invictissimo Rege congruentius judicaverint.—The second text in Hugonis Floriacensis (about 1120) tract. de regia potest. et sacerdotali dignitate in Baluzii miscell. lib. iv. p. 62 ss. and in Gratiani decret. dist. xxiii. cap. 1 : decernimus atque statuimus, ut obeunte hujus Romanae universalis Ecclesiae Pontifice imprimis Cardinales Episcopi diligentissime simul de electione tractantes mox ipsi Clericos

Cardinales adhibeant, sicque reliquus clerus et populus ad consensum
novae electionis accedat : nimirum praecaventes, ne venalitatis morbus
aliqua occasione subrepat.   Et ideo religiosissimi viri praeduces sint in
promovenda Pontificis electione, reliqui autem sequaces.   Certus vero
atque legitimus electionis ordo perpenditur, si perspectis diversorum
Patrum regulis s. gestis etiam illa b. Leonis praedecessoris nostri sententia recolatur : " Nulla," inquit, " ratio sinit, ut inter Episcopos habeantur, qui nec a clericis sunt electi, nec a plebibus expetiti, nec a
comprovincialibus Episcopis cum Metropolitani judicio consecrati."
Quia vero sedes apostolica cunctis in orbe terrarum praefertur Ecclesiis,
atque ideo supra se Metropolitanum habere non potest : Cardinales
Episcopi procul dubio Metropolitani vice funguntur, qui videlicet electum Episcopum ad apostolici culminis apicem provehant.   Eligatur autem de ipsius Ecclesiae gremio, si reperitur idoneus ; vel si de ipsa non
invenitur, ex alia assumatur : salvo debito honore et reverentia dilecti
filii nostri Henrici, qui impraesentiarum Rex habetur, et futurus Imperator Deo concedente speratur ; sicut jam sibi concessimus, et successoribus illius, qui ab apostolica sede personaliter hoc jus impetraverint.
Quodsi pravorum atque iniquorum hominum ita perversitas invaluerit,
ut pura, sincera atque gratuita fieri in Urbe non possit electio : Cardinales Episcopi cum religiosis clericis, catholicisque laicis, licet paucis,
jus potestatis obtineant eligere apostolicae sedis Pontificem, ubi congruere viderint.   The following, with a few unimportant deviations,
agrees in both texts : Plane postquam electio fuerit facta, si bellica
tempestas, vel qualiscumque hominum conatus, malignitatis studio re-
stiterit, ut si qui electus est in apostolica sede juxta consuetudinem in-
thronizari non valeat : electus tamen, sicut verus Papa, obtineat auctoritatem regendi Romanam Ecclesiam, et disponendi omnes facultates illius.
Quod b. Gregorium ante suam consecrationem fecisse cognovimus.
Quod si quis contra hoc nostrum decretum, synodali sententia promulgatum, per seditionem vel praesumtionem quolibet ingenio electus, aut
etiam ordinatus s. inthronizatus fuerit ; auctoritate divina et ss. Apostolorum Petri et Pauli perpetuo anathemate cum suis auctoribus, fautoribus et sequacibus a limine sanctae Dei Ecclesiae separatus, abjiciatur
sicut Antichristus, invasor etc.   It is generally assumed that the former
text is genuine, and that the second originated by interpolation, made
with a view to the papal interest, during the disputes about investiture.
But if we are to believe Anselm, bishop of Lucca, who contra Guibertum
P. lib. ii. (Bibl. PP. Lugd. xviii. 609), A. D. 1084, writes : Wicbertus
aut sui, ut suae parti favorem adscriberent, quaedam in eodem decreto
addendo quaedam mutando ita illud reddiderunt a se dissidens, ut aut
pauca aut nulla exemplaria sibi concordantia valeant inveniri : the first
text rather originated by an interpolation which the party of the antago-
nist pope, Clement III., had undertaken.   For this also the following
considerations may be alleged : 1. The cardinal bishops had certainly
received in the decree the privileges assigned to them in the second text.
Nicolaus II. himself assigns this determination in his synodical letter ap.
Mansi xix. 907. ut si quis apostolicae sedi sine concordia et canonica
electione, ac benedictione Cardinalium Episcoporum, ac deinde sequentium ordinum religiosorum clericorum inthronizatur, non Papa vel

Apostolicus habeatur. Petri Damiani lib. i. ep. 20, ad Cadolaum A. D. 1061: cum electio illa per Episcoporum Cardinalium fieri debeat principale judicium, secundo loco jure praebeat Clerus assensum, tertio popularis favor attollat applausum : sicque suspendenda est causa, usque dum regiae celsitudinis consulatur auctoritas. This position was also taken by the cardinal bishops at the next elections, for example, at that of Gregory VII. (Baron. 1073. no. 20) and Urban II. (chron. Casin. iv. 2). On the contrary, they had not co-operated in the choice of Clement III., and therefore his party had cause for undertaking this alteration. 2. The imperial rights are as indefinitely expressed in the second text, as one might expect from Hildebrand. The more precise considerations respecting them in the first text correspond entirely to the choice of Wibert, which took place in presence of Henry IV. in Brixa, A.D. 1080. 3. During the disputes about investiture, the papal party would not by any means have been satisfied with an interpolation of the decree, such as the changing of the first text into the second would have been ; on the contrary, the heads of this party, Desiderius, abbot of Cassino, Anselm, bishop of Lucca, Bonizo, declared it to be invalid. (See division 2 § 47. note pp). Comp. Ed. Cunitz de Nicolai II. decreto de electione Pontiff. Rom. diss. hist. crit. Argentor, 1837. 4.

[11] His right to Sicily he proved from a copy of the act of investiture of Otto I. (see above § 22. note 13) in which, in the passage necnon patrimonium Sicilae, si deus illud nostris tradiderit manibus etc. the last clause was left out. See Cenni monumenta dominationis pontificiae ii. 48. The two forms of the oath, ap. Baronius ad ann. 1059. no. 70 and 71, more complete in Borgia's breve istoria del dominio temporale etc. Append. nr. iii. p. 23 : First oath : Ego Robertus Dei gratia et s. Petri Dux Apuliae et Calabriae, et utroque subveniente futurus Siciliae ad confirmationem traditionis et ad recognitionem fidelitatis de omni terra, quam ego proprie sub dominio meo teneo, et quam adhuc ulli Ultramontanorum unquam concessi, ut teneat : promitto me annualiter pro unoquoque jugo boum pensionem, scilicet xii denarios papiensis monetae, persoluturum b. Petro etc. Second oath : Ego Robertus etc. ab hac hora et deinceps ero fidelis s. Romanae Ecclesiae, et tibi Domino meo Nicolao Papae. In consilio vel in facto, unde vitam aut membrum perdas, aut captus sis mala captione, non ero. Consilium, quod mihi credideris, et contradices, ne illud manifestem non manifestabo ad tuum damnum, me sciente. S. Romanae Ecclesiae ubique adjutor ero ad tenendum et ad acquirendum regalia s. Petri ejusque possessiones pro meo posse, contra omnes homines ; et adjuvabo te, ut secure et honorifice teneas Papatum Romanum, terramque s. Petri, et principatum : nec invadere, nec acquirere quaeram, nec etiam depraedari praesumam absque tua tuorumque successorum—certa licentia.—Omnes quoque Ecclesias, quae in mea persistunt dominatione, cum earum possessionibus dimittam in tua potestate. Et defensor ero illarum ad fidelitatem s. Romanae Ecclesiae. Et si tu, vel tui successores ante me ex hac vita migraveritis, secundum quod monitus fuero a melioribus Cardinalibus, clericis Romanis et laicis, adjuvabo ut Papa eligatur et ordinetur ad honorem s. Petri.

2 A 2

Alexander II. was even (1061) elected solely by the cardinals, without any regard to the young king. It is true that the Roman noblemen now sought for support at the imperial court, remembering their former influence over the choice of popes. *Honorius II.*[12] was chosen in Basel, and made a triumphal entry into Rome ; but when Anno, archbishop of Cologne, had taken on himself the regency (1062), the general endeavour to weaken the royalty led the German potentates to take Alexander II.'s side. Honorius II. was forsaken.[13] Alexander was able to appear even in Ger-

[12] Leo Ostiensis in chron. Casin. iii. c. 21 : defuncto apud Florentiam Apostolico—cum maxima seditio inter Romanos coepisset de ordinando Pontifice exoriri : Hildebrandus Archidiaconus cum Cardinalibus nobilibusque Romanis consilio habito, ne dissensio convalesceret, Anselmum tandem Lucensem Episcopum post iii. circiter menses in Romanum Pontificem eligunt, eumque Alexandrum vocari decernunt.—Quod cum ad aures Imperatricis ejusque filii pervenisset, indignatione nimia ducti, quod haec sine illorum consensu et auctoritate gesta fuissent, et ipsi nihilominus Cadolaum Parmensem Episcopum ultra montes—in Papam eligi faciunt, eumque Romam—cum valida manu militum et pecunia multa transmittunt. Bertholdus Constant. ad ann. 1061 : Romae Nicolao Papa defuncto Romani coronam et alia munera Heinrico Regi transmiserunt, eumque pro eligendo summo Pontifice interpellaverunt. Qui ad se convocatis omnibus Italiae Episcopis generalique conventu Basileae habito, eadem imposita corona Patricius Romanorum appellatus est. Deinde cum communi consilio omnium Parmensem Episcopum—elegit Pontificem. At this council at Basel also took place what Petrus Daminiani discept. synodalis (opp. iii. p. 31) makes the defensor Rom. Ecclesiae relate : Rectores aulae regiae cum nonnullis— Episcopis conspirantes contra Romam Ecclesiam concilium collegistis, quo Papam (Nicolaum) quasi per synodalem sententiam condemnastis, et omnia quae ab eo fuerant statuta cassare incredibili prosus audacia praesumpsistis. In quo nimirum non dicam judicio, sed praejudicio idipsum quoque privilegium, quod Regi praedictus Papa contulerat,— vacuastis. Those in favour of the kingly power asserted, according to Bonizo, p. 807 : eorum Dominum, ut heredem regni, ita heredem fore patriciatus, so that no particular papal conference with the latter was needed. Comp. Stenzel's Gesch. Deutschlands unter den fränk. Kaisern i. 203. Anales Allahenses von W. Giesebrecht S. 156. J. Voigt's Hildebrand S. 54.

[13] At the synod at Augsburg (Oct. 1062) for which Peter wrote the disceptatio synodalis inter Regis Advocatum et Romanae Ecclesiae defensorem (opp. iii. 25. ap. Baron. ann. 1062. no. 22 ss. Mansi xix. 1001), in which the relations of that time, and different views, are well explained. At the synod of Mantua (1064. see annales Altah. v. Giesebrecht S. 183) Alexander was generally acknowledged. Honorius remained confined to Parma, but never renounced his claims († 1072).

many, hierarchically ruling as none of his predecessors had done.[14] After Alexander's death (1073), Hildebrand himself assumed the papal dignity,[15] under the name of Gregory VII., to begin the great struggle of the papacy with the imperial power for the mastery.[16]

[14] He refused Henry IV.'s request for a divorce, by his legate Petrus Damiani (Lamberti annales ad ann. 1069. ap. Pertz vii. 174), then he summoned the archbishops of Mainz and Cologne and the bishop of Bamberg to Rome to answer for simony (Lambertus ad ann. 1070.)

[15] Lambertus ad ann. 1073 ap. Pertz vii. 194 :—Alexander Papa—decessit. Cui Romani protinus inconsulto Rege successorem elegerunt Hildebrandum.—Is quoniam zelo Dei ferventissimus erat, Episcopi Galliarum protinus grandi scrupulo permoveri coeperunt, ne vir vehementis ingenii et acris erga Deum fidei districtius eos pro negligentiis suis quandoque discuteret. Atque ideo communibus omnes consiliis Regem adorti, orabant, ut electionem, quae ejus injussu facta fuerat, irritam fore decerneret ; asserentes, quod nisi impetum hominis praevenire maturaret, malum hoc non in alium gravius quam in ipsum Regem redundaturum esset. On this account, Henry sent Count Eberhard to Rome. Hildebrand declared to him, se Deo teste honoris hujus apicem nunquam per ambitionem affectasse, sed electum se a Romanis, et violenter sibi impositam fuisse ecclesiastici regiminis necessitatem : cogi tamen nullo modo potuisse, ut ordinari se permitteret, donec in electionem suam tam Regem quam principes Teutonici regni consensisse certa legatione cognosceret ; hac ratione distulisse adhuc ordinationem suam, et sine dubio dilaturum, donec sibi voluntatem Regis certus inde veniens nuncius intimaret. Hoc ubi Regi est renunciatum, libenter suscepit satisfactionem, et laetissimo suffragio ut ordinaretur mandavit.

[16] How completely everything had hitherto bowed beneath the overbearing spirit of Hildebrand is seen from Petrus Damiani's epigrams († 1072), de Papa et Hildebrando (ap. Baron. ann. 1061. no. 34 and 35) :—

> Papam rite colo, sed te prostratus adoro :
> Tu facis hunc dominum, te facit ipse Deum.

and

> Vivere vis Romae, clara depromito voce:
> Plus domino Papae quam Domino pareo Papae.

Comp. ejusd. epist. ii. 8. ad Hildebrandum : tuis coeptis tuisque conatibus semper obtemperare contendi, et in omnibus tuis certaminibus atque victoriis ego me non commilitonem sive pedissequum, sed quasi fulmen injeci. Quod enim certamen unquam coepisti, ubi protinus ego non essem et litigator et judex ? Ubi scilicet non aliam auctoritatem canonum, nisi solum tuae voluntatis sequebar arbitrium, et mera tua voluntas mihi canonum erat auctoritas. Nec unquam judicavi, quod visum est mihi, sed quod placuit tibi. Peter's complaints against Hildebrand refer to the refusal of the latter to allow him to lay down his

SECOND CHAPTER.

HISTORY OF THE EPISCOPAL HIERARCHY.

§ 24.

RELATIONS OF THE PRELATES TO THE SECULAR POWER.

Planck's Gesch. d. kirchl. Gesellschaftsverfassung, iii. 411. K. O. Hüll-mann's Gesch. d. Ursprungs d. Stände in Deutschland. 2te Ausg. Berlin, 1830, S. 219. ff. C. Montag's Gesch. d. deutschen staatsbürgerl. Freiheit, ii. 79. Eichhorn's deutsche Staats u. Rechtsgesch. ii. 58.

The secular power of the prelates had been gradually increasing in the Frank empire, by the acquisition of royal prerogatives in times of disorder,[1] till at length the kings of Germany, especially since the time of *Otto I.*, found it to their advantage to balance

bishopric of Ostia, and retire to the desert. Thus, for instance, the passage, ep. i. 16. (ap. Baron. ann. 1061. no. 37) : Sed adhuc fortasse blandus ille tyrannus, qui mihi Nevoniana semper pietate condoluit, qui me colaphisando demulsit, qui me certe aquilino (ut ita loquar) ungue palpavit, hanc querelus erumpet in vocem : Ecce latibulum petit, et sub colore poenitentiae Romam subterfugere quaerit, accessum lucrari machinatur de inobedientia, et otium caeteris in bella ruentibus.—Sed ego sancto Satanae meo respondeo, quod filii Ruben et Gad Moysi ductori suo respondisse dicuntur : Nos, inquiunt, armati et accincti pergemus ad praelium ante filios Israel, donec introducamus in loca sua etc. (Num. xxxii. 17). Hoc itaque modo, comitaturus quidem vos arma corripio, sed vobis duce Christo post bella victoribus, mox recedo.

[1] Comp. § 9. note 5. Thus grants conferring privileges connected with markets, coinage, and tolls, and feudal judicature, were multiplied. Lewis the Infant, who was especially profuse in his gifts to the clergy (Gatterer comm. de Ludov. iv. Infante. Götting. 1759. p. 34), first conferred on the abbot of Corvey (900) the bishops of Treves (902. see Böhmer's regesta Karolorum S. 115) and of Tongern (908) and others, the privileges of counts (Gatterer l. c. p. 53.) Henry I., A. D. 928, bestows on the bishop of Toul the dukedom and dignity of the city Toul, the first instance of this sort. Böhmer's Regesta v. Conrad I. bis Heinrich vii. S. 3. Thomassinus P. iii. lib. i. c. 28 and 30. Montag i. ii. 41, 48; ii. 86. Hüllmann's Gesch. d. Ursprungs d. Regalien in Deutschland. Frankf. l. c. 1806.

the overgrown power of their nobles by transferring to the prelates whole counties as fiefs. By this means, for the present, the
dependence of the prelates on the kings was secured.[2] They were
for the most part appointed by the kings;[3] had constantly to be

[2] Otto I. invested his brother Bruno, archbishop of Cologne, with the
dukedom of Lorrain, but merely in his own person. Besides this he
bestowed on him the newly-founded bishoprics of Magdeburg, Brandenburg, &c., with the privileges of a count. In particular, the emperors Otto III. and Henry II. bestowed numerous counties on different
churches. See Thomassini vet. et nov. eccl. discipl. P. iii. lib. i. c.
26-32. Montag ii. 90. 197. Hüllmann's Gesch. d. Stände S. 276.
Comp. the old German chronicle in Leibnitii introd. in script. rer.
Brunsvic. T. i. p. 13. from the times of Otto I.: Da begunten zuerst
die Bischoffe weltliche Richte zu haben, das dauchte damals umbillig
manchen Manne. How such endowments were sometimes obtained
may be learned from the vita Meinwerci Ep. Paderb. c. 79. (Leibnit.
script. rer. Brunsv. T. i. p. 544.) Meinwerk beset the emperor Henry
II. to give him the estate Ervete (curtis Ervete sita in pago Westfalon),
and at length obtained it with the words: " Tu odium Dei omniumque
Sanctorum ejus habeas, qui me bonis concessis cum detrimento regni
spoliare non cessas." Episcopus autem privilegium cum manu in altum
exaltans: " Beatus es," ait, " Henrice, et bene tibi erit, cui pro hac
oblatione caelum patebit, cujus anima cum Sanctis sempiterna possidebit gaudia. Videte omnes populi, considerate fideles universi: talis
oblatio peccatorum fit abolitio; hoc sacrificium Deo acceptabile animabus fit propitiabile. Hoc quique fideles pro posse suae facultatis imitari
studeant; ut pro temporalibus aeterna, pro transitoriis mansura obtinere
valeant." Other instances of spiritual impudence, such as his wringing
from the emperor the gift of a goblet, of an altar-cloth, &c. may be seen
in the same work. Still farther, c. 82: Episcopus autem quoddam
Imperatoris tegmen egregium, praecipui decoris et mirifici operis pallium,
saepenumero obtinere desiderans, effectu caruit; donec · quadam die
Imperatori pluribus intento illud fortuito rapuit. Imperator vero Episcopum de rapinae incusans vitio talionem debitam suo se tempore red-
diturum perhibuit: he afterwards led him astray by a private alteration
in his missal, so that he prayed pro mulis et mulabus instead of famulis
et famulabus. On the gifts of Conrad II. see Stenzel's Gesch. Deutschlands unter den fränk. Kaisern ii. 127, during Henry Fourth's minority
ibid. p. 135 ff.

[3] For even the privilege of free choice, which many churches had,
were continually subject to the royal confirmation, and hence they were
for the most part apparent rather than real. The king often pointed
out to the electors the person to be chosen, as Henry II. did Tagino
1004 to be archbp. of Magdeburg (Thietmar v. 24, ap. Pertz v. 802),
1012 Walterd (Thietmar vi. 44): or he did not confirm a choice, but
appointed another, as Henry did in the cases of Meingaud, archbp. of
Treves, 1008 (Thietmar vi. 25) and Himmo abbot of Reichenau (Hermann. Contractus ad ann. 1006 ap. Pertz vii. 118.) At a disputed

installed in office by them ;[4] take the oath of allegiance to them, like other vassals ;[5] follow them to the wars in times of exi-

election in Halberstadt, Otto III. nominated a third as bishop, Arnulf, 995 (Thietmar iv. 17.) None doubted the right of the king. Pope John X. objects to Archbp. Hermann of Cologne that he had consecrated Hilduin, bishop of Tongern, contrary to the will of Charles the Simple, cum prisca consuetudo vigeat, qualiter nullus alicui clerico episcopatum conferre debeat, nisi Rex, cui divinitus sceptra collata sunt (Mansi xviii. 320 cf. Flodoardi hist. Eccl. Rhem. ad ann. 920.) Hüllmann S. 289. Montag. ii. 119. Planck iii. 406. Hence Sigismund, bishop of Halberstadt, when sick, advises his chaplain Bernhard (A. D. 923), whom he wished to succeed him (Thietmar i. 12) : vade ad curtem regiam, sumens ex mea parte, quae tibi sint ad haec necessaria, et acquire gratiam et auxilium ibi optime valentium, ut tibi liceat sine omni offensione mihi succedere. Bernhard follows his advice, et praedicti Regis (Henrici I.) munere, quod postulat consequitur.

[4] Even as early as Clovis in dipl. a. 508 (ap. Bouquet iv. 616) : quicquid est fisci nostri—per annulum tradimus. Of Clovis ii. 623, it is said in the vita s. Romani Ep. Rathomag. baculum illi contulit pastoralem. In like manner Lewis the German invested with the staff (vita Remberti c. 4. Act. SS. Febr. i. 562), and Arnulf (Adam. Brem. i. 39), and Otto I. (Thietmar ii. 16.) Henry II. gave Walterd the ring as a pledge that he would invest him with the staff (Thietmar vi. 44.) So also Conrad II. did to Bardo (vita Bardonis Archiep. Mogunt. c. 24. in the act. SS. Jun. ii. 381.) The custom of investire per baculum et annulum did not originate till a later time. Natal. Alex. hist. eccl. saec. xi. et xii. diss. iv. Mosheim institutt. hist. eccl. p. 408. not. r. Hüllmann S. 153. Montag i. ii. 186. ii. 127. Planck iii. 462.

[5] These oaths seem to have become customary under Charlemagne. It is true that the Episcopi apud Carisiacum congregati in epist. ad Ludov. Reg. Germ. ann. 858 cap. 15 (Baluzii capitt. ii. p. 119) complain of them : Et nos Episcopi Domino consecrati non sumus hujusmodi homines, ut sicut homines saeculares in vassalatico debeamus nos cuilibet commendare,—aut jurationis sacramentum, quod nos evangelica et apostolica atque canonica auctoritas vetat, debeamus quoquo modo facere. Manus enim chrismate sacro peruncta, quae de pane et vino aqua mixto per orationem et crucis signum conficit corpus Christi et sanguinis sacramentum, abominabile est, quicquid ante ordinationem fecerit, ut post ordinationem episcopatus saeculare tangat ullo modo sacramentum. Et lingua Episcopi, quae facta est per Dei gratiam clavis caeli, nefarium est, ut, sicut saecularis quilibet, super sacra juret in nomine Domini et Sanctorum invocatione.—Et si aliquando sacramenta ab Episcopis exacta aut facta fuerunt, contra Deum et ecclesiasticas regulas, quae Spiritu S. dictatae et Christi sunt sanguine confirmatae, irrita s. Scripturae paginis declarantur, et exigentes atque facientes medicamento exinde salutaris poenitentiae indigent. But Hincmar, probably the author of this letter, was himself obliged to take the oath a second time, 876, at the Synodus Pontigonensis (Baluz. ii. 250. Pertz iii. 533.) In proportion as the

gency ;[6] appear frequently at court ;[7] and were often deposed by them.[8] Besides, they drew on themselves the envy of the nobility ;[9] and were often, particularly the abbots, defrauded by their

prerogatives of the prelates were afterwards multiplied, those difficulties in the way of taking the oath disappeared. Thomassini vet. et nov. eccl. discipl. P. ii. lib. ii. c. 48. Montag Bd. 1. Th. 1. S. 180.

[6] They were even obliged to lead their troops in person. Ex. gr. Gerardus in vita Udalrici Ep. August. (in Mabillon act. SS. ord. Bened. saec. v. p. 415) cap. 3 : concessum est s. Udalrico Episcopo, ut Adalbero in ejus vice itinera hostilia cum militia episcopali in voluntatem Imperatoris perageret, et in curte Imperatoris ejus vice assiduitate servitii moraretur. Hence the prelates regularly accompanied the armies in the 10th century. Hüllmann S. 272. Montag ii. 111, 200. Planck iii. 465. How great the public calls were appears from the fact of the abbey of Lorch, in the 11th century, having to furnish 1200 men (cod. Lauresham. i. 183). It was even usual for them to take part in the battle in person. Thus Liutbert, archbishop of Mainz, fought against the Normans (annal. Fuld. ad ann. 872. Pertz i. 385); against the Sorabes (l. c. ad ann. 874) ; finally twice still against the Normans (l. c. ad ann. 883 and 885). Bishop Arno of Würzburg attacked the Slavonians (Regino ad ann. 892. Pertz i. 605), Henry, bishop of Augsburg, with many other bishops, and Werner, abbot of Fulda, 982, the Saracens (Lambertus ap. Pertz v. 65). Comp. Thietmar ii. 17, ap. Pertz v. 752. Michael, bishop of Ratisbon, accompanies the Bavarian princes against Hungary. The battle is lost. Episcopus autem abscisa suimet auricula, et caeteris sauciatus membris cum interfectis quasi mortuus latuit. A Hungarian is about to kill him. Tunc iste confortatus in Domino post longum mutui agonis luctamen victor hostem prostravit, et inter multas itineris asperitates incolumis notos pervenit ad fines. Inde gaudium gregi suo exoritur, et omni Christum cognoscenti. Excipitur ab omnibus miles bonus in clero, et servatur optimus pastor in populo, et fuit ejusdem mutilatio non ad dedecus, sed ad honorem magis.

[7] Hüllmann S. 274. Montag ii. 115, 202.

[8] The conc. Tribur. ann. 892. c. 10, after the example of the conc. Carthag. i. (see above, § 20, note 5), decrees ut nullus Episcopus deponatur nisi a xii. Episcopis, Presbyter a sex, Diaconus a tribus, without specifying the pope as sole judge of bishops according to Pseudo-isidore. However even that decree was not by any means adhered to as a form. The bishops were deposed at once by feudal lords for felony. Thus, by Henry II. were deposed the bishop of Asti (Arnulph. Mediol. i. 16), by Conrad ii., the archbishop of Milan, and the bishops of Vercelli, Cremona, and Piacenza (Wippo in vita Conradi ii. ed. Pistorii p. 441). The deposition of Arnulph, archbishop of Rheims (§ 22, not. 21), could only have been contested by the pope against a weak prince, and with imperial support. Planck iii. 443, 467.

[9] Hüllmann S. 237. Montag. ii. 17, 79.

bailiffs,[10] and were forced to bestow many church possessions in feudal tenure, which soon after became heritable, in order to obtain men fit for military service.[11] Spiritual places were conferred, especially by petty princes in Italy and France, from unworthy motives, or even sold.[12] The kings of Germany seldomer allowed themselves to incur the guilt of simony, and several of

[10] Abo, Abbas Floriacensis († 1004), canones § 2 (in Mabillonii vett. analecta p. 135): Defensores Ecclesiarum, qui dicuntur, hodie contra auctoritatem legum et canonum sibi defendunt quod fuerat juris Ecclesiarum : sicque violentiam Clericis et Monachis ingerendo, res Ecclesiarum seu Monasteriorum usufructuario diripiunt, colonos in paupertatem redigunt, possessiones Ecclesiarum non augent, sed minuunt : et quorum defensores esse debuerant, eos vastant. Patet rerum copia cunctis hostibus praedae, nec parant saltem vel verbis obviam ut resistant, qui se putant non jam Advocatos, sed dominos : dum post abscessum hostium consumunt quidquid fuerit residuum. Denique idcirco videmus ecclesias destructas, monasteria quaedam diruta, quaedam ad summam inopiam redacta,—quia multi se ultro offerentes sub advocationis obtentu de possessionibus, de reditibus, de oblationibus maximam portionem intercipiunt, quam Ecclesiastici capere debuerant. Hüllmann S. 250.   Montag. ii. 222.   Planck iii. 611.

[11] Hincmari epist. ad Carol. Calv. pro Hincm. Laudunensi (opp. ed. Sirmond ii. 324) : Porro Episcopus—cum de rebus Ecclesiae propter militiam beneficium donat, aut filiis patrum, qui eidem Ecclesiae profuerunt, et patribus utiliter succedere poterunt, quoniam, ut quidam scripsit, nisi vitulus nutriatur, bos aratro non jungitur, aut talibus dare debet, qui idonei sunt reddere Caesari quae sunt Caesaris, et quae sunt Dei Deo.   A quibus, vel ab eo, qui diu et Ecclesiae utilitatibus ac necessitatibus profuit, et reipublicae ac militiae utilis fuit, et infirmitate vel aetate confectus jam per se ipsum ea exequi non valet, praecipue autem sibi servientem filium habenti, qui pro eo haec valeat, exequi, si Episcopus beneficium quacunque occasione abstulerit ; non abhorret a ratione, si non accuset Episcopum ad publicos judices, quod non licet, sed ad vos se reclamat de beneficio militiae.   Egbert, archbishop of Treves, complains 981 (Honthemii hist. Trevir. i. 321) : Ipsius Episcopii (Trevirensis) maxima pars militibus in beneficium distributa, ita ut nulli lacorum propria hereditate prodesse possem.   Montag ii. 109.

[12] Comp. Attonis Ep. Vercellensis (about 950) lib. de pressuris ecclesiasticis (d'Achery spicileg. i. 414 ss.) p. 421 : Irreligiosi principes haec omnia parvipendentes, suum tantummodo in his [electionibus Episcoporum] parant praevalere edictum.   Solent etiam admodum indignari, si vel ab aliis aliquis, cujuscumque meriti sit, Episcopus eligatur, vel si a se electus, cujuscunque pravitatis sit, ab aliquo reprobetur. Illorum sane, quos ipsi eligunt, vitia, quamvis multa et magna sint, velut nulla tamen reputantur.   Quorum quidem in examinatione non charitas et fides vel spes inquiruntur, sed divitae, affinitas, et obsequium considerantur. p. 423 : Quidam autem adeo mente et corpore obcae-

them opposed it,[13] especially Henry III. ;[14] but during the minority of Henry IV., it was practised by his guardians in a scandalous manner.[15]

cantur, ut ipsos etiam parvulos ad pastoralem promovere curam non du-
bitent, quos nec mente nec corpore idoneos esse constet.   Rident plurimi, alii quasi de infantis honore gaudentes, alii tamen clarum et manifestum praestigium deridentes.   Ipse quoque parvulus de aliquibus
interrogatus capitulis, quae si praeparare poterit memoriter reddet, vel
in aliquo tremens leget pittacio, non episcopalem timens perdere gratiam, sed magistri incurrere virgam.   (Thus Count Heribert of Ver-
mandois, 925, forced his son, Hugo, five years old, as archbishop on the
church at Rheims, and got him confirmed by Pope John X.   Flodoardi hist. Eccles. Rhem. iv. c. 20.)   Hence Atto, p. 427, thus announces
the fortunes of the bishops : irreligiose eliguntur, inaniter ordinantur,
indifferenter accusantur, injuste opprimuntur, perfide dejiciuntur, crudeliter aliquando et necantur : and complains parte iii. p. 428 moreover
of this, quod res ecclesiasticae post mortem vel expulsionem Episcopi in
direptionem et rapinam saecularibus tradantur.

[13] Before the battle with the Hungarians, 933, Henry I. vowed
(Luitprandi antapod. ii. 27, ap. Pertz v. 294) : Simoniaca haeresis Deo
invisa,—quae a decessoribus nostris hactenus est temere custodita, modis
omnibus a nostro sit regno expulsa.   At the synod held in Ingelheim,
948, in presence of Otto I. (Flodoardi ann. ad h. a. ap. Pertz v. 307),
tractata sunt quaedam necessaria de—Ecclesiis, quae Presbyteris in
partibus Germaniae dabantur, immo vendebantur indebite, et aufere-
bantur a laicis illicite ; prohibitumque ac statutum, ne id omnino praesu-
meretur ab aliquo.   On Conrad II. Wippo in vita Conr. II. ap. Pistorius p. 431 : Civitatem Basileam invenit Rex vacuatam Episcopo.   Ibi
simoniaca haeresis subito apparuit, et cito evanuit.   Nam dum Rex et
Regina a quodam clerico, nobili viro, nomine Udalrico, qui ibi tunc
Episcopus effectus est, immensam pecuniam pro Episcopatu suscipe-
rent, postea Rex in poenitentia motus, voto se obligavit, pro aliquo
episcopatu vel abbatia nullam pecuniam amplius accipere.

[14] After he had introduced Clement II. into Italy, who began to oppose simony, he also assembled the German bishops 1047, made very
earnest representations to them about it, and issued the decree (Glaber
Radulphus v. 5), ut nullus gradus clericorum, vel ministerium ecclesiasticum pretio aliquo conquireretur ; ac si quis dare aut accipere praesumeret, omni honore destitutus, anathemate multaretur.   He added :
sicut mihi Dominus coronam imperii sola miseratione sua gratis dedit,
ita et ego quod ad religionem ipsius pertinet, gratis impendam.   Volo,
si placet, ut et vos similiter faciatis.   Comp. Stenzel's Gesch. Deutschlands unter d. fränk. Kaisern i. 117, ii. 130.

[15] Lamberti. ann. ad. ann. 1063 ap. Pertz vii. 166) : Hi duo (Adel-
bertus Bremensis Archiepisc. et Wernher comes) pro Rege imperita-
bant ab his episcopatus et abbatia, ab his quicquid ecclesiasticarum,
quicquid saecularium dignitatum est, emebatur : nec alia cuiquam, licet
industrio atque egregio viro, spes adipiscendi honoris ullius erat, quam

In France the prelates lost most of their regalia under the Capet family; but still they continued to be as dependent as ever on the kings, whose protection they needed against the attacks of the nobles.[16]   Thus the principles which were now spreading, by which the kingly dignity appeared to be subject to the bishops, were allowed to remain intact.[17]

ut hos prius ingenti profusione pecuniarum suarum redemisset.   Et ab Episcopis quidem et Ducibus metu magis, quam religione temperabant. In Abbates vero, quod hi injuriae obviam ire non poterant, tota libertate grassabantur, illud prae se ferentes, nihil minus Regem in hos juris ac potestatis habere, quam in villicos suos, vel in alios quoslibet regalis fisci dispensatores.   Et primo quidem praedia monasteriorum fautoribus suis, prout libitum erat, distribuebant, et quod reliquum erat, crebra regalium servitiorum exactione usque ad faeces ultimas exhaurie-bant.   Diendi convalescente audacia, in ipsa monasteria impetum facie-bant, atque ea inter se tanquam provincias partiebantur, Rege ad om-nia, quae jussus fuisset, puerili facilitate annuente, etc.   Ann. 1071, p. 184 : haec in Ecclesiam introducta est consuetudo, ut abbatiae publice venales prostituantur in palatio; nec quisquam tanti venales proponere queat, quin protinus emtorem inveniat, monachis inter se non de obser-vantia regulae zelo bono, sed de quaestibus et usuris zelo avaro conten-dentibus.   Comp. Stenzel i. 221. ii.58.

[16] Plank iii. 489.   Hence the royal influence in the occupation of bishoprics continued here also.   Ibid. S. 405, 408.   Striking examples of simony may be seen in Gallia christiana (opera monach congreg. s. Mauri T. xii.   Paris 1715—1770. fol.) T. i. Append. docum. p. 5, 23, 37. T. ii. p. 173, 179.

[17] Comp. particularly Gerberti philos (afterwards Sylvester II.) ser-mo de informatione Episcoporum (this is according to Mabillon ana-lect. p. 103, the true title of a work which is quoted so early as Gre-gory VII. lib. xi. epist. 2, under the appellation Ambrosii pastorale, and which appears in editions of Ambrose's works as lib. de dignitate sacer-dotali.)   Among other things we find cap. 2 : Honor igitur, fratres, et sublimitas episcopalis nullis poterit comparationibus adaequari.   Si Regum fulgori compares et principum diademati, longe erit inferius, quam si plumbi metallum ad auri fulgorem compares : quippe cum videas Regum colla et principum submitti genibus sacerdotam, et exos-culatis eorum dextris, orationibus eorum credant se communiri.   Quid jam de plebeja dixerim multitudine, cui non solum praeferri a Domino meruit, sed ut eam quoque jure tueatur patrio, praeceptis imperatum est evangelicis ?   The passage ep. Gelasii P. ad Anastasium Imp., was chiefly relied on, which passage the Paris council had already produced. See. above § 7, not 25 : Duo quippe sunt, Imperator Auguste (instead of this appears also the falsfied reading : Duae quippe sunt Imperatri-ces augustae, see Baluz. capitul. ii. 1213), quibus principaliter mundus hic regitur, auctoritas sacra Pontificum, et regalis potestas.   In quibus tanto gravius est pondus sacerdotum, quanto etiam pro ipsis Regibus Do-

§ 25.

PAPAL SUPREMACY.

Planck l. c. Bd. 3. S. 805 ff.

The ideas promulgated in the Pseudo-isidorian decretals[1] gradually pervaded the whole Western Church; and the metropolitans, so much injured, must have become reconciled to them the more readily, as their own power began to be traced to their investment with the pallium,[2] while the latter was bestowed, since

mino in divino reddituri sunt examine rationem. On this comments Conc. apud s. Macram a. 881 cap. 1. (Mansi xvii. 538): sicut in sacris legimus literis, duo sunt, quibus as above till regia potestas. Solus enim Dominus noster J. C. vere fieri potuit Rex. et sacerdos. Post incarnationem vero—ejus nec Rex Pontificis dignitatem, nec Pontifex regiam potestatem sibi usurpare praesumsit: sic actionibus propriis dignitatibusque ab eo distinctis, ut et christiani Reges pro aeterna vita Pontificibus indigerent, et Pontifices pro temporalium rerum cursu Regum dispositionibus uterentur. Et tanto est dignitas Pontificum major quam Regum, quia Reges in culmen regium sacrantur, a Pontificibus, Pontifices autem a Regibus consecrari non possunt: et tanto gravius pondus as above till rationem.—Conc. Troslejan. a 909 cap. 1. (Mansi xviii. 267): Sicut enim regalis potestas sacerdotali religioni se devote submittit: sic et sacerdotalis religioni se devote submittit: sic et sacerdotalis autoritas cum omni pietatis officio se regali dignitati subdere debet, sicut sanctus ostendit P. Gelasius ad Anastasium scribens Imp. " Duo sunt —rationem." Ergo quia et Rex pro aeterna vita indiget. Pontificibus, et Pontifices pro temporalium rerum cursu regali indigent dispositione: a Rege obediendum est Pontificibus, recta, sancta et justa suadentibus et vicissim a Pontificibus obediendum est Regi, pietatis cultui religione, jure et solatio servienti. Source of the notion that the regal dignity was conferred by the unction. See § 6. not. 14.—Comp. Planck iii. 477.

[1] Comp. § 20 not. 8.

[2] This had its source from the ancient custom of confirming the metropolitans in their office sive per manus impositionem, sive per pallii dationem episcopalis dignitatis firmitatem accipiunt (conc. Constant. oecum. viii. A.D. 869 can. 17). This patriarchal relation was now transferred to all metropolitans of the West. First Nicolaus i. in respons. ad consulta Bulgarorum c. 73 (Mansi xv. 426): [Archiepiscopum] Episcopi, qui ab obeunte Archiepiscopo consecrati sunt, simul congregati, constituant: sane interim in throno non sedentem, et praeter, corpus Christi non consecrantem, priusquam pallium a sede Romana percipiat, sicuti Galliarum omnes, et Germaniae, et aliarum regionum Archie-

the time of Nicolaus I., only under the condition of the receivers
vowing obedience on oath to the Romish institutions.[3]   The decretals designated the pope as universal bishop of the Church—
an idea as yet obscure and undeveloped—but on this account the
more dangerous—constantly stimulating the papal ambition, mis-
leading weak men and abused by the bad.[4]   That the popes alone

piscopi agere comprobantur.   In like manner Johannes viii. in ep. 94
ad Rostagnum Archiepisc. Arelat. A.D. 878 (Mansi xvii. 81) and in Syn.
Ravennensi a 877 can. 1 (see above § 21 not. 30. Can. i. and ii. of this
synod were soon ascribed to old popes: by Petrus Damiani l. 7, ep. 4,
Burchard and others to Damasus; by Ivo and Gratian P. i. dist. c. can.
1. to one Pelagius.   It is remarkable that even Boehmer has not observed the ψευδος.   See Jod. le Plat diss. de spuriis in Gratiano cann.
P. iii. sec. ii. c. 12 §. 2.)   A notable proof that though this view did
not immediately become general in the church, the bishops were notwithstanding already accustomed and prepared to receive with implicit
belief, hitherto unknown privileges of the Roman see, is given by Fulbert Episc. Carnotensis († 1028) ep. 47, ad. Archiepisc. Turon. (Bibl.
Max. PP. xviii. 17): Si pallium requisistis a Romano Pontifice, et ipse
vobis illud sine causa legitima denegavit, propter hoc non est opus dimittere ministerium vestrum : at si vestra tarditate nondum est requi-
situm, cautella est exspectare donec requiratur, ne vos ex improvisio prae-
sumptionis arguere possit.   Continentur enim quaedam reverenda nobis in
privilegiis Romanae Ecclesiae, quae propter negligentiam nostram non facile inveniuntur in armariis nostris.   Cf. Pertsch de origine et auctoritate
pallii archiepiscopalis, Helmst. 1754, 4. p. 145 ss.   On the cost of the
Pallium see Canuti Regis ep. ad Anglorum proceres, written from
Rome A.D. 1027 (Mansi xix. 499): Conquestus sum iterum coram
domina Papa, et mihi valde displicere dixi, quod mei Archiepiscopi in
tantum angariabantur immensitate pecuniarum, quae ab eis expetebant-
tur, dum pro pallio accipiendo secundum morem apostolicam sedem ex-
peterent : decretumque est ne id deinceps fiat.   It was the custom to
fetch the pallium in person from Rome, Thomassini eccl. disc. P. i. lib.
ii. cap. 57. no. 4.   Pertsch p. 222 ss.

[3] See above § 21. not. 19.

[4] Comp. conc. Triburiense under Hatto, archbp. of Mainz, a. 895,
c. 30. (Mansi xviii. 147, d'Achery spicileg. iii. 850): In memoriam
b. Petri Apostoli honoremus s. Romanam et apostolicam sedem, ut
quae nobis sacerdotalis mater est dignitatis, esse debeat magistra
ecclesiasticae rationis.   Quare servanda est cum mansuetudine
humilitas, ut licet vix ferendum ab illa s. sede imponatur jugum,
tamen feramus, et pia devotione toleremus.   Si vero, quod non decet, quilibet, sive Presbyter, sive Diaconus, aliquam perturbationem
machinando, et nostro ministerio insidiano, redarguatur falsam ab
Apostolico detulisse epistolam, vel aliud quid, quod inde non convenerit,
salva fide et integra circa Apostolicum humilitate, penes Episcopum sit
potestas, utrum eum in carcerem, aut in aliam detrudat custodiam, us-

were judges of bishops, was an idea not at all recognised :[5] their interference in the government of the dioceses of bishops was universally disapproved,[6] sometimes expressly repelled.[7] It was characteristic of the rude time to suppose, that the high priest in Rome could interfere in the name of the divine law, where the

quequo per epistolam, aut per idoneos suae partis legatos apostolicam' interpellet sublimitatem, ut potissimum sua sancta legatione dignetur decernere, quid de talibus justo ordine lex Romana statuat diffinire, ut et is corrigatur, et caeteris modus impŏnatur.

[5] See above § 24 not. 8. The synod of Altheim, A.D. 916, decrees repecting complaints against bishops, c. 13 (Pertz iv. 566), ut accusatus vel judicatus a comprovincialibus in aliqua causa Episcopis licenter appellet et adeat apostolicae sedis Pontificem.

[6] Comp. Caroli Calvi Const. ann. 878 above § 21, not. 32. Farther the narrative of Glaber Radulph. ii. c. 4. (Bouquet x. 15): A certain count, Fulco, of most abandoned character, for whom Hugo, archbishop of Tours, would not consecrate a church in honour of the cherubim and seraphim (about 1007) copiosa argenti et auri assumta peccunia Romam pergens Johanni P. causam suae profectionis exposuit : ac deinde reportans quod ab illo optaverat, plurima ei munerum dona obtulit. Qui protinus misit cum eodem Fulcone ad praedictam Basilicam sacrandam unum ex illis, quos—Cardinales vocant, nomine Petrum, cui etiam praecepit, veluti Romani Pontificis auctoritate assumta, quicquid agendum Fulconi videbatur, intrepidus expleret. Quod utique audientes Galliarum quique Praesules—pariter detestantes, quoniam nimium indecens videbatur, ut is, qui apostolicam regebat sedem, apostolicum primitus ac canonicum transgrediebatur tenorem : cum insuper multiplici sit antiquitus auctoritate roboratum, ut non quispiam Episcoporum in alterius Dioecesi istud praesumat exercere, nisi Praesule, cujus fuerit, compelente seu permittente. Licet namque Pontifex Romanae Ecclesiae ob dignitatem apostolicae sedis cateris in orbe constitutis reverentior habeatur non tamen ei licet transgredi in aliquo canonici moderaminis tenorem. Sicut enim nnusquisque orthodoxae Ecclesiae Pontifex, ac sponsus propriae sedis uniformiter speciem gerit Salvatoris, ita generaliter nulli convenit quippiam in alterius procaciter patrare Episcopi dioecesi. The narrative is indeed rectified from documents by de Marca lib. 4, c. 8. §. 2 : but Glabor's judgment always remains a notable testimony in favour of the views of that time.

[7] Chronicon Urspergense ad ann. 1052: When Leo IX. was in Worms, and Leutpold, archbishop of Mainz, read mass, the diaconus sang the lesson in the German manner. The pope, quia Romano more non agebatur, commanded him to cease. The deacon did not allow himself to be interrupted, et lectionem usque ad finem perduxit. Qua finita Papa illum ad se vocavit, et quasi pro inobedientiae contumacia degradavit. Archiepiscopus vero misit ad illum, ut suum sibi redderet ministrum. Quod ubi Papa abnuit, Pontifex, ut erat antiquae disciplinae, licet aegre, patienter tamen interim tacendo sustiuuit. But when

human was too weak or insufficient;[8] that, moreover, he could impart the most efficacious blessing,[9] and give the most effectual absolution for sins.[10]   The bishops, on the other hand, main-

[8] he should have continued the mass, in sede sua resedit, vere contestans, nec se, nec alium quempiam completurum illud officium, nisi reciperet processionis suae ministrum.   Quod ubi Apostolicus intellexit, Pontifici cessit, reindutumque ministrum continuo remisit.   Quo recepto, debito se praesul injunxit officio. Qua in re et Pontificis auctoritas, et Apostolici consideranda est humilitas : dum et ille officii sui dignitatem defendere contendebat, et iste, licet majoris dignitatis, Metropolitano tandem in sua dioecesi cedendum perpendebat.

[8] Pope Hadrian II. was required by the emperor Lewis II., to release him from a forced oath made to the Prince of Beneventa Adalgisus (annales Hincmari ad ann. 871 ap. Pertz. i. 493) and John VIII. loosed him (Regino add ann. 872 l. c. p. 584).   The emperor Charles the Corpulent, invited to him Pope Hadrian III. (annal. Fuldens. ad ann. 885 ap. Pertz. i. 402) : voluit enim, ut fama vulgabat, quosdam Episcopos irrationabiliter deponere, et Bernhardum, filium suum ex concubina, heredem regni post se constituere ; et hoc, quia per se posse fieri dubitavit, per Pontificem Romanum quasi apostolica auctoritate perficere disposuit.   Hatto, archbishop of Mainz, wrote to Pope John IX., A.D. 900 (Mansi xviii. 203) that in place of the deceased emperor Arnulf, his son, Lewis, seven years old, had been chosen, and explains in a tone of inculpation, cur hoc sine vestra jussione et permissione, factum sit.   Then he adds : Quia tandem occasio et tempus advenit, quo nostra epistola vestris obtutibus praesentaretur ; rogamus, nostram communem constitutionem vestrae Dominationis benedictione roborari.   In the year 916 the synod held at Altheim (Pertz iv. 555) : praesente domni Joannis Papae apocrisiario Petro,—misso ad hoc, quatenus aliquo modo diabolica semina in nostris partibus orta extirpare et nefandissimas machinationes quorundam perversorum hominum sedare et eliminando purgare deberet.   The decrees of the synod had for their object, partly the protection of the church, partly the confirmation of the kingly authority.   Under more powerful emperors, as the Ottos, the circumstances were reversed, and then the old imperial rights over the popes were again prominently adduced.

[9] Auxilius (about 894) de ordinationibus Formosi Papae (libb. ii. Bibl. PP. T. xvii. p. 1), lib. i. c. 29 : Qui de longinquis terrarum spatiis per mille, ut ita dicam, discrimina, tremebundi ad apostolicam sedem profecti sunt, et sacram ordinationem, ut moris est, magis ab Apostolo Petro, quam ab ejus vicario susceperunt.

[10] Nicolai i. ep. 20, ad Carol. Calv. ap. Mansi xv. 280 : Ad hanc sanctam Romanam—Ecclesiam—de diversis mundi partibus quotidie multi sceleris mole oppressi confugiunt, remissionem scilicet, et venialem sibi gratiam tribui supplici et ingenti cordis moerore poscentes (ep. 21 : et ab ea non solum animae, sed et corporis salvationem—humili prece suscipere precantur).   When Hatto, in the letter quoted note 8, announced to Pope IX. the death of the emperor Arnulph, he also added :

tained, they alone could exercise the ecclesiastical power of the keys in their dioceses.[11]

quod, quamdiu in hoc mundo subsistimus, per incerta ferimur, nescientes ubi quorundum animae post hanc lucem mansionem recipiant; vestris quasi provoluti vestigiis subnixe poscimus, ut animam ipsius vestrae auctoritatis potestate a vinculis peccatorum absolvatis, quia " quaecunque solveritis super terram, erunt soluta in caelo."

[11] Conc. Salegunstadiense (held in the year 1022, under the presidency of archbp. Aribo of Mainz), cap. 18 (Mansi xix. 398) : Quia multi tanta mentis suae falluntur stultitia, ut in aliquo capitali crimine inculpati poenitentiam a sacerdotibus suis accipere nolint, in hoc maxime confisi, ut Romam euntibus Apostolicus omnia sibi dimittat peccata: sancto visum est concilio, ut talis indulgentia illis non prosit, sed prius juxta modum delicti poenitentiam sibi datam a suis sacerdotibus adimpleant, et tunc Romam ire si velint, ab Episcopo proprio licentiam et literas ad Apostolicum ex iisdem rebus deferendas accipiant. Conc. Lemovicense a 1031, Sessio ii. (Mansi xix. 546). Complaints of some qui ignorantibus Episcopis suis a Romano Papa poenitentiam et absolutionem accipiunt :—dum quos isti juste ligant, ille injuste absolvit. So one Count Stephen excommunicated by his bishop, Romae a domno Papa absolutionem accepit, ignorante Papa eum excommunicatum. The bishop complaining of this, received for answer from the pope, " Quod nescienter egi, frater carissime, non mea, sed tua est culpa. Scis enim, quia quicunque de universa Dei Ecclesia—ad me causa remedii recurrit, impossibile est mihi ejus causam negligere, dicente Domino ad b. specialiter Petrum : ' Petre, pasce oves meas.' Debueras certe mihi—ejus causam tuis innotescere apicibus, et ego omnimodo abjicerem. Profiteor quippe omnibus consacerdotibus—adjutorem me et consolatorem potius esse, quam contradictorem. Absit enim schisma a me et a Coëpiscopis meis. Itaque illam poenitentiam et absolutionem, quam tuo excommunicato ignoranter dederam, irritam facio et cassam." Another excommunicated person had gone to Rome, Papae Romano subripuit poenitentiae legem, carrying with him letters, quibus Episcopum rogabat Apostolicus, quatenus illi poenitentiam, quam imposuerat, affirmaret. To them the bishop answered : Versa vice, quod ego postulare debueram ab Apostolico, Apostolicus postulat a me. Non credere possum hoc mandatum ab eo exortum: hoc tibi nihil utile est : et donec aut a me, vel ab hujus sedis Archidiacono, me jubente, accipias poenitentiam, permane in excommunicatione. Thereupon the synod determines: Parochiano suo Episcopus si poenitentiam imponit, eumque Papae dirigit, ut judicet, utrum sit an non poenitentia digna pro tali reatu: potest eam confirmare auctoritas Papae, aut levigare, aut superadjicere. Judicium enim totius Ecclesiae maxime in apostolica Romana sede constat. Item si Episcopus parochianum suum cum testibus vel literis Apostolico ad poenitentiam accipiendam direxerit, ut multoties pro gravissimis fieri solet reatibus, in quibus Episcopi ad dignam haesitant poenitentiam imponendam : hic talis licenter a Papa remedium sumere potest. Nam inconsulto Episcopo suo, ab Apostolico

The papal pretensions met with the greatest opposition from
the archbishops of Upper Italy, especially of Milan.[12] The Church
of Milan, indeed, had been compelled, A.D. 1059, to recognise in
form the Roman supremacy;[13] but still, aversion to the hierarchy
of Rome continued for a long time, and every opposition made to
that hierarchy found advocates there for a considerable period.[14]

poenitentiam et absolutionem nemini accipere licet. Comp. Planck
iii. 684.

[12] Schmidt's Kirchengesch. Th. 5. S. 4 ff.

[13] The party forming in Milan since 1056 against the married priests,
at the head of which stood Arialdux and Landulphus, were anxious for
their own ends to make the Milanese church as dependent as possible
on Rome. Comp. the contemporary works Arnulphi Mediol. rerum sui
temporis libb. v. (in Muratorii rer. Ital. scriptt. T. iv. p. 11) and Landulphi senioris Mediolanensis historiae libb. iv. (ibid. p. 47 ss.)—Cf.
Arnulph. iii. c. 11 : Romam proficiscitur Arialdus apologeticas ferens
literas. Ubi cum Ambrosianum accusaret clerum, affirmans omnes
Nicolaitas et Simoniacos, ac prorsus inobedientes Romanae Ecclesiae,
se autem cum Landulpho devotum, et pro sola veritate certantem, Romanorum celeriter adeptus est gratiam. Qui cum principari appetant
jure apostolico, videntur velle dominari omnium, et cuncta suae subdere ditioni, cum Doctor evangelicus suos doceat humilitatem Apostolos
dicens : " Reges gentium dominantur eorum,—vos autem non sic ; sed
qui major est in vobis, fiat sicut minor etc." (Luc. xxii. 25. 26.)   In
particular, the general opinion became prominent when Petrus Damiani
and Anselm, bishop of Lucca, appeared in 1059 as papal legates. Of
the following transactions a complete account is furnished by Petrus
Damiani opusc. v. to Hildebrand (opp. iii. p. 37. ap. Muratori l. c.
p. 25 ss.   Mansi xix. p. 887 ss.) As soon as they arrived, repente in
populo murmur exoritur, non debere Ambrosianam Ecclesiam Romanis
legibus subjacere, nullumque judicandi vel disponendi jus Romano
Pontifici in illa sede competere. Nimis indignum, inquiunt, ut quae
sub progenitoribus nostris semper extitit libera, ad nostrae confusionis
opprobrium nunc alteri, quod absit, Ecclesiae sit subjecta. A tumult
ensued, but Archbishop Guido submitted, and the Romish legates
triumphed. On this Arnulph iii. c. 13 : O insensati Mediolanenses,
quis vos fascinavit? Heri clamastis unius sellae primatum. Hodie con-
funditis totius Ecclesiae statum, vere culicem liquantes et camelum
glutientes.   Nonne satius vester hoc procuraret Episcopus ? Forte
dicetis : Veneranda est Roma in Apostolo. Est utique : sed nec sper-
nendum Mediolanum in Ambrosio. Certe, certe non absque re scripta
sunt haec in Romanis annalibus. Dicetur enim in posterum subjectum
Romae Mediolanum. Ecce Metropolitanus vester prae solito Romanam
vocatur ad Synodum etc.

[14] So the schism of Cadolus. See above § 23. not. 12. see annales
Altah. v. Giesebrecht S. 189 ; so too Henry IV. against Gregory VII.

§. 26.

RELATIONS OF THE BISHOPS TO THE CLERGY OF THEIR DIOCESES.

As the bishops became more involved in secular business, they neglected the spiritual care of their dioceses, and thus lost in proportion the completely monarchical power they had once exercised in them. *The chapters*, after the example of the chapter of *Cologne* (864),[1] received the independent right of managing

[1] The confirmation of the ordinatio Guntharii Archiep. Colon. issued on this subject by King Lothaire A. D. 866 (from the 11th year of King Lothaire, not of the emperor, therefore not 853 as Mastiaux has), see in Mastiaux diss. exhibens historiam turni Ecclesiarum collegiat. Coloniens. Bonnae 1786. 4. App. p. 1. (Gunthar probably wished, after his Roman deposal, see § 21. note 8. to bind his clergy more firmly to himself by that arrangement, see Gfrörer iii. ii. 994. 998.) The same arrangement is confirmed by the concil. Colon. a. 873 under Archbp. Wilibert (Mansi xvii. 275): Guntharius—monasteriis—ac canonice in eis commorantibus sumtuum suorum necessaria habenda delegavit atque contradidit: quatenus deinceps videlicet—perpetualiter inde consistere quivissent absque alicujus sumtus indigentia. Praeterea—illis concessit atque donavit, ultra licitum fore cum secura potestate et libero arbitrio inter se ordinare et facere tam de sua electione, quam de omnibus suis rebus absque ejus consultu et imperio; similiter—decrevit, ut Praeposito in sibi subjectis nullus nec praelatione nec potestate superponeretur, sed idem potius in ambobus super omnes praestantissimus haberetur, ac insuper eorundem subjectorum res communes—ipse solus cum consilio prudentum benevolentiumque fratrum gubernans—dispensaret.—Lege sancivit, ut nullus unquam Pontifex sine illorum conscientia sive consensu de ipsa substantia minimam unquam praebendam alicui per potentiam tribueret, aut item—quidquam eis per potentiam sive per aliquam vim destrueret;—hoc illis quasi in jus hereditarium firmiter concedens, quatenus quisque illorum, sive nobilis sive ignobilis esset, usque in sempiternum liberum haberet arbitrium, suam mansionem cum caeteris quibuscunque rebus donare, seu etiam tradere cuicumque suo confratri voluisset post obitum suum possidendam absque ullius Episcopi consultu sive contradictione. By degrees this ordinance was every where imitated, in many places very late. In Rätzeburg the division of goods between bishop and chapter first took place 1194, s. Westphalen monum. rerum Germ. praec. Cimbricarum iii. 2050, in Lyons about the year 1200. See Gallia christiana iv. 134. Planck iii. 641.

2 B 2

their own property, and then gradually discontinued their canonical life,[2] after the example of the chapter at *Treves* (973).[3]
The chapters,[4] and also the *archdeacons*,[5] acquired certain rights
in the management and rule of the dioceses. The benefices of
the parochial clergy were now fully fixed on an unalterable
basis.[6]

[2] Ivo Episc. Carnotensis (about 1092) epist. 215 : Quod vero communis vita in omnibus Ecclesiis paene defecit, tam civilibus quam dioecesanis, nec auctoritati, sed desuetudini et defectui adscribendum est,
refrigescente charitate, quae omnia vult habere communia, et regnante
cupiditate, quae non quaerit ea, quae Dei sunt et proximi, sed tantum
quae sunt propria. At the end of this period there were new attempts
to re-introduce the canonical life, conc. Rom. a. 1059 (ap. Mansi xix.
908), and conc. Rom. a. 1063, cap. 4. (ib. p. 1025), etc. (Cf. Thomassini vet. et nov. eccl. discipl. P. i. lib. iii. c. 11.—P. iii. lib. ii. c. 23.
no. 2.)

[3] Trithemii chron. Hirsaug. ad h. a. (ed. St. Galli 1690. T. i. p.
116) : Hoc tempore Heinrico, Trevirorum Archiepiscopo, mortuo Theo-
dericus de Moguntia successit, sub quo Canonici majoris Ecclesiae s.
Petri—abjecta pristinae conversationis norma desierunt esse regulares,
distributionibus inter se factis praebendarum : et qui prius more Apostolorum omnia habuere communia, coeperunt jam deinceps singuli possidere propria. Quorum exemplum postea secuti plures Canonici sicut
s. Paulini apud Treviros, s. Castoris in Confluentia, ss. Martini et
Victoris Moguntiae, in Wormatia quoque et Spira de communi ad propriam vitae rationem descenderunt. With the former account agree
also the Gesta Trevirorum (ed. Wyttenbach et Müller voll. iii. Aug.
Trev. 1836. 4.) i. 111 : sub eodem Pontifice regulares Canonici in Ecclesia s. Petri esse desierunt. At first they only began to live sepa-
rately, but still ate together; for in a document of Archbp. Poppo, A.D.
1017 (in Günther cod, dipl. Rheno-Mosell. i. 121), they are still designated as fratres cottidie manducantes in refectorio.

[4] Planck iii. 749.

[5] Thomassini P. i. lib. ii. c. 19 and 20.   Planck iii. 708.

[6] Thomassini P. iii. lib. ii. c. 8. 18. 19. 24.   Planck. iii. 650. 776.

THIRD CHAPTER.

HISTORY OF THEOLOGICAL AND RELIGIOUS-MORAL CULTURE.

§ 27.

ITS STATE IN THE TENTH CENTURY.

Cramer's fünfte Forts. von Bossuet or Th. 5. Bd. 2. S. 185 ff.

During the civil commotions which ensued on the partition of the great Frank empire, and the gradual disuse of the Latin tongue,[1] all science sank into decay, and a general barbarism prevailed, which characterises the tenth century in particular.[2] Unworthy persons took possession of the higher ecclesiastical situations, in order to vie with the nobles in rapacity and voluptuousness.[3] The grossest ignorance of religious subjects, and, as the effect of it, the rudest immorality, prevailed among the clergy,[4] as well as the people.[5] This was worst of all in Italy,[6]

---

[1] Dietz, Gramm. d. roman. Sprachen i. 74. 82. Bähr's Gesch. d. röm. Liter. im. karoling. Zeitalter. S. 59.

[2] Baronius ad ann. 900 no. 1 : novum inchoatur saeculum, quod sui asperitate ac boni sterilitate ferreum, malique exundantis deformitate plumbeum, atque inopia scriptorum appellari consuevit obscurum. Gatterer de Gunzone Italo ad illustrandum rei literariae statum saec x. Gottingae 1756. 4. On the other hand du Pin nouv. bibl. des aut. eccl. siècle 10. pr. p. 1, Leibnitius in praef. ad cod. juris nat. et gentium diplom. and Semler hist. eccl. vel. capita ii. 526, would prefer the 10th century to the 12th and 13th. But comp. Mabillon act. SS. ord. Ben. saec. v. praef. p. 2. Hist. lit. de la Fr. vi. 1. Cramer l. c. Heeren's Gesch. d. class. Literatur im Mittelalter i. 190. Bähr S. 49.

[3] Comp. § 24.

[4] Ex. gr. Ratherii itinerarium (in d'Achery spicil. i. 381) : Sciscitatus itaque de fide illorum (clericorum Veronensium) inveni plurimos neque ipsum sapere symbolum, qui fuisse creditur Apostolorum. Hac occasione Synodicam scribere omnibus Presbyteris sum compulsus etc. In this Synodica (ibid. p. 376 ss.) it is said among other things : Ipsam fidem—trifarie parare memoriae festinetis h. e. secundum symbolum— Apostolorum,—et illam quae ad Missam canitur, et illam s. Athanasii,

quae ita incipit : " Quicumque vult salvus esse." Quicumque vult ergo
sacerdos in nostra parochia esse, aut fieri, aut permanere, illa, fratres,
memoriter nobis recitet, cum proximo a nobis huc vocatus fuerit. Moneo
et jam vos de die dominico ut cogitetis aut si cogitare nescitis, interrogetis, quare ita vocetur.—ut unusquisque vestrum, si fieri potest, expositionem symboli et orationis dominicae juxta traditionem orthodoxorum penes se scriptam habeat, et eam pleniter intelligat, et inde, si
novit, praedicando populum sibi commissum sedulo instruat ; si non,
saltem teneat vel credat.   Orationes Missae et canonem bene intelligat,
et si non, saltem memoriter ac distincte proferre valeat.   Epistolam et
Evangelium bene legere possit, et utinam saltem ad literam ejus sensum posset manifestare etc. Cf. Baluzii not. ad Reginonem p. 540.
To what extent the morals of the clergy were corrupted may be seen
from the catalogue of crimes committed by Hugo, bishop of Langres,
in conc. Rhem. a 1049 (Mansi xix. 739.)
    [5] Conc. Troslejan. a. 909.   Praef. (Mansi xviii. 265) : iniquitates
nostrae multiplicatae sunt super caput, et delicta nostra creverunt usque
ad caelos.   Fornicatio et adulterium, sacrilegium et homicidium inun-
darunt, et sanguis sanguinem tetigit.   Sanguis quippe sanguinem tan-
git, cum peccator malis suis gravius aliquod malum adjungit—sed in
pejus quotidie proficit.—posthabito humanarum vel divinarum legum
timore, contemtis edictis episcopalibus, unusquisque quod vult agit :
potentior viribus infirmiorem opprimit, et sunt homines sicut pisces
maris, qui ab invicem passim devorantur : ac calcata iniquitate abundat
ac convalescit iniquitas.   Hinc est quod videmus per totum mundum
rapinas pauperum, depraedationes rerum ecclesiasticarum.   Hinc sunt
assiduae lacrymae, pupillorum luctus etc.   Denique ne nobis parcere
videamur, qui aliorum errata corrigere debemus, Episcopi dicimur, sed
episcopale officium non implemus.   Ministerium praedicationis relinquimus : eos, qui nobis commissi sunt, videmus Deum deserere, et in
pravis actibus jacere, et tacemus etc.   Cap. xv. (p. 305) : heu, proh
dolor ! nostris nostrorumque comministrorum, et qui jam discesserunt,
et qui adhuc supersunt, tam incuria quam inscientia perditi vitiis multi,
et paene innumerabiles adhuc inveniuntur in plebe ecclesiastica,—qui
ad usque sua tempora senectutis necdum, ut debuerant, percepere fidei
notitiam simplicis, usque adeo ut nec ipsius symboli verba salutaris, nec
saltem supplicationem dominicae noverint orationis.   Glaber Radulph.
iv. 5 relates how a great famine, 1033, had produced a general penance :
tunc primitus coepere—coadunari conciliorum conventus, ad quos etiam
multa delata sunt corpora Sanctorum.   Quod etiam tota multitudo universae plebis audiens, laetanter adiere maximi, mediocres ac minimi,
parati cuncti obedire, quicquid praeceptum fuisset a pastoribus Ecclesiae.   But with the extremity ceased also their penitence.   Nam ipsi
Primates utriusque ordinis in avaritiam versi, coeperunt exercere plurimas, ut olim fecerant, vel etiam eo amplius, rapinas cupiditatis : deinde
mediocres ac minores exemplo majorum ad immania sunt flagitia devoluti.   Quis enim ur quam antea tantos incestus, tanta adulteria audive-
rat etc.—impletum est Prophetae vaticinium, quod ait : " Et erit sicut
populus sic sacerdos" (Es. 24, 2), etc.
    [6] Comp. § 23, not. 2. So Ratherius de contemtu cann. P. ii.

where *Ratherius*, bishop of Verona († 974),[7] was at last forced to yield to the general corruption which he had ineffectually combated.

The religious ignorance of the times is plainly illustrated in the anthropomorphism of the clergy of Vicenza,[8] attacked by

(d'Achery spicil. i. 354): Quaerat et aliquis, cur prae caeteris gentibus baptismo renatis, contemtores canonicae legis et vilipensores clericorum sint magis Italici. Quoniam quidem libidinosiores eos et pigmentorum Venerem nutrientium frequentior usus, et vini continua potatio, et negligentior disciplina facit doctorum : unde ad tantam consuetudo et majorum eos exempla jam olim impulerunt impudentiam, ut solummodo barbirasio, et verticis cum aliquantula vestium dissimilitudine nudo, et quod in Ecclesia cum negligentia agunt non parva, unde tamen affectant magis placere mundo quam Deo, a ritu distare eos videas laico. Gerberti epist. 40, ad Stephanum Rom. Eccl. Diaconum (in du Chesne scriptt. Franc. ii. 798): Tota Italia Roma mihi visa est. Romanorum mores mundus perhorrescit.

[7] His writings (especially de contemtu canonum, partes ii. ; apologia sui ipsius: de discordia inter ipsum et clericos; liber apologeticus; itinerarium Ratherii Romam euntis; sermones; epistolae) collected in d'Achery spicileg. i. 345. To these add praeloquiorum libb. vi. in Martene et Durand ampl. coll. ix. 785. Opera emendata et ineditis aucta, cur. Petr. et Hier. fratr. Baleriniis. Verona 1765, fol. Comp. hist. liter. de la France vi. 339. Engelhardt's kirchengesh. Abhandl. Erlangen 1832. 8. 295. Bähr's Gesch. d. röm. Liter. im karoling. Zeitalter S. 546. Rather par Gantrel, in the Nouvelles archives historiques, philos. et litter, par MM. Hane, Huet, Lenz et Mone. Gand 1837, 8.

[8] Ratherii serm. i. de quadragesima (d'Achery i. 388) : Nudius enim tertius quidam nostratium retulit nobis, Presbyteros Vicentinae dioecesis, nostros utique vicinos, putare corporeum Deum esse : hac siquidem occasione inductos, quod in Scripturis legatur: " Oculi Domini super justos et aures ejus in preces eorum, etc." —(Ps. xxxiii. 16, then Hiob 10, 8. Genes. i. 26). Quod cum nos non modice permovisset, proh nefas ! nobis commisso gregi eandem adeo comperimus perfidiam inhaesisse, ut facto de periculo in populo sermone, et spiritum esse Deum—approbato, quidam, heu dolor ! nostrorum murmurando dicerent etiam sacerdotum : Quid modo faciemus ? Usque nunc aliquid visum est nobis de Deo scire, modo videtur nobis, quod nihil omnino sit Deus, si caput non habet, etc. (Comp. vol. i. Div. ii. § 95, not. 36.) Idola tibi in corde coepisti stultissime fabricare, immensitasque Dei oblitus, magnum quendam quasi Regem in throno aureo videlicet sedentem depingere, militiam Angelorum quasi quosdam homines alatos, ut in parietibus soles videre, vestibus albis indutos ei assistere, etc. Secunda, inquiunt, feria Michaël Archangelus Deo Missam celebrat. O caeca dementia, etc. And he was even compelled to defend himself for thus finding fault with them. Contra reprehensores sermonis ejusdem (ibid. p. 391) : Non dicit Ratherius, quod Deus Dei filius, Dominus noster J. Ch.—

Ratherius. The consciousness of their own corruption betrays
itself in the expectation which was becoming universal in the
tenth century, that the end of the world was at hand.[9]

The zealous efforts of *Alfred the Great* (871-901),[10] for the

non habeat caput, oculos, manus, et pedes, etc. Non dicit Ratherius,
quod malum faciat, qui vadit ad Ecclesiam s. Michaëlis, aut audit Missam s. Michaëlis, sed dicit Ratherius, quod mentitur ille, qui dicit, quod
conveniat alicui meliûs secunda feria ire ad Ecclesiam s. Michaelis vel
Missam s. Michaëlis audire, quam in alio die, etc.

[9] As early as Conc. Troslej, a. 909 (Mansi xviii. 266) : dum jam
jamque adventus imminet illius in majestate terribili, ubi omnes cum gre-
gibus suis venient pastores in conspectum pastoris aeterni, etc. According to Trithemii chron. Hirsaug. ad ann. 960, Bernhard an eremite from
Thuringia appeared at the diet of Würtzburg, and diem jamjam imminere
dicebat extremum, et mundum in brevi consummandum, idque sibi a Deo
revelatum constanter affirmabat. In cujus rei signum cruces Deum
praemisisse apparere in vestibus hominum asserebat, nec illas desituras,
donec mundi consummatio fiat. The gesta Episc. Leodiensium c. 21.
written about 1050, (in Martene ampl. coll. iv. 860), relate how Otto I.'s
army in Calabria was terrified by an eclipse of the sun : incredibili pa-
vore perterriti, nihil, aliud quam diem judicii putant imminere. Alii vasis
vinariis, alii cistis, alii sub carris turpiter sese recondunt : quisque pro
lucro reputat, si quod pro hac inusitata nocte sibi reperire queat latibulum. Abbo Abbas Floriacensis in apologetico ad Hugonem R. (about
990, appended to Fr: Pithoei cod. cann. Eccl. Rom. p. 401, and ap.
Gallandius XIV. 141) : De fine quoque mundi coram populo sermonem
in ecclesia Parisiorum audivi, quod statim finito mille annorum numero
Antichristus adveniret, et non longo post tempore universale judicium
succederet : cui praedicationi ex Evangeliis ac Apocalypsi et libro Danielis qua potui virtute restiti. Denique et errorem, qui de fine mundi
inolevit, Abbas meus b. memoriae Richardus sagaci animo propulit.
postquam literas a Lothariensibus accepit, quibus me respondere jussit.
Nam fama paene totum mundum impleverat, quod quando Annunciatio
Dominica in Parasceue contigisset, absque ullo scrupulo finis saeculi
esset. In the year 1010 the fear was renewed : Willelmi Godelli
(monk in Limoges about 1150) Chronica ap. Bouquet x. 262) : Anno
Dom. MX. in multis locis per orbem tali rumore audito (namely that
Jerusalem, 1009, had been taken by the Turks) timor et moeror corda
plurimorum occupavit, et suspicati sunt multi, finem saeculi adesse. Hence
the frequent endowments in the tenth century, beginning with : Appro-
pinquante mundi termina. In connection with this stands the passage,
Glaber Radulph. iii. c. 4 : infra millesimum tertio jam fere imminente anno contigit in universo paene terrarum orbe, praecipue tamen
in Italia et in Galliis, innovari Ecclesiarum Basilicas, licet pleraeque
decenter locatae minime indiguissent, etc. At this period were erected
the splendid cathedrals of Strassburg, Mayence, Treves, Speier, Worms,
Basel, Dijon, Toul, and many others.

[10] Some Anglo-Saxon poems of his, and translations of Orosius, Boe-

revival of letters in England, had no lasting influence. The most important schools were maintained in Germany, especially in Fulda, St Gallen,[11] Hirschau, and Corvey. *Roswitha*, a nun of Gandersheim (about 980), was eminent as a Latin poetess.[12]

§ 28.

NEW SPIRITUAL IMPULSES.

While all learning was become extinct among Christians of the West, the Arabs, from the time of the Chalifs *Harun Al Raschid* (786-808), and *Al Mamun* (808-833), had engaged with great ardour in the study of the sciences, which they had borrowed from the Greeks. Not only were many celebrated schools established in the East (*Bagdad*, Bassora, Damascus, &c.), but in Spain, under the Ommaiads, these studies were particularly patronised, and a college instituted at *Cardova* (founded by *Hakem* 980), for their encouragement.[1] As yet, however, only

thius, Gregory the Great, Bede, are extant. Cf. Asserii Schireburnensis (a contemporary) hist. de rebus gestis Alfredi Regis (best edited by Franc. Wise, Oxon. 1722, 8). Ant. Wood hist. et antiquitt. Univers. Oxoniensis, Oxon. 1674, fol. lib. i. p. 13 s. F. L. Graf zu Stolberg Leben Alfred des Grossen. Münster 1815, 8. Geschichte Alfred's d. G. übertragen aus Turner's Geschichte d. Angelsachsen von D. F. Lorentz. Hamburg 1828. Biographia britannica literaria. Anglo-Saxon period, by Thomas Wright. London, 1842.

[11] Here are particularly distinguished successively four Ekkehards and two Notkers (balbulus and labeo). See Ratperti († 900) casus monasterii s. Galli, continued by Ekkehardus iv. († about 1036) later by another, ap. Pertz ii. 59. cf. vita Udalrici, Ep. Augustani († 973), by Gerhard c. 1. (Pertz. vi. 386): (parentes) commendaverunt eum ad s. Galli monasterium, quia ibi nobilium Dei servorum multitudo et religiositas, discendi docendique studium tunc temporis habebatur. Ekkehardi iv. casus s. Galli c. 2. (Pertz ii. 94). On the time of the scholastic Hiso: Anhelabant ad illius doctrinam totius Burgundiae nec non et Galliae ingenia. See Ildefons v. Arx Geschichten des Cantons St. Gallen Bd. 1. (St Gallen 1810) S. 259 ff.

[12] Hroswitha or Helena of Rossow. Respecting her, see Schröckh's Lebensbeschr. ber. Gelehrten i. 3. Carmina; (Primordia coenobii Ganderscheimensis and Gesta Ottonis i., both ap. Pertz vi. 302. Comoediae sacrae vi., etc.) ed. C. Celtes. Norimb. 1501. fol. H. L. Schurzfleisch. Vitemb. 1707, 4. De Hroswitha poetria scripsit et comoediam Abraham inscriptam adjecit Dr G. Freytag. Vratisl. 1839, 8.

[1] Gesenius in Erich's u. Gruber's Encyclopädie Th. 5. S. 58 ff.

mathematics, astronomy, and medicine, were prosecuted.[2] For
this purpose individuals came hither even from the western
church ; though they were so few, and the field of those sciences
so confined, that the influence of them on general culture could
not have been considerable.   Yet the study of mathematics may
have given an impulse to individual minds, as it did to *Gerbert*, [3]
who owed to the Arabs such a knowledge of the science as excited universal astonishment at that time.   He opened up a better prospect for the degenerate condition of schools, by giving a
new impulse to the school at *Rheims ;* from which other schools
too soon received new teachers and a new spirit.[4] Hence the
school in Chartres, under bishop *Fulbert* († 1028),[5] acquired
high renown.   The art of medicine, which had for a long time
been chiefly cultivated in the convents of *Monte Cassino* and
Salerno, was enriched indeed with several important translations
of Arabic works, which *Constantine of Africa,* finally a monk at
Monte Cassino, about 1050, made ; but yet its character was too
superstitious and empirical to promote the general culture of the
age.[6]

Wachler's Gesch. d. Literatur Th. 2, (2te Umarb. 1823) S. 85 ff.   H.
Middeldorpf comm. de institutis literariis in Hispania, quae Arabes
auctores habuerunt, Goettingae 1810, 4.

[2] Jourdain recherches crit. sur. l'âge et l'origine des traductions latines
d'Aristote, Paris 1819 (translated with additions and corrections by Dr
A. Stahr, Halle 1831), nouv. édit. revue et augm. 1843, p. 86, 226.

[3] See above § 22, no. 19 and 27.   Hist. lit. de la France vi. 559.
Hüllmann's Städtewesen des Mittelalters iv. 317.   His mathematical
and astronomical writings have not been printed with the exception of the
geometry in B. Pezii thes. noviss. anecdot. iii. ii. 7.   De corpore et
sanguine Christi (prim. ed. Cellot. in hist. Gotteschalci, p. 541, but
without the author's name, therefore, till Pez discovered it, called Anonymus Cellotianus) and de. rationali et ratione uti, both in B. Pezii
thes. i. ii. 133.   Epistolae ed. Pap. Masson. Paris 1611, 4, more fully
in du Chesne scriptt. Franc. ii. 787 (on their historical connection, see
Wilmann's in den Jahrbüchern d. deutschen Reichs unter Otto iii. S.
141.)   On his league with the devil, see Illgen's Zeitschrift f. hist.
Theol. 1843. ii. 158.   Gerbert als Freund u. Förderer klassischer Studien, Schweidnitzer Schulprogr. für Ostern 1843.   Gerbert od. Papst
Sylvester ii. u. s, Jahrhundert v. Dr E. F. Hock, Wien 1837, 8.

[4] Hüllmann l. c. S. 322 ff.

[5] Opera (epistolas, sermones caet.) ed. Car. de Villiers. Paris, 1608.
8, and in the bibl. PP. Lugd. xviii. 1.

Among the German tribes, those works in the languages of the countries, which among the Franks proceeded from *Notker Labeo*, abbot of St Gallen († 1022),[7] and among the Anglo-Saxons from *Ælfric* (probably archbishop of York, from 1023-1051),[8] were important in tending to diffuse a spirit of general improvement. The intercourse with the Greek Church,[9] which had been renewed from the time of the Ottos, operated powerfully o n scientific, and especially on theological advancement, in additio n to the restoration of ecclesiastical order in the second half of th e 11th century; but, especially, the revival of a scientific study of the law, in the cities of Lombardy ;[10] the patronage of learnin g by the emperor Henry III. ;[11] and the renewed disputes with the

[6] K. Sprengel's Gesch. d. Arzneikunde Th. 2, (dritte Aufl. Halle 1823) S. 490. Jourdain l. c. p. 97. Wachler l. c. S. 54.

[7] Translation of the Psalms (in Schilter thes. antiquitt. teuton. more correctly in Hattemer, St. Gallens altdeutsche Sprachschätze B. 3), Martianus Capella (published by E. G. Graff, Berlin 1837, 8), Boethius (published by Graff, Berlin 1837, 8), the Categories and the work on Aristotle's sentences (published by Graff, Berlin 1837, 4). The following are lost ; the translations of Gregory's Moralia, Cato, single pieces from Virgil, Terence and others. Comp. v. Arx. Gesch. v. St. Gallen i. 276, 269. Raumer's Einwirkung des Christenth. auf die althd. Sprache. S. 38, 72.

[8] Ussher regards this writer as Ælfric who was archbishop of Canterbury 995, 1006. He wrote many works in the Anglo-Saxon tongue (Latin Grammar and Dictionary, translation of Gregory the Great's Dialogues, Homilies, in part his own, in part translated.) An Ælfric society has lately commenced to do something in the way of the Anglo-Saxon language : The homilies of the Anglo-Saxon Church, P. i. Homilies of Ælfric by Benj. Thorpe vol. i. London 1844, 8.

[9] Many Germans at this time were ignorant of Greek ex. gr. Luitprand, Hermannus Contractus. In St. Gallen it was assiduously cultivated, v. Arx Gesch v. St Gallen i. 258, 266, 271 ff. Schlosser's Weltgesch. ii. ii. 256. Concerning the revival of the sciences in the East under the Macedonian emperors, see below § 43.

[10] Savigny's Gesch d. röm. Rechts im Mittelalter iii. 75. Even clergymen applied themselves to it in great numbers, Petri Damiani ep. 15, ad Alex. ii. opp. i. 12 : Ecclesiarum rectores tanto mundanae vertiginis quotidie rotantur impulsu, ut eos a saecularibus barbirasium (the shorn beard) quidem dividat, sed actio non discernat, nec sacrarum meditantur eloquia Scripturarum, sed scita legum et forense litigium. Claustra vacant, Evangelium clauditur, per ora ecclesiastici ordinis forensia jura decurrunt.

[11] Stenzel's Gesch. Deutsch. unter d. fränk. Kaisern i. 132 ff.

Greek Church in the middle of the 11th century. The necessity of reflection led men back to a more earnest intercourse with translations of Boethius, and explanations of the logical writings of Aristotle.[12] *Lanfranc* (1042, monk in Bec, 1062, abbot in Caen, 1070, archbishop of Canterbury, † 1089),[13] prepared for such a task by previous legal studies, led the way in a new dialectic development of theology, the taste for which he spread far and wide by the monastic school which he founded in Bec. His rival was *Berengarius* (1031, a scholastic at Tours, 1040, archdeacon of Angers, † 1088),[14] and the first trial of the new science was in the dialectic dispute between them concerning the Lord's Supper.

§ 29.

BERENGAR'S CONTROVERSY CONCERNING THE DOCTRINE OF THE LORD'S SUPPER.

The most important authorities for the first part of the controversy are: Lanfranci de Eucharistiae sacramento contra Berengarium lib. (cum Philastrio prim. ed. Jo. Sichardus. Basil. 1528. 8. subsequently often published, among others in bibl. PP. Lugd. xviii. 763), and Berengarii de sacra coena

[12] The doubts which Heeren raised against the usual opinion, that Aristotle's writings were first known in the West by translations from the Arabic (Gesch. d. class. Lit. im Mittelalter, hist. Werke iv. 225), are partly confirmed, partly rectified, by Jourdain's inquiries referred to above (note 2) which furnish this result, that, till the thirteenth century, only the Organon of Aristotle was known in the West by the Latin translation of Boethius (vol. i. div. 2. § 114. not. 10.), or rather, only the introduction of Porphyry, and the first two treatises of the Organon, on the categories, and on the sentences, which alone were translated by Boethius. See Cousin ouvrages inédits d' Abélard. Introduction p. li. All these writings were known to, and used by, individuals even from the ninth century, as, for instance, Rabanus Maurus (Cousin l. c. p. lxxvi.), Gerbert, and an anonymous commentator on the Organon in the tenth century p. lxxx.: but now the acquaintance with them was more general. Notker Labeo translated both these treatises of Aristotle even into the Frankish-German. See note 7.
[13] Hist. lit. de la France viii. 260 ss. Opera (comm. in ep. Pauli; de corpore et sang. Domini epistolae etc.) ed. Luc. d'Archery. Paris. 1648. fol., prefixed to which is his life by his younger contemporary Milo Crispinus.
[14] Hist. lit. de la Fr. viii. 197.

adv. Lanfrancum lib. (MS. in Wolfenbüttel 228. S. in 8.)[1] primum edd.
A. F. et F. Th. Vischer, Berol. 1834. 8. (here cited according to the pages
of the MS. Comp. G. Ephr. Lessing's Berengarius Turon. od. Ankündig.
eines wichtigen Werks desselben, Braunschweig 1770. 4. in dess. sämmtl.
Schriften, Berlin 1825 ff. Th. 12. S. 143 ff. (according to which last edition
it is here cited). C. F. Stäudlin's Osterprogr. v. 1814: Annuntiatur editio
libri Bereng. Tur. adv. Lanfrancum, simul omnino de scriptis ejus agitur.
The same: Berengarius Tur. in Stäudlin's and Tzirschner's Archiv für
Kirchengesch. ii. i. 1.

For the later part of the controversy: acta concilii Rom. sub Gregorio P.
vii. ab ipso Berengario conscripta, prim. ed. Martene et Durand in thesaur.
nov. anecdotorum iv. 99. ap. Mansi xix. 761 (on its authenticity see Stäudlin im Archive l. c. S. 81 ff.)

A survey of all the treatises is given by Bernaldi Constantiensis[2] de Berengarii damnatione multiplici lib. written A. D. 1088 (the more important
part first published by P. F. Chiffletius in scriptorum vett. de fide catholica opusc. v. 1656. ap. Mansi xix. 757, complete by Matth. Rieberer in
in Raccolta Ferrarese di opuscoli scientifici e letterati T. 21. Venezia
1789. p. 37 ss.)

Neander's Kirchengesch. iv. 327. Dr A. Ebrard's Dogma v. heil. Abendmale
u. s. Geschichte, Bd. 1. (Frankf. a. M. 1845) S. 439.

Although Paschasius's sentiments concerning the Lord's Supper had been adopted by many,[3] and others taught at least the
corporeal presence of Christ without entering into a more subtle
development of the subject,[4] yet many still maintained a merely

[1] The conjecture of the late Stäudlin founded on the remarkable corrections (in the Archive Bd. 2. S. 65), that it may have been Berengar's own MS., is somewhat bold. Perhaps there were two editions of
that work, the MS. having been originally taken from the first, and then
improved and corrected after the second. Another MS. of a treatise of
Berengar's, probably the same treatise, was formerly in the library of
the Jesuits at Louvain, see Possevini apparatus sacer i. 211, from which
extracts have been given by Mabillon, Oudini comm. de scriptt. eccl. ii.
632. It is very desirable that this MS. should be found out again and
compared.

[2] In editions designated as anonymous. That Bernaldus was the
author, see in monumenta res Alemannicas illustrantia (ed. Ussermann,
St Blasii 1792) ii. 427.

[3] So by Gezo (abbot in Tortona about 950) lib. de corpore et sang.
Christi (in Muratorii anecdota iii. 237). It was confirmed especially
by miraculous stories, such as are found even in Paschasius's own writings. Comp. the proofs in Syn. Attrebatensi ann. 1025. c. 2. (Mansi
xix. 433).

[4] So Ratherius ep. vi. ad. Patricum (in d' Archery spicileg. i. 376):

spiritual presence.[5]   Thus Berengarius[6] also declared against
Paschasius, and in favour of the alleged John Scotus.[7]   He wrote

istud Dei benedictione vinum verus, et non figurativus efficitur sanguis,
et caro panis.—De caeteris, quaeso, ne solliciteris quandoquidem mysterium esse audis, et hoc fidei : nam si mysterium est, non valet com-
prehendi : si fidei, debet credi, non discuti. Gerbert de corp. et sang.
Christi (in Pezii thes. i. ii. 133. see § 28. not. 3.) regards the schism
between Paschasius and Ratramnus as not a great one, and is fired with
zeal only against the Stercoranists, particularly against Heribaldus and
Rabanus.

[5] Sigebert. Gemblac. de scriptt. eccles. c. 137. (Fabricii bibl. eccles.
p. 109) writes of Heriger, abbot of Laubes († 1007): Congessit etiam
contra Ratbertum multa catholicorum Patrum scripta de corpore et
sanguine Domini. Aelfric (see § 28. not. 8.) expresses decidedly the
Augustinian-ratramnian doctrine, that Christ's body is partaken of, not
corporeally, but spiritually (na lichamlice ac gastlice).   This opinion is
maintained in an Easter Homily, which has been preserved in the Anglo-
Saxon tongue, and is often opposed to the Catholics, as a testimony for
the faith of the Anglo-Saxon Church (prim. ed. Matth. Parker, London,
1567. 12. and also in Bedae hist. eccl. cum Alfredi Regis paraphrasi
Saxon. ed. A. Whelok. Cantabrig. 1644. fol. p. 462.   Comp. the Creed
of the Anglo-Saxon Church by H. Soames.   Oxf. 1835. 8).   Whether
the error of Leutherich, archbishop of Sens, censured by Robert, king
of France (Helgaldus in vita Roberti ap. Bouquet x. 100. Baronius
ann. 1004 no. 3), related to the use of the Eucharist as an ordeal, or to
the formula of administration : si dignus es, accipe, is obscure.   Praesul bene correctus, a Rege pio et bono sapienter instructus, quievit,
obmutuit, et siluit a dogmate perverso, quod erat contrarium omni bono,
et jam crescebat in saeculo.   But in a vita Johannis XVII. (Mansi xix.
279) it is said : Hujus tempore Leuthericus Senon. Archiep. haeresis
Berengarianae primordia et semina sparsit.

[6] Even Fulbert (see § 28. not. 5), Berengar's teacher, says : epist. 1.
(bibl. PP. Lugd. xviii. 5) : corporis et sanguinis sui pignus salutare
nobis reliquit, non inanis mysterii symbolum.   Ep. 2. p. 6 : panis ab
Episcopo consecratus—in unum et idem corpus Christi transfunditur.
Sed quodammodo aliud esse dicitur, quod virginali utero sumta carne
crucis injuriam sustinuit,—cujus memoriam in pane Presbyteris collato
Episcopus agere videtur : aliud, quod per mysterium agitur.   He cannot, however, have expressed himself decidedly against the transforma-
tion-doctrine, since Adelmann, in his letters, refers Berengar to their
common teacher.

[7] The first traces are afforded by the two works written to refute
him : Adelmanni de veritate corp. et sang. Dom. ad Bereng. epist. (of
which many though faulty editions, ex. gr. bibl. PP. xviii. 438. far more
complete ex Ms. Guelpherb. ed. C. A. Schmidt. Brunsv. 1770. 8.)
written before 1049 (hist. lit. de la Fr. vii. 542) ; and the notorious (see
§ 27. not. 4) Hugonis Ep. Lingonensis lib. de corp. et sang. Dom.
(prim. ed. d' Archery in opp. Lanfranci append. p. 68 ss. Bibl. PP.

a letter on the subject to Lanfranc,[8] on the strength of which
he was condemned without a hearing at *Rome*,[9] 1050 ; and the

Lugdun. xviii. 417), likewise written before 1049 (hist. lit. de la Fr. vii.
438). The first was answered by Berengar, as appears, after some time,
in his purgatoria epist. contra Adelmann. (Fragm. in Martene et
Durand thes. nov. anecdot. iv. 109 ss. and ap. Schmidt l. c. p. 34 ss.)

[8] Bereng. epist. ad Lanfr. (prim ed. d' Archery in opp. Lanfr. p. 22.
ap. Mansi xix. 768) : Pervenit ad me, frater Lanfranc, quiddam auditum ab Ingelranno Carnotensi, in quo dissimulare non debui ammonere
dilectionem tuam. Id autem est, displicere tibi, immo haereticas habuisse sententias Joannis Scoti de Sacramento altaris, in quibus dis-
sentit a suscepto tuo Paschasio. Hac ergo in re si ita est, frater,
indignum fecisti ingenio, quod tibi Deus non aspernabile contulit, prae-
properam ferendo sententiam. Nondum enim adeo sategisti in Scriptura divina cum tuis diligentioribus. Et nunc ergo, frater quantumlibet
rudis in illa Scriptura vellem tantum audire de eo, si opportunum mihi
fieret, adhibitis quibus velles, vel judicibus congruis, vel auditoribus.
Quod quamdiu non fit, non aspernanter aspicias quod dico. Si haereticum habes Joannem, cujus sententias de Eucharistia probamus : habendus tibi est haereticus Ambrosius, Hieronymus, Augustinus, ut de
caeteris taceam.—Guitmundus de corp. et sang. Chr. (comp. below, not.
15.) relates at the commencement : Postquam a dom. Lanfranco in
dialectica de re satis parva turpiter est confusus, cumque per ipsum d:
Lanfrancum virum aeque doctissimum liberales artes Deus recalescere
atque optime reviviscere fecisset : desertum se iste a discipulis dolens,
ad eructanda impudenter divinarum Scripturarum Sacramenta—sese
convertit.

[9] Lanfranc. de Euchar. cap. 4 : Tempore s. Leonis P. delata est
haeresis tua ad apostolicam sedem. Qui cum synodo praesideret,—
jussum est in omnium audientia recitari, quas mihi de corpore et sanguine Domini literas transmisisti. Portitor quippe earum legatus tuus,
me in Normannia non reperto, tradidit eas quibusdam clericis. Quas
cum legissent, et contra usitatissimam Ecclesiae fidem scriptas animad-
vertissent : zelo Dei accensi, quibusdam ad legendum eas porrexerunt.
plurimis earum sententias verbis exposuerunt. Itaque factum est, ut
non deterior de te quam de me fuerit orta suspicio, ad quem videlicet
tales literas destinaveris.—promulgata est in te damnationis sententia.
Posthaec praecepit Papa, ut ego surgerem, pravi rumoris a me maculam
abstergerem, fidem meam exponerem, exposita plus sacris auctoritatibus quam argumentis probarem. Itaque surrexi, quod sensi dixi, quod
dixi probavi, quod probavi omnibus placuit, nulli displicuit. On the
other hand, Berengarius de sacra coena Ms. p. 11 : Saepius me de falsitate tua scriptum tuum compellit ut loquar; qua enim fronte scribere
potuisti, suspicionem contra te de meo ad te scripto potuisse oriri ?—
nec sani ergo capitis fuit, aliquid contra te suspicari de scripto illo, in
quo ego reprehenderam, quod omnes, ut scribis te fecisse, approbabant.
—Quod promulgatam dicis in me damnationis sententiam, sacrilegae

council of *Vercelli,* immediately after, repeated the same sentence.[10]

sancto illi tuo Leoni notam praecipitationis affigis : injustum enim esse praescribunt tam humana jura, quam divina, inauditum aliquem condemnari.   Maxime cum me Leo ille accersisset : donec certum fieret, utrum praesentiam ejus adire suffugerem, suspendenda fuit sententia, ut revera cognosceret, quod falsissimum habet scriptum tuum, quaenam ego communi fidei adversa sentirem,—ut per me verbis audiretur aut scriptis, quae ego in Joh. Scoto approbarem, quae in Pascasio Corbejensi monacho condemnarem.—Milo Crispinus in vit. Lanfranci c. 3. says that he journeyed to Rome causa cujusdam clerici nomine Berengarii, qui de Sacramento altaris aliter dogmatizabat, quam Ecclesia tenet. The hist. lit. de la Fr. viii. 263. attempts to account for the journey in a different way.   See, however, on the other side, Lessing xii. 230.

[10] Lanfranc continues: Dehinc declarata est synodus Vercellensis. quae tunc proximo Septembri eodem praesidente Pontifice est celebrata Vercellis, ad quam vocatus non venisti.   Ego vero praecepto ac praecibus praefati Pontificis usque ad ipsam synodum secum remansi.   In qua in audientia omnium—Joannis Scoti liber de Eucharistia lectus est ac damnatus, sententia tua exposita ac damnata: fides s. Ecclesiae, quam ego teneo ac tenendam adstruo, audita, et concordi omnium assensu confirmata.   Duo clerici, qui legatos tuos se esse dixerunt, volentes te defendere, in primo statim aditu defecerunt et capti sunt.   On the other side, Berengarius p. 16 : Pervenerat ad me, praecepisse Leonem illum, ut ego Vercellensi illi conventui, in quo tamen nullam Papae debebam obedientiam, non deessem.   Dissuaserant secundum ecclesiastica jura, secundum quae nullus extra provinciam ad judicium ire cogendus est, personae ecclesiasticae, dissuaserant amici : ego ob reverentiam pontificatus multo Romam ita labore susceperam, et ut irem securius, ad Regem Franciae, Ecclesiae, cujus eram clericus, Abbatem (On this relation which Lessing misunderstands, p. 261, see Thomassinus P. i. lib. iii. c. 64. § 4), accesseram, nihil a regia dignitate, nihil ab Abbatis paternitate sinistrum exspectabam, cum me carcerandum ac rebus omnibus exspoliandum cuidam dedit.   Hoc Leo ille Vercellis audivit, non apostolica dignitate, non paterna miseratione, non humana motus est compassione,—haereticum me potius voce sacrilega—in conventu illo Vercellensi pronunciavit—p. 18 : Quod sententiam meam scribis Vercellis in consessu illo expositam, dico de rei veritate et testimonio conscientiae meae, nullum eo tempore sententiam meam exposuisse, quod nec mihi eo tempore tanta perspicuitate constabat, quod nondum tanta pro veritate eo tempore perpessus, nondum tam diligenti in Scripturis consideratione sategeram.   Duos clericos meos Vercellis affuisse scripsisti.—clerici illi mei revera non fuerunt, me defendere minime susceperunt. Alter Concanonicus mihi erat in ecclesia b. Martini,—hunc clerus ille b. Martini, cum me—Rex—carcerandum dedisset cuidam adolescentulo,—consilio communi ad Leonem illum misit Vercellis, si forte, infortunio meo compatiens, christiano rigore aliquid pro me adoriretur. Huic, cum esset in conventu illo Vercellensi, et quidam interrogatus a Papa responderet ad interrogata, quod respondendum putavit, visum

illi est, sicut mihi ipse narravit, dare illum sententiam, quod essem haereticus : quo viso perturbatissimus, ad quem nesciebat, inclamavit, quantum potuit : " per Deum omnipotentem mentiris :" Alter compatriota
tuus nomine Stephanus, ei, quem ab Ecclesia b. Martini missum dico
non ignotus, cum vidisset libellum Joh. Scoti ex nutu et libito tuo conscindi, nobili permotus zelo non tacuit, similiter posse conscindi librum
aliquem praeproperantur b. Augustini, non adhibita mora et lima,
utrum conscindendus esset, sufficientis considerationis. Ita factum
est, ut juberet Leo ille, utrumque teneri, non tamen, ut ipse postea ex-
ponebat, ut illis aliquid injuriae fieret aut molestiae, sed ne turba forte
in illos illicitum adoriretur aliquid. Ita indignum eruditione tua scriptum continuit tantam falsitatem tuum : " duo clerici tui te volentes defendere primo aditu defecerunt," etc. When Berengarius on the way
to Vercelli, went to Paris to ask permission for the journey, he took a
circuitous route through Normandy, probably for the purpose of making
friends there. But he found the universal voice against him, particularly in the conference at Brione (Durandi Abb. Troarn. de corp. et
sang. Ch. pars ix). So also at Bec, as appears from the letters of Bereng.
ad Ascelinum mon. Becensem and ap. Ascelini Bereng. (prim. ed.
d'Achery in opp. Lanfr. not. ad vit. Lanfr. p. 24, ap. Mansi xix. 775).
When Berengar writes to Ascil: Per vos igitur transiens disposueram
omnino nihil agere cum quibuscunque de Eucharistia, priusquam satis-
facerem in eo Episcopis, ad quos contendebam ; this passage so often
misunderstood refers (Stäudlin im Arch. S. 43) to the council of Vercelli. In the meantime Henry I. had summoned a council at Paris to
try Berengarius there, but Deoduinus (not Durandus) bishop of Lüttich
made objections, (Comp. his epist. ad Regem (first ed. complete in the
bibl. PP. Lugd. xviii. 531. Galandii bibl. PP. xiv. 244) : Fama supre-
mos Galliae fines praetergressa totam Germaniam pervasit, jamque omnium nostrum replevit aures, qualiter Bruno Andegavensis Episcopus,
item Berengarius Turon. antiquas haereses modernis temporibus intro-
ducendo, adstruant, corpus Domini non tam corpus esse, quam umbram
et figuram corporis Domini ; legitima conjugia destruant, et quantum in
ipsis est, baptismum parvulorum evertant. Quos ad revincendum ac
publice confutandum—ajunt, vos Concilium advocasse.—Sed despera-
mus id fieri, posse, cum Bruno existat Episcopus, Episcopum autem
non oportet damnationis subire sententiam praeter apostolicam auctoritatem. And at the conclusion : Quamobrem Brunonem et Berengarium
jam anathematizatos arbitramur. Quod si ita est, vere illis audientia
Concilii deneganda est, et cum vestris, cumque nostris Episcopis (si
vobis ita videtur) cum amico vestro Imperatore, cum ipso Papa, quae
vindicta in illos statuatur, deliberandum. By these arguments Henry
seems to have been induced to give up the council, and adopt the other
course described by Berengarius himself. For that Durand's (l. c.) account of a council actually held at Paris is wholly false, is proved incon-
trovertibly by Lessing p. 264 ff., though Stäudlin in the Archiv. p. 34
ff. opposes him. On the other hand, Durand's evidence in favour of Berengar's journey into Normandy is satisfactory authority, since he was
himself an inhabitant of that country. Lessing's doubts on this head,
(p. 276) are satisfactorily removed by the order of events given above.

2 c

By this means public opinion was turned against him, though he
still had many friends.[11]   He succeeded, however, in convincing
Hildebrand, the papal legate at *Tours* (1054) of his orthodoxy ;[12]
and relying on his powerful aid, he ventured to appear at the
synod of Rome (1059).   Here Humbert's rough violence forced

The letter of Deoduinus, Lessing had no right to question (p. 275) as
it is mentioned as early as by Guitmundus de verit. Euchar. lib. i.
init.

[11] Cf. Berengarii epist. ad Richardum (prim. ed. d'Achery in spicil.
iii. 400, ap. Mansi xix. 784), and the fragment in Mabillon. act. SS.
ord. Bened. saec. vi. P. ii. praef. n. 22, in which he prays interceding-
ly with the king, si forte—aliqua munificentia compensaret damnum,
quod in clerico Ecclesiae suae injustissime, ac regia majestate indignis-
sime tantum intulit.   Further, the very friendly epist. Frollanti Ep.
Silvanectensis ad Bereng. (prim. ed. d'Achery l. c. p. 399, ap. Oudinus
de scriptt. eccl. ii. 629), concluding: Illud volo Fraternitas tua noverit,
quod multum firmiter acquisivi tibi gratiam domini mei Regis.   Other
friends of Berengar's were Bruno, bishop of Angers (cf. Deoduinus not.
10), and Paulinus.   See below, note 20.

[12] Lanfranc. l. c.: Quae sententia (Leonis ix.) non effugit successorem quoque suum felicis memoriae P. Victorem.   Denique in concilio
Turonensi, cui ipsius interfuere ac praefuere legati, data est tibi optio
defendendi partem tuam.   Quam cum defendendam suscipere non auderes, confessus coram omnibus communem Ecclesiae fidem, jurasti te
ab illa hora ita crediturum, sicut in Romano concilio (see below, note
13), te jurasse est superius comprehensum.   On the other hand, Berengarius p. 23: Compellit me, velim nolim, longum facere continua scripti
tui monachatu tuo indignissima falsitas.   Sed quia adhuc superest Hildebrandus, qui de veritate consultus tota dignitate est adhuc respondere
idoneus ; visum est, de concilio Turonensi, quod rei veritas habuit, neque tamen eo nisi paucissimis tempore innotuit, palam facere.   Tempore non Victoris, sed Leonis ab Ecclesia Romana Hildebrandus, vices
in negotiis ecclesiasticis suppleturus apostolicas, Turoni adfuit.   Huic
contra calumniam in me insanorum, in quo adhuc, omisso me, audire
eum potest, qui voluerit, de Propheta, de Apostolo, de Evangelista, de
authenticis etiam scripturis satisfeci Ambrosii, Augustini, Hieronymi,
Gregorii.   Hildebrandus veritatis perspicuitate cognita persuasit, ut ad
Leonem P. intenderem, cujus auctoritas superborum invidiam atque
ineptorum tumultum compesceret.   The books were to be given to the
bishops, quos undecunque Hildebrandus ipse multos fecerat comportari,
in the meantime, however, they had expressed themselves satisfied with
Berengarius's confession, given orally and in writing : " Panis atque
vinum altaris post consecrationem sunt corpus Christi et sanguis," haec
me, sicut ore proferrem, juramento confirmavi corde tenere.   Ita Hildebrandus—tumultu compescito, alia—est prosecutus negotia.   During
this time nunciatum illi est, P. Leonem rebus decessisse humanis, quo
audito a proposito eundi Romam itinere supersedi.

him to subscribe a creed truly Capernaitic.[13] Berengarius re-

[13] Lanfranc. c. 5: Nicolaus P.—concessa tibi—respondendi licentia, cum non auderes pro tuae partis defensione aliquid respondere : pietate motus ad preces tuas praecepit tradi scripturam tibi, quam superius posui. Namely, c. 2 : " Ego Berengarius—anathematizo omnem haeresim, praecipue eam, de qua hactenus infamatus sum etc. Consentio autem s. Rom. Ecclesiae,—scilicet panem et vinum, quae in altari ponuntur, post consecrationem non solum Sacramentum, sed etiam verum corpus et sanguinem Domini nostri J. Chr. esse, et sensualiter non solum Sacramento, sed in veritate manibus sacerdotum tractari, frangi et fidelium dentibus atteri, jurans per s. et homousion Trinitatem," etc. Cum ergo venisses Romam, fretus iis, qui plus impensis a te beneficiis, quam ratione a te audita opem tibi promiserant, non ausus defensare, quod antea senseras, postulasti Nicolaum Pont, ejusque concilium, quatenus fidem, quam teneri oporteret, verbis tibi traderet, scriptura firmaret. Injuncta est hujus rei cura Humberto Episcopo. Itaque verba fidei superius comprehensa scripsit,—tu vero acquiescens accepisti, legisti, confessus es, te ita credere, jurejurando confirmasti, tandem manu propria subscripsisti. Cur ergo scriptum hoc magis adscribis Humberto Ep. quam tibi, quam Nicolao Pont., quam ejus concilio, quam denique omnibus Ecclesiis ?—c. 1 : Tu quoque inclinato corpore, sed non humiliato corde ignem accendisti, librosque perversi dogmatis in medio s. Concilii in eum conjecisti : jurans per id, quod rebus omnibus incomparabiliter majus est, fidem a Patribus, qui praesentes erant, traditam inviolabiliter te servaturum, veteremque doctrinam tuam de corp. et sang. Domini ab illa die aliis non praedicaturum. On the other side, Berengarius p. 43 : Ego longe verius te, quid cum Nicolao egerim, novi. Ego Nicolaum P. quanta potui objurgatione adortus, cur me quasi feris objecisset, immansuetis animis, qui nec audire poterant spiritualem de Christi corpore' refectionem, et ad vocem spiritualitatis aures potius obturabant ; minime ad hoc adducere potui, ut me ipse mansuetudine christiana paternaque diligentia audiret, aut, si id minus liceret, minusve liberet, idoneos ad negotium, qui scripturas ex mora et lima intenderent, eligeret. Solum mihi, ut in Hildebrandum ista conjicerem, Papa respondit. Ita nec mihi respondendi licentiam fecit, nec quia non auderem defendere partes meas—, sed quia comminatione mortis, et forensibus etiam litibus indignissima, mecum agebatur tumultuaria perturbatione, usquequaque obmutui, nec ullas, quod mentitur scriptum tuum, ad Papam ego preces feci. Tantum cum obmutuissem, ne mecum christianismo suo indignum agerent, corde convolvens humi procubui.—in eoque meam tecum infelicitatem confiteor maximam, quia instantis timore mortis atque insanorum perturbatione dejectus a protestatione veritatis et defensione mea obmutui, non quod a percepta unquam veritate desciverim ; quamquam nobilem quendam, mihique in immensum superiorem de quodam forsitan non dissimili, cui interfuisset, concilio dixisse non nesciam : " compressus indoctorum grege conticui, veritus, ne merito haberer insanus, si sapiens inter insanos videri contenderem."—p. 1.: manu, quod mendaciter ad te pervenit, non subscripsi, nam et de

nounced it with great bitterness as soon as he had regained his
liberty,[14] and became involved in an animated correspondence ;[15]
in which, during the progress of the controversy,[16] he had an

consensu pronunciarem meo, nullus exegit, tantum timore praesentis
jam mortis scriptum illud, absque ulla conscientia mea jam factum, manibus accepi.   p. 35 : ab asserenda veritate instantis mortis timore conticui, prophetica, evangelica et apostolica scripta in ignes ad vulgi jussionem conjeci.   p. 4 : Solus Humbertus ille, inconvento et inaudito me,
sine mora et lima diligentioris secundum scripturas considerationis, quod
voluit, scripsit, nimiaque levitate Nicolaus ille, de cujus ineruditione et
morum indignitate facile mihi erat non insufficienter scribere—, quod
dixerat Humbertus, approbavit.   p. 5 : Expertus in Humberto ego sum
non dei servum, sed Antichristi membrum.   p. 7 : Quod de humilitate
vitae et doctrinae Humberti confirmas, utinam non ex calumnia erga me
tua, sed ex veritate firmaveris : quantum ad experientiam hominis dico
meam, in negotio isto de mensa dominica, quoquo modo vixerit non
humiliter, sed superbissime docuit, quia ad praeferendum se mihi contra
ipsam veritatem, corruptibile adhuc esse Christi corpus, dicere non ex-
horruit.   Si humilitas in illo christiana fuisset, non me inauditum quasi
haereticum condemnasset ; potius—revera me audiens, si veritatis inve-
nisset inimicum,—mecum sub congruis judicibus, non cum gladiis et
fustibus, sed christiana mansuetudine constitisset.
   [14] Bernaldus de Bereng. damnat. multipl. : Sed Beringerius more
suo ad proprium vomitum redire non timuit, et ultra omnes haereticos
Romanos Pontifices et s. Rom. Ecclesiam verbis et scriptis blasphemare
praesumsit.   Nempe s. Leonem P. non pontificem, sed pompificem et
pulpificem appellavit, s. Rom. Ecclesiam vanitatis concilium et Ecclesiam malignantium, Romanam sedem non apostolicam, sed sedem Satanae dictis et scriptis non timuit appellare.   Unde venerabilis P. Alexander—literis eum satis amice praemonuit, ut a secta sua cessaret, nec
amplius s. Ecclesiam scandalizaret.   Ille autem ab incepto desistere noluit, hocque ipsum eidem Apostolico literis suis remandare non timuit.
   [15] Against Berengar's first writing, ad Lanfrancum et Richardum
(It is said to be in MS. in the Royal Library at Paris, hist. lit. de la Fr.
viii. 223.   Nothing more than the Fragments in Lanfranc's reply have
been published, collected in Stäudlin's Easter progamme of 1814, p. 8
ss.) wrote Lanfrancus de Euch. sacr. (not as the hist. lit. de la Fr. viii.
312 s. 279, would have it for the sake of converting Berengar in 1079,
but between 1063-1069, see Lessing S. 180 ff.)   In reply to this Berengarius de sacra coena adv. Lanfr.—Durandi Abb. Troarnensis lib. de
corp. et sang. Chr. contra Bereng. in ix. PP. (prim. ed. d'Achery in
opp. Lanfr. app. p. 71 ss. ap. Gallandius xiv. 245) was written after 1059,
and before Laufranc's production, and Guitmundi Archiep. Aversani de
corp. et sang. Chr. veritate in Eucharistia libb. iii. (in bibl. PP. Lugd.
xviii. 440) between 1073 and 1077.
   [16] Berengarii first work adv. Lanfr. (ap. Lanfr. c. 10) : Sacrificium
Ecclesiae duobus constat, duobus conficitur, visibili et invisibili, Sacra-

opportunity of developing his opinion more clearly, and also defending it with logical reasons ;[17] since the transformation-doc-

mento et re Sacramenti (i. e. Christi corpore).—Ibid. c. 9 : Per consecrationem altaris fiunt panis et vinum sacramentum religionis, non ut desinant esse, quae erant, sed ut sint, quae erant, et in aliud commutentur, quod dicit b. Ambrosius in libro de Sacramentis. De sacra coena Ms. p. 39 : sunt enim sicut secundum religionem sacramenta, ita secundum aliud alimenta, sustentamenta. p. 64 : fit panis, quod nunquam ante consecrationem fuerat, de pane, scilicet de eo, quod ante fuerat commune quiddam, beatificum corpus Christi, sed non ut ipse panis per corruptionem esse desinat panis, sed non ut corpus Christi esse nunc incipiat per generationem sui, but according to the illustrations of Ambrosius, as man becomes a nova creatura from a vetus creatura, and a filius fidelis from a filius perditionis. p. 65 : panis consecratus in altari amisit vilitatem, amisit inefficaciam, non amisit naturae proprietatem. p. 79 : omne quod sacratur necessario in melius provehitur, minime consumitur per corruptionem subjecti. Epistolae ad Adelmann. fragm. i. : Not the res sacramentorum, but the sacramenta are signa, figurae, similitudines, pignora, as also Augustin. de civ. Dei lib. x. explains sacramentum by sacrum signum : cum constet nihilominus, verum Christi corpus in ipsa mensa proponi, sed spiritualiter interiori homini : verum in ea Christi corpus ab his dumtaxat, qui Christi membra sunt, incorruptum, intaminatum, inattritumque spiritualiter manducari. Hoc Patres publice praeconantur, aliudque esse corpus et sanguinem, aliud corporis et sanguinis sacramenta non tacent ; et utrumque a piis, visibiliter sacramentum, rem sacramenti invisibiliter, accipi : ab impiis autem tantum sacramenta, commendant. Nihilominus tamen sacramentum secundum quendam modum res ipsas esse, quarum sacramenta sunt, universaque ratio et universa auctoritas exigit. Namely, de sacr. coen. Ms. p. 51 : non minus tropica locutione dicitur : panis, qui ponitur in altari, post consecrationem est corpus Christi, et vinum sanguis ; quam dicitur : Christus est leo, Christus est agnus, Christus est summus angularis lapis. On the other hand, Lanfranc's view de Euchar. c. 18 : Credimus terrenas substantias, quae in mensa dominica per sacerdotale ministerium divinitus sanctificantur, ineffabiliter, incomprehensibiliter, mirabiliter, operante superna potentia, converti in essentiam Domini corporis, reservatis ipsarum rerum speciebus, et quibusdam aliis qualitatibus, ne percipientes cruda et cruenta horrerent, et ut credentes fidei praemia ampliora perciperent, ipso tamen dominico corpore existente in caelestibus ad dexteram Patris immortali, inviolato, integro, incontaminato, illaeso ; ut vere dici possit, et ipsum corpus, quod de Virgine sumtum est, nos sumere, et tamen non ipsum ; ipsum quidem, quantum ad essentiam, veraeque naturae proprietatem, atque naturam : non ipsum autem, si spectes panis vinique speciem, caeteraque superius comprehensa.

[17] The distrust of dialectics still felt is shown by the demand of the Conc. Rom. on Lanfranc, ut plus sacris auctoritatibus, quam argumentis probaret (not. 9) Cf. Lanfranc. de Euch. c. 7 : Relictis sacris auctorita-

trine was also more definitely explained by his opponents.[18] He

tibus ad dialecticam confugium facis. Et quidem de mysterio fidei au-
diturus ac responsurus, quae ad rem debeant pertinere, mallem audire
ac respondere sacras auctoritates, quam dialecticas rationes. Verum contra haec quoque nostri erit studii respondere, ne ipsius artis inopia me
putes in hac tibi parte deesse. Fortasse jactantio quibusdam videbitur,
et ostentationi magis quam necessitati deputabitur. Sed testis mihi
Deus est, et conscientia mea, quia in tractatu divinarum Literarum nec
proponere, nec ad proposita respondere cuperem dialecticas quaestiones
vel earum solutiones. Et si quando materia disputandi talis est, ut hujus artis regulis valeat enucleatius explicari, in quantum possum per
aequipollentias propositionum tego artem, ne videar magis arte, quam
veritate, sanctorumque Patrum auctoritate confidere. Quamvis b. Augustinus—hanc disciplinam amplissime laudet, et ad omnia, quae in sacris literis vestigantur, plurimum valere confirmet, etc. On the other
hand, Berengarius Ms. p. 67: He does not neglect the sacras auctoritates where it is necessary: quanquam ratione agere in perceptione veritatis incomparabiliter superius esse, quia in evidenti res eet, sine vecor-
diae caecitate nullus negaverit: In support of this he cites Augustine:
" rationi purgatioris animae, quae ad perspicuam veritatem pervenit,
auctoritas nullo modo humana proponitur." Maximi plane cordis est,
per omnia ad dialecticam confugere, quia confugere ad eam, ad rationem est confugere: quo qui non confugit, cum secundum rationem sit
factus ad imaginem Dei,¦ suum honorem reliquit, nec potest renovari
de die in diem ad imaginem Dei. Examples of their dialectics: In his
first work, Berengar says (ap. Lanfr. c. 5-8), that in the proposition,
panis et vinum altaris solummodo sunt verum Christi corpus et sanguis,
lies also the proposition: panem et vinum superesse, just as the proposition Christus est angularis lapis, supposes of course that Christ is still
Christ. For: non constare poterit affirmatio omnis, parte subruta.
But an affirmation consists of the parts subject and predicate; if the subject be denied, so is the predicate. On this logical rule Lanfranc c. 7,
remarks: that instead of the particularis negativa, the universalis must
be inserted: nulla affirmatio constare poterit parte subruta, otherwise there
would be in the syllogism, duae particulares praecedentes, from which
it would be impossible to draw any regular conclusion. On the other
hand Berengarius Ms. p. 74: si quid secundum negligentiam dixi, non
me multum poenituerit: circa rem. ipsam nec transeunter agis. Another form of the same argument Ms. p. 50: Omne, quod est aliud, est
in eo, quod aliquid est, nec potest res ulla aliquid esse, si desinat ipsum
esse. As if should say: Socrates justus est, nullo modo Socrates justus
erit, si Socrates esse non contigeret.

[18] How loosely this was apprehended at first is proved by epist. Ascelini ad Bereng., where it is first said, panem et vinum vere carnem et
sanguinem potentialiter creari, next: hoc, quod in altari consecratur,
unitur corpori illi, quod ex Maria virgine redemtor assumsit. Berengarius ad Adelm. fragm. iii. thus sets forth the opposition of the two
opinions: Mea vel potius Scripturarum causa ita erat, panem et vinum

had still friends, it is true ;[19] but from the nature of the case they were not so fanatical as the adherents of the marvellous

mensae dominicae non sensualiter, sed intellectualiter ; non per absum-tionem, sed per assumtionem ; non in portiunculam carnis—sed in to-tum converti Christi corpus et sanguinem. That the portiuncula carnis is not a disfigurement (as Stäudlin in Arch. S. 70 ff. says), but that the dogma while in the course of development was frequently apprehended thus coarsely, is taught *inter alia* by the narration of the syn. Attreba-tensis ann. 1025 (Mansi xix. 434), that the host had once presented itself as partem digiti auricularis sanguine cruentatam. Here an ad-vancement is shown by the expositio canonis Missae secundum Petrum Damiani in A. Maji scriptt. vet nova collectio vi. ii. 211, (but which on account of its title cannot be looked on as a work of Peter, but was pro-bably composed soon after his death), where so much stress was laid on his authority, in this controversy, see below note 22. Comp. this expo-sitio § 4, p. 213 : Sicut et vidua Sareptana quotidie comedebat, et non diminuebatur farina de hydria et oleum de lecytho, sic universa Ecclesia quotidie sumit, et nunquam consumit carnem et sanguinem Domini nos-tri J. Chr. Verum an partes in partes, an totum in totum transeat, no-vit ille qui facit : ego quod residuum est, igne comburo : nam credere jubemur, distinguere prohibemur. Sed quia instat quaerentis improbi-tas, salva fide concedemus, quod talis panis in tale corpus commutatur, nec pars in partem. Reor tamen salva fidei majestate, quod ubi panis est consecratus, totus est Christus in tota specie panis, totus sub singu-lis partibus, totus in magno, totus in parvo, totus in integro, totus in fracto sacramento (so I read instead of scio tamen), quod dicitur a qui-busdam : quamdiu species integra est, sub totali specie totale corpus existit; ubi vero dividitur, in singulis divisionibus incipit esse totum : sicut in speculo, dum est integrum, una tantum apparet inspicientis imago ; sed ipso fracto tot apparent imagines, quot sunt fracturae. Here too we meet with the first occurrence of the word transubstantiatio c. 7, p. 215.

[19] Berengarius Ms. p. 27 : Quod nomen Ecclesiae totiens ineptorum multitudini tribuis, facis contra sensa majorum :—quod dicis, omnes tenere hanc fidem,—contra conscientiam tuam dicis, quam latere non potest, usque eo res ista agitata est, quam plurimos aut paene infinitos esse cujuscunque ordinis et dignitatis, qui tuum de sacrificio Ecclesia execrentur errorem, atque Pascasii Corbejensis monachi.

[20] Guitmundi de corp. et sang. Chr. lib. i. : Nam Berengariani omnes quidem in hoc conveniunt, quia panis et vinum essentialiter non mutan-tur, sed ut extorquere a quibusdam potui, multum in hoc differunt, quod alii nihil omnino de corpore et sanguine Domini sacramentis istis inesse, sed tantummodo umbras haec et figuras esse dicunt : alii vero rectis Ec-clesiae rationibus cedentes,—dicunt ibi corpus et sanguinem Domini revera, sed latenter contineri, et ut sumi possint, quodammodo (ut ita dixerim) impanari. Et hanc ipsius Berengarii subtiliorem esse sen-tentiam ajunt. Alii vero, non quidem jam Berengariani, sed acerrime Berengario repugnantes, argumentis tamen ejus, et quibusdam verbis

doctrine.   As is always the case in barbarous times, fanaticism
prevailed in the present instance also.[21]   Even the all-powerful
Gregory VII., who manifestly favoured Berengar, was not able

Domini paulisper offensi—solebant olim putare, quod panis et vinum ex
parte putentur, et ex parte remaneant.   Aliis vero—videbatur panem et
vinum ex toto quidem mutari, sed cum indigni accedunt ad communicandum, carnem Domini et sanguinem iterum in panem et vinum reverti.
This individual independence is also expressed in the letters of his two
friends.   Epist. Paulini primicerii Metensis ad Bereng. (in Martene et
Durand. thes. anecdot. i., 196): quod in scriptis tuis de Eucharistia
accepi, secundum eos, quos posuisti auctores, bene sentis et catholice
sentis.   Sed quod de tanta persona sacrilegum dixisti (see above note
9), non puto approbandum.—Rogamus etiam, ut sobrie in Domino semper sapias, neque profunditatem Scripturarum, quibus non oportet, mar-
garitas scilicet porcis projicias.   Comp. the excellent epist. Eusebii Bru-
nonis Ep. Andegavensis ad Bereng. (prim. ed. Claud. Menardus in
Augustini adv. Julian. libb. ii. posteriores.   Paris 1616, 8, p. 499 ss.):
Fratri et sincerae dilectionis cultu amplectendo consacerdoti Ber. salutem.   Scripsistis, ad vos pervenisse,—Gaufridum—praeconio publico
ineptiae atque insaniae Lanfrancii suffragari, et quibusdam interpositis
obtestati estis, ut vos et ipsum sub judice audiri faciam in libro b. Ambrosii de Sacramentis.   Super quod quid responsi—habeam patienter
aequanimiterque advertite.   Veritatis asserendae, an famae quaerendae
gratia, nescio, Deus [scit], sit haec orta motaque quaestio, quae, postquam Romani orbis maximam paene partem peragravit, ad ultimum nos
cum infami longinquorum ac vicinorum redargutione acerrime pulsavit.
Contra quod—tale responsionis elegi temperamentum : quod a veritatis
tramite nullo erroris diverticulo deviaret, et universalis Ecclesiae sublimioribus, et dignitate et eruditione, personis—scandalum jure incutere
minime deberet.—Relictis turbulentis disputationum rivulis de ipso veritatis fonte—necessarium dicimus haurire.   Quod est : Dominus Jesus
pridie quam pateretur, etc."   Panem post consecrantis in haec verba
sacerdotis sacrationem verum corpus Christi, et vinum eodem modo
verum sanguinem esse credimus et confitemur.   Quod se quis hoc qualiter fieri possit inquirat, non ei secundum naturae ordinem, sed secundum Dei omnipotentiam respondemus ;—si vero aliquis, quid de hac re
Patres Doctoresve nostri senserint,—a nobis requisierit, ad eorum libros
—eum mittimus, ut quid ibi invenerit, diligenter legat,—et quod acco-
modatius evangelicae veritati senserit, cum gratiarum actione et studio
fraternae concordiae sibi eligat.   Porro nos non Patrum scripta con-
temnentes, sed nec illa, ea securitate, qua Evangelium legentes,—eorum
sententiis—in tantae rei disceptatione abstinemus, ne si Patrum sensa
aut aliquo eventu depravata, aut a nobis non bene intellecta, aut non
plene inquisita, inconvenienter protulerimus, etc.

[21] Comp. the tumult at the council of Poitiers 1075, chron. s. Maxentii oder Malleacense (written about 1140) in Ph. Labbei nov. bibl.
Mss. Codicum ii. 212 : Anno aerae Christ. MLXXV. Pictavis fuit con-

to stem the tide. At the synod *of Rome* (1078) he attempted to restore Berengar's orthodoxy by means of a confession of faith couched in general terms;[22] but he was compelled *at a second*

cilium, quod tenuit Giraudus legatus de corp. et sang. Domini, in quo Berengarius—ferme interemtus est.

[22] Berengar. acta conc. Rom. (Mansi xix. 761): Juramentum Bereng. factum Romae in ecclesia Lateran. de Eucharistia temp. Gregorii P. vii.: " Profiteor panem altaris post consecrationem esse verum corpus Christi, quod natum est de Virgine, quod passum est in cruce, quod sedet ad dexteram Patris; et vinum altaris, postquam consecratum est, esse verum sanguinem, qui manavit de latere Christi. Et sicut ore pronuncio, ita me corde habere confirmo, sic me adjuvet Deus et haec sacra." Scriptum istud, cum Romae apud Papam moram facerem, in conventu Episcoporum, quem habuit in festivitate omnium Sanctorum, vociferatione multa omnibus pronunciari fecit, dicens sufficere debere his, quibus lac potus dandus esset, non cibus.—Inclamans populo, me non esse haereticum, ita me de Scripturis, non de corde meo habere; omnibus testificans, in audientia sua Petrum Damiani—non consensisse de sacrificio Ecclesiae dictis Lanfranni,—negligenda esse ea, quae diceret Lanfrannus, potius quam ea, quae diceret Petrus Damiani, Romanae Ecclesiae filius (but even the opposite party appealed to Peter Dam. who died 1072, see note 18). Ita Papa ille, cum quo moras paene per annum feceram, compescitam putare visus est et compositam vecordiam turbae turbatae etc. In the mean time the opposite party was not yet quiet: Cum tamen urgerent Papam illum quam maxime pestilentes et Scripturarum perversores, ut exigeret a me moras adhuc Romae facere usque ad conventum, qui futurus erat apud eum in Quadragesima Episcoporum,—sperantes tunc frequentiorem adfuturam turbam, et aliquid ulterius contra veritatem valiturum tumultum ineptorum etc. Et ita circa quaedam per Papae inconstantiam, quoad sperabat turba, rei exitus habuit. Yet Gregory assured Berengar only a few days before the second council p. 766: Ego plane te de Christi sacrificio secundum Scripturas bene sentire non dubito, tamen quia consuetudinis mihi est, ad b. Mariam de his, quae me movent, recurrere, ante aliquot dies imposui religioso cuidam amico—jejuniis et orationibus operam dare, atque ita a b. Maria obtinere, ut per eum mihi non taceret —quorsum me de negotio, quod in manibus habebam de Christi sacrificio, reciperem, in quo immotus persisterem. Religiosus vir—a b. Maria audivit,—nihil de sacrificio Christi cogitandum, nihil esse tenendum, nisi quod haberent authenticae Scripturae, contra quas Berengarius nihil habebat. Hoc tibi manifestare volui, ut securiorem ad nos fiduciam et alacriorem spem habeas. Ita erraticis consensum meum, ne secundum opinionem eorum quod legeram interpretarer, negavi. This was objected to Gregory particularly by Henry IVth's. party: Benno de vita Hildebrandi lib. i. (in Goldasti apologiae pro Henrico IV. Hanoviae 1611. p. 3): jejunium indixit Cardinalibus, ut Deus ostenderet, quis rectius sentiret de corpore Domini, Romanave Ecclesia an Beren

synod held at Rome (1079) to demand of him a confession of
faith acceptable to the stricter party.[23]   By this means he succeeded at least in procuring quiet for him;[24] for, though Berengar
immediately recalled his forced confession, he was allowed to re-

ganus, since dubius in fide, infideli sest.   Egilberti Archiep. Trevir.
epist. adv. Gregor VII. (Udalrici Babenb. cod. epist. no. 160. in Eccardi
corpus historicum medii aevi ii. 170) :   En verus pontifex et verus sacerdos, qui dubitat, si illud, quod sumitur in dominica mensa, sit verum
corpus et sanguis Christi.

[23] Berengarii acta l. c. p. 762 : Papa, qui in conventu illo in festivitate omnium Sanctorum, scriptum suprapositum multa vociferatione
fidei sufficere debere, omnibus pronunciari fecerat, nihil scripto demi,
nihil a calumniatoribus addi permiserat, usque eo dejectus est importunitate Paduani scurrae, non Episcopi, et Pisani non Episcopi, sed Antichristi ;—ut permitteret calumniatoribus veritatis in posteriori quadra-
gesimali concilio scriptum, a se firmatum in priori festivitate oo. 88.,
Episcoporum consessu, scripto mutari hujusmodi : " Corde credo et ore
confiteor, panem et vinum, quae ponuntur in altari, per mysterium
sacrae orationis et verba nostri Redemptoris substantialiter converti in
veram et propriam et vivificatricem carnem et sanguinem Jesu Christi
Domini nostri, et post consecrationem esse verum Christi corpus, quod
natum est de Virgine, et quod pro salute mundi oblatum in cruce pependit, et quod sedet ad dexteram Patris, et verum sanguinem Christi,
qui de latere ejus effusus est, non tantum per signum et virtutem Sacramenti, sed in proprietate naturae, et veritate substantiae."   Ego charta
correpta—perpendi, ad sanum intellectum utcunque posse reduci et
" substantialiter" et caetera verba, quae in scripto erratici posuissent suo,
respondi, quia ita placeret domino Papae, me "substantialiter" addi-
turum.   Namely substantialiter might also be understood salva sua substantia, therefore : panis sacratus in altari salva substantia est corpus
Christi, i. e. non amittens quod erat, sed assumens quod non erat.—
Quod in scripto suo erratici addiderunt "per mysterium orationis,"
revera contra se scripserunt, quia nihil per mysterium agi poterit, nisi
aliud expositum latens habuerit, et quod expositum in hoc negotio Sacramentum, et quod latet res Sacramenti accipitur.   After he had done,
however, ad interpretationem meam, non ad ipsorum me legere incla-
maverunt, ut etiam hoc juramento firmarem, nec (leg. me) secundum
eorum sensa scriptum, quod tenebam, deinceps interpretaturum.   But
he availed himself of the evasion : me ea, quae ante paucos dies mecum
inde Papa egerat, sola tenere.   See above note 22.

[24] See literae commendatitiae Gregorii VII. datae Beringario (in
d'Achery spicileg. iii. 413)—Omnibus h. Petro fidelibus.—Notum vobis
omnibus facimus, nos anathema fecisse—omnibus, qui injuriam aliquam
facere praesumserint Berengario, Romanae Ecclesiae filio,—vel qui eum
vocabit haereticum ; quem post multas, quas apud nos, quantas voluimus, fecit moras, domum suam remittimus, et cum eo fidelem nostrum
Fulconem nomine.

main quietly in retirement on the island *St Come* near Tours, till his death in the year 1088.[25]

FOURTH CHAPTER.

HISTORY OF MONACHISM.

Jo. Mabillonii annales ordinis s. Benedicti libb. xxxv.-lxii. Ejusdem acta SS. ord. s. Bened. saec. v. et vi.

§ 30.

CORRUPTION OF THE CONVENTS.

The monasteries suffered most in these rude times. The abuse of bestowing them as fiefs on persons not monks, reached its height.[1] From all sides rapacious hands were stretched out

[25] The respect in which the memory of Berengarius was held in Tours (comp. especially his disciple's Hildeberti epitaphium in Bereng. ap. Wilhelm. Malmsb., ap. Baron. ad ann. 1088), also the yearly festival at his grave (Mabillon act. SS. Bened. saec. vi. P. ii. praef. no. 68) gave rise in later times to the assertion that he had at last turned from his error. Mabillon l. c. no. 63 ss. Hist. lit. de la Fr. viii. 213 ss. On the other side Mosheim institutt. hist. eccl. p. 431. not. x. Lessing S. 177 ff. The contemporary Bernaldus in chron. ad ann. 1083 expressly asserts the contrary.—Of Berengar's doctrine we always find only one-sided views, as, Sacramentum non esse revera corpus Christi et sanguinem, sed veri corp. et s. figuram (Trithem. chron. Hirs. i. 194 etc.) Hence also he is considered a heretic by Luther (Bekenntn. v. Abendmal Christi 1528) and all the older Lutherans, but praised by the Calvinists. But after the discovery of many original documents even Mabillon l. c. no. 34 ss. and Martene and Durand (thes. nov. anecd. iv. 99), are of opinion that he only denied transubstantiation, but conceded the praesentia realis ; which might have been more accurately determined after his work was discovered. Lessing p. 152 ff.

[1] Comp. § 7. not. 10. Epist. Episc. e synodo apud Carisiacum missa ad Ludov. Reg. Germ. A. D. 858 (in Caroli Calvi capitul. tit. xxvii. ap. Baluz. ii. 101) cap. 8, that Charles the Bald bestowed many monasteries

towards the possessions of the monasteries; while those who
were abbots became worldly in their strivings after reputation
and power.[2]   Hence all discipline was neglected, disorders and
excesses of all kinds prevailed among monks and nuns.[3]

partim juventute, partim fragilitate, partim aliorum callida suggestione,
etiam et minarum necessitate, quia dicebant petitores, nisi eis illa loca
sacra douaret, ab eo deficerent, on laymen.   Afterwards they were even
bestowed by inheritance without distinction of sex.   Comp. Rudolf's
(King of Upper Burgundy) document of 888 in Mabillon. annal. app.
ad lib. 39. no. 36, where he bestows on his sister Adelaide abbatiam
Romanis in comitatu Waldense, ut haberet post discessum suum potestatem relinquendi cuicumque voluerit heredum suorum.   To another
Adelaide, daughter of Rudolf II., King of Upper Burgundy, Lotharius
King of Italy, 938, gave for dowry among other things three abbies
(Mabill. ann. lib. xliii. no. 95.)   Of the Emperor Conrad II. (from
1024-1039) his biographer Wippo says (scriptt. vi. rer. germ. ed. J.
Pistorius p. 432), Ernestus, Dux Alemanniae, aliquantulum Regi militans, Campidonensem Abbatiam—in beneficium accepit a Rege.   And
p. 437 : Manegoldus Comes, miles Imperatoris, de Augensi Abbatia
magnum beneficium (habebat) ab Imperatore.   The bishops followed
these examples, and Hatto, archbp. of Mainz (from 891-912) is said to
have possessed as many as twelve abbies.
   [2] Comp. § 24.
   [3] Conc. Troslejan. ann. 909. cap. 3. (Mansi xviii. 270): De monasteriorum vero non statu, sed lapsu quid dicere vel agere debeamus, jam
paene ambigimus.   Dum enim, mole criminum exigente,—quaedam a
Paganis succensa vel destructa, quaedam rebus spoliata, et ad nihilum
prope sint redacta, si tamen quorundam videntur superesse vestigia,
nulla in eis regularis formae servantur vestigia.   Sive namque monachorum, seu canonicorum, seu sint sanctimonialium, propriis et sibi
competentibus carent rectoribus, et dum contra omnem Ecclesiae auctoritatem praelatis utuntur extraneis, in eis degentes partim indigentia,
partim malevolentia, maximeque inhabilium sibi praepositorum faciente
inconvenientia, moribus vivunt incompositis : et qui sanctitati religion-
ique caelesti intenti esse debuerant, sui velut propositi immemores, ter-
renis negotiis vacant : quidam etiam, necessitate cogente, monasteriorum
septa derelinquunt, et volentes nolentesque saecularibus juncti saecularia exercent.—Nunc autem in monasteriis Deo dicatis monachorum,
canonicorum et sanctimonialium, Abbates laici cum suis uxoribus, filiis
et filiabus, cum militibus morantur et canibus.—Auditur, quod (monachi) spreta humilitate et abjectione monastica, ornamentis, et his etiam,
quae bonis laicis indecentia et turpia sunt, operam impendant ; et nequaquam contenti communibus rebus, propriis, et lucris turpibus inserviant
etc.   Hence Odo Abb. in collectionibus inveighs against the monks
who had isolated property, ex. gr. lib. ii. c. 34. 36. and against those,
qui ad saeculum relabuntur, lib. iii. c. 17 ss.   Of two nuns he relates
iii. c. 21 : Ad hoc autem egredi permissae sunt, ut de rebus parentum,

§ 31.

REFORMATION OF MONACHISM.

First of all the rules of Benedict were restored in the convent
Cluniacum (Clugny) that had been founded by Duke William of
Aquitania, by the abbot *Berno* A. D. 910.[1] But it was under
the second abbot *Odo* (927–941),[2] who sharpened those rules by

qui forte nuper obierant, aliquid monasterio reportarent. Sed hac occasione saeculum pergustantes oblitae sunt Deum.—Campo, abbot of
Farfa (about 930), and his assistant Hildebrand concubinis, quas prius
habuerant occulte, postmodum palam abuti coeperunt non solum ipsi,
sed et cuncti illorum Monachi hoc scelus non verebantur patrare : sed
nuptialiter unusquisque suam ducebat scortam. Campo himself vii.
filias et iii. filios habuit, quos et quas cunctos dotavit de rebus Monasterii, et alios parentes plurimos (see Hugo de destructione monast. Farfensis written about 1004 in Muratorii antiqu. Ital. med. aevi vi. 279.)
The same thing took place at this time in the monastery of Sens among
six abbots. See Richerii (about 1250) chronicon Senoniense ii. c. 18.
(in d'Achery spicilegium ii. 617) : Monachi—impudicis se actibus, comessationibus, ebrietatibus, ac caeteris mundi delectationibus implicabant,
nec erat qui corrigeret.—Quaesivit sibi quisque domunculam, ubi non
regulariter, sed voluntate propria sibi conversari quiret.—Victu defi-
ciente et vestitu decreverunt more rusticorum agricultores fieri, ut ita
saltim possent inopem defendere vitam.
[1] Bibliotheca Cluniacensis, in qua ss. Patrum Abbatum Cluniac.
vitae, miracula, scripta caet. cura Mart. Marrier et Andr. Quercetani.
Paris. 1614 fol. Planck iii. 697. Raumer's Gesch. d. Hohenstaufen
vi. 399. F. Hurter's Geschichte Papst Innocenz III. Bd. 4. (Hamburg 1842) S. 103. Essai hist. sur l'Abbaye de Cluny par M. P.
Lorain, Paris 1839. 8.—Bernonis vita in Mabillon act. SS. ord. Bened.
saec. v. p. 66 ss. Wilhelm's original document (testamentum) ibid.
p. 78. The conclusion is remarkable : sintque ipsi monachi cum omnibus praedictis rebus sub potestate Bernonis Abbatis: post cujus decessum monachi facultatem habeant alterius Abbatis eligendi, quemcumque
sui ordinis voluerint, secundum placitum Dei et regulam s. Benedicti,
ita ut nullius potestatis contradictione haec electio impediatur ; sitque
hic locus subjectus soli Romanae Ecclesiae, cui per singula quinquen-
nia X. solidi ad luminaria Apostolorum persolvantur.
[2] Odonis vita libb. iii. by his pupil John ap. Mabillon l. c. p. 150 ss.
comp. hist. lit. de la Fr. vi. 229. His ascetic writings (among them
collationum libb. iii. and moralium in Job. libb. xxxv. extracted from
Gregory the Great) in bibl. PP. Lugdun. xvii. 252. comp. Bähr's Gesch.
d. röm. Lit. im karol. Zeitalter S. 538.

additions of his own, that the fame of this convent became general.[3]   He and his successor (Aymardus till 948, Mayolus till 994, *Odilo* till 1048)[4] soon became objects of pious wonderment, and were constantly called to found new convents and to reform old ones.[5]   Thus originated, in the order of the Benedictines, the irst Congregation (Congregatio or Ordo Cluniacensis), a particular association of many convents under a common head, the abbot of Clugny.[6]   From this time lay abbots gradually disappeared in France.

In *Italy* the reformation of monachism was begun somewhat later by *Romualdus,* who founded the hermit order of Camaldulensians at *Camaldoli* (Campus Maldoli, Camaldulum in the Appenines near Arezzo) about 1018 († 1027);[7] and *John Gual-*

---

[3] The ritus et consuetudines Cluniacenses were first written down in the eleventh century, by Bernhard, monk at Clugny (ordo Cluniacensis per Bernardum libb. ii. in vetus disciplina monasterica s. collectio auctorum qui de monastica disciplina tractarunt (opera Marqu. Herrgott). Paris. 1726. 4. p. 133 : then about 1070 by Ulrich, monk in Clugny, for William, abbot of Hirschau (antiquiores consuetudines Cluniacensis monasterii lib. iii. in d'Achery, spicil. i. 641).   Particularly remarkable (ap. Ulrich lib. ii. c. 3.) the unbroken silence in ecclesia, dormitorrio, refectorio, et coquina.   Hence the novice opus habet, ut signa diligenter addiscat, quibus tacens quodammodo loquatur. c. 4. these signa loquendi are described.

[4] Odilonis vita by his pupil Jotsaldus (falsely called Lotsaldus) of which that of Petrus Damiani (in his opp. ed Cajetani ii. 193) is a mere extract.   Both in the act. SS. ad 1 Jan., that of Jotsaldus better in Mabillon act. SS. ord. Bened. saec. vi. i. 597.

[5] In doing which they often met with much opposition from the corrupt monks.   This was the case with Odo in Fleury, 930.   Mabillon ann. lib. xliii. no. 17.   Thus the monks at St Martialis, in Limoges, resisted still in 1063, and were obliged to be brought into order by Petrus Damiani, as papal legate. See Petri Dam. iter gallicum in Maji scriptt. vett. nova coll. vi. ii. 204.   Out of France also several convents assumed gradually the consuetudines Cluniac.   So Farfa near Rome 998.   Mabill. lib. lii. no. 72.

[6] The smaller convents, called cellae and obedientiae, were governed only by coabbates or proabbates. Mabillon lib. l. no. 19.   Clugny was Archimonasterium ; its abbots, Archiabbates.

[7] Romualdi vita by Petrus Damiani in P. Dam. opp. ed. Cajetani ii. 205 (according to the arbitrary alteration of Surius in Mabill. act. SS. ord. Bened. saec. vi. i. 247. comp. Pertz vi. 847).   The rules of the Camaldulensians in L. Holstenii cod. regularum monast. ii. 192. comp. Hurter's Innocentius iii. iv. 128.

bert, from whose hermitage in *Vallombrosa* (*Vallis umbrosa*, also in the Appenines, not far from Florence) († 1093) originated the coenobites of Vallombrosa, about 1038.[8]

In *Germany*, the attempts to bring about a similar reformation proved fruitless for a long time, from the obstinate attachment of the monks[9] to a free mode of life, and from the political

[8] Joan. Gualberti vita in Mabillonii act. SS. saec. vi. ii. 273. Comp. Jo. Lamii deliciae eruditor. ii. 238. 272. iii. 177. 212. &c. Hurter's Innoc. iii. iv. 133.

[9] Comp. Widukind's, monk in Corvey (about 960) characteristic narrative in his rebus gestis Saxon. ii. 37 (ap. Pertz v. 448): Gravis persecutio monachis oritur in diebus iliis [about 940], affirmantibus quibusdam Pontificibus, melius arbitrari, paucos vita claros, quam plures negligentes inesse monasteriis oportere: obliti, nisi fallor, sententiae patrisfamiliae prohibentis servos zizania colligere, sed utraque crescere oportere et zizania et triticum usque ad messem. Quo factum est, ut plures propriae infirmitatis conscii, deposito habitu, et relictis monasteriis, grave onus sacerdotum deviarent. Fuerunt autem quidam, qui summum Pontificem Fridericum (Archiep. Mogunt.) hoc non pure, sed ficte fecisse arbitrati sunt, quatenus venerabilem virum Regique fidelissimum Abbatem Hadumarum quoquomodo posset dehonestaret. Erluin, abbot of Gemblours, who wished to reform the abbey Laubes, in the diocese of Cambray, was nearly killed by the monks, and finally blinded (958), and Fulcuin (from 965 abbot of Laubes) de gestis Abbatum Lobiensium c. 26 (in d' Archery spicileg. ii. 739) seems to throw the blame only on Erluin, for which he was severely reproved by the Anonym. Gemblacensis (about 1100) (ibid p. 761 s). Abbot Godehard, about 1005, wishing to reform the monks in Hersfeld, primitus eis juxta regulare praeceptum duriora et aspera mandata proposuit, et licentiam eis ad preces Metropolitani, aut secum haec celebrandi, aut quo vellent discedendi contribuit. Qui statim unanimiter conspirati simul omnes, paucis tantum senioribus vel puerulis remanentibus, egressi per diversa loca varie sunt dispersi. However, they gradually returned, probably from necessity, vita Godehardi Ep. Hildesheimensis in Mabillon acta SS. ord. Bened. saec. vi. i. 356. and in Leibnitii scriptt. rer Brunsv. i. 486. Poppo, about 1025, at first abbot in Stablo, then in St Maximin at Treves, had to suffer much from the monks in both monasteries, because he attempted to reform them. Those in St Maximin went so far as to put his life in jeopardy. See vita Popponis ap. Mabillon l. c. p. 511: cumque sibi sub eo illicita jam non licere—conspexissent, de ejus morte plura machinantur, et quod palam non poterant, quibusdam praestigiarum suarum insidiis operantur. Ad quod, nefas dictu, sacrosancta Missarum sollemnia violando, suis occupant divinationibus, et quas preces credebant, in immunditia et sanguine manuum suarum execrandis admiscent incantationibus.—tam exsecrabili quam invida eousque perducuntur exagitatione, ut in apponendis beato viro cibis et potibus venenorum suorum uterentur admixtione. Even Theodorich, abbot of St

position of the convents.   At last, however, the examples furnished by France and Italy had their effect here also. *Hanno*, archbishop of Cöln, reformed the monastery of Siegburg (1068), which he had founded, and others besides ; and in this course he was pretty generally followed by the bishops on the left bank of the Rhine.[10]   *William*, abbot of Hirschau, established *the Congregation of Hirschau* (Congreg. Hirsaugiensis 1069) on the model of that of Clugny.   He died in 1091.[11]

To the new developments of monachism belonged the *donati*

Hubert in the Ardenne, had to contend violently against the open resistance of his monks, when he wished to restore order in his monastery, A.D. 1054, till a judicial miracle came to his aid.   See vita Theodorici in Mabillon act. SS. ord. Bened. saec. vi. P. ii. p. 369 ss.   Hence, too, we can explain the fact of there being men at this time, qui vel monachico, vel canonico, vel etiam graeco habitu per regiones et regna discurrunt.   See vita Godehardi no. 26. ap. Mabillon l. c. saec. vi. P. i. p. 363.

[10] Lambertus ad ann. 1075 ap. Pertz vii. 238.   Judgment of Lambert, an old Benedictine, ad ann. 1071 p. 188 : sicut vulgo assiduitate vilescunt omnia et popularium animi novarum rerum avidi magis semper stupent ad incognita, nos quos usu noverant, nihili aestimabant, et hos, quia novum inusitatumque aliquid praeferre videbantur, non homines sed angelos, non carnem sed Spiritum arbitrabantur.   Et haec opinio principum quam privatorum mentibus altius pressiusque insederat.   A quibus ad populum derivatus rumor tantum terroris plerisque in hac regione monasteriis injecit, ut ad ingressum illorum alias 30, alias 40, alias 50 monachi, austerioris vitae metu scandalizati de monasteriis abscederent.   Lambert had been for a long time in the monasteries of Siegburg and Saalfeld, for the purpose of learning the new discipline, and came to the conclusion, nostras quam illorum consuetudines regulae s. Benedicti melius congruere, si tam tenaces propositi, tamque rigidi paternarum nostrarum traditionum aemulatores vellemus existere.

[11] S. Wilhelmi constitutiones Hirsaugienses, in vetus disciplina monastica (ed. M. Herrgott), Paris. 1726. 4. p. 375 ss.   Respecting him see Bernoldi chron. ad ann. 1091 ap. Pertz vii. 451.   Jo. Trithemii († 1516) annales Hirsaugienses i. 225 : Hic est Wilhelmus Abbas,—qui Ordinem D. P. nostri Benedicti suo tempore paene collapsum in Germania, et deformatum insolentia monachorum, instaurare et reformare studuit, et plus quam C Monasteria tam per se quam suos, ad pristinam regularis disciplinae observantiam revocavit etc.   He adopted much from Clugny (see note 3).   A thank-worthy regulation was (ann. Hirsaug. i. 227) : xii. e monachis suis scriptores optimos instituit, quibus ut divinae auctoritatis libros, et ss. Patrum tractatus rescriberent, demandavit.   Erant praeter hos et alii scriptores sine certo numero, qui pari diligentia scribendis voluminibus operam impendebant.   Et his omnibus praeerat monachus unus in omni genere scientiarum doctissi-

or *oblati*, who yielded up themselves, and what belonged to them, to the service of a monastery ;[12] the *fratres conversi*, lay brethren, who had under their care the household department, and lived in part on the possessions of the monasteries, but apart from one another ;[13] and the *fratres conscripti, confratres*, to whom was allowed a share in the spiritual blessing of the brotherhood.[14]

mus, qui unicuique rescribendum opus aliquod bonum injungeret, mendaque negligentius scribentium emendaret.

[12] The first instance appears at Clugny, 948, Mabillon ann. lib. xlv. no. 4.   Later in Germany, Bernoldi chron. ad ann. 1091 ap. Pertz vii. 452 : His temporibus in regno Teutonicorum communis vita multis in locis floruit, non solum in clericis et monachis,—verum etiam in laicis. Nempe ipsi abrenunciantes saeculo, se et sua ad congregationes tam clericorum quam monachorum regulariter viventium devotissime contu-·lerunt, ut sub eorum obedientia communiter vivere et eis servire mererentur. So especially in the congregation of Hirschau (chron. Hirsaug. i. 229) see Dufresne glossar. s. v. oblati.

[13] Gualbert first permitted them (see not. 8), comp. his vita c. 21 : Deus—misit ad eum etiam laicos viros timoratos, qui legem Domini per omnia custodire cupientes, in bonis moribus fere nihil a monachis distabant, extra vestium qualitatem et silentium, quod in exterioribus occupati nequibant plenius observare.   Tales igitur tam probatos adversos Pater ad mercatum et omnia exteriora secure mittebat.   William immediately followed the example in the Hirschau congregation (chron. Hirsaug. i. 228).   Here they are called fratres barbati (the monks were not allowed to wear a beard), qui laboribus manuum insistentes, temporalium curam secundum praecepta seniorum agerent, et monachis contemplationi deditis hujus vitae necessaria providerent.   Among them were carpenters, smiths, stone-cutters, masons, tailors, shoemakers, &c. Other orders, too, soon followed this example, Mabillon acta SS. saec. vi. P. ii. praef. no. 89 s.   Alteserrae asceticῶν lib. iii. c. 5.

[14] Thus King Conrad I. 913, became a frater conscriptus in St Gallen (Ekkehardi iv. casus s. Galli ap. Pertz ii. 85), Henry II. in Clugny (fraternitate monachorum humiliter petita et accepta, vita Meinwerci c. 30 in Leibnitii scriptt. rer. Brunsv. i. 527), he and his successors in the monastery Fructuaria (Fructuariense coenobium—nos nostrosque in perpetuum successores, prout divae memoriae praedecessorem nostrum, Henricum, suo ac fratrum contubernio sociavit, diploma Conradi II. in Mabillonii act. SS. saec vi. i. 349).   Even the empress Gisela, spouse of Conrad II., monasterium s. Galli ingressa, xeniis benignissime datis, fraternitatem ibi est adepta, Hepidannus ad ann. 1033 in Goldasti scriptt. rer. Alem. i. i.   Comp. also the liber fraternitatum monasterii Sangallensis ap. Goldast l. c. ii. ii. 144.

2 D

§ 32.

EXEMPTIONS OF THE CONVENTS.

L. Thomassini vetus et nova eccl. discipl. P. i. lib. iii. c. 36 ss.   Planck iiі.
724.

The privileges granted to the convents by kings, popes, and
bishops, during this period, went no farther than merely to secure
them in the observance of the rules of their order,[1] and were not
meant to abridge the rights of the episcopal order.[2]   Hence

[1] Comp. the privilege given by Pope John XV. to the convents of
Corvey and Herford, 989, in Schaten annalium Paderborn. i. 335.
Mansi xix. 83 : Habeant praefata monasteria rerum suarum liberam in
omnibus disponendi regulariter potestatem :—confirmamus, ut nullus
Episcopus Patherbrunnensis aliquam ex eis vel accipiat vel exposcat
portionem ; neque vel in his, qui regiminis locum tenent, vel in ipsis
congregationibus, aut in ipsis coenobiis potestatem obtineat.   Nam
ipsius praefati monasterii Abbati suisque successoribus licentiam damus,
juxta altare sedendi populoque infra suum monasterium vel cellas secundum Deum praedicandi ac docendi ; ita ut nullus Episcopus per se
ad ipsa monasteria vel cellas eorundem—potestatem habeat accedendi,
nisi forte necessitatis causa vel dilectionis gratia vocatus advenerit,
ne importunitate sui ministorumque suorum inquietudine sacris locis fiat
molestia.   Ordinationes, quae necessariae fuerint ipsis monasteriis, agere
non differat ; altaris quoque et basilicarum benedictiones sive consecrationes libenter concedat ; chrisma quoque oleumque consecratum per
singulos annos praebere non differat, et pro his omnibus nullum munus
exigat.   Abbatem vero et Abbatissam in his locis semper eligendi habeant potestatem [monasteria] :—qui ordinati fuerint ad regimen sae-
pedictorum monasteriorum, nulla potestate praevalente dejiciantur, nisi
criminis causa fuerint deprehensi.   Infamiae vero maculis, sive criminis
alicujus denotatione si fuerint appetiti, non praeter canonicam aut regu-
larem deponantur examinationem.   Nos igitur nostram subscriptionem
annuli nostri impressione signantes, obsecramus Coëpiscopos nostros
omnes, in quorum manus ista devenerint, ut sua etiam auctoritate et
subscriptione haec confirmare velint, ut quicunque haec temerare prae-
sumpserit, generalitatis nostrae sententiis ita anathematis vinculo obli-
getur, ut neminem habeat, de cujus favore blandiatur, aut se tueri putet
a sententia damnationis.   On the alleged exemption-privileges of Fulda,
see Rettberg's Kirchengesch. Deutschl. i. 613.
[2] Therefore the superintendence of the morals, and the visitation of
the convents, was still made the duty of bishops by the concil. Tullense
apud Saponarias ann. 859 can. 9. (Mansi xv. 539), Rotomag. ann. 878

bishops still required canonical obedience[3] from abbots, and did not allow unusual privileges to the pope.[4] When the monastery of *Clugny*, which had been assigned to the care of the pope in particular by a Romish privilege attached to the original trust-deed at its foundation,[5] was about to be made completely independent of its bishop, the synod of *Anse* (1025) strongly opposed the first attempt to make it so.[6] A second was more fortunate.

can. 10. (in Harduin. act. conc. vi. i. 206), Augustanum ann. 952 can. 6. (Mansi xviii. 438).

[3] Thus the bishops of Orleans, Arnulf and Fulco, had a controversy with the abbots of Fleury, Abbo and Gauzlinus (between 970 and 1020), because the latter refused to promise this obedience. On this point Fulbertus, Episc. Carnotensis, ep. 41, ad Fulconem: Sacramenta et caetera, quae ad mundanam legem pertinent, propter amorem Regis domini missa faciatis, ut religionem potius quam saecularem ambitionem vos sectari cognoscat. At si Abbas in tantam superbiam intumuerit, ut ipsam quoque subjectionem canonicam vobis derogare contendat; superbiae, cui non parcit Deus, Dei servus quomodo parcat nescio. When after this Fulco excommunicated Gauzlinus, Fulbertus, ep. 73, wrote to the latter: Unde nunc, frater, commoneo, ut—Episcopo vestro subjiciamini sicut decet.—Ego enim neque legem, neque modum ratiocinationis invenire possum, quae vos ab jugo subjectionis hujus absolvat. Cf. Mabillon act. SS. ord. Bened. saec. vi. P. i. praef. § iii.

[4] Hermanni Contracti chron. ann. 1032: Bern Augiae Abbas missis Romam coenobii sui privilegiis, a Papa Joanne item privilegium cum sandaliis, ut episcopalibus idumentis missas ageret, accepit. Unde permoto Warmanno Constantiense Episcopo apud Imperatorem quasi sui pervasor officii et honoris accusatus eo usque ad utrisque coartatur, donec idem cum sandaliis privilegium ipsi Episcopo traderet, publice in synodo sua, i. e. in Coena Domini sequentis anni incendendum.

[5] Comp. §. 31, not. 1.

[6] Conc. Ansanum ann. 1025 (Mansi xix. 423): Gauslenus, bishop of Macon, complains of Burchard, archbishop of Vienne, qui sine licentia et assensu suo contra canonum instituta ordinationes de monachis fecerat in Episcopatu suo, scil. in Cluniacensi coenobio. Abbot Odilo desires to justify him, ostendit privilegium, quod habebant a Romana Ecclesia, quod eis talem libertatem tribuebat, ut nulli, in cujus territorio degebant, nec alicui aliquatenus subjacerent Episcopo: sed quemcumque vellent, vel de qualibet regione, adducerent, qui faceret ordinationes vel consecrationes in eorum monasterio. But the fathers relegentos s. Chalcedonensis, et plurimorum authenticorum, conciliorum sententias (comp. Vol. i. Div. 2, § 120, not. 2 and 4), quibus praecipitur, qualiter per unamquamque regionem Abbates et Monachi proprio subesse debeant Episcopo, et ne Episcopus in parochia alterius audeat ordinationes vel consecrationes absque licentia ipsius Episcopi facere: decreverunt, chartam non esse ratam, quae canonicis non solum non

Alexander II. pronounced (1063) the complete exemption of
Clugny from its bishop,[7] a privilege which was also granted to
many other convents, especially to those associated with that of
Clugny.

FIFTH CHAPTER.

HISTORY OF PUBLIC WORSHIP.

Martyrologies: Adonis martyrologium about 858 (see above pref. to § 18).
Usuardi (monk of St Germain about 876) martyrol. (Vgl. Bähr's Gesch-
d. röm. Lit. im karol. Zeitalter S. 501) castigatius ed J. B. Sollerius.
Antverp. 1714. fol. Notkeri balbuli, monk in St Gallen († 912 respecting
him s. Ildef. v. Arx Gesch. v. St Gallen i. 90. Bähr S. 531), martyrologium (written 893) published in Canisii lectt. ant. ed. Basnage ii. iii. 89
and in. Gallandii bibl. PP. xiii. 753.

§. 33.

The worship of saints at this period completely swallowed up
the worship of God, assuming the character to be expected from

concordaret, sed etiam contrairet sententiis. Thus the archbishop was
ratione convictus, petens veniam a Gausleno Episcopo etc.
   [7] While a new dispute between the bishop of Macon and the abbot
of Clugny was decided at the synod of Chalons (A. D. 1063), by the
papal legate, Petrus Damiani, in favour of the latter (Mansi xix. 1025),
Alexander P. ii. ep. ad Hugonem Abb. Cluniac. (l. c. p. 973), declared
himself to this effect : Sub divini judicii promulgatione, et confirmatione,
et anathematis interdictione corroborantes decrevimus, ut nullus Episcopus, seu quilibet sacerdotum in eodem veniat coenobio, pro aliqua
ordinatione, sive consecratione Ecclesiae, Presbyterorum, vel Diaconorum, Missarum celebratione, nisi ab Abbate ejusdem loci invitatus fuerit, venire ad agendum praesumat. Sed liceat monachis ipsius loci,
cujuscunque voluerint ordinationis gradum suscipere, ubicunque tibi
tuisque successoribus placuerit. Interdicimus autem sub simili anathematis promulgatione, ut idem locus sub nullius cujuscunque Episcopi
vel sacerdotis deprimatur interdictionis titulo, seu excommunicationis
vel anathematis vinculo (the date wanting here is supplied by Mabillon
ann. Ben. lib. lxii. no. 12 : Data in s. Lateranensi palatio VI. idus Maji

a rude, immoral, superstitious age.[1]   Great numbers of old saints
were discovered,[2] and new ones made.[3]   The world[4] was full of

—anno MLXIII. indictione i).   Cf. de gallica profectione domni Petri
Damiani, composed by a companion, in A. Maji scriptt. vett. nova coll.
vi. ii. 193.

[1] How deficient in moral character the worship of saints often was,
is proved by the two following cases.   Romualdus had lived as a hermit
in the neighbourhood of the abbey of Cusan, in Catalonia, and was held
in great repute as a saint, throughout the whole country round about.
When now he wished to return to Italy (vita s. Romualdi by Petr. Damiani c. 13, in his opp. ed. Cajetani ii. 212): audientes illius regionis
incolae, quia Romualdus abire disponeret, nimio moerore turbati sunt.
Et tractantes intra se, qualiter ab hac illum intentione reprimerent, hoc
illis tandem potissimum visum est, ut eum missis interfectoribus impia
pietate perimerent, quatenus quia eum non poterant retinere viventem,
haberent pro patrocinio terrae vel cadaver exanime.   Romualdus saved
himself by feigning madness.   Bishop Othwin of Hildesheim stole
(962), in Pavia, two saints' bodies, see hist. translationis s. Epiphanii c.
3 (ap. Pertz vi. 249): Venerabilis pater (Othwinus) respectu divini
amoris, quo semper animo sollicitus exstiterat, ossa sanctorum furtim
surripere—quasi praesumtionis ducebat.   Divinitus, ut credo, ecce adfuit Landwardi, Mindensis Episcopi, Presbyter,—qui illum adhuc titu-
bantem—sanctissimi Patris Epiphanii reliquias, sanctaeque virginis Spe-
ciosae uno ambitu templi inclusas auferre suasit; supervenientis noctis
tempus, nec in aliud protelandum, illis competere.   And so it took
place.

[2] Comp. the passio decem millium (al. MCCC.) Martyrum, apud
Alexandriam in Monte Ararath crucifixorum under Hadrian and Anto-
ninus (act. SS. Juni iv. 182), which Anastasius Biblioth. is said to have
translated from the Greek.   Papebroch puts it even in the 13th century (ibid. p. 179).

[3] Canonization of Ulrich, bishop of Augsburg, A. D. 993, by John
XV. (conc. Roman. ann. 993, ap. Mansi xix. p. 169), the first example
of papal canonization (Mabill. praef. ad acta SS. ord. Bened. saec. v.
no. 99 ss.   F. Pagi breviarium Pontificum Rom. ii. 257).   Besides, the
metropolitans, till 1153, still exercised the right of creating saints for
their provinces (Pagi l. c. iii. 115).

[4] Instead of many, take one graphic example by an eye-witness:
Glab. Radulph. iv. c. 3, A. D. 1027: Homo plebejus mangonum callidissimus, who had a different name in each different place,—effodiebat
e tumulis clancule ossa evellens a cineribus nuperrime defunctorum hominum; sicque imposita in diversis apophoretis venditabat apud plurimos pro ss. Martyrum seu Confessorum reliquiis.   Hic vero post innu-
meras hujusce illusiones in Galliis patratas perfuga venit ad loca Alpium.
Illic ergo more solito noctu colligens a loco abjectissimo ignoti ossa hominis, quae posuit in cassella et feretro, dicebat sibi angelica ostensione
revelatum fuisse, quem fingebat esse s. Martyrem nomine Justum.   Mox
quoque vulgus, ut se in talibus habere solet, ignavum, quicquid rusti-

relics and miracles,[5] the fruit of fraud and pious simplicity,[6]

canae plebis fuit, totum ad hanc famam confluit; poenitet insuper, si non est sibi morbus, quo curari deposcat. Tunc ducit debiles, confert munuscula, pervigil tenet excubias, praestolans repentina fore miracula, quae, ut diximus, aliquotiens permittuntur fieri a malignis spiritibus tentatorie, peccatis hominum praecedentibus ; quod tunc proculdubio evidentissime claruit. Multimodae quippe membrorum reformationes ibidem visae sunt exstitisse, ac insignia pendere oscillorum multiformia ; nec tamen—Praesules—diligentiam hujus inquirendae rei adhibuerunt : quin potius conciliabula statuentes, in aliquibus nihil aliud nisi inepti lucri quaesitum a plebe, simul et favorem fallaciae exigebant. Margrave Mainfried bought the body to deposit it in a church just erected at Suze. At the dedication the impostor appeared, and spondebat, se multa pretiosiora SS. pignora in proximo revelaturum, quorum scilicet gesta et nomina, atque passionum certamina, ut caetera, fallaciter confingebat. Glaber also was there, entered into conversation with him, and soon discovered the imposture. Still the pontiffs did not allow themselves to be in error, but went on, rite peragentes, ob quam venerant, Ecclesiae consecrationem, intromiserunt cum caeteris reliquiarum pignoribus ossa illius profani ; the elegantiores virorum personae sided with Glaber, and the people injusti nomen pro Justo venerans in suo permansit errore !

[5] Especially since so many churches were built, and many relics for them were required (comp. § 27, note 9, at the end).   Glab. Rad. iii. c. 6 : Candidato, ut diximus, innovatis Ecclesiarum Basilicis universo mundo, subsequenti tempore, i. e. anno MVIII. revelata sunt diversorum argumentorum indiciis, quorsum diu latuerant, plurimorum Sanctorum pignora. This began in Sens, where even a part of Moses' rod was found, virgae Moysi partem. To the more considerable relics of this time belong the s. lacryma Christi in Vendome in the 11th century. (J. B. Thiers diss. sur la sainte larme de Vendôme. Paris 1699. 12. Mabillon lettre à l'évéque de Blois. Paris 1700. 8. and in his oeuvres posthumes T. ii. p. 361 ss.)   Blood of Christ in Reichenau (Hermann. Contract. ad ann. 923 : Sanguis Domini in Augiam Insulam a quadam matrona defertur, sicuti literis inibi manifestatur) and in Mantua (according to Regino discovered as early as 804 ; the s. lancea (hallowed by nails from the cross of Christ, procured about 935 by the emperor Henry I., Luitpr. iv. c. 24, ap. Pertz v. 322, came among the crown-jewels, and was afterwards regarded as the spear of Longinus), &c.

[6] St Benedict was distinguished uniformly for miracles, a description of which is given by three writers of that age ; by Aimoinus Floriac. about 1000 (in Mabillon act. SS. saec. iv. ii. 356), Desiderius Abb. Casinensis, afterwards Pope Victor III. (ibid. p. 425 ss.) and Rodulfus Tortarius mon. Floriacens. about 1100 (ibid. p. 390).   That there was no want of imposture besides may be seen from vita Godehardi Episc. Hildesheimensis († 1038), by his disciple Wolferus, no. 48 (in Mabillon act SS. ord. Bened. saec. vi. i. 372) : quaedam vanae mentis personae in nostra patria usitato more per sacra loca discurrentes, se aut cae-

which were often a source of riches to the monasteries in particular, though at the same time they also led to irregularities.[7]

cos, aut debiles, aut elingues, vel certe obsessos temere simulant, et ante
altaria vel sepulcra Sanctorum se coram populo volutantes, pugnisque
tundentes, sanatos illico se proclamant, ea scilicet sola vesana voluntate,
ut sic tantum majorem stipem vel quaestum a plebe percipiant. Cum
in hujusmodi fallacia tales liquido deprehenduntur, etiam verae Sanctorum virtutes in periculosam desperationem hac dubietate retrahuntur ;
vel certe et hi qui vere sanantur etiam non solum a perfidis sed et interdum a fidelibus fallere creduntur.

[7] Hence strict abbots forbad all miracles in saints, comp above, §
18, not. 6. So the abbot Stephen in Lüttich (1026-1059) in the case
of St Wolbodo : hunc aliquando Sanctum per divinum nomen contesta-
tus est, quo temperaret a miraculis, quibus tantae fratribus fiebant per
occasionem infirmorum noctu et interdiu molestiae, see vita s. Wolbodo-
nis in Mabillon act. SS. ord. Bened. saec. vi. i. 165. Guntramnus,
abbot of St Tron (1034-1055), acted similarly. See chron. Abbatiae s.
Trudonis lib. i. (in d'Achery spicileg. ii. 662) : Hujus vitae ultimis annis
domini nostri Trudonis sepulcrum frequentissime coepit coruscare miraculis, quae ille studiosissime satagebat occultare ; sagaci enim pectore
concipiens quod futurum erat, signa data esse infidelibus non fidelibus
(1 Cor. xiv. 22.) dicebat : quod non longe post illum nonulli de nostris
experti sunt, qui inter ipsa quoque miracula Deum offendere non ti-
muerint. Namely, lib. ii. p. 664 : Defuncto eo [Guntramno] et suc-
cedente Adelardo II. (1055-1082) coeperunt haberi miracula et virtutes
sepulcri s. Trudonis non tam timori et reverentiae, quam ostentui et
populari gloriae. Frequentabat enim sepulcrum ejus infinitus peregrinorum numerus, neque diebus tantum singulis, sed singulorum dierum
horis superveniebat multitudo multitudini, atque noctis medio grandisona
faciebat venientium et abeuntium inquietatio. Vellent nollent fratres,
per omnes claustri irrumpebant partes : maxime quia aqua nostri—pu-
tei dicebatur potata in nomine s. Trudonis fieri medela atque fiebat ac-
cedentibus ad eam languidis. Sed et leprosi ibidem de ea loti referuntur nonnunquam fuisse curati. Quid multa ! Oratorium, chorus, templum, claustrum, pratum nocte dieque non inveniebatur a multitudine
vacuum, quorum perstrepentium continua inquietatio magnae fiebat
molestiae et ordinis impedimenti senioribus solitis et volentibus Deo
servire in quiete et silentio. Juniores vero, quibus taedio erat religio,
et disciplina odio, gratulabantur prius occulte, hac quasi necessitate se
magistrae Regulae mandata praeterire : accessu vero temporis, et fre-
quentissimo usu peregrinae multitudinis tandem inverecunda fronte coeperunt ad libitum cuncta agere, locorum indifferenter abutebantur qualitatibus, et horarum tam incompetentium quam competentium vicissi-
tudinibus ; seniorum increpationes indignanti supercilio respuere, in
ipsum quoque Abbatem interdum indecenter protervire etc.—Quanto
longius ferebatur relatione peregrinorum gloriosa celebritas miraculorum
s. Trudonis tanto et nostrorum reprehendebatur saecularitas ex levitate
morum et abusione indisciplinationis.

As the Church now began to admit the ordeal generally,[8] it also became usual to investigate the genuineness of relics by the fire-process.[9] This was the age of *the Legend* as well as *the Romance*,[10] and industrious monks dressed out the saints in the most arbitrary mode, with adventures and miracles.[11] After

[8] See below § 36. not. 2.

[9] Comp. vol. i. Div. 2. § 121. not. 4. Thus Meinwerk, bishop of Paderborn, had received the body of St Felix, a present from the patriarch of Aquileia A. D. 1030 (vita Meinwerci § 109 in Leibnitii scriptt. rer. Brunsvic. i. 560): et experiri volens, salutis ipsius auxilio si sibi suoque succurrere posset populo, rogum maximum in medio claustri sub dio fieri praecepit, in quem cum tertio corpus misisset, totiesque in favillam redactus ignis exstinctus fuisset, cum maxima omnium exsultatione et laudum jubilatione corpus manibus propriis excipiens, super principale altare detulit, et omnium venerationi solemnem sanctum illum deinceps habere instituit. Comp. Mabillon de probatione reliquiarum per ignem, appended to his lib. de cultu SS. ignotorum (also in his vetera analecta p. 568.)

[10] Comp. hist. lit. de la Fr. vi. 12.

[11] Letaldus mon. Miciacensis (about 980) in epist. dedicatoria ad Avesgaudum Episc. Cenoman. before his vita Juliani Episc. (in act. SS. Januar ii. 1152) :—cum magnae reverentiae gravitate dicenda et scribenda sunt, quae in conspectu veritatis recitari debent, ne, unde Deus placari creditur, inde amplius ad iracundiam provocetur; nihil enim ei placet, nisi quod verum est. Sunt autem nonnulli, qui dum attollere Sanctorum facta appetunt, in lucem veritatis offendunt, quasi Sanctorum gloria mendacio erigi valeat, qui, si mendacii sectatores fuissent, ad sanctitatis culmen nequaquam ascendere potuissent.—Cum ergo tam mira et speciosa de actibus hujus praecellentissimi Patris recito, non de meritis ejus diffido, nec de potentia Christi ambigo : sed cum haec eadem in aliis invenio, cui potius credendum sit, non perspicue video. Multa enim in actibus supradicti Patris conscripta sunt, quae et in bb. Clementis et Dionysii Martyrum et s. Furcaei Confessoris eodem sensu et paene iisdem verbis inveniuntur. Thus also he puts Dionysius and his company, among whom Julian, first bishop of Mans, was at that time reckoned, in the time of Decius, after the authority of Gregor. Turon. (vol. i. Div. i. § 57. note 2.) Quod vero s. Julianus dicitur a b. Clemente destinatus, neque ratio temporum, neque veterum consensit auctoritas. Comp. Herigerus Abb. Laubiensis about 990 in his gestis Pontiff. Tungrensium, Trajectens. et Leodiensium c. 23 (in Jo. Chapeavilli gest. Pontiff. Tungr. Traj. et Leod. scriptores i. 28), which are elsewhere filled with the most strange fables. St Servatius is said indeed to have descended from the family of Christ, but he was not able to discover any thing certain on the subject, idcirco nec faciles ad credendum esse possumus, nec tantae opinioni, quae fortasse ex pietate ingeritur, judicamus omnimodis derogandum, cum juxta Tullium non debeat pudere nos fateri nescire, quae nescimus, et hujus opinionis

Dionysius and his companions had been raised to the dignity of being disciples of the apostles,[12] a zeal arose among the French churches to procure like honour for their founders ; a task which they accomplished the more readily because in the stormy times, the older narratives were frequently lost.[13]   Very characteristic

assertoribus conveniat ignorantiam. potius verecunde fateri, quam irreverenter pro pietate mentiri.   Petrus Damiani de vita Romualdi in prologo (opp. ed. Cajetani ii. 206) : Nonulli Deo se deferre existimant, si in extollendis Sanctorum virtutibus mendacium fingant.   Thus it frequently happens that not only single actions of one saint are copied in the history of another, but whole legends are repeated with merely a change of the name.   In this way the legend of St Rictrudis is repeated as that of St Eusebia (hist. lit. de la Fr. vi. 259), the legend of St Ebrulfus for that of St Albertus (ibid. p. 557). also for St Ebremundus (ibid. p. 514).   Other examples ibid. p. 90. vii. 193. 194.

[12] See above § 18. note 15.   Comp. vol. i. Div. i. § 57. note 2.

[13] The Normans laid waste 881 Lüttich, Tongern, Cologne, &c. 882 Trier (Regino ad h. a.), by which, particularly at Trier, all the old records were lost.   Comp. auct. anonym. vitae s. Felicis (act. SS. Mart. iii. 622) : In hujus autem ter felicis Sancti mentione, sicut in omnium fere Trevirensium Sanctorum recordatione repetitam saepius hujus urbis vastationem cogimur plorare, per quam constat ingentia ss. Patrum nostrorum vitae volumina ita penitus esse consumta ; quod, nisi ex paucissimis, ut ita dixerim, tanti pelagi guttis, in vetustissimis aliorum locorum schedulis, vel etiam in plumbeis ac marmoreis tabulis, terrae penitus infossis, aliquatenus reformata fuissent, organa nostra, velut super flumina Babylonis nostrae suspensa, jam dudum in horum laude Sanctorum conticuissent.   (Similar complaints in the legends of bishops Modoaldus act. SS. Maj. iii. 52. and Maximinus Maj. vii. 32.)   What was the character of that reformatio vitarum may be seen in the promotion of the three first bishops of Trier, Eucharius, Valerius, and Maternus, to the dignity of apostle pupils, soon after that devastation at Trier (comp. vol. i. Div. i. § 57. not. 3).   Of these three the only mention in the older martyrologies was ad 29 Januar. Treviris depositio Valerii Episcopi, then in the martyrologies of Ado, Usuardus, and Notker : Treviris depositio b. Valerii Episcopi discipuli s. Petri Apostoli (on this addition see act. SS. Sept. iv. 362, probably in the same way as Boniface in epist. Caroli Martelli and capitul. lib. v. c. 2. is called Missus s. Petri.)   This was undoubtedly the foundation of the legend, first found in the vita SS. Eucharii, Valerii, Materni (act. SS. Januar. ii. 918, but not written as is said there by Goldscher, monk in Trier, about 1012, but probably) by Eberhard, monk and scholastic in Trier, † 909, (act. SS. Sept. iv. 358), then in the historia Trevir. (d'Achery spicileg. ii. 208), in Herigeri gesta Pontiff. Tungr. etc. (see note 10), and finally copied into all the chronicles of the middle age, for which even Methodius was afterwards adduced as voucher (first by Marianus Scotus ap. Pistorius-Struve T. i. p. 555. 563) (see above § 18. note 15).   Comp. Honthemii

of the time were the disputes concerning the apostleship of *St Martial*,[14] and the monks' quarrels concerning the place where

hist. Trevir. diplom. T. i. praef. p. ix ss. Acta SS. Sept. iv. 354. Walch de Materno uno in the commentationes Soc. Götting. vol. i. comm. hist. p. 1. Rettberg's Kirchengesch. Deutchlands i. 73. The example of Trier was soon followed by its suffragan see. Santinus, first bishop of Verdun, was looked upon as a disciple of St Dionysius, and was already elevated with him. In like manner Metz now raised its first bishop Clemens, and Toul its own Mansuetus to the rank of apostle disciples (first in the legend composed by abbot Adso about 980, acta SS. Sept. i. p. 615 ss.) Comp. histoire ecclésiastique et civile de Lorraine, par Ang. Calmet. T. i. Dissertation prélim. p. xi. ss. Rettberg i. 90. By Paul Crescens is said to have been sent to Vienne (Ado in chronico act. vi. ann. 59 et 101) and Mainz (Rupert. Tuitiensis about 1120 de divinis officiis lib. i. c. 27) according to 2 Tim. iv. 10 (cf. Eusebii h. e. iii. 4); see Rettberg i. 82. About the same time Linus is said to have come to Besançon, Memmius to Chalons, Sixtus to Rheims, Sinicus to Soissons, Ursinus to Bourges, Fronto to Perigueux, Altinus to Orleans, Lucianus to Beauvais, Nicasius to Rouen, Exsuperius to Bayeux, Taurinus to Evreux, Eutropius to Sainctes, Julianus to Mans, etc.

[14] After he had been put in the apostolic age with his companion Dionysius, and a correspondent life (vita) had been given him, his protegees, the monks of St Martial in Limoges, wanted even to exalt him to the rank of apostle; but the clergy of Limoges would only allow him the title of Confessor. Controversy on the point at the Syn. Pictav. ann. 1023 (Mansi xix. 413), Syn. Paris. ann. 1024 (ibid. p. 421). Jordanus, bishop of Limoges, epist. ad Benedictum P. viii. (Gallia christiana T. ii. app. p. 162), declared against the new apostle; but Johannes P. xix. (epist. ad Jordanum Episc. ap. Mansi xix. 417), and after him conc. Lemovicense ann. 1028 (not 1029, see Mabillon ann. Bened. lib. lvi. no. 49) decided in his favour; Ademarus mon. Cabanensis defended him (see epist. A. D. 1028 in Mabillon ann. append. ad tom. iv. no. 46), and the conc. Bituricense can. i. (Mansi xix. 503) and conc. Lemovicense, both A. D. 1031, at length settle the matter. Comp. particularly the copious acta of the latter (ibid. p. 507 ss.), ex. gr. p. 512: Plane si Apostolus nullus est exceptis duodecim, sicut Ebionitae haeretici praedicant,—ergo Paulus et Barnabas non sunt Apostoli etc—p. 525: Nos non sumus Ebionitae, qui non recipiunt praeter XII. Apostolos, et Paulum quasi transgressorem legis repudiant etc. Cf. acta SS. Jan. v. 535. This, however, did not prevent the monastic discipline in St Martial from utter extinction, nor the monks from offering violent opposition when the monastery was intended to be reformed (1063) externally by Clugny. See § 31. note 5. At a later period the monks of St Martial forged two letters in the name of their new apostle, ad Burdegalenses and ad Tolosanos (ed. Badius Ascensius, Paris. 1521, also annexed to Gennadius de dogm. eccl. ed. G. Elmenhorst, Hamburg 1614.)

the real bodies of *St Dionysius*[15] and *St Benedict*[16] were preserved.

The virgin *Mary*[17] was honoured above all saints. *Saturday*

[15] On this controversy between the monks of St Emmeran in Regensburg and of St Dionysius in Paris see Mabill. ann. Ben. lib. lx. no. 21
(where also the decision of Leo IX. in favour of the Regensburgians,
probably spurious, is printed) and no. 34.

[16] The convent Fleury near Orleans claimed the honour of possessing
them since the middle of the 7th century ; on the other hand Monte
Cassino claimed to have the grave and body. Leon. Ostiens. chronic.
Casin. lib. ii. c. 43. 44. 47. Mabill. ann. in many passages.

[17] Comp. especially Fulberti Ep. Carnotensis [+ 1029] Sermones
(opp. ed. Car. de Villiers. Paris. 1608. 8. Bibl. PP. Lugd. xvii. 1) and
Petri Damiani sermones (opp. ii. 1). In the latter's sermo xlv. or i. de
nativit. Mariae p. 107 it is said among other things : Etsi multa magna
facta sunt in creaturis mundi, nihil tamen tam excellens, tam magnificum fecerunt opera digitorum Dei,—Numquid quia ita deificata, ideo
nostrae humanitatis oblita es ? Nequaquam, Domina.—Data est tibi
omnis potestas in caelo et in terra.—Nil tibi impossibile, cui possibile
est desperatos in spem beatitudinis relevare. Quomodo enim illa potestas tuae potentiae poterit obviare, quae de carne tua carnis suscepit
originem ? Accedis enim ante illud aureum humanae reconciliationis
altare, non solum rogans, sed imperans, Domina, non ancilla. Sermo
xi. de annunciatione b. V. M. p. 25 : Cum fecerit Deus omnia opera
sua valde bona, hoc (Mariam) melius fecit, consecrans sibi in ea recli-
natorium aureum, in qua sola se post tumultus Angelorum et hominum
reclinaret, et requiem inveniret.—Peccant rationabiles creaturae.—Tacet
Deus omnipotens, et ordinans ejus omnipotentia tantam dissimulat confusionem.   Tandem nascitur Maria, et ad nubiles annos egrediens speciem induit speciosam, quae ipsum alliciat Deum, et divinitatis oculos
in se convertat.—Videt et ardet ille vehemens amator, et totum epitha-
lamium in laudibus ejus decantans (Song of Solomon), ubi manifeste
sponsus inducitur spirans amorem sincerissimum, nec ultra valens dissimulare quod patitur.   Evocatur statim caelestis ille conventus, et
juxta Prophetam (Jes. xvi. 3) init Deus consilium, cogit concilium, facit
sermonem cum angelis de restauratione eorum, de redemptione hominum, de elementorum renovatione, ac illis stupentibus et mirantibus
prae gaudio, de modo redemptionis. Et statim de thesauro divinitatis
Mariae nomen evolvitur, et per ipsam, et in ipsa, et de ipsa, et cum ipsa
totum hoc faciendum decernitur, ut sicut sine illo nihil factum, ita sine
illa nihil refectum sit.   Traditur epistola Gabrieli, in qua salutatio Virginis, incarnatio Redemptoris, modus redemptionis, plenitudo gratiae,
gloriae magnitudo, multitudo laetitiae continetur. Serm. xl. de assumtione b. M. v. p. 97 : Sublimis ista dies, in qua Virgo regalis ad thronum Dei Patris evehitur, et in ipsius Trinitatis sede reposita naturam
etiam angelicam sollicitat ad videndum. Tota conglomeratur Angelorum frequentia, ut videat Reginam sedentem a dextris Domini virtutum in vestitu deaurato etc.—Ascendenti Domino egressa est obviam

was devoted to her, and an *officium St Mariae* instituted in her

omnis illa beatorum Spirituum gloriosa societas.—Attolle jam oculos ad
assumptionem Virginis, et salva Filii majestate, invenies occursum hujus
pompae non mediocriter digniorem.   Soli quippe Angeli Redemptori
occurrere potuerunt, Matri vero caelorum palatia penetranti Filius ipse
cum tota curia tam Angelorum quam Justorum solemniter occurrens
evexit ad beatae consistorium sessionis, et ait: Tota pulchra et amica
mea, et macula non est in te (Cant. iv. 7).
[18] Both first began in convents.   The officium proceeded from the
hymns of praise in honour of Mary, of which the first trace is found in
the vita Udalrici (bishop of Augsburg from 923-973), written by a
contemporary, Gebhard, no. 14 (Mabillon acta SS. ord. Bened. saec. v.
p. 426): Cursus quotidianus cum matriculariis in choro ejusdem matriculae ab eo caute observabatur, quandocumque ei domi manendum aliae
occupationes consenserunt.   Insuper autem unum cursum in honore s.
Mariae genitricis Dei, et alterum de s. Cruce. tertium de omnibus
Sanctis, et alios psalmos plurimos, totumque psalterium omni die explere
solitus erat (cf. Mabillon ann. Bened. lib. xlii. no. 71). However, these
demonstrations of honour received a definite form and greater diffusion
in the eleventh century, and especially by means of Petrus Damiani.
Comp. his opusc. xxxiii. de bono suffragiorum c. 3: quam fideliter
aeterna sperabunt, qui beatae Reginae mundi quotidiana horarum omnium vota persolvunt!   Unde pulcher etiam mos in nonnullis Ecclesiis
inolevit, ut specialiter ad ejus honorem per omne sabbatum Missarum
celebrentur officia, nisi forte festivitas vel feria Quadragesimalis obsistat.
Nos etiam Eremis sive Monasteriis, quorum videlicet ad Christi gloriam
Ministri sumus, tres per hebdomadas singulas dies Sanctis assignatos habemus, ad quorum scilicet honorem Missas specialiter celebramus.—
Quod secundum virorum illustrium pias opiniones atque sententias quaelibet animae defunctorum in diebus dominicis requiescunt atque a suppliciis feriantur, secunda vero feria ad ea quibus assignata sunt poenarum
ergastula revertuntur: idcirco ipso potissimum die Angelis missarum
honor impenditur, ut et mortuis et morituris patrocinalis eorum defensio
procuretur.   Sexta quoque feria vivificae Cruci non inconvenienter
adscribitur, quae scilicet dies pendentis in Cruce Domini glorioso sanguine purpuratur.   Qua die omnes fratres nostri, quos utique monas-
terialis ordo connectit, hoc etiam ad cumulum propriae salutis adjiciunt,
ut et se mactent in Capitulo vicaria collisione scoparum, et insuper celebrent in pane et aqua jejunium.   Ad honorem quoque sanctae Crucis
eodem die Missas celebrant, ut sibi patrocinium Crucis in die necessitatis acquirant.   Cap. 4: Sabbatum enimvero, quod requies interpretatur, quo videlicet die Deus requievisse legitur, satis congrue beatissimae
Virgini dedicatur.   Quam nimirum sibi Sapientia domum aedificavit,
atque in ea per humilitatis assumptae mysterium, velut in sacratissimo
lectulo requievit.   Petrus Damiani also spread very zealously the Officium s. Mariae, but not without opposition, in the Italian monasteries.
See lib. vi. ep. 32: Statutum erat (in monasterio b. Vincentii), atque
jam per triennium fere servatum, ut cum horis canonicis b. Mariae sem-

praise.[18]   The festival of *all souls*, which arose in Clugny after 1024,[19] soon became general throughout the whole church.

per Virginis officia dicerentur.   However, a monk, Gozo, opposed it coepit conqueri, satis superque sufficere, quod sanctus praecepit Bene- dictus, nec novae adinventionis pondus debere superponi, nec nos esse antiquis Patribus sanctiores, qui videlicet haec superstitiosa ac superva cua judicantes psallendi nobis metam omnemque vivendi regulam prae- fixerunt : hac sane debere nos esse contentos, ne ab illa incautius decli- nantes per anfractus et invia ducamur erronei.   He actually succeeded in persuading the other monks, ut solitas b. Mariae laudes ulterius non offerent : but the convent met with great disasters, which did not cease till after they had solita Genitricis Dei praeconia unanimiter pollicentur. Petrus Damiani had himself composed an Officium s. Mariae, opp. T. iv. p. 9 ss.   According to Gaufridus Prior Vosiensis (1183) in chron. in Labbei biblioth. nova Mss. T. ii. p. 292. Urbanus II. established as early as the Council of Clermont (1095), ut horae beatae Mariae quoti- die dicerentur, officiumque ejus diebus sabbati fieret.   Mabillon annales lib. lviii. no. 15. lib. lx. no. 81.   Ejusd. acta SS. ord. Bened. saec. v. praef. p. lxxvi.

[19] The decretum by which the abbot Odilo prescribes this festival to all the monasteries of Clugny (ap. Mabillon act. SS. ord. Bened. saec vii. i. 385), mentions the Emperor Henry II. († 1024) as deceased.   On the solemnization of it see antiquiores consuetudines Cluniac. (§ 31. not. 3) lib. i. c. 42.   It was not till Odilo's death that the legend was formed for the purpose of procuring its permanence and greater diffusion, which is first met with in the vita s. Odilonis by Jotsaldus c. 14 (Mabillon l. c. p. 615) : Retulit mihi etiam domnus Richardus Episcopus (in Pannonia, who had previously been a disciple of Odilo) quandam visionem, quam et ego quondam audieram, sed tunc animo minime retinebam. Quodam tempore, inquit, vir quidam religiosus de pago Rotenensi (of Rodez) oriundus ab Jerosolimis revertebatur.   Transiens autem mare, quod a Sicilia versus Thessalonicam protenditur, pertulit cum pluribus aliis gravissimum ventum in medio positus, qui navim impellens, appulit ad quandam insulam sive rupem, ubi quidam servus Dei reclusus manebat. This person related to the other : Vicina loca sunt nobis, ex semetipsis manifesto Dei judicio gravissima eructantia ignis incendia, in quibus animae peccatorum ad tempus statutum diversa luunt supplicia.   Sunt vero ad eorum semper renovanda tormenta multitudo daemonum depu- tata, qui eorum poenas de die in diem restaurantes, intolerabiles magis ac magis exaggerant dolores.   Quos tamen saepius audivi lamentantes, et non parvam querimoniam facientes, quia orationibus religiosorum hominum, et eleemosynis pauperum, quae fiunt per diversa loca sanctorum, multotiens per Dei misercordiam ab eorum poenis liberarentur animae damnatorum.   Inter caetera vero mentionem et maximam querimoniam noveris illos praecipue fecisse de illa Cluniacensi congregatione et ipsius Abbate.   Quapropter per Deum te admoneo, si ad tuos cum prosperi- tate habueris reditum, ut haec omnia quae a me audisti nota facias prae-

SIXTH CHAPTER.

HISTORY OF ECCLESIASTICAL DISCIPLINE.

Contemporary chronicles: Reginonis, abbot of Prün, de disciplinis ecclesiasticis et religione christ. lib. ii. written 906-908 (according to the latest editors of the gesta Trevir. Wyttenbach and Müller, 899, see Tom. i. Adnotat. p. 27 at p. 99. ed. Jo. Hildebrand. Helmst. 1659, auctius St Balusius. Paris. 1671. 8. ad opt. codd. fidem rec. F. G. A. Wasserschleben, Lips. 1840. 8. Cf. Ballerini de antiquis collect. canonum P. iv. c. 11, Wasserschleben's Beiträge zur Gesch. d. vorgratian. Kirchenrechtsquellen. Leipz. 1839, S. 1. Bärh's Gesch. d. röm. Lit. im karol. Zeitalter S. 535.) Abbonis, abbot in Fleury († 1004) canones excerpti de aliis canonibus, written before 997 (in Mabillonii analect. ed. ii. p. 133 ss.) Burchardi, bishop of Worms († 1025), conlectarium canonum or decretorum volumen, written 1012—1023 (ed Colon. 1548. fol. Paris. 1549. 8. Cf. Ballerini l. c. P. iv. c. 12). Comp. Spittler's works published by K. Wachter, Stuttgart 1827 i. 270. (Fragment from a second part of the history of canonical law.

dictae congregationi, et ex mea parte denuncies, quatenus magis ac magis insistant orationibus, vigiliis et eleemosynis pro requie animarum in poenis positarum. The pilgrim, after his return, executed this commission. Hac igitur occasione sanctus Pater generale propositum per omnia monasteria sua constituit, ut sicut in capite kalendarum Novembrium festivitas agitur omnium Sanctorum, ita etiam in sequenti die memoria generaliter ageretur pro requie omnium fidelium animarum, privatim et publice Missae cum psalmis et eleemosynis celebrarentur, omnibus supervenientibus pauperibus eleemosyna multipliciter daretur; quatenus per haec jacturam sibi provenire magis ac magis doleret adversarius, et e contrario gratularetur sub spe misercordiae in hoc laborans Christianus. Nearly the same thing, but not without variations, is likewise related after the death of Odilo by a person belonging to Clugny, Burchardus, Dominis Patribus et senioribus Cluniacensis coenobii, told as something, quod veridicis testibus nuper audivimus (see Mabillon l. c. p. 684). From this expression as well as from the introduction of Jotsaldus, it is clear that the story was unknown at Clugny in Odilo's lifetime. The same is given in extract by Sigebert. Gemblac. ad ann. 998 who, however, transfers the scene to Sicily, to the places, quae vocantur ab incolis, Ollae Vulcani.

§ 34.

DISCIPLINE OF THE CLERGY.

Die Einführung der erzwungenen Ehelosigkeit bei den christl. Geistlichen und ihre Folgen, von D. F. A. Theiner und A. Theiner (2 Bde. Altenburg 1828) i. 444.

The impurity of the clergy caused by their celibacy, long a constant subject of legislation at the synods, increased during these times of rudeness to unnatural crimes.[1] The bishops, who were always becoming more worldly, led the way in evil example, and the inferior clergy followed with the less restraint as they had become so much more independent by the firm establishment of their benefices. While their office appeared to be privileged to commit the most scandalous excesses,[2] many began to

[1] Conc. Moguntiac. ann. 888 can. 10 (Mansi xviii. 67): Ut clericis interdicatur, mulieres in domo sua habere, omnimodis decernimus. Quamvis enim sacri canones quasdam personas feminarum simul cum clericis in una domo habitare permittant : tamen, quod multum dolendum est, saepe audivimus, per illam concessionem plurima scelera esse commissa, ita ut quidam sacerdotum cum propriis sororibus concumbentes, filios ex eis generassent. So too conc. Metense ann. 888, can. 5. Riculfi Ep. Suessionum constit. ann. 889, c. 14. Conc. Namnetense ann. inc. c. 3 (Mansi xviii. 167).
[2] Among the numerous synodal regulations, comp. conc. Aenhamense ann. 1009, c. 1. (Wilkins conc. Magn. Brit. i. 286. Mansi xix. 299): Omnes Dei ministros, et imprimis sacerdotes rogamus et docemus, ut Deo obediant et castitatem diligant, et caveant sibi ipsis ab ira Dei. Certissime norint, quod non debeant habere ob aliquam coitus causam uxoris consortium; ast pejus est, quod aliqui habeant duas vel plures : et quidam, licet dimiserit eam, quam nuper habuit, ipsa vivente tamen aliam ducit etc. Benedictus P. viii. in conc. Ticinensi (between 1014 and 1024), ap. Mansi xix. 345 :—sacerdotes Dei, ut equi emissarii, in feminas insaniunt:—toto vitae suae tempore summum bonum, ut Epicurus philosophorum porcus, voluptatem adjudicant. Neque id caute faciunt incauti : cum publice et pompatice lascivientes, obstinatius etiam quam excursores laici meretricari non erubescant (comp. below, note 5). A fearful description of priestly lewdness is given by Petrus Damiani opusc. vii. liber Gomorrhianus. Praef. : Vitium contra naturam velut cancer ita serpit, ut sacrorum hominum Ordinem attingat. Cap. 1. Alii siquidem secum, alii aliorum manibus, alii inter femora, alii denique consummato actu contra naturam delinquunt. Cap. 2. Quidam rectores

live in the ordinary state of marriage.   The violent measures

Ecclesiarum circa hoc vitium humaniores forsitan quam expediat, absolute decernunt, propter tres illos gradus, qui superius enumerati sunt,
neminem a suo Ordine debere deponi; hos autem solummodo non abnuunt degradari, quos ultimo actu cecidisse constiterit.   Cap. 6. Sed o
scelus inauditum!—quod dignum illis poterit excogitari supplicium, qui
cum suis spiritualibus filiis haec mala—committunt?—Quis jam sub
ejus imperio maneat,—qui de poenitente facit pellicem, et quem spiritualiter Deo genuerat filium,—per suae carnis immunditiam subjungat
servum? Comp. Leo IX.'s letter to Petrus Damiani, relating to this
subject, prefixed to the latter's work.   Ecce omnes illi, qui quavis quatuor generum, quae dicta sunt, foeditate polluuntur,—ab omnibus im-
maculatae Ecclesiae gradibus tam sacrorum canonum, quam nostro judicio depelluntur.   Sed nos humanius agentes, eos, qui vel propriis
manibus, vel invicem inter se egerunt semen, vel etiam qui inter femora
profuderunt, et non longo usu, nec cum pluribus, si voluptatem refrae-
naverint, et digna poenitudine probrosa commissa luerint, admitti ad
eosdem gradus, in quibus—fuerant,—volumus atque etiam jubemus.
(Cf. Baron. ad. ann. 1049, no. 10.)

   ³ Cf. § 23, not. 2.   Bonizo ap. Oefele ii. p. 799.   Guidonis disciplina Farfensis (about 1040) in vetus disciplina monastica (ed. M.
Herrgott).   Paris 1726, p. 37: Cum per universam Italiam Christi
praecepta annullarentur, et velut in fastidio versarentur: diabolicae sug-
gestiones coeperunt augmentari, et opere compleri, ita ut etiam in sacris
constituti ordinibus, sicut mos laicorum est, uxores acciperent, et sine
aliqua difficultate haeresim exercerent simoniacam.   Leonis VII. († 939)
ep. ad Gallos et Germanos (Mansi xviii. 379): [Gerardus s. Lauria-
censis Ecclesiae Archiepiscopus] intulit lamentabile et nimis lugendum,
ut Domini sacerdotes publice ducant uxores.   Aventinus, who also annal. Bojorum lib. iv. c. 23, p. 461, ed. Gundlingii mentions this epistle,
remarks, lib. v. c. 13, p. 541, of the times before Gregory VII: Sacerdotes illa tempestate publice uxores, sicuti caeteri Christiani, habebant,
filios procreabant, sicuti in instrumentis donationum, quae illi templis,
mystis, monachis fecere, ubi hae nominatim cum conjugibus testes citan-
tur, et honesto vocabulo Presbyterissae nuncupantur, invenio.   Thus
Presbyter quidam Gunduni nomine cum Presbyterissa sua Hiltigunde
makes a present of the Abbey of Ebersperg (Oefele scriptt. rerum Boicarum ii. 28, no. 82); So too quidam sacerdos nomine Perhcozus ac
ejus Presbyterissa Liutpurc (l. c. p. 29. no. 100).   In the year 1055,
Richolfus Presbyter makes a gift of the convent Benedictbeuern, and
among the witnesses we find first mentioned Froibirgis, uxor praelibati
Presbyteri (monum. Boica vii. 40).   In the case of another presentation
appears Gisila, quam Atto Presbyter duxerat uxorem (l. c. p. 42).
Wilhelm, Episc. Ausonensis, gives in fief with the approbation of his
chapter, 1052, Ermengando, canonico nostrae sedis, uxorique tuae et
filiis tuis a Castrum (Petr. de Marca Marca Hispanica, app. p. 1097,
no. 236).   Petri Damiani lib. iv. ep. 3, ad Cunibertum Ep. Taurinen-
sem (or opusc. xviii. contra Clericos intemperantes diss. ii.): Inter
nonnullos virtutum flores, venerabilis Pater, quibus tuae sanctitatis ver-

of *Dunstan*, from 961 archbishop of Canterbury († 988) in England, had only a temporary effect ;[4] still no yielding on the part

nat ingenium, unum mihi, fateor, valde displicuit.   Permittis enim, ut
Ecclesiae tuae clerici, cujuscunque sint ordinis, velut jure matrimonii
confoederentur uxoribus.   Praesertim cum et ipsi clerici tui, alias quidem satis honesti, et literarum studiis sint decenter instructi.   Qui dum
ad me confluerent, tamquam chorus angelicus, et velut conspicuus Ecclesiae videbatur enitere senatus.   Only a Petrus Damiani, although he
fully perceived the abominations of celibacy in his liber Gomorrhianus
could fail to see that this excellence of the Turin clergy coincided exactly with that permission of marriage, and could require the renuncia-
tion of it in the following time.   Worthy of remark is cap. 3 : Aliquando cum me Laudensis Ecclesia tauri pingues armata conspiratione val-
arent,—tamquam ructum fellis in os meum evomere, dicentes: Habemus
auctoritatem Triburiensis, si tamen ego nomen teneo, Concilii, quae
promotis ad ecclesiasticum ordinem ineundi conjugii tribuat facultatem.   Quibus ego respondi: Concilium, inquam, vestrum, quodcumque
vultis, nomen obtineat : sed a me non recipitur, si decretis Romanorum
Pontificum non concordat.   Even bishops were married (Æsopeja,
spouse of bishop Paschalis of Chur, is called in the documents episcopa
and Antistita Curiensis, Meier v. Knonau's schweizer. Gesch. i. 29).
At the time of Gregory VII., the bishop of Toul particularly (Gregor.
vii. lib. ii. ep. 10: quoniam—cum muliere quadam in publica fornica-
tione jaceret, de qua filium genuisset, quamque rumor esset sacramento
et desponsatione laicorum more sibi copulasse), and Burkard, bishop of
Lausanne (uxorem legitimam habuit; chartul. Lausann. in Müller's
Schweizergesch. i. 318.)

  [4] Eadmerus (about 1122) de vita s. Oswaldi Archiep. Eboracensis in
H. Wharton Anglia sacra ii. 200: Per id temporis ex sanctione et auctoritate Johannis apostolicae sedis Antistitis b. Dunstanus Archiepiscopus
Cantuariae et Primas totius Britanniae—coacto generali Concilio (ann.
969) statuit, et statuendo decretum confirmavit, videlicet ut Canonici
omnes, Presbyteri omnes, Diaconi et Subdiaconi omnes aut caste viver-
ent, aut Ecclesias quas tenebant una cum rebus ad eas pertinentibus
perderent. Habebat autem Regem Edgarum in hoc negotio fidelem fautorem, constantem adjutorem, firmum defensorem.   Qui rex ipsius patris consilio utens, curam exequendi decreti hujus super totum regnum
dobus viris injunxit, Oswaldo scilicet Episcopo Wigornensi et Athelwoldo
Wintoniensi. Quod illi zelo domus Dei succensi, et divinitatis amore sub-
nixi, et insuper praedicta auctoritate muniti, strenuissime sunt executi.
Nam ut de aliis taceam, b. Oswaldus septem monasteria in sua dioecesi re-
gulari disciplina, ejectis clericis feminarum consortium Ecclesiis antepo-
nentibus, instituit.—Post haec in aliis Angliae partibus ad parochiam
suam nil pertinentibus insignes Ecclesias ob praefixam causam clericis
evacuavit, et eas—viris monasticae institutionis sublimavit.   Comp. the
vita s. Dunstani by Eadmer ibid. p. 219, the other by Osbernus (about
1070) ibid. 112 and in Mabillon acta SS. ord. B. saec. v. p. 681 ; and
the vita s. Ethelwoldi Ep. Wintoniensis, written probably by his pu-

of the hierarchy could be expected here, because the church
estates were threatened by those disorders.[5]

pil Wolstanus ap. Mabillon l. c. p. 614. A document of King Edgar by
which the transference of a foundation in Worcester to the monks, eliminatis clericorum naeniis et spurcis lasciviis, is confirmed, ita ut jam
amplius non sit fas neque jus clericis reclamandi quicquam inde, quippe
qui magis elegerunt cum sui ordinis periculo et ecclesiastici beneficii dis-
pendio suis uxoribus adhaerere, quam Deo caste et canonice servire, see
in Usserii vet. epistt. hibernic. sylloge p. 121, and in Jo, M. Kemble
codex diplom. aevi Saxonici Tom. ii. (Lond. 1840, 8.) p. 404.   Comp.
Kemble ii. 402, 421, 429.   After Edgar's death the state of things was
changed († 975).   Matthaeus Westmonasteriensis (about 1307): Sicque post decessum Regis pacifici regni status perturbatus est, et in exe-
crationem commutatus.   Nam Principes plurimi et Optimates Abbates
cum monachis de monasteriis, in quibus Rex Eadgerus eos locaverat,
expulerunt, et clericos, ut prius, loco eorum cum uxoribus induxerunt.
The struggle between monks and secular clergy increased to be a con-
tention of political factions ; however, the old state of things again reap-
peared gradually (see conc. Aenham. above not. 2).   Stäudlin's Kirchengesch. von Grossbrit. ł. 92.   Theiner i. 533.   Lappenberg's Gesch.
von England i. 400.   Gfrörer iii. iii. 1609.
    [5] In an epist. canonica, quam debent adimplere Presbyteri, Diaconi
seu Subdiaconi, of the tenth century (in Maji scriptt. vett. nova coll.
vi. ii. 102) it is said: Ad nos perlatum est eo quod quidam conjugati
habentes titulos in quibus deserviant, de sacris vestibus, mulierum vel
filiarum suarum ornamenta faciant, et proprietario jure sibi defendant.
Benedictus P. viii. in conc. Ticinensi (between 1014 and 1024) ap.
Mansi xix. 343 : Omnes Ecclesiam pertranseuntes diripiunt, et hi maxime, qui videnter esse rectores, modis omnibus quibus possunt, concul-
cant et paupertant.   Praedia enim et possessiones aut tollunt, aut minuunt, aut quibusdam titulis et scriptis colludio fabricatis, a nomine et
a jure Ecclesiae alienant; servos libertant, licet non possint ; filiis con-
gerones infrontati omnia congerunt.   Ipsi quoque clerici, qui sunt de
familia Ecclesiae,—ex liberis mulieribus filios procreant; ancillas Ecclesiae hac sola fraude fugientes, ut matrem liberam filii quasi liberi pro-
sequantur.   Ampla itaque praedia, ampla patrimonia, et quaecunque
bona possunt, de bonis Ecclesiae, neque enim aliunde habent, infames
patres infamibus filiis adquirunt.   Sic Ecclesiae utrumque et servos per-
dit et conquisita.   Sic Ecclesiae olim ditissima—pauperrima nostris est
effecta temporibus.—hac fraude omnes filii servorum Ecclesiae ad clericatum aspirant, non ut Deo serviant, sed ut scortati cum liberis mulieribus, filii eorum de famulatu Ecclesiae cum omnibus bonis Ecclesiae
raptis quasi liberi exeant.   Hence the synod enacted, can. 3 : Filii et
filiae omnium clericorum, omniumque graduum de familia Ecclesiae,
ex quacunque libera muliere, quocunque modo sibi conjuncta fuerit,
geniti, cum omnibus bonis—servi proprii suae erunt Ecclesiae, nec unquam ab Ecclesiae servitute exibunt, which was confirmed by the emperor Henry I.   Comp. the remarkable enarratio eorum, quae perverse

Thus, then, under the last popes of this period, in addition to the other evil of the time viz., *Simony*,[6] the incontinence and marrying of the clergy were stamped as the *Nicolaitan heresy*,[7] and zealously opposed.[8] On the other hand, the first defenders of priest-

gesta sunt a custodibus Ecclesiarum s. Stephani et s. Donati in civitate Aretina, et quomodo Canonici tandem eas Ecclesias acquisierunt, written about 1092, in Muratorii antiquitt. Ital v. 217.

[6] Comp. § 23. not. 2. § 24. not. 12, 14. Cf. Girberti Phil. sermo de informatione Episcoporum § 8. (Mabillon analect. vet. p. 105, and ap. Galland. xiv. 135). Abbonis Abb. Floriacen. apologeticus § 9. [about 1000] ap. Galland. xiv. 139 : Nihil paene ad Ecclesiam—pertinere videtur, quod ad pretium non largiatur, scilicet episcopatus, presbyteratus, diaconatus, et reliqui minores gradus, archidiaconatus quoque, decania, praepositura, thesauri custodia, baptisterium, sepultura, et si qua sunt similia. Et hujusmodi negotiatores subdola responsione solent astruere, non se emere benedictionem, qua percipitur gratia Spiritus S., sed res Ecclesiarum, vel possessiones Episcopi, etc. Petrus Damiani in vita s. Romualdi c. 35 (opp. ed. Cajetani ii. 221) : Inter caeteros autem praecipue saeculares clericos, qui per pecuniam ordinati fuerant, durissima severitate corripiebat. Qui novam rem audientes, occidere illum moliti sunt. Per totam namque illam Monarchiam (i. e. Camerinam provinciam) usque ad Romualdi tempora vulgata consuetudine vix quisquam noverat, simoniacam haeresim esse peccatum. Est enim venenata illa haeresis, praesertim in episcopali ordine, tam dura, et ad convertendum rigida, ut semper promittens, semper de die in diem producens, atque in futurum procrastinans, facilius possit Judaeus ad fidem converti, quam haereticus latro plene ad poenitentiam provocari. The expression simoniaca haeresis first in Gregory the Great.

[7] First in Humberti responsio adv. Nicetam Pectoratum (ann. 1054) ap. Baronius xi. 1010 : arbitramur ab inferis emersisse principem hujus haeresis nefandum Diaconum Nicolaum, de quo Epiphanius vester sic scripsit (should rather be Augustini haer. 5, but is corrupted) : " Quarta Nicolaitarum a Nicolao haeresis est adinventa —. Iste—docere coepit, indifferentur debere uti conjugibus non solum laicos, sed etiam qui sacerdotis fungerentur officio." Petrus Damiani opusc. xviii. contra clericos intemperantes. Diss. ii. c. 13 : Qui dum corruunt, impudici ; dum defendere nituntur, merito judicantur haeretici. Unde et clerici uxorati Nicolaitae vocantur, quoniam a quodam Nicolao, qui hanc dogmatizavit haeresim, hujusmodi vocabulum sortiuntur.

[8] This too was begun by Leo IX.: Conc. Rom. ann. 1059 refers to his constitutum de castitate clericorum, as to the law that established a new order. At this council it was decreed by Nicolaus II. (Mansi. xix. 907) : ut nullus Missam audiat Presbyteri, quem scit concubinam indubitanter habere aut subintroductam mulierem. Still in this matter they were not yet so zealous as in regard to Simony. Petr. Dam. epist. ad Nicol. P. ii. ap. Baron. ann. 1059 no. 39 : Nostris quidem temporibus gemina quodammodo Romanae Ecclesiae consuetudo servatur, ut de caeteris quidem ecclesiasticae disciplinae studiis examen

ly marriage[9] reappear at the time, especially in Milan, where it had become quite customary.[10]

(prout dignam est) moveat; de clericorum vero libidine propter insulta-tionem saecularium dispensative conticescat. Si malum hoc esset oc-cultum, fuerat fortassis utcumque ferendum. Sed (oh scelus) omni pu-dore postposito pestis haec in tantam prorumpit audaciam, ut per ora populi volitent loca scortantium, nomina concubinarum, etc.

[9] To this time belongs the epist. Udalrici Ep. Augustani ad Nico-laum P. pro conjugio clericorum (prim. ed Matth. Flacius. Magdeb. 1550, 8, and in the catal. test. verit. no. 77. G. Calixtus de conjug. cleric. ed Henke p. 547. Martene collect. ampliis. i. 449, &c.) first mentioned about 1090 by Bernoldus in chron. ad. ann. 1079 (ap. Pertz vii. 436): In hac synodo Papa—scriptum quod dicitur s. Udalrici ad Papam Nicolaum de nuptiis Presbyterorum, et capitulum Paphnutii de eadem re, immo omnia sacris canonibus adversa damnavit. After-wards adopted into Udalrici Babeberg. codex epistolaris (collected about 1125, in Eccardi corp. historicum medii aevi ii. 23). The first Ulrich whom we find in the see of Augsburg is Ulrich, count of Dillingen, from 923-973. In the name of this long deceased bishop, who was in great repute as a saint in all Germany, this letter was addressed, pro-bably to Nicolaus II. Probably Ulrich was reckoned in the tradition as a defender of sacerdotal marriage. He speaks here as representative of the Augsburg Church. Many other opinions about this epistle may be seen in Theiner Bd. 1, S. 467 ff. In the letter it is said: Cum tua, o Pater et Domine, decreta super clericorum continentia nuper mihi transmissa a discretione invenirem aliena, timor quidem turbavit me cum tristitia.—non parum quippe a discretione deviasti, dum clericos, quos ad continentiam consiliis monere debebas, ad hanc imperiosa quadam violentia cogi volebas.—Domiuus quidem in veteri lege sacerdoti conju-gium constituit, quod ille postmodum interdixisse non legitur. Sed in Evangelio loquitur: " Sunt eunuchi," etc.—sed " non omnes hoc ver-bum capiunt: qui potest capere, capiat " (Matth. xix. 11, 12). Qua-propter Apostolus ait: " De virginibus praeceptum Domini non habeo, consilium autem do" (1 Cor. vii. 25). Quod, etiam juxta praedictum Domini. consilium non omnes capere posse considerans, sed multos ejus-dem consilii assentatores hominibus, non Deo, pro falsa specie conti-nentiae placere volentes, graviora praevidens committere, fratrum scili-cet uxores subagitare, masculorum ac pecudum amplexus non abhorrere, ne morbi hujus aspersione adusque pestilentiam convalescente nimium status labefactetur Ecclesiae totius: " Propter fornicationem," dixit, " unusquisque suam uxorem habeat" (1 Cor. vii. 2). Quod specialiter ad laicos pertinere, iidem mentiuntur hypocritae; qui, licet in quovis sanctissimo ordine constituti, alienis revera uxoribus non dubitant abuti. Illud apostolicum " unusquisque suam habeat uxorem" nullum excipit vere, nisi professorem continentiae, vel eum, qui de continuandi in Do-mino virginitate praefixit. Then follow proofs from 1 Tim. iii. 2. Isi-dor. de eccles. off. ii. c. 1, can. apost. 5, (Vol. i. Div. 2, § 97, not. 9), tri-partita hist. eccl. lib. ii. (Paphnutius, see Vol. i. Div. 2, § 97, not. 4).

Sunt vero aliqui qui s. Gregorium suae sectae sumunt adjutorium : quorum quidem temeritatem rideo, ignorantiam doleo. Ignorant enim, quod periculosum hujus haeresis decretum a s. Gregorio factum condigno poenitentiae fructu postmodum ab eodem sit purgatum. Quippe cum die quadam in vivarium suum propter pisces misisset, et allata inde plus quam millia infantum capita videret ; intima mox ductus poenitentia ingemuit,—suoque decreto prorsus damnato apostolicum illud laudavit consilium ; melius est nubere quam uri (1 Cor. ix. 7), addens ex sua parte: melius est nubere, quam mortis occasionem praebere. (A similar thing is related, ap. Landulphus Sen. Mediol. histor. lib. iii. c. 25 in Murat. scriptt. rer. Ital. iv. 112, by Andreas, a priest defending the marriage of priests, A.D. 1065 : Terrere te debent bella civilia, homicidia, sacramenta ac perjuria inenarrabilia : parvulorum multitudinem multorum necem sine baptismate incurrentium, quorum membra aequalia, et quanta hoc in anno in cisterna 'theatrali cum mundata a lutariis inventa sunt, paucis tamen condolentibus, ante tuos oculos habens. Such occurrences might easily have given rise to similar traditions respecting earlier times.) Quid vero per homines fieri potest stolidius, quid divinae maledictioni obligatius, quam cum aliqui, vel Episcopi videlicet, vel Archidiaconi, ita praecipites sint in libidinem, ut neque adulteria, neque incestus, neque masculorum (proh pudor !) turpissimos amplexus sciant abhorrere, quod casta clericorum conjugia sibi dicant foetere ; et ab eis non verae justitiae compassione clericos, ut conservos, rogent vel moneant continere, sed, ut servos, jubeant ac cogant abstinere ? Ad cujus imperii—tam fatuam tamque turpem addunt suggestionem, ut dicant: honestius est pluribus occulte implicari, quam aperte in hominum vultu et conscientia cum una ligari. On the passage, " vae vobis Pharisaeis, etc. [Matth. xxiii. 5]. Hi sunt homines, qui prius deberent nobis persuadere, ut in conspectu ejus, cui omnia nuda et aperta sunt, erubescamus peccatores esse, quam in conspectu hominum studeamus mundi esse. Finally 1 Tim. iv. 2, is explained of those false teachers, and a hope expressed that the pope would root out Pharisaicam doctrinam ab ovili Dei.

[10] A Milan chron. ms. flos florum relates even of archbishop Heribert (from 1019-1045): Hic Archiepisc. habuit Uxeriam, nobilem mulierem, uxorem : quae donavit dotem suam monasterio s. Dionysii, quae usque hodie Uxeria dicitur (cited in Murat. scriptt. rer. Ital. iv. 122). At the same time the Milanese clergy as well as the married Turin clergy (see Petr. Dam. lib. iv. ep. 3, above note 3), stood in high repute. A proverb was : Mediolanum in clericis, Papia in deliciis, Roma in aedificiis, Ravenna in Ecclesiis (Landulphi hist. Mediol. iii. c. 1). Even Anselm, bishop of Lucca (afterwards Pope Alexander II.) the author of the persecution of married priests confessed (ibid. c. 4) : Certe nisi feminas haberent omnes hujus urbis sacerdotes et Levitae, in Praedicatione et in aliis bonis moribus satis congrue valerent : and the Papal legate Petrus Damiani testatus est ad verum, nusquam se talem vidisse clerum (Arnulphi hist. Med. iii. c. 12). Arnulphus admits besides : ut caveatur mendacium, non ex toto fuerunt omnes ab objectis immunes : but the prejudicial descriptions of the Milanese clergy in Arialdus's partial biographers Andreas and Landulphus de s. Paulo in Puricelli's work

about to be quoted below, cannot be overborne by the above testimonies.
Concerning that persecution, comp. § 25, note 13. Archbishop Guido
first put off the authors of the trouble Landulphus and Arialdus (Landulph. iii. c. 6) : Vos dicitis, quia sacerdotes impossibile est adulterare
et sacrificare, et verum dicitis ; sed nostri sacerdotes, Deo gratias, nec
sunt nec nominati sunt adulteri ; sed curiose observant apostolicum
praeceptum, ut sint unius mulieris viri. Cf. id. iii. c. 25 : Dixisti :
Sacerdos, qui duxerit uxorem, deponatur. Bene dicis, et ego dico, si
post acceptum sacerdotium duxerit uxorem, sui ordinis periculo subjaceat : sin autem in sacerdotio unius uxoris virum inveneris, quid separas,
quod non licet ? (Comp. Vol. i. Divis. i. § 73, note 15). For the followers of Rome's example, the appellation, Patarini, was formed (Arnulph iii. c. 11, iv. c. 11. Muratori on the last passage, and antiqu.
Ital. med. aevi v. 83. Mosheim institutt. p. 406, not. m). Disputa-
tion between the two parties (ap. Landulph. iii. c. 21-25) : Cum diu per
Apostoli Pauli et canonum (effata) altercarentur, Arialdus et Landulphus proclamare coeperunt dicentes : vetera transierunt, et facta sunt
omnia nova, Quod olim in primitiva Ecclesia a Patribus sanctis concessum est, modo indubitanter prohibetur. Tantum b. magister et doctor
Ambrosius, cujus ordinem tenemus, vos damnet aut affirmet (c. 21).
The married priests then defended themselves actually with expressions
of Ambrose. They had even at that time the following story (Landulph.
i. c. 11) : Vivente b. Ambrosio gravissima dissensio inter sacerdotes mo-
nogamos et alios sub virginitate aut castitate degentes in Synodo coram
Apostolico orta est.—Apostolico imperante, et multis catholicis Episcopis exhortantibus in judicio b. patroni nostri Ambrosii a partibus amba-
bus datum est, affirmantes, quidquid ipse diceret, teneret et firmum atque sanctum haberent. At b. Ambrosius videns atque cognoscens sensus humanos, et sancta consilia et omnes pronos ad peccandum, maxime
propter incontinentiam, sciens aliquem neque virginitatem, neque castitatem, nisi a Deo, posse habere, os suum aperiens, quod in libro jam
dictaverat de officiis, ait : " de monogamia sacerdotum quid loquar ?
quin una tantum permittitur copula, et non repetita, et haec lex est non
iterare conjugium," etc. Itaque Graeci sacerdotes Ambrosianam tenentes sententiam, usque hodie, etc. (The passage is de officiis i. c. 50,
but refers to marriage before consecration as a priest). However even
the miracles which took place in favour of the married priests (Landulph.
iii. c. 27), were ineffectual. The older Milanese historians have frequently repeated this tradition about Ambrose ex. gr. Galvaneus Flamma (about 1340) in the manipulus florum c. 40. (Murat. scriptt. rer
Ital. xi. 570) : Clericis omnibus benedicens b. Ambrosius una uxore
posse uti concessit, qua defuncta et ipsi vidui in aeternum permanerent.
Quae consuetudo duravit annis 700 usque ad tempora Alexandri Papae.
Also Petrus Azarius (about 1360) and Bernardinus Corius (about 1500),
whom therefore the congreg. Indicis 1621, commanded to be expurgated.
To prevent mischief from these passages, Muratori has accompanied
them with (script. rer. Ital. iv. 121) J. P. Puricelli diss. utrum s. Ambrosius clero suo Mediolanensi permiserit, ut virgini nubere semel posset (from his dissertt. de Martyr. Arialdo, Alciato et Herlembaldo.
Mediol. 1657, fol.)

§ 35.

SYSTEM OF PENANCE.

The ecclesiastical punishment of public sinners was now regulated by the complete development of the *synodal judicature* (Synodus Placitum Episcopi) ;[1] though such pernicious moral

. [1] Placitum Episcopi, opposed to the placitum Comitis by the conc. Triburiense ann. 895. cap. 9.—Regino de discipl. eccles. lib. i. gives an account of the rule after which the bishop, in his ecclesiastical visitations, had to look in reference to the clergy, then he extracts, lib. ii., from the moral rule there to be assumed respecting the laity the following ex concilio Rotomagensi, which afterwards Burchardus lib. i. cap. 90-92, and in part Gratianus caus. xxxv. qu. 6. c. 7. repeat, but ascribe to pope Eutychianus. Lib. ii. c. 1 : Cum Episcopus suam dioecesim circuit, Archidiaconus vel Archipresbyter eum praeire debet uno aut duobus diebus per parochias, quas visitaturus est, et plebe convocata adnunciare debet proprii pastoris adventum, et ut omnes ad ejus synodum die denominata impraetermisse occurrant, omnimodis ex auctoritate ss. canonum praecipere, et minaciter denunciare, quod, si quis absque gravi necessitate defuerit, procul dubio a communione christiana sit repellendus. Deinde adscitis secum Presbyteris, qui illo in loco servitium debent exhibere Episcopo, quicquid de minoribus et levioribus causis corrigere potest, emendare satagat, ut Pontifex veniens nequaquam in facilioribus negotiis fatigetur, aut ibi immorari amplius necesse sit, quam expensa sufficiat. · Cap. 2. de juratoribus synodi (or testibus synodalibus) : Episcopus in synodo residens, post congruam allocutionem septem ex plebe ipsius parochiae, vel eo amplius aut minus, prout viderit expedire, maturiores, honestiores, atque veraciores viros in medio debet evocare, et allatis sanctorum pignoribus unumquemque illorum tali sacramento constringat : Cap. 3. Amodo inantea quidquid nosti, aut audisti, aut postmodum inquisiturus es, quod contra Dei voluntatem, et rectam christianitatem in ista parochia factum est, aut in futurum erit, si in diebus tuis evenerit, tantum ut ad tuam cognitionem quocunque modo perveniat, si scis, aut tibi indicatum fuerit, synodalem causam esse et ad ministerium Episcopi pertinere, quod tu nec propter amorem, nec propter timorem, nec propter praemium, nec propter parentelam ullatenus celare debeas Episcopo, aut ejus Misso, cui hoc inquirere jusserit, quandocunque te ex hoc interrogaverit. Sic te Deus adjuvet, et istae Sanctorum reliquiae. Then follows a long series of questions : Est in hac parochia homicida ? etc. Comp. the description in the vita Udalrici Ep. August. (from 923-973) in Mabillon act. SS. ord. Ben. saec. v. p. 431. Worldly power gave external force too to the procedure of the bishop. See Caroli Calvi cap. de statu Ecclesiae et de rebus eccl. reformandis ann. 853 c. 10 : ut Comites vel reipublicae ministri—sint in ministeriis illorum, quando Episcopus suam parochiam circumierit, cum

abuses in the system of penance as had been rejected by the
French synods in the first half of the ninth century (§ 19) pervaded general ecclesiastical practice in the second half of it.[2]
The *libri poenitentiales*[3] gave directions for substituting something more convenient for canonical punishments ;[4] and these ex-

Episcopus eis notum fecerit, et quos per excommunicationem Episcopus
adducere non potuerit, ipsi regia auctoritate et potestate ad poenitentiam
vel rationem atque satisfactionem adducant. Epistola Episcopp. syn.
Carisiac. ad Ludov. Reg. Germ. ann. 858 (Caroli Calvi capitull. tit.
xxvii.) c. 7 : Ut Episcopi quietam libertatem suas parochias circume-
undi, et praedicandi, ac confirmandi, atque corrigendi habeant, ordinate.
Ut Missus reipublicae, i. e. minister Comitis, cum ipsis, si jusserint,
eat, qui liberos homines incestuosos, si per admonitionem Presbyterorum venire ad Episcopum noluerint, eos ad Episcopi placitum venire faciat, commendate. Comp. Boehmer jus eccles. Protestantium
iii. 581. C. Ph. Kopp's Nachr. v. d. Verfassung der Geistl. u. Civil-
Gerichte in den Hessen-Casselischen Landen. (Cassel 1769. 4.) i. 118.
F. A. Biener's Beiträge zu d. Gesch. d. Inquisitions processes. Leipz.
1827. S. 32 ff. These synodal judicatures were certainly at that time
an important support of the public order, since the civil courts had only
to do with accusatorial not inquisitorial processes respecting crime. A
similar institute in civil judicature, originating since Charlemagne, did
not continue long, though perhaps it served as the model of the spiritual
synod. See Biener S. 130 ff.

[2] Regino de discipl. eccles. first spread more generally in the church
such regulations taken from the liber poenitentialis Romanus (cf. § 19.
not. 4) ; then Burchardus in his decretorum volumen.

[3] According to Regino de discipl. eccl. in the Inquisitio prefixed to
lib. 1. the bishop was to ask the parish in his ecclesiastical visitations :
Si habeat poenitentialem Romanum, vel a Theodoro Episcopo, aut a
venerabili Presbytero Beda editum ; ut secundum quod ibi scriptum est,
aut interroget confitentem, aut confesso modum poenitentiae imponat.
Comp. the mode in which conc. Cabilon. ann. 813 can. 38 (see above
§ 19. note 5), still declares itself against all libelli poenitentiales. But
even Atto, Cardinalis Presbyter, about 1080, before his capitulare declares the poenitentiale romanum to be apocryphum, and finds in it
turpissima quae sanctis viris solet esse pudor dicere, et pudor audire
(Maji scriptt. vett. nova coll. vi. ii. 60. 61.)

[4] The first trace of them is found perhaps in concil. Tribur. ann. 895,
cap. 56-58. In a fuller form in Regino de disc. eccl. lib. ii. c. 446.
De redemtionis pretio : Si quis forte non potuerit jejunare, et habuerit,
unde possit redimere ; si dives fuerit, pro VII. hebdomadis det solidos
XX. : si non habuerit tantum, unde dare possit, det solidos X.—Sed
attendat unusquisque, cui dare debeat, sive pro redemtione captivorum,
sive supra s. altare, sive Dei servis, seu pauperibus in eleemosynam.—
c. 447 : Pro uno mense, quod in pane et in aqua poenitere debet aliquis,
psalmos decantet MCC. genu flexo, et si non genu flexo, MDCLXXX.

changes soon degenerated into a proper sin-transaction, by which the Church was not a little enriched.[5]   Besides this, more fre-

---

—c. 449 : Qui vero psalmos non novit, et jejunare non potest, pro uno anno, quod jejunare debet in pane et aqua, det in eleemosynam XXVI. solidos etc.—c. 454 : cantatio unius Missae potest redimere XII. dies, X. Missae IV. menses etc.   In like manner in the cann. editis sub Edgaro rege ann. 960 (Wilkins conc. Magn. Brit. i. 237. ap. Mansi xviii. 525), and in the libris poenitential published by Morinus de discipl. poenit., Edm. Martene de ant. Eccl. rit. T. ii. and by Muratori ant. Ital. med. aev. v. 719.   This alms-giving was considered partly as in itself a good work, and partly as a mode of buying off penance. Poenitentiale ap. Murat. v. 726 : Et qui hoc facere non potest, quod superius dictum est, eligat sacerdotem justum, vel monachum, qui verus monachus sit, et secundum regulam vivat, qui pro se hoc adimpleat. et de suo justo pretio hoc redimat.   On the consequences of it see Petrus Damiani lib. i. ep. 15 ad Alexandrum ii. : dum afflictio carnis a cunctis poenitentibus paene respuitur, in praefigendis poenitudinum judiciis vigor canonum funditus enervatur.   Quamobrem aut liber omnino claudendus est canonum, aut a delegandae poenitentiae taxatione cessandum. Quis enim saecularium ferat, si vel triduo per hebdomadam jejunare praecipias ?   Modo stomachi laesionem simulant, modo splenis etc.— Comp. generally Muratori de redemtione peccatorum diss. in the antiqu. Ital. v. 710.

[5] Planck iii. 678, judges perhaps too favourably of the buying off of sins practised in these times.   Comp. Spittler's Werke i. 284.—Conc. Rotomag. ann. 1050 c. 18 : Ut poenitentes occasione avaritiae gravare aut levare nemo praesumat ; sed juxta modum culpae vel possibilitatem naturae moderentur poenitentiae.   The connection in which they stood with numerous endowments bestowed on churches and convents see in Petrus Damiani lib. iv. ep. 12. ad v. Episc. : Non ignoras, quia, cum a poenitentibus terras accipimus, juxta mensuram muneris eis de quantitate poenitentiae relaxamus, sicut scriptum est : divitiae hominis redemtio ejus (Prov. xiii. 8).   Hence the formulary used in documents of bequest at this period, especially in Upper Italy : Quisquis in sanctis ac venerabilibus locis ex suis aliquid contulerit rebus, juxta Auctoris vocem in hoc saeculo centuplum accipiat ; insuper, et quod melius est, vitam possidebit aeternam (Muratori antiqu. Ital. v. 628).   Comp. the donatio facta coenobio Casauriensi ann. 1032 (in Muratorii scriptt. rer. Ital. ii. ii. 994) : Cum quadam die cogitare coeperimus, qualiter impii et peccatores, qui peccata sua redimere (after Dan. iv. 24) negligunt, in illa poena perpetua cum diabolo damnabuntur ;—cum tremore et aestuatione cordis coepimus anxie quaerere consilium a sacerdotibus et religiosis viris, qualiter peccata nostra redimere, et iram aeterni judicis evadere possemus.   Et consilio accepto, quod nil sit melius aliud inter eleemosynarum virtutes, quam si de propriis rebus et substantiis nostris in monasterio dederimus etc.   In like manner the donatio facta Tremitensi coenobio ann. 1055, almost word for word in Muratori antiqu. Ital. v.

quent indulgences came to the aid of sinners.[6] Hence, even times
of penance could be imposed which reached far beyond the term
of human life.[7] For certain heavy crimes severer penances were
common ;[8] but in the eleventh century, rigid exercises of penance,

631. How earlier Catholic Christians were judged by Arians on account of such matters may be seen in vol. i. Div. 2. § 108. note 9.

[6] For example, the indulgence bestowed by Pontius, archbishop of
Arles, A. D. 1016, on a new conventual church, in d'Achery spicileg.
iii. 383, and Mabillon annal. Bened. lib. liv. no. 26 : A penitent ad jam
dictam ecclesiam si venerit, in die videlicet dedicationis ejus, aut semel
in anno cum sua vigilia, et adjutorium dederit ad opera. ecclesiae s.
Mariae,—sit absolutus ab ipso die, quo suam vigiliam fecerit, de tertia
parte majorum peccatorum, unde poenitentiam habet acceptam, usque
ad ipsam diem revertentis anni.—Denique illos, qui de minoribus peccatis sunt confessi, et habent acceptam poenitentiam,—absolvimus de
una medietate acceptae poenitentiae etc. In the 11th century the popes
too began occasionally to issue plenary indulgences. The infamous
Benedict IX. (Mabillon act. SS. ord. Bened. saec. v. praef. no. 109)
first bestowed on the church of St Victor at Marseilles, at its consecration, the privilege, that every one who repaired to it, omnium criminum
squaloribus absolutus libere ad propria laetus redeat, eo scilicet tenore,
ut transacta peccata sacerdotibus confiteatur, et de reliquo emendetur.
Afterwards the like practice is first met with again under Alexander II.
who in 1065 tam iis, quos tunc praesentes esse contigerat, quam omnibus, qui per octo continuos dies ob devotionem tantae solemnitatis
ibidem accurrere possent, confessorum peccatorum absolutione concessa,
dedicated a new church in Cassino (chron. Casin. iii. c. 31. in Muratorii
rer. Ital. scriptt. iv. 449), and A. D. 1070 at the consecration of a church
in Lucca concessit, ut octo dierum spatio dedicationis memoria perageretur annis singulis, concessa indulgentia poenitentiae (ex cod. Vatic. in
the propylaeum ad acta SS. Maji i. 132. no 8), where the expression
indulgentia first appears. Comp. Eus. Amort de origine, progressu,
valore ac fructu indulgentiarum. August. Vind. 1735. fol.

[7] So Petrus Damiani to Archbp. Guido of Milan (cf. § 25. not. 13).
Petri Dam. opusc. v. (ap. Mansi xix. 893) : Centum itaque annorum
sibi poenitentiam indidi redemtionemque ejus taxatam per unumquemque annum pecuniae quantitate praefixi.

[8] So for parricidium, cf. vita s. Conwojonis lib. iii. c. 1. (in Mabillon
acta SS. ord. Bened. saec. iv. ii. 215) : Tunc sanctus Praesul jussit
illum Diaconem ferro ligari per collum et brachia, sicut in lege parrici-
darum censetur, imperavitque ei, ut loca sancta circuiret, et indesinenter
Deum omnipotentem pro reatu suo postularet. Ibid. lib. iii. c. 8. p. 219 :
Episcopi jusserunt fabricare catenas ferreas, et ligare eos per brachia et
per lumbos strictim : et sic loca sancta circuirent in cinere et cilicio,
quousque Dominus reciperet poenitentiam eorum. Vita s. Wolfgangi
Ep. Ratisbon. by Othlonus monk in Hersfeld († after 1068) c. 41 (ap.
Pertz vi. 542) : Homo pauperculus quidam, qui ob criminum multorum
perpetrationem circulis ferreis in utroque brachio fuit constrictus, et ex

particularly pilgrimages to Rome and Palestine,[9] and the process

hoc gravissimis quotidie suppliciis afflictus, cum multa sanctorum loca pro ejusdem cruciatus remedio commissique sceleris abolitione perlustrasset, divina tandem miseratione respectus, ferri ligamen, quod in uno gestabat brachio, per sancti viri Adalperti merita amittere meruit. Deinde etiam quoniam s. Wolfgangi famam per longinquas audivit regiones, ad Ratisponam veniens, ibique ante sepulchrum ejus orationi insistens, alterius circuli cruciatu absolutus est.   Cf. Petrus Damiani de vita Romualdi c. 28 (opp. ed. Cajetani ii. 218).   Mabillon annal. Bened. lib. 48. no. 63. iii. 647.   However even here abuses had early made their appearance.   See Rabani Mauri epist. ad Clerum Argentin. in Kunstmann's Raban. Maurus S. 214 : Et quia parricidae aliqui vadunt per diversas provincias et civitates vagando, comessationibus atque ebrietatibus operam dando, dicentes, se ita poenitentiam agere debere ; cum in hoc non imminuunt scelera sed augent decrevit s. Synodus, ut in uno loco manentes districtae poenitentiae se subjiciant et orationibus vacent, si forte omnipotentis Dei bonitas veniam peccati aliquando illis tribuat.—Besides offences against the church were looked upon as requiring peculiarly severe penances ; for example, Lamberti ann. ad ann. 1046 (Pertz vii. 154) : Dux Gotefridus—civitatem Verdonensem cepit, majorem in ea Ecclesiam concremavit.   Sed post modicum facti in tantum poenituit, ut publice se verberari faceret, et capillos suos, ne tonderentur, multa pecunia redimeret, sumtus ad reaedificandam Ecclesiam daret, et in opere caementario per se ipsum plerumque vilis mancipii ministerio functus deserviret.

[9] Pilgrims Romei and Romipetae see du Fresne glossar. s. h. v.—Glab. Radulph. iv. c. 6 : Per idem tempus (about 1033) ex universo orbe tam innumerabilis multitudo coepit confluere ad sepulchrum Salvatoris Hierosolymis, quantam nullus hominum prius sperare poterat. Primitus enim ordo inferioris plebis, deinde vero mediocres, posthaec permaximi quique Regis et Comites, Marchiones ac Praesules : ad ultimum vero, quod nunquam contigerat, mulieres multae nobiles cum pauperioribus illuc perrexere.   Pluribus enim erat mentis desiderium mori, priusquam ad propria reverterentur.—multi ob vanitatem proficiscuntur, ut solummodo mirabiles habeantur.   In the year 1064 several German bishops travelled with a great retinue to Palestine (Lambert. ad ann. 1064 et 1065 ap. Pertz vii. 168).   From the ninth century the pious and curious were attracted thither by the lumen seu ignis sancti sepulchri (first mentioned by Bernardus Monachus 870 in Willelmi Malmesbur, de gestis Reg. Angl. iv. c. 2 ; and Monachus Gallus anonymus in the time of Nicolaus I. in his itinerarium in Mabillon act. SS. ord. Bened. saec. iii. ii. 523.) Cf. Mosheim de lumine s. sepulchri (ejusd. dissertatt. ad hist. eccl. pertin. ii. 211.)   The transition from symbolical discourse to symbolical action, which afterwards gave occasion to that false miracle, is indicated by the following passages : Eliae Cret. comm. in Gregorii Naz. orat. xix. (Gregorii opp. ed. Paris. 1630. ii. 738) : Splendidam autem noctem eam, quae diem hunc praecessit, appellat, ut quae peccati tenebras solverit : nam cum in ea per certam oeconomiam lux vera delituisset, ac postea e sepulchro exorta esset,

of flagellation recommended in particular by *Petrus Damiani*,
were very often undertaken spontaneously, with the idea that the
customary penance was too easy to propitiate Deity.[10]

peccati tenebrae deletae sunt.   Zachariae P. epist. ad Bonifacium (in
Bonif. epistt. ed. Würdtwein ep. 87. p. 250) : De igne autem paschali
quod inquisisti,—quinta feria Paschae, dum sacrum chrisma consecratur,
tres lampades magnae capacitatis—in secretiori ecclesiae loco ad figuram
interioris tabernaculi insistentes, indeficienter cum multa diligentia in-
spectae ardebunt, ita ut oleum ipsum sufficere possit usque ad tertium
diem.   De quibus candelis sabbato sancto pro sacri fontis baptismate
sumtus ignis per secerdotem renovabitur.   In the church of the ascension on the Mount of Olives there also appeared earlier a peculiar
miracle.   See Beda de locis sanctis c. 7 : In die ascensionis dominicae
per annos singulos, Missa peracta, validi flaminis procella desursum
venire consuevit, et omnes, qui in Ecclesia fuerint, terrae prosternere.
Proofs that in Palestine they had learned not only to sympathise with
the seeking after relics, but also the miracle-seeking of the pilgrims.
    [10] As early as Regino de discipl. eccl. ii. c. 442 ss. they are men-
tioned as proposed by individuals (quidam dixerunt, quidam judicave-
runt etc.), ex. gr. for one day xii. plagae or percussiones.   But they did
not become general till Petrus Damiani brought them forward.   Damian's pupil, Dominicus Loricatus († 1062) distinguished himself by
his voluntary exploits in this kind of penance.   Concerning him, Petri
Dam. vita SS. Rodulphi Ep. Eugubini, et Dominici Loricati (opp. ii.
233).   The tariff may be seen in Petr. Dam. opusc. li. de vita eremetica
et probatis Eremitis ad Teuzonem Eremitam c. 8. (opp. iii. 400) : Cum
tria scoparum millia unum poenitentiae annum apud nos regulariter expleant ; decem autem psalmorum modulatio, ut saepe probatum est,
mille scopas admittat ; dum cl. psalmis constare psalterium non ambigi-
tur, quinque annorum poenitentia in hujus psalterii disciplina recte
supputantibus invenitur.   Sed sive quinque vicies ducas, sive viginti
quinquies, centum fiunt.   Consequitur ergo, ut qui viginti psalteria
cum disciplina decantat, centum annorum poenitentiam se peregisse
confidat.   Quamquam et in hoc plerosque noster Dominicus superet ;
quia cum nonnulli unam manuum in disciplinis agendis exerceant, iste
ut revera Benjamin filius (Judic. iii. 16) contra rebelles carnis illecebras
utraque manu infatigabiliter pugnat.   Hanc autem centum annorum
poenitentiam, ut mihi ipse professus est, facile sex diebus ex more con-
summat.   On the spread of this penitential discipline see Petri Dam.
opusc. l., institutio monialis ad Blancam Comitissam c. 14 (opp. iii. 395) :
Hujus s. senis exemplo faciendae disciplinae mos adeo in nostris partibus
inolevit, ut non modo viri, sed et nobiles mulieres hoc purgatorii genus
inhianter arriperent.   Thus a woman of rank had told him, per praefixam
hujus disciplinae regulam centum annorum se poenitentiam peregisse.
Damiani, however, had still to defend his new discipline against various
opponents, particularly against a monk, Peter, and against Cardinal Stephanus.   Cf. Damiani epistt. lib. vi. ep. 27. ad Petr. cerebrosum monachum and opusc. xliii. de laude flagellorum et disciplinae ad Casin-

The authority of the Church to grant or refuse forgiveness of sins, was looked upon with the more awe, inasmuch as it had now extended for a long time even to the dead.[11]   *The interdict* was invented for the purpose of bending obstinate sinners.[12]

enses monachos.   Comp. Mabillon ann. Bened. lib. lx. no. 83 ss.   Die christlichen Geitzlergesellschaften, von D. E. G. Förstemann, Halle 1828. S. 9 ff.

[11] Supported particularly on Gregorii M. dial. ii. c. 23. iv. c. 55. Cf. Joannis viii. ep. 66. ad Episcopos in regno Ludovici constitutos ann. 878: Quia veneranda fraternitas vestra modesta interrogatione sciscitans quaesivit, utrum hi, qui pro defensione sanctae Dei Ecclesiae et pro statu christianae religionis ac reipublicae in bello nuper ceciderunt, aut de reliquo pro ea re casuri sunt, indulgentiam possint consequi delictorum; audenter Christi Dei nostri pietate respondemus, quoniam illi, qui cum pietate christianae religionis in belli certamine cadunt, requies eos aeternae vitae suscipiet, contra Paganos atque infideles strenue dimicantes etc.   Nostra praefatos mediocritate, intercessione b. Petri Apostoli, cujus potestas ligandi atque solvendi est in caelo et in terra, quantum fas est, absolvimus, precibusque illos Domino commendamus.   At the conc. Lemovicense ii. ann. 1031 Jordan, bishop of Limoges, defends this authority at length.   Sess. ii. (ap. Mansi xix. 539) especially with Gregorii M. diul. lib. ii.: Tantam Ecclesiae suae Christus largitus est virtutem, ut etiam, qui in hac carne vivunt, jam carne solutos absolvere valeant, quos vivos ligaverant.   Examples: Hattonis ep. ad Joh. P. ix. § 25. not. 10).   Count Erlebald is absolved, after his death, by the archbishop of Rheims, at the synod of Trosley (ann. 921) (Flodoard hist. Eccl. Rhem. iv. c. 16).

[12] We meet with even earlier individual cases, in which passionate hierarchs extended ecclesiastical punishment to entire societies to which the guilty belonged; but this was always disapproved.   Thus Augustinus, ep. 250, blamed one bishop Auxilius on account of such a proceeding, and shews him how unjust it is, aliquem cum omni domo sua anathematis sententia ferire, et animas innocentes pro scelere alieno, spiritali supplicio punire.   The interdict which Hincmar, bishop of Laon, inflicted on his diocese (869), was very much disapproved and removed by Hincmar of Rheims.   See Hincmari opusc. xxxiii. adv. Hincm. Laud. c. 28. 30-32.   The first example of an uncontradicted interdict is in Ademari Engolismensis (about 1029) chron. ad ann. 994 (ap. Bouquet x. 147): Aldninus Episcopus Lemovicensis pro nequitia populi novam observantiam constituit, scilicet Ecclesias et Monasteria cessare a cultu divino, a sacrosancto sacrificio, et populum quasi paganum a divinis laudibus cessare: et hanc observentiam excommunicationem censebat.   After this example the interdict was now introduced as the legal punishment against those who should disturb the peace of the country, at the instance of Odolricus, abbot of St Martial, at the conc. Lemovicense ii. ann. 1031 (ap. Mansi xix. 541).   The proposal of the abbot, which was adopted, was: Nisi (principes militiae Lemovicensis) de pace acquieverint, ligate omnem terram Lemovicensem pub-

§ 36.

INFLUENCE OF THE CHURCH IN THE PRESERVATION OF CIVIL ORDER.

From the middle of the ninth century, the clergy, yielding to the rude notions of the times, began to assume the superinten- dence of *the ordeal*,[1] an institute both ancient and important in

lica excommunicatione: eo videlicet modo, ut nemo, nisi clericus, aut pauper mendicans, aut peregrinus adveniens, aut infans a bimatu et infra, in toto Lemovicino sepeliatur, nec in alium episcopatum ad sepeliendum portetur. Divinum officium per omnes Ecclesias latenter agatur, et baptismus petentibus tribuatur. Circa horam tertiam signa sonent in Ecclesiis omnibus, et omnes proni in faciem preces pro tribulatione et pace fundant. Poenitentia et viaticum in exitu mortis tribuatur. Al- taria per omnes Ecclesias, sicut in parasceue, nudentur: et cruces et ornamenta abscondantur, quia signum luctus et tristitiae omnibus est. Ad Missas tantum, quas unusquisque sacerdotum januis Ecclesiarum obseratis fecerit, altaria induantur, et iterum post Missas nudentur. Nemo in ipsa excommunicatione uxorem ducat: nemo altari osculum det. Nemo clericorum aut laicorum, vel habitantium, vel transeuntium, in toto Lemovicino carnem comedat, neque alios cibos, quam illos, qui- bus in quadragesima vesci licitum est. Nemo laicorum aut clericorum tondeatur, neque radatur, quosque districti principes, capita populorum, per omnia sancto obediant concilio. Comp. Planck iii. 516.

[1] Charlemagne had allowed the ordeal to continue (capitulare iv. ann. 803 c. 3) and merely forbade the appeal to God by fighting (cap. i. ann. 804 c. 14: ad declarationem rei dubiae judicio crucis Dei voluntas et rerum veritas inquiratur, nec unquam pro tali causa cujuslibet generis pugna vel campus ad examinationem judicetur). Lewis the Debonaire forbade also capit. ann. 816 c. 27. examinationem crucis, ne quae Christi passione glorificata est cujuslibet temeritate contemptui habeatur, and though still Pope Eugenius II. prescribed ritus probationis per aquam frigidam (in Mabillon analect p. 161), yet Lewis ordained cap. Wormat. ann. 829 tit. ii. c. 12. (Baluz. i. 668), ut examen aquae frigi- dae, quod hactenus faciebant, a Missis nostris omnibus interdicatur ne ulterius fiat. Against the ordeal generally Agobard declared himself (see above § 10. not. 13). So also Pope Stephen V. epist. ad Leutbertum (not Heribertum, as Baron. ann. 890 no. 7. has) Episc. Moguntin about 888 (Mansi xviii. 25): ferri candentis vel aquae ferventis examinatione confessionem extorqueri a quolibet, sacri non censent canones: et quod ss. Patrum documento sancitum non est, superstitiosa adinventione non est praesumendum. Still later papal disapprovals see in d'Achery no- tae ad Guiberti Abb. opp. Paris. 1651. fol. p. 661.

German jurisprudence; though they had hitherto generally over-looked it, or in part directly discountenanced it.[2] By this means, they certainly rescued many a victim from superstition by their mild use of the instrument.[3] Of like utility in this rude and fierce age was *the truce of God* (trenga Dei),[4] first established in

[2] First defended by Hincmar. de divort. Loth. et Theutb. (see § 21. not. 5), especially with Num. v. 11 ss., and in his epist. 39. ad Hildegarum Ep. Meldensem. Conc. Wormat. ann. 868 can. 15. (Mansi xv. 872) decrees that, in cases of theft in convents, the suspected monks pro expurgatione sua corpus et sanguinem Domini nostri J. Chr. percipiant. Conc. Tribur. ann. 895 can. 21: Presbyter vice juramenti per s. consecrationem interrogetur: on the other hand, a suspected layman, can. 22. aut Episcopo vel suo misso discutiente, per ignem candenti ferro caute examinetur. But the ordeal by duel remained forbidden, conc. Valent. ann. 855 c. 12. Nicolai i. ep. 50. ad Carol. Calv. A. D. 867 (Mansi xv. 319). Directions for the hinderance of ordeals in Aethelstani R. Angl. constitutt. ann. 928 c. 5. (Wilkins conc. M. Brit. i. 206. Mansi xviii. 353). Ordo diffusior probandi homines de crimine suspectos per ignitos vomeres, candens ferrum, aquam ferventem s. frigidam in B. Pez. thes. anecdot. ii. p. 2. Comp. F. Maier Gesh. d. Ordalien. Jena 1795. 8. Zwicker über d. Ordale. Gött. 1818. 8. especially M. Gerbert. monum. veteris liturg. Alleman. ii. 553.

[3] William Rufus, king of England, said, in 1096, when fifty nobles had purified themselves in his presence by the fire-proof process (Spelmann codex legum Angliae in Houard anciennes loix des François. Rouen 1766. ii. 213): meo judicio amodo respondebitur, non Dei, quod pro voto cujusque hinc inde plicatur.

[4] Even before, the bishops had attempted to put an end entirely to private feuds. Thus A.D. 994, in a time of pestilence, at a council held at Limoges pactum pacis et justitia a Duce et Principibus vicissim foederata est(chron. Ademari written 1029, ap. Bouquet x. 147). Thus in 1016 King Robert proposed a council at Orleans de pace componenda (Fulberti carnot. ep. 21 ad Robert. ibid. p. 454). Comp. farther, Bouquet x. 172, 224, 379. Besides the bishops of Burgundy had made a decree, ut tam sese, quam omnes homines sub sacramento constringerent, pacem videlicet et justitiam servaturos (Balderici chron. Camerac. et Atrebat. written 1082, lib. iii. c. 27, ibid. p. 201): in like manner the Aquitanian bishops in conc. Lemovic ii. ann. 1031 (Mansi xix. 530, comp. § 35, not. 12), and their example was followed by the other French provinces, Glaber Radulph, iv. cap. 5, ap. Bouquet x. 49, and especially chron. Camerac. et. Atrebat. ap. Bouquet xi. 122: Istiusmodi decretum a Franciae Episcopis datum est servari subjectis sibi populis. Unus eorum caelitus sibi delatus dixit esse literas, quae pacem monerent renovandam in terra. Arma quisquam non ferret, direpta non repeteret: sui sanguinis vel cujuslibet proximi ultor minime existens, percussoribus cogeretur indulgere, etc. Here the language throughout relates to a total abolition of club-law; and therefore the pax, which was

Aquitania (1041), but soon adopted in the neighbouring countries also.[5]

the objects of all such attempts, has been erroneously confounded with
the later treuga. Gerardus Abb. (miracul. s. Adalhardi lib. i. written
about 1050, ap. Bouquet x. 379) thus describes one of these compacts
belonging to the year 1021 : Ambianensis et Corbeïenses cum suis Pa-
tronis (remains of patron saints) conveniunt, integram pacem, i. e., totius
hebdomadae (in opposition to the latter treuga) decernunt,—ut si qui
disceptarent inter se aliquo dissidio, non se vindicarent praeda aut incendio, donec statuta die ante ecclesiam coram Pontifice et comite fieret
pacificalis declamatio. As this complete peace could not be attained,
the Treuga Dei was substituted. Comp. Stenzel's Gesch. Deutschlands unter den fränk. Kaisern. i. 88.

[5] Glaber Radulph. v. c. 1. [Bouq. x. 59]: Anno MXLI. contigit, inspirante divina gratia, primitus in partibus Aquitanicis, deinde paulatim
per universum Galliarum territorium, firmari pactum propter timorem
Dei pariter et amorem : taliter ut nemo mortalium a feriae quartae ves-
pere usque ad secundam feriam incipiente luce, ausu temerario praesumeret quippiam alicui hominum per vim auferre, neque ultionis vindictam a quocumque inimico exigere, nec etiam a fidejussore vadimonium
sumere; quod si ab aliquo contigisset contra hoc decretum publicum,
aut de vita componeret, aut a Christianorum consortio expulsus patria
pelleretur. Hoc insuper placuit universis, veluti vulgo dicitur, ut Treuga Domini vocaretur : quae videlicet non solum humanis fulta praesidiis, verum etiam multotiens divinis suffragata terroribus. Contigit
enim, ut dum paene—per totas Gallias hoc statutum firmiter custodi-
retur, Neustriae gens illud suscipere recusaret. Deinde quoque occulto
Dei judicio coepit desaevire in ipsorum plebibus divina ultio : consum-
sit enim mortifer ardor multos, etc. Hugo Flaviniacensis in chron.
Virdunense (written 1102) ap. Bouquet xi. 145, relates the same more
briefly ad ann. 1041 and then adds : Superest adhuc domnus Eduensis
Episc.—qui et referre solitus est, quia cum a s. Odilone et caeteris ipsa
pax divinis revelationibus instituta, Treva Dei appellata, et ab Austra-
siis suscepta fuisset,—negotium hoc strenuitati hujus patris nostri Gratiae-
Dei ab omnibus impositum est, ut ejus studio et industria pax eadem in
Neustria servaretur, etc. The oldest document on the subject is the
sermo et confirmatio ss. Patrum, A.D. 1041, by Raginbaldus Arelat.
Archiep., Benedictus, Avenionensis, Nitardus Nicensis, Ab. Odilo and
all the Gallic clergy addressed to the clergy of Italy, recommending the
treuva Dei (in Martene et Durand thesaur. anecdot. i. 161, Mansi xix.
593) :—Quicumque hanc pacem et treuvam Dei observaverint, ac firmiter tenuerint, sint absoluti a Deo Patre omnipotente, it Filio ejus J,
Chr. et Spiritu S., de s. Maria cum choris virginum, et de s. Michaele
cum choris angelorum, et de s. Petro—cum omnibus Sanctis—. Qui
vero treuvam promissam habuerint, et se sciente infringere voluerint,
sint excommunicati a Deo Patre, etc., maledicti et detestati, hic et in
perpetuum, et sint damnati sicut Dathan et Abiron, et sicut Judas, qui
tradidit Dominum, et sint demersi in profondum inferni, sicut Pharao

SEVENTH CHAPTER.

SPREAD OF CHRISTIANITY.

§ 37.

IN THE NORTH OF EUROPE.

Chief authority: Adami Bremensis (wrote between 1072 and 1076 hist. eccles. praesertim Bremensis libb. iv. (prim. ed. A. S. Vellejus Hofniae, 1579) and ejusd. lib. de situ Daniae et reliquarum, quae trans Daniam sunt, regionum natura, moribus et religione ed. Erpold. Lindenbrogius. Lugd. Bat. 1595. 4. and in his scriptt. rerum germ. septentrionalium, Francof. 1609. fol. J. J. Maderus. Helmst. 1670. 4. translated with remarks by Carsten Misegaes. Bremen 1825. 8. Cf. Jac. Asmussen de fontibus Adami Brem. comm. Kiliae 1834. 4.

In *Denmark*, where Anschar had established Christianity in its weak beginnings (comp. above § 16), it had afterwards to ·suffer much persecution, till the German king, *Henry I.*, extorted toleration for it from *Gorm the old* (about 934). Accordingly, the number of the Christians increased under King *Harald Blaatand* (from 941-991), especially in Jutland. This was in a great measure owing to intercourse with the Normans, who had been longer settled and converted in *England* and *France*, especially

in medio maris, si ad emendationem non venerint. Afterwards adopted by William Duke of Normandy, 1042 (Mansi xix. 597) constitutt. pacis et treugae in vico Ausonensi (Marca Hispan. illustr. a. P. de Marca app. p. 1140, [and ap. Bouquet xi. 512), excerpta concilii apud s. Aegidium habiti 1042, (ap. de Marca de conc. Sac. et Imp. annexed to lib. iv. c. 14, ed Boehmer p. 416, ap. Bouquet xi. 513), conc. Tulugiense (Tulujes at Perpignan about 1845, ap. de Marca l. c. p. 409 and ap. Bouquet xi. 510.) Synod Helenensis (Perpignan) sub Oliba Ep. Ausonensi A.D. 1047 (ap. de Marco p. 411, Bouquet p. 514), where the time of the treuga is always brought down ab hora sabbati nona usque in die lunis hora prima. Conc. Narbonense A.D. 1054 (de Marca p. 412. Bouq. p. 514. Mansi xix. 827). Often renewed subsequently.

2 F

under *Rollo* or *Robert* (911).[1] On the other hand, it was checked
by the apparent connection of Christianity with German sovereignty, particularly after *Harald* had been compelled to submit
to baptism by *Otto I.*[2] (about 965).[3]   This was especially the
case in the islands, where the heathen were the more numerous.
At the head of the foes of Christianity appeared at first *Swen*,
heir to the throne; but after he had become king (991-1014),
and began to invade England, he tolerated and even favoured its
spread.   His son, *Knut the Great* († 1035) completed the work
by means of English priests.[4]

In *Norway*, Christianity had first been introduced from England, and was obliged, in the beginning, to encounter very severe
struggles, till *Olaf Trygvesen* (995-1000) undertook the conversion of his countrymen by force, which work was completed by
Olaf the Holy (1019-1033), in the same mode.[5] From Norway,
Christianity was carried, by Olaf Trygvesen's endeavours, to

---

1 Depping hist. des expeditions maritimes des Normands et de leur
établissement en France au dixième siècle.   Paris 1826, 2 voll. 8.

2 See Asmussen über die Kriegszüge der Ottone gegen Dänemark,
in Michelsen's and Asmussen's Archiv. f. Staats, u. Kirchengesh. v.
Schleswig, Holstein u. Lauenburg Bd. 1, (Altona 1833) S. 197.

3 Of what character Christianity had been up to this time in Denmark may be seen from the narration of Widukind the contemporary
monk of Corbey iii. 65 (Pertz v. 462) : Dani antiquitus erant Christiani,
sed nihilominus idolis ritu gentili servientes.   Contigit autem altercationem super cultura deorum fieri in quodam convivio Rege praesente,
Danis affirmantibus, Christum quidem esse deum, sed alios eo fore majores deos, quippe qui potiora mortalibus signa et prodigia per se ostenderent.   On the other hand, a cleric, Poppo, confessed the Christian
faith and stood the fire-proof for it (comp. on the transaction Giesebrecht's
Wendische Geschichten i. 197).   Ad haec rex·conversus, Christum deum
solum colendum decrevit, idola respuenda subjectis gentibus imperat,
Dei sacerdotibus et ministris honorem debitum deinde praestitit.   Otto
at that time erected the three bishoprics of Schleswig, Ripen and Aar-
hus in Jütland, and subordinated them to the Archbishop of Hamburg.
Adam. Brem. hist. eccl. lib. ii. c. 2, de situ Daniae. c. 1.

4 Annales Ecclesiae Danicae diplomatici zusammengetragen von
Erich Pontoppidan.   (Th. 1. bis Th. 4. Bd. 1. Copenh. 1741-1753, 4.)
Th. 1.   F. Münter's Kirchengeschichte v. Dänemark und Norwegen.
Th. 1, (Leipz. 1823, 8) S. 322 ff.

5 Chief authority is Snorro Sturleson's [† 1241] Heimskringla
(history of the Norwegian kings) translated into German by F. Wachter, Leipz. 1835, 36, 8), and in it especially Olaf. Trygvesens Saga u.
Saga af Olafi hin Helga.   Münter i. 429.

Iceland,[6] *the Faro and Shetland Isles,*[7] and even to *Greenland.*[8]

In Sweden, Christianity had increased its votaries in a more peaceful way, from the time of Anschar, though it was very often mingled with paganism. From the time of *Olaf SkautKonung* (baptized about 1008), the kings were Christians. King *Inge* at length forbade all worship of idols (1075), and obtained for Christianity complete victory in Sweden, after a severe contest with the rebellious heathen of his kingdom.[9]

All these countries belonged to the ecclesiastical province of the archbishopric *Hamburg-Bremen*, till, A. D. 1104, the archbishopric of *Lund* was founded, and the north subjected to it.[10]

§ 38.

CONVERSION OF THE MORAVIANS AND BOHEMIANS.

The conversion of the Slavonian nations dwelling to the east of Bavaria was looked upon as their official duty, both by the archbishop of Salzburg, to whom it had been entrusted by Charlemagne, and the bishop of Passau, who laid claim to the metropolitan rights of the ancient archbishopric of Lorch. But from the entire dissimilarity of language, Christianity could not attain to life in these lands; while the external condition of it always

Authorities are the Iceland-book of the priest Aredes Weisen [† 1148] c. 7 ss. translated in Dahlmann's Forschungen auf dem Gebiete der Geschichte. Bd. 1. (Altona 1822) S. 472 ff.; the Hungurvaka s. hist. primorum quinque Skalholtensium in Islandia Episcoporum (probably by Magnus, from 1215 bishop at Skalholt). Hafn. 1778, 8. (an extract in Schneider's Bibliothek d. Kirchengesch. i. 265; and the Kristni-Saga s. hist. religionis christ. in Islandiam introductae (of the 14th century). Hafn. 1773, 8. Fini Johannaei (Finnur Joensen, bishop of Iceland) hist. eccl. Islandiae, Hafn. 1772-75, 3 T. 4, (Comp. the Göttingen Geleh. Anz. A.D. 1777, S. 273 ff.) Münter i. 517.

[7] Münter i. 548.
[8] Münter i. 555.
[9] Claudii Oernhjalm historia Sueonum Gothorumque ecclesiasticae libb. iv. priores. Stockholm 1689, 4. Rühs Gesch. v. Schweden (also as the sixty-third part of the Allgem. Welthistorie Halle 1803). 2tes Buch.
[10] Münter ii. 76.

depended on the degree of German influence.[1]   Very different,
however, was the success of two Greek monks, *Constantine and
Methodius*,[2] who, after previous missionary labours in Chasaria

[1] Respecting Salzburg's endeavours, which were directed towards the
Slavonians dwelling south of the Raab-river, especially towards the state
of little Moravia Pannonia Savia (Slavonia, Croatia, and a part of Styria)
ruled since 830 by Priminna † 861, afterwards by Chozil under French
sovereignty, see de conversione Bojoariorum et Carentanorum, written
by a Salzburg priest, A.D. 873, (in Marquardi Freheri rer. Bohemica-
rum scriptt. p. 15 ; more complete, but from Aventin's copy, which is
not verbally accurate, in Oefelii scriptt. rer. Boic. i. 780.   First critical
edition in B. Kopitar Glagolita Clozianus, i. e. codicis glagolitici an-
tiquissimi λείψανον. Viennae 1836, fol. p. lxxii.)   The Salzburg archbishops from the time of Arno, maintained an Episc. regionarium for the
Slavonians, but Adelwin entirely took away this office (before 865) and
took the few churches under his own inspection.   Bishop Urolf of Passau even went so far as to appoint beforehand four suffragan bishops for
his portion, and had these confirmed by Eugenius II. about 824
(Eugen. ii. bulla in Goldast. comm. de regn. Bohem. juribus ed.
Schminck T. i. opp. p. 1, ap. Mansi T. xiv., and often with a commentary in Hageki, ann. Bohem. ed. Dobner ii. 486) : but his only object
in this was to have suffragans to keep up the appearance of being suc-
sessor to the old archbishop of Lorch.   We know nothing of the efforts
of the bishops of Passau to bring Christianity to Great Moravia, where
Rastislaw reigned till 870, and Swatopluk till 894.

[2] Sources : I. Latin : 1. vita Constant. cum translatione s. Clementis
(act. SS. Mart. ii. 19, composed perhaps by Guadericus bishop of Veli-
trae, a contemporary ib. p. 15, ap. Dobrowsky : the Italian legend).
2. Presbyteri Diocleatis [about 1161] regnum Slavorum c. 8 ss. (in Jo.
Lucii de regno Dalmat. et Croat. Amsteld. 1666. fol. p. 288 ss., in J.
G. Schwandtneri scriptt. rer. Hungar. iii. 479, and in Schlözer's Nestor
iii. 153).   3. Bohemian legends : a. vita s. Ludmillae (Dobner in the
Abhandl. d. böhm. Ges. d. Wiss. auf 1786, S. 417.   Dobrowsky krit.
Versuche i. 70).   b. Vita s. Ludmillae et s. Wenceslai auct. Christanno
de Scala mon. (partly in the act. SS. Sept. v. 354, and vii. 825.   The
extracts belonging here are also found Mart. ii. 24.   The author addresses the preface to Bishop Adalbert (about 985) and claims to be
great-grandson of Ludmilla.   Dobner ad Hageki ann. iv. 328).   According to Dobrowsky both legends, a. and b., belong to the first half of
the 14th century.   c. Vita ss. Cyrilli et Methodii.   (The first half is
borrowed from the Italian legend, the second from Christianity. ₁ According to Dobrowsky it was composed in the 14th century in Moravia,
hence called the Moravian legend, reprinted in act. SS. Mart. ii. 22. and
in Schlözer's Nestor iii. 154. best by Dobrowsky : Mähr. Legende von
Cyrill u. Method. Prag. 1826. 8.)   II. Greek.   Remarkable silence of
all Greek contemporaries.   Greek biography of Clement, archbishop of
Bulgaria, a disciple of Methodius, † 916 (fragment in Leon. Allatii in
R. Creyghtoni apparatum ad hist. conc. Florentini exercitationum i. 259,

and Bulgaria, came to great Moravia (862),[3] preaching in the language of the country, and bringing with them the holy Scriptures.[4] From a journey to Rome, where *Constantine* (Cyril) died, *Methodius* came back as bishop (868) to his Slavonians,[5] and

published entire by Ambros. Pampereus. Wien 1802. The author represents himself as a confidant of Clement, but Dobrowsky thinks he lived long after the eleventh century). III. Russian: 1. Nestor's annals cap. 10 (in Schlözer's extracts iii. 149, according to Dobrowsky inserted in the name of Nestor, in the 14th century). 2. Short Bulgarian legends, published by Kalajdowitsch (comp. Dobrowsky mähr. Legende S. 64 ff.) 3. Legends in the Russian menologium (ap. Schlözer iii. 233, late and of no value).—Works: Among the older uncritical collections is conspicuous J. G. Stredowsky sacra Moraviae hist. s. vita SS. Cyrilli et Methodii. Solisbaci 1710. 4.—Critical works: J. S. Assemani calendaria Ecclesiae univ. (Romae 1750-1755. T. vi. 4.) Tom. iii. Gelasii a s. Catharina [Gel. Dobner] Hageki annales Bohem. illustrati (Pragae 1761-1777. PP. v. 4.) Pars iii. Schlözer's commentary on Nestor's 10th chapter, l. c. Jos. Dobrowsky Cyrill u. Method., der Slaven Apostel, Prag 1823. 8. (Comp. Blumberger's review in the Wiener Jahrb. Bd. 26. 1824. S. 211 ff.) Dobrowsky mähr. Legende v. Cyrill und Method., Prag 1826. 8. (Comp. Blumberger's review in the Wiener Jahrb. Bd. 37. 1827. S. 41 ff.)

[3] Italian legend § 7 : audiens Rastilaus, Princeps Moraviae, quod factum fuerat a Philosopho in provincia Cazarorum : ipse quoque genti suae consulens ad praedictum Imperatorem (Michaelem) nuncios misit, nuncians hoc, quod populus suus ab idolorum quidem cultura recesserat, et christianam legem observare desiderabat ; verum doctorem talem non habent, qui ad logendum eos et ad perfectam legem ipsam edoceat : rogare se, ut talem hominem ad partes illas dirigat. Cujus precibus annuens Imperator eundem supernominatum Philosophum ad se venire rogavit : eumque illuc—simul cum Methodio germano transmisit.

[4] L. c. : Coeperunt itaque ad id quod venerant peragendum studiose insistere, et parvulos eorum literas edocere, officia ecclesiastica instruere, et ad corroptionem diversorum errorum, quos in populo illo repererant, falcem eloquiorum suorum inducere. Manserunt ergo in Moravia per annos quatuor et dimidium, et direxerunt populum illius in fide catholica, et scripta ibi reliquerunt omnia, quae ad Ecclesiae ministerium videbantur esse necessaria. Against Dobrowsky (Cyrill u. Method. S. 38. 52), according to whom Cyrill was the inventor of Slavonic writing, but that the Glagolitic alphabet was first invented in the 13th century for the Latin-Slavonian liturgy, it is asserted by Kopitar (Glagolita Clozianus p. x. lxxx. and in Chmel's österreich. Geschichtsforscher Bd. i. Heft 3. 1838), that Cyrill modelled the older Slavonic alphabet, which is substantially contained in the Glagoliza, after the Greek alphabet (Kiuriliza).

[5] According to the Italian legend they were invented by Nicolaus, but on their arrival found Hadrian II. in his place. Constantine delighted the Romans by producing the body of St Clement (who, accord-

began now, probably because great Moravia was distracted with wars,[6] to preach in the territory of the Moravian prince, *Chozil.* When every thing succeeded with him here also,[7] he became an object of hatred to the Salzburg clergy, and was accused at Rome as a heretic. By this means *Pope John VIII.* became suspicious of the use of the Slavonic language in public worship,[8] but

ing to a tradition first appearing in the Clementina epitome c. 166 ss., in Cotelerii Patr. apost. i. 799, is said to have been banished to the Pontic Chersonese under Trajan, and to have suffered martyrdom there), and they consecraverunt ipsum et Methodium in Episcopos, nec non et caeteros eorum discipulos in Presbyteros et Diaconos. Of the use of the Slavonic language in public worship we hear not a word as yet. The Bohemian legends first copy transactions under Hadrian similar to the later ones under John VIII. respecting the same object (see notes 8 and 9.) Constantine proclaimed himself the old opponent of Photius (comp. the story of Anastasius praef. ad syn. viii. ap. Mansi xvi. 6), besides at that time Constantinople appeared to bow beneath Rome, and there were Greek ambassadors with the pope. Why therefore mistrust the successfully working Greek ?

[6] Dobner ad Hageki annales P. iii. p. 118 ss.

[7] Anonym. de convers. Bojoar. et Carent.: As late as 865, Adelwin, archbishop of Salzburg, dedicated several churches in Chozil's dominions, and the Salzburg high-priest, Richbald, remained so long with Chozil, usque dum quidam Graecus, Methodius nomine, noviter inventis Slavinis literis, linguam Latinam doctrinamque Romanam atque literas auctorales Latinas philosophice superducens, vilescere fecit cuncto populo ex parte Missas et Evangelia, ecclesiasticumque officium illorum, qui hoc latine celebraverunt. Quod ille (Richbaldus) ferre non valens, sedem repetivit Juvaviensem. View of the papal see in Joh. viii. epist. ad Ludov. R. about 874 (in Sam. Timon imago ant. Hungariae lib. ii. c. 16): multis ac variis manifestisque prudentia tua poterit indiciis deprehendere, Pannonicam dioecesin ab olim apostolicae sedis privilegiis deputatam. ad Carolomann. (ibid.): reddito et restituto nobis Pannoniensium episcopatu, liceat praedicto fratri nostro Methodio, qui illic a sede apostolica ordinatus est, secundum priscam consuetudinem libere, quae sunt Episcopi, gerere. (Comp. the instructions given by John VIII. to the legate Paul, ap. Mansi xvii. 261 : Non enim solum intra Italiam ac caeteras Hesperiae provincias, verum etiam intra totius Illyrici fines consecrationes, ordinationes et dispositiones apostolica sedes antiquitus patrare consuevit, and therefore he even invited epist. 190 ad Salonitanos clericos this ecclesiastical province to unite itself again to Rome). This was probably in reference to the complaints of the Salzburg clergy.

[8] Johannis VIII. epist. 195. ad Method. Archiep. Pannoniensem A.D. 879 (Mansi xvii. 133): audivimus, quod non ea, quae s. Romana Ecclesia ab ipso Apostolorum principe didicit, et quotidie praedicat, tu docendo doceas, et ipsum populum in errorem mittas. Unde his apos-

Methodius justified himself at Rome, and obtained an express declaration from the pope in favour of the Slavonic worship (880).[9] In the meantime, however, *Swatopluk* had become still

tolatus nostri literis tibi jubemus, ut omni occasione postposita, ad nos de praesenti venire procures, ut ex ore tuo audiamus et cognoscamus, utrum sic teneas, et sic praedices, sicut verbis et literis te s. Romanae Ecclesiae credere promisisti, aut non ; ut veraciter cognoscamus doctrinam tuam. Audimus etiam, quod Missas cantes in barbara h. e. in Slavina lingua ; unde jam literis nostris per Paulum Ep. Anconitanum tibi directis prohibuimus, ne in ea lingua sacra Missarum solemnia celebrares ; sed vel in Latina, vel in Graeca lingua, sicut Ecclesia Dei toto terrarum orbe diffusa, et in omnibus gentibus dilatata cantat. Praedicare vero, aut sermonem in populo facere tibi licet, quoniam Psalmista omnes admonet Dominum gentes laudare (Ps. cxvii.), et Apostolus : " omnis," inquit, "lingua confiteatur, quia Dominus Jesus in gloria est Dei Patris" (Phil. ii. 11). In the same strain is the epist. 194. ad Tuventarum de Marauna contemporaneously issued (in the first syllable of Tuventarus the Slavonic princely title Zupan is unquestionably concealed, see Frähn's Ibn-Fotzlan über die Russen älterer Zeit. Petersb. 1823. 4. S. 167). But the most important point of suspicion against the Slavonians is clear from Joh. VIII. epist. 190. ad Salonitanos clericos :—si aliquid de parte Graecorum vel Slavorum super vestra ad nos reversione, vel consecratione, aut de pallii perceptione dubitatis etc.—At that time, therefore, Methodius was archbishop, and had other Episcopos regionarios under him (cf. epist. ad Tuvent.) So probably Gorasdos, see Dobrowsky Cyrill und Method. S. 121. Hence the later legend of the seven suffragans, see ibid. p. 105.

[9] Johannis VIII. epist. 247 ad 'Sfentopulcrum Comitem A. D. 880: Methodium venerabilem Archiepiscopum vestrum interrogavimus,—si orthodoxae fidei symbolum ita crederet,—sicut s. Romanam Ecclesiam tenere—constat.—Nos autem illum in omnibus ecclesiasticis doctrinis et utilitatibus orthodoxum et proficuum esse reperientes, vobis iterum ad regendam commissam sibi Ecclesiam Dei remisimus, quem veluti pastorem proprium ut digno honore et reverentia laetaque mente recipiatis jubemus.—ipsum quoque Presbyterum nomine Wichinum, quem nobis direxisti, electum Episcopum consecravimus s. Ecclesiae Nitrensis, quem suo Archiepiscopo in omnibus obedientem, sicuti ss. canones docent, esse jubemus. Presbyteros vero, Diaconos, s. cujuscunque ordinis clericos, sive Salvos, sive cujuslibet gentis, qui intra provinciae tuae fines consistunt, praecipimus esse subjectos et obedientes in omnibus jam dicto confratri nostro, Archiepiscopo vestro ut nihil praeter ejus conscientiam agant. Quodsi contumaces et inobedientes existentes, scandalum aliquod aut schisma facere praesumserint,—praecipimus esse procul abjiciendos secundum auctoritatem capitulorum, quae illi dedimus, et vobis direximus. Literas denique Slavonicas a Constantino quodam [quondam ?] philosopho repertas, quibus Deo laudes debite resonent, jure laudamus ; et in eadem lingua Christi Domini nostri praeconia et opera ut enarrentur, jubemus. Nequae enim tribus tantum, sed omnibus linguis Domi-

more estranged from Methodius; the German, *Wiching*, whom
he had appointed bishop of Neitra (880), ventured to be disobedient to his archbishop;[10] and after Methodius' death,[11] the
Greek-Slavonic clergy were even expelled from Moravia.[12] When
Swatopluk's son, *Moimar*, attempted to erect his kingdom into

num laudare auctoritate sacra monemur. (Reference to Ps. cxvii. Act.
ii. Phil. ii. 11. 1 Cor. xiv). Nec sanae fidei vel doctrinae aliquid obstat,
sive Missas in eadem Slavonica lingua canere, sive sacrum Evangelium,
vel lectiones divinas novi et veteris Testamenti bene translatas et inter-
pretatas legere, aut alia horarum officia omnia psallere: quoniam qui
fecit tres linguas principales, Hebraeam scilicet, Graecam et Latinam,
ipse creavit et alias omnes ad laudem et gloriam suam. Jubemus tamen,
ut in omnibus Ecclesiis terrae vestrae propter majorem honorificentiam
Evangelium latine legatur, et postmodum Slavonica lingua translatum
in auribus populi, latina verba non intelligentis, annuncietur: sicut in
quibusdam Ecclesiis fieri videtur. Et si tibi et judicibus tuis placet
Missas Latina lingua magis audire, praecipimus, ut latine Missarum tibi
solemnia celebrentur.

[10] Joh. VIII. ep. 268 ad Methodium Archiepisc. A.D. 881. Worthy
of note is the assurance, neque aliae literae nostrae (as those note 9.)
ad Sfentopulcrum ad eum directae sunt neque Episcopo illi palam vel
secreto aliud faciendum injunximus, et aliud a te peragendum decrevimus; quanto minus credendum est, ut sacramentum ab eodem Episcopo
exegerimus, quem saltem levi sermone super hoc negotio allocuti non
fuimus (Wiching, therefore, probably asserted that he had immediate
correspondence with the pope, and owed no obedience to Methodius).
Ideoque cesset ista dubietas etc. Caeterum et aliis tentationibus, quas
diverso modo perpessus es, noli tristari. Cum Deo duce reversus fueris,
quidquid enormiter adversum te est commissum, quidquid jam dictus
Episcopus contra suum ministerium in te exercuit,—legitimo fini trade-
mus, et illius pertinaciam judicii nostri sententia corripere non omitte-
mus. Blumberger's doubts of the authenticity of the letters of John
VIII. mentioned in notes 8-10. (see Wiener Jahrb. Bd. 26. S. 232, and
renewed in the same journal, vol. 37. p. 50 ff. against Dobrowsky mähr.
Legende p. 115 ff.), taken from the epistle of the German bishops
(note 13) lose their force when we consider that Method. was Archie-
piscop. regionarius.

[11] That letter (note 10) is the last we have with certainty concerning
Methodius. The older Latin legends say nothing of his death. Later
ones assume that he died in Rome, but fluctuate between the years 881
and 910. The Greek biographer of Clement states that he died in
Moravia, after he had been twenty-four years archbishop, consequently
in 892. Dobrowsky Cyrill u. Method. S. 115. 122 ff. According to
Palacky's Gesch. v. Böhmen i. 139. he died the 9th of April 885, and
was probably buried in the church of St Mary, at Welehrad, in Moravia.

[12] Biography of Clement see in Dobrowsky, Cyrill, and Method. S.
115 ff.

a separate diocese, with the pope's assistance, he was strongly opposed by the German bishops (900).[13] Soon after, however, Moravia was divided between Bohemia and Hungary (908), and the fate of Christianity now depended on the new rulers.

From Moravia Christianity was carried into *Bohemia*, where Duke Borziwoi (871?) is said to have been baptized by Methodius.[14] Yet neither the example of the holy *Ludmilla*, his spouse, nor the zeal of his grandson, saint *Wenzeslaus* (928-936), but the severe measures of *Boleslaus the pious* (967-999), were able to secure the triumphs of Christianity in Bohemia.[15]

[13] Comp. the two letters Hattonis Archiep. Mog. ejusque suffraganeorum, and Theotmari Archiep. Juvav. et suffrag. ad Johannem IX. A.D. 900 (ap. Goldast de regno Bohem. p. 5. Dobner iii. 343. Mansi xviii. 203). In the latter we read : Nequaquam credimus, quod coacti quotidie audimus, ut de illa s. et apostolica sede, quae nobis sacerdotalis mater est dignitatis, et origo christianae religionis, profluxerit quippiam perversitatis, sed doctrina et auctoritas ecclesiasticae rationis. Sed venerunt, ut ipsi promulgaverunt, de latere vestro tres Episcopi, videlicet Johannes Archiepiscopus, Benedictus et Daniel Episcopi, in terram Slavorum, qui Maravi dicuntur, quae Regibus nostris et populo nostro, nobis quoque cum habitatoribus suis subacta fuerat, tam in cultu christianae religionis, quam in tributo substantiae saecularis, quia exinde primum imbuti, et ex paganis Christiani sunt facti. Nunc vero, quod grave nobis videtur et incredibile, in augmentum injuriae jactitant se magnitudine pecuniae id egisse, qualia de illa apostolica sede nunquam audivimus exisse. Est enim unus Episcopatus [Pataviensis] in quinque divisus. Intrantes enim praedicti Episcopi in nomine vestro, ut ipsi dixerunt, ordinaverunt in uno eodemque episcopatu unum Archiepiscopum et tres suffraganeos ejus Episcopos. Antecessor vester, Zventibaldo duce imperante, Wichingum consecravit Episcopum, et nequaquam in illum antiquum Pataviensem opiscopatum eum transmissit, sed in quandam neophytam gentem, quam ipse dux domuit bello, et ex paganis Christianos esse patravit. Methodius and his assistants are not mentioned because they, as mere Episc. regionarii, did not endanger the rights of the German bishops.

[14] So first Cosmas Pragensis (about 1100) in chron, Bohemorum (libb. iii. best in Menckenii scriptt. rer. Germ. i. 1967. Cf. iii. 1771.) lib. i. then the Bohemian legends, note 2. Defended by Dobner (Abhandl. d. böhm. Gesellsch. d. Wissensch, auf 1786. S. 365 ff). Comp. Dowbrowsky krit. Versuche, i. Borziwoy's Taufe, Prag 1803. Same author's Cyrill und Method. S. 106. Also his mähr. Legende S. 114. F. Palacky's Gesch. v. Böhmen, Bd. i. (Prag 1836) S. 135. In the Koeniginhofer MS., a collection of old Bohemian songs, published by W. Hanka, put into German by W. A. Swoboda, Prag 1829, 8., several songs still belong to heathenism, and breathe hatred to Christianity. See particularly p. 73.

The strong attachment of all these nations to their Slavonic ritual, only made the German priests, now pressing in on every side, the more eager to suppress it. In *Bohemia*, John XIII., in founding the bishopric of Prague (973), made the use of the Latin ritual a condition.[16]   The Slavonic was only maintained here and there amid constant opposition, in addition to the Latin.[17]

[15] Dobner ad Hageki annal. P. iii. et iv.
[16] On the year of foundation see Giesebrecht's Jahrbücher unter Otto II. S. 123.   Joh. XIII. ep. ad Boleslaum A.D. 967 (in Cosmae chron. lib. i. in Dobneri annal. Hageki iv. 164) :—Unde apostolica auctoritate et s. Petri principis Apostolorum potestate—annuimus et collaudamus atque incanonizamus, quo ad Ecclesiam ss. Viti et Wenceslai Martyrum fiat sedes episcopalis.—Verumtamen non secundum ritus aut sectas Bulgariae gentis, vel Russiae, aut Slavonicae linguae ; sed, magis sequens instituta et decreta apostolica, unum potiorem totius Ecclesiae ad placitum eligas in hoc opus clericum, Latinis apprime literis eruditum etc.
[17] Comp. the narrative Cosmae chron. lib. i. appended to the cod. Dresdae by a monk of Sasawa (in Menckenii scriptt. rer. Germ. iii. 1782).   The convent Sasawa, founded by abbot Procopius about 1035, according to the Slavonic ritual, was already evil reported of to the Duke Spitignew (aures Principis favorabiliter compositis mendaciis obfuscantes, eos multifariis vituperiis publicabant, scilicet dicentes, per Slavonicas literas haeresis secta hypocrisique esse aperte irretitos ac omnino perversos ; quamobrem ejectis eis in loco eorum Latinae auctoritatis Abbatem et fratres constituere omnino esse honestum), who, therefore, 1058, introduced these Latin monks.   But Duke Wratislaw restored, 1063, the Slavonians, and applied to the pope for universal liberty to use the Slavonic ritual.   But Gregory VII., A. D. 1080, replied, (lib. vii. ep. 11, ad Vratisl, Bohem. Reg. ap. Mansi xx. 296) : Quia vero Nobilitas tua postulavit, quo secundum Slavonicam linguam apud vos divinum celebrari annueremus officium, scias nos huic petitioni tuae nequaquam posse favere.   Ex hoc nempe saepe volventibus liquet, non immerito sacram Scripturam omnipotenti Deo placuisse quibusdam locis esse occultam, ne si ad liquidum cunctis pateret, forte vilesceret et subjaceret despectui, aut prave intellecta a mediocribus, in errorem induceret.   Neque enim ad excusationem juvat, quod quidam religiosi viri hoc, quod simpliciter populus quaerit, patienter tulerunt, seu incorrectum dimiserunt ; cum primitiva Ecclesia multa dissimulaverit, quae a ss. Patribus, postmodum firmata christianitate, et religione crescente, subtili examinatione correcta sunt.   Unde ne id fiat, quod a vestris imprudenter exposcitur, auctoritate b. Petri inhibemus, teque ad honorem omnipotentis Dei huic vanae temeritati viribus totis resistere praecipimus.   The Slavonic monks in Sasawa were entirely expelled in 1097, et libri linguae eorum deleti omnino et disperditi, nequaquam ulterius in eodem loco recitabuntur.   Mon. Sazaviensis l. c. p. 1788.   Still, however, the Latin-Slavonian ritual was here and there retained after-

In the southern Slavonic countries, also, the Latins endeavoured to abolish it ;[18] but yet the *ritus slavo-latinus* has been continued in Illyria in many churches (the ritual books in the Glagolitic writing) down to the latest times.[19]

§ 39.

CONVERSION OF THE WENDS.

Sources: Widukindi [about 970] Corbej. res gestae Saxonicae, libb. iii. (ap.
Pertz v. 408). Thietmarus (see preface to section 2). Adamus Bremensis (see preface to § 37). Helmoldi [preacher at Bosow, † 1170] chronicon Slavorum ed. H. Bangert. Lübeck 1659. 4. and in Leibnit. script.

wards in Bohemia (Dobner Abhandl. d. böhmischen Gesellschaft der
Wiss. auf. 1786. S. 443) ; in the convent Emaus built by Charles IV.,
1347, in the suburbs of Prague, it is retained to this day.

[18] In the most southern part, the province of the metropolis Diaclea,
Alexander II. allowed it, probably on account of the nearness of the
Greek Church. Cf. Alex. ii. epist. iv. ad Petrum Dalmatiae et Slavon.
Archiepisc. A. D. 1062 (ap. Mansi xix. 943) : Monasteria quoque tam
Latinorum, quam Graecorum sive Slavorum cures : ut scias et haec omnia unam Ecclesiam esse. On the other hand, in the more western ecclesiastical province of Salona, it was to be extirpated. Cf. Thomae
Archidiac. Spalatens. († 1268) hist. Salonitanorum Episc. atque Spa-
latensium cap. 16. (ap. Lucius de regno Dalmat. p. 310 ss. and Schwandtneri scriptt. rer. Hung. iii. 552). Under Alexander II., the papal legate, Maynard, called a synod at Salona, where, among other things, it
was decreed : " ut nullus de caetero in lingua Slavonica praesumeret
divina mysteria celebrare, nisi tantum in Latina et Graeca, nec aliquis
ejusdem linguae promoveretur ad sacros ordines." Dicebant enim, Go-
thicas literas a quodam Methodio haeretico fuisse repertas, qui multa
contra catholicae fidei normam in eadem Slavonica lingua mentiendo
conscripsit : quamobrem divino judicio repentina dicitur morte fuisse
damnatus. (The Slavonians were at that time often called Goths. Comp.
Dobner in the Abhandl. d. böhm. Gesellsch. d. Wissensch. auf 1785, S.
109, and hence those enlightened fathers confound Methodius with Ul-
philas !!) Since now omnes sacerdotes Slavorum magno sunt moerore
confecti, omnes quippe eorum ecclesiae clausae fuerunt : the Slavonians
apply to Pope Alexander II. But their ambassadors receive the following reply : Scitote, filii, quia haec, quae petere Gothi student, saepenumero audisse me recolo, sed propter Arianos, inventores literaturae
hujusmodi, dare eis licentiam in sua lingua tractare divina, sicut praedecessores mei, sic et ego nullatenus audeo etc.

[19] Approved by Innocent IV. in 1248. See Dobnier in the Abhandl.
d. böhm. Gesellsch. d. Wissensch. auf. 1785. S. 174 s. Kopitar Glagolita Clozianus p. xiii. xvii.

Brunsv. li. 537.—L. Giesebrecht's wendische Geschichten aus den Jahren 780 bis 1182. 3 Bde. Berlin 1843. 8.

It was not to be expected that Christianity should meet with a friendly reception among the Wends, forced upon them as it was by German power, and in a foreign language. After *Henry I.* had conquered them, and erected the margraviates *Meissen*, *North Saxony* (Altmark), and *East Saxony* (Lausitz), about 931, *Otto I.* busied himself in the conversion of these people. The most enduring fruits of his efforts were among the *Sorbi* (in Meissen and Lausitz), where he founded the bishoprics *Meissen*, *Merseburg*, *Zeiz* (1029 transferred to *Naumburg*), and the arch-bishopric of *Magdeburg*, about 968.[1]

Otto had still earlier established among the *Wilzi* or *Lutizians* (between the Elbe and Oder), the bishoprics of *Havelberg* (946), and *Brandenburg* (949) ;[2] and among the *Obotrites* (in Meck-lenburg) the bishoprick of *Oldenburg* (952 not far from Lubeck, 1163 transferred to Lubeck) ;[3] but here the conversions did not

[1] Dönniges in Ranke's Jahrbüchern des deutschen Reichs i. iii. 137-222. Giesebrecht i. 192. The oldest history of these bishoprics relates much of endowments, but little of conversions. The religious state of the country may be illustrated by an anecdote of Boso, first bishop of Merseburg, one of the most zealous of their bishops. (Thietmar ii. 23, ap. Pertz v. 755) : Hic ut sibi commissos eo facilius instrueret, Slavonica scripserat verba, et eos Kirieleison cantare rogavit (see above, § 10. not. 37), exponens eis hujus utilitatem. Qui vecordes hoc in malum irrisorie mutabant Ukrivolsa, quod nostra lingua dicitur : Aeleri stat in frutecto (the Alder stands in the thicket); dicentes : sic locutus est Boso. Comp. chron. Episc. Merseburg (in J. P. a Ludewig reliquiae mss. omnis aevi diplomatum T. iv. p. 379) of bp. Werner from 1073-1101 : Quem tantus divini verbi seminandi fervor accenderat, ut studio praedicationis episcopalia plerumque negotia postponeret, et lucrandis animabus omni virtute quasi providus pastor intenderet. Verum quia Schlavonicae linguae admodum ignarus erat, et eum cura pastoralis Schlavorum genti, quorum multitudinem copiosam error adhuc idololatriae detinebat, verbum salutis credere cogebat ; libros Schlavonicae linguae sibi fieri jussit, ut Latinae linguae charactere idiomata linguae Schlavorum exprimeret, et quod non intelligeret, verbis stridentibus intelligendum aliis infunderet.

[2] Chr. W. Spieker's Kirchen- u. Reformationsgesch. der Mark Brandenburg Th. 1. (Berlin 1839) S. 17. Köpke in Ranke's Jahrb. d. deutschen Reichs i. ii. 64. 77. Giesebrecht i. 175. 176.

[3] Jul. Wiggers Kirchengesch. Mecklenburgs, Parchim und Ludwig-sluft 1840, S. 18.

reach farther than the Saxon garrisons extended their influence. The general insurrection of the Wends, under the prince of the Obotrites, *Mistui* or *Mistewoi* (983), was aimed alike at the German rulers and at Christianity.[4] Mistewoi's grandson, *Gottschalk*, founder of the great Wendian empire (1047), fell a victim to his efforts in favour of Christianity (1066) ;[5] and then all traces of it were effaced with wild rage for a long period.[6]

§ 40.

CONVERSION OF THE POLES AND HUNGARIANS.

In Poland, Christianity was propagated from the time of Duke *Mjesko*, or *Miecislav*, who had adopted it at the instance of his Bohemian spouse Dambrowka (966).[1] Among the *Prussians*,

[4] Helmold i. c. 14 ss. Kanngiesser's Gesh. v. Pommern i. 128. Giesebrecht i. 257. Wiggers S. 19.

[5] On Gottschalk's zeal Helmold i. c. 20: Sane magnae devotionis vir dicitur tanto religionis divinae exarsisse studio, ut sermonem exhortationis ad populum frequenter in Ecclesia ipse fecerit, ea scilicet, quae ab Episcopis vel Presbyteris mystice dicebantur, cupiens Slavicis verbis reddere planiora. Kanngiesser i. 233 ff. Giesebrecht ii. 85. Wiggers S. 22.

[6] Adam. Brem. iv. c. 11.—Helmold. i. c. 25: Slavi servitutis jugum armata manu submoverunt, tantaque animi obstinantia libertatem defendere nisi sunt, ut prius maluerint mori, quam christianitatis titulum resumere, aut tributa solvere Saxonum Principibus. Hanc sane contumeliam sibimet parturivit infelix Saxonum avaritia, qui—Slavorum gentes, quas bellis aut pactionibus subegerant, tantis vectigalium pensionibus gravaverunt, ut divinis legibus et Principum servituti refragari amara necessitate cogerentur (cap. 21 : Saxones—semper proniores sunt tributis augmentandis, quam animabus Domino conquirendis. Decor enim christianitatis, sacerdotum instantia, jamdudum in Slavia convaluisset, si Saxonum avaritia non praepedisset).

[1] Comp. Thietmar iv. 35, ap. Pertz v. 783, and the first Polish historian's Martini Galli (about 1130) chron. (ed. J. V. Bandtkie. Varsav. 1824. 8.) lib. i. c. 5. But when Martinus Gallus l. c. c. 11, and Vincentius Kadlubko (about 1200 bishop of Krakau, res gestae Principum et Regnm Poloniae per Vinc. Kadl. Varsav. 1824. 8. P. i. p. 92) make the two archbishoprics, Gresen and Krakau, with seven bishoprics, to be founded by Boleslaw, son of Mjesko ; and John Dlugossius (bishop of Lemberg, † 1480. Hist. Poloniae libb. xiii. ed. H. de Huyssen. Lips. 1711. fol. lib. ii. p. 91), even by Mjesko himself; it is more probable, according to Ditmar, that Posen had been the only Polish bishop-

on the contrary, nothing but martyrdom had yet been obtained.[2]

Among the *Hungarians*, the first and more important advances of Christianity began under their Duke *Geisa* (972-997)[3] *Stephen*, the first king (997-1038), rendered it victorious.[4]   These

ric for a long time.   Comp. Chr. G. v. Friese, Kirchengesh. des Königreichs Polen (2 Th. Breslau 1786. 8.) Th. 1.   Röpell's Gesch. Polens. Th. 1.   Hamburg 1840.   Giesebrecht's wend. Gesch. i. 196, 202. Epistola inedita Mathildis data 1027 ad Misegonem ii. s. vindiciae iv. primorum Poloniae latino-christinae Regum, auct. Ph. A. Dethier. Berol. 1842. 8.   Judicial laws for Christianity Thietmar viii. 2 : quicunque post septuagesimam carnem manducasse invenitur, abcisis dentibus graviter punitur.   Lex namque divina in his regionibus noviter exorta, potestate tali melius quam jejunio ab Episcopis instituto corroboratur. As the conversion of the Poles was achieved chiefly by Bohemian and Moravian priests, many peculiarities of the Greek-Slavonian ritual have also come to the Poles, and have long continued there.   Friese i. 61. Krasinski's Gesch. d. Reform. in Polen, übers. v. Lindau (Leipz. 1841.) S. 5.   Still, however, Poland connected itself immediately with Rome. As early as Miecislav's son, Boleslav, we find him complaining, about 1012, to the pope (Thietmar vi. 56), ut non liceret sibi propter latentes Regis (Henry II.) insidias promissum principi Apostolorum Petro persolvere censum.

   [2] Adalbert, bishop of Prague, murdered 997, cf. vita Adalberti in Canis. lectt. ant. ed. Basn. iii. i. 41, ap. Pertz vi. 574.   Voigt's Gesch. Preussens, i. 244, 650.   Palacky's Gesch. von Böhmen i. 233.   Bruno, slain 1009, see Thietmar vi. 58.   Voigt i. 281.   Giesebrecht ii. 19, 24.

   [3] The baptism of the Hungarian princes Bulosudes and Gylas (Vérbules and Gyula) in Constantinople A.D. 948 (Cedrenus p. 636. Zonaras lib. xvi. Tom. p. 194) was indecisive.   See Geschichte der Magyaren von Joh. Grafen Mailáth. Bd. 1.   (Wien 1828) S. 23, 32.   The spread of Christianity in Hungary under Geisa proceeded from Germany, favoured by the emperor Otto, promoted by Piligrin, bishop of Passau (see information to Benedict VII., A.D. 974, ap. Mansi. xix. 49. Since he considered himself as the successor of the old bishops of Lorch he asks here, that his metropolitan rights over Hungary might be restored), subsequently also by Adelbert, bishop of Prague, Mailath p. 31.   Theitmar viii. 3. ap. Pertz v. 862, respecting the Christianity of Geisa, whom he calls Deuuix : Hic Deo omnipotenti variisque Deorum illusionibus immolans, cum ab antistite suo ob hoc accusaretur, divitem se et ad haec facienda satis potentem affirmavit.   Comp. generally Gfrörer iii. iii. 1373.   Neander iv. 83.

   [4] The political character of this conversion shown in Schlosser's Weltgesch. ii. ii. 557.   Thietmar iv. 38, ap. Pertz v. 784 : Imperatoris autem (Ottonis iii.) gratia et hortatu gener Heinrici, ducis Bawariorum, Waic (i. e. Stephen) in regno suimet episcopales cathedras faciens, coronam et benedictionem accepit.   Bishop Chartvitius (about 1100) re-

violent conversions, however, still left in the people a very great inclination to Paganism.[5]

lates in his vita s. Stephani (in the act. SS. ad d. 2. Sept., and in Schwandtneri scriptt. rer. Hung. i. 417), that Stephen had sent Abbot Astricus to Rome A.D. 1001, to confirm the bishoprics already founded and to obtain for the Duke a regal crown. Just at that time a crown may have been ready for the Duke of the Poles, at Rome, but the Pope had received instruction by an angel to bestow it on the ambassador of an unknown people that appeared the next day. Thus, therefore, the Pope granted the wishes of the Hungarians, crucemque ante Regem, ceu apostolatus insigne, gestandum adjunxit, ego, inquiens, sum Apostolicus; at ille merito Christi Apostolus dici potest, cujus opera tantum populum sibi Christus acquisivit. Atque ea causa, quemadmodum divina gratia ipsum docebit, Ecclesias Dei, una cum populis, nostra vice ei ordinandas relinquimus. Accordingly, Stephen also says in the trust-deed of a convent, A.D. 1036 (in G. Fejér cod. diplom. Hungariae i. 328): sicut habui potestatem, ut ubicunque,vel in quocunque loco vellem, Ecclesias aut Monasteria construerem; ita nihilominus a Romanae sedis supremo Pontifice habui auctoritatem, ut quibus vellem Ecclesiis, seu Monasterriis libertates et dignitates conferrem. These rights over the church were always held fast by the Hungarian kings. See A. F. Kollar de originibus et usu perpetuo potestatis legislatoriae circa sacra apostolicorum Regum Hungariae. Vindob. 1764, 8, c. 24. The bull issued at that time, as is pretended, by Sylvester ii. (ap. Fejér i. 274) agrees for the most part word for word with Chartvitius, but adds besides, that Hungary was given over by Stephen to St Peter, and again received as fief. It is said to have been discovered again in 1550, but was first brought to light in the annal. ecclesiast. regni Hungar. Romae 1644, of the Jesuit Inchofer, to whom it was given by the Franciscan Raphael Levakovicz in Rome. From the latter's own letters it has been proved that he forged this bull, Kollár p. 157. Its authenticity, however, is defended by Gfrörer iii. iii. 1534.

[5] Reaction of paganism in the disturbances that followed Stephen's death. Schröckh Th. 21, S. 550. Schlosser Bd. 2, Th. 2, S. 578 ff. 665 ff.

SECOND PART.

HISTORY OF THE GREEK CHURCH.

FIRST CHAPTER.

RELATION OF THE GREEK CHURCH TO THE LATIN.

Partial, but useful as collections, are: Leo Allatius de Eccl. occid. et orient. perp. consensione, Colon. Agripp. 1648. 4. lib. ii. c. iv. ss. L. Maimbourg hist. du schisme des Grecs. Paris 1677. 4. and often reprinted.—Besides J. Gf. Hermann hist. concertationum de pane azymo et fermentato in coena Domini. Lips. 1737. 8. J. G. Walchii hist. controversiae Graecorum Latinorumque de processione Spiritus Sancti. Jenae 1751. 8. p. 32 ss.

§ 41.

CONTROVERSIES OF PHOTIUS WITH THE POPES.

Sources. Besides the acts cited in the notes below, the following works by contemporaries. By Greeks: Vita s. Ignatii by Nicetas David Paphlago (in the acts of the conc. viii. oecum. ap. Mansi xvi. 209), Metrophanis Ep. Smyrn. epist. ad Manuelem Patric. A. D. 870 (Latin translation by Baronius ann. 870 no. 45 ss.), Stiliani Mapae Ep. Neocaesar. epist. i. ad Stephanum P. v. A. D. 886 (ap. Mansi xvi. 425 ss., in an old Latin version xviii. 14.) By Latins: Anastasii bibl. praef. ad conc. viii. oec. (Mansi xvi. 1 ss.); ejesd. vit. cvii. Nicolai I. et cviii. Hadriani II., all unfair to Photius. Later historians: Theophanes continuatus (written at the instance of Constantine Porphyrogenn. about 940) lib. iv. de Michaele c. 30 ss. lib. v. de Basilio Mac. and Symeonis Magistri et Logothetae (about 967) annal. c. 28 ss. (Theophanes cont. Joannes Cameniata, Symeon Mag. Georgius Mon. ex recogn. i. Bekkeri. Bonnae 1838. 8.)—Cf. Mart. Hankii de Byzantinarum rerum scriptoribus liber. Lips. 1677. 4. p. 269 ss. Neander iv. 409. Gfrörer iii. i. 233.

The old jealousy between the hierarchs of *old and new Rome* broke forth afresh, when *Ignatius*, patriarch of Constantinople, was deposed at the instigation of Caesar *Bardas* by the Emperor *Michael III.*, and *Photius* appointed in his place (858). When an ecclesiastical schism took place on this account in Constantinople, and Pope *Nicolaus* was invited to adjust it,[1] instead of acting as mediator he immediately assumed the character of supreme judge.[2] The legates whom he sent to Constantinople

[1] The letter of the Emperor Michael is lost. Nicolaus relates (ep. i. ad univ. Cathol. ap. Mansi xv. 160): Imp. Michael—ad apostolatum nostrum legatis cum epistolis destinatis, accusationes quasdam adversus Ignatium deferentibus, petiit, ut a sede apostolica missos daremus, qui scandala illa sedarent et schismata dissiparent. In the same words ep. ix. ad Michael. Imp. p. 218 and ep. x. ad cler. Constant. p. 241.—Photius's writings (ap. Baron. ann. 859 no. 61 ss.) is a usual Enthronistica.

[2] Nic. ep. ii. ad Michael. Imp. and ep. iii. ad Photium. In the first, reproaches that Ignatius was deposed, without the knowledge of the pope, for a patribus et deliberatum ac observatum existit, qualiter absque Romanae sedis, Romanique Pontificis consensu, nullius insurgentis deliberationis terminus daretur. Then, that Photius a layman, should have been made bishop. So also ad Photium p. 168: Sed rectum vos ordinem minime continuisse dolemus, eo quod non per gradus Ecclesiae ductus ad tantum honorem de laici habitu vos prosiluistis.—Nam Sardicense concilium per omnia tantae temeritatis praesumtionem vetuit, pariter et ss. Pontificum Romanae sedis, Caelestini,—Leonis.—seu Gelasii doctrina.—Quapropter vestrae consecrationi consentire modo non possumus, donec nostri, qui a nobis Constantinopolim sunt directi, revertantur, qualiter per eos cognoscamus vestrae observationis actus, et ecclesiasticae utilitatis constantiam etc. Photius's reply (ap. Baron. ann. 861 no. 34 ss.) :—At canones, inquiunt, violati sunt, quod ad pontificatus fastigium e laicorum ordine adscendisti.—Quales autem canones hi, quorum asseritur praevaricatio ? quos ad hunc diem Constantinopolitanorum Ecclesia non accepit.—Multi canones aliis traditi sunt, aliis ne noti quidem sunt. Qui accipit et violat, dignus, qui in judicium inducatur: qui vero non novit, nec recipit, quomodo obnoxius est ?—Legitimis nuptiis Presbyter Romae uxori conjunctus non invenitur: nos vero eos, qui unico conjugio vitae suae moderati, sunt, edocti sumus in Presbyteri gradum efferre, eosque, qui hoc in discrimine ponunt, ac se secernunt, ne ab his Domini corporis participationem capiant, undique excludimus, eodem loco ducentes eos, qui legem aut fornicationis sanciunt aut nuptiarum tollunt.—Quaedam vero ne ab iis quidem, qui delinquunt (quod quidem sciam), quod fiunt, laudantur ob summam fortasse absurditatem.—Quis enim sabbatissare, qui in Christianis censeatur, etiam si millies his succumbat, non ejuret ? Quis se conjugium execrari legitimum, nisi quis impiorum ac sine Deo hominum sententiam opifici proponat ?— Quis autem dominicorum, et paternorum, et synodalium decretorum (ne sigillatim dicam) non revereatur confiteri, se moliri contemtum ?—testes apud nos et regulis nostris ad tres nume-

were indeed won over to declare for Photius (861) ;[3] but he annulled what was there transacted at *a synod in Rome* (863), and decided in favour of Ignatius.[4] Michael's threatening replies[5] could not of course terrify the pope, who had long been independent of Byzantine power.[6]

ramus, qui si caeteroqui vitio careant, satis sunt ad fidem veritati faciendam quamvis in Episcopi crimen adsciscantur: apud alios vero nisi testium numerus superet septuaginta quasi populum, qui accusatur, quantumvis in re ipsa fuerit deprehensus, omni crimine liber absolvitur. As there is a reference in this passage to a Roman regulation developed in the ninth century, and adopted also by Pseudo-Isidore (see § 20. note 5), so we must not overlook generally the bitter irony of this letter against Roman ecclesiastical customs, in order that a right view of Nicolaus' conduct and Photius' Encyclica may be obtained. Hear, however, the conclusion : Canonum custodia a quovis bono debetur : magis vero ab iis, divinae providentiae dignatione alios regunt : omnium sane maxime, quibus in horum numero primatus obtigit.—Quare vestra debet amabilis beatitudo, ecclesiasticam disciplinam ac modestiam in omnibus curae habens, et canonicam tenens rectitudinem, eos qui sine commendatitiis literis ad Romanam Ecclesiam hinc proficiscuntur (followers of Ignatius, namely), non temere ac fortuito recipere, nec sinere hospitalitatis specie odii fraterni jaci semina etc.

[3] Concerning the syn. Const. A. D. 861 see Nicol. ep. ix. ad Michael. Imp. (Mansi xv. 219), ep. x. ad clerum Const. (ib. p. 241), Nicetas David (Mansi xvi. 237), when the παριστάνουσιν ἑβδομήκοντα καὶ δύο ψευδομάρτυρας (comp. Photius not. 2) is worthy of notice.

[4] Acta syn. Rom. ann. 863 in Nicol. epist. vii. ad Michael.

[5] Michael's letter is lost, but its contents may be gathered from Nicolaus' answer. Nic. ep. viii. (Mansi xv. 189) : Dixistis, quod nullus antecessorum nostrorum a sexta synodo meruerit a vobis, quod nos meruisse dignoscimur:—quasi nostrum fuerit opprobrium, eo quod sedem apostolicam in nullo quaerere antecessores vestri dignati fuerint, cum magis eorum fuerit dedecus.—p. 192 : dicitis, non ideo ad nos misisse vos, ut secundum judicium Ignatius sustineret, p. 206 : noluisse vos, ut a missis nostris Ignatius judicaretur, eo quod fuerit jam judicatus et condemnatus, p. 203 : non eguisse vos in causa pietatis Romanae Ecclesiae. —p. 204 : si vestra fuerunt verba, quae in despectum b. Petri Apostolorum principis immo Dei, cujus ordinationi resistitis, scripta, et quasi detrahentia privilegiis hujus sacratissimae Ecclesiae missa sunt etc.— Ep. ix. p. 235 : epistola sub nomine vestro conscripta—tantis erat verbis contumeliosis, immo blasphemiis, respersa, ut scriptor ejus non nisi in gutture colubri calamum tinxisse putetur, et dictatoris labia pro dictionibus venena fudisse videantur.

[6] Nicol. ep. vii. et ix. ad Michael. Ep. x. ad clerum Constant. Ep. xi. ad Photium. Ep. xii. ad Bardam Caes. Ep. xiii. ad Ignatium. Ep. xiv. ad Theodorum Augustam. Ep. xv. ad Eudoxiam Aug. Ep. xvi. ad senatores Constant. All containing copious proofs of the privi-

These controversies were followed by a new one concerning church jurisdiction,[7] which embittered men's spirits to a much

legia Eccl. Rom. (but without mention of the Pseudoisidoriana, which yet he was at the same time defending against the Frank bisbops. See § 20, not. 15). For instance, that the judgment against Ignatius was null, because no one (Epist. viii. p. 200), qui minoris auctoritatis est, eum, qui majoris potestatis est, judiciis suis addicere potest. Hence aut nunquam omnino aut certe vix Constantinopolitanorum praesulum aliquis sine consensu Romani Pontificis reperitur ejectus. Remarkable that he even cites in his own favour the long rejected (at Rome) can. Chalced. ix. (Vol. i. Div. 2, § 93, not. 15), (ep. viii. p. 201): nunc Chalcedonensis concilii sanctiones ad memoriam reducamus, quae ita decernunt: " Si clericus habet causam adversus Episcopum proprium, vel adversus alterum, apud synodum provinciae judicetur: quod si adversus ejusdem provinciae metropolitanum Episcopus vel clericus habet querelam, petat primatem dioceseos, aut sedem regiae urbis Constantinopolitanae." Cum dixisset: " petat primatem dioeceseos," praeceptum posuit eadem s. synodus, regulamque constituit. Cum vero disjunctiva conjunctione addidisset: " aut sedem regiae urbis Constant." liquet profecto, quia hoc secundum permissionem indulsit. Quem autem primatem dioeceseos s. synodus dixerit, praeter Apostoli primi vicarium, nullus penitus intelligitur. Ipse est enim primas, qui et primus habetur et summus. Ne vero moveat, quia singulari numero dioeceseos dictum est, quia tantumdem valet dixisse primatem dioeceseos, quantum si perhibuisset dioeceseon etc. (! !) Ep. ix. p. 236 [of 866] he threatens: scitote, quoniam, postquam in hac vos pertinacia persistere fine tenus velle compererimus, primum quidem congregatis cunctarum occidentalium regionum ven. sacerdotibus dictatores et dispositores atque praeceptores tantae fallaciae etc.—diris anathematis vinculis innodabimus. Deinde vero—ipsam epistolam in stipite videntibus cunctis suspensam vasto supposito foco ad vituperium vestrum coram omnibus nationibus, quae penes memoriam s. Petri multiplices inveniuntur, extremae perditioni donabimus etc. Concerning these controversies see Nicolaus' own account in ep. lxx. ad Hincmarum et caeteros Episc. in regno Caroli constitutos A. D. 867, where he also mentions the view of the Greeks (Mansi xv. 358): gloriantur atque perhibent, quando de Romana urbe Imperatores Constantinopolim sunt translati, tunc et primatum Romanae sedis ad Constantinopolitanam Ecclesiam transmigrasse, et cum dignitatibus regiis etiam Ecclesiae Romanae privilegia translata fuisse. Quite analogous to the principles of the older Greek Church. See vol. i. Div. 2, § 93, not. 3. and 14.

[7] Even at the very beginning Nicolaus had referred to the subject, ep. ii. ad Mich. Imper. (Mansi xv. 167): Oportet vestrum imperiale decus,—ut antiquum morem, quem nostra Ecclesia habuit, vestris temporibus restaurare dignemini, quatenus vicem, quam nostra sedes per Episcopos vestris in partibus constitutos habuit, videlicet Thessalonicensem, qui Romanae sedis vicem habuit per Epirum veterem, Epirumque novam, atque Illyricum, Macedoniam, Thessaliam, Achaiam, Daciam

2 G 2

greater degree. The Byzantines had succeeded, after many vain attempts, in persuading *Bogoris*, king of the Bulgarians (about 861), to be baptised.[8] But immediately after, in order not to lose his independence by the influence of the too neighbouring Greeks, he sought to attach himself to the Western Church, and received forthwith from Rome (866) Latin teachers.[9] Enraged at this, *Photius* summoned a *synod at Constantinople* (867), by an *Encyclica*,[10] violent, and in the highest degree offensive to the

ripensem, Daciamque mediterraneam, Moesiam, Dardaniam, Praevalim, b. Petro Apostolorum principi contradicere nullus praesumat. Praeterea Calabritanum patrimonium et Siculum—vestris concessionibus reddantur. Inter ista et superius dicta volumus, ut consecratio Syracusano Archiepiscopo nostra a sede impendatur (comp. above, § 5, not. 3).

[8] On the preliminary steps by the sister of Bogoris and the picture of Methodius, see Theophanes continuatus iv. c. 13-15. The actual conversion is placed by a contemporary, Nicetas David (ap. Mansi xvi. 245), in the time when Nicolaus' legates return to Rome: Βούλγαροι δὲ τότε προνοίαις Θεοῦ, βιαίῳ κατακαέντες λιμῷ, ἅμα δὲ καὶ τοῖς δώροις τοῦ Αὐτοκράτορος θελχθέντες τὰ ὅπλα καταθέμενοι τῷ ἁγίῳ προσῄεσαν βαπτίσματι. On the contrary, it is said by Simeon Mag. c. 25 (followed by Leo Gramm. A. D. 1013, ed. Paris. p. 462), Michael undertook an expedition with Bardas against the Bulgarians, in the fourth year of his reign. τοῦτο μαθόντες οἱ Βούλγαροι, ἅμα δὲ καὶ λιμῷ τηκόμενοι—Χριστιανοὶ γενέσθαι τῷ Βασιλεῖ Ῥωμαίων ᾐτήσαντο. ὁ δὲ Βασιλεὺς τούτους ἐν τῇ πόλει ἀγαγὼν, ἐβάπτισε πάντας, καὶ τὸν Ἄρχοντα αὐτῶν Μιχαὴλ ἐπωνόμασεν. So too Photius in his epist. ad Michaelem Bulgarorum Regem (in Photii epist. ed. Rich. Montacutius. Londini 1651. fol. epist. i. also in H. Canisii lection. ant. ed. Basnage ii. ii. 379) calls the king καλὸν ἄγαλμα τῶν ἐμῶν πόνων (ap. Basn. p. 384) and τῶν ἐμῶν πνευματικῶν ὠδίνων εὐγενὲς καὶ γνήσιον γέννημα (p. 418). Comp. Schlosser's Weltgesch. ii. i. 519.

[9] Anastasius in vita cvii. Nicolai I. in praef. ad conc. oecum. viii. (Mansi xvi. 10), annales Bertiniani and Fuldenses ad ann. 866. At the same time Bogoris sent by his ambassadors a series of questions on ecclesiastical subjects to be laid before the pope, which called forth the responsa Nicolai P. i. ad consulta Bulgarorum (ap. Mansi xv. 401.)

[10] Encyclica ad Patriarch. orientales (Latin ap. Baronius ann. 863, no. 34 ss., more fully in Greek in edit. Montacutii ep. ii. p. 47 ss.) respecting the Latin teachers that had come among the Bulgarians : Οὕπω γὰρ ἐκείνου τοῦ ἔθνους, οὐδ' εἰς δύο ἐνιαυτοὺς, τὴν ὀρθὴν τῶν Χριστιανῶν τιμῶντος θρησκείαν, ἄνδρες δυσσεβεῖς καὶ ἀποτρόπαιοι,—ἄνδρες ἐκ σκότους ἀναδύντες (τῆς γὰρ ἑσπερίου μοίρας ὑπῆρχον γεννήματα), οἴμοι πῶς τὸ ὑπόλοιπον ἐκδιηγήσομαι; οὗτοι, πρὸς τὸ νεοπαγὲς εἰς εὐσέβειαν καὶ νεοσύστατον ἔθνος, ὥσπερ κεραυνὸς, ἢ σεισμὸς, ἢ χαλάζης πλῆθος, μᾶλλον δὲ οἰκειότερον εἰπεῖν, ὥσπερ ἄγριος μονιὸς (according to the lxx. Ps. lxxx. 13), ἐμπηδήσαντες, τὸν ἀμπελῶνα Κυρίου, τὸν ἠγαπημένον καὶ νεόφυτον καὶ ποσὶν καὶ ὀδοῦσιν, ἤτοι τρίβοις αἰσχρᾶς πολιτείας, καὶ διαφθορᾷ δογμάτων—κατανεμησάμενοι ἐλυμήναντο· ἀπὸ γὰρ τῶν ὀρθῶν καὶ καθαρῶν δογμάτων, καὶ τῆς τῶν Χριστιανῶν ἀμω-

Romish Church, and there pronounced sentence of condemnation
on the pope.[11] The Encyclica was answered in the West with
the same bitterness;[12] and from that time forward an insurmount-
able wall of separation remained between the two churches.

μήτου πίστεως παραφθείρειν τούτους, καὶ ὑποσπᾶν κατεπανουργήσαντο. Καὶ
πρῶτον μὲν αὐτοὺς ἐκθέσμως εἰς τὴν τῶν Σαββάτων νηστείαν μετέστησαν (see
vol. i. Div. 2. § 100. not. 4.) Οἶδε δὲ καὶ ἡ μικρὰ τῶν παραδοθέντων ἀθέτησις
καὶ πρὸς ὅλην τοῦ δόγματος ἐπιτρέψαι καταφρόνησιν. Ἔπειτα δὲ τὴν τῶν νηστειῶν πρώτην ἑβδομάδα τῆς ἄλλης νηστείας περικόψαντες, εἰς γαλακτοποσίας καὶ
τυροῦ τροφὴν, καὶ τὴν τῶν ὁμοίων ἀδδηφαγίαν καθείλκυσαν (see vol. i. Div. 2.
§ 100. not. 14.) Ἐντεῦθεν αὐτοῖς τὴν ὁδὸν τῶν παραβάσεων ἐμπλατύνοντες,
καὶ τῆς εὐθείας τρίβου καὶ βασιλικῆς διαστρέφοντες, καὶ δὲ καὶ τοὺς ἐνθέσμῳ
γάμῳ Πρεσβυτέρους διαπρέποντας οἱ πολλὰς κόρας χωρὶς ἀνδρὸς γυναῖκας δεικνύ-
οντες, καὶ γυναῖκας παῖδας ἐκτρέφουσας, ὧν οὐκ ἔστι πατέρα θεάσασθαι, οὗτοι
τοὺς ὡς ἀληθῶς Θεοῦ ἱερεῖς μυσάττεσθαί τε καὶ ἀποστρέφεσθαι παρεσκεύασαν,
τῆς Μανοῦ γεωργίας ἐν αὐτοῖς τὰ σπέρματα κατασπείροντες, καὶ ψυχὰς ἄρτι
βλαστάνειν ἀρξαμένας τὸν σπόρον τῆς εὐσεβείας τῇ τῶν ζιζανίων ἐπισπορᾷ λυμαινόμενοι. Ἀλλά γε δὴ καὶ τοὺς ὑπὸ Πρεσβυτέρων μύθῳ χρισθέντας ἀναμυρίζειν
αὐτοὶ οὐ πεφρίκασιν, Ἐπισκόπους ἑαυτοὺς ἀναγορεύοντες, καὶ τὸ τῶν Πρεσβυτέρων χρίσμα ἄχρηστον εἶναι, καὶ εἰς μάτην ἐπιτελεῖσθαι τερατευόμενοι.—Ἀλλὰ
γὰρ οὐχὶ μόνον εἰς ταῦτα παρανομεῖν ἐξηνέχθησαν, ἀλλὰ καὶ, εἴ τις κακῶν ἐστι
κορωνὶς, εἰς ταύτην ἀνέδραμον. Πρὸς γάρ τοι τοῖς εἰρημένοις ἀτοπήμασι καὶ τὸ
ἱερὸν καὶ ἅγιον σύμβολον, ὃ πᾶσι τοῖς συνοδικοῖς καὶ οἰκουμενικοῖς ψηφίσμασιν
ἄμαχον ἔχει τὴν ἰσχὺν, νόθοις λογισμοῖς, καὶ παρεγγράπτοις λόγοις, καὶ θράσους
ὑπερβολῇ κιβδηλεύειν ἐπεχείρησαν· ὢ τῶν τοῦ πονηροῦ μηχανημάτων, τὸ Πνεῦμα
τὸ ἅγιον οὐκ ἐκ τοῦ Πατρὸς μόνον, ἀλλά γε καὶ ἐκ τοῦ Υἱοῦ ἐκπορεύεσθαι καινο-
λογήσαντες!—Καὶ γὰρ δὴ καὶ ἀπὸ τῶν τῆς Ἰταλίας μερῶν συνοδικί τις ἐπιστολὴ
πρὸς ἡμᾶς ἀναπεφοίτηκεν, ἀρρήτων ἐγκλημάτων γέμουσα, ἅτινα κατὰ τοῦ οἰκείου
αὐτῶν Ἐπισκόπου οἱ τὴν Ἰταλίαν οἰκοῦντες μετὰ πολλῆς κατακρίσεως καὶ ὅρκων
μυρίων διεπέμψαντο, μὴ παριδεῖν αὐτοὺς οὕτως οἰκτρῶς ὀλλυμένους, καὶ ὑπὸ
τηλικαύτης βαρείας πιεζομένους τυραννίδος, καὶ τοὺς ἱερατικοὺς νόμους ὑβριζο-
μένους, καὶ πάντας θεσμοὺς Ἐκκλησίας ἀνατρεπομένους. Ἃ καὶ πάλαι μὲν
διὰ μοναχῶν καὶ πρεσβυτέρων ἐκεῖθεν ἀναδραμόντων εἰς πάντων ἀκοὰς διε-
φέροντο. Βασίλειος δ'ἆρα ἦν, καὶ Ζωσιμᾶς, Μητροφάνης τε, καὶ σὺν αὐτοῖς
ἕτεροι, οἱ τὴν τοιαύτην τυραννίδα ἀπωδύροντο, καὶ πρὸς ἐκδίκησιν τῶν Ἐκκλησιῶν
ἐξεκαλοῦντο δακρύοντες. Νῦν δὲ—καὶ γράμματα διάφορα καὶ ἐκ διαφόρων
ἐκεῖθεν ἀναπεφοίτηκεν,—ὧν τὰ ἴσα κατὰ τὴν ἐκείνων ἀξίωσίν τε καὶ ἐξαίτησιν
(καὶ γὰρ εἰς πάντας τοὺς ἀρχιερατικοὺς καὶ ἀποστολικοὺς θρόνους διαδοθῆναι
ταῦτα μετὰ φρικτῶν ὅρκων καὶ παρακλήσεων ἐδυσώπησαν) ὡς αὐτὰ ἐκεῖνα παρα-
στήσει ἀναγινωσκόμενα.

[11] Comp. Metrophanis epist. ad Manuelem and Anastassi praef. ad
conc. oecum. viii.

[12] The emperors Michael and Basil issued a letter to the king of the
Bulgarians, of like contents as the Encyclica. Bogoris communicated
this to the pope, and Nicolaus gives reply. lxx. ad Hincmar. et caeteros
Episc. in regno Caroli constitutos A. D. 867 (ap. Mansi xv. 355), from
it an extract, and admonishes the Frank bishops, who were always held
to be the most learned, to defend the Roman Church. In his list of

But no sooner had *Basil the Macedonian* ascended the throne, than Photius was compelled to yield to Ignatius (867), and the pope was invited to give a new decision.[13] Photius was condemned at a *synod* held *in Rome* (868),[14] and afterwards in *Constantinople* (oecumen. viii. 869).[15] But as Ignatius, in conse-

Greek objections still appear the following : Mentiuntur quoque, nos, sicuti per alia ipsorum conscripta indicatur, agnum in Pascha, more Judaeorum, super altare pariter cum dominico corpore benedicere et offerre. (That this was substantially true, see Walafridi Strab. lib. de rebus eccl. c. 18 : Illum dico errorem, quo quidam agni carnes in Pascha, juxta vel sub altari eas ponentes, benedictione propria consecrabant, et in ipsa resurrectionis die ante caeteros corporales cibos de ipsis carnibus praecipiebant. Cujus benedictionis series adhuc a multis habetur. The Benediction formula see in the ordo Romanus ap. Hittorp de divinis officiis p. 79. So also a lamb was solemnly eaten by the pope and eleven cardinals. See ordo Romanus auct. Benedicto in Mabillon museum Ital. p. 142, and ordo Rom. auct. Cencio, ibid. p. 186 f.) Quin et reprehendere satagunt, quia penes nos clerici barbas radere suas non abnuunt, et quia Diaconus non suscepto presbyteratus officio apud nos Episcopus ordinatur. (Certainly this took place, and was probably not abolished till these objections were adduced. See Mabillon comm. in ord. Rom. in the museum Ital. T. ii. p. cxix. ss.) Hincmar required Odo, bishop of Beauvais, to defend the Latin Church (ep. ad Odon. Belvac., opp. ed. Sirmond. ii. 809). He also furnished a work (Flodoardi hist. Eccl. Rhem. iii. c. 23), which has been lost. Probably, too, a lost work of Ado, archbp. of Vienne, was directed against the Greeks (hist. lit. de la France v. 473). There are still extant Ratramni Corbej. mon. contra Graecorum opposita libb. iv. (in d'Achery spicileg. i. 63), and Æneae Episc. Parisiensis liber adv. Graecos (ibid. p. 113). Recently Angelo Majus has published two anonymus writings belonging to this time, de Spir. S. processione a Patre Filioque in the scriptt. vett. nova coll. vii. i. 245. The Greeks appealed in favour of their view of this doctrine to Joh. xv. 26, the Latins to Joh. xx. 22; Act. ii. 33, xvi. 7; Gal. iv. 6; Phil. i. 19.

[13] Basillii Imp. epist. ad Nicolaum P. in the Acts of the eighth oecumenical synod actio iii. (ap. Mansi xvi. 46, 324).

[14] The acts of this synod in Anastasius in vita Hadriani ii. and in the Acts of the eighth oecumenical synod actio vii. (ap. Mansi xvi. 122 ss. and 371 ss.)

[15] The acts in a Latin translation by Anastasius bibl. (Mansi xvi. 1), and in a shorter Greek collection (prim. ed. Matth. Raderus. Ingolst. 1604. 4. ap. Mansi xvi. 209). The predominance of Rome was so evident here, that soon after a complaint was made by some Greek bishops to the emperor and the patriarch, non bene factum fuisse, quod Ecclesiam Constantinopolitanam tanta subjectione Romanae subdi Ecclesiae permiserint, ita ut hanc ei tamquam dominae ancillam tradiderint, whereon some of the acts are said to have been privately stolen from the papal legate, Anastasii annotatio ad act i. (Mansi xvi. 29). Thus the

quence of the decision of the other patriarchs, and favoured by Greek influence over Bulgaria resuscitated by Basil, again took ecclesiastical possession of this country,[16] the controversy between Rome and Constantinople still continued.[17]

Greek collection certainly appears to have proceeded from a new revision. The difference is most striking in the cann. which are firmly established act x., and of which 27·are found in Anastasius l. c. p. 160 ss. ; in the Greek collection, ibid. p. 397 ss., only 14. Almost all are directed against Photius. So, for instance, can. lat. xi. graec. x. the opinion is condemned, δύο ψυχὰς ἔχειν τὸν ἄνθρωπον (comp. vol. i. div. 2, § 83, not. 30, at the end), because it is supposed to have been held by Photius, cf. Anastasii praef. ad conc. p. 6 (which Schroeckh overlooks). Two canons extant in the Latin acts only, are remarkable for their evident attempt to modify the Pseudoisidorian principles to suit the East : can. xvii : Patriarchae—Metropolitanorum—habeant potestatem, videlicet ad convocandum eos, urgente necessitate, ad synodalem conventum, vel etiam ad coercendum illos et corrigendum etc. Consueverunt autem Metropolitani bis in anno synodos facere, ideoque, sicut dicunt, ad patriarchale penitus non posse concurrere caput. Sed sancta haec et universalis synodus, nec concilia quae a Metropolitanis fiunt interdicens, multo magis illa novit rationabiliora esse ac utiliora Metropolitanorum conciliis, quae a patriarchali sede congregantur; et idcirco haec fieri exigit etc. Can. xxvi. :—nullo modo quisquam Metropolitanorum vel Episcoporum a vicinis Metropolitis vel Episcopis provinciae suae judicetur, licet quaedam incurrisse crimina perhibeatur, sed a solo Patriarcha proprio judicetur. But in both collections is found the regulation (can. grace. xiii. lat. xxi) : si Synodus universalis fuerit congregata, et facta fuerit etiam de sancta Romanorum Ecclesia quaevis ambiguitas et controversia, oportet venerabiliter et cum convenienti reverentia de proposita quaestione sciscitari, et solutionem accipere,—non tamen audacter sententiam dicere contra summos senioris Romae Pontifices. It has been already remarked (§ 1, not. 28), that decrees were passed, at this council, against the enemies of image-worship, who began to be more active, cf. can. iii. and vii. Remarkable continues to be always the observation of the Continuator Aimoini hist. Francorum lib. v. (in Duchesne scriptt. rer. Franc. T. iii.) respecting this synod : In qua synodo de imaginibus adorandis aliter, quam orthodoxi doctores ante definierant, statuerunt ; quaedam etiam pro favore Romani Pontificis, qui eorum votis de imaginibus adorandis annuit, et quaedam contra antiquos canones, et contra ipsam synodum constituerunt, sicut qui eamdem synodum legerit, patenter inveniet. Cf. Richerii hist. concill. generall. i. 717, 740.

[16] Anastasius in vita cviii. Hadriani ii. After the conclusion of the council, the papal legates, the vicarii Patriarcharum, Ignatius and some others were assembled before the emperor. Then appeared the Bulgarian ambassadors, asking : Usque hodie pagani fuimus, et nuper ad gratiam christianitatis accessimus. Ideoque ne in aliquo errare videamur, cui Ecclesiae subdi debeamus, a vobis, qui vices summorum Patriarcha-

When *Photius* again took possession of the See of Constantinople after Ignatius's death (878), *John VIII.* was induced to acknowledge him in hope of regaining in this way jurisdiction over Bulgaria ;[18] and to appoint a *second conc. œcumen. viii. at*

rum geritis, nosse desideramus. The vicarii of the oriental patriarchs ask the legates : quando vos illam patriam cepistis, cujus potestati subdita erat, et utrum Latinos, an Graecos sacerdotes habuerit, dicite. The ambassadors : Nos illam patriam a Graecorum potestate armis evicimus, in qua non Latinos sed Graecos sacerdotes reperimus.   To this the vicarii : Si Graecos sacerdotes ibi reperistis, manifestum est, quia ex ordinatione Constantinopoleos illa patria fuit. The Roman legates declare on the contrary : Sedes apostolica—utramque Epirum, novam videlicet veteremque, totamque Thessaliam, atque Dardaniam—cujus nunc patria ab his Bulgaris Bulgaria nuncupatur, antiquitus canonice ordinavit et obtinuit. Ac per hoc etc.   Secondly : Bulgares,—sedis apostolicae semet—patrocinio—specialiter committentes, nobis debent, nec immerito, subjici, quos ultroneavoluntate magistros elegere. Thirdly : eosdem Bulgares s. sedes apostolica—a diversis erroribus ad catholicae fidei veritatem multo sudore—transferens—ultra triennium tenuit, tenet, ordinat ac disponit. Finally : S. sedes apostolica vos, quia revera inferiores estis, super sua causa judices nec eligit nec per nos elegit, utpote quae de omni Ecclesia sola specialiter fas habeat judicandi.   But to this the vicarii reply : Satis indecens est, ut vos, qui Graecorum imperium detrectantes, Francorum foederibus inhaeretis, in regno nostri Principis ordinandi jura servetis.   Quapropter [quod] Bulgarum patriam ex Graecorum potestate dudum fuisse, et Graecos sacerdotes habuisse comperimus, s. Ecclesiae Constantinopolitanae, a qua quia per paganismum recesserat, nunc per christianismum restitui judicamus.   And thus it was decided, Bulgares—Graecos sacerdotes—suscipientes, nostros ejiciunt.

[17] Continuation of the Roman claims to jurisdiction in Bulgaria in Hadriani ii. epist. ad Basilium (in append. ad conc. viii. ap. Mansi xvi. 206), Johannis viii. epist. 75, 77, 174, 189, 192, ad Michaelem Regem Bulgar. 76, ad Petrum Comitem. 78, ad Ignatium Patr. 79, ad Episc. et clericos Graecos, all in Mansi xvii. 62 ss.

[18] Joh. viii. epist. 199, ad Basilium et Alexandrum Imp. 200, ad clericos Constantinop. 201, ad Photium Patr. 202, ad Constantinopolitanos, all dated 16th August 879. To Photius he writes : Quod dicitur autem, s. Constantinopolitanam Ecclesiam in te convenire, teque privatam sedem recipere,—de adunatione omnium Deo gratias agimus. Verum super receptione privatae sedis nos debuimus ante consuli. Tamen quia obeunte fratre et coepiscopo nostro Ignatio, te Constantinopolitano throno praesidere audivimus : tantum ut pax augeatur, et jurgia cessent, multimodas Deo gratias agimus. Et cum non sit reprehensibilis erga correctum quantacumque miseratio, si satisfaciens coram synodo misericordiam secundum consuetudinem postulaveris, ac si evidenti correctione utaris, et peritiae non obliviscens nullius damna moliaris,—et si—omnes

Constantinople (879 and 880),[19] at which the first of 869 was re-

uno voto—in tua restitutione convenerint : veniam pro pace s. Constantinopolitanae Ecclesiae tibi concedimus etc.   Praeterea sicut vestra pars suum velle conatur vires accipere, ita et diocessim nostram Bulgariam, quam—P. Nicolai certamine sedes apostolica recepit, ac Hadriani— tempore possederat, summa nobis celeritate restitui volumus etc.

[19] Afterwards commonly called by the Latins Pseudosynodus Photiana.   The acts ap. Mansi xvii. 373 ss.   The Greeks succeeded in bringing over to their mind the papal legates, by flattery and artful management ; those papal letters to Basil and to Photius were laid before the synod in a Greek translation, in which all their rudeness was taken away.   That passage of the letter to Photius (note 18) ran thus for example (p. 413) : Ἔγραψας ἡμῖν, ὅτι ἡ ἁγιωτάτη τοῦ Θεοῦ Κωνσταντινουπολιτῶν Ἐκκλησία ἕν σοι συνεφώνησε,—καὶ ὅτι τὸν θρόνον, ὃν ἐστερήθης, ἀπέλαβες, ὃς ἦν ἴδιός σου· ὑπὲρ τούτων, λέγω δὴ τῆς Ἐκκλησίας καὶ τῆς ἀποκαταστάσεώς σου—Θεῷ τὴν εὐχαριστίαν ἐξ ὅλης ψυχῆς καὶ δυνάμεως ἀνεπέμψαμεν.—Ἀλλ᾽ αὐτὸς τῇ ἐνούσῃ σοι σοφίᾳ καὶ συνέσει—πάντας μετέρχου οἰκειοῦσθαι πρὸς σὲ κ. τ. λ.—Διὸ καὶ τὴν σὴν ἀδελφότητα ἀξιοῦμεν,—μὴ ἀπαξιῶσαι ἐπὶ τῇ συνόδῳ κηρύξαι τὸ εἰς σὲ τοῦ Θεοῦ ἔλεος, καὶ τὴν βοήθειαν, καὶ τῆς ἁγιωτάτης τῶν Ῥωμαίων Ἐκκλησίας τὸν ὑπερασπισμὸν κ. τ. λ.   Concerning Bulgaria not a word, but on the contrary there was interpolated : Τὴν δὲ γενομένην κατὰ τῆς σῆς εὐλαβείας σύνοδον ἐν τοῖς αὐτόθι ἠκυρώσαμεν καὶ ἐξωστρακίσαμεν παντελῶς, καὶ ἀπεβαλόμεθα, διά τε τὰ ἄλλα, καὶ ὅτι ὁ πρὸ ἡμῶν μακάριος πάπας Ἀδριανὸς οὐχ ὑπέγραψεν ἐν αὐτῇ.—Concerning the demands of the papal legates respecting Bulgaria it was said : ὁ περὶ ἐνορίας λόγος τῆς παρούσης διέστηκεν ὑποθέσεως, καὶ καιρὸν ἴδιον ἐπιζητεῖ.   Whatever the emperor may decide on the subject, στέργομεν καὶ συνευδοκοῦμεν καὶ ἡμεῖς (p. 420. 488.)   Finally actio vi. (p. 515) the Nicene-Constantinopolitan symbol was recognised, and respecting it the determination was : εἴ τις—ῥήμασι νόθοις ἢ προσθήκαις ἢ ἀφαιρέσεσι τὴν ἀρχαιότητα τοῦ ἱεροῦ τούτου καὶ σεβασμίου ὅρου κατακιβδηλεῦσαι ἀποθρασυνθείη·—εἰ μὲν τῶν ἱερωμένων εἴη τις, παντελεῖ καθαιρέσει τοῦτον καθυποβάλλομεν· εἰ δὲ τῶν λαϊκῶν, τῷ ἀναθέματι παραπέμπομεν.   By this only the Western addition could be meant.   As to what Baron. ad ann. 879, no. 73. and Bellarminus de concil. lib. i. c. 5. asserted, that the whole synod may have been a fabrication of Photius, Leo Allatius de octava synodo Photiana. Rom. 1662. 8. and de Eccles. occid. et orient. perpetua consensione p. 591, has expressed as a certainty.   On the contrary John viii. epist. 250 ad Photium : Ea, quae pro causa tuae restitutionis synodali decreto Constantinopoli misericorditer acta sunt, recipimus.   Et si fortasse nostri legati in eadem synodo contra apostolicam praeceptionem egerunt, nos nec recipimus, nec judicamus alicujus existere firmitatis.   In like manner epist. 251 ad Imperatores with the date Idibus Aug. Indict. xiii. (880.) Before open enmity had broke forth again, Photius sent a letter to the patriarch of Aquileia (Latin ap. Baronius ann. 883, no. 4), in which he proves at length to him that the Holy Spirit proceeds only from the Father.

versed. But he soon found himself deceived ; and no resource was left him but to retract every thing and condemn Photius.[20]

Photius was a second time deposed by *Leo the Wise* (886), though with less reference than before to the co-operation of Rome.[21]

The attempts of Photius (shortly before 866) to gain over *the Armenians* again to the Greek Church,[22] were as fruitless as those of *Nicolaus Mysticus*,[23] patriarch of Constantinople, from 895–925.

[20] In an an old work on the various condemnations of Photius, ap. Mansi xvi. 449 : Ἰωάννης—ἀνεθεμάτισε Φώτιον, ὅτε ἀπεπλάνησε τοὺς περὶ Εὐγένιον διὰ τὴν Βουλγαρίαν ἐλθόντας. Λαβὼν γὰρ τὸ Εὐαγγέλιον καὶ ἀνελθὼν ἐν τῷ ἄμβωνι, πάντων ἀκουόντων ἔφη· ὁ μὴ ἔχων τὸν θεοκρίτως ἀναθεματισθέντα Φώτιον, ὡς ἀφῆκαν αὐτὸν Νικόλαος καὶ Ἀδριανὸς οἱ ἁγιώτατοι Πάπαι, οἱ προκάτοχοί μου, ἔστω ἀνάθεμα. The Latins continued to count the council of 869 the viii. oecumenical one, the Greeks abide by that of 879, but reckon only seven general councils. Of the measures taken by the following popes against Photius, we have extant only Stephani v. epist. ad Basilium Imp. A. D. 885 (Mansi xviii. 11).

[21] It is true that even the emperor and Stylianus bishop of Neocaesarea (epist. ad Stephan. Mansi xvi. 425, and xviii. 14), applied this time to the pope, on which Stephanus epist. ad Episc. orient. (ib. xviii. 18) replied. With Styliani epist. ii. ad Stephan. A.D. 889 (ib. xvi. 437), to which Formosus (ib. xvi. 440, xviii. 101) replied, and a third letter of his A.D. 898, now lost, the answer to which, by John ix. Baronius ad ann. 905 no. 9, has, the correspondence closed without having had any effect.

[22] Photii ep. ad Zachariam, Patriarcham Armeniorum, and ep. ad Asutium, Principem Armeniae, both from the Armenian in the spicilegium Romanum x. ii. 449. It is remarkable that Angelo Majus has only given in brief the contents of the part of the first letter (p. 452) in which Photius praises very much the church of Constantinople, caeteroqui de Patriarchatuum aliquot origine malitiose et procul omni veritate loquitur. Photius seems to have been at first deceived by favourable replies and oriental flatteries from the Armenians; for in his Encyclica (ed. Montacutii p. 48 s.) he thinks he had converted them.

[23] A collection of his letters in the spicilegium Romanum x. ii. 161. In the same ep. 139 p. 417, to the ruler of Armenia comp. praef. p. xviii.

§ 42.

LATER CONTROVERSIES TILL THE ENTIRE SEPARATION OF THE TWO CHURCHES.

Michaelis Cerular. epist. ii. ad Petrum Patriarch. Antioch. (in Cotelerii
Ecclesiae Graec. monum. ii. 135 and 162.)

Since the *Encyclica* of Photius, doubts of Latin orthodoxy had
been gradually taking deeper root among the Greeks. And because, on the other side, the Pseudoisidorian principles, and the
continued claims of the popes to Bulgaria appeared in the way, the
ecclesiastical bond between the sees of Constantinople and Rome
was necessarily always becoming looser, and would have been
entirely broken earlier, had not the interest of the Greek emperors prevented the crisis. The little communication between
them had long been of a merely hostile character,[1] when at length

---

[1] Ex. gr. the fourth marriage of the emperor Leo Philosophus having
been condemned by the patriarch Nicolaus Mysticus, Pope Sergius III.
(904) declared it allowable (cf. Nicolai epist. ad Anastasiam P. A.D. 912
and ad Joannem x. A.D. 920, ap Mansi xviii. 243, more fully in Greek
in the spicilegium Rom. x. ii. 287, 326). Hence arose a division in the
Greek church: but the Synod Constant. A.D. 920, decided against the
pope (Acts ap. Mansi xviii. 331), cf. Theophanis continuati lib. vi. de
Leone, c. 23, 24. Symeon Logoth. in Leone c. 12, 17, 18. Schlosser's
Weltgesch. ii. ii. 226. Another remarkable transaction between the
two hierarchs is related by Glaber Radulph iv. c. 1: Circa annum igitur
Domini MXXIV. Constantinopolitanus Praesul cum suo Principe Basilio, aliique nonnulli Graecorum consilium iniere, quatenus cum consensu Romani Pontificis liceret Ecclesiam Constantinopolitanam in suo
orbe, sicuti Roma in universo, universalem dici et haberi. Qui statim mi-
serunt, qui deferrent multa ac diversa donorum xenia Romam, tam Pontifici, quam caeteris —. Ac licet pro tempore philargyria mundi regina
queat appellari, in Romanis tamen inexplebile cubile locavit. Mox
namque ut videre, Graecorum sibi deferri fulgidas opes, versum est cor
illorum ad fraudulentiae diverticula, pertentantes an forte clanculo concedere quiverant, quod petebatur: sed nequaquam.—Dum ergo adhuc leni
sub murmure hujusce machinatores in conclavi sese putarent talia trac-
tavisse, velox fama de ipsis per universam Italiam decucurrit. Sed qualis tunc tumultus, quam vehemens commotio per cunctos exstitit, qui audierunt, dici non valet. Willelmus Abbas Divionensis s. Benigni wrote
a severe letter of warning to the pope, concluding with these words:
De caetero quoque optamus, uti universalem decet Antistitem, vos acrius

Michael Cerularius, patriarch of Constantinople, renewed open
warfare, by his letter to *John*, bishop at *Trani* in Apulia[2] (1053),

in correctione ac disciplina sanctae et apostolicae Ecclesiae vigere.   So
also Hugonis Flaviniac. chron. Virdunense ad ann. 1024 (ap. Bouquet
x. 209).   The later Greeks pretend that Filioque was inserted in the symbol for the first time under Pope Christophorus (904) and that from that
time forwards the popes were erased from the Diptycha in Constantinople
(Allatii de Eccl. occid. et orient. perpet. consensu p. 606 ss.)   But this
is not true, since as late as John XVIII. († 1007) it was not so (Petri
Patr. Aut. ep. ad Michael. Cerul. in Cotelerii monum. Eccl. Gr. ii. 148).
At the time of Michael Cerul., however, it had long been so, for he
even supposes that it had been done since the sixth oecumenical council on account of the behaviour of Vigilius (!) ἡ ἐν τοῖς ἱεροῖς διπτύχοις ἀν-
αφορὰ—ἐξεκόπη τοῦ Πάπα (ep. ad Petr. Ant. l. c. p. 140), an error which
Peter corrects in this very passage.   Perhaps that difference respecting
the Patr. oecumenicus had given rise to such an idea.

[2] Only extant in Humbert's Latin translation (ap. Baronius ad. ann.
1853 no. 22 and Canis. lectt. ant. ed. Basnage iii. i. 281): Michael
universalis Patriarcha novae Romae et Leo Archiepiscopus Achridae
metropolis Bulgarorum dilecto fratri Joanni Tranensi Episc. Dei magna
dilectio et jucunda compassionis viscera flexere nos scribere ad tuam
Sanctitatem et per te ad universos principes sacerdotum et sacerdotes
Francorum, et monachos et populos, et ad ipsum reverendissimum Papam, et memorari de Azymis et Sabbatis, quae mystice indecenter cus-
toditis, et communicatis Judaeis.   Etenim Azyma et Sabbata ipsi custodire a Moyse jussi sunt: nostrum vero Pascha Christus est.   Reference to Matth. xxvi. 17, 18, 20, 26—28.—" hic est sanguis meus novi
Testamenti."   Dicendo enim " novi" ostendit, quomodo ea, quae veteris fuerunt Testamenti, cessavere.   Aspicite quomodo panem corpus
suum sub novo Testamento vocavit.   Vos quidem panem, nos ἄρτον dicimus Ἄρτος autem interpretatur elevatus et sursum portatus a fermento
et sale, calorem et elevationem habens.   Azymae autem nihil distant a
lapide sine anima, et luto lateris, deorsum conjunctae terrae et sicco luto
comparatae.   Aut non audistis Jesum dicentem discipulis suis: " Quia
vos estis sal terrae ?" (Matth. v. 13) et " quoniam simile est regnum
caelorum fermento, " quod accipiens mulier abscondit in farinae satis
tribus," etc. (Matth. xiii. 33).   Mulierem sanctam Ecclesiam vocat. Satis vero tribus [s.] modiis repletis, Patrem et Filium et Spiritum Sanctum, quorum nequaquam lutulentae azymae sunt participes.   (According to J. Sirmondi disquis. de azymo, semperne in usu fuerit apud
Latinos ? Paris 1651, 8, the Latins also used fermented bread in the
Lord's supper till the eighth century ; with whom agrees J. Bona, rerum liturg. lib. i. c. 23.   On the other side is J. Mabillon diss. de pane
eucharistico, azymo ac fermentato.   Paris 1674, 8, also in his analectis ed. ii. p. 522 and J. Ciampini conjecturae de perpetuo azymorum
usu in Ecclesia latina.   Romae 1688, 4).   Sabbata vero quomodo in
Quadragesima Judaice observatis ?   An allusion to Matth. xii. 1 ss.
Marc. ii. 27. Joh. ix. 16. Luc. xiii. 15.   Et ideo hi, qui Sabbata cum
azymis custodiunt, neque Judaei neque Christiani sunt, sed similes sunt

filled with invectives against the alleged errors of the Latin Church. The Emperor *Constantine Monomachus* used indeed every means in his power to prevent the entire rupture, and fortunately succeeded in persuading Pope Leo IX. to enter on the preliminaries of a reconciliation;[3] but the extravagant demands of the Roman legates[4] sent to Constantinople, the bitterness of the writings which *Humbert* composed in refutation of that letter of the patriarch,[5] and another of a later opponent of the Latin

leopardo, sicut dicit magnus Basilius, cujus capilli nec nigri sunt, nec albi omnino. Quomodo autem et suffocata hi tales comedunt, in quibus sanguis tenetur? An nescitis, ut omnis animalis sanguis anima ipsius sit, et qui comederit sanguinem, animem, comedit? (Cf. Jo. Rud. Kiesling hist. concertationis Graec. Latinorumque de esu sanguinis et carnis morticinae. Erlang. 1763, 8). Item Alleluja in Quadragesima non psallitis, sed semel in Pascha tantumodo, etc. Cur tantam deceptionem horum talium non aspicitis, nec intelligitis, neque corrigitis populos et vosmetipsos, sicut qui debent judicari ex his a Deo? Non derelinquitis, quod dicitur, quod hoc Petrus, et Benedictus, et Paulus et caeteri docuerunt? Decipitis vos ipsos et populum in istis. Quae vero scripsi, ea sunt, quae Petrus et Paulus et caeteri Apostoli et Christus docuit; et sancta Ecclesia catholica suscepit et custodit religiose. Quae et vos correcti custodite. Azymas vero et custodias sabbatorum projicite miseris Judaeis: similiter et suffocata barbaris gentibus, ut fiamus puri in recta et immaculata fide, et unus grex unius pastoris Christi. Cujus in cruce divino sanguine inebriati laudamus puri pure Patrem et Filium et Spiritum Sanctum, universa Mosaicae legis et ab eo custodita derelinquentes sine Deo Judaeis, qui velut caeci perquirentes Christum lumen amiserunt, permanentes in umbra, sicut insipientes perpetuo. Haec autem homo Dei et multotiens ipse cum populo agnoscens docuisti esse, et correctus scripsisti multis similem consuetudinem habentibus. Et ut habeas salutem animae tuae, mitte principibus sacerdotum et sacerdotibus, et adjura, ut per haec seipsos corrigant et Dei populum, ut Dei mercedem in istis habeas. Et si hoc feceris, propono et per secundam scriptionem majora et perfectiora his tibi scribere, fidei vera ostensione et firmamento animarum, pro quibus Christus posuit animam suam. A larger work of Michael against the Latin church is found in MS. in the Imperial library at Vienna (Lambec. comm. de bibl. Vindob. lib. iii. p. 160).

[3] Cf. Leonis ix. epist. i. et vi. ad Michaelem Constantinop. Patr., epist. vii. ad Constant. imp. (ap. Mansi xix. 635 ss.)

[4] Their names see below not. 7.

[5] Humberti responsio instar dialogi ab ipso latine conscripta—et jussu Imp. Constant. graece edita sub nominibus Constantinopolitani et Romani (prim. ed. Baronius in append. T. xi. in Canisii lectt. ant. ed. Basn. iii. i. 283). The epist. Michaelis ad Joannem Trauensem is expressed piece by piece from the Constantinopolitan, and is then refuted by the Roman. Ex. gr. in the beginning: Ex hac vestra praefatione,

Church, *Nicetas Pectoratus*,[6] in Constantinople, and the mode in

sicut profitemini, crederemus, vos salutem totius Latinae seu occidenta-
lis Ecclesiae pro sola magna Dei dilectione quaerere: si sciremus vos
vestram vestrorumque non negligere. Cum vero vos ipsos et vobis
commissos negligatis, ut nefandos Jacobitas, imo Theopaschitas, seu
alias haereticorum pestas, inter vos et penes vos habeatis (Comp. vol. i.
Div. ii. § 111. not. 6, below § 45, not. 3), neque eorum consortia, neque
colloquia, neque convivia seu pariter orare devitetis: quomodo saltem
suspicabimur, vos aliqua dilectione Dei aut proximi praemonitos compati nostrae perditioni, sicut putatis ? etc.   Ast vos, quasi omnia munda
immunda sint vobis, oculis contra vos et vestra clausis, s. Romanam et
omnem occidentalem Ecclesiam pollutam haeresi et Judaismo proclama-
tis, et velut quandam abominationem devitatis. Ex qua tam caeca et
hactenus inaudita audacia ad hoc prorupistis, ut cunctorum haereticorum, quos adhuc deprehendere voluimus, temeritatem transcendatis.
Quamvis omnino singulae haereses suis adinventionibus aliqua Ecclesiae
membra fatigaverint: nulla tamen adhuc ad tantam vesaniam erupit, ut
opinionem suam primae et apostolicae sedi ingerere praesumsisset cum
interpositione anathematis. Recensete si placet ab initio Christianitatis usque ad nostra tempora cunctarum haereseon molimina, et videbitis,
an aliqua earum praesumserit talia. Et cum non inveneritis, saltem
tunc resipiscite, ne, quod absit, permaneatis viciniores praecursores illius
Antichristi, qui adversatur et extollitur supra omne, quod dicitur Deus
aut quod colitur. The conclusion : Haeccine sunt illa majora et perfectiora, ut tanta oblatio imponatur altari, quanta nequeat a ministris,
vel a populo sumi, et idcirco debeat subterrari, aut in puteum ad hoc
praeparatum projici ? Haeccine quoque sunt illa majora et perfectiora,
ut novus maritus, et recenti carnis voluptate resolutus, et totus marcidus
Christi ministret altaribus, et ab ejus immaculato corpore sanctificatus
manus confestim ad muliebres transferat amplexus ? Haeccine sunt
illa perfectiora, ut mulieribus christianis in partu vel in menstruo peri-
clitantibus communio denegetur ? aut paganis baptismus interdicatur ?
et parvulis morituris ante octo dies regeneratio per aquam et Spiritum
Santum subtrahatur ?   In quo utique crudeliores Herode, non tantum
in corpore, sed et in anima quotidie trucidatis parvulorum innumerabi-
lem populum, et destinatis ad ignem aeternum.   Numquid etiam inde
est, quod hominis morituri imaginem affigitis crucifixae imagini Christi,
ita ut quidam Antichristus in cruce Christi sedeat, ostendens se adorandum tanquam sit Deus ? Numquid et illud inde est, quod pejus sit,
monachos femoralibus indui et carnibus vesci, quam fornicari ? Ideone
clauditis ecclesias Latinorum, et dirigitis scripta per totum orbem, ut ad
haec majora et perfectiora pertrahatis omnem christianum populum ?
Non sunt haec talia ostensio verae fidei, sed adinventio Diaboli. Nec
sunt firmamentum, sed destructio animarum. Pro quibus omnibus et
aliis, quos longum est scripto prosequi, erroribus, nisi resipueritis, et digne satisfeceritis, irrevocabile anathema hic et in futuro eritis a Deo et
ab omnibus catholicis, pro quibus Christus animam suam posuit.

   [6] Nicetae Presb. et monachi monasterii Studii lib. contra Latinos
(ap. Baron. l. c. and Canis. l. c. p. 308). This work touches also other

which the latter had been humbled with the aid of the emperor,[7] must have prevented all adjustment of the dispute. Michael, supported by his clergy and the people, remained immoveable ;

peculiarities of the Latins. Quis ille est, qui tradidit vobis, prohibere et abscindere nuptias sacerdotum ? Quis ex doctoribus Ecclesiae hanc vobis tradidit pravitatem ? Referring to can. apost. 5. (vol. i. Div. 2. § 73, not. 9) and Conc. sexti can. 13, (ibid. § 129, not. 3). Unde igitur vobis, et ex quibus hae horribiles infirmitates supervenerunt, o viri Romanorum sapientissimi, et omnium aliarum gentium nobilissimi ? Aestimo, quod quidam ex Judaeis in tempore Apostolorum credentes, vana lucra cupientes, et pecuniarum amatores reperti, volentes multos fidelium abstrahere ex Evangelio :—in hoc et Christianitas et Judaismus corrupta sunt. On the other hand Humberti responsio contra Nicetam (ll. cc.) ex. gr. in the beginning: Vae tibi, Sarabaita, qui nulla coenobitali examinatus disciplina, voluntate atque voluptate ductus propria, contra sanctam et Romanam et apostolicam Ecclesiam et omnium ss. Patrum concilia horribiliter latrasti, stultior asino, frontem leonis et murum adamantinum frangere tentasti. In quo utique conatu non es victor erroris, sed victus errore :—puer centum annorum maledictus, potius dicendus Epicurus, quam monachus : nec credendus es degere in monasterio Studii, sed in amphitheatro aut lupanari, etc.

[7] Brevis commemoratio eorum, quae gesserunt Apocrisarii s. Rom. sedis in regia urbe (written by Humbert ap. Baron. ann. 1054 no. 19, Canis. l. c. p. 325) : Anno xl. imperii Constantini Monomachi, Ind. vii. ipso die nativitatis b. Joannis Baptistae, advenientibus a domino Papa Leone IX. Apocrisariis s. Romanae sedis, Humberto scilicet Cardinali Episcopo Sylvae Candidae, et Petro Amalphitanorum Archiepiscopo Friderico quoque Diacono et Cancellario, ad monasterium Studii intra urbem Constantinoplitanam : Niceta monachus, qui et Pectoratus, ante praesentiam praefati Imperatoris et procerum ejus, insistentibus ipsis Nuntiis Romanis, anathematizavit quoddam scriptum sub suo nomine contra sedem apostolicam et omnem Latinam Ecclesiam editum, et praetitulatum : De azymo, de subbato, de nuptiis sacerdotum. Insuper anathematazavit cunctos, qui ipsam s. Ecclesiam Romanam negarent primam omnium Ecclesiarum esse, et qui illius fidem semper orthodoxam prasumerent in aliquo reprehendere. Post haec statim in conspectu omnium, ad suggestionem eorundem Nuntiorum Romanorum, jussit idem orthodoxus Imperator praefatum incendi scriptum, sicque fuit discessum. Sequenti autem die praedictus Niceta urbe est egressus, ultro adiit legatos ipsos intra palatium Pigi. A quibus accipiens perfectam suarum, propositionum solutionem, iterum sponte anathematizavit omnia dicta et facta vel tentata adversus primam et apostolicam sedem. Sic ab eis in communionem receptus, effectus est eorum familiarus amicus. Porro dicta vel scripta eorundem Nuntiorum adversu diversas calumnias Graecorum, et maxime contra scripta Michaëlis Constantinopolitani Episcopi, et Leonis Acridani Metropolitani Episcopi, et saepedicti Nicetae monachi, jussu Imperatoris in Graecum fuere translata, et in eadem urbe hactenus conservata.

the legates (on the 16th July 1054) laid upon the altar of St Sophia an act of excommunication against him,[8] which, however,

[8] Brevis commem proceeds: Tandem Michaële praesentiam eorundem et colloquium devitante atque in stultitia sua perseverante, praefati Nuntii xvii. kal. Aug. adierunt Ecclesiam s. Sophiae, et super obstinatione illius conquesti, clero ex more ad Missas praeparato, jam hora tertia, die sabbathi, chartam excommunicationis super principale altare posuerunt sub oculis cleri et populi. Inde mox egressi, etiam pulverem pedum suorum excussere in testimonium illis, dictum Evangelii proclamantes: "Videat Deus et judicet." (Michaël epist. i. ad Petr. Ant. admits, after much complaint of the presumptuous pride of the legates: ἡμεῖς μὲν τὴν αὐτῶν συντυχίαν παρῃτησάμεθα καὶ τὴν ἔντευξιν διά τε τὸ ἀμεταθέτως ἔχειν αὐτοὺς τῆς δυσσεβείας πεπεῖσθαι· καὶ ὅτι ἄνευ τῆς σῆς μακαριότητος καὶ τῶν ἄλλων ἁγιωτάτων Πατριαρχῶν, περὶ τοιούτων λόγους πρὸς τοὺς τοποτηρητὰς τῆς Ῥώμης ἀνακινεῖν, καὶ ἀνάξιον ὅλως, καὶ τῇ κατὰ τοὺς ἄνω χρόνους ἐν τοῖς τοιούτοις κρατησάσῃ συνηθείᾳ ἐναντίον καὶ ἀκατάλληλον ἐνομίζομεν). Hinc ordinatis Ecclesiis Latinorum intra ipsam Constantinopolim, et anathemate dato cunctis, qui deinceps communicarent ex manu Graeci Romanum sacrificium vituperantis, in osculo pacis accepta orthodoxi Imperatoris licentia donisque imperialibus s. Petro et sibi, alacres coepere reverti xv. kal. Augusti; sed nimia instantia precum Michaëlis, spondentis tunc demum, se conflicturum cum eis, Imperator compulsus a Solembria literis suis eos revocavit xiii. kal. Augusti. Quo etiam die festinantes regressi devenerunt ad palatium Pigi. Quos praefatus Michaël haeresiarcha comperiens redisse, quasi ad concilium conabatur adducere in Ecclesiam s. Sophiae, sequenti die ut ostensa charta, quam omnino corruperat transferendo, obruerentur ibidem a populo. Quod prudens Imperator praecavens noluit haberi aliquod concilium, nisi et ipse adesset praesens. Cumque hoc ei omnimodis Michaël contradiceret. jussit Augustus ipsos Nuntios confestim arripere iter. Quod et factum est. (On the other hand, Michaël l. c., says there was no intention of punishing the bold, however, τοὺς τὴν ἀσεβῆ κατὰ τῶν ὀρθοδόξων ἐκθεμένους γραφὴν, προστάξει βασιλικῇ ἐν τῷ μεγάλῳ σεκρέτῳ ὑπερβάλομεν ἀναθέματι πολλὰ μὲν μετὰ τὴν τῆς γραφῆς ταύτης ὑπόθεσιν, περὶ τοῦ εἰς ὄψιν ἡμῖν ἐλθεῖν, καὶ τοῖς τε ἄλλοις τῶν ἐν αὐτῇ, καὶ τῇ διαστροφῇ τοῦ ἁγίου συμβόλου ἀποτάξασθαι παραινέσαντες· ὡς δὲ οὐκ ἠνείχοντο, ἀλλὰ καὶ διαχειρίσασθαι ἑαυτοὺς, εἰ μὴ παύσονται περὶ τούτου ὀχλούμενοι, διηπείλουν, εἰς τὸ κατὰ τῆς αὐτῶν βλασφημίας συνείδομεν χωρῆσαι ἀνάθεμα). Porro vesanus Michaël dolens suas non procedere insidias, concitavit Imperatori vulgi seditionem maximam, velut Nuntiis cooperata fuerit ejus voluntas. Unde Imperator coactus, interpretes Latinorum Paulum ac filium ejus Smaragdum, caesos et detonsos Michaëli tradidit: sicque tumultus ille conquievit. Verum Imperator post Nuntios Romanos directis suis, exemplar excommunicationis verissimum a civitate Russorum remissum sibi accepit, civibusque exhibuit, ac tandem Michaëlem falsasse chartam legatorum comperit atque convicit. Itaque commotus amicos et affines ipsius honoribus privatos a palatio eliminavit, contraque ipsum usque nunc graves iras retinuit. Denique exemplar chartae excommunicatoriae est tale: Humbertus,

was immediately answered by the patriarch with a like anathema.[9] The other oriental patriarchs joined with the Constan-

—Petrus,—Fredericus,—omnibus catholicae Ecclesiae filiis : Sancta
Romana prima et apostolica sedes—nos Apocrisarios suos facere dignata
est, ut juxta quod scriptum est, descenderemus et videremus, utrum
opere completus sit clamor, qui sine intermissione ex tanta urbe conscendit ad ejus aures. Quantum ad columnas imperii, et honoratos
ejus atque cives sapientes, christianissima et orthodoxa est civitas.
Quantum autem ad Michaëlem abusive dictum Patriarcham, et ejus
stultitiae fautores, nimia zizania haereseon quotidie seminantur in medio
ejus. Quia sicut Simoniaci donum Dei vendunt : sicut Valesii hospites
suos castrant, et non solum ad clericatum sed insuper ad episcopatum
promovent : sicut Arriani rebaptizant in nomine s. Trinitatis baptizatos,
et maxime Latinos : sicut Donatistae affirmant, excepta Graecorum Ecclesia, Ecclesiam Christi et verum sacrificium atque baptismum ex toto
mundo periisse ; sicut Nicolaitae carnales nuptias concedunt et defendunt sacri altaris ministris ; sicut Severiani maledictam dicunt legem
Mosis : sicut Pneumatomachi vel Theomachi absciderunt a symbolo
Spiritus Sancti processionem a Filio : sicut Manichaei inter alia quodlibet fermentatum fatentur animatum esse : sicut Nazareni carnalem
Judaeorum munditiam adeo servant, ut parvulos morientes ante octavum
a nativitate diem baptizari contradicant, et mulieres in menstruo vel in
partu periclitantes communicari, vel si paganae fuerint, baptizari prohi-
beant, et capillos capitis ac barbae nutrientes, eos qui comam tondent,
et secundum institutionem Rom. Ecclesiae barbas radunt, in communione non recipiant.—Therefore : Michaël —et Leo Acridanus Episcopus dictus, et sacellarius ipsius Michaëlis Constantinus, qui Latinorum
sacrificicium profanis conculcavit pedibus, et omnes sequaces eorum in
praefatis erroribus et praesumtionibus, sint Anathema Maranatha, cum
Simoniacis, Valesiis etc. et cum omnibus haereticis, imo cum Diabolo et
Angelis ejus, nisi forte resipuerint. Amen, amen, amen.

[9] A synod summoned by Michael issued in July 1054, in opposition
to that excommunication—writing a ζημείωμα (edictum) (see in Allatii de
libris ecclesiasticis Graecorum diss. ii. Paris. 1645. 4. p. 161. Instead of μηνὶ ᾽Ιουνίῳ ᾽Ινδικτ. ζ΄. it must be read ᾽Ιουλίῳ, as p. 170 the
reading twice appears). There it is said that those legates were ταῖς
παρὰ τοῦ ᾽Αργυροῦ (a Greek dux in Lower Italy, see Schlosser's Weltgesh. ii. ii. 602 ff. 647 ff.) δολεραῖς ὑποθήκαις καὶ συμβουλαῖς, αὐτοί τε ἀφ᾽
ἑαυτῶν ἀφικόμενοι, καὶ μήτε παρὰ τοῦ Πάπα ἀποσταλέντες, ἀλλὰ καὶ τὰ γράμματα, ἃ ὡς ἀπ᾽ ἐκείνου δῆθεν ἐπεφέροντο, πλασάμενοι. This was proved in
particular by the false seal. Having departed immediately after their
daring act, the emperor, at the instance of the patriarchs, sent to bring
them back, but οὐ βούλονται δὲ τῇ ἡμετέρᾳ μετριότητι προσελθεῖν, ἢ τῇ ἱερᾷ
καὶ μεγάλῃ συνόδῳ εἰς ὄψιν ἐλθεῖν, καὶ ἀπόκρισίν τινα δοῦναι, περὶ ὧν ἀσεβῶν
ἀπηρεύξαντο,—αἱρεῖσθαι δὲ θανεῖν μᾶλλον, ἢ εἰς ὄψιν ἡμῶν καὶ τῇ συνόδῳ ἐλθεῖν. According to his letter inserted here, the emperor was entirely on
the side of the patriarch, and only withheld from violent measures
against the legates διὰ τὸ δοκοῦν περικεῖσθαι τούτους τῆς πρεσβείας ὀφφίκιον.

tinopolitan;[10] and thus the Christian East separated from the West for ever.[11]

The conclusion is, that on the 24th July, ἐπ' ἀκροάσει τοῦ πλήθους ἀναθεματισθῆναι τὸ αὐτὸ ἀσεβὲς καὶ αὖθις·ἔγγραφον· πρὸς δὲ καὶ τοὺς τοῦτο ἐκθεμένους καὶ γράψαντας, καὶ συναίνεσίν τινα, ἣ βουλὴν εἰς τὴν τούτου ποίησιν δεδωκότας. τὸ δὲ πρωτότυπον τοῦ ῥιφέντος παρὰ τῶν δυσσεβῶν ἀνοσίου ἐγγράφου καὶ μισαροῦ [οὐ] κατεκαύθη, ἀλλ' ἐν τῷ εὐαγεῖ τοῦ χαρτοφύλακος ἀπετέθη σεκρέτῳ εἰς ἔλεγχον διηνεκῆ τῶν τηλικαῦτα τοῦ Θεοῦ ἡμῶν βλασφημησάντων.

[10] Cf. Michaëlis epist. i. ad Petrum Antioch. in which an account of the affair is given, and of the errors of the Latins. To those already recounted new ones are added : ἐν τῇ λειτουργίᾳ κατὰ τὸν καιρὸν τῆς μεταλήψεως εἰς τῶν λειτουργούντων ἐσθίων τὰ ἄζυμα τοὺς λοιποὺς ἀσπάζεται (above § 18. not. 8). καὶ δακτυλίους φοροῦντες ἐν ταῖς χερσὶν οἱ Ἐπίσκοποι, ὡς δῆθεν γυναῖκας τὰς Ἐκκλησίας λαμβάνοντες, τὸν ἀρραβῶνα φορεῖν λέγουσι (above § 24. not. 4). καὶ εἰς πολέμους δὲ ἐξιόντες, αἵμασι τὰς ἑαυτῶν χεῖρας χραίνουσι (above § 24. not. 6)—ὡς δέ τινες ἡμᾶς διεβεβαιώσαντο, καὶ τὸ θεῖον βάπτισμα ἐπιτελοῦντες, τοὺς βαπτιζομένους βαπτίζουσι εἰς μίαν κατάδυσιν (this was really a custom in Spain, Gregor. Magni lib. i. epist. 41. Conc. Tolet. iv. ann. 633 can. 6., approved by Alcum epist. 75., justified by Walafrid Strabo de reb. eccl. c. 26.)—ἀλλὰ καὶ ἅλατος πρὸς τοῦτο τὰ τῶν βαπτιζομένων πληροῦσι στόματα.—Instead of Μικρὰ ζύμη ὅλον τὸ φύραμα ζυμοῖ, they read, 1 Cor. v. 6. and Gal. v. 9, φθείρει (Vulg. has corrumpit), for the purpose of defending their unleavened bread. Ἀλλ' οὐδὲ τὰ λείψανα τῶν Ἁγίων ἀνέχονται προσκυνεῖν· τινὲς δὲ αὐτῶν οὐδὲ τὰς ἁγίας εἰκόνας (see above § 11). οὔτε μὴν τοὺς ἁγίους καὶ μεγάλους Πατέρας ἡμῶν,—τόν τε θεολόγον φημὶ Γρηγόριον καὶ τὸν μέγαν Βασίλειον καὶ τὸν θεῖον Χρυσόστομον τοῖς λοιποῖς συναριθμοῦσιν Ἁγίοις, ἢ ὅλως τὴν διδαχὴν αὐτῶν καταδέχονται. More rational and moderate is the judgment of Peter, patriarch of Antioch, in his reply to Michael (ap. Cotelerius l. c.p. 145 ss.) respecting this controversy : p. 149 : ὅσα δέ σοι καὶ ἀπηρίθμηται Ῥωμαϊκὰ ἐλαττώματα μετήλθομεν καὶ τὰ μὲν τούτων ἐδόκει ἀπευκταῖα καὶ φευκτὰ, τὰ δὲ ἰάσιμα, τὰ δὲ παροράσεως ἄξια. τί γὰρ πρὸς ἡμᾶς τὸ ξυρᾶσθαι τοὺς ἀρχιερεῖς τοὺς πώγωνας, καὶ δακτυλιοφορεῖν αὐτοὺς κ. τ. λ. ;—p. 152 : κακὸν δὲ καὶ κακῶν κάκιστον, ἡ ἐν τῷ ἁγίῳ συμβόλῳ προσθήκη. p. 153 : ἀλλ' ὡς ἔοικεν ἀπώλεσαν Ῥωμαῖοι τὰ ἀντίγραφα τῆς ἐν Νικαίᾳ πρώτης συνόδου, οἷα τῆς Ῥώμης ἐπὶ πολὺ τοῦ τῶν Οὐανδάλων ἔθνους κυριαρχήσαντος· παρ' ὧν ἴσως καὶ ἔμαθον ἀρειανίζειν, καὶ εἰς μίαν κατάδυσιν, εἰ τοῦτο ἀληθὲς, ὡς ἐδήλωσας, τὸ βάπτισμα ἐπιτελεῖν. p. 154 : Καλὸν γὰρ πρὸς τὸ καλοθελὲς ὁρῶντας ἡμᾶς, καὶ μᾶλλον ἔνθα μὴ θεὸς ἢ πίστις τὸ κινδυνευόμενον, νεύειν ἀεὶ πρὸς τὸ εἰρηνικόν τε καὶ φιλάδελφον· ἀδελφοὶ γὰρ καὶ ἡμῶν οὗτοι, κἂν ἐξ ἀγροικίας ἢ ἀμαθίας συμβαίνῃ τούτους πολλάκις ἐκπίπτειν τοῦ εἰκότος, τῷ ἑαυτῶν στοιχοῦντας θελήματι. καὶ μὴ τοσαύτην ἀκρίβειαν ἐπιζητεῖν ἐν βαρβάροις ἔθνεσιν, ἣν αὐτοὶ περὶ λόγους ἀναστρεφόμενοι ἀπαιτούμεθα. p. 157: Περὶ γὰρ τῆς ἐν τῷ ἁγίῳ συμβόλῳ προσθήκης, καὶ τοῦ μὴ κοινωνεῖν αὐτοὺς τῶν ἁγιασμάτων διὰ τὸ γεγαμηκότος ἱερέως, καλῶς καὶ θεοφιλῶς ἡ ἁγιωσύνη σου ἐνίσταται· καὶ μὴ παύσαιτό ποτε περὶ τούτου ἐνισταμένη καὶ πείθουσα,—μέχρις ἂν αὐτοὺς ἕξεις συντιθεμένους τῇ ἀληθείᾳ.—τὰ δ' ἄλλα περιφρονητέα μοι εἶναι δοκεῖ, τοῦ τῆς ἀληθείας λόγου μηδὲν ἐξ αὐτῶν καταβλαπτομένου. In like

manner Theophylact, archbp. of Bulgaria, about 1078, in his lib. de iis in quibus Latini accusantur (prim. ed. in Jo. Aloys. Mingarelli anecdotorum fasc. Romae 1756. 4. p. 257 ss.), with bitter complaints both against the passionateness of the Greeks, and the proud obstinacy of the Latins.   Ex. gr. p. 283 : Καὶ τοῖς δυτικοῖς τοίνυν εἴ τι μὲν περὶ τὸ δόγμα διαμαρτάνεται τὴν πατρικὴν πίστιν σαλεῦον, οἷον δὴ τὸ ἐν τῷ συμβόλῳ περὶ τοῦ ἁγίου Πνεύματος προστιθέμενον· ἔνθα ὁ κίνδυνος μέγιστος, καὶ τοῦτο μὴ διορθώσεως ἀξιούμενον ὁ συγχωρῶν, ἀσυγχώρητος· κἂν ἀπὸ τοῦ θρόνου τοὺς λόγους ποιῶνται, ὃν ὑψηλὸν ὑψηλοὶ προτιθέασι· κἂν τὴν τοῦ Πέτρου ὁμολογίαν προβάλωνται· κἂν τὸν ἐπ' ἐκείνῃ μακαρισμὸν περιφέρωσι· κἂν τὰς κλεῖς τῆς βασιλείας ἡμῖν ἐπισείωσιν· οἷς ὅσῳ τιμᾷν ἐκεῖνον δοκοῦσι, τοσοῦτον ἑαυτοὺς ἀτιμάζουσιν, ἃ ἐκεῖνος ἤδρασεν αὐτοὶ καταλύοντες, καὶ τοὺς θεμελίους ὑποσπῶντες τῆς ἐκκλησίας, ἣν ἐκεῖνος ἀνέχειν πιστεύεται.—p. 286 : οὐ τοίνυν οὔτε περὶ τῶν ἀζύμων, οὔτε περὶ τῶν νηστειῶν ἀντισκληρυνθησόμεθα τῷ ἀκαμπεῖ τοῦ ἔθνους φρονήματι·—οὐδὲ πολλοῦ δεῖ περὶ τῶν ἀπηριθμημένων λοιπῶν, ἅπερ ὁμολογοῦντες καὶ αὐτοὶ τηρεῖν—δοκοῦσι πολλοῖς ἀσύγγνωστα σφάλλεσθαι. Ὧν μὴ συντίθεσθαι τοῖς λόγοις, ἀνδρός ἐστιν, ὡς οἶμαι, ταῖς ἐκκλησιαστικαῖς ἱστορίαις ἐγγυμνασθέντος, καὶ μαθόντος, ὡς οὐ πᾶν ἔθος ἀποσχίζειν Ἐκκλησίας ἰσχύει, ἀλλὰ τὸ πρὸς διαφθορὰν ἄγον δόγματος. κ. τ. λ.

[11] The views of the Greeks of the highest rank in the hierarchy are expressed by the Patrician Baanes, imperial plenipotentiary at the genuine oecumenical council of 869, in the Latin Acts, act. viii. (Mansi xvi. 140) : Posuit Deus Ecclesiam suam in quinque patriarchiis, et definivit in Evangeliis suis, ut nunquam aliquando penitus decidant, eo quod capita Ecclesiae sint. . Etenim illud quod dicitur : et portae inferi non praevalebunt adversus eam (Matth. xvi. 18), hoc denunciat, quando duo ceciderint, currant ad tria ; cum tria ceciderint, currant ad duo ; cum vero quatuor forte ceciderint, unum, quod permanet in omnium capite Christo Deo nostro, revocat iterum reliquum corpus Ecclesiae. Cf. Petri Antioch. epist. ad Dominicum Archiep. Gradensem (in Cotelerii mon. Eccl. Gr. ii. 114) : πέντε ἐν ὅλῳ τῷ κόσμῳ ὑπὸ τῆς θείας ᾠκονομήθη χάριτος εἶναι Πατριάρχας,—ἀλλ' οὐδὲ τούτων ἕκαστος κυρίως Πατριάρχης καλεῖται· καταχρηστικῶς δέ. ἀνακηρύττονται δὲ, ὁ μὲν ἀρχιερεὺς τῆς Ῥώμης Πάπας, ὁ δὲ Κωνσταντινουπόλεως Ἀρχιεπίσκοπος, ὁ δὲ Ἀλεξανδρείας Πάπας, καὶ ὁ τῶν Ἱεροσολύμων Ἀρχιεπίσκοπος· μόνος δὲ ὁ Ἀντιοχείας ἰδιαζόντως ἐκληρώθη Πατριάρχης ἀκούειν καὶ λέγεσθαι.—τὸ σῶμα τοῦ ἀνθρώπου ὑπὸ μιᾶς ἄγεται κεφαλῆς, ἐν αὐτῷ δὲ μέλη πολλά· καὶ πάντα ὑπὸ πέντε μόνον οἰκονομεῖται αἰσθήσεων.—καὶ τὸ σῶμα δὲ πάλιν τοῦ Χριστοῦ, ἡ τῶν πιστῶν λέγω Ἐκκλησία,—ὑπὸ πέντε αἰσθήσεων οἰκονομούμενον, τῶν εἰρημένων μεγάλων θρόνων, ὑπὸ μιᾶς ἄγεται κεφαλῆς, αὐτοῦ φημὶ τοῦ Χριστοῦ. About 870 this comparison was also allowed in Rome, see Anastasii praef. in conc. viii. generale (Mansi xvi. 7) : Cum Christus in corpore suo, quod est Ecclesia, tot patriarchales sedes, quot in cujusque mortali corpore sensus, locaverit ; profecto nihil generalitati deest Ecclesiae, si omnes illae sedes unius fuerint voluntatis, sicut nihil deest motui corporis, si omnes quinque sensus integrae communisque fuerint sanitatis. Inter quas videlicet sedes quia Romana praecellit, non immerito visui comparatur : qui profecto cunctis sensibus praeeminet, acutior illis existeus, et communionem, sicut nullus eorum, cum omnibus habens. But the Greeks did not acknowledge such a pre-eminence of the Romish patriarch, comp. Nilus Doxo-

SECOND CHAPTER.

INTERNAL CONDITION OF THE GREEK CHURCH.

§ 43.

The dependence of the church on the court gave countenance to its cabals and alterations (see above § 2),[1] and therefore it could never regain a peculiar life of its own.

When science, or more properly only scientific industry in compilation, was favoured once more under the Macedonian emperors *Basilius Macedo* (867–886), *Leo Philosophus* († 912), *Alexander* († 913), *Constantine Porphyrogennetos* († 959), theology also gained by that means useful collections ;[2] but no

patrius, in his (written A.D. 1143) τάξις τῶν πατριαρχικῶν θρόνων (in Stephle Moyne varia sacra ed. 2. Lugd. Bat. 1694, i. 211 ss.), who also uses that comparison, but in reference to that Roman pretension remarks, p. 242: 'Ορᾷς ὅπως ἀπὸ τοῦ παρόντος κανόνος (can. Chalced. 28, see Vol. i. Div. 2, § 93, not. 14), προφανῶς ἐλέγχονται ληροῦντες οἱ λέγοντες προτιμηθῆναι τὴν 'Ρώμην διὰ τὸν ἅγιον Πέτρον. 'Ιδοὺ γὰρ, προφανῶς ὁ κανὼν οὗτος— φησὶ " διὰ τὸ εἶναι τὴν 'Ρώμην βασιλείαν, ἔχειν τὴν προτίμησιν"—ἐπεὶ δὲ ἐπαύσθη τοῦ εἶναι βασίλισσα—ἐκπεσοῦσα τῆς βασιλείας ἐκείνης, ἐκπίπτει καὶ τῶν πρωτείων. p. 245 : διὸ καὶ ὁ Πατριάρχης Κωνσταντινουπόλεως ὑπογράφει 'Αρχιεπίσκοπος Νέας 'Ρώμης καὶ οἰκουμενικὸς Πατριάρχης· ἐπεὶ γὰρ ἔλαβε τὰ πρεσβεῖα καὶ τὰ προνόμια τῆς 'Ρώμης· βασίλισσα λὰρ ἡ 'Ρώμη ἦν τῆς οἰκουμένης πρότερον, εἶτα πάλιν ὕστερον ἡ Κωνσταντινούπολις (cf. Nicol. i. ep. lxx. ad Hincmar. above, § 41, not. 6). This is also the view of the later Greeks. See Anna Comnena Alexiados lib. i., Joannes Cinnamus histor. lib. v. c. 10, Nilus Archiepisc. Thessal. de Papae primatu lib. ii., Barlaamus Mon. de Papae principatu c. 5 et 6, and also Joannes Zonaras, Theodorus Balsamo, and Alexius Aristenus in their scholia on the conc. Chalced. xxviii.

[1] The new civil legislation of Basil and Leo (βασιλικαὶ διατάξεις or βασιλικά in 60 books) comprehended, like the older, ecclesiastical relations also. Soo too the 113 novellae constitutiones or ἐπανορθωτικαὶ καθάρσεις of Leo (among others in the corpus juris civilis ed. Spangenberg ii. 673 ss.) and the διατάξεις of the following emperors (ibid. p. 773 ss.)

[2] Heeren's Gesch. d. klass. Literatur in Mittelalter. Th. i. (Histor. Werke Th. 4.) S. 138 ff.

independent or new impulses. *Photius* († about 891)[3] deserves distinction beyond all scholars of the time. *Simeon Metaphrastes* (about 900)[4] devoted himself to the history of the saints ; *Eutychius (Said Ibn Batrik)*, patriarch of *Alexandria* († 940),[5] to general and ecclesiastical history ; *Oecumenius*, bishop of Tricca (about 990),[6] to exegesis.

[3] His works are Bibliotheca (prim. graece ed. Dav. Hoeschelius. August. Vind. 1601 fol. gr. et lat. Andr. Schott. Genev. 1613 and Rothom. 1653. fol. ex rec. Imm. Bekkeri. Berol. 1824. T. ii. 4.)—Σύνταγμα κανόνων (in the spicilegium Rom. vii. ii. 1), put together according to an arrangement of subjects in 14 titles. To it is attached the Νομοκανών (cum comm. Theod. Balsamonis in H. Justelli biblioth. juris can. vet. ii. 785 ss.), in which there is first a short reference to the canons in the Syntagma, but afterwards the laws relating thereto are adduced, and explanations appended. It is according to Biener in his Zeitschrift für geschichtliche Rechtswissenschaft vii. ii. 148, the revision of an older work. Comp. his Gesch. d. Novellen Justinian's, Berlin 1824. 8. 202 ff. Ejusd. de collectionibus canonum Eccl. Graecae schediasma, Berol. 1827, p. 21 ss.—Διήγησις περὶ τῶν νεοφάντων Μανιχαίων ἀναβλαστήσεως libb. iv. (see above before § 3.) Epistolae ed. Rich. Montacutius. Lond. 1651. fol.—Ἀμφιλόχια or Ἀμφιλόχεια, 313 theological elucidations, mostly of passages from the Bible, addressed to Amphilochus, metropolitan of Cyzicus, have been in part published, about a half, viz. 65 in the collection of letters ed. Montacutii, 7 in Canissi lect. ant. ed. Basnage ii. ii. 420, 2 by Combefis, 4 in Montfaucon catal. bibl. Coisl. p. 346, 46 in Wolfi curae philol. et crit. V. 651, 18 by Angelus Scotus in Naples, 20 in Angeli Maji scriptorum vett. nova collectio i. 193, comp. Fabricius-Harles xi. 25. A Maji praef. p. xxxvi. ss. Among the unprinted works of Photius several controversial ones against the Latins (see Cave hist. lit. ii. 49 s. A. Majus l. c. p. xliv.) and his commentarius in Pauli epistt. (Ms. in Cambridge) are to be noted. Cf. Fabricii bibl. Graeca ix. 369 ss. (ed. Harles x. 670 ss.)

[4] He has left 122 vitae Sanctorum, many more are spuriously ascribed to him (see Leo Allatii diatr. de variis Simeonibus et Simeonum scriptis. Paris. 1664, 4. p. 124), in part Latin, ap. Surius, Greek and Latin in the actis SS. Antverp., partly still unprinted. Different opinions about Simeon's period : Oudinus de scriptt. eccl. ii. 1302 ss. places him in the 12th century. On the other side, Cave scriptt. eccl. hist. liter. ed. Basil. 1745, ii. 88. Comp. Hanke de Byzantinarum rerum scriptt. p. 418 ss. Fabricii bibl. Gr. ix. 48 (ed. Harles x. 180).

[5] From him we have the Arabic contextio gemmarum s. annales ab orbe cond. ad annum usque 940. An extract from it origines Alexandrinae ed. J. Seldenus. Lond. 1642, 4. The whole ed. E. Pocockius. Oxon. 1659, 4.

[6] Comm. in acta Apost., epist. Pauli et epist. catholicas ed. Frid. Morellus. Paris, 1631, T. ii. fol. Cf. Rich. Simon hist. crit. des principaux commentateurs du N. T. c. 32, p. 460.

THIRD CHAPTER.

SPREAD OF CHRISTIANITY.

§. 44.

Muhammedanism now thwarted the farther progress of Christianity even in the Eastern boundaries of Europe. The *Bulgarians* at *the Danube* had, indeed, been won over to the gospel;[1] but those at *the Wolga* were soon after gained to Islamism.[2] Among *the Chazari*, both religions took root about the same time.[3] On the other hand, *the Slavonians* dwelling in the inte-

---

[1] See above, § 41, not, 8.

[2] The Chalif Muktedir sent thither 921 Ibn-Fosslan, to complete the introduction of Muhammedanism, agreeably to the request of the Bulgarian king. Comp. the accounts of Ibn-Fosslan and other Arabians respecting the Russians of older time by C. M. Frähn, Petersburg 1823, 4. Vorr. S. lii. ff. and lvi.

[3] Regarding the spread of Christianity among them by Cyril, about 850, see the contemporaneous vita Constantini cum translat. Clementis (see above, § 38, not. 2), § 1. To the emperor Michael, Cazarorum legati venerunt, orantes ac supplicantes, ut dignaretur mittere ad illos aliquem eruditum virum, qui eos fidem catholicam veraciter edoceret, adjicientes inter caetera, quoniam nunc Judaei ad fidem suam, modo Saraceni ad suam nos convertere e contrario moliuntur. The emperor had sent Constantinus Philosophus (Cyril), and the latter, § 6, praedicationibus et rationibus eloquiorum suorum convertit, omnes illos ab erroribus, quos tam de Saracenorum quam de Judaeorum perfidia retinebant. On this account they had thanked the emperor, affirmantes se ob eam rem imperio ejus semper subditos et fidelissimos de caetero velle manere. However, Ibn-Fosslan in his journey 921 among the Chazari, found as many Muhammedans as Christians, and, besides, Jews and idolaters. Their prince (Chakan) was a Jew. See Fraehn in the Mémoires de l'Académie des sciences de St Petersbourg. Tome viii. (1822) p. 589 ss. The same thing is related by the geographers, Massudi, A.D. 943, and his contemporary, Ibn Hhaukal, whose paragraphs concerning the present topic are translated in Jul. v. Klaproth's description of the Russian provinces between the Caspian and Black Seas. Berlin 1814.

rior of Hellas and the Pelloponnesus, gradually subdued since 783, now adopted Christianity, especially after the conversion of the Bulgarians;[4] in like manner, too, *the Mainots*.[5] The Byzantines were not less successful in the conversion of *the Russians* to Christianity. The baptism of the grand Duchess *Olga* (955)[6] did not decide the matter; but after her grandson *Wladimir* (Wassily) had become a Christian (988), he caused his Russians to be baptised in crowds in the Dnieper.[7] Under his successors *Jaroslav* (1019–1054)[8] and *Isaeslav* (1054–1077), Christianity was firmly established in Russia. Under the latter, the celebrated hollow monastery at Kiew was founded by *Anthony*;[9] in which the first Russian annalist *Nestor* appeared.[10]

S. 196 ff. 262 ff. comp. Jost's Gesch. d. Israeliten vi. iii. According to Elmacin († 1273) hist. Sarac. p. 62, Islamism had been urged as early as 690 p. C. on a part of the army of the Chazari, vanquished by the Arabians. According to Ibn el-Asir († 1233) they adopted it first in 868, for the purpose of obtaining help against the Turks. See Frähn in the mémoires de Petersb. viii 598, and the same writer's Ibn-Fosslan, preface. S. ix.

[4] Comp. vol. i. div. 2, § 109, not. 3. On their subjugation see Fallmerayer's Gesch. der Halbinsel Morea während des Mittelalters i. 216. Zinkeisen's Gesch. Griechenland's i. 752. On their conversion, Fallmerayer i. 230. Zinkeisen i. 767.

[5] Constantini Porphyrog. de administr. imperio c. 50 (Constant. Porphyr. recogn. Imm. Bekker, vol. iii. Bonnae 1840 p. 224): Οἱ τοῦ κάστρου Μαΐνης οἰκήτορες—μέχρι τοῦ νῦν παρὰ τῶν ἐντοπίων Ἕλληνες προσαγορεύονται διὰ τὸ ἐν τοῖς προπαλαιοῖς χρόνοις εἰδωλολάτρας εἶναι καὶ προσκυνητὰς τῶν εἰδώλων κατὰ τοὺς παλαιοὺς Ἕλληνας, οἵτινες ἐπὶ τῆς βασιλείας τοῦ ἀοιδίμου βασιλείου βαπτισθέντες Χριστιανοὶ γεγόνασιν. Fallmerayer i. 137. Zinkeisen i. 769.

[6] Nestor in Schlözer's Uebers. v. 58 ff. (his commentary especially should be compared). Zonaras lib. xvi. c. 21, ed. Paris, p. 194. Cedrenus p. 636, in whom she is called Ἔλγα. Karamsin's Geschichte des Russ. Reichs, übers. v. F. v. Hauenschild (Riga 1820 ff. 5 Bde.) i. 136 ff. Ph. Strahl's Geschichte der russischen Kirche, (Halle 1830) S. 51 ff.

[7] According to Nestor, see Karamsin i. 168 ff. Strahl S. 58 ff.

[8] Karamsin ii. 21 28. Strahl S. 86 ff.

[9] Karamsin ii. 71. Strahl S. 96 ff.

[10] Nestor's annals with translation and remarks by A. L. v. Schlözer. Göttingen 1802-1809. 5 Th. 8. (The edition unfortunately extends only to the commencement of the reign of Wladimir.) On Nestor's life see Schlözer i. 3 ff. On the state of his annals i. 10, v. 4, remarks. They reach to 110. Schlözer i. 15. Karamsin ii. 61, remarks.

THIRD PART.

§ 45.

HERETICS IN THE EAST.

(See the literature before § 3).

After *Karbeas*, the Paulicians received in his son-in-law *Chrysocheres*, an equally bold leader, who continued to invade the Byzantine territories, at first with no less success; and in 867 reached as far as Ephesus.[1] But after he had been overpowered by the Greeks on returning from such an invasion, and cut off with his army (871); the Paulicians were compelled to be subject to the emperor *Basil*, the Macedonian.[2] Finally, *John Tzimisces* removed a great part of them to the neighbourhood of Philippopolis, in Thrace, (970) as border-watchers, where they were allowed religious freedom.[3]

[1] Jos. Genesii (about 940) Regum lib. iv. (ed. Lachmann, Bonnae 1834, p. 120 ss.)

[2] Theophanes contin. lib. v. de Basilio Mac. c. 37 ss. Genesius p. 123 ss.

[3] Zonaras lib. xvii. p. 209. ed. Paris. This is copiously described by Anna Comnena [1148] in Alexiade lib. xiv. p. 450 ss. ed. Paris, especially p. 453: Ὁ δὲ Τζιμισκῆς Ἰωάννης τοὺς ἐκ Μανιχαϊκῆς αἱρέσεως ἀντιμάχους ἡμῖν ποιησάμενος συμμάχους, κατά γε τὰ ὅπλα, ἀξιομάχους δυνάμεις τοῖς νομάσι τούτοις Σκύθαις ἀντέστησε, καὶ τὸ ἐντεῦθεν ἀπὸ τῶν πλειόνων καταδρομῶν ἀνέπνευσε τὰ τῶν πόλεων. Οἱ μέντοι Μανιχαῖοι φύσει ὄντες ἐλεύθεροι καὶ ἀνυπότακτοι, τὸ εἰωθὸς ἐποίουν, καὶ εἰς τὴν φύσιν ἀνέκαμπτον. Πᾶσα γὰρ ἡ Φιλιππούπολις, πλὴν ὀλίγων, ὄντων Μανιχαίων, τῶν τε αὐτόθι Χριστιανῶν ἐτυράννουν, καὶ τὰ τούτων διήρπαζον, μικρὰ φροντίζοντες ἢ οὐδὲν τῶν ἀποστελλομένων παρὰ βασιλέως· Ηὔξανε τοίνυν, καὶ τὰ κύκλῳ Φιλιππουπόλεως πάντα ἦσαν αἱρετικοί. Συνεισέβαλε δὲ καὶ τούτοις ἕτερος ποταμὸς ὁ τῶν Ἀρμενίων ἁλμυρὸς, καὶ ἄλλος ἀπὸ τῶν βολερωτάτων πηγῶν Ἰακώβου, καὶ ἦν, ὡς οὕτω γε φάναι, κακῶν ἁπάντων μιγάγκεια. Καὶ τὰ μὲν δόγματα διεφώνουν, συνεφώνουν δὲ ταῖς ἀποστασίαις οἱ ἄλλοι τοῖς Μανιχαίοις.

Thus not only the Paulicians spread themselves thence,[4] but that country became the asylum of all parties who were persecuted elsewhere. Among them the *Euchites* or *Messalians* now emerged once more ; a party who had given evidence of their existence for centuries past only in individual traces.[5] It was a necessary consequence that the near residence of these parties should have an influence on their internal development also.

[4] That they did much for this purpose may be seen in Petri Siculi's dedication of his history (see preface to §. 3) to the archbishop of the Bulgarians : χρονοτριβήσας τοίνυν—πρὸς τοὺς Παυλικιανοὺς ἐν Τιβρικῇ (nine months 868)—τῶν ἀσεβῶν ἐκείνων ἀκούσας φληναφούντων, ὡς μέλλουσιν ἐξ αὐτῶν ἐκείνων ἀποστέλλειν ἐν τοῖς τόποις Βουλγαρίας τοῦ ἀποστῆσαί τινας τῆς ὀρθοδόξου πίστεως, καὶ πρὸς τὴν οἰκείαν καὶ μεμιαμμένην αἵρεσιν ἐπισπάσασθαι· τῇ ἀρχῇ τοῦ θείου κηρύγματος θαρρούντες καὶ οἰόμενοι, ὡς εὐκόλως δυνήσονται, τῷ ἀδήλῳ καὶ ἀληθινῷ σίτῳ τὰ οἰκεῖα σπεῖραι ζιζάνια. Εἰώθασι γὰρ τοῦτο πολλάκις ποιεῖν οἱ ἀνόσιοι, καὶ πολλοὺς κόπους καὶ κινδύνους προθύμως ἀναδέχεσθαι πρὸς τὸ μεταδιδόναι τῆς οἰκείας λοίμης τοῖς παρατυγχάνουσι.

[5] The basis of the Euchite doctrine was the opinion, that a demon dwells in every man from his birth, who can only be expelled by unceasing prayer (Vol. i. Div. 2, § 95, not. 39), an opinion, which, so far as it led to an excessive estimate of the power of the devil, and to a contempt of ecclesiastical worship, certainly bordered on Monachism. As it originated with the monks who believed that they continually had to fight with the devil and to conquer him by prayer, and who accustomed themselves in their solitude to dispense with ecclesiastical worship (comp. l. c. note 37); it subsequently too was fostered by an overstrained monachism, and had its secret firm points in the concealment of many convents (Theodoreti hist. eccl. iv. 10 : Letojus saw πολλὰ τῆς νόσου ταύτης σπάσαντα μοναστήρια· hist· religiosa c. 3. opp. ed. Halens. iii. 1146 : Εὐχίτας ἐν μοναχικῷ προσχήματι τὰ Μανιχαίων νοσοῦντας. Concil. Ephesini ann. 431 definitio contra Messalianos, act. vii. Mansi iv. 1477 : [Messaliani] convicti non permittantur habere monasteria, ut ne zizania diffudantur et crescant. Jo Damasc. de haeresibus c. 80 : Μασσαλιανῶν, τῶν μάλιστα ἐν μοναστηρίοις εὑρισκομένων)· The Euchites arose in Mesopotamia, withdrew to Syria, and from thence, towards the end of the fourth century, to Pamphylia (Theodoreti hist. eccl. iv. 10). In the fifth century, they were found in Syria (Hieron. dial. adv. Pelagian. prooem.), in Pamphylia and Lycaonia (Conc. Ephes. definitio l. c.) ; in the sixth and seventh centuries among the Nestorians in Mesopotamia (Assemani bibl. orient. iii. ii. 172), and under Justinian and Justin II. in the Greek empire (Timoth. Presb. de. receptione haereticorum in Cotelerii monum. Eccl. Graecae iii. 400). In the eighth century, John Damascenus speaks of them as still existing (de haeresibus c. 80 in Cotelerii monum. Eccl. graecae i. 302). In like manner in the 9th century, Photius (bibl. cód. 52 : καθὼς καὶ ἡμεῖς—πολλὴν σηπεδόνα παθῶν καὶ κακίας τὰς ἐκείνων ψυχὰς ἐπιβοσκομένην ἑωράκαμεν). Comp. generally Walch's Ketzerhist. iii. 500. Engelhardt's Kirchengeschichte Abhand-

lungen S. 191. Amid their concealment one can scarcely wonder, when in
the sixth century, the western Facundus pro defens iii. capitul. viii. 7.
(Gallandii bibl. xi. 755) reckons the Messalians as heretics, quorum nomina abolita sunt cum haeresibus suis. In the eleventh century they again
appear openly in Thrace. Georg. Cedrenus (about 1060) historiarum
comp. ed Bonn. i. 514, relates how Flavianus, bishop of Antioch, towards
the end of the fourth century, expelled the Euchites, ἀφ᾽ ὧν ὁ μέγας
Φλαβιανός μοναχοὺς συναθροίσας πολλούς—διήλεγξεν, from Syria: εἰς δὲ
τὴν Παμφυλίαν ἀνεχώρησαν καὶ ταύτην τῆς λώβης ἐπλήρωσαν, νῦν δὲ σχεδὸν
εἰπεῖν καὶ τὴν πλείονα δύσιν, i. e., the west of the Greek imperial empire,
particularly Thrace. About the same time more definite particulars
are given by Michael Psellus περὶ ἐνεργείας δαιμόνων διάλογος (cur J. F.
Boissonade. Norimbergae 1838, 8). Here a Thracian coming to
Constantinople relates the following, p. 2, respecting the party that had
newly arisen there : Εὐχίτας αὐτοὺς καὶ Ἐνθουσιαστὰς οἱ πολλοὶ καλοῦσιν.
—Ἔχει μὲν τὸ παλαμναῖον τοῦτο δόγμα παρὰ Μάνεντος τοῦ μανέντος τὰς ἀφορ-
μάς· ἐκεῖθεν γὰρ αὐτοῖς αἱ πλείους ἀρχαὶ, καθάπερ ἐκ πηγῆς τινος δυσώδους, ἐρ-
ρύησαν. Ἀλλὰ τῷ μὲν ἐπαράτῳ Μάνεντι δύο ὑπετέθησαν τῶν ὄντων ἀρχαί·
Εὐχίταις δὲ τούτοις τοῖς κακοδαίμοσι καὶ ἑτέρα τις ἀρχὴ προσελήφθη τρίτη.
Πατὴρ γὰρ αὐτοῖς, υἱοί τε δύο, πρεσβύτερος καὶ νεώτερος, αἱ ἀρχαί, ὧν τῷ μὲν
πατρὶ τὰ ὑπερκόσμια μόνα, τῷ δὲ νεωτέρῳ τῶν υἱῶν τὰ οὐράνια, θατέρῳ δὲ τῷ
πρεσβυτέρῳ τῶν ἐγκοσμίων τὸ κράτος ἀποτετάχασιν·—Οἱ μὲν—νέμουσιν ἀμφοῖν τοῖν υἱοῖν τὸ σέβας· κἂν πρὸς ἀλλήλους διαφέρεσθαι φασὶ νῦν, ἀλλ'
ὅμως ἄμφω σεβαστέον. ὡς ἐκ πατρὸς ἑνὸς καταλλαγησομένους ἐπὶ τοῦ μέλλοντος.
Οἱ δὲ θατέρῳ τῷ νεωτέρῳ λατρεύουσιν, ὡς τῆς κρείττονος καὶ ὑπερκειμένης μερί-
δος κατάρχοντι· τὸν πρεσβύτερον οὐκ ἀτιμάζοντες μὲν, φυλαττόμενοι δ' αὐτὸν ὡς
κακοποιῆσαι δυνάμενον. Οἱ δὲ χείρους αὐτῶν τὴν ἀσέβειαν τοῦ μὲν οὐρανίου
δῦστῶσιν ἑαυτοὺς ἐπὶ πᾶν, αὐτὸν δὲ μόνον τὸν ἐπίγειον Σαταναὴλ ἐνστερνίζον-
ται, τῶν τε ὀνομάτων τοῖς εὐφημοτέροις ἀποσεμνύνοντες, πρωτότοκον τὸν ἀλλό-
τριον ἐκ πατρὸς καλοῦσι, φυτῶν τε καὶ ζώων καὶ τῶν λοιπῶν συνθέτων δημιουργὸν τὸν φθοροποιὸν καὶ ὀλέθριον. Ἀποθεραπεύειν δ' αὐτὸν καὶ μᾶλλον ἔτι βουλόμενοι, φεῦ ! ὁπόσα παροινοῦσιν εἰς τὸν οὐράνιον, φθονερόν τε λέγοντες εἶναι, τἀδελ-
φῷ παραλόγως διαφθονούμενον εὖ διακοσμοῦντι τὰ ἐπὶ γῆς, καὶ φθόνῳ τυφόμενον
σεισμοὺς καὶ χαλάζας καὶ λοιμοὺς ἐπάγειν· Διὸ καὶ ἐπαρῶνται αὐτῷ ἄλλα τε καὶ
τὸ παλαμναῖον ἀνάθεμα. Then it is related of them, that in their assemblies
they practised lewdness, murdered and burned the children there begot-
ten, and partook of blood and ashes ; a report which even the heathen circulated against the first Christians, the Catholics against many heretical
sects, and which has always been revived where secret meetings consisting
of both sexes appeared. How the doctrine which Psellus attributes to
the Euchites, was developed among them, whether by the influence of
the Zend religion, already in Syria, or by Gnostic influences, is uncertain. In the addictedness to contemplation which was peculiar to the
Euchites, a manifold fantastic development of doctrine could not fail to
appear. Hence even towards the end of the eleventh century the Bogomiles took their rise from them. Comp. Walch and Engelhardt, l. c.
Schnitzer : die Euchiten im 11ten Jahrb. in Stirm's Studien der evangel. Geistlichkeit Wirtembergs xi. i. 169.

§ 46.

MANICHAEANS IN THE WEST.

J. C. Füesslin's Kirchen = u. Ketzerhist. der mittlern Zeit. i. 31. H. Schmid
der Mysticismus des Mittelalters in seiner Entstehungsperiode darges-
tellt, Jena 1824. 8. S. 387 ff. D. Chr. U. Hahn's Gesh. d. Ketzer im Mittelalter, Bd. 1. Gesch. d. neumanichäischen Ketzer, Stuttgart 1845, 8.

Encouraged by the apparent downfall of the church, and doubts
of its soundness which were spreading in consequence, *the Manichaeans*[1] again emerged from their obscurity, after the com-

---

[1] Contemporaries looked upon these heretics as sprung from the
Manichaeans, and they themselves declared it as their own opinion.
According to Roger, bishop of Chalons, between 1043 and 1048 (see
below note 7) they taught that the Holy Spirit is only vouchsafed
through Manes. Comp. Ekberti (about 1163) adv. Catharos serm. 1.
(Bibl. PP. Lugd. xxiii. 602): indubitanter secta eorum—originem
accepit a Manichaeo haeresiarcha. Albericus (about 1241) chron. ad
ann. 1239 ed. Leibnit. p. 570: invenit etiam frater Robertus, et secundum hoc publica terit opinio, quod ille Fortunatus Manichaeus pessimus,
quem b. Augustinus de Africa expulit, venit eodem tempore ad illas
partes Campaniae, et invenit Widomarum Principem latronum in eodem
monte cum suis latitantem ; hunc ad suam sectam cum sociis convertit,
et a tempore illo circa montem illum in proximis villulis nunquam de-
fuit semen istud pessimum Chanaan et non Juda. That in Italy, from
which country this party had certainly transplanted themselves in the
first place to France (see Glaber Radulphus iii. c. 8. below not. 3. and
acta syn. Attrebat. below note 4), the Manichaeans also existed, according to Leo the Great (see vol. 1. Div. 2. § 86. not. 6.), which is also
testified by the notices in the biographies of Gelasius († 496), Symmachus († 514), and Hormisdas († 523) belonging to Anastasii liber
pontificalis, purporting that the popes had had to contend against the
Manichaeans. Besides, their continuance till the time of Gregory the
Great is established. See his lib. v. ep. 8. ad Cyprianum Diaconum :
De Manichaeis, qui in possessionibus nostris sunt, frequenter Dilectionem tuam admonui, ut eos persequi summopere debeat, atque ad
fidem catholicam revocare. lib. ii. epist. 37 ad Joh. Episc. Squillacinum :
Afros passim vel incognitos peregrinos ad ecclesiasticos ordines tendentes
nulla ratione suscipias : quia Afri quidam Manichaei, aliqui rebaptizati.
This last passage has been repeated for centuries at the induction of
bishops. See liber diurnus cap. iii. tit. ix. 3. Gregorii ii. ep. ad
clerum et plebem Thuringiae A. D. 723 (Mansi xii. 239), and also in
the institution-documents set forth by Gerbert, archbp. of Capua, in
the year 978 (in Ughelli Italia sacra vi. 564), Athenulph, archbp. of

Capua, A. D. 1032 (ibid. p. 676), and Alfanus, archbp. of Salerno, A. D. 1066 (Ughelli vii. 802). In every case it is clear that even after Gregory the Great the Manichaeans were in Italy, and threatened danger to the Church; but the general account of this period agrees, to the effect that they again emerged from their obscurity about the year 1000, and spread themselves from Italy into other countries. It has been attempted, however, to deduce them from other sources. These new Manichaeans are derived from the Priscillianists in the histoire générale de Languedoc i. 148, and by H. Leo Lehrbuch der Gesch. des Mittelalters S. 79. It is the most common opinion, however, after Muratori antiquitt. medii aevi v. 83. Mosheim institt. hist. eccl. p. 463. E. Gibbon's decline and fall of the Roman Empire, chap. 54, that these new western sects sprung from the Paulicians. Neander (Kirchengesch. iv. 457) has modified this view by considering the Euchites as their proper progenitors. The origin of the new Manichaeans from a Greek party appears to be favoured by Evervini epist. ad Bernardum A. D. 1146 (Mabill. annal. p. 473) : Illi vero, qui combusti sunt, dixerunt nobis in defensione sua, hanc haeresin usque ad haec tempora occultatam fuisse a temporibus Martyrum, et permansisse in Graecia et quibusdam aliis terris. So also Reinerius (+ 1259) summa de Catharis et Leonistis in Martene thesaur. anecdot. v. 1767, where he mentions the 16 Catharian churches, and among them last of all the Ecclesia Bulgariae and the Eccl. Dugunthiae (s. Dugunithiae s. Dugranicae) adding : et omnes habuerunt originem de duabus ultimis. Then it may be also adduced in favour of this opinion that in the 13th century Bulgari, Bulgri, Bogri, French Bougres, were the usual appellation of these heretics. See Monachus Antissidorensis, Albericus and Matthaeus Paris. On the other hand it is to be observed, that at the first appearance of the sect in France it was derived from Italy, and not till more than a century later, from Greece and Balgaria. Farther, that the new western Manichaeism was very different from Paulicianism in many essential points, and rather approached the old Manichaeism by the rejection of marriage and flesh-eating, the distinction of the Electi and Auditores, and a proper hierarchy, for even Manes, whom the Paulicians cursed (Petrus Sicul p. 42 : προθύμως ἀναθεματίζουσι Σκυθιανὸν, Βουδδᾶν τε καὶ Μανέντα, cf. Photius i. c. 4), stood in high repute among the western Manichaeans. It is not the less to be remarked, that even the Euchites of the 11th century are distinguished from the western Manichaeans in this, that according to them the perfect had to abstain from no food (Cedrenus i. 515, μηκέτι δεῖσθαι λοιπὸν νηστείας): and that the Bogomiles who sprung from them subsequently, first adopted the principles of the western Manichaeans on this point. Since then these sects, in such times as they vegetated in retirement, without progress, would naturally abide most firmly by such external usages, we may certainly conclude from those relations that their origin was different. It is not till after the crusades that the western Manichaeans and those Greek sects appear to have become known to one another as cognate parties, and to have borrowed many things from one another, so that in the 12th century in the east, the Bogomiles, and among the western Manichaeans the Concorrezensians appeared to agree completely in doctrine and usages.

mencement of the eleventh century; a few remains of them having been still preserved in Italy; and diffused themselves in the West. Similar manifestations present themselves in earlier times.[2] But the *Manichaeans*, properly so called, were first

Hence therefore the tradition might originate among the western Manichaeans that their party had existed in the East from the beginning, in the same manner as similar false traditions respecting their own origin arose among the Waldenses.—The western Manichaeans, when they emerged from their obscurity in the 11th century, had only preserved the most general features of their creed in addition to external usages; but by degrees the old Manichaean doctrinal system again appeared among them in greater completeness, though occasionally with peculiarities. If the source from which they may have derived it again be inquired after, none other can be pointed out than Augustine's writings against the Manichaeans. Since, very early, ecclesiastics are found among the heads of the party, to whom the writings of Augustine were accessible, since they could not be indifferent to the Manichaean fragments preserved in these writings, and to Augustine's account of the Manichaean doctrine (comp. Ekberti adv. Catharos sermo i. in fine, A. D. 1163, in the bibl. PP. Lugd. xxiii. 600: Produnt autem semetipsos quod sint de errore Manichaei, in eo, quod dicere solent, quod b. Augustinus prodiderit secreta eorum), a restoration and new development of the system from this source is very probable. As the Catholic Church honoured in Augustine its chief teacher, so those who renounced that church, for this very reason, sought for the truth among his most decided opponents.

[2] Glab. Rudulph. lib. ii. c. 11. relates of one Leutardus in the village Virtus in pago Catalaunico A. D. 1000: Terrified by a dream he had in the field, he came home, dimittens uxorem, quasi ex praecepto evangelico fecit divortium: egressus autem velut oraturus intrans ecclesiam, arripiensque crucem et Salvatoris imaginem contrivit. He was looked upon as insane, but he maintained, universa haec patrare ex mirabili Dei revelatione. He taught, decimas dare esse omnimodis superfluum et inane,—Prophetas ex parte narrasse utilia, ex parte non credenda. But against a bishop coepit—de Scripturis sacris testimonia sibi assumere.—In brevi ad se traxit partem non modicam vulgi. Finally, semet puteo periturus immersit.—Cap. 12. of a Grammarian Vilgardus, who coepit multa turgide docere fidei sacrae contraria, dictaque poetarum per omnia credenda esse asserebat. He was executed. Plures etiam per Italiam tunc hujus pestiferi dogmatis sunt reperti, qui et ipsi aut gladiis aut incendiis perierunt. Ex Sardinia quoque insula, quae his plurimum abundare solet, ipso tempore aliqui egressi, partem populi in Hispania corrumpentes, et ipsi a viris catholicis exterminati sunt. In Sardinia paganism sustained itself for a very long time (vol. i. Div. 2. § 109. note 9.) The confession of faith which Gerbert, as archbp. of Rheims 991 issued (ep. 75. ap. Bouquet x. 409), does not prove, as Hahn (Gesch. d. neumanichäischen Ketzer S. 31) thinks, that Manichaeism existed in that country. Gerbert was doubtless accused in

discovered in *Aquitania* and in *Orleans* (1022),[3] much about

many ways by his numerous opponents, and therefore he set forth this confession against many heresies, expressly rejecting not only Manichaean but also Origenist and Novatian errors.

[3] Three accounts by contemporaries. Ademarus (monk in Angouleme about 1029) chronic. (ap. Bouquet x. 154) alone relates : Pauco post tempore (after 1018) per Aquitaniam exorti sunt Manichaei, seducentes plebem, negantes baptismum sanctum et crucis virtutem, et quidquid sanae doctrinae est : abstinentes a cibis quasi monachi, et castitatem simulantes, sed inter seipsos luxuriam omnem exercentes.   Then p. 159, the discovery and burning of ten canonici in Orleans, A.D. 1022, not 1017 (see A. Pagi ad ann. 1017 no. 1), concerning which see also Glab. Radulph. iii. c. 8. (ap. Bouquet x. 35) and gesta syn. Aurelianensis a. 1017 (rather 1022, in d'Archery spicileg. i. 604. ap. Mansi xix. 376).—Glaber Rad. : Fertur a muliere quadam ex Italia procedente haec insanissima haeresis (he says of it before : diutius occulte germinata) in Galliis habuisse exordium, quae—seducebat quoscumque volebat, non solum idiotas et simplices, verum etiam plerosque, qui videbantur doctiores in clericorum ordine.   (Ademarus : those Canonici, qui videbantur aliis religiosiores, were decepti a quodam Rustico Petragoriensi).—Qui non solum in praedicta urbe, sed etiam in vicinis urbibus malignum dogma spargere tentabant, dum quendam sanae mentis in Rotomagorum civitate Presbyterum cupientes suae consortem facere vesaniae, missis legatis, qui ei omne secretum hujus perversi dogmatis explanantes docerent : dicebant nempe fore in proximum, in illorum scilicet dogma cadere populum universum.   Thus they expressed themselves subsequently in the hearing they had before the king : Hoc enim diu est, quod sectam, quam vos jam tarde agnoscitis, amplectimur ; sed tam vos quam caeteros cujuscunque legis vel ordinis in eam cadere exspectavimus : quod etiam adhuc fore credimus.   Concerning their doctrines see gesta synodi Aurelianensis, though merely from the relation of a novice, Arefastus.   It was taught by the two heads of the sect, Stephanus and Lisojus : Christum de virgine Maria non esse natum, neque pro hominibus passum, nec vere in sepulcro positum, nec a mortuis resurrexisse.—in baptismo nullam esse scelerum ablutionem : neque sacramentum corporis et sanguinis Christi [effici] in consecratione sacerdotis.   Sanctos Martyres atque confessores implorare pro nihilo ducebant.   They had addressed him thus : Tractandus es a nobis ut arbor silvestris, quae translata in viridario, tamdiu aquis perfunditur, donec humo radicetur, dehinc spinis et rebus superfluis emundatur, ut postmodum terrae tenus truncata sarculo, meliori inseratur ramusculo, quae postmodum fertilis sit mellifluo pomo.   Itaque tu simili modo translatus de iniquo saeculo, in nostro sancto collegio aquis perfunderis sapientiae, donec informeris, et gladio verbi Dei vitiorum spinis carere valeas, ac insulsa doctrina tui pectoris ab antro exclusa, nostram doctrinam a s. Spiritu traditam mentis puritate possis excipere.   Then : Procul dubio, frater, in charybdi falsae opinionis hactenus cum indoctis jacuisti.—Pandemus tibi salutis ostium, quo ingressus per impositionem videlicet manuum nostrarum, ab omni peccati labe mundaberis, atque

sancti Spiritus dono replęberis, qui Scripturarum omnium profunditatem
ac veram dignitatem absque scrupulo te docebit. Deinde caelesti cibo
pastus, interna satietate recreatus, videbis persaepe nobiscum visiones
angelicas, quarum, solatio fultus cum eis quovis locorum sine mora vel
difficultate, cum volueris, ire poteris : nihilque tibi deerit, quia Deus
omnium tibi comes nunquam deerit, in quo sapientiae thesauri atque
divitiarum consistunt. Respecting the preparation of the heavenly food
it is related : Congregabantur certis noctibus in domo denominata, singuli lucernas tenentes in manibus, ad instar letaniae daemonum nomina
declamabant, donec subito daemonem in similitudine cujuslibet bestiolae
inter eos viderent descendere. Qui statim ut visibilis illa videbatur visio
omnibus exstinctis luminaribus, quam primum quisque poterat mulie-.
rem, quae ad manum sibi veniebat, ad abutendum arripiebat. Sine
peccati respectu, et utrum mater, aut soror, aut monacha haberetur, pro
sanctitate et religione ejus concubitus ab illis aestimabatur. Ex quo
spurcissimo concubitu infans generatus, octava die in medio eorum—in
igne cremabatur. Cujus cinis tanta veneratione colligebatur atque cus-
todiebatur, ut christiana religiositas corpus Christi custodire solet, aegris
dandum de hoc saeculo exituris ad viaticum. Inerat enim tanta vis
diabolicae fraudis in ipso cinere, ut quicumque de praefata haeresi im-
butus fuisset, et de eodem cinere, quamvis sumendo parum, praeliba-
visset, vix unquam postea de eadem haeresi gressum mentis ad viam
veritatis dirigere valeret. So Ademar relates, l. c. Rusticus—pulverem
ex mortuis pueris secum deferebat, de quo si quem posset communicare,
mox Manichaeum faciebat. Adorabant Diabolum, qui primo eis in
Aethiopis, deinde Angeli lucis figuratione apparet etc. (On this report
see § 45. not. 5., comp. Baur, d. neuen manich. Religionssysteme S.
138). At this council these two heads say, respecting the birth of Christ
from a virgin, and his resurrection : Nos neque interfuimus, neque haec
vera esse credere possumus.—Quod natura denegat, semper a creatione
discrepat. Quibus praesul respondit, dicens : Antequam quicquam
fieret per naturam, non creditis per filium Deum patrem fecisse omnia
ex nihilo ? Cui alienati a fide dixerunt: Ista illis narrare potes, qui
terrena sapiunt, atque credunt figmenta carnalium hominum scripta in
membranis animalium : nobis autem qui legem scriptam habemus in
interiori homine a Spiritu sancto, et nihil aliud sapimus, nisi quod a Deo
omnium conditore didicimus, incassum superflua et a divinitate devia
profers : idcirco verbis finem impone, et de nobis quidquid velis facito.
Jam regem nostrum in caelestibus regnantem videmus, qui ad immortales
triumphos dextera sua nos sublevat, dans superna gaudia.—Glaber Radulph l. c. : Dicebant deliramenta esse quicquid in veteri ac novo Canone certis signis ac prodigiis veteribusque testatoribus de trina unaque
Deitate beata confirmat auctoritas : caelum pariter ac terram, ut conspi-
ciuntur, absque auctore initii semper exstitisse asserebant. Et cum
universarum haeresum insanientes canum more latrantes deterrima, in
hoc tantum Epicureis erant haereticis similes, quoniam voluptatum flagitiis credebant non recompensari ultionis vindictam : omne Christianorum opus, pietatis dumtaxat et justitiae, quod aestimatur pretium remunerationis aeternae, laborem superfluum judicabant esse.

the same time in *Arras* (1025),[4] in *Monteforte*, near Turin

---

[4] The only authority is acta syn. Attrebatensis ann. 1025 (in d'Achery
spicil. i. 607, ap. Mansi xix. 423). These reply at the council, se esse
auditores Gundulfi cujusdam ab Italiae partibus viri, et ab eo evangelicis mandatis et apostolicis informatos, nullamque praeter hanc scripturam se recipere, sed hanc verbo et opere tenere. But the bishop had
heard, illos sacri baptismatis mysterium penitus abhorrere, dominici
corporis et sanguinis sacramentum respuere, negare, lapsis poenitentiam
post professionem proficere, Ecclesiam annullare, legitima connubia
·execrari, nullum in ss. Confessoribus donum virtutis spectare, praeter
Apostolos et Martyres neminem debere venerari. In the praefatio this
is expressed thus: dicebant, baptismatis mysterium et dominici corporis
et sanguinis sacramentum nullum esse, et idcirco rejiciendum, nisi si-
mulationis causa non intrare [leg. ministrarentur]: poenitentiam nihil
ad salutem proficere: conjugatos nequaquam ad regnum pertinere
(hence the charge brought against them ap. Mansi xix. 449: De con-
nubiis vero, quae vos contra evangelica et apostolica decreta sacrilega
mente abominanda judicatis, dicentes conjugatos in sortem fidelium nequaquam computandos etc.) They themselves reply to the bishop, to
his questions regarding baptism (l. c. p. 425): Lex et disciplina nostra, quam a Magistro accepimus, nec evangelicis decretis, nec apostolicis sanctionibus contraire videbitur, si quis eam diligenter velit intueri.
Haec namque hujusmodi est, mundum relinquere, carnem a concupis-
centiis fraenare, de laboribus manuum suarum victum parare, nulli laesionem quaerere, charitatem cunctis, quos zelus hujus nostri propositi
teneat, exhibere. Servata igitur hac justitia, nullum opus esse baptismi;
praevaricata ista, baptismum ad nullam proficere salutem. Haec est
nostrae justificationis summa, ad quam nihil est, quod baptismi usus
superaddere possit, cum omnis apostolica et evangelica institutio hujusmodi fine claudatur (hence the charge against them l. c. p. 457: falsae
justitiae doctrinam introducere tentatis, quam divinae gratiae adeo prae-
ponitis, ut omnia propriis meritis adscribatis). Si quis autem in baptismate aliquod dicat latere sacramentum, hoc tribus ex causis evacuatur.
Una, quia vita reproba ministrorum baptizandis nullum potest praebere
salutis remedium. Altera, quia quidquid vitiorum in fonte renunciatur,
postmodum in vita repetitur. Tertia, quia ad parvulum non volentem
neque currentem, fidei nescium, suaeque salutis atque utilitatis ignarum,
in quem nulla regenerationis petitio, nulla fidei potest inesse confessio,
aliena voluntas, aliena fides, aliena confessio nequaquam pertinere videtur. Unfortunately the bishop did not allow them to answer the other
charges again. Remarkable, however, are the objections that they
taught (ap. Mansi xix. 436): in templo dei nihil esse, quod sit aliquo
cultu religionis dignum magis, quam proprii domicilii cubiculum,—
mensam Domini—nullum—in se aliud praeter acervum lapidum retinere
sacramentum, p. 453: ex errore hominum venisse, quod venerantur
crucem, cum nullam magis in se virtutem contineat, quam caetera ligna
sylvarum etc. They returned to the Catholic Church. Schmid S.
415 ff.

(1030),[5] not long after, and even in *Goslar* too (1025)[6] *Wazon*, bishop of Lüttich († 1048), lifted up his voice in vain against the universal practice of putting these heretics to death.[7]

[5] Glaber Radulph iv. c. 2. Respecting their doctrine the only authority is Landulph. Sen. Mediol. histor. lib. 2. c. 27. (Murat. scriptt. rer. Ital. iv. 88.) One of them, Girardus, thus expresses himself before Herbert, archbishop of Milan : Deo omnipotenti, Patri et Filio, et Spiritui Sancto gratias refero immensas, quod tam studiose me inquirere satagitis. Et qui vos ab initio in lumbis Adae cognovit, annuat, ut sibi vivatis, sibique moriamini, et cum ipso per saeculorum saecula regnantes gloriemini. Vitam meam, et meorum fratrum fidem qualicunque animo ea sciscitetis, vobis edicam : Virginitatem prae caeteris laudamus, uxores habentes.—Nemo nostrum uxore carnaliter utitur, sed quasi matrem aut sororem diligens tenet (afterwards : si universum genus humanum sese conjungeret, ut corruptionem non sentiret, sicut apes sine coitu genus humanum gigneretur). Carnibus nunquam vescimur, jejunia continua et orationes indesinenter fundimus ; semper die nocte nostri majores vicissim orant, quatenus hora oratione vacua non praetereat, omnem nostram possessionem cum omnibus hominibus communem habemus. Nemo nostrum sine tormentis vitam finit, ut aeterna tormenta evadere possimus (afterwards : si nos ad mortem natura perducit, proximus noster, antequam animam damus, quoquomodo interficit nos). Patrem et Filium et Spiritum Sanctum credimus et confitemur (namely Pater Deus est aeternus—Filius animus est hominis a Deo dilectus et Jesus Chr. animus sensualiter natus ex Maria Virgine, videlicet natus est ex s. Scriptura,—Spiritus Sanctus divinarum scientiarum intellectus, a quo cuncta discrete reguntur). Ab illis vero, qui potestatem habent ligandi et solvendi, ligari ac solvi credimus (to the question whether he meant the pope to be bishop or priest : Pontificem habemus non illum Romanum, sed alium, qui quotidie per orbem terrarum fratres nostros visitat dispersos, et quando Deus illum nobis ministrat, tunc peccatorum nostrorum venia summa cum devotione donatur. This is not, as Schmid thinks, a human pope, but the Holy Spirit who was given by the imposition of hands : according to Baur, das manich. Religionssystem S. 305, Christ, as the sun surrounding the earth). Vetus ac novum Testamentum ac ss. Canones quotidie legentes tenemus.

[6] Hermanni Contr. chron. ad. ann. 1052 (ap. Pertz vii. 130) : Imperator Natalem Domini Goslare egit, ibique quosdam haereticos inter alia pravi erroris dogmata, Manichaea secta, omnis esum animalis execrantes—in patibulis suspendi jussit.

[7] Gesta Episcopp. Leodiensium c. 59 (in Martene et Durand ampliss. collectio iv. 898 ss.) : Roger, bishop of Chalons, wrote to Wazon between 1043 and 1048 : in quadam parte dioecesis suae quosdam rusticos esse, qui perversum Manichaeorum dogma sectantes, furtiva sibi frequentarent conventicula, nescio quae obscoena et dictu turpia quadam sua solemnitate actitantes, et per sacrilegam manuum impositionem dari Spiritum Sanctum mentientes, quem ad adstruendam errori suo fidem

non alias a Deo missum, quam in haeresiarcha suo Mani (quasi nihil aliud sit Manes nisi Spiritus Sanctus) falsissime dogmatizarent : incidentes in illam blasphemiam, quam juxta veritatis vocem et hic et in futuro impossibile est remitti.   Hi tales, ut dicebat, cogebant quos possent in suam concedere turbam, nuptias abominantes, esum carnium non modo devitantes, sed et quodcunque animal occidere profanum dicentes ; tutelam errori suo assumere praesumentes sententiam Domini in veteri lege occidere prohibentis.   Si quos vero idiotas et infacundos hujus erroris sectatoribus adjungi contingeret, statim eruditissimis etiam catholicis facundiores fieri asseverabat, ita ut sincera sane sapientium eloquentia paene eorum loquacitate superari posse videretur.   Addidit etiam plus de quotidiana perversione sese aliorum dolere, quam de ipsorum perditione.   Quid de talibus praestet agendum, anxius praesul certum sapientiae consuluit secretarium, an terrenae potestatis gladio in eos sit animadvertendum necne : modico fermento, nisi exterminentur, totam massam posse corrumpi.   The reply of Wazon is preserved entire c. 60 : Haec licet christiana abhorreat religio,—tamen imitata Salvatorem suum —jubetur interim tales quodammodo tolerare.   A reference to Matth. xiii. 24 ss. particularly, v. 29 and 30.   Quid his verbis nisi patientiam suam Dominus ostendit, quam praedicatores suos erga errantes proximos exhibere desiderat ?   Maxime cum hos, qui hodie zizania sunt, possible sit, cras converti et esse triticum.   Cesset ergo judicium pulveris, audita sententia condemnatoris ; nec eos quaeramus per saecularis potentiae gladium huic vitae subtrahere, quibus vult idem creator et redemtor Deus, sicut novit, parcere : ut resipiscant a diaboli laqueis etc. Meminisse debemus, quod nos qui Episcopi dicimur, gladium in ordinatione—non accipimus ; ideoque non ad mortificandum, sed potius ad vivificandum auctore Deo inungimur.   The historian adds : Haec tantopere vir Dei exemplo b. Martini (Vol. i. Div. 2, § 104, not. 11) studebat inculcare, ut praecipitem Francigenarum rabiem caedes anhelare solitam a crudelitate quodammodo refraenaret.   Audierat enim, eos solo pallore notare haereticos, quasi quos pallere constaret, haereticos esse certum esset (Vol. i. Div. 2, § 86, note 6) ; sicque per errorem simulque furorem eorum plerosque vere catholicorum fuisse aliquando interemtos.   He then finds fault with the executions in Goslar cap. 61 : Wazonem nostrum, si haec tempora contigisset, huic sententiae assensum nequaquam praebiturum, exemplo b. Martini etc.   Haec dicimus, non quia errorem haereticorum tutari velimus ; sed quia hoc in divinis legibus nusquam sancitum [nos] non approbare monstremus.   Concerning Wazon see hist. lit. de la France vii. 588.